Survey of
Historic
Costume

Survey of
Historic
Costume
A History of Western Dress

FOURTH EDITION

Phyllis G. Tortora
Queens College of the City University of New York

Keith Eubank
Queens College of the City University of New York

I.C.C. LIBRARY

Fairchild Publications, Inc.

New York

o'size
GT
580
T67
2005

Executive Editor: Olga T. Kontzias
Assistant Acquisitions Editor: Jason Moring
Production Editor: Elizabeth Marotta
Editorial Services: Barbara Chernow
Art Director: Adam B. Bohannon
Production Manager: Ginger Hillman
Associate Development Editor: Suzette Lam
Copy Editor: Chernow Editorial Services, Inc.

Cover Design: Adam B. Bohannon

Color plate photographs copyright The Metropolitan Museum
of Art: Figure 1 © 1980; Figure 4 © 1979; Figure 8 © 1981; Figure 13
© 1993; Figure 22 © 1988; Figure 24 © 1990; Figure 28 © 1982; Figure
39 © 1988; Figure 40 © 1986; Figure 41 © 1983; Figure 53 © 1986;
Figure 58 © 1999; Figure 68 © 1999.

Fourth Printing, 2006
Third Printing, 2006
Second Printing, 2006
Fourth edition, copyright © 2005
Fairchild Publications, Inc.

Third edition, copyright © 1998
Fairchild Publications, Inc.

Second edition, copyright © 1994
Fairchild Publications, Inc.

First edition, copyright © 1989
Fairchild Publications, Inc.

All rights reserved. No part of this book covered by the copyright
hereon may be reproduced or used in any form or by any means—
graphic, electronic, or mechanical, including photocopying,
recording, taping, or information storage and retrieval systems—
without written permission of the publisher.

Library of Congress Catalog Card Number: 2005926652

ISBN: 1-56367-345-2

GST R 133004424

Printed in the United States of America

CH01, TP08

8/08 Emery Pratt 106.00

CONTENTS

Extended Contents **vii**

Preface **xvii**

Acknowledgments **xviii**

Some Notes on Using This Book **xxi**

CHAPTER ONE — Introduction **1**

PART ONE — The Ancient World c. 3000 B.C.–A.D. 300 **11**

CHAPTER TWO — The Ancient Middle East c. 3500–600 B.C. **15**

CHAPTER THREE — Crete and Greece c. 2900–300 B.C. **43**

CHAPTER FOUR — Etruria and Rome c. 800 B.C.–A.D. 400 **63**

PART TWO — The Middle Ages c. 300–1500 **83**

CHAPTER FIVE — The Early Middle Ages c. 300–1300 **87**

CHAPTER SIX — The Late Middle Ages c. 1300–1500 **121**

PART THREE — The Renaissance c. 1400–1600 **147**

CHAPTER SEVEN — The Italian Renaissance c. 1400–1600 **151**

CHAPTER EIGHT — The Northern Renaissance c. 1500–1600 **169**

PART FOUR — Baroque and Rococo c. 1600–1800 **193**

CHAPTER NINE — The Seventeenth Century 1600–1700 **199**

CHAPTER TEN — The Eighteenth Century 1700–1790 **225**

PART FIVE — The Nineteenth Century 1800–1900 **253**

CHAPTER ELEVEN — The Directoire Period and the Empire Period 1790–1820 **261**

CHAPTER TWELVE — The Romantic Period 1820–1850 **279**

CHAPTER THIRTEEN — The Crinoline Period 1850–1869 **303**

CHAPTER FOURTEEN — The Bustle Period and the Nineties 1870–1900 **327**

PART SIX — The Twentieth Century 1900–1996 **357**

CHAPTER FIFTEEN — The Edwardian Period and World War I 1900–1920 **361**

CHAPTER SIXTEEN — The Twenties, Thirties, and World War II 1920–1947 **387**

CHAPTER SEVENTEEN — The New Look: Fashion Conformity Prevails 1947–1960 **427**

CHAPTER EIGHTEEN — The Sixties and Seventies: Style Tribes Emerge 1960–1980 **457**

CHAPTER NINETEEN — The Eighties and Nineties: Affluence, Information, and a New Millennium 1980–2003 **499**

Bibliography **552**

Index **559**

E X T E N D E D   C O N T E N T S

Preface xvii

Acknowledgments xviii

Some Notes on Using This Book xxi

CHAPTER ONE
Introduction 1

The Origins of Dress 1

Limitations to the Design of Garments 1

Common Themes in Costume History Across Time 2

Functions of Dress in the Social Context 2

Clothing as a Means of Social Communication 4

The Historical Context 4

Cross-Cultural Influences 5

Geography, the Natural Environment, and Ecology 5

Clothing as an Art Form 5

The Phenomenon of Fashion in Western Dress 6

Sources of Evidence for the Study of Historic Costume 7

Summary 8

Notes 8

Selected Readings 9

PART ONE
THE ANCIENT WORLD C. 3000 B.C.–A.D. 300 11

Table I.1 Civilizations of the Ancient World 12

CHAPTER TWO
The Ancient Middle East c. 3500–600 B.C. 15

Chronology 14

Historical Background: Mesopotamia 16

Historical Background: Egypt 16

*Differences in the Development of Egyptian
and Mesopotamian Civilizations* 17

Mesopotamian Civilization 18

Social Structure 18

The Family 18

Fabrics and Cloth Production 18

Sources of Evidence About Sumerian Costume 19

*Mesopotamian Costume/Sumerian Costume
for Men and Women: c. 3500–2500 B.C.* 19

Costume Components for Men and Women 19

*Mesopotamian Costume/Later Sumerians
and Babylonians: c. 2500–1000 B.C.* 20

Costume Components for Men/Military Dress:
c. 2500–1000 B.C. 20

Costume Components for Men/Civilian Dress:
c. 2500–1000 B.C. 20

Costume Components for Women: c. 2500–1000 B.C. 21

*Mesopotamian Costume/Later Babylonians
and the Assyrians: c. 1000–600 B.C.* 21

The Tunic 22

Costume Components for Men: c. 1000–600 B.C. 22

Costume Components for Men/Military Dress 23

Costume Components for Women: c. 1000–600 B.C. 23

Mesopotamian Costume for Children: c. 3500–600 B.C. 24

Egyptian Civilization 24

Social Structure 24

Sources of Evidence for the Study of Egyptian Costume 25

Egyptian Art 25

The Contents of Tombs 25

Egyptian Decorative Motifs 26

Contributions of Artisans to Costume 26

Textile Production and Technology 26

Jewelry 27

Egyptian Costume: c. 3000–300 B.C. 27

Costume Terminology 27

Egyptian Costume for Men: c. 3000–300 B.C. 27

Costume Components for Men 27

*Table 2.1 Garments Worn by Egyptian Men and Women
During Various Historical Periods* 28

Contemporary Comments 2.1 29

Egyptian Costume for Women: 3000–300 B.C. 31

Costume Components for Women 31

Costume Components for Men and Women 32

Egyptian Costume for Children: 3000–300 B.C. 35

Egyptian Costume for Specialized Occupations 35

Military Costume 35

Religious Costume 35

Illustrated Table 2.1 Some of the Headdress Worn in Ancient Egypt 36

Costume for Musicians, Dancers, and Acrobats 38

Summary 38

Themes 38

Visual Summary Table 39

Later Survivals of Mesopotamian and Egyptian Dress 40

Notes 40

Selected Readings 41

CHAPTER THREE

Crete and Greece c. 2900–300 B.C. 43

Chronology 42

Minoan and Mycenaean Civilizations 44

Historical Background 44

Social Organization and Material Culture of Minoan and Mycenaean Civilizations 44

Art and Technology of Minoan and Mycenaean Civilizations 45

Minoan Costume for Men and Women: 2900–1150 B.C. 45

Costume Components for Men and Women 45

Minoan Costume for Children: 2900–1150 B.C. 47

Transitions in the Dominant Styles 47

Greek Civilization 47

Historical Background 47

Social Organization of the Greek Civilization 48

Fabrics and Cloth Production 49

Sources of Evidence for the Study of Greek Costume 49

Greek Art 49

Greek Costume for Men and Women: 800–300 B.C. 50

Costume Components for Men and Women 51

Table 3.1 Types of Chitons Worn by Greek Men and Women 51

Illustrated Table 3.1 Examples of Hairstyles and Headdress Worn by Men and Women in Greece 53

Contemporary Comments 3.1 55

Greek Costume for Children: 800–300 B.C. 55

Contemporary Comments 3.2 56

Costume Components for Children 56

Greek Costume for Specialized Occupations or Occasions 57

Wedding Dress 57

Military Costume 58

Theatrical Costume 58

Summary 58

Themes 58

Visual Summary Table 59

Later Survivals of Greek Dress 59

Notes 60

Selected Readings 60

CHAPTER FOUR

Etruria and Rome c. 800 B.C.–A.D. 400 63

Chronology 62

The Etruscans 64

Historical Background 64

Social Life of the Etruscans 64

Art and Trade of the Etruscans 64

Etruscan Costume for Men and Women: c. 800–200 B.C. 65

Costume Components for Men and Women 65

Etruscan Costume for Children: c. 800–200 B.C. 67

The Romans 67

Historical Background 67

Social Life in the Roman Empire 68

Fabrics and Clothing Production 68

Table 4.1 The Appearance and Significance of Various Types of Togas 69

Sources of Evidence for the Study of Roman Costume 69

Roman Costume for Men and Women 70

The Toga 70

Contemporary Comments 4.1 73

Costume Components for Men: 500 B.C.–A.D. 400 73

Costume Components for Women: 500 B.C.–A.D. 400 74

Costume Components for Men and Women: 500 B.C.–A.D. 400 75

Illustrated Table 4.1 Examples of Hairstyles and Headdress Worn by Men and Women During the Roman Empire 76

Roman Costume for Children: 500 B.C.–A.D. 400 77

Military Costume for Men During the Roman Empire 78

Roman Costume for Special Events 78

The Synthesis 78

Bridal Costume 78

Religious Garb 78

Changes in Costume During the Declining Years of the Roman Empire 79

Summary 79

Differences Between Greek, Etruscan, and Roman Costume 79

Themes in Etruscan and Roman Dress 79

Visual Summary Table 80

Survivals of Etruscan and Roman Dress 80

Notes 81

Selected Readings 81

PART TWO

THE MIDDLE AGES C. 300–1500 83

CHAPTER FIVE

The Early Middle Ages c. 300 – 1300 87

Chronology 86

The Byzantine Period c. 330–1453 88

Historical Background 88

Social Organization in the Byzantine Period 88

Culture, Art, and Technology in the Byzantine Period 88

Byzantine Costume for Men: A.D. 300–1450 90

Costume Components for Men 90

Byzantine Costume for Women: A.D. 300–1453 92

Costume Components for Women 92

*Byzantine Costume for Men and Women:
    A.D. 300–1450 93*

Costume Components for Men and Women 93

*Western Europe from the Fall of the Roman Empire
    to A.D. 900 94*

Historical Background: The Fall of the Roman Empire 94

Historical Background: The Merovingian and Carolingian
    Dynasties 94

Sources of Evidence About Costume 95

*Costume in Western Europe: Fall of the Roman
    Empire to A.D. 900 95*

The Production of Cloth 95

*Costume for Men: The Merovingian and Carolingian
    Dynasties 95*

Contemporary Comments 5.1 96

Costume Components for Men: The Merovingian Period 96

Costume Components for Men: The Carolingian Period 96

*Costume for Women: The Merovingian and Carolingian
    Dynasties 96*

Costume Components for Women: The Merovingian Period 96

Costume Components for Women: The Carolingian Period 97

Clerical Costume in the Early Middle Ages 97

Dress of Priests 98

Monastic Dress 98

Historical Background: The 10th–13th Centuries 99

The Feudal Monarchies 99

Political Developments in Europe: 900–1300 99

The German Dynasties 99

Anglo-Saxon and Norman Britain 99

The French Kings 101

Factors Related to Developments in Costume 101

The Crusades 101

Medieval Castles and Courts 101

Town Life 101

Fabric Production 101

Art 102

Costume in the 10th and 11th Centuries 102

Costume Components for Men: 10th and 11th Centuries 102

Costume Components for Women: 10th and 11th Centuries 104

Costume for Men and Women: 12th Century 105

Costume Components for Men: 12th Century 105

Costume Components for Women: 12th Century 107

Problems of Costume Terminology in the 13th Century 108

Costume in the 13th Century 108

Costume Components for Men: 13th Century 108

Contemporary Comments 5.2 109

Table 5.1 Old English and French Costume Terms 110

Costume for Women: 13th Century 113

*Accessories of Dress for Men and Women:
    10th–13th Centuries 114*

Military Costume 114

Summary 115

Themes 115

Visual Summary Table 116

Origins, Developments, and Survivals of Byzantine
    and Early Medieval Styles 117

Notes 118

Selected Readings 118

CHAPTER SIX
The Late Middle Ages c. 1300 – 1500 121

Chronology 120

Historical Background 122

Medieval Social Structure 122

The Peasant 122

The Nobility 123

The Bourgeoisie 124

Fabrics and Tailors 124

Sources of Evidence for the Study of Costume 124

Art 124

Contemporary Comments 6.1 125

Documentary Sources 125

Fashion Change Becomes Evident 125

Costume for Men: 14th Century 126

Costume Components for Men: 14th Century 126

Costume for Women: 14th Century 129

Costume Components for Women: 14th Century 129

Costume for Men and Women: 15th Century 131

Costume for Men: 15th Century 131

Contemporary Comments 6.2 132

Costume for Women: 15th Century 134

Costume for Children: 14th and 15th Centuries 136

Mourning Costume for Men and Women 137

Costume for Specialized Occupations 138

Student Dress 138

*Illustrated Table 6.1 Evolution and Styles of 15th-Century
    Headdress for Women 139*

Military Dress 140

Illustrated Table 6.2 Late Middle Age Accessories 141

Summary 142

Themes 142

Survivals of Styles from the Late Middle Ages 142

Visual Summary Table 143

Notes 144

Selected Readings 145

PART THREE
THE RENAISSANCE C. 1400–1600 147

CHAPTER SEVEN
The Italian Renaissance c. 1400–1600 151

   Chronology 150

   Historical Background 152

   The Political Organization in Renaissance Italy 152

   Life in Renaissance Italy 152

   The Production and Acquisition of Textiles 153

   The Cloth Industries in Renaissance Italy 153

   The Manufacture and Acquisition of Clothing 153

   Cross-Cultural Influences from the Middle East 153

   Sources of Evidence About Costume 154

   Costume for Men and Women: 1400–1600 154

   Costume for Men: 1400–1450 154

   Costume for Women: 1400–1450 154

   Costume for Men: 1450–1500 154

   Contemporary Comments 7.1 156

   Costume for Women: 1450–1500 159

   Costume for Men and Women: 16th Century 159

   Costume for Men: 16th Century 160

   Illustrated Table 7.1 Italian Renaissance: Accessories 162

   Costume for Women: 16th Century 162

   Regional Distinctions in Costume for Men
      and Women: 15th and 16th Centuries 163

   Distinctive Venetian Costume for Women 163

   Distinctive Venetian Costume for Men 163

   Venetian Dress for Officials 163

   Contemporary Comments 7.2 164

   Costume for Children During the Italian Renaissance 164

   Summary 165

   Themes 165

   Visual Summary Table 166

   Survival of Italian Renaissance Styles 167

   Notes 167

   Selected Readings 167

CHAPTER EIGHT
The Northern Renaissance c. 1500 – 1600 169

   Chronology 168

   Historical Background 170

Developments in Germany 170

Developments in Spain 170

Developments in England 171

Developments in France 171

Factors in the Dissemination of Fashion Information 171

Table 8.1 Royal Intermarriages During the 16th Century 172

Cross-Cultural Influences from the Middle East 172

Textiles 172

Changes in Technology 172

Decorative Techniques of the 16th Century 172

Sources of Evidence for the Study of Costume 173

Art 173

Documentary Sources 173

Actual Garments 173

Costume for Men and Women: 16th Century 173

Costume for Men: 1500–1515 174

Costume for Men: 1515–1550 175

Costume for Men: 1550–1600 175

Costume for Women: 16th Century 178

Costume for Women: 1500–1530 179

Contemporary Comments 8.1 180

Costume for Women in Germany: 1530–1575 180

Costume for Women in Other Northern European
    Countries: 1530–1575 181

Costume Components for Women: 1575–1600 183

Costume Accessories for Men and Women:
   16th Century 185

Illustrated Table 8.1 Northern Renaissance: Accessories 186

Costume for Children: 16th Century 187

Summary 188

Themes 188

Visual Summary Table 189

Survivals of 16th Century Dress 190

Notes 190

Selected Readings 190

PART FOUR
BAROQUE AND ROCOCO C. 1600–1800 193

   The Arts During the Baroque and Rococo Periods 193

   Expanding Trade with the Far East 194

   The Cotton Trade with India 195

   The Industrial Revolution 196

   The Consumer Society and the Acceleration
      of Fashion Change 196

CHAPTER NINE
The Seventeenth Century 1600–1700 199

   Chronology 198

   Historical Background 200

France 200

England 200

Social Life During the 17th Century 201

The French Court 201

England 201

Holland 201

America 202

Some Distinctive Costume Traditions 202

Puritan Costume 202

Spanish Costume 202

Production and Acquisition of Textiles and Clothing 203

Sources of Evidence of Historic Costume 204

Costume for Men: 17th Century 204

Table 9.1 Terms Describing Men's Trouser-Type Garments: 16th Century to 19th Century 205

Costume for Men: 1625–1650 206

Costume for Men: 1650–1680 207

Costume for Men: 1680–1710 208

Contemporary Comments 9.1 209

Costume for Women: 17th Century 210

Costume for Women: 1630–1660 210

Illustrated Table 9.1 9th–17th Centuries Accessories 211

Costume for Women: 1660–1680 213

Costume for Women: 1680–1700 213

Contemporary Comments 9.2 216

Costume for Men and Women: 17th Century 217

Costume for Children: 17th Century 217

Costume Components for Children 219

Summary 220

Themes 220

Survivals of 17th Century Styles 220

Visual Summary Table 221

Notes 222

Selected Readings 222

CHAPTER TEN
The Eighteenth Century 1700–1790 225

Chronology 224

Historical Background 226

The Arts 226

Social Life in 18th Century France 226

Social Life of the Affluent in 18th Century England 227

Contemporary Comments 10.1 228

Production and Acquisition of Clothing and Textiles 228

Advances in Textile Technology 228

Home Versus Factory Production of Cloth 228

Clothing Manufacture and Sale 228

Sources of Information About Costume 229

The American Colonies in the 18th Century 229

Urban Clothing Styles 229

Working Class and Rural Dress 229

Some Influences on Costume in the 18th Century 229

Costume for Men: 18th Century 230

Costume for Men: Up to Mid-18th Century 231

Contemporary Comments 10.2 232

Changes in Men's Costume After the Mid-18th Century 233

Costume for Men: After the Mid-18th Century 233

Costume for Women: 18th Century 235

Illustrated Table 10.1 Typical Women's Hairstyles and Headdress in the 18th Century 236

Costume for Women: 1715–1730 237

Costume for Women: 1730–1760 239

Costume for Women: 1760–1790 239

Contemporary Comments 10.3 240

Other Costume Components for Women: The 18th Century 243

Costumes for Active Sports for Men and Women: The 18th Century 244

Costume for Children: The 18th Century 244

First Half of the 18th Century 244

Second Half of the 18th Century 244

Illustrated Table 10.2 18th Century Accessories 245

Summary 248

Themes 248

Survivals of 18th Century Dress 248

Visual Summary Table 249

Notes 250

Selected Readings 250

PART FIVE
THE NINETEENTH CENTURY 1800–1900 253

Historical Background 253

France 253

England 253

Italy and Austria 253

The United States 254

Industrialization 255

Cross-Cultural Influences on Fashion 256

Textiles from India 256

Resumption of Trade with Japan 257

Morality and Values in the 19th Century 257

Dress Reform for Women 258

Changes in Clothing for Men 258

The End of an Age 259

CHAPTER ELEVEN
The Directoire Period and the Empire Period 1790–1820 261

Chronology 260

Historical Background 262

France: The Revolution and the Directory 262

France: The Empire 264

England 264

The United States 264

The Arts and Costume Styles of the Period 265

The Revolution in Men's Clothes 265

Contemporary Comments 11.1 266

Production and Acquisition of Clothing and Textiles 267

Sources of Information About Costume 267

Costume for Women: Directoire and Empire Periods 267

Costume for Men: Directoire and Empire Periods 270

*Illustrated Table 11.1 Typical Women's Hairstyles and
    Headdress in the Empire Period* 271

Illustrated Table 11.2 Empire Period: Accessories 272

Costume for Children: The Empire Period 274

Costume for Girls 274

Costume for Boys 275

Summary 275

Themes 275

Survivals of Empire Style Costume 275

Notes 276

Visual Summary Table 277

Selected Readings 277

CHAPTER TWELVE
The Romantic Period 1820–1850 279

Chronology 278

Historical Background 280

England 280

France 280

The United States 281

Women's Social Roles and Clothing Styles 281

Manufacture and Acquisition of Clothing and Textiles 282

Sources of Evidence About Costume 282

Costume for Women: The Romantic Period 282

Costume for Women: 1820–1835 282

Costume for Women: 1836–1850 286

*Illustrated Table 12.1 Examples of Women's Hairstyles and
    Headdress: 1820–1850* 288

Costume Components for Women: 1820–1850 289

Costume for Men: The Romantic Period 290

Costume for Men: 1820–1840 290

Costume for Men: 1840–1850 291

Costume for Men: 1820–1850 292

Illustrated Table 12.2 Romantic Period: Accessories 294

Costume for Children: The Romantic Period 295

Costume Components for Girls 295

Costume Components for Boys 295

Clothing for Slaves in North America 295

Contemporary Comments 12.1 297

Summary 298

Themes 298

Visual Summary Table 299

Survivals of Romantic Period Costume Styles 300

Notes 300

Selected Readings 300

CHAPTER THIRTEEN
The Crinoline Period 1850–1869 303

Chronology 302

Worth and the Paris Couture 304

Historical Background 304

England 304

France 304

The United States 305

Production of Clothing: The Sewing Machine 306

*Early Attempts at Dress Reform: The "Bloomer"
    Costume* 307

Gymnastics for Women 307

Contemporary Comments 13.1 308

Sources of Evidence About Costume 308

Costume for Men and Women: The Crinoline Period 309

Costume for Women: 1850–1870 309

*Illustrated Table 13.1 Selected Undergarments for Women, Men,
    and Children from the Second half of the 19th Century* 310

*Illustrated Table 13.2 Typical Women's Hairstyles and
    Headdress: 1850–1870* 314

Costume for Men: 1850–1870 316

Illustrated Table 13.3 Crinoline Period, 1850–1860: Accessories 317

Costume for Children: The Crinoline Period 320

Costume for Boys and Girls: 1850–1870 321

Costume for Boys: After Age Five or Six 321

Summary 323

Themes 323

Survivals of Crinoline Period Costume Styles 323

Visual Summary Table 324

Notes 325

Selected Readings 325

CHAPTER FOURTEEN
The Bustle Period and the Nineties 1870–1900 327

Chronology 326

Historical Background: 1870–1890 328

Historical Background: 1890–1900 328

Social Life: 1870–1900 328

Sports for Women 329

*The Manufacture and Acquisition of Clothing
    and Textiles* 329
Textile Technology 329
Ready-to-Wear Clothing 329
Merchandising of Ready-to-Wear 330
The Visual Arts and Costume 330
Aesthetic Dress 331
Art Nouveau 331
Sources of Evidence About Costume 332
Costume for Women: The Bustle Period, 1870–1890 332
General Features of Women's Costume: 1870–1890 332
Specific Features of Women's Dress Styles During Different
    Phases of the Bustle Period 333
*Illustrated Table 14.1 Selected Undergarments for Men, Women,
    and Children: 1870–1900* 336
Contemporary Comments 14.1 339
*Illustrated Table 14.2 Selected Hats and Hairstyles for
    Women: 1870–1900* 340
Illustrated Table 14.3 Selected Footwear for Women: 1870–1900 342
Costume for Women: The Nineties 343
Costume Components for Women 343
Costume for Men: 1870–1900 347
*Illustrated Table 14.4 Bustle Period and Nineties
    Accessories: 1870–1900* 349
Costume for Children: 1870–1900 350
Costume Components for Girls 350
Costume Components for Boys 350
Costume for Boys and Girls 351
*Table 14.1 Typical Stages in the Acquisition of Adult Clothing
    in the Late 19th Century* 352
*Mourning Costume in the Second Half of the 19th
    Century* 352
Summary 353
Themes 353
Survivals of Bustle and Nineties Costume Styles 353
Visual Summary Table 354
Notes 355
Selected Readings 355

PART SIX
THE TWENTIETH CENTURY 1900–1996 357
    Art and Costume in the 20th Century 358
    New Sources of Evidence for the Study of Costume 359

CHAPTER FIFTEEN
The Edwardian Period and World War I 1900–1920 361
    Chronology 360
    Historical Background 362
    The United States 362

Great Britain and France at the Turn of the Century 362
World War I 362
The Effect of the War on Fashions 362
Influences on Fashion 363
The French Couture and Paul Poiret 363
Fortuny 363
Contemporary Comments 15.1 364
Oriental Influences on Art and Fashion 365
The Changing Social Roles of American Women 365
The Automobile 365
American High Society 365
The Production and Acquisition of Clothing 366
Sources of Information About Costume 366
Costume for Women: 1900–1920 366
Costume Components for Women: 1900–1908 366
*Illustrated Table 15.1 Selected Undergarments for Women, Men,
    and Children: 1900–1920* 368
Costume for Women: 1909–1914 370
Costume for Women: 1914–1918 372
*Illustrated Table 15.2 Selected Hairstyles and Hats for Women:
    1900–1920* 373
Costume for Women: 1918–1920 375
Costume for Men: 1900–1920 375
*Illustrated Table 15.3 Selected Examples of Footwear for Women:
    1900–1920* 376
*Illustrated Table 15.4 Edwardian and World War I, 1900–1920:
    Accessories* 380
Costume for Children: 1900–1920 381
Costume for Girls 381
Costume for Boys 382
Costume for Boys and Girls 382
Summary 383
Themes 383
Survivals of Edwardian and World War I Styles 383
Visual Summary Table 384
Notes 385
Selected Readings 385

CHAPTER SIXTEEN
The Twenties, Thirties, and World War II 1920–1947 387
    Chronology 386
    Historical Background 388
    The Twenties 388
    Changes in the Social Life of the Twenties 388
    The Thirties 389
    World War II 389
    Contemporary Comments 16.1 390

Some Influences on Fashions 390
The Movies 390
Royalty and Cafe Society 391
Sports 391
The Automobile 391
Production and Acquisition of Textiles and Clothing 391
Technological Developments Affecting Fashion 391
The French Couture 392
Table 16.1 Designers of the French Couture: 1920–1947 394
Contemporary Comments 16.2 395
American Designers 395
Théâtre de la Mode 397
Art Movements and Their Influence on Fashion 398
Art Deco 398
Surrealism 398
Sources of Information About Costume 398
Costume for Women: 1920–1947 399
Costume for Women: 1920–1930 399
Illustrated Table 16.1 Selected Undergarments for Women, Men, and Children: 1920–1947 400
Illustrated Table 16.2 Selected Hairstyles and Hats for Women: 1920–1947 404
Costume for Women: 1930–1947 405
Illustrated Table 16.3 Selected Examples of Footwear for Women: 1920–1947 407
Costume for Women: 1920–1947 409
Illustrated Table 16.4 1920–1947: Accessories 411
Costume for Men: 1920–1947 413
Costume for Children: 1920–1947 420
Costume for Girls 420
Costume for Boys 420
Costume for Boys and Girls 420
Illustrated Table 16.5 Children's Clothing Styles: 1920–1947 421
Costume for the Teenage Market 422
Summary 423
Themes 423
Survivals of Styles of the 1920s and 1930s 423
Visual Summary Table 424
Notes 425
Selected Readings 425

CHAPTER SEVENTEEN
The New Look: Fashion Conformity Prevails 1947–1960 427
Chronology 426
Historical Background 428
International Developments: 1947–1960 428
The United States: 1947–1960 429
Influences on Fashion 430
The Silent Generation Moves to the Suburbs 430
Fashion Influences from the Young 430

The Impact of Television 431
Internationalism 432
Production and Acquisition of Clothing and Textiles 433
The Fabric Revolution 433
The Changing Couture 433
Table 17.1 Influential Paris-Based Designers, 1947–1960 434
The American Mass Market 435
New Centers of Fashion Design 435
Costume for Women: 1947–1960 435
Style Features of the New Look 435
Table 17.2 Some Major American Fashion Designers Who Came to Prominence During World War II and Were Important in the 1950s 436
Costume for Women: 1947–1954 437
Illustrated Table 17.1 Selected Undergarments for Women, Men, and Children: 1947–1960 438
Contemporary Comments 17.1 439
Illustrated Table 17.2 Typical Hats for Women: 1947–1960 444
Signs of Silhouette Changes: 1954–1960 444
Costume for Men: 1947–1960 444
Illustrated Table 17.3 Selected Examples of Popular Footwear for Women: 1947–1960 446
Illustrated Table 17.4 1947 to 1960: Accessories 448
Clothing for Active Sports 450
Costume for Children: 1947–1960 451
Costume for Infants and Preschool Children 451
Costume Components for Girls 451
Illustrated Table 17.5 Children's Clothing Styles: 1947–1960 452
Costume for Boys 452
Costume for Boys and Girls 452
Summary 453
Themes 453
Visual Summary Table 454
Survival of New Look Styles 455
Notes 455
Selected Readings 455

CHAPTER EIGHTEEN
The Sixties and Seventies: Style Tribes Emerge 1960–1980 457
Chronology 456
Historical Background 458
Europe and the Soviet Union 458
The Middle East 458
Africa and the End of Colonialism 458
The Emergence of Japan as an Economic Power 458
The United States 459
The Impact of Social Change on Fashion 461
Style Tribes and Street Styles 461
Some Style Tribes of 1960–1980 462

The Women's Movement 463

The Civil Rights Movement 463

Other Influences in Fashion 464

The White House Influences Styles 464

Political Events 464

Table 18.1 Some Media Influences on Fashion: 1960–1980 464

The Space Age 464

The Fine Arts 465

Ethnic Looks 466

The Changing Fashion Industry 466

Increasing Variety in Fashion Segments 467

Attempts to Curb Fashion Changes 467

Changes in Fashion Design 467

Contemporary Comments 18.1 468

Labeling and Licensing 469

Designers of Men's Clothing 469

Costume for Women: 1960–1980 469

Costume for Women: 1960–1974 469

*Table 18.2 Influential Designers in Paris and Other Fashion
    Centers: 1960–1980* 470

*Illustrated Table 18.1 Selected Undergarments for Women,
    Men, and Children: 1960–1980* 473

*Illustrated Table 18.2 Typical Hairstyles and Hats for
    Women: 1960–1980* 475

The Introduction of the Midi: 1970–1974 480

Changes in Costume for Women: 1974–1980 481

*Illustrated Table 18.3 Selected Examples of Popular Footwear
    for Women and Men, 1960–1980* 482

Illustrated Table 18.4 1960–1980: Accessories 484

Contemporary Comments 18.2 485

Costume for Men: 1960–1980 488

Costume for Children: 1960–1980 492

Infants and Toddlers 492

Preschool and School-Age Children 492

Costume for Girls 492

Illustrated Table 18.5 Children's Clothing Styles: 1960–1980 493

Costume for Boys 494

Costume for Boys and Girls 494

Summary 494

Themes 494

Visual Summary Table 495

Survivals of Styles of 1960–1980 496

Notes 496

Selected Readings 496

CHAPTER NINETEEN
*The Eighties and Nineties: Affluence, Information,
and a New Millennium 1980–2003* 499

Chronology 498

Historical Background: International 500

The Cold War Ends 500

Progress Continues Toward European Union 500

War and Peace 500

The Middle East 500

Japanese Economic Influences 501

Historical Background: United States 501

Political and Economic Developments 501

Gore–Bush Presidential Campaign 501

Energy and Environmental Issues 502

The Changing American Family 502

Changes in the Roles of Women 502

The Computer Revolution 503

The New Immigrants 503

AIDS 503

The Fashion Industry Undergoes Changes 504

Postmodernism 504

Elements of the Fashion System 504

*Table 19.1 Some Style Tribes and Their Impact on Mainstream
    Fashion* 506

Changes in the Production and Retailing of Apparel 511

*Table 19.2 Some Prominent Designers Working in Paris and
    Other Fashion Centers: 1980–2003* 512

*Table 19.3 Some American Designers Who Became Prominent
    in the Period 1980–2003* 514

Contemporary Comments 19.1 516

The Fashion Industry in the New Millennium 516

The Origins of Major Fashion Trends of 1980–2003 516

Retro Fashions 516

Various Social Groups Influence Fashion 517

Current Events 518

The Media as a Fashion Influence 519

Table 19.4 Some Media Influences on Fashion: 1980–2003 520

Influences from the Fine Arts 520

Demographic Changes 521

The Trend to Casual Dress 521

Fabrics Old and New 521

Sports 523

Costume Components for Women: 1980–1995 523

Contemporary Comments 19.2 526

*Illustrated Table 19.1 Selected Undergarments for Women
    and Men: 1975–1996* 527

*Illustrated Table 19.2 Typical Hairstyles and Headcoverings
    for Women and Men: 1980–2003* 532

Costume Components for Women: 1995–2003 533

*Illustrated Table 19.3 Selected Examples of Popular Footwear
    for Women, Men, and Children: 1980–2003* 538

Illustrated Table 19.4 Accessories: 1980–2003 539

Costume for Men: 1974–2003 540

Costume Components for Men 540

Costume for Children: 1980–2003 544

Infants and Preschool-Age Children 544

Illustrated Table 19.5 Children's Clothing Styles:
*   1980–2003 545*

School-Aged Children: Trends Affecting Boys and Girls 547

Costume Components for Girls 547

Costume Components for Boys 547

Summary 548

Visual Summary Table 549

Notes 550

Selected Readings 550

Bibliography 552

Index 559

PREFACE

Each new edition of a book provides opportunities to satisfy needs that earlier editions did not address. The fourth edition brings this survey of Western dress to 2003 and adds a number of new features.

Survey of Historic Costume is intended for use as a basic text for readers who desire an overview of the history of costume in the West. We continue to emphasize the subtitle, *A History of Western Dress*, so that readers will recognize that the book focuses on historic costume in the Western world and makes no attempt to survey the vast topic of historic costume in all parts of the world. Our purpose is to present a *survey* of this vast subject rather than an infinitely detailed picture. At the same time, it is our intention to make that picture as complete as possible within the limitations of space.

Dress of each era must be viewed within the context of the period. To assist readers who may have a limited background in history, a brief summary of the major historical developments related to the chapter is provided. Clothing is a part of the basic equipment for everyday life and so in each chapter, brief note is made of some of the important aspects of the life of people of the time. Where the arts, specific individuals, events, or societal values can be seen to influence styles, these are discussed. The technology and economy of the production and distribution of fabrics often influences clothing, therefore changes in technology for the making of cloth and clothes and in the economic systems of production and distribution are noted where these are appropriate. As the fashion industry becomes more complex in the twentieth century, changes in its organization and function are stressed.

After the setting has been delineated, specific styles of each period worn by men, by women, and by children are described. Organization and contents are parallel in all chapters, and all elements of dress, ranging from undergarments to accessories, are included for every period. In this way a rather detailed picture of costume can be provided even within the space limitations imposed on a single volume.

We also believe that it is important for readers to have depictions of costume from original source materials available not only to illustrate some of the unfamiliar terms, but also to supplement the general, survey approach of the text. The captions of the illustrations not only identify various parts of the costume and provide the contemporary names for elements of the styles, but also identify the aspects of the pictures that provide supporting evidence to the costume historian of the nature of costume at this period. The material in the captions of illustrations is as important as the contents of the book and should be read as carefully as the text.

Tables and illustrated tables are utilized throughout the book in an attempt to summarize material more briefly and effectively. Each chapter includes at least one box in which comments from contemporary sources on some aspect of clothing are reproduced. These quotations are intended to provide readers with a flavor of the attitudes toward clothing of individuals of the period as well as contemporary descriptions.

Historic costume reference books and materials (particularly for some of the early periods where actual records are confusing, contradictory, and scarce) show marked differences in terminology and content. We have attempted to present as accurate a summary as possible and one that we hope is free from the tendency to present largely apocryphal stories of the origins of styles as fact. When such material is introduced, it is clearly labeled as questionable or as legend.

In this text, the terms **clothes** and **clothing** are synonymous and mean wearing apparel. **Dress** is a general term that includes not only garments, but also aspects of personal appearance that can be changed, such as grooming. **Style** is the predominant form of dress of any given period or culture. Styles may persist for very long or shorter periods of time. **Fashion** is synonymous with style after the latter part of the Medieval period but implies styles of relatively short duration. **Costume** is the style of dress peculiar to a nation, a class, or a period.

Bibliographies at the end of each chapter are intended to serve three purposes. They list books that contain a good cross-section of illustrations of original source materials for costumes of the period covered in that chapter. They identify books that provide a more complete picture of life in the period covered so that those who desire can learn more about the period. Finally, periodical articles dealing with costume or related topics are cited. The purpose of including such articles is to introduce students to some of the journals that are sources of further information about costume and also to provide some of the detailed analyses of costume topics that are not possible in a text that surveys so broad a topic.

A bibliography at the end of the book lists some of the many books written about historic costume, organized by topic. This bibliography does not duplicate materials listed at the end of each chapter, nor does it include books dealing with techniques of theatrical costuming or sociocultural aspects of dress.

Several tools have been provided for readers. Each chapter contains a chronology listing important dates and events in the order in which they occurred. Many of the words for items of historic costume are foreign terms. Where the pronunciation of these terms is not obvious, a phonetic pronunciation of the word is provided in parentheses just after the word.

New features in this edition are many. The text and illustrations have been updated to 2003. The results of recent research have been incorporated in the text where they are relevant. New illustrations have been added throughout. The most important of these are the Visual Summary Tables that present a visual and verbal summary for each chapter. The idea of recurring themes or concepts in dress introduced in the third edition continues, as do the sections that identify and illustrate later revivals of styles from each period.

The index is organized so that it can be utilized as a glossary of terms. Terms printed in boldface type are defined within the text; the page numbers printed in bold type immediately after these words in the index are the pages on which these words are defined or explained.

Two supplementary publications are available for those using this book as an academic textbook. One is an *Instructor's Guide*, the other is a *Power Point Program*. Both can be obtained from the publisher. The *Instructor's Guide* provides information about sources of slide and video materials that complement and amplify this book and Websites that provide information about costume, as well as suggested teaching strategies and evaluative techniques.

The PowerPoint program is an interactive visual presentation. Beginning with early civilizations in Mesopotamia and Egypt and ending in 2003, the program parallels the organization of the book as it reviews the geographic, economic, and artistic context for each culture and period in the history of Western dress. Visuals provide users with a wide array of primary source images, many in color, from all periods in combination with drawings and diagrams showing the structure of clothing, and photographs of actual garments. A special feature is the inclusion of links to the Internet for additional visuals and further research and study.

ACKNOWLEDGMENTS

No person, even after a lifetime of study, can be expected to be knowledgeable in all aspects of historic costume solely on the basis of his or her own research. Fortunately there are many individuals who have specialized in certain countries or periods and whose work has been invaluable in the preparation of a broad survey of this type. It is important that these sources be given special acknowledgment beyond a citation in footnotes or a listing in the bibliography.

Elizabeth Barber's books on prehistoric textiles, which contain both the results of the most recent scholarship and her interesting insights, were very useful. For materials dealing with costume of the ancient world, the books of Mary Houston and Lillian Wilson were of inestimable help, while the work of Gillian Vogelsang-Eastwood on Egyptian dress and of Judith Sebesta and LarissaBonfante (editors) on Roman dress added new information. The work of Larissa Bonfante served as a basis for much of the material on Etruscan costume and related Greek styles.

For the Medieval period, Joan Evans' work on costume of the Middle Ages and the fine handbook by Phillis and Cecil Willet Cunnington were invaluable. Goddard's work on French costume of the 11th and 12th centuries also provided useful information, as did works by Piponnier and Mane and by Koslin and Snyder.

Elizabeth Birbiri's fine study of Italian Renaissance costume provided not only detailed information but a wealth of excellent illustrative materials, as did the work of Heard. For the 16th through the 19th centuries, the several volumes of handbooks on costume by the Cunningtons, and that by Mrs. Cunnington and Alan Mansfield for the 20th century, were among the most useful of the materials cited. Not only were they a superlative source for detailed information, but they were also a helpful tool for cross-checking conflicting information.

For men's wear of the 20th century the *Esquire Encyclopedia of Men's Clothing* was by far the most useful secondary source an author or researcher could find with its wealth of detailed information quoted directly from the fashion press and its many illustrations from the periods covered in this book. For women's fashions in the 20th century, probably the most extensive reference prepared to date is *Vogue History of 20th Century Fashion*. For information about fashion designers, *Who's Who in Fashion* by Anne Stegemeyer were invaluable.

Underclothing has been thoroughly illustrated and explored in the books by C. W. Cunnington, Nora Waugh, and Elizabeth Ewing. Waugh's work is especially helpful in its inclusion of quotations from the literature of various periods concerning different types of undergarments. For some specialized material in the area of bathing costume, Claudia Kidwell's monograph was useful, as was the work she and Marjorie Christman did on American ready-to-wear.

The works of François Boucher and Millia Davenport should be noted for their wealth of illustrative material drawn from sources from the various periods, although we recommend that readers approach these books armed with a magnifying glass.

A number of scholars have explored the many complex changes that fashion has undergone in the twentieth and twenty-first centuries. We note particularly the work of Ted Polemus, Amy de la Haye, and Cathie Dingwall on "style tribes," Diana Crane's insightful work on the contemporary fashion system, as well Valerie Steele's corpus of work.

Books on subjects related to fashion and fashion design in the recent past have proliferated. There are too many to cite specifically, but we do note that the beautiful color illustrations in these books are a boon to students of dress.

Having begun by citing some of the books to which we are indebted, it is perhaps appropriate to acknowledge next the various libraries that were especially helpful. Because the new edition is built on the foundations of the first and second editions, persons instrumental in the preparation of those editions should be acknowledged once again. The resources of the Costume Institute Library of the Metropolitan Museum of Art were most helpful from the first edition, when the late Gordon Stone, formerly librarian, gave the project much time and energy to this edition when the staff was again most helpful. Librarians from the following institutions have assisted with all editions: the Pierpont Morgan Library in New York City, the research library of the New York Public Library, the Queens College Library, the Port Washington Public Library, the library of the Fashion Institute of Technology, Alderman Library and Darden Graduate School of Business Administration Library, University of Virginia, and the Charlottesville branches of the Jefferson-Madison Regional Library. For this edition, we also thank the Briarcliff Public Library, the Westchester Public Library system, and the library of Westchester Community College.

Some individuals also deserve special recognition. The late Vincent Tortora took many of the photographs used in this and previous editions and also reviewed and corrected phonetic pronunciations. His encouragement and contributions from the first to the present edition made completion of this book possible. We will miss his assistance in future editions.

Don Kurka, artist and Emeritus Professor, University of Tennessee, offered invaluable advice on illustrative material for the chapter opening pages for the 20th Century. We appreciate the willingness of designers Rob Hillested and Charles Kleibacker to provide photographs of their fine work. The late Mitzi Caputo of the Huntington Historical Society,

Huntington, New York, was most helpful in locating photographs for the first to the third editions. We are grateful that Huntington has continued to permit reproduction of images from its collection. Other important assistance in finding illustrative material came from the Cleveland Museum, the Metropolitan Museum of Art Photographic Services Department, and Jeffrey Ryan of the Museum of Modern Art. We express gratitude to the New York Public Library for maintaining the superlative picture collection that is available to researchers. Dover Publications has been very generous in permitting reproduction of images from its books.

We cannot thank individually all of our colleagues and friends who contributed in many ways, but we would like to note that the International Textiles and Apparel Association (ITAA), and the Costume Society of America have consistently provided settings for the reporting of new research and the interchange of ideas with colleagues from around the world, and these opportunities have been much appreciated.

A number of anonymous reviewers had offered suggestions over the many years during which the first edition was developed, and their input continues to influence subsequent editions. Prior to publication of the first edition, Elizabeth Ann Coleman, curator, author, and scholar, did a careful reading and made excellent suggestions to the chapters on the 19th and 20th century.

We express grateful thanks, also, to the many users and readers of previous editions who have made helpful suggestions for revisions. Among those who have consistently offered sound advice are included Patricia Warner of the University of Massachusetts at Amherst, Patricia Cunningham of the Ohio State University, and Linda Welters of the University of Rhode Island who not only offered valuable critiques and suggestions, but willingly shared resources. Other readers selected by the publisher were also very helpful.

Working with Fairchild Books was, as always, a pleasure. Sincere appreciation is due to Olga T. Kontzias, Executive Editor, who once again smoothed the way for this project. Elizabeth Marotta, Production Editor, always displayed cheerful efficiency and skill as she facilitated a variety of tasks. Suzette Lam organized and managed the preparations for the PowerPoint program, while Claire King, of CVK Engineering, designed, crafted, and produced the handsome PowerPoint program, a valuable new supplement to this text. Barbara Chernow of Chernow Editorial Services and her staff, especially Kathy Cleghorn who helped to organize the art for the compositor, moved the book quickly and efficiently from manuscript to finished product. They made the final stages of production seem easy.

2005

Phyllis Tortora
Keith Eubank

Briarcliff Manor, NY and Charlottesville, VA

SOME NOTES ON USING THIS BOOK

Humans select the clothing they wear for many reasons. When one studies the dress of various historical periods one may focus on any or all of a variety of aspects. For some individuals, it is the item of costume itself that is important: How did it look? Of what materials was it constructed? How was it worn? For others the object itself is of lesser importance. Instead, the interest lies in its relationship to the world in which it was worn. What symbolic meaning did it have? What status did it confer? How does it reflect its times? Or, it may be that aesthetic aspects are foremost in the mind of the reader who may be viewing dress as an art form.

For the most part, one looks at costume for some combinations of these reasons. The task of a text of this kind, a survey of the subject, is to attempt to satisfy the needs of all readers. In doing so, some depth is necessarily sacrificed. From this introduction to the topic, individuals can go on to pursue their special interests more intensively, and we have provided lists of resources in each chapter as well as an extensive bibliography at the end of the book. These should enable readers to move beyond this survey to a more specialized look at areas of particular interest.

The first chapter of the book provides a general introduction to dress, to theories about its origins, and to its functions. Common themes (recurring or unifying subjects or ideas) that can be seen in many costume periods are identified and discussed. Readers will encounter many of these themes in subsequent chapters.

To guide readers, we have organized each of the Chapters 2 through 19 in much the same way. An opening page of illustrations of objects from the fine and applied arts such as buildings, furniture, paintings, sculpture, and the like is intended to give readers a sense of the aesthetic of the period. Chronologies summarize important events, developments in the fine or applied arts, and other developments relative to costume history. Chapter textual material begins by providing a brief summary of historical developments in the period under study. Where those periods extend for thousands of years, this summary is written in very broad strokes. With shorter periods, especially those from the recent past, the picture is presented in more detail. Following the setting of historical context, we introduce those sociocultural, artistic, political, economic, and/or technological developments of the period that are relevant to or have influenced costume.

Each chapter also includes one or more readings from contemporary sources about some aspect of dress. From these materials, readers should be able to get a glimpse of attitudes and values about clothing as they were expressed by individuals of that period.

A detailed presentation of the specifics of costume for each period for men, women, and children follows the contextual materials. These details begin with a description of the silhouette or predominant lines. From silhouette, the reader moves on to a comprehensive review of types of clothing in the period under study.

Each chapter ends with a summary that identifies some of the themes that are most evident in that chapter, as well as a discussion of revivals of style elements that are evident in later periods.

In any work dealing with costume, the illustrations are particularly important. This work contains several different types of illustrations. In the body of each chapter, illustrations come as much as possible from works of art, drawings, or, photographs made at the time being discussed. Where such material is not readily available, re-drawings are based on original sources or work by scholars.

Several types of illustrations in earlier editions have been expanded. Beginning in Chapter 6, illustrated tables that depict important accessory items have been added to illustrated tables of footwear and headwear.

Photographs of works of art from early periods are often difficult to interpret; therefore, visual summaries that consist of clear line drawings had been added at the end of Chapters 2 through 5. When compared to the photographs illustrating the chapters, these drawings should make it easier to understand what scholars believe the silhouette and construction of garments to have been.

Fashion change begins in the late Middle Ages (chapter 6), and styles start to change more rapidly. Beginning with Chapter 6, new *Visual Summary Tables* have been added that consist of brief verbal summaries of the major styles within each period along with a sketch of typical styles. These tables serve as a summary for the period covered in the chapter and are intended to clarify the duration and features of the various fashion trends in each century or decade. By comparing a *Visual Summary Table* from one chapter to that of previous and/or subsequent chapters, changes of fashions over time should be clear.

The aforementioned list of references can lead readers to additional illustrations of the period from primary source materials, books that illuminate the sociocultural context of the period more completely, and some research, scholarly, or other writings about some narrower aspect of costume in this period.

The index has been organized for use as a glossary of terms. Immediately after each term in the index is a page notation in boldface italic type. Readers will find a definition of this term on that page. Words that are defined are printed in boldface type in both the index and the text. Also, as an aid to readers, when new terms for which the pronunciation is not clear are introduced in the text, a phonetic rendering of the pronunciation is provided in parentheses after the word.

Our objective throughout has been to provide a comprehensive survey of historic costume in the Western world, one that can serve as a basis for looking at dress from a variety of perspectives.

INTRODUCTION

THE ORIGINS OF DRESS

The earliest depictions of dress are found in prehistoric cave paintings from the Old Stone Age, or Early Paleolithic Period, some 30,000 years ago. These paintings show little detail. One can say only that clothing appears to have taken the form of draped skirts, cut and sewn trousers, and capelike garments, probably all of which were made from animal skins. Supporting evidence for this conclusion comes from archeologists who have found needles for sewing, bone scrapers for preparing skins, and bone devices that were probably used for fastening clothing in sites dating from the same general period.

The earliest evidence of textile fabrics dates from about 27,000 years ago and consists of imprints of woven material on clay pots (Fowler 1995). The oldest actual textile yet discovered by archeologists dates from about 7000 B.C. It is a white fabric tentatively identified as linen (Wilford 1993). Other remains of woven fabrics from Turkey date from 8,500 years ago. These fabrics were made by rather complex weaving techniques (Mellaart 1963). As a result, archeologists have concluded that for production of textiles to have evolved to the relatively sophisticated level of skill needed to make these particular fabrics, weaving of fabrics must have begun well before this time. If cloth was woven, it was probably made into articles of dress, but no records have been found that describe the form these articles took.

Psychologists and sociologists have attempted to identify the motivations that cause people to dress themselves. There are places in the world where clothing is not essential for survival, and yet most cultures do use some form of dress. The most basic reasons that have been suggested for the wearing of clothing are these: (1) clothing was worn for protection, (2) clothing was worn for decoration, (3) clothing was worn out of modesty, (4) clothing was worn to denote status. Of these four reasons, that of decoration is generally acknowledged to be primary.

Most cultures use dress to denote status, but it is argued that this function probably became attached to dress at some time after it first came into use. Just what constitutes modesty differs markedly from society to society, and what is modest in one part of the world is immodest in another. Modesty, too, may have become associated with dress after its use became widespread.

Protection from the elements is needed, it would seem, for survival, but humans seem to have had their origins in warm, not cold, climates. Not only clothing, but also shelter and fire can provide warmth. Furthermore, people from various geographic areas have differing responses to the temperature of their surroundings.

Another type of protection may be related to the origins and functions of dress: supernatural protection, or protection against the spiritual dangers that are thought to surround each individual. Good luck amulets and charms are worn in most cultures. Aprons to protect the genitals not only from physical harm but also from witchcraft may have evolved into skirts or loincloths in some areas.

The reasons given for believing decoration to be a primary if not *the* most primary motive in human dress are compelling. Although using dress as protection against the elements and evil spirits is not universal, decoration of the human body is. There are cultures in which clothing as such does not exist, but there are no cultures in which some form of decoration does not exist. The logical conclusion is that decoration of the self is a basic human practice. Dressing the body may have grown out of this decoration of the self, and protection, modesty, and status may have been important motivations for the elaboration and development of complex forms of dress.

LIMITATIONS TO THE DESIGN OF GARMENTS

As with any medium, the design of clothing is subject to limitations. Garments have some functional aspects. Except for costumes that have only a ceremonial purpose, the wearer must be able to move, to carry the weight of the costume, and, often, to perform certain duties while wearing the garment. The duties assigned to an individual will have a direct influence on the kind of costume he or she can wear. Affluent men and women with servants to do the work of the household were able to dress in one way, while the servants dressed in costumes more appropriate to the labors they performed.

There are other limitations as well. Although paint and ornaments alone can serve as the prescribed dress in some cultures, more complex dress evolved in most societies. Early peoples may have used skins. The draping qualities of skins are different from that of cloth, and would therefore impose certain restrictions on the shapes of garments that could be constructed.

Once people learned to spin yarns and weave fabrics, these techniques were employed to make clothing. Before the advent of manufactured fibers in the 20th century, only natural materials were available for use. Each of these had inherent qualities that affected the characteristics of fabrics that could be made from it. Some materials such as raffia, made of fibers from an African palm tree, are relatively stiff; other fibers such as cotton, wool, or linen are more flexible.

People in isolated regions were limited to the use of local materials. Trade between regions could bring materials from one part of the world to another. Silk was little known in Europe until the Romans imported it from India and China about the beginning of the Christian era. Cotton plants do not grow in the cool northern climate of Europe and so it was not until after the Crusaders imported limited quantities of cotton fabrics from the Near East that cotton cloth was known in Medieval Europe.

Dress is generally constructed by either draping or tailoring. **Draped dress** is created by the arrangement around the body of pieces of fabric that are folded, pleated, pinned, and/or belted in different ways. Draped clothing usually fits the body loosely. It is thought that draped garments were developed after people learned to weave cloth.

By contrast, the use of skins or leather is thought to have led to the development of **tailored dress.** In tailored garments, pieces are cut and sewn together. They fit the body more closely and provide greater warmth than draped garments; hence they are more likely to be worn in cool climates. Draped costume is more characteristic of warm climates. Some costume combines elements of both draping and tailoring.

Technology has an important impact on costume. Some regions developed spinning and weaving skills to a far greater extent than did others. Many of the changes in costume that came about in Europe and North America after the 18th century can be directly or indirectly attributed to developments such as mechanized spinning and weaving, the sewing machine, and the emergence of the American ready-to-wear industry. The resulting mass production probably helped to simplify styles and speed up fashion changes.

Costume is also limited by the mores and customs of the period. The word "costume" derives from the same root as the word "custom." Persons who violate the dress customs of their culture or even those of their socioeconomic class are often considered to be deviant or asocial—perhaps even mad. George Sand, a French female writer of the 19th century who dressed in men's clothing, was considered to be decidedly eccentric. Psychologists report that mental disturbance often first manifests itself in lack of attention to clothing or in bizarre dressing behavior.

COMMON THEMES IN COSTUME HISTORY ACROSS TIME

A **theme,** in the sense that the word is used here, is "a recurring or unifying subject or idea" (Webster 1988). One can identify many themes that are related to dress. Although the ways in which various themes emerge, develop, and have an impact on dress differ from period to period, a thematic approach to the study of dress may facilitate the comparison of historical periods and can aid in understanding how and why styles developed and changed.

In the pages that follow, specific themes are identified and discussed. These themes are printed in bold type and small capital letters so that they will be readily identifiable. The themes that emerge from what is known of costume in any period are often most clear when that period is viewed retrospectively. For this reason, although each chapter will touch on many themes, a final section of each chapter will summarize, highlight, and discuss some of the themes that stand out for that period.

Individual humans rarely live in isolation, but gather together in social groups. The interactions of individuals living together and communicating on a number of levels have strong influences on how people dress. **SOCIAL LIFE, SOCIAL CLASS STRUCTURE, SOCIAL ROLES** (including those related to **GENDER**), and **CHANGES** and/or **PATTERNS IN SOCIAL BEHAVIOR** (what modern terminology might call **LIFESTYLES**) comprise one set of important themes in the study of dress. In the playing out of these themes many of the functions of dress are evident.

Functions of Dress in the Social Context

Throughout history clothing has served many social purposes. It has been used to differentiate between the sexes, and to designate age as well as occupational, marital, and socioeconomic status, group membership, and other social roles that individuals played.

DESIGNATION OF GENDER DIFFERENCES

One of the most fundamental aspects of dress in most societies is that custom decrees that the dress of men and women be different. These differences reflect culturally determined views of the social roles appropriate to each sex. No universal customs exist that dictate the specific forms of dress for each gender. What is considered appropriate may differ markedly from one civilization or one century to another. From the late Middle Ages until the 20th century in Western Europe, for example, skirted garments (with a few exceptions such as kilts) were designated as feminine dress and breeches or trousers as male dress.

Understanding the part clothing plays in reflecting gender-related issues requires some knowledge about relationships between the sexes in a particular cultural context. Costume historians have explored the topic of gender and dress, paying attention to the complex and intricate interplay of attitudes toward gender roles and the dress of men and women (Kidwell and Steele 1989).

DESIGNATION OF AGE

Sometimes clothing serves to mark age-associated changes. In Western Europe and in European settlements in North America, for example, boys and girls often were dressed alike in their earliest years, but once they reached a designated age, a distinction was made between the dress of boys and girls. In England during the Renaissance, this stage was celebrated in a ritual called **breeching,** when the five- or six-year-old boy was given his first pair of breeches.

Age differentiation may, as in the preceding example, be an established procedure, but it is often less a ritual than an accepted part of the mores of a society. Throughout the 19th century, for example, younger girls wore shorter costumes than their adolescent sisters. During the 1920s and 1930s the wearing of knickers marked a stage of development between childhood and adult life for many young men.

DESIGNATION OF STATUS

A uniform or a particular style of dress frequently designates occupational status. In England, even today, lawyers wear an established costume when they appear in court. The police, fire fighters, postal workers, and some of the clergy are but a few of those whose dress may identify them as members of a particular profession. Sometimes the uniform worn also serves a practical function, as, for example, the fire fighter's waterproof coat and protective helmet or the construction worker's hard hat.

Dress designating occupational status is not limited to a "uniform." For many years, particularly during the 1950s and 1960s, men employed by certain companies in the United States were required to wear white shirts with ties to work. Colored shirts were not permitted. Young lawyers who, on first entering the practice of law, went to a menswear store and requested "a lawyer's suit" found that the salespersons knew exactly what they wanted.

Marital status may be indicated by customs of dress. In Western society, a wedding ring worn on a specific finger may signify marital status. Among the Amish, an American religious group, married men wear beards while unmarried men do not. For many centuries, it was customary for married women to cover their hair, while young unmarried women were permitted to go without head coverings.

In some cultures or during some historical periods certain types of clothing have been restricted to persons of a particular rank and social and economic status. These restrictions were sometimes codified into **sumptuary laws.** Sumptuary laws restrict the use of or expenditures on luxury goods such as clothing and household furnishings. During the 14th century in England persons who worked as servants to "great men" were required to limit the cost of their clothing, nor were they permitted to wear any article of gold or silver, embroidery, or silk (Scott 1975).

In Ancient Rome only the male Roman citizen was permitted to wear the costume called the toga, which identified his sociopolitical status.

IDENTIFICATION OF GROUP MEMBERSHIP

Dress is also used to identify an individual as belonging to a particular social group. A uniform or insignia may be adopted formally by that group and kept for its members alone, as in the uniforms of fraternal groups such as the Masons or Shriners, or religious groups such as the Amish of today or the Puritans of the 17th century. At other times, group identification is demonstrated by an informal kind of uniform, such as those adopted by adolescents who belong to the same clique, or the "zoot suits" affected by certain groups of young persons during the early 1940s.

CEREMONIAL USE OF CLOTHING

Ceremonies are an important part of the structure of most societies and social groups. Designated forms of dress are frequently an important part of any ceremony. Sociologists speak of rites of passage, ceremonies marking the passage of the individual from one status to another. Often these require the wearing of designated garments. Specific costumes exist in modern American society that are considered appropriate for weddings, baptisms, burials, to designate mourning, and for graduation. Other ceremonies that serve to strengthen the community, called rites of intensification, may involve special clothing. For example, when the bicentennial of the founding of a town is celebrated, townspeople often dress in the costumes of the period of the founding of the town. Many significant moments of life are accompanied by the wearing of culturally specified ritual costume.

ENHANCEMENT OF SEXUAL ATTRACTIVENESS

Clothing is also a means of enhancing sexual attractiveness of individuals. In some cultures this is quite explicit, with clothing focusing attention on the breasts of women or genitals of men. In many periods women have padded dresses to make the bosom appear larger or have worn dresses with very low necklines designed to call attention to the breasts. At other times the waist, the hips, or the legs have been emphasized. James Laver (1950), a well-known costume historian, believed that fashion changes in women's dress were a result of "shifting erogenous zones." His theory was that women uncovered different parts of the body selectively in order to attract men; for example, as men became used to seeing more of the breasts, this area lost its interest and power to excite and so was covered while another area, such as the hips, was emphasized.

Laver also suggested that sexual attractiveness might lie in other aspects of dress. Men in modern, Western society, he said, are considered attractive when they appear from their dress to be affluent and successful.

Clothing as a Means of Social Communication

The foregoing discussion of the functions of dress leads to the conclusion that dress serves as a means of communication. To the person who is knowledgeable about a particular culture, dress is a silent language. It tells the observer something about the organization of the society in which it is worn. It discloses the social stratification of the society, revealing whether there are rigid delineations of social and economic class or a classless society. For example, the political leaders in the African Ashanti tribe wore distinctive costumes marking their special status. Any subject who wore the same fabric pattern as the king would be put to death. In contrast, the costume of American political leaders does not differ from that of most of the rest of the population. The political distinctions between the two cultures—the one an absolute monarchy, the other a democracy—are mirrored in the clothing practices.

Other aspects of social organization may be manifest in dress. The garments worn by religious leaders may distinguish them from worshippers or may show no differentiation. The roles of men and women may be distinctly identified by dress (as in some Islamic countries that require women to be veiled). Alternatively, when the social roles of men and women are not clearly defined, there may not be sharp distinctions in the customary dress of the sexes. For example, since the 1920s in Europe and North America women have been free to wear trousers, a garment previously reserved for men.

The Historical Context

Most writing about historic dress provides modern readers with some context for the period in which costumes were worn. In this text, the introductory historical background sections set that context. Within the historical background of each period, one of the recurring themes is POLITICS, a term

meaning "of or concerned with government." Governments and political leaders often have a strong impact on the lives of individuals under their influence and can affect clothing styles either directly or indirectly. Such political influences may range from laws restricting wearing of actual items of dress or regulation of clothing-related industries, to the desire of individuals or groups to imitate clothing worn by a charismatic political leader. Examples of the impact of politics on dress include the banning of imported kashmir shawls by the Emperor Napoleon in the early 19th century, the revival of interest in homburg hats that followed President Eisenhower's wearing of this hat to his inauguration, or the popularity of the fashion designer Charles Worth in the mid-1800s after the Empress Eugenie began wearing clothes he had designed.

Unfortunately another common theme in history is POLITICAL CONFLICT, often the cause of wars. Warfare may restrict access to the raw materials needed for apparel or produce the opposite effect and by introducing new materials and ideas, result in the expansion of apparel alternatives. The disappearance of nylon from the consumer market during World War II when it was diverted for use in wartime equipment, or the adoption of the trench coat, an item of military dress, after World War I are examples.

Another important theme in history is ECONOMIC EVENTS, which include TRADE. Economic events may be the result of political policy or may be shaped by unexpected occurrences such as disease or the discovery of valuable natural resources. Such themes were evident when the economic Depression of the 1930s was accompanied by a shift from ornate, decorative clothing to more subdued styles, or when the opening of the silk trade with China by the Romans by the end of the first century B.C. made this fabric available to the upper-class Romans.

Another theme closely related to economics is the PRODUCTION AND ACQUISITION OF TEXTILES AND APPAREL. Textiles are the raw materials from which many elements of dress are created. This is a theme that is quite literally woven throughout the history of costume. One dramatic example from the 19th and early 20th centuries was the development of mass production of clothing in the United States, which made possible the modern fashion industry.

The theme of TECHNOLOGY is often related to the production of textiles and apparel. Technology may also have an impact on areas such as transportation, communications, or production of consumer goods, each of which, in turn, may influence dress. Examples range from the invention of the sewing machine, without which mass production would have been impossible, to the development of the automobile, which probably encouraged the wearing of shorter skirts by women.

As has been noted, dress can be a form of communication. But it is also the subject of communication. Information about dress can be transmitted through a variety of MEDIA OF

COMMUNICATION. Over the centuries, the media by which information has been transmitted have changed. The impact of those changes on dress is another theme to be explored. Photography, motion pictures, and television can be cited as examples of 19th and 20th century media that both communicated information about dress and also influenced it.

Cross-Cultural Influences

In an article suggesting new approaches to the teaching of history of costume, Jasper and Roach-Higgins remind us that unless we include the historical traditions of Asia, the Near East, Africa, and North and South America before Columbus, we are studying the history of Western costume (Jasper and Roach-Higgins 1987). Although many non-Western areas have adopted Western dress to a greater or lesser extent, most of these regions retain distinctive traditions in dress. From the first to the last chapters of this text, readers will see how when one culture comes into contact with another, "foreign" styles can be influential. Cross-cultural influences may come about through war, trade, travel, immigration, or through the medium of communication.

Roach and Musa (1980) call styles that incorporate components from several cultures **mixtures.** Erekosima and Eicher (1981) suggest the term **cultural authentication** to identify the process "whereby elements of dress of one culture are incorporated into the dress of another." Usually the culturally authenticated style is changed in some way. Only rarely are entire garments adopted. The steps in this process that were identified by Erekosima and Eicher include *selection* of an item of dress from another culture, *characterization* of the item by giving it a name, *incorporation* of the item into its possessions by a particular group, and *transformation* of the item by making some changes from the original.

The fashion designer who incorporates ethnic styles into fashionable garments is participating in cultural authentication of the styles that inspired the design, just as the fashionable ladies of the Empire period did when they "borrowed" Middle Eastern turbans for their head dress in the early 19th century.

Many cultures and ethnic groups have contributed to and influenced all aspects of life in the Western world. The study of historic costume can sometimes provide a visual representation of some of these "multicultural" contributions. Hence the theme of CROSS-CULTURAL INFLUENCES IN DRESS grows out of a recognition that Western society, or any one country or other political entity within that society, cannot exist in isolation. As cultures come into contact there is a reciprocal infusion of new ideas, and much of this cross-cultural material is culturally authenticated, resulting in styles that are mixtures. Examples of cross-cultural influences are present in almost every costume period. They include the introduction of tunics to ancient Egypt from abroad, Middle Eastern influences on Renaissance dress, and Chinese influences on American fashions after President Nixon visited China in the early 1970s.

Geography, the Natural Environment, and Ecology

Factors such as GEOGRAPHIC LOCATION, the NATURAL ENVIRONMENT, and ECOLOGY (the relationship of humans to their physical environment) may emerge as themes that are evident in dress. Examples can be seen in preferences for tailored clothing in cold climates and draped clothing in warm environments, or in contemporary avoidance of fur by some consumers as a means of protecting endangered species.

Clothing as an Art Form

Expression through the arts is rooted in a particular culture and historical period. Conventions or customs determine the form and content of art in any given period. Although the human impulse toward expressing feelings through art is universal, the specific expression of an era is determined by a complex mixture of social, psychological, and aesthetic factors often called the *zeitgeist* or spirit of the times.

Artists or designers of a given period all experience many of the same influences; therefore it is not surprising that different art forms from the same era may display similar qualities. These similarities may occur in the decorative motifs that are used, in scale, form, color, and proportion, and in the feelings evoked by works of art. This is certainly true of clothing, and likenesses between dress and architectural forms, furnishings, and the other visual arts are often pointed out. Writers speak of the visual resemblance of the tall, pointed headdresses of northern European women of the late Middle Ages to the tall spires of Gothic cathedrals. The elaborate trimmings applied to Victorian women's dresses have been likened to some of the decoration applied to Victorian furniture. The spare, straight lines of early modern architecture and the work of cubist painters are seen as related to the straight, somewhat square lines of women's clothing in the 1920s, clothing that is frequently ornamented with Art Deco designs similar to those used in architecture and interior design of the period. The result may be expressed as yet another theme for examination: THE RELATIONSHIPS BETWEEN COSTUME OF A PARTICULAR ERA AND DEVELOPMENTS IN THE FINE AND APPLIED ARTS

The modern apparel industry assigns the role of creating new design ideas to fashion designers. Some designers are exceptionally innovative, generating exciting new ideas that the public finds to be in keeping with the current zeitgeist. When this happens, a designer may help to move current fashion in a new direction, a theme that might be called THE RELATION-

SHIP BETWEEN COSTUME AND THE WORK OF INDIVIDUAL ARTISTS AND DESIGNERS. Examples of such influential designers include Paul Poiret before World War I, Gabrielle Chanel in the 1920s, Madeleine Vionnet in the 1920s and 30s, and Christian Dior in the post–World War II period.

At the same time, clothing offers the designer or the wearer a medium of expression with its own forms and techniques. The lines, textures, colors, proportions, and scale of fabric designs and the shapes of garments can and have varied enormously at different times and in different places throughout history. Ideals of human beauty change with changes in the *zeitgeist*. Often individuals use clothing to attempt to conform to the physical ideal of human beauty at a particular time.

Another theme in historic costume grows out of the tendency for dress to play a role in REVIVALS of interest in earlier styles. This phenomenon of deriving contemporary styles from those of an earlier time period may result from factors such as a culture-wide interest in ideas and/or art of an earlier period, from the popularity of films or books, or from political events. Whatever the cause, revivals in clothing styles have been especially notable over the past two centuries and deserve attention. For this reason, each chapter will close with a discussion of how and where the styles of the period under study survived and were later revived.

The Phenomenon of Fashion in Western Dress

The word "fashion" is often used interchangeably with the words "costume," "dress," or "clothing." **Fashion** is more precisely defined as a taste shared by many for a short period of time. Although fashion as a social phenomenon is not limited to clothing (it can be observed in such diverse aspects of modern life as the design of automobiles, houses, or furniture; in literary styles; and in vacation destinations), it is very much a feature of 20th-century clothing styles. It is also a characteristic of **Western dress,** the dress prevalent in Western Europe and Euro-America since the Middle Ages.

Although acceptance of a style by a large and influential part of the population is characteristic of all costume periods, frequent change of these styles is not. Although occasional exceptions can sometimes be observed in earlier periods, it is generally agreed that fashion as a pervasive social phenomenon first appeared in Western Europe in the Middle Ages. The precise date when fashions began changing more rapidly is debated, but it is clear that by the end of the 15th century, style changes were occurring at least every several decades instead of taking a hundred or more years.

Scholars who have investigated fashion as a social phenomenon agree that for fashion change to occur, a society must have sufficient affluence for a reasonably large number of persons to participate in the fashion process, a class structure that is open enough to allow movement from one social class to another, and a means of communication of fashion information. The history of Western dress in the late Middle Ages and after is a history of fashionable dress worn by affluent people.

As a social phenomenon FASHION is a theme that is integral to all periods after the Middle Ages. This focus on fashionable rather than utilitarian dress is particularly true of the centuries preceding the French Revolution, which began in 1789. Little documentation existed in earlier times of the clothing worn by the poor. Their clothing was worn until it was no longer serviceable. Their portraits were not painted, and they rarely appeared in other art works of these periods. For the 19th and 20th centuries, far more evidence of costume for all levels of society has been preserved, especially after the invention of photography in the 1840s. Then, too, a far wider proportion of the population was wearing fashionable dress. Recent scholarship has shed some light on the dress of slaves, of the rural and urban poor, and of others who by necessity or by choice did not follow fashion.

By the early 20th century, clothing was being mass-produced and, especially in the United States, a complex industry developed that linked together textile production, clothing design and manufacture, and retail distribution of clothing. This **fashion system** has made fashionable clothing available in a wide variety of price ranges. As a result, for most of the 20th century, men and women of all income levels tended to follow current fashions. Consequently, the history of costume in the 20th century is a history of fashionable clothing.

The tendency of most consumers to follow one predominant style line began to change in the decades after the 1960s, leading some to predict "the end of fashion." Fashion did not disappear, but rather became more segmented. As a result, the fashion production and distribution system underwent changes. In such periods and in periods when fashion changes are abrupt or radical, certain aspects of the theme of FASHION may demand special attention.

FASHIONABLE DRESS AND FOLK DRESS

Folk costume is, for purposes of this discussion, defined as the dress of the European peasant class. European **folk costume** had its major flowering and development in the 18th and 19th centuries. The European peasant was the farmer or agricultural worker who lived in rural areas or villages (Webster 1988). Like urban dwellers, peasants could be quite affluent, moderately well off, or very poor. The terms ethnic costume or traditional costume are sometimes used to refer to folk dress.

During the 18th and 19th centuries and in some areas into the 20th century, local communities used traditional textiles and dress forms as a means of setting themselves apart from others. Through the vocabulary of folk dress individuals proclaimed themselves as part of a region or town. Conservative and traditional in its outlook, peasant society stressed conformity and stability rather than change. The Romantic movement in the arts in the 19th century and the adoption of folk costume by royalty in some countries helped to reinforce interest in local dress (Snowden 1979). While folk dress has sometimes influenced fashionable dress and while fashionable elements may appear in folk styles, folk dress in Western Europe diverges from the mainstream of fashionable dress and is not covered in this book. Like non-Western dress, it is too complex and varied a subject to be included in a general survey of Western dress.

SOURCES OF EVIDENCE FOR THE STUDY OF HISTORIC COSTUME

The study of costume, then, must take into account the socioeconomic structure of a society, the customs relating to dress, the art of the period, and the technology available for the production of both fabrics and clothing itself. To obtain this information, the costume historian must utilize the evidence he or she can garner from a variety of sources. Because these SOURCES OF INFORMATION ABOUT COSTUME, another ongoing theme in the study of costume, so often determine what is known about costume, this topic will be given special attention in each chapter.

The sources of evidence used by the costume historian are plentiful for some periods and relatively scarce for others. The further back one goes in history, the less clear and abundant is the historic record. For periods before the 16th century, the major sources of information are sculpture and painting, and, sometimes, written records. Rarely does fabric remain, although there are a few examples of fabrics or clothes from burial sites. Archeological evidence is usually limited to durable items: jewelry, buttons, pins, and/or decorations.

After the invention of printing in the 1500s, written and pictorial records of European costume became more abundant, with even more material being added after the invention of photography in the 19th century. Fabrics and individual items of costume have been preserved since the early Renaissance, although the supply becomes plentiful only around the 18th century. Many items of dress from the early 19th century up to the present have been preserved in museums and costume collections.

To obtain a complete picture of costume in a given era historians must assemble evidence from all of the sources available. These sources must be checked against others, including written as well as pictorial records. Even so, the student of historic costume should be aware of some of the problems involved in obtaining accurate dates for particular styles.

Since many of the representations of costumes from the 18th century and earlier periods come from art works, the artistic conventions of a given period may interfere with accurate representation of dress. For example, it is believed that Egyptian artists depicted women in tight-fitting garments that in actuality were probably worn in a less form-fitting version. Artists such as Gainsborough and Rembrandt enjoyed dressing the persons who were sitting for portraits in fanciful, imaginary costumes. Some paintings done at a later date of earlier historical scenes dressed the figures in costumes the artist imagined were those worn at the time, as when French painters of about 1800 showed scenes from Greek and Roman history and dressed the figures in those paintings according to their perceptions of Greek or Roman styles, with varying historical accuracy.

Sometimes the attribution of a painting to a particular country or date may be in error. Also, standards of modesty may preclude the depiction of certain items of costume, such as underclothing, leaving the costume historian without a record of the appearance of such garments.

Even when fashion magazines of the 19th or 20th centuries are consulted, one must remember "proposed" styles were often shown that may not necessarily have been actually worn at the time. It is a fairly safe assumption that many women copied the fashion plates shown therein, and yet Elizabeth Ann Coleman, Curator Emeritus, Boston Museum of Fine Arts points out that even though skirts with lavish panels of decoration are depicted in fashion magazines of the Crinoline period, few, if any, costumes in collections show this characteristic. Fashion magazines stress the "ideal" and not necessarily the "real."

Nor can written material always be so easily interpreted. Fashion terms with one meaning may take on a different meaning at a later time. The term "pelisse" when used before 1800 usually implied an outdoor garment with some fur trim or lining. In the 19th century, a pelisse was still an outdoor garment, but did not necessarily have fur associated with it. The precise meaning of some terms is lost. The words "kalasiris" in Egypt and "cotehardie" in the Middle Ages are examples of words that have been given a number of different definitions by various costume historians. Writers of earlier periods often used color and fabric names that are no longer understood.

The interpretation of written material cannot always be taken literally. This is particularly true of writing about sumptuary laws that restricted the use of spending on luxury items. These laws were often passed, but were not always enforced. Although such laws may express a certain attitude toward social stratification, society was not always prepared to obey or impose them.

Even photographs must be viewed with a skeptical eye. Many photographs are not reliably dated. People generally dressed in their best clothing to be photographed, so these pictures may not be representative of all types of clothing.

Fashion photographs share some of the problems of fashion drawings in showing "proposed" styles. In addition, camera angles may purposely distort the proportions of garments.

Finally, one must treat even actual garments that remain with some degree of skepticism. Dating of some items may be inaccurate. Persons who donate items to costume collections may give the date of an item on the basis of the ages of the owners during the last years of their lives rather than at the time garments were actually worn. Then, too, a garment may have been remodeled several times, thereby making it difficult to assign an accurate date.

The dating of historic costume, therefore, requires corroborative evidence from a variety of sources. For this reason, one may often encounter conflict between different writers about historic costume as to the precise practices in periods where evidence is scarce or fragmentary.

SUMMARY

Readers can follow the themes identified in the foregoing discussion through the chapters of this text. Headings within each chapter may help to identify material related to some of these themes; however, not all themes will be evident or important in all periods. This is especially true of periods in which data about costume are lacking or unclear or where the historical record is incomplete.

Finally, it must be noted that such recurring topics as have been identified in the preceding discussion do not exist in isolation. Factors that influence dress are often the result of many interconnecting themes. A brief look at one rather simple example may serve to illustrate this point. In 1947, following the end of World War II, designer Christian Dior showed a collection that came to be known as the New Look because it represented a pronounced change from the styles of the wartime years. In considering the speed with which these stylistic changes were adopted, one can identify a number of themes that, working together, helped to promote the new style. Among the themes that can be identified are these: THE RELATIONSHIP BETWEEN COSTUME AND THE WORK OF AN INDIVIDUAL DESIGNER, evident in the presence of a talented and perceptive designer Christian Dior; ECONOMIC EVENTS, which made possible the renewal of production of luxury textile fabrics and their availability to Dior; and the active participation of various MEDIA OF COMMUNICATION, as the fashion press not only named the style but promoted its adoption world wide.

Far more complex relationships can be identified in each of the periods examined in this text. It is these complex interactions that help to make the study of historic costume so fascinating.

NOTES

Barber, E. J. W. 1991. *Prehistoric Textiles*. Princeton, NJ: University Press.

Erekosima, T. and J. Eicher. 1981. "Kalabari 'Cut-thread' and 'Pulled-thread' Clothing: An Example of Cultural Authentication." *African Arts*, Vol. 14, No. 2, p. 48.

Fowler, B. 1995. "Find Suggests Weaving Preceded Settled Life." *New York Times*, May 9, C1.

Kidwell, C. B. and V. Steele, eds. 1989. *Dressing the Part*. Washington, D.C.: Smithsonian Institution Press. See this publication for a lengthy exploration of the topic of gender and dress.

Laver, J. 1950. *Dress*. London: Albemarle.

Mellaart, J. 1963. "Catal Huyuk in Anatolia." *Illustrated London Daily News*, Feb. 9.

Scott, A. F. 1975. *Everyone a Witness: The Plantagenet Age*. New York: Thomas Crowell Company, p. 85.

Snowden, J. 1979. *The Folk Dress of Europe*. New York: Mayflower Books.

Waugh, N. 1964. *The Cut of Men's Clothes, 1600–1900*. New York: Theatre Arts Books, p. 11.

Webster's New World Dictionary. 1988. Cleveland: Simon & Schuster.

Wilford, J. N. 1993. " Site in Turkey Yields Oldest Cloth Ever Found." *New York Times*, July 13, C1.

SELECTED READINGS

Barber, E. J. W. 1994. *Women's Work: The First 20,000 Years.* New York: W.W. Norton.

Boodro, M. 1990. "Art and Fashion: A Fine Romance." *Art News,* Vol. 89, No. 7 (Sept.), p. 120.

"Forum: Research and Publication." 1988. *Dress,* Vol. 14, including:

- Rexford, N., "Studying Garments for Their Own Sake," p. 69.

- Cunningham, P. "Beyond Artifacts and Object Chronology," p. 76.

- Kaufman, R. "Given the Wide Range of Approaches and Emphases, How Does/Can a Librarian Know What to Collect as 'Costume,'" p. 79.

- Trautman, P. "Commentary," p. 81.

Jasper, C. R. and M. E. Roach-Higgins. 1987. "History of Costume: Theory and Instruction." *Clothing and Textile Research Journal,* Vol. 5, No. 1 (Summer), p. l.

Nochlin, L. 1987. "Art: A Sense of Fashion." *Architectural Digest,* Vol. 44, No. 2 (Feb.), p. 110.

Roach, M. E. and K. E. Musa. 1980. *New Perspectives on the History of Western Dress.* New York: Nutri-guides.

Tortora, P. 1993. "Is a Picture Really Worth a Thousand Words? An Exploration of the Problems Inherent in the Use of Visual Images for the Study of Historic Costume in the Western World." *Proceedings of the International Textile and Apparel Association, Inc.,* Monument, CO.

THE ANCIENT WORLD

C. 3000 B.C. — A.D. 300

The roots of Western Civilization are to be found in the area around the Mediterranean Sea, a region that gave rise to a series of civilizations that formed the artistic, religious, philosophical, and political basis of Western culture. The valley of the Nile River and the land between the Tigris and the Euphrates Rivers were the locations of some of the earliest agriculturally based urban societies.

About 3500 years before Christ, a civilization flourished in the region that the Greeks would later call Mesopotamia, "the land between the waters" (the Tigris and Euphrates Rivers), which approximates modern-day Iraq. This region became the home of a people called the Sumerians. Over the next 2500 years, the center of civilization and the site of political power in this area spread gradually northward into Babylonia and Assyria.

The first civilization that was established at Sumer developed the city-state, the first example of urban planning, including cobbled streets and multistory buildings (the Tower of Babel); a system of canals for irrigation; and, most important, a form of writing. During the Babylonian domination of Mesopotamia, the first written collection of laws was drafted, the Code of Hammurabi antedating the laws in the Bible, and a level of mathematics was achieved that would be unsurpassed until the Renaissance.

Concurrently about 3000 B.C. in the Nile River Valley the Egyptians were developing another center of culture, a civilization that endured for almost 3000 years. And also between 2000 and 1400 B.C., the island of Crete (the home of a people known as the Minoans) became the center of an important Mediterranean civilization. Minoan civilization was marked by a high standard of housing and material possessions; organized production of food, textiles, and other products; and a vigorous trade with remote regions. The Minoans eventually extended their cultural influence to mainland Greece. This mainland area included the town of Mycenae, home of a people called the Mycenaeans. After about 1400 B.C., the Mycenaeans, in reversal of power, came to dominate Crete.

Soon after 1200 B.C., the Dorians, a wave of invaders historians believe came from regions to the north, overwhelmed the Mycenaean civilization, and Greece entered a Dark Age about which little is known. During the Archaic Age of the 8th and 7th centuries B.C., the period of the poet Homer, Greek colonists left their homes to found colonies in the Mediterranean area. The Classical Age of Greece in the 5th and 4th centuries B.C., the period of the great philosophers and playwrights and Greek democracy, ended in the early 300s after the Greeks, led by Alexander the Great, had conquered much of the eastern Mediterranean regions.

The westward colonization that extended Greek art and culture influenced the Etruscans, who were a people living in the Italian peninsula. The Etruscans dominated central Italy from 800 B.C. until they were absorbed by the Romans in the third century B.C. The Romans went on to triumph over the other civilizations surrounding the Mediterranean. Eventually the Roman legions conquered not only North Africa and the Middle East but also the lands extending as far north in the east to the Danube River and northwest into much of Britain.

Table I.1 compares the periods and duration of each of these civilizations. As the table shows, some of these peoples

Table I.1

CIVILIZATIONS OF THE ANCIENT WORLD

Time Period	Mesopotamia	Egypt	Crete	Greece	Etruria	Rome
B.C. 4000–3000	Sumerian Civilization	Unification of Egypt				
3000–2000		Old Kingdom				
2000–1000	Rise of Babylonia	Middle Kingdom New Kingdom	Minoan Civilization Mycenaean	Mycenaean Civilization		
1000–800	Rise of Assyria			Dark Age		
800–600		Decline of Native Egyptian Civilization	Greek Civilization	Homeric (archaic) Period	Rise of Etruscan Civilization	
600–500	Neo-Babylonian Period					Etruscan Kings of Rome
500–400	Persian conquests of Asia and Middle East			Golden Age		Roman Republic
400–300	Greek Conquests	Greek Conquests		Alexander the Great		
300–200					End of Etruscan Confederation	
200–A.D. 0					Roman Empire	Roman Empire
0–300	Roman Domination	Roman Domination	Roman Domination	Roman Domination		

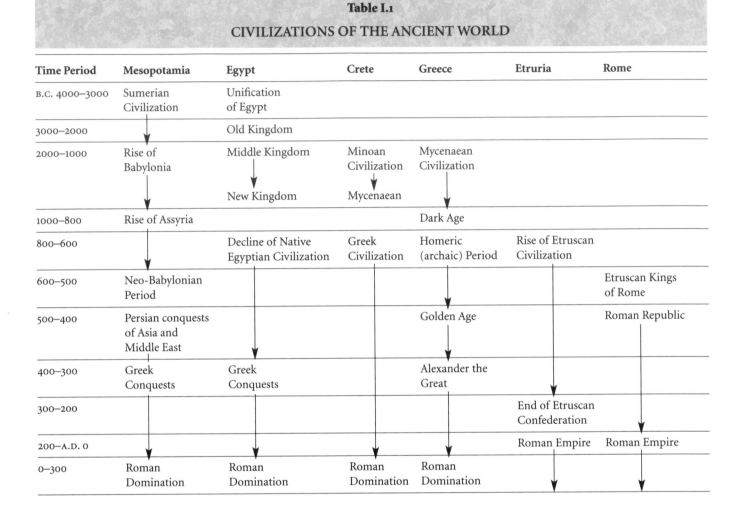

reached their peak of power and development at the same time. Others flowered and then declined while new centers of influence were rising. Some cultures borrowed liberally from each other, such as the Greeks, the Etruscans, and the Romans, while others such as Egypt and Mesopotamia, although in contact, evolved in separate directions.

Figure I.1 shows the locations of the most important of the civilizations of antiquity.

Although each of the Mediterranean cultures had its own distinctive forms of various items of dress, a number of basic garment types can be identified that were common to most of these cultures. The Mediterranean basin possesses a warm climate in which draped clothing is more comfortable than fitted clothing. With a few notable exceptions, garments of the region consisted of a draped length of square, rectangular, or semicircular fabric. When fastening was required,

these draped garments were closed with pins or by sewing. The general term used by archeologists for a pin that was used in holding a garment together is a Roman word, **fibula.**

These draped garments can be further subdivided into loincloths, skirts, tunics, shawls, cloaks, and veils.[1] The skirt,

[1] Costume terminology from these periods can be confusing, as different authorities use different phonetic terms for words which modern people have never heard pronounced, and with which readers are unfamiliar. For this reason descriptions of costume must rely upon using the closest modern equivalent for the costume in order that the reader can relate the unfamiliar term to one that is more familiar. Sometimes modern costume terms have taken on connotations that are misleading or confusing when that term is applied to historic costume. For example, the term "skirt" is associated in modern usage with women's costume, whereas in the ancient world men and women both wore "skirts." As a result, many costume sources will refer to the skirt as worn by men as a "kilt," even though "kilt" is actually a Scottish word for a specific skirt worn by men. For this reason the authors have chosen to use the nearest equivalent modern word that will be descriptive of the form of the ancient costume, except in those instances where an ancient word has come into modern usage, such as *toga* (from Latin) or *chiton* (from the Greek.)

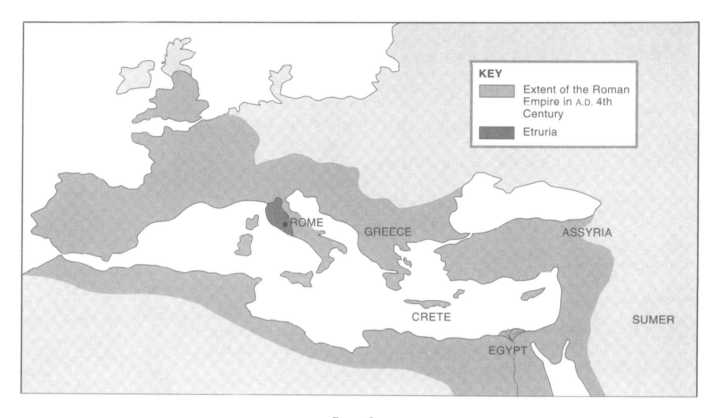

FIGURE I.1

Locations of the civilizations of the ancient world in the Mediterranean region.

in the ancient world, began at the waist or slightly below and hung loosely around the body. Skirts were worn by both men and women and varied in length. The loincloth was a length of cloth wrapped to cover the genitals. Tunics were simple one-piece and often T-shaped garments with openings for the head and the arms. Tunics were usually long enough to cover the torso and, like skirts, were made in many different lengths.

Rectangles, squares, or ovals of fabric were commonly combined with skirts or tunics. These shawllike garments ranged from pieces that covered only the upper body to larger squares that were wrapped to cover the entire body. As a cloak or outdoor covering large squares of fabric tied or pinned at the neck, rather like a modern cape. Veils, smaller rectangles than either shawls or cloaks, were worn to cover the head, and sometimes part of the body. Veils were worn almost exclusively by women.

CHRONOLOGY

3500 B.C.

Founding of cities in southern Mesopotamia

Development of cuneiform writing

3500–2800 B.C.

Sumerian civilization

3200–2620 B.C.

Early dynastic period in Egypt

Uniting of Lower and Upper Egypt

Building of the first step pyramid

Development of hieroglyphic writing

2620–2260 B.C.

Old Kingdom in Egypt

Building of the first "pure" pyramids

2334–2279 B.C.

Conquest of Sumerian civilization by Sargon and Akkadians

2260–2134 B.C.

First intermediate period in Egypt

2134–1786 B.C.

Middle Kingdom in Egypt

Influence extended into Palestine and south along the Nile

1792–1786 B.C.

King Hammurabi and development of Hammurabi's code of laws

1786–1575 B.C.

Second intermediate period in Egypt

1750 B.C.

Conquest of Egypt by Hyksos

1575–1087 B.C.

Expansion under Thutmose III

12th century B.C.

Decline of Egyptian power

1000–612 B.C.

Assyrian dominance in Mesopotamia

10th century B.C.

Libyans on the throne of Egypt

8th century B.C.

Nubians on the throne of Egypt

670 B.C.

Assyrian conquest of Egypt

612–539 B.C.

Chaldean Babylon

525 B.C.

Persian conquest of Mesopotamia

332 B.C.

Greek conquest of Egypt

THE ANCIENT MIDDLE EAST

c. 3500–600 B.C.

A.

Assyrian Decorative motif

B.

Assyrian Decorative motif

C.

Assyrian Chair

D.

Egyptian Chair

E.

Egyptian temple

F.

Top of Egyptian column

G.

Egyptian decorative motif

Figures A, B, F from Rettelbusch, E. 1996. *Handbook of Historic Ornament.* New York: Dover, pp. 5, 8. Figures C, D, G from Hottenroth, F., 1884. *Trachten Der Völker,* Vol. 1. Stuttgart: Verlag Gustav Wiese, p. 8. Figure E from Harris, C. M. *Illustrated Dictionary of Historic Architecture.* New York: Dover, p. 187.

HISTORICAL BACKGROUND: MESOPOTAMIA

The first civilizations in the Middle East were located in Mesopotamia (the name means "between rivers"), the region between the Tigris and Euphrates Rivers. The greater part of ancient Mesopotamia is now contained in present-day Iraq. The area extended from the Persian Gulf to near the borders between modern Iraq and Turkey. Towns and cities first developed in the southern parts of the region in the rich, fertile plains created by the deposits from the two rivers where agriculture and herding had produced sufficient food to enable people to establish more permanent residences. Town and city residents gradually developed complex social organizations.

The people called the Sumerians who founded the first cities in southern Mesopotamia entered the area from the northeast about 3500 B.C. The complexity of the Sumerian civilization (3500–2500 B.C.) led to the invention of a form of writing that enabled them to keep records of their activities, codify laws, and transmit knowledge. The Sumerians, however, never developed a strong political organization and remained only a loose confederation of city-states. Sumer came under the domination of a northern neighbor, Akkad, led by a ruler called Sargon (c. 2334–2279 B.C.), whose dynasty extended Akkadian influence into Asia Minor. Then new invaders from the west, the Amorites, conquered Sumer and Akkad, and established a new empire with the capital at Babylon. These Babylonians created an autocratic state, extending their control northward during the reign of King Hammurabi (c. 1792–1750 B.C.). His famous law code, dealing with almost every facet of life, influenced later Middle Eastern law codes, including the Mosaic law.

After about 1700 B.C. Babylonian power declined as a series of invaders attacked the Empire. Control of the region seesawed back and forth among the invaders until after 1000 B.C., when a powerful Assyrian army from the upper Tigris River conquered Babylonia. The Assyrians, once the vassals of the Babylonians, developed the first great military machine consisting of a large standing army equipped with superior weapons, including iron swords. Their Empire, the largest the Near East had seen, stretched into Syria, Palestine, and even Egypt. The cruelties of the Assyrian armies made them so hated and feared that their enemies, conspiring against them, eventually brought about their downfall. In 612 B.C. the armies of the Chaldeans, who now ruled Babylonia, destroyed Nineveh, the capital of Assyria, thereby ending the Assyrian Empire. In time, Chaldean Babylon fell to a new and greater power, the Persians under Cyrus in 539 B.C.

Chaldean Babylon, notorious for its luxury and wealth, became the site of the Hanging Gardens, a terrace roof garden, considered one of the seven wonders of the ancient world. Motivated by their religion, the Chaldeans became the most competent astronomers in Mesopotamian history. Their records of the movements of the heavenly bodies were maintained for more than 350 years.

HISTORICAL BACKGROUND: EGYPT

At much the same period that the early Mesopotamian civilization was developing between the Tigris and Euphrates Rivers, the Nile River became the site of the Egyptian civilization. The development of an advanced civilization in Egypt was aided by the deserts and the seas, which helped protect the land from foreign invaders. In addition, agriculture flourished thanks to the annual flooding of the Nile which left behind a rich deposit of soil that made fertilizers unnecessary.

The ancient Egyptian kingdoms flourished from about 3200 B.C. until about 300 B.C., when Greeks led by Alexander the Great conquered Egypt. Historians have divided Egyptian history into six periods: the early dynastic period, the Old Kingdom, the first intermediate period, the Middle Kingdom, the second intermediate period, and the New Kingdom. Within each period are a number of dynasties or sequences of rule by members of the same family.

During the early dynastic period (c. 3200–2620 B.C.) two separate kingdoms that bordered the Nile River were united under the first pharaoh or king. The first pyramid, a step pyramid, was constructed. Pyramids were intended not only to be the tombs of the pharaohs but also a sign that the Egyptian state was indestructible. In addition to building the first pyramids, the needs of the newly unified state required the keeping of records. This resulted in the invention of the earliest form of Egyptian writing.

By the time of the Old Kingdom (2620–2260 B.C.), the powers of the pharaohs had become unlimited, and pyramid building had become the chief activity of the monarchy. The pyramids were astounding feats of engineering, dwarfing monuments from other eras. The great pyramid of Cheops, which reached the height of 481 feet, contained more than two million limestone blocks that were fitted together with great precision. Some weighed more than fifteen tons. But pyramid building exhausted the government's revenues. Weak pharaohs lost control of the government, and local nobles, usurping power, began to act like petty kings.

The succeeding first intermediate period (c. 2260–2134 B.C.) was a time of troubles, civil war, and disorder. Tombs of the pharaohs were looted and bandits robbed travelers; desert tribes invaded Egypt.

Pharaohs of the 11th and 12th dynasties established the Middle Kingdom (c. 2134–1786 B.C.) and united the country after ending the period of anarchy. A stronger central government was restored; public works that benefited the population replaced pyramid building, which lacked any practical use. Egyptian influence was extended into Palestine and south along the Nile. As prosperity returned, wealth became more widespread among the Egyptian people. This period ended with the first serious threat from abroad.

Another time of troubles came in the second intermediate period (c. 1786–1575 B.C.) when the nobility again revolted and the pharaohs' power grew weak. About 1750 B.C., a nomadic people from western Asia, the Hyksos, seized control of Egypt. The Hyksos, who brought horse-drawn chariots and new weapons, soon adopted Egyptian customs and ways, including the power and title of pharaoh.

Hatred of the Hyksos stimulated the Egyptians to launch a revolt under the leadership of the founder of the 18th dynasty who finally drove the Hyksos out of Egypt. In the period of the New Kingdom (1575–1087 B.C.), also called the period of Empire, Egypt became a strong, military power under the pharaoh Thutmose III (1504–1450 B.C.). After leading seventeen campaigns, he expanded Egyptian rule eastward as far as the Euphrates and made Egypt a powerful force in the eastern Mediterranean region. The new monarchy restored temples and built luxurious palaces. Art forms, which had been formal, stylized, and monumental, became more natural and realistic.

By the 12th century, Egyptian power had declined and society had decayed; the empire was disappearing. Libyans occupied the throne of the pharaohs in the 10th century only to be followed by Nubian conquerors in the 8th century. In 670 B.C. Assyria conquered Egypt but remained for only eight years. Regaining independence, Egypt enjoyed a national renaissance until the Persians invaded in 525 B.C. Egypt stagnated, its glory far in the past. In 332 B.C., Alexander the Great, a Greek from Macedonia, conquered Egypt, ending Persian rule. Successive periods of Egyptian history were marked by domination first by Greece and then by Rome. A truly native Egyptian civilization had been ended.

Details of the life and history of Egypt are more complete than those for Mesopotamia over the same period. Like the Mesopotamians, the Egyptians had a form of writing, known as hieroglyphic, that has been deciphered by historians. Written records provide an abundant source of information about Egyptian life and religion. The Egyptians not only believed in life after death, but also buried personal possessions with the dead so that they might use them in the afterlife. These included tools, furniture, food, and drink. The hot dry climate of the desert where prominent Egyptians were buried preserved these objects, often in excellent condition. In addition, many of the temples and tombs contained paintings and sculpture, but unlike the Mesopotamians whose art generally emphasized the ceremonial aspects of life, the Egyptians painted and sculpted individuals engaged in a variety of daily tasks.

DIFFERENCES IN THE DEVELOPMENT OF EGYPTIAN AND MESOPOTAMIAN CIVILIZATIONS

One of the most outstanding aspects of Egyptian civilization was the relative slowness with which changes occurred. It is not that there were no significant changes in the 3,000 years during which this civilization existed, but that they took place so gradually that they seemed almost imperceptible even over several hundred years. For almost 3,000 years, Egyptian civilization was scarcely affected by foreign cultural and political influences. "Between the Egypt of the Pyramid Age and that of Cleopatra were many differences, but many of these seem superficial, for much of the hard core of Egyptian thought and institutions was comparatively unchanged after some 25 centuries" (Fairservis 1962).

The civilizations of Mesopotamia displayed greater diversity when viewed over a period of 3,000 years. One of the reasons for these differences may have been the geographical unity of the landscape in Egypt, in contrast to a variety of landscapes and types of terrain in Mesopotamia. Egypt was a narrow strip of land set in the valley of the Nile where annual floods maintained the fertility of the land. Deserts on either side provided security from invasion, while throughout Egypt farmers carried on the ceaseless routine of agriculture. In Mesopotamia, regions differed more. Each area supported specific crops, and each crop required special skills and care. The necessary labor force, the investment of capital, and the organization of agriculture were different in each region. For example, flocks had to be moved seasonally, but grain crops required long-term storage and distribution throughout the year. Some crops required long-range planting and planning, while others could be sown and harvested in a short time.

These differences also accounted for some variations between the costume of the two cultures. While the climate in Egypt was relatively warm and uniform throughout the year, that of Mesopotamia was more variable, including both areas at higher altitudes where warm clothing was required at some times of the year and hot, desert areas.

Ecology, then, was a factor contributing to the differences between Egyptian and Mesopotamian civilizations. Another was the degree to which each culture was subjected to outside influences. Both traded abroad to obtain raw materials unavailable within the boundaries of the region. With trade came outside influences. Egypt, however, was less open to outside influences because of natural barriers, the sea and the desert, which provided security from foreigners. Because natural barriers to invasion were lacking, foreign invaders periodically entered Mesopotamia. Some of them came to dominate the region. These groups adopted many traditions of the native peoples so there was a perpetuation of tradition, but at the same time new ideas were also incorporated into the culture. Egypt maintained a continuity in political and religious tradition that was seriously threatened from outside only once, by the Hyksos.

MESOPOTAMIAN CIVILIZATION

For convenience the history of the Mesopotamians will be subdivided into three periods: Early Sumerian (c. 3500–2500 B.C.), Later Sumerian and Babylonian (c. 2500–1000 B.C.), and Assyrian (c. 1000–600 B.C.). Relatively little is known of the earliest period of Sumerian history. The record is clearer during the latter part of the period and it is possible to obtain a better picture of some aspects of life in general and of costume in particular.

Social Structure

The Babylonian culture was based on the earlier Sumerian civilization, and the social structure of the Babylonians was similar to that of the Sumerians. Social classes were clearly defined. In addition to the nobility who stood far above all the rest of society, there were three major classes in Babylonian society: free men; an intermediate class of people who might be called "the poor" who were "worth little;" and the slaves, who were "worth nothing." The free men made up a sort of middle-class of artisans, tradesmen, lesser public officials, and laborers. Farmers were generally part of the "intermediate" or "poor" class. Slaves were relatively few in Sumer, but by the time of the Babylonians had grown in number as they became an increasingly necessary part of the work force. Slaves could be foreign captives, the children of slaves, or wives and/or children of free men sold into slavery to meet the debts of the father of the family. Adopted children who disgraced their adoptive parents could also be sold into slavery (Contenau 1954).

The Family

The family was patriarchal in structure. Marriage was a contractual arrangement generally made to cement an economic alliance between two families. By this contract a man had a principal wife, but could, and usually did, keep one or more concubines as well. Divorce was easily obtained if the principal wife was unable to have children.

The art that remains from Sumer and Babylonia indicates that the position of women was subordinate. Representations of men predominate, and illustrations of women–usually goddesses, priestesses, or queens–are relatively rare. Women were not completely without rights, however, as Baby-

lonian law codes extended to them the right to testify in court cases and provided some degree of economic protection in the case of the death of a husband.

Although children had no legal rights, letters written on clay tablets and sent from children of the upper classes to their parents reveal that they felt free to demand the clothing or jewelry that they considered appropriate to their rank. One boy wrote to his mother:

From year to year the clothes of the young gentlemen here become better, but you let my clothes get worse from year to year. Indeed you persisted in making my clothes poorer and more scanty. At a time when in our house wool is used up like bread, you have made me poor clothes. The son of Adid-iddinam whose father is only an assistant of my father has two new sets of clothes while you fuss even about a single set of clothes for me. In spite of the fact that you bore me and his mother only adopted him, his mother loves him, while you do not love me (Oppenheim 1967).

Another boy wrote to his father:

I have never before written to you for something precious I wanted. But if you want to be like a father to me, get me a fine string full of beads, to be worn around the head it should be full [of beads] and it should be beautiful. If I see it and dislike it, I shall send it back! Also send the cloak, of which I spoke to you (Oppenheim 1967).

Fabrics and Cloth Production

The cloak and the new sets of clothes these boys asked for were most likely made of wool. The chief products of Mesopotamia are described as barley, wool, and oil. These fabrics were produced not just for domestic consumption, but were traded to other regions as well. Flax is occasionally mentioned in the ancient records, but although fragments of linen have been found in excavations and there were skilled linen weavers, linen was clearly less important than wool, which is mentioned often along with quotes for current prices. Clothes, tapestries, and curtains were made of wool. One contract has been found that describes the period of apprenticeship for a weaver as five years, an exceptionally long time when compared with the training of other artisans. However, the variety of fabrics and the decorations applied to them seem to have been quite complex, so the weaver may have had to master quite a complicated system of manufacture (Leix *CIBA Review*, No. 1).

In writing about women's work in the ancient world, Barber (1994) notes that in the 19th century B.C. women often played an important role in producing Mesopotamian textiles. Women seem to have been responsible for spinning and weaving, while men may have done the dyeing and finishing. Although men traveled long distances to trade in textiles, women often supervised local textile production and took care of aspects of business close to home.

SOURCES OF EVIDENCE ABOUT SUMERIAN COSTUME

The evidence for details of the costume of Mesopotamia is largely derived from visual materials. Depictions of persons are found on seals (small engraved markers used to press an identification into clay and wax). These seals had scenes of Sumerian mythology incised or cut into them. A few wall paintings survive, as do small votive statuettes of worshipers left at shrines as substitutes for the worshipers themselves, to provide a sort of perpetual presence of the individual at the temple. From these rather limited remains and the excavation of Sumerian tombs, some impressions of Sumerian dress can be gained.

MESOPOTAMIAN COSTUME/ SUMERIAN COSTUME FOR MEN AND WOMEN:
C. 3500–2500 B.C.

Costume Components for Men and Women

GARMENTS

Skirts, worn by both men and women, were the major item of dress seen in the art of this era. In the earliest period these were probably made of sheepskin with the fleece still attached. A Greek word, **kaunakes,** has been applied to this fleece or fleecelike fabric. Lengths varied: servants and soldiers wore shorter lengths; royalty and deities wore longer lengths. Skirts apparently wrapped around the body. When fabric ends were long enough, an end of the fabric length was passed up, under a belt, and over one shoulder. (See *Figure 2.1.*) Even after sheepskin had been supplemented by woven cloth, the cloth was fringed at the hem or constructed to simulate the tufts of wool on the fleece. (See *Figure 2.2.*) Fragments of cloth from an excavation of the tomb of a queen showed that she and her attendants wore a bright red, heavy woolen fabric.

Belts were located at the waist to hold skirts in place. They appear to have been wide and padded.

Cloaks were probably made from animal skins, leather, or heavy, felted cloth, and covered the upper part of the body.

HAIR AND HEADDRESS

Shaving the head was a practice of several Mediterranean cultures, including the early Mesopotamian and the Egyptian. Very likely this was a means of discouraging vermin and for comfort in the hot, humid climate. Mesopotamian men are depicted both clean-shaven and bearded. Sometimes their

FIGURE 2.1

Praying Figure. Mesopotamian, Sumerian, c. 2200 B.C. Sumerian man wearing kaunakes garment in the form of a wrapped skirt. The end of the skirt is thrown over his left shoulder. Both men and women wore the same type of garment. His head is shaven. (Photograph courtesy, The Metropolitan Museum of Art, Harris Brisbane Dick Fund, 1949.)

heads are bald. (See *Figures 2.1* and *2.2.*) Both men and women might pull their long hair into a **chignon** (*sheen'yon*), a bun of hair at the back of the neck, which was held in place by a **fillet** (*fil'ay*), another name for a headband. Alternatively, they also wore their hair falling straight to the shoulders and held in place by a fillet. Over their heads soldiers wore close-fitting helmets with pointed tops that may have been made of leather.

JEWELRY

From archeological evidence it appears that some royal women apparently wore elaborate gold jewelry. An excavation at the city of Ur from about 2800 B.C. unearthed a beautiful gold and jeweled crown, made with delicate leaves and flowers and massive gold necklaces and earrings. Compara-

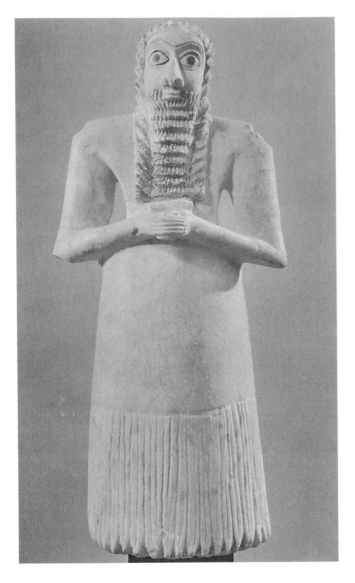

FIGURE 2.2

Praying Figure. Mesopotamian, Sumerian, c. 3000 B.C. Bearded Sumerian man wears fringed skirt. (Photograph courtesy, The Metropolitan Museum of Art, Fletcher Fund, 1940.)

ble items have not been found for later periods, nor are they depicted in the art of the period.

MESOPOTAMIAN COSTUME/ LATER SUMERIANS AND BABYLONIANS: C. 2500–1000 B.C.

Styles evolved slowly, and sharp distinctions cannot be made between costume of the later Sumerian and early Babylonian

periods. Costume generally increased in complexity. Although men's and women's dress continued to utilize similar elements, evidence indicates a trend toward greater distinctions in the clothing for each gender. Skirts continued in use. Shawls, woven rectangles or squares of fabric, were draped in various ways. Tunics were worn.

Costume Components for Men/Military Dress: *c. 2500–1000 B.C.*

From depictions of armies and military leaders one can identify these elements of the dress of soldiers. Skirts were probably made of woven fabric. Fringed decoration around the lower edge persisted in military dress. Shawls were worn with skirts. The center of the shawl was placed across the left shoulder, with the ends crossing the chest and carried back to be knotted over the right hip.

Military men wore helmets made of leather or metal, sometimes with horn-shaped decorations. Footwear consisted of sandals, which were worn when rough terrain made foot coverings necessary.

Costume Components for Men/Civilian Dress: *c. 2500–1000 B.C.*

GARMENTS

Skirts, loincloths, and tunics probably made up the most common items of dress for the poor. The nobility or mythological figures wore a draped garment described by Houston (1964) as being made from a square of fabric about 118 inches wide and 56 inches long and draped as shown in *Figure 2.3,* which depicts Ur-Ningirsu, son of Gudea, a ruler of about 2120 B.C. Sumerian and Babylonian art depicts these garments as smooth-surfaced, without draped folds, but this is probably an artistic convention. Not only do the woven fabrics appear to fall without folds, but even faces, skin, and arms have smooth planes and lack detail. Fabrics are fringed and/or have woven or embroidered edging.

HAIR AND HEADDRESS

Before 2300 B.C., men are shown both clean-shaven and with beards. Later men are depicted only with beards. Hats are turbanlike and close-fitted at the crown, with a small brim or padded roll at the edge. (See *Figure 2.3*.)

FOOTWEAR

Feet usually are shown as bare or with sandals, which would have provided covering in rough terrain. Archeologists have found a clay model of a leather shoe that dates from about 2600 B.C., with a tongue, upward curve to the toe, and a pompom on the toe. Born (*CIBA Review,* No. III) suggests that such shoes may have originated in mountainous areas where there

FIGURE 2.3

Statuette of Ur-Ningirsu, Son of Gudea. Mesopotamia, Neo-Sumerian. c. 2100 B.C. The garment shown here was probably made from a rectangular length of fabric wrapped around the body. On his head is a close-fitting hat with a small brim or padded roll. (Photograph courtesy, The Metropolitan Museum of Art, Rogers Fund, 1947 (head). Body on loan from the Louvre Museum, L1977.23.1.)

was snow, and that they may have been brought from there to Mesopotamia. This style of shoe seems to have taken on a ceremonial function, being reserved in sculpture for a heroic figure representing the king. "The peaked shoe with a pompom," says Born, "is probably to be regarded as a regal attribute."

Costume Components for Women: c. 2500–1000 B.C.

GARMENTS

The kaunakes garment persisted for a time for women, but gradually became associated with religious figures (goddesses, priestesses, or minor deities). In this period, garments were cut to cover the entire body, not just one shoulder as in earlier periods. Evidence is inadequate to be certain of the specific design, but possible constructions were a skirt in combination with short cape cut with an opening for the head or a tunic with openings for the head and arms.

Figure 2.4, based on Houston's reconstruction, shows two additional women's garment forms utilizing a long piece of fabric wrapped around the body in slightly different ways.

HAIR AND HEADDRESS

The chignon held in place with a fillet continued in use; in some representations hair appeared to be confined in a net.

FOOTWEAR

Bare feet were common. The well-to-do wore sandals.

JEWELRY

A tight-fitting, dog-collar type of necklace made from several rings of metal was shown most often.

MESOPOTAMIAN COSTUME/ LATER BABYLONIANS AND THE ASSYRIANS: c. 1000–600 B.C.

The Assyrians adopted Babylonian costume; thus a clear break between the late Babylonian and early Assyrian styles cannot be seen. Patterns of change in costume history are generally evolutionary. In these early periods lack of detailed knowledge gives the impression that changes occur slowly over time.

Although the Assyrian leaders adopted the styles of the Babylonians, they added to their decoration. Woven or embroidered pattern is seen in great profusion on the costumes of the king and his chief officials. Cross-cultural contacts through trade or warfare may have the effect of introducing new style ideas or new materials, thereby having an impact on dress. Although the Assyrians continued the tradition of wearing wool garments, King Sennacherib (c. 700 B.C.) is said to have introduced cotton to Assyria. He speaks of having "trees bearing wool" in his botanical garden, but there is no solid evidence for the use of cotton by the Assyrians (Barber 1991).

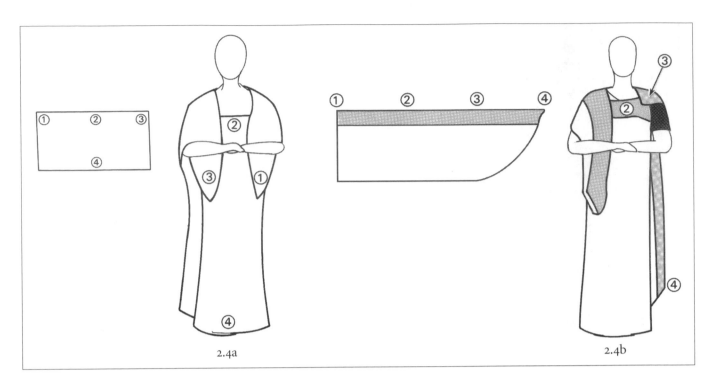

2.4a   2.4b

FIGURE 2.4

Houston suggests these reconstructions for Babylonian women's costume. (Drawings adapted from Houston, M.G. 1964. *Ancient Egyptian, Mesopotamian, and Persian Costume*. New York: Barnes and Noble, Chap. 10.)

2.4a   Costume is draped from a rectangle of fabric. Point 2 is placed at center front, points 1 and 3 are drawn under the arms, segment 2–3 crossing over 1–2 in back. Points 1 and 3 are pulled over the shoulder to hang down at each side in front.

2.4b   Costume is draped from a rectangle with one end curved. A small fold of fabric, (shaded area) is made at the top. Square corner at point 1 is draped across the right shoulder to the back, across the back and under the left arm, across the front again, passing under the drape of point 1. Point 3 is pulled across the back again and pinned over the shoulder to point 2 in the front. Section 3–4 falls in a drape behind the shoulder to the ground.

The Tunic

The word "tunic" has come into English from the Latin, and is used here, and subsequently, as a generic term for a T-shaped garment with openings at the top for the head and arms. Textile historian and linguist Elizabeth Barber (1994) suggests that the Latin word *tunica* derived from a Middle Eastern word for linen. She notes that the earliest tunics seem to have been made of linen and that in some areas tunics first appeared just after wool came into use. She concludes that linen tunics were probably adopted as an under layer to prevent irritation of the skin by wool garments.

Tunic-type garments were an essential part of dress in all of the civilizations of antiquity. Tunics from different civilizations showed variations in cut, construction, and fit; in length; in whether or not they had sleeves; and in the length of those sleeves. Tunics could be made from any type of fabric, although when worn next to the body, they were more likely to be linen.

At some point, the Assyrians replaced the skirts and draped garments characteristic of the earlier Babylonian period with tunics. Perhaps the tunic, a closely fitting garment more suitable for cooler climates, was borrowed from nearby mountain peoples. (See *Figure 2.5*.)

Costume Components for Men: c. 1000–600 B.C.

GARMENTS

Royalty wore floor-length tunics beneath several long, fringed shawls. Draping of shawls around the body juxtaposed horizontal, vertical, and diagonal arrangement of fringes and was sufficiently complex to inhibit movement. It is likely that these costumes were for state occasions and that everyday clothing, even for royalty, may have been simpler. In scenes depicting hunting or warfare, the king's costume has less encumbering drapery.

In any civilization, the dress of royal figures is set apart by differences in style, costlier materials, greater elaboration in its decoration, or by the emblems of power in the form of a special headdress, a staff, or a scepter. Often the costume of royalty is specified by tradition and does not necessarily re-

FIGURE 2.5

Winged being (a mythological figure) from Mesopotamia, Assyrian period, 9th century B.C. This figure wears a short tunic over which a fringed shawl has been placed. Other aspects of his costume that are characteristic of Assyrian dress are the sandals with wedge-shaped heels, jewelry, including that worn on the arms and ears, and elaborately arranged curls in the hair and beard. (Photograph courtesy, The Metropolitan Museum of Art, gift of John D. Rockefeller Jr., 1932.)

flect current styles. Mesopotamian artists depict the garments of the king as covered with what appears to be embroidery, although some authors suggest that these designs may have been woven. Priests determined the specific garment worn by the king on any given day. The Assyrians believed that some days were favorable and some unfavorable; therefore, a priest would prescribe the most auspicious garment, including its

color and fabric. On some unfavorable days, the king was not permitted to change his clothing at all.

Tunics for the laboring classes were worn with a belt and little decoration and ended above the knee. Soldiers wore them knee length with armor.

HAIR AND HEADDRESS

Men were bearded, with the hair and beard arranged in small curls thought to have been achieved with the help of curling irons. The king's beard was longer than that of other men, and supplemented with a false section. Lower-class men had shorter beards and hair. (See *Figure 2.5*.)

Among the hat styles was a high brimless hat similar to the **fez** or **tarbush,** a modern-day, traditional Arab style worn in southwest Asia or northern Africa that is shaped like a truncated cone. In Assyrian art this hat is sometimes depicted with broad bands of fabric hanging down the back. The king wore a higher, straighter version similar to hats worn in later centuries by Persian royalty and by Eastern Orthodox Christian priests in the 20th century.

FOOTWEAR

Sandals, depending on whether they were to be given heavier or lighter use, had thicker or thinner soles. (See *Figure 2.5*.) Closed shoes are depicted, though less commonly than sandals. High boots are shown on horsemen, probably as protective footwear for the aggressive Assyrian military forces.

JEWELRY

Earrings, bracelets, and armlets were worn. Decorative motifs used for jewelry often resembled those seen on patterned fabrics. (See *Figure 2.5*.)

Costume Components for Men/Military Dress

Soldiers wore a short tunic, a corselet of mail, and a wide belt. The mail was probably made by sewing small metal plates onto leather or heavy cloth. Representations of soldiers indicate that sometimes mail covered only the upper torso, while at other times entire tunics were covered in mail. Helmets fit the head closely, coming to a peaked point at the back of the head. Both sandals and high boots were worn.

Costume Components for Women: c. 1000–600 B.C.

Few representations of women are found in Assyrian art. Although the status of women in Sumer and Babylon had been relatively low, Babylonian wives did participate actively when families were engaged in commercial production of textiles. Under Assyrian law the right to testify in court was taken away, and some of the protection extended to women in re-gard to property rights in Babylon was removed. Historians see this as evidence of a possible influx of new people whose customs differed from those of the native population.

Customs surrounding the wearing of veils by women may also be related to such population and attitude changes. References to the wearing of veils are found in Assyrian law codes. In Assyrian and late Babylonian times, the veil was considered to be the distinguishing mark of a free, married woman. Slaves and prostitutes were not permitted to wear veils, and a concubine could wear a veil only when she accompanied the principal wife. Some representations show the veil hanging over the hair on either side of the face, but apparently veils often covered the face in public. This custom persists today in some areas of the Middle East, and although the reasons for veiling women are no longer related to marital status, one can see that wearing the veil is a tradition of long duration in the area.

GARMENTS

Women wore tunics that were cut with somewhat longer sleeves than those for men. Fabrics used for women's tunics were elaborately patterned. Women also wore fringed shawls draped around the body.

HAIR AND HEADDRESS

Hair styles show considerable variety. Earlier styles for Assyrian women are elaborately arranged. Later styles were simplified to curly, shoulder-length hair.

FOOTWEAR

Both sandals and closed shoes are depicted.

JEWELRY

Jewelry consisted of necklaces, earrings, bracelets, and armlets.

MESOPOTAMIAN COSTUME FOR CHILDREN: C. 3500–600 B.C.

Sources do not provide any solid information about children's clothing. Children occupied a subservient position in the family. In Babylonia, the father of the family had the right to sell his children into slavery or leave them on deposit with a creditor as security for repayment of a loan! Their costume was probably minimal. When clothing was worn, it may have consisted of the simplest of the adult garments: a loincloth, a skirt, or a tunic. Children of the upper classes probably wore clothing like that of their parents.

EGYPTIAN CIVILIZATION

Egyptian culture and dress developed in quite different ways from that of the Mesopotamian civilizations. More evidence in the form of works of art, real objects, and written records is available to researchers.

Social Structure

The hierarchy of Egyptian society has been compared to the shape of the pyramids. The pharaoh, or hereditary king, was at the apex of this pyramid. At the next level were his chief deputies and the high priests. Below them were a host of officials of lesser status who were associated either with the court or the administration of towns and cities.

Other important positions were occupied by the scribes, comparable to the "white collar" workers of today such as department managers, bookkeepers, accountants, clerks, and bureaucrats. They were attached to the courts, city administrations, religious organizations, and the military. These occupations provided an avenue of upward mobility within Egyptian society.

A step below the scribes were the artisans, a vast throng of skilled workers such as painters, sculptors, architects, furniture-makers, weavers, and jewelers. Servants and laborers and the huge number of peasants who tilled the land provided the agricultural base on which the upper levels of the social pyramid rested. Slavery existed. Slaves were foreign captives, not native Egyptians. Some, like the Hebrew slave Moses, were able to attain freedom and rise to relatively high station, but this was rare.

THE UPPER CLASSES

Costume served to delineate social class, even though much of Egyptian costume was relatively simple. The draping, the quality of the fabrics, and the addition of costly jewelry and belts distinguished the garments of the upper from those of the lower classes.

Upper-class families lived in luxuriously furnished houses. By 20th century standards, the quantity of furniture was small, but pieces were decorated with beautiful inlays and worked metal. Homes were spacious with carefully tended gardens.

Artists often depicted social gatherings at home during the New Kingdom. Men and women dressed lavishly for these occasions, wearing long, full, pleated gowns, vivid cosmetics, and brightly colored jewelry and headdress. Musicians, acrobats, and dancing girls entertained. Cones of scented wax were set on the heads of guests. As the evening progressed these wax cones would melt, run down over the wigs, and perfume the air. (See *Figure 2.7.*)

The hot, humid climate made cleanliness essential for comfort. Upper-class Egyptians had high standards of personal cleanliness, bathing two or more times each day. In some periods, heads were shaved and wigs worn, possibly as a means of keeping the head clean and free from vermin. Class distinctions in grooming practices are evident in Egyptian art. Higher standards of grooming were expected of the upper classes. Workmen are shown in paintings with a stubbly growth of beard while upper-class men are invariably clean shaven.

THE FAMILY

Marriage was a civil contract; divorce was easy. Multiple marriages were not common, although many well-to-do men had a harem or at least several concubines. Some wall paintings show scenes of warm, close family life. Fathers and mothers caress the young, and small children play happily with toys or pets.

SOURCES OF EVIDENCE FOR THE STUDY OF EGYPTIAN COSTUME

Egyptian Art

Many of the buildings of ancient Egypt are gone, the stones used by subsequent generations for building later structures. The massive pyramids remain, as do a number of temples. Among the artistic expressions still to be found in these buildings are statues and carved wall reliefs.

Although art historians identify various styles that changed over time in Egyptian art, to the nonspecialist these changes are hard to detect. Fortunately for the costume historian, Egyptian artists continued to be interested in the depiction of humans going about their daily activities, as it is through the art of Egypt that much of the information about Egyptian costume has been gained.

Artists probably did not always depict costume with absolute fidelity. Artists followed strict guidelines that governed the proportions of sculpture and relief depictions of important figures. These conventions derived from the Egyptian system of measurement. In relief carvings and wall paintings the conventional pose shows shoulders to the front, head and legs facing to the right or left. Clothing is often shown frontally, while legs face to one side (Iversen 1991). (See *Color Plate 1.*) It is likely that the representation of some costume forms in art may have lagged behind their actual adoption; others may not have been depicted at all.

Then, too, artists depicted figures of persons of lower status as smaller in size than those who were more important.

As a result these figures sometimes have been mistakenly identified as those of children.

The Contents of Tombs

Much of Egyptian art has been preserved in tombs where painters decorated the walls with scenes from daily life and the afterlife, and where personal possessions and models of useful objects were placed. The dead, awakening to the afterlife, would be well supplied with everything necessary for a comfortable existence.

Private housing was made from mud brick and therefore these structures have not survived. It is possible to have some idea about homes and workplaces and the activities that took place there because the paintings in the tombs do show private housing.

Archeologists made a particularly valuable discovery when the tomb of King Tutankhamen was excavated in the 1920s. The tombs of many pharaohs had been robbed of much of their treasure, but this tomb of a young king dating from about 1350 B.C. had remained undisturbed for thousands of years.

Egyptian tombs have sometimes yielded items of dress that seem to have no counterpart in paintings or statuary, such as the multicolored garments and elaborately decorated sandals found in the excavation of the tomb of Tutankhamen. These might have been ceremonial garments, special funeral garments, or actual items from the King's wardrobe.

During the periods of Greek and Roman dominance, pharaohs were represented in art as dressed in the styles of the Old Kingdom, and yet records indicate that the rulers of the period actually dressed in Greek and Roman styles (Mertz 1990). One of the basic costumes for women is a straight, fitted garment of tubular form. Paintings and statues show this garment as fitting so tightly around the body that the wearer would be virtually unable to walk. Woven fabrics do not cling so closely to the body, and as far as research can ascertain, the Egyptians had not developed techniques such as knitting that would permit such a close fit; consequently one may hypothesize that artistic convention required the garment be shown as exceptionally tight fitting.

Recent research by Gillian Vogelsang-Eastwood (1993), a textile archeologist, has added significantly to what is known of Egyptian costume. Combining evidence from actual garments excavated by archeologists with a careful study of Egyptian artists' depictions of clothing, she has published the most complete summary of what is known about Egyptian clothing to date. Vogelsang-Eastwood also reproduced and had students put on copies of garments in order to see how they might actually have been worn. The result has been some new ideas that challenge certain of the prevailing views of Egyptian dress. Many of her proposals will be discussed later

in this chapter. In spite of the wealth of evidence available and continuing research, our knowledge about the clothing of Egypt is still incomplete.

Egyptian Decorative Motifs

In any historic period certain similarities may be observed in the various art forms. (See *Chapter 1, page 5,* for a discussion of clothing as an art form.) In Egypt these are most obvious in decorative motifs, most of which are derived either from the natural world or from religious symbolism. These motifs appear in the decoration of temples and tomb chambers, on furniture and utilitarian objects, and in clothing, most often in jewelry or decorative accessories of clothing.

The Egyptians had an abiding faith in magic and believed that by representing symbols of religious figures in jewelry, the positive qualities of the deity would be transferred to the wearer. The scarab, a symbol of a beetle that represented the sun god and also rebirth, was a popular motif. The hawk appears often as another symbol of the sun god. The sacred cobra, called the uraeus, was the symbol of Lower Egypt, and the vulture of Upper Egypt. Used together on royal headdress and in jewelry, the two symbolized the unification of Lower and Upper Egypt under the pharaohs. The "eye of Horus," a stylized representation of the human eye, symbolized the moon. The lotus blossom, papyrus blossom, and animal forms that were native to the area were also translated into decorative motifs.

CONTRIBUTIONS OF ARTISANS TO COSTUME

The workmanship of artisans was of exceptional quality. Of special interest to the study of historic costume are the weaving and jewelry-making crafts.

Textile Production and Technology

Thanks to the hot, dry climate of Egypt, actual pieces of fabric have been preserved from the burial places of Egyptians. Linen was the fiber most used by Egyptians. (Linen is a fiber that is removed from the stems of the flax plant.) Wool was considered ritually unclean and was not worn by priests or by visitors to sanctuaries, or for burial. Herodotus, a Greek historian of the 5th century B.C. who traveled in Egypt, reported that wool was used for some outer garments. Although a recent archeological find indicated that silk may have been present in Egypt as early as 1000 B.C., silk was not widely used in Egypt until the 4th century A.D., well after the periods discussed here (Wilford 1993). Cotton cloth, too, reached Egypt only after Egyptian power had declined.

Linen is difficult to dye to colors that will not fade unless substances called mordants are used to fix the colors. Egyptian dyers were apparently unfamiliar with mordants until the New Kingdom period; therefore most Egyptian clothing was made in the natural, creamy-white color of linen or bleached to a pure white.

Spinning and weaving techniques were well developed as early as the Old Kingdom. During the Old and Middle Kingdoms, Egyptians used a horizontal ground loom to weave fabrics of varying widths. Weaving cloth consists of interlacing lengthwise (called **warp** yarns) and crosswise (called **weft** or **filling**) yarns. The place at the sides of a fabric where a weft yarn turns to make its return trip across the fabric is called the **selvage.** By looping or adding extra yarns, decorative elements can be introduced at the selvage. At each end of the cloth, where the weaving has stopped, the ends of the warp yarns remain. These can be cut off, can remain as fringe, or can be tied into tassels. Egyptian weavers used these decorative selvages, fringes, and tassels to ornament their clothing.

Flax was raised on the large estates owned by wealthy Egyptians where the cloth needed by the estate was also woven. Because the Egyptians did not have a cash economy, woven textiles were "a sort of money for barter" (Barber 1994). Men processed the flax stems to remove linen fibers, then women spun the fibers into yarns and wove the yarns into cloth. Men did a final cleaning of the finished cloth, by either boiling or washing in the river, where they had to be on the lookout against attack by dangerous crocodiles.

Some fine, closely woven fabrics had been found with thread counts as high as 160 threads in the lengthwise direction and 120 threads in the crosswise direction (Casson 1975). The finest sheer organdy fabrics of the 19th and 20th centuries rarely have thread counts as high as 150 in the lengthwise and 100 in the crosswise directions (*American Fabrics Encyclopedia* 1972).

Pleated linen fabrics appear in art and in actual garments. Pleats were probably made on a grooved board or other surface. Cloth would have been pressed into the grooves, and the pleats fixed by the application of starch or sizing (Stead 1986). Pleats were made horizontally, vertically, or in a sort of herringbone effect that was produced by pleating a fabric in one direction, then turning the fabric and pleating it again in the other direction.

The earliest fabrics decorated with ornamental tapestry-woven designs date from after 1500 B.C., as do wall paintings of a new type of loom, a vertical loom. Barber (1994) suggests that this new technology may have been taught to the Egyptians by foreign captives. While the vertical looms did not replace the older horizontal looms, they did make weaving of more elaborately patterned fabrics possible.

The items excavated from the tomb of King Tutankhamen included robes made of beaded fabric, others with wo-

ven and embroidered patterns, and still others with appliqué. These artifacts reveal that the arts of fabric construction included skill in beading, pattern weaving, embroidery, and appliqué.

Jewelry

Gold jewelry was prized by the Egyptians; silver, however, was not found in Egypt and had to be imported so that its use was limited. The Egyptians did not make glass, but natural volcanic glass and imported glass were used in jewelry. Semiprecious and precious stones such as carnelian, lapis lazuli, feldspar, and turquoise were worked into large, multicolored round collars, pectorals (decorative pendants), earrings, bracelets, armlets, and hair or head ornaments. Religious symbols appear often in jewelry, as well as in art. Archeological finds attest to the high level of skill of jewelers, and to the widespread use of jeweled personal ornaments.

EGYPTIAN COSTUME:
C. 3000–300 B.C.

Costume may express the relationships between the individual and his or her natural and social environments. As the social structures of society evolved, dress was one means of manifesting visually one's personal power, dignity, or wealth. The climate of Egypt did not require clothing for warmth. Most garments consisted of pieces of fabric, usually square or rectangular, that were draped and tied around the body. Raw, unfinished edges of cut cloth were turned under and hemmed. Clothing forms for all ages and classes were relatively simple, with minimal sewing and construction required. Only a few garments actually had **seams** (places where one piece of cloth was joined to another by sewing).

Clothing identified distinctions in social status. These were evident not so much in the types of clothing worn, but rather in the quality of the materials used and in the amount of clothing owned by the individual. Slaves, peasants, and lower-class people lacked personal wealth, power, and status (hence they would not have needed a great variety of clothing items). But what clothing they did have was not different in shape or construction from that of the upper classes.

Table 2.1 summarizes the types of garments worn during the various Egyptian periods.

Costume Terminology

Although the Egyptians had a written language called hieroglyphics, it is not possible to ascertain what names Egyptians gave to individual garments. Costume historians have as-

signed names to some of these garments. In some cases those names derive from words that have been associated with Egyptian civilization in some way; in other cases names have been made up based on the style or the function of garments. In this text the authors will use descriptive modern English terms for costume items, but will also mention those names that appear frequently in costume histories so that readers will know what is meant if they encounter these words in other publications.

The term **kalasiris** or **calasiris** serves to illustrate some of the problems of terminology. As readers can see in *Contemporary Comment Box 2.1, page 29,* the Greek historian Herodotus mentioned a garment which he said the Egyptians called a **calasiris.** He described it as a fringed tunic. Many costume historians apply this term to a close-fitting garment, also called a **sheath dress,** which was worn by women; others apply it to tunics; and still others apply it to both tunics and closely fitting dresses.

EGYPTIAN COSTUME FOR MEN:
C. 3000–300 B.C.

Costume Components for Men

GARMENTS

loincloth Linen loincloths were under or outer garments shaped and worn like triangular diapers. Strings were attached for tying the garment around the waist, although sometimes a separate sash was also wrapped around the waist. Often loincloths were the sole garment worn by laborers. (See *Figure 2.6.*) Actual examples of leather loincloths have also been found. A few are solid leather, but most consist of a network of leather with solid sections of leather as reinforcement at the waist and over the buttocks. These network loincloths are generally depicted as being worn over cloth loincloths.

apron Vogelsang-Eastwood (1993) defines aprons as separate items that cover the genital area and are worn alone over a skirt or some other garment, or over a loincloth and under a skirt. She describes them as being made of one or more pieces of cloth attached to a belt, sash, or band that fastens around the waist. No actual examples of this garment have been found in Egypt, although examples exist in the nearby region of Nubia, which was subject to Egyptian influences. Illustrations show men dressed only in aprons, but when these garments are combined with skirts (see *Figure 2.6*) it is difficult to ascertain whether they are separate garments or a part of the skirt construction. This is especially true of art from the Middle and New Kingdoms that frequently showed men wearing skirts with large, projecting triangular aprons. Since

Table 2.1

GARMENTS WORN BY EGYPTIAN MEN AND WOMEN DURING VARIOUS HISTORICAL PERIODS

Periods	Men	Women
Old Kingdom (2620–2260 B.C.)	cloth loincloths short wraparound skirts long, narrow aprons long cloaks sashes and straps sandals	cloth loincloths wraparound skirts of various types wraparound sheath dresses bead-net dresses V-necked dresses shawls and long cloaks sashes and straps sandals
Middle Kingdom (2134–1786 B.C.)	cloth and leather loincloths wraparound skirts of various lengths long, narrow and triangular aprons short shawls and long cloaks sashes and straps sandals	cloth loincloths wraparound skirts of various types wraparound sheath dresses bead-net dresses V-necked dresses shawls and long cloaks sashes and straps sandals
New Kingdom (1575–1087 B.C.)	cloth and leather loincloths wraparound skirts of various lengths, sometimes layered sashed, wraparound skirts triangular aprons bag tunics knotted and wraparound cloaks of various kinds sashes and straps sandals	cloth loincloths wraparound skirts of various types wraparound sheath dresses wraparound dresses of more complex construction bag tunics shawls and long cloaks sashes and straps sandals

Based on material in data from G. Vogelsang-Eastwood. 1993. *Pharaonic Egyptian Clothing.* Leiden, The Netherlands: E. J. Brill, p. 180.

no actual examples of such garments have been found, the question of whether these were separate aprons or simply the way that the ends of the wrapped skirt were arranged remains unanswered.

wrapped skirt　A wrapped skirt, the length, width, and fit of which varied with different time periods and social classes, served as a major garment for men throughout all of Egyptian history. Costume historians have called this costume a **schenti, shent, skent,** or **schent.** Others use the term **kilt.** (A kilt is a short skirt worn by Scotsmen, and authors may use this term as a means of distinguishing between male and female dress, calling the same garment a skirt when worn by women.) A number of different skirts for men can be seen in *Figures 2.6, 2.7,* and *Color Plate 1.* The following variations can be identified:

- In the earliest periods, the skirt was generally knee length or shorter, and fitted closely around the hips. There were pleated skirts and some with a diagonal line across the front, which sources have suggested was achieved by rounding one end of the fabric. No curved fabrics have been found, however, and Vogelsang-Eastwood (1993, p. 53) points out that by taking the end of a square piece of fabric and pulling it up to tuck into the waist, a curved shape is produced. Thus, it seems likely that the ornamental effect was achieved through draping.

- Middle Kingdom styles show the skirt elongated, sometimes reaching to the ankle, with shorter versions for work, for soldiers, or for hunters. A double skirt, the under layer opaque and outer layer sheer, appears, and continues in use into the New Kingdom. Some depictions show what appear to be pleats.

- New Kingdom styles have pleated skirts, both shorter examples that tend to fit more closely and long skirts that are quite full. Large, triangular decorative panels are located at the front of some skirts.

By following the lines of pleats in garments shown on statues, it is possible to gain some understanding of how the fabrics were draped. In one version, a length of fabric ap-

CONTEMPORARY COMMENTS 2.1

Egyptian Costume as Described by Herodotus

The Greek historian Herodotus (484?–425? B.C.) traveled extensively. One of the places that he visited was Egypt. The following are his observations on the clothing practices of the Egyptians.

In other countries the priests have long hair, in Egypt their heads are shaven; elsewhere it is customary, in mourning for near relatives to cut their hair close; the Egyptians, who wear no hair at all at any other time, when they lose a relative, let their beards and the hair of their heads grow long....

... Their men wear two garments apiece, their women but one. [Book II, Chapter 36.]

... They wear linen garments, which they are specially careful to have always fresh washed....

... [Of priests] Their dress is entirely of linen, and their shoes of the papyrus plant: it is not lawful for them to wear either dress or shoes of any other material.... [Book II, Chapter 37.]

... They wear a linen tunic fringed about the legs, and called calasiris; over this they have a white woollen garment thrown on afterwards. Nothing of woollen, however, is taken into their temples or buried with them, as their religion forbids it. [Book II, Chapter 81.]

From *The Persian Wars by Herodotus*, translated by George Rawlinson. Copyright 1942 by Random House, Inc.; reprinted by permission of Random House, Inc.

FIGURE 2.6

Egyptian wall painting, c. 1415 B.C. A variety of costume types. Within the picture can be seen a woman in a sheath dress, various examples of schentis worn without upper body coverings, two workers dressed only in loincloths, sheer long and short tunics of varying lengths worn over or under a schenti. (Photograph courtesy, the Metropolitan Museum of Art.)

FIGURE 2.7

Apuy, a sculptor of the New Kingdom period, and his wife receiving an offering. Men and women wear sheer, pleated linen gowns with wide bead collars. Man making the offering wears a leopard skin with a pleated linen schenti. All wear wigs, those of the men are shorter than those of the women. A scented cone of wax is placed on their heads. The fingernails and toenails of both men and women are polished, their eyes outlined in kohl. The men wear sandals. (Photograph courtesy, The Metropolitan Museum of Art, copy in tempera of wall paintings from a tomb.)

peared to have been pleated along its long direction. The pleats were arranged horizontally across the back, then pulled up, diagonally, to the waistline in front where the ends were tied or passed over each other. They hung downward at center front to form a pleated panel (Houston 1964).

upper body coverings　In very early representations, one may see the skin of a leopard or lion fastened across the shoulders of men. In later periods, fabric replaced skins for the construction of upper garments. Wearing animal skins was reserved for the most powerful element in society: kings and priests. (See *Figure 2.7*.) Finally, even the skins were no longer worn, but were replaced by ritual garments made from cloth simulating animal skins. Leopard spots were painted onto the cloth. The Egyptian belief in magic seems to underlie this practice. The Egyptians believed that by wearing the skin of a fierce beast the powers of the animal were magically transferred to the wearer.

In the Middle and New Kingdoms men wore a short fabric cape that fastened at center front. Not unlike a cape, a wide necklace made from concentric circles of precious or semiprecious stones might be worn alone, over a linen gown, over a short cape, or with a corselet. (See *Figure 2.7*.) The **corselet** was sleeveless, probably a decorative form of armor, and might be either strapless or suspended by small straps from the shoulders (See *Visual Summary Table, page 39*).

Men were sometimes depicted wearing narrow straps wrapped around the upper part of the body. The method of wrapping varied. Sometimes straps ran diagonally over one shoulder, sometimes across both shoulders, sometimes they were also wrapped around the waist or at various points on the chest. They were most likely a practical garment used to prevent perspiration from running down the body. Women were only rarely shown wearing straps, and then usually when engaged in physical activity such as dancing or acrobatics.

tunic　During the New Kingdom a number of new elements entered dress, probably as a result of cross-cultural contacts with the near East, the invasion of the Hyksos, and/or the expansion of the Egyptian empire into the area west of Egypt.

Longer tunics, similar to those of Mesopotamia, appeared in Egypt about the time of the New Kingdom. As depicted on wall paintings, they are made with or without sleeves and often of sheer almost transparent linen. Artists show loincloths or a short skirt underneath or skirts wrapped over tunics. (See *Figure 2.6* and *Color Plate 1*.)

long wrapped garments　The earliest wrapped garments appeared on depictions of both men and women of all classes from the earliest period up until the Middle Kingdom. Later wrapped garments seem to be associated only with women, gods, and kings. A possible way of wrapping the fabric is depicted in *Figure 2.10*.

During the New Kingdom men appeared in long, loose flowing garments of sheer pleated linen. (See *Figure 2.7*.) The precise construction of these garments is not clear from most of their representations. The following alternatives have been suggested:

• Full tunic worn loose or belted.

• Skirt with cape or shawl.

• Wrapped shawl.

shawls and cloaks　Shawls, consisting of squares or rectangles of fabric that wrapped around the upper part of the body and did not extend below the waist, were shown on both men and women. Longer cloaks, which probably were worn for warmth, also appeared. Some of these were wrapped around the body in various ways, while others had ends tied together over one shoulder.

EGYPTIAN COSTUME FOR WOMEN: 3000–300 B.C.

Costume Components for Women

GARMENTS

skirts Paintings often show skirts on lower-class women at work. Slaves and dancing girls are also depicted occasionally without clothes or with a small cloth strip covering the genitals and held up with a narrow waistband. (See *Figure 2.11.*)

wrapped dress or sheath and bead net dresses Costume historians have described the most common garment for women of all classes as a **sheath** dress. This garment appears as a close-fitting tube of fabric beginning above or below the breasts and ending around the lower calf or ankle (see *Figure 2.8*). It appears to have one or two straps holding it over the shoulders. Many authors have commented about the tightness of this garment, and have noted that it fits so tightly that it would have been difficult not only to get into, but also to wear. For this reason it has been suggested that artists depicted the garment in a conventional rather than a realistic manner.

Dr. Vogelsang-Eastwood (1993, 96) argues persuasively that this garment was probably a wraparound dress (see *Figures 2.8 and 2.10a*), and that the shoulder straps were separate garments. As evidence she notes that no sheath dresses have been found in any excavations, but that lengths of cloth with patterns of wear consistent with wrap-around dresses have been found in fairly substantial numbers. This also solves the problem of the varying placements of the top of the garment, as the cloth could have been wrapped around the body at any point above or beneath the breasts or at the waist. Separate straps could have been placed in any of a variety of ways.

Scholars are uncertain about the techniques used to decorate the fabrics of sheath dresses, which are often elaborately patterned. Speculations include painted designs, appliqués, leather, feathers, beadwork or woven designs. From the evidence in the Tutankhamen tomb we know that skill in beadwork was well-developed. A pair of gloves of woven fabric with a design similar to those seen on many of the sheaths was discovered in the same tomb. Actual beaded net dresses have been found in tombs (see *Figure 2.9*). Some of the patterned effects seen on closely fitting dresses (*Figure 2.8*) could have been achieved by placing a beaded net dress over a wrapped dress.

FIGURE 2.8

Models of girls of the Middle Kingdom (XI Dynasty) bearing baskets of offerings for a funeral. Both wear closely fitted sheath dresses and wide, faience collars. (Photograph courtesy, The Metropolitan Museum of Art, Museum Excavations, 1919–1920; Rogers Fund, supplemented by contribution of Edward S. Harkness.)

pleated and draped wrapped long dress Though at first glance the sheer, pleated robes of men and women look alike, careful examination reveals that their draping and arrangement were different. Some women's styles cover the breasts, and others leave them exposed. (See *Figure 2.7*.) These garments are the most complex worn by Egyptian women. A number of scholars have suggested ways in which these sheer, pleated garments may have been wrapped. See *Figure 2.10* for some of these suggestions.

tunics and v-necked dresses Women, like men, wore loosely fitted tunics. Women of a lower economic class, such as musicians, often wore these garments. (See *Figure 2.11*.)

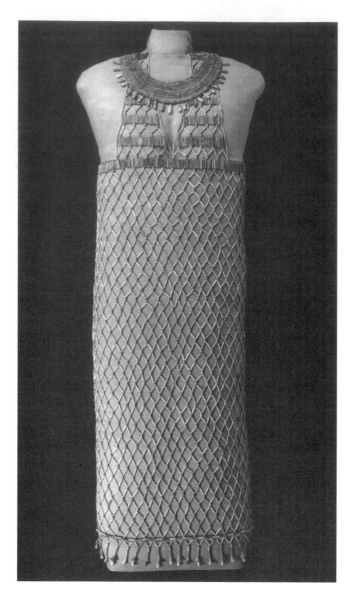

FIGURE 2.9

Bead-net dress from Giza. It has been suggested that these dresses were placed over a wraparound garment such as that shown in Figure 2.10a. (Photograph courtesy, Museum of Fine Arts, Boston. u27.1548.)

Among the most numerous garments found in women's tombs are V-necked dresses with or without sleeves. The simple sleeveless version of this dress, which may be either pleated or plain, appeared beginning with the Old Kingdom. The sleeved version is more complex, with a tubular skirt joined to a yoke. *Figure 2.12* shows two examples of this dress.

Shawls and cloaks of similar types were worn by women and men.

With so much of Egyptian clothing being made from lengths of cloth wrapped around the body, sashes helped to hold clothing in place. Both men and women are depicted wearing sashes; however, men seem to wear sashes more often. Surviving examples are made of rope; plain weave linen, sometimes with fringes or tassels; and elaborately designed tapestry or double weave fabrics. For upper-class individuals dressed in white linen, sashes and men's decorated aprons are sometimes the only ornamentation and color, other than that provided by jewelry.

Costume Components for Men and Women

HAIR AND HEADDRESS

Men were usually clean shaven. However, the beard was a symbol of maturity and authority and was, as a consequence, worn (or at least depicted on paintings and sculpture) not only by adult male rulers but also by young kings and even by Queen Hatshepsut, who ruled around 1500 B.C. A king with a false beard is shown in *Color Plate 1*. During some periods, men shaved their heads as well. It was less common, though not unknown, for women to shave their heads.

Wigs were worn over the shaved head or over the hair. The shape, length, and arrangement of wigs varied from period to period. More expensive wigs were of human hair; cheaper ones were made of wool, flax, palm fiber, or felt. Most wigs were black in color, although blue, brown, white, or some gilded examples exist. Even when wigs were relatively short, women's tended to be longer than men's. Their styling ranged from simple, long flowing locks to complex braiding, curls, or twists of "hair." It is likely that wigs were worn because they were decorative and could more easily be made into complicated styles than real hair. Furthermore, in the hot Egyptian climate some individuals probably found it comfortable and convenient to wear wigs over shaved heads or short hair. This also made it easier to avoid getting head lice. (See wigs in *Figures 2.7, 2.8,* and *Color Plate 1.*)

Much of Egyptian headdress was ceremonial and/or symbolic. See *Illustrated Table 2.1, page 36,* for depiction and summary of the major head covering styles and their functions.

FOOTWEAR

Only high-status persons wore sandals, while low-status individuals went barefoot. Sandals were made of rushes woven or twisted together. Some examples from royal burials are elaborately decorated. The status of the wearer was demonstrated by superior workmanship, increased decoration, and finer materials. (See *Figures 2.7* and *2.13.*)

JEWELRY

With New Kingdom gowns, jewelry or jeweled belts were the main sources of color. Belts and decorated aprons often provided the only touches of color on clothes made of plain white linen. Beads, leatherwork, appliqué, and woven designs could all be used to construct the highly ornate deco-

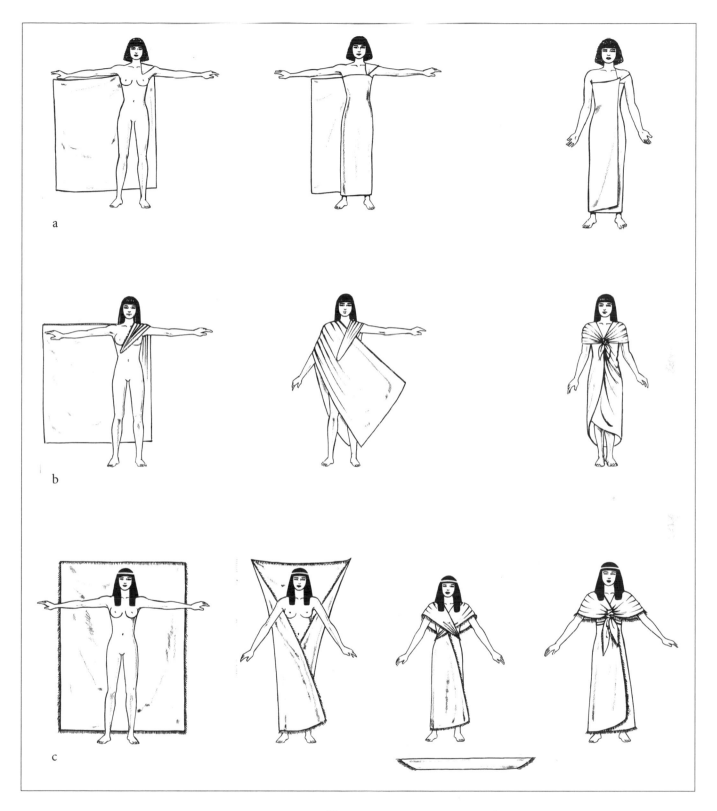

FIGURE 2.10

Suggested ways of draping some items of Egyptian wrapped costume. (a) The wrap-around garment for men or women. (b) and (c) Two alternatives for creating a woman's draped gown. (Adapted from Vogelsang-Eastwood, G. 1993. *Pharaonic Egyptian Clothing*. Leiden, The Netherlands: E. J. Brill.)

FIGURE 2.11
Wall painting of musicians from the New Kingdom (Dynasty VIII.) Figures on the extreme left and right wear sheath dresses and have cones of wax on their heads. The flute player wears a kalasiris. (Photograph courtesy, The Metropolitan Museum of Art.)

FIGURE 2.12

V-necked linen dresses from Deshasha, Egypt. (Photograph courtesy, Petrie Museum, London. UC31182 and 31183.)

FIGURE 2.13

From left to right: Shawl, of linen, from the Late Period (Dynasty XX1); kerchief from the New Kingdom (Dynasty XVII); child's linen garment, made like the description by Herodotus of the kalasiris, from the Late Period; sandals for a child and for an adult from the New Kingdom, (Dynasty XVIII). (Photograph courtesy, The Metropolitan Museum of Art.)

rative belts and aprons that were an integral part of Egyptian costume.

Wide jeweled collars covered most of the chest and had a counterweight at the back to balance the heavy section in front. These collars appear in art from the Old Kingdom up to and beyond the New Kingdom. Other ornaments worn at the neck were **pectorals** (ornaments that hung down on the chest), single **amulets** (charms worn around the neck to ward off evil), or plaques with mounted amulets.

Some **diadems** (crowns) or fillets placed on the head held flowers. Others copied flowers in metal and polished stones. Armlets, bracelets, and anklets were all worn, though only in the New Kingdom were they all worn simultaneously.

Possibly another of the contributions of the Hyksos to Egyptian styles, earrings are a late addition to Egyptian jewelry. First worn by women, they seem eventually to have also been used by men. In the 1977–78 exhibit of artifacts from the tomb of Tutankhamen, it was suggested that earrings may have been worn by young boys, but abandoned in manhood (*Treasures of Tutankhamen 1972*).

COSMETICS

Both men and women decorated their eyes, skin, and lips. Red ochre pigment in a base of fat or gum resin was used to color lips. Fingernails and toenails were polished and buffed. Henna, a reddish hair dye, may have been used to color nails. Scented ointments were applied to the body.

Eye paint had cosmetic, symbolic, and medicinal functions. Eye painting represented the eye of the god Horus, considered a powerful charm, and the line formed around the eye helped to protect against the glare of the sun. Some written records include medical prescriptions for eye paints. In the Old Kingdom green eye paint predominated; in the Middle Kingdom both green and black paints were used; by the New Kingdom black **kohl** (made of galena, a sulfide of lead) had replaced green. (See *Color Plate 1*.)

EGYPTIAN COSTUME FOR CHILDREN: 3000–300 B.C.

The children who are depicted in Egyptian paintings are generally the offspring of wealthy or royal families. These representations and the numerous toys found in Egyptian tombs indicate that children were regarded with interest and warm affection. Education was provided for boys—the very rich had private tutors, the less affluent went to temple schools. Children of the lower classes were taught a trade or craft, while sons of peasants labored in the fields with their fathers.

Dress for the very young was minimal. Little boys are depicted as naked except for an occasional bracelet or amulet;

little girls wear necklaces, armlets, bracelets, anklets, and sometimes earrings. Some pictures show girls wearing a belt at the waist. (See *Figure 2.11*.) After beginning school, boys apparently were dressed in skirts or tunics (see *Color Plate 1*), or among the lower classes probably in a loincloth. Girls apparently continued to go naked until close to the time they reached puberty, when they were dressed like their mothers.

Special hairstyles for children appear. In some representations, the head is completely shaved; in others part is left unshaven. The long locks of hair that grew in the unshaven part of the head were arranged in curls or braids. The children of the pharaoh wore a distinctive hairstyle called the **lock of Horus** or the **lock of youth** in which one lock of hair remained on the left side of the head. This lock was arranged carefully in braids over the ear. (See *Illustrated Table 2.1, page 37*, and *Color Plate 1*.)

EGYPTIAN COSTUME FOR SPECIALIZED OCCUPATIONS

Costume for specialized occupations showed some minor variations from the basic Egyptian styles.

Military Costume

The ordinary foot soldier of Ancient Egypt wore a short skirt. In the New Kingdom representations, an additional stiffened triangular panel is shown at the front, possibly to protect the vulnerable genitals. A helmet, made of padded leather, covered the head. The soldier carried weapons and a shield. In some instances a sleeveless armored corselet supported by straps was shown. This garment covered the chest and is thought to have been made of small plates of bone, metal, or leather sewn to a linen body. Most soldiers are depicted as barefooted.

When the pharaoh dressed for war, he wore the costume typical of his era plus the special insignia of his rank: a special crown called the blue war crown (see *Illustrated Table 2.1, page 36*) and a false beard. When at war the king carried weapons. After the adoption of chariots for warfare the pharaoh was often represented riding in a chariot while a servant preceded him, carrying his sandals.

Religious Costume

The costume of priests does not differ much from that of ordinary Egyptians. Priests were usually depicted with shaven heads. One of the insignias of the priesthood was either a real or simulated leopard skin draped over the shoulders.

Illustrated Table 2.1

SOME OF THE HEADDRESS WORN IN ANCIENT EGYPT

Illustration	Name of Style	Worn by
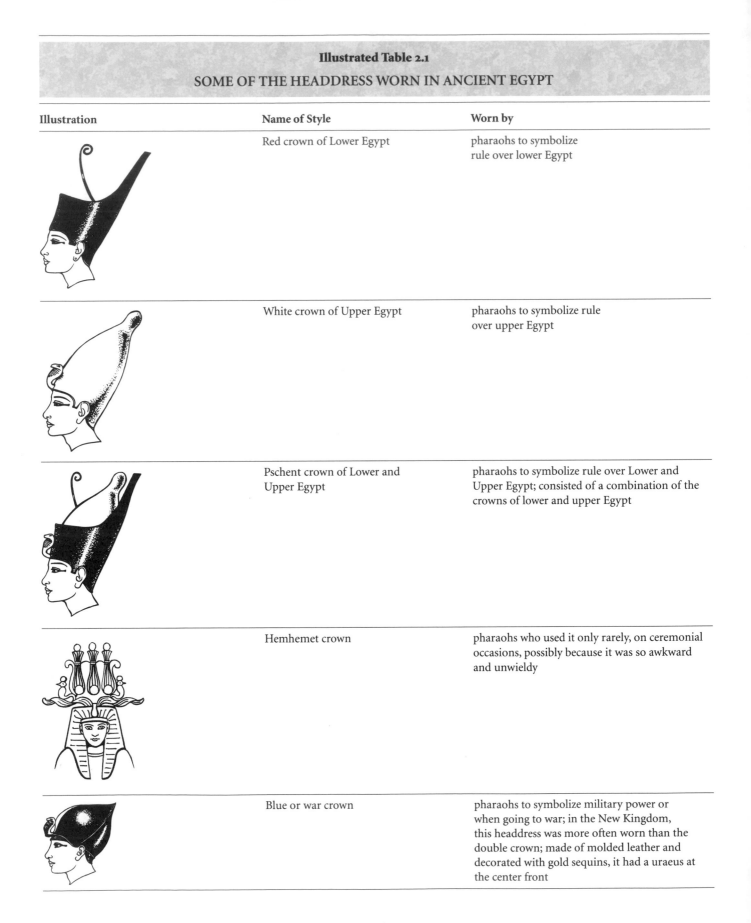	Red crown of Lower Egypt	pharaohs to symbolize rule over lower Egypt
	White crown of Upper Egypt	pharaohs to symbolize rule over upper Egypt
	Pschent crown of Lower and Upper Egypt	pharaohs to symbolize rule over Lower and Upper Egypt; consisted of a combination of the crowns of lower and upper Egypt
	Hemhemet crown	pharaohs who used it only rarely, on ceremonial occasions, possibly because it was so awkward and unwieldy
	Blue or war crown	pharaohs to symbolize military power or when going to war; in the New Kingdom, this headdress was more often worn than the double crown; made of molded leather and decorated with gold sequins, it had a uraeus at the center front

Illustrated Table 2.1

SOME OF THE HEADDRESS WORN IN ANCIENT EGYPT

Illustration	Name of Style	Worn by
	Uraeus	kings and queens; a representation of a cobra, which was a symbol of royal power; could be worn on a headband, or as part of another headdress
	Nemes Headdress	rulers from the Old to the New Kingdom; a scarflike construction that completely covered the head, was fitted across the temple, hanging down to the shoulder behind the ears, and with a long tail at center back that symbolized a lion's tail; the shape of the Nemes head covering is similar to a simple, scarflike headcovering owned by the Metropolitan Museum (See *Figure 2.13*)
	Falcon or vulture headdress	queens or goddesses; shaped like a bird of prey with the wings falling down at the side of the head and framing the face
	Flat crown	appears on depictions of Queen Nefertiti, a New Kingdom queen, who apparently wore this head covering over a shaved head
	Lock of Youth	children of the royal family

Gods and goddesses are shown in Egyptian art dressed as ordinary mortals, but wearing special headdresses or carrying symbols of their divinity. In the New Kingdom, goddesses were dressed in the older, fitted sheath style and they often appeared alongside mortals dressed in the pleated robe. It may have been a convention to show these divinities in costumes that emphasized their timelessness. The pharaoh, who was considered to be divine, frequently appears wearing the special headdress or insignia of the gods.

Costume for Musicians, Dancers, and Acrobats

Entertainers, such as dancers and acrobats, are often shown as naked or wearing only a band around the waist. Musicians, both male and female, wore the simpler costume forms of the period. During the New Kingdom this would have been a full, very sheer tunic or calasiris. (*See Figure 2.11.*)

SUMMARY

VISUAL SUMMARY

The accompanying *Visual Summary Table* illustrates the most important apparel items from the Mesopotamian and the Egyptian periods.

THEMES

Although we are separated from the Mesopotamian and Egyptian cultures by thousands of years and we do not have a complete view of the lives of these ancient peoples, some of the themes discussed in Chapter 1 emerge from this broad overview of 3,000 years of Mesopotamian and Egyptian costume.

The stability of costume in Egypt as compared with more frequent changes in Mesopotamia can be related to themes such as POLITICAL CONFLICT with its accompanying wars and invasions, ECONOMIC EVENTS such as patterns of trade, and the CROSS-CULTURAL CONTACTS that resulted from warfare and trade. Mesopotamia, more open geographically to both invaders and traders, shows the results in its more frequent costume changes, whereas Egypt, more geographically isolated, experiences important changes only in relatively rare instances such as the adoption of the tunic after the invasion of Egypt and subsequent political control by the Hyksos, a foreign people.

SOCIAL LIFE, SOCIAL ROLES, SOCIAL CLASS STRUCTURE, and CHANGES AND/OR PATTERNS IN SOCIAL BEHAVIOR undoubtedly shaped clothing practices in both of these civilizations. The most obvious examples are in the differences in the quality and variety of apparel worn by upper classes and

lower classes and in those items such as headdresses that designated status. (See *Illustrated Table 2.1, page 36.*) However, because our knowledge of social life of these periods is limited in many ways, we undoubtedly overlook nuances in dress that must have been obvious to people living at the time.

In Egypt and Mesopotamia, the themes of PRODUCTION OF TEXTILES, ECOLOGY, and THE ARTS AND DRESS come together. Linen, a fabric that was comfortable in the heat of a tropical climate and that could be made into soft, sheer, drapable fabrics, was the primary material from which garments were made throughout the history of this civilization. Mesopotamian costume, too, continued to utilize one fiber to a considerable extent: wool, which made a fabric of greater bulk and warmth than linen. (In the later periods, both cotton and linen seem also to have been added to the materials from which Mesopotamians made their clothes.)

Egyptian costume began with the simple loincloth or skirt for men and a straight, close-fitting wrapped dress (sheath) or a skirt for women. Throughout the history of this civilization, although the forms of these costumes grew more elaborate and more decorative and although additional types of garments were added, the basic aesthetic preference for clothing that complemented the natural lines of the body was retained. By contrast, Mesopotamian clothing was designed not to complement the body, but to cover it. The early kaunakes skins and full-length garments, the draped styles of the later Babylonians, and the shawls that wrapped the Assyrian kings covered the body with layers of fabric that obscured its natural lines. These differences have been attributed not only to geographical or ecological differences, but also to differences in standards of taste. Leix (*CIBA Review*) pointed out that Egyptians loved clarity of form in life and art, while the Babylonians loved pomp and luxury. This latter preference is reflected in the heavy fabrics, rich patterns, and elaborate fringes of Mesopotamian styles. Furthermore, moral reasons, possibly expressed as different views of modesty in dress, may

Visual Summary Table

MAJOR MESOPOTAMIAN AND EGYPTIAN GARMENTS

Sumerian man and woman in kaunakes
type garments (3500–2500 B.C.)

Babylonian man
(2500–1000 B.C.)

Assyrian ruler
(1000–600 B.C.)

Royal Egyptian boy in
draped skirt, corselet, and
wearing his hair in the lock
of youth. (New Kingdom)

Egyptian women in (a) draped gown
(New Kingdom) and (b) sheath dress
(Old Kingdom through New Kingdom)

Egyptian wearing a tunic
(New Kingdom)

also have influenced styles. Mesopotamian religions show a greater preoccupation with ethical problems than do those of Egypt.

LATER SURVIVALS OF MESOPOTAMIAN AND EGYPTIAN DRESS

The decline of the Assyrian civilization did not totally obliterate all traces of Mesopotamian costume. At least one element of dress persisted in the region and, eventually, found its way into other parts of the world. The high crowned headdress worn by Assyrian kings was adopted by the Persians. From its use in Persia it eventually found its way into the costume of the Eastern Orthodox Christian priests.

Certain other aspects of Mesopotamian costume utilized not only by the Sumerian, Babylonian, or Assyrian peoples, but also more generally throughout the Near East have survived into more recent times. The custom of requiring women to wear a veil outside of the home is one example. It has also been suggested (although it cannot be documented) that the kaunakes fabric in the form of a garment worn by shepherds and other rustic peoples may have come into European art to symbolize people from little known or distant lands of the Middle East.

Egyptian costume did not long survive the Greek and Roman domination of Egypt, although it was used for the formal portraits of the last pharaohs and Queen Cleopatra. Instead the Egyptians adopted first Greek, then Roman styles. In several instances, however, ancient Egyptian fashions have influenced 20th century styles. The first was in 1920 when the discovery of the tomb of King Tutankhamen gave rise to a

FIGURE 2.14

After the discovery of the tomb of King Tutankhamon in 1922, Egyptian influences appeared in fashions of the 1920s such as this evening dress from 1923. (Reproduced courtesy Dover Publications, Inc. from *Authentic French Fashions of the Twenties*).

short-lived vogue for Egyptian-inspired fabrics, jewelry, and to a lesser extent, women's fashions. (See *Figure 2.14*.) The exhibit of artifacts from this same tomb in 1977–78 also motivated fashion and jewelry designers to orchestrate a revival of Egyptian inspired products. This, too, proved to be a short-term fashion.

NOTES

American Fabrics Encyclopedia of Textiles. 1972. Englewood Cliffs, NJ: Prentice-Hall.

Barber, E. J. W. 1991. *Prehistoric Textiles*, Princeton, NJ: Princeton University Press.

Barber, E. J. W. 1994. *Women's Work: the First 20,000 Years.* New York: W. W. Norton.

Born, W. "Footwear of the Ancient Orient," *CIBA Review,* p. 1210.

Casson, L. 1975. *Daily Life in Ancient Egypt.* New York: American Heritage.

Contenau, G. 1954. *Everyday Life in Babylon and Assyria.* London: Edward Arnold.

Fairservis Jr., W. A. 1962. *The Ancient Kingdoms of the Nile.* New York: New American Library, pp. 84–85.

Herodotus on Egypt reprinted in J. Hawkes, ed. *The World of the Past. Vol. I.* 1963. New York: Knopf.

Houston, M. G. 1964. *Ancient Egyptian, Mesopotamian, and Persian Costume.* New York: Barnes and Noble. Houston made an analysis of pictorial and sculptural representation of Mesopotamian and Egyptian costume and, based on her analysis, draped and sketched styles.

Iversen, E. 1991. In *Canon and Proportions in Egyptian Art.* United Kingdom: Aris and Phillips.

Leix, A. "Babylon-Assur: Land of Wool." *CIBA Review,* p. 406.

Mertz, B. 1990. *Red Land, Black Land.* New York: Peter Bedrick Books.

Oppenheim, A.L. 1967. *Letters from Mesopotamia.* Chicago, IL: University of Chicago Press, pp. 67, 85.

Stead, M. 1986. *Egyptian Life,* Cambridge, MA: Harvard University Press.

Treasures of King Tutankhamen. 1972. Catalog of the exhibition of the British Museum. London: British Museum, p. 39.

Vogelsang-Eastwood, G. 1993. *Pharaonic Egyptian Clothing.* Leiden, The Netherlands: E.J. Brill.

Wilford, J. N. 1993. "New Finds Suggest Even Earlier Trade on Fabled Silk Road." *New York Times,* March 16, C1.

S E L E C T E D   R E A D I N G S

Books Containing Illustrations of Costume of the Period from Original Sources

Al-Misri, et al. 1999. Egyptian Treasures from the Egyptian Museum in Cairo. New York: Harry N. Abrams.

Arnold, S., J. Allen, and L. Green. 1996. *The Royal Women of Amarna. Images of Beauty in Ancient Egypt.* New Haven, CT: Yale University Press.

Collon, D. 1995. *Ancient Near Eastern Art.* Berkeley, CA: University of California Press.

Curtis, J. et al., eds. 1995. *Art and Empire: Treasures from Assyria in the British Museum.* New York: Harry N. Abrams.

Egypt's Golden Age: The Art of Living in the New Kingdom, 1558–1085 B.C. 1982. Boston: Museum of Fine Arts.

Lloyd, S. 1961. *The Art of the Ancient Near East.* New York: Frederick A. Praeger.

Parrot, A. 1961. *The Arts of Assyria.* New York: Golden Press.

———. 1961. *The Dawn of Art (Sumer).* New York: Golden Press.

Vassilika, E. 1995. *Egyptian Art.* New York: Cambridge University Press.

Wilkinson, C. K. 1983. *Egyptian Wall Paintings.* New York: Metropolitan Museum of Art.

Periodical Articles

Barber, E. J. 1982. "New Kingdom Egyptian Textiles: Embroidery vs. Weaving." *American Journal of Archeology,* Vol. 86, No. 3, July.

Bass, G. F. 1970. "A Hoard of Trojan and Sumerian Jewelry." *American Journal of Archeology,* Vol. 74, No. 4, Oct., p. 335.

Cox, J. S. 1977. "The Construction of an Ancient Egyptian Wig (c. 1400 B.C.) in the British Museum." *Journal of Egyptian Archeology,* Vol. 63, p. 57.

Francis, M. 1978. "Form Follows Fashionable Function: The Look of the Egyptian XVIII Dynasty." *Dress,* p. 1.

Hall, R. and J. Barnett. 1985. "A Fifth Dynasty Funerary Dress in the Petrie Museum of Egyptian Archeology: its Discovery and Conservation." *Textile History,* Vol. 16, No. 1, p. 5.

Jastrow, M. "Veiling in Ancient Assyria." *Review of Archeology,* Vol. XIV, p. 209.

Larson, J. 1981. "The Het-sed Robe and the 'Ceremonial Robe' of Tutankhamen." *Journal of Egyptian Archeology,* Vol. 67, p. 180.

Reifstahl, E. 1970. "A Note on Ancient Fashions: Four Early Egyptian Dresses in the Museum of Fine Arts, Boston." Boston, MA: Museum of Fine Arts Bulletin, Vol. 67 (354), p. 244.

Daily Life: Mesopotamia

Oppenheim, A. L. 1977. *Ancient Mesopotamia: Portrait of a Dead Civilization.* Chicago: University of Chicago Press.

———. 1967. *Letters from Mesopotamia.* Chicago: University of Chicago Press.

Saggs, H. W. F. 1995. *Babylonians (Peoples of the Past, 1).* Norman, OK: University of Oklahoma Press.

Snell, D. C. 1997. *Life in the Ancient Near East.* New Haven, CT: Yale University Press.

Nemet-Nejet, K. 2002. *Daily Life in Ancient Mesopotamia.* Peabody, MA: Henrickson Publishing.

Daily Life: Egypt

Casson, L. 2001. *Everyday Life in Ancient Egypt.* Baltimore: Johns Hopkins University Press.

David, R. 1999. *Handbook to Life in Ancient Egypt.* New York: Oxford University Press.

Harris, N. 2002. *History of Ancient Egypt: The Culture and Lifestyle of the Ancient Egyptians.* New York: Barnes and Noble.

James, T. G. H. 1984. *Pharaoh's People.* Chicago: University of Chicago Press.

Mertz, B. 1990. *Red Land, Black Land.* New York: Peter Bedrick Books.

Romer, J. 1990. *Ancient Lives: Daily Life in Egypt of the Pharaohs.* New York: Henry Holt & Co.

Scott, N. 1973. *The Daily Life of the Ancient Egyptians.* New York: Metropolitan Museum of Art Bulletin, Vol. XXXI, No. 3, Spring.

White, J. M. 2002. *Everyday Life in Ancient Egypt.* (reprint). Mineola, NY: Dover.

CHRONOLOGY

2900–2100 B.C.
Early Minoan period

2000 B.C.
Development of the city of Knossos

2100–1600 B.C.
Middle Minoan period

1600–1150 B.C.
Late Minoan period

1571–1521 B.C.
Minos, legendary ruler of Crete

1450 B.C.
Eruption of volcano on the island of Thera, (now called Santorini),
destroying Cretan cities, including Knossos

1400–1200 B.C.
Domination by Myceneans

1100–800 B.C.
Dark Age of Greece

800–500 B.C.
Archaic period

776 B.C.
First Olympic games in Greece

500–323 B.C.
Classical Age
Flowering of Greek philosophy, art, drama, literature

356–323 B.C.
Alexander the Great

after 323 B.C.
Hellenistic period
Decline of Greek power

CRETE AND GREECE

c. 2900 – 300 B.C.

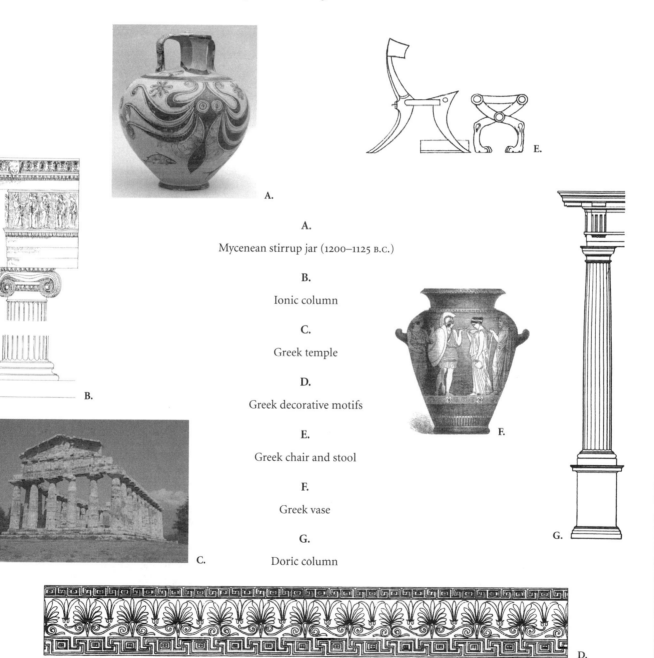

A.

Mycenean stirrup jar (1200–1125 B.C.)

B.

Ionic column

C.

Greek temple

D.

Greek decorative motifs

E.

Greek chair and stool

F.

Greek vase

G.

Doric column

Figure A courtesy of the Metropolitan Museum of Art, Louisa Eldridge McBurney Gift Fund (55.11.6). Figures B, D from Rettelbusch, E. 1996. *Handbook of Historic Ornament.* New York: Dover, pp. 13, 17. Figure C courtesy of V. R. Tortora. Figures E, F from Hottenroth, F. 1884. *Trachten Der Volker,* Vol. 1. Stuttgart: Verlag Gustav Wiese, p. 38. Figure G from Harris, C. M. 1977. *Illustrated Dictionary of Historic Architecture.* New York: Dover, pp. 127.

MINOAN AND MYCENAEAN CIVILIZATIONS

Historical Background

On the narrow island of Crete in the eastern Mediterranean, another civilization flourished over much the same period of time as that of the Egyptians and Mesopotamians. Named for their legendary king, Minos, the Minoan people enjoyed peace and prosperity from about 2900 to 1450 B.C. and developed an elegant culture. The Minoans were a prosperous seafaring people who carried on an active trade with Egypt, Syria, Sicily, and even Spain. The Minoan people are depicted in the wall paintings of Egypt; their pottery and other traces of their contact with foreign lands have been discovered in Asia Minor, mainland Greece, and islands in the Aegean Sea. Their cities had no fortifications because they depended on their fleet for protection. The pleasure-loving, secure life of the Minoan people was caught by their artists in delicate, brightly colored frescoes that have been found on the walls of excavated palaces in Crete and on the island of Thera. The crowning achievement of Crete was the palace of Knossos. Its many rooms gave rise to the legend that a labyrinth under the palace housed a fearsome creature, half man and half bull, that devoured prisoners.

Sir Arthur Evans, the English archeologist who first revealed the rich civilization of Crete, divided Minoan history into three main periods: Early Minoan (c. 2900–2100 B.C.), Middle Minoan (c. 2100–1600 B.C.), and Late Minoan (c. 1600–1150 B.C.). During most of the Middle Minoan period, the Minoans maintained political control not only over Crete, but also over what is today mainland Greece. The mainland people, named for their most powerful city-state, Mycenae, gradually grew stronger. By about 1400 B.C., in a reversal of political control, the Mycenaeans (*My-seh'-ne-ans*) had come to dominate Crete and the Minoan people. Archeologists had believed that this reversal of power probably resulted from a volcanic eruption on the island of Thera that caused earthquakes, fires, and tidal waves that wrecked Cretan cities. Recent discoveries, however, place this eruption about 200 years earlier than the fall of Crete and it is now thought that the Mycenaeans probably invaded and overcame the Minoans.

The Mycenaean civilization extended throughout Greece, centered in more than 300 towns. The towns spread out around the palaces, which each king tried to make a monument to his power and glory. The palaces were decorated with magnificent frescoes of great artistic and technical quality. The remains of these towns reveal works of architecture and large-scale engineering projects, which so astounded later generations of Greeks that they thought the walls of the Mycenaean cities and palaces had been built by giants. Other sources of information about the Mycenaeans include grave sites in which the artifacts of gold and silver reveal a wealthy and sophisticated civilization.

At the end of the 13th century, the mysterious "Sea People" (whose origins are not known by historians) devastated the Eastern Mediterranean area and ruined trade in a series of piratical raids. Many Mycenaean cities and towns suffered. The people were driven within the city walls for safety while their houses outside the fortifications were destroyed. Mycenae survived another century before it was destroyed, probably by the Dorians, invaders from the north. Some settlements were abandoned because they had depended on trade that no longer existed. Throughout Greece the population declined. Among the Mycenaean cities, Athens survived although it was somewhat impoverished. At the beginning of the 12th century, Greece entered a Dark Age about which little is known; the Minoan civilization disappeared at about the same time.

SOCIAL ORGANIZATION AND MATERIAL CULTURE OF MINOAN AND MYCENAEAN CIVILIZATIONS

Evidence about the organization and structure of Minoan and Mycenaean society is fragmentary. Apparently the Minoans had what amounted to a two-class society, with the ruling classes separated from the common people by a great gulf. No genuine middle class developed in ancient Greece.

Women occupied a higher place in society than in most early cultures. They enjoyed equality with men, and they were not secluded in the household but participated with men in public festivals. They engaged in athletics, often joining men in a favorite Minoan sport, vaulting over bulls. The position of women in Minoan civilization was an exception in the ancient world, possibly reflecting the importance of female deities. The major figure in Minoan religion was the "mother goddess." At the same time, unlike Egypt where queens did rule as pharaohs in some periods, the rulers of Crete were invariably men.

For the wealthy standards of material comfort were high. Several palaces have been excavated and their remains reveal that the private apartments in the palace were well lighted, decorated with wall paintings (frescos), and even had running water piped into bathrooms.

The Mycenaeans imitated many aspects of Minoan decoration and styles, but their social organization seems to have differed somewhat. Little is known of the manner of life of the ordinary citizen. Wealth apparently was concentrated in the king's court. There was a lesser nobility and a large group of lower-class craftsmen, peasants, and shepherds.

Art and Technology of Minoan and Mycenaean Civilizations

ART AS A SOURCE OF INFORMATION ABOUT COSTUME

As a result of the close contacts between Mycenaeans and Minoans, the styles of clothing utilized by both groups were essentially the same from the Middle Minoan period until the Later Minoan period. Most of the evidence for costume during the Minoan civilization comes from the statuary and wall paintings discovered in Crete. Some frescos and statuary of the period have also been found in mainland Greece.

The costume of the small statuettes of Minoan goddesses and priestesses is depicted in good detail. The dress of these statues has been taken to be characteristic of the dress of upper-class women. Wall paintings of general scenes of Minoan life confirm these details. Men's costume is more often shown on wall paintings than in statuary. Many of the wall paintings have been restored, with details reconstructed from fragments of the original paintings, so that inaccuracies may have been incorporated into the restorations.

TEXTILE PRODUCTION AND TECHNOLOGY

Barber (1994) describes a Minoan village in which evidence has been uncovered for spinning, weaving, and dyeing both linen and wool textiles. Minoan wall paintings and other art forms such as clay figurines depict brightly colored, elaborately patterned garments. Barber's (1991) careful analysis of evidence about Minoan textiles shows that many of the design motifs seen in Minoan art could have been woven easily. Many others, more difficult and time-consuming, are also technically possible with the types of looms in use. A few could have been achieved only by tapestry weaving, by embroidery, or by painting on textiles. Color was used lavishly, and skill in dyeing textiles must have been well developed. (See *Color Plate 2.*)

Egyptian wall paintings of traders dressed in Minoan garments provide evidence of trade between Egypt and Crete. Archeological evidence shows that chemicals used to fix dyes on linen were imported to Crete. A seafaring people, the Minoans undoubtedly traveled widely around the Mediterranean trading their textiles for other goods.

MINOAN COSTUME FOR MEN AND WOMEN: 2900–1150 B.C.

In commenting on many of the objects from the early Greek civilizations that archeologists have found, a Greek archeologist George Mylonas (1966) said "... these may be likened to the illustrations of a picture book for which the scholar must provide the text." This text, however, can be widely divergent in its interpretations and highly subjective. Precisely the same comment can be made about the representations of costume from the Minoan period. The lack of any body of literature, legal texts, or religious writings and even the fragmentary nature of many of the paintings from this period leave the costume historian at a loss as to the precise function of many items of dress and the conclusions that are drawn are, therefore, somewhat tentative.

Minoan costume is often described as tailored, cut and sewn to fit the body more closely, rather than draped. In a detailed study of Minoan costume, Houston (1966) suggests that the tailored costume of the Minoans may have evolved from the early use of leather for clothing.

Costume Components for Men and Women

GARMENTS

The garment worn closest to the skin was the loincloth, a fitted garment that covered much the same area as a pair of modern athletic briefs. A similar costume (called the *perizoma* in Greek) was worn by Greeks and Etruscans. (See *Figure 4.1, page 65*) Loincloths were depicted as worn by men and by women athletes. Men and women performed athletic leaps over the horns of bulls. For this activity they both wore loincloths, which, when used for this purpose, were reinforced at the crotch to protect against the horns of the bulls.

Men wore skirts. Some were short, ending at the thigh. These apparently wrapped around the body and generally ended in a point with a suspended, weighted tassel at center front and/or center back. They are shown as being made of elaborately patterned fabric. (See *Figure 3.1.*) Other skirts were depicted in longer lengths, ending either below the knee or at the ankle.

Women's skirts were bell shaped and had at least two, and possibly three, different forms. (See *Figure 3.2.*) One version was fitted at the waist, and flared gently to the ground. Another style seemed to have been made of a series of horizontal or V-shaped ruffles, with each successive ruffle wider in circumference than the one above it. In drawings and sculpture a third form shows a line down the center of women's skirts. Some scholars have interpreted this as a bifurcated garment similar to modern culottes. This may, however, have been an artistic convention used to depict V-shaped ruffles.

Women's costume had a unique aspect. Smoothly fitted bodices laced or otherwise fastened beneath the breasts, leaving the breasts exposed. (See *Figure 3.2a.*) Because most depictions of this breast-exposing style are of priestesses, some authorities believe ordinary women covered the breasts with sheer fabric (Boucher 1987). Most bodices had sleeves that fitted the arms closely. A few examples have small puffs at the shoulders.

Paintings and sculpture show apronlike garments worn by women on top of skirts. (See *Figures 3.2 c and d.*) They ex-

FIGURE 3.1

Restored frescoes from the palace at Knossos depict men from Crete who wear wrapped skirts with a tassel at the front.

HAIR AND HEADDRESS

Curly hair was apparently an ethnic characteristic. Probably much of the headdress had religious significance and may have served as a symbol designating priest or priestess status.

Men wore their hair long and curly or short, cut close to the head, and curly. Sometimes men tied their hair into a braid or lock at the back of the head; sometimes they held it in place with a fillet. Hat styles include elaborate, possibly ritual types: high, round and crownlike with a tall plume; turbans; small caps; and wide-brimmed hats.

Women's long, curled hair was often held in place with a fillet or elaborate arrangement of plain or jeweled bands. (See *Illustrated Table 3. 1, page 53.*) Hats ranged from high, tiered, brimless styles to beretlike flat hats.

FOOTWEAR

Men and women wore sandals or shoes with pointed toes that fitted the foot closely and ended at the ankle. Athletes (bull-leapers) wore a soft shoe with what appears to be a short sock

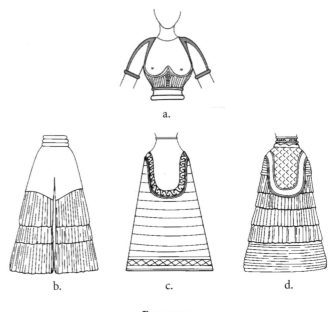

FIGURE 3.2

Redrawing of elements of Minoan costume for women: (a) Depicts bodice cut with short, fitted sleeves, a tight bodice which is open to below the breasts, made from patterned fabric and trimmed with bands of braid or embroidery. Whether all women bared their breasts is not clear, but figurines showing either priestesses or goddesses are represented with this bodice style. (b) Probably a skirt, but some scholars suggest that this garment may have been made in the form of wide-legged trousers. The exact construction is not clear. (c) A flared skirt with decorative horizontal bands. (d) Apparently made from rows of ruffles. Both (c) and (d) are depicted with an apronlike covering that extends from below the waist to the hip area. All drawings show tightly fitting wide belts.

tend in front and back to about mid-thigh. Archeologist Arthur Evans (1963) believed that this garment was a costume worn in religious rituals by women and that it derived from a primitive loincloth worn originally by members of both sexes.

Poncholike capes were usually worn by men in combination with skirts. These capes covered the upper part of the body and appeared to consist of a rectangle of fabric, folded in half, with an opening cut for the head. Both men and women wrapped shawllike garments made from animal skins or heavy wool around the body in cold weather.

Tight, rolled belts were apparently made from fabric or leather and decorated with metal. Belts were worn by men and boys from the earliest periods and adopted by women during later Minoan periods. Because Minoan men are shown with abnormally small waists (which may have been an artistic convention), some authorities speculate that these belts may have been placed on young boys from age 12 or 14 in order to constrict the development of the waist.

Men and women wore T-shaped tunics with long or short sleeves. Women's tunics were long; men's were long or short. Tunics were generally decorated with patterned bands at the hem, along the sides, and following the shoulderlines. These bands may have been decorative selvages, woven tapes, or embroidery. (See *Figure 3.3.*) Mycenaean men are more likely to be depicted in tunics rather than skirts or loincloths.

46

FIGURE 3.3

Redrawing of figures depicted on a sarcophagus from the 14th century B.C. at Hagia Triada, Crete, showing a procession of two women and a man. The woman at the left wears a sheepskin skirt and a fitted bodice. The man and woman at the right are wearing long tunics decorated with trimming that may be woven braid.

or ankle support. Archeologists have found that the floors of Minoan palaces show little wear from shoes, while entrance stairs are worn away from the passing of shod feet. This has led to the conclusion that people went barefoot indoors but wore shoes out-of-doors.

JEWELRY

Men and women wore rings, bracelets, and armlets. Women wore necklaces. Although earrings were found in Minoan graves, they are not generally depicted in the art.

COSMETICS AND GROOMING

Women apparently used eye makeup and, probably, lip coloring. Men were clean shaven.

MINOAN COSTUME FOR CHILDREN: 2900–1150 B.C.

Little evidence exists for the costume of children. Boys depicted in the paintings found on Thera wore little clothing: a fishing boy wore nothing; those boxing had strings around their waists. Their heads were shaven except for some locks of hair. One statuary group from Mycenae shows a small boy of perhaps about three or four years of age dressed in a floor-length skirt and wearing a necklace and a padded, rolled belt. Probably children wore simple costumes such as skirts or tunics. After puberty they undoubtedly assumed adult clothing.

TRANSITIONS IN THE DOMINANT STYLES

Some costume historians have pointed out parallels between the tiered skirts of Minoan women and the fringed kaunakes garments of Mesopotamia. Similarities also exist in language elements between Crete and the Middle East. Cretan traders traveled extensively throughout the Mediterranean area both to the East and to Egypt in the South. Certainly the Cretan traders reached the areas of Asia Minor where the kaunakes garments were worn, but even if the origin of the tiered skirt for Minoan women was to be found in the Middle East, the forms that evolved during the height of Minoan civilization differed markedly from the costume of Mesopotamia and Egypt during concurrent periods.

Sometime during the Dark Ages after the close of the Minoan–Mycenaean period, the fitted, full-skirted costume for women disappeared. Just how long it persisted after the beginning of the Dark Ages and how it came to be supplanted by the later Greek styles is unknown. By the time political control of Crete had passed to the Mycenaeans the elaborately patterned fabrics declined in use, giving way to plain cloth with simpler edgings. Barber (1991) speculates about this development, saying "One wonders if the Mycenaeans cheerfully bought up and wore the sumptuous Minoan fabrics as they began to take over affairs on Crete, but then allowed the local native industry to fade" (p. 330).

After a period of almost 400 years mainland Greece emerged from the Dark Ages into the Archaic period. By this time costume in general and the costume of women in particular had altered dramatically.

GREEK CIVILIZATION

Historical Background

Written records vanished during the Dark Ages. The political history of the period does not exist. Intellectual achievements were limited to epic ballads, sung perhaps by wandering bards, which were eventually woven into a cycle familiar to modern readers from the poems attributed to Homer, *The Iliad* and *The Odyssey*. Although he related stories about the heroes of the Trojan War, which occurred during the Mycenaean period, his epic poems describe the life and customs of his own times, probably before 700 B.C.

As the Dark Ages ended and Greece entered the Archaic period, c. 800 to 500 B.C., the Greek people began to prosper as their culture revived. Village communities began to evolve into independent city-states that would provide the first type of democratic government with elections, juries, and government by citizens of the city-state.

In the Classical Age, c. 500–323 B.C., Greece enjoyed a golden age, one of the most creative eras in the history of Western civilization. Greek philosophers such as Socrates, Plato, and Aristotle pondered the nature of the universe, the meaning of life, and ethical values. Tragic dramatists such as Aeschylus, Sophocles, and Euripides wrote dramas for the public dealing with the nature and fate of man. The Greeks developed "history," a new literary form, which related and analyzed past experiences. Greek sculpture glorified the human body; using new techniques to build in marble, the Greeks created architectural masterpieces.

Even before the Classical Age, Greeks had for centuries been establishing colonies throughout the Mediterranean. The first were on the western coasts of present-day Turkey, which the Greeks called Ionia. Greek settlements had also been established in Sicily, throughout southern Italy, and as far west as southern France. These centers of Greek culture and trade helped to spread Greek culture. Etruscan costume (the Etruscans were a people living on the Italian peninsula whose civilization predated the Roman) shows many resemblances to that of the Greeks, as do the later Roman styles. At the same time Greek costumes borrowed from the regions with which the Greeks came into contact, particularly from the Middle East.

Greek influence was spread also by the conquests of Alexander the Great of Macedonia (356–323 B.C.) whose father had brought Greece under his control. Alexander carved out an empire that stretched from Greece and Egypt in the west to the shores of the Indian Ocean in the east. After Alexander's death his empire fell apart; Greek influence waned while that of the Romans began to expand. Gradually the Romans supplanted the Greeks as the dominant force in the Mediterranean region, although the art and the wisdom of Greece continued to influence the world long after its political power was eclipsed.

Social Organization of the Greek Civilization

Society in the time of Homer was made up of nobility and commoners. Households were largely self sufficient, each one producing its own food and clothing textiles. A man's home was, quite literally, his fortress, protected by walls against the raiders who frequently attacked the Greek settlements, which were located near the sea.

By the Classical Age, a period for which written and art records abound, Greek communities had grown into city-states, and had developed a far more sophisticated and urban organization. A quite detailed picture of daily life in ancient Greece can be painted. Athens, the most famous city-state in Greece, was composed of a population of adult men (the active citizens), their dependent women and children, resident foreigners, and slaves.

An ordinary Athenian lived in a small, unpretentious house made of sun-dried brick that lacked central heating and running water. When not engaged in work, a man might attend the assembly of the law courts. "His recreation was found in the festivals and public facilities like gymnasiums which were provided by the city. Luxuries of diet, clothing, and furniture were for the very rich, although they, too, lived relatively simply. In democratic Athens extravagance and ostentation were quick to attract attention and draw censure" (Roebuck 1966).

In Homeric times, women occupied a subordinate position, but judging from the writings of Homer they had a rather open, companionable relationship with men. By the Classical Age, all this had changed. Women of good families not only lacked political power, but they also quite literally had no control over their own destinies. From birth to death they were under the control of some man. Even widows or divorced women, although they retained title to their inherited property, had to be supervised by their nearest male relative.

Marriages were arranged, and monogamy was the rule. Girls married at about age 14 to men who were usually about age 30. Scholars believe the average life span for women was about 40 years. Husbands did not consider their wives as equals, socially or intellectually, and did not appear with them in public. Secluded in the household, the wife oversaw the running of the home, where she was responsible for the children, food, and clothing. Through the spinning and weaving of fabrics and the making of clothing, she made a very real contribution to the economy of the household.

Scholars differ as to how freely women could move around the city outside the home. The current belief is that women were able to carry out at least some activities outside the home. They had to obtain water from the town fountains, attended public speeches, visited religious sanctuaries, and participated in religious festivals. Some of these activities included members of both sexes, but others were strictly for women. They could visit close friends and were permitted to attend tragic plays but not comedies, perhaps because these tended to be bawdy. As Reeder (1995) notes, "In all movements outside the home, a woman was supposed to be inconspicuous to the point of invisibility, and although the use of the veil is not yet well understood, she was probably expected upon leaving her house to wrap her mantle or a veil around her head so that it obscured part of her face and neck."

This practice may have come to Greece from Ionia and the Near East about 530 B.C., along with such styles as the Ionic form of dress. This veiling symbolized the subjugation of women to their husbands. Scholars see evidence for this custom in a large number of statues of women that have been found in which veils are pulled down at least partially over the face (Galt 1931) and in references in the writing of poets such as Homer.

There were exceptions to the strict regulation of women's activities. In Sparta, the largest and the most militaristic Greek city-state, women were less restricted, a state of affairs other Greeks found disquieting. The historian Plutarch described Spartan women as bold, masculine, and overbearing and seemed shocked at the notion that they spoke openly "even on the most important subjects" (Durant 1966).

One group of women was not subject to these constraints: the prostitutes. The lowest class of prostitutes lived in brothels, often in seaports. They dressed in such lightweight clothing that literary references described them as "naked." Nudity for women was not socially acceptable. A slightly higher class of courtesans were the "flute girls" who entertained with music and dancing at the otherwise all-male parties that were customary. These women are often depicted on vase paintings where some are shown clad in ordinary dress, some in special short dancing costumes, and others in the nude. The highest class of courtesans were the *hetairi*, the literal translation of the word is "companions." These women moved freely among men. They were often better educated than ordinary women, and some were known for their skill in philosophical disputation or for their literary efforts. A few became quite famous. Many dyed their hair blonde (the predominant hair color among Greek women was dark), and it appears that the law required them to wear specially decorated robes to distinguish them from respectable women.

In the Hellenistic period (after the death of Alexander the Great, 323 B.C.) the status of women seems to have risen somewhat. Female nudity in art increased (although it is not likely that women ever appeared nude), women were treated more openly and sympathetically in drama, and, interestingly, the influence of the *hetairi* on Athenian life diminished.

Fabrics and Cloth Production

Spinning and weaving were considered fit occupations for queens and goddesses. In Homer's *Odyssey*, Ulysses' faithful queen, Penelope, promises to choose a new king for Ithaca after she has completed the weaving of a shroud or burial sheet. After each day of weaving she secretly, at night, unravels the work that she has done. In this way she avoids taking a new husband. Athena, goddess of wisdom, patroness of the city of Athens, and patroness of artisans, is credited in Greek mythology as being the first woman to work with wool. As part of the religious ceremonies held in Athens every four years in honor of the goddess, a magnificently patterned garment, the sacred peplos, was carried in procession to the temple to be placed upon her statue. It had been woven by two women selected from those who participated in fertility rites associated with the cult of Athena.

Sheep herding was practiced in the mountainous Greek peninsula, and from those sheep wool for weaving was obtained. The Greeks also used linen, particularly after the 6th century B.C. Linen use seems to have come to Greece from Egypt by way of Asia Minor, particularly from the Ionian region where many Greeks had settled. Most of the linen used

in Greece was imported from the Middle East and Egypt. The island of Cos was known, in the late Greek period, for the production of silk, but scholars believe that the silk produced there was made from fabrics imported from China by way of Persia. Weavers unraveled the fabrics, turning them into fibers by untwisting the yarns. They combined silk fibers with linen fibers in order to make the precious silk go farther. Cotton fiber was apparently brought to Greece by the soldiers of Alexander the Great. For the most part, however, Greek clothing was made from wool or from linen (Faber *CIBA Review*).

The visual evidence for Greek styles often comes from marble statues that have been bleached white over the centuries or from vase paintings that do not show color. As a result it is often mistakenly assumed that Greek clothing had little color. (See *Color Plates 3* and *4*.) Fabrics were colored with dyes obtained from plants, minerals, and shellfish. Decoration of fabrics during weaving or by embroidery was common. Greek women were gifted weavers, and they were talented in embroidery.

Skill was developed in pleating fabrics, and some sort of clothes press existed for smoothing and flattening fabrics and pressing in pleats. Fabrics were bleached with the fumes of a sulfur compound. Because Greek costume was draped, not cut and sewn, the fabric was probably woven to the correct size and did not require cutting. (See *Figure 3.4.*)

Women manufactured all of the family clothing and covers for beds, cushions, and chests. Women making cloth at home generally carried out all of the steps in the process with the possible exceptions of dyeing and fulling. (See *Figure 3.4.*) Fulling is a process whereby wool fabrics are washed and shrunk to produce a dense, close weave. Dyeing and fulling were both processes that produced strong, unpleasant odors and required both space and a good supply of water; therefore they were not especially suited to urban households. When textiles were produced commercially for sale in the marketplace, the labor was divided into specialties that included wool combers, preparers of flax, spinners of yarn, dyers, fullers, and, when necessary, tailors to do the cutting and sewing.

SOURCES OF EVIDENCE FOR THE STUDY OF GREEK COSTUME

Greek Art

The sculpture and vase paintings of Greece provide evidence concerning the costume of ancient Greece. However, records from the early Archaic period are unclear. The art of that time was highly stylized (it is called "geometric art"), and provides little information about dress. The statuary of the 7th century B.C. begins to be sufficiently representational to permit some

FIGURE 3.4

Athenian women, c. 560 B.C., (left to right) preparing wool, folding cloth, spinning yarn, weaving on an upright loom, and weighing wool fiber. These women are dressed in the form-fitting Dorian peplos of the Archaic period. (Photograph courtesy, The Metropolitan Museum of Art, Fletcher Fund, 1931.)

conclusions to be drawn about costume. The later periods, particularly the Classical period, abound in representations of costume in sculpture and painting.

The Greeks developed the concept of ideal human form and proportions. Polyclitis, a sculptor (c. 450 B.C.), wrote an influential treatise about his view of the appropriate standard of proportions for sculptors. Through Greek art and writings this Greek ideal, a figure about seven and a half heads high with the hipline at wrist level halfway down the body, continued to influence ideas about perfect male and female proportions in subsequent periods and became a part of the heritage of classical influences in the Western world.

Although Greek vase painting and sculpture provide plenty of evidence about the construction of clothing, the conventions of Greek art limit information about color in dress. Greek marble statues had been colorfully painted, but over the centuries that color has been bleached away. Major Greek vase painting styles include black figure painting, with black figures on an orange-red background; red figure painting, with red figures on black background; and white ground vases. Only on these latter vases (see *Color Plate 4*) can one see color.

The Greek attitude toward nudity should be mentioned in this context. Nudity was not acceptable to the Minoans, the Mycenaeans, or the Homeric Greeks. Tradition records the date at which Greek men began to participate in athletic events in the nude as around 720 B.C. (Bonfante 1977). Athletic games in Greece were part of religious ritual. Athletes performing in the nude therefore had a religious context. Furthermore, the Greek ideal stressed not only perfection of the soul but perfection of the body as well. At about the same time that nudity came into athletics, artists began to make representations of the male nude.

Depiction of female nudity did not, however, follow. Although in earlier periods the ideal of the well-formed female body was clearly visible beneath the softly flowing draperies of the costume, only in Sparta did women participate in ath-

letics or attend the games. Women dancers and acrobats wore, at the minimum, a perizoma (a loincloth) and usually also a band covering the breasts. It is only after 400 B.C., when attitudes toward women seem to have become somewhat less restrictive, that artists sculpted some of the now famous nude or partially nude statues of women such as the Venus de Milo.

GREEK COSTUME FOR MEN AND WOMEN: 800–300 B.C.

The garment called the tunic heretofore was called a **chiton** *(ky′tn)* by the Greeks. Although many of the earliest depictions of Greek chitons give the impression of a garment sewn together at the shoulders and under the arms, later versions were not necessarily sewn, but often were created by taking a single rectangle of fabric and wrapping it around the body, securing it at the shoulders with one or more pins. Variations in the appearance of chitons were often achieved by belting the chiton at any of several locations, by creating and manipulating a fold over the top of the fabric, and by varying the placement of the pins at the shoulder.

Full-length chitons were woven to the same size no matter how tall or short the person who was to wear the garment. Lengths could be easily adjusted by increasing or decreasing the size of the overfold.

Over the chiton Greek men and women placed shawls or cloaks. Some of the overgarments were decorative; others were utilitarian. The summary and illustrations that follow describe the major costume forms in use during the Archaic, Classical, and Hellenistic periods of ancient Greek history. Various authors use conflicting terminology to identify different types of chitons. The terms used here are those that seemed to the authors to be most consistently used by reliable sources.

Costume Components for Men and Women

THE CHITON

Greek art and literature indicate that the chiton underwent a number of changes over time. *Table 3.1* summarizes the variations in the type of chitons worn by men and women at various times. Chitons are shown in *Figures 3.4, 3.5, 3.6, 3.7,* and *3.9.*

The Greek author Herodotus claims the Doric peplos style of the Archaic period was abandoned because of an incident toward the beginning of the 6th century B.C. in which Athenian women supposedly used their dress pins to stab to death a messenger who brought the bad news of the almost total destruction of an Athenian military force in battle. According to Herodotus, the wearing of the Ionic chiton, which did not utilize these large, sharp pins, was mandated as a result. *Contemporary Comments 3.1, page 55,* contains Herodotus's description of the scene.

Geddes (1987) relates men's change from the Ionic chiton to the Doric chiton in the Classical period to changes in social and political attitudes. He believes that the luxurious fabrics and elaborate draperies of the full Ionic chiton had offered many opportunities for the display of a man's wealth. But beginning in the late 5th century B.C., Greek political thought and practices encouraged values such as fitness, equality, and a sense of "thinking alike" that required, at the least, less flaunting of wealth. The Doric chiton, which had simple, relatively straight lines, was seen to best advantage on a fit body and did not lend itself to ostentatious display. It was, therefore, more in keeping with these new values.

THE HIMATION

Just when the term **himation** (*hi-mat'e-ahn*) came to be applied to a large rectangle of fabric that wrapped around the body is not entirely clear. (See *Figures 3.8* and *3.9.*) This garment has been compared to the wrapped shawls of Mesopotamia. An earlier version worn in the Archaic period seems to have been called a *chlaina* (Evans 1964). Under the name himation, this garment was in wide use by the late 5th century B.C. Various methods of draping the himation are depicted by artists, but the most common way of wearing it seems to have been with the upper corner covering the left shoulder, the bulk of the fabric wrapped across the back, passed under the right arm, and draped over the left shoulder or carried across the left arm. Both women and men wore this garment over a chiton. Philosophers and older gods are depicted in the himation alone, without a chiton beneath, but whether this was an artistic convention or actual practice is unclear. Geddes (1987) suggests that the popularity of the himation may have been related to an emphasis on athletic fitness because it was easily taken off for sports, and just as easily put back on.

Table 3.1

TYPES OF CHITONS WORN BY GREEK MEN AND WOMEN

Name of Style	Worn by	Length	Fit	Fabric	Duration
chitoniskos	men	usually short, between hip and thigh	close to body, similar in shaping to the doric peplos	usually patterned wool	Archaic period to c. 550 B.C.
doric peplos (See *Figure 3.4.* and *Color Plate 3*)	women	to ankles	close to body, fastened with large straight pin at shoulder	usually patterned wool	Archaic period to c. 550 B.C.
ionic chiton (See *Figure 3.5*)	men	short or long	full, longer sleeves, fastened with many small brooches at shoulder	lightweight wool or pleated linen	550 B.C. to 480 B.C., less often from 480 B.C. to 300 B.C.
	women	long, to ground			
doric chiton (See *Figure 3.6*)	men	short, with few exceptions	narrower than ionic, without sleeves, fastened with one brooch (fibula) at shoulders	wool, linen, or silk	400 B.C. to 100 B.C.
	women	long			450 B.C. to 300 B.C.
hellenistic chiton (See *Figure 3.7*)	women	long	similar to doric chilton, but narrower, often belted just below bosom	lightweight wool, linen, or silk	300 to 100 B.C.
exomis (see *Visual Summary Table*)	working class men and slaves	short	fastened over one shoulder	sturdy, durable fabric, probably wool	throughout all Greek periods

was a more complicated form of the woman's diplax in which fabric was pleated into a fabric band. (See *Figure 3.5.*)

Various styles of cloaks and capes were worn for cool weather. The most notable example was the **chlamys** *(kla'mis)*, a rectangular cloak of leather or wool pinned over the right or left shoulder. Worn by men over a chiton, especially for traveling, it could be used as a blanket for sleeping at night. (See *Figure 3.9.*)

HAIR AND HEADDRESS FOR MEN

See *Illustrated Table 3.1,* for a cross section of hairstyles for the period.

In the Archaic period, long or medium length hair and beards predominated, whereas in the Classical period, young men wore short hair and no beards and older men longer hair and beards.

Types of hats often shown in art included fitted caps and the **petasos** *(pet'a-sos)*, usually worn with the chlamys. Its wide brim provided shade in summer or kept rain off the head. Though not Greek styles, **Phrygian** *(frig'ee-an)* **bonnets,** brimless caps with a high padded peak that fell forward, were often depicted. Phrygian bonnets in Greek art identify

FIGURE 3.5

Woman in Ionic chiton over which she wears a chlamydon. (*Atalanta Lekythos, Funerary Oil Jug,* attributed to Douris, Greek, Athenian, 1st half 5th century B.C. Painted white ground terra-cotta, H. 31.8 cm, 500–490 B.C. © The Cleveland Museum of Art, Leonard G. Hanna, Jr., Fund, 1966.114.)

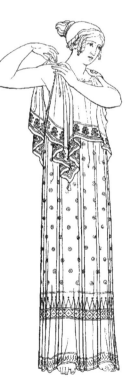

FIGURE 3.6

Redrawing of figure from a Greek vase by Thomas Hope (18th century). Woman fastens the shoulder of her Doric chiton. Notice the small weights at the end of the drapery that falls from her right shoulder. (Reproduced courtesy, Dover Publications, Inc.)

OTHER GARMENTS

The **perizoma** *(per-i-zo'ma)*, Greek for a loincloth, was a garment worn by men either as an undergarment or for athletic contests. (See *Figure 4.1, page 65.*) The type of undergarments worn by women is not entirely certain. Some Greek vases show women with bands of cloth that wrapped around the upper torso and, depending on how the bands were placed, either bound or supported the breasts.

The **diplax** *(dy'plax)*, a small rectangle of fabric worn by women, especially over the Ionic chiton, was draped in much the same way as the himation. The **chlamydon** *(kla'mi-don)*

Illustrated Table 3.1

EXAMPLES OF HAIRSTYLES AND HEADDRESS WORN BY MEN AND WOMEN IN GREECE

Youthful male figure with short, curly hair from Classical period

Bearded philosopher from Classical period

Youth wearing a petasos

Youth wearing a Phrygian bonnet

Woman's hair style depicted in Minoan wall painting

Women's hairstyles depicted on Archaic Greek sculpture

Women's hairstyles and headdress from Classical period depicted on vase paintings

Thomas Hope, Reproduced courtesy, Dover Publications, Inc.

FIGURE 3.7

Greek woman wears the Hellenistic chiton which is belted typically high under the breasts, and made of lightweight fabric that molds the body lines. (*Dancing Lady,* Greek, c. 50 B.C. Marble, H. 85.4 cm (with base). © The Cleveland Museum of Art, John L. Severance Fund, 1965.24.)

FIGURE 3.8

Greek youth wearing himation. (Photograph courtesy, Photo Arts Company.)

FIGURE 3.9

5th century B.C. Greek vase shows (from left to right) a woman in an Ionic chiton with a shawl drawn over her head; a naked cupid; a goddess in a Doric chiton; a woman in an Ionic chiton, a veil over her head and a cloak over her shoulders; two men in chlamys and petasos; and a man in a himation. Older men are bearded, the youth is clean shaven. (Photograph courtesy, The Metropolitan Museum of Art, Rogers Fund, 1907.)

CONTEMPORARY COMMENTS 3.1

Herodotus Describes the Origins of the Change from Doric to Ionic Chitons.

In his history of the Persian Wars, Book V, Herodotus recounts the story of how the women of Athens were required to change the style of their dress. Only one Athenian warrior escaped death in battle and returned, to tell the story of the defeat.

. . . When he came back to Athens, bringing word of the calamity, the wives of those who had been sent out on the expedition took it sorely to heart, that he alone should have survived the slaughter of all the rest; they therefore crowded round the man, and struck him with the brooches by which their dresses were fastened[1]—each, as she struck, asking him where he had left her husband. And the man died in this way. The Athenians thought the deed of the women more horrible even than the fate of the troops; as however they did not know how to punish them, they changed their dress and compelled them to wear the costume of the Ionians. Till this time the Athenian women had worn a Dorian dress [see *Figure 3.4.*], shaped nearly like that which prevails at Corinth. Henceforth they were made to wear the linen tunic, which does not require brooches.[2] [Book V, Chapter 87.]

[1]These "brooches" are not like modern brooches with safety clasps, but long, sharp, daggerlike pins.
[2]Ionic styles (see *Figure 3.5.*) were fastened with small, button-shaped closures of *fibulae*, probably closing more like a small safety pin. The later revival of Dorian styles did not include the use of the daggerlike pin for fastening.

From *The Persian Wars*, by Herodotus, trans. by George Rawlinson. Copyright 1942 by Random House, Inc.; reprinted by permission of Random House, Inc.

wearers as foreigners from the Middle East. This type of hat reappears in European styles in the Middle Ages.

Both men and women wore the **pilos** (*pi'los*), a narrow-brimmed or brimless hat with a pointed crown.

HAIR AND HEADDRESS FOR WOMEN

See *Illustrated Table 3.1, page 53*, for a cross section of hairstyles for the period.

In the Archaic period, women wore their hair long in curling tresses with small curls arranged around the face. In the Classical period, it was pulled into a knot or chignon at the back of the head.

Fillets, scarves, ribbons, and caps were used to confine the hair. Paintings and sculpture of women depict veils that were worn over the head and are sometimes shown pulled across to cover the face.

FOOTWEAR

Both men and women wore sandals. Men also wore fitted shoes, ankle high or high mid-calf length; or, for travel or warfare, leather boots that laced up the front. (See *Figures 3.8* and *3.9.*)

JEWELRY

More often worn by women than men, jewelry consisted of necklaces, earrings, rings, decorative pins for fastening the chiton, and brooches.

COSMETICS

Statues and vase paintings do not reveal the extent to which makeup was worn. Writings of the period do record the use of perfumes. *Contemporary Comments 3.2, page 56*, reprints passages from *The Iliad and The Odyssey* that describe not only some of the clothing worn by women, but also cosmetics and jewels.

GREEK COSTUME FOR CHILDREN:
800–300 B.C.

Infants were wrapped in **swaddling clothes** (bands of fabric wrapped around the body) and wore close-fitting, peaked

CONTEMPORARY COMMENTS 3.2

Homer Describes Women's Grooming and Dress

In the Iliad, [Book 14, lines 169–186], Homer describes how Hera, a goddess, beautifies herself so that she may persuade the god Zeus to do something she wishes.

She went to her chamber.... there entering she drew shut the leaves of the shining door, then first from her adorable body washed away all stains with ambrosia,[1] and next anointed herself with ambrosial sweet olive oil, which stood there in its fragrance beside, ... When with this she had anointed her delicate body and combed her hair, next with her hands she arranged the shining and lovely and ambrosial curls along her immor-

tal head, and dressed in an ambrosial robe that Athene [another goddess] had made her carefully, smooth, and with many figures upon it, and pinned it across her breast with a golden brooch, and circled her waist about with a zone [belt] that floated a hundred tassels, and in the lobes of her carefully pierced ears she put rings with triple drops in mulberry clusters, radiant with beauty, and, lovely among goddesses, she veiled her head downward with a sweet fresh veil that glimmered pale like the sunlight. Underneath her shining feet she bound on the fair sandals.

In the Odyssey, an epic describing the adventures of Odysseus, a Greek

warrior, suitors who believe Odysseus is dead give presents to his wife Penelope. These gifts include clothing and jewels.

. . . every man sent a squire to fetch a gift—Aninoos a wide resplendent robe, embroidered fine, and fastened with twelve brooches, pins pressed into sheathing tubes of gold; Eurymakhos, a necklace wrought in gold, with sunray pieces of clear glinting amber. Eurydamas's men came back with pendants, eardrops in triple clusters of warm lights; and from the hoard of Lord Polyktor's son, Peisandros, came a band for her white throat, jewelled adornment.

The Iliad of Homer. [N.D.] Translated with an introduction by Richmond Lattimore. Chicago: University of Chicago Press. Homer: The Odyssey. 1961. Translated by Robert Fitzgerald. Garden City, NY: Doubleday.
[1] A sweet-smelling substance.

---

caps. Swaddling of babies was a common practice throughout Europe until the 19th century and was thought to prevent deformity of children's limbs. As the Greeks emphasized bodily perfection, it may be that they held similar beliefs. A few representations of infants, perhaps older ones, show them wrapped in loose cloth draperies rather than in swaddling bands.

Costume Components for Children

Sometimes small boys are depicted in the nude. School-age boys wore short, belted or unbelted chitons. Girls' chitons were arranged much as those of older women and belted in a variety of ways. Boys and girls wore himations; those for girls were worn over a chiton and for boys, either alone or over a chiton.

For protection outdoors, art of the period depicts small, rectangular cloaks with clasps on the right shoulder. Another warm garment was a long cape with a pointed hood that either closed in front or had an opening through which it could be slipped over the head.

HAIR AND HEADDRESS

Small children and boys had short hair. Older girls dressed their hair the same ways as women. Boys and girls wore a flat-crowned hat with a heavy roll as a brim. Girls wore a high, peaked hat with a flat, stiff brim.

FOOTWEAR

Children were often shown barefoot. Foot coverings included sandals and closed shoes.

JEWELRY

Children wore earrings, necklaces, and bracelets, especially those in the form of a serpent.

GREEK COSTUME FOR SPECIALIZED OCCUPATIONS OR OCCASIONS

Wedding Dress

The Greek bride's costume for weddings was laden with symbolism. (See *Figure 3.10.*) The wedding garment had some areas that were dyed purple with a costly dye obtained from a rare type of mollusk called the murex. The bride wore a belt tied with a double knot known as a bridal or Hercules knot. The loosening of this knot, which took place on the wedding night, was both a symbol of and a necessary preface to the sexual union of the bride and groom. Her veil, which was either a mantle pulled up over the back of the head or a separate veil, was colored yellow-orange with the dye from the saffron plant. Saffron was associated with women because of its use as a medicine for menstrual problems. Over the veil was placed the **stephane** or bridal crown. Before and during the ceremony, the veil covered the bride's face until the ritual unveiling of the bride, the **anakalypteria,** took place. Not until this unveiling had either the bride or groom seen each other, and this part of the ceremony is thought to have symbolized the bride's willing acceptance of the groom.

Both bride and groom were also crowned with laurel wreaths, a religious symbol with divine associations that was intended to glorify the weddings of mortals. The bride also wore special sandals called **nymphides** and decked herself

FIGURE 3.10

Woman preparing for her wedding. The attendant at the left is handing her the *stephane* or bridal crown. The bride, on the right, has a belt, tied with a bridal knot, around her waist and is in the process of donning her bridal veil. (Photograph courtesy, Museum of Fine Arts, Boston.)

FIGURE 3.11

Greek soldier wearing leather cuirass with suspended leather panels. Note that the cheek guards of the helmet are raised. When in use, these panels would fold down to protect the side of the face. The soldier wears greaves on his legs. (Thomas Hope, 18th century, drawn from a Greek vase. Reproduced courtesy, Dover Publications, Inc.)

with elaborate jewelry. (See *Figure 3.10.*) Finally, the bride presented the groom with a tunic, a **chlanis,** she had woven herself. This gift probably symbolized her mastery of an essential housewifely skill.

Military Costume

Military costume during both the Archaic and Classical periods varied from one city-state to another but usually included some form of protective clothing worn over a tunic. In the Archaic period, soldiers wore cloaks of rough wool. They protected themselves with such devices as breast plates made from metal plates or disks mounted on fabric corselets and held up by shoulder straps. Helmets made of either leather or bronze that had chin straps and high crests were intended to make warriors look more fearsome. **Greaves,** shaped leather or metal protectors for the lower legs, and wide metal belts and shields provided additional protection.

In the Classical period, chlamys-style cloaks were worn. Protective devices for common soldiers included a leather **cuirass** *(kwi-ras')* (a modern term for a close-fitting, shaped armor that covered the body), a metal belt, and greaves. Heavily armed infantry wore a metal or leather cuirass with a row of leather tabs hanging down from the cuirass at the waist to protect the lower part of body. (See *Figure 3.11.*) Helmets, worn either with or without crests, became more protective. They had extended pieces to cover the cheekbones, nose, jaws, and neck. In both periods men either went barefoot, or wore high boots.

Theatrical Costume

The theater was important in Greece and eventually acquired a traditional style of costume through which the theater-goer could immediately identify the characters. Male actors played all of the parts in both comedies and tragedies. Tragic actors wore a tragic mask, with either tall wigs or tufts of hair fastened to the mask, and thick-soled platform shoes. Kings, queens, gods, goddesses, happy characters, tragic figures, and slaves were each identified by a specific style of dress, special insignia, or color. For those who are interested in a more lengthy exploration of Greek theatrical costume, several references are listed in the *Selected Readings* at the end of this chapter.

SUMMARY

VISUAL SUMMARY

The accompanying *Visual Summary Table* illustrates the major styles of Greek costume. Major items of Minoan dress can be seen in *Figures 3.2* and *3.3.*

THEMES

Although lack of precise information about Minoan life and culture limits our ability to explore themes related to social life, we can readily see the impact on dress of themes such as the **PRODUCTION OF TEXTILES** and related **TECHNOLOGY.** Skills related to weaving and dyeing, especially of wool fibers, made possible the wide variety of highly ornamented fabrics used in Minoan dress. **TRADE,** exporting textiles and importing dyestuffs to and from other Mediterranean countries, was another factor that contributed to the development of Minoan styles. The resulting **CROSS-CULTURAL** interchanges may also have influenced some specific garments, such as shoes.

Minoan **POLITICAL CONTROL** of Mycenae helped to spread Minoan-influenced styles to the mainland of Greece. Eventually **POLITICAL CONFLICT** in the form of the conquest of the Minoans and the Mycenaeans by outside forces closed off information about these peoples for a number of centuries.

The Archaic and Classical Greek periods provide more fertile territory for identification of important themes. Some of the variations in the forms of the chiton illustrate themes such as **POLITICS, CROSS-CULTURAL INFLUENCES,** and changes in **SOCIAL VALUES.** The Ionic chiton was a style with non-Greek origins, most probably a Middle Eastern style adopted by Greeks in Ionia, a settlement at the far eastern end of the Mediterranean. From Ionia the style spread to the mainland, where it supplanted the Doric peplos. About 480 B.C., as a result of war with Persia, a period of intense interest in the Greek past and a denigration of oriental styles apparently led to a rejection of the Ionic chiton in favor of a new style, the Doric chiton, which represented a sort of revival of the older, native Dorian peplos. For men the simpler Doric chiton was more compatible with the social value of equality than the more elaborate Ionic chiton.

The shape and construction of costume for men and for women in Greece was not markedly different. Nevertheless

Visual Summary Table

MAJOR GREEK GARMENTS

Doric peplos (c. 550 B.C.)   Ionic chiton (c. 550–480 B.C.)   Doric chiton (c. 400–100 B.C.)

Himation   Chlamys (cloak) and petasos (hat)   Exomis

the theme of **GENDER ROLES** does appear in the dress of brides and in veiling of married women.

Many writers have commented on similarities between certain aspects of Greek **ARTS AND DRESS.** These similarities are especially notable in architecture. Decorative motifs often appear both on buildings and as ornamentation on garments. Tall, slender Doric and Ionic building columns with their fluted surfaces have been compared to the long, pleated tubular chitons worn by the Greeks.

LATER SURVIVALS OF GREEK DRESS

The travels of the chiton do not end with the decline of Greek power. The spread of Greek settlements and Greek culture throughout the Mediterranean world resulted in the adoption of many elements of Greek costume by contemporary Egyptians, by the Etruscans, and later, by the Romans in Italy.

By way of Roman costume, Greek costume can be said to have served as a basis for the costume of Romanized Europe for the six centuries following the death of Alexander the Great. It can even be argued that its influence in certain aspects of dress can be felt until the latter part of the Middle Ages. Moreover, Greek influence on dress was not limited to the civilizations that coexisted with Classical Greece. Elements of classical art have been revived during the Renaissance (15th and 16th centuries), the Neoclassical period (18th century), and the Empire period (early 1800s.) In this latter period a method of belting the dress high, under the bustline, was copied from Hellenistic chiton styles. (See *Figures 11.1* and *11.2, pages 263* and *265.*) Called the **empire waistline,** this Greek-inspired style was revived periodically by fashion designers of the 20th century, many of whom looked to historic periods for design inspiration. The soft, flowing lines of the Greek styles seem to appeal particularly to lingerie designers and designers of evening dress.

NOTES

Barber, E. J. W. 1991. *Prehistoric Textiles.* Princeton, NJ: Princeton University Press.

Barber, E. J. W. 1994. *Women's Work: the First 20,000 Years.* New York: W. W. Norton.

Bonfante, L. 1977. *Etruscan Dress.* Baltimore, MD: Johns Hopkins University Press.

Boucher, F. 1987. *20,000 Years of Fashion.* London: Thames and Hudson.

Durant, W. 1966. *The Life of Greece. The Story of Civilization. Vol. 2.* New York: Simon and Schuster, p. 84.

Evans, A, 1963. "Scenes from Minoan Life." In J. Hawkes, ed. *The World of the Past.* New York: Knopf.

Evans, M. M. 1964. "Greek Dress." In M. Johnson, ed. *Ancient Greek Dress.* Inc.: Chicago, IL: Argonaut.

Faber, A. "Dress and Dress Materials in Greece and Rome." *CIBA Review,* p. 297.

Galt, C. 1931. "Veiled Ladies." *American Journal of Archeology,* Vol. 35, No. 4, p. 373.

Geddes, A. G. 1987. "Rags and Riches: The Costume of Athenian Men in the Fifth Century." *Classical Quarterly,* Vol. 37, No. ii, pp. 307–331.

Houston, M. G. 1966. *Ancient Greek, Roman, and Byzantine Costume.* London: Adam & Charles Black.

Mylonas, G. 1966. *Mycenae and the Mycenaean World.* Princeton, NJ: Princeton University Press, p. 136.

Reeder, E. D. 1995. "Women and Men in Classical Greece." In E. Reeder, ed. *Pandora: Women in Classical Greece.* Princeton, NJ: Princeton University Press, p. 20.

Roebuck, C. 1966. *The World of Ancient Times.* New York: Charles Scribners Sons, p. 366.

SELECTED READINGS

Books Containing Illustrations of Costume of the Period from Original Sources

Charbonneaux, J., R. Marlin, and F. Villard. 1972. *Classical Greek Art.* New York: George Braziller.

———. 1973. *Hellenistic Art.* New York: George Braziller.

Hale, W. H. 1985. *The Horizon Book of Ancient Greece.* New York: Random House.

Higgins, R. 1997. *Minoan and Mycenaean Art.* New York: Thames and Hudson.

Kaltsas, N. 2003. *Ancient Greek and Roman Sculpture in the National Archaeological Museum, Athens.* Los Angeles: Getty Trust.

Mylonas, G. 1966. *Mycenae and the Mycenaean Age.* Princeton, NJ: Princeton University Press.

Richter, G. 1994. *A Handbook of Greek Art.* New York: Phaidon.

Periodical and Other Articles

Alexander, S. M., ed. 1978. "Information on Historical Techniques, Textiles: 1. The Classical Period." *Art and Archeology Technical Abstracts,* Vol. 15, No. 2.

Blundell, S. 2002. "Clutching at Clothes." In L. Llewellyn-Jones, ed. *Women's Dress in the Ancient Greek World.* London: Duckworth, p. 143.

DeBrohun, J. 2001. "Power Dressing in Ancient Greece and Rome." *History Today,* February, p. 18.

Faber, G. A. "Dress and Dress Materials in Greece and Rome." *CIBA Review,* Vol. 1, p. 296.

Galt, C. 1935 "Veiled Ladies." *American Journal of Archeology,* Vol. 35, p. 373.

Geddes, A. G. 1987. "Rags and Riches: The Costume of Athenian Men in the Fifth Century." *Classical Quarterly,* Vol. 37, No. II , p. 307.

Jones, B. 2000. "Revealing Minoan Fashions." *Archeology.* May/June, Vol. 53, No. 3, p. 36.

Llewellyn-Jones, L. 2002. "A Woman's View? Dress, Eroticism, and the Ideal Female Body in Athenian Art." In L. Llewellyn-Jones, ed. *Women's Dress in the Ancient Greek World.* London: Duckworth, p. 171.

Peterson, S. 1981. "A Costuming Scene from the Room of the Ladies on Thera." *American Journal of Archeology,* Vol. 85, No. 2, April, p. 211.

Rebak, P. 1996. "Aegean Breechcloths, Kilts, and the Keftiu Paintings." *American Journal of Archeology.* Jan, Vol. 100, p. 35.

Daily Life

Browning, R., ed. 2000. *The Greek World.* New York: Thames and Hudson.

Castleden, R. 1993. *Minoans: Life in Bronze Age Crete.* New York: Routledge.

Chadwick, J. 1976. *The Mycenaean World.* New York: Cambridge University Press.

Garland, R. 1998. *Daily Life of the Ancient Greeks.* Westport, CT: Greenwood Press.

Grant, M. 1992. *A Social History of Greece and Rome.* New York: Scribner: Maxwell Macmillan International.

Hawkes, J. 1968. *Dawn of the Gods.* New York: Random House.

Lefkowitz, M. R. and M. B. Fant, eds. 1992. *Women's Life in Greece and Rome.* Baltimore, MD: Johns Hopkins University Press.

Pomeroy, S.B. 1995. *Goddesses, Whores, Wives, and Slaves: Women in Classical Antiquity.* New York: Schocken Books.

Robinson, C. E. 1989. *Everyday Life in Ancient Greece.* Westport, CT: Greenwood Press.

Greek Theater Costume

Brooke, I. 2003. *Costume in Greek Classic Drama.* Mineola, NY: Dover.

Simon, E. 1982. *The Ancient Theatre.* New York: Methuen.

Stone, L. M. 1981. *Costume in Aristophanic Poetry.* Salem, NH: Ayer.

CHRONOLOGY

800 B.C.

Major Etruscan civilization

Etruscan wall paintings in tombs

753 B.C.

Founding of the city of Rome

753 B.C.–509 B.C.

Kings rule Rome

Etruscan kings of Rome

509 B.C.–27 B.C.

Roman Republic

396 B.C.–88 B.C.

Romans subdue and conquer Etruscan cities

44 B.C.

Assassination of Julius Caesar

31 B.C.–A.D. 395

Roman Empire

A.D. 79

Eruption of Mt. Vesuvius covers Pompeii and Herculaneum

A.D. 395

Division of Rome into Eastern and Western Empires

A.D. 476

Last Western emperor of Rome deposed

CHAPTER FOUR

ETRURIA AND ROME

c. 800 B.C. — A.D. 400

A.

B.

E.

A.

Etruscan collar

B.

Etruscan horse

C.

Etruscan urn

D.

Roman aqueduct

E.

Roman brasier

F.

Roman table

G.

Roman sarcophagus

C.

F.

D.

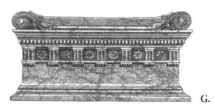

G.

Figure A from Hart, H. H. 1977. *Jewelry: A Pictorial Archive of Woodcuts & Engravings.* New York: Dover, p. 105. Figures B, D courtesy of V. R. Tortora. Figures C, E, F, G from Hottenroth, F. 1884. *Trachten Der Völker,* Vol. 1. Stuttgart: Verlag Gustav Wiese, plates 54, 55.

Prehistoric human occupants of the Italian peninsula migrated to Italy from such different places as Africa, Sicily, Spain, France, the Danube Valley, and Switzerland. Because they left no written records, they are known only through archeological remains, which tell us that they were pastoral people who tilled the soil, wove clothing, and made pottery and bronze implements. Among the pre-Roman peoples who migrated into Italy, none left a deeper impression than the Etruscans.

In certain areas of the Italian peninsula, by about 800 B.C. a culture had developed that was superior in skills and artistic production, and more complex in organization than the culture of the neighboring tribes. The Romans called the people who created this culture **Etruscans.** Eventually their territory stretched as far north as the region near the present-day city of Venice, but the most important settlements in Etruria were concentrated in the western area that today is bounded on the north by Florence and on the south by Rome, the current Italian province of Tuscany.

Another group of immigrants also entered Italy. By the latter part of the 8th century, Greek colonies had been established in Sicily and in southern Italy. By the 6th century the Greeks reached the northern limits of their colonization, the southern boundary of Etruria. (It was the Greeks who gave the name "Italy" to the region, naming it after an early king of one of the native tribes.)

In addition to the Etruscans and the Greeks, other native tribes populated the Italian peninsula. One of these tribes, the Latins, lived in an area near the mouth of the Tiber River. At some point, possibly in the 8th century, on one of the hills near the river, a colony of these people established a settlement on the Palatine Hill that grew into the city of Rome. But the Romans, as these people were to be known to history, did not become an important political force in the Mediterranean until about the 3rd century B.C. when they subjugated the Etruscans.

THE ETRUSCANS

Historical Background

The origins of the Etruscans (*ih-trus'cans*) are shrouded in mystery. They may have emigrated from Asia Minor, or they may have been an indigenous people, native to the Italian peninsula. Because of their superiority in arms and fighting ability, they were able to seize strategic points along the coast. From there they pushed inland, conquering vital sites from which they could control the local population. Eighteen fortified cities have been found. The twelve most important cities, ruled by kings and nobles, formed a loose confedera-

tion. The Etruscans were in the minority—a dominant, military, aristocracy.

The Etruscans left abundant records of their lives in wall paintings, statues, and in the objects that they placed in their elaborate necropoli or grave cities. Although they had a written language using a Greek alphabet, the limited numbers and types of inscriptions have not allowed full understanding of grammar and vocabulary. Consequently, terms related to Etruscan costume will be given in Greek- or Latin-based words.

The chief Etruscan towns had been founded by the middle of the 7th century B.C. Not only did the Etruscans improve the arable land and plant vineyards and olive groves, but they also mined and smelted iron ore, exploited deposits of copper, traded throughout the Mediterranean area, and amassed great wealth. In building their cities, they utilized a form of city planning. When a new site for a city was selected, they laid out the towns in a checkerboard pattern with two main streets intersecting at right angles.

Social Life of the Etruscans

We know relatively little of Etruscan family life. Women seem to have occupied a position of greater importance in Etruscan society than did either Greek or Roman women. Roman writers frequently sneered about the foolishness of the Etruscans in granting their women such privileged status. Many of the funerary statues and paintings show men and women reclining together on couches at banquets with expressions and in attitudes of warm affection. When family groups are shown they are depicted in relaxed, informal poses. Some recently excavated terra cotta statues of children are among the most delightfully realistic statues from antiquity of infants and small children.

Art and Trade of the Etruscans

The art of the Etruscans showed strong Greek influences, particularly during the 6th and 5th centuries B.C. when Greek colonies were well established in southern Italy. Clearly Greece and Etruria had an active and close trading relationship. The scenes of daily life depicted by the Etruscans, however, portrayed Etruscans, not Greeks. This is indicated not only by the inclusion of some dress styles and conventions that are peculiar to the Etruscans but also by the way in which respectable women are depicted as dining and appearing with men in public. The Etruscan tomb paintings were done in color so the observer can see the characteristic use of vivid color and pattern in clothing. (See *Color Plate 5.*) Although much of the art of Etruria was of local production, rich Etruscans also purchased imported art objects from abroad, especially from Greece, and many of these were placed in the tombs with their owners.

ETRUSCAN COSTUME FOR MEN AND WOMEN: C. 800–200 B.C.

Costume Components for Men and Women

GARMENTS

The Etruscan **perizoma** (*par-e-zo-ma'*) was a loincloth (like that worn by Minoans and Greeks) that was worn alone as an outer garment by laborers or other physically active men. When worn as an undergarment it was placed under a short, shirtlike chiton; or a slightly longer chiton. (See *Figure 4.1*.) The Etruscans apparently did not share Greek acceptance of male nudity.

The Etruscan versions of the chiton worn by men and women were essentially the same as those worn by Greeks. The most common length for men was to the thighs, but longer versions were also depicted. The Doric peplos was made in woven plaid or decorated with what may have been embroidery. (*Figure 3.4, page 50* shows the general shape and form of the Doric peplos.) Subsequently a chiton cut fuller than the Doric peplos and with pleats appears in Etruscan art. According to Bonfante (1975) this may be a forerunner of the later Ionic chiton. She points out that the Ionic chiton appeared in Etruria slightly earlier than in mainland Greece and suggests that both Greece and Etruria may have adopted the style independently from a third source, the Ionian region of the Near East.

Both Ionic and Doric chitons were worn between 580 B.C. and the beginning of the Roman period, around 300 B.C. Although Greek and Etruscan chitons are often difficult to tell apart. (See *Figure 4.2*.) Etruscan chitons consistently tend to be shorter and less voluminous than Greek. Some appear to have sleeves cut and sewn into the garment, giving garments a closer fit and a less draped appearance. (See *Figure 4.3*.) During the Classical period,[1] upper-class Etruscan ladies wore a badge of status consisting of a fringe or tassel that hung down at the front and back of each shoulder.

Wraps for the body were among the most distinctive styles developed by the Etruscans. Varieties included a heavy woolen cloak for men, which was similar to the Greek chlamys. It fastened at one shoulder. Etruscans wore the himation, adopted after it first appeared among the Greeks. The most original of the Etruscan mantles was the **tebenna** (*ta'ben-a*), a rounded mantle worn by men and women. Tebenna is a Greek rendering of what was probably an Etruscan word. This garment seems to have been woven with curved edges in a roughly semicircular or elliptical form. It was draped in various ways: either (1) like a chlamys, (2) worn back-to-front with the curved edge hanging down in front

[1]The terminology for periods used in the discussion of Etruscan civilization, i.e., Archaic, Classical, etc., is the same as that used in discussing Greek civilization.

FIGURE 4.1

Figure from the land of Cyprus, c. 7th–6th centuries, B.C., wears a perizoma (loincloth) of the type worn by both the Greeks and the Etruscans. (Photograph courtesy, The Metropolitan Museum of Art, The Cesnola Collection, purchased by subscriptions, 1874–76.)

and the two ends thrown back over the shoulder, or (3) like an himation. (See *Figure 4.4*.) This garment is thought to have been a forerunner of the Roman toga (*to'ga*), a semicircular draped garment symbolizing Roman citizenship.

HAIR AND HEADDRESS

Men in the Archaic period wore medium-length hair and pointed beards; in the post-Archaic period hair was short and faces were clean shaven. During the Archaic period women arranged their hair in a single braid at the back or in long, flowing tresses. In post-Archaic periods women's hairstyles were like those of Greek women.

FIGURE 4.2

Reclining Etruscan figure dressed in Doric chiton with shawl draped around her body, over her shoulders, and drawn over her hair. She wears a small fillet in her hair. (Photograph courtesy, Photo Arts.)

FIGURE 4.3

Etruscan garments such as this one often show more shaping in the cut of the sleeves and a more fitted line through the body than the Greek costume of a comparable period. This figure also wears characteristic Etruscan pointed-toed shoes and the tutulus, a high-crowned, small-brimmed hat. (*Dancer of maenad* [a mythological figure in the form of a young girl], Italy, Etruscan, late 6th century, B.C. Bronze, H. 18.7 cm. © The Cleveland Museum of Art, 1997, purchase from the J. H. Wade Fund, 1953.124.)

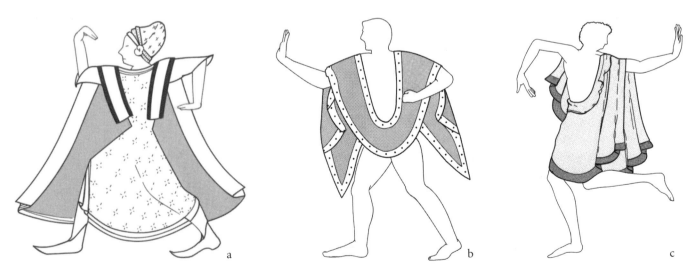

FIGURE 4.4

Three of the varied styles of mantles worn by the Etruscans: (a) a capelike garment worn by women that had long tabs hanging down in the front; (b) a tebenna, worn with the curved edge hanging down in the front and the two ends thrown over the shoulders; (c) a tebenna, draped over one shoulder, in a manner much like the himation. Compare the draping of 4.4c to that of the toga in Figure 4.6. The tebenna is thought to have been the precursor of the toga.

Distinctive styles of headwear included wide-brimmed hats similar to the petasos for men and fillets to confine the hair for both men and women. On festive occasions men and women wore a crownlike headpiece. Both wore high-crowned brimless hats; men's styles often were peaked, while women wore the tutulus, with a rounded crown. (See *Figure 4.3.*)

FOOTWEAR

Both men and women wore sandals. Another style, often red in color, covered the foot up to the ankle and had an elongated toe that curled upward. (See *Figure 4.3.*) Bonfante (1975) suggests this style may have survived from Mycenae and come by some unknown route to Etruria from Greece in the 6th century, when they first appear.

JEWELRY

More often worn by women than men, necklaces, earrings, decorative brooches, and fibulae appear in painting and sculpture. Jewelry was either of local origin or imported from abroad.

ETRUSCAN COSTUME FOR CHILDREN: C. 800–200 B.C.

So far as one can tell there were no specialized costumes for children. Small children went naked in warm weather. Young boys dressed in short tunics. (See *Figure 4.5.*) Specific evidence of the dress of young girls is lacking, but probably they wore chitons similar to those of Greek girl children.

FIGURE 4.5

Etruscan statue of boy wearing chiton (tunic). This tunic is seamed at the shoulders and carries a band of decoration down either side at the front. These decorations were called clavi by the Romans. (Photograph courtesy, Photo Arts.)

THE ROMANS

Historical Background

Early Roman history was closely intertwined with that of Etruria. During the early years of Roman history, kings ruled Rome. Several of the early kings were Etruscan, but in 509 B.C. revolution ended the reign of Etruscan kings in Rome. Following the revolt, Etruscans and Romans battled each other until, one by one, the cities of Etruria became a part of the growing Roman confederation, losing their independence and becoming another of the many ethnic strands woven into Roman Italy.

The Roman Republic (509 B.C.–27 B.C.) had a conservative government with two consuls elected annually who exercised the executive powers and in time of war commanded the armies. Rome also had a senate and a popular assembly.

Under this form of government, Rome fought a series of wars that expanded Roman control over all of Italy. Rome and Carthage, whose empire stretched across North Africa, quarreled over Sicily. This led to the first wars of conquest beyond the Italian peninsula that, in time, produced the Roman Empire. (See *Figure 1.1, page 13.*) Ultimately under the Republic, Roman-dominated lands included much of North Africa, large areas of the Middle East, eastern Europe up to the Danube River, and most of continental Europe.

Rome became a wealthy, complex society. However, the strain of the war on the society and the economy, the resulting social strife, and the rivalries of ambitious generals led to civil war and to the appointment of a dictator for life, Julius Caesar.

After Caesar's assassination in 44 B.C., Augustus, his grandnephew and adopted son, won out over all rivals in a struggle for power and he became the first Roman emperor in 27 B.C. Augustus laid the foundations for an empire that would give the Mediterranean world 200 years of prosperity and peace, the *Pax Romana* (Roman Peace). Augustus and his successors added territory to the Empire in Arabia, Africa, Germany east of the Danube, and in Britain. Not until the 3rd century (A.D.) would decline set in, culminating in the fall of the Roman Empire. Among the causes for the decay of the Roman Empire were the flawed quality and competence of the emperors, military anarchy and civil wars, the failure of the economy, and the collapse of Roman society. A major cause for the fall of the Roman Empire was the migration of the German tribes into the empire in search of land and provisions.

The construction of a new capital in the eastern portion of the empire, Constantinople (now called Istanbul), by the Emperor Constantine about A.D. 325 signaled the decline of the Western Empire. In A.D. 395, the naming of two Roman emperors, one for the east and one for the west, in effect split the Empire; each portion became involved in separate struggles for survival. In the west, where German chieftains had begun to establish Germanic kingdoms, a barbarian chieftain deposed the last emperor in A.D. 476. The Eastern Roman Empire, wealthy and secure, grew into the powerful and influential Byzantine Empire.

Social Life in the Roman Empire

During the early imperial period the population of the city of Rome is estimated to have been more than a million people consisting of Roman citizens, their families, their slaves, and foreigners (Friedlander 1936). Only men were citizens, but citizens could be rich, middle class, or poor. By the 2nd century, perhaps 90 percent of the residents of Rome were of foreign extraction; however, many foreigners were provincials to whom citizenship had been extended (Casson 1975).

The well-to-do population lived in town houses built around a sunny courtyard and decorated with colorful frescos, or in large, comfortable apartments located on the ground floor of buildings that rose from four to nine stories high. The less affluent and the poor lived in the tall apartment buildings on the higher floors, sometimes under crowded conditions, with poor lighting, bad ventilation, and the constant threat of disastrous fires.

Members of the aristocracy lived in large households composed of relatives, servants who were often freed slaves, and household slaves. Heading every Roman family was the oldest male member, the *pater familias*. The pater familias was the sole owner of family possessions, including not only those of his children but also of his grandchildren. He decided whom his children would marry. If a marriage was not a success, it could be dissolved very easily. Married women of middle class or higher status supervised the children and the household, the size and complexity of which depended on the family's socioeconomic status.

SOCIAL DISTINCTIONS AND DRESS

"Dress for a Roman often, if not primarily, signified rank, status, office, or authority" (Bonfante 1994, 5). Roman literary sources indicate that a married Roman woman wore a distinctive item of costume: the *stola*. (See *page 74*.) When her husband became a *pater familias,* she became the *mater familias.* On achieving this status, she then began to dress her hair in a distinctive hairstyle called the *tutulus.* If she were widowed, she wore a dark, square cloak for at least a year after her husband's death.

In spite of socioeconomic differences among Romans, the primary distinction made in Roman society for men was between the citizen and the non-citizen. This status was clearly marked by dress. The male citizen was entitled to wear the **toga,** a draped, elliptically shaped mantle that probably had evolved from the Etruscan tabenna. Slaves, foreigners, and chaste adult women were prohibited from wearing this costume.

The Emperor and the imperial court were at the very top of Roman society, and the upper classes more or less faithfully mirrored the manners and customs of the court of the day. Upper-class men generally belonged to one of the civil and military orders. The most important of these were the senators. Second in importance were the knights (referred to by historians as the equestrian orders). Beginning in Republican times, senators were distinguished by their dress. Their tunics (and those of the Emperor) had broad purple bands that extended vertically from hem to hem across the shoulders. These bands were called **clavi** (*clah'vee*) (plural) or **clavus** (*clah'vus*) (singular).[2] Furthermore, they wore shoes with laces that wrapped around the leg halfway to the knee. The tunics of knights had slightly narrower purple bands and they wore a gold ring that signified their rank. After the end of the 1st century A.D., however, it became customary for all male members of the nobility to wear clavi on the tunic.

The remainder of the citizenry had no special insignia aside from the toga, although a number of special types of togas were worn for certain occasions or to designate particular roles. (See *Table 4.1.*) Foreigners wore the costume of their native land, and slaves wore tunics.

Fabrics and Clothing Production

Throughout Roman history wool was the major fiber used for clothing and flax the second most important. It is clear from literary sources that by the time of the Roman Republic, quite varied types of fabrics and ready-made garments were available in the marketplace. Used clothing was cut into patches and made into cloaks or quilts for slaves.

---

[2]For the pronunciation of **clavi** (*clah'vee*): although standard Latin pronounces *v* as *w,* this text has chosen an anglicized version in which v is pronounced as the English v.

Linen or wool fabrics could be gauzelike or tightly woven. Some may have had a soft pile or a tapestrylike weave. Well-to-do individuals could purchase luxurious linen goods from Egypt. Cotton was first mentioned in Roman writings around 190 B.C., although it was probably imported earlier. It was often mixed with linen to make a fabric that draped better than linen but that had a handsome, fairly lustrous surface when pressed. Wool and cotton blends were also made.

By the end of the first century B.C., silk was available to the wealthy. Imported from China through Northern India, silk was so expensive that is was generally mixed with other fibers, especially linen. On those very rare occasions when a garment was made entirely of silk, it was valued at its own weight in gold (Sebesta 1994b).

Fabrics were dyed to a wide range of colors. Among the most important dyestuffs were those used to produce the shade of purple required for the clavi of men's tunics and the borders of certain togas.

Although women were closely associated with fabric production and many Roman women did weave cloth for their families, the textile industry was not a home craft, as it had been in Greece. Large estates often produced their own cloth. Here the work was done mostly by women, many of whom were slaves (Herlihy 1990). Much of the weaving, dyeing, and finishing was carried out in business establishments that might employ as many as fifty or one hundred people, both men and women. These "factories" were located in many towns throughout the Empire. Both fabrics and garments were imported to Rome from all parts of the empire and beyond. Some cities were especially well known for making certain types of cloth or items of clothing. A cloak from Modena was considered superior to one from Laodicia or a tunic from Scythia better than one from Alexandria (Jones 1960).

Wealthy families probably had their clothing needs provided by the slaves of the household, but evidence concerning trades in Roman times indicates that there was also a thriving "ready-to-wear" business. A dialogue in a Greek–Latin book reflects the nature of bargaining that went on in these shops (Friedlander 1936):

> "I am going to the tailor."
> "How much does this pair cost?"
> "One hundred denarii."
> "How much is the waterproof?"
> "Two hundred denarii."
> "That is too dear; take a hundred."

Tailors are accused of adjusting their prices for winter garments according to the severity of the season.

Specialization among shoemakers was apparently sufficiently great that differentiation was made between shoemakers, bootmakers, sandal-makers, slipper-makers, and ladies' shoemakers. Jewelry crafts members included workers

in pearls and diamonds, gold and silversmiths, and ringmakers. In Rome, each craft was concentrated in a different district of the city.

Table 4.1

THE APPEARANCE AND SIGNIFICANCE OF VARIOUS TYPES OF TOGAS

Type of Toga	Appearance	Significance
toga pura or *toga viriles*	plain white, undecorated wool	worn after the age of sixteen by the ordinary male Roman citizen
toga candida	this was the *toga pura* lightened to an exceptional white	worn by candidates for office; the word "candidate" derives from this term
toga praetexta	with a purple border about two to three inches wide	worn by the young sons (until age sixteen) and daughters (until age twelve) of the nobility and by certain adult magistrates and high priests
toga pulla	black or dark-colored toga	said to have been worn for mourning
toga picta	purple with gold embroidery	assigned on special occasions to victorious generals or other persons who distinguished themselves in some way
toga trabea	apparently multi-colored, striped toga	assigned to augurs (religious officials who prophesied the future) or important officials

Based on material in Wilson, L. M., 1924. *The Roma Toga.* Baltimore, MD: Johns Hopkins University Press.

SOURCES OF EVIDENCE FOR THE STUDY OF ROMAN COSTUME

Information about Roman dress comes from Roman art, Roman literature, and archeological excavations. Remarkable artifacts were preserved when the cities of Pompeii and Herculaneum were buried by the eruption of Mt. Vesuvius, a nearby volcano, in A.D. 79.

Greek artists were brought to Rome to work, often as slaves. Many Roman statues were copies of sculpture created by earlier Greek artists. As a result, Roman art showed strong Greek influences, and it is not always clear whether the individuals depicted are actually Roman. On the other hand, Roman portrait sculpture (often executed by Greek sculptors working in Rome) emphasized a realism not to be found in the more idealized copies of Greek works. Many of these statues are portraits of individuals and depict the appearance, hairstyles, and garb of upper-class Romans.

Very sophisticated painting techniques had also developed. **Frescos,** paintings on plaster, were extensively utilized in decorating the interiors of buildings, but relatively few of these art works survived. Those that have been found provide some indication of the colors used in Roman costume, although artists may have been limited in the pigments available for painting or colors may have faded. (See *Color Plates 6 and 7.*) One of the favorite ways of decorating buildings was with mosaics, pictures created from small pieces of colored stone. Here, too, people might be depicted.

Literary works, especially plays and satires, provide the names of garments; insight into current attitudes toward particular styles; and how they were bought, worn, or used to create an impact on friends. (See *Contemporary Comments 4.1, page 73.*)

Written material also reveals some of the uncertainties about Roman costume. This is especially true for the costume of Roman women. Although a number of authors make reference to specific elements of women's dress, visual sources are confusing and individual scholars have interpreted this material differently.

ROMAN COSTUME FOR MEN AND WOMEN

The basic form of the chiton, called a tunic by the Romans, was adopted from the Greeks, possibly by way of Etruscan dress. The most distinctive Roman costume form, the toga, was apparently Etruscan in origin. These adopted costumes, however, took on Latin names and elements that reflected the Roman character.

In describing clothing the Romans made a distinction between garments that were "put on" (*indutus*) and garments that were "wrapped around" (*amictus*). Indutus was worn underneath or closest to the skin (the tunic, for example), and amictus might be considered outerwear (for example, the toga or the himation).

The Toga

Over time the toga took on symbolic meaning and its use became increasingly restricted. Roman sources indicate that initially both women and men wore togas, men wearing theirs over a loincloth. By the 2nd century B.C., the toga was a garment worn over a tunic by adult males. Laws passed in the middle of the first century restricted its use to male Roman citizens. The earlier usage for both men and women was preserved in the practice of having freeborn boy and girl children wear togas with purple borders (**toga praetexta**); girls until they reached puberty (around twelve years) and boys until age fourteen to sixteen, after which they donned the white **toga virilis** of the citizen (Stone 1994). At the time of the Emperor Augustus, any adult female wearing a toga was considered a prostitute, and women who had been divorced for infidelity were required to wear togas (Sebesta 1994). Togas for special uses had distinctive names, shapes, modes of decoration, colors, or forms of draping. (See *Table 4.1.*)

The earliest toga, the basis of later styles, was draped from a length of white wool fabric, roughly semicircular in shape, with a band of color around the curved edge. Wilson (1924), in a lengthy study of the Roman toga, determined that the early toga was shaped as depicted in *Figure 4.6a.*

By the Imperial period the shape of the toga had evolved to that shown in *Figures 4.6b* and *4.7* and its draping had become more complicated. Two new features were added. (See *Figure 4.7.*) The **sinus** was formed from the overfold of the Imperial toga. The overfold was rolled into loose folds as it crossed the back of the body, then as it emerged from under the right arm the folds were loosened, causing the overfold to fall almost to the knee, rather like a draped apron. The other new feature was the **umbo** (literally translated as "the knob"). Created by pulling a clump of fabric up from the first and invisible part of the toga that had been placed vertically from floor to shoulder, the umbo may have helped to hold the toga drapery in place, but seems ultimately to have become a decorative element. In its first development, before it became too large and open, the sinus was used as a sort of pocket in which to carry things. After the sinus enlarged, the umbo served this purpose. Before entering a sacred area, men sometimes pulled the overfold up and over the head at the back to form a sort of hood (Stone 1994). (See *Color Plate 6.*)

It required care to apportion the folds of a toga properly and to balance the bulk of the fabric. Carcopino (1940) comments:

> *The toga was a garment worthy of the masters of the world, flowing, solemn, eloquent, but with over-much complication in its arrangement and a little too much emphatic affectation in the self-conscious tumult of its folds. It required real skill to drape it artfully. It required unremitting attention if the balance of the toga were to be preserved in walking, in the heat of a discourse, or amid the jostling of a crowd.*

Step 1

Step 2

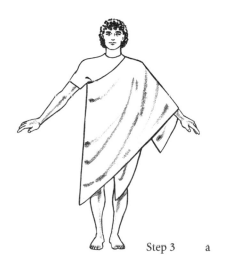

Step 3   a

FIGURE 4.6A

(left) Steps in draping the early form of the toga. Step 1: The toga is placed over the shoulder with point 1 below the knee. Step 2: Point 3 is drawn across the back, under the right arm and up to the left shoulder. Step 3: Point 3 is thrown across the left shoulder and arm to hang down in back of the left shoulder. Point 1 is obscured by draping the bulk of the toga across the front of the body. SOURCE: (Drawings adapted from drawings and photographs in Wilson, L. M. 1938. *The Roman Toga.* Baltimore, MD: Johns Hopkins University Press.)

_____

FIGURE 4.6B

(below) The imperial toga was draped in essentially the same way, except that the fold created an extra drapery at the front of the body. The fold, the sinus, and the umbo (pockets formed by pulling part of the side fold to the front) can be seen in Figure 4.7. SOURCE: (Drawings adapted from drawings and photographs in Wilson, L. M. 1938. *The Roman Toga.* Baltimore, MD: Johns Hopkins University Press.)

_____

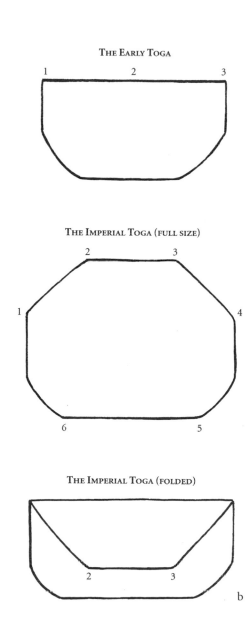

THE EARLY TOGA

THE IMPERIAL TOGA (FULL SIZE)

THE IMPERIAL TOGA (FOLDED)

b

style. The over-fold was folded back-and-forth upon itself until a folded band of fabric was formed at the top of the semicircle. These folds were probably held in place by stitching or pinning. When draped around the body, the folds created a smooth, diagonal band across the breast to the shoulder. (See *Figure 4.8.*)

When etiquette grew more lax during the late Empire, men felt free to wear garments other than the toga for important occasions. Many Roman men preferred an evolved form of the Greek himation (called in Latin, **pallium**), which was a broad rectangle that was draped around the shoulders, crossed in front, and was held in place with a belt.

FIGURE 4.7

Roman wearing the imperial toga over a tunic. The draped pouch at the front is the sinus. (Photograph courtesy, Photo Arts.)

FIGURE 4.8

Toga with the folded bands. (Redrawn by Thomas Hope from the Arch of Constantine, courtesy, Dover Publications, Inc.)

The toga was required dress during most of the Imperial period for audiences with the Emperor, at the spectacles that were staged in the Roman arena, and for any event where a citizen appeared in an official capacity. The heavy garment was probably uncomfortably hot in summer. To keep it white required frequent cleaning, which must have caused the toga to wear out quickly. Martial, a satirical poet, is constantly complaining about having a threadbare toga that he must replace.

It is not surprising, then, to learn that less cumbersome versions of this garment gradually developed. One variant, called the **balteus** (meaning "belt"), developed after 2nd century A.D. Bringing the section under the right arm higher and twisting the top into a sort of beltlike band eliminated the umbo. The **"toga with the folded bands"** evolved from this

CONTEMPORARY COMMENTS 4.1

In The Art of Love, *the Roman poet Ovid offers advice on grooming and dress in order to attract the opposite sex.*

To men he says:

Don't be crimping your locks with the use of the curling iron,

Don't scrape the hair off your legs, using the coarse pumice stone, . . .

Men should not care too much for good looks; neglect is becoming . . .

Let your person be clean, your body tanned by the sunshine,

Let your toga fit well, never a spot on its white,

Don't let your sandals be scuffed, nor your feet flap around in them loosely,

See that your teeth are clean, brush them at least twice a day,

Don't let your hair grow long, and when you visit a barber,

Patronize only the best, don't let him mangle your beard,

Keep your nails short, and don't ever let them be dirty,

Keep the little hairs out of your nose and ears,

Let your breath be sweet, and your body free from rank odors . . .

To women:

. . . I do not recommend flounces,

Do not endorse the wools reddened with Tyrian dye.

When you have such a choice of cheaper and pleasanter colors

You would be crazy to use only one costly display.

There is the color of sky, light-blue, with no cloud in the heavens,

There is the hue of the ram, rearing the golden fleece,

There is the color of wave, the hue of the Nereids' raiment,

There is the saffron glow worn by Aurora at dawn,

All kinds of colors: swans-down, amethyst, emerald, myrtle,

Almond, chestnut, and rose, yellow of wax, honey-pale—

Colors as many as flowers born from new earth in the springtime,

When the buds of the vine swell, and old winter has fled,

So many colors, or more, the wool absorbs; choose the right ones—

Not every color will suit everyone's differing need.

If your complexion is fair, dark-gray is a suitable color; . . .

If you are dark, dress in white . . .

Also, I need not remind you to brush your teeth night and morning.

Need not remind you your face ought to be washed when you rise.

You know what to apply to acquire a brighter complexion—

Nature's pallidest rose blushes with suitable art.

Art supplies the means for patching an incomplete eyebrow,

Art or a beauty-spot, aids the cheeks that have never a flaw.

There's nothing amiss in darkening eyes with mascara,

Ash, or the saffron that comes out of Cilician soil. . . .

Don't let your lover find the boxes displayed on your dresser,

Art that dissembles art gives the most happy effect.

Who wants to look at a face so smeared with paint that it's dripping,

Oozing sluggishly down into the neck of the gown?

Ovid, *The Art of Love*. 1957. Translated by Rolfe Humphries. Bloomington: Indiana University Press. Book One, pp. 120–121 (men and Book Three, pp. 158–159 (women).

COSTUME COMPONENTS FOR MEN: 500 B.C.–A.D. 400

GARMENTS

In Latin the loincloth was referred to as **subligar** (*sub-li'-gar*), and was probably comparable to the Greek perizoma, serving as an undergarment for middle- and upper-class men and a working garment for slaves.

Roman versions of the tunic ended around the knee, were short-sleeved and T-shaped. Tunics served as underclothing or a night shirt for upper-class men; belted tunics served as the usual street costume for poor men. By the 1st century A.D. of the Empire these variations are noted: (1) tunics cut shorter in front than back; (2) shorter versions for manual laborers and the military.

Several layers were worn in cold weather, one as an undergarment (interior tunic) and one as an outer garment (superior tunic). Those sensitive to cold wore two under tunics. The Emperor Augustus is said to have worn four layers! Personal style also affected wearing of the tunic. Horace, a Roman writer, describes two extremes: "Maltinus minces about with his tunic trailing low, another has it hoisted obscenely up his crotch" (Rudd 1973, p. 33).

During the 3rd century A.D. tunics had lengthened and covered the lower leg, reaching to the shin. This longer length continued in use to the end of the Empire, although the military and working men wore the practical, shorter length. The toga, that essential garment for male citizens, was worn over a tunic.

Cloaks and capes served as outdoor garments for cold weather and were made with or without hoods. The most important cloaks cited by various sources were:

- **paenula** (*pie-new′-la*): a heavy wool cloak, semicircular in shape, closed at the front, with a hood

- **lacerna** (*la-cer′na*): rectangular, with rounded corners and a hood

- **laena** (*lie′-na*): a circle of cloth folded to a semicircle that was thrown over the shoulders and pinned at the front

- **birrus** (*beer′rus*) or **burrus** (*bur′-rus*): resembling a modern, hooded poncho, cut full and with an opening through which the head was slipped

- **paludamentum** (*pa-lu-da-men′-tum*): a large white or purple cloak similar to the Greek chlamys, worn by emperors or generals

COSTUME COMPONENTS FOR WOMEN: 500 B.C.–A.D. 400

The individual elements of costume for adult women were similar to those of Greek women and consisted of undergarments, several layers of tunics, and outer mantles. Roman literary sources provide the Latin names of these garments, but it is not always possible to tell precisely how the garments appeared, and individual scholars have come to different conclusions concerning some aspects of women's clothing.

GARMENTS

Undergarments for women consisted of a loincloth (called *subligaria*—the feminine form of subligar) and a band of fabric, the *strophium,* that supported the breasts. A mosaic in Sicily shows female athletes in what looks like a two-piece, modern bathing suit. It is thought these women are each wearing the subligar and the strophium. There are also works of art in which cupids help the goddess Venus to tie her strophium. Goldman notes that in attempting to reproduce Roman costume she experimented with a long, narrow piece of fabric. She found that "the band would be most efficiently used as a brassiere by bringing the ends around the body from the back so that each long end crossed in front, supporting the breasts. These ends then continue around to the sides to the back, where they are tucked inside the wrapping to be held securely in place" (Goldman 1994, p. 235).

The tunic (Latin: *tunica*) was the basic garment for women in Rome and had much the same appearance as the Greek chiton. Women's tunics reached to the ankle or to the floor. Like men, women wore an under tunic and an outer tunic. The under tunic was not seen in public. It served as a night dress and was worn alone in the privacy of the home.

A draped shawl (counterpart of the Greek himation), the **palla** (*pal′la*) was placed over the outer tunic. (See *Figure 4.9* and *Color Plate 7.*) The palla is depicted as draped either similarly to the toga, casually pulled across the shoulder or pulled over the head like a veil.

For outdoor wear women wrapped themselves in cloaks, including the paenula, which was worn when traveling in bad weather.

GARMENTS DESIGNATING SOCIAL STATUS FOR WOMEN

Literary sources make it clear that specific garments were associated with women at various stages of their adult lives. Often the terms for these garments are known, but their precise form may not be. The following are the major garments designating social status for women as described by Sebesta (1994).

stola Roman literary sources speak of the stola as a garment reserved for free, married women. Like the toga, it was a garment that denoted status. Scholars have disagreed about its construction. Roman writers use the term *instita* in describing the distinctive dress of a Roman matron. Some scholars have interpreted this as a ruffle at the bottom of the stola that covered the feet, others as a dress suspended from sewed-on straps. Sebesta argues that this latter description is accurate and she describes the stola as resembling "a modern slip, though made of fuller material which hung in distinctive folds..."

Roman art does show some examples of a sleeveless outer tunic with straps worn over an undertunic (see *Figure 4.10*), but there are also many other representations of women dressed in garments without these straplike shoulders. Assuming that Sebesta is correct, a number of reasons could account for the relatively small number of images of the traditional stola, and the lack of clarity about its construction. Mythological characters appear frequently in Roman art and such women would not be dressed as Roman matrons. Depictions of women at home usually show them in informal situations where the formal "status" garment would most likely not have been worn, and when women are depicted outside the home, they frequently are shown with cloaks (see *Figure 4.10*) that obscure the precise construction of their garments.

FIGURE 4.9

Woman is wearing an under tunic, an outer tunic that may be a stola, and, draped over these, a palla. Her hair is dressed in the simple style of the Republican period. In her hand she carries a folded linen handkerchief, a symbol of rank. (Photograph courtesy, Photo Arts.)

FIGURE 4.10

Statue from early 1st century A.D. of a woman wearing a stola and palla. Note the clear depiction of the strap at the shoulder of the stola. The under tunic is visible at the neck. (Museo Archeologico, Naples. Photo courtesy, DAI, Rome, neg. 56.232.)

veil Although the palla was not worn exclusively by Roman matrons, they were expected to cover their heads with their pallas when they left their homes.

vitta A woolen band used to bind her hair was another element of the prescribed dress for Roman matrons.

tutulus A Roman matron became the *mater familias* only when her husband became the *pater familias*. This special status was designated by a special hairstyle, the tutulus. Probably created by drawing the hair to the top of the head and wrapping it in vittae, the effect was a conical shape similar to the Etruscan women's headdress of the same name. (See *Figure 4.3, page 66.*)

rincinium According to literary sources, widows wore this garment instead of a palla for a year of mourning. It was probably dark colored, but its precise form is unclear.

toga A women who was divorced on the grounds of adultery was no longer permitted to wear the stola and vittae. Instead she was required to wear a plain toga. There is no indication of how a woman who was divorced for other reasons dressed, nor do we know how unmarried adult women dressed.

COSTUME COMPONENTS FOR MEN AND WOMEN: 500 B.C.–A.D. 400

HAIR AND HEADDRESS

See *Illustrated Table 4.1* for illustrations of typical Roman hairstyles.

Illustrated Table 4.1

EXAMPLES OF HAIRSTYLES AND HEADDRESS WORN BY MEN AND WOMEN DURING THE ROMAN EMPIRE

Bearded Roman of the
Republican period

Clean-shaven Roman man with
carefully arranged hair, depicted on
Trajan's column, 1st century A.D.

Depiction of the Emperior
Constantine, 4th century A.D.

Roman women's hairstyles before 1st century A.D.

Elaborate hair arrangements of Roman women from after 1st century A.D.

Simpler hairstyles from after 2nd century A.D.

Thomas Hope. Reproduced courtesy, Dover Publications, Inc.

In the Republican period women had softly waved hair. By the end of the 1st century, complex—almost architectural—forms were built up of curls, braids, and artificial hair. Blonde hair was fashionable, and since dark hair is a common ethnic characteristic among many Mediterranean people this had to be achieved through bleaching or wearing wigs made from the hair of northern European blonde captives.

Roman writers ridiculed the custom of elaborately dressing the hair. Juvenal (quoted in Carcopino, 1940) said, "So numerous are the tiers and stories piled one upon another on her head: in front you would take her for an Andromache; she is not so tall behind; you would not think it was the same person."

During the later Empire, women's hairstyles became simplified, with braids or locks doubled up in back and pinned to the top of the head.

Men's hair was cut short and arranged by a barber. Sometimes straight hair was favored; at other times, curls. Men who wished to appear more youthful dyed their hair. Beards predominated in the Republican years; clean-shaven faces during the Empire until the reign of Hadrian (c. A.D. 120), an Emperor who was bearded.

Without sharp-edged steel razors, shaving was a painful and sometimes dangerous experience. Penalties were established for barbers who scarred their clients. A really good barber could become very prosperous. A Roman poet commemorated one barber for his skill. A man's first shave was a rite of passage, celebrated with a religious ceremony. The shaven hairs were deposited in a special container and sacrificed to the gods at a festival to which family and friends were invited (Carcopino 1940).

Instead of wearing hats, women tended to pull the palla or a scarf over the head. They wore fillets and coronets. Men's hat styles included those similar to the Greek petasos, hoods, and rounded or pointed caps.

FOOTWEAR

Men and women wore sandals (in Latin, **solae** [so'lay] or **sandalis**), boots, and a slipperlike shoe reaching to the ankle (**soccus**).

ACCESSORIES

Women carried fans and handbags. Sun shades were needed for the games held in the arenas, and for this purpose women used either wide hats or parasols that did not fold.

White linen handkerchiefs had different names and functions. The **sudarium** was for wiping off perspiration, veiling the face, or holding in front of the mouth to protect against disease. An **orarium** was a slightly larger version of the sudarium. (See *Figure 4.9.*) It became a symbol of rank, and in the late Empire was worn by upper-class women neatly pleated across the left shoulder or forearm. A **mappa** was a table napkin. (Guests brought their own napkins when invited for dinner.)

JEWELRY

Women wore expensive and beautifully crafted rings, bracelets, necklaces, armlets, earrings, diadems, as well as less costly versions. Of the types of jewelry, men wore only rings.

COSMETICS AND GROOMING

According to the satirists, cosmetics were used lavishly by both men and women. Practices reported for women included whitening the skin with lead, tinting the lips red, and darkening the eyebrows. One disgruntled lover makes this charge about his mistress, "You lie stored away in a hundred caskets; and your face does not sleep with you" (Carcopino 1940).

Appearance-conscious men were said to use makeup cream on the cheeks and to paste small circles of cloth over skin flaws. Members of both sexes used perfume.

Large public baths were frequented not only for cleanliness and exercise, but also as a place to socialize and do business. In some periods baths were segregated by sex; in others men and women bathed together.

Contemporary Comments 4.1, page 73, presents excerpts from the Roman writer Ovid's *The Art of Love,* a book in which he offers advice to both men and women as to how to improve one's appearance in order to please the opposite sex.

ROMAN COSTUME FOR CHILDREN: 500 B.C.–A.D. 400

Children dressed much like adults of the same sex: boys wearing short tunics and girls a garment similar to the stola. At first only the children of noble families wore the toga praetexta, but by 200 B.C. legislation had extended the right to wear this costume to all freeborn children. When boys reached the age of fourteen to sixteen, they gave up the praetexta in favor of the toga pura. Girls apparently ceased wearing the toga praetexta after puberty. Some sources indicate this was after age twelve; others say at age sixteen or when they married, whichever came first.

Croom (2002) notes that young girls may have worn a garment called a *supparum.* She points to depictions of girls wearing a belted linen garment that looks very much like a chiton with an overfold and suggests that the garment could easily have been lengthened by shortening the overfold.

Infants were swaddled. At the time a freeborn boy was named, a locket, called a **bulla,** made of gold, silver, bronze, or leather and containing charms against the evil eye was placed around the infant's neck. This was worn throughout childhood. (See *Figure 4.11.*) From infancy until they reached adult status, girls wore their hair braided and tied with a single woolen band.

FIGURE 4.11

Male and female children of the family of the Emperor Augustus, 1st century A.D., wear the toga praetexta. A bulla can be seen around the neck of the smallest child at the left. (Photograph courtesy, Photo Arts.)

MILITARY COSTUME FOR MEN DURING THE ROMAN EMPIRE

One of the distinctive elements of the dress of Roman soldiers was body armor that was worn over a tunic. Such armor might be made from leather bands, from corselets of metal plates, or from disks mounted on fabric or leather. Some armor consisted of large metal plates hinged at the shoulders and molded to fit the body. A wide band of leather rectangles might be suspended from the waist to cover the lower torso. Greaves protected the legs, and helmets protected the head.

During the Imperial period Roman soldiers adopted knee-length trousers that were placed under the tunic in cold weather. These garments were similar to those worn by the Gauls, a northern European tribe. Cloaks provided protection from the weather. Distinctions existed between the dress of officers and ordinary soldiers. Officers wore the **abolla** (*ah-bol'-la*), a folded rectangle fastening on the right shoulder. The **sagum** (*sa'gum*), like the abolla, was a single layer of thick wool, generally red. Ordinary soldiers wore it, and in time of war so did Roman citizens. The phrase "to put on the sagum" was synonymous with saying "to go to war." Generals leaving the city of Rome for a military campaign donned the afore-

mentioned paludamentum, larger and thicker than the cloaks of either officers or common soldiers.

Footwear for the military included boots that laced up the front, covering the leg to above the ankle; sandals; and open- and closed-toed shoes.

ROMAN COSTUME FOR SPECIAL EVENTS

The Synthesis

The synthesis (*sin-the'-sis*) was a garment worn by men at dinner parties, the precise form of which is a matter of debate. After a careful analysis of the Latin texts, McDaniel (1925) concluded that the synthesis was a lightweight garment worn instead of the toga for dining because the toga was too heavy and cumbersome to wear when the Romans reclined to eat. The texts that refer to the synthesis imply that the garment had two parts, and McDaniel suggested that these two parts probably consisted of a tunic plus a shoulder garment, such as the pallium. Latin authors speak of the synthesis as bright and colorful.

The synthesis was never seen outside of the home except during the Saturnalia, a public festival in December. One of the characteristics of the Saturnalia was that everything was turned "upside down." For example, masters waited upon their slaves, and gambling games that were normally forbidden were allowed. The wearing of the synthesis out-of-doors may be another example of the upsetting of tradition that was part of the Saturnalia.

Bridal Costume

Roman bridal costume for women introduced certain elements that have continued to have traditional association with weddings even until the present day: the veil and orange blossoms. The bridal costume consisted of a tunic woven in a traditional way, and tied around the waist with a knotted belt of wool; a saffron-colored palla and matching shoes; and a metal collar. The bride's hair was arranged with six pads of artificial hair, each separated by narrow bands and over this a veil of bright orange—the **flammeum** (*fla-may'um*). The veil covered the upper part of the bride's face. On top of the veil a wreath made of myrtle and orange blossoms was placed.

Religious Garb

Religious garb differed little from the costume of ordinary persons. Vestal virgins, a group of unmarried women assigned to guard the sacred flame kept burning in the temple of Vesta, wore veils that fastened under the chin and six pads of artificial hair separated by bands like those worn by brides. Augurs wore the multicolored, striped toga trabea.

CHANGES IN COSTUME DURING THE DECLINING YEARS OF THE ROMAN EMPIRE

During the closing century of the Roman Empire, some changes in costume highlighted the erosion of Roman control over the outer limits of its Empire. Throughout the Imperial period, articles of local, non-Roman dress had tended to survive or be incorporated into Roman clothing in out- lying regions. The Gallic cloak; a loose, unbelted tunic worn in Roman Gaul (now France); and trousers, worn by north- ern barbarian tribes, provide examples of this tendency. As Roman control over the provinces declined, local styles and Roman costume tended to merge even more.

In Rome itself a new variant of the tunic, called the **dalmatic** (*dal-mat'ik*), was adopted. It was fuller than earlier tu- nics, and had long, wide sleeves. Citizens wore the toga less and less. After the fall of the Roman Empire, the practice of wearing a draped shawl over a tunic survived during the Byzantine Empire and the early Middle Ages in Europe in modified form. This garment was, however, more like a Greek himation than a toga.

When the Western Roman Empire fell, at the close of the 5th century, the focus of Roman styles shifted eastward to the court in Constantinople where elements of Roman style blended with influences from the East to produce Byzantine styles (discussed in *Chapter 5*).

SUMMARY

VISUAL SUMMARY

The *Visual Summary Table* presents major costume forms of the Romans. Major Etruscan forms can be seen in *Figure 4.4*.

DIFFERENCES BETWEEN GREEK, ETRUSCAN, AND ROMAN COSTUME

Much of what were originally Greek clothing styles came to the Romans by way of the Etruscans. Comparisons of Greek, Etruscan, and Roman styles may serve not only to summarize the material in *Chapters 3* and *4*, but also to point up differ- ences in these three cultures that are reflected in their costume.

Most Greek garments are based on rectangular forms. Roman and Etruscan styles used a greater variety of shapes, with particular emphasis on rounded or elliptical forms. (In this context it is interesting to note that the Etruscans are thought to have originated the round arch, now called the "Roman arch," whereas the Greeks tended to use the rectan- gular post-and-lintel construction in their buildings.) Both Roman and Etruscan styles rely less than Greek styles on the draping of a single piece of fabric and make greater use of cut- ting and sewing, although draped elements are also present in the styles of the Italian region. This and the tendency of the Romans in particular to use wool fabrics in preference to linen helps to account for the difference in appearance be- tween the free flow of Greek clothing and the heavier draperies of Etruscan and Roman clothes.

Both the Etruscans and Romans used more ornamenta- tion and accessories, and in general they also wore more clothing. The climate may have been a factor (the climate of northern Italy is cooler than that of Greece), but it also re- flects a cultural attitude. The Etruscans and Romans did not share the Greek appreciation of nudity or the lightly clad hu- man body.

THEMES IN ETRUSCAN AND ROMAN DRESS

From the visual images, which are the major source of infor- mation about Etruscan dress, it is obvious that the theme of CROSS-CULTURAL INFLUENCES played a major role in Etrus- can styles. Indeed, during the period when Classical Greek

Visual Summary Table
MAJOR ROMAN GARMENTS

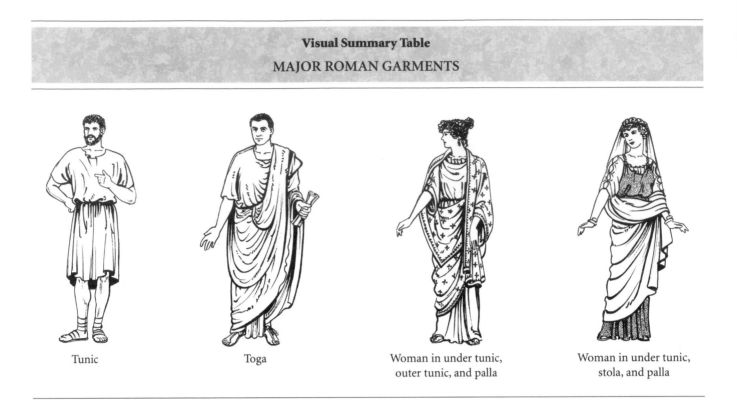

| Tunic | Toga | Woman in under tunic, outer tunic, and palla | Woman in under tunic, stola, and palla |

culture dominated the Mediterranean region, Etruscan styles hardly differed from the Greek.

Roman dress continues the CROSS-CULTURAL theme. Although the terminology for the basic garment changes from the Greek term *chiton* to the Roman *tunica,* the form of this garment does not change much. To this garment the Romans added the toga, probably derived from their neighbors, the Etruscans.

POLITICAL CONFLICT played a role in Roman dress, as well. The conquest of enormous territories brought both the raw materials for textiles and the finished products to Rome and the Romans.

The major theme that plays out in Roman dress, however, it that of the delineation of SOCIAL ROLES. Throughout Roman costume one finds evidence of the use of costume to set the individual or the occasion apart. One thinks in this context of the special garment for dining, the synthesis; the special costume of senators and of knights; the stola of the Roman matron; and the variety of togas, each with special significance. From childhood to widowhood Roman dress was full of well-defined symbols.

SURVIVALS OF ETRUSCAN AND ROMAN DRESS

Greek, Etruscan, and Roman styles are often called "classical styles." Except where a garment, such as the toga, is unique to one civilization, or where terminology assigned to styles makes that connection explicit, the similarities in garment styles of these periods make it difficult to identify revivals of classical styles as specifically Greek or Roman. For example, a hairstyle of the Directoire Period (see *Chapter 11*) was called the Titus. Titus is the name of a Roman Emperor, and the hairstyle was similar to Roman men's haircuts. Artists of the 18th century sometimes dressed the subjects of portraits in some version of a Roman toga, but few revivals of this garment can be found in fashionable dress. However, the name *toga* is often used as a fashion term that describes garments that cover one shoulder and leave the other bare.

The far-reaching influence of classical styles on subsequent periods is discussed on *page 59*.

N O T E S

Bonfante, L. 1975. *Etruscan Dress.* Baltimore, MD: Johns Hopkins University Press.

———. 1994. "Introduction," pp. 3 10. In J.L. Sebesta, and L. Bonfante, eds., *The World of Roman Costume.* Madison, WI: University of Wisconsin Press.

Carcopino, J. 1940. *Daily Life in Ancient Rome.* New Haven, CT: Yale University Press, pp. 155, 160, 169.

Casson, L. 1975. *Daily Life in Ancient Rome.* New York: Heritage, p. 12.

Croom, A. T. 2002. *Roman Clothing and Fashion.* Charleston, SC: Tempus.

Friedlander, L. 1936. *Roman Life and Manners under the Early Empire. Vol. 1.* New York: Dutton, p. 148.

Goldman, N. 1994. "Reconstructing Roman Clothing," pp. 213–237. In J. L. Sebesta and L. Bonfante, eds. *The World of Roman Costume.* Madison, WI: University of Wisconsin Press.

Herlihy, D. 1990. *Opera Muliebria: Women and Work in Medieval Europe.* Philadelphia: Temple University Press.

Jones, A. H. M. 1960. "The Cloth Industry under the Roman Empire." *Economic History Review,* Vol. 13, No. 2, p. 183.

McDaniel, W. B. 1925. "Roman Dinner Garments." *Classical Philology,* Vol. 20, p. 268

Rudd, N., translator. 1973. *The Satires of Horace and Persius.* Baltimore, MD: Penguin Books, p. 33.

Sebesta, J. L. 1994. "Symbolism in the Costume of the Roman Woman," pp. 46–53. In J. L. Sebesta and L. Bonfante, eds. *The World of Roman Costume.* Madison, WI: University of Wisconsin Press.

Sebesta, J. L. 1994. "Tunica Ralla, Tunica Spissa," pp. 65–76. In J. L. Sebesta and L. Bonfante, eds. *The World of Roman Costume.* Madison, WI: University of Wisconsin Press.

Stone, S. 1994. "The Toga: From National to Ceremonial Costume," pp. 13–45. In J. L. Sebesta and L. Bonfante, eds. *The World of Roman Costume.* Madison, WI: University of Wisconsin Press.

Wilson, L. M. 1924. *The Roman Toga.* Baltimore, MD: Johns Hopkins Press.

S E L E C T E D   R E A D I N G S

Books Containing Illustrations of Costume of the Period from Original Sources

Beard, M. and G. Henderson. 2001. *Classical Art: from Greece to Rome.* New York: Oxford University Press.

Becatti, G. 1968. *The Art of Ancient Rome and Greece.* Englewood Cliffs, NJ: Prentice Hall.

Bonfante, L. 1975. *Etruscan Dress.* Baltimore, MD: Johns Hopkins University Press.

Casson, L. 1975. *The Horizon Book of Daily Life in Ancient Rome.* New York: Simon and Schuster.

Heintze, H. 1990. *Roman Art.* Universe Books.

Pallotino, M. 1955. *The Art of the Etruscans.* New York: Vanguard Press.

Spivey, N. 1997. *Etruscan Art.* New York: Thames and Hudson.

Von Matt, L. 1970. *The Art of the Etruscans.* New York: Harry N. Abrams.

Periodical Articles

Bonfante, L. 1971, "Etruscan Dress as an Historical Source." *American Journal of Archeology,* July, p. 277.

———. 1978. "The Language of Dress: Etruscan Influences." *Archeology,* Jan./Feb., p. 14.

Braun-Ronsdorf, M. "The Sudarium and Orarium of the Romans." *CIBA Review,* No. 89, p. 3298.

DeBrohun, J. 2001. "Power Dressing in Ancient Greece and Rome." *History Today.* February, p. 18.

Jones, A. H. M. 1960. "Cloth Industry Under the Roman Empire." *Economic History Review,* December, p. 183.

Wild, J.P. 1963. "Byrrus Britannicus." *Antiquity,* September, p. 193.

———. 1976. Chapter 13: "Textiles." In D. Strong and D. Brown, eds. *Roman Crafts.* New York: New York University Press.

Daily Life

Aries, P. and G. Duby. 1987–1991. *A History of Private Life. Vol. 1.* Cambridge, MA: Belknap Press of Harvard University Press.

Bonfante, L. 1987. *Etruscan Life and Afterlife.* Detroit, MI: Wayne State University Press.

Brilliant, R. 1984. *Visual Narratives: Storytelling in Etruscan and Roman Art.* Ithaca, NY: Cornell University Press.

Cornell, T. and K. Lomas, eds. 1994. *Urban Society in Roman Italy.* Palgrave Macmillan.

Carcopino, J. 1960. *Daily Life in Ancient Rome.* New Haven, CT: Yale University Press.

Caselli, G. 1985. *History of Everyday Things: The Roman Empire and the Dark Ages.* New York: Peter Bedrick Books.

Connolly, P. and H. Dodge. 2000. *The Ancient City: Life in Classical Athens & Rome.* New York: Oxford University Press.

Dupont, F. 1994. *Daily Life in Ancient Rome.* Cambridge, MA: Blackwell.

Haynes, S. 2000. *Etruscan Civilization: A Cultural History.* Los Angeles: J. Paul Getty Museum Publications.

Heurgon, J. 2002. *Daily Life of the Etruscans.* New York: Phoenix Press.

Nichols, R. and K. McLeish. 1976. *Through Roman Eyes.* New York: Cambridge University Press.

Shelton, J. 1997. *As the Romans Did: A Source Book in Roman Social History.* New York: Oxford University Press.

PART TWO

THE MIDDLE AGES

c. 300–1500

The founding of Constantinople, the new capital of the Roman Empire, signaled the decline of Rome and the western portion of the empire. It also meant two cultures would develop in the empire, in addition to two imperial lines of emperors. The advantage belonged to the wealthier, more populous Eastern Empire whose capital, Constantinople, was well situated to defend the eastern portion of the empire and to dominate the Eastern economy. The Western Empire, ruled from Rome, was overwhelmed by the mass migration of German tribes, which began at the close of the 4th century and continued on throughout the 5th century.

Because of its geographical location, the city of Rome was sacked in A.D. 410 and several times later in the century. The western emperors, however, moved the capital of the Western Empire from Rome to Ravenna in A.D. 403, hoping that this city on the Adriatic coast, south of Venice, would be less easily attacked than Rome. In 476 when Odovacar, king of an obscure German tribe, deposed the emperor of the West, Roman power disappeared from Italy.

Certain elements that had been part of Roman civilization and culture survived. The Christian church, which had endured persecution, became the official state church of the Empire in the 4th century, exercising a unifying force in western Europe and converting the barbarians[1] to Christianity. The church had continued to function because its organization paralleled that of the Roman Empire. The head of the church was not the emperor (as in the Byzantine Empire) but the bishop of Rome, the pope. In each important city across Europe, bishops loyal to the pope administered the affairs of the church. Over the bishops in each capital city of the province were archbishops (called "metropolitans" in the Eastern Em-

pire). The level of the bishops corresponded to the position held by the governors of the Imperial Roman provinces. After Christianity became the official state religion, some Christians sought a more ascetic form of Christianity; they found satisfaction in monasticism. Originating in the east, it became the way of life for those who wanted only to seek salvation for their souls. Because the monks had to be occupied with some form of work, the copying of books by hand became an appropriate form of labor for them. Through the centuries monastery libraries would preserve not only Christian but also earlier Greek and Roman classical literature which otherwise would have been lost forever.

The early Middle Ages, from the fall of the Roman Empire until the 9th century, have often been called the Dark Ages because of the decline in cultural standards as people lost command of the Latin language. Education for laymen disappeared, producing generations who could neither read nor write. In much of the period depopulation, poverty, and isolation affected many areas of Europe; the quality of life declined seriously. A major cause of the decline in Roman civilization was the decay of the cities and towns, which had been the centers of Roman culture. Written records from the period are often sparse, leaving gaps that cannot be filled. Information about costumes is especially scarce. With the decline in living standards and the decrease in wealth, works of art were rarely commissioned, except for those intended for the church. Literary production decreased as well because of illiteracy. Nevertheless enough evidence remains to construct a general, if not too detailed, picture of life in the early Medieval period.

Throughout the Middle Ages the Eastern Roman Empire (more often called the Byzantine Empire) survived, helping to preserve ancient Greek thought and creating magnificent works of art. The survival of the Byzantine Empire was based on an efficient bureaucracy and a sound economy. Although

[1]The term barbarian today has a pejorative connotation. As used here, it means those tribes from Northern Europe who were not citizens of the Roman empire.

trade and urban life almost ceased in the West, cities and commerce flourished in the Byzantine Empire. With money obtained from trade, the Byzantine officials recruited, trained, and equipped armies that held off one attacker after another. A period of expansion ended in the 7th century when Arab armies invaded Byzantine territories.

Islam, a new religion, founded by Mohammed in Mecca in the early 7th century, inspired the Arab allies. Mohammed's successors united the Bedouin tribes in Arabia into a military force that soon swept across the Middle East. Arab armies, inspired by their new faith and seeking booty and land, conquered Iraq, Syria, and Palestine, and pressed on to seize territories as far to the east as India. On more than one occasion their armies besieged Constantinople. After conquering North Africa, they moved northward through Spain and into southern France, where their expansion was halted at the battle of Tours in 732.

Throughout its history, the Byzantine Empire was menaced by attacks from both the East and West. In spite of constant pressure from hostile forces, the Empire survived until 1453, when the city of Constantinople and the remains of a once-powerful empire fell to a conquering force of Ottoman Turks. In its history of more than a thousand years, the Byzantine Empire developed an artistic and intellectual atmosphere in which styles and ideas of both East and West were merged. Records and traditions from Greek and Roman antiquity were preserved in the libraries and in the Byzantine art collections even though the Turks destroyed many of the manuscripts and works of art.

In the Western Roman Empire, Roman government disappeared by the end of the 5th century to be replaced by Germanic kingdoms. These kingdoms helped to fuse Roman and Germanic cultures into a new civilization. One of the Germanic kingdoms that retained its political identity was the kingdom of the Franks. In the year 800, the pope crowned the king of the Franks, Charlemagne, emperor of the Romans. The ceremony symbolized a declaration of independence from the Byzantine Empire and a revival of the Roman Empire, but it was in fact more German than Roman. After his death in 814, Charlemagne's empires, which extended over much of western Europe, disintegrated under the impact of new and more destructive invasions. From the wreckage of the Carolingian Empire emerged a feudal society in which petty, local lords controlled small areas. These leaders pledged their personal loyalty to more powerful lords in return for their protection, and above them all was the supreme overlord, the king.

Under feudal monarchies Europe revived so much that by the 11th century a great military expedition, the First Crusade, was launched to regain the Holy Land from the Moslems. Originally preached by Pope Urban II, it was a call for the unruly feudal knights to do battle for a righteous cause. Thousands, both knights and poor people, responded to the pope's call. For centuries Christians had done penance for their sins by going on pilgrimages to holy places. Now the crusade became a superpilgrimage. The crusaders captured Jerusalem in 1099 and slaughtered the inhabitants. In this region the crusaders established feudal states, which were soon under attack from the Moslems, prompting a series of crusades continuing for 200 years until the crusading spirit vanished. From the Middle East the crusaders returned to Europe bringing back new products: spices, fabrics, perfumes, jewelry, and new ideas.

By the 12th century trade among the nations of Europe again flourished, and their once-stagnant economies experienced a remarkable revitalization. While the Crusades brought Middle Eastern styles and ideas to Europe, other developments extended European contacts beyond the Mideast to the Far East.

The Muslim conquests in the 7th century closed the land routes to Asia until the Mongols swept out of northern China, across western Asia and into Russia in the 13th century. The Mongols, eager for trade and cultural relations with Europe, welcomed enterprising Europeans who dared to travel across Asia to the Mongol capital at Peking. Two Venetian merchants, Nicolo and Matteo Polo, traveled eastward across Asia in 1260 hoping to contact traders from the Orient and profit from the reopening of the land route to Asia. Eventually they met envoys from the Mongol ruler Kublai Khan, who brought them to his court where they received a cordial welcome. No Western Christians before the Polo brothers had ever visited China. Kublai Khan asked them to return to Europe and to bring back a hundred teachers to teach his people Christianity. The Polo brothers returned to Europe but could recruit only two Dominican friars, who soon decided they had no wish to make the long trip.

The Polo brothers set out for China again in 1271 accompanied by Nicolo's 17-year-old son Marco. The three men journeyed across the deserts and mountains of central Asia for three and a half years until they reached Shangtu, the summer capital of Kublai Khan. The young Marco Polo so impressed Kublai Khan that he was permitted to enter the Mongol civil service. He governed a Chinese city for three years and traveled on numerous missions for Kublai Khan. In his travels Marco Polo visited Burma, Indochina, and South China. Marco Polo, his father, and uncle remained in China and did not return to Europe until 1295.

Following a sea battle between Venice and Genoa in 1298, Marco Polo became a prisoner of war. While in prison he began to dictate his memoirs, *The Travels of Marco Polo,* which appeared in 1307. The book circulated in manuscript form until it was printed in 1477. It became one of the most widely read books in Europe in the 14th and 15th centuries, arousing great interest in the Orient among merchants eager to trade in cassia, ginger, pepper, and cinnamon. His book fascinated sailors who were attracted to the idea of sailing to the Far East, where they hoped to make their fortune with a cargo of spices. The sea route to the Far East had become more important following the death of Kublai Khan in 1294 and the breakup of his empire. These two factors made it impossible for caravans of merchants to repeat the Polo's feat of crossing Asia by land.

Marco Polo was the first European ever to cross the continent of Asia and leave a record of what he had seen and heard. Because he wanted his book to be a description of Asia for Europeans, he dealt with animals, land forms, inventions, plants, customs, governments, religions, and manufacture of garments. Marco Polo portrayed the Chinese civilization as being far superior to Europe in technology and culture. Because of his unflattering contrasts, Polo's book was dismissed as fiction or at best exaggeration. Not until the 19th century were scholars and explorers able to confirm Marco Polo's observations and to verify that his book was the first to present an accurate idea of China and other Asian countries. Columbus read Marco Polo's book and made notes on his copy. *The Travels of Marco Polo* became a strong impetus to European trade with the Orient and stimulated the European search for the spices and luxuries of the Far East, a search that was to lead in 1492 to the accidental discovery of the lands of the Western Hemisphere.

By the 1400s the arts, the intellectual life, and the social structure of Europe had been virtually transformed. During this transformation of society, a change had come about in the speed with which clothing styles changed. Many costume historians and social scientists believe that the phenomenon of fashion in dress in Western society began during the Middle Ages.

Fashion has been defined as "a pattern of change in which certain social forms enjoy temporary acceptance and respectability only to be replaced by others" (Blumer 1968). Bell (1948) pointed out that the increasingly rapid change of dress styles characteristic of Europe after the Middle Ages contrasts with the more static nature of clothing in earlier and in non-Western civilizations. *The Dictionary of Social Sciences* (Gold 1964) describes fashion as "a recurring cultural pattern, found in societies having open-ended class systems" and notes that "fashion becomes a matter of imitation of higher by lower classes in the common scramble for unstable and superficial status symbols." By the early 21st century fashion change is no longer originating solely with the upper classes. But at the time of its beginnings, it is generally agreed that those who sought to be in fashion were copying the dress of royalty and the wealthy.

These two elements, an open-ended class system and the imitation of higher classes by lower classes, are both aspects of medieval life in the 13th through the 15th centuries. Peasants who moved from rural areas to cities often became part of the growing middle class. A wealthy merchant, Jacques Coeur, adviser to the king of France in the 1400s, was made a nobleman by that king in reward for his service. The passage of sumptuary laws regulating dress and other luxuries in the 13th to the 15th centuries is good evidence of the vain attempts of the nobility to prevent the increasing affluent commoners from usurping those status symbols the nobility considered to be their own (Nicholas 1974).

Two other conditions contributed to the spread of fashion. In order to imitate those of higher status, the imitator must have sufficient means to afford the latest fashions. A newly affluent middle class, largely merchants and artisans, was emerging. This development not only provided social mobility, but also increased affluence for a substantially larger proportion of the population. Finally, if fashions are to be more than a merely local style, fashion information must be carried from one place to another. Increased trade and travel satisfied this condition.

As the Middle Ages drew to a close, the phenomenon called fashion was firmly established and the duration of the periods that fashionable styles endured grew shorter and shorter. No longer can one speak of styles, such as those of the Egyptians, that lasted for thousands of years. Instead, by the close of the Medieval period one speaks of fashions that lasted less than a century.

NOTES

Bell, Q. 1948. *On Human Finery.* London: Hogarth Press, p. 41.

Blumer, H. 1968. "Fashion." In the *International Encyclopedia of the Social Sciences,* V. New York: Macmillan, p. 142.

Gold, R. L. 1964. "Fashion." In *The Dictionary of the Social Sciences.* New York: Free Press, p. 262.

Nicholas, D. 1974. "Patterns of Social Mobility." In *One Thousand Years: Western Europe in the Middle Ages.* New York: Houghton-Mifflin, p. 45.

CHRONOLOGY

A.D. 330
Constantinople becomes capital of the Eastern Roman Empire

481–511
Clovis founds the Merovingian dynasty

6th century
Secrets of the process of silk production smuggled back to Byzantium from China

527–565
Reign of Justinian

early 7th century
The founding of Islam by Mohammed

732
Defeat of Arabs at the battle of Tours halts their expansion in Europe

751
Pepin the Short deposes Merovingian king and founds the Carolingian dynasty

800
Charlemagne, son of Pepin, crowned Emperor of the Romans by the pope

871–899
Alfred the Great, Anglo-Saxon king whose dynasty united Britain under one king

962
Otto I of Saxony crowned Holy Roman Emperor by the pope

987
Hugh Capet ascends the French throne and begins
Capetian dynasty that rules France for 300 years

1066
William the Conqueror, a Norman, invades England and becomes king

1095
Pope Urban declares the First Crusade

mid-11th to mid-12th centuries
Romanesque architecture styles predominate in Europe

after 1150
Gothic styles develop in architecture

1125–1268
Hohenstaufen dynasty attempts to rule Germany, Italy, and Sicily

1215
King John of England compelled to sign the Magna Carta

1271–72
The Ninth and last crusade

1273
First Hapsburg emperor of German states

1296
Marco Polo dictates the story of his travels to the Far East

1453
Constantinople conquered by the Ottoman Turks

CHAPTER FIVE

THE EARLY MIDDLE AGES

c. 300 – 1300

A.

Byzantine chair

B.

Interior of St. Apollinaire in Ravenna

C.

Small decorated box

D.

Windows, Serrabone monastery, 11th c.

E.

Chest

F.

St. Martin de Canigou monastery, 12th c.

G.

Sculpted figures, Chartres, 12th c.

Figure A, from Hottenroth, F. 1884. *Trachten Der Völker,* Vol. 1. Stuttgart: Verlag Gustav Wiese, plate 69. Figure C, from Hottenroth, F. 1884. *Trachten Der Völker,* Vol. 2. Stuttgart: Verlag Gustav Wiese, plate 22. Figures B, E, from Lavisse, E. 1905. *Album Historique, Le Moyen-Age.* Paris: Librairie Armand Colin, pp. 74, 226. Figures D, F, G courtesy of V. R. Tortora.

The first section of this chapter will deal with the Byzantine Empire, which lasted from A.D. 330 to 1453. The latter section will deal with Europe from about 300 to 1300. In the years between 400 and 900, styles of the Byzantine Empire influenced all of Europe. Byzantium was the greatest cultural center of the period, while in the remainder of Europe literacy was barely kept alive in the monasteries. After the 10th century, however, Europe began an economic recovery and Byzantine influences became somewhat less important.

THE BYZANTINE PERIOD
C. 330–1453

Historical Background

The capital of the Byzantine Empire was Constantinople, a Greek city that had been selected by the Roman Emperor Constantine in 330 to be the capital of the eastern part of the Roman Empire. Located at the entrance of the Black Sea, the city and its surrounding territories commanded both land and sea trade routes between the West and central Asia, Russia, and the Far East. At the same time, the city was protected by the rugged Balkan Mountains from the invading barbarians who overran Rome and the Italian peninsula.

As a result, Constantinople was the metropolis of the Mediterranean economy until 1200. But while the location of the capital ensured its survival, it also altered its character. Situated at the literal crossroads between East and West, the city and the empire of which it was the capital became a rich amalgam of Eastern and Western art and culture. In costume, one sees this reflected in a gradual evolution of Roman styles as they added increasingly ornate Eastern elements.

By the year 565 the Byzantine Empire stretched north through the Balkans to the Danube; east into Asia Minor, Syria, and Palestine; and west into Egypt and North Africa, Italy, and Southern Spain. (See *Figure 5.1.*) During the 7th and 8th centuries its size was reduced, and by the mid-9th century it comprised only the Greek peninsula and much of modern-day Turkey. This diminished empire was separated from the rest of Europe to such an extent that Greek replaced the Latin language, and Middle Eastern influences on life and styles became pronounced.

Throughout its history, Byzantium was constantly at war with a series of enemies: the Persians, Arabs, Bulgars, Avars, Seljuq Turks, and, at the end, the Ottoman Turks. Even the crusaders became enemies. On the Fourth Crusade, the crusaders were unable to pay the price Venetians charged to transport them to the Holy Land. After more bargaining, the crusaders agreed to capture the city of Zara for the Venetians, but after taking Zara the crusaders were still short of cash to pay for the passage to Jerusalem. Urged on by the Venetians, the crusaders accepted the offer of a pretender to the throne of the Byzantine Empire to supply the necessary cash if they helped him take Constantinople. The crusaders obliged, but when he reneged on the bargain in 1204 they seized Constantinople; sacked the city, destroying manuscripts and priceless works of art; and declared a crusader emperor. In 1261 a Byzantine emperor retook Constantinople but the once-great empire had vanished. Byzantium was reduced to little more than a Balkan state. The artistic and intellectual life of the city revived, but the menace of invasion by the Turks continued. Finally, in 1453, the Ottoman Turks captured Constantinople, destroying the Empire.

Social Organization
in the Byzantine Period

At the head of the Byzantine state was the emperor, who was not only the absolute ruler who could make law as he wished, but also the head of the Eastern church. The Eastern church separated from the Christian church in the West in 1054. The emperor lived with the empress in an elaborate palace in Constantinople. But the finest example of Byzantine architecture was to be found in the church of Hagia Sophia (Holy Wisdom) constructed by the Emperor Justinian (527–565). The interior was decorated with gold leaf, colored marble, bits of glass, and colored mosaics. Similar motifs and decorative elements appear in Byzantine costume.

A landed nobility made up an important element in the provincial economic life and the government of the empire. A well-developed civil service helped the imperial administration function by collecting taxes, administering justice, raising armies, and putting them into the field. The aristocracy was one of wealth, rather than blood line, so ambitious young men could rise from one social group to the next, unlike the process in Western society. Education was important to wealthy families, most of whom had tutors for their sons. There were schools in some provincial areas and Constantinople had a well-known university.

The status of women was rather advanced, although more so in the earlier empire period than in the later phase when ideas from the Near East predominated. Empresses were known to reign alone or as regents for minor sons, and a number of them exercised great power. At the other end of the social scale were the slaves, both foreign captives and poor people who sold themselves into slavery in order to survive.

Culture, Art, and Technology
in the Byzantine Period

Throughout its history, the city of Constantinople saw itself as a center for the preservation of the "antique" (i.e., Greek and Roman) culture. Writings and works of art were con-

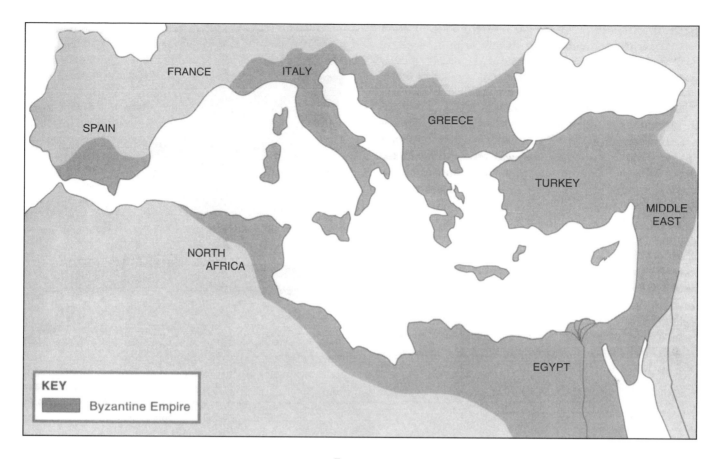

FIGURE 5.1

This map shows the extent of the Byzantine Empire under Justinian, in the 6th century A.D.

sciously preserved. Many of these treasures were destroyed when the crusaders and the Turks sacked the city. Others were saved or were carried away by raiders to other places where they escaped destruction.

ART AS A SOURCE OF INFORMATION ABOUT COSTUME

The art of the Byzantine Empire provides the major record from which costume information comes. Artists decorated churches with mosaics (pictures or designs made from small, colored stones), many of which still exist. Other special skills included carving of ivory and illumination (hand painting and lettering) of manuscripts. Byzantine art displays a blending of classical and Middle Eastern motifs and forms of decoration.

Much of the art that remains from the Byzantine period has a religious motif. Religious art often utilized traditional rather than realistic representations of people. For example, early in the Byzantine tradition artists began to depict the evangelists in the classical costume worn in Rome of the 4th century. This convention persisted to such an extent that many 8th and 9th century depictions of these figures in man-

uscripts appear to be derived from versions that first appeared almost four centuries before (Calkins 1993). Other conventions also developed in Byzantine art: Christ was represented as a king, Mary as a queen. They were dressed in royal robes, which symbolized their status. Like portrayals of the evangelists, these stereotypes continued in use during the remainder of the Middle Ages and even beyond. For these reasons, depictions of religious scenes in Byzantine art must be evaluated carefully to ascertain whether figures are actually wearing costumes that are contemporary with the period in which the art was created.

TEXTILE PRODUCTION AND TECHNOLOGY

The Byzantines wove fine textiles. From the 4th to the 6th centuries, linen and wool were the predominant fabrics. Production of silk fabrics had been a secret process held first by the Chinese and later by the Koreans and Japanese. Gradually knowledge of how silk was produced spread westward. Trade routes had brought silk fabrics and possibly some raw silk fiber to Greece and Rome before the 1st century B.C., but silk production had been possible only on a very limited scale. It is reported by Byzantine historians that in the 6th century a pair of monks brought the secret of sericulture (silk production) to the Byzantine emperor. Not only did they learn how the silkworm was bred, raised, and fed, but it was also reported that they smuggled a number of silkworm eggs out of China in a hollow bamboo pole (Heichelheim 1973).

From this point until the 9th century when Greeks in Sicily also began to produce silk, the Byzantines produced silk for all of the Western world. The emperor exploited his monopoly by charging enormous prices for the fabrics; therefore, only the wealthiest Europeans could afford the fabric. Brocades woven in Byzantium were especially desirable. Often the designs used in these fabrics were Persian in origin. Christian subjects were also depicted in complex woven patterns. When made into garments or wall hangings, these luxurious fabrics might be adorned with precious and semi-precious stones, small medallions of enamel, embroidery, and/or appliqués.

FIGURE 5.2

Tunic from the Byzantine period in Egypt, c. 6th to 7th centuries. Tunic has tapestry-woven decorations in colors on a red ground in the form of clavi over the shoulders, segmentae on either side of the skirt and over the shoulders, and on the sleeves. Woven decorative bands are attached at the cuffs and hem. (Photograph courtesy, The Metropolitan Museum of Art, gift of Maurice Nahman.)

BYZANTINE COSTUME FOR MEN:
A.D. 300–1450

Early Byzantine and late Roman costumes are virtually indistinguishable. When the Emperor Constantine moved his capital to Constantinople, the Roman administrators carried with them Roman costumes and customs. With time, Roman influences eroded and Oriental influences prevailed. The evolution of the toga is an example of this process. The toga, diminishing in use by Romans from the 3rd century on, was by the 4th century used only for ceremonial occasions by the emperor and the consuls, who were important state officials. Finally, only a vestige of the toga remained—a narrow band of folded fabric that wrapped around the body in the same way as the toga. Eventually even this was transformed into the emperor's narrow, jeweled scarf.

Costume Components for Men

GARMENTS

The basic garment for men was a tunic. (See *Figure 5.2*.) Tunics could be either short, ending below the knee, or long, reaching to the ground. Byzantine art shows the Emperor Justinian and other men of the 6th century in tunics that ended below the knee. (See *Color Plate 9*.) In later centuries emperors and important court officials appear to have worn full-length tunics (see *Figure 5.3*), while less important persons wore short tunics.

Some long tunics were cut with sleeves fitted to the wrist. Others with long, close-fitting sleeves were worn beneath an outer tunic or dalmatic with shorter, fuller sleeves. Outer tunics generally had belts.

Short tunics usually had long sleeves, wider at the top and tapering to fit closely at the wrists. Working men frequently caught up the hem of the tunic and fastened it to the belt at a point just over each leg in order to make movement easier. Some tunics were decorated with clavi (by now these stripes that originated in Roman dress on either side of the tunic had become ornamental rather than indicative of wearer's status) and **segmentae** (*seg-men'-tie*), square or round decorative medallions that were placed in different areas of the tunic.

Tunics of the wealthy were decorated with vertical and horizontal bands that were elaborately patterned with embroidery, appliqué, precious stones, or woven designs. (See *Color Plate 8*.) In the early part of the Empire, fabrics were usually plain in color and decoration was achieved by use of clavi, segmentae, and banding but as Oriental influences gained, fabrics developed overall patterning. (See *Figure 5.3*.)

After A.D. 1000 the silhouette changed and tunics were more closely fitted to the body. Under tunics had fitted sleeves;

fabric with an opening for the head, sometimes with a round collarlike construction at the head opening. (See *Figure 5.4.*)

HAIR AND HEADDRESS

From the 4th to 10th centuries men tended to be clean shaven. (See *Color Plate 9.*) Later, men were more likely to have beards. (See *Figure 5.3.*)

On their heads emperors wore jeweled crowns, often with suspended strings of pearls. Other head coverings portrayed in art included a Phrygian bonnetlike style shown in a mosaic depicting the Magi, and several versions of a high hat with an upstanding brim surrounding either a high-crowned turban, a smooth, close-fitting crown, or a soft crown with a tassel at the back.

FIGURE 5.3

Byzantine man's costume of the end of the 11th century and after. (19th century redrawing by Jacquemin. New York City Public Library, Picture Collection.)

FIGURE 5.4

Enameled picture of Archangel Michael, in the Byzantine style, c. 10th to 12th centuries or later. The Archangel wears a jeweled lorum or pallium over an ankle-length tunic. (Photograph courtesy, The Metropolitan Museum of Art, gift of the Estate of Otto H. Kahn, 1952.)

outer tunics had wide sleeves and were shorter than under tunics. When the tunic was belted, some of the fabric bloused out and over the belt. Fabrics had overall patterns and bands of jeweled decoration were placed at hems and on sleeves, with wide, decorative yokes at the neck. (See *Figure 5.3.*)

Hose were worn with short tunics as a leg covering. Some had horizontal bands of geometric patterns.

The **pallium,** also called a **lorum** (*pal-ee'-um; lo'rum*), was a long, narrow, heavily jeweled scarf, possibly evolved from the toga with the folded bands, that became part of the official insignia of the emperor. The empress was also permitted to wear this garment. Initially draped up center-front, around the shoulders, across the front of the body, and carried over one arm, it eventually became a simpler panel of

BYZANTINE COSTUME
FOR WOMEN: A.D. 300–1453

Costume Components for Women

GARMENTS

The tunic and palla of the Romans continued in use during the early Byzantine Empire. Gradually the wide, long-sleeved tunic called the dalmatic, which was decorated with clavi and segmentae, replaced the outer tunic and was worn over an under tunic with closely fitted sleeves. A simple veil worn over the head replaced the palla for a time. Eventually the palla returned to use in a modified form that wrapped around the body and covered the upper part of the skirt, the bodice, and either one or both shoulders. (See *Figure 5.5.*)

Although occasional outer garments with long fitted sleeves are depicted in art in the 7th century and after, for the most part women wore double-layered tunics. The under tunic had long fitted sleeves and the outer tunic had full, open sleeves cut short enough to display the sleeve of the under tunic.

Noble and wealthy women's garments were made from elaborately patterned fabrics that might also be decorated with jewels. Women of this class also wore jeweled belts and collars. (See *Color Plate 9.*)

After A.D. 1000 ornamentation of tunics increased. Variations in sleeve styles included wide, hanging sleeves or sleeves with long bands of fabric forming a sort of pendant cuff. Occasionally what appears to be a skirt and long, knee-length over-blouse is depicted, though this may be just an especially short outer tunic.

HAIR AND HEADDRESS

Some early representations show women with hair parted in the center, soft waves framing the face, and the bulk of the hair pulled to the back or knotted on top of the head. Otherwise, women's hair is usually covered.

FIGURE 5.5

Mosaic from the church of St. Apollinarus in Ravenna depicting women who each wear a white under tunic of the 6th century. A white palla is draped across the shoulders. (Photograph courtesy, Edizione Alinari.)

Characteristic hair coverings included veils and tur- banlike hats that appeared from the 4th century to the 12th century. This latter style has been described as looking like a cap surrounded by a small tire. (See *Figure 5.6.*) It evolved from having a fairly large hat crown with a smaller roll sur- rounding it to a smaller crown with a much larger roll. The hat itself might be trimmed with jewels. Empresses set their royal crowns on top of the hat. Royal crowns were heavily jeweled diadems with pendant strings of pearls. (See *Color Plate 9.*) Very late representations of empresses may show them wearing a crown over their own hair, which is dressed close to the face.

BYZANTINE COSTUME FOR MEN AND WOMEN: A.D. 300–1450

Costume Components for Men and Women

CLOAKS

Upper-class men and the empress wore the **paludamentum** (*pa-lud-a-men'tum*), which fastened over the right shoulder with a jeweled brooch. This cloak was distinguished by a large square decoration, the **tablion** (*tab-lee'on*), in contrasting colors and fabric that was located at the open edge over the breast. (See *Color Plate 9.*) After the 11th century, upper-class men and the imperial family no longer wore the paludamen- tum out-of-doors, wearing semicircular cloaks fastened at center front instead.

For common people and women other than the empress, a simple, square cloak replaced the hooded paenula of Roman times for general wear. After the 7th and 8th centuries, a semi- circular cloak pinned at the shoulder or at center front came into general use.

FOOTWEAR

Shoes, made of cloth (including silk) or leather, were often quite open in construction and ornamented with decorations cut out of the material. Some tied and others buckled at the ankle. Many were ornamented with stones, pearls, enameled metal, embroidery, appliqué, and cutwork. Red apparently was a favored color for empresses and their retainers. (See *Color Plate 9.*) Hose were worn under shoes.

Although a few boots are depicted as high at the front and lower behind the knee, most ended just below the calf. Some decorated styles were worn by the wealthy. Military fig- ures from the early Byzantine Empire wear Roman-like, open-toed boots; later a closed boot was worn. Boots seem to have been worn by men, not women.

FIGURE 5.6

Byzantine sculpture, 2nd half of the 5th century. Marble bust of a lady of rank who wears a large, turbanlike haircovering. (Photograph courtesy, The Metropolitan Museum of Art, the Cloisters Collection, purchase, 1966.)

JEWELRY

Jewels were not just accessories but an integral part of the cos- tume. Empresses wore wide, jeweled collars over the paluda- mentum or at the neck of the dress. (See *Color Plate 9.*) Other important items of jewelry included pins, earrings, bracelets, rings, and other types of necklaces. Jewelers were skilled in techniques of working gold, setting precious stones, enamel- ing, and making mosaics.

WESTERN EUROPE FROM THE FALL OF THE ROMAN EMPIRE TO A.D. 900

Historical Background: The Fall of the Roman Empire

Even though Constantinople was nominally the capital of the eastern and western sections of the Roman Empire when Constantine moved the capital there in A.D. 300, events soon caused each part of the empire to develop along separate lines. For centuries, the Germans had been filtering into the Roman Empire in search of land. Many enlisted in the Roman armies, rising to high rank, often becoming commanders. Eventually entire German tribes migrated into western Europe and North Africa. Other tribes were also on the move. Those in the north had been attracted by the Roman standard of living, and those from east of the Danube sought new homelands.

The tribes from the East were migrating because the Huns had dispossessed them. The Huns were fierce, nomadic warriors who had pushed westward from their Asiatic homeland, driving Germanic tribes into the Roman Empire. One group, the Visigoths, were admitted into the Empire in 376, but after being mistreated by corrupt Roman officials, they rebelled, and in 378 defeated a Roman army and killed the emperor in the battle of Arianople. The defeat shattered the prestige of the hitherto invincible Roman armies. After wandering through the Eastern Roman Empire, the Visigoths invaded Italy and sacked Rome in 410, an event that shocked the entire Empire.

Elsewhere other tribes entered the Empire and finally settled down to live alongside the Romans. They intermarried with the Romans, adopting many of their customs, converted to Christianity, and established German kingdoms in the lands once ruled by Augustus. The fusion of Roman and Germanic cultures would make up medieval civilization. After the establishment of Germanic kingdoms in the West and the end of any semblance of a Roman Empire, the Eastern and Western sections drifted farther apart, divided by religion, culture, and political systems.

During the reign of the Emperor Justinian (527–565) Byzantium had gained control over Italy and southern Spain at enormous expense, all part of Justinian's dream of restoring the Roman Empire to its former greatness. His dream was doomed to failure, but he left behind an important legacy: the codification of the Roman law, which became the basis of civil law in European countries. After Justinian's death, the Byzantine Empire suffered a series of losses as a result of attacks by barbarians and the Moslems, thereby reducing the Empire to a small territory in Europe and in Asia that centered on Constantinople.

Historical Background: The Merovingian and Carolingian Dynasties

In the West, the early Germanic kingdoms were soon destroyed, but one of these, the Franks, survived. Their kingdom was founded by the brutal Clovis (481–511), who conquered most of modern France and Belgium and founded the Merovingian dynasty. Eventually the Merovingian line degenerated into "do-nothing" kings who allowed the chief minister, titled "mayor of the palace," to actually rule. In 751 a mayor of the palace, Pepin the Short, deposed the Merovingian king with the blessing of the pope and himself became king.

King Pepin was succeeded by his son, Charles the Great, known to history as Charlemagne (768–814), who expanded the kingdom into central Europe and southward into central Italy. He became the dominant figure in western Europe. His contemporaries compared him to the ancient Roman emperors. His greatest achievement was encouraging the establishment of schools to teach reading and writing. He founded a palace school to which he invited scholars from all over Europe. The climax of his reign came with his coronation on Christmas Day 800, when the pope crowned him emperor of the Romans. For a time Charlemagne hoped to arrange a marriage between himself and a Byzantine empress and to unite the eastern and western empires, but he failed. Nevertheless, throughout this period, contacts between the eastern and western empire continued, with Byzantine styles exercising a strong influence on European dress.

A new culture entered western Europe when the Moors, Berbers from Morocco who were Moslem, invaded Spain in 711. Within several years they overran Spain except for northern mountainous areas. Near Tours in southern France, the defeat of a small Moslem force in 732 marked the most northerly advance of Islam in Western Europe. Spain now became part of a form of free trade area stretching across the Islamic world from the Middle East through North Africa. Consequently many new ideas and products entered Europe through Spain, including citrus fruits, almonds, figs, and cotton.

Charlemagne, as well as his heirs, failed to conquer Islamic Spain. His success in uniting the Western European Empire lasted for only a little while after his death in 814. His successors were not strong enough to hold the Empire together and it was once again divided. No single power emerged to replace the ineffective Carolingian kings, the last of whom was deposed in 888. The remnants of Carolingian rule gradually collapsed under the impact of new and more destructive invasions. From the east, hordes of Magyar horsemen devastated the eastern lands of the Carolingian Empire. From the south came the Saracens, Arab raiders, who plundered southern France and coastal Italy. The most destructive of the invaders, the Northmen or Vikings, came from Scandinavia, attracted by the wealth of the Christian churches and the monasteries. They looted and burned, ruthlessly killing their victims. Britain and France suffered the worst spoliation, but about the middle of the 9th century the annual expeditions in search of plunder gradually ended.

Many areas in the West were depopulated and ruined. However, a new Europe began to appear. Commerce and town life began to revive; improvements in agriculture helped produce an increase in population. The Carolingian Empire was followed by feudal monarchies, the nations of the future.

SOURCES OF EVIDENCE ABOUT COSTUME

Relatively few images from western Europe that depict costume remain from the centuries after the fall of Rome. From the 5th to the 8th centuries, these sources are mostly two-dimensional images depicted in illuminated manuscripts, mosaics, and some rare frescoes in churches. Early Christian art in the West, like that of the Byzantine East, derived from Roman art. As late as the 7th and 8th centuries, religious figures, saints, and angels are often depicted in draped garments borrowed from Roman art. The relatively few surviving illuminated manuscripts, like the famous *Book of Kells* or others painted by Celtic monks in the 8th and 9th centuries, often contain little figurative art and no clear information about costume.

COSTUME IN WESTERN EUROPE: FALL OF THE ROMAN EMPIRE TO A.D. 900

During the Roman era the people residing in the provinces had become Romanized in their dress. Men wore tunics and women wore layered tunics covered by pallas. After the fall of Rome costumes retained these Roman elements, but added other components derived from the dress of the barbarian tribes that had moved west. The barbarians, too, utilized a tunic cut to the knee, but combined it with a type of trousers. Coming as they did from colder climates, they used more fur, often as a sleeveless vest worn over a tunic. Gartered hose, which became part of Western, medieval dress, were also derived from barbarian costume. But the most pronounced change came as garments made from pieces that were cut and sewn together replaced draped garments characteristic of the classical era.

The Production of Cloth

The Roman tradition in which women were the major producers of textiles continued. Although free women and serfs must have made fabrics at home to meet family needs, large quantities of cloth were produced in a *gynaceaum* or women's workshop. References to women's textile workshops indicate that very young slave and lower-class girls worked at this trade until they reached adulthood, when they left to marry or enter a convent. Most of these workshops were on large estates in rural areas (Herlihy 1990).

Linen and wool were the principal textiles produced, and women sheared wool from the sheep or crushed the flax to remove linen fibers. They spun the yarns by hand, wove the fabric on upright looms, and cut and sewed the clothing. Although the Moors had introduced cotton manufacture to Spain in the 9th century, it had not yet spread to the non-Moslem West. Like silk, it was largely an upper-class, luxury, imported fabric.

COSTUME FOR MEN: THE MEROVINGIAN AND CAROLINGIAN DYNASTIES

Evidence for the costume of the Merovingian and Carolingian periods is sparse, so that what is known about costume is of a very general nature. Royal figures were described by contemporary writers, but very little is known of the clothing of commoners.

Clovis, the first of the Merovingian kings of northern France, was crowned in 493. He married a Christian, converted to Christianity, and adopted Byzantine style dress for his court as a symbol of his change from the status of tribal chief to Christian king. He wore a short tunic, decorated with bands of embroidery or woven design, but without the lavish jeweled decoration of the Byzantine emperors. His hose were tied close to the leg with garters. The paludamentum and a crown completed his regalia. He retained one earlier Frankish practice. The king wore his hair long as a symbol of his rank, while the rest of the men in his court and other subjects cut their hair short. Costume in the Carolingian period showed few differences from costume of the Merovingian period, as elements of Byzantine influence continued to be apparent in the dress of the wealthy and powerful. See , *Contemporary Comments 5.1*, for a contemporaneous description of Charlemagne and his way of dressing.

CONTEMPORARY COMMENTS 5.1

In his Life of Charlemagne, *Einhard, a Frankish historian who lived at the court of Charlemagne, describes the appearance of the emperor.*

He wore the national dress of the Franks. The trunk of his body was covered with a linen shirt, his thighs with linen pants. Over these he put on a tunic trimmed at the border with silk. The legs from the knee downward were wound with leggings, fastened around the calves with laces, and on his feet he wore boots. In winter he protected his shoulders and chest with a vest made of otter skins and marten fur, and over that he wrapped a blue cloak. He always carried a sword strapped to his side, and the hilt and belt thereof were made either of gold or silver. Only on special holidays or when ambassadors from foreign nations were to be received did he sometimes carry a jewel-studded saber. He disliked foreign clothes, no matter how beautiful they were, and would never allow himself to be dressed in them. Only in Rome was he seen on two occasions in a long tunic, chlamys, and Roman shoes[1]: the first time at the entreaty of Pope Hadrian and the second by request of his successor [Pope] Leo. On high festival days he wore a suite of golden cloth ornamented with jewels. His cloak was fastened by a golden brooch, and on his head he carried a diadem of gold, embellished with gems. On other days, however, his dress was not much different from the common people.

Einhard. *The Life of Charlemagne.* A new English translation by E. S. Scherabon Firchow and E. H. Zeydel. 1972. Coral Gables, FL: University of Miami Press, p. 89.
[1]The translators note that this is the costume traditionally worn by Byzantine emperors.

Costume Components for Men: The Merovingian Period

Tunics worn by Merovingians ended below the knee. Like the tunic worn by King Clovis, they sometimes had bands of ornamentation, but for general wear were not likely to have been elaborately decorated. They were worn with or without belts. (See *Figure 5.7.*)

Their cloaks were shaped like the Greek chlamys, fastening over one shoulder. They also wore hooded capes, which may have been a later version of the Roman paenula.

The Merovingian king wore his hair long; his subjects had short hair. Gartered hose were worn with boots or shoes.

Costume Components for Men: The Carolingian Period

Changes in dress from the Merovingian to the Carolingian period were minor. The shapes and styles of cloaks did not undergo any important changes. Tunics changed slightly, narrowing through the upper body and widening in the skirt. Belts were worn over tunics, which remained short except for ceremonial occasions. When tunics were ornamented, clavii and decorative bands were used around the neckline and sleeve edges.

Carolingian kings no longer wore long hair. Men cut their hair below the ears and adult men wore beards. Footwear included boots, which ended below the calf, or shoes.

COSTUME FOR WOMEN: THE MEROVINGIAN AND CAROLINGIAN DYNASTIES

Costume Components for Women: The Merovingian Period

Presumably (evidence is sparse) women placed loose-fitting shawls or pallalike draperies over tunics. Archeological excavations of a tomb in Paris have brought to light a burial of a Merovingian queen of the 6th century. Enough clothing remained to permit determination of the various layers of her costume and their general form.

A linen shift or chemise was closest to the body. Over this was placed a knee-length under tunic of violet silk, with a jewel-decorated belt. Outermost was a long, outer tunic of dark red silk, opening at the front and closed with richly jeweled pins. A red silk veil was on her head. The thin leather slip-

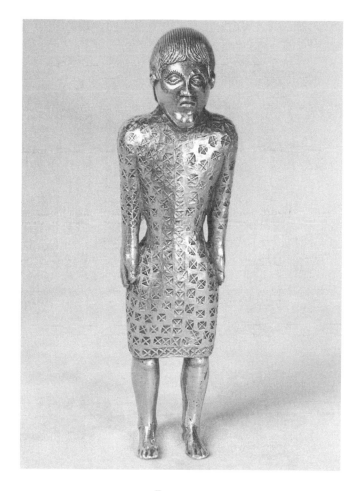

FIGURE 5.7

Late 4th or early 5th century statuette of a man from the region of Gaul. He wears a knee-length tunic that has an overall pattern and a braid decoration at the neck, the hem, and down the center front. (Photograph courtesy, Dumbarton Oaks, Byzantine Collection, Washington, DC.)

pers on her feet were worn with cross-gartered linen stockings. Her jewelry included earrings, brooches, silver belt ends and buckles, and a long gold pin. A signet ring identified her as Arnegunde, a queen known to have lived about A.D. 550 (Rice 1965).

From the foregoing description it is clear that royal families were importing silk from Byzantium. Common people would have worn linen, which grew well in damp northern climates, or wool from local sheep herds. Cotton was not yet being imported into Europe.

Jewelry-making techniques and styles were greatly influenced by Byzantine jewelry. Archeologists have found a number of fine enameled pieces and mountings of large stones.

Costume Components for Women: The Carolingian Period

Carolingian costume shows strong Byzantine influences. Under tunics were made with fitted sleeves. Outer tunics often had wider sleeves and bands of ornamentation. (See *Figure 5.8*.) Garments were cut full with pallalike shawls draped over outer tunics. Adult women placed veils or shawls over their heads, thereby covering their hair.

CLERICAL COSTUME IN THE EARLY MIDDLE AGES

Much of the clerical costume that was to become traditional for the Roman Catholic priests, monks, and nuns originated during the early Middle Ages. Both members of the priesthood, with its ceremonial costume, and the monks and nuns who separated themselves from the world evolved a distinctive form of dress that changed relatively little until the mid-20th century.

FIGURE 5.8

Women of 8th-century Italy wear costumes showing strong Byzantine influences. (Photograph courtesy Città di Cividale del Friuli.)

Dress of Priests

Ecclesiastical costume worn by priests and higher church officials developed gradually from the 4th century to the 9th century. Before the 4th century priests wore no special costume. Throughout the Medieval period the parish priest who lived in the community was more clearly distinguished by his tonsure (haircut) than by his everyday costume. Either of two distinctive haircuts was adopted. In one style the top of the head was shaved and a fringe of hair grew around the shaved area. In the other, the forehead was shaved from ear to ear.

Higher-ranking prelates wore more distinctive costume on ceremonial occasions or during church services. By the 9th century a number of items had been established as part of the liturgical costume of the Roman Catholic Church. (See *Figure 5.9a* and *b*.) Briefly summarized these were:

amice (*am'is*)   A strip of linen placed around the shoulders and tied in position to form a collar, which was worn by priests saying mass.

alb   A long white tunic with narrow sleeves and a slit for the head, tied with a belt. The name derived from the Roman *tunica alba* (white tunic).

chasuble (*chahz'you-bul*)   An evolved form of the paenula. This round Roman cape was given up by the laity, but continued to be worn by clergy in a form with sides cut shorter to allow movement of the arms. A Y-shaped band of embroidery called the **orphrey** extended from each shoulder to meet and form a vertical line in the back and front of the chasuble.

stole   A long, narrow strip of material, which was worn over the shoulder during the mass.

pallium   A narrow band of white wool that was worn by popes and archbishops. Prelates wore the band with one end falling to the front and the other to the back. This band evolved from the Greek himation, which lost its shawl-like form and became a narrow band that was a symbol of learning in Roman and then Byzantine styles.

cope   A voluminous cape that was worn for processions. (See *Figure 5.9b*.)

Other refinements of costume specific to particular clerical rank or ceremonies, such as colors or garments assigned to certain days within the liturgical year, were made at different periods of the history of the Catholic Church. For those interested in a more detailed exploration of clerical costume some references are included at the end of this chapter.

Monastic Dress

The practice of leaving the world to devote oneself to prayer and self-denial began early in the history of the Christian

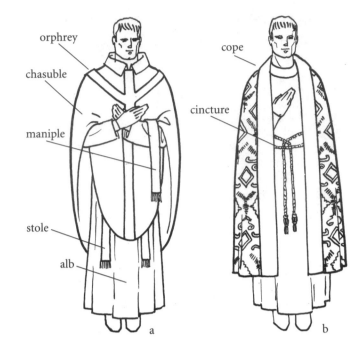

FIGURE 5.9A AND B

(a) Clerical dress of priest with various components of the garments labeled. (b) Cope and cincture worn by clerics. (From *The Fairchild Dictionary of Fashion.* Courtesy of Fairchild Publications.)

church. After the 4th century entire communities were formed, often around the person of a particularly holy man or woman. These monasteries or convents did not require specialized costume; their members dressed in the ordinary costume of the poor. Although the costume of most people changed over time, the monks and nuns retained their original dress, thereby distinguishing themselves from the "worldly." Both men and women wore a loose-fitting tunic with long, fairly wide sleeves. This tunic reached to the ground and was belted. Specific colors and cuts showed some variations from order to order, but the usual colors employed were brown, white, black, or gray.

The monk's costume included a cowl, a hood that either was attached to the tunic or was a separate garment. Nuns covered their heads with veils. On first entering convents, women cropped their hair closely. Members of some orders went barefoot; most wore sandals. Eventually the distinctions among the various orders became quite pronounced, and even the most casual observer could identify the order with which the individual was associated. Some Catholic religious orders still wear garments of the type first adopted in the Middle Ages.

HISTORICAL BACKGROUND: THE 10TH–13TH CENTURIES

The Feudal Monarchies

The feudal system developed out of the need for protection as the Carolingian Empire collapsed under the attacks of the Vikings, Magyars, and Saracens. Central government vanished; law and order disappeared. Security could be found only in military might. Much as chiefs in the Germanic tribes had assembled their warriors in war bands, leaders gathered around them who trained fighting men. Then a new invention, the stirrup, revolutionized warfare by combining human and animal power to produce mounted warriors with sword and lance capable of shock combat. The warriors became the armored knights on horseback. Knights, who were professional warriors, needed years of training to learn how to handle the horse and the weapons. Such training began in youth, and it was not cheap. The knight needed not just one horse, but a number especially trained and bred for warfare. In addition, there must be someone to look after the horses for the knights. So knights become elite, professional fighters.

Knights were also vassals of a lord. The word "vassal" came from a Celtic word meaning "one who serves." These sworn military retainers were just like the warriors in the German war band who swore to be faithful to their chief. To maintain his vassals, a lord granted each of them land, called a fief or fiefdom, in exchange for military services. The knight lived on his fief when he was not off fighting on behalf of his lord. Along with the fief came serfs, who worked the land for the lords and knights. Serfs had lost their freedom years before when an ancestor surrendered his freedom and that of his family to a lord in return for protection.

In theory, the feudal king was the supreme lord and theoretical owner of all the land within his kingdom. His great vassals owed him allegiance, but if a powerful independent vassal challenged him, the monarch could only call on his other vassals to assemble their knights to help discipline the unruly noble. If they chose to be disloyal, he had no national army that could be mobilized. On the local level, the lord and his vassals enforced whatever law and order existed.

The feudal lords not only fought invaders, but also went to war with other feudal nobles. Fighting, however, was not as dangerous as in modern warfare. The armored knight was more likely to be captured and held for ransom than killed. The serfs and peasants suffered more because their lives, homes, and crops could be destroyed in a battle.

Feudal lords and knights built castles on their lands to serve as places of protection. At first these castles were structures of wood intended only for defense, but by the 12th century they had become very elaborate. Castles were not only defensive structures; they were also homes for the lord and his family. They were uncomfortable, cold, damp, dark, and very windy because the windows in the outer walls were nothing more than slits without glass.

Feudalism took various forms in different parts of Europe because it developed from local practices and customs. Originating in northern France, it spread from there into southern France, Germany, and into northern Italy. England did not develop a feudal organization until after Duke William of Normandy invaded England in 1066 and became king of England.

POLITICAL DEVELOPMENTS IN EUROPE: 900–1300

Political developments in Europe over the period from 900 to 1300 were far too complex to describe in detail in this survey. The reader may be best served by a brief note of some of the more important developments in the different areas of Europe. See *Figure 5.10*, a map showing the major political divisions of Europe by the mid-14th century.

The German Dynasties

In Germany, after the German line of the Carolingian emperors had died out, a new dynasty emerged from the duchy of Saxony. Otto I (936–973) halted the Magyar threat to Europe, forcing them to settle in Hungary. He spent years battling rebellious dukes. He made alliances with archbishops and bishops, whom he chose. By granting them large estates, he made them his vassals. After invading Italy he proclaimed himself king and had the pope crown him Holy Roman Emperor in 962. Although the empire was thoroughly German, it was considered to be a continuation of the ancient Roman Empire. Otto's heir encountered opposition from the popes, who sought independence from the emperor. After Otto's line ended in 1125, the Hohenstaufen emperors ruled until the last one was executed in 1268. The task of trying to rule Germany, Italy, and Sicily while at the same time fighting off rebellious dukes and hostile popes had proved too much for the Hohenstaufen dynasty. When the nobles elected the first Hapsburg emperor in 1273, Germany had become a collection of semi-independent principalities instead of a united empire.

Anglo-Saxon and Norman Britain

After the Roman legions had been withdrawn from northwestern Germany, Angles, Saxons, and Jutes invaded Britain in the 5th century, driving the original Britons, the Celts,

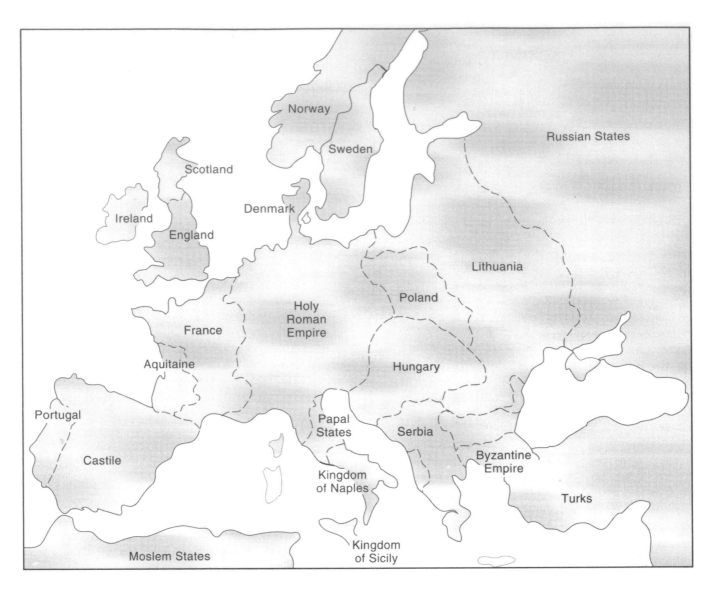

FIGURE 5.10

This map shows the major political divisions of Europe during the mid-14th century.

westward into Wales, Devon, Cornwall, and north into Scotland. The Anglo-Saxons settled down, intermarried, converted to Christianity, and established seven Anglo-Saxon kingdoms. In the 9th century, the Anglo-Saxons suffered an invasion by the Danes (Vikings) who came to plunder and settle. The Anglo-Saxon king, Alfred the Great (871–899), halted the Danes, and his dynasty united Britain under one king. When Alfred's line died out in 1066, William the Conqueror, Duke of Normandy, claimed the throne. He invaded England and defeated the Anglo-Saxon claimant to the throne in the battle of Hastings. William I established a feudal system in England that was better organized and more centralized than on

the continent of Europe. Under Henry II (1154–1189), one of the greatest of English kings, whose mother was a granddaughter of William I and whose father was of the Plantagenet family, England laid claim to large areas of France. These claims were based on the fact that William the Conqueror had ruled Normandy and Henry II had married Eleanor of Aquitaine, an heiress who controlled a large area of southwestern France. For many years thereafter France and England battled over these claims. The struggle climaxed in the Hundred Years' War (1337–1453), which ended with the English being driven from France except for a foothold in Calais. The Plantagenet family ruled over England until 1399.

The French Kings

In France, after the death of Charlemagne, the title of king carried with it little actual wealth or power. The kings were often less powerful than their feudal vassals. The election of Hugh Capet (987–996) as king marked the beginning of the famous Capetian dynasty, which ruled France for more than 300 years. But not until the 1100s would the French kings begin to increase the power and wealth of the monarchy and to weaken their mighty vassals. By the time that the Capetian line died out in 1328, the French king had become a genuine force in European power politics by consolidating his holdings, subjugating the powerful dukes, and replacing provincialism with unifying national patriotism.

FACTORS RELATED TO DEVELOPMENTS IN COSTUME

Political, social, and economic events may have both direct and indirect influence on clothing styles. The availability of the raw materials from which garments are made, the social stage on which they are worn, and even the practical needs they must satisfy will each play a part in their development.

The Crusades

In the 11th century, under the urging of Pope Urban II, the European powers launched the first of seven Crusades against the Moslems. Ostensibly intended to free the holy places of Christendom from the Moslems who now controlled them, the actual motivations for each of the Crusades varied from genuine religious fervor to outright mercenary designs for accumulating wealth and power.

By the end of the Crusades in the 13th century, many new products and processes had been imported to Europe. The crusaders learned the technique of printing patterns on textiles from the Moslems, who had learned it from the Coptic people of Egypt. Foods, spices, drugs, works of art, and fabrics were brought back by the crusaders. New fabrics such as muslin, dimity, and silk damask came into use, as did a new fiber, cotton. Many crusaders stopped in Constantinople on their way to and from the wars, thereby continuing the strong Byzantine influences on the costume of the nobility of western Europe.

These cross-cultural contacts did not end with the end of the Crusades. Trade expanded, especially between the Italian seaports and the Middle East.

Medieval Castles and Courts

The feudal lord and his family had private quarters in the large, fortified castles. Rooms were poorly ventilated. In winter only a large fireplace provided heat. Woolen garments were desirable not only in winter to combat the cold, but also in summer when castles continued to be damp and chilly. By modern standards, furnishings were simple and not very comfortable; however, more luxurious items such as carpets, wall hangings, and cushions were brought back from the East as a result of the Crusades. In spite of these improvements, multiple layers of clothing provided the most practical way of dressing for comfort.

The institution of knighthood and chivalry, the system for training knights, required that boys learn not only the arts of war, but also the manners and customs of the upper classes. Generally to do this the young knight had to leave his home and reside in the castle of a powerful lord. These courts, especially those of the dukes and kings, attracted artists, poets, troubadours or wandering singers, musicians, and other entertainers. The courts of southern France were especially noted as centers of artistic, musical, and literary expression. Moreover, they provided a stage for the display of fashion.

Town Life

After the fall of Rome, many formerly thriving urban centers had been severely depopulated. During the 10th and 11th centuries, urban life revived. Europe experienced an economic upturn in agriculture, manufacturing of goods, and trade, so that by the 12th and 13th centuries major cities had become lively centers that attracted an increased population. Among those residing in towns were wealthy merchants whose affluence was such that they could dress themselves in clothing styled after that worn by the nobility. The clergy disapproved of this blurring of class distinctions, saying that "Jesus Christ and his blessed mother, of royal blood though they were, never thought of wearing the belts of silk, gold, and silver that are fashionable among wealthy women" (Gies and Gies 1974).

Fabric Production

A major evolution in the organization of textile manufacture took place. In the early Middle Ages women working in the gynaeceum or at home had produced most of the textiles. By 1300 the weaving was done by men and the fiber preparation and spinning by women. Dyeing and fulling (compacting of wool cloth by pounding) were specialized crafts, practiced outside the home. In a study of women's work in the Middle Ages, Herlihy (1990) sees the decline in slavery and the movement of population from rural to urban centers as one of the reasons for these changes. As a result, the women's workshops disappeared and textile production moved into the household. Men, formerly employed in agriculture, needed to find work in the urban centers, and took over work that had formerly been done by women.

These developments were accompanied by technological changes. Water-powered mills had been providing the power for fulling wool since the 10th century. By the 12th century, a horizontal loom that allowed the weaver to sit rather than stand replaced the vertical loom. The horizontal loom had foot treadles for moving the lengthwise yarns and added a carrier, called a shuttle, for the crosswise yarn. The old hand-spinning method was supplanted by the spinning wheel in the 13th century. This machine apparently came to Europe from India by way of Moslem Spain (Gies 1994).

By the 12th century European craftsmen had established a number of centers for the manufacture of cloth for export. Trade guilds had first been established in the 11th century, not by workers but by merchants who wanted to prevent the importation of competing goods. By the 12th century the craftsmen had begun to form their own guilds. Only by apprenticing himself to a guild could a young boy become a practitioner of a craft, so that guilds were able to regulate the number of artisans and to set quality standards, rates of pay, and regulate working conditions.

Textile trade guild members were permitted to hire their wives and daughters to spin and weave. The widow of a guild member could herself become owner of her late husband's business and a member of the guild. However, pay scales for women were consistently lower than those for men.

Wool was an especially important fiber in the European textile trade. Wool grown in England was considered to be the finest available. Much English wool was exported to Flanders, where skilled weavers made it into high-quality cloth. Cloth merchants were by no means limited to wool cloth. Linen was grown throughout Europe and used for household textiles and for clothing. Silk production was, by the mid-1200s, a major industry in Italy, Sicily, and Spain. Cotton, originally a product from India, was introduced into Spain by the Moors, so that it, too, was available for spinning.

The merchant purchased the raw fiber. After cleaning, carding, and combing it, he sold it to the weaver. The weaver's wife spun the yarn with spindle and distaff or, after the 13th century, with a spinning wheel. The weaver created the cloth on a hand loom. Some finishing steps were given to the fabric, and if color had not been added to either the fiber or the yarn, the fabric might be dyed. In some cases, the fabric was sold undyed to skilled dyers from Italy who added the color.

Art

Europe underwent marked changes in the arts at the same time it experienced this economic awakening. Most of the public art produced was intended not solely as decoration, but told the generally unlettered population the stories of the Christian faith. Although some of the traditions of dressing Christ, Mary, the angels, and saints in the stereotypical garments that had been depicted in the art of earlier centuries continued, other factors led artists to include more figures dressed in the costume of the artist's own time. Manuscripts incorporated calendars that showed ordinary people doing the work of the various seasons. After the 13th century more manuscripts were produced in urban workshops, not in monasteries, and created by lay artists rather than monks. Then, too, some of these manuscripts dealt with secular themes. Sometimes costumes were based on imagination or on the reports of costume brought back by the returning crusaders. In spite of these limitations, scholars are able to use these works of art as the major source of visual evidence of 12th and 13th century costume.

Important art forms included manuscript illumination and the carving of miniatures in ivory and wood. Romanesque architecture of the 10th and 11th centuries, characterized by rounded arches and massive, well-proportioned buildings, utilized the work of sculptors as an important element of decoration. After the 1150s Romanesque architecture was superseded by the Gothic style, which predominated until the end of the 1400s. Gothic churches with their pointed arches and soaring, graceful structures used not only sculpture but also beautiful stained glass windows to tell stories to the faithful.

COSTUME IN THE 10TH AND 11TH CENTURIES

Costume Components for Men: 10th and 11th Centuries

GARMENTS

Underclothing consisted of undershirts and underdrawers. The garment that eventually evolved into the modern man's shirt originated as an undergarment. Worn next to the skin, this garment was usually either not seen at all or only partially visible. In the chapters that cover periods before the 19th century this text will discuss shirts as undergarments. After the 19th century, shirts were no longer considered as underwear.

Undershirts, sometimes referred to as chemises, were short-sleeved linen garments. Underdrawers, called **braies** (*brays*), were loose-fitting linen breeches fastened at the waist with a belt. (See *Figure 5.16.*) Lengths varied, ranging from knee-length to longer ankle-length variations, which were wrapped close to the leg with gartering.

Men often wore two tunics, one over the other: an outer tunic and an under tunic. Usually both were the same length although sometimes the under tunic was slightly longer and therefore visible at the lower edge of the garment. (See *Figure 5.11.*)

When short in length, outer tunics were almost always made with close-fitting sleeves. Sometimes sleeves extended

FIGURE 5.11

Page from a manuscript c. 1050. Men at left wear short tunics with gaitered hose, over which they wear cloaks. The long sleeves of their tunics are pushed up into folds above the writst. Their hats are in the Phrygian bonnet style. Women on the page wear long tunics and cover their hair with veils. (Photograph courtesy, The Pierpont Morgan Library, manuscript G44 f2v.)

over the hand with the excess fabric pushed up into folds above the wrist. (See *Figure 5.11.*) Long outer tunics were made either with fitted sleeves, or (more often) cut wide and full, allowing the sleeve of the under tunic to show.

Tunic necklines were round or square. These garments were usually belted at the waist. The fabrics most frequently used were linen and wool. The poor wore wool almost exclusively. Silk was imported by the very well-to-do.

Social class distinctions were evident in length of the tunic and its decoration. Outer tunics of the wealthy were decorated with bands of silk embroidery at neck, sleeves, and hem. (See *Color Plate 10.*) The nobility and the clergy wore long flowing robes for ceremonial occasions. For hunting and warfare men of all classes wore more practical short tunics.

Mantles for men were either open or closed. **Open mantles** were made from one piece of fabric that fastened on one shoulder (see *Figure 5.11*), while **closed mantles** were a length of fabric with a slit through which the head could be slipped. (See *Figure 5.12.*)

Tenth-century mantles were usually square; in the 11th century semicircular mantles began to appear. Men in im-

portant political or religious positions wore mantles draped like Greek himations for ceremonial events.

HAIR AND HEADDRESS

Young men were clean shaven; older men were bearded. (See *Figure 5.11.*) Hair was parted in the middle, falling naturally either straight or in waves at the side of the face to the nape of the neck or below.

Except for helmets worn in war, hoods and Phrygian bonnet styles were the predominant styles of headcoverings. Hats with small round brims and peaked crowns were depicted on Jewish men as early as the 11th century in works of art. These hats, and also beards, seem to have been part of tra-

FIGURE 5.12

Twelfth-century manuscript illustration depicts woman in closed mantle with a light-colored veil over her head. The outer tunic has been raised up to display the under tunic, which is of a contrasting lighter color. The garb of the angel is similar, except that he wears an open mantle. (Photograph courtesy, The Pierpont Morgan Library, manuscript M44f. 1v.)

ditional dress worn voluntarily by Jews. Rubens (1967) suggests that they probably derived from a conical hat worn by non-Moslems in Moslem countries and were introduced into Europe by way of Spain or Byzantium.

FOOTWEAR AND LEG COVERINGS

To cover their legs men wore either braies extending to the ankle or hose. Hose were made of woven fabric, cut and sewn to fit the leg, ending either at the knee or thigh. **Leg bandages** (also called gaiters) were strips of linen or wool wrapped closely around the leg to the knee and worn either over the hose or alone. (See *Figure 5.11.*)

Socks, shorter than hose, were usually brightly colored. Some socks with decorative figures around the upper edges might be placed over the end of the braies, over hose, or worn with leg bandages.

Boots might be either short to the ankle or longer, reaching to mid-calf, and they were frequently decorated. Flat shoes of the Middle Ages did not have raised heels. Shoes were cut with a slight point at the front opposite the big toe. Closely fitted, shoes generally ended at the ankle, fastening when necessary with thongs of leather or fabric. (See *Figure 5.11.*) Some clergymen wore Byzantine-style slippers that were cut low over the instep.

Costume Components for Women: 10th and 11th Centuries

Costume of men and women showed relatively few differences during the 10th and 11th centuries.

GARMENTS

Women wore a loose-fitting linen garment very close to the skin. Called a **chemise** (*chem-eze'*) in French, it was cut longer but otherwise was much like a man's undershirt.

Over this women wore floor-length under tunics with close-fitting sleeves and an embroidered border at neck, hem, and sleeves. Outermost they placed floor-length outer tunics made with wide sleeves that allowed the under tunic sleeves to show. Usually the outer tunic was pulled up and bloused over a belt. (See *Figure 5.12.*) Some under tunics had decorative borders at the wrist and hem.

For outdoors, women wore either open or closed mantles. (See *Figure 5.12.*) Some were made as **double mantles** lined in contrasting colors. **Winter mantles** could be fur lined.

HAIR AND HEADDRESS

Young girls wore their hair loose, flowing, and uncovered. Married (and older) women covered their hair with a veil, which was pulled around the face under the chin; or was open, hanging close to the sides of the face and ending about mid-chest. (See *Figure 5.12.*) The rich had silk or fine linen veils; people in the lower classes used coarser linen or wool.

FOOTWEAR AND LEG COVERINGS

Hose (stockings) tied into place around the knee. Women's shoes were similar to those of men. Women also wore open slippers with bands across the ankle, similar to those worn by some clergymen. Clogs were wooden platforms that raised shoes out of the water, mud, or snow. These were placed over leather shoes.

JEWELRY

Rarely is jewelry depicted on paintings and sculpture of the period; however, written records indicate that wealthy

FIGURE 5.13

First half of the 12th century. Fashionable tunics, both short and long, are more closely fitted through the torso in the 12th century, whereas the monk's costume retains the fit and characteristics of an earlier period. With their short tunics, the servants wear hose, over which they place short, striped stockings, and shoes that end at the ankle. (Photograph courtesy, The Pierpont Morgan Library, manuscript 736 f21.)

women wore head bands (circlets) of gold and neck bands or beads, bracelets, rings, and earrings. Jeweled belts (often called **girdles**) are sometimes depicted in art.

COSTUME FOR MEN AND WOMEN: 12TH CENTURY

At least some of the styles of the 12th century were viewed as radical departures from customary dress. Snyder (2002) identifies three types of garments in the courtly dress of the period that are shown in art. The first is a tunic that fits a little more closely than in the previous century. Lower class men and women wore this tunic. (See *Figure 5.13.*) The second is a tightly fitted one-piece garment, which she calls a **bliaut** (man standing at center, *Figure 5.14*). The third is a close-fitting garment with an upper section joined to a skirt, the **bliaut gironé.** (See *Figure 5.15.*)

Waugh (1999) analyzes the evidence from art and from an extant garment that belonged to a Spanish prince (c. 1146). Earlier garments were straight. Openings were left in the underarm seams and were closed by lacing. Waugh concludes that the closer fit of the bliaut was achieved by curving the seams of the section close to the upper body section. Gores (triangular wedges of fabric) were set into the skirt in order to make the skirt widen gradually.

Waugh does not distinguish between the bliaut and the bliaut gironé. Snyder (2002) describes the latter form as more complex in cut than earlier garments, having a fuller skirt that was joined to a separate bodice section. It, too, laced shut at the sides. The skirt and bodice joined below the anatomical waistline. The bodice and skirt were sewn together and an inset bias (diagonal) fabric piece may have been used to ensure a better fit at the hips. Seams were concealed by applied pieces of decorative tape. There is no evidence, however, that sleeves were set in. The bliaut gironé, an elaborate, closely fitted garment, was limited in its use to upper-class men and women. (See *Figure 5.15.*) It was made of costly silk fabrics such as satin or velvet, embroidered with gold thread, and decorated with precious stones.

Another distinctive feature of the bliaut that demonstrated radical changes in attitudes toward modesty was the way it closed. Both the bliaut and the chemise laced shut. These lacings sometimes fell one above the other, revealing the bare flesh beneath. (See *Figure 5.16.*)

Costume Components for Men: 12th Century

GARMENTS

Mantles were worn outdoors; no major changes took place in the customary styles. (See *Figure 5.14.*)

As noted, men of high status wore the bliaut. Both the under tunic and outer tunic continued to be the basic elements of dress for most men, although in some representations no

FIGURE 5.14

Manuscript illustration for a bible from before 1185 depicts a variety of costumes, including women (left side) with wide, pendant cuffs on their outer tunics. The sleeves of the under tunics are visible at the wrist. Woman at far left wears a closed mantle; the one at the right an open mantle. The man in the center panel wears a bliaut under a mantle lined in fur. (Photograph courtesy of the Pierpoint Morgan Library, Manuscript M619 Detail lower 1/3 recto.)

evidence can be seen of an under tunic, which leads to the conclusion that in some instances only a single tunic was worn. Sleeves became more varied, the major types being:

- close-fitting sleeves with decorative, turned-back cuffs
- elbow-length sleeves

FIGURE 5.16

Garment (possibly a chainse) of crinkled fabric shows a row of lacing up the side, under the arm. (German manuscript, c. 1200. Photograph courtesy, The Pierpont Morgan Library, manuscript 710 f110.)

FIGURE 5.15

French sculpture, 12th century. This bliaut gironé, worn by a figure representing a king, is fitted through the waist to the hip where a finely pleated skirt joins the top. The sleeves are slightly pendant. Both sleeves and neckline are edged in decorative fabric. (Photograph courtesy of the Metropolitan Museum of Art, purchase 1920, Joseph Pulitzer Bequest.)

- full sleeves on the outer tunic that revealed fitted sleeves on the tunic underneath
- sleeves cut fairly close at the shoulders and widening to a full bell shape at the end

HAIR AND HEADDRESS

Most men were bearded and had moustaches. Hair length varied, but usually was not longer than to the shoulder. Clergymen railed against the hairstyles adopted by some men who grew their hair long and had small, clipped, and pointed beards. Many viewed these men as effeminate.

For outdoors men wore hoods or small round hats that had a small stem or tab at the top. The **coif,** a cap that tied under the chin and was similar to a modern baby's bonnet in shape, began to be used in the latter part of the century. (See *Figure 5.17.*)

FOOTWEAR

Shoes and boots much like those of the previous century continued in use. Among the innovations that brought down the wrath of moralists were the long, pointed-toed shoes adopted by some upper-class men. See *Contemporary Comments 5.2, page 109,* for a description by a clergyman who disapproves of the new styles of clothing and the introduction of shoes with extremely long toes.

FIGURE 5.17

Manuscript of about 1240–1260. Lower left panel shows three men harvesting wheat. The man on the right wears only his braies and a small, white coif on his head. His fellow workers wear short tunics or cotes, the man on the left has tucked his into his belt, thereby revealing his braies and the top of his hose, which fasten to the top of his braies. Women in the upper panel wear (from left to right) a cote; a cote with a sideless surcote (which is lifted up to reveal her patterned stockings); cotes and mantles. The woman at the far right is wearing a fur lined mantle. (Photograph courtesy, The Pierpont Morgan Library, manuscript M638 fi8.)

Costume Components for Women: 12th Century

While costume for lower-class women changed very little, upper-class women's costume underwent the changes described earlier. The chemise, the under tunic, and the outer tunic all fitted the body more closely. Some sculpted representations of the bliaut gironé of this period show fabric that looks as if it may have been pleated, smocked, or crinkled.

GARMENTS

Sleeves of women's bliauts or tunics were even longer and more exaggerated in their cut than those of men. Some illustrations show closely fitting sleeves ending in long, pendant cuffs or bands that hang all the way to the floor. If both under and outer tunics were worn, the sleeves of the garment underneath were usually long and fitted while outer garments had either pendant cuffs, wide cuffs with decorative banding, or sleeves narrow at the top and flaring gradually to end in a bell shape. (See *Figure 5.14*.)

The **chainse** (*shens*) was another distinctive type of outer garment for upper-class women. Made of washable material, probably linen, it was long and seems to have been pleated. (See *Figure 5.16*.) Many costume historians have confused the terms chainse and chemise. However, Goddard (1927), in a study of costume terminology for women's styles of the 11th and 12th centuries, found that contemporary texts state clearly that the chainse was worn over the chemise and that it was definitely a separate garment. The chainse seems to have been worn alone, without an outer tunic, as a "house dress" and seems to have been especially used in the late 12th century. It is possible that it may have been a summer garment, since it was washable and made of lightweight fabric.

The old French word *mantel* (from which the English word "mantle" derives) was originally applied to cloaks worn out-of-doors by upper-class women. Medieval mantles for the upper classes were long, capelike garments that opened down the front and fastened with a long ribbon that was attached to clasps placed on either side of the front.

Some of these mantles were exceedingly luxurious. One is described as being made of rose and white cloth from India, woven or embroidered with figures of animals and flowers, cut in one piece, and lined with scented fur. It had a collar and a border spotted with dark blue and yellow and fastened with jeweled clasps on the shoulder that were made from two rubies (Poet of the *Roman de Troie*, quoted in Goddard 1927).

Some cloaks were fur lined or decorated with fur. Peliçon (*pel′ee-son*) or pelice (*pel′eese*) are terms applied to any of a number of fur-trimmed garments including outer wraps, under tunics, and outer tunics.

HAIR AND HEADDRESS

Women of the highest classes adopted a style in which hair was arranged in two long plaits that hung down on either side of the face. These braids sometimes reached almost to the floor, and contemporary records indicate that hairpieces were added in order to reach the fashionable length. Decorative bands of ribbon might be intertwined in the braids or the end of the braid held in a jeweled clasp. Over this a loose veil was placed; however, the hair was quite visible.

Most women covered their hair entirely and wrapped veils so closely that only the face showed. New developments in headcoverings included barbettes, fillets, and wimples. A barbette was a linen band that passed down from one temple under the chin and up to the other temple. Barbettes were worn with fillets. A fillet was a standing linen band, rather like a crown (see *Figure 5.20*) over which a veil might be draped. A wimple was a fine white linen or silk scarf that covered the neck, the center placed under the chin and each end pulled up and fastened above the ear or at the temple. A wimple was generally worn in combination with a veil. (See *Figure 5.17.*) Not worn by lay women after the Middle Ages, wimples became part of the dress of many orders of Roman Catholic nuns and continued to be worn until the 1960s.

PROBLEMS OF COSTUME TERMINOLOGY IN THE 13TH CENTURY

Increasing variety in types of dress is evident in the history of costume of the later Middle Ages. This tendency, which began to accelerate in the 13th century, presents the costume historian with difficulties in terminology. The written records of the period abound in descriptions of items of luxurious dress, but these descriptions are not accompanied by illustrations of the garments or accessories that they describe. The application of these terms to costume leaves the reader with a maze of terms in several languages that cannot be attached to particular garments with complete accuracy. For these reasons textbooks, costume histories, and journal articles dealing with costume of the late Middle Ages may be in conflict as to the names applied to particular items, or the definition of terms. Furthermore, modern English words frequently derive from the early names for costume items, but the modern usage of the term is often markedly different from its original use.

Table 5.1 represents an effort to clarify the meaning of some of the terms that the student may encounter and also to point out some of the modern English words that derive from the old English and French words. The table is restricted to English and French, as these are the languages most often chosen in writing about historic costume in English.

COSTUME IN THE 13TH CENTURY

Costume Components for Men: 13th Century

Throughout the 13th century men would have dressed in garments of functions similar to those described previously; however, the terminology used to describe this clothing un-

FIGURE 5.18

Drawing of a man and woman, c. 1225–1250. Both wear garments cut full under the arm. Man wears cote and mantle, woman wears cote, sideless surcote, and mantle. From Bowie, T., ed. 1982. *Sketchbook of Villard de Honnecourt.* Reproduced courtesy, Indiana University Press.)

📖

CONTEMPORARY COMMENTS 5.2

Fashionable Dress of Men in the 12th Century

Orderic Vitalis, a monk writing in the early 12th Century, writes disparagingly of the fashionable styles of the period. In his diatribe against the new styles, he gives one version of the origins of the long, pointed toes for shoes that appear periodically throughout the Middle Ages.

Count Fulk[1] was a man with many reprehensible, even scandalous, habits, and gave way to many pestilential vices. Being a man with deformed feet he had shoes made with very long and pointed toes, to hide the shape of his feet and conceal the growths that are commonly called bunions. This encouraged a new fashion in the western regions, which delighted frivolous men in search of novelties. To meet it cobblers fashioned shoes like scorpions' tails, which are commonly called 'pulley-shoes' [poulaines], and almost all, rich and poor alike, now demand shoes of this kind. Before then shoes always used to be made round, fitting the foot, and these were adequate to the needs of high and low, both clergy and laity. But now laymen in their pride seize upon a fashion typical of their corrupt morals....

Robert, a certain worthless fellow at King Rufus's court, first began to stuff the long 'pulley-toes' and in this way bend them into the shape of a ram's horn.... The frivolous fashion he had set was soon imitated by a great part of the nobility as if it had been an achievement of great worth and importance. At that time effeminates set the fashion in many parts of the world . . . They rejected the traditions of honest men, ridiculed the counsel of priests, and persisted in their barbarous way of life and style of dress. They parted their hair from the crown of the head to the forehead, grew long and luxurious locks like women, and loved to deck themselves in long, overtight shirts and tunics.... They add escrescences like serpents' tails to the tips of their toes where the body ends, and gaze with admiration on these scorpion-like shapes. They sweep the dusty ground with the unnecessary trains of their robes and mantles; their long, wide sleeves cover their hands whatever they do; impeded by these frivolities they are almost incapable of walking quickly or doing any kind of useful work. They shave the front part of their head, like thieves, and let their hair grow very long at the back, like harlots. Up to now penitents and prisoners and pilgrims have normally been unshaven, with long beards, and in this way have publicly proclaimed their condition of penance or captivity or pilgrimage. But now almost all our fellow countrymen are crazy and wear little beards . . . They curl their hair with hot irons and cover their heads with a fillet or cap. Scarcely any knight appears in public with his head uncovered and decently shorn according to the apostle's precept.

Quoted from Orderic Vitalis, *The Ecclesiastical History,* translated by M. Chibnall. 1973. Oxford: Clarendon Press, 1973. Vol. 4, pp. 187, 189.
[1]Count Fulk le Rechin was from France.

---

derwent some changes. To summarize, a man would wear knee-length or shorter braies (breeches) and a linen chemise (under shirt). Over this he placed a **cote** (under tunic) and over the cote, a **surcote** (outer tunic). In cold weather or for protection out-of-doors he added yet another garment, some form of cloak with a more or less fitted cut.

An emphasis on greater modesty in court dress came at the time that Louis IX was king of France. Louis, a very pious man, was the only French king ever to be declared a saint by the Catholic Church. During his reign, court dress became more austere and luxurious display was discouraged.

GARMENTS

Upper-class men wore long cotes; working men wore them short. Two types of sleeves are depicted most frequently. One is long and tightly fitted. (See *Figure 5.19.*) The other is cut very full under the arm, tapering to a close fit at the wrist. Some costume references call this a **magyar sleeve.** (See *Figure 5.18.*)

Table 5.1.

OLD ENGLISH AND FRENCH COSTUME TERMS

Type of garment	Definition	Old French term	Old English term	Modern English term derived from:
underwear	undergarment for men, worn next to the skin and covering the lower part of the torso and upper legs. (See *Figure 5.17.*)	braies	brech	breeches
	undergarment for both men and women worn next to the body and cut as loose, linen garment with sleeves. (See *Figure 6.12, page 135.*)	chemise	shirt	shirt chemise
under tunic	under tunic worn by both men and women and placed over chemise or shirt. (See *Figure 5.17.*)	cotte	cote	coat[1] petticoat[2]
outer tunic	top most garment (excluding garments worn for out-of-doors to protect against weather). Worn either over or under tunic or when no under tunic is worn, worn over chemise or shirt. (See *Figure 5.17.*)	sorcot	surcote	overcoat[2]
		rogue	roc	frock
		sorquenie	sukkenie	smock
		bliaud	bliaut	blouse[2]
		cuertel	kirtel or kirtle	none currently in use
		cotte-hardie cotardie	cotehardie	none currently in use
		gonele[1]	goune or gowne or gonne[1]	gown
outdoor garments	cloak or cape designating high rank. (See *Color Plate 11.*)	mantel	mantel	mantle
	wide cape with hood	chape	cope	cape
	hood, cut and sewed to a chape (See *Figure 6.3, page 127.*)	chaperon	chaperon	chaperon[3]
	long cloak with capelike sleeves (See *Figure 6.5, page 128.*)	garnache or gamache or ganache	garnache	none currently in use
	cloak with long, wide sleeves having a slit below the shoulder length through which the arm could be slipped, leaving the long, full sleeve hanging behind. (See *Figure 5.20.*)	herigaut	herigaut	none currently in use
		gardecorps	gardcors	none currently in use
sets of garments	a set of garments consisting generally of under tunic, outer tunic, and mantel, however, the same term is also used to refer to a single garment.	robe	robe	robe

[1]Seems to have been first applied to the dress of elderly priests and to that of nuns.
[2]Modern term differs markedly from term of origin but is a fashion term.
[3]No longer a clothing term, but is applied to another item altogether.

Table 5.1

OLD ENGLISH AND FRENCH COSTUME TERMS

Type of garment	Definition	Old French term	Old English term	Modern English term derived from:
head coverings or parts of head coverings	hood	coul	couel	cowl[2]
	veil worn around the side of the face and under the chin (See *Figure 5.17.*)	guimpe	wimpel or wimple	none currently in use
	circlet worn around head	chapel or chapelet	chapelet	chaplet
	small white cap that tied under the chin (See *Figures 5.17* and *5.19.*)	coif	coif	coif[2]
	long tube of fabric hanging down from the back of a hood (See *Figure 6.3, page 127.*)	cornette	liripipe	none
leg coverings	garment that fits the foot and leg up to the knee or thigh (See *Figure 5.13.*)	chausses	hose	hose
other terms	fur-trimmed garment	peliçon	pellison	pelisse (19th century)
	narrow band of cloth attached to hood, headdress, or sleeve (See *Figure 6.3, page 127.*)	coudieres	tippet	none

[2]Modern term differs markedly from term of origin but is a fashion term.

Some costume historians use the term **cyclas** in referring to sleeveless and other surcotes. Sources vary in defining precisely what the cyclas was; how, when, and by whom it was worn; and its variations in style. Therefore we have chosen to use the more general term surcote.

Depictions of surcotes (the outermost tunics) show variations in cut. Some were sleeveless with a round or wide horizontal neckline and wide armholes, the garment being sewn closed under the wide armhole. (See *Figure 5.18.*) Others had sleeves to the elbow or three-quarters of the way down the arm (see *Color Plate 11*) or long sleeves cut full and wide under the arm, tapering to the wrist (as described for the cote).

Long surcotes were often slit to the waist to make riding and other movement easier. Even short surcotes and cotes worn without a surcote sometimes had these slits at the front. (See *Figure 5.19.*)

Distinctions between the surcote and some of the cloaks and mantles worn out-of-doors blur. No surcote was worn over some outdoor garments. Major items of outdoor wear included open or closed cloaks or mantles. Mantles placed over the shoulders and fastening across the front with a chain or ribbon remained a symbol of high rank or status.

The **garnache** (*gar'nosh*) was a long cloak with capelike sleeves. Often lined or collared with fur, this garment was open at the sides under the arms. (See *Figure 5.19.*)

The **herigaut** (*er-ee-go'*) was a full garment with long, wide sleeves and a slit below the shoulder in front through which the arm could be slipped, leaving the long, full sleeve hanging behind. In some instances the top of the sleeve was pleated or tucked to add fullness to the sleeve. (See *Figure 5.20.*) (From descriptions, the **gardcors** or **gardecorps** [*gard'-corz*] seems to have been the same kind of garment.)

The **tabard** (*tab'erd*) was originally a short, loose garment with short or no sleeves that was worn by monks and lower-class men. In some instances it fastened for only a short distance under the arms either by seaming or with fabric tabs. In later centuries this garment became part of military dress or the dress of servants in lordly households. (See *Figure 5.21.*) Decorations were applied to the tabard that identified the lord to whom the wearer owed allegiance.

Slits or **fitchets,** which to the modern eye look like pockets, were made in some of the more voluminous outdoor garments so that one could put his hands inside for warmth or to reach a purse hung from the belt around the waist of the garment beneath.

FIGURE 5.19

Manuscript of about 1240–1260 shows a variety of costumes including a garnache, a cloak with wide, capelike sleeves depicted both in lower left panel and upper right-hand panel. (Photograph courtesy, The Pierpont Morgan Library, manuscript M638 f16.)

HAIR AND HEADDRESS

Hair length was moderate and hair was parted in the center. Younger men wore shorter hair than their elders. If beards were worn, they were short. Many men were beardless because of the development of a new closed military helmet that completely covered the face. It was uncomfortable if worn over a beard.

The most important headcoverings were the coif and hoods. (See *Figure 5.19.*) Some hoods no longer had attached capes. By the end of the 13th century, hoods fitted the head more closely and some were made with a long, hanging tube of fabric at the back. The French called this a **cornette** (*kor′net*); the English, a **liripipe** (*leer′-eh-pip*). (See *Figure 6.3, page 127.*)

By the 13th century many Jewish men had ceased to wear the traditional Jewish pointed hat and could no longer be clearly distinguished from other Europeans by their dress. Prejudice against Jews led leaders of the Catholic Church to pass edicts requiring that Jews dress in ways that made them clearly identifiable, and wearing of this hat now became a requirement, rather than a voluntary act. Many artists creating works of art for an illiterate audience used symbols such as the pointed hat and beard to enable viewers to identify Jewish characters in biblical stories more easily. (See the man in the upper right corner of *Figure 5.23.*) During the late Middle Ages these hats gradually went out of use; anti-Semitic attitudes continued, however. In many communities Jewish men and women were required to wear either distinctive items of clothing or some sort of badge.

FOOTWEAR

Closed shoes that buckled or laced, open slippers, shoes open over the top of the foot and having a high tab behind the ankle, and loose-fitting boots rarely above calf height were all worn. (See *Figure 5.19.*)

Both long hose and short stockings were worn and footed hose increased in use.

FIGURE 5.20

Manuscript illuminated after 1262 depicts donors of the manuscript each shown wearing an herigaut. The woman on the right has her hair enclosed in a net, a barbette around her chin, and fillet around her head. (Photograph courtesy, The Pierpont Morgan Library, Manuscript 756 fiov.)

FIGURE 5.21

Kneeling Carthusian Monk wearing a tabard, which closes with cloth tabs under the arm. (France c. 1380–1400. Marble, H. 24.15 × 12 cm. © The Cleveland Museum of Art, John L. Severance Fund, 1966.113.)

Costume for Women: 13th Century

While women did not wear braies, the other garments in their wardrobes corresponded to those of men: a chemise, cote, surcote, and, out-of-doors, a mantle or cloak.

GARMENTS

Cotes had either fitted sleeves or sleeves cut full under the arm. Surcotes were either sleeved or sleeveless. Sleeved surcotes ended somewhere between the elbow and the wrist and were generally quite wide and full. Sleeveless surcotes were cut with wide armholes through which the cote beneath was visible. (See *Figure 5.18.*)

The loose, enveloping garments considered proper during the time of Saint Louis were replaced by more fitted styles toward the end of the 13th century. In warm summer months some women wore the surcote over the chemise, but this was considered daring and a sign of immoral behavior. Some women laced the cote (under tunic) tightly to emphasize their figures, which were visible through the wide armholes of the surcote.

The ceremonial open mantle worn by women of high rank was worn indoors as well as outside. (See *Color Plate 11.*) Cloaks such as those of the 11th and 12th centuries continued in use, some of them were hooded for cold weather. Women occasionally wore the herigaut and less often the garnache, which was for the most part a man's garment. (See *Figure 5.20.*)

HAIR AND HEADDRESS

Young girls continued to wear their hair uncovered while adult women covered their heads. Long braids (such as those of the 12th century) were no longer seen. Veils and hair nets covered the hair. Barbettes, fillets, and wimples remained, although sometimes they were placed over a hair net instead of a veil. (See *Figure 5.20.*)

FOOTWEAR

No major changes were to be seen in footwear from that worn in the preceding century.

ACCESSORIES OF DRESS FOR MEN AND WOMEN: 10TH–13TH CENTURIES

Accessories were largely limited to jewelry, wallets, purses or other devices for carrying valuables, and gloves.

According to Cunnington (1952), until the 13th century, only the nobility and the clergy wore gloves. Kings are sometimes represented wearing jeweled gloves. By the close of the 13th century, gloves seem to have been used more commonly by both men and women. Some were elbow length, others wrist length. Some women were said to have worn linen gloves to protect their hands from sunburn.

Purses and pouches or wallets were suspended from belts (and, rarely, from the shoulder), or were sometimes worn underneath outer garments and reached through an opening or slit.

JEWELRY

Rarely visible in pictures or statuary, jewelry is described in literary sources. Most important items were rings, belts, clasps used to hold the ribbon that fastened the mantle, and a round brooch—**fermail** (*fair'my*) or **afiche** (*a'feesh*)—used to close the top of the outer tunic, bliaut, or surcote.

COSMETICS

After the Crusades, perfumes and ointments imported from the Middle East came into general use. The Cunningtons (1952) say English women of higher ranks used rouge in the 12th century. If it was imported for use in England where the nobility retained close ties to France and to English territories on the continent, one can be sure it was used on the continent as well. The same source mentions hair dyes and face creams.

MILITARY COSTUME

Entire books have been devoted to the subject of military costume and armor. The discussion that follows touches on only highlights of this topic. For those interested in more detailed information about military costume, a section of the bibliography provides several specific references.

Blair (1972), an authority on armor, suggests that armor be divided according to types of construction: (1) soft armor, made of quilted fabric or leather that has not been subjected to any special hardening process; (2) mail, made of interlocked metal rings; and (3) plates of metal, hardened leather, whalebone, or horn. The third category can also be divided

into large plates that completely cover areas of the body and are flexible only where necessary for movement of the body; or small plates fastened together to provide more flexible covering.

In the Greek and Roman armies all three of these forms were utilized. During the early Middle Ages in Europe the plate type of armor seems not to have been used. Blair (1972), in a lengthy study of European armor, says that although some forms of small plate armor were used by the Franks and the Vikings, "it is probably safe to say that during the period c. 600–1250 when anything other than soft armor was worn, it was in ninety-nine cases out of a hundred made of mail." (See *Figure 5.22*.) Mail in medieval Europe was made of circular rings, each ring having four other rings hooked through it.

The Bayeux Tapestry is one of the earliest and most important sources of information about the appearance of medieval armor. Dated from the second half of the 11th century, or slightly later, the tapestry depicts the events leading to and the actual Battle of Hastings, which took place in 1066. In the tapestry many figures wear knee-length shirts of mail, which are split in front for riding. This mail shirt was called a **hauberk** (*ho'berk*) or **byrnie** (*burr'neh*). A hood of mail was worn to protect the neck and head. This may have been a separate piece, but in most later armor the hood is made in one

FIGURE 5.22

Mail shirt, 15th century. This shirt typifies the construction of chain mail garments, which were the major form of armor in the early Middle Ages and continued to be used in conjunction with plate armor in the later Middle Ages as well. (Photograph courtesy, The Metropolitan Museum of Art, Bashford Dean Memorial Collection, gift of Edward S. Harkness, 1929.)

with the body of the hauberk for maximum protection of the neck. Some figures also wore leg protectors of mail, or **chausses** (*shos*). Some chausses merely covered the front of the leg while others were more like hose and fitted all around. On the head and over the mail hood, the warrior placed a cone-shaped helmet with a barlike extension that covered the nose.

In the mid-12th century men began wearing a surcote over the armor. (See *Figure 5.23*.) Possibly the practice originated during the Crusades in an attempt to protect the metal armor from the heat of the Mediterranean sun, a custom that may have been copied from Moslem soldiers. In later periods soldiers wore surcotes decorated with a coat of arms that identified the force to which they belonged, a necessary step when faces were covered by helmets.

In the 12th and 13th centuries, armor consisted of a coat of mail—sometimes quite long, other times shorter—hose and shoes of mail. The sleeves reached over the hands to form a sort of mail mitten. The whole outfit weighed from 25 to 30 pounds and was worn over a padded garment. In the early 13th century, a closed form of helmet developed. Blair (1972) compares it to a modern welder's helmet, except that it was closed in the back, with eyeslits and breathing holes, sort of like wearing a large, inverted can over the head. Placed over the chain mail coif and a small padded skull cap that protected the head from the ridges of the mail, the helmet was worn only for combat as it was too uncomfortable for general wear. In the last half of the 13th century, large crests in animal or birdlike shapes were placed on top of the helmet so as to identify the knight.

The use of closed helmets brought about changes in hair styles. Men wore their hair shorter and were clean shaven in order to avoid the heat and discomfort that came from wearing a closed helmet over a full beard or long hair.

FIGURE 5.23

Soldiers in chain mail with colorful surcotes placed over the mail. The mail covers all parts of the body except the face. (Photograph courtesy, The Metropolitan Museum of Art, the Cloisters Collection, purchase 1968.)

Common foot soldiers were not equipped with chain mail. Their protection was most likely limited to reinforced, quilted coats such as those worn under the armor to which they might add quilted leg guards.

By the end of the 13th century, a change from mail to plate armor had begun. (See *Chapter 6, page 140.*)

SUMMARY

VISUAL SUMMARY

The accompanying *Visual Summary Table* shows the major garment styles of the Byzantine and Early Medieval periods.

THEMES

Byzantine dress, with its blending of Eastern and Roman styles, clearly plays out the theme of CROSS-CULTURAL IN-FLUENCES. One can also see here the connections between ART AND DRESS. In the decoration of Byzantine styles with brightly colored embroideries and jeweled ornamentation one can find an echo of the jewel-like, brightly colored mosaics that decorate Byzantine churches.

CROSS-CULTURAL themes play a dominant role in the history of dress in western Europe from the early Medieval period onward. Byzantine decorative elements in dress traveled across Europe to influence the dress of the rich and powerful Merovingian and Carolingian kings and their courts. Even the dress of the common people results from a merging of Roman with barbarian dress.

It is often through POLITICAL CONFLICT that CROSS-CULTURAL contacts occur. Crusaders traveling to the Middle East brought back new textiles and garments. The Moorish

Visual Summary Table

MAJOR GARMENTS OF THE BYZANTINE AND EARLY MEDIEVAL PERIODS

Byzantine man,
c. 6th century

Byzantine woman,
c. 6th century

Byzantine man,
c. 11th century

Byzantine woman,
c. 11th century

Medieval European man,
12th century

Medieval European woman,
12th century

Medieval European man and
woman, 13th century

Outer garment called the garnache,
late 13th/early 14th century

Medieval outer garment called herigaut
or gardecorps, mid-13th century

conquest and occupation of Sicily and Spain helped to spread new **TECHNOLOGIES** important for dress, such as the cultivation and processing of cotton and silk fibers or the introduction of the spinning wheel. New garments associated with armor were adopted by civilians as a result of **POLITICAL CONFLICT** and warfare.

One can also see hints of the theme of **SOCIAL CLASS.** Thorstein Veblen (1953), a 19th century economist, argues in his *Theory of the Leisure Class* that clothing can be an important means of displaying social class. He speaks of demonstrating that affluence through "conspicuous consumption," the acquisition of items that display the wealth of the wearer, and "conspicuous leisure." In the 10th to the 13th centuries upper-class men wore long tunics, and lower-class men wore short tunics. These more encumbering garments, in which it would be difficult to do any menial work, could be said to demonstrate conspicuous leisure. Women's garments of the 12th century were even more restrictive, with their voluminous sleeves.

ORIGINS, DEVELOPMENTS, AND SURVIVALS OF BYZANTINE AND EARLY MEDIEVAL STYLES

Styles during the early Middle Ages might be characterized as Roman forms in combination with local forms. In Byzantium, the non-Roman elements came from the Middle East, whereas in Europe the non-Roman elements came from barbarian dress. In both cases, however, the chief components of dress were layered tunics combined with a mantle of some sort.

Byzantine styles influenced European styles among the upper classes. Byzantine silks were purchased, and rulers in Europe adopted Byzantine styles. By copying the Byzantine styles these rulers brought to their courts a reflection of the wealth and status associated with the court at Constantinople, which had become the most cultured center of the period. (See *Color Plates 9* and *10.*)

Except for the introduction of sericulture into the West by way of the Byzantine Empire, neither technology for the production of cloth nor basic styles took any great leap forward in Europe during the period before 900. The major changes of the Middle Ages in western Europe were yet to come.

In the years between 900 and 1300, costume had evolved gradually from loosely fitted, T-shaped tunics and loose mantles to more closely fitted styles of a more complex cut. As medieval courts became centers of fashionable life, special court dress developed. Made of more costly materials, clothing was often so extreme in cut that it clearly demonstrated that the wearer belonged to a more leisured class. As the economy improved, the manufacture and distribution of fabrics multiplied, and new types of cloth became available. As the merchant class in the towns increased in wealth and numbers, fashionable dress was adopted not only by the nobility but also by the bourgeoisie.

Some elements of styles from the late Middle Ages served as an inspiration to fashion designers of the 19th and 20th centuries. Notable revivals of medieval styles include parti-colored clothing, sideless surcoats, cowl necklines, and hanging sleeves. The magyar sleeve, cut full under the arm, was revived in the 1930s and the World War II period as the "bat wing" or "dolman" sleeve. During the late Romantic through the Crinoline periods, hanging sleeves appeared again.

Changes in styles in the High Middle Ages were gradual. A young woman of modest means might be married and, many years later, buried in the same dress, or she might pass it to her daughter in her will. After the end of the 13th century, this was less likely to occur. Fashion, with its rapid changes, was becoming an important aspect of dress, and styles began to change at what must have seemed like a dizzying pace. No wonder that a writer of 1350 was to look back on the styles at the end of the 1200s and lament that "Once upon a time women wore white wimples, surcotes with hanging sleeves, long full skirts, and decent hoods of cloth or silk. A woman had only three dresses. One for weddings and great feasts, one for Sundays and holidays, and one for every day. Narrow laced shoes and buttoned sleeves were for courtesans; decent women tied their bodices with ribbons and sewed their sleeves, wore their belts high and plaited their hair round their heads" (Evans 1952).

NOTES

Blair, C. 1972. *European Armour*. London: Batsford, p. 19.

Calkins, R. 1993. *The Illuminated Books of the Middle Ages*. New York: Cornell University Press.

Cunnington, C. and P. Cunnington. 1952. *Handbook of Medieval Costume*. London: Faber and Faber, p. 41.

Durant, W. 1950. *The Age of Faith*. New York: Simon and Schuster, p. 287.

Evans, J. 1952. *Dress in Medieval France*. Oxford: Clarendon Press, pp. 24–25.

Gies, C. and F. Gies. 1974. *Life in a Medieval Castle*. New York: Thomas Y. Crowell, p. 47.

Gies, F. and J. Gies. 1994. *Cathedral, Forge, and Water Wheel*. New York: HarperCollins.

Goddard, E. R. 1927. *Women's Costume in French Texts of the 11th and 12th Centuries*. Baltimore, MD: Johns Hopkins University Press.

Heichelheim, F. M. 1975. "Byzantine Silk Fabrics." *CIBA Review*, p. 2761.

Herlihy, D. 1990. *Opera Muliebria: Women and Work in Medieval Europe*. Philadelphia: Temple University Press.

Rice, D. T., ed. 1965. *The Dawn of European Civilizations*. New York: McGraw-Hill.

Rubens, A. 1967. *A History of Jewish Costume*. New York: Funk and Wagnalls.

Snyder, J. 2002. "From Content to Form: Court Clothing in Mid-Twelfth-Century Northern French Sculpture," p. 85 ff in D. Koslin and J. E. Snyder, eds. *Encountering Medieval Textiles and Dress*. New York: Palgrave Macmillan.

Veblen, T. 1953. *The Theory of the Leisure Class*. New York: New American Library.

Waugh, C. F. 1999. "'Well-Cut through the Body:'" Fitted Clothing in Twelfth Century Europe." *Dress*, Vol. 26, p. 3 ff.

SELECTED READINGS

Books Containing Illustrations of Costume of the Period from Original Sources

Aubert, M. 1952. *Le Cathedral de Chartres*. France: B. Arthaud.

Backhouse, J. et al., eds. 1985. *The Golden Age of Anglo Saxon Art. 966 to 1066*. Bloomington, IN: Indiana University Press.

Beckwith, J. 1992. *Early Christian and Byzantine Art*. New Haven, CT: Yale University Press.

Cormack, R. *Byzantine Art*. 2000. New York: Oxford University Press,

Duby, G., X. B. Altet, and S. G. deSuduiraut. 1990. *Sculpture: The Great Art of the Middle Ages from the Fifth to the Fifteenth Century*. New York: Rizzoli.

Hollander, H. 1990. *Early Medieval Art*. New York: Universe Books.

Hubert, J., J. Porcher, and W. F. Volbach. 1970. *Carolingian Renaissance*. New York: George Braziller.

Kessler, H. L. and M. S. Simpson, eds. 1986. *Pictorial Narrative in Antiquity and the Middle Ages*. Washington, D.C.: National Gallery of Art.

Lucas, D. 1975. *A Gallery of Great Paintings*. New York: Hamblyn.

Mutherich, F. and J. E. Graehde. 1977. *Carolingian Painting*. New York: Braziller.

Periodical Articles

Alexander, S. M. 1979. "Information on Historical Techniques. Textiles, 2: The Medieval Period." *Art and Archeology Technical Abstracts*, Vol. 16, No. 1, p. 198.

Backhouse, J. 1968. "Manuscript Sources for the History of Medieval Costume." *Costume*, No. 2, p. 3.

Cameron, A. 1973. "A Byzantine Imperial Coronation of the Sixth Century." *Costume*, No. 7, p. 4.

Effros, B. 2002. "Appearance and Ideology: Creating Distinctions between Clerics and Lay Persons in Early Medieval Gaul," p. 7 in

D. Koslin and J. E. Snyder, eds. *Encountering Medieval Textiles and Dress*. New York: Palgrave MacMillian.

Herchelheim, F. M. "Byzantine Silk Fabrics." *CIBA Review*, No. 75, p. 8761.

Hughes, M. J. 1975. "Marco Polo and Medieval Silk." *Textile History*, p. 119.

King, D. 1996. "Roman and Byzantine Dress in Egypt." *Costume*, No. 30, p. 1.

Sencer, Y. J. 1985. "Threads of History" (Woolen textiles in ancient Ireland). *The F.I.T. Review*, Vol. 2, No. 1, Oct. p. 5.

Staniland, K. 1991. "Clothing Provision and the Great Wardrobe in the Mid-Thirteenth Century." *Textile History*. Vol. 22, p. 239.

Waugh, C. F. 1999. "'Well-Cut through the Body:'" Fitted Clothing in Twelfth Century Europe." *Dress*, Vol. 26, p. 3.

Daily Life

Aries, P., et al. 1987. *History of Private Life: From Pagan Rome to Byzantium*. Cambridge MA: Belknap Press of Harvard University Press.

Duby, G., ed. 1988. *A History of Private Life: Revelations of the Medieval World*. Cambridge MA: Belknap Press of Harvard University Press.

Gies, F. and J. Gies. 1980. *Women in the Middle Ages*. New York: Barnes and Noble.

Gies, F. and J. Gies. 1999. *Daily Life in Medieval Times*. New York: Black Dog and Leventhal.

Goetz, H. 1993. *Life in the Middle Ages: From the Seventh to the Thirteenth Century*. Notre Dame, IN: University of Notre Dame Press.

Herlihy, D. 1990. *Opera Muliebria: Women and Work in Medieval Europe*. Philadelphia: Temple University Press.

Howarth, D. 1981. *1066: The Year of the Conquest*. New York: Penguin.

Hussey, J. 1982. *The Byzantine World.* Westport CT: Greenwood Press Reprint.

Kraus, H. 1967. *The Living Theatre of Medieval Art.* Philadelphia: University of Pennsylvania Press.

Labarge, M. 1980. *A Baronial Household of the Thirteenth Century.* New York: Barnes and Noble.

Riche, P. 1988. *Daily Life in the World of Charlemagne.* Philadelphia: University of Pennsylvania Press.

Stuard, S. M. 1976. *Women in Medieval Society.* Philadelphia: University of Pennsylvania Press.

Todd, M. 1988. *Everyday Life of the Barbarians, Goths, Franks and Vandals.* New York: Fromm.

Ecclesiastical Dress

Butler, J. T. "Ecclesiastical Vestments of the Middle Ages." *Connoisseur,* Vol. 177 (714), August 1971, p. 297.

Davenport, M. 1972. "The Roman Catholic Church." In *The Book of Costume.* Vol. 1. New York: Crown, p. 93.

Mayo, J. 1984. *A History of Ecclesiastical Dress.* New York: Holmes and Meier.

CHRONOLOGY

1300s

Introduction of gunpowder and cannon to warfare

1337–1453

Hundred Years War between France and England

1348

First appearance of the plague in Europe

c. 1416

Portugal initiates exploration of the west coast of Africa

1453

Ottoman Turks conquer Constantinople

1454

First record of printing with moveable type in Europe

1488

Portuguese round the Cape of Good Hope

1492

Columbus reaches America

Spain expels its Jewish citizens

Reconquest of Spain from the Moors completed

1498

Vasco da Gama, Portuguese explorer, reaches India

CHAPTER SIX

THE LATE MIDDLE AGES

c. 1300 – 1500

B.

A.

E.

C.

D.

F.

A.

Reims cathedral door (12th–15th c.)

B.

Sideboard

C.

Hotel de Dieu, Beaune, 15th c.

D.

Cabinet

E.

Chair

F.

Chest decoration, Spanish, 14th c.

Figures A, C courtesy of V. R. Tortora. Figures B, D, E, F from Lavisse, 1897. *Album Historique, Le Fin Du Moyen-Age.* Paris: Armand Colin & Cie Editeurs, pp. 17, 134, 208.

HISTORICAL BACKGROUND

As medieval monarchs succeeded in centralizing the government, the power of nobles and knights declined. Feudalism began to wane before the 14th century because kings found new sources of revenue by taxing cities and towns. The income gained enabled them to hire knights who fought as long as they were paid. Monarchs had learned that a paid army was more dependable than feudal nobles who, under the usual feudal practice, were expected to serve only forty days once a year at their own expense.

Changes in warfare hastened the decline of the armored knight on horseback. In the Hundred Years' War the English longbow decimated French knights. In the 15th century, the introduction of gunpowder and the cannon gave an even greater advantage to the infantry over the armored knights on horseback. Gunpowder and the cannon also ended the security of medieval castles.

As kings brought law and order to their realms, the revival of trade, commerce, and industry that had begun in the 12th century continued. Although the towns lost some independence as the royal government grew stronger, kings had to protect the cities since they were centers of business, which were a most important source of taxes. Within the cities, as commerce became more capitalistic, the medieval guilds, which had apportioned business among the members of the guild, declined in importance. The merchant class, however, became more influential by turning to new fields, particularly banking, which made them welcome by their rulers. In France, Jacques Coeur (1395–1456), son of a lowly artisan, made his fortune through investing in commerce and mining. He became treasurer to Charles VII (1403–1461), who later had him imprisoned and confiscated his wealth. In the late 15th century the Fugger family of Ausgburg built a vast financial empire based on silver, copper, and iron mines. They became papal bankers as well as bankers to the Emperor Charles V (1500–1558), to whom they lent money enabling this Spanish king to bribe the electors and win election as Holy Roman Emperor.

Free peasants who no longer owed their lord services in return for the use of his land gradually replaced serfs. Instead of providing services, peasants paid rent. With the funds gained, the lord could hire landless peasants to work the land. The vast majority of the population consisted of peasants. They were the farmers, day laborers, millers, bakers, cattle dealers, and domestic servants. In time of war they were the foot soldiers of the king.

As freemen they were also more mobile. Increased commercial activity in the towns drew people from the countryside in search of work and higher salaries. These new townspeople could, if they had the talent and the opportunity, move up in social status. As a result, the population of the rural areas declined after the middle of the 14th century, while some towns and cities continued to grow.

Another reason for the increase in urban population was the flight of peasants from the countryside because of a series of famines resulting from poor harvests in the early years of the 14th century. Heavy rainstorms and cold weather ruined the crops on which people and cattle depended. The result was catastrophe: famine and starvation.

A population already weakened by famine suffered another scourge, the Black Death, a plague that struck Europe in 1347 and repeatedly throughout the 14th and 15th centuries. As late as 1665 London was devastated by an outbreak of the plague. The Black Death was probably a combination of bubonic and pneumonic plague. This devastating disease killed a third of the population in the regions that it struck. The densely populated Italian cities suffered heavy losses. As a result of this depopulation, labor became scarce and aspiring workers from the lower classes were, thereby, afforded opportunities for advancement that had not existed before the Black Death (Herlihy 1974).

Wages rose sharply. Landlords and merchants had to grant concessions to peasants and workers. When they tried to restrict wages and raise rents, social unrest and popular insurrections followed, lasting throughout the century.

MEDIEVAL SOCIAL STRUCTURE

Late medieval society can be divided into three classes: the nobility, the bourgeoisie, and the peasants. The clergy were regarded as a separate class. An early medieval bishop once said that society was divided into those who prayed, the clergy; those who fought, the nobles; and the rest of society, which labored (Nicholas and De Molen 1974).

The Peasant

The rural peasant is frequently depicted at his labors in the *Books of Hours* painted during the Middle Ages. These prayer books, illustrated by the artists of the day, show the farmer and his wife at work. (See *Figure 6.1.*) Men and women worked side by side on the land, planting, harvesting, and clipping the fleece from sheep. Women tended their children and prepared simple food in a house of two or three rooms furnished with utilitarian tables, benches or stools, chests or cupboards, and beds.

Everyday clothing for the peasant was plain and serviceable, and very like that described for men of the earlier medieval period: a homespun tunic, belted at the waist, with stockings for cold weather, and a cloak. Wooden clogs or

FIGURE 6.1

Upper-class men look on while peasants harvest grain. Illumination from a book depicting agricultural techniques, French, c. 1470. (Photograph courtesy, The Pierpont Morgan Library, manuscript M232 f201v.)

heavy boots (for muddy weather) and a hat to keep off the sun in summer or a hood to protect against the cold in winter completed his workaday wardrobe. His wife wore a gown with a close-fitting bodice and a skirt with moderate fullness. When the task required protection of the garment beneath, an apron was placed over the dress. If she worked in the field where her long skirts hampered her movement, the skirt was tucked up into the belt and the chemise underneath exposed.

Although many of the peasants were poor and lived a hand-to-mouth existence, others were better off and some even reasonably affluent. The poorest were, of course, able to clothe themselves only in coarse cloth that was either left undyed or dyed with readily available natural dyestuffs such as the blue dye, woad. The more affluent were not unaware of current fashions and for festive occasions their dress reflected somewhat the fashionable lines of upper-class dress.

The Nobility

If one were to judge from the painted miniatures, the life of the nobles was an endless round of entertainment: riding and hunting, feasting and talking, music and dancing—and, of course, warfare. Intermittent fighting in France between the French and English marked the 1300s, as the Hundred Years' War continued off and on between 1337 and 1453.

Entertainment among the nobility provided a stage for the display of fashion. Wealthy noblemen and women dressed in rich silk brocades and velvets trimmed with fur. The Court of Burgundy was especially notable for luxurious dress during the 14th and 15th centuries. The kingdom of France did not then control all of the regions that are part of the present country of France. Powerful autonomous dukes, who sometimes allied themselves with and sometimes against France, governed regions such as Brittany to the northwest and Burgundy to the northeast.

The court of the dukes of Burgundy was renowned for its splendid costume. The garments worn by the dukes, their families, and members of the court have been described at length in the chronicles of the period and painted by artists of the time. Some of the costumes of Philip the Bold, Duke from 1363 to 1404, indicate the costliness of Burgundian dress. One of his doublets was described as scarlet, embroidered in pearls in a design of 40 lambs and swans. The lambs had little gold bells around their necks and the swans held bells in their beaks (Wescher, *CIBA Review*).

The fabrics of which Burgundian clothing was made were imported from all over Europe. Inventories list silk from Italy, wool from Flanders, and felt from Germany.

Headgear of men and women could be quite extreme. An inventory made in 1420 of the clothing of Philip the Good mentions a silk hat with peacock and other feathers, flowers, and gold spangles. At the close of the 14th century Burgundian women adopted a tall, exaggerated, steeple-shaped headdress style which some costume historians call a **hennin** (*hen'in*). The word hennin derives from an old French word meaning "to inconvenience," and certainly a tall, peaked hat a yard high must have been a considerable inconvenience. Some authors believe the word hennin was not used as a fashion term, but rather to poke fun at this extreme style. Sumptuary laws regulated the size of these hats. Princesses could wear steeple headdresses a yard in height, while noble ladies were permitted no more than 24 inches. Jirousek (1995) suggests that the hennin may have been yet another borrowing from the Orient. She points out similarities between tall Ottoman Turkish headdress for women and the steeple-shaped headdress of Burgundy and France.

The Dukes of Burgundy and their retinues traveled to other parts of Europe for royal weddings, funerals, councils, and other events. As a result others copied the styles they affected.

Much of the color and pageantry of costume of this period derives not only from the dress of royalty with its vivid colors and fanciful headdresses, but also from the costume of the dependent nobles and servants. Kings, dukes, and feudal lords had established the practice of presenting robes or sets of clothing to men and women of their household. The French word for "to distribute" is *livraison* and the items distributed became known as the *liveree* or, in English, **livery.** Eventually the word livery came to mean special uniforms for servants; however, during the 14th and 15th centuries livery was worn not just by servants, but also by officials of the court and ladies-in-waiting to queens or duchesses. Although subject to the wishes of the queen or duchess, a lady-in-waiting was not a servant, but a well-born woman who lived and took part in the life of the court as part of the queen's retinue. The garments that were distributed were decorated with special devices or symbols associated with the noble or his family. The search for unique patterns had led to the practice of sewing together sections of different-colored fabrics within one garment. Garments decorated in this way were called **mi-parti** (*me-partee*) or **parti-colored.** Some examples of parti-colored hose show as many as four different colors in a single pair of hose. Parti-colored effects were utilized in both men's and women's costume.

The Bourgeoisie

Merchants were part of a kind of "middle" class, not of the nobility and yet far wealthier than the peasant. Some of these men, such as the previously discussed Jacques Coeur, became rich and powerful and achieved high offices under kings whom they helped to finance.

By far the larger numbers of merchants were men of more modest incomes who lived in the towns and who achieved the means to live comfortably in houses that were furnished with well-crafted furniture, linen, and china. They lacked none of the necessities and had the means to obtain some of the luxuries of the period. The wives of these merchants were expected to run these homes efficiently.

The wife of the merchant supervised the household, but did not do the housework herself. If she lived up to the standards of behavior for a woman of her class, she conducted herself discreetly and modestly. If her dress followed the ideal expressed by clergy and by others such as the "Goodman of Paris" it was free from extravagance. The "Goodman of Paris" was an elderly husband of a very much younger wife. This gentleman wrote out a book of instructions for his 15-year-old wife on how to conduct herself in every aspect of management of the home. He even included some recipes for her. *Contemporary Comments 6.1* presents his advice as to her dress and comportment when out-of-doors.

Not all merchants, however, agreed with the "Goodman of Paris." Some merchants demonstrated their affluence through lavish dress for themselves and their wives. The passage of numerous sumptuary laws during this period testifies to the growing tendency of well-to-do burghers to imitate the nobility. For example, one set of sumptuary laws from the time of Edward IV of England (c. 1450) was entitled "For the

Outrageous and Excessive Apparel of Divers [different] People, against their Estate and Degree [status] to the Great Destruction and Impoverishment of All the Land."

FABRICS AND TAILORS

The technology of cloth manufacture underwent no major changes, although the spinning wheel gradually replaced the distaff and spindle for the making of yarn. Trends in textile manufacture cited in *Chapter 5* continued to accelerate, as the "putting out" system became the normal way of doing textile business. A merchant became the middleman for textile workers, selling the workers the fiber, then buying back the finished cloth, followed by selling it to the fuller, then buying it back. The merchant arranged for dyeing, then sold the completed fabric to agents who sold it at one of the medieval trade fairs (Gies and Gies 1994).

Tailors underwent a lengthy and rigorous apprenticeship to become skilled in the construction of clothing. Different craftsmen made different items of dress: tailors made garments, professional lingerie makers made wimples and veils, and bootmakers or shoemakers made boots or shoes.[1] The variety of materials and colors was considerable. Fabrics were traded all over Europe, and imported from Turkey and Palestine. Furs were used as both trimmings and linings. One king of France, Philip the Tall (1294–1392), who was described as "anything but extravagant," used 6,364 skins of gray squirrel in three months just to fur his own robes (Evans 1969).

SOURCES OF EVIDENCE FOR THE STUDY OF COSTUME

Art

The variety of sources of information available to the costume historian for this period is considerably greater than for the earlier periods. Secular romances and religious works such as Bibles and prayer books were hand lettered and illustrated with vividly colored, painted miniatures. These miniatures depicted scenes from the romances, from the Bible, or from church history in terms of everyday medieval life. Un-

---

[1]The word lingerie, which will be encountered frequently in subsequent chapters, derives from the French and originally meant "making of linen cloth." Over the years this meaning has changed. The term is now applied to women's underclothing, an application made because until the 19th century linen was the fabric most often used for women's underwear.

CONTEMPORARY COMMENTS 6.1

Advice on Dress

The Menagier (translated "householder") of Paris, a well-to-do older man provided the following instructions on how to dress for his young, fifteen-year-old wife.

Have a care, that you be honestly clad, without new devices and without too much or too little frippery. And before you leave your chamber and house, take care first that the collar of your shift [chemise], and of your *blanchet, cotte,* and *surcote,* do not hang out one over the other as happens with certain drunken, foolish, or witless women, who have no care for their honor, nor for the honesty of their estate or of their husbands, and who walk with roving eyes and heads horribly reared up like a lion, their hair straggling out of their wimples, and the collars of their shifts and *cottes* crumpled the one upon the other, and who walk mannishly and bear themselves uncouthly.... Therefore, fair sister, have a care that your hair, wimple, kerchief and hood and all the rest of your attire be well arranged and decently ordered that none who see you can mock at you, but that all the others may find in you an example of fair and simple and decent array....

Reprinted from E. Power. 1968. *Medieval People.* New York: Barnes and Noble, p. 102.

fortunately these two-dimensional art works often show only the front views of costumes.

Stone sculpture on the facades of Gothic cathedrals, the tombs of the rich and high-born, and painted wooden statues for churches show the three-dimensional form of costume. However, as Scott (1986) points out, it was not uncommon for tombs to have been made well after the lifetime of the deceased.

Only a few individual items of dress from the period have survived, such as a *pourpoint* (a sort of man's jacket) worn in the second half of the 14th century by a French noble, Charles of Blois, or a jacket worn by the Burgundian, Charles the Bold, around 1476.

Documentary Sources

In France and England annual inventories were kept of the clothing given to or purchased by the royal families, and these inventories not only described fabrics from which clothing was made, but also gave their cost. Often the introduction of a style can be dated quite precisely from these lists. Even so, the precise meaning of many terms from the 14th and 15th centuries is still in doubt. Apparently, too, similar terms were applied to different items in each country or region.

A number of literary works survive from the 14th and 15th centuries. They sometimes make reference to clothing and may provide valuable information, especially about attitudes or customs related to clothing. Many documents, however, may not have been translated into modern English and are therefore not easily accessible. Dating of written material can also be a problem, as some authors borrowed liberally from original works written as much as a century and a half earlier (Scott 1986).

FASHION CHANGE BECOMES EVIDENT

Many costume historians point to the 14th century as the point at which fashion change begins. Although one can see instances in the early Middle Ages when the affluent appear to be following fashion, by the close of the 15th century it is obvious that periodic changes in the predominant style are taking place and that those who can afford to do so are dressing according to the current mode. Piponnier and Mane (1997, p. 65) note that the duration of fashion change can be seen on two levels. Details, they say, were in "a constant state of change, while big modifications of the silhouette took place only about every fifty years."

It is convenient to organize information so that it fits neatly into periods such as centuries or decades. Unfortunately, changes in the predominant styles in historic costume and the arts do not always fit into such convenient packages. Nor do stylistic changes come about with the same frequency in all periods. In order to help to clarify the changes of styles that will come with increasing rapidity in subsequent chapters, from this chapter forward the visual summary tables at the end of each chapter will contain illustrations of the most typical garments of the period together with a brief description of the major elements of styles and their duration. See *Visual Summary Table 6.1, page 143,* at the end of this chapter.

COSTUME FOR MEN:
14TH CENTURY

For the first 40 years of the 14th century styles for men continued to be much the same as those of the previous century. These were the chemise (see *Figure 5.17, page 107*) and braies as undergarments and the cote worn with a surcote. About 1340, styles for men changed markedly. Short skirts, always a part of peasant dress, returned to fashion for men of all classes. A number of new garment (pourpoints, cote-hardies, houppelandes) came into use, along with modifications of earlier forms.

Costume Components for Men: 14th Century

GARMENTS

The **pourpoint** (*pour-pwant'*) was also called a **doublet** (*dub'let*) or **gipon** (*jhi-pahn'*). This close-fitting, sleeveless garment with a padded front originated as military dress. Padded garments were worn alone as armor by ordinary soldiers, as padding under armor, or over armor after the turn of the century. About 1340 men began wearing a sleeved version of the pourpoint for civilian dress, together with a pair of long hose. Worn over the undershirt and cut to fit the body closely, the pourpoint closed down the front with laces or closely placed buttons. Strings sewn to the underside of the pourpoint skirt below the waist allowed attachment of hose to the pourpoint rather than to the waistband of the braies, the underwear worn under the hose. This mode of attachment of hose gave the pourpoint its name. **Points** were laces or ties, which ended in small, metal tips or "points," and the garment was "*pour les points*" or "for the points."

The pourpoint neckline was round. Sleeves fitted the arm and fastened with buttons at the wrist. (See *Figure 6.2.*) Initially pourpoints tended to be worn unbelted beneath another garment, but after about 1350 they were often the outermost garment, and were belted. Those seen in the second half of the century become increasingly shorter, barely covering the hips. Some had sleeves extending below the wrist in a point as far as the knuckles. In English usage the term doublet replaced the word pourpoint after 1400.

Hose covered the legs. Footed hose with leather soles were worn instead of shoes. Hose cut with a strap under the instep were worn with shoes or boots.

FIGURE 6.2

Short doublet or pourpoint is depicted in panel showing a detail of *The Passion of Christ* from Austria, Styria, c. 1400. The laces that close the doublet are visible on the second figure from left, who also wears parti-colored clothes. The hose of one man at the right have been undone revealing his braies. His doublet is unbuttoned. (Tempera and gold on wood, diptych, each wing 45.7 × 27 cm. © The Cleveland Museum of Art, Mr. and Mrs. William H. Marlatt Fund, 1945.115.)

When worn over the pourpoint, surcotes were shaped close to the body, short in length, and either sleeveless or with sleeves. Men who dressed conservatively continued to wear the surcote over a longer cote.

Other influences on civilian dress from military garments probably included the adoption of set in (sewn in) sleeves. Earlier tunics had been cut T-shaped, with sleeves being an extension of the body of the garment. To keep the underarm fullness from bunching up when worn under armor, sleeves had to be cut separately and sewn into the body of the tunic (Pipionnier and Mane 1997).

the cote-hardie The **cote-hardie** (*koat'-har'de*) is thought to have been a variant of the surcote or outer tunic. The term "cote-hardie" shows the differences in usage of the same term from one country to another and the variation in definition of terms that are encountered from one costume historian to another. Evans (1969), a specialist in French medieval history, says that in France the cote-hardie was always a sleeved garment for outdoor wear that was first worn by the lower classes and later became a more elegant, often fur-trimmed or fur-lined, garment. Boucher (1987), a French costume historian, notes the confusion surrounding the terminology, and suggests that the term seems to have been applied variously to the first short outer garments for men, to a gown, and to a surcote for men that was open in front and that buttoned at the sides. The Cunningtons (1952), who have compiled a handbook of English medieval costume, identified the cote-hardie in England as a very specific garment that replaced the older form of surcote for use over the pourpoint.

The Cunningtons provide quite a complete description of the English cote-hardie in the first half of the 1300s. It included these features: It was fitted through the waist, where it buttoned; then it flared to a full skirt that was open at the front and, usually, knee-length. The sleeves were apparently its major distinguishing feature. These ended at the elbow in front, while hanging down in back as a short tongue or longer flap. In some versions, however, both the sleeve and the flaps were absent. The English belted the cote-hardie low, on the hip. (Italian paintings also depict cote-hardies with belts at the hip.) For the lower classes, a variation is described that is looser, not buttoned but slipped on over the head. Its skirt and sleeves were like the more fashionable garment. This garment was either unbelted, belted at the waist, or belted at the hip. (See *Figure 6.3.*)

In the second half of the 14th century buttons extended from neck to hem, instead of from neck to waist. Hanging flaps at the elbows became longer and narrower. The length shortened. The edges of skirts and hanging sleeve flaps were often decorated with **dagging,** a form of decoration in which edges of the garment were cut into pointed or squared scallops.

Belts, worn at hip level, were commonly seen with cote-hardies. They were either long, with hanging ends, or short, made of metal plaques with an ornamental buckle.

the houppelande The **houppelande** (*hoop'land*) is first mentioned in French royal inventories in 1359. This important garment seems to have come to England slightly later. Apparently originating as a man's house coat worn over the pourpoint, the garment was fitted over the shoulder, then widened below into deep, tubular folds or pleats, which were held in place by a belt. (See *Figure 6.4.*) It was constructed from four long pieces that were sewn together at the sides, center front, and center back. Houppelandes were put on over the head. Sometimes seams were left open at the bottom for a short distance to form vents. The style was especially suited to heavy fabrics such as velvet, satin, damasks, brocades, and wool fabrics. It is often depicted as fur trimmed.

FIGURE 6.4

Two older, more conservative kings on the left from a French manuscript of about 1420 wear ermine fur-lined mantles. A third, younger and more fashionable, king at the right wears a houppelande a mi jambe (mid-calf and also fur-lined) with wide, funnel sleeves, parti-colored hose, and a short, "bowl crop" haircut. (Photograph courtesy, The Pierpont Morgan Library, manuscript M105 f37.)

FIGURE 6.3

Man on stilts wears a cote-hardie, and over his head a chaperon with a long liripipe hanging down the back. The pages of manuscripts were often decorated with playful figures in scenes from games or other aspects of life such as this one. (Photograph from an illuminated manuscript, c. 1350, courtesy, The Pierpont Morgan Library, manuscript G24 f40.)

Styles were either short, to the thighs, or long, for ceremonial occasions. A mid-calf version **houppelande a mi-jamb** (*hoopland-ah-mee-zhamb*) appeared in the 1400s.

Most versions had a high, standing collar that encircled the neck. Collar edges might be dagged or the collar lined in contrasting color. When the houppelande first appeared, sleeves were funnel shaped, with the upper edge ending at the wrist and the lower edge extending, in the most extreme versions, as far as the ground. (See *Figure 6.6*.) Sleeve edges might also be finished in dagging or lined in contrasting color.

For outdoors the garnache, herigaut, and varied capes and cloaks continued in use. Several new forms appeared. One was the **houce** or **housse** (*oose*). In French accounts, the houce is described as a wide-skirted overcoat with winged cape sleeves and two, flat, tongue-shaped lapels at the neck. From descriptions this appears to be a French variation of the garnache, which also had these tongue-shaped tabs. (See *Figure 6.5*.) Another was the **corset** or round cape, which buttoned on the right shoulder and left the right arm free or closed at the center with a chain or ribbon. Round capes ranged from full-length to mid-thigh. Some capes buttoned to close down the front. There were also short, shoulder-length capes. After mid-century many of these were finished at the edge with dagging.

FIGURE 6.5

Man at right wears a garnache or houce, with two, flat, tongue-shaped lapels at the neck. Man at the left wears a cote-hardie with a chaperon. (Photograph from a manuscript c. 1360, courtesy, The Pierpont Morgan Library, manuscript G52 f24.)

HAIR AND HEADDRESS

Hair was cut moderately short, below the ears. Faces were most often clean shaven.

In the first half of the century there were few changes in the styles of coifs, berets, or caped hoods with liripipes. The new styles that appeared were a hat with a low, round crown and an elongated, pointed brim at the front and one with a high, domed crown and small rolled or turned-up brim.

In the second half of the century, hat styles grew more varied and fanciful. Some were made of decorative brocades and trimmed with plumes and colored hat bands. Hoods were transformed into turbanlike styles by varying the way they were worn. The face opening was placed around the head, the cape extended on one side and the liripipe on the other, and both of these could be draped or tied into various positions. (See *Illustrated Table 6.2, page 141*.)

FOOTWEAR

Lower-class men wore stockings that reached to the knee or just below the calf. Long hose were often made in colors that contrasted with rest of costume or might be parti-colored, each leg made of a different color.

Shoes covered the foot entirely or were cut away, closing with a strap over the ankle. Points at toes grew increasingly longer. (See *Illustrated Table 6.2, page 141*.)

Wearing of the **poulaine** (*poo-lan'*) or **crackowe** (*crak'ow*), an elongated, exaggeratedly pointed-toed shoe resumed toward the end of the century. The name derived in French (poulaine) from the word for Poland and in English (crackowe) from the name of the capital city of Poland, Krakow. As has been noted (see *page 106*), the style for pointed-toed shoes had appeared earlier. Some reports place it as early as the 10th century. The lengthy passage quoted in *Chapter 5* describes its use in the 12th century. Some authorities suggest that it traveled to Poland, where pointed toes continued in use while the style was abandoned in the rest of Europe, then returned to western Europe from Poland c. 1360 (Chevalier, *CIBA Review*). Although the toes of all shoes of this period were pointed, only nobles and the rich wore the extreme forms. As one writer put it, "The crackowe was a badge of rank; it was the characteristic of a man whose mode of life did not require him to perform physical labor" (Born, *CIBA Review*). The style was followed in France, England, Portugal, and Spain but never took hold in Italy to any great extent. By 1410 poulaines were out of fashion, but a revival of the style was seen later in the 15th century.

Boots ranged from ankle length to calf length, or extended to the thighs for riding, and included both fitted and loose styles. Working class men wore clogs when weather made streets muddy.

ACCESSORIES

In addition to belts such as those worn with the cote-hardie (see *Illustrated Table 6.2, page 141*), some belts had suspended daggers or pouches for carrying valuables. Gloves were now worn by members of all classes, and were usually cuffed. More elaborate styles were embroidered.

COSTUME FOR WOMEN: 14TH CENTURY

Costume Components for Women: 14th Century

GARMENTS

In English the term gown superseded the term cote. Changes in the first half of the 1300s were mostly confined to alterations of fit with the gown conforming closely to the body through the torso and flaring out to a full skirt below. (See *Figure 6.8* and *Color Plate 12.*)

Surcotes were made with or without sleeves and were worn over the gown as an outer layer. These also followed body contours. One type of surcote was a mark of status. By the second half of the century a traditional form of dress for French royal women had evolved. From this point on to the end of the Middle Ages this garment in painting or sculpture marked the wearer as a French queen or princess. Its major features were:

- **gown**—fitting smoothly through the body and with tight-fitting, long sleeves.

- **surcote**—sideless, with a low décolletage (neckline) giving the appearance of straps across the shoulders. A stiff-

ened panel with a rounded lower edge (in French, the **plastron** and in English, the **placard**) extended to the hip where it joined a wide band encircling the hips to which the skirt was attached.

- **skirt**—so long and so full that it had to be lifted when walking.

- A vertical line of decorative brooches was placed on the front of the placard. (See *Figure 6.6.*)

Adopted for wear by women only after 1387, women's houppelandes reached their fullest development in the 1400s. The English version of the cote-hardie for women had a low, round neckline and sleeves ending at the elbow, with a dangling lappet falling from behind the elbow. (See *Figure 6.7.*) French styles of this garment appear to have been garments for outdoors. Their exact form is unclear. The Italian houppelande seems to have been like that of the English. Pistolese and Horsting (1970) claim that the cote-hardie originated in Italy.

Royal women wore ceremonial mantles for state occasions. They were open and clasped across the front, and worn with a matching gown. Capes, cloaks, and the herigaut were worn for warmth. Fur linings were common for winter, although sumptuary laws attempted to regulate the type of fur that could be used for lining or trimming according to social status. For example, ermine and a fur resembling ermine called lettice were reserved for women of the nobility, while the lower classes were allowed to use fur of foxes, otters, and conys (small burrowing rodents).

HAIR AND HEADDRESS

Hairstyles and head coverings were wide rather than high. The hair of adult women was hidden under a veil or held in-

FIGURE 6.6

Queen Isabelle of England at the center of a manuscript illumination of 1388 wears traditional dress of queens: a sideless surcote over a closely fitted cote. The bodice has a plastron or placard decorated with a vertical row of decorative brooches. King Richard II is shown receiving a copy of a manuscript of Froisart's chronicles from the author. King Charles VI of France, brother of Isabelle greets her and prince Edward whom she holds by the hand. The child is dressed like an adult. The figure behind Queen Isabelle wears a long houppelande with extremely long sleeves. Other men in the illustration wear a variety of doublets and robes. (Photograph courtesy, The Pierpont Morgan Library, manuscript M804 f1.)

FIGURE 6.7

Three women in cote-hardies with sleeves that end in long, hanging lappets. Second quarter of the 15th century. (Photograph courtesy, The Pierpont Morgan Library, manuscript M396 f113v.)

---

side hair nets. If visible, hair was plaited, and either coiled around the ears (first half of the century) or arranged parallel to the vertical direction of the face. (See *Figure 6.6* and *Illustrated Table 6.2, page 141.*) But it was unusual for women's hair to be uncovered.

The barbette with the **fillet** worn during the first part of the century gradually went out of use. The wimple continued in use somewhat longer, but by the end of the century was worn only by widows and members of religious orders. A narrower fillet was worn over a net or, as nets were called, **fret.**

Veils, often held in place by a fillet or chaplet, were not so closely wrapped as in earlier periods. One veil style featured a pleated section of the veil close to the face, which formed a frame for the top and both sides of the face. (See *Figure 6.8.*) Fillets of metal, for royal ladies in the form of a small crown or coronet, were important accessories with all kinds of veils. The inventory of belongings of a French queen of 1372 included 60 such chaplets.

With the ceremonial placarded surcote, royal women arranged the hair in a jeweled net over the ears; a coronet or fillet was set on the head over the net. (See *Figure 6.6.*)

Hoods or wide-brimmed hats were used for bad weather.

FOOTWEAR

Stockings ended at the knee and tied in place. Although women's shoes were similar to those of men, the toes of women's shoes never elongated to the same extent.

ACCESSORIES

Women wore gloves.

JEWELRY

Specific types of jewelry included necklaces, bracelets, earrings, rings, decorative brooches; jeweled belts and buttons and clasps for mantles. (See *Illustrated Table 6.2, page 141.*)

COSMETICS AND GROOMING

Late in the 1300s it became fashionable to have a broad-looking, high forehead, achieved by plucking the hair growing around the face on the forehead. Eyebrows were also plucked. Although not common practices, dyeing the hair, especially to a blonde shade, as well as "face painting" were occasionally reported. In the *Contemporary Comments 6.2, page 132,* an Italian writer, Sacchetti, complains about 14th century fashions.

FIGURE 6.8

Scene from the life of Alexander the Great from a manuscript of the 14th century depicts woman in pleated veil. The man wears a closely fitted doublet and the pointed-toed shoes called poulaines or crackowes. (Photograph courtesy, The Pierpont Morgan Library, manuscript M268 f22.)

COSTUME FOR MEN AND WOMEN: 15TH CENTURY

The styles of the 1400s described in the following section are those of northern Europe, especially France and England. Italian styles of the 15th century will be examined in *Chapter 7*, which deals with the Italian Renaissance, which began in Italy and spread slowly northward.

Variations also existed between styles worn in France and those worn in England. These differences have been attributed not only to the less abundant supply of rich fabrics in England, but also to differences in social organization in these two countries. The French court and the nearby court of Burgundy provided a stage for the display of costume that was not equaled in England. Evans (1969) pointed out, "England had a lower standard of luxury, and the life of its upper classes was based on the castles and manors of the countryside rather than on the court at Windsor or Westminster. Fashions were less splendid and changed less rapidly."

Costume for Men: 15th Century

GARMENTS

The doublet was worn as an underlayer after the first decade of the century and was placed over the under shirt and beneath the jacket. It was short, barely reaching to the thighs and in some cases extending only a little below the waist. Often the sleeves and collars of doublets were the only sections visible. When this was true, these sections were made with decorative fabrics, while plain, less expensive fabrics were used for the invisible body of the garment. Detachable sleeves appeared at the close of the 15th century.

The hose covering the lower part of the body were exposed for almost their whole length. They were constructed in a new form, comparable to modern tights. Into the crotch of this garment a pouch of fabric, called a **codpiece,** was sewn to accommodate the genitals. It tied shut with laces. Hose laced to doublets by means of a series of small eyelets around the lower edge of the doublet and the upper edges of the hose. Points, laces made of leather and with plain or decorated metal tips, connected the eyelets.

For the first two thirds of the 15th century the houppelande continued to be an important garment for men. After mid-century it was called a gown or robe in England. The term does not appear in royal accounts in France after 1470, although it appears often in the reign of Charles VII who died in 1461. (See *Figure 6.9*.)

Houppelandes were fitted across the shoulders, then full from that point. From 1410 to 1440, fullness was arranged all around the body with an equal number of pleats (often two) spaced at the front, back, and each side. After 1440, fullness

FIGURE 6.9

Men and women in a tapestry dated from 1435–1440. Short versions of the houppelande worn by men show a variety of sleeve constructions and include those with slits through which the arm could be placed, leaving the sleeve hanging behind. Women's gowns have V-shaped revers. Elaborately patterned fabrics are used for both men's and women's styles. (Photograph courtesy, The Metropolitan Museum of Art, Rogers Fund, 1909.)

was concentrated at front and back; garments were smooth at the sides. Although the houppelande closed down the front, the fastening was generally not visible.

Sleeve styles were either open at the end or closed at a cuff. Open styles included wide funnel-shaped sleeves (stylish until c. 1450) and plain cylindrical sleeves, often lined in contrasting colored fabric and turned back at the wrist. Closed styles included "bagpipe" shapes (exceedingly popular after 1410) that widened from the shoulder to form a full, hanging pouch below a tight cuff. (See *Figure 6.11*.) After 1445, sleeve caps were given increased height by small pleats. Sleeves narrowed somewhat, tapering to the wrist and hanging sleeves

CONTEMPORARY COMMENTS 6.2

Fourteenth-Century Fashions

Fashions at the close of the 14th century are described by Sacchetti, an Italian writer.

And what more wretched, dangerous, and useless fashion ever existed than that of wearing such sleeves as they do, or great sacks as they might rather be called? They cannot raise a glass or take a mouthful without soiling both their sleeves, and the tablecloth by upsetting the glasses on the table. Likewise do many youths wear these immense sleeves, but still worse is it when even sucklings [infants] are dressed in them. The women wear hoods and cloaks. The young men for the most part go without cloaks and wear their hair long; they need but divest themselves of their breeches and they will then have left off everything they can, and truly these are so small that they could easily do without them. They put their legs into tight socks and upon their wrists they hang a yard of cloth; they put more cloth into the making of a glove than into a hood. . . . The Lord created our feet free, yet many persons are unable to walk on account of the long points of their shoes. He created legs with joints, but many have so stiffened them with strings and laces that they can scarcely sit down; their bodies are drawn in tightly, their arms are burdened with a train of cloth, their necks are squeezed into their hoods and their heads into a sort of nightcap, whereby all day they feel as though their heads were being sawn off. Truly there would be no end to describing the women's attire, considering the extravagance of their dress from their feet up to their heads, and how every day they are up on the roofs, some curling their hair, some smoothing it, and some bleaching it, so that often they die of the colds they catch!

Quoted in *The Portable Medieval Reader,* edited by J. B. Ross and M. M. McLaughlin. 1977. New York: Penguin Books, pp. 168–169.

had either wide or tight-fitting wrists. The wearer placed his arm through an opening above the elbow. The rest of the sleeve then hung down behind the arm.

Houppelandes worn in winter had fur linings. Decorations ranged from dagging to embroidery. Often the garments were constructed from colorful, woven, patterned fabrics. Shorter versions were worn, the lengths ranging from mid-leg (houppelande a mi-jambe) to hip length, though longer styles were more common.

During the early part of the 15th century the cote-hardie was gradually replaced by the shorter houppelande or by an alternative style called a **jacket.** (See *Figure 6.10* and *Color Plate 15.*) For the first part of the century in England the terms jacket and cote-hardie were used interchangeably; after 1450 the term "cote-hardie" was no longer used. In France, the term pourpoint was still applied to what the English called the jacket.

The 15th-century jacket was somewhat similar in function (though not in cut) to the modern suit jacket, although it was worn with hose rather than with trousers. It was the outermost garment worn on the upper part of the body, except for a cape or cloak. The most popular lengths barely covered the hips. In other versions, skirts reached mid-thigh. Whereas short houppelandes went out of fashion, jackets continued to be important garments.

Jackets had vertical pleats at front and back, and shoulders built up over pads to produce a broad, full sleeve cap. Usually collarless, the jacket typically had a rounded neck shaping to a shallow V-shape at front and back; or was cut with a deep V to the waist that was held together with lacings.

Jacket sleeve styles were numerous. Among the various sleeve types were those with shoulders that narrowed gradually to the wrists, full sleeves gathered to small wrist bands, tube shapes with wide turned-back cuffs, and hanging sleeves. Toward the end of the century slashes were made in parts of the sleeves through which the undersleeves of the doublet or shirt were visible.

Although similar in appearance to the short houppelande, the jacket was constructed differently. Jackets had a seam at the waist to join the top and the skirt sections, a feature that houppelandes lacked. The jacket skirt flared out sharply from the hip.

Cloaks or full capes with hoods were the chief outdoor garment for working men. The huke (French, *huque*) was a garment worn by upper-class men. Like the cote and surcote, the huke originated as a covering for armor. It was shaped much like a tabard, being closed over the shoulders and open at the sides. In short versions it had a slit at the front for ease when riding. In longer versions for walking there was no slit. Worn unbelted, belted, or with the belt passed across the front

FIGURE 6.10

Men of all classes, including criminals, are depicted in this scene from a French manuscript of 1480. Fighting men at lower left seem to be wearing padded jackets. Criminals are executed in their chemises or undergarments. Fashionable gentlemen looking on wear robes and jackets cut in many styles. (Photograph courtesy, the Pierpont Morgan Library, manuscript M457 f85v.)

while the back hung free, hukes were more fashionable in the first half of the century than the second. (See *Figure 6.11*.) Shoulder capes and a variety of short capes that were about the same length as the jacket were also part of men's dress for outdoors.

HAIR AND HEADDRESS

Hair was worn in a style frequently described by costume historians as the **bowl crop** because it gives the appearance of an inverted bowl around the top of the head. Below the cut hair the neck was shaved. (See *Figure 6.11*.) After mid-century the shortness of the cut modified somewhat, to be replaced after 1465 by longer styles similar to what in modern terminology would be called a **page boy** cut. Faces were generally clean shaven.

Art of the period depicts an enormous variety of head coverings, many quite fanciful. To describe them all is not possible; however, see *Illustrated Table 6.2, page 141*, for examples of some of the most popular styles.

The coif gradually disappeared except in the dress of clergy and professions such as medicine. Caped hoods went out of style except for country folk, although a number of the hats that developed were derived from hoods.

FOOTWEAR

Lower-class men wore knee or mid-calf length stockings. The preferred leg coverings were hose. Joined hose predominated, although separate hose continued in use. Joined hose made with leather soles were worn both indoors and out. Often dyed to bright colors, many were parti-colored. (See *Color Plate 15*.)

Even though paintings may show hose as fitting the leg quite closely, hose of this period were made of woven cloth, usually wool, and cut on the bias for greater stretch. They were seamed together up the back. Knitted hose did not take the place of woven cloth stockings until the 16th century. Knitted stockings are listed in the records of the English city of Nottingham as early as 1519 and the oldest guild of stock-

FIGURE 6.11

Man at far right wears a huke, open at the sides under the arm. The man at the center wears a houppelande with bagpipe sleeves. The seated figure, a king, wears a robe and mantle. (Photograph of manuscript of 1438, courtesy, The Pierpont Morgan Library, manuscript M442 f1.)

ing knitters was not founded until 1527 in Paris ("The Knitted Stocking," *CIBA Review*).

Foot coverings were pointed, some with exaggerated or piked toes, the length waxing and waning over the century. For the first ten years, while pointed in shape, they were relatively short; after mid-century piked poulaines were revived, persisting in use until about 1480 when shoe forms became more rounded. Very long points were stuffed and stiffened, some even rolled up. As in the 14th century, the extremes of this style were limited to the affluent. Shoes laced or buckled at the side to fit the foot closely.

Pattens were raised wooden platforms (or sometimes leather for the upper classes) that fastened over the shoe with a strap for protection during bad weather. (See *Illustrated Table 6.2, page 141*.)

For general wear boots were close fitting, ended at the calf, and closed with laces or buckles. Long, thigh-length boots with a turned-down cuff at the top that had been worn for riding in the first half of the century became fashionable for general pedestrian wear in the second half.

ACCESSORIES

Accessories included jeweled collars, daggers, pouches or purses (see *Illustrated Table 6.2, page 141*), gloves, and decorative belts. In the first half of the 1400s, a man's belt was one of

his most important possessions, and to deprive a man of his belt was a symbol of degradation. In the second half of the century belts became a less essential part of the costume.

Costume for Women: 15th Century

Terminology tends to become somewhat confusing as styles become more varied and as the same garments are called by different names in different countries. As before, women tended to wear linen undergarments and one or two layers of outer garments.

GARMENTS

The undermost garment for women was called a **smock** or a shift in English; *chemise* in French. (See *Figure 6.12*.)

Women's houppelandes were always long, belted slightly above the anatomical waistline, and had soft, natural shoulderlines, but otherwise were similar in cut to those of men. Collar styles on these garments included high standing collars, usually open at the front to form a sort of winged effect (see *Figure 6.13*), or flat, turned-down collars around a round or V-shaped neckline. Sleeve variations consisted of huge funnel shapes, lined in contrasting colors or fur, and reaching to the ground; bagpipe sleeves; plain tubular sleeves turned

FIGURE 6.12

Detail from a tapestry of the third quarter of the 15th century has a rare depiction of woman and man clad in chemises. Woman's chemise is embroidered at the neck and armscye. Man's garment has embroidery at the armscye. (Photograph courtesy, The Metropolitan Museum of Art, gift of J. Pierpont Morgan, 1907.)

being replaced by a soft, gathered fullness. The bodice developed a deep V, sometimes reaching all the way to the waist, and sometimes not so far. The edges of the V were turned back into revers, which were generally lined in a contrasting color or in fur. The skirt was long and trained, usually so long that it had to be lifted up in front to avoid treading on it when one walked. (See *Color Plate 14*.) Often the skirt was bordered in the fabric of which the revers were made. The deepness of the V generally required that a modesty piece or filler be placed across the bodice. A wide, stiff belt encircled the waist.

In the earliest of these styles, the cut of the bodice was soft with fullness caught in by the belt. (See *Figure 6.9* and *Color Plate 13*.) As the style evolved, the cut became more tailored and the bodice fitted the body more closely. (See *Figure 6.15* and *Color Plate 14*.) When the V shaped revers were set further out on the shoulders, women wore a transparent linen

FIGURE 6.13

Woman's houppelande with fur trimming at the hem (c. 1430). (Photograph courtesy, The Pierpont Morgan Library, manuscript M785 f16.)

back at the end to show contrasting cuffs; or hanging sleeves, usually tubular in shape.

The English used the term gown when referring to women's dresses; the French called this garment a cote or cotte. In one style variation two gowns were worn, one over the other. Gowns were worn with sideless surcotes. In England, where styles generally were less revealing than in France, women wore cote-hardies with hanging tippets, while upper-class women in France appeared in gowns cut with low necks, closely fitted bodices that emphasized the breasts, and full, long skirts (see *Figure 6.14*). Sleeves on dresses might be close fitting from shoulder to wrist or hanging sleeves that were wide, full, and funnel shaped.

Gown styles evolved in the second half of the century. Rigid, tube-shaped pleats disappeared from women's dresses,

FIGURE 6.14

Gown of 1400 shows the low-necked, close-fitting style worn in France at this period. Over it is placed an open mantle. (Photograph courtesy, The Metropolitan Museum of Art, gift of J. Pierpont Morgan, 1916.)

---

fabric piece pinned to the garment at the neckline, shoulders, and back to secure it in place. If one looks very closely at some of the Flemish portraits of the period, one can see that artists often give a hint of this fabric and sometimes depict the pins at the front of the bodices.

The **roc** was a loose-fitting gown. This style appears infrequently, seemingly most often in Flemish and German paintings. The bodice was cut with a round neckline with a cascade of gathers or pleats at the very center of the front and back. Unbelted and made in soft fabric, the dress fell loose and unfitted to the ground. Sleeves were long and fitted or short. When sleeves were short, the gown was worn over a long-sleeved under dress. (See *Figure 6.15* and *Color Plate 15.*) Although this gown appears fairly frequently in northern European paintings, few costume historians discuss it. Even the name, roc, may be another form of the general term **frock.**

Hooded cloaks were worn for bad weather. Open mantles, often worn over matching gowns and fastened with chains at the front, remained unchanged.

HAIR AND HEADDRESS

Unmarried girls, brides, and queens at their coronations could bare their heads and show their hair. All other respectable adult women placed some covering over the hair. High, smooth foreheads, achieved through plucking out the hair, remained popular; therefore little or no hair was visible around the edges of the fanciful headdresses that became fashionable.

For the first half of the century headdresses were wide from side to side. If the headdress did not fully cover the hair, the hair was generally placed in a net. Various structural forms were placed on the head. Often veils were draped over the entire structure. In the second half of the century headdress grew taller. Its size ranged from a flat-topped, high-crowned, brimless hat that was four or five inches high to what has come to be known as the hennin, which was an enormous cone-shaped, peaked hat that was as much as a yard high. This latter style was limited in use to France and Burgundy. See *Figure 6.16* and *page 123* for a longer discussion of the hennin. Veils, ideally sheer and gossamerlike, were pinned and draped over the headdresses.

Illustrated Table 6.1, page 139, depicts the various types of headdress and suggests the way in which headdresses may have evolved in the 15th century.

FOOTWEAR

Stockings, which ended at the knee, tied around the leg. Shoes fitted the foot closely. Although toes were pointed and somewhat elongated, shoes for women never adopted the exaggeratedly piked cut characteristic of some men's shoes. Wooden pattens were worn in bad weather.

ACCESSORIES

Accessories consisted of jewelry, gloves, pouches or purses, and girdles (belts). With lower necklines, necklaces became more important. (See *Figure 6.16* and *Illustrated Table 6.2, page 141.*)

COSTUME FOR CHILDREN:
14TH AND 15TH CENTURIES

What evidence is available shows that throughout the Middle Ages, children, except during infancy, were dressed in the same fashions as adults. The infant was swaddled, wrapped in bands of linen from head to foot. It was believed that swad-

FIGURE 6.15

Women dressed in a variety of styles from the second half of the 15th century, including the full gown, the roc, that appears often in Flemish or German painting. Two of the figures have raised the skirts of their gowns so that the underdress in a contrasting fabric is visible. (Photograph courtesy, The Pierpont Morgan Library, manuscript M222 f39 detail.)

---

dling prevented deformity when the child grew older. There is no clear evidence as to how long infants were swaddled, but apparently the swaddling grew looser as children grew older, and by the time they became more active, the practice was discontinued.

During the first four or five years, both boys and girls dressed in loose gowns. Those of royal children were of rich fabrics, elaborately trimmed. When children were old enough to leave the nursery and take part in the work or other activities of the family, they were dressed as miniature adults. (See *Figure 6.6*.)

Boys' tunics were generally somewhat shorter than those of adult men, except of course in periods when the male jacket became extremely short. Girls always wore long gowns.

The major difference in the dress of girls and women was in the hairdressing. Young girls went about with their hair uncovered until they married.

MOURNING COSTUME FOR MEN AND WOMEN

Special costume practices during the mourning period after the death of an individual were not well established until the close of the 15th century, when the etiquette of mourning became more fixed and elaborated. By the mid-1300s, black had become recognized in northern Europe as a symbol for grief.

Previously a dark drab-colored garment worn with an enveloping dark hood and placed over ordinary colored clothing had been all that was required. The mourner did not have to give up color for a long period of time. A mother of the 1300s is cited as wearing black on the death of her son in the fall, but by the following spring she was dressing in colors again.

FIGURE 6.16

Fragment of a tapestry depicts headdress of men and women of the second half of the 15th century. Woman at center wears a tall, pointed hennin. Man at center of bottom row of figures wears a "sugar loaf" hat. (Photograph courtesy, The Metropolitan Museum of Art, bequest of George Blumenthal, 1941.)

The dress of widows, however, was more fixed by tradition. After secular women gave up the wimple in the 1400s, it was traditional for widows to wear this veil. Bereaved wives also avoided bright hues, often wearing shades such as violet and gray for the rest of their lives.

It was not considered fitting for men to wear the short pourpoint or jacket during the mourning period. Robes had to be long and black. In France the long, hooded cloak was worn by members of both sexes for mourning. Servants of great men were issued these black garments on the deaths of their masters.

COSTUME FOR SPECIALIZED OCCUPATIONS

Student Dress

Toward the close of the Middle Ages, certain items of dress that had once been part of "fashionable" dress, but had since gone out of style, became traditional for particular professions or categories of persons. During the 1400s students retained the cote and surcote after it had been abandoned for general wear.

Illustrated Table 6.1

EVOLUTION AND STYLES OF 15TH-CENTURY HEADDRESS FOR WOMEN

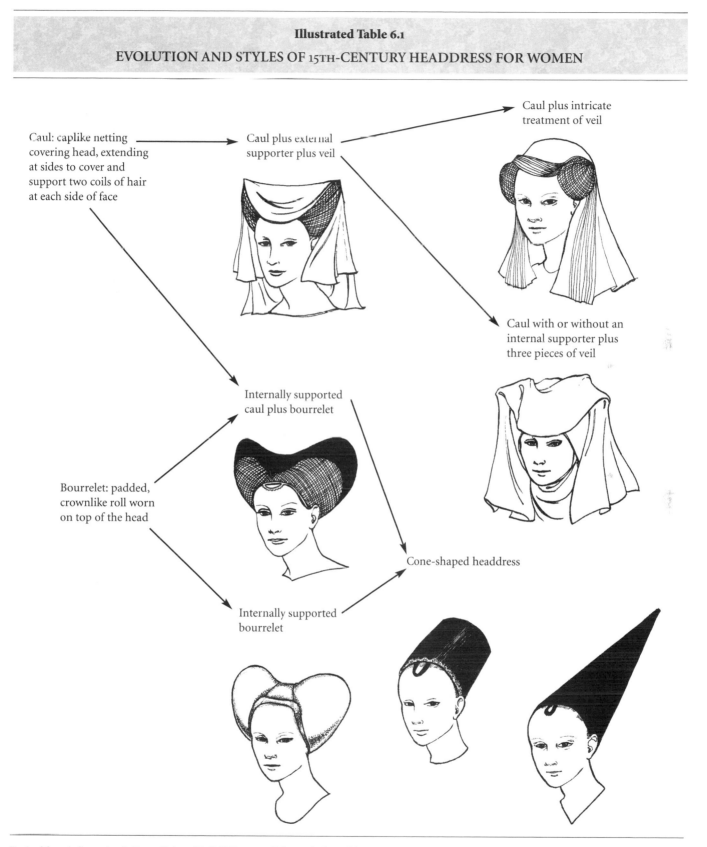

Caul: caplike netting covering head, extending at sides to cover and support two coils of hair at each side of face

Caul plus external supporter plus veil

Caul plus intricate treatment of veil

Caul with or without an internal supporter plus three pieces of veil

Internally supported caul plus bourrelet

Bourrelet: padded, crownlike roll worn on top of the head

Internally supported bourrelet

Cone-shaped headdress

Derived from information in Song, C. A. and L. R. Sibley, 1990. "The Vertical Headdress of Fifteenth Century Northern Europe," *Dress, The Journal of the Costume Society of America*, Vol. 16, pp. 4–15.

A variant of this long robe has been passed down over the intervening years and is still part of official academic dress, worn by students and faculty at graduation ceremonies.

Military Dress

During the 14th and 15th centuries, the chain mail armor that had characterized the armor of the earlier medieval periods was gradually replaced by armor made from large, rigid plates. The first step in this direction came with the development of solid metal defenses for the legs, elbows, and knees. By the third decade of the 14th century, these were universally adopted. Subsequently solid armor for the trunk developed. This was first a cloth or leather garment lined with metal plates, called a **coat of plates.**

About 1350 when a knight put on his armor, he would first don a close-fitting shirt, braies, and hose. His arms and legs would be covered with metal protectors. Then he added a padded undercoat, called a **gambeson** (*gam'bee-sun*), and over this his hauberk (or the shorter coat of mail called the **haubergeon** (*ho'bear-zhun*). Next came a coat of plates, and over all went a surcote, often belted, and a sword belt. When going into action, he added his helmet, and a pair of metal gloves or gauntlets.

The coat of plates, actually a plate-lined, close-fitting surcote, opened in front and fastened with buckles. As Nickel (1991) notes, "Before the development of plate armor, knights charged with their left (shield) side turned toward their enemies. Even after shields were abandoned this practice continued, and impacts of lance and sword were expected to hit primarily on the knight's left side. To let these blows slide off, the left plate had to overlap the right." He concludes that it is likely that the origin of the practice for men's jackets to buckle left over right is to be found in the construction of this garment.

By 1400 the shape of the helmet had become more rounded. It still covered the entire face, but usually had a hinged visor, a face-guard that could be opened. Craftsmen skilled in making armor varied this construction and the shape of helmets according to their individual techniques. Local differences are also evident in sizes, shapes, and construction of all parts of the suit of armor. (See *Figure 6.17*.)

The breast plate and back plate were constructed to protect these areas, and it was a logical step from this point to the complete suit of armor that could be constructed to protect all areas of the body. The armor was worn over a haubergeon

FIGURE 6.17

Complete suit of armor, Italian, 15th century. Mail protection is visible at those areas not covered by the plate armor. (Photograph courtesy, The Metropolitan Museum of Art, Bashford Dean Memorial Collection, gift of Edward S. Harkness, 1929.)

until the second half of the 1400s, when the coat of mail was replaced by an arming coat, a padded coat made with mail in those areas not protected by the armor

Until about 1420 a padded jacket, often sleeveless, was worn over the armor, but after this date "white" armor, or highly polished metal armor, was rarely covered except by a tabard or huke that served to identify the wearer by its colors or decoration.

The forms of armor that developed were many and were varied in their specific construction. For persons interested in further exploration of this topic several books about armor are cited in the bibliography at the end of the book.

Illustrated Table 6.2

LATE MIDDLE AGES ACCESSORIES

Brooches, 15th century

Necklace, c. 1483

Man's belt,
late 14th or early 15th century

Purse, c. 1340

Purse, 15th century

Poulaine, or crakows, 15th century

Wooden clog worn with poulaine
to keep feet dry

Man's hat made from
draped hood,
14th century

Man's hat,
first half of 15th century

Sugarloaf hat,
second half of 15th century

Fillet worn over coiled braids

SUMMARY

VISUAL SUMMARY

The accompanying *Visual Summary* shows the major style changes of the late Medieval period.

THEMES

New costume forms for both men and women, and more distinctions between dress for men and dress for women highlight the theme of GENDER DIFFERENCES in clothing. At the beginning of the 14th century both men and women wore cotes and surcotes that, though different in fit, were not especially different in their basic construction. By the second half of the century men had adopted short styles: the pourpoint and hose. These styles came to men from military dress, an example of the theme of POLITICAL CONFLICT. When contrasted with the long, flowing gowns of women, men's dress served to dramatize SOCIAL ROLE differences between the active life of men and the more passive lives of women. Many historians have pointed out that women of the later Middle Ages had lost many of the economic and social privileges they had in the High Middle Ages. Herlihy (1978) suggests that it was because the life expectancy of women increased in the 14th and 15th centuries. In the earlier periods, because many women died young, the value to society of a young woman of child-bearing age was much greater.

An important theme of the late Middle Ages was FASHION, as the 14th and 15th centuries were marked by increasingly rapid changes in styles. The increased emphasis on fashionable dress was seen in the accession to popularity for men of first the cote and surcote, then the cote-hardie or pourpoint, followed by the long and short houppelande, and finally giving way to the jacket. For women comparable changes in fashion were demonstrated by the popularity of the gown and sideless surcote, the cote-hardie or fitted gown, the houppelande, and finally the high-belted fitted gown of the second half of the 1400s, together with a multitude of changes in headdress styles.

ECONOMIC CHANGES of the late Middle Ages were in large part responsible for an increased interest in fashionable dress. Greater prosperity had brought fashionable clothing within the reach of an enlarging middle class, especially the merchant class. SOCIAL CLASS themes appear as the nobility, wanting to set themselves apart from the newly rich and lower classes, passed sumptuary laws to restrict luxurious dress, but historians tell us that these laws were generally ignored. Increased trade was one of the reasons for the greater prosperity of the period. Trade, with its concomitant CROSS-CULTURAL INFLUENCES, also brought a wide variety of fabrics from all over the world to the population centers of Western Europe. The availability of these fabrics made possible the construction of colorful and elaborate garments characteristic of upper-class dress of this period.

At home, changes in the textile manufacturing processes, an aspect of the theme of PRODUCTION AND ACQUISITION OF CLOTHING, not only led to greater prosperity for the textile trades but also to more variety in the raw materials of fashion. Tailors were gaining skill in cutting and sewing more and more sophisticated garments. (See *Color Plate 17.*)

SURVIVALS OF STYLES FROM THE LATE MIDDLE AGES

Revivals of earlier styles are sometimes intended to make a philosophical statement, rather than to provide a precise reproduction of the earlier style. This is true of the attempt of several groups of artists of the second half of the 19th century to revive medieval styles. These artists believed that craftsmanship of the Medieval period was superior to that of the Victorian era. As part of their attempt to revive interest in an earlier period, which they saw as having superior design values, they also created clothing which was very loosely based on medieval and Renaissance styles. See *page 331* for a fuller discussion of the Aesthetic movement of the 19th century.

Fashion designers of the 20th century often turned to earlier historical periods for inspiration for their designs. One example of a late 20th century style that can be compared to a medieval garment is tights worn as outer garment (see *Figure 6.18*). Hat designers of the 1940s based some designs on medieval hoods. Parti-colored designs, which are referred to in the 1990s as color blocking, appeared from time to time, and in the 1993 fashion design collections, a number of designers cited the Middle Ages as their design inspiration.

c. 1300–c. 1340

Man: cote and surcote, long except for military men. Woman: long cote and surcote. Distinctions between men's and women's dress are minimal

c. 1340–1400

Man: short close-fitting garments (pourpoints, doublets), worn with hose. Long garments, such as the houppelande (see below), still used for some occasions. Woman: Long gowns, closely fitted to the body. Distinctions between men's and women's dress are pronounced.

c. 1340–1400

Women: Sideless surcotes over fitted gowns. Men: Cote-hardie an important garment for working men.

c. 1400–c. 1450

Man: short upper body garments (doublets; jackets) worn with hose. These continue to grow shorter, some ending at the waist.

c. 1400–1450

Houppelande made in full, mid-calf, and short lengths. Women now adopt houppelande. Cote-hardie no longer in fashion.

c. 1400–1500

Woman: Fitted gowns. Distinctions between men's and women's dress clear. Specific details of styles keep changing.

c. 1450–1500

Women: V-necked gowns predominate, but fit becomes less full, bodice has closer fit. Wide belt. Overall styles do not change so much, but details of fit and cut change.

c. 1450–1500

Men: jacket, worn with hose, develops distinctive large shoulder. Long robes also have broad shoulders.

FIGURE 6.18

Tights, a modern version of hose, seen here with a matching long jacket and short skirt made with a looped hem. The overall effect, even to the belt that rides low on the hip of this 1992 design by Valentino, is quite medieval. (Photograph courtesy, Fairchild Publications, Inc., *Women's Wear Daily*, March 18, 1992.)

NOTES

"The Knitted Stocking," *CIBA Review,* No. 106, p. 3800.

Born, W. "The Development of European Footwear from the Fall of Rome to the Renaissance." *CIBA Review,* No. 3, p. 1229.

Boucher, F. 1987. *20,000 Years of Fashion.* London: Thames & Hudson, p. 428.

Chevalier, A. "The Most Important Articles of Dress in the Middle Ages." *CIBA Review,* No. 5, p. 2078.

Cunnington, C. W. and P. Cunnington. 1952. *Handbook of Medieval Costume.* London: Faber and Faber, p. 55ff.

Evans, J. 1969. *Life in Medieval France.* London: Phaidon.

Gies, F and J. Gies. 1994. *Cathedral, Forge, and Water Wheel.* New York: HarperCollins.

Herlihy, D. 1974. "Ecological Conditions and Demographic Change." In D. Molen, ed. *One Thousand Years: Western Europe in the Middle Ages.* Boston: Houghton-Mifflin, p. 34ff.

Herlihy, D. 1978. "The Natural History of Medieval Women." *Natural History,* March, p. 56.

Jirousek, C. 1995. "More than Oriental Splendor: European and Ottoman Headgear; 1380–1580." *Dress,* Vol. 22, p. 22.

Nicholas, D. 1974. "Patterns of Social Mobility." In D. Molen, ed. *One Thousand Years: Western Europe in the Middle Ages.* Boston: Houghton-Mifflin, p. 45.

Nickel, H. 1991. *Arms and Armor.* New York: The Metropolitan Museum of Art Bulletin, p. 15.

Piponnier, F. and P. Mane. 1997. *Dress in the Middle Ages.* New Haven, CT: Yale University Press.

Pistolese, R. and R. Horsting. 1970. *History of Fashion.* New York: John Wiley & Sons, p. 148.

Scott, M. 1996. *A Visual History of Costume: The Fourteenth & Fifteenth Centuries.* London: Batsford.

Wescher, H. "Fashion and Elegance at the Court of Burgundy." *CIBA Review,* No. 5, p. 1842.

SELECTED READINGS

Books Containing Illustrations of Costumes of the Period from Original Sources

The Art of Chivalry. [N. D.] New York: Metropolitan Museum of Art.

Avril, F. 1978. *Manuscript Painting at the Court of France.* New York: George Braziller.

Duby, G., X. B. Altet, and S. G. deSuduiraut. 1990. *Sculpture: The Great Art of the Middle Ages from the Fifth to the Fifteenth Century.* New York: Rizzoli.

Europe 1492. 1989. New York: *Facts on File.*

Evans, J., ed. 1966. *The Flowering of the Middle Ages.* New York: McGraw-Hill.

———. 1952. *Dress in Medieval France.* Oxford: Clarendon Press.

Holmes, B. 1987. *Medieval Pageant.* New York: Thames and Hudson.

Newton, S. M. 1980. *Costume in the Age of the Black Prince.* Totowa, NJ: Rowan and Littlefield.

Nickel, H., et al. 1991. *Arms and Armor.* New York: Metropolitan Museum of Art.

Scott, M. 1986. *A Visual History of Costume: The Fourteenth and Fifteenth Centuries.* London: Batsford.

See also reproductions of *Books of Hours* such as:

* *Tres Riche Heures of the Duc de Berry*
* *Tres Belle Heures of the Duc de Berry*
* *King Rene's Book of Love*
* *The Hours of Anne of Cleves*

Periodical Articles

Abbott, R. 1994. "What Becomes a Legend Most?: Fur in the Medieval Romance." *Dress,* Vol. 21, p. 5.

Bell, C. R. and E. Ruse. 1972. "Sumptuary Legislation and English Costume: an Attempt to Assess the Effect of an Act of 1336." *Costume,* No. 6, p. 22.

Blanc, O. 2002. "From Battlefield to Court: The Invention of Fashion in the Fourteenth Century." In D. Koslin and J. E. Snyder, eds. *Encountering Medieval Textiles and Dress.* New York: Palgrave Macmillan, p. 157.

Dufresne, L. R. 1990. "A Woman of Excellent Character: A Case Study of Dress, Reputation, and The Changing Costume of Christine de Pizan in the Fifteenth Century." *Dress,* Vol. 17, p. 105.

Jirousek, C. 1995. " More than Oriental Splendor: European and Ottoman Headgear; 1380–1580. *Dress,* Vol. 22, p. 22.

Nevinson, J. L. 1977. "Buttons and Buttonholes in the Fourteenth Century." *Costume,* No. 11, p. 38.

Nockert, M. 1987. "The Bocksten Man's Costume." *Textile History,* Vol. 18, No. 2, p. 175.

Parker, L. 1971. "Burgundian Court Costume from a Norwich Tapestry." *Costume,* No. 5, p. 14.

Song, C. and L. R. Sibley. 1990. "The Vertical Headdress of Fifteenth Century Northern Europe." *Dress,* Vol. 16, p. 4.

Staniland, K. 1980. "Medieval Courtly Splendor." *Costume,* No. 14, p. 6.

Van Uytven, R. 1999. "Showing off One's Rank in the Middle Ages." In W. Blockmans and A. Janse, eds. *Showing Status: Representations of Social Positions in the Late Middle Ages.* Turnhout, Belgium: Brepolis.

Daily Life

Britnell, R. 1998. *Daily Life in the Late Middle Ages.* Wolfboro, NH: Alan Sutton.

Duby, G., ed. 1988. *A History of Private Life: Revelations of the Medieval World.* Cambridge MA: Belknap Press of Harvard University Press.

Goldberg, P. J. P. 1992. *Women, Work, and Life Cycle in a Medieval Economy: Women in York and Yorkshire, c. 1300 1520.* New York: Oxford University Press.

Loomis, R. S. 1978. *A Mirror of Chaucer's World.* Princeton, NJ: Princeton University Press.

Newman, P. 2001. *Daily Life in the Middle Ages.* Jefferson, NC: McFarland & Company.

Nicholas, D. 1985. *The Domestic Life of a Medieval City: Women, Children, and the Family in Fourteenth-century Ghent.* Lincoln, NE: University of Nebraska Press.

Rigby, S. H. 1995. *English Society in the Later Middle Ages: Class, Status, and Gender.* New York: St. Martin's Press.

The Secular Spirit: Life and Art at the End of the Middle Ages. 1975. New York: E. P. Dutton.

Tuchman, B. 1978. *A Distant Mirror.* New York: Alfred Knopf.

Virgoe, R. 1989. *Private Life in the Fifteenth Century.* New York: Weidenfeld & Nicolson.

PART THREE

THE RENAISSANCE

c. 1400–1600

Exciting cultural changes began in Italy about mid-14th century when sculptors, painters, and writers began to identify with the ancient civilizations of Greece and Rome. These Italians believed that 1000 years of darkness and ignorance separated the Roman era and their times. They believed that there had been a "re-birth" of classical arts and learning, a Renaissance, a term derived from the Italian word "renascere" meaning to be reborn. Modern historians in general do not consider that there was "re-birth" of the arts, but rather that Europe underwent a chaotic change, a period of profound transition as medieval institutions crumbled and a new society and culture began to appear. The Renaissance could be viewed as a time of transition from the medieval to a modern view of man and the world.

The Renaissance began around the middle of the 14th century in Italy and lasted until the end of the 16th century. Dates assigned to artistic and to costume periods are of necessity arbitrary. In this book, the dates 1400–1600 are assigned to Renaissance costume style. While this is a useful device for separating one period from another, it should be noted that the intellectual and artistic trends leading to the first flowering of the Renaissance style in Italy actually appeared before 1400, during the late Middle Ages. In the preceding chapter, the costume styles of the 15th century in northern Europe have already been discussed as part of medieval styles. Not only do costume and artistic periods fail to fit into neat, clearly defined time periods, they also begin and end at different times in different parts of the world. While the rest of Europe was following a line of political, economic, and artistic development that was an extension of trends begun during the Middle Ages, a new perception of life had begun to emerge in Italy in the 15th century and from there spread to the rest of Europe.

Even during the Medieval period, between 400 and 1300, Italy was in some ways different from the rest of Europe. Its ties with the Byzantine Empire were closer than those of northern Europe. Until the 11th century, northeastern Italy and Sicily were part of the Byzantine Empire. During the Middle Ages, before the economic revival in Europe, urban life in most of northern Europe was severely disrupted, but in Italy urban centers remained more vigorous. Moreover, feudalism had relatively shallow roots in Italy because it flourished best in a more rural society. Italian feudal lords seldom exercised the independent powers of the great barons of France, England, and the Holy Roman Empire. Italian seaports declined to some extent during the early Middle Ages. Nevertheless, owing to Italy's geographical position in the Mediterranean Sea, they continued to carry on overseas trade. Consequently, thanks to a more thriving economy, much of Italy enjoyed a higher standard of living throughout the early Middle Ages than did the men and women living in the more depressed northern lands. There, cities had declined, international trade had slowed to a trickle, and literacy was preserved only in the monasteries.

When the European economic revival began in the 11th century, Italy benefited first. By the 12th century, city-states with large seaports, such as Venice and Genoa, carried on a large volume of trade with the Middle East and with northern Europe. Crusaders bought provisions for their expeditions and sailed from Italian ports for the Near East. In addition, improvements in ship construction allowed the Venetians and Genoese to carry more cargo, and even to sail into the stormy Atlantic Ocean. The money generated by this trade enriched the merchants and rulers of these states with enormous profits. The Italian merchants became financiers and bankers as well as traders, chiefly in textiles.

Not only merchandise but also ideas traveled the routes of trade. The 12th and 13th centuries in Italy witnessed an intellectual ferment that radically altered philosophy, literature, and art in the 14th and 15th centuries. By the 15th century a fresh vitality in the arts and a new attitude toward man and his place in the world had emerged: the Renaissance.

At the same time Europe also experienced a revival of interest in studying and reading the Greek and Roman classics. The learning, the arts, and the philosophy of the Romans and the Greeks had not been lost during the Middle Ages because medieval scholars had continued to study and to read the ancient writers in order that they might know God. Medieval Christianity had emphasized the spiritual, the need for man to prepare himself for the next world. When Renaissance scholars turned to the writings of Greek and Roman philosophers, many of which had been preserved in the monastery libraries, they focused on the humanistic aspect of classical thought, which emphasized the interests, achievements, and capabilities of human beings. From the spirituality of the Middle Ages, artists and scholars turned toward a more secular emphasis on man, his abilities, and his place in the world. Even within the Roman Catholic Church, St. Francis of Assisi and his followers brought a new spirit of emphasis on human and earthly problems.

In the Renaissance, unlike during the Middle Ages when people thought of themselves as part of a social or religious group, there was a strong sense of individualism. Italians with unusual talents were not afraid of being unique. There was a stress on the fullest development of a person's potential whether painter, writer, scholar, or sculptor.

During the 14th and 15th centuries, the Renaissance was largely confined to Italy. The increasing growth of international trade throughout Europe along with contacts between nations that came through warfare promoted the exchange of ideas. Students from northern Europe flocked to Italy to imbibe the learning of the Renaissance and to carry it back to their countries. Kings and wealthy nobles brought back Ital-

ian scholars and artists, and many Italians were given prominent positions at northern courts and in the church. Consequently, during the 15th century the Renaissance in the arts and learning spread into northern Europe. There the new Renaissance learning would strongly influence the challenge to the established religious beliefs that produced the Protestant Reformation.

And it was during the Renaissance that the configuration of present-day Europe as characterized by a number of independent nations gradually became established. During the Medieval period strong nations with distinct national identities and strong hereditary monarchies such as France, England, and Spain had emerged. By the close of the Renaissance in 1600 the general outlines of European nations had begun to emerge. Germany and Italy were exceptions. In Germany the many separate states owed little allegiance to the Holy Roman Emperor, who by this time was always the head of the Austrian house of Hapsburg. Italy also remained a set of independent city-states or territories, which were often under the domination of one or the other of the great European powers.

The styles that developed during the Renaissance in art and architecture, textiles, clothing, music, literature, and philosophy were not forgotten, but continued to influence Western culture. The artistic, literary, and philosophical works of the Renaissance are studied in colleges and universities of the 21st century. The plays of William Shakespeare and Christopher Marlowe are still performed, museums contain large numbers of Renaissance paintings, Renaissance music is performed in concerts, and Renaissance textile designs are often reproduced in fabrics for drapery or upholstery materials or copied for wallpaper designs. Renaissance furniture and architectural styles experienced a number of revivals in the centuries that followed the close of the Renaissance. The term "a Renaissance man" is still applied to the ideal of the cultured, learned person of many talents.

Moreover some of the discoveries and inventions of the Renaissance had a profound impact on the history of subsequent periods. Among the most important of these was the voyage to America by Christopher Columbus in 1492. His discovery opened up new areas of the world for expansion and colonization by European peoples and shifted the center of European economic power away from Italy and the Mediterranean to the Atlantic. These discoveries also opened up new opportunities to make fortunes. The Renaissance also saw a revolution in science, with one of the most revolutionary developments being the theory developed by Copernicus that the earth revolved around the sun.

Another invention with far reaching historical consequences was Johann Gutenberg's invention of printing from moveable type. Heretofore all books had to be hand-lettered or hand printed by a laborious, expensive process. The new method of printing reduced substantially the cost of books, thus making them more readily available and consequently enabling more people to read them.

Although the Chinese, the Hindus, the Greeks, the Arabs, the English, and the Germans all claim to have invented gunpowder, it was only during the Renaissance that it was used as a propellant first in guns and then in cannons, thus helping to end feudalism and begin a revolution in warfare.

CHRONOLOGY

---

c. 1266–1377
Life of Giotto, thought to have changed the course of Italian painting

1304–1374
Life of Petrarch, Italian poet interested in the humanistic approach of the classics

15th and 16th centuries
The Medici, rulers of Florence, encourage the arts through their patronage

1452
Birth of Leonardo da Vinci

1475
Birth of Michelangelo

1492
Italian explorer Christopher Columbus, sailing for Spain, reaches the Americas

1494–1549
The Italian Wars: Northern Europeans contest for control of large parts of Italy

CHAPTER SEVEN

THE ITALIAN RENAISSANCE

c. 1400–1600

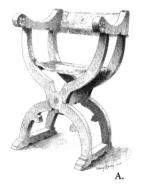

A.

Dante chair

B.

Sgabello chair

C.

Pazzi chapel, Florence, 15th c.

D.

Villa Rotonda, Vicenza, 16th c.

E.

Tomb effigies, Pavia, 16th c.

F.

Chest, 16th c.

Figures A, B from Hart, H. H. 1977. *Chairs Through the Ages, A Pictorial Archive of Woodcuts & Engravings.* New York: Dover, pp. 36, 46. Figure C from Lavisse, E. 1897. *Album Historique, Le Fin Du Moyen-Age.* Paris: Armand Colin & Cie Editeurs, p. 215. Figure D, E courtesy of V. R. Tortora. Figure F from Lavisse, E. 1907. *Album Historique Le XVIII Le XIX Siècle.* Paris: Librairie Armand Colin, p. 87.

HISTORICAL BACKGROUND

Italy had been the center of the largest and most influential of the civilizations of classical antiquity. All around the Italians were imposing ruins, physical reminders of the grandeur of ancient Rome. Roman and Greek manuscripts had been copied by monks and priests, and thereby preserved in the libraries of the monasteries and churches.

The actual cause of a renewed interest in the writings of the Classical period seems to have come from the work of the lawyers and notaries in Italian city-states who looked to Roman law for justification of the independence of these territories. Many of the earliest Renaissance writers, such as Petrarch, a gifted Italian writer who lived from 1304 to 1374, were trained in the law. Petrarch contrasted the humanistic approach of the classics with what he saw as a narrow, academic philosophy in the medieval universities. Others followed Petrarch's lead, and by the early years of the 15th century a revival of interest in the classics in literature and the arts was under way (Gundersheimer 1965).

The Political Organization in Renaissance Italy

At the time of the Renaissance the word "Italy" referred not to a country but to a geographic area made up of a number of small city-states. A powerful prince ruled each city-state. These princes were sometimes members of ancient noble families, sometimes *condottieri* or hired military commanders who had taken over the reins of government in the states that they were hired to defend, and sometimes wealthy merchant families that had come to political as well as financial leadership.

Many of these princes were violent men, oppressive and cruel to their subjects. Others were more benevolent. Fortunately for the advancement of art, many rulers commissioned art works to display their wealth. They dressed lavishly in expensive clothing, and the artists who painted or sculpted their portraits depict these garments in considerable detail.

Even the most benevolent of the princes often engaged in warfare with other princes. And it was this failure to unify under a single leader as had France, Spain, and England that resulted in the loss of large parts of Italy to other nations. From 1494 to 1549 the countryside was the scene of the "Italian Wars," a series of wars for control of large segments of Italy by the northern powers.

At the same time, the occupation of Italy by the northern countries had the effect of spreading the Renaissance more quickly through the rest of Europe. It is from the beginning of the 16th century that the Northern Renaissance is generally dated.

LIFE IN RENAISSANCE ITALY

The population of Renaissance Italy was roughly divided among the aristocracy, the merchant class, artisans and artists, the town laborers, and the peasants of the countryside. Some families owned slaves from Mongolia, Turkey, or Russia. Most of these were women who served as domestic help.

Men of aristocratic or noble families made up the ruling class in most Italian city-states. In some areas, however, merchants had gained great power and political control. These men generally sought to become more respectable by marrying into the noble families. In wealthy or noble families, sons inherited the family wealth. Girls could take only a small portion of the family holdings even if they had no brothers. The family estate passed to the brother of the man who left no male heirs. Much of the family wealth had to be invested in equipping a marriageable daughter with a sufficiently large dowry to enable her to marry well. When a family had been blessed with too many daughters, some of them were packed off to convents where no dowry was required. A woman such as Caterina Sforza (c. 1463–1509), who ruled and defended the town of Forli against the assassins of her husband and later against other attacking forces, was an exception and "existed outside of the general social framework of the Renaissance" (Gage 1968).

Although the merchants were often the wealthiest members of the city population, in some towns they were considered to be of lower status than the aristocracy. This was not so in Florence and Genoa, however, where the ruling families came out of merchant backgrounds. The sons of merchant families were educated to succeed their fathers in running the family business. Most large businesses were in some way related to the textile industry, weaving, dyeing, finishing, or trading cloth. Even bankers had first been traders in cloth.

Skilled artisans could do well and were more fortunate than unskilled laborers, who often had difficulty managing to feed and clothe themselves and their families. The attitude of those who were better off toward these people was expressed by one Matteo Palmieri, a rich merchant who said ". . . If the lowest order of society earn enough food to keep them going from day to day, then they have enough" (quoted in Gage 1968).

At the very bottom of the social scale were the peasants who farmed the land, working on a sharecropping basis with the landowner. Not only were they dependent on the vagaries of the weather, but also their lives were disrupted by the armies that constantly ravaged the countryside fighting for one city or another.

In spite of the economic difficulties involved, many of those from lower levels of society tried to imitate the upper classes in their dress. Records indicate that an enormous number of sumptuary laws regulating dress were passed during this period. The Renaissance author of a book outlining the appropriate conduct for gentlemen put the prevailing attitude of the authorities this way: "Everyone should dress well, according to his age and his position in society. If he does not, it will be taken as a mark of contempt for other people" (Della Casa, *Galatea*, quoted in Gage 1968). The sumptuary laws that can be found in all Italian cities whose archives have survived regulated the numbers of items of clothing an individual could acquire. The **guardaroba** (*gwar-da-ro′ba*) was a set of clothing made up of three garments: two layers of indoor clothing and a mantle for outdoors. (The term is comparable to the word "*robe*" in medieval French.) In middle-class Italian families, one new set of clothing was ordered each year. Discarded clothing was then passed along to the poor either by outright donation or by sale through secondhand clothing dealers (Birbari 1975).

The head of a household had the responsibility for clothing the members of the household, which was usually made up of knights and squires committed to fight for him, pages, grooms, and valets. The mistress of the household had to supply the clothing for her lady attendants.

THE PRODUCTION AND ACQUISITION OF TEXTILES

The Cloth Industries in Renaissance Italy

By the beginning of the Renaissance, Italian textiles were widely used throughout Europe. Wool and silk were the primary fabrics loomed in Italy. Many of the Italian wool fabrics were made from fiber imported from as far away as Britain, but the silk was cultivated locally. Silk, wool, cotton, and linen were used in Italian dress.

A description of the organization of the wool trade in the city of Prato around 1400 provides a brief overview of the production system for textiles. Entrepreneurs, providing the capital and controlling the production, employed a number of different craftsmen and women. Washers and carders prepared the fiber for spinning. Those who spun the yarn, prepared the yarn for the loom, and wove the wool cloth were almost all women working at home. Dyers were members of a cloth guild, and also subject to control by the entrepreneur, while the finishers who did the fulling, clipping, mending, and folding had their own workshops and tools and were more independent (Origo 1957).

Although little documentary evidence exists, most scholars agree that the increase in the complexity of decoration of Italian silk fabrics of the 15th century indicates that improvements in silk weaving looms must have been made at about this time.

Renaissance painters depict many of these luxurious fabrics so realistically that one can identify them as satins, cut velvets, plain velvets, or brocades, simply by looking at the pictures. These fabrics were especially suited to the almost sculptural lines of fashions of the Renaissance in Italy. In pointing out the superiority of Italian textiles and noting that Italy was the center of the most important and luxurious textile manufacture in all of Europe, Birbari (1975) says, "Her [Italy's] woolen cloth was unsurpassed for quality; her woven silks were unique in their splendor." (See *Color Plate 19.*)

Many of these fabrics utilized patterns and decorative motifs that were Chinese, Indian, or Persian in origin, a reflection of the close trading contacts between Italy and the Far East. Some Renaissance painters are thought to have designed textiles; others sketched textile designs to incorporate into their paintings (Herald 1981).

The Manufacture and Acquisition of Clothing

Those who were well off ordered their clothing from tailors, who made garments for both men and women, or doublet-makers, who made men's doublets. Tailoring skills had been refined during the 14th century once tailors had mastered the making of buttoned closures (Herald 1981). (See *Color Plate 17.*)

The less affluent might make their own clothing at home or could purchase used clothing. There was apparently a large market in second-hand clothing and such dealers are listed among the categories of tradesmen. Some ready-made garments may have been available. Paintings do show garments hanging in stalls in the street, but these may have been used clothing.

CROSS-CULTURAL INFLUENCES FROM THE MIDDLE EAST

The Ottoman Turks, conquerors of the Byzantine Empire in 1453, remained a military threat to Austria and eastern Europe until the end of the 17th century. At the same time, because the Turks controlled trade routes to the Orient, treaties were made with the Italians, the French, and later with the English to permit the safe passage of trading caravans through Turkish-controlled lands.

As a result many Italian merchants passed to and from the Middle East, bringing back goods and tales of the Orient. Probably the most obvious influences on fashion that emerged from these contacts were the aforementioned elaborate silk fabrics. The many Eastern-influenced designs probably originated as copies of silk fabrics imported from the Orient. Castiglione, an Italian who wrote a book of advice about courtly behavior, noted that there was no shortage of people who ". . . clothe themselves like Turks" (quoted in St. Clair 1973).

One of the most important styles that seems to have originated in Turkish-dominated lands was the turbanlike hat style that is often seen in the portraits painted by many Italian Renaissance artists. (See *Figure 7.9.*)

SOURCES OF EVIDENCE ABOUT COSTUME

The Renaissance artist painted realistically, and this realistic approach extended into the representation of clothing. Not only are the external folds and draping of the garment shown, but the artist also depicts gussets, eyelets for laces, and even the wrinkles on a pair of ill-fitting hose. (See *Figure 7.4.*)

In addition to the pictorial and sculptural representations of costume, some actual items of dress remain. Written documents such as letters, diaries, and inventories of personal possessions shed some light on the quantity as well as the variety of garments commonly owned. The first books about costume were printed in the 16th century. Several books by Venetian authors depict authentic contemporary dress along with some historic and foreign costumes that scholars have found to be at the best inaccurate and at the worst, imaginary. A passage that gives a contemporary comment on dress is reproduced on *page 156.*

Drawing conclusions about dress from the costumes on certain of the religious figures depicted by Renaissance artists requires caution. The Virgin Mary is almost always dressed more conservatively and less fashionably than other women. A veil usually covers her hair. Angels are frequently dressed in what appears to be a Renaissance version of the Greek chiton. Figures from classical mythology are garbed as the Renaissance artist believed ancient Greeks and Romans dressed. Furthermore, Newton (1975), in her extensive study of Renaissance theatrical costume, argues persuasively that figures such as the Wise Men in the Christmas story are shown wearing the types of clothing worn by actors in religious pageants, rather than realistic costume of the time.

COSTUME FOR MEN AND WOMEN: 1400–1600

Costume for Men: 1400–1450

Italian costume of the first half of the 15th century had many of the characteristics described in *Chapter 6* for the rest of Europe. (See *Figure 7.1.*) A few differences can be noted.

Many doublets worn with hose were knee length, not so short as in the north. Hukes were placed over doublets. Whether they were long or short, most houppelandes had either wide, funnel-shaped or hanging sleeves. Although they were pointed, Italian shoe styles did not have the extreme piking seen in other parts of Europe. Although hair was cut short, the bowl cut does not seem to have been adopted in Italy.

Costume for Women: 1400–1450

Many houppelandes for women had imaginatively cut sleeves. Foreheads were bared and fashionably high, as in the rest of Europe, but Italian women covered their hair less completely than women elsewhere. A distinctive Italian women's headdress style of the second quarter of the century was a large, round, beehive shaped hat. (See *Figure 7.1.*) These headcoverings were somewhat turbanlike, possibly a reflection of contacts with the Middle East.

About the beginning of the second half of the century, Italian costume and that of Northern Europe diverged, with distinct differences evident until the early 1500s. Neither the V-necked gown with wide revers nor the tall hennin, with which it was so often worn in France and Flanders, spread to Italy. The houppelande was supplanted by new and distinctly Italian styles, although even within the Italian styles regional variations were evident, especially in Venice.

Costume for Men: 1450–1500

The components of men's costume in Italy from 1450 to 1500 will not be new to readers. They are the same as those discussed for men in *Chapter 6, pages 131–134,* and include linen drawers, undershirts (the Italian word for shirt was **camicia**[1] (*cah-mee′cha*), doublets to which hose were attached, and outer jackets. Italian versions of these garments show some stylistic differences from those worn elsewhere at the same time, as well as similarities.

GARMENTS

Worn next to the skin as an undergarment, shirts were visible at the edges or openings of the outermost garments. Lower-class men sometimes wore only shirts and underpants for hard labor. (See *Figure 7.2.*) Shirts were made of coarse, heavy linen for lower-class men, and finer, softer linen for upper-class men. Sleeves and body were cut in one piece with gussets (small triangles of fabric) inset under the sleeve to permit ease of movement. Lengths ranged from between waist and hip to above the knees. (See *Figures 7.2 and 7.3.*)

[1] The Italian word for a man's shirt and the word for a woman's chemise are the same: camicia. The plural form of camicie is camecie (*ca-mee′chay*).

FIGURE 7.1

Costume of men and women in Italy in the first half of the 15th century. Female figures at the lower left-hand corner of the painting are wearing houppelande-style gowns with long, full sleeves. The edges of the sleeves are finished in dagging. The sleeves are lined in a contrasting fabric. They wear the high, round, beehive-shaped headdress favored by Italian women of the second quarter of the century. Just above and to the right are two men wearing knee-length jackets with full, hanging sleeves. Their hose are slightly piked. Men in fashionable dress in the rest of the picture wear variations of the same style in jackets; and a variety of fashionable hats. Monks, priests, and nuns are dressed in typical religious garb. Angels wear slightly bloused outer tunics that derive from ancient Greek and Roman styles. (*Paradise*, by Giovanni de Paolo; photograph courtesy, The Metropolitan Museum of Art, Rogers Fund, 1906.)

CONTEMPORARY COMMENTS 7.1

Appropriate Attire for a Renaissance Court

The Courtier, a book published in 1528, the author Baldassare Castiglione instructs readers in appropriate attire for a Renaissance court and comments on the importance of dress in making an impression on others.

. . . I should prefer them not to be extreme in any way, as the French are sometimes in being over-ample and the Germans in being overscanty—but be as the one and the other style can be when corrected and given a better form by the Italians. Moreover, I prefer them always to tend a little more toward the grave and sober rather than the foppish. Hence, I think that black is more pleasing than any other color; and if not black, then at least some color on the dark side. I mean this of ordinary attire, for there is no doubt that bright and gay colors are more becoming on armor, and it is also more appropriate for gala dress to be trimmed, showy, and dashing; so too on public occasions, such as festivals, games, masquerades, and the like. For such garments, when they are so designed, have about them a certain liveliness and dash that accord very well with arms and sports. As for the rest, I would have our Courtier's dress show that sobriety which the Spanish nation so much observes, since external things often bear witness to inner things.

. . . what I think is important in the matter of dress, I wish our Courtier to be neat and dainty in his attire, and observe a certain modest elegance, yet not in a feminine or vain fashion. Nor would I have him more careful of one thing than of another, like many we see, who take such pains with their hair that they forget the rest; others attend to their teeth, others to their beard, others to their boots, others to their bonnets, others to their coifs; and thus it comes about that those slight touches of elegance seem borrowed by them, while all the rest, being entirely devoid of taste, is recognized as their very own. And such a manner I would advise our Courtier to avoid, and I would only add further that he ought to consider what appearance he wishes to have and what manner of man he wishes to be taken for, and dress accordingly; and see to it that his attire aid him to be so regarded even by those who do not hear him speak or see him do anything whatever.

I do not say . . . that by dress alone we are to make absolute judgments of the characters of men, or that men are not better known by their words and deeds than by their dress, but I do say that a man's attire is no slight index of the wearer's fancy, although sometimes it can be misleading. . . .

Castiglione. *The Courtier.* Translated by C. S. Singleton. 1959. Garden City, NY: Anchor Books, pp. 121, 122–123.

Doublets ended anywhere from the waist to below the hip. In longer lengths, doublets were sometimes cut with a small skirt. Four seams (front, back, and both sides) allowed for a close fit. (See *Figures 7.2* and *7.3*.) Doublets (and jackets) often had a distinctive neckline finish that displayed the high level of skill of Italian tailors. At the front, the garments appear to have a collarless neckline. At the center of the back a deep U-shaped piece was cut out. Into the U-shaped opening was inserted a curved, U-shaped piece with a straight top edge. The result was a neck edge that stood away from the neck, and a smooth unwrinkled back to the doublet from waist to neck without using darts or gathers. (The man at the far left of *Figure 7.3* wears a garment with this design feature.)

Hose, which were tied to the doublet, were cut either as two separate pieces or seamed together at the crotch. Doublet and hose were worn by working men and soldiers. By the end of the century fashionable young men began to wear the doublet and hose without an outer jacket. Most hose were still apparently made from woven fabrics and cut in the bias direction. Tight lacing of hose to the doublet helped attain a smooth fit, but hampered physical activity. Renaissance painters frequently depict men involved in physical activity with their laces untied and their hose hanging loosely at the back. (See *Figure 7.2*.)

Around mid-century, jackets fitted smoothly through the torso. They had a flared skirt that attached at the waist and ended below the hip. In the last half of the century, jackets were usually fitted over the shoulders and upper chest, then fell in full pleats from a sort of yoke. Fullness was belted in at the waistline. (See *Figure 7.4*.) Toward the end of the century sleeveless jackets, looking much like hukes, were seamed at the shoulder and open under the arms. Full and pleated, this

FIGURE 7.3

A variety of different jacket, doublet, and sleeve styles. Figure on the left wears a dark red doublet with fitted sleeves under a jacket of green with hanging sleeves. The doublet sleeve is slit at the back seam and the edges of the split tied together with laces. A thin line of white from his camicia shows at the opening. The figure behind him wears a doublet of dark blue with a sleeveless hukelike jacket that is belted. The sleeve of the doublet is full to the elbow, where it gathers to fit the tight lower portion of the sleeve which closes with a row of small buttons. The man emerging from the well wears a jacket with a full sleeve gathered to fit the armscye then narrowing gradually to the wrist. The standing figure wears the hukelike jacket over a green doublet. His flat, round hat is typical of the period as are the hairstyles of all men. (Photograph courtesy, Edizione Alinari.)

FIGURE 7.2

Workman. This laborer wears his jackets open and detached from his hose in order to allow him to move freely. Under his jacket one can see his camicia, and at the hip, under his camicia, one gets a slight glimpse of his short drawers. The loosened hose are rolled below the knee and over the hose he wears shoes, probably leather, that come to the ankle. (Photograph courtesy, Edizione Alinari.)

version was worn belted or unbelted. (See the second man from the left in *Figure 7.3*.)

Sleeve styles were among the distinctive aspects of Italian styles. Their construction could be quite complex. Sleeves tended to become more fitted in the second half of the century, and identifiable sleeve types seem to show a type of evolution. Early in the century, the sleeves were cut in two sections. One section was full and somewhat puffed from shoulder to elbow, and the other section was fitted from elbow to wrist. (See *Figures 7.2* and *7.3*.) Slightly later, one-piece sleeves were full at the shoulder and tapered gradually to the wrist. (See *Figure 7.3*.) Even later, sleeves narrowed to fit

appeared mostly in costume for ceremonial occasions. Jackets with hanging sleeves were worn over doublets so that the sleeves of the doublet were exposed. (See *Figure 7.3.*)

Ceremonial robes worn by state officials and lawyers were usually full-length gowns. Placed over doublet-and-hose and jacket as a third, outermost layer, robes often had hanging sleeves.

For outdoors and for warmth, men wore open and closed capes. These always covered the jacket completely, varying in length to correspond with the length of the jacket. Often they were trimmed in fur or lined in contrasting colors. (See *Figure 7.5.*)

HAIR AND HEADDRESS

Younger men cut their hair in medium to longer lengths that tapered gradually from below the ears in front to about the shoulders in the back. Hair might be either straight or curly. Older men cut their hair shorter. Men were generally clean shaven.

FIGURE 7.4

Bowman in the entourage of the Medici princes wears a green, pleated jacket. His undershirt is visible at the neckline of his jacket, and his hose are parti-colored. Detail from painting c. 1460 by Benozzo Gozzolo of the *Journey of the Magi.* (Reproduced courtesy, Alinari Art Resource, NY.)

smoothly for the length of the arm. If sleeves were too tight to allow easy movement, one or more openings were left through which the long, white shirt sleeve could be seen. Some ways of permitting this ease included leaving seams open at various places and closing them with laces, or making a horizontal seam at the elbow and leaving it open at the back where the elbow bends. (See *Figure 7.3.*)

Attachment of sleeves could be done either by sewing them into the body of the doublet or jacket or by lacing them into the armhole. The fabric of the camicia was then pulled through the openings between the laces to form decorative puffs. If laced, sleeves were interchangeable from one garment to another.

Hanging sleeves that were generally nonfunctional, purely decorative, and attached to the jacket were still seen. This style

FIGURE 7.5

Saint Anthony distributing his wealth to the poor, painted by Sassetta, second quarter of the 15th century. This painting contrasts the ragged, torn clothing of the poor, dressed in long gowns, with the fashionable, fur-trimmed costume of the Saint. Children are dressed as the adults, except that the skirt of the boy's garment is short. (Photograph courtesy, The National Gallery of Art, Samuel H. Kress Collection. 1952.)

A variety of hat styles are seen in paintings, including turbanlike styles, brimless pillbox styles, either soft or rigid high toques, and hats with soft crowns and upturned brims or round crowns and narrow brims. (See *Illustrated Table 7.1, page 162.*)

FOOTWEAR

Pointed toes begin to round off at the front toward the end of the century. Leather soled, footed hose were by far the most popular footwear for men. When worn, shoes fitted closely and were cut high across the instep, and below the anklebone. Boots, generally worn for out-of-doors in bad weather or for riding, tended to have turned-down cuffs and ended at mid-calf.

Costume for Women: 1450–1500

The most common combination of garments for women during the Italian Renaissance was a chemise worn as an undergarment beneath a dress, and a second overdress on top. There are also a number of examples of women's dress in which only the chemise and an outer dress are worn.

GARMENTS

The chemise, called a **camicia** in Italian, was made of linen. The quality of the fabric of which it was made varied with the status of the wearer. The fullness of the cut related to the weight of the fabric, with sheerer fabrics being cut more fully. A camicia was made full length, to the floor. Sleeves were generally long; some were cut in raglan style (i.e., seams running from below the arm at front and back to the neck rather than being set into the armhole). In the last part of the century, large sections of the neckline of the camicia were displayed at the necklines of gowns and fine embroidery, bindings, smocking, or edgings were added. (See *Figure 7.9.*) Although the camicia was an undergarment, peasant women are shown in some paintings wearing camicie to work in the fields, and apparently during hot weather women wore the garment in the privacy of their own quarters.

Lavish use of opulent fabrics for the dresses of upper-class women gave garments of relatively straight cut a splendid appearance. By carefully manipulating the layers of camicia, dress, and overdress and choosing contrasting fabrics for each layer, rich decorative effects were achieved.

Dresses without an obvious overdress were usually either straight from shoulder to hem with a smooth-fitting, yokelike construction over the shoulder, which opened into full pleats or gathers over the bustline. These full gowns we generally belted. (See *Color Plate 18.*) Alternatively, gowns could be made with a bodice section joined to a full gathered or pleated skirt. These dresses usually closed by lacing up the front and also sometimes at the side. (See woman at bottom left, *Figure 7.6.*)

At mid-century necklines were usually rounded, but cut relatively high. Toward the end of the century necklines tended to be lower, some more square than round, or with deep Vs held together by lacing that showed off the upper part of the chemise.

When two layers of dresses were obvious, underdresses were usually made with bodices and skirts joined. They were fitted fairly closely and were visible at the neckline, sleeves, and/or under the arm of the outer dress. Outer dresses were often cut like a man's huke, i.e., sleeveless, seamed at the shoulders, and open under the arm to display the underdress. (See *Figure 7.6.*)

Sleeve styles for women were similar to those for men. The most common forms were sleeves that were wider above the elbow and fitted below (see woman in background of *Figure 7.6*), or close fitting sleeves with openings to display the sleeves of the camicia (see *Figure 7.7*), or hanging sleeves. (See *Color Plate 18.*)

Mantles or capes worn outdoors were both open and closed, often lined in contrasting fabric and sometimes matching the dresses with which they were worn. A purely decorative cape, fastening to the dress at the shoulder but not covering the shoulder or upper arms, and extending into a long train at the back was also used.

HAIR AND HEADDRESS

A major distinction is seen between Italian hairdressing and that of northern Europe. While northern European women covered the hair, Italian women arranged their hair elaborately, wearing a "token" head cover in the form of a small jeweled net set at the back of the head or a sheer, small veil. (See *Figure 7.6.*) Young girls dressed their hair simply, curled into long tresses. Women placed a loose, curling tress on either side of the face and pulled the rest into a bun or a long braid or made more elaborate arrangements that combined braids, loops of hair, and curls. (See *Figure 7.7.*)

FOOTWEAR

Rarely seen in paintings, women's shoes appear to have been cut along the same lines as those of men.

JEWELRY

Highly skilled jewelers created masterpieces from precious stones, pearls, gold, and silver. They made necklaces, earrings, brooches, and interesting hair ornaments. One of the latter that became especially popular was a chain or band of metal or pearls worn across the forehead with a jeweled decoration located over the center of the forehead. This chain was called a **ferroniere** (*fehr′ ohn-yair*). (See *Illustrated Table 7.1, page 162.*)

COSTUME FOR MEN AND WOMEN: 16TH CENTURY

The distinctiveness of Italian costume persisted until about midway through the 16th century, after which, except for women's dress in Venice, styles became subject to Spanish and French influences as a result of the occupation of large areas of Italy by

FIGURE 7.6

Domestic scene following the birth of a child shows women dressed in a variety of costumes. To the far right are two women, one an older woman in a simple dress and mantle with a white veil over her head. To her left a fashionable matron in a brocade outer gown worn over a gold gown which can be seen at the neckline and at the end of the sleeves of the outer gown. The third figure to the left, a young woman, wears a fashionable under gown of blue brocade with red flowers. At the elbow of the sleeve and down the lower part of the arm her camicia is visible through the slits in the sleeve. Her sleeveless outer gown is of pink brocade and open at the sides. She carries a handkerchief. Her hair, which is uncovered, is of the fashionable blond shade. Other women in the room all wear two-layered gowns except for the mother whose camicia is visible at the neckline of her simple blue gown. The dress of the wet nurse, seated at the center, opens down the front so she can suckle the baby. The laces that close the dress of the seated figure at far left are visible under the arm. She, too, wears a split sleeve with her camicia bloused through below the elbow. Her mantle, the lining of which matches the sleeves of her under gown, has slipped off her shoulders and fallen to the ground. She wears a small, sheer cap denoting her status as a young matron. (Photograph courtesy, Edizione Alinari.)

these two powers. Venice remained independent, and Venetians continued to wear some styles that had unique qualities.

Costume for Men: 16th Century

GARMENTS

White linen camicie often had embroidered necklines and cuffs. Black work, a black-on-white Spanish embroidery, was especially popular. (See *Figure 8.10, page 182.*)

Over the camicia a man placed a close-fitting doublet that was sometimes worn without a jacket to create an extremely narrow silhouette. This style persisted only until shortly after the end of the first decade, after which men's doublets became fuller, though never so full as in France, England, or the German lands. Some had deep, square necklines to show off embroidered camicie. Decorative slashing, sometimes with puffs of contrasting fabric pulled through the slits, was more restrained than in other parts of Europe. (Contrast *Figure 7.8* with *Figure 8.3, page 176.*) Some jackets had short

FIGURE 7.7

Portrait of Bianca Maria Sforza, painted about 1493 by Ambrogio de Predis. The jeweled haircovering reveals more of the hair than was customary in northern Europe. The dark band that crosses her forehead is a ferroniere. Puffed areas of a white camicia, show through the openings where the sleeve and the bodice lace together and at the back where the two sides of the close-fitting sleeve are laced together. A fine black line running from behind the neck to under the neckline probably marks the edge of the sheer fabric of the camicia, which is so fine that it seems to be transparent. (Photograph courtesy, The National Gallery of Art, Washington, DC, Widener Collection.)

sleeves, ending just below the shoulder line, which allowed a contrast between the jacket and the sleeve of the doublet. (See *Figure 7.8.*) Hose, which were attached to doublets, had a distinct, usually padded, codpiece.

The introduction of a codpiece into joined hose had been a practical solution to making the hose fit properly and to enable men to relieve themselves. But by 1500, the codpiece had grown to enormous proportions and had become a very obvious feature of men's clothing. (See *Figure 7.8.*) Vicary

(1989) suggests that this feature may have been a response to an epidemic of syphilis in Europe that began about 1494 and spread rapidly. She notes that treatment of the disease required the use of medications that would have stained the clothing, and that a padded codpiece would have provided protection. In explaining why the style was so widespread, she argues that because of the social stigma attached to this illness, almost universal adoption of the codpiece made it impossible to single out individuals as being infected. The codpiece disappeared in the later 16th century, Vicary says, possibly because as the population built up some level of immunity, the epidemic subsided.

HAIR AND HEADDRESS

Men began to wear beards again.

FIGURE 7.8

Portrait of Lodovico Capponi by Agnolo Bronzino, middle of the 16th century. A row of buttons closes the closely fitted black jacket. The jacket sleeves end just below the shoulder, so that the slashed sleeves of the doublet are visible. At the wrists and around the neck, the edges of the camicia are visible. A prominent codpiece is seen at the top of the paned trunkhose. (Photograph courtesy, The Frick Collection, New York.)

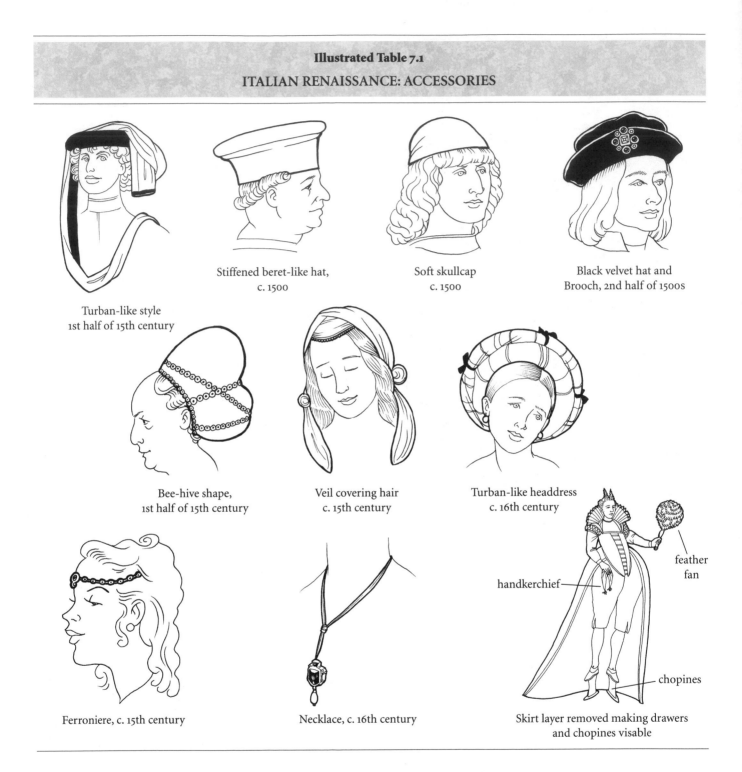

Illustrated Table 7.1

ITALIAN RENAISSANCE: ACCESSORIES

Turban-like style
1st half of 15th century

Stiffened beret-like hat,
c. 1500

Soft skullcap
c. 1500

Black velvet hat and
Brooch, 2nd half of 1500s

Bee-hive shape,
1st half of 15th century

Veil covering hair
c. 15th century

Turban-like headdress
c. 16th century

Ferroniere, c. 15th century

Necklace, c. 16th century

handkerchief

feather
fan

chopines

Skirt layer removed making drawers
and chopines visable

Costume for Women: 16th Century

GARMENTS

Camicie were sometimes cut high, to show above the neck-line of the gown. (See *Figure 7.9.*) Sometimes this was just high enough to form a small border at the edge of the neckline. Camicie were often embroidered or otherwise decorated, and sometimes finished with a small neckline ruffle.

Silhouettes of dresses grew wider and fuller. (See *Figure 7.9.*) Bodices became more rigid, a reflection of the increasing Spanish influences on Italian styles. Square, wide, and low necklines predominated. Sleeves widened. Often they had a full, wide puff at the top, and were more closely fitted from above the elbow to the wrist. Many were decorated with puffs and slashes. Waistlines were straight in the early part of the century. Spanish-influenced V-shapes in the front gradually began to appear as the century progressed.

HEADDRESS

Turbans became quite fashionable. (See *Figure 7.9.*) The turban style derived from Turkish headdress and reflected Italian trading contacts with the Turks of the Ottoman Empire.

FIGURE 7.9

A young woman and her little boy by Agnolo Bronzino, first half of the 16th century. The woman's decoratively embroidered camicia extends well beyond the neckline of her red brocade dress, and the ends of the camicia sleeve can be seen at her wrist. The turban-like headdress was especially popular at this time. She carries a pair of gloves in her hand, which at this period were often perfumed. (Photograph courtesy, The National Gallery of Art, Washington, DC, Widener Collection, 1942.)

REGIONAL DISTINCTIONS IN COSTUME FOR MEN AND WOMEN: 15TH AND 16TH CENTURIES

Basic clothing forms (i.e., layers worn, construction techniques, etc.) were similar in the various city-states of Italy, but regional difference did exist. The clearest and most distinctive differences were evident between the costumes of Venice and those of other parts of Italy, particularly those of areas under Florentine influence.

Distinctive Venetian Costume for Women

Venetian women of the 15th century wore gowns with the waistline located just below the bosom. Fabrics utilized appear to have been less heavy and rigid than in other regions. **Chopines** (*sho'peen*), very high platform-soled shoes, were worn throughout Italy and in northern Europe, but visitors to Venice reported that those worn in Venice were exceptionally high. Women bleached their hair to light blonde shades. Drawings of women also showed them wearing underdrawers, garments that were not common elsewhere in Europe until later centuries. (See *Figure 7.10* and *Illustrated Table 7.1, page 162.*)

By the last half of the 16th century, Venetian gowns typically had normal waistlines in back, and dipped to a deep U-shape in front. Women arranged their hair at the front above the forehead in little, twin "horns." This style also appeared in some other parts of Europe, but it seems to have been most extreme in Venice. Chopines grew even taller.

The description of Venetian styles by an English traveler who visited Venice in the 16th century is reprinted on *page 164.*

Distinctive Venetian Costume for Men

Venetian men of the 15th century wore garments with waistlines located at the anatomical waist or slightly below at the back, V-shaped in front. Long outer tunics were preferred to jackets, although jackets were also worn.

By the 16th century men's dress in Venice, like the styles for men elsewhere in Italy, was being influenced by Spanish and French styles.

Venetian Dress for Officials

The Doge, the highest official in Venice, together with an hereditary ruling class of nobles, wore a long-established, traditional long robe with wide sleeves. The wider the sleeve, the more important was the rank. Colors varied according to rank

CONTEMPORARY COMMENTS 7.2

Dress of Venetian Women

A Frenchman, Villemont, visiting Venice toward the close of the 16th century described the exaggerated forms of these styles worn by Venetian women:

They have their blond hair for the most part hanging nicely and arranged at the forehead in the shape of two horns half a foot high, without any iron mounting or any other thing to hold them up, unless it were the charming braiding which they do themselves . . . They apper a foot taller than the men because they are mounted on patens of wood covered with leather, which are at least a foot high so that they are obliged to have a woman to aid them walk, and another to carry their train . . . But the Romans, Milanese, Neapolitans, Florentines, Ferrarans and other ladies of Italy are more modest, for their patens are not so high, and also they do not bare their breasts.

Quoted by H. K. Morse, 1934. *Elizabethan Pageantry.* New York: Studio Publication, p. 19.

and office. The Doge's headdress was worn over a coif and had something of the shape of a Phrygian bonnet, the point at the back stiffened and rigid. (See *Figure 7.11*.) Venetian nobility did not give up these costumes until the 18th century.

COSTUME FOR CHILDREN DURING THE ITALIAN RENAISSANCE

Once out of swaddling clothes, children started to wear clothing that was not distinctive from that of adults. The numerous paintings of the Madonna and infant Jesus confirm this. In some paintings the Christ child wears a camicia, in others a loose-fitting under tunic and an over tunic. Boys of nursery years wore skirts; older boys wore doublets, jackets, and hose. Little girls wore dresses similar to those of older women. (Compare *Figures 7.9* and *7.12*.) (See *Color Plate 19*.)

FIGURE 7.10

Venetian women in a painting by Carpaccio wear typical high-waisted Venetian women's dresses. Notice the high-soled chopines visible just in front of the peacock. Their hair is of the fashionable blonde color. (Photograph courtesy, Museo Correr, Venice.)

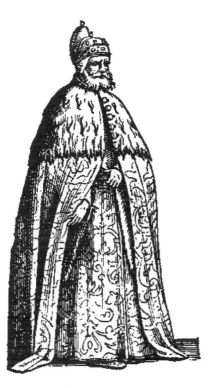

FIGURE 7.11

Costume of the Doge of Venice. Drawing was made in the 16th century, but the style of the garments is of much earlier origin. Under his fur-trimmed cape it is possible to make out wide sleeves. On his head is the traditional Phrygian-style bonnet. (Reproduced from *Vecellio's Renaissance Costume Book*, first published in 1598 and reprinted by Dover Publications, Inc., 1977.)

FIGURE 7.12

Child in costume of the early 16th century. Compare this to the dress worn by the woman in Figure 7.9 in order to see how similar were the costumes of adults and children. The full, puffed sleeve at the shoulder joined to a section that fits the rest of the arm. The edge of her camicia is just barely visible around the square neck of the dress. Even the type of jewelry she wears is similar in its type and arrangement to that of the adult woman. (Photograph courtesy, Photo Arts.)

SUMMARY

THEMES

The history of Italian dress is marked throughout by the theme of CROSS-CULTURAL INFLUENCES, many of which resulted from POLITICAL CONFLICTS or POLITICAL ALLIANCES between the Italian city states and France and Spain. In the first half of the 15th century, fashions were clearly shaped by the International Gothic style, and in the northwestern regions influences from neighboring French and Burgundian regions were especially prominent.

Styles in Italy during the last half of the 15th century differed markedly from those of northern Europe. The distinctions were evident in the cut of clothing and in the types of fabrics used. Here, too, design motifs from the Far East can be seen in elaborate brocades, attractive cut velvets, and other sumptuously decorated textiles produced by Italian weavers, as well as in individual items of dress such as the turbanlike headdresses favored by Italian ladies.

These costumes developed at a time when a new and independent spirit in the arts, literature, and philosophy was abroad in Italy. Moreover, ECONOMIC CHANGES brought powerful families, many of them merchants, to levels in the SOCIAL CLASS STRUCTURE where they could purchase luxurious clothing and accessories. Such materials were readily available through industries focused on the PRODUCTION OF TEXTILES, an important theme in Italian Renaissance dress.

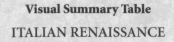

Visual Summary Table

ITALIAN RENAISSANCE

Man: 1400–1450
Doublet and hose

Woman: 1400–1450
Houppelandes and fitted gowns

Man: 1450–1500
Doublet under skirted
jacket and hose

Woman: 1450–1500
Gowns worn either as a single layer or two layers

Man: (c. 1510) 1500–1550
Clothes grow wider, often
decorated with puffs and slashes

Woman: 1500–1550
Gowns are full, have puffed
sleeves; are decorated with
puffs and slashes

Man: 1550–1600
Silhouette widens, jackets take
on rigid shape, puffs and
slashes increase

Woman: late 1500s
Spanish influences appear
in more rigid bodices,
V-shaped waistlines

The **ARTS AND THEIR RELATION TO DRESS** are notable because painters originated designs for textiles and for actual garments worn in pageants and theatrical presentations. The arts, too, made a most important contribution to costume history as **SOURCES OF INFORMATION ABOUT COSTUME.** Depictions by artists clearly show details of the actual construction of dress and of daily life as they portrayed individuals from a wide range of social classes.

CROSS-CULTURAL themes return to the fore in the 16th century when Italy was overpowered by the Spanish, the French, and the Austrians and the period of innovation in dress ended. Foreign influences came to dominate the Italian city-states. After 1500 fashions took on a more international cast. This was a result not only of the imposition of foreign rule on most parts of Italy, but also of the increasing movement among peoples and the improvements in **COMMUNICATIONS** that took place throughout Europe in the 16th century.

SURVIVAL OF ITALIAN RENAISSANCE STYLES

The textile designs for which Italian Renaissance weavers were famous have had a lasting impact not only on clothing for luxury garments, but also on fabrics for interior design. Fortuny, a textile and fashion designer of the early 20th century, based many of his textile designs on these fabrics. (See *pages 363–365.*)

Another area in which Renaissance designs frequently exert strong influence is that of jewelry. The ferroniere, often seen in Renaissance portraits, appeared again in the Romantic and Crinoline periods of the 19th century.

The high, platform shoes called chopines never again reached such dramatic heights, but platform soles in shoes did return. Their most notable revivals were in the period of World War II, the 1960s, and again in the 1990s and after.

NOTES

Birbari, E. 1975. *Dress in Italian Painting 1460–1500.* London: John Murray. See for a fully developed discussion of realism in depicting costume in Italian renaissance paintings.

Gage, J. 1968. *Life in Italy at the Time of the Medici.* New York: G. P. Putnam's Sons, p. 179.

Gundersheimer, W. L. 1965. *The Italian Renaissance.* Englewood Cliffs, NJ: Prentice-Hall, p. 6.

Herald, J. 1981. *Renaissance Dress in Italy 1400–1500.* Atlantic Highlands, NJ: Humanities Press.

Newton, S. M. 1975. *Renaissance Theatre Costume.* New York: Theatre Arts Books.

Origo, I. 1957. *The Merchant of Prato.* New York: Alfred A. Knopf.

St. Clair, A. N. 1973. *The Image of the Turk in Europe.* New York: The Metropolitan Museum of Art, p. 11.

Vicary, G. "Visual Art as Social Data: The Renaissance Codpiece." *Cultural Anthropology.* 1989, Vol. 4, No. 1, p. 3.

SELECTED READINGS

Books Containing Illustrations of Costume of the Period from Original Sources

Birbari, E. 1975. *Dress in Italian Painting, 1460–1500.* London: John Murray.

Brock, M. 2002. *Bronzino.* Paris: Flammarion.

Christiansen, K. 1983. *Early Renaissance Narrative Painting in Italy.* New York: Metropolitan Museum of Art Bulletin, Vol. XLI, No. 2.

Herald, J. 1981. *Renaissance Dress in Italy, 1400–1500.* New York: Humanities Press.

Ketchum, R. M. et al. 1961. *The Horizon Book of the Renaissance.* New York: American Heritage.

Waugh, E. S. 2001. *Art in Renaissance Italy. 1350–1500.* New York: Oxford University Press.

Also see any of the many books of reproduction of works of art by Italian Renaissance artists, especially Bronzino, Carpaccio, Ghirlandaio, Piero Della Francesca, Pisanello, and the like.

Periodical Articles

Bridgeman, J. 1992. "Belle Considerazioni: Dress in the Works of Piero della Francesca." *Apollo,* No. 136 (368), p. 218.

Deruisseau, L. G. "Extravagance in Renaissance Dress." *CIBA Review,* No. 2, p. 604.

———. "Velvet and Silk in the Italian Renaissance." *CIBA Review,* No. 2, p. 595.

Newton, S. M. 1971. "Homage to a Poet." *Metropolitan Museum of Art Bulletin,* August/September, p. 33. (This article is an analysis of the costume in a painting by a Renaissance artist in order to determine whether the painting was done by a follower of the master Giorgione.)

Daily Life

Chamberlin, E. R. 1965. *Everyday Life in Renaissance Times.* New York: G. P. Putnam's Sons.

Cohen, E. S. and T. V. Cohen. 2001. *Daily Life in Renaissance Italy.* Westport, CT: Greenwood Press.

Gage, J. 1967. *Life in Italy at the Time of the Medici.* New York: Putnam.

Mee, C. L. Jr. 1975. *Daily Life in Renaissance Italy.* New York: McGraw-Hill.

Origo, I. 1957. *The Merchant of Prato.* New York: Alfred Knopf.

Pierotti-Cei, L. 1987. *Life in Italy During the Renaissance.* Geneva: Liber.

Rabb, T. 2001. *Renaissance Lives: Portraits of an Age.* New York: Basic Books.

CHRONOLOGY

1509
Henry VIII becomes king of England

1517
Martin Luther's debate with the Roman Catholic Church begins

1519
Charles V elected Holy Roman Empire, thus adding rights over Germany and
northern Italy to his rule of Spain, the Low Countries, and Austria
Death of Leonardo da Vinci in France

1535
Reign of Suleyman the Magnificant, Sultan of the Ottoman Empire, begins

1542
Death of Francis I and accession to throne of his son Henry II
brings Italian influences to court through his wife Catherine de Medici
First European contact with Japan by Portuguese sailors

1543
Nicholas Copernicus publishes *Revolution of the Heavenly Bodies*

1547
Henry VIII dies and his son Edward becomes Edward VI

1553
Death of Edward VI brings Mary Tudor to the throne

1556
Charles V abdicates, dividing his territories between his son Philip
(Spain, Low Countries, and the New World) and his brother
Ferdinand (Austria and the Holy Roman Empire)

1557
Portuguese settlement in Macao establishes contact with Chinese

1558
Queen Elizabeth I succeeds to the throne on death of Mary Tudor

1560–1589
France wracked with religious strife

1564
Death of Michelangelo

1578
Spanish lose control of the Dutch Provinces

1589
Henry of Navarre becomes King Henry IV of France

1590
Shakespeare begins writing plays

1603
Death of Elizabeth I of England

CHAPTER EIGHT

THE NORTHERN RENAISSANCE

c. 1500 — 1600

A.

A.

Elizabethan house

B.

Elizabethan wainscot chair

C.

Tudor chair

D.

Château des Tuileries, 16th c.

E.

Table, 16th c.

F.

Painting by Breugel, *The Harvesters*, c. 1559

Figure A from Harris, C. M. 1977. *Illustrated Dictionary of Historic Architecture*. New York: Dover, p. 191. Figures B, C from Hart, H. H. 1977. *Chairs Through the Ages, A Pictorial Archive of Woodcuts & Engravings*. New York: Dover, pp. 23, 22. Figures D, E from Lavisse, E. 1907. *Album Historique Le XVIII Le XIX Siècle*. Paris: Librairie Armand Colin, p. 237. Figure F courtesy of the Metropolitan Museum of Art (19.164).

HISTORICAL BACKGROUND

By the beginning of the 16th century, northern Europe had experienced a gradual transition to participation in the new spirit of the Renaissance. Along with these changes in arts and letters came profound changes in religious attitudes, which culminated in a revolution against the Roman Catholic Church. This revolution, the Protestant Reformation, had a major impact on the European nations and split Europe into two hostile religious camps. It began in the German states of the Holy Roman Empire.

The Hapsburg territories, the Low Countries, and Spain came under the rule of one man, the Emperor Charles V (1500–1558), at the beginning of the 16th century. From his grandparents he inherited a vast array of lands and claims. From his paternal grandfather, Emperor Maximilian, he inherited the Hapsburg lands, including Austria, and from his grandmother, Mary, the Burgundian lands, including the Low Countries. From his maternal grandparents, Ferdinand of Aragon and Isabella of Castile, he received Spain and the Spanish empire in America as well as the kingdoms of Sicily, Naples, and Sardinia. In 1519, after having inherited all of these lands and kingdoms, Charles V was elected Holy Roman Emperor and thus gained imperial rights over all of Germany and northern Italy. At the age of 19, he ruled over a larger territory than any ruler had ever attempted to govern.

So vast a territory made up of such a variety of peoples and lacking geographical unity was difficult to rule effectively. Moreover, the extent of Charles's empire meant that he was continually involved in wars with rival monarchs who feared Hapsburg domination of Europe. Eventually Charles found his burden so heavy that he abdicated. In 1556 he divided his territories between his brother Ferdinand (1503–1564), who received Austria and the Holy Roman Empire, and his son Philip (1527–1598), who inherited Spain, the Low Countries, and the New World.

Developments in Germany

German artists, rejecting the Gothic style of the Medieval period, adopted the new Renaissance forms. Scholars turned toward an interest in science, philosophy, and morality. The artistic and intellectual ferment of the Renaissance in Germany coincided with an increasing dissatisfaction on the part of many people with certain practices within the Roman Catholic Church. This dissatisfaction culminated in the Protestant Reformation.

Among the major causes of the Reformation in Germany were papal financial abuses (profiting financially from religion), corruption and moral laxity among some of the clergy and religious orders, and the secular spirit of the Renaissance. The study of the Bible from the original sources led to dissatisfaction with medieval Catholic theology and a growing nationalism rejected the political influence of the papacy. The printing press played a major role in the Reformation because it became easier to publish and disseminate the arguments of the reformers, including the first translation of the New Testament into German.

The translator was Martin Luther (1483–1546), a priest and university professor, who became the spokesman and theorist for the dissenters. Luther would not have succeeded without the support of local political leaders who saw in religious dissent an opportunity to break away from the control of Charles V, who was Catholic. The leaders also recognized the opportunity to confiscate the great wealth of the Christian church in Germany. Luther's argument with the Church began in 1517; it soon spread throughout much of Europe. And with it, as often enough happens, came war and revolution.

Developments in Spain

Areas of Spain, which had been under control of the Moors from northern Africa until late into the 15th century, were finally united in the late 1400s under Ferdinand and Isabella. (She is famous as the patroness of Columbus's voyage to the New World.) Charles V inherited the Spanish throne in 1506.

As a result of its exploitation of the American territories, which Spanish explorers had conquered, Spain became incredibly wealthy from the influx of gold and silver from Mexico and Peru. Spain dominated Europe because of Charles' political interests in so much of Europe and the wealth acquired through trade in goods from the Americas. The 16th century could well be called "The Golden Age of Spain." But the wealth proved a curse. There was so much gold that Spain suffered inflation, and the gold was spent on the expensive foreign wars of Charles V. When the wealth was exhausted, there was nothing left for the Spanish people.

Charles was a devout Catholic, and Spain the most orthodox nation in Europe. Consequently the Reformation had little effect on Spain. Nevertheless it prevented Charles from maintaining control over the Holy Roman Empire and preserving the unity of the Christian faith in Europe. The strain of attempting to maintain the empire led Charles V to abdicate the throne of Spain and the Low Countries in favor of his son, Philip II. A fervent Catholic who bore proudly the traditional title of the Spanish monarch, "The Most Catholic King," Philip II antagonized the 17 prosperous provinces that made up the Low Countries by levying high taxes and by the appointment of haughty Spanish administrators. Moreover, he stationed Spanish troops among them, and attempted to repress Protestantism, which had made deep inroads among the people of the Low Countries. In 1568 revolution had broken out, and by the end of the century, Philip had lost the seven northern provinces that formed the Dutch Republic or Holland. Again Philip failed in 1588 when he dispatched the ill-fated Armada of 130 ships to conquer England and restore that land to the Roman Catholic faith. His intervention in the

French religious wars also failed. The increasing decline in Spanish political influence helped to contribute to the end of the "Golden Age" of Spain.

Developments in England

The 16th century in England was divided between the great Tudor monarchs Henry VIII (reigned 1509–1547) and his second child Elizabeth I (reigned 1558–1603). Henry split with the church of Rome over the Pope's refusal to permit him to divorce his Spanish Queen, Katharine of Aragon, to whom he had been married for 18 years. Because Henry and Katharine had only one sickly daughter, Mary Tudor, Henry had unsuccessfully sought a divorce in order that he might remarry and father a male heir to preserve the Tudor line. Breaking with Rome, Henry established a national Church of England, but maintained the basic beliefs and practices of the Roman Catholic faith. During the short reign of his son Edward VI (reigned 1547–1553), the child of his third marriage, England became Protestant. Mary Tudor (reigned 1553–1558), who succeeded Edward, tried and failed to restore England to the Church of Rome. After Mary's death, Elizabeth became queen.

Henry's reign saw the climax of the Gothic style in England and the beginning of the English Renaissance. During the Elizabethan era, England enjoyed a literary Renaissance, chiefly in dramatic poetry. English theater was born in the Renaissance thanks to dramatists such as William Shakespeare, Christopher Marlowe, and Ben Jonson. Shakespeare surpassed his contemporaries with the vast range of his plays—comedies, topical dramas, histories, profound tragedies—and filled them with characters who became immortal. Elizabethan music profited from the genius of Thomas Tallis and William Byrd.

Both Henry and Elizabeth brought painters and sculptors to England from other parts of Europe to decorate their palaces. Elizabeth, who was well educated and enjoyed reading Latin verse, was praised in Edmund Spenser's great epic poem filled with national feeling, "Faerie Queene." She patronized the arts, thereby stimulating music and literary productions.

Developments in France

During the first half of the 16th century, the French Renaissance in the arts began under the monarch Francis I (reigned 1515–1547). He invited Italian artists and artisans—including Leonardo da Vinci and Benvenuto Cellini—to the French court to work. His son, Henry II, married an Italian, Catherine de Medici, who brought her Italian tailors and dressmakers, perfumers, cooks, and other craftsmen to France where they found ample opportunity to employ their talents. Catherine's Italian perfumers are said to have started the French perfume industry.

After her husband's sudden death in 1559, and the death of her son Francis II, in 1560, Catherine became the regent for her weak son, Charles IX, remaining the power behind the throne until 1588. In the reigns of Charles IX (reigned 1560–1574) and his brother Henry III (1574–1589), France was wracked by religious civil war as powerful Protestant and Catholic noble families struggled for political control. Catherine helped create a climate of revolt and political dissension for most of the rest of the century by throwing the royal support behind the Catholic faction.

The accession of the Protestant Bourbon Henry IV (1589–1610) brought an end to religious persecution of the French Protestants. To appease the Roman Catholics who were in the majority, Henry IV converted to Roman Catholicism and settled the religious problem by issuing the Edict of Nantes guaranteeing freedom of conscience and full political rights to all Protestants. In the economic sphere, Henry encouraged French industry, and the cloth industries especially benefited. French linen rivaled that of Holland, and her silk weaving industry challenged what had formerly been an Italian monopoly on the manufacture of silk.

FACTORS IN THE DISSEMINATION OF FASHION INFORMATION

One of the factors in the spread of fashion information from one part of Europe to another was the intermarriage of the royal families from different countries. These marriages were usually arranged to cement alliances between two powers, and the brides were sent from their own countries to their new homes equipped with not only a substantial dowry, but also a trousseau of the latest fashions and accompanied by a group of fashionably gowned ladies-in-waiting. Table 8.1 highlights the intermarriages between royal families during the 16th century and illustrates the cross-influences of styles that accompanied such weddings.

The intermarriage of members of royal families from one country with those of another was only one of the ways that fashion information could be spread from one locality to another. Other sources of fashion information included imported garments and fabrics, books dealing with costume, and travelers who brought back information about and examples of foreign styles. Peasants tended to use functional and simple clothing rather than fashionable dress, but among the upper classes a more or less internationalization of styles occurred in which the predominant silhouettes and features had substantial similarities. At the same time, distinctive local styles often traveled abroad, as this 16th century poem attests (quoted in Chamberlin 1969):

Table 8.1
ROYAL INTERMARRIAGES DURING THE 16TH CENTURY

England and Scotland	France	Spain	Austria-Germany	Italy
Henry VIII		Katharine of Aragon	Anne of Cleves	
	Henry II			Catherine de Medici
Mary, Queen of Scots	Francis II			
Mary I of England		Philip II		

Behold a most accomplished cavalier,
That the world's ape of Fashion doth appear.
Walking the streets his humours to disclose,
In the French doublet and the German hose,
The muff, cloak, Spanish hat, Toledo blade,
Italian ruff, a shoe right Flemish made.

CROSS-CULTURAL INFLUENCES FROM THE MIDDLE EAST

Francis I of France had found it politically expedient in the early 1500s to make an alliance with Sultan Suleyman, leader of the Ottoman Turks. Although the Turks still menaced eastern Europe, other European powers interested in stimulating trade with the Orient also made treaties. Style ideas brought back by diplomats, merchants, and travelers from the Middle East entered the European courts. The first illustrated travel book showing Middle Eastern scenes and styles appeared in 1486.

The Turks were viewed as fierce and exotic. Ballets, masques, and dramas featured Turkish characters, but often portrayed them in a derogatory manner. Nonetheless, their costume fascinated many in Europe, although direct influence on fashion appears to have been somewhat limited. In 1510 the English Earl of Essex appeared at a banquet dressed in what was described as "Turkish fashion." He wore long robes powdered with gold, a hat of crimson velvet with great rolls of gold (probably like a turban), and two scimitars (curved, Turkish-style swords) (St. Clair 1973). There is one portrait of Henry VIII of England dressed in what appears to

be a Turkish robe, and some researchers believe the garment called the **ropa,** a loosely fitted overdress, derives from Middle Eastern styles.

TEXTILES

Changes in Technology

Only a few advances in textile technology took place during the 16th century. A treadle-powered spinning wheel in combination with a device called a bobbin-and-flyer mechanism made spinning easier. Some sources credit Leonardo Da Vinci with this invention; others say he simply sketched what he had seen in use. The device speeded up the process of spinning by doing away with the necessity of stopping to wind up the yarn after each length was spun. It was improved by a German inventor and came into use in the mid-1500s.

Hand knitting seems to have begun in Europe only after the 15th century. By the latter part of the 16th century it was being used to make stockings. When an inventor, William Lee, sought a patent for a knitting machine for stockings in 1589 Queen Elizabeth refused the patent because she feared it would put the hand-knitters out of business, so Lee took his invention to France (Derry and Williams 1961).

Decorative Techniques of the 16th Century

The 16th century brought new techniques for decorating fabrics into style. Embroidered decorations were applied not only to outer garments, but also to visible neck and sleeve edges of undergarments such as shirts and chemises. (See *Figure 8.1* and *Color Plate 20*.) **Spanish work,** an especially fashionable embroidery, originated in Spain and spread throughout the rest of Europe. This embroidery consisted of delicate black silk figures worked on fine, white linen, often being applied to the neck band and wrists of men's shirts and women's chemises. (See *Figure 8.9*.)

A variety of Italian drawn and cutwork techniques were also employed. Threads were removed from the fabric and embroidery applied to the now open areas. Cutwork was created by embroidering designs on solid cloth, then cutting away sections of the cloth between the decorations. In another decorative technique called **filet** or **lacis,** the artisan embroidered patterns on a net background. Both cutwork and filet are considered to have been forerunners of lace.

Lacemaking probably began in Europe just before the beginning of the 16th century. **Lace** differs from either cutwork or filet in that it is constructed entirely from threads, dispensing with any backing fabric. Two types of lace were made: **needlepoint lace,** which seems to have originated in Italy, and **bobbin lace,** which may have originated in the Low

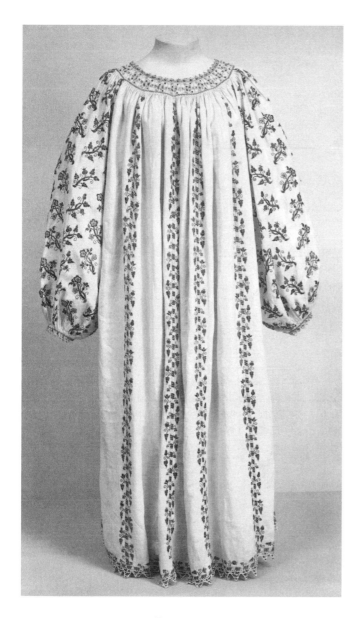

FIGURE 8.1

Woman's chemise from the late 16th century, probably from Venice. The white linen garment is embroidered with lavender floss silk and gold thread. Notice that the placement of embroidered designs on this chemise is similar to those on the neck and sleeves of the chemise in Figure 8.9. (Photograph courtesy, The Metropolitan Museum of Art, gift of Mrs. Edwin O. Holtzer, 1941.)

lace to decorate garments of both men and women was almost universal. (See *Figures 8.7, 8.10,* and *8.12.*)

SOURCES OF EVIDENCE FOR THE STUDY OF COSTUME

Art

Art is the primary source of information about what people wore in the 15th century. Portraits, drawings, and tapestries abound, and from these one can gain a wealth of information about upper class dress. A number of books about costume were published; however, these tend to mix accurate and inaccurate drawings and must be approached with care.

Documentary Sources

Scholars can find many more inventories and other documentary records for the 1500s than for earlier periods. Such records can confirm or supplement evidence from portraits. Nevinson (1968), for example, compared the portrait of Prince Edward (see *Figure 8.14*) to royal household accounts of the time. He concluded that the portrait was a reasonably accurate representation of the Prince's clothing. He also noted that the household accounts also provided information about the undergarments and types of fabrics that was not clear in simply viewing the portrait.

Actual Garments

Costume historians also have access to more surviving garments from the 16th century. The illustrations in this chapter include several examples. Such materials help enormously in learning about details of clothing construction and cut.

COSTUME FOR MEN AND WOMEN: 16TH CENTURY

The speed with which styles changed continued to increase in the 16th century. Costume of men and women in this century can be said to have gone through three different phases. In each phase, styles differed markedly from the preceding phase. The general dates of these phases, however, are not the same for the dress of women and men. Moreover, styles of accessory items and underclothing did not necessarily vary as the overall silhouette did. For these reasons the summary of details of costume in this chapter is organized as follows: cos-

Countries. Needlepoint lace is made by embroidering over base threads arranged in a pattern, and connecting these base threads with a series of small intricate stitches. Bobbin lace, also called **pillow lace,** created a complex pattern by twisting or knotting together a series of threads held on bobbins. These laces could be made of any fine thread—linen or silk or cotton. During the last half of the 16th century the use of

tume for all three phases will be discussed first for men, then for women, and finally accessory items for men and women will be given a century-long overview.

The three phases seen in men's styles might be summarized as consisting of an early phase in which a transition was made from medieval styles to the styles of the Renaissance (c. 1500–1515); a second phase concentrated in the second to the fourth decades of the century in which strong German influence can be seen (c. 1515–1550); and a final phase in which Spanish influences predominated (1550–1600).

Throughout the century men wore an evolved form of the earlier braies, which the English tended to refer to as **drawers.**

Costume for Men: 1500–1515

GARMENTS

Shirts, made of white linen, were cut full and gathered into a round or square neckline. The neckline was often decorated with embroidery or cutwork. Shirts had long, raglan sleeves.

Doublets and hose were laced together, the doublet being only waist length. Hose were seamed into one garment with a codpiece at the front. (See discussion of origin of the codpiece in *Chapter 7, page 161.*) In one version the doublet (also called a **paltock** in England) was cut with a deep V at the front, which sometimes had a filler (or **stomacher**) of contrasting color inserted under the V. (See *Figure 8.2.*) Laces

could be used to hold the open area together, and also to hold the sleeves in place. Following the Italian styles, sleeves of shirts were bloused through openings in the sleeves.

Jackets, sometimes worn over doublets and cut the same length, were like doublets in shaping. They were made either with or without sleeves. In England the term **jerkin** was used synonymously with the word jacket after 1500. Often it is difficult to make out from period illustrations whether men's outermost garments are doublets or jackets, especially after bases gained in popularity.

Bases were separate short skirts worn with a jacket or doublet for civil dress or over armor for military dress. Made from a series of lined and stiffened gores (wedge-shaped pieces), bases persisted in civilian dress until well into the mid-century, and over armor for even longer. (See *Figure 8.2.*) The term probably derives from the fact that this was the lower part, or the "base" of the jacket. The term seems to have been applied to this lower section of the garment and also to separate skirts that became popular in the early 16th century. The metal skins of some suits of armor are made to simulate bases. It was not uncommon for armor to incorporate details of contemporary fashion for men.

Gowns or robes were long, full garments with huge funnel-shaped or large hanging sleeves that opened down the front. The front facings were made of contrasting fabric or fur and turned back to form wide, decorative revers. Younger and more fashionable men wore shorter gowns, ending below the

FIGURE 8.2

Lady with Three Suitors, France, c. 1500. The two more visible suitors wear, respectively, a short jacket with wide lapels and a skirt or bases, and a long robe. Both dress their hair in the predominant straight-cut style and wear French bonnets. Their shoes have broad, rounded toes. The lady wears a wide-sleeved gown with a typically square-cut neckline. Her headdress is a coif with lappets hanging down on either side of the face. (Anonymous artist, pen and brown ink, brown wash, over traces of black chalk, 23 × 19.3 cm. © The Cleveland Museum of Art, John L. Severance Fund, 1956.40.)

hips. Gowns were worn over doublets or jackets. (See *Figure 8.2.*) This garment seems to have been distinctively northern European and had no precise counterpart in Italian styles. In a painting by the Italian artist Carpaccio, dated from the first part of the 16th century, entitled "Reception of the English Ambassadors," and set in Venice, the ambassadors are clearly distinguishable by their robes.

Circular cloaks, open at the front and with a slit up the back to facilitate horseback riding were worn over doublets and hose for warmth out-of-doors.

Costume for Men: 1515–1550

Whereas the earlier styles had relatively slender silhouettes, the second phase emphasized fullness in the construction of the costume with large, bulky, puffed areas. Garments were ornamented with decorative **slashings** or **panes** (narrow strips of fabric), under which contrasting linings were placed. (See *Figure 8.3* and *Color Plate 20.*)

This story is told of the origins of these slashes. A ragged but victorious Swiss army was said to have stuffed the colorful silk fabrics they had looted from the enemy camp under their badly torn clothes for warmth. This impromptu fashion was supposedly picked up and imitated by the general population. Whether the style actually had its origin in this way or not, it is true that the Swiss and German soldiers' uniforms were made with multi-colored fabrics and decorated with a variety of cuts and slashes, panings, and layers. These same features were evident in men's costume almost everywhere, although German influences were more muted in Italy. Reade (1951) suggests that these garments may have had a practical value as well, allowing men to lift and swing heavy weapons without placing too great a strain on the seams.

GARMENTS

Shirts, doublets, and jackets continued much as before, with marked increases in the aforementioned slashed decoration. Instead of having separate bases, some doublets and jackets were cut with gored skirts. Some had no sleeves; some had wide U- or V-shaped necklines beneath which the wide neck, the doublet, and part of the shirt were often visible. Bases were still worn with armor. Sleeves of the outermost garment were cut very full, often with a puff from armhole to elbow and a closer fit from elbow to wrist. (See *Figure 8.4.*)

Men held up their hose by lacing them to the doublets. Some hose were divided into two sections: **upper stocks** and **nether stocks,** which were sewn together. (See *Figure 8.3.*) Codpieces, the pouches of fabric for the genitals sewn at the front of the upper stocks, were sometimes padded for emphasis. (See *Figure 8.3.*) Although upper stocks and nether stocks continued to be attached, upper stocks (also called **breeches**) eventually took on the appearance of a separate garment, and were cut somewhat fuller than the lower section. Style variations included long breeches, fitting the leg

closely and ending at the knee, and breeches ending at the hip and more rounded. Any of these variations might be paned, with contrasting fabric placed beneath the panes.

Slight alterations in cut and trimming of gowns or robes made them wider. Wide revers extended into a wide collar. Sleeve types included those that were sleeveless but with wide, extremely deep armholes lined in contrasting fabric and turned back upon themselves to show off the lining. Other sleeves were short, very full, puffed-and-slashed or paned sleeves (see *Figure 8.4*), or long, hanging sleeves.

Costume for Men: 1550–1600

By mid-century the width of the shoulders had narrowed somewhat and during the remainder of the century one can see gradual decreases in the width of the shoulders and gradual increases in the width of the hip area. By the beginning of the third phase a new combination of garments had evolved, and men no longer appeared in short jackets or longer skirted jackets and hose. Instead the upper hose and nether hose had evolved into a large, padded breech (called **trunk hose**), which was joined to nether or lower stocks. (See *Figure 8.5.*) Alternatively, separate breeches were worn with hose kept in place by garters. The codpiece gradually went out of style after mid-century.

GARMENTS

Around mid-century men displayed the small, square collar of the shirt at the neck edge of the doublet. Next the collar of the shirt became a small ruffle, and in the final stage of evolution the **ruff** developed as an individual item of costume, separate from the shirt. Very wide, often of lace, and stiffly starched, the ruff became one of the most characteristic features of costume during the second half of the 16th century and persisted into the first decades of the 17th century as well. (See *Contemporary Comment 8.1, page 180* and *Figures 8.5* and *8.7.*)

The neck of the doublet was cut high, its shape and finish varied. A row of small, square flaps called **pecadils** was placed just below the waist. (See *Figure 8.5.*) Sleeves, though padded, followed the shape of the arm and narrowed as the century progressed until by 1600 sleeves were unpadded and closely fitted. Waistlines followed the natural waist at the back, but dipped to a point at the front, where padding emphasized the shape. By 1570 the amount of padding increased and the point at the front of the doublet became so pronounced that it was called a **peascod belly** as it resembled the puffed-out chest of a peacock. (See *Figures 8.5* and *8.7.*)

The jacket was similar in shaping to the doublet, over which it was worn. It usually had short puffed sleeves or pecadils at the arm and no sleeve, thereby making the sleeve of the doublet the outermost sleeve.

Breeches were separate garments worn together with separate stockings. They included skintight versions, those wide at the top and tapering to the knee (called **Venetians**),

FIGURE 8.3

The *Landesknecht* and the *Lady Holding Pansies* by Lucas Cranach, early 16th century. The knight on the left wears the decoratively slashed costume of a German soldier. The slashed upper stocks over his hips contrast with the nether stocks, which cover his legs. Strips of cloth are tied around his leg at the knee. A codpiece is visible at the front of his upper stocks. His hat is an exaggeration by the artist of the military headdress of the period. The lady wears typical German dress with sleeves made in alternatively wider and narrower sections having V-shaped cuffs that cover the backs of her hands. She has several gold chains around her neck. Her headdress is also a fanciful exaggeration of the current style of hats for women. (Photograph courtesy, The Metropolitan Museum of Art, Harris Brisbane Dick Fund, 1926.)

FIGURE 8.4

In this miniature of 1520, François I of France and his courtiers wear skirted jackets cut with differing necklines, short robes, wide shoes, and a variety of plumed hats with beretlike shapes. Two men (at the right) wear caps under their hats. (Photograph courtesy, The Pierpont Morgan Library, manuscript M948, F4.)

and those wide and full throughout (called **open breeches**). (See *Figures 8.6* and *8.7.*)

Trunk hose were made in several shapes. Melon-shaped trunk hose were usually paned, heavily padded, and ended at the hip or somewhat below. They were approximately the shape of a pumpkin. (See *Figure 8.5.*) Others sloped gradually from a narrow waist to fullness concentrated about mid-thigh, where they ended. (See *Figure 8.6.*) This type may have been called gallygaskins or slops. One form had limited use outside

of very fashionable court circles. It was made of a short section, not much more than a pad around the hips, worn with very tight-fitting hose. (See *Figure 8.7.*) Boucher calls them **culots.**

Trunk hose and, to a lesser extent, doublets were heavily padded with **bombast,** a stuffing made of wool, horsehair, short linen fibers called tow, or bran. Excessive use of bombast led one chronicler to suggest that a man was carrying the whole contents of his bed and his table linen as stuffing in his trunk hose. It was said that the English parliament house had

FIGURE 8.5

Prince Hercule-François, Duc d'Alençon, 1572. The Duke wears wide, somewhat melon-shaped, paned trunkhose with a codpiece. His jacket with its high collar surrounded by a small ruff has the fashionable peascod belly shape, and finishes below the waistline in a row of pecadils. His hat is in the capotain shape, decorated with a jeweled band and a plume. The short cape is fur-lined. (Photograph courtesy, The National Gallery of Art, Samuel H. Kress Collection, 1961.)

to be enlarged to accommodate the bulky trunks of the members (Wescher, *CIBA Review*).

Canions were extensions from the end of the trunk hose to the knees or slightly below that were either made in the same color or a contrasting color to trunk hose.

FIGURE 8.6

Close-up photograph of slashed satin breeches of about 1600 shows the way in which this garment was constructed. (Photograph courtesy, The Victoria and Albert Museum.)

Canions fastened to separate stockings at the bottom. (See *Figure 8.7.*)

Stockings were more often used with trunk hose and canions than the long, joined hose. Stockings and hose were either cut and sewn or knitted. References to knitting begin to appear around 1530.

After the middle of the century shorter and longer capes for outdoors largely replaced the aforementioned gowns. Short capes were cut very full, flaring out sharply from the shoulder.

Costume for Women: 16th Century

During the Classical and Medieval periods, undergarments helped provide warmth and protected the skin from the garments worn closest to the body and the garments from being soiled by perspiration. By the 16th century there had been changes in the function of undergarments—changes that had their beginnings in previous centuries, but that became especially obvious during the 1500s.

Just when undergarments took on the function of shaping the body is not entirely clear. Ewing (1981) sees the forerunner of the corset in the tightly laced cote of the Medieval period and cites evidence of a linen under-bodice made from two layers of fabric stiffened with glue. By the 17th century this garment had taken on the name **stays** in English. Earlier it had been known as a **pair of bodys** as it was cut into two sections and fastened at the front and back with laces or tapes. This garment appears not only as an undergarment, but occasionally as an outer garment as well.

FIGURE 8.7

Engraving of 1581 shows men who all wear peascod belly-shaped doublets and neck ruffs. The man at left wears very full Venetian breeches, the men second from left and at the far right wear short trunks attached to full-length hose, and the man third from the left wears short trunks with canions. The engraver, de Bruyn D'Anvers, has identified them as Spanish. (Courtesy Fairchild Publications.)

A few examples of steel or iron "corsets" dating from the 16th century can be found in museums. These are regarded as either orthopedic garments or later, fanciful reconstructions. There is no evidence that these iron corsets were worn as fashionable dress. The stays that were worn seem to have followed the pattern described earlier: made of cloth, shaped as an under-bodice and laced together at front, back, or both. The stiffening was provided by a **busk,** a device made from a long flat piece of wood or whalebone that was sewn into one or more casings provided in the stays. When gowns were constructed with a V-shaped section, called a stomacher, at the front of the bodice that extended to the waist or beyond, this removable busk could be placed in a sort of pocket sewn in the back of the stomacher.

The shaping and support of the outer garment is yet another function of undergarments, and was a particularly important element in women's clothing of the 1500s. Beginning with the **verdugale,** continuing with the **bum roll,** and culmi-

nating in the huge **wheel farthingale,** undergarments henceforth are important elements in the shape of Western costume.

Costume for Women: 1500–1530

The first phase of women's costume was a transition from the styles of the Medieval period.

GARMENTS

The chemise continued to be the undermost garment. The gowns worn over the chemise were fairly plain; somber colors predominated. Bodices were fitted. Skirts were long and full, flaring gently from the waistline to the floor in the front and trailing into long trains at the back. (See *Figure 8.2.*)

Women wore either a single dress or two layers consisting of an outer and an under dress. If two dresses were worn, the outer skirt might be looped up in front to display the contrasting skirt of the under dress. Trains on outer gowns

CONTEMPORARY COMMENTS 8.1

Puritan View of 16th-Century Fashion

Philip Stubbes, a Puritan writer of the Elizabethan period, published Anatomy of Abuses in England *in 1583. Included within a lengthy section in which he decries contemporary fashions is the following discussion of ruffs, an important part of the fashions of his times.*

Of ruffs worn by men, Stubbes says:

They have great and monstrous ruffs, made either of cambric, holland, lawn, or else of some other the finest cloth that can be got for money, whereof some be a quarter of a yard deep, yea some more, very few less; so that they stand a full quarter of a yard (and more) from their necks, hanging over their shoulder points instead of a veil. . . . The devil first . . . invented these great ruffs. . . . the one arch or pillar whereby his kingdom of great ruffs is underpropped, is a certain kind of liquid matter which they call starch, wherein the devil has willed them to wash and dry their ruffs well, which, when they be dry, will then stand stiff and inflexible around their necks. The other pillar is a certain device of wires, created for the purpose, whipped over either with gold, thread, silver, or silk and this he [the devil] calls a supportasse, or underpropper. This is to be applied round their necks under the ruff, upon the outside of the band, to bear up the whole frame and body of the ruff from falling and hanging down.

Of women's ruffs, Stubbes says:

The women there use great ruffs and neckerchiefs of holland, lawn, cambric, and such cloth, as the greatest thread shall not be so big as the least hair that is: then lest they should fall down they are smeared and starched . . . ; after that dried with great diligence, streaked, patted, and rubbed very nicely, and so applied to their goodly necks. [*Stubbes describes the styles of ruffs*] three or four degrees of minor ruffs, placed *gradatim,* step by step, one beneath another, and all under the master devil ruff. The skirts then, of these great ruffs are long and fall every way, pleated and crested full curiously . . . . Then, last of all, they are either clogged with gold, silver, or silk lace of stately price, wrought all over with needle work, speckled and sparkled here and there with the sun, the moon, the stars, and many other antiques, strange to behold. Some are wrought with open work down to the midst of the ruff and further, some so cloyed with pearled lace, and so pestered with other gewgaws as the ruff is the least part of itself. Sometimes they are pinned up to their ears, sometimes they are suffered to hang over their shoulders, like windmill sails fluttering in the wind, and thus every one pleaseth herself with her foolish devices.

P. Stubbes. 1877. *Anatomy of Abuses in England in Shakespeare's Youth* A.D. *1583.* London: New Shakespeare Society.

often had decorative underlinings. The train was buttoned or pinned to the waist at the back in order to show the lining fabric.

Most often dress necklines were square, with the edge of the chemise visible, or they might be cut with smaller or larger V-shaped openings at the front or at both front and back. Lacings held the V-shaped opening together.

Sleeve styles included smooth-fitting narrow sleeves with decorative cuffs, wide funnel shapes with contrasting linings, and hanging sleeves. When two layers were worn, the under dress usually had closely fitted sleeves and the outermost large, full, funnel-shaped sleeves or hanging sleeves.

Except for ceremonial occasions when the open mantle fastening with a chain or braid at the front was still worn, women wore long, full cloaks outdoors.

Costume for Women in Germany: 1530–1575

Although costume of the 16th century had become more international with styles from one country or another often predominating, regional differences continued to exist. This is particularly evident in German women's styles of the first half of the century. (See *Figure 8.3.*)

A brief summary of the major features of German women's styles of the first half of the 16th century follows. During the second half of the century, German styles were subject to Spanish influence and lost much of their unique character.

Softly gathered skirts were joined to closely fitted bodices that had low and square or rounded necklines. The neckline was usually filled in, most often by the chemise. Bodices were elaborately decorated or embroidered across the bosom. Sleeves were close fitting, with tight horizontal bands alternating with somewhat enlarged, puffed areas. The cuff extended into a point over the wrist. (This sleeve style does appear in other northern countries over the same period, but may itself derive from the Italian sleeves of the latter half of the 15th century in which the chemise puffed through openings in a tightly fitted sleeve.)

Hair was often held in a net, over which was placed a wide-brimmed hat trimmed with plumes. Gold chains, frequently worn along with a wide jeweled "dog collar," were important status symbols.

Costume for Women in Other Northern European Countries: 1530–1575

The second phase of costume for women outside of Germany was marked by Spanish influences (see *Color Plate 21*), whereas men's styles of this period had been more directly influenced by German styles. Spanish influence was not evident in men's clothing until the second half of the century. One important aspect of the Spanish influence was a tendency to emphasize dark colors, especially black.

The changes in women's clothing after 1530 represent a gradual evolution in style, not a radical change.

GARMENTS

Significant changes took place in the construction of dresses. Instead of an under dress and an outer dress, women wore a **petticoat** (an underskirt) and an over dress. The overall silhouette was rather like an hourglass. Bodices narrowed to a small waistline. Skirts gradually expanded to an inverted cone shape with an inverted **V** opening at the front. (See *Figure 8.8.*)

Bodices and skirts of dresses were sewn together. The bodice narrowed and flattened, becoming quite rigid and the waist dipped to an elongated **V** at the front. A rich, jeweled belt outlined the waistline, and from the dip in front its long end fell down the center front of the gown almost to the floor.

At first most necklines were square. Later more closed styles were preferred. Such dresses had closed necklines with standing, wing collars or necklines filled in by the chemise, which closed up to the throat and ended in a small ruffle.

FIGURE 8.8

Dress in the style that developed after the third decade of the 16th century. The ruffled cuff of the chemise is visible at the end of the sleeve. Large, detachable undersleeves match the fabric of the petticoat. The flared skirt was supported underneath by a hoop called a verdugale or Spanish farthingale. The painting by an unknown artist is of Queen Elizabeth I as a princess. (Photograph provided and printed by the gracious permission of Her Majesty the Queen Elizabeth II. Copyright reserved.)

(See *Figure 8.10.*) Ruffs, of moderate size at this phase of their development, were worn with high, fitted collars. (See *Color Plate 21.*)

The first of many changes in sleeve styles came early in the period when the previously described German and Italian style sleeves were adopted. Subsequently other styles developed. Many sleeves were narrow at the shoulder and expanded to a huge, wide square cuff that turned back upon itself. This cuff was often made of fur or of heavy brocade that matched the petticoat. A detachable, false sleeve decorated with panes and slashes through which the linen of the che-

FIGURE 8.9

Portrait of a Young Lady, Flemish, c. 1535. The chemise, elaborately embroidered in black work, worn by the young lady shows clearly at the neck and below the sleeves of her gown. Her sleeves, fitted at the shoulder, widen at the bottom. The small coif is decorated with jewels. The hair is enclosed in a dark, possibly velvet, hood at the back. (Photograph courtesy, The Metropolitan Museum of Art, The Jules S. Bache Collection, 1949.)

FIGURE 8.10

Portrait of Margaretta of Parma by Anthonis Mor von Dashorst, second half of the 16th century. This lady wears a Spanish-style, sleeveless ropa. Small ruffles, probably on her chemise, extend above the high collar and below the ends of her sleeves. Her coif dips slightly at the front. (Photograph courtesy, The Philadelphia Museum of Art, John G. Johnson Collection.)

mise was visible might be sewn to the underside of the cuff or, if the chemise were richly decorated, the sleeve of the chemise might be seen below the cuff. (See *Figures 8.8* and *8.9.*)

Another style had a puff at the shoulder and a close-fitting, long extension of the sleeve to the wrist. Though worn elsewhere as well, this style was especially popular in France. A relatively simple style was full from shoulder to wrist where it was caught into a cuff. Some sleeves were remarkably complex, especially those worn at the Spanish court, as they utilized combinations of fitted, full, and hanging sleeves. (See *Color Plate 21.*)

Sleeve decorations included cutting and paning with decorative fabrics, and fastening the panes with **aiguillettes**

(small, jeweled metal points). Padded rolls of fabric were sometimes located at the joining of bodice and sleeve and these served to hide the laces fastening separate sleeves to bodices.

Skirts became more rigid. Many dresses were untrained and floor length. Although the petticoat was separate from the dress, its visibility through the inverted V at the front of the skirt made it an integral part of the ensemble. Petticoats were usually cut from rich, decorative fabric (often brocade or cut velvet). The back of the petticoat was covered by the skirt of the dress, which made it possible to make the front of the petticoat of expensive fabric, and the invisible back of lighter weight, less expensive fabric.

The flared, cone-shaped skirt required support to achieve the desired rigidity of line. A Spanish device called the **verdugale** (in Spanish, verdugado) or **Spanish farthingale** provided that support. The verdugale was a construction of whalebone, cane, or steel hoops graduated in size from the waist to the floor and sewn into a petticoat or underskirt. Formerly a visible part of the construction of traditional Spanish dress of the region of Catalonia, the hoops were at first sewn into the dress itself. English chroniclers report that Katharine of Aragon, the first wife of King Henry VIII, wore such a skirt in the early part of the century when she came to England from Spain; however, at that time it was noted as a foreign and atypical style.

The **ropa** was a garment of Spanish origin. It was an outer gown or surcote made either sleeveless or with one of several types of sleeve: a short puffed sleeve, or with a long sleeve, puffed at the top and fitted for the rest of the arm's length. The ropa fell from the shoulders, unbelted in an A-line to the floor. Some versions closed in front, but most were open to display the dress beneath. Some researchers have suggested that this garment originated with the Moors who had occupied Spain in the preceding centuries—it has the loose fit of a Middle-Eastern caftan—and that it can be seen as another instance of Middle Eastern influences on European styles. (See *Figure 8.10.*)

Costume Components for Women: 1575–1600

The first changes in the last quarter of the century came in the shape of the skirt, which grew wider at the top. (See *Figure 8.11.*) Instead of the cone-shaped Spanish farthingale, a padded roll was placed around the waist in order to give skirts greater width below the waist. The English called these pads **bum rolls,** "bum" being English slang for buttocks. For better support of dresses than these rolls provided and to attain greater width, a modification of the farthingale was made. Instead of using graduated circles of whalebone, cane, or steel sewn into a canvas skirt, the circles were made the same diameter top to bottom. Steel or cane spokes fastened the topmost hoop to a waistband. It was called the wheel, drum, or **French farthingale.** (See *Figures 8.11* and *8.12,* and *Color Plate 23.*)

This style was not used in Italy, nor, to any great extent, in Spain at this period. Instead the older, hourglass shape of the Spanish farthingale with a slightly padded roll at the waist predominated. The wheel farthingale was essentially a northern European style. Even in northern Europe, some women continued to wear Spanish farthingales, or dresses widened slightly at the waist with bum rolls, or small, wheel farthingales.

Dresses worn over wheel farthingales had enormous skirts that were either cut and sewn into one continuous piece all around, or open at the front or sides over a matching underskirt. A ruffle the width of the flat shelf-like section of the farthingale was sometimes attached to the skirt. To avoid having the body appear disproportionately short in contrast with the width of

FIGURE 8.11

Portrait of a Young Lady by Marcus Gheeraerts the Younger, c. 1600. The lady wears a wheel farthingale. The skirt of the farthingale opens at the front, but the petticoat beneath it is not visible. Around the waist is placed a ruffle the width of the farthingale. She wears a standing lace ruff at the neck. Her hair is dressed high with jeweled decorations. (Photograph courtesy, The Metropolitan Museum of Art, gift of Kate T. Davidson, in memory of her husband, Henry Pomeroy Davidson, 1951.)

the skirt, sleeves were made fuller and with very high sleeve caps. The stomacher at the front of the bodice was elongated, ending in a deep V at the waist. Additional height came from high standing collars and dressing the hair high on the head.

FIGURE 8.12

FIGURE 8.12

Portrait of a Lady, c. 1600, by an unknown British painter. Over a farthingale-style dress, the lady wears a conch, a sheer headdress, and cape edged in pearls. Her lace ruff is in the open style. In her right hand she holds a feathered fan. Her brocade dress is decorated with jeweled rosettes. (Photograph courtesy, The Metropolitan Museum of Art, gift of J. Pierpont Morgan, 1911.)

Skirts of Spanish women of the late 16th and early 17th centuries often had a horizontal pleat going around the skirt. Explanations of its functions differ. It may have been placed there to allow enough fabric for the dress to be repaired if the skirt hem frayed, or it may have allowed the skirt to bend when the woman was seated, thereby modestly covering her legs (Read 1951).

Ruffs grew to enormous widths. Made of sheer linen or of lace they had to be supported by a frame called the **supportasse** (see *Figure 8.13*) or by starching. Methods of constructing ruffs included gathering one edge of a band of fabric or lace to the size of the neck to form a frill of deep folds or placing several layers of round lace pieces one over the other. Some ruffs were simply round, flat lace pieces without depth or folds, more like a wide collar. Open ruffs, almost a cross between a collar and a ruff, stood high behind the head and fastened in front into a wide, square neckline. (See *Figure 8.12*.) During the 18th and 19th centuries, revivals of this style were called Medici collars after the Medici Queens of France, Catherine and Marie, in whose reigns this style was popular.

The **conch,** known in French as a conque, was a sheer, gauzelike veil so fine that in some portraits it can just barely be seen. It was cut the full length of the body from shoulder to floor and worn capelike over the shoulders. At the back of the neck it was attached to a winglike construction that stood up like a high collar behind the head. Some writers consider the conch to have had some significance as a widow's costume, and this may be true in France; however, in England it seems to have been more widely worn as a purely decorative element of dress by women, such as Queen Elizabeth, who were never widowed. (See *Figure 8.12*.)

FIGURE 8.13

Drawing shows a ruff "underpropped with a supportasse," a frame which holds the ruff in place. (Based on drawing from Phillip Stubbes, *Anatomy of Abuses,* Queens College Library Collection.)

COSTUME ACCESSORIES FOR MEN AND WOMEN: 16TH CENTURY

Changes in the styles of many accessories did not precisely parallel changes in overall silhouettes. Therefore the discussion of accessory items for men and women is not divided into phases, but extends across the entire century. See *Illustrated Table 8.1* for depictions of some of the most widely worn accessory items.

HAIR AND HEADDRESS FOR MEN

At the beginning of the century men cut their hair straight across the back in a length anywhere from below the ears to the shoulder and combined this with a fringe of bangs across the forehead. (See *Figure 8.2.*) Among the fashionable hat styles was a pillbox-like shape with a turned-up brim. Some versions had decorative cutout sections in the brim. This hat was sometimes referred to as a **French bonnet.** (See *Figure 8.2.*) Men also wore a skull cap or hair net holding the hair close to the head over which they placed a hat with a basin-shaped crown and wide brim, the brim turned up at one point. Many hats were decorated with feathers.

After 1530 beards became fashionable, and the hair was cut short. (See *Figure 8.4.*) Hat styles included a moderately sized, flat crowned hat with a small brim and a feather plume and beretlike styles with feather plumes. (See *Figure 8.4.* and *Illustrated Table 8.1.*)

After mid-century men allowed their hair to grow longer; beards and mustaches remained popular. (See *Figure*

8.7.) Hats were made with increasingly high crowns, some with soft shapes, others with stiffer outlines. Brims tended to be narrow. The high-crowned, narrow brimmed hat was called a **copotain** and this style remained popular until well into the 17th century. (See *Figure 8.5.*) Trimmings for hats included feathers, braid, and jewels.

HAIR AND HEADDRESS FOR WOMEN

The custom of having married and adult women cover the hair continued. One of the most important headcoverings was the coif—a cap of white linen or more decorative fabric, usually with long lappets or short square or pointed extensions below the ears that covered the side of the face. Coif shapes ranged from round to heart-shaped or **gabled,** an English style shaped like a pointed arch. (See *Illustrated Table 8.1.*) Over the coif, women placed a band about 40 inches long and 4 inches wide was pinned. The ends either hung down at either side of the face or were arranged in decorative folds. Some of these bands had hoods of semicircular fabric attached at the back. As the century progressed, the coif was set further back on the head, allowing more hair to show. Decorative overcaps might be placed on top of the coif, some trimmed with jewels or metallic netting. (See *Figures 8.8, 8.9,* and *8.10.*)

In the last two thirds of the century more hair was visible. The hair was combed back from the forehead, puffed up slightly around the face, then pulled into a coil at the back of the head. Local differences arose. The French combed the hair up, over small pads on either side to form a heart-shaped frame for the face. The English imitated the hair color of the Queen, which was red, so that among ladies of the court red, auburn, and varying shades of blonde hair were fashionable. (Toward the end of her reign, Queen Elizabeth's hair had become so thin that she generally wore a red wig.) To balance the width of the wheeled farthingale, women gained extra height by dressing the hair high and decorating it with jeweled ornaments. (See *Figures 8.11* and *8.12.*)

Hats popular toward the end of the century were generally small, with high crowns and narrow brims, and trimmed with feathers. (See *Illustrated Table 8.1.*) Jeweled nets and caps were also worn.

FOOTWEAR

With a few exceptions, trends in styles of footwear were similar for men and for women. Often because they were more visible, men's styles tended to greater exaggeration. Square-toed shapes expanded as the period progressed, especially for men's shoes. By mid-century, when Mary I was Queen of England, shoes had become so wide that a law was passed limiting the width to six inches. Decorations included slashing with puffs of fabric pulled through the openings. Costume historians of the 19th century called these shoes **duck-bills** because their shape resembled the bill of a duck. (See *Illustrated Table 8.1.*)

Illustrated Table 8.1

NORTHERN RENAISSANCE: ACCESSORIES

Ruff

Necklace

Cuff

Bum roll

Purse

Late 1500s. Woman with bum roll
at waist, purse, lace ruff and cuffs,
necklace and earrings

Feather Fans, 16th century and a square face shield

Elizabethan gloves

Women's headdress

English hood,
16th century

French hood,
16th century

German hat and hairnet,
16th century

Hat, late 1500s

Jeweled collar
King Henry VIII

Duckbilled shoes,
1st half 1500s

Small pins in king's hat

Undecorated cap
of ordinary citizen

Early 1500s,
Jeweled and feather
trimmed beret style hat

During the second half of the century, toes remained square, but width decreased and shoes conformed more closely to the shape of the foot. Shoes were also slashed at this time, but instead of puffs had a contrasting lining underneath that showed when the foot was bent.

Among the shoe styles worn by men and women were backless shoes called mules. Some shoes had a tongue and tied shut with laces (called **latchets**) that crossed the tongue from either side. High-heeled shoes for men and women first appeared sometime during the 1570s. The heels were about one and a half inches high. Sometimes ribbon rosettes were placed at the front of the shoe or decorative stones were set into them.

Styles worn only by women included low-cut slippers with a strap across the ankle and chopines. These high, platform-soled shoes can be seen first in Italy, from where their use spread to other parts of Europe.

Boots were worn out-of-doors when riding horseback.

JEWELRY

Although lavishly used by royalty and wealthy men and women during the first half of the century, jewelry use by men declined during the second half of the century. Men did not give up wearing jewelry, but rather wore smaller quantities and more restrained pieces. Women continued to wear large quantities of extravagant jewels. Men wore wide jeweled collars that were not a part of the garment but a separate circular piece made of ornamental plates joined together. Both men and women wore neck chains of gold or other precious metals that were wrapped several times around the neck. Women wore pendant necklaces.

Jeweled decorations were applied to almost any part of the costume. Men and women pinned brooches to hats, hoods, and other parts of the clothing. During the time when large, lacy ruffs were worn, some of which looked somewhat like spider webs, women wore jeweled pins made in the shape of spiders among the folds of the ruff. Aiguillettes (*ay-gwe-laze*), small, jeweled points mounted on laces that served to hold panes or slashes together, were placed on hats. Sleeve clasps, small jeweled pins, were also used to hold together paned segments of sleeves. (See *Illustrated Table 8.1.*)

Earrings, seen in paintings of women, and occasionally of men, were popular in countries and periods when the hair or headdress did not cover the ears. Rings were worn everywhere. Bracelets were obscured by the large sleeves, and so were not much worn.

Some items of jewelry were worn exclusively by women. Women wore ferronieres in France, but this forehead ornament was not especially popular in England. Jeweled belts with long cords hanging down the front became popular for women after the second decade. On the cord were mounted such things as a jeweled tassel, a perfume holder (pomander), a purse, or a mirror.

ACCESSORIES

Both men and women carried purses, which were often suspended from belts. Middle- and lower-class persons used leather pouches. Purses of the wealthy were ornamented with embroidery, beading, metalwork, jewels.

In their earliest form, fans were squares of embroidered fabric mounted on a stick. Later fans included ostrich or peacock feathers mounted on ornamental sticks and circular folding fans.

Both men and women carried handkerchiefs and wore gloves. Fashionable gloves often had decorated cuffs.

Women wore masks out-of-doors when riding to protect the complexion against the sun. Amateur performers in theatrical productions also used them, as did persons who wanted to remain disguised.

COSMETICS

Many cosmetics were made from potentially dangerous chemicals such as mercuric salts, which were used to whiten the complexion. Red coloring was applied to lips and cheeks. Perfumes were used. Puritans railed against these "evil practices," predicting that men and women would pay dearly for their concessions to vanity when they reached the afterworld. Philip Stubbes, writing in 1583, said "It must be granted that the dyeing and coloring of faces with artificial colors, and unnatural ointments is most offensive to God and derogatory to his Majesty. . . . And what are they [artificial colors] else than the Devil's intentions, to entangle poor fools in the nets of perdition."

COSTUME FOR CHILDREN: 16TH CENTURY

The pattern of dressing children in the same kind of costume as their elders continued during the 16th century. Small children, both boys and girls, were dressed in skirts until they passed the age of five or six and then boys donned doublet and hose and whatever other garments were fashionable for men at the time. They did not escape even the large ruffs, which must have been especially awkward and ungainly for active children. Royal children wore elaborate, costly silks made into heavy velvets and brocades. (See *Figure 8.14.*) Children of the poor and middle class dressed more simply, just as lower- and middle-class adults dressed more simply than the wealthy.

FIGURE 8.14

Edward VI (son of Henry VIII) as a child, by Hans Holbein the Younger, c. 1540. The young prince is dressed in a miniature version of adult styles of the time, including an embroidered shirt which is visible at the neck and sleeves. Both his hat and sleeves are decorated with aiguillettes. Although the lower half of his garment is not visible, it is likely that at this early age the prince would have been wearing long skirts. (Photograph courtesy, The National Gallery of Art, Washington, DC, Andrew Mellon Collection, 1937.)

PARVVLE PATRISSA, PATRIÆ VIRTVTIS ET HÆRES
ESTO, NIHIL MAIVS MAXIMVS ORBIS HABET.
GNATVM VIX POSSVNT COELVM ET NATVRA DEDISSE,
HVIVS QVEM PATRIS, VICTVS HONORET HONOS.
ÆQVATO TANTVM, TANTI TV FACTA PARENTIS,
VOTA HOMINVM, VIX QVO PROGREDIANTVR, HABENT
VINCITO, VICISTI. QVOT REGES PRISCVS ADORAT
ORBIS, NEC TE QVI VINCERE POSSIT, ERIT.

SUMMARY

THEMES

Clothing styles of the 16th century took on an increasingly international flavor, and fashion played an ever more important role. Styles often originated in one country or another, making communication an important means of spreading fashion information. **COMMUNICATION** of information about new styles became easier with printed books.

New **TECHNOLOGY** contributed to costume. The development of lacemaking provided important decorative touches, while the technique of knitting lent itself to the making of better fitting stockings.

CROSS-CULTURAL INFLUENCES continued to come from the East. Some may have been indirect, as in the Spanish ropa, which probably was a reminder of the Moorish occupation of the Iberian peninsula. Others may have been more direct, coming from actual garments sent as gifts to European monarchs or in trade.

Patterns in social behavior can perhaps be related to developments in Spanish styles. Standards of social behavior and religious practice were rigorously enforced in Spain. At this

Visual Summary Table

NORTHERN RENAISSANCE

Man: c. 1500–1515
Doublet laced to hose, worn under jacket with short skirt (bases).

Man: c. 1515–1550
Wider garments that may be puffed, slashed, or paned. Breeches appear separate from the lower stocking.

Man: 1570 (c. 1550–1600)
Doublet and waist-length jacket with narrow shoulders and wide ruff. Many types of now wider trunk hose.

Woman: c. 1500–1530
Fitted bodices usually with square necklines and long sleeves. Skirts long, full, and trained. Similar to late Medieval styles.

Woman: c. 1530–1575
German style.
Fitted bodice, with sleeves that have tight bands alternating with puffed areas, is attached to gathered skirt.

Woman: c. 1530–1575
Northern
European countries
Hourglass-shaped gown with stiff, tight bodice and inverted cone-shaped skirt. Sleeves large and full, necklines often square.

Woman: c. 1575–1600
Skirts widen at the top; bodices elongate into a V-shape and ruffs grow exceptionally wide or high.

same time, clothing style lines were stiff and rigid. Reade (1951) asks, "How much, too, of the Spanish temperment betrayed itself in the conception of devices like the verdugado, which brought about rigidity in women's clothes analogous to that firm restraint imposed on behavior by the Inquisition?"

The theme of **POLITICAL INFLUENCES** emerges when the dress of monarchs such as Charles I and Catherine di Medici of France or Elizabeth I of England was imitated. This theme and its accompanying **CROSS-CULTURAL INFLUENCES,** can be seen again as the rise and fall of fashion leadership parallels gains and losses of international prestige during the century. In the first half of the century fashion leadership came from Germany, Italy, and then, as Spain gained ascendency, chiefly from Spain in the second half. By the end of the century, Spanish fashion influence decreased just as Spanish political power was also waning.

SURVIVALS OF
16TH CENTURY DRESS

A considerable number of details of costume that originated in the 16th century have become part of the repertory of fashion design in subsequent centuries. Some examples include the ruff and the open, standing collar, later named the Medici collar. From the 16th century onward an undergarment for supporting skirts appeared at least once in every century. The precise form of these garments is not the same in each instance, but once the basic idea that skirt shapes could be supported by a hoop or paniers was accepted, that idea was revived periodically. (See *Figures 10.10* and *19.17a* and *Illustrated Tables 13.1* and *17.1.*)

N O T E S

Boucher, F. [N.D.] *20,000 Years of Fashion.* New York: Harry Abrams, p. 233.

Chamberlin, E. R. 1969. *Everyday Life in Renaissance Times.* New York: G. P. Putnam's Sons, p. 54.

Derry, T. K. and T. L. Williams. 1961. *A Short History of Technology.* New York: Oxford University Press.

Ewing, E. 1981. *Dress and Undress.* New York: Drama Books, p. 21 ff.

Nevinson, J. L. 1968. "Prince Edward's Clothes." *Costume,* p. 3.

Reade, B. 1951. *Costume of the Western World: The Dominance of Spain.* London: George C. Harrap and Company.

St. Clair, A. N. 1973. "The Image of the Turk in Europe." *Metropolitan Museum of Art Bulletin,* p. 11.

Stubbes, P. 1877. *Anatomy of Abuses in England in Shakespeare's Youth A.D. 1583.* London: New Shakespeare Society, p. 66. (Put into modern English by the author.)

Wescher, H. [N.D.] "Dress and Fashion at the Court of Queen Elizabeth." *CIBA Review,* No. 78, p. 2846.

S E L E C T E D   R E A D I N G S

Books Containing Illustrations of Costume of the Period from Original Sources

Ashelford, J. 1983. *A Visual History of Costume: The Sixteenth Century.* London: Batsford.

Ashelford, J. 1988. *Dress in the Age of Elizabeth I.* New York: Holmes and Meier.

Bartrum, G., et al. 2003. *Albrecht Durer and His Legacy.* Princeton, NJ: Princeton University Press.

Chastel, A. 1995. *French Art: The Renaissance, 1430-1620.* Paris: Flammarion.

Mellon, P. 1971. *Jean Clouet.* New York: Phaidon.

Plumb, J. H. and H. Weldon. 1977. *Royal Heritage: The Treasures of the Royal Crown.* New York: Harcourt, Jovanovich.

Rowlands, J. 1985. *Holbein.* Boston: David R. Godine.

Strong, R. 1968a. *The Elizabethan Icon: Elizabethan and Jacobean Portraiture.* London: Her Majesty's Stationery Office.

Strong, R. 1968b. *Tudor and Jacobean Portraits.* London: Her Majesty's Stationery Office.

Periodical Articles

Acton, B. 1976. "Portrait of a Swaddled Baby-16th Century." *Costume Society of Scotland Bulletin,* No. 17, Autumn p. 13.

Arnold, J. 1975. "Decorative Features: Pinking, Snipping, and Slashing." *Costume,* No. 9, p. 22.

Arnold, J. 1989. "The 'Armada' Portraits of Queen Elizabeth I." *Apollo,* April, No. 129 (326), p. 242.

Buck, A. 1990. "The Clothing of Thomasine Petre 1555–1559." *Costume,* No. 24, p. 25.

Cocks, A. S. 1980. "Princely Magnificence: Jewelry at the Renaissance Court." *Connoisseur,* Vol. 205 (825), p. 210.

Hayward, M. 1996. "Luxury or Magnificence? Dress at the Court of Henry VIII." *Costume,* No. 30, p. 37.

Nevinson, J. L. 1967. "Shakespeare's Dress in His Portraits." *Shakespeare Quarterly,* Spring, p. 101.

Olian, J. 1977. "Sixteenth Century Costume Books." *Dress,* Vol. 3, p. 20.

Warner, P. C. 1990. "Fetters of Gold: The Jewelry of Renaissance Saxony in the Portraits of Cranach the Elder." *Dress,* Vol. 16, p. 17.

Wescher, H. "French Fashions in the Sixteenth Century." *CIBA Review,* No. 69, p. 2552.

Daily Life

Braudel, F. 1981. *The Structure of Everyday Life. The Limits of the Possible. Civilization and Capitalism, 15th–18th Centuries.* New York: Harper and Row.

Burton, E. 1977. *Pageant of Tudor England: 1485–1558.* New York: Encore Editions.

Chartier, R., ed. 1988. *A History of Private Life: Passions of the Renaissance.* Cambridge MA: Belknap Press of Harvard University Press.

Febvre, L. 1979. *Life in Renaissance France.* Cambridge, MA: Harvard University Press.

Fussell, G. E. 1975. *The English Rural Labourer: His Home, Furniture, Clothing and Food from Tudor to Victorian Times.* Westport, CT: Greenwood Press.

Singman, J. L. 1996. *Daily Life in Elizabethan England.* Westport, CT: Greenwood Press.

PART FOUR

BAROQUE AND ROCOCO

c. 1600–1800

During the 17th century, Europe endured a crisis—a series of social and political upheavals involving civil war, revolts, peasant uprisings, and a rebellion of the nobility. This continent-wide crisis so shook the European nations that a form of stronger government—absolute monarchy—became necessary to overcome it. By the 18th century, absolute monarchy had been generally accepted everywhere in Europe except Great Britain, where the monarch's power had been limited as a result of the Glorious Revolution of 1688.

Nearly every year during the 18th century, there was either a war in progress or a rumor of an impending war. The wars between European powers had also become global, with the fighting spreading to involve India and the continent of North America. The century concluded in an era of revolution, commencing with the American Revolution and ending with the cataclysm of the French Revolution.

The Reformation had ended, but religious strife continued. Late in the 1500s, the Roman Catholic Church mounted a Counter-Reformation, which halted the spread of Protestantism. In many areas, Protestantism was firmly established and from this point on Catholics and Protestants coexisted more or less peaceably. France and Spain were the major Roman Catholic powers; Britain, northern Germany, Scandinavia, and Holland remained Protestant.

Religious toleration had been established in France in 1598 with the Edict of Nantes, which ended a series of religious wars. However, in 1685 Louis XIV revoked the Edict of Nantes and resumed the persecution of French Protestants. Many of these people, called Huguenots, fled from France to other European countries or to America. Large numbers of them worked in the textile trades, especially the silk industry, and their exodus had drastic effects on the French economy.

In England, a branch of Protestantism appeared that opposed the Church of England and sought to cleanse the Church by purifying it from rituals that were "Roman." Nicknamed "Puritans," members of this branch became the leading faction in opposing the Stuart kings of England. Eventually Puritans would settle in New England.

Germany had become a patchwork of small principalities after the Thirty Years' War (1618–1648). The war began as a conflict between Lutherans and Roman Catholics but before it ended all of the great powers of Europe had become involved. As a result of the Peace of Westphalia, which ended the terrible struggle, each German state gained the right to determine its own religion.

THE ARTS DURING THE BAROQUE AND ROCOCO PERIODS

The Baroque style, generally dated from the end of the 16th century to the middle of the 18th century, is the name given to the artistic style that developed during this period. The Baroque style emphasized lavish ornamentation, free and flowing lines, and flat and curved forms. It was massive rather than delicate. The patrons for this art form included the Catholic and Protestant churches, the aristocracy, and the affluent bourgeoisie. Because the courts of Europe were the center for royal patronage, artists and artisans often clustered around these centers.

Clothing styles were affected by these changes in the arts, and one can see in the lines of garments, particularly those of the first half of the 1600s, reflections of the Baroque emphasis on curvilinear forms. Squire (1974) speaks of artists who drew fashion plates in which they "caught the characteristic manner of bunching up the skirt when walking, to emphasize that exuberant ballooning drapery so beloved of artists like Bernini far away in Rome. Such a gesture was surely not accidental, but the unconscious spirit of an age working to achieve a recognizable style in every aspect of life."

Of the second half of the century, and its stylistic changes, Squire comments, "The fashionable dress of men and women in the second half of the seventeenth century interpreted the regimented ceremonial, the disciplined restraint and the academic precision of French modifications of an earlier exuberant Baroque."

From about 1720 to 1770, the Rococo style supplanted the Baroque. Rococo is considered by art historians to be a trend within the overall classification of Baroque, a refinement of the heavier, more vigorous Baroque expression. Rococo styles were marked by "S" and "C" curves, tracery, scrollwork, and fanciful adaptations of Chinese, classical, and even Gothic lines. They were also smaller and more delicate in scale. Rococo found a reflection in the fashions of the times: in the curving lines of the hoop-supported skirts, the delicate lace and flower decorations of dresses, and the pastel shades favored by women as well as in the men's waistcoats ornamented with delicate, Rococo embroideries.

The final phase of the 18th century was marked by a revival of interest in classical styles. While this neoclassical art was expressed in architecture, painting, sculpture, interior design, and furnishings during the second half of the 18th century, its influence in costume was not really felt strongly until the last decade of the century during the Directoire period (see *Chapter 11*).

EXPANDING TRADE WITH THE FAR EAST

Although overland trade with the East had existed for centuries, the sea voyages that opened the way to merchant shipping were not made until the late 15th and early 16th centuries when the Portuguese voyaged around South Africa to India. The Portuguese established a colony in Macao and Portuguese sailors also made the first European contacts with Japan in 1542. A limited trade between Europe and Japan developed, but in the 1600s the Japanese government chose a policy of seclusion for its people and barred all foreigners from its shores. The few remaining trading posts were abandoned. When two Portuguese envoys came to negotiate the question, they were put to death. Japanese citizens were preventing from traveling abroad, and those Japanese living abroad were forbidden to return home. Although Japan was closed to trade, the European nations quickly began to compete for other lucrative commerce with the Far East.

For centuries trade with the East had involved commodities that were of small bulk but high value, usually either luxuries purchased by kings and nobles or articles used in religious cults. The oldest and best known of the oriental products were spices, particularly pepper, which were used to season the bland European diet, and silk. Silk, which had made its way over the so-called Silk Road as early as Greek and Roman times, had originated in China. By 300 B.C., sericulture (the production of silk) had spread to Korea and from there to Japan. A commodity that eventually found a mass market was cotton, a native product of India, which had been imported into Europe by the Arabs as early as the 1st century. Dyed cotton colors were relatively durable, and the fabric was comfortable when worn either as under or outer clothing, as well as easy to clean. It became one of the major products shipped by the East India Company.

Late in the 16th century, English merchants encountered stiff competition from the Dutch, who were on the verge of cornering the spice trade. Spices were the most valuable commodities shipped from Asia. English merchants were too weak to compete individually; consequently they joined to form the East India Company in 1599. The following year Queen Elizabeth I granted a charter to the East India Company that gave them a monopoly of English trade from the Cape of Good Hope (southernmost point in Africa) to the Straits of Magellan (southern South America). By 1600, the East India Company had become a joint stock company and with a small fleet of five ships began trading with the Spice Islands of Indonesia. Once again the company encountered such stiff competition from the Dutch and Portuguese that

India soon appeared to be a more promising market. In 1608 the Company set up a "factory" at Surat. It was not until 1615 that the Company's first ship brought a cargo of cotton goods and indigo to England.

THE COTTON TRADE
WITH INDIA

The East India Company handled trade on the Indian subcontinent through "factories," which were armed outposts with their own government and military establishment. The first were established early in the 17th century. Originally goods had been bought and sold whenever ships put into port. As voyages became more regular, it made financial sense to have a permanent representative called a "factor" who would collect goods throughout the year and have a full load ready whenever a ship put into port. Having a place for storage, the factor could also sell the imported goods brought from England whenever they would bring higher prices. Specific orders could be placed for export items. In the textile trade, patterns and designs could be distributed and the particular quality of goods could be specified. The factory could even finance some of the orders by advancing money. Goods that were substandard could be rejected. The factory could even take over the organization of production through a putting out system and by setting up workshops within the compound.

In Europe cotton quickly became popular. Chintz was a particularly important fabric among the imports. Chintz in 17th century India was a hand-painted or printed fabric that was sometimes glazed.[1] When the English and the Dutch realized that these fabrics might find a market in Europe, they did not select materials with local patterns, but rather provided patterns that were currently in vogue in Europe. Oriental designs, both authentic and imaginary, were fashionable, and these were among the designs produced on Indian chintz fabrics. There are even examples of Japanese-inspired designs that probably traveled from Japan to Europe by way of the Dutch trade with Japan, then back to India where the textiles were painted. First used as table and bed linens, by the latter half of the 17th century chintz was much in demand as material for clothing. Colorful Indian printed calicos[2] made of cotton were also becoming popular in England. Women were willing to pay exorbitant prices for very fine muslin[3] from Bengal which became enormously popular in the late 18th and early 19th centuries. Indian trade in cotton goods prospered in England in spite of a succession of parliamentary laws prohibiting certain materials in an effort to protect the domestic woolen trade. The demand for cotton goods was so strong that smuggling and evasion of laws was widespread. By 1719, it was estimated that of the calicoes worn in England more had no duty paid than those on which duty had been paid.

Unlike the Dutch, who used middlemen in the textile business, the British preferred to deal directly with producers, calling their system the "thread and money systems." The manager of the factory warehouse sent agents to the weavers, supplied them with yarn, and paid them daily wages for their work. The cloth was taken to the factory workshop where it was washed, bleached, and processed. In the bargaining for work the British offered low wages and often pressured the weavers to get the lowest possible prices for the cloth.

After the restoration of the monarchy, Charles II granted a new charter in 1661 that gave the East India Company wide ranging powers, including the right to wage war and conclude peace, and to appoint governors who with their councils could exercise civil and criminal jurisdiction over the company's settlements. In addition, the company could acquire territory, coin money, conclude alliances, command fortresses, and administer troops. The company had in effect become almost a sovereign state. When the wars with France came in the 18th century, the company often loaned money to the British government. In the Seven Years' War (1756–1763), the French, who still had a foothold in India, were defeated and obliged to withdraw. The East India Company was now supreme.

[1]At the present time, the term chintz is defined differently, and generally refers to a printed or dyed cotton or cotton-blend fabric with a shiny, glazed surface. Eighteenth-century chintz fabrics were not necessarily glazed, although they could be.

[2]The name calico was first applied to fine quality, printed, cotton fabrics from Calcutta, India. Later the term came to be generally applied to a wide variety of colorful, printed cotton fabrics of all qualities.

[3]Muslins were very fine, soft, lightweight, plain-weave cottons, usually white or with a printed design on a white background. The characteristics of this fabric (its softness and drapability) probably made a significant contribution to changes in the style of women's clothing that came about at the end of the 18th century.

THE INDUSTRIAL REVOLUTION

The Industrial Revolution began in England partly as a result of attempts to mechanize production of English cottons so that they would be more competitive with the cheaper imports from India, which were threatening English industry. Although it had its first stages during the 18th century and before, the most far-reaching effects of the changes resulting from industrialization were not felt until the following century. Its full impact on the textile industry was, however, a significant factor influencing textiles of the 1700s.

Technological innovations and industrial capitalism developed together in the textile industry, largely as a result of the high cost of some of the innovative machinery. For centuries weaving had been a cottage industry. The weaver, often a man, owned his own loom and worked at home. As more complex looms were made the weaver could no longer afford to buy his own machine. Instead, the industrialist purchased a number of looms, placed them together in one, long room, then hired people to come in to work. Gradually something close to factory organization developed in which the loom house was placed beside a bleaching and dyeing operation. The use of water power to operate looms in the silk industry led to increased production of silk. Silk looms, which were expensive, required outside capitalization.

But the true transformation of the clothing industry depended on an increase in and efficiency of carding and spinning, and in the perfection of completely mechanized looms. The spinning mule, the spinning jenny, and the Arkwright water spinning frame had been developed by the end of the 18th century and they provided the necessary speed in carding and spinning, but the mechanized loom was yet to come.

THE CONSUMER SOCIETY AND THE ACCELERATION OF FASHION CHANGE

Fashionable behavior as has been noted earlier had been evident in western Europe since the Middle Ages (see discussion, *page 85*). But participation in the fashion process had been limited, for the most part, to an affluent elite consisting of royalty and their courts, the nobility, professionals, and the well-educated. McKendrick, Brewer and Plumb (1992) argue convincingly that all this changed in the 18th century in England when, they believe, the "consumer society" was born.

The economic benefits of expanding consumer demand in late 17th century England appear to have been manifested first in the "epidemic" of demand for the cheap cottons from India, imported by the East India Company. Gradually commercial interests recognized the benefits inherent in stimulating demand for consumer goods and the ways in which the desire to follow fashion, not only in clothing but also in furnishings, houses, and art objects such as pottery, fed the economy. Participants in the consumer revolution were located at all levels of society where there was enough cash income to allow the purchase of non-essential consumer goods. The English class structure, more compact and open than elsewhere in Europe, the rise of wage rates, the large proportion of the population living in the urban center of London, and the growth of an aggressive retailing industry all facilitated an increase in consumer demand. The desire to be "in fashion" was exploited by commercial interests.

McKendrick states, "Once this pursuit [of fashion] was made possible for an ever-widening proportion of the population, then its potential was released, and it became an engine for growth, a motive of power for mass production. Explaining the release of that power, in terms of release of a latent desire for new consumption patterns, goes a long way towards explaining the coming of the Industrial Revolution and the birth of a consumer society" (*pages 65–66*).

Although McKendrick and colleagues focus on English society, it is safe to assume that similar patterns of behavior would have been transplanted to Britain's American colonies. France maintained its leadership in innovating dress fashions, but it was not until after the French Revolution that French society, in which social classes were more widely separated than in England, became more open to fashion participation at varying social levels.

Among the results of the consumer revolution and increased commercialization of clothing production were the increases in the speed of fashion change and a wider variety of styles. In the 21st century, we have become used to seasonal promotion by the fashion industry and the fashion press of the "latest" innovations. From this perspective, the changes of the 18th century may not seem so dramatic. However, writers of the period testify to contemporary amazement at the rapidity with which new fashions were introduced. The great burst of growth in fashion terminology provides additional evidence of the proliferation of new styles.

To interest consumers in new styles, fashion information had to be communicated to a broad audience. Sellers of new styles advertised their wares. Engraved drawings of fashions—many hand-colored—could be purchased. Fashion dolls, prepared by Parisian dressmakers, dressed in the latest fashions, and sent abroad had existed since the 14th century, but these dolls had originally been sent to the court and circulated only among the elite. By the 18th century in England, such dolls could be viewed for two shillings and taken away temporarily (probably so that the costume could be copied more accurately) for seven shillings (McKendrick, Brewer, and Plumb 1982).

An even less expensive variant on the fashion doll was developed in England in the 1790s. Printed cardboard dolls and wardrobes, comparable to modern "paper dolls," were sold for a few pence, making information about current styles available to those with more modest incomes.

By the close of the 18th century, the commercialization of fashion was well established. Throughout western Europe and in North America, most of the population adopted fashionable dress and followed fashion trends. Notable exceptions were peasants who maintained regional folk dress, slaves who had no control over the provision of their own clothing, the abject poor, religious orders, and some religious sects.

NOTES

McKendrick, N., J. Brewer, and J. H. Plumb. 1982. *The Birth of a Consumer Society: The Commercialization of Eighteenth Century England.* Bloomington, IN: Indiana University Press.

Squire, G. 1974. *Dress and Society: 1560–1970.* New York: Viking Press, p. 86.

CHRONOLOGY

1601

Birth of Rembrandt

1607

First permanent English settlement in New World established at Jamestown, in Virginia

1610

Louis XIII becomes king of France

1611

King James version of the Bible

1613–1691

English East India Company establishes trading centers on the Indian subcontinent

1616

Death of Shakespeare

1619

First African slaves brought to the American mainland

1620

Pilgrims establish settlement at Plymouth, Massachusetts

1624

Dutch establish settlement of New Amsterdam (now New York)

1625

Charles I becomes king of England

1642

Civil War breaks out in England

1643

Louis XIV becomes king of France

1649

Charles I of England executed
The Commonwealth proclaimed in England

1653

Oliver Cromwell becomes Lord Protector of England

1660

Monarchy reinstated in England and Charles II,
son of Charles I, becomes king

1666

Charles II of England introduces new garment: a "vest"

1669

Death of Rembrandt

1682

French court moves to the Palace at Versailles, built by Louis XIV

1685–1688

James II rules England

1689–1702

William of Orange and Mary, daughter of James II, rule England

1699

Disintegration of the Ottoman Empire begins

THE SEVENTEENTH CENTURY

1 6 0 0 – 1 7 0 0

A.

B.

C.

E.

A.

Baroque ornamentation

B.

Louis XIII chair

C.

Carolean chair

D.

Versailles

E.

Baroque painting by Gerard de Lairesse,
Apollo and Aurora, c. 1671

F.

Early American house, c. 1670

D.

F.

Figure A from Rettelbusch, E. 1996. *Handbook of Historic Ornament from Ancient Times to Biedermeier.* New York: Dover p. 162. Figures B, C from Hart, H. H. 1977. *Chairs Through the Ages, A Pictorial Archive of Woodcuts & Engravings.* New York: Dover, pp. 51, 25. Figures D, F courtesy of V. R. Tortora. Figure E courtesy of the Metropolitan Museum of Art, gift of Manuel E. and Ellen G. Rionda (43.118).

HISTORICAL BACKGROUND

The major powers in 17th century Europe were France, England, and Spain. Italy remained divided into small political units dominated by other countries. Holland had become not only independent of Spain, but also wealthy and prosperous. The German princes, technically within the Holy Roman Empire, were sovereign powers, independent, free to make war or peace. The head of the Austrian Hapsburgs still had the title of Holy Roman Emperor, but this was an illusionary honor. In reality, the Austrian Hapsburgs had only their hereditary lands in eastern Europe.

The Renaissance styles in the arts had given way in the late 16th century to the Mannerist style. Mannerist styles stressed realistic representation of religious themes painted to appeal to the emotions of the beholder. Mannerism served as a bridge between the Renaissance and the Baroque styles. During the 17th century, the Italians again led the artistic transition from Mannerism to the vigorous Baroque style. Like the Renaissance, the Baroque style spread across the Alps and into the rest of Europe.

France

In France, the figure of Louis XIV dominated the Baroque period. After the assassination of Henry IV in 1610, Henry's young son became King Louis XIII. During a reign lasting until 1643 Louis XIII entrusted the government of France to Cardinal Richelieu, who sought to centralize authority in the monarchy and to raise France to a dominant position in Europe. After Richelieu's death in 1642, Cardinal Mazarin carried on his work into the reign of Louis XIV, who succeeded his father on the throne in 1643 at the age of five years. At his death in 1715, after a reign of 72 years, Louis XIV's court had established a standard of grandeur to which other European monarchs would aspire, but never equal.

During his youth, some of the high-ranking nobility engaged in an open rebellion. This rebellion, called the *Fronde* (a Parisian child's game), was undertaken in an effort to ruin Cardinal Mazarin and to undermine absolute government. The episode, which endangered his life, left a strong impression on young Louis. As an adult, he resolved to forestall rebellions by the nobility and to bring them to court where they could not endanger the security of France.

Because the *Fronde* had also made Louis wary of the city mobs, he moved his court away from Paris. At great expense, he had an enormous palace constructed outside of Paris at Versailles, where his father had a hunting lodge. The Palace of Versailles became the symbol of the glory and the majesty of Louis XIV's reign, serving as a stage on which he played the role of an absolute monarch, the epitome of a divine-right king surrounded by fawning nobles.

Members of the nobility who were out of favor with the king were forced to live on their ancestral estates in the provinces instead of close to the court. Furthermore, they were deprived of pensions and sinecures, which could be bestowed only on those at court. By this tactic, Louis kept his nobles busy at court where he could keep an eye on them.

To be at Versailles, a nobleman had to either live at the palace in the royal apartments or in squalid lodgings. To maintain appearances at court, a nobleman needed an expensive, varied wardrobe and funds to spend on life at court. Furthermore, nobles competed to participate in a complicated court ritual that included helping the king get up in the morning and prepare for bed at night. As a result, Louis XIV kept the nobles so busy waiting on him and spending money that they had neither the time nor the funds to plot against him.

In 1589, Louis XIV's grandfather, Henry IV, had issued the Edict of Nantes, a political arrangement intended to bring peace between the warring Protestant minority, the Huguenots, and the Roman Catholic majority in France. Because the Edict contravened Louis XIV's ideal of "one faith, one law, one king," his government gradually whittled away the rights enjoyed by the Huguenots. Louis formally revoked the Edict of Nantes in 1689. Following the revocation, it is estimated that as many as 200,000 Huguenots left France and settled in England, the Netherlands, Prussia, and even Boston and Charleston. Among those who left were skilled artisans from the textile industries. Many silk workers settled in Spitalfields, England, an important textile center, where this influx of new labor stimulated this important English industry.

In his search for glory Louis tried to dominate Europe through a series of wars. The European powers, however, reacted to his aggressions by forming alliances to thwart his ambitions. In the end, Louis's efforts at dominating Europe resulted only in exhausting the nation and impoverishing the people. Despite his sins and errors, Louis XIV set the style for absolute monarchy, a style that was copied throughout Europe.

England

While the French king grew more powerful, the English monarchy across the Channel was in difficulty. After the death of Elizabeth I, her cousin James VI of Scotland was crowned James I of Great Britain. The son of the ill-fated Mary Queen of Scots, James talked about divine-right monarchy but backed away from real confrontation with Parliament over the question. During his reign, a radical Protestant religious faction within the Church of England, called the Puritans, continued to grow. Appearing in England during the reign of Elizabeth I, the Puritans, imbued with John Calvin's teachings, wanted to "purify" the Church of England of the remnants of Roman Catholic ritual and practice. Some Puritans, known to American history as "the pilgrims," were sufficiently unhappy with James's religious policies that they fled to Holland, and from there in 1620 they sailed on the Mayflower to the New World.

James I's son, Charles I (1625–1649), a king who took very seriously the theory of divine right, could not escape a showdown with Parliament over money and religion. The royal income could keep up neither with inflation nor with the growing royal expenses. Moreover, Charles antagonized Puritans and other Englishmen by trying to compel religious conformity to the practices of the Church of England and by levying taxes without consent of Parliament. Civil war broke out in 1642, and by 1646 the king was a prisoner. In 1649 Charles I was beheaded, the monarchy abolished, and a republic, called the Commonwealth, proclaimed.

Oliver Cromwell, commander of the New Model Army which had defeated the royal forces, led the Commonwealth and later the Protectorate, a form of military dictatorship, until his death in 1659. In 1660, with civil war threatening, no Puritan leader could fill Cromwell's place. There was no alternative but to restore the monarchy and to invite the eldest son of Charles I, who had taken refuge in France at the court of Louis XIV, to return.

The new monarch, Charles II, brought to the throne a taste for French styles and a bevy of royal mistresses. A witty, shrewd politician, Charles schemed, plotted, and bribed to gain absolute power. With victory almost assured, he died suddenly in 1685 leaving no legitimate children. His brother James II succeeded to the throne.

A Roman Catholic, but an incompetent politician, James II pursued policies that frightened all political factions. The birth of a son who would be raised in the Roman Catholic faith led leaders of English political parties to invite William of Orange to come over from Holland and help end the reign of James II. Deserted by his supporters at the news that William had landed with a Dutch army, James was allowed to escape to France in 1688.

William and his wife, Mary, the Protestant daughter of James II, accepted the throne offered them by Parliament. During their reign (1689–1702), Parliament, through the Bill of Rights, limited the power of the monarch and protected the rights of individuals. Through the Toleration Act, Parliament granted freedom of worship to Protestant dissenters but not to Roman Catholics. Nevertheless, religious persecution ended for English men and women.

SOCIAL LIFE DURING THE 17TH CENTURY

The French Court

The French court at Versailles was the hub of upper-class activity. Courtiers lodged either in the Palace, where housing accommodations except for the quarters of the royal family were neither spacious nor luxurious; in their own houses nearby; or in Paris. Those of sufficient rank attended the king when he arose in the morning. The king lived most of his life in public, including dressing in the morning. He donned his breeches, then was handed his shirt by the highest ranking person present. Washing consisted of rubbing his face with cotton soaked in diluted, scented alcohol—washing in water was considered dangerous. (Baths were rarely taken.) The rest of his day was just as ritualized, and the activities of each and every person were carefully prescribed by court etiquette. Rules even governed the length of the trains of dresses ladies could wear. The queen's train was 11 ells long (one ell equaled about 28 inches), a daughter of the king, nine; his granddaughter, seven; a princess of the blood (i.e., related but not a direct descendant of the king), five; and a duchess, three (Levron 1968).

Clothing was one of the major items of expense for courtiers. One writer of the period, St. Simon, speaks of spending 800 louis d'or for clothes for himself and his wife for the wedding of the Duke of Burgundy. One louis d'or is equal to about $5.00, so that St. Simon must have spent around $4,000 for costumes for this one occasion! Obviously not all clothing was so luxurious, nor should it be assumed that this is the cost of one or two items of clothing. The festivities of an elaborate wedding would have required many different changes of clothing.

England

In England during the reign of Charles I, the court was less important than it was to become under his son, Charles II. In the first half of the 17th century, England was still largely rural, and many of the aristocracy lived on their country estates. Those members of Parliament who lived in the country went to London for Parliamentary sessions, but returned home when Parliament had ended. Others lived in houses in London or in towns. After the end of the Civil War and during the Commonwealth, life continued to center in the rural areas, but when Charles II was restored to the throne, social life of the upper classes began to center more at Court, and London society became more important as a leader of fashion.

Holland

In Holland, where a prosperous middle class had developed as a result of Dutch interests in trade, the number of items of clothing owned by some individuals is remarkable. For example, a dowry for the daughter of a wealthy Amsterdam family was reported to include 150 chemises and 50 scarves. One upper-class widow of the first half of the century was said to have 32 different ruffs and the inventory of the wardrobe of the mayor of one town listed 40 pairs of drawers,

150 shirts, 150 collars, 154 pairs of ruffled cuffs, 60 hats, 92 night-caps, 20 dressing gowns worn as informal attire during the day, a dozen nightgowns, and 35 pairs of gloves (Zumthor 1963).

America

Among the early Puritan settlers of New England, one might expect to find a population with little interest in fashion, living under somewhat primitive conditions. Indeed, the earliest settlers in New England did live in temporary structures under difficult conditions, but these structures were gone by 1660, replaced by more permanent houses. Wills of the period show that some houses were well equipped while others had more frugal belongings.

An invoice of English goods shipped to New England about 1690 includes many fashionable accessories and fabrics for making suits and dresses. Cargo listed included felt and castor (beaver) hats for men and boys, hair powder, looking glasses, periwigs, wool hose, lace, girdles (belts), caps, fringe, cornette and fontange wires (supports for fashionable head-dresses), and a wide range of fabrics including "worsted fancies," "striped silk crepes," "silk fancies," "camblett" (camlet—a wool fabric), as well as more mundane fabrics such as kerseys (a coarse, rib-weave, woolen cloth) in brown, gray, and drab; linsey-woolsey (a linen and wool fabric), and cottons in shades of white, red, blue, and yellow. One well-to-do woman was sent a feather fan with a silver handle and "two tortoise fans, 200 needles, five yards of calico, silver gimp, blank sarindin (a white fabric), a cloak, a damson leather skin, and two women's ivory knives" (Dow 1925).

Religious and secular leaders did not always approve of such "fancies." In some communities sumptuary laws were passed that included provisions that neither men nor women "should wear clothing with more than one slash on each sleeve and another on the back." Cutwork, embroidery, needlework caps, bands (lace collars), and head rails (scarves) were among the items prohibited, as were ruffs, beaver hats, and long, shoulder-length, curled hair. One minister disinherited his nephew because he wore his hair fashionably long. That these laws were more ignored than observed is likely. Captain George Corwin, a merchant of Salem, Massachusetts, included in his large wardrobe a cloth coat trimmed with silver lace, a velvet coat, and accessories such as golden topped gloves, embroidered and fringed gloves, a silver hat band, and a silverheaded cane (Dow 1925).

SOME DISTINCTIVE COSTUME TRADITIONS

Costume worn by the upper classes in the 17th century was fairly consistent from country to country. Nevertheless within this trend toward greater international style, some distinctive costume traditions did develop. In England, the clothing of Puritans reflected their spiritual and political values. In Spain, distinctive styles were probably more a result of conservatism and resistance to change.

Puritan Costume

Descriptions by later historians of the civil strife between the Puritans and Cavaliers (or Royalists) in England often imply that these two parties wore styles of garments that separated one group from the other. The reality is that the Puritans followed much the same styles as the rest of the population. Distinctions between these factions were chiefly those of degree. Puritans decried excesses of dress and the wearing of more stylish clothes than was appropriate to one's station, whereas Cavaliers and their ladies stressed lavishly decorated costumes in vivid colors.

Puritan dress is often described as "sad-colored." As generally understood, "sad colors" were drab. Wealthy Puritans wore clothing of fine quality albeit more restrained in decoration and color than those of their Cavalier neighbors. Soldiers who followed the Puritan cause cut their hair shorter, and avoided the elaborate curls of the Cavaliers, thereby earning themselves the nickname of "roundheads."

Cavalier or royalist sympathizers tended to wear broad-brimmed, flat-crowned hats trimmed with plumes, while the Puritans favored high-crowned, narrower brimmed copotains, but neither faction followed this pattern slavishly. Puritan women and Cavalier women alike wore aprons for every day, but those of the Puritans were less ornate as a rule.

The Puritan settlers in New England brought with them the styles current in England at the time of their sailing, 1620. Like their English counterparts, the New England clergy stressed restrained and simple styles. In spite of the preaching of the clergy and the time required for fashion information to travel across the Atlantic, these colonists tried to keep up with the major developments in European fashions. (See *Color Plate 26*.)

Spanish Costume

Although Spain had been the major fashion leader of western Europe during the latter half of the 16th century, by the beginning of the 17th century Spanish styles were beginning to lag behind those of other countries. The Spanish tended to be more conservative than other nations, and this conservatism had the effect of prolonging styles like the ruff and the Spanish farthingale (in Spanish, **verdugado,** pronounced *vair-du-ga'do*) even after the rest of Europe had abandoned them.

Even the Spanish **mantilla** (*man-teel'ya*), the veil worn to cover the hair that has come to be associated with traditional Spanish costume is a smaller version of the mantle worn by women during the Medieval period and carried over into later times. Custom was strong in Spain and tradition regulated the length of this veil according to the status of the woman as either widow, married woman, or unmarried girl. In some regions, an unmarried girl was expected to cover her face when outside of the house. This practice may have been borrowed from the Moors who occupied Spain for such a long time during the Middle Ages.

But the most notable of the Spanish costume practices in the 17th century was the belated adoption of a style somewhat similar to the wide, French farthingale. Obsolete in the rest of Europe after the second decade of the 17th century, wealthy Spanish women took up the style only around the mid-1600s. The Spanish called the style the **guardinfante** (*gward-in-fahn'tay*). (See *Figure 9.1*.) The skirt was more oval than the French farthingale, with greater width from side to side. The bodice had a long, wide **basque** (a basque, pronounced "*bask,*" is the extension of the bodice below the waistline) that extended down over the top of the wide skirt. The bodice shoulderline was usually horizontal and showed similarities to necklines of costumes then being worn in the rest of Europe. (See *Figure 9.10*.) Sleeves were full and slashed to show contrasting underlinings and generally ended in fitted cuffs.

With these dresses women wore high chopines with wooden or cork soles that helped to elongate the figure somewhat to compensate for the width of the guardinfante. Not all Spanish women wore these excessively wide skirts, which were a feature of court dress. As Reade (1951) points out, " Since exertion was difficult for anyone wearing it, the vogue emphasized social distinctions." Other women often placed a pad around the waist, which slightly widened skirts.

Spanish men's styles also changed slowly. They retained the ruff and trunk hose somewhat longer than men in the rest of Europe. However, men's styles were never so extreme in their regional differences as women's. By 1700, the Spanish had re-entered the mainstream of European fashion.

PRODUCTION AND ACQUISITION OF TEXTILES AND CLOTHING

The technology for producing fine textiles did not change radically, but gradual improvements in machinery were made. Elaborately figured silk fabrics had to be produced on

FIGURE 9.1

Princess dressed in the Spanish court style called the guardinfante. (Portrait by Velasquez, c. 1659–1660. Photograph courtesy, The Prado Museum.)

a special loom called a draw loom. Use of this loom required that a small boy sit on top of the loom and manually raise and lower sets of yarns in order to create a pattern. It is believed that the draw loom was invented in China. By the late Middle Ages it was in use in Italy and by 1600 was being used wherever complicated patterns in silk fabrics were being woven. Around 1600, improvements were made that allowed the drawboy to sit at the side of the loom and lift the patterned yarns more easily and also made possible the weaving of more complex patterns. As a result figured silk fabrics were readily available and quite popular throughout the century.

Siamese ambassadors wore sumptuous garments when visiting the court of Louis XIV in 1684, and these garments are said to have inspired imitations called *siamoises,* which were made of cotton with colorful silk stripes (Montgomery 1984). In the last decades of the 17th century, fine English woolens somewhat eclipsed the popularity of silks, this vogue even extending as far as Egypt (Braudel 1982).

For the upper classes, a hired professional tailor made clothing; for the lower classes, women of the family did the work. Most professional tailors were male, although women frequently did ornamental and fine hand sewing. Women began to move into this profession after 1675. A group of French women seamstresses applied for the right to form a guild of female "tailors" for making women's clothes. The application was approved. Hollander (1994) believes that as a result, "A difference in the way clothes were conceived and made for the two sexes came into existence for the first time, a separation that profoundly affected both the character and reputation of fashion for the next two centuries, and that still survives."

SOURCES OF EVIDENCE OF HISTORIC COSTUME

Although more garments survive from the 17th century than from earlier periods, works of art make up the largest part of sources of information about costume in the 17th century. These works include painted portraits and drawings of actual individuals and paintings and drawings of scenes of everyday life.

Hand-colored fashion plates began to be produced in Paris in the late 17th century (and on into the 18th century). These were accompanied by brief written descriptions. Cumming (1985, p. 14) cautions that these plates are ". . . more akin to modern fashion photographs in glossy magazines than to styles of dress which were generally worn," produced as they apparently were in consultation with tailors, seamstresses, and milliners. As for verbal descriptions, they are often hard to interpret. Words were coined, and specialized fashion terms proliferated.

Marshall (1981) evaluated 17th century Scottish portraits as a source of costume information, and found that these images could be valuable sources of information. She points out, however, that some examples are misleading because (1) some artists invented garments, (2) some portraits were painted after the death of the subject and were dressed in clothing of later dates, and (3) some examples are of persons long dead and dressed in purely imaginary garments.

Cumming (1985) lists the questions that should be asked when looking, for example, at a painting from the mid-1600s. "Are the figures depicted in it fashionable city dwellers or provincial conservatives? Are they elderly, wearing a style once fashionable which they cling to for sentimental reasons, or have they adopted a current fashion . . . ? Are they young, rich, experimental? Are they from the lower orders in society, or do they practice a profession which dictates a certain style of dress which overlays or distorts a contemporary fashion? Or are they subscribing to an artistic and social admiration for a form of stylized dress, perhaps pseudo-classical or 'antique' or pastoral, which they and/or their chosen artist wish to translate into timeless fashion . . . ?"

Works by great artists may often be less useful than those of lesser artists. We know, for example, that Rembrandt collected Near Eastern paraphernalia that he used to dress the subjects of his paintings (Jansen 1991). It is rare to find a Rembrandt portrait that is useful in illustrating costume.

Sometimes figures in the background of a painting may be quite useful. Hollander (1978, p. 319) observes, "From such representations one may learn how bodies in their clothes not only were supposed to look, or were conceived by the privileged eyes of artists, but undoubtedly how they actually did look in the eyes of the epoch."

COSTUME FOR MEN: 17TH CENTURY

Men's costume in the first two decades of the century retained the major elements characteristic of costume of the latter part of the 1500s. In these two decades major elements of costume were the shirt, the doublet, the jacket or jerkin, and trunk hose or knee-length breeches called Venetians. Trunk hose became baggy and full, extending to the knees. By the close of the third decade, however, a different style had emerged, the first of three fairly distinct phases in men's clothing styles.

A number of variants in the style of and the terminology used to describe garments that cover men's bodies below the waist developed in the 17th and subsequent centuries. *Table 9.1* summarizes these developments.

Table 9.1

TERMS DESCRIBING MEN'S TROUSER-TYPE GARMENTS: 16TH CENTURY TO 19TH CENTURY

Terms	Origins of Terms	Dates in Use	Description
breeches	probably derived from term "braies"	beginning about 1570; by the 1620s breeches replaced trunk-hose in England	made with seams on outside and inside of each leg, hung from waist, and had varying degrees of fullness; the term continues in use until the present but shape and cut has varied over time (For example, see *Figures 9.2* and *10.6*.)
slopp (also spelled sloppe)	seems to originate with the Dutch; eventually the meaning changes and the term is applied to any ready-made clothing	from 16th century to 19th century	seems to apply to breeches that appear wide at the knees; the Dutch were said generally to wear wider breeches (See *Figure 8.6*.)
petticoat breeches or rhinegraves	had a skirtlike shape, hence the name "petticoat" breeches	c. 1658–1680	wide, bifurcated garment that has the appearance of a skirt (See *Figure 9.4*.)
trowsers or trousers	origin uncertain; appears to derive from an Irish term for garment similar to breeches	in 17th century as sailors' clothing, possibly over breeches as a protective garment in America in the 18th century; from c. 1800 to the present for fashionable dress	initially cut as short as the knee and full for sailors; later long but fairly full; in 18th century, generally a working man's garment, long and fairly loose; by 19th century, has come to have the modern meaning of a generic bifurcated garment (See *Figure 12.13, page 292*.)
pantaloon	derives from the name of St. Pantaleon, from Venice, and is named after an Italian comic character called Pantalone who always appeared dressed in ankle-length breeches or "trowsers"	for civilian dress, late 18th century; used earlier for military dress	garment cut from waist to ankle in one piece; at various times was cut to fit either close to the leg or fuller; by the 19th century, the terms "pantaloons" and "trousers" were sometimes used interchangeably
pants	shortened form of the word "pantaloons," which is used mostly in the United States	19th century and after	in modern usage is used interchangeably with trousers
overalls	derives from practice of wearing this garment to cover or protect other garments	c. 18th century and after	worn as outer layer over a second garment; trousers also were sometimes used as protective, outer garment and in early usage, distinction between overalls and trousers is not clear; eventually a bib was added; "bib" and overalls came to be work clothing
sherryvallies	probably derived from Polish *szarawary*, a term for a similar garment	during the American Revolution, c. 1776 to about 1830	a legcovering generally worn by horseback riders over trousers or pantaloons that buttoned up on the outside of the leg
knickerbockers, more often shortened to knickers	derived from the name of the pretended author of Washington Irving's *History of New York;* the term came into usage to describe the descendants of the original Dutch settlers of New York, and was applied to full, loose-fitting breeches, gathered at the knee, which looked like the garments in the illustrations in the aforementioned book	term originates in the mid-19th century and has been used ever since	breeches, full and loose, and gathered into a band at the knee; a garment for sports in the 19th century, and until the 1940s; also worn by preadolescent boys; this style is revived occasionally and is also worn for cross-country skiing (See *Figure 15.16, page 379*.)

Information derived from Murray, A. 1976. "From Breeches to Sherryvallies." *Dress,* Vol. 2, No. 1, p. 17.

Costume for Men: 1625–1650

GARMENTS

Now less an undergarment and more an integral part of the whole costume, the shirt was cut very full, was made of white linen and had a flat collar (**falling band**) that replaced the ruff. Sleeve cuffs and collars were often of lace or decorated with cutwork embroidery.

The doublet was worn over the shirt and tied (laced) to breeches. Evolving forms, all with the waistline set somewhat above the anatomical waistline, included a short tabbed extension below the waist, which was the earliest form, carried over from the previous century. The new style had a skirtlike extension reaching to the hip. (See *Figures 9.2* and *9.3*.) Some doublets had panes or slits through which the shirt or a colored lining was visible. (See *Figure 9.2* and *Color Plate 24*.)

Breeches, cut full throughout or cut more closely and tapering gradually to the knee, began at the waist and extended to the knee. The lower edges might be decorated with ribbons and lace. (See *Figures 9.2* and *9.3*.)

For outdoors, men wore capes and cloaks, which often had wide collars. One type of cape was convertible into a coat. Larger, more enveloping cloaks were worn over both shoulders, while circular capes, which hung over one shoulder, were often secured with a cord that passed under the wide collar (see *Figure 9.3*). In France, such capes were called **Balagny** (*bal-ahn'-yee*) cloaks after a popular military hero. **Cassocks** (English term) or **casaques** (*kazaks'*) (French term) were coats cut with wide, full sleeves that were wide throughout the body and ended at thigh height or below.

HAIR AND HEADDRESS

Most men wore their hair long and curling. Beards were trimmed to a point; moustaches were large and curled. French and English men of fashion grew one lock of hair (a "**love lock**") longer than the rest. (See *Figure 9.2*.) Large-brimmed hats had full feather plumes. (See *Figures 9.2* and *9.3*.)

FOOTWEAR

Both shoes and boots had high heels and **straight soles,** without shaping for left or right feet. Prior to the appearance of high heels, shoes were shaped for either right or left feet. It appears that when shoes began to have high heels, shoemakers found it too difficult to make both high heels and shaped soles, and so straights were made until the early 19th century when shoes might be, once again, shaped to fit each foot (Swann 1991).

Some boots and shoes had **slap soles,** a flat sole attached only at the front, not at the heel. These soles "slapped" the ground as the wearer walked. These were intended to keep the heel of the shoe or boot from sinking into soft ground. (See the man in the foreground of *Figure 9.3* and *Illustrated Table 9 .1, page 211*.)

FIGURE 9.2

Painting of Henri, Duc de Guise, by Van Dyck. The Duke wears a doublet over a white shirt, which can be seen at the front of his doublet and through the slashes in its sleeves. His collar, a falling band, and cuffs are decorated with lace and embroidery. His breeches extend below the knee and are decorated with lace where they meet his high boots. One lock of his hair is grown longer than the rest, tied with a ribbon and called a "love lock." He carries a wide-brimmed, plumed hat and a cloak over his arm. (Photograph courtesy, The National Gallery of Art, Washington, DC, gift of Cornelius Vanderbilt Whitney, 1947.)

The most important items of footwear were boots extending to the knee, where they met the breeches (see *Figure 9.2*), and shoes with large, open sides and extensions (called **latchets**) that tied across the instep. Until the 1630s toes were rounded; afterward, toes were more square with very large rosettes and ribbon decorations over a high square tongue. (See *Figure 9.3*.) Hose or stockings were knee-length and worn under shoes or boots.

FIGURE 9.3

The Ball, by Abraham Bosse, depicts fashionable men and women of the third and fourth decades of the 17th century. Note the coat worn over the shoulder in the manner of a cape by the gentleman in the right foreground. (Photograph courtesy, The Metropolitan Museum of Art, Rogers Fund, 1922.)

Costume for Men: 1650–1680

GARMENTS

Changes in the doublet caused shirts to become more visible and more important. Collars or bands were either a part of the shirt or a separate piece. These enlarged at the front to form a bib-like, often lace-trimmed, construction. After 1665, a long linen tie served as an alternative to the collar.

The doublet shortened, ending several inches above the waist. It was straight and unfitted through the body. Although its sleeves ended at the elbow, there were also some sleeveless forms. (See *Figure 9.4* and *Color Plate 25.*)

Knee length breeches were either short and straight or full and drawn in to tie at the knee. An alternative form was made in a style called **petticoat breeches** or **rhinegraves.** These breeches were actually a divided skirt, rather like a

modern culotte, that was cut so full that it gave the appearance of a short skirt. (See *Figure 9.4.*) The origin of these breeches, popular from about 1650 to 1675, is uncertain, but the name rhinegraves would indicate that they may have originated in Germany. Full, wide ruffles attached at the bottom of breeches were called **canons.**

THE VEST

The origin of the prototype of what eventually evolved into the three-piece suit is thought to be a garment that was introduced to the English court by Charles II in 1666 (Kuchta 1990). The actual costume consisted of below-the-knee-length coat and what we would call a vest or a waistcoat of the same length, worn over narrow breeches. (Petticoat breeches, the predominant style of the time, were too full to fit beneath the vest and coat.)

FIGURE 9.4

Man dressed in the style (popular between 1650 and 1680) called petticoat breeches or rhinegraves, a divided skirt cut so full that it has the appearance of a skirt. His short jacket allows a large expanse of his white shirt to show. Over this he wears a cape. (Drawing by Sebastien LeClerc, "Album of 472 Engravings." Print Collection, Miriam and Ira D. Wallach Division of Art, Prints, and Photographs, The New York Public Library, Astor, Lenox and Tilden Foundations.)

———

Called by contemporaries a "vest," a term used in describing some Persian garments of a similar cut, it is thought to have oriental antecedents. The king, contrary to a promise he made never to change from this style, did not wear this type of garment for the rest of his life. The basic pattern of a long coat and a long vest underneath worn over a shirt and breeches did, however, become the basic components of men's dress not only in England but also in France by around 1680. (*Contemporary Comments 9.1* reproduces reactions to and comments about the king's vest.) (Also see *Figue 9.5*.)

OUTDOOR GARMENTS

Outdoor garments included cloaks or capes and coats that were cut full, some versions ending at the knee and obscuring the costume beneath.

HAIR AND HEADDRESS

Some men shaved their heads and wore long, curling wigs. Others dressed their own hair in long, curling styles. In England, alternative hat styles demonstrated the wearer's political affiliations. A wide-brimmed, low-crowned, feather trimmed hat was associated with "Cavaliers" or supporters of the British royal family. High-crowned, small-brimmed copotains were associated with supporters of the Puritan faction, opposed to the King. Men wore hats indoors and out and in church. (See *Illustrated Table 9.1, page 211.*)

FOOTWEAR

Shoes had elaborate rosette, ribbon, and buckle trimmings. Shoes were preferred to boots for fashionable dress and boots were worn for riding and in bad weather. The term **galosh** (or golosh) appears in contemporary records. Swann (1991) defines it as a flat-soled overshoe with a toe cap for keeping it in place. Although Swann notes the use of red-heeled and soled shoes as early as 1614 and speaks of them for court wear in England in the 1640s, Louis XIV is often credited with originating the style during his reign. Whatever the origin, this style was very popular in court circles in France and England for the remainder of the century, and on into the 18th century.

Costume for Men: 1680–1710

GARMENTS

Shirts were little changed from the forms worn earlier in the century. **Cravats,** long, narrow, scarflike pieces separate from the shirt were worn instead of collars. (See *Figure 9.5.*) Of one "dandy" with an excessively long cravat it was said, "his cravat reached down to his middle and had stuff enough in it to make a sail for a barge" (Edwards and Ramsey 1968).

Knee-length coats replaced doublets as outer garments. Called **surtouts** (*surtu'*) or **justacorps** (*jewst-a-cor'*) by the French and cassocks by the English, such garments had fitted straight sleeves with turned back cuffs, and buttoned down the front. They completely covered the breeches and waistcoat. (See *Figure 9.6.*)

By the late 17th century the terms vest and waistcoat were being used interchangeably. These garments were cut along the same lines as outer coats, but slightly shorter and less full. Before 1700 most were sleeved; later some were made without sleeves. These coats and waistcoats can be seen as developing from the "vest" introduced by Charles II of England.

Cut with less fullness than in earlier periods, breeches ended at the knee.

HAIR AND HEADDRESS

Wigs grew larger, the hair built up somewhat on the top of the head. Some wigs were dusted with powder to make them white, but most were worn in natural colors.

CONTEMPORARY COMMENTS 9.1

Charles II of England's Vest

Comments about Charles II of England's introduction of a new style of men's dress to the English court. From the Diary of Samuel Pepys, *October 1666.*

October 8th.

The King hath yesterday in Council declared his resolution of setting a fashion for clothes, which he will never alter. It will be a vest, I know not well how; but it is to teach the nobility thrift and will do good.

October 13th.

To White Hall, and there the Duke of York . . . was just come in from hunting. So I stood and saw him dress himself and try on his vest, which is the King's new fashion, and will be in it for good and all on Monday next, and the whole Court: it is a fashion the King says he will never change.

October 15.

This day the King begins to put on his vest, and I did see several persons of the House of Lords and Commons too, great courtiers, who are in it; being a long cassocke close to the body, of black cloth and pinked [cut] with white silk under it, and a coat over it, and the legs ruffled with a black riband like a pigeon's leg; and upon the whole I wish the King may keep it, for it is a very fine and handsome garment.

From the Diary of John Evelyn, *October 1666.*

October 18.

To Court. It being the first time his Majesty put himself solemnly into the Eastern fashion of vest, changing doublet, stiff collar, bands and cloak into a comely dress after the Persian mode, with girdle or straps, and shoe strings and garters into buckles, of which some were set with precious stones, resolving never to alter it, and to leave the French mode, which had hitherto obtained to our great expense and reproach. Upon which various courtiers and gentlemen gave his Majesty gold by way of wager that he would not persist in this resolution [i.e., to wear only this costume henceforth]. I had sometime before presented an invective against that unconstancy, and our so much affecting the French fashion, to his Majesty, in which

I took occasion to describe the comeliness and usefulness of the Persian clothing, in the very same manner his Majesty now clad himself. This pamphlet I entitled "Tyrranus, or the Mode," and gave it to the King to read. I do not impute to this discourse the change which soon happened, but it was an identity [coincidence] that I could not but take notice of.

October 30th.

To London to our office, and now had I on the vest and surcoat and tunic as 'twas called, after his Majesty had brought the whole Court to it. It was a comely and manly habit, too good to hold, it being impossible for us in good earnest to leave the Monsieurs vanities [i.e., the French styles] long.

Quoted from *Diary and Correspondence of Samuel Pepys, F.R.S., Volume 2.* [N.D.,] New York: National Library Company, pp. 467, 471, 473, and *Diary of John Evelyn.*

Hats were somewhat superfluous given the large scale of wigs and were more often carried under the arm than worn. Flat hats with brims turned or "cocked" up at one or more points were often seen, especially one with the brim turned up at three points to form a triangle. Nineteenth century writers called this a tricorne; however, that term does not appear in the 17th or 18th centuries.

FOOTWEAR

Styles were similar to those from earlier in the century. Shoes were preferred for general wear over boots. Shoe buckles, which could be quite costly, were made to transfer from one pair of shoes to another. High, rigid boots made of heavy leather and called **jack boots** were worn for horseback riding in the latter 1600s. (See *Illustrated Table 9.1, page 211.*)

FIGURE 9.5

Man's long vest worn under an outer coat that is just slightly longer and breeches, which are almost invisible. The long vest probably derives from the style introduced by Charles II in 1666, and this three-piece outfit is considered to be the forerunner of the modern three-piece suit. (Drawing by Sebastien LeClerc, "Album of 472 Engravings." Print Collection, Miriam and Ira D. Wallach Division of Art, Prints, and Photographs, The New York Public Library, Astor, Lenox and Tilden Foundations.)

Knee-length stockings, also called hose, were worn with knee breeches.

COSTUME FOR WOMEN: 17TH CENTURY

The wheel farthingale retained its hold on fashion in the first years of the 17th century. Gradually, however, the farthingale flattened in front and the whole line of the costume grew

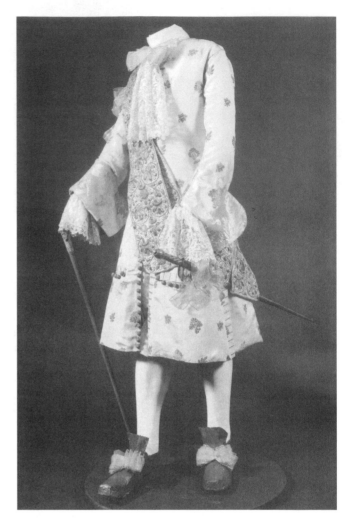

FIGURE 9.6

Costume made for the wedding of Sir Thomas Isham in 1681. Men's outer coats had lengthened to the extent that they hid the knee-breeches beneath. (Photograph courtesy, The Victoria and Albert Museum.)

softer and more square. Necklines were low and rounded. In Spain and Holland the stomacher of the dress elongated into a rigidly boned U-shape. The sides of the gown remained wide and full. Sleeves were multilayered with fitted sleeves under hanging sleeves, and the ruff became even more enormous. (See *Figure 9.7.*)

Although the farthingale lingered on at the Spanish court, it went out of style elsewhere in Europe and the transition to a new style was complete by about the end of the third decade.

Costume for Women: 1630–1660

GARMENTS

The undermost garment continued to be the white linen chemise.

Falling band, man's collar 1st half
of the 1600s

Lace cravat, c. 1640

Cavalier style man's hat, c. 1640

Copotain style hat, c. 1650

Boot with slap sole, c. 1st half
of the 1600s

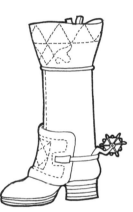

Jackboot, 17th century

Mule style shoe, called a Pantofle,
17th century

Fontange or commode headdress,
c. 1680

Child's protective head
covering called a Pudding,
17th century

Fan, 17th century

Woman's mask for outdoors,
worn with hood, c. 1640

Sleeves, which were often very full on gowns and fashionable jackets, were puffed out and frequently paned. Writers of the period refer to stylish sleeves that were paned and tied into a series of puffs as **virago sleeves.**

While necklines tended to be low, some were V-shaped, some square, and others horizontal in shape. Stiff ruffs had been replaced by falling ruffs, which were gathered collars that sloped from neck to shoulder, or wide collars tied under the chin with strings. Also seen were large neckerchiefs. Horizontal necklines were often edged with a wide, flat collar that in present-day fashion terms would be called a bertha. (See *Color Plate 25.*)

Capes, cut full and with flat turned-down collars, were worn out-of-doors. Some were fur-lined.

HAIR AND HEADDRESS

A part was made behind the ears and the back hair was drawn into a roll or chignon at the back of the head, while the front hair was arranged in curled locks around the face. Although hats were worn indoors and out, women also went bareheaded. Styles included wide-brimmed, "cavalier-style" hats (see Figure 9.9) and copotains, which were frequently worn over a white, close-fitting small cap or coif. Squares of fabric were tied under the chin (see *Color Plate 26*) or sewn or pinned to form a cap. Hoods provided head coverings for out-of-doors. (See *Illustrated Table 9.1, page 216.*)

FIGURE 9.7

Portrait of a Genoese Noblewoman, an Italian Marquise, painted by Van Dyck, wears costume characteristic of Spain and the Low Countries in the first several decades of the 1600s. (Photograph courtesy, The Frick Collection, NY.)

Generally gowns were made with bodices and skirts seamed together at the waist, which was slightly elevated. Gowns, open at center front, served as one of several layers. The outer layer was worn over an underbodice, a boned, stiffened garment like a corset that had a long, U-shaped stomacher at the front and this filled in the upper part of the gown.

Skirts were separate garments worn under gowns, visible at the front when gowns were open or seen when the outer skirts were carried looped up over the arm. Even when the skirts of outer gowns were closed in front, a second layer or under skirt was worn. The French called the outer layer the **modeste** (*mow-dest'*) and the under layer the **secret** (*sek-ray'*). (See *Figure 9.8.*)

Jackets could be worn in combination with skirts instead of gowns. These bodices had short tabs (basques) extending below the waist. Jackets worn at home were often quilted, looser in fit than fashionable dress and without elaborate sleeve constructions. (See *Figure 9.9* and *Color Plate 22.*)

FIGURE 9.8

Lady of the mid-17th century has pulled up her outer skirt (*modeste*) to reveal her underskirt (*secret*). (Courtesy, Picture Collection, New York Public Library.)

FIGURE 9.9

Queen Henrietta Maria with her dwarf, by Van Dyck. The tabs of the jacket in the style of 1625–1660 can be seen where they extend below the waistline. (Photograph courtesy, The National Gallery of Art, Washington, DC, Samuel H. Kress Collection.)

FOOTWEAR

Shoes were similar in shape to those described for men. For bad weather one could wear clogs with toe caps, instep straps, no heels, and wooden soles that protected the shoes and raised them out of the wet streets.

Costume for Women: 1660–1680

GARMENTS

As undergarments women wore chemises and under-petticoats (not to be confused with visible, decorative, outer petticoats or skirts). Drawers, which had been worn by women

for some time on the continent, were not worn in England at this period. Chemises usually showed slightly at the neckline and the edge of sleeves.

The silhouette and shaping of women's gowns changed somewhat. Bodices lengthened and narrowed, becoming long-waisted and more slender with an extended V-shaped point at the front. Heavy satin fabrics seem to have been fashionable for formal dresses. Pastel colors predominate in paintings, but actual fabrics of the period are also brightly colored. (See *Figures 9.10* and *9.11*.)

Frequently edged by a wide lace collar or band of linen called a whisk, necks tended to be low, wide, and horizontal or oval in shape. (See *Figures 9.10* and *9.11*.) Most sleeves were set low on the shoulder, opening into a full puff that ended below the elbow. Some skirts fell straight to the floor and were closed all round, and others were split at the front and pulled back into puffs or looped up, over the hips. Decorations for gowns often consisted of a row of ruffles down the front or lines of jeweled decoration or braid placed on top of seam construction lines. (See *Figure 9.10*.)

Costume for Women: 1680–1700

GARMENTS

Undergarments showed no major changes from the preceding 20 years.

Styles of gowns evolved. Necklines revealed less bosom and became more square. This may have been as a result of the influence of Madame de Maintenon, conservative widow whom King Louis XIV of France is believed to have married secretly in 1684.

Corsets were now visible at the front of the bodice. They were heavily decorated, ending in a pronounced V at the waist. Separate stomachers could be tied or pinned to the front of the corset to vary the appearance of a dress. (See *Color Plate 30*.)

Skirts composed of several layers were often so heavy that they required additional support from whalebone, metal, or basket-work supports. Overskirts were generally split at the front and looped up in complex drapery with a long, back train. The underskirt, which could be seen through the split overskirt, was ornamented with embroidery, ruffles, pleated edgings, and other trimmings. (See *Figure 9.12*.)

A new construction for women's dresses appeared. Instead of cutting the bodice and skirt as separate pieces that were sewn together, bodice and skirt were cut in one length from shoulder to hem. The shaping of this garment, called a **mantua** or **manteau** (pronounced *man-too-a'* or *man-toe'*), is thought to derive from the construction of Middle Eastern robes that were imported into Europe. The resulting garment, however, was quite different from its supposed ancestor. Full in both back and front, the garment was worn over a corset and an underskirt. For casual wear it was loose (the

FIGURE 9.10

The Intruder, by Gabriel Metsu. The lady at the center of the picture is partially undressed. Her braid-decorated outer skirt is draped across the chair in the foreground, as is her characteristically Dutch, velvet, fur-trimmed outer jacket. On her head is a linen nightcap. She has just taken off her backless shoes, which are on the floor. The woman seated by the window wears a jacket similar to the one on the chair. (Photograph courtesy, The National Gallery of Art, Washington, DC, Andrew Mellon Collection, 1937.)

FIGURE 9.11

Dutch woman from after 1660. Her open overskirt displays the decorative underskirt beneath. The panel of ribbons at the front is a typical feature of many women's costumes of this period. (Gerard ter Borch, Dutch, 1617–1681. *Portrait of a Woman,* c. 1663. Oil on canvas, 63.3 × 52.7 cm. © The Cleveland Museum of Art. The Elizabeth Severance Prentiss Collection, 1944.93.)

FIGURE 9.12

Lady of the Court of Versailles (c. 1680) wears a dress with draped overskirt. (Courtesy, Picture Collection, New York city Public Library.)

style is thought to have originated to provide a less confining costume for women), but for more formal wear it was pleated to fit the body at front and back and belted. Front skirt edges were sometimes pulled to the back and fastened to form a draped effect. (See *Figure 9.13*.)

For outdoors, capes in shorter or longer lengths still predominated. Coats, cut like men's cassocks, were worn for riding or walking. Long, broad scarves were placed around the shoulders, as were lappets or short, waist-length capes.

HAIR AND HEADDRESS

Hair was built up high, on top of the head, with long curling locks at the back and sides. On top of the hair women placed a device made of a series of ruffles held in place with wire supports and known as the **fontange** (*fone-tanj'*) in France and the **commode** in England and the American colonies. Over a period of about 30 years, the style evolved from a small bow tieing up the hair in front to an elaborate, tall structure of three or four lace tiers in front and a cascade of ruffles and bows in the back. (See *Illustrated Table 9.1, page 211* and *Color Plate 27*.) It is said that the fontange was named after one of the mistresses of Louis XIV. She supposedly emerged from the woods during a royal hunt in a somewhat disheveled state,

FIGURE 9.13

Mantua-style dress, c. 1690–1695, worn with the headdress called the fontange. (Photograph courtesy, The Metropolitan Museum of Art, Rogers Fund, 1933.)

probably as the result of an amorous encounter with the King. Using her lace garter to tie up her hair, she is supposed to have begun this fashion. See *Contemporary Comments 9.2*, on the rise and fall of the fontange style.

FOOTWEAR

Shapes changed, as shoes became more pointed at the front, and heels became higher and narrower. Brocades and decorated leathers were used for fashionable shoes. Although men

CONTEMPORARY COMMENTS 9.2

The Rise and Fall of the Fontange

The following series of quotations from letters written at the French court and from the English newspaper The Spectator *provide a contemporary account of the rise and fall of the headdress called the* fontange *in France and the* commode *in England.*

Versailles to June 1687. It doesn't surprise me to hear that you are wearing coiffures of ribbon—everyone here does, from little girls to old ladies of eighty, the difference being that young people wear bright colours and old ones dark shades or black. The reason I don't wear them is that I can't bear anything on my head during the day, and at night I find the rustling of the ribbons too noisy; I should never get any sleep, so I have given this fashion a miss.

Versailles 26 January 1688. . . . No one at court wears a fichu. The coiffures grow taller and taller every day. The King told us at dinner today that a fellow by the name of Allart, who used to do people's hair here, has dressed all the ladies of London so tall that they can't get into their sedan-chairs, and have been obliged to have them heightened in order to follow the French fashion.

Versailles 11 December 1695. We don't dress our hair so very high now, still high but not so high as before. The headdresses are now worn bent forward and not so straight up as they used to be. It isn't true that a tax has been put on the coiffure, someone must have invented that tale as a joke.

The Spectator, *an English daily periodical, remarked on the abandonment of the style:*

Friday, June 22, 1711. There is not so variable a thing in Nature as a Lady's Head-dress: Within my own Memory I have known it rise and fall above thirty Degrees. About ten Years ago it shot up to a very great Height, insomuch that the Female Part of our Species were much taller than the Men. . . . At present the whole Sex is in manner dwarfed and shrunk into a race of Beauties that seems almost another Species. I remember several ladies, who were once very near seven Foot high, that at present want some inches of five. . .

Apparently the style changed first in England. St. Simon, in his Memoires of the Court of Louis XIV, *describes the reaction of the English Duchess of Shrewsbury to the style in his memoirs for the year 1713.*

. . . it was not long before she had pronounced the ladies' style of hairdressing to be perfectly ridiculous—as indeed it was, for they then wore erections of wire, ribbons, and false hair, supplemented with all manner of gewgaws, rising to a height of more than two feet. When they moved, the entire edifice trembled and the discomfort was extreme. The King, so autocratic in small details, detested this fashion, but despite his wishes it continued to be worn for more than a decade.

What the monarch could not command, the taste and example of an eccentric old foreigner achieved with surprising speed. From those exaggerated heights the ladies suddenly descended to an extremity of flatness, and the new style, so much simpler, more practical, and infinitely more becoming, has lasted to the present day.

A Woman's Life at the Court of the Sun King. Letters of Liselotte von der Pfalz. 1984. Baltimore: Johns Hopkins University Press, pages 47, 48, 71. Norton, L. ed. and trans. *Historical Memoirs of the Duc de Saint-Simon. Vol. II, 1710–1715.* (Shortened Version) 1984. New York: McGraw-Hill, p. 284. St. Simon wrote his memoirs, based on notes taken the time of which he wrote, between 1739 and 1751.

used buckles to close shoes, women tended to use ties as the buckles were likely to catch on dresses or petticoats.

Pantofles (*pan-toff'-ahl*) were heel-less slippers or mules that, though worn throughout the century, became especially fashionable toward the end of the period. (See *Illustrated Table 9.1, page 211*) The word *pantofle* derives from the Greek word *pantophellos*, which means "cork." Apparently the earliest versions of these backless slippers were made with cork soles, and were used as overshoes. By the 17th century they were made with leather soles and worn indoors as well.

Knitted both by machine and by hand from wool or silk, some stockings had knitted or embroidered decorations.

Costume for Men and Women: 17th Century

ACCESSORIES

Accessories of dress, use of cosmetics, and grooming practices are not easily separated into the same time periods as clothing. Also, both men and women used many of these items. For these reasons the following section summarizes the major trends in accessories, etc., for the 17th century for both men and women. (See *Illustrated Table 9.1, page 211*.)

Among the more widely used accessories were:

- gloves worn by men and women and sometimes scented with perfume
- handkerchiefs and purses carried by men and women
- purses made of beaded leather or embroidered
- fans for women, made of feathers or of the folding type
- muffs made of silk, velvet, or satin, fur, or fur-trimmed fabrics and carried by ladies
- face masks worn by ladies who wanted to protect their faces against the weather or to engage in flirtations without being recognized
- aprons: The practical cotton or linen varieties were worn to protect the garment beneath as women went about their household tasks; decorative ones made of silk or lace and lavishly embroidered were worn as an attractive accessory to fashionable dress.

JEWELRY

Men wore neck chains, pendants, lockets, rings, and, in the first part of the century, earrings. Women wore necklaces, bracelets, earrings, and rings. They also placed mirrors and pomander balls around their waists on chains. Pomander balls were small balls of perfume enclosed in decorated, perforated boxes that might be shaped like an apple. The French word *pomme*, from which the word pomander derives, means apple.

COSMETICS AND GROOMING

Women and some men used cosmetics. Perfume was applied to the person and to articles of clothing. Lead combs were used to darken the eyebrows; paint, and powder to tint the face. Some women colored their lips and fingernails red. (The Cunningtons [1972] report that artificial eyebrows made of mouse skins are mentioned by contemporary satirists.)

Patches, small fabric shapes, were glued to the face to cover imperfections or skin blemishes. Ladies wore night masks to protect, soften the skin, and remove wrinkles. From 1660 to 1700 some women placed "**plumpers**," small balls of wax, in the cheeks to give the face a fashionably rounded shape.

COSTUME FOR CHILDREN: 17TH CENTURY

Many costume historians identify the first changes in clothing for children that reflect changes in attitudes toward them as taking place in the late 1700s. Aries (1962), in a social history of the family and childhood, disagrees, arguing that the first important changes in costume for children come as early as the beginning of the 16th century. The changes he identifies were well established and had become common practice during the 17th century at least for upper-class children (Aries 1962).

The practice for many centuries had been to dress children, once they were released from their swaddling clothes, in the same styles as the adults of their region and class. Starting in the 16th century, this changed for small boys, but not for girls. The nursery-age boy was first dressed not in the clothing of his elders but in the same dress as his sisters, who were, in turn, dressed like small women. Later he was dressed in a long robe that buttoned or fastened down the front. As a result, the sequence of costumes worn by boys was: first swaddling clothes, and then a skirt, robe, and apron. About age three or four the boy donned the long robe, and at six or seven he was first dressed in adult male styles. Louis XIII received his first doublet and breeches at age seven. In England the occasion on which a young boy was presented with his first pair of breeches was called his "breeching" and was an occasion for celebration by all of the family and their friends.

Aries points out that the distinctive item of costume for small boys was the robe, which was not worn by adults or by girls. Here, he says, was a clear example of a costume exclusively for a child, and it had its origins in costume of the past. During the High Middle Ages men wore long robes. When these robes went out of general use, replaced by shorter jackets, they continued to be used by priests, certain professions, and in upper-class families by children. This was not a universal practice in western Europe. Children in Renaissance Italy seem not to have followed it, but French, German, and English children did.

Other vestiges of earlier styles were also preserved in children's dress. The infants' cap worn by children is almost identical with the medieval coif. Attached to the shoulders of the robes for boys and dresses for girls was a broad ribbon of

FIGURE 9.14

Toddler, probably a boy, standing beside his mother wears a padded protective cap called a pudding and a pinafore over a long skirt. Kneeling girl has wide "ribbons of childhood" attached to the back of her dress. Standing older boy wears petticoat breeches of the type worn by adult men of the period. Girl child being carried wears a dress cut in adult woman's style and a white cap. (Jacob Ochterveldt. c. 1664, *Dutch Family Portrait.* Photograph courtesy, Wadsworth Atheneum, Hartford. Gift of Robert Lehman, accession no. 1960.261.)

fabric that hung down the back. Many writers identify these ribbons as "leading strings," small strings used to help hold the child upright when he or she learned to walk and retained for another two years or so to help control the child's movements. Aries disagrees, pointing out that in many portraits of the time both leading strings and these ribbons are depicted. Leading strings were narrow, rope-like in construction, as compared to the flat ribbons of childhood. Instead, he argues convincingly, they are probably a stylized or atrophied form of the hanging sleeves that were part of the medieval costume. (See *Figures 9.14* and *9.15.*)

Of the origins of these archaic styles for children, Aries says it was obviously out of the question to invent a costume out of nothing for them, yet it was felt necessary to separate them in a visible manner by means of their dress. They were accordingly given a costume of which the tradition had been maintained in certain classes, but which adults no longer wore. The adoption of a special costume for children, which became generalized throughout the upper classes from the end of the 16th century, corresponded with the beginnings of the formation of the idea of childhood as a separate stage of life.

FIGURE 9.15

Front and back views of a dress for a boy or a girl from after 1690 that has "ribbons of childhood" behind the sleeves. (Photograph courtesy, Division of Costume, American Museum of National History.)

Costume Components for Children

LAYETTE

For an infant in the 17th century a layette would have consisted of swaddling bands, bibs, caps (also called **biggins**), shirts, mittens and sleeves, and what the English called **tail-clouts** or **nappies** and Americans called **diapers.** This latter term derived from the use of linen cloth made in a checked pattern and called a "diaper weave." Diapers were usually made from unbleached linen or cotton. One Englishwoman, Lady Anne Clifford, used her husband's old shirts (Kevill-Davies 1991).

SWADDLING BANDS

Infants were swaddled for the first two or three months, tightly wrapped in bands of linen that inhibited movement. When these bands were removed, they were replaced by thick corded or quilted material that was tied tightly around the body. These pieces called **stays, staybands,** or **rollers** were probably intended to prevent umbilical hernias or to promote an upright posture.

CHRISTENINGS

The major occasion in the baby's first year of life was the christening. Christening robes and accessories differed little from those of later centuries. Charles I of England's christening clothes have been preserved and they consisted of undershirts open at the front and closed by small crossed tabs, binders for the stomach, bibs, a small cap, and a long, embroidered christening gown.

GOWNS

Infants unable to walk were dressed in long gowns, called "**carrying frocks.**" Children old enough to walk wore shorter dresses or "**going frocks.**" During the 17th century aprons or pinafores replaced bibs. The term **pinafore** derived from the practice of pinning this garment to the front or forepart of the gown. Sometimes a handkerchief, called a **muckinder,** was pinned to the front of the dress for extra protection (Kevill-Davies 1991). (See *Figure 9.14.*)

Toddlers who were learning to walk and might fall and bump their heads wore a special padded cap, which was called a **pudding.** (See *Illustrated Table 9.1, page 211.*)

During the 17th century one other form of dress for young boys can be observed in a few portraits. It is almost a compromise between the dress of adult and child. Boys of age five to seven sometimes wore the waistcoat of the first half of the century with a long, full, gathered skirt.

CORAL TEETHING RINGS OR NECKLACES

Infants and very young children are often depicted in paintings with small pieces of coral mounted in silver or gold and suspended around their necks. From as early as the Roman era, coral had been thought to have magical power to ward off evil. It also provided a cool, hard surface for babies to bite on to relieve the pain of teething.

SUMMARY

THEMES

The themes of **POLITICS AND POLITICAL CONFLICT** are evident in costume throughout the 17th century. In England, the **POLITICAL CONFLICT** between those who supported King Charles I and those who opposed him was reflected in the differences between the dress of the "cavaliers" and the "round-heads." In the second half of the century, Louis XIV of France centralized the power of government and focused attention on the court at Versailles as a stage on which to display fashion. Courtiers who had to spend vast sums of money keeping up with the latest styles had little time and few resources for plotting against the government. Charles II of England sought asylum in France during the English Civil War. When he returned to claim the throne of England, French court styles became a major influence on English styles.

Another theme, **SOCIAL CLASS STRUCTURE,** was intimately related to French court dress. Social rank helped to determine such specific aspects of dress such as the length of women's trains. In England and Spain **SOCIAL VALUES** were expressed through dress. The English Puritans avoided lavish sartorial display, and Spanish traditionalism and rigid social conventions contributed to the social distinctions evident in the dress of upper and lower classes.

ECONOMIC EVENTS that had an impact on styles included the expansion of trade with the Middle and Far East. Both the famous vest of Charles II of England and the mantua gown of the late 1600s are thought to have originated in the Middle East, examples of **CROSS-CULTURAL INFLUENCES** that stemmed from trade.

Styles were all the more easily spread both at home and abroad because of the expansion of a new **TECHNOLOGY,** printing. This **MEDIUM OF COMMUNICATION** made printed descriptions and drawings of fashionable dress readily available.

At the same time, regional differences in dress persisted. Clothing worn at the court of Spain, which clung to the styles of the late 16th century for more than 50 years, is the most obvious example of localized dress, but styles that were preferred by and associated with the Italians, the Dutch, the French, and the English can also be identified.

For the costume historian, the 17th century, the theme of **SOURCES OF INFORMATION ABOUT COSTUME,** is particularly worthy of note. The many portraits painted and drawings made, not only of the well-to-do but also of everyday life among the lower classes, are supplemented by the aforementioned printed materials that touch on current fashion. Also, greater numbers of actual garments remain in museums, particularly in England.

The theme of **RELATIONSHIPS BETWEEN COSTUME AND DEVELOPMENTS IN THE FINE AND APPLIED ARTS** is evident in all periods. In the 17th century these relationships are relatively easy to see, as one looks at architecture, sculpture, painting, and textiles. The scale, lines, and proportions of baroque styles of the fine and applied arts are remarkably similar.

SURVIVALS OF 17TH CENTURY STYLES

Portraits painted in the 17th century, especially those painted by Anthony Van Dyck, exercised a considerable influence on styles of the 18th century. To what extent these revivals were limited to fancy dress for masquerades or worn by sitters when they had their portraits painted is not entirely clear.

In the 1880s Oscar Wilde, the English poet and playwright, adopted a style of dress that included knee breeches, a wide collar, and long curling hair that he said was based on Cavalier men's dress. Although adults other than those in

Visual Summary Table
BAROQUE

Man: 1600–1620
Shirt, wide trunk hose
or Venetians, worn with
doublet, jacket or jerkin.

Man: 1625–1650
Shirt, doublet, ending
with tabs or skirt-like
section below the waist,
worn with knee breeches.

Man: 1650–1680
Shirt, waist-length
doublet, and knee-length
breeches cut to look like a
skirt or straight or full and
drawn in to knee.

Man: 1680–1710
Shirt, a knee-length vest, and
a knee-length outer coat that
hid knee-length breeches.

Woman: 1600–1630
Skirt flat in front, sides
wide and full. Bodice
has elongated U-shaped
stomacher and complex
sleeves.

Woman: 1630–1660
Low necked bodice
with puffed and paned
sleeves has U-shaped
stomacher and slightly
elevated waist. Open
front of skirt shows
underskirt.

Woman: 1660–1680
Elongated bodice has
V-shaped point at the
bottom of the front.
Skirts are either closed
or open at front to
show underskirt.

Woman: 1680–1900
Bodice front opens
showing decorative stomacher.
Trained and heavy skirts
need support. New cut is
called a mantua.

Wilde's aesthetic circle never adopted these styles, they were used as the basis of a style for boys called "Little Lord Fauntleroy" suits. This name derived from a popular children's book. (See *Figure 14.22, page 352.*)

Neckwear of the 17th century often appears in later centuries. Ruffs, standing lace collars, and wide lace collars can be found throughout the 19th century and on into the early 20th century. (See *Figures 14.13, page 346* and *14.18, page 350.*)

NOTES

Aries, P. 1962. *Centuries of Childhood: A Social History of Family Life.* New York: Knopf, p. 52ff.

Braudel, F. 1982. *The Wheels of Commerce.* New York: Harper & Row.

Cumming, V. 1985. *A Visual History of Costume: The 17th Century.* New York: Drama Books.

Cunnington, C. W and P. Cunnington. 1972. *Handbook of English Costume in the Seventeenth Century.* London: Faber and Faber.

Dow, G. F. 1925. "Domestic Life in New England in the Seventeenth Century." Lecture delivered at the opening of the American Wing of the Metropolitan Museum of Art.

Edwards, R. and I. Ramsey, eds. 1968. *The Connoisseur & Complete Period Guides.* New York: Bonanza Books, p. 448.

Hollander, A. 1978. *Seeing through Clothes.* New York: Viking Press.

———. 1994. *Sex and Suits.* New York: Knopf, p. 67.

Jansen, H. W. 1991. *History of Art,* 4th ed. New York: Abrams.

Kevill-Davies, S. 1991. *Yesterday's Children.* Woodbridge, Suffolk, England: Antique Collector's Club.

Kuchta, D. M. 1990. "'Graceful, Virile and Useful:' The Origins of the Three-Piece Suit." *Dress,* Vol. 17, p. 118. This reference provides a full discussion of the evolution of the three-piece suit.

Levron, J. 1968. *Daily Life at Versailles in the 17th and 18th Centuries.* New York: Macmillan, p. 108.

Marshall, R. K. 1981. "Scottish Portraits as a Source for the Costume Historian." *Costume,* No. 15, p. 67.

Montgomery, F. 1984. *Textiles in America, 1650–1870.* New York: Norton.

Reade, B. 1951. *Costume of the Western World: The Dominance of Spain.* London: Harrap.

Swann, J. 1991. *Shoes.* London: Batsford, pp. 7, 14.

Zumthor, P. 1963. *Daily Life in Rembrandt's Holland.* New York: Macmillan, p. 61.

SELECTED READINGS

Books Containing Illustrations of Costume of the Period from Original Sources

Blum, A. 1951. *Costume of the Western World: Early Bourbon.* London: Harrap.

Brown, C. et al. 1999. *Van Dyck: 1599–1641.* New York: Rizzoli.

Brown, C. 1993. *Dutch Painting.* New York: Phaidon.

Cumming, V. 1985. *A Visual History of Costume: The 17th Century.* New York: Drama Books.

DeMarly, D. 1988. *Louis XIV and Versailles.* New York: Holmes and Meier.

Hart, A. 1998. *Fashion in Detail: From the 17th and 18th Centuries.* New York: Rizzoli.

Reade, B. 1951. *Costume of the Western World: The Dominance of Spain.* London: Harrap.

Thienen, F. V. 1951. *Costume of the Western World: The Great Age of Holland.* London: Harrap.

Also see art books that reproduce the paintings and drawings of artists such as Callot, Rubens, Gerard Ter Borch, Van Dyke, Velazquez, and others.

Periodical Articles

Chapman, D. L. and L. E. Dickey. 1990. "A Study of Costume Through Art: An Analysis of Dutch Women's Costumes from 1600 to 1650." *Dress,* Vol. 16, p. 29.

DeMarly, D. 1981. "Indecent Exposure." *Connoisseur,* Vol. 206, No. 827, p. 1.

Kuchta, D. M. 1990. "'Graceful, Virile and Useful:' The Origins of the Three-Piece Suit." *Dress,* Vol. 17, p. 118.

Marshall, R. K. 1974. "Seventeenth Century Babies." *Costume Society of Scotland Bulletin,* Spring, No. 13, p. 2.

———. 1981. "Scottish Portraits as a Source for the Costume Historian." *Costume,* No. 15, p. 67.

Murray, A. 1976. "From Breeches to Sherryvallies." *Dress,* Vol. 2, p. 17.

Ribero, A. 1977. "Some Evidence of the Influence of Dress of the 17th Century on Costume in the 18th Century Female Portrait. *Burlington Magazine,* December, p. 834.

Strong, R. 1980. "Charles I's Clothes for the Years 1633–35." *Costume,* Vol. 14, p. 73.

Swan, S. B. 1979. "The Pocket Lucy Locket Lost." *Early American Life,* Vol. 10, No. 2, p. 40.

Daily Life

Chartier, R., ed. 1988. A *History of Private Life: Passions of the Renaissance.* Cambridge, MA: Belknap Press of Harvard University Press.

Defourneaux, M. 1979. *Daily Life in Spain in the Golden Age.* Stanford, CA: Stanford University Press.

Earle, P. 1994. *A City Full of People: Men and Women of London 1650 1750*. London: Methuen.

Earle, P. 1989. *The Making of the English Middle Class: Business, Society, and Family Life in London: 1660–1730*. Berkeley, CA: University of California Press.

Erlanger, P. 1967. *The Age of Courts and Kings. Manners and Morals, 1558–1715*. New York: HarperCollins.

Hanson, N. 2002. *The Great Fire of London: In That Apocalyptic Year, 1666*. New York: John Wiley & Sons.

Levron, J. 1968. *Daily Life at Versailles in the 17th and 18th Centuries*. New York: Macmillan.

Zumthor, P. 1994. *Daily Life in Rembrandt's Holland*. Stanford, CA: Stanford University Press.

C H R O N O L O G Y

1709
Discovery of the ruins of Herculaneum

1714–1820
Georgian period in England

1715
Death of Louis XIV, Louis XV, his great-grandson, becomes king

1733
John Kay patents the flying shuttle

C. 1720–C. 1770
Rococo styles in the arts predominate

C. 1770–mid-1800
Neoclassical styles in the arts predominate

1740–1786
Frederick the Great rules in Prussia, builds rococo and neoclassical palaces

1745
Madame Pompadour becomes mistress of King Louis XV and
influences arts and fashions of the French court

1748
Discovery of the ruins of Pompeii, which along with excavations at
Herculaneum, helps to stimulate neoclassical revival

1756
Birth of Mozart

1764
James Hargreaves invents spinning jenny

1769
Richard Arkwright develops the spinning machine

1774
Death of Louis XV
Louis XVI, his grandson, becomes king

1776
American Revolution

1789
French Revolution

1791
Death of Mozart

1796
James Watt invents the steam engine

CHAPTER TEN

THE EIGHTEENTH CENTURY

1700–1790

A.

D.

B.

A.

Louis XV bombe chest

B.

Queen Anne–style chair

C.

Rococo clock

D.

Chippendale chair

E.

Louis XVI chair

F.

Monticello, late 1700s

E.

C.

F.

Figures A, C, E from Lavisse, E. 1907. *Album Historique Le XVIII Le XIX Siècle*. Paris: Librairie Armand Colin, pp. 70, 109, 71. Figures B, D from Hart, H. H. 1977. *Chairs Through the Ages, A Pictorial Archive of Woodcuts & Engravings*. New York: Dover, pp. 106, 68. Figure F courtesy of V. R. Tortora.

HISTORICAL BACKGROUND

Upon the death of Louis XIV in 1715, his great-grandson, Louis XV, became king of France at the age of five. During the period of the Regency (1715–1723), when the king was too young to reign alone, a gradual change in the Baroque art styles that had predominated in the previous century had taken place. The new style lines were less massive, the curves more slender and delicate, and an emphasis was placed on asymmetrical balance. This new style, Rococo, reached its height during the reign of Louis XV.

The king, at whose court these styles flourished, lacked the intelligence and the common sense needed for the task of governing France. Lazy, egotistical, bored with affairs of state, he sought entertainment through hunting as often as possible. His other great passion was women. Perhaps the most famous of his mistresses and paramours was Madame de Pompadour, who encouraged authors and helped artists while also serving as the king's political advisor.

During much of Louis XV's reign, France engaged in costly wars, which brought little but defeat and debts. Louis's half-hearted efforts never succeeded in solving the nation's mounting fiscal crisis. The lifestyle enjoyed at his lavish court contrasted sharply with the lives of the ordinary citizens. Louis XV died in 1774, more hated and despised than any other French king for many generations.

Despite the lamentable condition of the finances of the nation, France dominated the culture of western Europe. France still set the style in fashion, literature, decorative arts, and in philosophical theories. French had become the international language of Europe, preferred by royalty and aristocracy.

The grandson of Louis XV succeeded him on the throne. Louis XVI was a well-meaning and pious king. As a hobby he made and repaired locks. He also enjoyed hunting. But he was unfit for the heavy task that confronted him. His wife was of little help to him, for he had married an attractive young Austrian princess, Marie Antoinette. In her first years as queen, she was immature and frivolous. She had an intense dislike for the customs and etiquette of the French court, which was not surprising since she was only fourteen when she married Louis. Her unpopularity with both the older nobles and the people did little to support the monarchy.

At the same time, writers called *philosophes,* who believed that the application of reason and science would create a better world, used the press to unleash a wave of criticism aimed at the abuses in French society and government. The success of the American Revolution, which France helped finance, encouraged Frenchmen who wanted to reform government and society. Their opportunity came in 1789 when the bankruptcy of the French government forced the calling of the Estates General, which declared itself a National Assembly, abolished feudalism, and began to write a constitu-tion. France was undergoing a revolution. After the country suffered defeats in war with Austria and Prussia, the revolution was taken over by radicals who ended the monarchy, and eventually executed the king and queen in 1793. The old regime was abolished.

The Arts

The mid-century changes in philosophy brought related changes in styles of art. The Rococo styles were replaced by a neoclassical revival. Excavations in Italy, in 1719 and 1748, uncovered the ruins of two Roman cities, Pompeii and Herculaneum, which had been destroyed in A.D. 79 by the eruption of Mt. Vesuvius near Naples. The discovery of these remains fueled a revived interest in classical antiquity. Although neoclassical style influences on women's dress did not appear until near the close of the century, neoclassical styles in art and architecture were evident from mid-century onward.

For the first half of the 18th century, the influence of the French court styles was also felt elsewhere in continental Europe. In Prussia, Frederick the Great (ruled 1740–1786) patterned his court on the French court, building Rococo and neoclassical palaces. Empress Maria Theresa of Austria, whose daughter Marie Antoinette became queen of France, maintained loose links with France. Spain, too, was closely tied to France because the great-grandson of Louis XIV, Philip V, became Spain's first Bourbon king in 1700. He and his successors would attempt modest reforms. First Spain and then Austria dominated the Italian peninsula. Only the Venetian Republic remained independent, and at the end of the 18th century even Venice lost its autonomy when it was handed over to Austria by Napoleon.

In England, the Georgian era had begun. Except for a short period at the beginning of the century when Queen Anne, daughter of James II, reigned, the Hanoverian kings—George I, George II, and George III, who were of German extraction—ruled England. Late in the 18th century, English ideas would exert strong influence on France, particularly in the field of reforming the government and civil rights. English influences extended to fashions as well. A veritable Anglomania took hold in the 1780s.

SOCIAL LIFE IN 18TH CENTURY FRANCE

During the minority of Louis XV, Versailles was abandoned and the center of the French administration was moved to nearby Paris. After Louis came of age in 1723 at thirteen, he returned to Versailles and for most of the rest of the 18th century, the palace was again the center of royal life. Madame Pompadour, an official mistress of King Louis XV, was a major influence on styles in costume and the arts during his reign. Her patronage assured artists and artisans of success. In return, they named styles in such diverse areas as fans, hairdos, dresses, dishes, sofas, beds, chairs, ribbons, and the rose pattern of her favorite porcelain after her (Durant and Durant 1965).

The court became somewhat less important during the reign of Louis XVI, in large part because Queen Marie Antoinette, an Austrian, found the French court etiquette stifling. No wonder, when ceremony required that, when the queen arose, not only did one person hand her the chemise and a different person her petticoat and dress, but also if a person of higher rank entered the room, the task had to be turned over to her. The queen changed this procedure after the cold winter day on which the following incident (described by her attendant) took place:

> . . . the Queen, quite undressed, was about to slip on her chemise. I was holding it unfolded. The Lady-in-waiting entered, hastened to remove her gloves and took the chemise. Someone scratched at the door, which was opened; it was the Duchesse de Chartres. She had removed her gloves and came to take the chemise, but the lady-in-waiting handed it, not to her, but to me. I gave it to the Duchesse. Someone else scratched at the door: it was the Comptesse de Provence; the Duchesse de Chartres passed her the chemise. The Queen had folded her arms over her bosom and looked cold. Madame [the Comptesse] saw her strained attitude, just dropped her handkerchief, kept on her gloves and while passing the chemise over the Queen's head, ruffled her hair (Levron 1968).

The queen's dispensing with this and some other traditional court etiquette added to the strains between the royal family and the older, more conservative nobility. Furthermore, the queen was extravagant at a time when the economy of France was in difficulty. She spent a great deal on jewelry, and on an average she ordered 150 dresses a year and spent the equivalent of about $40,000 on clothes. In one year, when she wished to wear a dress that matched her ash blonde hair, she sent a lock of hair to Lyons, a city in the south of France where the silk industry was located, in order to be sure the fabric was dyed precisely the right color (Levron 1968). *Contemporary Comments 10.1*, describes the costume worn for presentation at court.

For a period she abandoned the palace at Versailles for life at the Petit Trianon, a small chateau on the grounds of the palace built to simulate a country farmhouse where she and the rest of her court favorites played at being "country folk." There they started a fashion for peasant-style dresses and hats. Although the importance of the queen's lifestyle as a cause of the French Revolution is often overemphasized, it is true that her lack of popularity with both the old nobility and the people were factors in the decline of support for the monarchy.

SOCIAL LIFE OF THE AFFLUENT IN 18th CENTURY ENGLAND

The organization of society in England was less centered on the court than that of France. Even though the center of fashionable life was London, small towns and country estates also had their own social class structure and took an interest in fashionable dress. A brief review of the apprenticeships to which a young man of the provinces could apply himself shows the diversity of occupations related to clothing and fashion: clothiers, collar-makers, cordwainers (shoemakers), glovers, lacemakers, linen drapers, mantua-makers (dressmakers), peruke (wig) makers, tailors, weavers, wool combers, wool winders, and woolen drapers (Marshall 1969).

Fashionable clothing was divided into categories according to the time of day the costume was worn or the sort of occasion for which it was appropriate. A man divided his garments among "undress" or lounging clothes; "dress," slightly more formal outfits for daytime or evening wear; and "full dress" or the most formal evening dress. His "nightgown" was not a sleeping garment in the modern sense, but a dressing gown or informal robe worn indoors. He also had a "powdering jacket," which he wore to keep the powder off his clothing while having his wig powdered.

The clothing a woman wore around the house was her "undress," "half dress," or "morning dress." Her "habit" was either a riding costume or a tailor-made costume. Her "coat" was not for out-of-doors, but was her petticoat. The garment we call a "coat" today, she would have called a "greatcoat." She never called a dress a "frock," because that term was applied to a type of man's coat ("frock coat") or to children's dresses. And although by the end of the century she was wearing what the 19th century fashion magazines would call a "bustle," she called it a "false rump."

The man of means who did not have to work for a living got up late, breakfasted, and received his friends at home (wearing his "nightgown") in the morning. In the afternoon he went out to a popular spot or to the shops, and then on to dinner; after dinner, to a play or coffee house. During the summer season he might go to a spa, a fashionable resort, to take the curative waters for real or imagined ailments. A man who paid a great deal of attention to his dress was called a "beau," a "coxcomb," or a "fop." Those men who adopted French and Italian-inspired fashions during the last half of the century were called "macaronis." The name derived from the Macaroni Club, a club formed by young men who affected an interest in Continental culture and who were noted for their brightly colored silks, lace-trimmed coats in the latest silhouette, and fashionable wigs and hats. When the English sang of "Yankee Doodle Dandy" who "stuck a feather in his hat and called it 'macaroni,'" they were commenting on his attempt to appear fashionable.

CONTEMPORARY COMMENTS 10.1

Costume for Presentation at Court

In her memoirs Madame de la Tour du Pin, a member of the French nobility, described her costume for presentation at court in 1787.

I was presented on Sunday morning, after Mass. I was 'en grand corps,' that is to say, wearing a special bodice without shoulders, laced at the back, but narrow enough for the lacings, four inches wide at the bottom, to show a chemise of the finest lawn through which it could easily be seen if the wearer's skin was not white. This chemise had sleeves, but they were only three

inches deep and the shoulders were uncovered. From the top of the arm to the elbow fell three or four flounces of blonde lace. The throat was bare. Mine was partly covered by the seven or eight rows of large diamonds which the Queen [Marie Antoinette] had kindly lent me. The front of the bodice was as if laced with rows of diamonds and on my head were more diamonds, some in clusters and some in aigrets [feathers].

The gown itself was very lovely. On account of my half-mourning, it was all in white and the entire skirt was embroidered with pearls and silver.

Excerpted from the *Memoirs of Madame de La Tour du Pin*, trans. by Felice Harcourt. 1971. New York: McCall Publishing Company, p. 69.

Fashionable ladies spent their mornings in bed, where they reclined while receiving guests. Several hours were required for the late-rising lady to dress. In the afternoon she either visited friends or drank tea. Dinner was taken about 4 p.m., and her evenings were spent in card playing and dancing.

Not only the wealthy aristocrats, but also the middle class, which was a growing segment of English society, kept up with fashion. The middle class as well as the upper classes traveled to spas for vacations. In addition to the spas there were many other places where the middle-class lady or gentleman could observe the most recent styles. Many of the forms of entertainment, especially the outdoor amusement parks and the theater, provided opportunities for the mingling of the social classes. Nor was it uncommon for the rich daughters of merchants to marry into upper-class families.

PRODUCTION AND ACQUISITION OF CLOTHING AND TEXTILES

Advances in Textile Technology

Textile manufacturing technology advanced rapidly in the 18th century. The flying shuttle, a device that automatically carried yarn across the fabric was invented in 1733. The resulting increase in the speed of weaving meant that the weaver consumed yarn more rapidly. Inventors searching for

speedier methods of spinning soon produced a number of mechanized spinning devices. By 1800, both steam and water power were being used to run this new machinery.

Most of these advances were applied to the spinning of cotton. As a result, cotton fabrics became available at much lower prices than heretofore, and this stimulated the use of cotton fabrics. In the 19th century these advances would be extended to spinning other fibers.

Home Versus Factory Production of Cloth

Textiles with elaborate and sophisticated patterns were produced in Europe. The American colonies were an important market for English manufacturers who sold handsome fabrics to well-to-do colonists and poor quality, cheap cloth to those less well off. Most of the poorer families living in rural areas or small towns produced their own textiles, especially those made of linen or wool. Professional weavers also produced cloth. Some traveled from home to home to weave; others had their own shops.

Clothing Manufacture and Sale

By the 18th century the practice of having male tailors make men's suits and coats and women make dresses for women was well established. Although affluent individuals had their clothing made for them by skilled professionals, women working at home, whose skills were probably limited, made much of the clothing for those of ordinary means. As Kidwell and

Christman (1974) say of the 18th century American housewife, "Although she might sew a fine seam, she was ignorant of the variety of stitches as they were employed by the trained tailor. Her mandate was not to create fashionable shapes out of unfashionable figures, but merely to be sure that her family was clothed against the elements. Homemade clothing must have looked homemade" (p. 27). Limited quantities of ready-made clothing had always been and were still available.

Among the poor, simply keeping dressed was a problem. In the country, women could obtain wool, spin, and weave or knit garments, but in town clothing had to be purchased and for those on a small income prices were very high. In his autobiography, W. H. Hutton described how it took him two years to save enough money to purchase a good suit of clothes. Unfortunately the suit was stolen, and it took him another five years to save for a replacement. Thefts of clothing were common. Some thieves were even so enterprising as to cut holes in the backs of carriages through which they grasped a passenger's wig and whisked it away (Marshall 1969).

The poor purchased clothing from secondhand clothes dealers. These dealers obtained their stocks from the servants of good families, to whom castoff clothing was routinely given, or from thieves. In some towns, breeches clubs were formed where each member contributed a small amount to a common fund. When the fund was large enough, a name was drawn and that person received a pair of breeches. The club continued to function until a pair had been obtained by every member.

SOURCES OF INFORMATION ABOUT COSTUME

Museum collections include many more garments dating from this period. For the most part these are upper-class clothes.

Portraits painted during the 18th century abound. Many are excellent sources of information, but individual artists sometimes felt that portraits demanded timeless rather than fashionable dress. One of the most prominent English portraitists, Sir Joshua Reynolds, "despised fashion" and "exhorted young artists to rise above it," advising young artists to "change the dress from a contemporary fashion to one more permanent, which has annexed to it no ideas of meanness from its being familiar to us." He urged artists to "disregard all local and temporary ornaments, and look only on those general habits which are everywhere and always the same . . ." (Reynolds 1891).

Some English portraits of the 18th century also reflect the interest of fashionable people in masquerades. The portraits of Van Dyck were one popular source of inspiration for masquerade costume, and some individuals had their portraits painted in these 17th century inspired styles.

THE AMERICAN COLONIES IN THE 18TH CENTURY

Urban Clothing Styles

Americans living in towns and nearby areas imported British goods and followed European fashions, many of which originated in Paris. Some clothes were imported; others were made in the colonies by copying styles shown on fashion plates or on the fashion dolls (called **fashion babies**) made in Paris.

American Quakers, like their English counterparts, dressed somewhat differently from the rest of the population. Quaker men wore plain hats and no wigs. Women wore simply shaped hats, which were later replaced by unadorned bonnets. By the end of the 18th century, some Quakers were tending to give up their distinctive dress.

Working Class and Rural Dress

Working class dress was designed for convenience. A common costume for working class women consisted of a chemise and over this a petticoat skirt and a hip-length garment called a **short gown,** which was like a jacket or an over blouse. To these were added a serviceable apron and a kerchief at the neck, together with some kind of a cap covering the hair. (See *Figure 10.1.*)

Farmers and artisans wore loose smocks over breeches. Made of coarse linen for summer and wool in winter, these garments were pulled over the head and tied at the neck with strings. Laborers often placed a leather apron over the smock. On the frontier men adopted a costume derived, in part, from Native American styles. They, too, wore a loose smock or a shirt made of fringed deerskin or, sometimes, of coarse homespun decorated with fringes. For traveling through wooded regions, Native American-style deerskin leggings were worn. Close-fitting caps of coonskin, fox, bear, or squirrel often had a long, hanging tail sewn to the back.

SOME INFLUENCES ON COSTUME IN THE 18TH CENTURY

Styles of the 18th century, like those of the 17th century, reflected the increasing European trade with the Far East. Specific clothing items that originated abroad, such as men's dressing gowns and the mantua cut for women's dresses, were relatively rare, but Eastern textiles were very important. Not only imported Oriental silk brocades and damasks and Indian chintz, calico, and muslin fabrics, but also European copies of these fabrics were made into handsome garments.

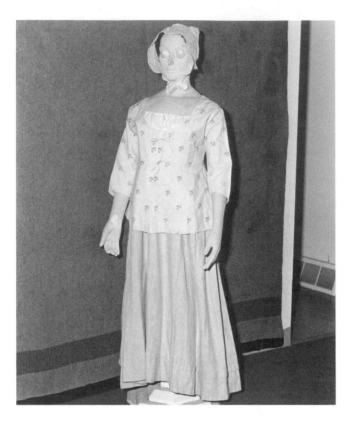 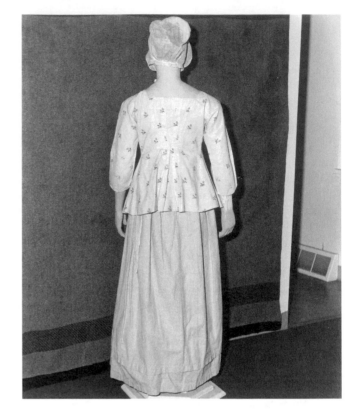

FIGURE 10.1

Petticoat and short gown, front and back views. Late 18th century. (Photograph courtesy, The Germantown Historical Society, Philadelphia, PA; photographer: Philip Mossburg, Ill.)

During the last quarter of the century English styles for both men and women had a significant impact on Parisian fashion. In women's clothes, **Anglomania** (a French fad for things English) became evident in a vogue for simpler styles, for English riding habits, and for coat-dresses derived from English men's riding coats, which were called **redingotes.** Frenchmen copied Englishmen's tailoring, and, except for court functions, wore simpler, undecorated suits and affected a more casual mode of dress. Mercier in *Contemporary Comments 10.2* on *page 232* pokes fun at Anglomania and at current French excesses in dress.

COSTUME FOR MEN: 18TH CENTURY

The major elements of men's costume consisted of under drawers, a shirt, waistcoat, an outer coat, knee-length breeches, hose, and shoes. Hats and wigs were added on appropriate oc-

casions, along with other accessories and outdoor wear. Although these elements remained constant throughout the century, the styles of the first and second halves of the centuries do show some differences.

The underwear worn next to the body remained much the same for most of the 18th century. Shirts were considered to be part of "underclothing."

GARMENTS

Drawers, which were worn next to the skin beneath the breeches, were the functional equivalent of modern undershorts or medieval braies. They closed at the waist with drawstrings or buttons, were made of white cotton or wool, and ended at the knee. (See *Figure 10.2.*)

Shirts were cut much like those of preceding centuries. They had a ruffled frill at the front of the neck and at the end of the sleeves. Collars and cravats were generally made of white cotton or linen. During the first half of century, collars were gathered to a neckband. Neck cloths or cravats wound around the neck and knotted under the chin, concealing the collar. In the second half of the century neckbands lengthened, evolving into a collar that was sewn to the shirt. The **steinkirk**

FIGURE 10.2

Undergarments of the 18th century from England. Made of flannel for warmth, they include (left) underdrawers, (center) a shirt, and (right) an undervest. (Photograph courtesy, The Metropolitan Museum of Art.)

was a style of the cravat in which the tie pulled through the buttonhole and twisted loosely. It was named after a battle in 1692 in which soldiers were supposed to have twisted their cravats loosely around the neck. Evidence, however, indicates that the style originated several years before the battle for which it was supposed to have been named. (See *Color Plate 27.*)

During cold weather some men wore a second waistcoat either over or under the shirt. Waistcoats worn over the shirt were sometimes made with a collar that was visible. Others were strictly utilitarian garments to provide warmth and these were hidden from view.

Costume for Men: Up to Mid-18th Century

Whether an item of clothing was classified as either "dress" or "full dress" depended on the degree of formality of the item. Dress coats, breeches, and waistcoats were usually made from less decorative fabrics; full dress garments were made from elaborate brocades and trimmed with handsome embroidery and lace. (See *Color Plate 29.*)

By 1700 extra fullness was added to the straighter cut that had been characteristic of the 1680s. Coats were knee length and until about 1720 buttoned to the hem. After 1720, they only closed to the waist. (See *Figure 10.3* and *Color Plate 28.*) Buckram stiffening was used to hold out the full skirts of coats. Side seams were usually left open from below the waist to accommodate swords. Pockets were generally positioned at hip level and pocket flaps had scalloped edges.

Until the 1730s most sleeves tended to end in large full attached cuffs that either closed all around or were open at the back. Cuffs that reached to the elbow were called **boot cuffs.** An alternative style had no cuffs and was slit at the back to expose the sleeve ruffle.

Waistcoats followed the lines of outer coats, ending close to the knee. They were made either with or without sleeves and usually matched the outer coat in color and fabric. Men wore sleeveless waistcoats over shirts but without an outer coat at home as casual wear or "undress."

The cut of breeches was moderately full. The seat was cut very full and gathered to a waistband that rode, loosely fitted, below the waist. Breeches ended at the knee, often being just barely visible when the coat was closed. They closed at the front with buttons or, after 1730, with a **fall,** a square, central flap that buttoned to the waistline. (See *Figure 10.6.*)

CONTEMPORARY COMMENTS 10.2

Anglomania in France

Louis-Sebastien Mercier, slightly tongue-in-cheek, exhorts his fellow-countrymen to abandon English styles and return to those that are French.

Just now English clothing is all the wear. Rich man's son, sprig of nobility, counter-jumper—you see them dressed all alike in the long coat, cut close, thick stockings, puffed stock; with hats on their heads and a riding-switch in their hands. Not one of the gentlemen thus attired, however, has ever crossed the Channel or can speak one word of English.... No, no, my young friend. Dress French again, wear your laces, your embroidered waistcoats, your laced coats; powder your hair to the newest tune; keep your hat under your arm, in that place which nature,

in Paris at any rate, designed for it, and wear your two watches, with concomitant fobs, both at once.

Shopkeepers hang out signs—"English Spoken Here." The lemonade-sellers even have succumbed to the lure of punch [an English drink], and write the word on their windows. English coats, with their triple capes, envelop our young exquisites. Small boys wear their hair cut round, uncurled and without powder. Older men walk with the English gait, a trifle round-shouldered. Our women take their headgear from London. The racecourse at Vincennes is copied from that at Newmarket. Finally, we have Shakespeare on our stage, rhymed, it is true, by M. Ducis [a French poet], but impressive nevertheless.

Excerpted from Louis-Sebastien Mercier, trans. by Helen Simpson. 1933. *The Waiting City, Paris 1782–88.* Philadelphia: Lippincott, pp. 29–30.

FIGURE 10.3

Ditto suit, first half of the 18th century. Of mauve silk with a design of white flowers with green stems, this suit shows the sleeve cuff construction and long waistcoat characteristic of the first half of the century. (Photograph courtesy, The Metropolitan Museum of Art.)

Frock coats were cut looser and shorter than dress coats and they had flat, turned-down collars. After 1730, frock coats were considered suitable for country wear and after 1770, they were accepted for more formal wear as well. They were not embroidered and usually were made from such fabrics as serge, plush, or sturdy woven cloth. (See *Figure 10.4.*)

The origin of the term frock coat, like the origins of so many costume terms, is not entirely clear. Before being applied to the coat style described earlier, the word **frock** had been applied to several other garments—among these a woman's undergarment, a priest's gown, a child's dress, and a loose-fitting riding coat. A garment worn by Spanish shepherds that was a loosely fitted, washable linen outer garment seems to have traveled to England by way of the Spanish Netherlands. In England it was adopted by laborers and farmers and called a **smock frock** (DeMarly 1986). The smock frock (later called a **smock**) continued in use for English agricultural workers up until the 19th century, when it was frequently decorated with a type of embroidery that is now called **smocking.** Given that most other garments to which the term "frock" was applied were loosely fitted, it may be that the designation "frock coat" came about because of the looser fit of this garment.

Suit and coat fabrics for daytime or less formal evenings included plain, woven wool, plush, velvet, and silk, which included satin trimmed with lace, braid, or fur. Full dress clothing was usually made of cloth of gold, silver, brocade, flow-

FIGURE 10.4

Three gentlemen in a country scene are dressed in informal frock coats. The figure at the right holds a three-cornered hat in his hand and wears what appear to be knee-length spatterdashers or gaiters over his shoes. (Painting of *The Honorable Henry Fane, with His Guardians, Inigo Jones and Charles Blair*, painted by Sir Joshua Reynolds.) (Photograph courtesy, The Metropolitan Museum of Art, gift of Junius S. Morgan, 1887.)

ered velvet, or embroidered materials. (See *Color Plate 29.*) Breeches utilized sturdy woven cloth, plush, or serge for casual wear; silk satin or velvet for evening; and leather, especially buckskin, for riding. Coats did not necessarily match breeches or waistcoats. When all three items were made of the same fabric, the suit was called a **ditto suit.** Cunnington notes that this term is first encountered after 1750, although such suits were seen earlier. (See *Figure 10.3.*)

Changes in Men's Costume
After the Mid-18th Century

In the second part of the century fullness of coats decreased, side pleats were eliminated, and the front of the coat curved toward the side. By 1760 a narrow stand-up collar appeared. The silhouette narrowed, as did sleeves, which were longer and generally cuffed. (See *Figure 10.5.*)

Now sleeveless and shorter, waistcoats were both single and double breasted. Since coats were worn open, the waistcoat fabric became a center of attention and more brocades, or elaborately embroidered silks, were used. Breeches fit more closely. The fall or flap closing predominated. (See *Figure 10.6.*)

After 1730 cravats tended to be replaced by stocks, a linen square folded to form a high neck band that was stiffened with buckram, and fastened behind the neck. Often a length of black ribbon tied in a bow at the front was worn over the stock.

Costume for Men:
After the Mid-18th Century

Until mid-century, capes or cloaks for outdoors were cut full and gathered at the neck under a flat collar. After mid-cen-

FIGURE 10.5

Moss green velvet embroidered coat, embroidered waistcoat, and satin breeches worn between 1774 and 1793. This costume reflects the shorter waistcoat style and standing collar characteristic of the second half of the century. (Photograph courtesy, The Metropolitan Museum of Art, gift of Henry Dazian, 1933.)

FIGURE 10.6

Man's knee-breeches. c. 1780–1790. The front closing is of the fall or flap type. (Photograph courtesy, Division of Costume, American Museum of National History.)

tury, full wide-skirted greatcoats (**surtouts**) ended below the knee. Coat sleeves were generally cuffed. Some coats had as many as three broad, falling, capelike collars, each shorter than the one below.

Comfortable loosely fitted garments variously known as nightgowns, morning gowns, dressing gowns, Indian gowns, or banyans (*ban'-yan*) were worn throughout the century as casual or undress at home. Cunningham in a detailed study identifies several variations. A loose, full kimono style was more widely worn in the early part of the century. (See *Figure 10.16, page 246*.) Another type was more form fitting, similar to a man's coat, with set-in sleeves. (See *Figure 10.7*.) Each of these basic styles could have additional variations (Cunningham 1984). Fabrics preferred for banyans included cotton calicos; silk damasks, brocades, velvets, taffetas, or satins; and wool worsteds and calamancos (glazed, wool worsted fabric with raised stripes of the same color).

Writings of the period indicate these garments were worn out-of-doors as well as at home. Many men had their portraits painted in these handsome garments. They appear to derive from full, loose Oriental garments, and several of the names given to them—Indian gown, banyan—reflect these origins. They are yet another example of the strong Asian and Middle Eastern influences on fashions of the 18th century.

HAIR AND HEADDRESS

Most men who could afford them wore wigs. Styles varied. Until the 1730s, long, "full-bottomed" wigs such as those of

the 1600s were favored, although fullness gradually shifted to the back. (See *Color Plate 28*.) Brushing the hair straight back from the forehead and into a slightly elevated roll called in French **toupee** (*too-pay'*) or in English **foretop** began in the 1730s. (See *Figure 10.8*.) Hair was dressed higher after 1750 and wider in the 1780s, paralleling women's hairstyles.

Other popular styles included wigs with **queues** (a lock or pigtail at the back), and **club wigs** or **catogans** (*ka-toe'gan*) in which queues were doubled up on themselves and tied at the middle to form a loop of hair. Colors varied, but powdered wigs were preferred for formal dress. Wigs were made of human hair, horsehair, or goat hair. (See *Illustrated Table 10.2*)

Widespread use of wigs made hats less important. The most common styles were three-cornered hats; large flat hats called **chapeau bras** (*shap-po brah*) that were carried under the arm, rather than being worn; and two-cornered hats, which appeared about 1780. In the 19th century, three-cornered hats were named **tricornes** and two-cornered hats **bicornes** by costume historians. Three-cornered hats and jockey caps were worn for riding and, after the 1770s, the hats that would be called top hats today were worn for riding. They were called round hats. (See *Illustrated Table 10.2*)

Men wore caps at home instead of wigs. Two of the styles most frequently depicted were a cap with round crown and

FIGURE 10.7

Seated man wears a striped satin banyan with matching waistcoat. His manservant combines a ruffled and embroidered waistcoat with purple and black figured silk breeches. He holds a nightcap of embroidered silk in his hand. (Photograph courtesy, The Metropolitan Museum of Art, The Costume Institute.)

FIGURE 10.8

Satirical drawing of 1777 pokes fun at the tight lacing of corsets and the hair styles of that period. (Photograph courtesy, Division of Costume, American Museum of National History.)

flat, turned-up brim that fit close against the crown (see *Figure 10.7*) or one with a shapeless crown and rolled brim, somewhat turbanlike.

FOOTWEAR

Stockings were long, ending above the knee. After 1770 those men who considered their calves not fashionably shaped might wear "artificial calves," padding strapped to hose or strapped to the leg. (See *Figure 12.11, page 290.*)

Until 1720 shoes had square toes, high square heels, and large square tongues. Later shapes were rounder, and the heels not so high. Young men of the late 18th century nicknamed older, more conventional and conservative men "square toes," using the phrase in much the same way as young people today might use the term "square" (Swann 1982).

Decorative buckles were placed at the base of shoe tongues. Red heels were favored for court dress and for fashionable men before 1750 and after 1770. Slippers and dress shoes had low heels and flat soles. (See *Illustrated Table 10.2, page 245.*)

When sturdy shoes were worn outdoors, **spatterdashers** (also called **spats** or gaiters), separate protective coverings that extended from the top of the shoe to some point below the knee, were worn to protect the legs. (See *Figure 10.4.*)

Various sizes and shapes of boots were worn for riding, traveling, hunting, and by the military. As boots were not worn indoors, they tended to be sturdy and practical. Jack boots made of rigid, stiff leather were knee length, and protected the legs of horseback riders. Boots of softer leather and shorter lengths were also adopted, some copied from jockeys' boots and others from military styles.

ACCESSORIES AND JEWELRY

Men used such accessories and jewelry as muffs, walking sticks, watches, pocketbooks, and decorated snuff boxes for carrying powdered tobacco, which was inhaled. They wore rings, some brooches, and jeweled shoe buckles. (See *Illustrated Table 10.2, page 245.*)

COSMETICS AND GROOMING

Men used powder and perfume. Most were clean shaven.

COSTUME FOR WOMEN: 18TH CENTURY

A variety of supporting undergarments determined the shape of women's costume during the 18th century. The silhouette described in Chapter 9 of a long slender bodice and a skirt with back fullness continued until about 1720. (See *Color Plate 27.*) Wide hoops (in French, *paniers*) were used first in England about 1720 and slightly later in France. By the end of the second decade their use was widespread, and hoops remained a part of everyday costume until about 1770–1780.

The French called these hoops **paniers** (*pahn-yay'*), which means basket. Some hoops did produce the visual effect of perching a basket on either hip; however, the term was derived from the fact that both baskets and paniers might be made of wicker. In England, they were more likely to be called hoops.

Extreme width made it necessary for ladies to enter rooms sideways. Small railings were built around the edges of table tops and other furniture to prevent the sweeping of teacups and *object d'art* from the tables to the floor. Some paniers were hinged so that they could be folded up under the arms when necessary for mobility.

Caricatures and contemporary literary sources are full of gibes at ladies for wearing such an "outrageous" style. Male commentators in English journals (quoted by the Cunningtons 1957) offer these observations:

Illustrated Table 10.1

TYPICAL WOMEN'S HAIRSTYLES AND HEADDRESS IN THE 18TH CENTURY

Hairdress tyle of the first decade of the 18th century[1]

Hairdress and indoor cap of about 1725[1]

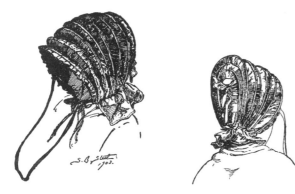

Calash, a folding hood of about 1765

Tall headdress popular after about 1775[2]

c. 1789: hair dressed *à la hedgehog*[3]

Late 18th-century hairstyle and hat[3]

[1]Comptesse Marie de Villemont, *Histoire de la Coiffure Feminine*, 1891.

[2]Author's collection of fashion plates.

[3]New York Public LIbrary Picture Collection.

- *The Spectator* of 1711: "... the hoop petticoat is made use of to keep us [i.e., the male sex] at a distance."
- *The Weekly Journal,* in 1717 appealed to women to "...find one tolerable convenience in these machines."
- *The Salisbury Journal* noted that the swaying hoops revealed ankles and legs, scolding ladies whom they accused of making their petticoats short so "... that a hoop eight yards wide may indecently show how your garters are ty'd."

Between 1720 and 1780, the shape of the hoop varied, thereby causing changes in the silhouette of the garments it supported. Although all classes adopted hoops, not every woman wore hoops. Between 1770 and 1780, as part of the focus on less formal English styles, hip pads and bustles supplanted hoops as support garments. The French did continue to wear the robe à la Française for ceremonial occasions and even after the French Revolution, when hoops were entirely out of style, they were preserved in the required formal dress at the English court.

UNDERGARMENTS

As undergarments women wore chemises, under petticoats, and the aforementioned hoops. Drawers were not yet universally worn. Chemises, which were worn next to the body, were knee length and cut full, with wide necklines edged with lace. This lace often showed at the neckline of the outer dress. Sleeves were full, to the elbow, but not visible.

Placed over the chemise but under the hoop, under petticoats were fairly straight garments made of cambric (a plain-weave, fine, white linen fabric), dimity (usually of cotton with a woven, length-wise cord or figure), flannel (a soft wool with a napped surface), or calico (see *page 195*). In winter they were often quilted for warmth.

Corsets, commonly called **stays,** were made of coarse fabric unless they were intended to be a visible part of the costume, in which case they were covered at least in front by dress fabric. Both the front and back were boned. Most laced up the back, although some laced at the front and back, and for stout and pregnant women, side lacings were sometimes added. (See *Figure 10.8.*) Some had fronts constructed to allow the insertion of a decorative, V-shaped stomacher. (See *Color Plate 30.*) The term **jumps** was applied to loose, unboned bodices worn at home to provide relief from tight corseting.

The hoop that shaped the skirt had a construction that was similar to that of the farthingale of the 16th century. From around 1710, they were cone shaped and made of circles of whalebone sewn into petticoats of sturdy fabric, each hoop increasing in size as it moved nearer the floor. In the 1720s the shape became rounded like a dome; in the 1730s the favored shape was narrower from front to back and wider from side to side, and by the 1740s extremes of width were reached. Some hoops reached a width of two and three-quarters yards; these wide styles remained until the 1760s.

The earliest hoops were made of whalebone. As the style persisted, the materials used expanded to include metal hoops and wicker basketlike shapes, one worn over each hip. Some metal or whalebone hoops were sewn into a petticoat while others were made as a frame held together with tapes and tied around the waist. (See *Figure 10.10b.*) Some dress bodices were so heavily boned as to make stays superfluous, in which case they were not worn.

Costume for Women: 1715–1730

OUTER GARMENTS

Gowns and two-piece garments were constructed to be either open or closed at center front. Gowns could be either loose or fitted. **Sacque** (*sahk*), **robe battante** (*ba-tahnt*), **robe volante** (*vo-lahnt*), and **innocente** (*in no-sahnt*) are all names for a gown that was unbelted, loose from the shoulder to floor. Made with pleats at the back and at the shoulder in front, sacques were worn over a dome-shaped hoop and might either have a closed front or be worn open over a corset and petticoat. (See *Figure 10.9.*) From the time of the death of Louis XIV until Louis XV reached adulthood, rigid court etiquette relaxed somewhat. The loose-fitting gown is sometimes cited as evidence of this lack of formality.

Other important styles included the **pet-en-lair** (*pet-ahn-lair*), which was a short, hip-length version worn with a separate, gathered skirt, and a **mantua-style gown,** cut in one piece from shoulder to hem that was fitted to the body in front and back. These gowns were more popular in England than in France. Many were open in front and the petticoat visible. Petticoats were often decorated with quilting.

HAIR AND HEADDRESS

See *Illustrated Table 10.1* for some examples of hairstyles and headdress in the 18th century.

Fairly simple hairstyles replaced the fontange styles, which went out of fashion about 1710. Waved loosely around the face, the hair was twisted into a small roll or bun worn at the top of the head, toward the back, or, alternatively, arranged around the face in ringlets or waves. Women, like men, might powder their hair for formal occasions.

Hats were worn both indoors and out. For indoors women wore **pinners,** circular caps with single or double frills around the edge that were placed flat on the head, or **mob caps.** These had high, puffed-out crowns at the back of the cap and wide, flat borders that encircled the face. Lace trimming was much used. Long lace or fabric streamers (lappets) hung from the edge or tied under the chin. White indoor caps might also be worn out-of-doors, under other hats. Outdoors, women covered their heads with hoods or wore small straw or silk hats with narrow brims and trimmed with narrow ribbon bands.

FIGURE 10.9

Both the lady in the foreground of the painting and her maid who gives the alarm in the background wear loose sacque garments, also known as *robes battante, volante, or innocente.* (Photograph of painting *The Alarm* by Troy, 1823, courtesy of the Board of Trustees of The Victoria and Albert Museum.)

Costume for Women: 1730–1760

GARMENTS

Two new styles replaced the loose sacque. The **robe à la Française** (*frahn-says'*) had a full, pleated cut at the back and a fitted front. (See *Figure 10.10a.*) The term **Watteau back** (*wat-tow'*) came to be attached to the loose-fitting, pleated back styles in the 19th century when similar styles were revived. The term was not used in the 18th century. Watteau was an 18th century painter who often depicted women wearing such gowns. The **robe à l'Anglaise** (*lahn-glays'*), had a close fit in the front and at the back. (See *Figure 10.11.*) The *robe à la Française* was more popular in France, a l'Anglaise with the English, though both styles were worn in both countries and in America.

Most gowns had open bodices and skirts that allowed the display of decorative stomachers and petticoats. (See *Color Plate 30.*) The stomacher, a triangular piece had tabs on the sides and was pinned either to the bodice or to the stays. Some stomachers were decorated with embroidery; others were covered with ribbons (**eschelles,** *eh-shell'*) or masses of artificial flowers or lace. Formal gowns and their petticoats were usually made from the same fabric thereby giving them the appearance of being a single garment. The extremely wide skirts effectively showed off the elaborately patterned fabrics used for full dress. *Contemporary Comments 10.3* describes the decorative fabrics worn in English court circles in the 1730s.

The necklines of these gowns were usually low and square or oval in shape. Sleeves ended below the elbow, finishing in one or more ruffles (called **engageants** *'on-gaj-ahnt'*).

When garments consisted of separate tops worn over petticoats or skirts, the skirts were full, supported by paniers. Fashionable tops included the short sacque or pet en lair and a jacket (in French, casaquin, pronounced *cas-ah-can'*) that was fitted through the bodice and flaring out below the waist almost to the knee. Sleeves were tight, with a small, turned-back cuff. (See *Figure 10.14.*)

HAIR AND HEADDRESS

Hair styles began to change by 1750 when hair was combed back from the face, smooth and high on top in toupee fashion, then arranged in a bun at the top of the head or a plait at the back. Another style was achieved by close, tight curls called **tête de mouton** (*tet-duh-moo-tahn'*), which translated into English means sheep's head.

The caps worn indoors remained much the same. For outdoors women wore either large flat straw hats with low crowns and wide brims, called **bergere** (*bear-jere'*) or **shepherdess hats,** that tied under or over the brim; three-cornered hats; or, for riding, jockey caps of black velvet with a peak at the front.

a

b

FIGURE 10.10 A AND B

(a) *Robe à la Française* of the mid-18th century, made of yellow flowered silk. (b) The wide skirts of the dress are supported by a frame called panniers, depicted in this drawing. (Photograph in (a) courtesy, The Metropolitan Museum of Art, bequest of Mrs. Maria P. James, 1911. Sketch in (b) courtesy, Fairchild Publications.)

Costume for Women: 1760–1790

GARMENTS

After 1770, the *robe a la Francaise* modified, as paniers were replaced by hip pads. Excess fabric was pulled through pocket

CONTEMPORARY COMMENTS 10.3

Elaborate English Fashions of 1738–1739

The contemporary description by Mary Granville of clothing worn in English court circles in the years of 1738 and 1739 provides a glimpse of the lavishness of English upper-class costume during this period. In her letter to her sister of January 23, 1738–9.

I never saw so much finery without any mixture of trumpery in my life. Lady Huntington's, as the most extraordinary I must describe first:—her petticoat was black velvet embroidered with chenille, the pattern a *large stone vase* filled with *ramping flowers* that spread almost over a breadth of the petticoat from the bottom to the top; between each vase of flowers was a pattern of gold shells, and foliage embossed and most heavily rich; the gown was white satin embroidered also with chenille mixt with gold ornaments, *no vases* on the sleeve, but *two or three on the tail;* it was a most labored piece of finery, the pattern much properer for a stucco staircase than the apparel of a lady—a mere shadow that tottered under every step she took under the load. . . .

In another letter to her sister of January 22, 1739–40(?)
. . . Lady Dysart was in a scarlet damask gown. Facings [trimmings] and robings [bands of decoration] embroidered with gold and colours, her petticoat white satin, all covered with embroidery of the same sort, very fine and handsome . . . The Princess's clothes were white satin the petticoat, robings and facings covered with a rich gold net, and upon that flowers in their natural colours embroidered, her head crowned with jewels and her behavior, (as it always is,) affable and obliging to everybody. . . . The Duchess of Bedford's petticoat was green padusoy [peau de soie], embroidered very richly with gold and silver and a few colours; the pattern was festoons of shells, coral, corn, corn-flowers, and sea weeds; everything in different works of gold and silver except the flowers and coral, the body of the gown white satin, with a mosaic pattern of gold facings, robings and train the same of the petticoat; there was an abundance of embroidery, and many people in gowns and petticoats of different colours. The men were as fine as the ladies . . . My Lord Baltimore was in light brown and silver, his coat lined *quite throughout* with ermine.

From *The Autobiography and Correspondence of Mary Granville, Mrs. Delany. Vol. II. 1861. London: Richard Bentley.*

slits in such a way that the bunched fabric hung through the pocket to form a drapery. By 1780 this robe was no longer fashionable. The *robe a l'Anglaise,* with slight modifications in waistline placement and a fuller bodice, continued to be worn into the 1780s. (See *Figure 10.11.*) Skirt fullness swung from sides to back in the late 1770s, and a "false rump" pad tied at the back of the waist supported the fullness. Contemporary references indicate **false rumps** were filled with cork or other light cushioning materials. The *London Magazine* of 1777 issued this warning to prospective bridegrooms:

> *Let her gown be tuck'd up to the hips on each side*
> *Shoes too high for to walk or to jump;*
> *And to deck the sweet creature complete for a bride*
> *Let the cork-cutter cut her a rump.*
> *Thus finish'd in taste, while on Chloe you gaze*
> *You may take the dear charmer for life;*
> *But never undress her—for out of her stays,*
> *You'll find you have lost half your wife.*

In the late 1770s and 1780s some skirts shortened, revealing the leg above the ankle. (See *Color Plate 31.*) The many gown styles include the **polonaise** (*po-lohn-ays'*)(fashionable from about 1770–85), which was an overdress and petticoat in which the overskirt was puffed and looped by means of tapes and rings sewn into the skirt. A hoop or bustle supported the skirt. (See *Figure 10.12.*) In subsequent periods the term polonaise will be used very broadly to refer to any overskirt that is puffed or draped over an under layer. Other gowns that were seen frequently were closed or "**round" gowns,** that is, gowns closed all the way down the front. Redingote dresses resembled buttoned greatcoats or English riding coats with wide lapels or revers at the neck. The **chemise a la reine** (*chem-eze ah la rehn*) was a white muslin gown that resembled the chemise undergarment of the period, but, unlike the chemise, had a waistline and a soft, fully gathered skirt. This garment, made of muslin imported from India, was a forerunner of styles of the beginning of the 19th century. (See *Figure 10.13.*)

FIGURE 10.11

Standing woman wears a *robe à l'Anglaise*, which is fitted close to the waist at front and back. Seated woman wears a bergere or shepherdess hat (*Young Woman with Servant*. Stephen Slaughter; English, 1697–1765. Photograph courtesy, Wadsworth Atheneum, Hartford. The Ella Gallup Sumner and Mary Catlin Sumner Collection Fund.)

Fashionable two-piece garments included skirts worn with a long, fitted jacket (the **caraçao** (*kara-sow*) bodice) similar in style to the aforementioned casaquin in cut (see *Figure 10.14*) and jackets based on English men's riding dress, worn with men's hats.

HAIR AND HEADDRESS

See *Illustrated Table 10.1* for some examples of hairstyles and headdress in the 18th century.

Hair styles expanded to extreme sizes. In the 1760s hair was dressed higher and frizzed around the face. This changed to an arrangement of sausage curls flat against the head, running from ear to ear. In the 1770s, maximum size was reached when towering structures were supplemented by feathers, jewels, ribbons, and seemingly almost anything a lady could perch on top of her head. (See *Illustrated Table 10.1, page 236.*) In 1768 the *London Magazine* was talking about hairstyles raised "a foot high and tower-wise." In the 1780s height diminished, but fullness was retained in the hedgehog fashion,

with hair curled, full and wide around the face and long locks hanging at the back. (See *Figure 10.13.*)

For indoors, small day caps were discarded when hairstyles grew to exaggerated sizes, although some mob caps were enlarged to accommodate high hairstyles. For outdoors, hoods were made large enough to cover the hair. These included **calashes** or **caleches** (*cal-eshes*), which were made of a series of semi-hoops sewn into the hood at intervals. These hoops supported the hood without crushing the hair, and folded flat when not in use. Other hats perched on top of the tall headdress. When the flatter hedgehog hairstyle developed, women set enormous hat structures with great quantities of lace, ribbons, feathers, and flowers were set flat on the head or at an angle. (See *Illustrated Table 10.1, page 236.*)

FIGURE 10.12

Brocade overdress dated from c. 1775 to 1789 has skirt with puffed draperies that are often referred to as a polonaise. (Photograph courtesy, Division of Costume, American Museum of National History.)

FIGURE 10.13

Antoine-Laurent Lavoisier and his wife, 1788, painted by Jacques-Louis David. Madame Lavoisier wears a muslin dress of the *chemise de la reine* style. Her hair is dressed *à la herisson* or "hedgehog" fashion. (Photograph courtesy, The Metropolitan Museum of Art, purchase, Mr. and Mrs. Charles Wrightsman Gift, 1977).

FIGURE 10.14

Day dress, 1778. Gown of yellow-gold satin with a caraçao bodice, in the pseudo-shepherdess style popular at the court of Louis XVI. This dress is said to be from the wardrobe of Queen Marie Antoinette. The child's dress of the 18th century is probably of an earlier date, and is made of green and gold flowered silk. (Photograph courtesy, The Metropolitan Museum of Art.)

Other Costume Components for Women: The 18th Century

OUTDOOR GARMENTS

Cloaks were cut full, to fit over wide skirts. These varied in lengths, some being full length and others ending at the waist or hip. Some were hooded. Fabrics included velvet and wool, with fur trims for cold weather and silk or other lightweight fabrics for warm weather. (See *Figure 10.15*.) Overcoats, cut like a man's greatcoat, though more closely fitted, were used in the last two decades after the style for hoops had passed.

Other garments worn outdoors included large scarves, shawls, and wraps, with or without sleeves, which covered the upper part of the body or smaller shawls and short capes covering the shoulders and upper arms. Narrow fur or feather pieces like a modern-day stole but called **tippets** were worn around the shoulders.

FOOTWEAR

Stockings extended to the knee and were held in place with garters. Fabrics used included cotton, wool, or silk knits.

Shoes had pointed toes, high heels, tongues, and side pieces called latchets that fastened over the instep. Backless slippers (**mules**) were popular. In the late 1880s Chinese influences were evident in slippers with small, low heels and turned-up toes that were held on the foot by a drawstring in a casing around the top of the shoe. Such Oriental influences are evident in all the decorative arts of the 18th century, although in clothing they are most evident in men's dressing gowns and in fabric decoration.

Clogs or pattens, overshoes that protect against wet and muddy surfaces, were made of matching or other fabrics and had sturdy leather soles, built up arches, and latchets that tied across the instep to hold the clog in place. Country people wore wooden clogs or metal pattens to raise the shoe

FIGURE 10.15

Silk satin cloak from the 18th century. (Photograph courtesy, Division of Costume, American Museum of National History.)

out of the mud. (See *Illustrated Table 10.2*, for some examples of footwear.)

ACCESSORIES

See *Illustrated Table 10.2* for examples of some types of 18th century accessories. Items for covering the hands included gloves, mittens, and muffs. Gloves usually extended to the elbow. Mittens were gloves without thumb and finger coverings. Muffs were small until the 1770s, after which they enlarged. They were most often made of feathers, fabric, or fur (and often had matching tippets).

Pockets were not yet sewn into dresses. Instead they were bags sewn onto a ribbon and tied around the waist and reached through a slit in the skirt. After 1760, some women carried small bags, as well as wearing clothes with pockets.

Other accessories included folding fans of various sizes and shapes, parasols, black masks mounted on sticks that were held up before the face to cover the full or half face. These masks were often worn to balls.

JEWELRY

Among the more commonly used items of jewelry were necklaces, often with matching earrings, gold watches worn around the neck; jeweled hair pins and hair ornaments; and jeweled buckles for shoes. Among the popular necklaces were rows of pearls, chains, lockets, pendants, and crosses.

COSMETICS AND GROOMING

Lips, cheeks, and fingernails could be colored red with rouge. Eyebrows were shaped with scissors or by plucking, and blackened with combs of soft lead. Patches and plumpers (noted in the 17th century) continued in use. Perfumes were used, as were creams. Creams were smeared on bands of cloth, wrapped around the head, and worn at night to remove wrinkles. In place of soap, women used "wash balls"—a combination of rice powder, flour, starch, white lead, and orris root. The lead was probably injurious to the skin.

COSTUMES FOR ACTIVE SPORTS FOR MEN AND WOMEN: THE 18TH CENTURY

There were no special riding or hunting costumes. Men wore frock coats, breeches (preferably of buckskin), and high boots. Toward the end of the 18th century the first top hats developed as part of men's riding costume.

For women a costume for riding was adapted from everyday styles worn by men. It consisted of a shirt, waistcoat, outer coat, and skirt. Coat and waistcoat reached almost to the knees until after mid-century, when they shortened and

became fuller and more flared. By the end of the 18th century a variation modeled on men's greatcoats appeared. Women wore three-cornered hats, black velvet jockey caps, and high-crowned, narrow-brimmed hats for riding.

Both men and women were bathing in the sea in England by the 18th century, and written evidence together with engravings indicates that nude bathing took place in segregated areas. At most resorts, however, a special costume was worn. Cunnington and Mansfield (1969) describe this as jackets and petticoats of brown linen or long, loose sacks of flannel. Sea bathing was not popular in America until after 1800, but bathing at spas and springs was considered beneficial to health. A blue and white checked bathing gown exists that is said to have belonged to Martha Washington. Its cut is similar to that of a chemise, although the sleeves are narrower and the neck higher. Lead disks are wrapped in linen and attached to the gown near the hem, which probably served to keep the gown in place when the bather entered the water (Kidwell 1968).

Tennis, skating, and in England golf and cricket as well, were played by men and, more rarely, women, but no special costume had developed for these activities.

COSTUME FOR CHILDREN: THE 18TH CENTURY

First Half of the 18th Century

Babies were wrapped in swaddling clothes. After infancy to age six or seven, both boys and girls wore skirts. After age six or seven both boys and girls wore adult styles (see *Figure 10.16*), although the ribbons of childhood were still appearing on young and even adolescent girls' dresses until about 1770.

Some children were sent away to boarding schools, and some ran away from school. Descriptions of runaway children provide some descriptions of how children were dressed. One boy aged eleven or twelve was wearing "sad color kersey coat trim'd with flat new gilded brass buttons, a whitish callamanca waistcoat with round silver buttons, silver edging to his hat, rolled white worsted stock. Sad color sagathy stuff britches with silver plate buttons" (Ashton 1929).[1]

Second Half of the 18th Century

Styles especially for children, different from either previous or current adult dress, came into being. Jean-Jacques Rousseau, a French philosopher, is often given credit for inspiring

---

[1] Sad color was any dull color; kersey, a closely-woven twill cloth; callamanca, a glazed fabric with raised stripes of the same color; and sagathy, a lightweight serge. Stuff was a synonym for "cloth."

Illustrated Table 10.2

18TH CENTURY ACCESSORIES

Tie pocket

Man's pocketbook

S.L. GORDON

Woman's stockings
with embroidered clocks

Fan, c. 1780

Parasol, c. 1715

Umbrella, c. 1715

Woman's shoe,
early 18th c.

Woman's shoe
with matching clog
early 18th c.

Man's three-cornered hat

Man's club wig,
c. 1760–1790

Man's black shoe with gold buckle,
late 1700s

FIGURE 10.16

Informal family group at home. The child wears a dress in the style *à l'Anglaise*. The mother, in a combing jacket, has not yet had her hair arranged. The father, in a banyan with a matching waistcoat, is already wearing his powdered wig. (Group portrait by Drouais [1727–1775]. Photograph courtesy, The National Gallery of Art, Washington DC, Samuel H. Kress Collection, 1964.)

this change. His writings do stress the importance of modifying current clothing practices in the direction of greater freedom for children, but Macquoid (1925) points out that changes in English styles for children had already begun to take place before the publication in 1760 of *Emile*. Macquoid notes that portraits of little girls in sacques after 1720 are very rare, in spite of the fact that they were popular for wear among adult women, and that boys were dressed in straighter, less full coats than their elders (Macquoid 1925). Moore (1953) suggests that paintings by the artist Joshua Reynolds may have helped to spread styles from England to the continent, because he liked to paint children in unadorned costume or in costumes from his own stock of clothes, which were not necessarily part of actual street dress (Moore 1953).

The importation of muslin from India may also have had an impact on children's dress. This sheer white fabric was at first very expensive and artists enjoyed painting wealthy children dressed in the soft folds of the fabric.

But even if the less restrictive styles for children were not a result of Rousseau's philosophy of child rearing, his recommendations must have lent this trend considerable support. In the light of previous practices, his counsel was quite revolutionary. Summarized briefly, the guidelines he laid down for children's dress included:

1. For infants, "No caps, no bandages, no swaddling clothes." Instead he recommended loose and flowing flannel wrappers that were neither too heavy to check the child's movements, nor too warm to prevent feeling the air.

2. For older children, nothing to cramp or hinder the movement of the limbs of the growing child. No tight, closely fitting clothes, no belts.

3. Keeping children in frocks (skirts) as long as possible.

4. Dressing children in bright colors. He says, "Children like the bright colors best, and they suit them better too."

5. ". . . the plainest and most comfortable clothes, those which leave him most liberty" (Rousseau 1933, pages 27, 91, 92).

Although clothing for children did not reach the ideal recommended by Rousseau, it did improve significantly during the second half of the century. One of Rousseau's strongest statements was about the detrimental effects of swaddling infants. Whether a result of his influence or not, the practice was, at least in England and the United States, pretty well given up by the end of the century.

The usual clothes for toddlers up to age six or seven were dresses or robes. After 1780 boys over six or seven wore long

FIGURE 10.17

Children, late 18th century. Girls are dressed in white muslin dresses; the boy wears a skeleton suit. (Photograph of painting by John Hoppner, courtesy of The Metropolitan Museum of Art, bequest of Thomas W. Lamont, 1948.)

straight trousers, a white shirt with a wide collar that finished in a ruffled edge and, over the shirt, a jacket that was either a shorter, simplified version of those of adults or cut to the waist and double-breasted. This costume was called a **skeleton suit**. (See *Figure 10.17*.)

Just how boys came to wear trousers is not clear. In the adult world trousers were worn in the 17th and 18th centuries by Italian comic actors, and by city laborers in the 18th century. English sailors seem to have been the first Englishmen to wear long trousers. Moore suggests that it may have been by way of copying the sailor's costume for young boys that they first were used (Moore 1953).

Girls wore simple straight dresses, often of white muslin. Dresses tended to have slightly elevated waistlines. (See *Figure 10.17*.) Out-of-doors, girls wore long or short cloaks. Small, white linen mob caps were worn indoors and out. Some small girls appear in portraits in large, decorative hats, similar to those of adult women, but this may have been the artist's choice and not common practice.

After age 11 or 12 boys and girls assumed adult dress.

SUMMARY

THEMES

The themes of SOCIAL LIFE, SOCIAL CLASS STRUCTURE, and SOCIAL ROLES stand out clearly against the background of 18th century dress. Costume history before the 19th century generally focuses on the clothing of the well-to-do. Pictorial evidence as well as the clothing that is preserved in museums leads to this upper-class bias. As can be seen from *Figure 10.1,* clothing of less affluent people and servants was relatively simple and practical, with some general reflection of the lines of fashionable dress. These differences in style also served to reinforce the class distinctions that permeated society. The fairly decorative dress of servants of the nobility (see *Figure 10.7*) was a statement of a sort of reflected glory, as if the status of the master would be diminished if his servant were inadequately attired.

Related to the theme of ECONOMICS is Thorstein Veblen's *Theory of the Leisure Classes* (1936), which can easily be applied to the styles of the 18th century. His view was that clothing can be a means of showing one's wealth through the owning and display of valuable objects (conspicuous consumption) and through demonstrating that one does not need to work (conspicuous leisure.) The lavishness of 18th century clothing illustrates the principle of conspicuous consumption. Conspicuous leisure is evident in the inconvenience of the tall headdresses and wide panniers, because the wearers could not possibly be accused of doing any productive work!

It is rarely possible to point to clear, unambiguous parallels between costume and current events, but it is tempting to see the variability of styles, the extremes of size and shape, and the lavishness of decoration as evidence of a frantic attempt on the part of the French nobility to escape the POLITICAL CONFLICTS that will shortly lead to the bloody French Revolution.

If such analogies were so clear cut, however, then one would expect to see quite different styles in America following 1776, and yet women of the American democracy also powdered their hair and donned paniers. One can note that American styles were less extreme and lagged a little behind those of the European courts.

The themes of INTERNATIONAL TRADE and CROSS-CULTURAL INFLUENCES on costume appear not only in the styles of some shoes and in men's robes or dressing gowns, but also in the use of Indian chintzes, muslins, and in the Oriental designs of woven brocades and damasks. TECHNOLOGY, another recurring topic, is important as advances within the textile industry served to expand textile availability and to lower costs.

SOCIAL ATTITUDES toward children, shaped by the writings of Rousseau, seem to have been changing at about the same time that clothing for children changed. Greater freedom in both child rearing methods and in clothing for children shows interesting parallels.

Challenges to SOCIAL NORMS were expressed through clothing as well. Quaker men avoided wearing fashionable wigs, and both men and women of the Quaker faith wore subdued colors without elaborate embellishments.

Clearly a major role of clothing was the establishment of SOCIOECONOMIC STATUS. Although advances in the technology for manufacturing cloth were beginning to have an impact on the availability of fine fabrics, the enormous amount of hand labor required to make both men's and women's clothing shows not only the wealth of the owner, but also the ready availability of low-paid men and women who spent hours in sewing and embroidering these garments.

The French Revolution in 1795 marked the end of the *Ancien Regime,* a way of life in which the aristocracy was separated from the rest of the population. It has long been held that radical changes in costume accompanied the political upheavals of the Revolution, mirroring the contrasts between pre-Revolutionary and post-Revolutionary eras. Steele has argued that these changes were already underway before the Revolution, and that the "roots of the change in fashion precede the great event" (Steele 1988, p. 40).

Both points of view (that the end of the 18th century saw revolutionary fashion changes paralleling the revolutionary political changes or that these fashion changes had their roots in earlier style changes) can be seen as analogous to the sociopolitical developments of the 18th century. The Revolution brought an abrupt and violent end to one regime, but the roots of the Revolution, like the roots of fashion change, preceded the great event.

SURVIVALS OF
18TH CENTURY DRESS

Pompadour, polonaise, Watteau back, tricorne, and bicorne are all names assigned to costume items of the 18th century long after that century had passed. That these terms were coined and have continued in use today is evidence of costume survival. The hairstyle worn by Madame Pompadour has entered the repertory of hairdressing, and was especially notable in the Edwardian period (1900–1910) (see *Illustrated Table 15.2, page 373*) and during the late 30s and World War II.

Visual Summary Table
ROCOCO

Man: 1700 to c. 1750
Shirt, waistcoat and coat, ending just below the knee, with full skirts; knee-length rather full breeches.

Man: c. 1750–1800
The line narrows. Shirt under shorter waistcoat; slender coats, worn open, angle toward the side. Narrower breeches are knee-length.

Woman: 1700–1715
Continuation of styles of 1680–1700.

Woman: 1715–1730
Gowns either full from shoulder to floor or fitted. Hoops hold out wide skirts.

Woman: 1730–1760
Open bodices have decorative stomachers. Skirts grow very wide. Gowns with full backs called *à la Francaise*; if fitted in back *à l'Anglaise*.

Woman: 1760–1790
Hoops replaced by hip pads to support skirts, which are less wide. Skirt fullness gradually swings toward back.

The Watteau back, the construction of the back of the robe à la Française, has been especially popular in dressing gowns in a number of subsequent periods. The polonaise had extensive revival in the Crinoline (see *Figure 13.5*) and Bustle periods (*Figure 14.7*) and has been used in wedding and ball gowns in the 20th century. Although men gave up tricorne and bicorne hats after the early 19th century, women's hat designers have continued to employ these forms.

NOTES

Ashton, J. 1929. *Social Life in the Reign of Queen Anne.* New York: Scribners, p. 50.

Cunningham, P. 1984. "Eighteenth Century Nightgowns: The Gentleman's Robe in Art and Fashion." *Dress,* Vol. 10, p. 2 ff.

Cunnington, P. and A. Mansfield. 1969. *English Costume for Sports and Outdoor Recreation.* New York: Barnes and Noble, p. 261.

Cunnington, C. W. and P. Cunnington. 1957. *Handbook of English Costume in the Eighteenth Century.* London: Faber and Faber.

DeMarly, D. 1986. *Working Dress: A History of Occupational Clothing.* New York: Holmes and Meier, p. 10.

Durant, W. and A. Durant. 1965. *The Age of Voltaire.* New York: Simon and Schuster, p. 282.

Kidwell, C. and M. Christman. 1974. *Suiting Everyone: The Democratization of Clothing in America.* Washington, DC: Smithsonian Institution Press, p. 27.

Kidwell, C. B. 1968. *Women's Bathing and Swimming Costume in the United States.* Washington, DC: Smithsonian Institution Press, p. 14.

Levron, J. 1968. *Daily Life at Versailles in the 17th and 18th Centuries.* New York: Macmillan, p. 194.

Macquoid, P. 1925. *Four Hundred Years of Children's Costume.* London: Medici Society, p. 100.

Marshall, D. 1969. *English People in the 18th Century.* London: Longmans, p. 84.

Moore, D. L. 1953. *The Child in Fashion.* London: Batsford, p. 12.

Reynolds, J. 1891. *Sir Joshua Reynolds' Discourses.* Chicago: A. C. McClurg.

Rousseau, J. J. 1933. *Emile.* London: J. M. Dent, pp. 27, 91, 92.

Steele, V. 1988. *Paris Fashion: A Cultural History.* New York: Oxford University Press, p. 40.

Swann, J. 1982. *Shoes.* London: Batsford, p. 26.

Veblen, T. 1936. *Theory of the Leisure Class.* New York: Viking.

SELECTED READINGS

Books Containing Illustrations of Costume of the Period from Original Sources

Baumgarten, L. 2002. *What Clothes Reveal: The Language of Clothing in Colonial and Federal America.* Williamsburg, VA: The Colonial Williamsburg Foundation.

Blum, S. 1982. *Eighteenth Century French Fashion Plates.* New York: Dover.

Cobban, A. 1969. *The 18th Century.* New York: McGraw-Hill.

Gaunt, W. 1971. *The Great Century of British Painting: Hogarth to Turner.* New York: Phaidon.

Halls, Z. 1970. *Men's Costume: 1580–1750.* London: Her Majesty's Stationery Office.

———. 1973. *Men's Costume: 1750–1800.* London: Her Majesty's Stationery Office.

Hart, A. 1998. *Fashion in Detail: From the 17th and 18th Centuries.* New York: Rizzoli.

Little, N. F. 1976. *Paintings by New England Provincial Artists: 1775–1800.* Boston: Museum of Fine Arts.

Maeder, E. 1983. *An Elegant Art.* New York: Abrams.

Shesgreen, S., ed. 1973. *Engravings by Hogarth.* New York: Dover.

Schonberger, A. and H. Soehner. 1960. *The Rococo Age.* New York: McGraw-Hill.

Periodical Articles

Bryant, N. O. 1988. "Buckles and Buttons: An Inquiry into Fastening Systems Used in Eighteenth Century Breeches." *Dress,* Vol. 14, p. 27.

Benhamou, R. 2001. "Who Controls This Private Space? The Offense and Defense of the Hoop in Early Eighteenth-Century France and England." *Dress,* Vol. 28, p. 13.

Clark, G. 1994. "Infant Clothing in the Eighteenth Century: A New Insight." *Costume,* No. 28, p. 47.

Cunningham, P. 1984. "Eighteenth Century Nightgowns: The Gentleman's Robe in Art and Fashion." *Dress,* Vol. 10, p. 2.

Kidwell, C. 1978. "Short Gowns." *Dress,* Vol. 4, p. 30.

Lemire, B. 1991. "Peddling Fashion: Salesmen, Pawnbrokers, Taylors, Thieves, and the Second-hand Clothes Trade in England, c. 1700–1800. *Textile History,* Vol. 22, p. 67.

Ribeiro, A. 1978. "The Macaronis." *History Today,* Vol. 28, No. 7, p. 463.

Trautman, P. 1985. "An 18th Century American Tailor: Myth and Reality as Seen Through One Tailor's Surviving Records." *Clothing and Textiles Research Journal,* Vol. 3, No. 2, p. 25.

Winner, V. H. 2001. "Abigail Adams and the 'Rage of Fashion.'" *Dress,* Vol. 28, p. 64.

The following pages provide color photographs of costumes from various historical periods. From these depictions, readers can gain some understanding of the colors utilized in costumes during these periods.

FIGURE 1

Egyptian works of art depict individuals clad in white, solid, and multicolored fabrics. It is not clear whether multicolored effects were created by weaving, appliqué, or beading. (Courtesy, The Metropolitan Museum of Art, Rogers Fund, 1933, 33.8.7.)

FIGURE 2

Minoan woman from a fresco in Knossos, Crete, c. 1300–1250 BC is wearing a bodice of yellow with blue figured braid trim. Her dark, curly hair is dressed in styles typical of Minoan women. (National Archaeological Museum. Athens, Greece. Courtesy, Scala/Art Resource, NY.)

FIGURE 3

Depiction of a family performing sacrifices, c. 530 B.C. Women are dressed in blue Doric peplos with red cloaks. Young boys wear himationlike draped cloaks. (National Archeol. Museum, Athens, Greece. Courtesy, Nimatallah/Art Resource NY.)

FIGURE 4

Only rarely does Greek art show colors of costumes. Here a woman wearing a gold-colored Ionic chiton has a lavender chlamydon over her shoulder. (Courtesy, The Metropolitan Museum of Art, Classical Purchase, Fletcher, and Rogers Funds, 1979, 1979.11.15.)

FIGURE 5

Etruscan dancers from the Tomb of the Triclinium, Tarquinia, Italy, wear colorful garments. On the left is a dancer wearing a blue tabenna draped like a himation. On the right the dancer, with a tabenna draped to the front, wears a tunic that has a woven or printed design. (Courtesy, Scala/Art Resource, NY.)

FIGURE 7

Wall painting depicting Roman women at home. They are wearing tunics in a variety of different colors with pallas draped over them. (Museo Archeologica, Naples. Courtesy, Erich Lessing, Art Resource NY.)

FIGURE 6

Roman man at center is participating in a religious rite and wears his toga pulled over his head, according to custom. His tunic bears two broad purple clavii, and the purple border on his toga indicates that he may have been a magistrate. Two figures on either side wear special religious garb. (Courtesy, Photo Arts.)

FIGURE 8

Child's tunic and hood of green wool with bands of gold tapestry decoration on hood, sleeves, and body of garment. 5th century A.D., Coptic Egypt. (Courtesy, The Metropolitan Museum of Art, gift of George D. Pratt, 1927, 27.239.)

FIGURE 9

The Byzantine Empress Theodora wears a paludamentum of purple, a color associated with royalty, while her female retainers are dressed in colorful brocades probably woven from silk produced by the Byzantine silk industry (A.D. 6th century). (Corte de Teodora. Ravenna S. Vitale. Courtesy, Scala/Art Resource, NY.)

FIGURE 10

Byzantine influences appeared in European dress of the upper classes during the early Middle Ages. Bands of embroidery on the tunic of the second figure on the left show Byzantine influence, while other figures wear under tunics, and mantles of various solid colors (11th century). (Courtesy, The Pierpont Morgan Library/Art Resource NY, M.641, F.18.)

FIGURE 11

Manuscript page, c. 1230, shows a king and queen on the upper panel. The queen, Blanche of France, wears a cote, cut full under the arm, and over it a fur-lined mantle. The king who is her son, St. Louis IX, wears a cote with long, fitted sleeves and a surcote that ends below the elbow with wider sleeves. His mantle closes at the front with a decorative brooch. The author of the book and scribe on the lower panel each wear sideless surcotes. (Courtesy, The Pierpont Morgan Library/Art Resource, NY, M.240, F.8.)

FIGURE 12

The Butler Family at Mass, an English miniature c. 1340, shows husband and wife in typically tight–fitting garments of this period with fur trimming. The prelate celebrating the Mass wears religious dress of the period. (Courtesy, Walters Gallery, Baltimore, MSW.105f.15)

FIGURE 13, 14

Love of color, says Umberto Eco, is evident not only in medieval art, but also in everyday life, clothing, ornament, and weapons. (See Eco, U. 1986. *Art and Beauty in the Middle Ages.* New Haven: Yale University Press, Chapter IV.) Paintings of the 15th century not only show color variations, but subtle fashion variations, as well. In Figure 11, a bride and groom of about 1449 consult a goldsmith. (Courtesy, The Metropolitan Museum of Art, Robert Lehman Collection, 1975, 1975.1.110.) Contrast her elaborately patterned gown with its wide sleeve and her double-horned headdress with the tall, pointed hennins, predominantly solid-colored fabrics, and narrow sleeves of the ladies of the late 1400s in Figure 14. (Courtesy, Beinecke Rare Book and Manuscript Library, Yale University.)

FIGURE 15

It is evident that white was not traditional for weddings during the Middle Ages. The bride in this bridal couple, c. 1470, wears red, the groom wears parti-colored jacket and hose. (*A Young Couple,* German, oil on wood, 62.2 cm. × 36.5 cm. © The Cleveland Museum of Art, Delia E. and L. E. Holden Funds, 1932.179.)

FIGURE 16

Fifteenth century wedding banquet. Bride, at center of table, wears traditional dress of royal women, the women who flank her wear tall headdresses called hennins and gowns typical of the late 1400s. Serving men in wide-shouldered jackets and hose wear long-pointed shoes, called poulaines. The man directing the serving who is older and more conservative in his dress wears a short houppelande. (Bibliotheque de l'Arsenal, Paris, France. Courtesy, Erich Lessing/Art Resource, NY.)

FIGURE 17

A tailor's shop of the late 15th century has colorful bolts of cloth stacked on the counter. Garments in various stages of manufacture hang over the rod at the back of the shop. The tailor at far left sits cross-legged on the counter to sew; to his right, another cuts a garment piece while two others measure cloth. (Castle of Issogne, Italy. Courtesy, Photo Arts.)

FIGURE 18

Italian women c. 1450–1465 in Renaissance dresses made of richly-colored fabric that may be velvet. Their headdresses are simpler than those in northern Europe (see Figure 16). (S. Francesco. Arezzo, Italy. Courtesy, Scala/Art Resource, NY.)

FIGURE 19

Renaissance patrons often commissioned paintings that depicted their families. Here members of the fashionably dressed Sforza family of Milano (c. 1490) kneel in worship before the Madonna, the Christ child, and saints who wear various forms of religious dress. Even an infant in swaddling clothes and cap is shown kneeling in prayer, an impossible position for a child so young. (Brera Museum, Milan, Italy. Courtesy, Art Resource.)

FIGURE 20

Henry VIII, king of England (1497–1543) is depicted wearing a doublet that is ornamented with slashes through which puffs of fabric are pulled. A prominent codpiece is visible at the front of the skirt-like bases. Over this is a fur-trimmed short robe. (Petworth House. Petworth, Sussex, Great Britain. Courtesy, National Trust/Art Resource, NY.)

FIGURE 22

Embroidery in multicolored yarns decorates this jacket for a girl of the late 16th or early 17th century. (Courtesy, The Metropolitan Museum of Art, Rogers Fund, 1923, 23.170.1.)

FIGURE 21

Stiffly rigid styles, often in black or white with elaborate embroidery and lace, were characteristic of the Spanish styles that influenced all of Europe in the 16th century (c. 1584). (*Infanta Isabella Clara Eugenia with Magdalena Ruiz* by Felipe de Liano. Courtesy, Prado Museum.)

FIGURE 23

Women in farthingales and men wearing jackets with wide ruffs, breeches, and hose participate in a ball at the court of the French king, Henri III c. 1582. (Musée du Louvre, Paris. Courtesy, Art Resource.)

FIGURE 24

Man's doublet, c. 1625, is elaborately constructed with paned sections on sleeves and chest. Made of silk brocade. (Courtesy, The Metropolitan Museum of Art, purchase, The Costume Institute Fund, in memory of Polaire Weissman, 1989, 1989.196.)

FIGURE 25

Dutch men, c. 1665, wear petticoat breeches with waist-length jackets over white shirts. The man at the right has a pair of canons, a wide ruffle, at his knees. (*A Game of Skittles* (detail) by Pieter de Hooch, copyist. Courtesy, Cincinnati Art Museum, gift of Mary Hanna.)

FIGURE 26

These Massachusetts settlers dressed for their portraits in light and bright colors, contrary to the stereotype of the drab and dark-colored dress of the Puritans. (*Mrs. Elizabeth Freake and Baby Mary*, by an unidentified artist, c. 1674. Courtesy, Worcester Art Museum, Worcester, MA, gift of Mr. and Mrs. Albert W. Rice.)

FIGURE 27

Styles of about 1700 are shown on a "dressed" fashion print, one which has had actual fabrics glued in place. (*Cavalier and Lady Drinking Chocolate*, a dressed costume print, France between 1690–1710, though "dressed" about 50 years later. Courtesy, The Pierpont Morgan Library/Art Resource, NY.)

FIGURE 28

Although white wedding dresses had not yet become customary in the 18th century, this bride wore cream satin and gold (1729). (*Wedding of Stephen Beckingham and Mary Cox* (detail) by William Hogarth. Courtesy, The Metropolitan Museum of Art, Marquand Fund, 1936, 36.111.)

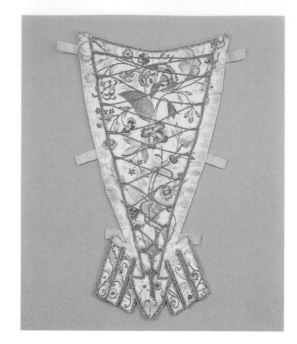

FIGURE 30

Embroidered silk satin stomacher, c. 1740. These elaborately decorated fillers for the front of 18th century dresses were removable and could be worn with different garments. (Cora Ginsburg image, Embroidered, ivory, silk, satin stomacher polychrome silk flowers, gilt cord lacing; English, ca. 1740. Courtesy, Cora Ginsburg LLC.)

FIGURE 29

Men's outer coats and waistcoats of the 18th century were often heavily embroidered with silk in vivid colors (c. 1770). Contrast the cut of the men's coats in Figure 28 with the narrower cut of the second half of the century in Figure 29. (Courtesy, Philadelphia Museum of Art, gift of Charles F. Saake.)

FIGURE 31

Silk brocades with floral patterns in pastel and light colors were among the more widely used fabrics for women's dresses in the 18th century (England, 1775–1785). (Courtesy, Cincinnati Art Museum, John J. Emery Endowment.)

FIGURE 32

The red cap of freedom was one of the important symbols worn by the *sans culottes*. These men also wore trousers, a garment of the lower classes, rather than the knee-breeches that upper-class men wore in the 18th century. (Courtesy, New York Public Library, Picture Collection.)

FIGURE 33

The simple white dress with puffed sleeves of the Empire period was frequently worn together with a long, narrow shawl with a multi-colored paisley design like the one draped over the arm of this woman. (*Comtesse Daru* by Jacques-Louis David, 1748–1825. Copyright The Frick Collection, New York.)

FIGURE 34

Men's dress in the 19th century lost much of its color. As a result, neckwear took on more importance, showing off stiffly starched, white collars and carefully tied black cravats. (American 19th century. *Portrait of a Black Man* © 1993 National Gallery of Art, Washington, DC. Photograph by Richard Carafelli.)

FIGURE 35

Of all the items of men's wear, waistcoats were most likely to provide touches of brightness. Man at left wears an opera cloak over his evening clothes and carries a chapeau bras. Man at right wears a frock coat and carries a top hat. (1834, Italian fashion plate.)

FIGURE 36

Both the pelisse and the dress are made in colors that fashion commentators of the period called "amber," "apricot," or "citron." The white, embroidered pelerine is a typical feature of dresses of the period, and its shape is echoed in the collar of the pelisse. (Courtesy, Cincinnati Art Museum: United States, 1830, day cloak, gift of Chase H. Davis. United States, 1930s, pelerine, gift of the Ohio Mechanics Institute, by exchange. English, 1830–1832, dress, Museum Purchase, gift of Mr. and Mrs. J. G. Schmidlapp, by exchange. Photograph by Richard Carafelli.)

FIGURE 38

While the silhouette of Crinoline period styles was achieved through the use of the hoop, some of the more vivid colors in fabrics and trimmings were often due to the growing use of coal tar dyes, first synthesized in 1856 (United States, 1856–1858). (Courtesy, Cincinnati Art Museum, gift of Mrs. Jesse Whitley.)

FIGURE 37

Paisley patterned fabrics were widely used in the 19th century, and the garments that were made from them ranged from women's paisley shawls to men's dressing gowns, this one from c. 1845. (Harding, Chester. *Portrait of Amos Lawrence*, c. 1845. Given in memory of the Reverend William Lawrence by his children. © 1993 National Gallery of Art, Washington, DC.)

FIGURE 39

Traditional mourning customs of the Victorian era were closely followed. Black fabrics, trimmed in black crape were worn for specified periods, and the amount of black as well as the duration of its wearing varied according to the relationship of the wearer to the deceased (c. 1876). Note the mourning handkerchief embroidered in white with a black-printed design. (Courtesy, The Metropolitan Museum of Art, gift of Theodore Fischer Ells, 1975, 1975.227.4. Photograph by Sheldan Collins.)

FIGURE 40

Art Nouveau designs, such as this one made by the house of Worth in 1898, appeared in many evening gowns of the period between 1890 and 1910. (Courtesy, The Metropolitan Museum of Art, gift of Miss Eva Drexel Dahlgren, 1976, 1976.258.lab. Photograph by Sheldan Collins.)

FIGURE 42

The pleated gowns of Fortuny (1915–1935) were usually made in bright solid colors, while his patterned fabrics were in rich, often dark shades influenced by Renaissance and Oriental designs. (Courtesy, Cincinnati Art Museum, Left: tea dress, gift of Mrs. James Morgan Hutton, evening jacket, gift of Mr. and Mrs. Charles Fleischmann. Right: tea dress, gift in honor of the birthday of Margery B. Behr; evening coat, gift of Patricia Cunningham in memory of Mrs. Alfred Lewis Flesh.)

FIGURE 41

Paul Poiret (1879–1944), designer of exotic and dramatic clothes for women, may have been influenced by the Ballet Russe which appeared in Paris in 1909, when he designed this garment in 1911. (Courtesy, The Metropolitan Museum of Art, purchase, Irene Lewisohn Trust Gift, 1983, 1983.8.)

FIGURE 43

The duster in tan would show the effects of dirt kicked up by open automobiles less than if it were made in a darker or lighter shade (c. 1905). The small boy wears a sailor suit. (Photographed at Fashion Institute of Technology Galleries, "All-American: A Sportswear Tradition.")

FIGURE 44

Men's wear was rarely lightened with color in the 20th century. Dark pin-striped suits in dark blue were worn for business before World War I. For leisure and sports, however, more colorful shirts could be worn. (Illustrated by J. C. Leyendecker, 1912. Courtesy, The Arrow Company. 1988. Cluett, Peabody & Co., Inc.)

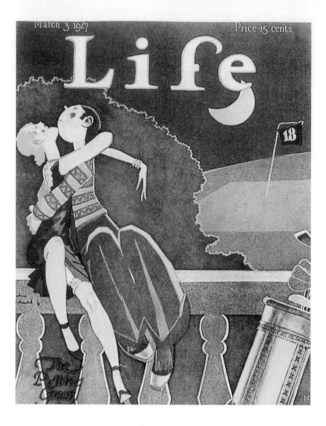

FIGURE 45

The "flapper" and the "sheik" as drawn by John Held Jr. became the personification of "flaming youth" and 1920s styles: he is in his colorful argyle pullover and she with her stockings rolled and her lips and checks roughed. (Courtesy, Jones, Brakeley, & Rockwell, Inc.)

FIGURE 46

Evening dresses in the 1920s were short, and often made from heavily beaded fabrics with elements of Art Deco style in the geometric patterning. (Courtesy, Philadelphia Museum of Art, gift of Mrs. Basil R. Beltran.)

FIGURE 47

Colorful lounging pajamas and beach pajamas were two of several ways in which women were able to wear the trousers that had heretofore been worn exclusively by men (c. 1929). (Courtesy, Belding Hemingway Company, Inc.)

FIGURE 48

Dinner dress and jacket, mid- to late-1930s, is made in bias cut of silk crepe. The metal zipper used to close the jacket was an innovation not previously seen in high fashion. (Courtesy, Texas Fashion Collection, University of North Texas.)

FIGURE 49, 50

Schiaparelli (1890–1973) used many surrealist elements in her couture collections in the 1930s. In this jacket (49) the surrealist embroidered decoration was provided by artist Jean Cocteau. (Courtesy, Philadelphia Museum of Art. Given by Mme. Elsa Schiaparelli.) Schiaparelli was most closely associated with the color called "shocking pink," but others (50) such as the American designer Norman Norell (1900–1972) also used this color for dramatic effect (1941). (Illustration by Eric. Courtesy Vogue. Copyright 1941 [renewed 1969] by the Condé Nast Publications, Inc.)

FIGURE 51

When World War II caused silk supplies to dry up, many women preferred to paint their legs with leg makeup rather than wear ill-fitting rayon stockings. (Courtesy, Elizabeth Arden Inc.)

FIGURE 53

Evening dresses from Christian Dior's 1949 collection show typical New Look silhouette and feature the popular strapless bodice. (Courtesy, The Metropolitan Museum of Art, gift of Mrs. Byron C. Foy, 1953, CI 53.40.5, .7.)

FIGURE 52

Hawaiian shirts made a strong impact on the men's wear market in the late 1940s and the late 1950s. At left: 1940s rayon Kabe crepe, a fabric often used for early Aloha shirts. At right: 1950s cotton broadcloth border print showing Hawaiians working in the fields. (Courtesy, CTAHR Historic Costume Collection, University of Hawaii. Research by Dr. Linda Boynton Arthur; photographer: Bob Chinn.)

FIGURE 54

The vivid colors characteristic of the mid-1960s are seen in this short "cocktail" dress (1965). (Courtesy, The Goldstein: A Museum of Design, University of Minnesota.)

FIGURE 55

Not only dresses, but also underwear utilized bright prints in the late 1960s. (Illustration by Phillip Castle. Courtesy, *Vogue.* Copyright 1968 by The Condé Nast Publications, Inc.)

FIGURE 57

Hippie influences led young people to adopt eclectic styles that often combined both contemporary and used clothing. (Courtesy, David Hurn/Magnum Photos, Inc.)

FIGURE 56

Surrealist, cubist, and op art all influenced fashion in the 1960s. These garments draw on the style of Dutch abstract painter Piet Mondrian.

FIGURE 58

Although the origin of hippie styles was with young counterculture youth in the late 1960s, high fashion designers such as Giorgio di Sant Angelo drew inspiration from these colorful clothes. This type of dress was sometimes called a "hippie-gypsy" design. It was part of his 1971 collection. (Courtesy, The Metropolitan Museum of Art, gift of Martin F. Price, 1988, 1998.493.189.)

FIGURE 59

By the late 1960s, men were able to choose from more colorful items. From left to right: cotton slacks by Catalina Martin, man's slacks by Corbin, trousers by Moyer, and shirt by Oleg Cassini. (*GQ*, Winter 1968–69. Courtesy, *GQ*. Copyright © 1968 [renewed 1996] by the Condé Nast Publications, Inc.)

FIGURE 61

Spiked, pink hair and black leather jacket with metal trim that were characteristics of punk styles of the early 1980s provide a marked contrast with the more conservative men's dress of the period. (Courtesy, Chris Steele-Perkins/Magnum Photos.)

FIGURE 60

Emilio Pucci (1914–1992), Italian designer, was well-known in the 1960s for his unique, colorful printed fabrics. The dress shown here was made from velour in 1966. (Courtesy, Texas Fashion Collection, University of North Texas.)

FIGURE 62

Traditional clothing and textiles from various ethnic groups inspired designers of the 1970s and 1980s. Here, Yves Saint Laurent shows a Peruvian-derived pattern in an evening dress for his fall/winter collection of 1980–1981. (Courtesy, Fairchild Publications.)

FIGURE 63

By the 1980s, traditional pastel colors for the very young had been augmented by vivid, multicolored designs. (*Children's Business*, November 1986. Courtesy, Fairchild Publications.)

FIGURE 64

Clothing for active sports was increasingly worn as casual sportswear in the 1980s. The man at left wears warm-up pants and a cotton T-shirt. Although the clothing worn by the woman at right is casual in style, the white pullover is silk, the pants and long cardigan are cashmere. (Designed by Zoran in 1981–1982. Courtesy, Fairchild Publications.)

FIGURE 65

Wearable art, consisting of original pieces by innovative designers, first became important in the 1965–1975 period and has continued to be a distinctive part of modern fashion. Shown here is Celebration Cape # 1, an original design by Robert Hillestad. (Courtesy, Robert Hillestad; photographer, John Nollendorfs.)

FIGURE 66

Colorful kente cloth patterns, like this printed fabric from Senegal, were being incorporated into the highly original designs by many African-American designers. These dresses were created by Therez Fleetwood for Phe-Zula in 1993. (Courtesy, Therez Fleetwood.)

FIGURE 67

Men continued to have the option of selecting from a wide variety of brightly colored clothing items. Shown here is a colorful ensemble from Christian Dior's Fall 1996 show. (Courtesy of *Daily News Record,* Fairchild Publications.)

FIGURE 69

This 1993 acrylic microfiber shirt and pants ensemble was typical of the use of manufactured fiber microfibers in activewear. (Courtesy of Jack Mulqueen, manufacturer.)

FIGURE 68

By 1994 Japanese designers had left the dark designs with which they first came on the fashion scene and Issey Miyake created the "Flying Saucer Dress" in colorful, pleated, polyester. (Courtesy, The Metropolitan Museum of Art, gift of Issey Miyake, 1994, 1994.603.1.)

FIGURE 70

Knitted cotton dresses, 1996, made from Fox Fibre™ naturally colored cotton. These are the two colors in which this fiber grows. (Photograph courtesy of Ruth Huffman, designer, of Ruth Huffman Designs, Dallas, TX.)

FIGURE 71

The surge of patriotic feeling after the 9/11 attack was evident in both mass and high fashion. (Courtesy, Fairchild Publications.)

FIGURE 73

A reflection of fashion interest in military styles in 2003 and after is seen in an increase of prints that derive from camouflage prints, however they were transformed by using non-traditional colors. (Courtesy, Victoria Shiroma.)

FIGURE 72

Furs took on new colors and textures, especially in the years after 2000, as new techniques for handling fur developed. (Photograph © Jean-Claude Lussier, Fur Council of Canada.)

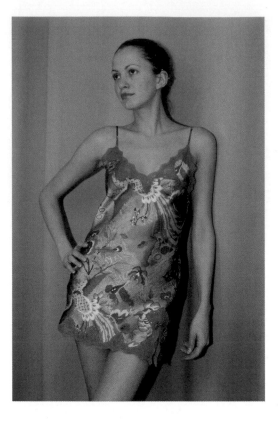

FIGURE 74

By the turn of the millennium underwear was available in vivid colors and patterns. (Samantha Chang design slip. Courtesy, Fairchild Publications.)

FIGURE 76

One way of participating in the fashion for tattooing without getting permanently tattooed was to wear a shirt like this one that simulates tattoos. (Courtesy, Fairchild Publications.)

FIGURE 75

Children wore styles similar to those of adult women. (Courtesy, Wai Ng. www.waing.com).

Daily Life

Douville, R. and J. Casanova. 1968. *Daily Life in Early Canada.* New York: Macmillan.

Earle, P. 1989. *The Making of the English Middle Class: Business, Society, and Family Life in London: 1660–1730.* Berkeley, CA: University of California Press.

———. 1994. *A City Full of People: Men and Women of London 1650–1750.* London: Methuen.

Fairchilds, C. 1984. *Domestic Enemies: Servants and Their Masters in Old Regime France.* Baltimore: Johns Hopkins University Press.

Jarett, J. 1986. *England in the Age of Hogarth.* New Haven, CT: Yale University Press.

Levron, J. 1968. *Daily Life at Versailles in the 17th and 18th Centuries.* New York: Macmillan.

Marshall, D. 1980. *English People in the 18th Century.* Westport, CT: Greenwood Press.

Memoirs of Madame de la Tour du Pin, trans. by F. Harcourt. 1971. New York: McCall.

Taylor, D. 2002. *Everyday Life in Colonial America.* Cincinnati, OH: F & W Publications.

A Woman's Life at the Court of the Sun King. Letters of Liselotte von der Pfalz. 1984. Baltimore, MD: Johns Hopkins University Press.

PART FIVE

THE NINETEENTH CENTURY

1800—1900

HISTORICAL BACKGROUND

Political events in Europe and the United States provided an almost kaleidoscopic backdrop against which the fashions of the 19th century should be viewed.

France

In France the Revolution of 1789 and the Republic shortly gave way to the First Empire, founded by Napoleon Bonaparte. He re-established a court and made Paris the center of power and fashion. After his overthrow, the Bourbon monarchy was restored under Louis XVIII in 1814. For the remainder of the century France experienced a variety of governments: kings (Charles X, 1824–30, and Louis Philippe, 1830–48); another Republic, the Second, with Louis Bonaparte as President, who then became Napoleon III. After 1870, France had the Third Republic, lasting through the remainder of the 19th century.

England

In Great Britain, the unlucky King George III was periodically deranged as the result of an inherited disease called porphyria. As a result, his ministers and his son, the Prince Regent, had to govern for him. The Prince gathered around him a fashionable circle of men and women who set the styles for the upper classes. On the death of his father in 1820, the Prince became George IV. His scandalous personal life helped make him an unpopular king. After his death in 1830, William IV succeeded him, and he in turn was followed by a niece, Victoria, who came to the throne in 1837 at the age of 18 and ruled Great Britain and the Empire until her death in 1901. Through her personality she helped to restore the popularity of the monarchy. So strong was her influence that her name has often been used to describe the greater part of the 19th century—"the Victorian Age."

Italy and Austria

In the mid-19th century, the forces of nationalism altered the map of Europe. For centuries Italy had been a geographical expression, a land controlled by stronger powers. Under Napoleon Italy was treated as a vassal state but enjoyed many beneficial reforms, only to have them disappear after Napoleon's fall when Austria became dominant. This experience impelled some Italians to think about establishing an independent Italy, freed of reactionary forces. Revolutionary movements to establish a republic failed. However, in an alliance with Napoleon III of France, Piedmont, the only genuinely independent Italian state, defeated Austria, and established an independent Italy in the north in 1859. A military expedition under Giuseppe Garibaldi conquered southern Italy. By 1861, the unification of Italy was completed except for Venice and Rome, and Victor Emmanuel became the first king of Italy.

In central Europe, Austria dominated the German states, until defeated by Prussia in 1866 in a short war. In 1870, after defeating France, Prussia united the German states in the German Empire.

The United States

The 19th century in the United States was the era of westward expansion as new territories were added. In 1800 the United States were composed of sixteen states, all east of the Mississippi River. After a bloody Civil War (1860–1865) over slavery, a united country of forty-five states stretched from the Atlantic Ocean to the Pacific Ocean. At the same time, the expanding nation, which offered so many opportunities for a new life, attracted millions of immigrants who came primarily from Europe.

IMMIGRATION DURING THE 19TH CENTURY

In one of the greatest folk movements in history, thirty-three million immigrants came to the United States between 1865 and 1930, bringing a unique cultural heritage and making possible the great westward expansion. After the Civil War the largest number of immigrants came from northern and western Europe. By the 1870s immigrants were coming from the Austro-Hungarian Empire (Poles, Bohemians, Hungarians), Italy, and Russia. Immigrants from northern Europe tended to settle in the Middle West, taking up the farmlands on the Great Plains. Most of the Irish immigrants settled in cities, particularly in the East. Later immigrants from southern and eastern Europe—Russians, Jews, Poles, and Italians—were too poor to buy farms and the necessary machinery; consequently they settled in the towns and cities of the East. Many became unskilled laborers, working in mines, mills, and factories.

Most of these immigrants gave up their loyalties to their native land and took on the customs and ways of their new homeland, including language. The political system promoted naturalization and voting. One of the greatest agents in assimilating the newcomers to American life was the public school, which was free. Soon the immigrants were making a major contribution to American life. Among them were Alexander Graham Bell, inventor of the telephone; Andrew Carnegie, financier; and Joseph Pulitzer, newspaper publisher.

CLOTHING OF ETHNIC MINORITIES IN THE UNITED STATES

As has been noted previously, the history of costume is in general a history of fashionable dress. Little attention has been paid to the dress of those either unwilling or unable to wear current fashions. Voluntary immigration, described earlier, brought populations that did attempt to preserve some of the clothing unique to their cultures, but for the most part these people freely chose to adopt currently fashionable dress.

The European colonization of the Americas brought several other groups into contact with Western fashions: Native Americans living in the Western Hemisphere; Native Hawaiians living on the islands of Hawaii; and African slaves, brought to America against their will.

While it is true that European nations also colonized other parts of the world and that Western dress was adopted to some extent by some of the people native to the regions that were colonized, Western dress never became the dominant style in Asian, African, or Indian colonies. In North America, Western dress became the norm as the Europeans gained dominance over the indigenous peoples.

NATIVE AMERICANS

Native Americans had their own form of dress, made with local materials and adapted to regional conditions. When the Europeans arrived, the Native Americans acquired new textiles, garments, and decorative materials such as beads and ribbons and incorporated these into their dress. (This is an example of the process of cultural authentication discussed on *page 5*.) At the same time, European settlers found some of the clothing worn by indigenous people to be practical for the climate and geography of the new world and they, in turn, adapted elements of Native American dress for their own use.

THE HAWAIIANS

Although the indigenous inhabitants of the Hawaiian Islands had been in contact with Western traders and familiar with Western textiles since 1778, the arrival of American Congregationalist missionaries in 1820 had a long-lasting effect on clothing worn by the islanders. Missionary women were shocked by the dress of Hawaiian women, which covered only the lower half of the body. At the same time, royal Hawaiian women were fascinated by the dress of the missionaries, which was that of the Empire period.

When the Queen Dowager Kalakua asked for a dress like that of the missionaries, the missionary women made her a dress, but because the queen was exceptionally large, they modified the style somewhat. The final result was a full-length dress with a loose fit that fell from a yoke, had a high neck, and long sleeves. (See *Figure 11.9*.) This garment, called a **holoku,** became a traditional part of Hawaiian dress. Two variations, one loose and one more fitted, are worn to this day by persons of Hawaiian descent. In 1820, the missionaries also gave Hawaiian women chemises to wear under the holoku, but the women, who called this garment **mu'umu'u** (meaning cut off), wore them for swimming and sleeping (Arthur 1996). (See chemises on *Illustrated Table 13.1, page 310,* for an example of the cut of a chemise.)

By the mid-19th century, the holoku was worn by most Hawaiian women. The nobility wore western dress for formal occasions and the holoku as leisure wear. When the mu'umu'u was made in Hawaiian print fabrics in the 1930s, it became acceptable for street wear. In the 20th century, the holoku became a formal gown (Arthur 1996).

AFRICAN-AMERICAN SLAVES

African slaves, on the other hand, had little autonomy when it came to clothing. Until recently relatively little attention has been paid to the clothing worn by slaves. Some researchers have now turned their attention to the question of how slaves were dressed, and gradually more is being learned. These researchers indicate that there were regional differences in clothing for slaves, but at the same time some broad generalizations can be made.

Owners provided clothing for slaves. Those slaves who worked in the houses of their owners were dressed so as to make a decent appearance to those whom they served. As Warner and Parker (1990) noted, "Field hands wore minimal clothing, but house servants wore livery or hand-me-downs. It is interesting to realize that those slaves who did their work in the Big House, close to their white owners, were well-dressed so that the owners would not be constantly reminded of the inhuman conditions of the field laborer."

What clothing the field hands had was made of coarse, harsh cloth. Although African slaves were forcibly deprived of the right to wear the dress of their native lands, it is thought that they may have preserved some elements of hair styles and headgear (Simkins 1990).

From the arrival of the first African slaves on the North American continent in 1619 until the emancipation of the slaves during the Civil War, the dress of slaves was imposed on them by others. The slave owner even determined the differences in dress between the "house slaves" and the "field slaves." Warner and Parker (1990) observe, "Clothing has the power to establish commonalties and draw wearers together even as it has the power to separate. The obvious differences in clothing among the slaves themselves must have also heightened the awareness within the slave community of the differences between the 'haves' and the 'have nots,' at least in some measure serving to keep the slaves separated from each other. Throughout the history of slavery in the United States, owners feared the possibility of united rebellion from their slaves. Clothing then would act as a constant visual separator of black from white, even black from black."

Warner (1992) notes that some house slaves who were the valued seamstresses on plantations fashioned their own clothes—or were able to buy them from the towns nearby. Others got them as gifts from freed family members.

Slaves who had been freed or who managed to escape to the North after slavery had been abolished there (in 1803) adopted fashionable dress. After emancipation their clothing was like that of any other Americans of the same economic level, except that many women in the rural south chose to continue wearing head cloths. It was not until the Civil Rights movement of the 1960s that African-Americans made a conscious effort to return to the wearing of styles that originated on the continent from which they were so brutally and forcibly expatriated.

INDUSTRIALIZATION

The Industrial Revolution, which had begun in the preceding century, accelerated during the 19th century. The Industrial Revolution brought a fundamental change to industry, resulting in increased production of goods at lower prices, and ultimately a higher standard of living. But in the process it reshaped the pattern of life of men and women. The transition from an economy that had been primarily agricultural with household industries to an economy dominated by great factories was harsh and often cruel.

The Industrial Revolution produced the factory system, which involved the migration of people from rural areas to towns and cities that were unprepared to receive them. At the same time, industrial changes produced squalor and misery for many workers who were required to work long hours under unsafe conditions for low pay. Because of the factory system, workers gravitated to towns in which crowding and poor housing conditions gave rise to large slum areas. The crowding, poor sanitation, overwork, and poor nutrition contributed to the spread of disease.

The laborers in factories who were most abused were the women, children, and the unskilled. Even those who worked at home were subjected to exploitation. An anonymous author described a swindle perpetrated on sewing girls in New York in the 1850s. One of these girls was given pantaloons to sew, but only after depositing a security payment. When the garments were finished, she brought them back, expecting to be paid. The man behind the counter examined the bundle, and declared that she had ruined them, and refused to pay her. When the frightened girl asked for the return of her deposit, she was told that she had ruined seven or eight dollars worth of merchandise, and was not entitled to the return of the deposit. The "ruined" garments were subsequently pressed, sorted, and packed up for sale (Tryon 1952).

For the industrial capitalists, however, industrialization brought wealth and luxury. The early Victorian period in England also saw the middle class achieve greater numbers and a more important place in society.

CROSS-CULTURAL INFLUENCES ON FASHION

Textiles from India

In the 18th century much of the influence of Oriental styles on Western dress had been seen in textile materials. Many of the handsome brocades and printed cottons used for garments had beautiful designs copied from or derived from Chinese, Japanese, and Indian textiles. This continued to be true in the 19th century.

The importation of fine linen muslins from India, first seen in the soft chemise dresses of the late 18th century, continued. White muslin, sometimes printed or embroidered, was used extensively in the first two decades of the 1800s. Imported fabrics of this sort were very costly, and soon European manufacturers were producing cheaper imitations.

The production of these fabrics seems to have operated as follows. First came the importation of foreign textiles or costume items. As novelties they were costly and exclusive. Once demand was established, European textile manufacturers began to produce these items in large quantities. Generally the European imitations were of lower quality and sold for cheaper prices. The Kashmir shawl is a particularly good illustration of this practice.

Indian men wore Kashmir shawls (spelled cashmere in the anglicized form). Made from the soft hair of the cashmere goat, they were woven in Kashmir, a northern province on the Indian subcontinent. Beginning in the late 1600s, these shawls had incorporated a decorative motif thought to derive from the *boteh*, a stylized representation of the growing shoot of the date palm. Shrimpton (1992) notes that the first appearance of this shawl in Europe is not certain, but that some scholars relate it to the arrival in London in 1765 of a young English woman who had been in Bombay, India.

The rapid growth of interest in the style, in spite of its enormously high cost, led European manufacturers to begin imitating the design of these shawls, not in cashmere but in less costly (and harsher-feeling) wools and in silk. The traditional designs also underwent changes.

The Scottish town of Paisley began producing large quantities of shawls, many of which utilized stylized versions of the traditional palm design that had, by now, taken on more of the shape of a pine cone. So closely was the motif associated with the textile mills of Paisley that the design came to be known as a "paisley" design, and the shawls themselves were often called "paisley shawls" even if they were not manufactured in the Paisley mills.

The fashion for Kashmir or paisley shawls continued for almost 100 years. The most fashionable shapes, decorations, and preferences for colors changed from time to time, but the basic style had a long life during the 19th century. The so-called paisley pattern has become a classic style, and its Indian origins are rarely recognized today.[1]

[1] For a detailed historical study of these shawls see V. Reilly, *The Paisley Pattern*. Salt Lake City, UT: Peregrine Smith Books, 1987.

Resumption of Trade with Japan

By the 19th century Russia, Britain, and the United States were all interested in seeking reentry into Japan to trade. Americans were particularly interested in establishing relations with Japan because American clipper ships engaged in the China trade passed close to Japan on the great circle route, as did whaling ships. Unable to take on provisions or fuel for newly developed steamships, the Americans saw the isolation of Japan as a threat to their economic interests.

The American government decided to force the Japanese to end their policy of seclusion. In July of 1853 an American naval force, under the command of Commodore Matthew Perry, dropped anchor in what is now Tokyo Bay. Perry brought a letter from President Millard Fillmore requesting that Japanese ports be opened for trade, that ships be permitted to take on water and supplies, and that shipwrecked sailors be properly cared for. Perry informed the Japanese officials that if these terms were not met, he would return later with a larger naval force.

The Japanese government had been shocked at the size and power of the American naval force, and when Perry returned they accepted the American demands. Two ports were opened to American ships. Later the Japanese signed similar treaties with the British, Russian, and Dutch governments. Subsequently additional ports were opened. Soon foreign merchants set up business concerns in Japanese port cities.

One of the first Japanese industries to profit from the opening of trade was the silk industry. A silk blight in Europe in 1860 created a demand for Japanese silk and silk eggs. In the 1870s the Japanese enterprises developed methods of reeling silk by mechanical power. They produced more uniform and superior silk thread than other Asian competitors. As a result, Japan soon had the major portion of the silk market in Europe and the United States. Cotton also became a valuable export. Because Japan was the first non-Western nation to adopt Western industrial techniques on a large scale, by the end of the 19th century textiles dominated Japanese exports.

Once Japan opened its ports, collectors obtained examples of Japanese prints, lacquer, porcelain, glass, and textiles. Impressionist painters were inspired by Japanese woodblock prints. In 1862, the British Minister in Japan showed his personal collection of lacquer, bronze, and porcelain at the International Exhibition in London. A. L. Liberty opened a shop in London in 1875 specializing in Japanese goods that included carpets, embroideries, porcelain, dress fabrics, and a wide variety of decorative objects.

Japanese art had an immediate and major impact on European fine and decorative arts in the second half of the 19th century. Aslin (1969), writing about Japanese influences on English styles, noted, "Directly or indirectly Japan was the strongest external design influence in England from the mid-sixties until the end of the century."

Japanese, and other Asian, influences on costume in the 19th century were most often to be seen in the textiles utilized or in decorative accessories such as fans. It was not until the early 20th century that Asian garments can be seen to exert major influences on the cut and styling of women's garments in the West.

MORALITY AND VALUES IN THE 19TH CENTURY

The reign of the Prince Regent, later King George IV, in the first three decades of the century was "memorable for the dissolute habits" of the monarch. "Regency life was characterized by expensive flamboyance of costume and endless sessions with one's tailor, barber, and valet preparatory to attending glittering salons, gambling halls, prize fights, modish brothels, and, in extreme cases, early morning duels" (Altick 1973).

The Victorian period is often contrasted with the Regency period. Historians have long taken the view that the remainder of the century was marked by a code of conduct that was determined by "rigid notions about the right ordering of society and individual behavior" (Reader 1964). Because these standards were set by the increasingly influential middle classes, the term "middle-class morality" is often applied to a code of behavior which stressed obedience, male authority, religious piety, thrift, hard work, and sexual morality.

Until recently, when revisionist historians such as Peter Gay and Valerie Steele have questioned this view, Victorian women have been seen as sexually repressed and Victorian men hypocritical. The accepted view has held that any references that might have an even vaguely sexual connotation were improper. That classics such as Shakespeare's plays were published with "off color" sections removed is cited as evidence of Victorian prudery. The following incident is often used to demonstrate that Americans of the Victorian era were even more proper than their British counterparts. British Captain Marryat recalled an incident during a visit to upper New York State in the 1840s. While walking with a lady over some rough terrain, the lady slipped and obviously hurt her leg. When he inquired as to whether she had injured her "leg," she was visibly offended and upset. When he asked what he should have said, "her reply was, that the word "limb" was used; "Nay," continued she, "I am not so particular as some people are, for I know those who always say limb of a table or of a pianoforte" (Nevins 1969).

The charge of hypocrisy arises from the sharp contrast of middle class moralizing with reality. Prostitution was common. Working class women were often driven to the streets by poverty. Their patrons were from all classes of society.

Many scholars have held that respectable women were expected to marry and to bear children as a "duty." Sexual pleasure, especially for women, was held to be sinful. Recent scholarship, however, has tempered this view of Victorian sexual attitudes. Utilizing evidence ranging from personal diaries and letters to Victorian medical surveys, historian Peter Gay (1984) suggests that the public image and private practices of Victorian women were at odds, and that many women had happy and fulfilling sex lives. Valerie Steele (1985) writes of the erotic nature of much of Victorian costume and the willingness of middle- and upper-class women to wear obviously seductive clothing. The notion of complete Victorian conformity to a strict and monolithic set of values is undoubtedly an oversimplification. The reality is obviously more complex, with significant differences between public and private lives.

DRESS REFORM FOR WOMEN

The role of respectable women for most of the 19th century was limited by tradition to that of wife and mother. Even so, at the mid-century feminists had begun to agitate for more rights. Being denied the right to vote was a symbol of oppression of women in the eyes of the suffragists. Another symbol of the oppression of women to some feminists was fashion, particularly those fashions that tended to confine and hamper women.

Several efforts at dress reform were mounted. The first of these was attempted by the suffragists between 1851 and 1854. The costume they saw as preferable to fashionable dress was called the "Bloomer costume" after Amelia Bloomer, one of the women who wore this full skirted, short dress that was placed over full trousers. Other feminists such as Susan B. Anthony, Lucy Stone, and Elizabeth Cady Stanton also adopted the style. The Bloomer costume, however, gained few adherents and provoked a good deal of ridicule, and was given up as an alternative to fashionable dress.

Garments similar to the Bloomer costume were retained in styles for athletic activities for women. They were evident in clothing for physical education, which was added to the curriculum at Vassar in 1865, and in bathing dress (Cunningham 1993).

Although feminists abandoned the Bloomer dress, they did not abandon their belief in the need for dress reform. Throughout the remainder of the 19th century they continued to publish calls for less encumbering clothing for women.

Other attempts at dress reform marked the second half of the century. Emphasis on reform of underwear styles focused on the dangers of tight corseting, the ill effects of the weight of too much heavy underwear, and promoted the supposed health benefits of wearing wool next to the body.

Beginning with the Pre-Raphaelite artists in the 1860s, continuing into Aesthetic Dress of the 1870s and 1880s, and the "rational-artistic dress" of the Arts and Crafts movement near the turn of the century, reformers based their concepts of appropriate dress on this artistic ideal. They also saw aesthetic or artistic dress, with its looser fit, diminished draperies, and less restrictive corseting, as more healthful than fashionable dress (Cunningham 1993).

CHANGES IN CLOTHING FOR MEN

Although they had different characteristics, the clothing styles of men and women shown in the preceding chapters have been equally grand. With the coming of the French Revolution (see *pages 262–263*) and with changes in occupations for men that stemmed from the Industrial Revolution, this changed.

With the elimination of ornamentation, the essence of fine clothing for men was in the cut and tailoring. Variety of choices decreased and decoration diminished. It would be a mistake, however, to assume that fashion change had disappeared from men's clothes. Although men's clothing style changes became less obvious, styles did continue to evolve. By contrast, however, the more dramatic and flamboyant style changes in women's clothing move women's dress to the forefront of any consideration of fashionable dress. For this reason, in all of the remaining chapters of this book, women's clothing is discussed before that of men

THE END OF AN AGE

Queen Victoria died in 1901. The Victorian Era had actually ended before her death, if one defines that era by the attitudes discussed heretofore. By the end of the 19th century the sense of an absolute code of correct behavior, the self-confidence and self-righteousness that had characterized Victorian attitudes, had passed. The era that followed, shortened though it was by the First World War, "... was electric with an exultant and slightly self-conscious sense of liberation—liberation, that is, from the stuffiness, the obscurantism, the false verities, the repressions and taboos now attributed, fairly or not, to the Victorian mind" (Altick 1973).

NOTES

Altick, R. D. 1973. *Victorian People and Ideas.* New York: W. W. Norton, pp. 9, 301.

Arthur, L. 1996 *Design Evolution of the Hawaiian Holoku.* Video Script. University of Hawaii at Manoa.

Aslin, E. 1969. *The Aesthetic Movement.* New York: Frederick A. Praeger, p. 96.

Cunningham, P. 1993. "Healthy and Artistic Alternatives to the Fashionable Ideal." *With Grace and Favor.* Cincinnati, OH: Cincinnati Art Museum, Spring.

Gay, P. 1984. *The Bourgeois Experience, Victoria to Freud,* Vol. 1: *Education of the Senses.* New York: Oxford University Press.

Nevins, A. 1969. *American Social History as Reported by British Travelers.* New York: Augustus M. Kelley, pp. 245–246.

Reader, W. J. 1964. *Life in Victorian England.* New York: G. P. Putnam's Sons, p. 6.

Shrimpton, J. 1992. "Dressing for a Tropical Climate: The Role of Native Fabrics in Fashionable Dress in Early Colonial India." *Textile History,* Vol. 23, No. 1, p. 67.

Simkins, A. 1990. "Function and Symbol in Hair and Headgear Among African American Women" in Starke, et al., *African American Dress and Adornment.* Dubuque, IA: Kendall/Hunt, pp. 166 ff.

Steele, V. 1985. *Fashion and Eroticism. Ideals of Feminine Beauty from the Victorian Era to the Jazz Age.* New York: Oxford University Press.

Tryon, W. S. 1952. *A Mirror for Americans: Life and Manners in the United States 1790–1870. Glimpse of New York City.* Vol. 1: *Life in the East.* Chicago: University of Chicago Press, pp. 222 ff.

Warner, P. C. 1992. "Had on When He Ran Off. . . . Slave Clothing and Textiles in North Carolina, 1775–1835." Paper presented at the meeting of the Costume Society of America, San Antonio, Texas, May. c.f. H. A. Jacobs. *Incidents in the Life of a Slave Girl.* Cambridge, MA: Harvard University Press, 1987.

Warner, P. C. and D. Parker. 1990. "Slave Clothing and Textiles in North Carolina, 1775–1835." in Starke, et al., *African American Dress and Adornment.* Dubuque, IA: Kendall/Hunt, p. 90.

CHRONOLOGY

1789

Convening of the Estates General in France

Storming of the Bastille

Declaration of the Rights of Man

1792

Abolition of the French monarchy

1793

Eli Whitney invents the cotton gin

1793–1794

"Reign of Terror" in France

1795

French "Directoire," executive council of five men, is established

1799

Napoleon stages a "coup d'etat" and becomes First Consul

1803

Louisiana Purchase, acquisition of approximately 828,000 square miles
of territory from France, by the United States

1804

Napoleon crowned Emperor of France

Slavery abolished in the states north of the Mason-Dixon Line

1810

Prince of Wales named Regent to act for his father, the ailing George III

1811–1820

Regency period in England

1812

War between the United States and Britain

1813

Publication of Jane Austen's *Pride and Prejudice*

1814

Napoleon abdicates and goes into exile

Louis XVIII, grandson of Louis XV, becomes king of France

1815

Napoleon escapes from exile, returns to Paris, takes command of the army,
and is defeated by the English Duke of Wellington and the Prussians
under Marshal Blucher at Waterloo

CHAPTER ELEVEN

THE DIRECTOIRE PERIOD AND THE EMPIRE PERIOD

1790 – 1820

A.

B.

D.

C.

E.

F.

A.

Empire period chair

B.

Duncan Phyfe chair

C.

Painting by Pierre Paul Prud'hon,
Between Love and Riches, c. 1804

D.

Empire period table

E.

Empire period interior

F.

Decorative relief

Figures A, E, F from Lavisse, E. 1907. *Album Historique Le XVIII Le XIX Siècle.* Paris: Librairie Armand Colin, pp. 161, 178. Figures B, D courtesy of J. Curcio in Federico, J. T. 1988. *Clues to American Furniture.* Washington: Starrhill, pp. 40, 39. Figure C courtesy of the Art Institute of Chicago, Mr. and Mrs. Martin A. Ryerson Collection (1933.1090).

The Directoire and the Empire periods encompass the years from 1790, just after the beginning of the French Revolution, until 1820. The dates assigned to the Directoire (c. 1790–1800) include major events of the French Revolution and the establishment of the Directory, a government by a five-man executive. The Empire period coincides generally with the period during which Napoleon Bonaparte was the head of state in France. Indeed, the name of the period is derived from the title of his era, the Napoleonic Empire.

HISTORICAL BACKGROUND

France: The Revolution and the Directory

Social, political, and economic grievances, high unemployment and high prices, along with a bankrupt government combined to produce conditions ripe for revolution in France in 1789. Peasants, who bore the heaviest load of unjust taxation, did not lead the revolution. That role belonged to the urban bourgeoisie who resented the nobility's privileges and monopoly of high offices in government, church, and the armed forces.

Unable to solve the national financial crisis, Louis XVI summoned the Estates General, a representative assembly of French citizens, to meet in 1789. This body had not met in more than a century and a half. Upon the convening of the Estates General for May 5, 1789, the Grand Master of Ceremonies sent instructions to participants as to the costume to be worn for the meeting. Each Estate was assigned a specific mode of dress. The clergy, the First Estate, were to wear the various forms of dress that were traditional for their ecclesiastical ranks. The Second Estate, the aristocrats, wore black silk coats and waistcoats trimmed with gold braid, black silk breeches, white stockings, lace cravats, hats with feathers of the Order of St. Esprit (a special order open only to the nobility), and black silk cloaks. The aristocrats of the Second Estate carried swords. The Third Estate (the largest group of deputies comprised of individuals ranging from upper middle class to peasants) were instructed to dress simply, in suits of black cloth (not silk), short black silk capes, black stockings, plain muslin cravats, and black three-cornered hats. They were not permitted to wear swords, as this right was limited to "gentlemen." Members of the Third Estate objected to these dress regulations, many refusing to comply, and when the Estates convened on October 15, the regulations were abolished (Ribero 1988).

Soon after its opening session the Estates General proclaimed itself a National Assembly and began to reform France by abolishing feudalism, adopting the Declaration of the Rights of Man, and by drafting the first written constitution in French history. War broke out in 1792 and began to go badly for France. Parisian rioters, frightened by the defeats on the battlefield, overthrew the monarchy and established the first French republic. The king was tried and executed in 1793. Doctrinaire radicals, the Jacobins, resorted to a "Reign of Terror," 1793–1794, in an effort to save the nation from defeat. Although they saved France, the Jacobins were overthrown in 1794 and a new government established: the Directoire (*dye-rec-twar'*), an executive of five men. The Directoire (in English, Directory) ruled France for the next five years.

During the Revolution the silhouette of fashions for women did not change radically from those of the pre-Revolutionary period. Styles had already simplified somewhat, and English-influenced styles were popular. Neckcloths, similar to those worn by peasants and working class women, became popular. Citizens were expected to declare their revolutionary ardor by displaying the revolutionary colors—red, white, and blue—so these colors were fashionable and appeared often in dresses. Red, white, and blue flowers or ribbons were seen on costumes or hats. Beginning with September 21, 1793, wearing a tricolor ribbon cockade was mandatory.

For a time men's costumes took on a number of symbolic meanings. The most obvious and most visible symbols of the Revolution were the **bonnet rouge** (*buhn-ay' ruhze*)(the red cap of liberty) and the costume of the **sans culottes** (*sahn koo-lot'*). Ribero (1988) notes, "It is easier to define what the sans culottes wore than what they were, the vocal element of the working classes with, from the summer of 1792, hitherto unheard-of access to power at the highest levels."

Culotte was the French word for knee breeches. For many generations, men of the laboring classes had worn trousers, while the nobility and the more affluent wore knee breeches. This group of working class men, who supported the Revolution, wore trousers—hence the name "sans culottes," meaning "without knee breeches." Other elements of sans culotte dress included the **carmagnole** (*kar-man-yole'*), a short woolen or cloth jacket of a dark color. It was hip length with fullness at the back, cut rather like a smock. Trousers were made of the same material, or of red, white, and blue striped drill. A red waistcoat was worn, and wooden shoes called clogs or sabots. A soft woolen peasant's cap of red color (the bonnet rouge) was worn with this costume. (See *Color Plate* 32.)

The bonnet rouge became synonymous with the Revolution. Its origins have been debated. Ribero, in a footnote to her excellent and detailed study of Fashion in the French Revolution, cites a French source of 1796 that says the cap has Roman origins. The sans culottes apparently believed the cap to have been worn in Greece and Rome as a "symbol of freedom and a rallying cry for all those who hated despotism." Ribero continues, "In the Middle Ages a similarly shaped cap was worn to celebrate the end of apprenticeship, and by the sixteenth century there are a few references to it as a general item of working-class/peasant dress in France." Whatever its origins, the cap became a widely used symbol. Jacobin speakers donned the bonnet rouge at their political meetings.

Fashionable men gave up knee-breeches for long, tight-fitting, ankle-length trousers called pantaloons. These garments bore little resemblance to the baggy, loose-fitting trousers of the sans culottes.

When the Terror ended and the Directoire was established, the passions aroused during the Revolution began to cool. At this point in France, the silhouette of women's dresses changed radically. A new style, elements of which are thought to have appeared first in England, became fashionable. Based on Ancient Greek forms and cut with little or no sleeve, a low, round neckline, and a high waist, the dress fell straight to the floor. Soft clinging fabrics such as muslin or linen were employed. Many were sheer and under these dresses some women wore little underwear aside from the chemise and no corseting. Others who were quite bold wore pink tights to give the illusion of flesh.

Steele (1988) sees the antecedents of this style in the muslin chemise dresses worn by aristocratic women before the French Revolution, in the neoclassical revivals in the decorative and fine arts, and in the interest in the philosophy and politics of the ancient Greeks and Romans. Men's dress was similar in its basic aspects to that from before the Revolution: a fitted coat, a waistcoat, and knee breeches. Extremists in fashion were assigned nicknames. The **merveilleuse** (*mere-vay-use'*) (the marvelous ones) were women who affected the most extreme of the Directoire styles, with long flowing trains, the sheerest of fabrics, necklines cut in some extreme cases to the waistline, and huge, exaggerated jockeylike caps. The men, known as **incroyables** (*ahn-kroy-ab-luh'*) or "incredibles" wore waistcoats of loose fit at the shoulders, excessively tight breeches, and cravats or neckties and collars that covered so much of their chins that one wonders if they could be heard or understood when they spoke. Both the men and women affected a shaggy, unkempt hairdress. (See *Figure 11.1.*)

FIGURE 11.1

Styles of the early Empire period. Women's dresses are cut low, from fabrics that cling and reveal the body. Their hairstyles show strong Greek and Roman influences. The man on the left wears an exaggeratedly high collar and cravat; his coat cut full and somewhat loose over the shoulder. Such styles were associated with fashion extremists, the *incroyables* and *merveilleuse* of about 1800. (Photograph courtesy, The Metropolitan Museum of Art, Harris Brisbane Dick Fund, 1938.)

France: The Empire

The French Revolution had opened careers to young men of talent. A young Corsican, Napoleon Bonaparte, a second lieutenant in artillery in 1789 and a brigadier general by 1795, saved the Directoire from a mob with a "whiff of grapeshot." Promoted to major general, his victories over the Austrians in Italy (1796–1797) and his victories in Egypt against the British and the Turks (1798–1799) made him the hero of Paris.

The Directoire governed ineffectively; the war again went badly. Because they feared another Terror, conspirators joined with Napoleon in staging a coup in 1799, overthrowing the Directoire. An executive group consisting of Napoleon and two other consuls replaced it, but Napoleon as First Consul had dictatorial power. By 1804, after consolidating his power, he was crowned "Emperor of the French." In the next 10 years, Napoleon instituted legal and educational reforms, reorganized the government, making it more efficient, competent, and honest. Napoleon extended his hegemony over all of Europe, defeating all but Great Britain. In 1812, finding it necessary to attack Russia, his armies marched to Moscow but the Tsar refused to surrender. With winter coming Napoleon had to retreat. Harassed by Russians, the retreat became a rout. It was the beginning of the end for Napoleon. In 1814 he abdicated and went to the Island of Elba.

After the establishment of the Empire, the basic style lines that had been worn by both men and women during the Directoire continued, but the extremes of nudity and the styles of the merveilleuse and incroyable disappeared. In part this may have been because Napoleon was somewhat conservative in his attitudes, and considered the more extreme styles as immoral. The newly established court also provided a stage for the display of fashions, and more elaborate fabrics and styles began to appear as the Emperor attempted to recreate the elegance of the old regime.

Napoleon tried to encourage French industry by stimulating the demand for French goods, and he restricted the importation of fabrics from abroad, particularly muslin and printed cottons from India. Shawls were a popular fashion item imported from India. Napoleon ended their importation and ordered that they be copied in France. His first wife, Josephine, however, continued to have her own shawls imported without his knowledge. She must have helped to stimulate French industry almost single-handedly, as an inventory of her wardrobe in 1809 included 666 winter dresses, 230 summer dresses, and 60 cashmere shawls.

Napoleon himself had an extensive wardrobe. See *Contemporary Comments 11.1*, his letter instructing one of his staff about the items he wished to have ordered.

England

In England, King George III reigned throughout this period. A pious, virtuous man, who enjoyed the simple life, he wrote articles on farming under the byline, "Farmer George." This unlucky gentleman, who had to preside over the loss of the American colonies in 1776, suffered from a hereditary disease, porphyria, which periodically incapacitated him. By 1810 his condition had become permanent; he could no longer rule. The Prince of Wales had to be named as Regent to act for his father. During the Regency Period (1811–1820), the English court and fashionable society were organized around the Prince Regent, who had an eye for the ladies and for whom the pursuit of pleasure was possibly his most active pastime. His cleverness and gracious manners gave him the title, "the first gentleman of Europe." As a result, the court became the center of fashion in England.

For the greater part of the period the English remained at war with France, resolved to block Napoleon's ambition to become supreme in Europe. The defeat of the French fleet at Trafalgar in 1805 ended any danger of French invasion of the British Isles. Final peace came only with the defeat of Napoleon at Waterloo in 1815.

For a time, at the beginning of the Empire period, English and French women's dress styles diverged. While the French were narrowing the silhouette as it fell from the elevated Empire waist, the English placed a padded roll under the waistline to create a fuller, rounded line to the skirt. It is thought that these differences developed because England and France were at war, and trade and dissemination of ideas were restricted. After about a year or two, the English line narrowed and became like that of the French. (See *Figure 11.2*.)

The United States

The continuing expansion of the American frontier brought Native American and European populations into frequent contact. As noted previously, many Native Americans added goods gained in trade to their apparel items, and the European settlers also adapted some items of Native American dress, a further example of the process of cultural authentication. (See *page 5*.)

Some of these interchanges produced garments that have persisted in use for long periods of time. For example, the Europeans traded blankets bordered with colored bands (so-called "Indian blankets"). Native Americans in Canada appear to have cut these blankets into coats, placing the colored borders at the bottom of the coat. Rural settlers and the Canadian military adopted these coats, cutting them along the lines of fashionable dress of this and subsequent periods. Over time not only in Canada but also in the United States these warm, hooded coats were adopted for outdoor sports. Their descendants can still be found today (Beaudoin-Ross 1980).

The footwear of Native Americans, moccasins, was also adopted by settlers. Canadian settlers in French-speaking Canada found the soft deer and moose skins used by native people for these shoes too fragile for daily use and wear. In-during the Empire period. This interest accelerated as a result of the military campaigns of Napoleon in Italy, where Roman ruins abounded, and because of the political emphasis on the revival of the republican ideals of ancient Greece and Rome. Many French painters depicted events in ancient history on huge canvasses. Architecture emphasized classic styles. When Napoleon took his armies to Egypt, his staff included artists who sketched the ruins of Egyptian civilization, and a number of Egyptian influences began to find their way into furniture and design.

The renewal of interest in the arts and philosophy of the ancient world paralleled the revival of many classical elements in the new costume style for women that was based on an interpretation of the styles worn by women of Greece of the Golden Age. Taken largely from statuary and from Greek vase painting, the dress styles were predominantly white in color. Over the years since their creation the color of Greek and Roman statues had been bleached away, leaving them completely white. This led to the incorrect assumption that classical costume had been white.

Many costume historians have viewed the styles that so closely followed the Revolution as revolutionary. When images of these new styles are placed beside images from the pre-Revolutionary period (compare *Color Plates* 31 and 33), the marked differences are obvious. The seeds of the new style may have been sown in the preceding decades, yet the flowering of the Empire styles was sudden. Ribero (1988) notes, "In some respects, it [the Revolution] acted as a catalyst for styles already in the pipeline, but which were pushed to the forefront by the impact of politics." It is not far-fetched to see in these styles a visible symbol of the political ideals of the period in which they flowered. Their obvious inspiration came from Greek and Roman styles. They were visible evidence of the ascendancy of a political ideal; an ideal that the population believed had originated in classical antiquity.

FIGURE 11.2

White embroidered cotton dress of the round gown type, which exhibits the fullness at the elevated waistline that characterized English styles of 1800. (Photograph courtesy, Division of Costume, American Museum of National History.)

stead, the settlers constructed them from the sturdier hides of farm animals (Beaudoin-Ross 1980). Over time, moccasin-style shoes have become one of the "classic" shoe styles and are used worldwide.

Styles in the United States paralleled those of Europe. Imported fashion engravings provided information about current fashions in Paris and London.

THE ARTS AND COSTUME STYLES OF THE PERIOD

The revival of interest in the arts of classical antiquity that had begun in the second half of the 18th century continued

THE REVOLUTION IN MEN'S CLOTHES

The revolution in men's clothing was more subtle, but also more long lasting, than that in women's dress. While neither the components of men's dress (coat, waistcoat, breeches or, later, trousers) nor the silhouette were radically altered, gone were the colors, the lavish embroideries, and the luxurious fabrics. Ribero (1988) effectively summarizes the impact of the political revolution on men's dress.

For most of the eighteenth century there was a sartorial harmony in the dress of men and women; they were united in their love of colour, elegant design and luxurious materials. One of the results of the French Revolution was to divide the sexes in terms of their clothing. Men's dress becomes plain in

CONTEMPORARY COMMENTS 11.1

Napoleon's Wardrobe

In August of 1811, Napoleon wrote to General Duroc, the Grand Marshall of the Palace, about his wardrobe, providing a complete list of the items he wished to have ordered.

Inform Count Rémusat that he is to have nothing more to do with my Wardrobe, and that I have deprived him of the title of Master of the Wardrobe. You are to carry on his functions until I find a substitute for him. . . .

have an inventory made of my things: see that they are there, and check them off. . . . See that the tailor arranges to send in no bad work, and not to exceed his estimates. Whenever any new clothes are delivered, bring them to me yourself, so that I may see whether they fit me properly: if they do, I will have them. Regularise all this, so that, when I appoint a Master of the Wardrobe, he will find his duties cut and dried. . . .

Estimate for the Emperor's Wardrobe
Uniforms and Greatcoats
1 Grenadier's tail coat on January 1st with epaulettes, etc.

1 Chasseur's tail coat on April 1st with epaulettes, etc.

1 Grenadier's tail coat on July 1st with epaulettes, etc.

1 Chausseur's tail coat on October 17, with epaulettes, etc. (Each tail coat will have to last 3 years.)

2 Hunting coats: one for riding, in the Saint-Hubert style, the other for shooting, on August 1st. (These coats will have to last 3 years.)

1 Civilian coat on November 1st (to last 3 years.)

2 Frock coats: one grey, and the other another color. (They will be supplied on October 1st every year and will have to last 3 years.)

Waistcoats and Breeches
48 pairs of breeches and white waistcoats at 80 francs (They are to be supplied every week, and must last 3 years.)

Dressing Gowns, Pantaloons, and Vests
2 dressing gowns, one quilted, on May 1st and one of swansdown, on October 1st.

2 pairs of pantaloons, one quilted and one of wool, supplied in the same way. (The dressing gowns and pantaloons will have to last 3 years.)

48 flannel vests (one a week) at 30 francs. (The vests will have to last 3 years.)

Body Linen
4 dozen shirts (a dozen a week)

4 dozen handkerchiefs (a dozen a week)

2 dozen cravats (one a fortnight [two weeks])

1 dozen black collars (once a month) which must last a year.

2 dozen towels (a dozen a fortnight)

6 Madras night caps (one every 2 months) to last 3 years

2 dozen pairs of silk stockings at 18 francs (one pair a fortnight)

2 dozen pairs of socks (one pair a fortnight) (All this linen, except the black collar and night caps will have to last 6 years.)

Footwear
24 pairs of shoes (one pair a fortnight, which must last 2 years)

6 pairs of boots, to last 2 years

Headwear
4 hats a year, supplied with the tail coats

Miscellaneous
Scents slimming mixture, eau de Cologne, etc.

Washing the linen and silk stockings

Various expenses. (Nothing to be spent without His Majesty's approval.)

Reprinted from Thompson, J. M. 1934. *Napoleon Self-Revealed.* Oxford, England: Blackwell, p. 294ff.

---

design and sober in colour; it is unadorned with decoration. It symbolizes gravitas and an indifference to luxury—essential elements of republican austerity; its virtual uniformity emphasizes the revolutionary ideal of equality.

The change to more sober attire for men had begun in England, where dress had been for some time less formal and more "egalitarian." English tailors for men had a fine reputa-

tion. During the Regency period in England a favorite companion of the Prince Regent became an arbiter of men's styles. George "Beau" Brummel was famous for his impeccable dress. He wore beautifully tailored coats, the linen of his shirts and cravats was immaculate, and he personified the Regency "dandy," a fashionable man who dressed well, circulated in the "best" society, and who was always ready with a witty comment. One of the dandy's chief preoccupations was fashion, and Beau Brummel set the fashions until he fell out of favor with the Prince.

PRODUCTION AND ACQUISITION OF CLOTHING AND TEXTILES

The growth of the textile industry accelerated as the Industrial Revolution continued. The invention of the cotton gin (patented 1794) had an enormous impact on cotton production in the American South. Within 16 years the annual output of raw cotton had risen from 2 million to 85 million pounds (Cipolla and Birdsall 1979). With this increase in the supply of cotton and gradual adoption of water or steam to power textile mills, prices dropped making this fabric both affordable and available.

In 1801, Joseph Marie Jacquard, a Frenchman, developed a type of mechanized loom for weaving patterned fabrics. Based on the draw loom, Jacquard's machine provided a means of raising and lowering yarns that formed the pattern automatically. More than 10,000 of these looms were sold within the next 10 years (Cipolla and Birdsall 1979.)

Most women's clothing continued to be made at home or by seamstresses. By the 1820s, however, tailors were beginning to produce men's clothing that was "ready made," as well as custom-made clothing. Kidwell and Christman (1974) quote from an 1827 advertisement by one T. S. Whitmarsh of Boston who "keeps constantly for Sale, from 5 to 10,000 Fashionable ready-made Garments, comprising every article of apparel to a Gentleman's Wardrobe."

SOURCES OF INFORMATION ABOUT COSTUME

A substantial quantity of actual garments from the Empire period is available for study. When using this material, however, some care must be taken. As Newton (1975) cautions, "Surviving clothes in our museums are those which were saved in the past because their condition was too good for them to have been thrown away; they are not the most representative nor the most interesting of their period."

Individual garments provide detailed information about construction and fabrics, but they rarely furnish insights into just how individuals were supposed to look when these garments were placed over undergarments, and combined with accessories, headdress, and grooming to create a "total" look.

For this information one must go to such other sources as paintings, drawings, or fashion plates.

COSTUME FOR WOMEN: DIRECTOIRE AND EMPIRE PERIODS

Men could no longer compete with women in the arena of fashion. Women's clothing, in comparison to that of men, was more complicated and more subject to change. For this reason the order in which clothing styles will be discussed changes with this and all subsequent chapters, with women's styles being discussed before those of men.

GARMENTS

During the Directoire period (c. 1795–1800), very fashionable women ceased wearing corsets and wore, at most, a lightweight chemise as underclothing. Most women, however, wore a chemise made of cotton or linen as close as possible to the body. It had short, set-in sleeves with a gusset under the arm and a low square neck, and it was cut full and straight from the neck to the knees. Women did not give up their corsets, but placed them over the chemise. Corsets, more commonly known as stays, were cut in a straight line without waistline indentation and pushed the breasts up and out. Use of false bosoms is noted; these were made of wax or cotton. One disgruntled lover lamented (*The Oracle* 1800):

My Delia's heart I find so hard, I would she were forgotten
For how can hearts be adamant when all the breast is cotton.

While drawers were new to England and the American colonies, continental European women seem to have worn cotton or linen drawers much earlier. From the Empire period on, they became a basic part of women's underclothing. Unlike modern underpants, they were usually open through the crotch area, an important convenience when women wearing long, bulky skirts needed to relieve themselves.

Some women placed petticoats over their chemises. Poor women and African slaves in the Americas often wore petticoats in combination with short gowns (see *Figure 10.1, page 230*.) as street clothing. While the skirts of dresses remained narrow, undergarments were cut fairly straight, but as skirts widened toward the end of the Empire period, both the chemise and petticoat gained in breadth.

Pantalettes were long, straight, white drawers trimmed with rows of lace or tucks at the hem that became fashionable for a short time around 1809. While the fashion did not long continue for adult women, young girls wore them throughout this and subsequent periods.

Bustlelike padded rolls were placed under dresses at the back of the waistline during the closing years of the period.

The result was to give a peculiar forward slant to the body, which was known as the "Grecian bend."

Dresses had a tubular shape, with a waistline placement just under the bosom. Skirts reached to the floor. To achieve the straight line and incorporate the gathered fullness, supple and lightweight fabrics had to be used. A small concentration of gathered fabric at the back of the skirt was a vestige of the back-fullness characteristic of the last part of the 1700s. Both trained and untrained dresses were made until about 1812 when skirts shortened.

Several different constructions were utilized. Dresses open at the front to display an elaborate, decorated "petticoat," which was not an undergarment but a visible underskirt, were often worn for evening. Daytime or evening dresses that did not open at the front to show a petticoat were called round gowns. (See *Figures 11.2* and *11.3*.) In tunic dresses an underdress was placed beneath a loose shorter (ranging from hip to ankle) tunic or outerdress.

The apron or **high stomacher dress** had a complex construction in which the bodice was sewn to the skirt at the back only. Side front seams were left open to several inches below the waist and a band or string was located at the front of the waist of the skirt. The lady slipped the garment over her head, put her arms into the sleeves, and then tied the waist string around the back like an apron. The bodice often had a pair of underflaps that pinned across the chest, supporting the bust. The outer bodice closed in front either by wrapping it across the bosom like a shawl or lacing it up the front over a short undershirt (called a **habit shirt**), or by buttoning it down the front.

Low-cut necklines on the aforementioned dresses were either round or square. Higher necklines often finished in a small ruff or ruffle or with a drawstring that tied around the neck.

The most common types of sleeve styles on these dresses were short, puffed or fitted. (See *Figures 11.1* and *11.2*.) Sometimes sheer oversleeves were placed over the aforementioned short sleeves. Long sleeves were either fitted or full. (See *Figures 11.3, 11.4,* and *11.5*.) Some full, long sleeves tied into sections of short puffs and others had a single puff at the shoulder, with the rest of the sleeve fitted to the arm. (See *Color Plate* 33.)

These styles showed to best advantage in lightweight cotton and linen muslins and soft silks. In the Directoire period, plain white, undecorated "Grecian-style" gowns were fashionable, but with the coming of the Empire pastel shades or white with a variety of delicate embroideries were more often used.

OUTDOOR GARMENTS

Garments worn outdoors, over dresses, were shawls, stoles, cloaks, and capes. Shawls or stoles were made in square or oblong shapes. (See *Color Plate* 33.) In winter these provided relatively little protection. A flu epidemic during the Directoire

FIGURE 11.3

Printed cotton round gown of 1800. (Photograph courtesy, Division of Costume, American Museum of National History.)

period gained the nickname "muslin fever" after the practice of wearing lightweight muslin dresses with so little covering over them. The terms mantle, cloak, and cape were used interchangeably.

The **spencer** was a short jacket (worn by both men and women) that ended at the waistline, which in the case of women's styles was just under the bosom. Made with sleeves or sleeveless, the color usually contrasted with the rest of the costume. Spencers were worn indoors as well as out. (See *Figure 11.4*.) The term "spencer" provides a good illustration of the many stories told about origins of costume terms. There are at least three different stories of how the spencer came into being. In the first anecdote, Lord Spencer is supposed to have made a bet with a friend that he could start a new fashion within two weeks. The bet was taken. On the spot, Lord

FIGURE 11.4

From left to right: Empire dress of embroidered muslin with a spencer of figured silk; small child in embroidered muslin dress and wearing pantalettes; ribbed silk dress, c. 1807–1812; muslin dress (1804–1814) with multicolored bead embroidery and embroidered muslin scarf. (Photograph courtesy, The Metropolitan Museum of Art, Costume Institute.)

Spencer cut off his coat tails and by starting a new fashion won his bet. Another version relates how Lord Spencer was standing too close to an open fire at a party and his coat tails caught on fire; after the fire was put out Lord Spencer cut off the singed coat tails, thereby beginning a new fashion. The final version has the same Lord Spencer being thrown by his horse, and in the accident his coat tails were torn off. He did not want to leave the races, and so simply went about wearing the shortened coat. One—or none—of these stories may be true.

The **pelisse** was similar to a modern coat. It was generally full length and followed the typical Empire silhouette. For winter, especially when made of silk or cotton, pelisses had warm linings. (See *Figure 11.5*.)

HAIR AND HEADDRESS

See *Illustrated Table 11.1* for depictions of some hairstyles and headdress of the Empire period.

Hairstyles were often based on Greek prototypes, with the hair combed back from the face and gathered in ringlets or coils at the back of the head, while the hair around the face was arranged in soft curls. Other modes included a short, curly style called **à la victime** or **à la Titus.** The former term

FIGURE 11.5

On the left a silk walking dress (c. 1805–1810) in chestnut brown faille and green-gold satin worn with a leghorn hat tied "gypsy" fashion and at the right a red, silk taffeta pelisse (c. 1816–1818). The pelisse is padded throughout for warmth; the hat is a poke bonnet. (Photograph courtesy, The Metropolitan Museum of Art.)

was a reference to the short haircuts given to victims about to be guillotined during the French Revolution; the latter to short hair, depicted on statues of Roman men.

Hat styles included jockey caps, especially for riding. Riding was one of the few sports in which women could participate. Turbans were especially fashionable after Napoleon's invasion of Egypt. Influences from ancient Greece and Rome were evident in small fabric hats similar to military helmets of classic antiquity.

Bonnets had crowns of fabric or straw and wide brims. Toques were high, brimless hats, and "gypsy hats," with a low crown and a moderately wide brim, were worn with ribbon tied over the outside of the brim and under the chin. Mature women wore small muslin or lace caps, called **day caps,** indoors. Hats were worn not only out-of-doors but also for evening events such as the theater or balls.

FOOTWEAR

Shoes in colors matching dresses or pelisses were usually made of leather, velvet, or satin. They had no heels; were flat. With the return of flat shoes, soles of some shoes were once again shaped to fit right and left feet. Some slippers had crisscross lacings that ran up the leg to below the knee. (See *Illustrated Table 11.2.*)

Short boots reached to the calf. Boots closed at the sides with laces or buttons or at the back with laces. For bad weather women wore pattens with small platforms of wood or steel that fastened over shoes.

ACCESSORIES

See *Illustrated Table 11.2* for depictions of some accessories of this period.

Long gloves, ending on the upper arm or above the elbow, were worn with short-sleeved dresses. Gloves were made of leather, silk, or net.

Reticules or **indispensibles** were small handbags, often with a drawstring at the top. In earlier periods, when skirts had been full, pockets placed under the skirt were used for carrying small personal objects. The narrow silhouette of the Empire period made such pockets impractical, so the reticule replaced the pocket. Some found the device amusing and took to calling it a "ridicule."

Other hand-carried accessories included muffs that were large in size, often of fur, swansdown, or fabric; parasols moderate to small in size, some of which were pagoda shaped; fans; and decorative handkerchiefs.

JEWELRY

Popular jewelry items were necklaces, earrings, rings, small watches that pinned to the dress, and brooches, some of which served the function of closing the dress. Bracelets were worn high on the arm in imitation of those on Greek and Roman statues and vases.

COSTUME FOR MEN: DIRECTOIRE AND EMPIRE PERIODS

GARMENTS

Drawers were similar to those shown in *Figure 10.2, page 231,* and were usually made of linen or cotton. Cotton or linen fabrics were used to make full-cut shirts with high, standing collars that reached to the cheek. The front of the shirt was generally pleated or ruffled. Around the neck of shirts men wrapped **cravats,** large squares of fabric folded and wrapped several times around the neck and tied in front or **stocks,** stiffened neck bands that buckled or tied behind the neck.

Illustrated Table 11.1

TYPICAL WOMEN'S HAIRSTYLES AND HEADDRESS IN THE EMPIRE PERIOD

Haircut *à la victime* or *à la Titus*[1]

Hairstyles and hats of 1802[2]

Headcoverings of 1806[2]

Bonnets

Indoor day caps

Turbans

[1] *Le Journal de Dames et des Modes,* s c. 1801.

[2] Comptesse Marie de Villemont, *Histoire de la Coiffure Feminine,* 1891.

Illustrated Table 11.2

EMPIRE PERIOD: ACCESSORIES

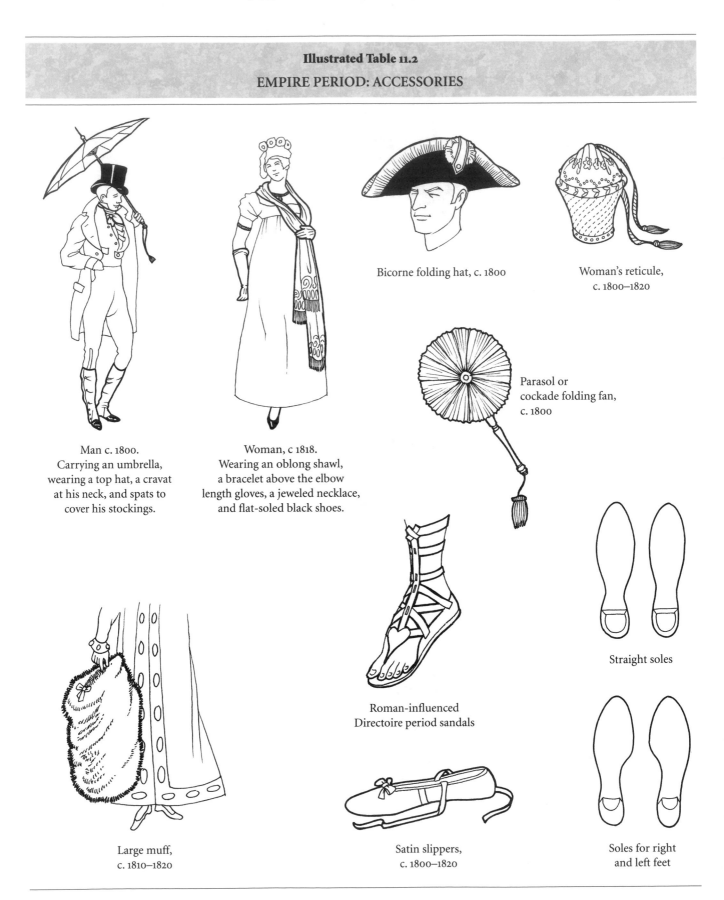

Bicorne folding hat, c. 1800

Woman's reticule,
c. 1800–1820

Man c. 1800.
Carrying an umbrella,
wearing a top hat, a cravat
at his neck, and spats to
cover his stockings.

Woman, c 1818.
Wearing an oblong shawl,
a bracelet above the elbow
length gloves, a jeweled necklace,
and flat-soled black shoes.

Parasol or
cockade folding fan,
c. 1800

Straight soles

Roman-influenced
Directoire period sandals

Large muff,
c. 1810–1820

Satin slippers,
c. 1800–1820

Soles for right
and left feet

A coat, a waistcoat worn beneath the coat, and either breeches or trousers made up the suit. Clothing for "dress" (formal occasions) and "undress" (less formal occasions) usually differed only in color or quality of fabric, buttons, and accessories. Rarely were the three parts of the suit the same color. Generally they contrasted. Colors were light or dark, bright or subdued. Wool was used in a variety of weights and qualities. For formal occasions and especially at the French or English courts, lavishly decorated velvets and silk fabrics were suitable.

Coat fronts generally ended at the waist, either curving gradually back from the waist into two tails that ended slightly above the knee, or with a cut-in, a rounded or square space at the front where no skirt was attached. The tails began where the cut-in ended. (See *Figures 11.6* and *11.7*.) Coat collars generally had a notch where the collar joined the lapel. Some coats had velvet facings applied. Closings were both single and double breasted. Pockets were located in the pleats of the coat tails, or at the waist. Some coats had false pocket flaps.

Only the front of the sleeveless waistcoat was visible when a coat was worn; therefore the back was made of plain cotton or linen fabric or of the waistcoat lining fabric. Collars generally stood upright. Some were cut so that the upper and lower edges formed a steplike structure, that is, were "stepped." About two inches of waistcoat were visible at the bottom of the coat when it was closed, and only a small edge of the waistcoat was visible at the open neck of the coat. (See *Figure 11.7*.) Several waistcoats worn one over the other provided more warmth.

Until about 1807 breeches were worn extensively. Breeches ended at the knee, trousers extended to the ankle. (See *Figure 11.7*.) **Pantaloons** at this period were generally defined as fitting the leg more closely than trousers, which were made in close-fitting, moderately full, or very full styles. The extremely full trousers were based on the dress of Russian soldiers and fashion publications called them **cossacks**. Tight pantaloons or trousers had an instep strap to keep them from riding up the leg. Trousers had been introduced for fashionable wear during the French Revolution, but were discarded again by fashion leaders immediately following the Revolution. After 1807 they returned as acceptable fashions.

OUTDOOR GARMENTS

Overcoats or great coats worn for cold weather were very full, single or double breasted, knee or full length. Coats had collars and lapels. Some had one or more capes at the shoulder. Cloaks were no longer fashionable, but were sometimes worn for travel.

Spencers were worn by men, as well as by women, but for men they took the place of the coat with a suit.

DRESSING GOWN OR BANYAN

The dressing gown or banyan was usually ankle length, cut with a full, flared skirt and was made in fabrics such as deco-

FIGURE 11.6

Gentleman of 1806 in tail coat, knee-breeches, and two-cornered hat. One waistcoat is visible between the end of his coat and the beginning of his breeches. At the open neck of his jacket two waistcoats and ruffled shirt front are visible. His companion wears a dress with short, puffed sleeves, and a closely fitted bonnet, and carries a small parasol. (Fashion plate, courtesy, the Cooper Hewitt Museum.)

rative damasks or brocades of wool, cotton, or silk. Some had matching waistcoats. According to Coleman (1975), "in the eighteenth and early nineteenth centuries this outfit was not confined to 'at home' wear as its descendant the robe or dressing gown, is today. It was accepted for street and office wear."

HAIR AND HEADDRESS

Men cut their hair short. Faces were clean shaven, although side whiskers were somewhat long.

FOOTWEAR

Early in the period shoes closed with decorative buckles. A tie closing at the front gradually supplanted buckles. Shoes had low, round heels and rounded toes. The French Revolution may have helped to end the fashion for buckles, as one of the revolutionary slogans was "down with the aristocratic shoe buckle" (Swann 1982).

Many boot styles were named for military heroes or well-known army units. (Examples: Napoleons, Wellingtons, Bluchers, Cossacks, and Hessians.) True military boots were high in front, covering the knees, and scooped down behind the knee in back so that the knee could be bent easily. Other boot styles had turned-down tops with contrasting linings. Shorter boots were worn over close-fitting trousers.

ACCESSORIES

Gloves were short, and made of cotton or leather. Hand-carried accessories included canes and **quizzing glasses,** that is, magnifying glasses mounted on a handle and worn around the neck. Some authors claim that the fad for quizzing glasses led some dandies to have their optic nerves loosened surgically in order to justify the acquisition of a glass, but this is undoubtedly an example of the exaggerated claims often made for the impact of fad or fashion.

JEWELRY

For men jewelry was mostly limited to rings and decorative watch fobs and occasionally decorative brooches worn on the shirt or neck cloth.

COSMETICS

Some very fashion-conscious men used rouge to heighten their color, bleached their hands to whiten them, and used substantial quantities of eau de cologne.

FIGURE 11.7

Gentleman of 1815 wearing fashionable trousers with a tail coat. A strap that holds the trousers in place is visible at the instep of his shoe. He carries a top hat. His companion's dress shows changes in hem length and additional ornamentation characteristic of women's dress in the late Empire period. (Fashion plate, courtesy, the Cooper Hewitt Museum.)

Top hats were the predominant hat style. (See *Figure 11.7.*) These hats had either taller or shorter crowns and medium-sized brims that rolled up slightly at the sides and dipped in front and back. The **bicorne** was a two-pointed hat worn with the points from front to back or from side-to-side. (See *Figure 11.6.*) When worn for evening and carried flattened, under the arm, the two-pointed hat was called a *chapeau bras* (a French phrase meaning "hat for the arm"). Hats were made from silk, wool felt, or beaver (felted beaver fur mixed with wool).

COSTUME FOR CHILDREN: THE EMPIRE PERIOD

Costume for Girls

GARMENTS

Dresses were cut along same lines as those of adult women, but shorter for both little girls and young adolescents. Girls wore pantalettes under dresses. For out-of-doors, girls wore shawls and pelisses.

HAIR AND HEADDRESS

Although small girls wore simple, natural styles; adolescents adopted fashionable adult styles, particularly Grecian styles. Bonnets were among the most popular hat styles.

FOOTWEAR

Girls wore slippers or soft boots made of leather or fabric.

Costume for Boys

GARMENTS

From infancy to about four or five years, boys wore dresses with skirts similar to those of little girls, although generally slightly shorter. By age four or five, they usually wore trousers under skirts. After age six or seven, boys donned skeleton suits, which consisted of a loose shirt with wide, frilled collar and ankle-length trousers that began high, with the trousers generally buttoned to the shirt. This style was very popular for young boys. After age 11 or 12, boys dressed much the same as men.

For cold weather boys wore overcoats.

HAIR AND HEADDRESS

Boys' hair was either long or short.

FOOTWEAR

Either slippers or soft boots were usually worn.

SUMMARY

THEMES

POLITICS AND POLITICAL CONFLICT were themes expressed through dress in France at the beginning of the years covered in this chapter. As the French Revolution accelerated, clothing made obvious political statements. The revolutionaries traded their aristocratic knee breeches for trousers and donned the "red hat of liberty," while women ornamented their dresses with revolutionary colors. The revival of classical Greek and Roman styles in women's dresses during the Directory paralleled the interest in the political ideals of the Greek and Roman republics.

Intertwined with the political overtones of dress one can observe the theme of **RELATIONSHIPS BETWEEN COSTUME AND DEVELOPMENTS IN THE FINE AND APPLIED ARTS.** Classical revivals, which had begun in the late 18th century, not only continued to influence dress, but also architecture, interior design, furnishings, and the fine arts.

The soft, white muslins that were so suitable to these classical revival styles were also related to the themes of **TRADE** and **CROSS-CULTURAL** contacts that, in turn, interacted with **TECHNOLOGY** and the **PRODUCTION AND ACQUISITION OF TEXTILES AND APPAREL.** These fabrics were brought to Europe from India during the 18th century. By the early 19th century the technological advances of the Industrial Revolution permitted European and American manufacturers to imitate these and other foreign products in cotton.

Yet another theme important in dress in this and subsequent periods was that of **GENDER DIFFERENCES** which reflected changes in **SOCIAL ROLES** of men and women after the Industrial Revolution. Clothing for men and women during the Directoire and Empire periods provides a marked contrast with the styles of the preceding century. For men the acceptance of trousers in place of knee breeches represented the triumph of a style that had once been associated with working class men. Moreover, the accepted styles for men for the rest of the 19th century, and on into the 20th century, that will be described in the coming chapters will continue to utilize the more somber color range and plainer fabrics that had become acceptable for upper-class men in these first two decades. By comparison with men's costume, women's dress utilized more decorative fabrics, a greater variety of colors, and many different style details. This will continue in subsequent periods.

SURVIVALS OF EMPIRE STYLE COSTUME

Subsequent revivals of empire styles for women are, in a sense, a revival of a revival. The inspiration for the empire style lay in the styles of classical antiquity. However, with time and the evolution of fashion, these styles developed very distinct characteristics of their own. The so-called empire waistline for women's dresses was revived for several years in the period around 1910 (see *Figure 15.6, page 371.*), and again just before 1960. With the popularity in 1996 of films based on the novels of Jane Austen (published 1811–1818), designers of 1996 were, once again, reviving empire period styles. (See *Figure 11.8.*)

In the Hawaiian Islands the Empire period dress of the first American missionaries was transformed into the holoku. This garment is still worn in Hawaii, a direct descendant of Empire period styles. (See *Figure 11.9.*)

FIGURE 11.8

Evening gown from the Givenchy Fall collection of 1996 designed by Galliano that takes its inspiration from Empire period styles. (Photograph from *W* magazine, September 1996, courtesy, Fairchild Publications.)

FIGURE 11.9

Princess Kaiulani of Hawaii photographed in the 1890s wearing a holoku, a traditional Hawaiian costume that derives from Empire style dresses worn by American missionaries in Hawaii about 1820. (Photograph courtesy, Hawaii State Archives.)

NOTES

Beaudoin-Ross, J. 1980. "A la Canadienne: Some Aspects of 19th Century Habitant Dress." *Dress*, p. 71.

Cipolla, C. and D. Birdsall. 1979. *The Technology of Man.* New York: Holt, Rinehart and Winston.

Coleman, E. A. 1975. *Of Men Only, A Review of Men's and Boy's Fashion, 1750–1975.* New York: The Brooklyn Museum, p. 6.

Kidwell, C. and M. Christman. 1974. *Suiting Everyone: The Democratization of Clothing in America.* Washington, DC: Smithsonian Institution Press.

Newton, S. M. 1975. *Renaissance Theatre Costume and the Sense of the Historic Past.* London: Rapp and Whitney.

The Oracle, an English periodical of 1800.

Ribero, A. 1988. *Fashion in the French Revolution.* London: B. T. Batsford, pp. 45, 140, 141.

Steele, V. 1988. *Paris Fashions: A Cultural History.* New York: Oxford University Press, pp. 36–41.

Swann, J. 1982. *Shoes.* London: B. T. Batsford, p. 29.

Visual Summary Table

DIRECTOIRE AND EMPIRE PERIOD

Man: 1790 to c. 1807	Man: c. 1807–1820	Woman: 1790–1800	Woman: 1816
Shirts, under waist-length waistcoats. Over these, tailcoats, worn with knee breeches or trousers.	Men more likely to wear trousers than knee-breeches. Otherwise, little change.	Elevated waistline, soft gathered skirt with narrower silhouette. Sleeves tend to be short; necklines low.	Sleeve variations and necklines appear and gradual widening of skirt hem and rising of waistlines as the period progresses.

S E L E C T E D   R E A D I N G S

*Books Containing Illustrations of Costume of the Period
from Original Sources*

Ackermann's Repository of the Arts. 1979. Reprinted by Dover Publications, New York, *Catalogue of the drawings of Horace Vernet. Incroyables et Merveilleuses.* 1991. New York: Didier Aaron.

Coleman, E. A. 1972. *Changing Fashions: 1800–1970.* New York: The Brooklyn Museum.

———. 1975. *Of Men Only, A Review of Men's and Boy's Fashion, 1750–1975.* New York: The Brooklyn Museum.

Garlick, K. 1989. *Sir Thomas Lawrence.* New York: New York University Press.

Gibbs-Smith, C. H. 1960. *The Fashionable Lady in the 19th Century.* London: Her Majesty's Stationery Office.

Rosenblum, R. 1985. *Ingres.* New York: Harry Abrams.

White, W. J. 1971. *Working Class Costume from Sketches of Characters, 1818.* London: Costume Society and Victoria and Albert Museum.

Periodical Articles

Anninger, A. 1982. "Costume of the Convention: Art as Agent of Social Change in Revolutionary France." *Harvard Library Journal,* Vol. 30, No. 2, April, p. 179.

Baumgarten, L. 1992. "Under Waistcoats and Drawers." *Dress,* Vol. 19, p. 5.

Bradfield, N. 1973. "Studies of an 1814 Pelisse and Bonnet." *Costume,* p. 60.

Cocuzza, D. 2000. "The Dress of Free Women of Color in New Orleans, 1780–1840. *Dress,* Vol. 27, p. 78.

Deslandres, Y. 1977. "Josephine and La Mode." *Apollo,* Vol. CVI, No. 185, July, p. 44.

Harris, J. 1981. "The Red Cap of Liberty: A Study of Dress Worn by French Revolutionary Partisans, 1789–94." *Eighteenth Century Studies,* Vol. 14, No. 3, Spring, p. 283.

Daily Life

Ashton, J. 1968. *Social England Under the Regency.* Gale.

Langdon, W. C. 1981. *Everyday Things in American Life, 1776–1876.* New York: Macmillan.

Laver, J. 1972. *The Age of Illusion: Manners and Morals 1750–1848.* New York: David McKay.

Low, D. A. 1977. *That Sunny Dome: A Portrait of Regency Britain.* Totowa, NJ: Rowman.

Murray, V. 1999. *An Elegant Madness: High Society in Regency England.* New York: Viking.

Peterson, H. L. 1986. *Americans at Home: From the Colonists to the Late Victorians.* New York: Ayer.

Pool, D. 1993. *What Jane Austen Ate and Charles Dickens Knew.* New York: Simon and Schuster.

Robiquet, J. 1963. *Daily Life in France Under Napoleon.* New York: Macmillan.

CHRONOLOGY

1820

Prince Regent becomes King George IV of England

1823

United States announces in the Monroe Doctrine that the
Western hemisphere is no longer open to colonization

1824

Death of Lord Byron

1830

Publication of first American fashion magazine, *Godey's Lady's Book*
Revolution in France, ending with installation of King Louis Philippe

1837

Queen Victoria ascends the throne in England

1839

Louis Daguerre announces that he has found a method for making photographic images

1840

Wedding of Queen Victoria to Prince Albert

1842

Publication of *Peterson's Magazine,* second American fashion magazine

1845

The United States annexes Texas

1846

Elias Howe invents the lock stitch sewing machine

1848

Revolution in France, Louis Napoleon elected President of France
Declaration of the Rights of Women, issued in Seneca Falls,
NY, proposes that women be granted the right to vote

1849

Gold Rush to California where gold was discovered at Sutter's Mill

CHAPTER TWELVE

THE ROMANTIC PERIOD

1820 – 1850

A.

B.

D.

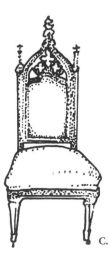

C.

A.

Biedermeier chair

B.

Greek revival building

C.

Gothic revival side chair

D.

Grace Church:
Gothic revival architecture

E.

Painting by William Sidney Mount,
Barroom Scene, 1835

E.

Figure A from Lavisse, E. 1907. *Album Historique Le XVIII Le XIX Siècle.* Paris: Librairie Armand Colin, p. 238. Figures B, D courtesy of V. R. Tortora. Figure C courtesy of J. Curcio in Federico, J. T., 1988. *Clues to American Furniture.* Washington: Starrhill, p. 47. Figure E. courtesy of the Art Institute of Chicago, the Goodmen Fund (1939.392).

The name assigned in this text to the period in costume from about 1820 to 1850 is the Romantic period. The term "Romantic" has been applied to the literature, music, and graphic arts of this same era. Romantic art and literature emphasized emotion, sentiment, and feeling. Romanticism represented a reaction against the formal classical styles of the 17th and 18th centuries. Romantics rejected the classical insistence on rules governing creative work. Romantics were concerned more with content and less with form; they preferred to break rules. Romantic writers assumed that "empirical science and philosophy were inadequate as a means of answering all the most important questions concerning human life" (Harris 1969). Romantic artists appealed to the emotions.

Romanticism was a form of rebellion against restrictions on artistic expression. The artists or the writers should express their innermost feelings in any form they chose. Romanticism had a new set of values—the innermost emotions should be fully expressed. Art should please the senses. Imagination was more important than reason.

Romantics ignored social conventions, including marriage. They resorted to tears and violent emotions, loving and hating fiercely. A true romantic heroine fainted easily because of inner spiritual turmoil. The Romantic lifestyle included wearing beards, long hair, and unusual clothing. English poets such as Lord Byron, Shelley, and Keats were nonconformist in their lifestyles, as well as in their poetry.

Romantics preferred other times and places, and one of their favorite times was the Middle Ages. The Romantic Movement invented the historical novel. Writers such as Walter Scott wrote popular historical novels filled with the legends and history of Scotland and medieval England. In France, Alexander Dumas the Elder wrote swashbuckling historical novels, including *The Three Musketeers* and *The Count of Monte Cristo*. Subjects of Romantic paintings were often events from the past, as well as Oriental and Mediterranean scenes of violent action. Some Romantic artists painted moonlit ruins, ghosts, and mysterious forms. Tales such as Mary Wollstonecraft Shelley's *Frankenstein* exemplified the romantic love of the unusual and fantastic.

These trends in the arts were reflected in costume. After 1820, elements that can be related to Romanticism in the arts began to appear, especially in women's dress. Many costumes showed conscious attempts to revive certain elements of historical dress, such as neck ruffs, the ferroniere (a chain with a jewel worn at the center of the forehead), or sleeve styles from earlier costume periods. Costume balls at which men and women appeared dressed as figures from the past were in vogue. The leading Romantic poet, Lord Byron, through exotic costume, inspired some styles or names of styles in men's dress. Fashionable colors were given names such as "dust of ruins" or "Egyptian earth."

After the revolution in France of 1848–49, Romanticism declined. Although some artists and writers continued to work in the Romantic vein, the period of major influence of the Romantics was over.

HISTORICAL BACKGROUND

The Romantic Movement was played out against the following political background.

England

In England, the Prince Regent finally became King George IV in 1820, but the scandals surrounding his marital life made him unpopular. During his reign, the first professional police force was created with headquarters at Scotland Yard, and Roman Catholics were permitted to sit in Parliament. William IV, an eccentric old sailor with little political sense, succeeded his brother on the throne in 1830. During his reign, Parliament enacted the famous Reform Bill, which redistributed the seats in the House of Commons and extended voting rights to more men. When William died without an heir in 1837 his 18-year-old niece, Victoria, became queen. Victoria ruled until 1901, and gave her name to an age. She restored the prestige of the monarchy, recapturing for it the respect and admiration of the English people.

France

In France after the fall of Napoleon, the Bourbon monarchy was restored. Louis XVIII, brother of the executed Louis XVI, became king and granted the nation a written constitution. The restoration of the Bourbons contributed (along with the historicism of the Romantic writers) to the revival of styles from earlier monarchical periods and to an interest in costume balls.

In 1824, Louis's brother succeeded him as Charles X. A king lacking in common sense, he attempted to restore royal absolutism, which led to revolution in July 1830. The revolution was led by an alliance of journalists, republicans, unemployed working men, and students who had been enthusiastic supporters of the rebellious spirit of Romanticism. They expressed their rebellion not only through political actions but also in their style of dress, wearing clothes deliberately different from those of fashionable men. They wore working class clothes, and they rejected stiff collars and neck cloths.

At the end of three days of fighting Charles X abdicated in favor of his grandson, but the Parisians wanted no more of the Bourbon dynasty. Leaders of the bourgeoisie (middle class), fearing another republic, succeeded in having the crown offered to Louis Philippe, the Duke of Orleans, who was the head of the younger branch of the Bourbon family, and whose father had been an aristocratic supporter of the French Revolution. He now became the king of the French. But his reign was filled with social and economic unrest because he proved too conservative. His unwillingness to make reforms in the electoral system led to the outbreak of revolution in 1848. France established a Second Republic and the voters elected Louis Napoleon as president, but in 1852, the Second Republic became the Second Empire. Meanwhile, the revolution in France led to a tidal wave of revolution that swept over Austria, the German states, and Italy.

The United States

In the United States during the same period, the westward expansion had begun. Texas was annexed in 1845, and after a war with Mexico, New Mexico and California were ceded to the United States. The Oregon territory was also acquired, giving the United States government control over virtually all of the territory now part of the continental United States.

By the mid-19th century, the cultivation of cotton dominated the economy of the Southern states. Cotton brought high financial returns, greater than those of any other commodity. With cotton so important to the Southern economy, slavery flourished. Because of cotton, the South was identified with slavery, a condition that separated the South from the North.

By 1840 almost half of the population in Louisiana and Alabama and more than half the population in Mississippi were slaves. According to the Census of 1860, there were 3,521,111 slaves in the Southern states and 429,401 in the border states (Delaware, Maryland, Kentucky, and Missouri). However, nearly three fourths of the families in the South owned no slaves, and the great majority of slaveholders possessed only a few slaves.

Slaves worked not only in the fields tending the cotton crop, but also as skilled artisans and in textile mills, mines, and tobacco factories. Slaveholders received a good return from their "investment" in slaves.

Slavery did not exist without challenge. Those who vehemently opposed slavery were known as abolitionists. Local abolitionist societies became the basis for a movement with a membership of two million members by 1840. They opposed slavery, denying the validity of any law that recognized slavery as an institution, and they dwelt on the cruelties of slavery. Northerners at first thought abolitionists were wild fanatics. Eventually, however, abolitionists convinced many Northerners that slavery was immoral and consequently could not be accepted as a permanent institution in the United States. They attracted support in the battle to prevent slavery from being introduced into new territories and states. Abolitionists were active in the underground railroad by which runaway slaves were concealed, fed, clothed, and helped on their way to Canada. (Although slavery had been abolished in the North, the Fugitive Slave Acts made it possible for escaped slaves captured in the North to be returned to their masters in the South.)

The abolitionists tried to use "moral suasion" and political influence to end slavery. Although they did not favor the use of force to end slavery, their efforts in publicizing the evils of slavery helped to prepare Northerners for the terrible struggle that divided the country when the Civil War came in 1861.

In the Monroe Doctrine of 1823, the United States had also given notice to the European powers that the Western hemisphere was no longer open to colonization. But although Americans were becoming politically independent of Europe, American people continued to follow the fashions in dress that were originated abroad.

WOMEN'S SOCIAL ROLES AND CLOTHING STYLES

Romantic poets often emphasized the maiden who died for love or the one whose hard-heartedness caused despair in her lover. According to one analysis of women's attitudes in the 19th century, it was distinctly unstylish to appear to be in good health. Circles under the eyes were cultivated and rice powder was liberally applied to produce a pale look. The middle-class woman was expected, furthermore, to be a "perfect lady" (Cunnington 1935).

With industrialization and the growing movement of business out of the home and into an external workplace, women's roles were increasingly confined to the home. Affluent women were severely limited in their activities. The home was the center of entertainment, and well-to-do women served as hostesses for their husbands. For this role, they required a substantial wardrobe of fashionable clothes. They supervised the servants, who did all of the household tasks. Women who dressed in the most stylish gowns of the 1830s and 1840s, when sleeves were set low on the shoulder, would not have been able to raise their arms above their heads, and were virtually incapable of performing any physical labor. Accomplishments such as sewing, embroidering, modeling in wax, sketching, painting on glass or china, or decorating other functional objects were encouraged. Most women had seamstresses who would come to the home to make the more complicated garments.

Women from working class families and rural areas, and women pioneers, however, did toil at a wide variety of tasks. Their garments were less hampering, more practical in form, and made from less expensive fabrics. Even so, their dresses followed the basic style lines and silhouette of the period. (See *Figure 12.7*.) Farm and pioneer women transformed the fashionable bonnet of the Romantic period into a sunbonnet, a practical covering to protect the face and head from the hot sun.

MANUFACTURE AND ACQUISITION OF CLOTHING AND TEXTILES

The advances in the technology for producing woven textiles were now well established. Machines for producing lace had been gradually growing more sophisticated. By about 1840, most of the traditional handmade lace patterns could be made by machine in both narrow and wide widths, making lace trimmings and fabrics available at relatively low cost. Another advance in the 1840s was the development of a power-driven knitting frame that could make seamless hosiery.

The variety and types of ready-made clothing available for men continued to expand; however, women could buy few ready-made garments other than corsets and cloaks.

SOURCES OF EVIDENCE ABOUT COSTUME

A major source of fashion information was women's magazines, which carried a number of features about current styles. Introduced in Europe in the late 18th century, these periodicals included hand-colored prints showing the latest styles, together with a printed description. The major American fashion magazines of the 19th century, *Godey's Lady's Book* and *Peterson's Magazine,* began publication in 1830 and 1842, respectively. From the 1830s up to the present time, fashion magazines have served as an excellent primary source of information about what was considered to be the newest fashion.

Fashion magazines clearly demonstrated the influence of Paris styles on women's fashions. Descriptions of plates in both English and American magazines usually emphasized that these were the "latest Paris fashions." Descriptions were heavily larded with French phrases and French names for garments or fabrics.

In using fashion plates as sources of fashion information, it is important to remember that a fashion plate represents the "proposed" style, and this style may not always have found its way into mainstream fashion. Also, fashion plates were made by tinting an engraved picture with water colors. The representation that resulted is quite different from that produced by the painter working in oils. The result provides much less information about the texture and even the type of fabric than a painting might provide.

The colors of fashion plates may be misleading, too. Fashion plate descriptions sometimes describe colors different from those shown on the plate. Individuals hired to hand-tint these plates may have run out of one color and substituted another.

The 1840s also marked the beginning of photographic portraiture. Louis Daguerre of France perfected his photographic process and it immediately became fashionable for individuals to sit for their "daguerreotypes." These pictures provide not only a record of styles actually being worn but also allow comparison of the idealized fashion plates and artists' painted portraits with real clothing. From 1849 on, when the process became established in the United States, there is a wealth of photographic material documenting costumes.

Items from the period between 1820 and 1850 in historic costume collections are more plentiful than those from earlier periods, although the largest number of items tend to be wedding dresses, ball gowns, and other "special" clothing. Everyday dresses, men's, and children's costumes are rarely represented in quantity in collections.

COSTUME FOR WOMEN: THE ROMANTIC PERIOD

The period between 1820 and 1825 was a period of transition between the Empire styles and the newer Romantic mode. A change in the location of the waistline took place gradually. By 1825, the waistline had moved downward from just under the bust to several inches above the anatomical location of the waist. (See *Figure 12.1.*) Along with the changes in waistline placement, women's dresses had, by 1825, developed large sleeves, which continued to grow larger, and gored skirts, which were widening and becoming gradually shorter. (See *Figure 12.2.*)

Costume for Women: 1820–1835

GARMENTS

Women's undergarments included chemises, drawers, stays, and petticoats. Chemises were wide, about knee length, and usually had short sleeves. (See *Figure 12.3.*) No substantive changes took place in the construction of women's drawers. Women of all social classes were increasingly likely to wear them. As dress silhouettes placed greater emphasis on a small waist, stays shortened and laced tightly to pull in the waist. Multiple layers of petticoats supported the ever-wider skirts of dresses. **Bustles,** which were small down or cotton-filled pads that tied on around the waist at the back, held out skirts in back. (See *Figure 12.3.*)

Dresses were frequently identified in fashion magazines according to the times of day or the activities for which they were intended. As a result, fashion plates generally carried captions such as "morning dresses," "day dresses," "walking" or "promenade dresses," "carriage dresses," "dinner dresses,"

FIGURE 12.1

Dress of 1824 shows transition from Empire to early Romantic period styles. Waistline has been moved to a somewhat lower level than during the Empire, the skirt is more bell-shaped, and sleeves are growing a little larger. (Courtesy, Picture Collection, New York Public Library.)

FIGURE 12.2

Plum-colored silk dress with gigot or leg-of-mutton sleeves, 1830. (Photograph courtesy, Division of Costume, American Museum of National History.)

or "evening" or "ball dresses." **Morning dresses** were generally the most informal, often being made of lingerie-type fabrics such as white cotton or fine linen with lace or ruffled trimmings. **Day dresses, promenade** or **walking dresses,** and **carriage dresses** are often indistinguishable one from the other, especially in summer.

Daytime dresses with their lower waistlines, wide sleeves, and full skirts fastened either in front or in back. They were not trained. Necklines varied, with many being V-shaped. Others were high, ending at the throat, and finished off with a small collar or ruff. Draped necklines had crossover folds arranged in various ways. Open necklines might have white linen or cotton fillers.

In the 1820s and 1830s, many bodices had wide, V-shaped revers extending from shoulder to waist in front and back. Wide, capelike collars in matching colors or white-work also were popular.

Sleeves were exceptionally diverse. Fashion periodicals gave many different names to the styles they showed. The following are the major varieties identified by Cunnington and Cunnington (1970):

- Puffed at the shoulder then attached to a long sleeve, which was fitted to the wrist. Others consisted of a small puff covered by a sheer oversleeve. Decorative epaulettes— **mancherons** (*mahn-sher-ohng'*)—were sometimes placed at the shoulder.

FIGURE 12.3

Caricature of 1831 shows the down-filled hip pad called a bustle that was worn under full-skirted dresses. Other garments depicted include a corset, worn over a chemise. The sleeves of the chemise are puffed and stiffened to support the large sleeves of dresses of the period. Several layers of petticoats are visible. The lady is tucking a handkerchief into a pocket suspended from the waist. These pockets were reached through openings in the skirt seams. (Photograph courtesy, Division of Costume, American Museum of National History.)

- **Marie sleeve:** full to the wrist, but tied in at intervals with ribbons or bands. (See *Figure 12.4*.)

- **Demi-gigot** (*demi-ghe-go'*): full from shoulder to elbow, then fitted from elbow to wrist, often with an extension over the wrist.

- **gigot** (*ghe-go'*), also called **leg-of-mutton sleeves:** full at the shoulder, gradually decreasing in size to the wrist where they ended in a fitted cuff. (See *Figure 12.2* and *Color Plate 36*.)

- **imbecile** or **idiot sleeves:** extremely full from shoulder to wrist, where they gathered into a fitted cuff. (See

Figure 12.6.) The name "imbecile" derived from the fact that its construction was similar to that of sleeves used on garments for confining mad persons—a sort of "strait jacket" of the period.

Waistlines remained straight, with buckled belts or sashes at the waist, until about 1833 after which V-shaped points were used at the front of the waistline. Skirt lengths changed gradually. At first long, ending at the top of the foot, they shortened about 1828. From the end of the 1820s until about 1836, skirts were ankle length or slightly shorter, then in 1836 they lengthened again, stopping at the instep. From about 1821 to 1828, skirts were fitted through the hips with gores, gradually flaring out to ever-greater fullness at the hem. (See *Figure 12.1*.) After 1828, skirts were fuller through the hips, and this fullness was gathered or pleated into the waist. (See *Figures 12.2* and *12.4*.)

FIGURE 12.4

Dress of gray silk with detachable pelerine and Marie sleeves. (Photograph courtesy, The Metropolitan Museum of Art, gift of Mrs. Frank D. Millet, 1913.)

Pelisse-robe was a name given to a dress for daytime that was adapted from the pelisse that was worn out-of-doors. A sort of coat dress, it closed down the front with buttons, ribbon ties, or, sometimes, hidden hooks and eyes.

The most popular fabrics for daytime dresses included muslins, printed cottons, challis, merinos (wool), and batistes.

Dresses for evening differed from daytime dresses in details, but not in basic silhouette. Necklines were lower, sleeves were shorter, and skirts were shorter. In the 1820s necklines tended to be square, round, or elliptical; in the late 1820s and 1830s, they were more likely to be off-the-shoulder. (See *Figure 12.5.*) Fabrics for evening dresses included silk satins or softer gauzes and organdy held out by full petticoats.

ACCESSORY GARMENTS FOR DRESSES

A number of separate garments were used as accessories to dresses. By varying these, the same dress could be given different appearances.

Fillers, also called **chemisettes** (*shem-eze-zet′*) or **tuckers**, raised the necklines of daytime dresses. They were separate from the dress and could be worn with different bodices. Wide, capelike collars that extended over the shoulders and

FIGURE 12.6

Fichu-pelerine. (*Petite Courrier des Dames*, April 15, 1834. Courtesy, Picture Collection, New York Public Library.)

down across the bosom called **pelerines** (*pel-er-eens′*) were especially popular. (See *Figures 12.4* and *12.15.*) A variant of the pelerine, the **fichu pelerine** (*fee-shu′ pel-er-een*) had two wide panels or lappets extending down the front of the dress and passed under the belt. (See *Figure 12.6.*)

Other popular accessories were the santon (*sahn-tohn′*), a silk cravat worn over a ruff, and the canezou (*can-eh-zoo′*). In some fashion plates, the canezou appears as a small, sleeveless spencer worn over a bodice, and in others as a garment synonymous with the pelerine.

HAIR AND HEADDRESS

See *Illustrated Table 12.1, page 288,* for some examples of hairstyles and headcoverings for the Romantic Period.

Generally women parted their hair at the center front. In the early 1820s, hair around the forehead and temples was arranged in tight curls, and the back pulled into a knot, bun, or (for evening) ringlets. After 1824, elaborate loops or plaits of false hair were added. The style called **à la Chinoise** (*ah la shen-wahs′*) of about 1829 was created by pulling back and side hair into a knot at the top of the head, while hair at forehead and temples was arranged in curls.

FIGURE 12.5

Woman in evening dress of 1835. Her full-skirted white dress, trimmed with pink rosettes and sash, is typical of the period. Her companion is dressed in white trousers, a brown checked vest, and blue coat. (Italian fashion plate from the author's collection.)

Day caps were worn indoors by adult women. These caps were made of white cotton, linen, or silk and often had lace or ribbon trimming. Hats were usually large brimmed with high, round crowns and large feather and lace decorations. Others were bonnet styles that framed the face and tied under the chin. One bonnet, the **capote,** had a soft fabric crown and a stiff brim.

Many hair ornaments were used, and these included jewels, tortoise shell combs, ribbons, flowers, and feathers. For evening, hair ornaments were favored over hats, although berets and turbans were also worn.

Costume for Women: 1836–1850

DRESSES

The silhouette of dresses gradually became more subdued. The change in sleeve shaping has been compared to a balloon that started to deflate. While fullness in the sleeves did not entirely disappear, it moved lower on the arm until about 1840 when sleeves became narrower and more closely fitted. At the same time, skirts lengthened. The result was a subtle change in the feeling of the costume from one of lightness to one of a heavier, almost drooping quality. (See *Figure 12.7.*) Bodices

FIGURE 12.7

On the left is a daytime dress of the 1840s made of barège, a fabric made from a blending of silk and wool fiber. Contrast the more elaborate fabric and garment details of this garment with the one on the right, an everyday dress belonging to a woman of more modest means, which is made of cotton fabric and worn with an embroidered apron. (Photographs courtesy, Division of Costume, American Museum of National History.)

generally ended at the waist, which was likely to come to a point at the front and to close with hooks, buttons, or laces down the front or back. Although dresses were predominantly one piece, there were also some two-piece jacket and skirt styles. Some front-buttoning jacket bodices had short basques (extensions of the bodice below the waist). One popular style was the **gilet corsage** (*jhe-lay kor-sajhe'*), made in imitation of a man's waistcoat. French terms appear frequently in descriptions of fashions on fashion plates or in women's magazines. *Gilet* is French for waistcoat and *corsage* means bodice.

Most sleeves were set low, off the shoulder after 1838. The Cunningtons (1970) identify several sleeve constructions and their fashion names. The **bishop sleeve,** which at this period was made with a row of vertical pleats at the shoulder that released into a soft, full sleeve gathered to a fitted cuff at the wrist, was popular until about 1840. The **sleeve en bouffant** (*ahn boo-fahn*) or **en sabot** (*ahn sah-bow'*) alternated places of tightness with puffed out expansions. A variation of this construction, the **Victoria,** had a puff at the elbow. There were also tight sleeves with decorative frills above the elbow, those with short oversleeves, and others with epaulettes at the shoulder. A new style, seen early in the 1840s, fitted at the shoulder and widened about halfway between the elbow and wrist into a funnel or bell shape. White lace or embroidery-trimmed cotton or linen **undersleeves** were sewn into the wide, open end of the sleeve and could be removed for laundering.

The shape of skirts (whether attached to bodices or separate) was full, that fullness gathered into the waist. Innovations in skirt constructions dating from about 1840 included edging skirt hems with braid to prevent wear and sewing pockets into skirts. Prior to this time, pockets were made separately from dresses and tied around the waist. They were reached through slits in the skirts.

Trimmings included **ruchings** (*roo'shing*) (pleated or gathered strips of fabric), flounces, scallops, and cordings. Many fashion plates show skirts with one, two, or multiple rows of flounces for the entire length of the skirt. The styles depicted on fashion plates are not necessarily representative of the styles worn by ordinary women. For example, although fashion magazines of the 1840s show skirt decorations arranged in a vertical panel at the front or horizontally around the skirt, most extant examples of costumes in collections lack such trims.

The silhouette of evening dresses was similar to that of daytime dresses. Evening dresses were most often made with off-the-shoulder necklines that extended straight across or **en coeur** (*ahn kour*), made with a dip at the center. Many had **berthas** (wide, deep collars following the neckline).

Some gowns had overskirts that were open at the front or puffed up. Silks, especially moiré, organdy, and velvet, were used. Trimmings were more extensive on evening dresses, with lace, ribbon, and artificial flowers being the most popular. (See *Figure 12.8*.)

FIGURE 12.8

Evening dress of 1837 made of gold brocade. The sleeves show the shifting of fullness to a lower position on the arm, which took place in the latter half of the 1830s. (Photograph courtesy, Division of Costume, American Museum of National History.)

HAIR AND HEADDRESS

See *Illustrated Table 12.1*, for some examples of hairstyles and headdresses for the Romantic period, c. 1848.

Parted in the middle, the hair was pulled smoothly to the temples where it was arranged in hanging sausage-shaped curls or in plaits or with a loop of hair encircling the ears. At the back, hair was pulled into a bun or chignon.

Adult women continued to wear small white cotton or linen caps indoors. Some had long, hanging lappets. The predominant hat shape was the bonnet, and both utilitarian and decorative types were worn, including sunbonnets to keep the sun from the faces of women who worked outdoors. These were made of quilted cotton or linen with a **bavolet**

Illustrated Table 12.1

EXAMPLES OF WOMEN'S HAIRSTYLES AND HEADDRESS: 1820–1850

Turban, 1825

Hat, 1825

Hairstyle *à la Chinoise,* c. 1830

Front view of bonnet, 1834

Back view of bonnet, 1834

Hairstyle, 1839

Bonnet with veil over it, 1848

Bonnet, 1848

Contemporary fashion plates.

(*bah-vo-lay'*) or ruffle at the back of the neck to keep the sun off the neck. Fashionable bonnets were often worn with bonnet veils attached to the base of the crown, the veil worn either hanging over the brim or thrown back over the crown.

Fashionable bonnet styles included **drawn bonnets,** made from concentric circles of metal, whalebone or cane and covered in silk; **capotes** (with soft crowns and rigid brims), and small bonnets that framed the face.

For evening, hair decorations were preferred over hats.

Costume Components for Women: 1820–1850

While women's dress silhouettes showed major differences during the years 1820–1836 and 1836–1850, differences in other costume components were less complex and less marked. Therefore, components such as outdoor garments, footwear, and accessories can be discussed for the entire period from 1820 to 1850. See *Illustrated Table 12.2, page 294* for examples of commonly worn accessories.

OUTDOOR GARMENTS

The pelisse followed the general lines of dress and sleeve styles until the mid-1830s (see *Figure 12.9*), when it was replaced by a variety of shawls and mantles that were worn out-of-doors during the day or in the evening. Until about 1836, full-length mantles predominated; later they shortened. Evening styles were made in more luxurious, decorative fabrics such as velvet or satin and trimmed with braid.

Fashion terminology for mantles proliferates. Some of the more commonly seen terms in ladies' magazines include:

· **mantlet** or **shawl-mantlet:** a short garment rather like a hybrid between a shawl and a short mantle with points hanging down at either side of the front.

· **pelerine-mantlet:** with a deep cape, coming well over the elbows and having long, broad front lappets worn over, not under, a belt. (See *Figure 12.10.*)

· **burnous:** a large mantle of about three-quarter length with a hood, the name and style deriving from a similar Arab garment

· **paletot** (*pal-to'*): about knee-length and having three capes and slits for the arms.

· **pardessus** (*par-duh-sue'*): a term applied to any of a number of garments for outdoor wear that had a defined waistline and sleeves and were from one half to three quarters in length.

FOOTWEAR

Generally stockings were knitted of cotton or silk or worsted wool. For evening in the 1830s and 1840s, black silk stockings were fashionable.

Most shoes were of the slipper type. Toes became somewhat square after the late 1820s. (See *Illustrated Table 12.2.*) Very small heels were applied in the late 1840s. Black satin

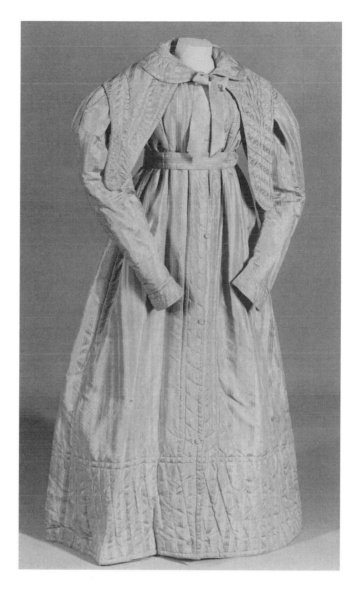

FIGURE 12.9

Striped silk quilted pelisse, c. 1830. (Photograph courtesy, The Metropolitan Museum of Art, gift of Mrs. Frank D. Millet, 1913.)

slippers seem to have predominated for evening until about 1840, when ribbon sandals and white satin evening boots appeared.

In cold weather women wore leather shoes or boots with cloth gaiters (a covering for the upper part of the shoe and the ankle) in colors matching that the shoe. Rubber **galoshes** or overshoes were introduced in the late 1840s.

ACCESSORIES

Gloves were worn for both daytime and evenings. Daytime gloves were short and made of cotton, silk, or kid. Evening gloves were long until the second half of the 1830s, after which

FIGURE 12.10

Pelerine-mantlet. (*Petite Courrier des Dames,* June 1834. Courtesy, Picture Collection, New York Public Library.)

they were shortened. Gloves, cut to cover the palm and back of the hand but not the fingers, were called **mittens** or **mitts.**

Hand-carried accessories included reticules, handbags, purses, fans, muffs, and parasols. When hats were very large (1820s and 1830s) parasols were often carried unopened. Parasols of the 1840s were small and included **carriage parasols** with folding handles.

JEWELRY

In the 1820s and 1830s, women wore gold chains with lockets, scent bottles, or crosses attached. **Chatelaines** (*shat'-te-lehn*) were ornamental chains worn at the waist from which were suspended useful items such as scissors, thimbles, button hooks, and penknives. Other items in wide use were brooches, bracelets, armlets, and drop earrings.

In the 1830s a narrow tress of hair or piece of velvet ribbon was used to suspend a cross or heart of pearls around the neck (called a **Jeanette**). By the 1840s, less jewelry was being worn. Watches were suspended around the neck or placed in a pocket made in the skirt waistband.

COSMETICS AND GROOMING

Rice powder was used to achieve a pale and wan appearance, but obvious rouge or other kinds of face paint were not considered "proper."

COSTUME FOR MEN: THE ROMANTIC PERIOD

Although men's clothing had become more subdued in color and ornamentation, there were subtle details in cut and style that marked the dress of men who wanted to be fashionable. The variety of fashion terms applied to items of men's wardrobes, as well as for women's, increased substantially.

Costume for Men: 1820–1840

GARMENTS

No major changes took place in the kinds of undergarments being worn. Some men used corsets and padding to achieve a fashionable silhouette. (See *Figure 12.11.*)

Shirts were cut with deep collars, long enough to fold over a cravat or neck cloth wrapped around the neck. Daytime shirts had tucked insets at the front; insets for evening shirts were frilled. Sleeves were cuffed, closing with buttons

FIGURE 12.11

Caricature of 1822 depicts the artificial assistance required by some men to achieve a fashionable silhouette: pads at the shoulder, chest, hip, and calf, and a tight corset. (*Monsieur Belle Taille.*) (Photograph courtesy, Division of Costume, American Museum of National History.)

or studs. With these shirts men wore either stocks (wide, shaped neckpieces fastening at the back that were often black) or **cravats** (square cloths folded diagonally into long strips and tied around the neck, finishing in a bow or knot). (See *Illustrated Table 12.2* and *Color Plate 34.*)

Coat, waistcoat, and trousers were the components of a suit. Tail coats and frock coats were the most common types of coats. (See *Figures 12.12, 12.13*, and *Color Plate 35.*) Variations of the frock coat included "military" frock coats that were worn by civilians but with evident military influences. They had a rolled or standing collar and no lapel. Riding coats had exceptionally large collars and lapels.

At least one, sometimes more, waistcoats were worn under the outer or suit coat. These were arranged so as to show only at the edge of the outer coat. Waistcoats were sleeveless and had either straight, standing collars or small, rolled collars without a notch between the collar and lapel. The roll of the collar extended as far as the second or third waistcoat but-

FIGURE 12.12

Left to right: Boy in tunic suit. The jacket has large, demi-gigot sleeves and is worn over contrasting trousers. Man in frock coat, top hat, and trousers. Man dressed in riding coat, knee-breeches, and boots. (*Petite Courrier des Dames*, March 1834. Courtesy, Picture Collection, New York Public Library.)

ton. Both single- and double-breasted waistcoats were worn, although in the 1820s single-breasted styles predominated for daytime wear. Evening waistcoats were white or black, and often made of velvet (see *Color Plate 35*). The ultra-fashionable English "dandies" of the 1820s wore waistcoats in colors contrasting with dark, evening dress suits.

The terms trousers and pantaloons were used interchangeably. Most were close fitting, with an ankle strap or slit that laced to fit the ankle. (See *Figures 12.12* and *12.13.*) In the 1820s it was fashionable to use a different color, or at the least a different shade of the same color, for each part of the costume.

Costume for Men: 1840–1850

The components of a suit (coat, waistcoat, and trousers) underwent some changes. Coat styles were usually either of the tail coat or frock coat types. The tail coat was either single or double breasted. Double-breasted coats had large lapels; single-breasted styles had smaller lapels. Collars were cut high behind the neck, with the rolled collar joined to a lapel to form either a V-shaped or M-shaped notch.

Until 1832 coat sleeves were cut full through the armscye, and gathered into the armhole opening, which made a full puff at the joining. In the 1840s this gathering disappeared, and sleeves fit into the armhole more smoothly. The most fashionable of men's coats had padding in the shoulder and chest areas, the width helping to emphasize a narrow, sometimes corseted, waist. This heavy padding disappeared after about 1837.

A more casual garment than tail coats, frock coats fitted the torso. Its collar, lapel, sleeve construction, and chest and shoulder padding were as described previously, but at the waist a frock coat had a skirt flared out all around ending at about knee level. (After c. 1830, the skirts were somewhat shorter.) After 1830, frock coats were more generally worn during the day, while tail coats were more often used for evening dress. Frock coats were worn for "undress" or casual wear. Coats became longer waisted, skirts narrower and shorter, and sleeves fitted into armholes without gathers. (See *Figures 12.13.*)

New coat styles included a riding coat or **newmarket,** which differed from the tail coat in that the coat sloped gradually to the back from well above the waist, rather than having a squared, open area at the front. Jacket styles were single breasted, with or without a seam at the waist. Jackets had side pleats and no back vent. The front closing was fairly straight, curved back slightly below the waist to stand open. Collars and lapels were small, and pockets placed low, with or without flaps.

Waistcoats lengthened and developed a point at the front (called a **Hussar front** or **beak**). Lapels narrowed and were less curved. By the end of the 1840s, however, lapels grew wider again and were sometimes worn turned over the edge

FIGURE 12.13

Left to right: Boy's coat is made of plaid cotton, his hat of silk. The gentleman wears a green wool tailcoat, linen trousers with a fall front closing, and a top hat of straw. The girl is dressed in a dark green silk pelisse and a white dimity cap (second quarter of the 19th century). (Courtesy, The Metropolitan Museum of Art, The Costume Institute.)

of coat collars and lapels. Wedding waistcoats were white or cream colored; evening waistcoats were made of silk satin, velvet, and cashmere.

By 1840, breeches were limited to sportswear and ceremonial full dress and trousers were daily wear. The name "trousers" gradually superseded the term "pantaloons." Fly-front closures were replacing fall closures for trousers.

Dressing gowns were worn at home, especially in the mornings. They were made of vivid colors. The cut did not change markedly from styles of the Empire period. (See *Color Plate 37.*)

Costume for Men: 1820–1850

OUTDOOR GARMENTS

After the 1820s, the spencer went out of fashion but many other garments were quite similar to those of the Empire period and included:

- **greatcoats:** a general term for overcoats. (See *Figure 12.14.*) Single- or double-breasted, often to the ankle, their collars had a deep roll. Coats were made with and without lapels.

- **box coats:** large, loose greatcoats with one or more capes at the shoulder. (In the 1840s this coat was likely to be called a **curricle coat.**)

Some new terminology developed.

- **paletot:** a term first used in the 1830s. The styles to which the term was applied vary over time. At this period it appears to have been a short greatcoat, either single or double breasted, with a small flat collar and lapels. Sometimes it had a waist seam, sometimes not.

- **chesterfield:** The chesterfield was named after the Sixth Earl of Chesterfield, who was influential in English social life in the 1830s and 1840s. This term is used first in the 1840s and then applied to a coat with either a single- or double-breasted closing, although the double-breasted closing has since been more closely associated with this term. The coat had no waistline seam, a short vent in the back, no side pleats, and often had a velvet collar.

- **mackintosh:** a waterproof coat made of rubber and cut like a short, loose overcoat. Invented at this time, the mackintosh was named after its inventor. Waterproof cloaks and paletots are also mentioned. These early mackintoshes did not meet with universal approval. The

FIGURE 12.14

Overcoat of the 1830s. Note fullness in sleeve cap and close fit through the body, characteristics that disappeared in the 1840s. (Photograph courtesy, Division of Costume, American Museum of National History.)

Cunningtons (1970) quote complaints that "... the mackintosh is now becoming a troublesome thing in town from the difficulty of their being admitted to an omnibus on account of the offensive stench which they emit."

Cloaks were especially used for evening dress. (See Color Plate 35.) Cut with gores and fitting smoothly at the neck and shoulder, capes had both large flat collars and semi-standing collars. Some had multiple capes at the shoulders. Late in the period, evening cloaks became more elaborate, many with large sleeves with slits in front that allowed the sleeve to hang behind the arm like a medieval hanging sleeve. Lengths var-

ied. In the late 1830s and the 1840s, a short, round, full so-called Spanish cape lined in silk of a contrasting collar was worn for evening.

HAIR AND HEADDRESS

Most men wore their hair in loose curls or loosely waved, short to moderate in length, and cut short at the back. Beards, beginning with a small fringe of whiskers, returned to fashion around 1825, and gradually grew to larger proportions.

The **top hat** was the predominant headwear style for day and evening. Different names were applied to top hats, based on subtle differences in shape. The crown was a cylinder of varying height and shape, ranging from those that looked like inverted pots to tubes with a slight outward curve at the top. Brims were small, sometimes turned up at the side. The **gibus hat**, a collapsible top hat for evening named for its inventor, was fitted with a spring so that the hat could be folded flat and carried under the arm. Hats that were called **derby hats** (in the United States) or **bowlers** (in England) began to be worn at the close of the period. These hats had stiff, round, bowl-shaped crowns with narrow brims. Caps were favored for sports. (See Illustrated Table 12.2.)

FOOTWEAR

Most stockings were knitted from worsted, cotton, or silk. Shoes had square toes and low heels. Shoes lacing up the front through three or four eyelets came into use in the 1830s. Formal footwear was open over the instep and tied shut with a ribbon bow. Boots were important for riding. The first rubber soles for shoes were made about 1832. By the 1840s rubber overshoes, galoshes, and elastic-sided shoes were available.

Bedroom slippers were worn at home. Women's magazines frequently included patterns for making needlepoint slippers as a gift for gentlemen.

Gaiters made of sturdy cloth and added to shoes for bad weather or for hunting were called **spatterdashers** or **spats.** Those worn for sports ended below the knee; those for every day were ankle length. Elastic gaiters were invented in the 1840s.

ACCESSORIES

The most important accessories for men were gloves, usually made of doeskin or kid leather, of worsted wool, or of cotton for daytime; and of silk or kid for evening. Men who took snuff (a tobacco that was inhaled) carried pocket handkerchiefs because inhaling snuff caused sneezing. Canes and umbrellas were used for rainy weather.

JEWELRY

Men wore little jewelry other than such items as cravat pins, brooches worn on shirt fronts, watches, jeweled shirt buttons and studs, and decorative gold watch chains and watches.

Illustrated Table 12.2

ROMANTIC PERIOD: ACCESSORIES

Woman's chatelaine,
an ornamental cluster
of small tools worn
hanging from the waist

Small beaded handbag,
c. 1820–1840

Variously shaped
men's top hats
c. 1830–1840

Women's shoes of the 1840s:
(A) Flat heel with a squared toe
(B) Low-heeled laced boot
(C) Boot with an elastic inset gusset

Cravat that wraps
around neck and ties
in front with a bow,
c. 1830

Parasol, c. 1830s

Women's gloves, c. 1830s and 1840s
(A) Fingerless glove called a mitt or mitten, made of black silk net
(B) Short kid glove

COSTUME FOR CHILDREN: THE ROMANTIC PERIOD

Children of the late 18th century through the Empire period seem to have escaped from wearing uncomfortable, burdensome clothing. This was thanks to the relative simplicity of adult women's clothing and the tendency to dress children in less constricting styles than in adult styles. During the Romantic period, the clothes for children reverted to some extent to less comfortable clothes based on adult fashions.

Both boys' and girls' costumes in fashion plates of the period are curiously like fashion plates of adult styles. When narrow waists for both men and women were emphasized in the drawings, the children were likewise given abnormally small waists. During the time that women's sleeves ballooned out to enormous proportions, not only little girls but also little boys were depicted in the awkward, large sleeves. (See *Figure 12.12*.)

Although the clothing depicted in the fashion plate may be somewhat exaggerated, a comparison of the clothes of the boy drawn in the plate in *Figure 12.12* with the actual tunic suit in *Figure 12.15* does indicate that real garments could be very much like those drawn in fashion magazines.

Costume Components for Girls

Girls' dresses were like those of women, but shorter and with low necklines and short sleeves. White, lace-trimmed drawers, or leglets, a sort of half-pantalette that tied around the leg, were worn under dresses.

Some kind of hat, bonnet, or starched lingerie cap was worn out-of-doors.

Costume Components for Boys

Until age five or six most boys were dressed in skirts, after which they were put into trousers. Boys, like men, wore suits. The skeleton suit, a carryover from the Empire period (see *Figure 12.15*), was worn until about 1830. The **Eton suit** consisted of a short, single-breasted jacket, ending at the waist. The front was cut square, the lapels wide with a turned down collar. The suit was completed with a necktie, vest or waistcoat, and trousers. This style derived from the school boy clothing worn at Eton School in England. This suit, with minor variations, remained a basic style for young boys for the rest of the century.

The **tunic suit** consisted of a jacket, fitted to the waist where it attached to a full, gathered or pleated skirt that ended at the knee. It buttoned down the front, often had a wide belt. Usually worn with trousers, some versions for small boys aged three to six combined the tunic jacket with frilled, white drawers. (See *Figures 12.12* and *12.15*.)

FIGURE 12.15

Left to right: Boy's tunic suit and matching trousers, c. 1838; woman's dress of moiré silk with gigot sleeves and a double pelerine of white, embroidered mull, c. 1836; boy's wool skeleton suit, c. 1830. Note that the children's sleeve constructions are similar to the styles popular for adult women. (Photograph courtesy, The Metropolitan Museum of Art, The Costume Institute.)

Jackets, in combination with trousers, were cut like those of adult men. Boys did not wear frock or dress coats, however.

FOOTWEAR FOR BOYS AND GIRLS

Both boys and girls wore ankle-high boots. Slippers were more often seen on girls than on boys. Both boys and girls wore white cotton stockings.

CLOTHING FOR SLAVES IN NORTH AMERICA

Recent scholarly interest in clothing of the enslaved has provided some insights into the dress of slaves in the decades before the Civil War. Few depictions of slaves exist. Those that do often reflect the bias for or against slavery of the individual who created the picture. Several garments that may have been worn by slaves have been preserved and studied (Tandberg 1980).

Advertisements for runaway slaves always described what they had been wearing in detail. (See *Contemporary Comments 12.1* for newspaper notices.) Oral histories were taken in the 1930s from former slaves. Some former slaves, slave owners, and visitors to the South kept diaries and journals. Plantation inventories and financial records exist that listed purchases of cloth or clothing for slaves. From these various sources, researchers have gleaned some information and more is certain to be added as research proceeds.

Warner and Parker (1990), describing North Carolina practices, reported that most owners issued two outfits of clothing a year to slaves. One outfit was for the warm months and one for the cold. This usually amounted to an allotment of materials to make the clothes. One plantation owner entered these amounts into his diary: for the winter: "six yards of woolen cloth, six yards of cotton drilling [which later became a fabric used for summer uniforms for the army and navy], a needle, a skein of thread, and 1/2 dozen buttons." Information collected from former slaves, however, indicates this practice was not universal. As Thomas H. Jones, an enslaved man from North Carolina reported, "Once a year [the master] distributed clothing to his slaves . . . The slaves were obliged to make up their own clothes, after the severe labor of the plantation had been performed. Any other clothing, beyond this yearly supply, which they might need, the slaves were compelled to get by extra work, or do without" (quoted in Foster 1997).

Fabrics were coarse and harsh, either homespun or purchased from manufacturers in Rhode Island and Europe who provided the "cheapest, meanest cloth for slave purposes" (Warner 1993). The name **negro cloth** was given to a coarse, white homespun used for slaves in the West Indies and the American South.

While house slaves were dressed more fashionably, perhaps even in hand-me-downs from white owners, no attention was wasted on the niceties of style for field hand clothing. Fabrics were generally not dyed, unless the wearers

themselves were able to dye the fabric with natural dyestuffs and slave accounts speak of dyeing with materials such as indigo, which had to be purchased, and tree bark, poison ivy, sumac, and other plants (Foster 1997).

Tandberg (1980) describes the dress of slave women as being of two types. One consisted of a "frock" or "robe" with a simple, sleeveless and collarless bodice joined to a skirt. If the bodice had sleeves, they were short and "set into loose armscyes." The neck was V shaped, skirt lengths ranged from below the knee to the top of the foot. The other type had a semi-fitted bodice with a round neckline (sometimes an attached collar), long, loose sleeves, and a gathered skirt. Some pictures show a shortened version of this frock worn over a skirt, and quite similar to short gowns (see *page 230*).

Men wore loose-fitting shirts, cut to require as little sewing as possible, over loose pantaloons or short breeches. Children wore a sort of long shirt. At least one diary entry does indicate that little girls may sometimes have been given dresses, and some examples of boys' pantaloons and sleeveless shirts have been preserved at one Mississippi plantation (Tandberg 1980).

Whenever possible, slaves decorated their clothing items and tried to personalize them. Baumgarten (1992) notes that they did this by trimming and dyeing clothing in an individualistic style, by making some of their own clothing, and by purchasing extra clothing or accessories with money earned through tips and sale of farm products that they grew. Clearly attempts were made to conform to current fashion. Reports from formerly enslaved men and women tell of the ways women attempted to conform to fashion when hoopskirts became fashionable in the late 1850s. Some apparently made hoops from grapevines, from flexible thin limbs of trees, or used stiff paper to support skirts (Foster 1997).

Even so, active and free participation in the fashion process was not possible for slaves. Their clothing generally served to mark their status. (See *Figure 12.16*.) Escape to the North, especially to Canada, could bring freedom. Runaway slaves knew that they must dress like freed slaves in order to avoid capture. For this reason, they often took more fashionable clothing to wear or to sell on their journey. Once free, they dressed as did other Americans. (See *Color Plate 34*.)

Clothing of Runaway Slaves

Antebellum period descriptions of clothing worn by African-Americans, whether slaves or free, are rare. One place that contemporary records of their clothing is to be found is in newspapers. Owners of runaway slaves or prison officials who had arrested individuals suspected of being escaped slaves placed notices in local newspapers. Such listings generally included a description of the clothing they wore.

The Globe, a semi-weekly newspaper in Washington, D.C. regularly printed notices of apprehended slaves. The following reprints one such notice, to provide the flavor of the context in which the clothing descriptions appeared.

October 12, 1831. NOTICE		
Was committed to the prison of Washing County, D.C., on the 17th of September, 1831, as a runaway Negroman, who calls himself Jacob Johnson: he is 5 feet 5 inches high, had on when committed a bang-up roundabout[1] and pantaloons. he says he is a	free man; he is very light complected, and has a black mole on the right side of his nose; he has a very heavy black beard on his upper lip and chin; he has a very large square-looking face, a pleasant look when spoken to, he is about 37 years of age. The owner or	owners of the above described negroman are requested to come forward and prove him and take him away or he will be sold for his prison and other expenses, as the law directs.

A number of descriptions quoted from other similar notices in The Globe are listed below:

July 16, 1831: . . ."had on when committed, an old drab peacoat, and dark colored pantaloons." August 10, 1831: "She had on when committed, a light colored calico dress." September 14, 1831: "Had on when committed a Grey Virginia Cassimere[2] coatee, a pair of Black	Ratinett[3] Pantaloons and an old Fur Hat." September 21, 1831: . . ."had on, when committed, linen pantaloons, domestic roundabout and vest, black hat, very much worn." October 26, 1831: "His clothing were cassinet[4] coat and cordury [sic] pantaloons—hat and shoes."	"Her clothing consisted of a striped cotton frock, bonnet, shoes and stockings." "His clothing when committed were cassinet coatee, and pantaloons, palm leaf hat—and wears rings in his ears." November 12, 1831: . . ."had on when committed a striped linsey dress and check apron."

The Georgia Advertiser of Augusta, Georgia, March 2, 1822 carried an advertisement for two "runaway slaves" who were described as wearing:

Of the first person it was said, ". . . and wore away a blue broadcloth coat, with covered buttons, black cloth waistcoat,	and blue jeans pantaloons." The second person wore, ". . . blue broadcloth	coat, yellow striped waistcoat, and black cassimere pantaloons."

The Globe, Washington, DC and *Georgia Advertiser*, Augusta, GA
[1]A roundabout is a jacket.
[2]Cassimere was a wool cloth, of medium weight with a twill weave.
[3]A cheap, coarse worsted wool cloth.
[4]A modified form of cassimere, sometimes also called "negro cloth."

FIGURE 12.16

Men and women who have just been freed from slavery during the American Civil War. The women are dressed in similar simple, unornamented one-piece cotton dresses of a cut like that which predominated between 1848 and 1865. All wear headcloths. The men's dress varies from suits to shirts and trousers, sometimes worn with vests. (Collection of the J. Paul Getty Museum, Los Angeles, California, Henry P. Moore, "Slaves of General Thomas F. Drayton," 1862.)

SUMMARY

THEMES

The theme of **RELATIONSHIPS BETWEEN COSTUME AND DEVELOPMENTS IN THE FINE AND APPLIED ARTS** continued to be evident as classical styles gave way to those of the Romantic movement. Literary works, as well as the visual arts, contributed to a broad interest in and **REVIVAL** of styles from the past. **POLITICS** also contributed to this interest in the past. The French monarchy had been restored and the population, at least for a time, glorified past monarchs such as the 17th century Henry IV. Costume recalled history with such features as hanging sleeves, neck ruffs, and standing lace collars.

Toward the end of this period, a new **MEDIUM OF COMMUNICATION**, photography, was invented, adding to the variety of **SOURCES OF INFORMATION ABOUT COSTUME**. The

Visual Summary Table

ROMANTIC PERIOD

Man 1820–1840
Shirt, waist-length waistcoat, trousers,
worn under a frock style or tailcoat
often with nipped-in waistline and
slightly puffed sleeve cap.

Man: 1840–1850
Shirt, waistcoat, trousers worn
with tailcoats for dress; frock coats
for everyday. Skirts of coats narrow
slightly, waistline falls.

Woman: 1820–1835
Waistline closer to anatomical
waistline, skirts wider, and short
enough that ankles may show. Sleeves
may be very large.

Woman: 1836–1850
Full, less buoyant appearing skirts
lower to floor. Waistline at anatomical
placement. Dropped shoulder line
for narrower sleeves.

number of publications for women that carried fashion news and hand-colored fashion plates also increased.

Looking at these plates it is clear that the Romantic period was one of evolution, which brings in another persistent theme, FASHION. For women this evolution can be seen in the gradual shift of the waistline from the Empire placement to a lower position, slightly above the natural, anatomical waist, and finally by the close of the period to the natural position. Sleeves, too, evolved year by year, first enlarging gradually until they reached maximum dimensions, then collapsing with the fullness moving gradually down the arm. Hemlines shortened gradually, then lengthened just as gradually.

In men's styles there were echoes of the changes in women's styles and an evolutionary development. The sleeves of men's coats grew larger, then smaller again. The skirts of frock coats widened, then narrowed. At the same time the GENDER DIFFERENCES of subdued colors and styles for men and more fanciful styles for women that had been established at the beginning of the century continued.

By the end of the period a new fashionable look had been established that was a marked contrast to that seen in the early years of the 1820s. This new style can also be seen as a reflection of the theme of PATTERNS OF SOCIAL BEHAVIOR. Women were expected to be "genteel instead of jolly" (Cunnington 1935)—"the bounce was gone, replaced by a sensitive fragility" (Squire 1974).

SURVIVALS OF ROMANTIC PERIOD COSTUME STYLES

Romantic period styles in women's dress incorporated a number of elements from earlier periods. Even so, a few distinctive elements from this period did appear again later in the century. The leg of mutton sleeve made its first appearance in the early Romantic period. It was revived in the 1890s, although its shape was not precisely the same as in the 1830s. (See *Figure 14.12, page 345.*) Many wedding dresses of the late 1980s also utilized large, leg-of-mutton style sleeves.

The bertha, a neckline style of the 1840s, continued in use into the 1850s and 60s, then disappeared. It was revived again in the 40s and 50s, especially for evening wear.

NOTES

Baumgarten, L. 1992. "Personal Expression in Slaves' Clothing and Appearance before 1830." Costume Society of America: Symposium Abstracts, May 22–30, San Antonio, TX, p. 17.

Cunnington, C. W. 1935. *Feminine Attitudes in the 19th Century.* London: Heinemann.

Cunnington, C. W. and P. Cunnington. 1970. *Handbook of English Costume in the 19th Century.* London: Faber and Faber, pp. 142, 385 ff.

Foster, H. B. 1997 *"New Raiments of Self:" African American Clothing in the Antebellum South.* New York: Berg, pp. 112–113, 137, 170.

Harris, R. W. 1969. *Romanticism and the Social Order.* New York: Barnes and Noble, p. 19.

Squire, G. 1974. *Dress and Society.* New York: Viking, p. 159.

Tandberg, G. G. 1980. "Field Hand Clothing in Louisiana and Mississippi During the Ante-Bellum Period." *Dress,* Vol. 5, p. 90.

Warner, P. C. 1993. Information provided in correspondence.

Warner, P. C. and D. Parker. 1990. "Slave Clothing and Textiles in North Carolina, 1775–1835." in B. M. Starke, L. O. Holloman, and B. Nordquist, eds., *African American Dress and Adornment: A Cultural Perspective.* Dubuque, IA: Kendall/Hunt, p. 84.

SELECTED READINGS

Books Containing Illustrations of Costume of the Period from Original Sources

Fashion Magazines: *Godey's Lady's Book, Peterson's Magazine.*

Coleman, E. A. 1972. *Changing Fashions: 1800–1970.* New York: Brooklyn Museum.

Dalrymple, P. 1991. *American Victorian Costume in Early Photographs.* New York: Dover.

Gibbs-Smith, C. H. 1960. *The Fashionable Lady in the 19th Century.* London: Her Majesty's Stationery Office.

Holland, V. B. 1955. *Hand Coloured Fashion Plates, 1770–1899.* London: Batsford.

Johnson, J. M. 1991. *French Fashion Plates of the Romantic Era in Full Color.* New York: Dover.

Severa, J. 1995. *Dressed for the Photographer. Ordinary Americans and Fashion 1840–1900.* Kent, OH: Kent State University Press.

Tarrant, N. 1983. *The Rise and Fall of the Sleeve 1825–1840.* Edinburgh: Royal Scottish Museum.

Periodical and Short Articles

Back, A. M. 1983. "Clothes in Fact and Fiction, 1825–1865." *Costume,* No. 17, p. 89.

Coleman, E. J. 1979. "Boston's Atheneum for Fashions." *Dress,* Vol. 5, p. 25.

Finkel, A. 1984. "Le Bal Costume: History and Spectacle in the Court of Queen Victoria." *Dress,* Vol. 10, p. 64.

Tandberg, G. G. 1980. "Field Hand Clothing in Louisiana and Mississippi During the Antebellum Period." *Dress,* Vol. 5, p. 90.

Tandberg, G. G. and S. G. Durand. 1981. "Dress-up Clothes for Field Slaves of Antebellum Louisiana and Mississippi." *Costume,* No. 15, p. 40.

Warner, P. C. and D. Parker. 1990. "Slave Clothing and Textiles in North Carolina 1775–1835." In B. M. Starke, L.O. Holloman, and B. Nordquist, eds., *African American Dress and Adornment: A Cultural Perspective.* Dubuque, IA: Kendall/Hunt.

Daily Life

Burton, E. 1978. *Pageant of Early Victorian England, 1837–1861.* New York: Scribners.

Eisler, B. 1977. *The Lowell Offerings: Writings by New England Mill Women (1840–1845).* New York: Lippincott.

Lacour-Gayet, R. 1969. *Everyday Life in the United States Before the Civil War.* New York: Frederick Ungar.

Larkin, J. 1989. *The Reshaping of Everyday Life. 1790–1840.* New York: Perennial.

Laver, J. 1972. *The Age of Illusion.* New York: David McKay.

Page, T. N. 1897 (reprint). *Social Life in Old Virginia Before the War.* New York: Scribners.

Wright, L. B. 1972. *Everyday Life in the New Nation: 1787–1860.* New York: Putnam's.

CHRONOLOGY

1850–1870
Queen Victoria continues to occupy the British throne

1851
Isaac M. Singer invents the first practical sewing machine

1852
Louis Napoleon becomes Napoleon III and the
Second French Republic becomes the Second Empire

1857
Hoopskirt or cage crinoline is introduced

1858
Charles Worth opens couture establishment in Paris

1859
Charles Darwin publishes his theory of evolution in *Origin of Species*

1860
Charles Worth meets the Empress Eugenie and begins to design her clothes

1861
Reunification of Italy

1861–1865
Civil War in the United States

1862
Congress passes the Morill Act, establishing Land Grant Colleges

1863
Emancipation Proclamation ends slavery in the United States
Ebenezer Butterick patents the first sized, paper patterns for clothing

1865
Abraham Lincoln is assassinated

1867
The United States purchases Alaska from Russia
Harper's Bazaar, fashion magazine, begins publication

1869
Transcontinental railroad completed

THE CRINOLINE PERIOD

1850 – 1869

A.

D.

B.

A.

Lyndhurst:
Gothic revival house

B.

Rococo revival furniture

C.

Gothic revival cottage

D.

Renaissance revivval furniture

E.

Early impressionist painting
by Claude Monet, *Garden at Sainte-Adresse*, 1867

C.

E.

Figures A, C courtesy of V. R. Tortora. Figure D from Lavisse, E. 1907. *Album Historique Le XVIII Le XIX Siècle*. Paris: Librairie Armand Colin, p. 238. Figure B courtesy of J. Curcio in Federico, J. T., 1988. *Clues to American Furniture*. Washington: Starrhill, p. 47. Figure E courtesy of the Metropolitan Museum of Art (67.241).

The **cage crinoline,** the major fashion innovation for women in the 1850s, provided the name for this period. The increasing width of women's skirts had led to the use of more and more stiffened petticoats. When the hoop skirts of the 18th century were revived to hold out these voluminous skirts, the editor of *Peterson's Magazine* hailed its revival in September 1856:

> There can be no doubt that, so long as wide and expanded skirts are to be worn, it is altogether healthier to puff them out with a light hoop than with half-a-dozen starched cambric petticoats as has been the practice until lately. Physicians are now agreed that a fertile source of bad health with females is the enormous weight of skirts previously worn. The hoop avoids that evil entirely. It also, if properly adjusted, gives a lighter and more graceful appearance to the skirt.

WORTH AND THE PARIS COUTURE

The person who invented the hoop skirt—or rather who chose to revive it, for it had been used in much the same form in the early 1700s and 1500s—is not known. Many sources have given the credit to Charles Frederick Worth, but there is no evidence that he actually originated the style. Charles Worth was an Englishman who could claim to be the founder of the French couture. With only 117 francs and unable to speak a word of French, he came to Paris to work in the fabric houses. While an employee of the Maison Gagelin, he began to have his attractive French wife wear dresses he had designed. Soon customers began to request that similar designs be made for them. After leaving Gagelin in 1858, he set up his own establishment. He was aware that to be successful he must gain the patronage of influential women, and so he presented his designs to the Princess Pauline Metternich, wife of the Austrian ambassador. She was an important figure at the court of Emperor Louis Napoleon III and the arbiter of Paris fashion. The success of the gowns Worth made for the Princess helped him to win the favor of the Empress Eugenie, and soon all of fashionable Paris waited in the anterooms of his salon.

Worth dressed the most respectable as well as the most notorious women of the world. His clients ranged from Queen Victoria to Cora Pearl, a well-known courtesan. He sold designs wholesale for adaptation by foreign dressmakers and stores. A unique aspect of Worth's talent was his engineering. He designed clothes so that each part would fit interchangeably with another. For example, each sleeve could fit any number of different bodices and, conversely, each bodice any number of sleeve styles. Bodices could fit any number of skirts.

Until the 1880s Worth worked as a couturier. After his retirement his sons continued the business, organizing the couture, which had expanded since their father opened his salon, into the **Chambre Syndicale de la Couture Parisienne,** an organization of couturiers that is still active in the French haute couture. In the 1920s and 1930s, the House of Worth declined in importance. It closed after World War II, although a perfume bearing the name of Worth is still sold.

HISTORICAL BACKGROUND

England

In this era, the accepted ideal of womanhood was the virtuous wife and mother. The British found the perfect example of their ideal in their young queen, Victoria. In 1840 she married a German prince, Albert, and became the model of sedate, respectable motherhood for the British. She brought to the throne a sense of a loving family, something especially lacking among British monarchs of that period.

In mid-century, Britain enjoyed prosperity marked by increasing imports and exports, expanding production of iron and steel, and industrial growth. Other nations not only envied Britain's industry, but also tried to emulate its success. Nothing symbolized the well-being of Britain so much as the Great Exhibition of 1851, which was held in a specially designed great glass building in Hyde Park. There more than 7,000 British exhibitors demonstrated their products as evidence of Victorian progress.

France

Worth helped Paris once again become the fashion center of Europe. The city had passed through bloody days: revolutions in 1830 and again in 1848 with fighting in the streets. A Second Republic, proclaimed after King Louis Philippe had abdicated in 1848, enjoyed a short life. The French president, Louis Napoleon, who was the nephew of Napoleon Bonaparte, staged a coup d'etat. In 1852, following a carefully staged election that approved a Second Empire, he assumed the title of Emperor Napoleon III.

During the Second Empire France regained the leadership of Europe and Paris again became a world capital. The Tuileries Palace became the center of social life in the glamorous city where the beautiful Empress Eugenie presided over a glittering court. Kings, princes, princesses, statesmen, and their ladies flocked to the court, bejeweled and dressed in the best of Paris fashion. Once again masked balls became the rage, offering ladies opportunities to display fanciful gowns.

Although his glittering court was the most brilliant and colorful since the old monarchy, Louis Napoleon was himself a man of conservative and simple tastes. In the morning he dressed in a dark blue coat, a waistcoat, and gray trousers. The ribbons of the Legion of Honor and a military medal were the only symbols of authority that he wore. In the evening for concerts and official dinners he wore the typical evening dress of the period: a tail coat with black knee breeches and silk stockings, and for really gala events he dressed in a general's uniform with his tunic covered with orders and crosses.

His wife, Eugenie de Montijo, a Spanish countess who was much younger than he, was considered quite beautiful. Although she dressed lavishly for state occasions, Eugenie really had little interest in clothes. Actually she was reluctant to adopt new fashions even after they had become popular. At home she wore a plain black dress. Eugenie followed fashion; she was not a fashion setter.

Nevertheless the arrangements for the storage of her wardrobe were formidable. Her dressing room was located directly beneath a group of rooms in which wardrobes with sliding panels were located. Here her clothing was arranged in perfect order. Four dressmaker forms with the exact measurements of the empress served a twofold purpose. They made it unnecessary for Eugenie to try on her clothes too often when they were being made. When her costume for the day had been selected, the figure was dressed, and the form—complete with all parts of the costume—was lowered by elevator through an opening in the ceiling of her dressing room.

To be a guest at the court or one of the royal residences required a considerable wardrobe. A visiting American socialite described her wardrobe for a week at one of the royal residences.

> I was obliged to have about twenty dresses, eight day costumes (counting my traveling suit), the green cloth dresses for the hunt, which I was told was absolutely necessary, seven ball dresses, five gowns for tea (Hegermann-Lindencrone 1912).

But the glamorous Second Empire had to end. Although Napoleon III did much for the economic life of the Empire, including the rebuilding of Paris, his foreign adventures led to his downfall. In the 1860s his fortunes began to decline. After Prussia defeated France in 1870, the emperor abdicated and fled to Britain, where he spent the remainder of his life in exile with Eugenie and their son. The Second Empire vanished to be replaced by the more somber Third Republic. Paris, however, never conceded its position as the fashion center of Europe.

The United States

In the United States the Crinoline period coincided with the Civil War. The American population was about twenty-three million, and a little more than half of these people lived west of the Alleghenies. Twelve percent of the population was foreign born. In 1850 there were 141 cities of more than 8,000 residents, containing 16 percent of the population.

By this time, thanks to the Industrial Revolution, the annual output of mills and factories had surpassed the value of agricultural products, and manufacturing was concentrated in the northeastern states. Already the nation was bound together by a network of turnpikes, rivers, canals, and railroads. By 1870 East and West were connected by transcontinental railroads.

Although education remained predominantly private, the foundations of public school education had been laid. In 1862 Congress passed the Morill Act establishing the land grant system of higher education. The new colleges were intended to emphasize a more practical education in agriculture and industry.

The women's rights movement had begun and would get increased impetus through an alliance of this movement with the anti-slavery and temperance (anti-alcohol) movements. Women still lived under many legal and social restrictions. They had no legal control over property; they lacked the vote; and as late as 1850, some states allowed a husband to beat his wife with a "reasonable instrument."

Religion had a strong influence in pre-Civil War America; some forms of religious expression were allied with an interest in Utopian societies. Some of these groups even developed their own form of dress. The costume worn by women of the Oneida colony in New York State, composed of a bodice, loose trousers, and a skirt ending slightly above the knees, was similar to the Bloomer costume (see page 307).

THE GOLD RUSH AND THE
ORIGINS OF LEVI'S

The discovery of gold at Sutter's Mill in California in 1848 brought more than 40,000 prospectors to California within the next two years. Along with the miners came entrepreneurs who saw potential markets for selling products the miners would need. According to tradition, the garment called **Levi's** originated when one Levi Strauss took a supply of heavy-duty canvas to San Francisco in 1850 to sell to Gold Rush miners for tents. The miners complained that their pants didn't last long under the rough wear of mining and Mr. Strauss, seeing an unanticipated use for his canvas, hired a tailor to make "sturdy, close-fitting work pants." The success of the first pants meant that Strauss needed more fabric, and this time he requested **denim,** and had the fabric dyed blue with indigo. Miners liked the pants, telling others about "those pants that Levi made for us," and thus the term Levi's, often used synonymously with **blue jeans,** was born (Ratner 1975). The generic term "blue jeans," eventually shortened to "jeans," derives from the color and name of the fabric of which these work pants were made. Jean is a heavy twill-weave cotton fabric, very much like denim, and indigo blue dye produced dark blue, a color with good fastness (durability of the color).

The firm established by Levi Strauss flourished. Blue jeans became a basic item of work clothing for farmers, cowboys, and laborers. The features now associated with the trademarked Levi's® were gradually added: riveted pockets and stitching a double arc design on the back pockets with orange thread in 1873, a leather patch with two horse brands in 1886, belt loops in 1922, a red tab trademark on back pockets in 1936, and concealed back pocket rivets in 1937. Zippers were added to some styles in 1954. From their beginnings in 1850 up to the present day, Levi's have remained important costume components.

THE CIVIL WAR AND COSTUME

National divisions over slavery came to a head in the war between the North and South, the bloodiest conflict in American history. The Civil War had profound and far-reaching effects on American society, the political system, and the economy. The conflict halted secession and ended slavery. It strengthened the central government at the expense of the states, which were no longer members of a voluntary confederation but now belonged to a nation. The Civil War also accelerated the spread of mechanization and the factory system. The number of sewing machines doubled between 1860 and 1865. The production of shoes increased during the war with the development of machines to sew the uppers to the soles.

Although the war had little direct influence on the continuity of Western fashion, which in any event was being set abroad, women living in the beleaguered South were forced to rely on their ingenuity to keep up with fashion. Because the Union fleet was blockading Southern ports, the importation of foreign goods ceased. Moreover, the major manufacturers of textiles were located in the North so that even domestically produced goods were unavailable. In addition, fashion magazines were printed in Northern cities such as Philadelphia and Boston.

For one Southern woman the first year of the war presented little difficulty because "most of us had on hand a large supply of clothing." But Southern women continued the practice of giving away clothing they had tired of only to regret it later, wondering how they "could ever been so foolish as to give away anything so little worn." They were grateful for the popularity of skirts and blouses, which could be made from scarves, aprons, or shawls, and for tight sleeves, which could be cut down from the wide ones so popular in preceding years.

Women had to patch their clothes and piece them with scraps cut from worn-out clothes. Inflation also took its toll. Milliners paid $150 in Confederate dollars for an old velvet bonnet that they then renovated and sold for $500. In the final year of the war, $1,000 was not considered an unreasonable price for a hat (Hay 1866).

An extended excerpt from a Southern woman's account of the problems Southern women encountered with their clothing as a result of the Northern blockade of Southern ports is reprinted in *Contemporary Comments 13.1*.

PRODUCTION OF CLOTHING: THE SEWING MACHINE

The first patents on the sewing machine were taken out in the 1840s. Public response to the new device was not overwhelming because the cost was relatively high, at least $100. In 1857, James Gibbs, a Virginia farmhand, devised a simpler, less expensive type of sewing machine that he marketed for about $50.

But it was Isaac Singer, mechanic, unemployed actor, and inventor who developed one of the most successful sewing machines. Singer's sewing machines became one of the first domestic appliances manufactured on a production line basis using interchangeable parts. Consequently, the Singer sewing machines could be produced in quantities sufficient to reduce the price substantially.

Singer also pioneered innovative sales methods. He displayed his sewing machines in elaborate showrooms where pretty young ladies not only demonstrated the sewing machines but also taught purchasers how to operate them. Singer sold his machines to seamstresses on the installment plan: five dollars down and the remainder, with interest, in monthly installments. To interest respectable ladies in purchasing sewing machines, Singer sold his machines at half price to church-connected sewing societies in the hope that each member would soon want to own her own sewing machine. The Singer Company also allowed $50 credit on an old sewing machine when a customer purchased a new one.

But it was the Civil War that demonstrated the usefulness of the sewing machine. The war generated an immediate and enormous demand for ready-to-wear uniforms: the Northern Army wore out over a million and a half uniforms a year. Such quantities could be supplied only by using sewing machines.

During the war, the Northern army collected statistics on the form and build of American males. These statistics were useful to manufacturers of civilian clothing in developing the ready-to-wear clothing industry after the Civil War. The sewing machine became a vital factor in the development of this industry. Without the sewing machine, it would have been impossible to produce sufficient quantities of clothing to meet the needs of the growing American population.

Seamstresses, particularly those who were hired by clothing manufacturers to do piece work in their homes, soon saw the benefits of the increased speed of the sewing machine. The first major savings in time were in simple items: men's shirts, aprons, calico dresses. These were the first items to be mass produced.

Soon sewing machines were used in the production of men's and boys' suits and overcoats. In the 1860s, a first rate overcoat that required six days of steady sewing by hand could be finished in three days with the help of the sewing machine.

The sewing machine also contributed to the popularity of fashions such as ready-made women's cloaks and the hoopskirt, inasmuch as these garments could be manufactured cheaply and in quantity by using sewing machines instead of hand-sewing. Attachments for sewing machines made possible the easy addition of braiding, tucking, and pleating to fabrics, and the use of these trimmings increased accordingly.

EARLY ATTEMPTS AT DRESS REFORM: THE "BLOOMER" COSTUME

The increasing numbers of petticoats required to support the skirts of the late 1840s were certainly uncomfortable and hindered easy movement. A group of American feminists combined their interest in women's rights with a desire to reform a costume that they saw as confining and impractical. "Women are in bondage; their clothes are a great hindrance to their engaging in any business which will make them pecuniarily independent," said Lucy Stone, a leader of the movement.

Elizabeth Smith Miller had seen women in health sanitariums in Europe wearing short skirts over **turkish trousers.** (Turkish trousers had full legs that were gathered to fit tightly at the ankle.) She adopted the style, wearing it on a visit to her cousin, the feminist leader Elizabeth Cady Stanton, in Seneca Falls, New York. Mrs. Stanton, Mrs. Stone, Susan B. Anthony, and Amelia Bloomer all adopted the style. Even though Mrs. Bloomer did not originate the style, it was named after her. She endorsed it, wrote favorably about it in 1851 in a journal she edited, and she wore it for lectures. (See *Figure 13.1*.)

The Bloomer costume consisted of a pair of full trousers gathered in at the ankle, over which a dress with a knee-length skirt was placed. The style was not limited to the United States, but was also seen in Germany, England, the Netherlands, and Sweden. English cartoonists in the humor magazine *Punch* had great fun caricaturing the style.

Few women outside the feminist movement took up bloomers, which provoked a great deal of ridicule, leading some feminists to conclude that emphasizing the costume was counter-productive. When the hoop skirt became fashionable, Mrs. Bloomer found the cage crinoline a "comfortable and practical garment," and she and others willingly discarded the Bloomer costume. The cut of the trousers, however, retained the name "bloomers," and as some women's undergarments had a similar cut, they were nicknamed "bloomers." Today the term is often applied to any full pants gathered in at the bottom.

FIGURE 13.1

Amelia Bloomer wearing the so-called "Bloomer costume." The contemporary drawing is based on a daguerreotype of Mrs. Bloomer. (Courtesy, Picture Collection, New York Public Library.)

GYMNASTICS FOR WOMEN

Although the Bloomer costume had a short life as fashionable dress, it survived in athletic costume for women. The exercise movement, given impetus by an exceptionally successful book of the 1860s called the *New Gymnastics for Men, Women and Children,* endorsed an exercise outfit for women consisting of turkish trousers with shorter skirts.

Women's seminaries or colleges of the period included calisthenics or some type of exercise program. In 1863, Mount Holyoke College adopted the overskirt and turkish trouser as appropriate dress for physical education. Vassar College also adopted a similar style (Warner 1993).

CONTEMPORARY COMMENTS 13.1

Rebel Dress During the Civil War

After the end of the Civil War, Godey's Lady's Book *printed the following description of "Dress Under Difficulties: Or Passages from the Blockade Experience of Rebel Women" By Elzey Hay.*

We managed pretty well during the first year of the war, for although we were too "patriotic," as we called it, to buy any "new Yankee goods," most of us had on hand a large supply of clothing. Planters were rich men in those days; and their wives and daughters always had more clothes than they could wear out.... Before the blockade was raised all learned to wear every garment to the very last rag that would hang on our backs.... there began to be, however, a marked change in our style of dress. Instead of kid gloves, we wore silk or lace mitts; we had no fresh new ribbons; our summer dresses were no longer trimmed with rich Valenciennes lace, and our hats and bonnets were those of the last season "done over." In a word, we began to grow seedy....

... We knew very little of the modes in the outer world. Now and then a *Godey* or a *Bon Ton* [fashion magazines] would find its way through the blockade, and create a greater sensation than the last battle ... I remember walking three miles once to see a number of the *Lady's Book* only six months old.

... The blessed *Garibaldi* [blouse] came in, which must have been invented expressly for poor blockaded mortals, whose skirts had outlasted their natural bodies [bodices].... Black silk was the favorite material for piecing out old clothes, because it suited everything. ... An old black silk skirt with nine flounces was a treasure in our family for nearly two years, and when that store was exhausted, we fell back on the cover of a worn-out silk umbrella. The finest traveling dress I had during the war, was a brown alpaca turned wrong side out, upside down, and trimmed with quillings made of that same umbrella cover. I will venture to say that no umbrella ever served so many purposes or was so thoroughly used up before. The whalebones served to stiffen corsets and the waist of a homespun dress, and the handle was given to a wounded soldier for a walking stick.

Hay, E. 1866. "Dress Under Difficulties: Or Passages from the Blockade Experience of Rebel Women," *Godey's Lady's Book,* July p. 32.

Existing examples of bathing dress also appear to be modeled on the bloomer styles. As Warner (1993) notes, none of these variations, however, "used the term 'Bloomer' in describing these outfits at that time, probably avoiding it because of the disastrous connotations the term had come to suggest." Even in subsequent decades of the 19th century the term "turkish trousers" was apparently preferred over the rejected "bloomers."

SOURCES OF EVIDENCE ABOUT COSTUME

Many costume collections have substantial numbers of garments dating from this period of time. Women's magazines regularly printed hand-colored fashion plates and their descriptions. As a result, a wealth of detailed information about fashions from this period is available to the fashion historian.

The practice of photography was so widespread that it was the rare family that had not immortalized its members in photos. (See *Figure 13.2.*) The carte de visite, and other portrait photographs, show us (black-and-white only, of course) how thousands of people wanted to be seen. They do not, generally, show us undergarments, how people dressed for outdoors in winter, or workday clothing. Some of these gaps can be filled in by non-portrait photography, but the record is not complete.

Even with the advent of photography, portraits and other paintings also continue to be an important source for the 19th century, especially because they provide a record of color in clothing. Foster (1984) notes the usefulness of genre or modern-life paintings, although she observes that working class individuals are not often depicted, and that if poor people appear, they may have been "cleaned up."

weaving one color in the lengthwise yarns and another in the crosswise yarns. Washable cotton or linen was used for everyday clothing (very little of which has been preserved), for underwear, and for much of the clothing for children. Wool fabrics appear in everyday and dressier clothing for women and suits for men. Outerwear for men, women, and children is usually made of wool. One also sees an attractive silk and wool blended fabric, relatively sheer, crisp and lightweight, called **barege.**

The first synthetic coal tar dyes were synthesized in 1856. A vivid magenta shade, called mauve, was the first dye to be made, but the development of other colors followed rapidly. This technological advance increased not only the range of colored fabrics readily available, but also their intensity. (See *Color Plate 38.*)

Although knowledge of silhouette and costume detail is useful in dating historic costume, clues as to dates can sometimes be found within the costume itself. For example, men's waistcoats or trousers in this period and later may have buckles that are used to adjust their fit. Some of these buckles will contain a patent number and even the date of the patent. Other closures such as hooks and eyes, snaps, and some buttons are marked with patent numbers and the dates of patents can be ascertained.

FIGURE 13.2

Woman of about 1866 wears a one-piece dress with jacket-type sleeves. The wide braid-trimmed skirt is pleated into a narrow waist. Skirt fullness is supported by a hoop beneath. Her hair is dressed typically, parted in the middle and apparently held in a net. Her husband wears a frock coat. His watch chain is visible at the front of his vest. His shoes have rather high heels. The photograph was taken on this couple's wedding day. (Courtesy, Washington State Historical Society, Tacoma.)

COSTUME FOR MEN AND WOMEN: THE CRINOLINE PERIOD

The basic silhouette of women's costume (and also, therefore of children up to age five or six and girls older than six) fits closely through the bodice to the waist, then the skirt immediately widens into a full round or dome shape. Armhole seams are placed below the natural shoulder on the upper part of the arm. (See *Figure 13.4c and d.*)

Fabrics used are fairly crisp, with enough body to enhance the fullness of the skirt, even though a hoop supports it. Among the silks used for better dresses, one sees a great many taffetas, particularly plaid and striped patterns (see *Color Plate 38*) and "shot" or iridescent fabrics created by

Costume for Women: 1850–1870

GARMENTS

As undergarments, a woman wore a chemise and drawers under a corset and a hoop. She placed a petticoat on top of the hoop. Undergarments were made of cotton or linen. (See *Illustrated Table 13.1*) The chemise was a short-sleeved, knee-length garment, short and full without much decoration. Drawers were knee length and trimmed at edges with tucking, lace, or embroidery. The crotch was left open and unseamed. In winter some women wore colored, flannel drawers for warmth.

A **camisole** or **corset cover** was placed over the corset. This waist-length garment was shaped to the figure, had short sleeves, and buttoned down the front. Less whalebone was now being used in corsets. Instead they were shaped with gores of fabric and inset gussets of elastic. After the introduction of the crinoline, corsets shorted, as there was no need to confine the hips. When the crinoline declined in size, corsets became tighter. Reference to "stays" declined; the term "corset" was more widely used.

A series of either whalebone or steel (only after 1857) hoops were sewn onto tapes or into a fabric skirt to make a hoop skirt or "cage crinoline," as it was called. (See *Figure 13.3.*) Shapes varied with changes in the fashionable silhouette, which was round in the 1850s and flatter in front and fuller at the back in the 1860s. A single petticoat decorated with lace, embroidery, or small tucks was placed over the

Illustrated Table 13.1

SELECTED UNDERGARMENTS FOR WOMEN, MEN, AND CHILDREN FROM THE SECOND HALF OF THE 19TH CENTURY

Woman's chemise, 1870[1]

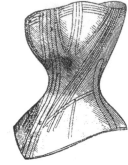
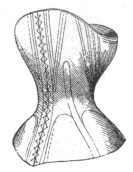

Woman's corset, front and back views, 1862[2]

Woman's corset cover, 1864[2]

Woman's knitted wool underpetticoat, 1864[2]

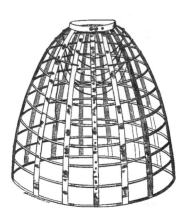

Woman's hoopskirt, 1858[2]

Woman's drawers, 1862[2]

Bodice and drawers for a boy, age 3 or 4, 1869[2]

Man's shirt, 1870[1]

Man's drawers, 1869[2]

[1]*Harper's Bazaar,* 1870, reprinted in Schroeder, J. S. 1971. *The Wonderful World of Ladies Fashion.* Northfield, IL: Digest Books.
[2]Blum, S., ed. 1985. *Fashions and Costumes from Godey's Lady's Book.* New York: Dover.

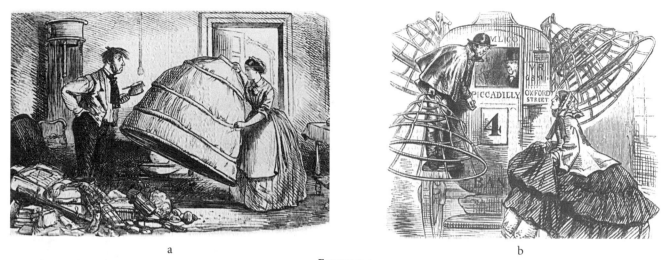

a   **FIGURE 13.3**   b

Cartoonists found the hoop an irresistible target. Drawing (a) shows a harried husband of 1858 being asked by his wife's maid if he can find room for her hoop in his suitcase. In drawing (b), the hazards of public transportation for hoop-wearing ladies are noted. (Courtesy, Picture Collection, New York Public Library.)

hoop. Additional layers, flannel, or quilted petticoats could be worn in winter for warmth.

Daytime dresses (see *Figure 13.4*) were either one piece, with bodice and skirt seamed together at the waist; princess style, without a waistline seam; or, increasingly, two piece with matching but separate bodices and skirts. Bodice shaping was often achieved through curved seams in back and darts in front. Armholes were placed low on the arm, below the natural shoulderline in a so-called "dropped" shoulder. Silk or wool garment bodices were usually lined with cotton or linen fabric and occasionally had some whalebone pieces stitched to seams.

Separate bodices worn for daytime generally ended at the waist and fastened up the back or front with buttons or hooks and eyes. Some were cut like a jacket and had extensions of the bodice below the waist, called **basques,** which flared out below the waist. Before 1860, the bodice was generally cut longer in order to form basques. Later they were often made by sewing separate pieces to the bodice at the waist. Some extended about six inches below the waist and were even all around; others were short in front, long in back.

Necklines were high, without attached collars and usually finished in bias piping. Removable, washable collars and cuffs were usually worn with daytime dresses. (See *Figure 13.4.*) Many sleeves were open at the end and were worn with removable lace or muslin undersleeves (called in French and in some fashion magazines **engageantes,** pronounced *ahn-gahj'-eh-ahnt.*) The following are some sleeve styles that are often seen in photographs and fashion plates. Bell-shaped sleeves, which were narrow at the shoulder and gradually widened, ended between elbow and wrist. (See *Figure 13.4a.*)

Pagoda sleeves were narrow at the shoulder and expanded abruptly to a wide mouth at the end. They were sometimes shorter in front, longer in back. Some sleeves consisted of double-ruffles, the second ruffle ending about three quarters of the way down the arm. In the 1860s, sleeves were frequently closed at the end. (See *Figure 13.4d* and *e.*) Variations of closed sleeves included sleeves pleated into the armhole with released fullness gathered into a wristband; sleeves close-fitting to the wrist with epaulettes at the armhole; or sleeves made up of a series of puffs from shoulder to wrist. Jacket-type sleeves were made like a man's coat sleeve, with an inner seam under the arm and an outer seam down the back of the arm. These sleeves had no gathers at the shoulder and were relatively fitted for the length of the arm. (See *Figure 13.2.*)

Separate blouses were worn with skirts. These generally had high necks and the aforementioned closed sleeves. The red **garibaldi** (*gar-ee-bal'-dee*) blouse was especially popular in the 1860s. (See *Figure 13.5.*) Red shirts worn by Italian soldiers who fought to unify Italy under General Giuseppe Garibaldi inspired the fashionable garibaldi blouses.

Skirts widened throughout the 1850s and into the 1860s (some were twelve to fifteen feet in circumference). In the early 1850s, skirts were dome shaped. In the 1860s, they were more pyramid shaped with fullness toward the back. By the late 1860s, there was less fullness at the waist, skirts were gored instead of gathered, and the waistline was located somewhat above the natural anatomical placement. (See *Figure 13.15.*) Skirts were usually lined completely, halfway, or with a band of lining around the underside of the hem to keep the skirt from being soiled. Braid placed at the hem edge helped to reinforce and keep the edge of the hem from fraying as it touched the

FIGURE 13.4

Carte de viste-type photographs from the Crinoline period. The first two figures, (a) and (b) upper left, wear open sleeves with engageants. The woman on the left wears her hair in a chenille snood, the one on the right has on a small lingerie cap. The young woman (c) at upper right has sleeves of the jacket type, which is decorated at the top with epaulettes. The outlines of the hoops underneath their skirts can be seen clearly in the photographs of the women and child at lower left (d and e). The woman on the right (f) wears her hair in sausage curls or ringlets around her face. On her head is a small cap with hanging ribbon lappets. All of the figures part their hair in the center. All except the little girl wear detachable white collars. (Photographs from the author's collection.)

ground. Some skirts were plain and undecorated. Others consisted of two or more flounces sewn onto an under skirt. A similar effect could be achieved by layering skirts, with each layer being cut shorter than the last to form a flounce. Decorative skirts were made of rows of narrow frills or of double skirts on which the outer skirt layer was puffed or looped up.

The **princess dress** was a new, one-piece style that was cut without a waistline seam. Long gored sections, extending from the shoulder to the floor, were shaped to fit at the waist through the curved cut of the sections.

To protect garments or to vary their appearance women wore dress accessory garments such as washable aprons. Elaborately embroidered silk aprons were worn for decoration, not practicality. The aforementioned separate collars and undersleeves were generally white and washable and trimmed in lace and/or embroidered. **Fichus** appear in pictures as being worn crisscrossed and tied in back. **Canezou** is a fashion term that is applied to a variety of accessories including fichus, muslin jackets worn over bodices and chemisette neck fillers. The term canezou seems to go out of use after this period.

Differences in dresses worn for evening from dresses worn for daytime were seen mostly in the cut of the neck, sleeves, types of fabrics used, and elaborateness of decoration. Frequently two-piece, some evening dresses were made in the princess style.

Most evening dresses had "off the shoulder" necklines, either straight across or with a dip at the center (*en coeur*), and often with a wide bertha trim (a folded band of fabric around the neckline). (See *Figures 13.5, 13.6,* and *Color Plate 38.*) Sleeves were short, straight, and often obscured by the bertha. (See *Figure 13.6.*) In the late 1860s, some sleeveless dresses had shoulder straps or ribbons tied over the shoulders. Double skirts might have decorative effects created by looping or puffing up the outer layer. Skirts were trimmed with artificial flowers, ribbons, rosettes, or lace. (See *Figure 13.5.*)

OUTDOOR GARMENTS

Outdoors women wore either sleeved, unfitted coats of varying lengths (see *Figure 13.7a*); sleeved, fitted coats of varying lengths; or sleeveless loose capes, cloaks, and shawls. (See *Figure 13.7a.*)

The tendency of fashion magazines to assign names to each of a number of different styles tends to confuse terminology. The following are some of the names reported by Cunnington and Cunnington (1970) for these garments:

- **pardessus:** sleeved outdoor garment.
- **paletot:** sleeved outdoor garment that fitted the figure.
- **pelisse-mantle:** double-breasted, sleeved, unfitted coat with wide, flat collar and wide, reversed cuffs.
- **mantle:** three-quarter-length coat, fitted to waist in front, full at the back, with either long loose sleeves or full, shawl-like sleeves cut as part of the mantle.

FIGURE 13.5

Fashion plate depicts young woman, on left, wearing a red Garibaldi blouse with a black taffeta skirt. Her hair is enclosed in a red, net snood, possibly of chenille, and her small, flat hat with feathers at the side is tipped forward. Her companion is wearing an evening dress with horizontal bands of pleated fabric at the neckline and short, puffed sleeves. The bodice dips to a deep V at the waist. The underskirt, visible beneath the puffed up overskirt, is made with horizontal tiers of small pleats. In one hand the lady carries a folding fan, in the other a small bouquet. Both were popular accessories for evening dress. (Courtesy, Picture Collection, New York Public Library.)

- **shawl-mantle:** loose cloak, reaching almost to the skirt hem.
- **talma-mantle:** full cloak with tasseled hood or flat collar.
- **rotonde:** shorter version of the talma-mantle.
- **burnous:** a hooded cape.
- **zouave:** short, collarless jacket, trimmed with braid and often worn over a Garibaldi shirt (see *Figure 13.8*). Zouave jackets derived from the uniforms of Algerian troops that fought as part of the French army. During the American Civil War, a regiment called the Zouaves

Illustrated Table 13.2

TYPICAL WOMEN'S HAIRSTYLES AND HEADDRESS: 1850–1870

Hairstyles

1851[1]   1859[1]   1864[1]   1866[1]

Headcoverings

Bonnet, 1850[1]   Bonnet, 1858[1]   Bonnet, 1864[1]

Snood, 1864[1]   Hat, 1865[2]   Hat, 1867[1]

Indoor cap, 1866[1]

[1] Fashion magazines, 1850–1870
[2] Blum, S., ed. 1985. *Fashions and Costumes from Godey's Lady's Book.* New York: Dover.

FIGURE 13.6

Evening dress of about 1860 with wide bertha collar. The lady wears a pair of black lace mitts; her hair is arranged in long ringlets. Her companion wears what appears to be a dark frock coat, dark vest, and light trousers. The photograph may be a wedding portrait. (Photograph from a glass plate negative, Courtesy, Huntington Historical Society, Huntington, NY.)

---

fought for the North and adopted, in part, the costume of the French Zouaves.

HAIR AND HEADDRESS

See *Illustrated Table 13.2* for examples of hairstyles and head coverings for the Crinoline period.

Women generally parted their hair in the center and drew it over the ears smoothly or in waves and then into a bun or plaits at the back of the head. Pads, placed under the hair at the side, helped to give a wider appearance. For evening, curls were arranged at the back of the neck. In the 1860s, the quantity of hair massed at the back enlarged. False hair supplemented natural hair as required. In daytime, hair was usually confined in a net, called a **snood.** This was frequently made of colored silk or chenille.

Small, muslin "day caps" with long lappets or ribbons were still worn by some older or married ladies. Although bonnets continued to be worn, small hats were more fashionable by the 1860s, especially hats with low, flat crowns and wide brims. Other popular styles were hats with flexible brims; bergere straw hats, similar to those of the 18th century; sailor hats; and "pork pie" hats with low, round crowns and small brims turned up at one side. Beaded hair nets, lace kerchiefs, hair ornaments made of flowers or fruit, and jeweled hair ornaments were worn for evening.

FOOTWEAR

See *Illustrated Table 13.3,* for examples of some accessories of the period.

Stockings were made of cotton or silk. White was the preferred color, but colored and plaid stockings were also worn.

Most shoes worn for daytime had square toes and low heels. Some styles had rosette trimming over the toes. Shoes worn for evening were made of white kid or satin. In the 1860s, evening shoes were often colored to match the gown. Boots were cut to above the ankle and closed with lacing, buttons, or with elastic sides.

ACCESSORIES

Gloves tended to be short and fitted for daytime, except for "sporty" gauntlets with wide cuffs. White gloves, short in the 1850s and long and elbow length in the 1860s, were worn with evening dress. Fingerless mitts, often of lace, were worn for day or evening. (See *Figure 13.6.*)

Popular hand-carried accessories included handkerchiefs, folding fans of moderate size, and small muffs. Parasols were small, dome shaped, often of silk, and lined inside. Carriage parasols had folding handles. (See *Illustrated Table 13.3.*)

A **Swiss belt,** cut wide with a triangular piece in front, was a popular accessory.

JEWELRY

Most commonly worn jewelry items were bracelets, earrings, brooches, and necklaces. Fashionable materials included coral, cameos, cabochon stones (i.e., cut in convex form but without facets), colored glass, and jet.

COSMETICS

Use of "paint" was considered to be in bad taste among "ladies of quality," but fashion magazines did offer regular advice about homemade cosmetic remedies. Examples of such recommended cosmetics were "a tablespoon of gin thrown into lukewarm water will remove redness in the face produced by exertion" (*Godey's* 1854). "Water to thicken hair and prevent

a

FIGURE 13.8

Zouave jacket of white pique trimmed with black braid. Worn with a Garibaldi shirt. (Fashion drawing, c. 1860.)

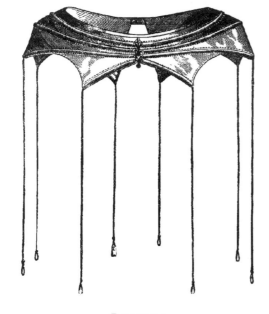

b

FIGURE 13.7

(a) Outdoor garments from 1863. On the right, a full, plaid mantle trimmed with cording and tassels, worn over a dress with a skirt having a band of matching plaid around the hem. On the left, a coat of the pardessus type, closed with frogs. The skirt under the jacket is raised from the ground by means of a porte jupe or dress elevator. (b) A dress elevator, which was placed under the skirt and fastened to the hem of the skirt with loops that enclose buttons. A tab at the front of the elevator pulled to raise the device in much the same way that one would raise a modern-day Venetian blind. (Courtesy, Picture Collection, New York Public Library.)

its falling out: distil [sic] and cool as slowly as possible two pounds of honey, a handful of rosemary, and twelve handfuls of the curlings or tendrils of grapevines, infused in a gallon of new milk" (*Godey's* 1864).

Costume for Men: 1850–1870

GARMENTS

Men wore long or short cotton or linen underdrawers and an undervest of cotton or linen next to the skin in the warm months and, sometimes, wool in the winter. (See *Illustrated Table 13.1, page 310.*) Shirts showed no major changes in shape from earlier styles. Points of the collar extended to the jaw. (See *Figure 13.12.*) With less of the shirt front exposed at the neck, shirts worn in the daytime lost their decorative tucking or ruffles. Evening shirts, however, had embroidered or ruffled fronts. Most shirts were white; some shirts for country or sportswear were colored. Ties and cravats were wrapped around the collar. (See *Figures 13.11* and *13.12.*)

As before, suits were made up of coats, waistcoats (vests), and trousers. Coats did not button shut but were worn open leaving the waistcoat visible. (See *Figure 13.9.*) Dress coats (formerly called tailcoats) were cut with a short, square "cut-in" in front and tails at the back. Although they were worn for both day and evening for formal occasions in the 1850s, by the 1860s tailcoats were strictly evening dress. Evening coats were black, some with velvet-faced lapels.

Construction of the frock coat was the same as in the previous decade. It was fitted through the torso. The skirt was not

Illustrated Table 13.3

CRINOLINE PERIOD, 1850–1860: ACCESSORIES

Woman c. 1860 wearing necklace,
bracelets, and rings

Women's footwear, c. 1860s

Men's footwear, c. 1860s

Miser's purse, netted
and beaded, c. 1850s

Ladies muff,
c. 1860s

Parasols
(A) and (B) Marquise parasol,
that tips at the top, c. 1850s
(C) Carriage parasol that folds, c. 1860s

Decorative undersleeve,
made for wearing under a
wide dress sleeve, c. 1860s

Derby or bowler hat

of fabric covered side seams of some styles. Men commonly wore suspenders (called in England, **braces**) to hold their trousers in place. As an alternative, some pants were constructed with a tab and buckle at the back of the waistband and did not require suspenders. An embroidered or needlepoint pair of suspenders was considered an appropriate gift from a lady to a gentleman.

A new sportswear garment called **knickerbockers** appeared after 1850. They were cut with loose legs and belted into a band that buckled just below the knee. The term was later shortened to **knickers.** Wearing knickerbockers for sports seem to have originated from the practice of wearing fitted knee breeches for riding, shooting, and hunting. (See *Table 9.1, page 205,* for a discussion of the origin of the term "knickers.")

Some garments were worn only in the privacy of one's home. These included dressing gowns, which were made in decorative fabrics and worn with nightcaps, and smoking jackets, which were loose jackets cut like a sack jacket and made in velvet, cashmere, or other decorative fabrics and worn with small, tasseled caps.

OUTDOOR GARMENTS

The trend toward looser, more comfortable clothing was evident in overcoats. Some overcoats were fitted with a defined

FIGURE 13.9

Men and boys dressed for a formal occasion. (*Gentleman's Magazine,* January 1854.)

---

overly full. In the 1860s the frock coat waistline dropped somewhat, and the waistline was less well defined. These coats lengthened after 1855, and remained longer for the rest of the period. (See *Figures 13.10, 13.12,* and *13.13.*)

There were other popular coat styles as well. Morning coats (also called riding coats or Newmarket coats) curved back gradually from the waist, the curve becoming less pronounced in the 1860s. The **sack jacket** (called a lounging jacket in England) was a loose, comfortable jacket with no waistline. Sack jackets had straight fronts, center vents in back, sleeves without cuffs, and small collars with short lapels. (See *Figure 13.11.*) **Reefers** or **pea jackets** were loose, double-breasted jackets with side vents and small collars. These were also worn as overcoats.

Waistcoats for daytime ended above the natural waist. (See *Figure 13.12.*) Both single- and double-breasted styles were worn; the latter had wider lapels. For evening waistcoats were single breasted and longer.

Instep straps disappeared after 1850, but trousers fitted close to the leg. Pegged-top styles, which were wider at the top and narrowed gradually to the ankle, were also seen. After 1860, legs widened somewhat. For daytime some were made of striped or checked fabrics. Bands made from colored strips

FIGURE 13.10

Left to right: Hunting garb, a paletot, and a frock coat, vest, and trousers. (*Modes de Paris,* c. 1850.)

FIGURE 13.11

Man wearing sack jacket, a loosely fitted coat, introduced in the late 1840s for casual wear. (Fashion plate, c. 1850.)

waist while others were loose, with no clear waistline definition. Combined coat-capes had a loose fit and capelike or full sleeves, and/or an over-cape. (The term paletot continued to be used to refer to the general category of overcoats.) (See *Figure 13.10*.)

Named coat styles included:

- The **chesterfield,** either single- or double-breasted.

- The **frock overcoat,** cut along the same lines as the frock coat, but longer.

- **Inverness cape,** a large, loose overcoat with full sleeves and a cape ending at wrist length.

- **Raglan cape,** in spite of the name, a full overcoat with an innovative sleeve construction. Instead of setting the sleeve into a round armscye, it was joined in a diagonal hole seam running from under the arm to the neckline.

In addition, there was a wide variety of capes or cloaks with sleeves. A man's cloak similar to the lady's talma mantle was worn for evening. Waterproof coats, such as the mackintosh, continued in use. Men also wore large shawls over suits for out-of-doors. Some of the most famous photographs of President Abraham Lincoln show him wearing a dark shawl outdoors.

HAIR AND HEADDRESS

Men wore their hair fairly short, and either curly or waved. Long, full side whiskers were stylish. Mustaches became more popular in the 1850s; by the 1860s being clean shaven was no longer fashionable. (See *Figures 13.9 to 13.13*.)

FIGURE 13.12

Gentlemen of about 1860 wears a plaid waistcoat which is double-breasted and has a wide lapel. His collar stands upright, the points reaching to his jaw. Around the collar he has wrapped a cravat which is tied in a knot, the ends hanging. (Photograph courtesy, Huntington Historical Society, Huntington, NY.)

The top hat was the predominant style of headcovering. (See *Figures 13.9, 13.10,* and *13.11.*) Other styles included the **wide awake,** with a low crown and wide brim and made of felt or straw; caps for casual wear; derbies (bowlers); and straw hats with flat crowns and narrow brims. The Stetson hat was born in 1865 when John B. Stetson, who was traveling in the western United States, made himself a broad-brimmed, high-crowned felt hat of beaver and rabbit skins. Cowboys adopted this practical, water-repellent, wide-brimmed, crushable hat, and Stetson began to manufacture these hats on his return to New Jersey (Watson 1994).

FOOTWEAR

Important types of footwear included laced shoes, half or short boots with elastic sides or buttoned or laced closings, and long boots. Short or long gaiters or spatterdashers (spats) were added to shoes for sportswear.

ACCESSORIES

Men carried canes, umbrellas with decorative handles, and wore gloves.

JEWELRY

For men, jewelry was largely confined to watches and watch chains, tie pins, rings, and a variety of ornamental buttons and studs.

COSTUME FOR CHILDREN: THE CRINOLINE PERIOD

Infants unable to walk were dressed in long gowns. Once they were able to walk and until the age of five or six, boys and girls both wore short skirts. (See *Figures 13.13* and *13.14.*)

a   b

FIGURE 13.13 A AND B

(a) Boy and girl wear similarly cut zouave jackets; the girl with a gathered skirt, the boy with a pair of trousers. Their leather boots reach to the ankle. (b) A small boy still dressed in skirts wears a white shirt, with belt and band of trim in velvet, lace-trimmed drawers, knee length stockings, and ankle-high boots. The man standing beside him wears a frock coat and light-colored trousers. (Photographs from the author's collection.)

Infants wore caps indoors and out, which were intended to keep them from losing heat from their heads. Many infants' caps were quite decorative, made of cotton or linen and trimmed with elaborate embroidery and lace. Others were knitted or crocheted.

COSTUME FOR BOYS AND GIRLS: 1850–1870

Girls wore shorter versions of the styles adopted by adult women. Skirts lengthened as girls grew. At four years, girls and boys wore dresses ending just below the knee. Skirts for girls age sixteen had gradually lengthened to two inches above the ankle. Older girls wore hoops to hold out their skirts. Pan-

talettes continued in use until the end of the period, after which they were no longer worn. (See *Figure 13.14.*)

FOOTWEAR

Children were generally dressed in ankle-high boots or slippers. (See *Figures 13.13* and *13.14.*) They wore striped or plain colored stockings.

HAIR AND HEADDRESS

Boys generally had short hair; girls' hair was often dressed in tight ringlets around the face. Boys wore caps, straw sailor hats, small pillboxes, and smaller versions of men's hats. Girls' hats resembled those of adult women.

Costume for Boys: After Age Five or Six

After they were taken out of skirts, boys wore trousers or short pants cut similarly to adult men's clothing. (See *Figure*

FIGURE 13.14

Left to right: Child's dress in wool with soutache braid trim, c. 1869; mother's dress, c. 1860; infant's christening gown, c. 1860; and girl's dress, c. 1869. (Photograph courtesy, The Metropolitan Museum of Art, The Costume Institute.)

FIGURE 13.15

Children in this picture wear clothing of the late 1860s with narrower, gored skirts. Younger girls wear shorter skirts while the older girl in the center wears a skirt reaching to the ground. The boy in the center wears a modified form of the tunic suit with knickers and a sailor hat. The boy and girl at left, rear, wear jackets of the unfitted cut that was popular at the time and pill box hats. (Courtesy, Picture Collection, New York Public Library.)

13.9.) Specific styles for boys included knickerbockers, which were cut full to the knee where they gathered into a band and buttoned or buckled to close. (See *Figure 13.15.*) Knickerbocker suits added a short, collarless jacket to these pants, and for older boys, a vest as well. Sailor suits were made up of trousers or knickers, a blouse with a flat, square collar and a V-shaped neck opening. The sailor blouse style was known as a "middy," the word derived from "midshipman." Eton suits, tunic suits, and jackets plus trousers were all similar to those of the preceding period. (See *Figures 13.10* and *13.15.*)

Outdoor garments were mostly smaller versions of adult men's coats, and they included inverness, chesterfield, and Ulster styles.

Knitted wool jersey suits were worn for the beach.

SUMMARY

THEMES

During the Crinoline period we first encounter the theme of THE RELATIONSHIP BETWEEN COSTUME AND THE WORK OF AN INDIVIDUAL DESIGNER. That designer was Charles Worth, father of the French couture, who not only determined what would be fashionable, and what would not through his fashion designs, but who also played a significant role in changing the ACQUISITION OF APPAREL. With the founding of the *Chambre Syndicale* in Paris by Worth's sons, the hegemony of Paris over fashion innovation was established.

Other changes in the PRODUCTION AND ACQUISITION OF APPAREL also have their beginnings in this period. During the Crinoline period, fashion changes in women's clothing were concentrated more in variations of details than in major silhouette alterations. To be sure, the shape of the hoop-supported skirts did evolve from a dome like shape to one more pyramidal. The period might be considered a product of the Industrial Revolution and TECHNOLOGY. Surely it would have been difficult for so many women of all social classes to adopt the hoop so quickly without the factories to produce the steel from which the hoops were made and the sewing machines that permitted their assembly at relatively low prices and in great quantities.

The invention of the sewing machine radically altered the way in which clothing was made. POLITICAL CONFLICT gave impetus to this new technology in the United States when huge numbers of uniforms were required for soldiers of the Civil War.

The themes of POLITICAL CONFLICT and FASHION came together when Garibaldi blouses, named for an Italian general; Zouave jackets, named for a French military regiment; and raglan sleeves, named for an English Crimean War hero became fashionable.

POLITICAL LEADERS and their families also appeared as influences on dress. Empress Eugenie of France was admired for her style of dressing. Queen Victoria, not a fashion innovator, exemplified SOCIAL ATTITUDES that placed a high value on family life and reinforced GENDER DIFFERENCES in dress. While women were being confined inside the steel structure of the hoop, men were gaining greater comfort and freedom in their clothing. The sack suit, the closest 19th century ancestor of the men's sport jacket of today, was a comfortable, non-confining jacket that men accepted readily and have made a staple in their wardrobes ever since.

SURVIVALS OF CRINOLINE PERIOD COSTUME STYLES

The term crinoline took on a new definition in the 1850s that it has retained to this day. Crinoline was a stiff fabric used in petticoats to hold out skirts. When hoopskirts were introduced, people took to calling them "cage crinolines" and then finally shortened the term to "crinoline." Today the term crinoline is applied to any stiff petticoat, whether or not it includes a hoop of any kind. The crinoline experienced a revival with the introduction of the New Look in 1947 (see *Illustrated Table 17.1, page 438*) and again when "mini-crinolines" were shown in the late 1980s (*Figure 19.17a*). It appears in any period when wedding dresses have long, full skirts.

Knickers, themselves a descendant of the knee breeches of the 18th century, have been fashionable for men, for boys, or for women ever since their introduction in the 1860s. (See *Illustrated Table 16.4, page 397,* and *Figure 18.5*.) Levi's, a by-product of the 1849 Gold Rush, have had a long life as work clothing, but also experienced several fashion revivals as sports clothing, children's play clothing, and finally as fashionable dress for almost any occasion.

Visual Summary Table
CRINOLINE

Man: 1850–1870
Shirts with suits made up of coats
(tailcoats for dress, frock coats for
daytime) waistcoats, and trousers.
Sack jackets now used more.

Woman: 1850–late 1860s
Fitted bodices have sleeves set in
at a dropped shoulder. Waistline is close
to the anatomical waistline.

Woman: after 1857
Hoopskirts support full gathered or
pleated skirts. At first concentrated all around,
fullness gradually moves toward the back.

Woman: late 1860s
Skirts are gored, have higher waistlines.

NOTES

Cunnington, C. W. and P. Cunnington. 1970. *Handbook of English Costume in the 19th Century.* London: Faber and Faber, p. 453 ff.

Foster, V. 1984. *A Visual History of Costume: The Nineteenth Century.* New York: Drama Book Publishers.

Godey's Lady's Book, July 1854, p. 91.

Godey's Lady's Book, November 1864, p. 439.

Hay, E. 1866. "Dress Under Difficulties; or Passages from the Blockade Experiences of Rebel Women." *Godey's Lady's Book,* July, p. 36ff.

Hegermann-Lindencrone, L. 1912. *In the Courts of Memory.* New York: Harper & Brothers, p. 60.

Ratner, E. 1975. "Levi's." *Dress,* Vol. l, p. 1.

Warner, P. C. 1993. "The Gym Suit: Freedom at Last. In P. A. Cunningham and S. V. Lab, eds., *Dress in American Culture.* Bowling Green, OH: Bowling Green State University, Popular Press.

Watson, B. 1994. "In the Heyday of Men's Hats, Fashion Began at the Top." *Smithsonian,* Vol. 24, No. 3, p. 72.

SELECTED READINGS

Books and Other Materials Containing Illustrations of Contemporary Styles from Original Sources

American Fashion Magazines: *Godey's Lady's Book, Graham's Magazine, Peterson's Magazine.*

Blum, S. 1985. *Fashions and Costumes from Godey's Lady's Book.* New York: Dover.

Dalrymple, P. 1991. *American Victorian Costume in Early Photographs.* New York: Dover.

Ginsburg, M. 1983. *Victorian Dress in Photographs.* New York: Holmes and Meier.

The House of Worth: The Gilded Age in New York. 1982. New York: Museum of the City of New York.

Nuncio, R., ed. 1971. *Mr. Godey's Ladies.* New York: Bonanza Books.

Of Men Only. 1975. Brooklyn, NY: Brooklyn Museum.

Rosenblum, R. [N. D.]. *Jean-August-Dominique Ingres.* New York: Abrams.

Severa, J. 1995. *Dressed for the Photographer. Ordinary Americans and Fashion 1840–1900.* Kent, OH: Kent State University Press.

Periodical Articles

Adler, S. 1980. "A Diary and a Dress." *Dress,* Vol. 5, p. 83.

Beck, J. F., P. Havlane, and T. Harding. 1986. "Sewing Techniques in Women's Outerwear 1800–1869." *Clothing and Textiles Research Journal,* Vol. 4, No. 2, p. 20.

Dupont, A. 1992. "Textile and Apparel Management Functions Performed by Women in the 19th Century Plantation South." *ASR Textron.* No. 18, December, p. 51.

Footer, S. 1980. "Bloomers." *Dress,* Vol. 5, p. 1.

Hollander, A. 1982. "When Worth Was King." *Connoisseur,* Vol. 212, December, p. 113.

Levitt, S. 1993. "From Mrs. Bloomer to the Bloomers: The Social Significance of the Nineteenth Century English Dress Reform Movement." *Textile History,* Vol. 24, No. 1, p. 27.

Magill, D. 2000. "Luxuriant Crowns: Victorian Men's Smoking Caps, 1850–1890. *Dress,* Vol. 27, p. 9.

Richmond, R. 1971. "When Hoops Did Tilt and Falsehood Was in Flower. Women's Fashions of the 1860s." *American History Illustrated,* Vol. 6, No. 1, p. 23.

Daily Life

Hubert, C. 1975. *The Horizon Book of Daily Life in Victorian England.* New York: McGraw-Hill.

Lacour-Gayet, R. 1969. *Everyday Life in the United States Before the Civil War 1830–1860.* New York: Frederick Ungar.

Magneton, S. 1969. *Leisure and Pleasure in the 19th Century.* New York: Putnam Publishing Group.

Peterson, H. L. 1971. *Americans at Home. From the Colonists to the Late Victorians.* New York: Scribners.

Roger, J. P. 1997. *Life in the South During the Civil War.* San Diego, CA: Lucent Books.

Richardson, J. 1971. *La Vie Parisienne.* New York: Viking.

Sclerite, T. J. 1992. *Victorian America : Transformations in Everyday Life, 1876–1915.* New York: Perennial.

Wilson, L. 1993. *Daily Life in a Victorian House.* New York: John Wiley & Sons.

CHRONOLOGY

1870–1900
Queen Victoria continues to occupy throne of England

1870–1871
Franco-Prussian War; Napoleon III surrenders to Prussians and abdicates

1871
Civil War in France

1872
Steam-powered machine for cutting multiple layers of cloth introduced

1874
Impressionist artists show their work at the *Salon des Independents* in Paris

1880s and 1890s
Aesthetic movement in the arts
English writer Oscar Wilde lectures about Aestheticism in the United States

1890–1910
Art Noveau styles develop

1892
Daily News Record begins publication, being
printed under the title *Daily Trade Record* until 1916
Vogue magazine begins publication

1893
Sigmund Freud publishes the first of his papers
that lead to the development of psychoanalysis

1896
Klondike gold rush

1898
Spanish-American War
United States annexes Hawaii

1899–1902
Boer War between Britain and South Africa

THE BUSTLE PERIOD AND THE NINETIES

1870 – 1900

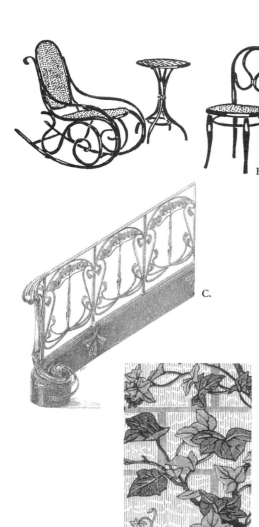

A.

Art Nouveau jewelry

B.

Bentwood furniture

C.

Art Nouveau staircase railing

D.

William Morris wallpaper

E.

Victorian Renaissance revival house

F.

Eastlake furniture

G.

Painting by Vincent van Gogh, *The Starry Night,* 1889

Figures A, C from Lavisse, E. 1907. *Album Historique Le XVIII Le XIX Siècle.* Paris: Librairie Armand Colin, p. 278. Figure B courtesy of J. Curcio in Federico, J. T. 1988. *Clues to American Furniture.* Washington: Starrhill, p. 52. Figures D, F from Eastlake, C. L. 1969. *Hints on Household Taste in Furniture, Upholstery and Other Details.* New York: Dover, p. 182, 122. Figure E courtesy of V. R. Tortora. Figure G courtesy of the Museum of Modern Art, New York, acquired through the Lillie P. Bliss Bequest.

Two costume periods are included in this chapter. The first, the Bustle period, derives its name from the bustle, a device that provided the shaping for a silhouette with marked back fullness. The concentration of fullness at the back of the costume that had evolved gradually during the late 1860s at first required a modification of the hoop and eventually led to the construction of devices that, either alone or in combination with the hoop, supported the fullness, which came to be concentrated more and more at the back of the skirt.

In the 1890s this silhouette altered. The name most often given to the last decade of the 19th century in the United States is "the Gay Nineties." In France, the period is frequently called "La Belle Epoque." Both names convey a sense of fun, good humor, and, indeed, the Western world seemed to be emerging from the serious moralistic tone of the Victorian era.

HISTORICAL BACKGROUND:
1870–1890

By the time that the bustle became a popular fashion, Queen Victoria had been ruler of Great Britain for just over 30 years, and would remain Britain's ruler for 30 more. During the earlier years of Victoria's reign, the British people had come to share a common ideal with particular emphasis on the importance of morality and high standards of conduct. The British Empire had grown to include lands across the world. In 1870 when the Bustle period began, industrial England was in the midst of a great economic boom. During the following 20 years there was a gradual extension of voting rights, and passage of legislation to clean up the slums and to improve sanitary conditions. These years were not marked by any major internal or international upheavals for England.

In France, the period began with the shock of the Franco–Prussian war, when French armies were defeated and Napoleon III surrendered to the victorious Prussian armies. Peace did not come to France until after a revolution that ended the Second Empire and replaced it with the Third Republic. In the spring of 1871, the people of Paris endured a bloody civil war—the Commune—a struggle of Paris radicals against conservative France.

In the United States the Civil War had ended, the country was united from east to west by the railroads, and settlers were moving westward in ever-increasing numbers. Industrialization, urbanization, and immigration were continuing apace, and with them the corresponding problems of labor strife, poverty, and exploitation of laborers. But Americans remained optimistic and the long peace and economic expansion that followed the Civil War provided opportunity for many native and immigrant Americans to improve their economic status.

HISTORICAL BACKGROUND:
1890–1900

The decade of the 1890s in the United States saw the continuation of trends cited in the preceding decades. The frontier was closing and urban centers were expanding as the country moved toward the new century.

In Europe, too, the social conventions of the Victorian era continued, but there were signs of changes in attitude. In England, the Prince of Wales, heir to the throne, was enormously popular, while the Queen was considered somewhat old-fashioned. The prince, a ladies' man, lived a lifestyle of which his mother disapproved. One of his favorite spots for escaping from parental constraints was Paris, then considered the pleasure capital of Europe. In popular dance halls like the Moulin Rouge, risqué dances and songs were performed. The Folies Bergere had opened and a new form of entertainment called the strip tease became popular. Houses of prostitution flourished. They ranged from the lavish, beautifully furnished houses visited by the Prince of Wales to rooms in the most degraded quarters of the city.

For those who came to Paris for more sedate pleasures there were the fashion houses of Worth, Paquin, and others, as well as outdoor cafes, the theater, and tree-lined boulevards for strolling.

SOCIAL LIFE: 1870–1900

It is difficult for urban dwellers today to realize that the first apartment house in New York City was built in 1870. It was a five-story walk-up, patterned after the apartment buildings of Paris. With increased pressure for housing that developed as urban centers grew, it was not long until this first luxurious building had inspired a host of imitations, including the notorious, crowded tenements that housed the poor.

But whether people lived in sprawling suburban Victorian houses, on farms, or in city apartments, Western society in the 1870s was family oriented, and the father was the head of the household. Even so, increasing numbers of American women were entering the work force. In 1890, 3,704,000 women were employed in a variety of jobs outside the home. By 1900 that figure had reached 5,319,000. The Census of 1890 shows that women were concentrated in occupations such as teaching, domestic and personal services (i.e., as nurses, laundresses, servants, and waitresses), bookkeeping and account-ing, selling, and dressmaking. Many were employed in agri-culture. More than 226,000 were farm-owners or overseers and 447,000 were listed as hired help on farms. There were even 60 female blacksmiths and more than 4800 physicians and surgeons. Seven out of every ten colleges had become co-educational by 1900.

The tendency for women to go out of the home to work was probably responsible for the development of less cum-bersome clothing for women, which was particularly evident in the 1890s. Fashion magazines do not always accurately re-flect this trend, whereas photographs of women at work show clearly that they wore their skirts shorter than those shown in magazines and with relatively little decoration. Many of the items in historic costume collections reinforce the notion of excessive decoration and elaborate construction because most women did not save their "everyday" clothing. Everyday clothing is more readily seen in mail-order catalogs and can-did photographs of the period.

Bicycles first appeared in the early 19th century but had not really caught the public fancy. The English bicycle with a front wheel five feet high and a rear wheel of eight inches in-trigued a few manufacturers when it was shown in the Philadelphia Centennial exhibition of 1876. By 1885 more than 50,000 Americans had taken up cycling and by 1896 the number swelled to an estimated 10 million.

The first lady cyclists pedaled decorously in their long skirts, even while wearing bustles, but in the 1890s a bifur-cated garment, a sort of full knicker, was devised as a practi-cal costume for the sport. (See *Figure 14.15, page 347.*) While relatively few women actually adopted knickers (called **ratio-nals** in England), the style did mark the first use of bifurcated garments for women that had achieved some modest success. Once these knickers had been accepted for a particular sport they were also adopted for other activities such as mountain climbing. It was not until the late 1920s, however, that large numbers of women began to wear anything approximating men's trousers.

SPORTS FOR WOMEN

If sport is defined as recreational activity that requires more or less vigorous bodily exertion, women did not enter into real participation in active sports until well into the 19th century. True, women had ridden horses for recreation as well as for transportation for a number of centuries. They also ice skated and played croquet, but it was after 1870 that women increas-ingly participated in tennis, golf, rollerskating, hiking, and even mountain climbing. Women also "bathed" in lakes or the sea, but few did any real swimming. Bathing and riding re-quired special costumes. Other sports needed only slight modifications of daytime costume. Except for shortening skirts a little, tennis or croquet players and skaters or golfers tended to follow the fashions of the period. When cycling be-came the rage, however, a special costume was devised.

Calisthenics or gymnastics had been part of the curricu-lum in most women's seminaries and colleges since the 1860s. In the 1870s and 1880s, some colleges added team sports such as crew and baseball. The clothing worn for these sports was apparently made at home or by a dressmaker. After women in colleges began playing basketball in the 1890s, physical educa-tion uniforms appeared. By the early 20th century, the "gym suit" uniform had replaced the individually selected outfit for physical education. These were more practical than the turk-ish trousers that had heretofore been worn in combination with either short, skirted dresses or bloused bodices. Warner (1993) describes them as follows: "The bloomers shortened and widened to give the appearance of a short skirt and the separate blouse buttoned onto the bloomer waistband."

THE MANUFACTURE AND ACQUISITION OF CLOTHING AND TEXTILES

Textile Technology

The technological advances in textile production, which had matured during the 19th century, resulted in fabrics that were better and often less expensive. Power looms replaced hand-looms and the not always dependable natural dyestuffs gave way to more reliable synthetic dyes.

Various chemical processes were applied to textiles. To give silk fabric greater body, a process called **weighting** was used in which silk was treated with chemical salts. Unfortu-nately, excessive weighting made the fabric wear out much more quickly. Many weighted garments dating from the 1870s, when weighting first became common, to the late 1930s, at which point weighting was regulated and limited by law, show this damage in split or broken yarns. The performance of cotton fabrics could be improved by **mercerizing,** treating it with sodium hydroxide, which improved strength, recep-tivity to dyes, and luster.

Ready-to-Wear Clothing

By 1879 most men bought at least part of their clothing in stores. Corsets, crinolines, bonnets, and cloaks were about the only ready-made items that most ladies bought through the 1860s. The average housewife counted sewing among her many skills, and for the more affluent, a dressmaker was easily employed. The entry of more women into the work force after 1870 made for changes in clothing production and consumption, as did the development of department stores. The first women's garments to become available in stores were underclothes and "wrappers." Soon after, dresses, suits, and walking costumes were being advertised. A vogue for shirtwaists and skirts in the 1890s gave a tremendous impetus to manufacturing and by 1910 "every article of female clothing could be purchased ready-made" (Kidwell and Christman 1974).

A number of technological developments had made the move to mass production possible. The invention of the sewing machine was a major factor. In 1863 Ebenezer Butterick, a tailor, had patented a special type of tissue paper pattern that he sold successfully. The unique feature of these patterns was that they were made in different sizes. Prior to this time seamstresses had to enlarge small patterns printed in fashion magazines and adjust them to the correct size. The sized paper dress pattern helped to standardize sizes, a necessity for ready-to-wear clothing.

Cutting out each garment by hand was a time-consuming process. Unless some way could be found to speed up this step, no great quantity of garments could be made efficiently. The first device for cutting large numbers of pattern pieces at the same time was a long knife that was worked up and down through slots in the table. This device could cut 18 thicknesses of cloth at one time. A cutting machine powered by steam was introduced about 1872, but the device was stationary and the fabric had to be brought to it, making it awkward and cumbersome to use. After 1890, use of electricity for manufacturing allowed the development of smaller, more efficient cutting machines. The first of these cut 24 thicknesses of fabric; later models could do up to 100.

The efficiency of the garment industry was also based on the piecework concept in which each operator completed only one step in the manufacturing process. The division of labor among a number of different workers that was characteristic of less expensive clothing made it possible for even a novice to acquire sufficient skill to handle a single component of garment manufacturing.

Sociological factors also contributed to the development of the garment industry. The absorption of more women into the work force on a full-time basis decreased the amount of time they had available for dressmaking for themselves and their families and at the same time created more of a demand for clothing to wear to work. The industry developed over a period of time when great waves of immigrants, many of whom possessed excellent tailoring and dressmaking skills, were entering the United States and seeking work. Even the American ideal of a society in which "all men are created equal" helped to foster acceptance of ready-made clothing that, as Kidwell (1974) put it, "served to obliterate ethnic origins and blur social distinctions." Nothing comparable evolved in western Europe, where not only was the immigrant labor force lacking, but where the more clearly defined social class structure did not lend itself so readily to the acceptance of a mass-produced supply of clothing suitable for all but the wealthiest. Even in the United States the rich continued to purchase their clothing in Paris or from custom dressmakers and tailors.

Merchandising of Ready-to-Wear

Department stores, which first appeared in the 1860s, stocked a wide variety of goods, including ready- and custom-made clothing. For customers who could not come to the city to shop, many stores published mail-order catalogs. In 1872 Aaron Montgomery Ward prepared and sent a catalog to farmers, offering them a variety of products available for purchase by mail. The success of the Montgomery Ward catalog inspired other companies to enter the mail-order business. Sears, Roebuck, and Co. began operation in 1893.

THE VISUAL ARTS AND COSTUME

The entire Victorian period in the arts was markedly eclectic, featuring many styles that derived from earlier historical periods. In architecture, Gothic and Renaissance styles were among the more important examples of this tendency. Most of the important styles in furniture or interior design were also based on earlier furniture or architectural styles and included not only Gothic and Renaissance revivals, but also revivals of Rococo, Louis XVI, and neo-Greek forms.

Revivals of historic styles were also evident in women's dress, particularly in the years between 1870 and 1890. Some dresses had hanging sleeves similar to those of the Middle Ages or the Renaissance, others had "Medici" collars, derived from the 16th and early 17th centuries, and many skirts were cut with polonaises inspired by the costumes of the 18th century. Shoes were made with "Louis" heels, modeled after those worn at the court of Louis XIV, and garments were given fashion names such as the "Marie Antoinette fichu" or the "Anne Boleyn paletot."

A reaction against the traditional and conservative nature of art was stirring, however. Artists such as Courbet and Manet had begun to challenge the traditional painting styles as early as the 1860s. The Impressionists, who received a hostile reaction not only from the traditional salon painters and critics, but also from the public, followed them in the 1870s and 1880s. In 1874, their work was refused admission to the official French salon, a show of art works approved by the established art world. In response they set up a separate show called the *Salon des Independents,* which became an annual event. By the 1890s the Impressionists had gained a substantial following among the public and had become the acknowledged leaders of the art world. The direct influence of Impressionist art on costume of the period was, however, minimal.

Aesthetic Dress

In the 1880s and 1890s, a dress reform movement directly related to attempts to reform the arts in England did have some impact on clothing styles. The dress reforms of the Bloomer movement proposed by the American women's rights proponents had been based chiefly on the premise of a need for more comfortable and convenient clothing for women. "Aesthetic dress," of the latter part of the 19th century, had different philosophical origins.

Its origins lay in the Pre-Raphaelite Movement, a group of painters who opposed the direction of English art of the 1840s. They took their themes from Medieval and Renaissance stories. Not only did they make costumes for their models to wear, but the women of the group also adopted these dresses for themselves. The costumes, while not wholly authentic, were based on drawings from books on costume history published in the 19th century. After the opening of Japan to the West in the 1850s, Japanese influences also appeared in Pre-Raphaelite art. From the 1850s through the 1870s, Pre-Raphaelite dress was limited to this group of artists and a few others. By the 1880s and 1890s, the costume had begun to catch on with those who espoused the Aesthetic Movement in the arts, a popularized form of Pre-Raphaelite philosophy that attracted painters, designers, craftsman, poets, and writers. Japanese and Asian influences became more pronounced, especially in textiles and other decorative arts.

One of the major proponents of Aestheticism was the poet and playwright Oscar Wilde. During his lectures on Aestheticism, Wilde sometimes wore his own version of Aesthetic costume: a velvet suit with knee breeches and a loosely fitting jacket, worn with flowing tie and a soft, wide collar.

Women's Aesthetic costume generally had no stays. Sleeves were of the puffed, leg-of-mutton style. Dresses were made of Liberty prints or oriental silks and worn without petticoats. The wearer had a languid, drooping appearance that contrasted with the stiffly constructed lines of fashionable, bustle-supported dresses. The satirists of the period had great fun mocking the Aesthetes with their emphasis on "art for art's sake." Most of the illustrations of Aesthetic dress come from the cartoons of George DuMaurier whose work appeared regularly in the British humor magazine *Punch.* (See *Figure 14.1.*) The operetta *Patience,* written by Gilbert and Sullivan, also poked fun at the Aesthetes. Indeed, its leading character was modeled on Oscar Wilde.

FIGURE 14.1

Couple in aesthetic dress, 1880s. Although the dress has some back fullness, it lacks the full bustle of the period and has sleeves that are not found in mainstream fashions. The man's velvet jacket and shirt with a soft collar and tie are also part of aesthetic dress, as is his long hair. (Drawing from Appelbaum, S., and R. Kelly, eds. 1981. *Great Drawings and Illustrations from Punch: 1841–1901,* p. 31, reproduced courtesy, Dover Publications.)

Art Nouveau

In the period between 1890 and 1910 yet another European reform movement in the arts had some influence on costume for women. **Art Nouveau** was an attempt by artists and artisans to develop a style with no roots in earlier artistic forms. Its proponents saw it as a revolt against the eclectic nature of art and design of the Victorian period.

Art Nouveau designs emphasized sinuous, curved lines, contorted and stylized forms from nature, and a constant sense of movement. The silhouette of some women's dresses, especially in the first decade of the 20th century, echoed these lines. The stylized natural forms appeared in some dress fabrics, and embroidered patterns in Art Nouveau motifs were often applied to garments. (See *Color Plate 40.*) Jewelry, the metal clasps of handbags, hat pins, and parasol and umbrella handles often show Art Nouveau influences.

In a sense the Art Nouveau movement formed a bridge between the artistic styles of the 19th century and those of the 20th century. Although Art Nouveau artists did not succeed in making a sharp break with traditional styles, this artistic philosophy that stressed the need for art to be divorced from the past led eventually to the true revolution in art that arrived with modern, abstract art after World War I.

SOURCES OF EVIDENCE ABOUT COSTUME

The previously cited sources—clothing in museum collections, photographs, works of art, and magazines—continue to provide most of the information we have about costume at the end of the 19th century.

Portraits of men and women from these periods present more or less faithful renderings of clothing. Impressionist painters, active in these decades, did not pay a great deal of attention to details of dress. Depictions of dress in women's portraits of the late 19th century can present other problems, too. In the late 19th century, exhibits of 18th century portraits of women were held in New York and London. These portraits inspired women of the upper classes to have themselves painted in garments modeled after the 18th century dress in these portraits.

Hand-tinted fashion plates gradually disappeared as fashion magazines in the 1880s and 90s adopted color printing. Fashion magazines began to use fewer drawings and more photographs, but color photographs of good quality were not available until the 1930s. When color was wanted, the magazines reproduced color drawings. In a study of proportions of fashion illustrations, Warner (1992) showed how fashion drawings often exaggerate proportions to provide a longer, leaner look, and that even photographs can be shot from angles that provide a fashionable distortion.

COSTUME FOR WOMEN: THE BUSTLE PERIOD, 1870–1890

General Features of Women's Costume: 1870–1890

The confining nature of women's clothing, the heavy draperies and long trains, encumbering bustles, and the tight corseting

necessary to achieve the fashionable silhouette prompted intense activity on the part of those promoting dress reform. *Contemporary Comments 14.1* quotes the views of some proponents of dress reform. (See *page 339.*)

Back fullness was a feature of women's dress for most of the period. To support this fullness a number of different structures called bustles were devised.

THE BUSTLE

Initially the new back fullness was supported by the cage crinoline of the preceding period, which was worn with an added bustle. Some crinolines were shaped with greater fullness at the back. Subsequently other bustle-support constructions developed. These ranged from padded, cushion-like devices to half hoops of steel. See *Illustrated Table 14.1, page 336* for examples of undergarments from the period 1870–1900.

The shaping of the back fullness, however, was not consistently the same for the entire period and three somewhat different subdivisions can be identified within the overall Bustle period:

1. 1870–1878: a full bustle created by manipulation of the drapery at the back of the skirt (*Figures 14.2* and *14.3*).

2. 1878–1883: the sheath or cuirass-bodice. During the period when the narrow, **cuirass bodice** (*kwi-ras'*) was fashionable, fullness dropped to below the hips, and a semicircular frame supported the trailing skirts (*Figure 14.4*).

3. 1884–1890: large, rigid, shelf-like bustles (*Figure 14.5*).

GARMENTS

See *Illustrated Table 14.1, page 336,* for examples of undergarments from the period 1870–1900.

Drawers changed very little from those of earlier periods. Chemises, made of cotton or linen, were generally short sleeved and round necked, and extended to the knee. They became more decorative, with trimmings at the neck and sleeve and, often, ornamental tucks at either side of the front opening.

A garment combining the chemise and drawers into one was called a **combination**. At least one example of a combination was depicted in *Godey's Lady's Book* as early as 1858. It was described thus: "This garment combining the chemise and drawers has very many advantages. We recommend it to ladies traveling, to those giving out their wash, and to ladies boarding. It is also decidedly cooler for summer." Some models were knitted, others woven. In winter, wool was preferred. Widespread acceptance of combinations after 1870 was probably related to a desire for less bulky underclothing to wear beneath dresses that fit quite closely. (See *Illustrated Table 14.1, page 336.*)

Now long, curved, and supported with strips of whalebone, steel, or cane, corsets were shaped to achieve a full, curved bustline, narrow waist, and smooth, round hip curve.

The fullness of petticoats increased and decreased as skirt widths changed.

In the early 1870s a new form of dress called a **tea gown** was introduced. Intended to provide some relief from the tight lacing, it was worn without a corset, loosely fitted, and softer in line than daytime or evening dresses. Ladies wore tea gowns at home with other women friends. Tea gowns were also viewed as rational or reform garments.

Other negligee items that were worn before the day's toilette was complete or before retiring included wrappers, dressing saqucs, combing mantles, and breakfast jackets.

Throughout the period two-piece dresses consisting of bodice and matching skirt predominated. The princess dress, cut in one piece from shoulder to hem, without a waistline seam, was an exception. To achieve a fit that followed body contours through the torso, princess dresses were cut with many vertical seams and vertical darts (long, shaped tucks).

Skirts and blouses, although seen less frequently than dresses, were also worn. Most were overblouses, cut loosely and belted at the waistline. Women wore Norfolk jackets (a men's coat style) with skirts. Princess-style overdresses were sometimes combined with a separate underskirt. When the outer fabric was looped up or draped over the hip the style was known as a **princess polonaise.**

Specific Features of Women's Dress Styles During Different Phases of the Bustle Period

DAYTIME DRESSES: 1870–1878 (See *Figure 14.2.*)

Bodices were generally of the fitted jacket type with either shorter basques (i.e., extensions of the bodice below the waist) at front and/or back or longer basques forming a sort of overskirt at the back of the costume. Necklines were high and closed, square, or V-shaped. Open necklines were generally filled in with a decorative chemisette or lace frill. Even when the front of the bodice was cut low, the back neckline was high.

Close-fitting sleeves ended about three quarters of the way down the arm or at the wrist. Coat sleeves were fitted sleeves ending in a deep cuff. Sleeves were now set into the armhole higher, without a dropped shoulder.

Unless worn with a blouse rather than a bodice, skirts generally matched bodices in color and fabric. Often overskirts were draped to produce an apronlike effect at the front. Both skirts and long basques were made with plenty of fabric, which was then looped or draped in various ways at the back of the skirt, thereby achieving considerable back fullness. This fullness was supported by the bustle.

EVENING DRESSES: 1870–1878 (See *Figure 14.3.*)

Many women had two bodices made for each skirt; one for daytime, one for evening wear. Because evening dresses followed the same lines as daytime dresses, the chief differences between them were in the use of more decorative fabrics,

FIGURE 14.2

Daytime dress of 1874. Pleated and fringed trimmings were applied to the sleeves, to the bodice and its elongated basques, and to the skirt. (Photograph courtesy, Division of Costume, The American Museum of National History.)

greater ornamentation, and cut of sleeves and necklines. Many evening bodices had off-the-shoulder sleeves, were sleeveless, short sleeved, or had elbow-length sleeves finishing in ruffles. Necklines for evening were square, V-shaped, or round and low.

DAYTIME AND EVENING DRESSES: 1878–1883

The silhouette (see *Figure 14.4*) modified continually, with gradual year-by-year diminishing of bustle dimensions. The

FIGURE 14.3

Evening dress of 1873; this pink silk gown has elbow-length sleeves. (Photograph courtesy, Division of Costume, The American Museum of National History.)

change began as early as 1875, with the **cuirass bodice,** a long jacket ending in a point at the front and fitting smoothly over the hips. This cut required less back fullness, and as a result bustle fullness decreased gradually. The decoration applied to many costumes became more asymmetrical.

Cut of necklines, sleeves, and trimmings showed no radical changes. Long heavily trained skirts fitted smoothly over the hips. Their decoration was concentrated low, at the back of the skirt. Skirts were held close to the knee in front by ties, restricting women's movements to small, mincing steps.

DAYTIME DRESSES: 1883–1890 (See *Figure 14.5.*)

Bustles returned, but they differed from earlier styles in that the back fullness had more the appearance of a constructed, shelflike projection rather than the softer, draped construction of the 1870–1878 styles.

The bodices most frequently seen were fitted, jacket-style with short basques, polonaise bodices, or belted over blouses. (See *Figures 14.6* and *14.7.*) Almost all daytime dresses of the 1880s had high, fitted, boned collars. The collars were either part of a blouse worn under a jacket, part of the jacket, or a part of the dress. Generally close fitting, most sleeves ended above the wrist. As early as 1883 some sleeves developed a small puff at the sleeve cap. In 1889 this puff (called a **kick-up**) grew, becoming more pronounced, a forerunner of the extremely full sleeves that characterized the 1890s. Skirts usually ended several inches above the floor and only rarely had trains.

EVENING DRESSES: 1883–1890

Evening dresses had the same silhouette as daytime dresses, but had increased trimming. Some were trained. Sleeves on ballgowns were short, covering just the shoulders. By the

FIGURE 14.4

Styles from the second phase of the bustle period. Princess-style dresses, front and back views, on adults show focus of decoration at hem, particularly at the back. The child's dress, though shorter, is cut along similar lines. (Print from *Demorest's Monthly Magazines,* April 1878.)

FIGURE 14.5

Bustle dress of the third phase (c. 1882) worn in New York City. (Photograph courtesy, The Metropolitan Museum of Art, The Costume Institute.)

close of the 1880s, some evening dresses had broad or narrow shoulder straps in place of sleeves. Conservative ladies wore elbow-length sleeves.

OUTDOOR GARMENTS (See *Figures 14.8* and *14.9.*)

The variety of outdoor garments increased. Whereas Crinoline period styles relied heavily on cloaks and capes, the bustle silhouette was more easily accommodated by coats or jackets. Jackets were close fitted at the back, loose or fitted in front, generally extending below the waist. Some were knee length. They were cut to accommodate the bustle configuration of the particular year. Sleeves generally were coat style with turned-back cuffs.

"Paletot," "sacque," and "pelisse" are terms applied to a variety of coatlike garments, most of which were three-quarter length or reached to the floor. Another long coat was the **ulster,** a long, belted coat often made with a removable shoulder cape or hood. Full-length chesterfield-style coats usually had velvet collars.

The **dolman** was a semifitted garment of hip to floor length that was shaped like a coat but had a wide-bottomed sleeve that was part of the body of the garment (a sort of coat/cape). Cloaks and capes were cut in varying lengths, fitted to the shoulder, and some were fitted in the back and loose in the front.

CLOTHING FOR ACTIVE SPORTS

Although women were beginning to take more interest in active sports, the costumes worn for tennis, golf, yachting, or walking were made with bustles and elaborate draperies. The only concession to the activity of these pastimes was that dresses worn were cut slightly shorter.

A vogue for wearing wool knit fabric began when Lillie Langtry, an internationally famous stage personality, adopted a wool knit fabric as a tennis costume. Langtry was born on the British island of Jersey and was nicknamed "the Jersey Lily." As a result the fabric became known as "jersey," the name by which it is still called today.

Bathing costumes consisted of bloomers or trousers with an overskirt and bodice. Gradually the trousers shortened to the knee and stockings covered the lower part of the leg. Bathing shoes or slippers and a cap completed the outfit. Sleeves decreased in size, and in 1885 some bathing costumes were sleeveless. Even with these modifications ladies could do little real swimming and their activity in the water was generally limited to a little splashing about in the shallower areas. (See *Figure 14.10.*)

HAIR AND HEADDRESS

See *Illustrated Table 14.2, page 340* for some examples of hairstyles and headdress for the period from 1870 to 1900.

Usually hair was parted at the center, waved around the face and pulled to the back of the head. Bangs or curled fringe covered the forehead. In the early 1870s, long hair was arranged in large braids, a chignon, or long curls cascading down the back of the head. False hair was used lavishly. As the costume silhouette grew more slender, hair was worn closer to the head and arranged in a confined bun or curls at the nape of the neck. High-boned collars were worn so widely after 1884 that most women dressed their hair off the neck and high on the top of the head in a bun or curls.

By the end of the 1880s only elderly women still wore day caps indoors. Hats and bonnets were exceedingly elaborate, with ribbons, feathers, lace, flowers, and flounces as trimming. When masses of large curls or chignons were concentrated at the back of the head, hats were worn either tilted up, or perched on the front of the head, or set back, resting on the

Illustrated Table 14.1

SELECTED UNDERGARMENTS FOR MEN, WOMEN, AND CHILDREN: 1870–1900

A variety of bustle styles illustrated in fashion magazines of the 1870s and 1880, including:

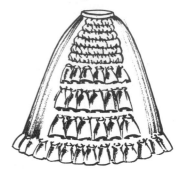

Horsehair bustle

Bustle of hoops sewn into cambric

Horsehair ruffles attached to petticoat

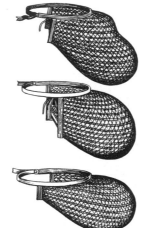

BVD spiral bustle, "the only bustle that will not break down."

Three braided wire bustles of differing shapes

Taylor's star folding bustle, described as "light, cool, and comfortable."

Corset cover, 1880s[1]

Lady's muslin drawers, 1886[2]

[1]Grafton, C. B. 1993. *Victorian Women's Fashion Cuts.* New York: Dover.
[2]Bloomingdale Brothers. 1988. *Bloomingdale's Illustrated 1886 Catalog.* New York: Dover, p. 26.

Illustrated Table 14.1

SELECTED UNDERGARMENTS FOR MEN, WOMEN, AND CHILDREN: 1870–1900

Knitted combination underwear of the type
recommended by advocates of dress reform, 1897[3]

Lace-trimmed muslin
chemise, 1886[2]

Lady's lace-trimmed petticoat, 1890s[1]

Boy's drawers with
attached underwaist[5]

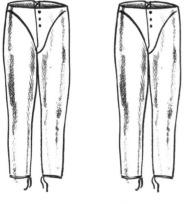

Men's drawers[5]

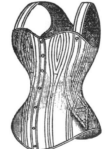

Corsets for children age one year
up to adult, 1893[4]

Child's vest[2]

[3]Picture Collection, New York Public Library.
[4]*The Delineator,* May 1893.
[5]Bryk, N. V. 1988. *American Dress Pattern Catalogs, 1873–1909.* New York: Dover.

FIGURE 14.6

Women and men of the 1880s. Women's jacket-style bodices have basques extended below the waist and high collars typical of the period. Their hair is dressed on top of the head, off the neck. Most of the men wear frock coats. (Courtesy, Huntington Historical Society, Huntington, NY.)

FIGURE 14.7

At a concert in Japan c. 1889, women wear elaborately draped polonaise-style dresses with high collars that are typical of the period, while the male musicians wear dark tailcoats as formal evening dress. (Courtesy, The Kyoto Costume Institute Collection, Japan.)

📖

CONTEMPORARY COMMENTS 14.1

The Effect of Fashionable Garments on Women's Health

The Arena, a periodical published in the late 19th and early 20th centuries, campaigned vigorously for women's dress reform. One of their often-voiced concerns was the effect of contemporary garments on the health of women.

In the issue of August 1891, Mrs. Abba B. Gould is quoted as saying of what The Arena calls the "long, heavy, disease-producing skirts" of the bustle period.

"Do what we will with them, they still add enormously to the weight of clothing, prevent cleanliness of attire about the ankles, overheat by their tops the lower portion of the body, impede locomotion, and invite accidents. In short, they are uncomfortable, unhealthy, unsafe and invite accidents." (p. 402.)

In the same article, Mary A. Livermore is quoted as observing:

"The invalidism of young girls is usually attributed to every cause but the right one: to hard study—co-education—which it is said, compels overwork that the girl student may keep up with the young men of her class; too much exercise, or lack of rest and quiet at certain periods when nature demands it. All the while the physician is silent concerning the glove-fitting, steel-clasped corset, the heavy, dragging skirts, the bands engirdling the body, the pinching, deforming boot, and the ruinous social dissipation of fashionable society." (pp. 402–403.)

Emily Bruce, M.D., participating in a symposium on dress reform in the February 1894 issue, notes:

"The long, heavy skirt is scarcely less dangerous than the right bodice. It impeded free and graceful movements by embarrassing and entangling the lower extremities, and picks up all sorts of evil things from the street and elsewhere, carrying them home to be distributed to all the family without their knowledge or consent. It aids the wicked bodice in compressing the waist, and drags upon spine, hips, and abdomen, producing a state of exhaustion very conducive to the development of disease." (p. 318.)

FIGURE 14.8

Outdoor garments for adult women and young girls. The garment at the far right is a dolman mantle. (Italian fashion magazine, November 1874.)

FIGURE 14.9

Ladies of 1889 dressed for winter. The lady at far left wears her dress jut slightly shorter than the others for ice skating. (Courtesy, Picture Collection, New York Public Library.)

Illustrated Table 14.2

SELECTED HATS AND HAIRSTYLES FOR WOMEN: 1870–1900

Hat, 1874, front view

Hat, 1874, side view

"Waterfall" hairstyle, 1876

Hat, 1885

Hat, 1885

Hairstyle, 1888

Hat and hairstyle, 1894

Contemporary fashion plates.

FIGURE 14.10

Group of women and children by the sea from *Der Bazar*, a German publication, of 1874. The three figures in the center are dressed in bathing costume. (Courtesy, Picture Collection, New York Public Library.)

chignon. When hairstyles simplified, hats and bonnets were built up higher, crowns enlarged, and brimless toques were in style. For sportswear, a straw sailor hat with low flat crown and wide stiff brim was a popular fashion.

FOOTWEAR

See *Illustrated Table 14.3* for some examples of footwear for the period from 1870 to 1900.

Usually stockings matched the color of the dress and/or shoes. Embroidered and striped patterns were popular. For evening in the 1870s, white silk stockings with colored clocks (a small design) were preferred, whereas black became more popular in the 1880s.

For both shoes and boots, pointed toes and medium high heels predominated. Daytime shoes often matched dresses; evening slippers were of white kid or satin, often with flower or ribbon ornaments at the toe. Boots, less fashionable than

shoes, were usually cut to the lower calf, closed with laces and shaped similarly to shoes. Rubber-soled shoes with canvas or buckskin tops were worn for sports such as tennis and boating, boots for hiking and skating.

ACCESSORIES

See *Illustrated Table 14.4, page 349* for examples of some popular accessories.

Glove lengths varied with sleeve lengths, longer gloves being worn with shorter sleeves. Evening dress required elbow or longer lengths. Although there were some large, fur muffs, most were small. (See *Figure 14.9.*)

Popular fan styles for evening included folding fans of gauze with painted decorations or large ostrich plumes mounted on tortoise shell or ivory sticks. Parasols were large in size, with ornate handles, long points, and they were trimmed with lace and ribbons.

Illustrated Table 14.3

SELECTED FOOTWEAR FOR WOMEN: 1870–1900

Congress-style boot, 1876

Black kid shoe, 1876

Ball slipper, 1881

Mule-type house slipper, 1881

Boots, 1882

Boots and shoes, 1892

Blum, S., ed. 1974. *Victorian Fashions and Costumes from Harper's Bazaar: 1867–1898*. New York: Dover.

Illustrated Table 14.3

SELECTED FOOTWEAR FOR MEN: 1870–1900

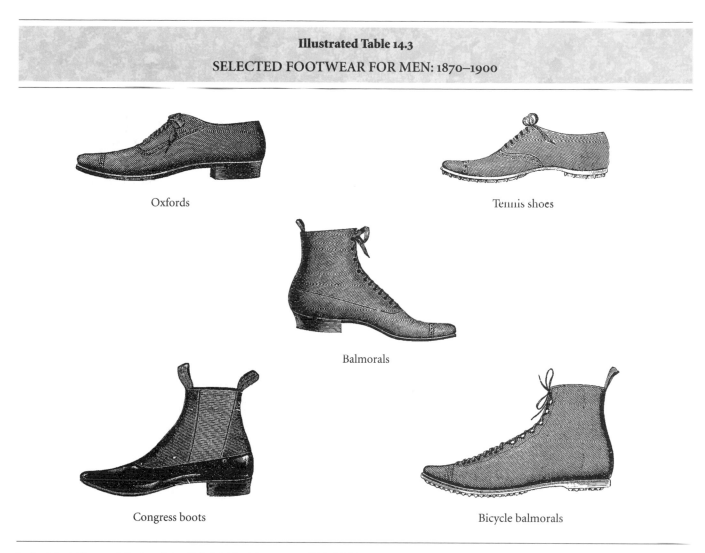

Oxfords

Tennis shoes

Balmorals

Congress boots

Bicycle balmorals

Jordan Marsh Illustrated Catalog of 1891. Philadelphia: Athanaeum of Philadelphia.

Boas, which were long, narrow, tubular scarves of feathers or fur, were an important and decorative accessory.

JEWELRY

Utilized for evening more than for day, popular items included bracelets, earrings (usually small balls or hoops), necklaces, and jeweled hair ornaments. With daytime dresses women sometimes wore brooches.

COSMETICS AND GROOMING

Rouge and "paint" were unacceptable in polite, middle-class society, but face creams, beauty soaps, rice powder, and light scent were used.

COSTUME FOR WOMEN: THE NINETIES

Costume Components for Women

GARMENTS

See *Illustrated Table 14.1, page 337,* for examples of undergarments from the period 1870–1900.

Most underwear was trimmed with quantities of lace, tucking, embroidery, or other decoration. Drawers, chemises, or combinations were the layer of garments worn next to the body. They changed little from those worn during the Bustle period.

Although the traditional style of corsets continued in use, a new corset shape was introduced that confined the waist and ended just below the bust. This removed the support that had previously been provided for the bosom and helped to make a garment to support the bust desirable. Farrell-Beck and Gau (2002), in an exploration of the history of the brassiere in America, show that breast supporters had been patented as early as 1863. They note that although the early designs were intended to provide a "more comfortable and healthful alternative" to contemporary corsets, they apparently failed to produce the desired fashionable silhouette and none achieved commercial success. By the 1890s, however, women's magazines were carrying advertisements for garments known variously as short stays, bust girdle, bust corset, bust bodice, and strophium (a Latin name for the breast supporters of ancient Rome). These garments can be seen as forerunners of the brassiere.

"Bust improvers" designed to fill out a deficient figure were commonly worn. Some were made of "flexible celluloid," others of fabric and stuffed with pads of cotton. Caroline Newell, one of the suppliers of bust supporters, advertised "All Deficiency of Development Supplied" (Farrell-Beck and Gau 2002).

What had been called corset covers were now known as camisoles. It was usual to wear one or two petticoats.

Although vestiges of the bustle remained in pleats or gathers concentrated at the back of the skirt, the silhouette of the 1890s could be described as hourglass shaped. By mid-decade sleeve styles were large and wide at the top for both day and evening. Waists were as small as corsets could make them, and skirts flared out into a bell-like shape. (See *Figures 14.11, 14.12,* and *Color Plate 40.*)

Two-piece dresses were constructed with lined and boned bodices that usually ended at the waist and had round or slightly pointed waistlines. A few had short basques, extending below the waist. Shoulder constructions included yokes or revers with width at the shoulder produced by ruffles or frills. (See *Figures 14.12* and *14.13.*)

The expansion that had begun in the late 1880s with enlargement of sleeve caps continued. Sleeves were still larger by 1893 and by 1895 had become enormous. The **leg-of-mutton sleeve** had a full puff to the elbow, then a fitted sleeve from elbow to wrist or a wide top that narrowed gradually to the wrist. Other sleeves made of softer fabric were full for the length of the arm, ending in a cuff. After 1897 sleeve size generally decreased and reminders of the larger sleeve styles could be seen in small puffs or epaulettes at the shoulder, the rest of the sleeve being fitted. (See *Figure 14.20.*)

Most skirts were gored, fitting smoothly over the hips. They had some back pleating or fullness. The gores flared out to a wide bell shape. Skirts were lined with fabric. Some had bands of linen or buckram around the hem for stiffness. Fashion magazines and costume historians speak of skirts to the floor. However, candid photographs of women working show

FIGURE 14.11

Couple of 1890s dress for the photographer, she in leg-of-mutton sleeved bodice and bell-shaped skirt; he in a sack jacket, waistcoat, and matching trousers. His "handlebar" moustache was a popular fashion in this decade. (Photograph courtesy, Huntington Historical Society, Huntington, NY.)

that for practical purposes, skirts of three or four inches from the floor were more often worn. Dresses for sportswear were also shorter.

The name for blouses, **shirtwaist,** was often shortened to **waists.** Styles ranged from blouses with leg-of-mutton sleeves tailored to look like a man's shirt to styles covered with lace, embroidery and frills. (See *Figure 14.12.*) Shirtwaists were among the first products of the growing American ready-to-wear industry.

Artists can sometimes capture the ideal look for a particular period. Charles Dana Gibson's pen and ink sketches of young men and women at the turn of the century—the Gib-

a

b

FIGURE 14.12 A AND B

Shirtwaists. (a) Young woman of the 1890s wears a decorative lace-trimmed shirtwaist blouse and skirt of brocade. (b) Simple shirtwaist (1894), cut like a man's shirt except for the leg-of-mutton sleeves. (a) Photograph courtesy, Huntington Historical Society, Huntington, NY. (b) Drawing from Blum, S., ed. 1974. *Victorian Fashions and Costumes from Harper's Bazaar: 1867–1898*. New York: Dover.

---

son girls and the Gibson men—did just that. Young people throughout the United States strove to imitate that look. Revivals of shirtwaists with leg-of-mutton sleeves in the late 1940s were called Gibson Girl blouses.

Tailor-mades (see *Figure 14.13*) were matching jackets and skirts, worn with a blouse. These were the predominant fashion for wear outside the home. Styles ranged from severely tailored costumes modeled after men's suits to elaborately decorated models with ruffles and lace trimmings. Even the most severely tailored, however, had the enlarged sleeves of the period. Tailors rather than dressmakers made these garments, hence the name.

Evening dresses had low necklines that were either V, square, or round shaped. After 1893, off-the-shoulder lines were more common. These gowns had full sleeves, ending above or at the elbow, and were usually large and balloon shaped. When daytime sleeves grew smaller (c. 1897), evening dress sleeves also diminished to short, small puffs.

Evening dresses were frequently trained. The shape of skirts was like that of daytime dresses. (See *Figure 14.14*.)

OUTDOOR GARMENTS

Capes, many with high puffs at the shoulder to accommodate the large sleeves of dresses, were the most common outdoor garments. Styles included full capes of velvet or plush trimmed with fur or jet beading. Collars were high and standing or the neck finished in a ruffle. Those coats that were worn could be fitted or full, had large sleeves, and ranged in length from short, hip length to three-quarters or floor length. Chesterfield-style and ulster coats remained popular. The terms sacque and dolman gradually went out of use.

CLOTHING FOR ACTIVE SPORTS

Knickers (called rationals in England) worn with a fitted jacket were proposed as cycling costume in fashion magazines. (See *Figure 14.15*.) Some of these knickers were constructed with considerable fullness so that when a lady dismounted from her bicycle they gave the appearance of a full skirt. Other cycling costumes included divided skirts or a skirt worn over knickers and blouses. Many women simply cycled in their shirt-

costumes were cut with knickerbockers instead of skirts, but even these were very full.

HAIR AND HEADDRESS

See *Illustrated Table 14.2, page 340*, for some examples of hairstyles and headdress for the period from 1870 to 1900.

Many women wore their hair in a curled fringe at the front and twisted and arranged the rest of the hair in a coil or curl at the top. The "Gibson Girl" favored an arrangement with deep, soft waves around the face. Hair was built up at the front in a "pompadour." The ears were uncovered.

Now worn only out-of-doors, hats were small to medium in size; some had no brim. Trimming tended up-

FIGURE 14.13

Tailor-made costume of 1895 has large, leg-of-mutton sleeves. The bell-shaped skirt would have had some fullness at the back, generally in the form of pleats or gathers. (Author's collection.)

FIGURE 14.14

Evening gown from the couture house of Worth. Appearing in *Harper's Bazaar* in 1894, the gown was made of light-blue satin bordered with black fur and decorated with bead embroidery in iris designs. The fan is made of black lace appliquéd on tulle. Blum, S., ed. 1974. *Victorian Fashions and Costumes from Harper's Bazaar: 1867–1898*. New York: Dover.

waists and skirts or tailor-mades and maintained a dignified, if somewhat strained, upright position.

Bathing costumes of the nineties were not only no more practical for swimming than those of the Bustle period, but were perhaps even more cumbersome since, by following the lines of the dresses, they contained more fabric. As a result, they often had large, puffed sleeves of elbow length, narrow waistlines, and full, bell-shaped skirts ending at about knee length. All this was worn over bloomers of the same length and with dark stockings that came to the knee. A few bathing

FIGURE 14.15

Velveteen bicycling costume of 1894. Sleeves are leg-of-mutton shape fashionable at the time. The fashion magazine caption used the term "Turkish trousers," not bloomers, in describing the garment. (Blum, S., ed. 1974. *Victorian Fashions and Costumes from Harper's Bazaar: 1867–1898*. New York: Dover.)

ward, with lace, feathers, ribbons as the favored trims. For sportswear or work, women wore men's styles including the fedora and the straw boater. Face veils were popular. For evening, hair decorations such as feathers, combs, and jeweled ornaments were worn.

FOOTWEAR

See *Illustrated Table 14.3, page 342*, for some examples of footwear for the period from 1870 to 1900.

For daytime, stockings were made of cotton; for evening of black or colored silk. Shoes generally had slightly rounded toes, medium high heels. Boots either laced or buttoned to close.

ACCESSORIES

Gloves were worn short during the day; long in the evening. Hand-carried accessories changed little from those of the Bustle period. Boas remained popular.

JEWELRY

Art Nouveau design influence was strong in many items of jewelry. Watches that pinned to the dress were a fashionable accessory item.

COSMETICS

Although only face powder and face creams were acceptable cosmetic items, a little tinting was sometimes added to these materials.

COSTUME FOR MEN: 1870–1900

GARMENTS

See *Illustrated Table 14.1, page 337*, for examples of undergarments from the period 1870 to 1900.

Men's drawers were usually made of wool, although cotton knits were worn in the summer. They buttoned closed in front and had a drawstring at the back that could adjust the fit around the waist. When worn under trousers, drawers ended at the ankle, but those worn under knickers for sportswear were knee length.

Undervests, also called undershirts, were usually of wool, although more expensive silk versions were also available. Hip length, and with long sleeves, they buttoned in front.

Men also could purchase combinations or **union suits** that united drawers and undervests into one garment.

Frock coats remained fashionable until the late 1890s when they were supplanted for formal daytime wear by morning coats. Morning coats curved back from well above the waist, thereby displaying the lower part of the waistcoat. Lounge coats or sack coats continued to gain in popularity. (See *Figures 14.11* and *14.16*.) These had no waist seam. They were cut straight or slightly curved in front and could be either single or double breasted. Reefers, similar in cut, were always square and the front double breasted, with slightly larger lapels and collar than the sack jacket. After 1890, reefers went out of use as suit jackets and were chiefly worn as overcoats. Another popular style was the **Norfolk jacket,** a belted sport jacket.

At this period trousers were straight and fairly narrow, with daytime trousers cut slightly wider than those for evening. Knickerbockers were worn for golf, hiking, tennis, and shooting, together with knee-length stockings and sturdy shoes or high boots or gaiters.

Coats tended to button high in the 1870s and early 1880s; therefore waistcoats became less important. Often they were

FIGURE 14.16

A double-breasted jacket with contrasting trousers for the yachtsman; a tuxedo for dress; and a light-colored, double-breasted suit with a sack jacket and worn with a straw "boater" hat; all were appropriate for summer wear in 1896. (*Sartorial Arts Journal*, July 1896.)

made of the same fabric as suits. When patterned, waistcoats were made from plaids, checks, and woven figures. By the 1890s, coats were often worn open, and as waistcoats had now become more visible, some were made from quite decorative fabrics.

Shirts for formal daytime wear had stiff, starched shirt fronts, which after 1870 were plain, rather than pleated. Just how much of the shirt front was visible through the coat front opening varied from year to year. Standing stiff collars gradually grew wider, the widest being close to three inches high in the 1890s. Removable, starched collars and cuffs were common by the 1880s, and came in a variety of shapes ranging from straight collars to those that folded over. Bow ties were popular. Longer neckties were knotted, the ends often held in place with a decorative tie stud. Fancy-colored shirts appeared in the 1890s, most of them striped. Some had plain white collars.

Evening dress for men consisted of tail coats, which had tails about knee length that were slightly narrower at the bot-

tom than at the top. In the 1880s the cut of the dress tail coat altered somewhat, and a continuous, rolled collar faced in satin or some other silk fabric replaced the notched collar.

Evening waistcoats most often matched the rest of the suit and were usually double breasted. Formal shirts were white, generally plain, with two studs at the front. After 1889, some dress shirt fronts were pleated. Collars fit closely and narrow bow ties were the fashionable evening wear. Fairly narrow trousers matched coats in color, and generally had bands of braid covering the outer, side seams.

In the 1880s, a dress version of the sack suit jacket was introduced. It was called a tuxedo (after its origin in Tuxedo, New York) in the United States, and a dinner jacket in England. (See *Figure 14.16*.)

OUTDOOR GARMENTS

To follow fashion in outdoor wear, men had to pay attention to the length of these garments. They were shorter in the 1870s, longer in the 1880s, and still longer in the 1890s. Major styles were chesterfield or top frock coat styles. (See *Figure 14.17*.) The **inverness cape** was a garment with full cape covering the shoulders and arms, or a cape in front that fitted

FIGURE 14.17

Front and back views of the Chesterfield coat; at center the frock-style overcoat. Hats worn include a derby (left), a top hat (center), and a homburg (right). (*Sartorial Arts Journal*, 1896.)

Illustrated Table 14.4

BUSTLE PERIOD AND NINETIES ACCESSORIES: 1870–1900

Jewelry and watches, c. 1870–1890

(A) Brooch at neck and small, hanging earring

(B) Watch that pinned to the dress bodice

(C) Man's pocket watch

New hat styles for men   (A) Deerstalker, c. 1870s
(B) Homburg, c. 1870s   (C) Fedora, c. 1880s

Lady's embroidered lace fan. c. 1890

Men's neckwear
(A) Striped knotted necktie, c. 1880s
(B) Ascot, c. 1880s

Feather boa, 1890

Lady's bags
(A) Handbag
(B) Travel bag

Parasol, c. 1876

into the armscye in the back so that from the front the cape was visible but from the back the coat looked like a conventional overcoat with full sleeves. The **ulster,** a long, almost ankle-length coat, had a full or half belt and, sometimes a detachable hood or cape.

HAIR AND HEADDRESS

Generally men cut their hair short and used a side or, less often, center part. Mustaches were popular, worn with side whiskers or a beard, although over this time period the trend moved toward clean-shaven faces with mustaches.

Most hat styles had been seen in earlier periods. Top hats were the favored dress hat and folding top hats were used for the opera or theater. Evening top hats were black, silk plush. Light gray, fawn and white were all used in the daytime. Other styles included bowlers or derbies, **fedoras** (low, soft hats, with the crown creased front to back), **homburgs** (a variant of the fedora made popular by the Prince of Wales), and a variety of caps worn for sports.

Straw boaters, made of shellacked straw, were worn for sports. The **deerstalker cap** was made famous through the illustrations of Conan Doyle's Sherlock Holmes stories. (See *Illustrated Table 14.4, page 349.*)

FOOTWEAR

See *Illustrated Table 14.3, page 343,* for some examples of footwear for the period from 1870 to 1900.

Patent leather shoes were used with both day and evening dress. They laced up the front. Elastic-sided shoes, sturdy high shoes for work or hunting, oxfords, and gymnastic shoes of canvas or calf with rubber soles were all popular styles.

ACCESSORIES

Accessories for men included such items as gloves and walking sticks.

JEWELRY

It was not considered masculine for men to wear jewelry except for such things as tie pins, watches, shirt studs, and cuff links.

COSTUME FOR CHILDREN:
1870–1900

The basic approach to dressing children remained constant throughout the 19th century. Infants and young children of both sexes were dressed alike. (See *Figure 14.18.*)

Costume Components for Girls

Girls' dresses were like those of adult women in silhouette, but were shorter in length. As a result, early in the Bustle

FIGURE 14.18

A mother, her small son, still dressed in skirts, and young daughter from about 1885. The boy's draped skirt and long buttoned bodice show a resemblance to the style of his mother's dress. (Photograph courtesy, Huntington Historical Society, Huntington, NY.)

period they had large bustle constructions. About 1880, when adult cuirass style was worn, girls had dresses cut straight from shoulder to hem with a belt located just a few inches above the hemline, at the knee. When bustles enlarged again, young girls wore bustles. In the 1890s large leg-of-mutton sleeves also appeared in girls' dresses. (See *Figure 14.19.*) Other style features included Russian blouses, Scotch plaid costumes, smocked dresses, and sailor dresses. (See *Figure 14.20.*)

Costume Components for Boys

After age five or so, boys no longer wore skirts but changed to trousers or knickers. By 1890, the age of breeching had dropped to about age three (Paoletti 1983). Boys' knickers of the 1870s became more fitted, resembling knee breeches of 18th century. In the 1880s they were like short trousers ending at the knee. (See *Figure 14.21.*)

Suit styles for boys included Eton suits, like those of the Crinoline period, sailor suits (see *Color Plate 43*), and tunic

FIGURE 14.19

Nez Perce Native American girls, c. 1900, wear dresses with sleeves that resemble adult women's leg-of-mutton sleeves. (Photograph courtesy, Idaho State Historical Society. Photo 63.221.317 by E. Jane Gay.)

FIGURE 14.20

Adult and child from the late 1890s. The little girl's dress falls from a wide, ruffled plaid yoke. (Photograph courtesy, Huntington Historical Society, Huntington, NY.)

suits, but with a narrower skirt and slightly lower waistline than earlier styles.

Boys wore reefers, cut like those of adult men; blazers, made of striped or plain colored flannel, loosely fitted, with patch pockets, and generally worn for sports; and Norfolk jackets, especially with knickers. Usually shirts had stiff, high collars.

Boys wore smaller versions of adult men's outerwear.

Costume for Boys and Girls

Table 14.1 summarizes typical stages in the acquisition of adult clothing by children in the late 19th century.

INFLUENCES FROM AESTHETIC DRESS

The aesthetic movement influenced children's clothing. **Kate Greenaway styles** (based on illustrations by Kate Greenaway, an Aesthetic Movement illustrator of children's books who showed little girls in dresses derived from Empire styles) became popular and were imitated in girls' dresses for the 1880s

and 1890s. Kate Greenaway styles have been revived periodically ever since for children and have influenced women's styles as well. **Little Lord Fauntleroy suits** consisted of a velvet tunic, ending slightly below the waist, tight knickerbockers, a wide sash, and a wide, white lace collar. This outfit was based on clothing worn by the hero of the children's book of the same name. (See *Figure 14.22.*) The similarity of this costume to that worn by Oscar Wilde was no coincidence. According to Cunnington and Beard (1972) the author of *Little Lord Fauntleroy* was influenced by the comments of Wilde on his trip to the United States in 1882, when he declared that the Cavalier dress on which he based his "aesthetic" costume was the most artistic male dress ever known. With this costume some boys wore long, curling locks. Many children's books of the time characterized the wearers of Fauntleroy costume as "mama's boys" or "sissies," while boys forced to wear the costume are depicted as hating every moment and longing for the day when the barber would relieve them of these obnoxious curls. The truth is that relatively few boys actually wore Little Lord Fauntleroy suits.

FIGURE 14.21

Boy dressed in knee-length knickers, c. 1860. (Author's collection.)

Table 14.1		
TYPICAL STAGES IN THE ACQUISITION OF ADULT CLOTHING IN THE LATE 19TH-CENTURY		
	Boys	**Girls**
Infant	Long white dresses	Long white dresses
Toddler	Short dresses	Short dresses
Small child	Dresses or tunic suits	Short dresses
School-age child	Suit with short trousers	Somewhat longer dresses
Adolescent	Suit with long trousers No adult formal wear	Somewhat longer dresses No revealing formal evening dresses
Adult	Formal wear permitted	Hair worn up dresses to ankle décolletage for formal evening dress

A survey of childcare manuals, etiquette books, and advice. Reprinted from Paoletti, J. 1983. "Clothes Make the Boy." *Dress, The Annual Journal of the Costume Society of America,* Vol. 9, p. 19.

FIGURE 14.22

Boy dressed in "Little Lord Fauntleroy suit." Although the suit is made from wool rather than velvet, the wide lace collar and cuffs, knickers, bow at the neck, and the long hair are typical of the style. (Author's collection.)

HAIR AND HEADDRESS

Boys wore their hair slightly longer until they were out of skirts, then their hair was cut short like adult men's. Girls' hair was long, natural waves were encouraged. Large bows were a popular hair ornament. Boys wore caps. Boys and girls wore sailor hats, both wore other styles modeled on adults' hats.

MOURNING COSTUME IN THE SECOND HALF OF THE 19TH CENTURY

Wearing special dress that signifies bereavement is not unique to any period. However, social custom in the second half of the 19th century did seem to place far greater emphasis on conforming to a rigid and far-reaching code of etiquette for mourning than in most previous or subsequent periods. Taylor (1983), in an extended study of mourning costume and customs, indicates that several factors were influential in the increased emphasis on appropriate mourning costume in the 19th century.

One factor was the more widespread imitation of royal and upper-class behavior and dress by the middle class. When

Prince Albert, husband of Queen Victoria, died in 1861, the queen put on mourning not only for the requisite period, but also for the rest of her life. In so doing, she set a highly visible example for others to follow. Another important influence was the widespread availability of fashion magazines, which frequently published articles about proper mourning etiquette and reported on the mourning dress of famous persons.

Custom prescribed not only colors and fabrics for mourning, but established stages and gradations of mourning. Although men were not required to do much more than wear a black armband, widows had to wear deep mourning for a year and a day. Deepest or first mourning consisting of black crape-covered dresses,[1] black accessories, and even, in

[1] Mourning crape was a black, silk fabric with a crinkled or uneven surface texture. The preferred modern spelling for similar fabrics in various colors is "crepe," however, when used for mourning in the 19th century, it was spelled "crape."

some cases, black underwear! Widows wore second mourning for 21 months (black with crape trimming), and ordinary mourning (in which crape could be omitted altogether and black clothing trimmed in black was worn), for at least three months. (See *Color Plate 39.*) Even children wore black or white trimmed in black.

After the first decade of the 20th century, the rigid etiquette surrounding mourning diminished. Taylor (1983) explains,

> It was the terrible slaughter of the First World War that undoubtedly caused the major breakdown in funeral and mourning etiquette. . . . As the war continued the survivors had somehow to face up to the loss of almost a whole generation of young men and the creation of a new army—this one of widows and fatherless children. . . . The sight of millions of women of all ages shrouded in crape would have been too much to bear.

SUMMARY

THEMES

Important themes of the late 19th century include PRODUCTION AND ACQUISITION OF TEXTILES AND APPAREL AND TECHNOLOGY. The budding American women's ready-to-wear industry, born in the last decades of the 19th century as a result of socioeconomic changes and technological advances in the United States, was beginning to be a factor in women's fashion. It made possible the mass production and distribution of fashionable items such as the shirtwaist.

The more rapid movement of fashion changes for women, the more static nature of styles for men, and the transformation of certain segments of the ready-to-wear industry into a "fashion industry" foreshadowed important trends that would continue in the 20th century.

FASHION, a constant theme since the Middle Ages, stands out as styles for women in the years between 1870 and 1900 went through a more rapid series of changes than did styles of any preceding period of comparable length. None of the distinct phases of costume can be said to have lasted even ten years. These changes were gradual, progressing year-by-year as the silhouette changed from one emphasizing the draped bustle, narrowing to the slim cuirass bodice with both decorative detailing and training at the back, and returning to back fullness again in the rigid structure of yet another sort of bustle. When the bustle finally subsided, it was superseded by the hourglass silhouette of the 1890s.

Men's costume, contrariwise, showed little change in silhouette. The items of a man's wardrobe remained constant and varied little from year to year, except in details such as the length of coats, or the width of trousers or lapels.

The theme of CHANGES IN SOCIAL BEHAVIOR is also reflected in women's apparel. The movement of more women into the workplace was evident in such practical styles as tailor-mades and shirtwaists. Bicycling bloomers, bathing costume, and gymnastic clothing demonstrated that women were beginning to feel free to participate in active sports.

As has been true so often before, RELATIONSHIPS BETWEEN COSTUME AND DEVELOPMENTS IN THE FINE AND APPLIED ARTS are evident. Not only do the enormously elaborate Bustle period dresses find a parallel in the Victorian parlors with their wealth of pattern and knick-knacks, but costume also shares the tendency of furniture and architecture to revive styles of the past. As new artistic movements emerged, clothing styles reflected these as well. Those who shared this artistic philosophy adopted Aesthetic dress. And as the century ended, Art Nouveau motifs could be seen not only in fabrics, jewelry, and accessories, but also in a sinuous, S-shaped silhouette that was developing in women's dress.

SURVIVALS OF BUSTLE AND NINETIES COSTUME STYLES

Although the bustle in its fullest form has not truly returned since 1890, the focus of fullness at the back of women's skirts is an idea that comes and goes. It most frequently appears in

Visual Summary Table

BUSTLE AND NINETIES

Man: 1870–1900
Shirts and neckties, vests, coats, and trousers. Coat alternatives were frock coats, morning coats, sack coats, and Norfolk jackets.

Man: 1870–1900
The tuxedo, an evening suit with a sack jacket, appeared in the 1880s.

Woman: 1870–1878
Mostly two-piece dresses, close-fitting bodices, sleeves set in at the shoulder. Fullness concentrated at the back of the skirt falls in ruffles and draperies supported by a bustle.

Woman: 1878–1883
The bustle diminishes and skirt fullness drops toward the floor. Bodices lengthen, fitting smoothly over the hip, then becoming wider below the knee.

Woman: 1883–1890
The bustle returns as a shelf-like, rigid form at the back. Skirts are rarely trained. Details include high, standing collars, long fitted sleeves for daytime.

Woman: 1890–1900
A few pleats at the back of the skirt replace bustles. Dresses are hourglass shaped, with very large sleeves, small waistlines and skirts shaped like an inverted cone.

evening or wedding gowns. The figure revealing styles of the 1990s even produced their own version of the bustle, a padded girdle called the "wonderbutt." (See *Illustrated Table 19.1, page 528.*)

Norfolk jackets, with their distinctive cut, are revived from time to time. Their most recent revival in men's dress was in the late 1960s and 70s.

Although the leg-of-mutton sleeves of the 90s show remarkable similarities to sleeve styles of the 1830s, their incorporation into shirtwaist blouses was something new. Styles, often called the "Gibson Girl" look, that derive from shirtwaist blouses have experienced revivals. Around 1947 they became a fad for adolescents, and returned again, with less sleeve fullness, in blouses of the latter part of the 1980s.

NOTES

Cunnington, C. W. and C. Beard. 1972. *A Dictionary of English Costume 900–1900.* London: Adam and Charles Black, p. 127.

Farrell-Beck, J. and C. Gau. 2002. *Uplift: The Bra in America.* Philadelphia, PA: University of Pennsylvania Press, pp. 1, 12, 14.

Kidwell, C. B. and M. C. Christman. 1974. *Suiting Everyone.* Washington, DC: The Smithsonian Institution Press, p. 137.

Paoletti, J. 1983. "Clothes Make the Boy, 1860–1910." *Dress,* Vol. 9, p. 17.

Taylor, L. 1983. *Mourning Dress.* London: George Allen and Unwin, pp. 266, 267.

Warner, P. C. 1992. "The Thin Ideal: A Matter of Proportion and History." *ITAA Proceedings.* Monument, CO: International Textile and Apparel Association, p. 56.

Warner, P. C. 1993. "The Gym Suit: Freedom at Last." In P. A. Cunningham and S. V. Lab, eds., *Dress in American Popular Culture.* Bowling Green, OH: Bowling Green State University, Popular Press.

SELECTED READINGS

Books and Other Materials Containing Illustrations of Costume of the Period from Original Sources

Fashion Magazines: *The Delineator, Godey's Lady's Book, Harper's Bazaar, Peterson's Magazine.*

Blum, S., ed. 1974. *Victorian Fashions and Costumes from Harper's Bazaar: 1867–1898.* New York: Dover.

Foster, V. 1985. *A Visual History of Costume: The 19th Century.* New York: Drama Books.

Gersheim, A. 1963. *Fashion and Reality.* London: Faber and Faber.

Hall, L. 1992. *Common Threads: A Parade of American Clothing.* Boston: Bulfinch Press.

The House of Worth. 1962. Brooklyn, NY: Brooklyn Museum.

Severa, J. 1995. *Dressed for the Photographer. Ordinary Americans and Fashion 1840–1900.* Kent, OH: Kent State University Press.

Waller, G. 1966. *Saratoga: Saga of an Impious Era.* Englewood Cliffs, NJ: Prentice-Hall.

Articles

Helveston, S. 1990. "Fashion on the Frontier." *Dress,* Vol. 17, p. 141.

Johns, M. J. and J. Farrell-Beck. 2001. "'Cut Out the Sleeves' Nineteenth-Century U.S. Women's Swimmers and Their Attire." *Dress,* Vol. 28, p. 53

Ormond, L. 1968. "Female Costume in the Aesthetic Movement of the 1880s and 1890s." *Costume,* No. 2, p. 33.

Paoletti, J. 1980. "The Role of Choice in the Democratization of Fashion: A Case Study, 1875–1885." *Dress,* Vol. 5, p. 47.

Richards, M. L. 1995. "Memories of Girlhood Apparel from the United States Indian Territory, 1850-1907." *Costume,* No. 29, p. 68.

Schonfield, Z. 1972. "The Expectant Victorian (Late 19th Century Maternity Clothes)." *Costume,* No. 6, p. 36.

Sims, S. 1991. "The Bicycle, the Bloomer, and Dress Reform in the 1890s." In P. A. Cunningham and S. V. Lab, *Dress and Popular Culture.* Bowling Green, OH: Bowling Green State University Popular Press.

Walsh, M. 1979. "The Democratization of Fashion: The Emergence of the Women's Dress Pattern Industry." *The Journal of American History,* Vol. 66, No. 2, p. 299.

Warner, P.C. 2001. "'It Looks Very Nice Indeed.' Clothing in Women's Colleges, 1837–1897." *Dress,* Vol. 28, p. 23.

Daily Life

Andrist, R. K. 1972. *American Century: One Hundred Years of Changing Life Styles in America.* New York: McGraw-Hill.

Cooper, S. F. 2001. *The Victorian Woman.* New York: Harry N. Abrams.

Horn, P. 1997. *The Rise and Fall of the Victorian Servant.* New York: Sutton Publishing.

Mitchell, S. 1996. *Daily Life in Victorian England.* Westport, CT: Greenwood Press.

Schlereth, T. 1991. *Victorian America: Transformations in Everyday Life, 1876–1915.* New York: Harper Perennial.

Smith, S. H. and M. Dawson, eds. 2000. *The American 1890s: A Cultural Reader.* Chapel Hill, NC: Duke University Press.

This Fabulous Century. 1870–1900. 1972. New York: Time-Life Books.

I dreamed I was

WANTED
in my Maidenform bra

Name: Star Flower*   **Reward:** Just wearing it!

Distinguishing characteristics: Circular stitched cups in pretty petal pattern. Twin elastic bands beneath cups. Upper bands adjust to make bra fit like custom-made. Lower bands make bra breathe with wearer.

Physical description: White broadcloth. A, B, C cups. 2.50.

Last seen: In stores everywhere. Looking *ravishing*.

THE TWENTIETH CENTURY

1 9 0 0 – 1 9 9 6

The beginning of the new century was, for many, almost a magical period. It seemed to mark a turning point, a new era, and it was marked by special celebrations, expositions, pronouncements by public officials, and a rash of predictions about what the world would be like by the turn of the next century. And yet, had people been able to look into the future to see the events of the next 100 years, it is likely they would have chosen 1914 rather than 1900 as the beginning of a new era.

For it was in 1914 that World War I began, and it was after 1914 that nothing ever seemed the same again. For Americans, particularly, World War I marked the beginning of an expanded role in international politics and economics from which the country, try as it might, could never pull back.

In the 1920s, general prosperity was the norm for most Americans, the single largest exception being the farmers. The country entered a period of reaction to the war that brought with it a revolution on the part of the young against traditional mores and values. Technology expanded, the buying power of individuals increased, and life for most people, though more frenetic, was marked by a higher standard of material comfort than ever before.

When the stock market crash in 1929 ushered in the Depression of the 1930s, all this changed. Not only the farmers but also large numbers of middle-class Americans experienced varying degrees of poverty. The Depression was not confined to the United States; its impact was worldwide. The stage was slowly being set for another international conflict when Fascist dictator Benito Mussolini rose to power in Italy in the 1920s and Adolf Hitler in Germany in the 1930s. War

began in 1939 when Germany invaded Poland. The United States managed to stay out of the war until December 7, 1941, when the Japanese bombed Pearl Harbor.

The end of the war in 1945 was marked by yet another 20th century milestone, the development of atomic power. The United States emerged from the war as a "super power," along with the Soviet Union. The older European powers that had exercised Western world leadership for so many centuries had been devastated by the war and had to begin to rebuild.

The postwar period was marked politically by the "Cold War" between the Soviet Union and the United States and economically by a period of prosperity. In the United States, the returned veterans flooded the colleges, married or took up married life again, produced a bumper crop of babies and moved to the suburbs in large numbers. The Korean War (1950–1953) disturbed the return to peacetime life for some Americans.

In 1957 the Russians announced that they had launched the first earth-orbiting satellite and thus began what has been called "The Space Age." The Americans made intense efforts to catch up. When John Kennedy was elected President in 1960 he vowed that Americans would reach the moon by 1970, and indeed the first manned moon landing was successfully accomplished July 20, 1969.

The 1960s in the United States could be referred to as the decade of protest and demonstrations. The Civil Rights Movement pressed its demands for racial equality through passive resistance and mass demonstrations in the early 1960s and when students of the late 1960s first began to oppose the escalating war in Vietnam, they borrowed these same tactics.

In the 1970s the United States government resumed diplomatic relations with China, and an American president resigned from office. By the 1980s American consumers and manufacturers became aware of the expanding Japanese economy, while at the same time a new wave of immigration and the computer revolution changed American life.

In Europe the Economic Community continued to grow and to prosper in the 1970s and into the 1980s. The Soviet Union maintained its control over eastern Europe until the strain of the Cold War undermined the Soviet economy and forced the Soviet system to collapse. While the Soviet economy had been deteriorating, the economies of Asian countries that followed the Japanese model had been booming. That boom ended when the Japanese economy went into a severe decline in the last decade of the 20th century.

As the 21st century approached, individuals and businesses feared that computers, which had assumed a great many routine functions, would encounter problems that would cause malfunctions in a host of essential services. Technologists worked feverishly to prepare for anticipated problems and ready the world for the year 2000. The problems never happened and the world passed easily into a new millennium.

The decade preceding the millennium was far from peaceful, with conflicts in the former Yugoslavia and in the Middle East. The years after 2000 brought terrorists attacks to the heartland of the United States and American-led wars in Afghanistan and Iraq.

Visible differences between 1900 and 2000 were many, but changes in attitudes and values were even more dramatic—as dramatic as the contrast between the corseted Gibson Girl of the turn of the century in her long, softly flowing skirts and soft pompadour and the woman of the new millennium dressed for cycling in her spandex activewear.

One of the major changes that has taken place is a fundamental change in the makeup of the student body in American colleges and universities. Women are applying in greater numbers for admission to colleges and universities. With better high school records, women outnumber men in colleges and universities. This disparity has affected applications because students prefer an equal ratio of the sexes in co-ed colleges and universities. According to the United States Department of Education, in another decade 42 percent of undergraduates will be men. As a result, college and university administrators are struggling to maintain a gender balance.

ART AND COSTUME IN THE 20TH CENTURY

With the advent of photography, drawings, paintings, and sculpture were no longer the only images depicting contemporary clothing. Indeed, in the century following the invention of photography, artists themselves moved away from representing photographic-like reality and moved gradually from impressionist representations of the world toward greater abstraction. In earlier centuries the work of artists showed how clothing appeared, and at the same time the lines, proportions, and decoration of clothing embodied the artistic spirit or zeitgeist of the times. In the 20th century, much of the art does not show us how clothing appeared, but we can still see many connections between the visual arts and dress in areas such as line and proportion, and in the design of textiles. These parallels are sometimes quite obvious, as in the Art Nouveau and Art Deco periods, and at other times more subtle, tenuous, or even superficial.

Whether clothing can be considered an art has been hotly debated. In earlier centuries this issue was not even considered. It arose only after the establishment of the haute couture and the elevation of the fashion designer to the role of a creative genius shaping new and original styles. If we accept the idea of the designer as an artist working in the medium of clothing, then it is not surprising to find that like other artists of any period the designer will be sensitive to the *zeitgeist*, the spirit of the age, and that the creations of the designer will reflect that period. The designer, however, is required to produce at least two new lines of clothing each year. The designer must also work within the constraints of what is wearable. Designers often turn to current art, events, and media for design ideas, and reflections of all frequently appear in their creations.

NEW SOURCES OF EVIDENCE
FOR THE STUDY OF COSTUME

Two additional media sources became available in the 20th century through which to learn about costume: motion pictures and television. By the 1920s motion pictures were playing in urban and rural areas. When leading actors and actresses wore contemporary clothing, they were seen by millions of individuals. Although some trends began after they were seen "in the movies," it is not entirely clear whether, as a general rule, the styles shown in films followed current trends or initiated them. If the costume designer for a film was effectively using costume to delineate character, the clothing could have been selected in order to make a specific point, and does not necessarily simply reproduce current styles. The viewer should be alert to the purposes of the designer in any film, and how motion pictures can be a useful source of information about clothing of the years in which the film was made.

Styles shown in films set in earlier periods, however, may be less trustworthy. Even when garments are reasonably authentic, makeup and hairstyles often bear little resemblance to the styles of the historic period depicted, but rather reflect the period in which the film was made. When a famous actress appears in a period film she may have her own designer whose task it is to set off the star's physical charms, rather than to produce authentic costumes.

As a record of contemporary costume, the dramatic programs on television have some of the same problems as motion pictures. It should be noted, however, that costume designers for soap operas generally selected the costumes from styles available in stores or from manufacturers. If one uses dramas from television or motion pictures as a source of information about costume, these should be evaluated carefully, and insofar as is possible, one should ascertain whether clothing was designed and intended to serve a specific dramatic purpose or purchased for use.

On the other hand, once the motion picture camera was available to the press many actual events were photographed, and these accurately depict the clothing being worn by real people. Such film footage was seen in newsreel films, and a great deal of early film material has been utilized in documentary motion pictures. With the advent of television after World War II, the amount of film and video material increased dramatically. Future generations studying costume should have no difficulty determining what was worn in public during the second half of the 20th century!

CHRONOLOGY

1900
Exposition Universelle held in Paris; couturiers display their designs
International Ladies Garment Workers Union (ILGWU) founded

1901
Queen Victoria's death, Edward VII assumes the throne
First Paris exhibit by Pablo Picasso

1903
First successful flight by Orville and Wilbur Wright at Kitty Hawk, North Carolina
The Great Train Robbery, first feature film, released

1905
Einstein formulates the theory of relativity

1908
Henry Ford makes first Model T Ford

1909
First newsreel film shown in Paris
The Russian Ballet appears in Paris

1910
Women's Wear Daily begins publication
Death of Edward VII, George V succeeds to the throne
Mexican Revolution
Vernon and Irene Castle's success as a dance team helps
to launch a dance craze in the United States

1911
Cubists exhibit in *Salon des Independants* in Paris
Fire in Triangle Shirtwaist Company, New York

1912
Henry Ford introduces the assembly line in Detroit for manufacturing cars
Poiret designs costumes for show *Le Minaret* in which he uses hobble skirts
Woodrow Wilson elected President

1913
16th Amendment, establishing the income tax, is ratified.
G. Sunderback invents the slide fastener—later called the zipper

1914
Outbreak of World War I

1917
The United States enters World War I
Russian Revolution overthrows Czarist government

1918
World War I ends

1919
The Bauhaus is established as a center for contemporary design in Germany

THE EDWARDIAN PERIOD AND WORLD WAR I

1 9 0 0 – 1 9 2 0

A.

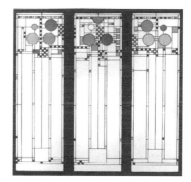

D.

A.

Mission furniture

B.

Flatiron building by Daniel H. Burnham, 1902

C.

Painting by Pablo Picasso,
Les Demoiselles d'Avignon, 1907

D.

Window by Frank Lloyd Wright

E.

Tiffany Candelabrum

F.

Robie house
by Frank Lloyd Wright, 1908

B.

C.

E.

F.

Figure A courtesy of J. Curcio in Federico, J. T. 1988. *Clues to American Furniture.* Washington: Starrhill, p. 52. Figure B courtesy of V. R. Tortora. Figure C courtesy of the Museum of Modern Art, New York, acquired through the Lillie P. Bliss Bequest. Figure D courtesy of the Metropolitan Museum of Art, gift of Edward C. Moore, Jr., and Edgar J. Kaufman Charitable Foundation (67-231.1–3). Figure E courtesy of the Art Institute of Chicago, gift of the Antiquarian Society through William Y. Hutchinson Fund (1985.221a–c). Figure F courtesy of AP/Wide World Photos/Robie House by Wright.

HISTORICAL BACKGROUND

The United States

Writers have called the years preceding World War I in America "the good years," "the confident years," "the age of optimism," "the innocent years," and even "the cocksure era." These appellations reflect a sense of well-being that seemed to pervade the country.

The total population of the United States in 1900 was something over 76 million, 40 percent of whom lived in urban areas. Only 41 million of these Americans were native born, and almost half a million new immigrants entered the country each year. There were 45 states, New York the largest in population and Nevada the smallest.

The country was coming to depend more and more on a host of useful devices. The telephone, the typewriter, the self-binding harvester, and sewing machines were commonplace. Electricity was installed in many of the homes of America. And 8,000 automobiles were registered in the United States by 1900.

At the drug store soda fountain, ice cream sodas were 10 cents, and orangeade was a nickel. Beef was 10 cents a pound and spring chicken 7 cents a pound. Ladies could buy a tailor-made suit at the department store for $10.00 and a pair of shoes for $1.50. At the same time the average wage was $12.00 a week or 22 cents an hour. Five percent of the population were unemployed; almost 11 percent were illiterate.

The Wright brothers made the first successful flight in 1903. In the same year a 12-minute movie, *The Great Train Robbery,* was released, and a new industry was on its way.

Great Britain and France at the Turn of the Century

The accession of Edward VII to the throne of the British Empire in 1901, after the almost 70-year reign of his mother Queen Victoria, raised in some of the British hopes for a fresh approach in politics. Britain was involved in the Boer War in South Africa when Edward became King, and the war dragged on until 1902.

Edward was a genial and worldly man with a wide range of interests. While Prince of Wales, he had displayed an especially keen interest in women and led such an active social life that his lifestyle earned the disapproval of the queen. One of the most popular cartoons of the era showed a rotund Prince of Wales standing in the corner while the queen scolded him.

Edward's name is generally applied to the first decade of the century—the Edwardian period. He brought to the English throne an emphasis on social life and fashion that had been absent during the long years of Victoria's widowhood.

In France in the period from 1900 to just before World War I, a political system emerged that permitted a high degree of individual freedom. A remarkable number of creative artists and scientists who were active at the time can be cited. Important authors of the period included Zola, de Maupassant, Anatole France, Verlaine, and Mallarmé. Monet, Manet, Renoir, Degas, Cezanne, and Gauguin were among the important painters of the era, and in music the composers Massenet, Saint-Saëns, Bizet, Debussy, and Ravel were active. In science the names of Pierre and Marie Curie and Louis Pasteur stand out.

WORLD WAR I

Events that led to the beginning of World War I developed rapidly and unexpectedly. The major European powers confronted each other in two heavily armed alliance systems. Germany feared encirclement by hostile powers. However, because of Germany's rise to power, other nations feared German domination of Europe. Indeed, some German leaders dreamed of such a goal.

The assassination of the Archduke Franz Ferdinand, heir apparent to the Austro–Hungarian throne, provided the spark for war. The Austro–Hungarian government, convinced of Serbian responsibility for the assassination, used the assassination as an excuse to declare war on Serbia. After Russia refused to stop mobilizing in defense of Serbia, Germany declared war on Russia and two days later on France, Russia's ally. Germany took these actions because the war plan required attacking first France and then Russia. To attack France, German armies marched through Belgium, whose neutrality had been guaranteed by the European powers. Consequently, Britain entered the war as an ally of France and Russia in defense of Belgium.

To Americans the war was far away. The average man and woman on the street, though likely to sympathize with the French and British and aghast at "the rape of Belgium," thought the United States was well out of it. But as the war dragged on, American sentiment changed and on April 2, 1917, President Woodrow Wilson called for a declaration of war against Germany.

When the fighting stopped on November 11, 1918, more than 10 million soldiers had been killed and more than 20 million wounded. Three great empires had collapsed. Western civilization had been forever changed.

The Effect of the War on Fashions

The War influenced styles of the period in Europe and America from 1914 to 1918 in a number of ways. The most obvious of these was in a move by women into more comfortable, practical clothes that were required for their more active participation in the variety of jobs that they had taken over from men. The prevailing costume during World War I had a relatively short skirt, several inches above the ankles. The skirt was fairly wide around the hem, a distinct change from the hobble skirt that had been the rage about 1912. The fit through the body was comfortable. Military influences were evident in the cut of some jackets and coats that followed the lines of officers' tunics. (See *Figure 15.11*.)

The War also affected colors and fabrics. Wool was in short supply, as it was diverted to the manufacture of uniforms for fighting men. And the scarcity of chemicals used for certain dyestuffs restricted somewhat the use of dark colors. *Contemporary Comments 15.1* describes the impact of fabric shortages.

After the War, some of the clothing worn by soldiers passed into use by the general public. Sweaters were issued to soldiers, and the men who had become used to wearing these comfortable garments adopted them for general sportswear. For warmth, the army issued a sleeveless vestlike garment to wear under the uniform. After the War, these were sold as army surplus. The success the surplus stores had in selling these garments led manufacturers to add sleeves and make jackets over the same general pattern, and the buttoned, and later, zippered jacket for outdoor wear was born. Another postwar style that originated during the War was the trench coat. This water-repellent coat of closely woven cotton twill was belted at the waist. It became a standard item of rainwear for men and after several decades was also adopted by women.

INFLUENCES ON FASHION

The French Couture and Paul Poiret

The turn of the century was marked, as such events often are, by a major exposition in Paris, the *Exposition Universelle*. In one of the exhibit halls members of the Parisian haute couture, the leading fashion houses of the era, presented exhibits showing their designs. These were the most important design houses of the time: Doucet, Paquin, Rouf, Cheruit, Callot Soeurs, Redfern, and Worth.

The original Worth, Charles, had died in 1895, and had been succeeded by his two sons, Gaston and Jean Philippe. In the early part of the century Gaston engaged a young designer named **Paul Poiret** (*Pwar-ray'*). Gaston saw in Poiret's work the kind of change he felt was needed for styles, but Jean Philippe and Gaston disagreed and Poiret left the House of Worth and in a few years opened his own establishment. In any fashion period there may be designers whose influence is so great or whose work so captures the spirit of the age that they seem to serve as a focal point for style in that time. Poiret was such a figure. He was not only an outstanding designer,

but also a colorful character whose personal idiosyncrasies help to perpetuate his legend.

Between 1903 and World War I Poiret reigned supreme in the Paris couture. His customers submitted to his every wish, and he altered their way of dressing. The first radical step that he took was to do away with corsets. But while making gowns that were loose and free through the body, he put women into skirts with hems so narrow that they could hardly move. He is quoted as saying, "I freed the bosom, shackled the legs, but gave liberty to the body" (Lyman 1972).

One of Poiret's major talents was for the use of vivid colors. Many writers have credited the color and Oriental-influenced styles he devised to the popularity of the Russian Ballet and the costumes designed for the ballet by the artist Leon Bakst. The Russian Ballet took Paris by storm in 1909, but Poiret disclaimed the influence of Bakst, saying that he had already begun to use vivid colors and a new style with strong Oriental overtones before the arrival of the ballet. No matter which version of the development of these styles is accurate, the two complemented each other and helped to reinforce the popular lines and colors of the time. (See *Color Plate 41*.)

In 1912 Poiret designed costumes for a show called *Le Minaret*. He put the women into hobble skirts over which he placed wide tunics. The tunic and hobble skirt became the rage. One of his designers was an artist named Erté who, in turn, became a prominent fashion artist and designer for the stage as well as for women's clothing.

In addition to the styles he created, Poiret was an innovator in other ways. He traveled abroad with a group of fashion models on which he showed his designs. He was also the first of the couturiers to begin marketing perfume, which he named after his daughter.

During and after World War I, the theatrical, colorful styles so characteristic of Poiret's work became outmoded. He never adjusted to the newer lines and look, and although his business continued into the 1920s, he grew less and less successful. Eventually he dropped from public sight, and died in 1943. Some say that he died in poverty; others claim that he lived quietly but comfortably.

Fortuny

While Poiret was a designer whose work seems to be uniquely suited to his times, the Spanish-born Mariano Fortuny y Madrazo (generally called Fortuny) was one of those rare designers whose work seems timeless. An artist who had begun exhibiting in the 1890s and who continued to paint for all of his life, Fortuny designed clothing and textiles from 1906 to 1949. His biographer, Guillermo de Osma, writing in the catalog of a 1981 exhibition of his work, says:

Fortuny's clothes, like the rest of his work, were quite outside accepted convention. He was not a couturier but rather a creative artist of dress. . . . His fabrics were conceived like

CONTEMPORARY COMMENTS 15.1

Impact of World War I on Textile Supplies

The First World War disrupted fiber supplies. In the Journal of Home Economics *for March 1918, Amy L. Rolfe of the Department of Home Economics, University of Missouri, analyzes the impact of the war on "What We Shall Wear This Year and Next" (pp. 125–129).*

Few persons realize the very small amount of textile fibres which can be purchased by our clothing manufacturers or the causes which have brought about such conditions. . . . there is so little raw wool on the market, and so much of that is being commandeered by the government for soldier's uniforms and blankets. . . .

Before the war the United States grew only two-thirds of the wool used in our mills and the remaining third came from abroad. Now none is imported except from South America for the Allies have use for all they can get. Besides that used for uniforms and blankets, millions of yards of worsted cloth, costing $3 a yard and known as shalloon and shell cloth are being used in bagging or covering both the propelling and explosive charges for the big guns. Every bit of wool used in this way is entirely destroyed.

. . . The draft has taken spinners from the mills in great numbers and new workers must be trained before they can use their hands skillfully. . . .

For these and various other reasons it seems very improbable that there will be much wool to be worn by the civilian population next year. . . .

The cotton situation is almost as bad as the wool situation, although the United States has the advantage as it grows more than half the cotton in the world. . . . the price of raw cotton has risen to alarming heights. . . . a bale of cotton is needed to fire one of the large guns, vast quantities are used for the unbleached muslin and gauze used in Red Cross work, and a still greater amount is commandeered by the government for khaki uniforms and tents. . . .

The use of linen as a substitute is more impossible still. Millions of yards of linen are needed for aëroplane wings . . . The reason for the shortage of linen is that much of the flax of the world has been grown near the German border and has been trampled down and broken by the warfare that has been going on there. . . .

Most of our silk comes to us from China and Japan and so the supply of that material should be little influenced by the war. . . . a series of experiments being conducted at the front . . . may result in the use of all of the silk which it is possible to procure. As the boys "Somewhere in France" are sent into the trenches they are provided with silk underwear. It is thought that silk will prove to be gas resisting and also will be less irritating to the wounds than cotton . . .

As wool, cotton, linen, and silk comprise the list of fibres which are commonly used for clothing, . . . we in the United States . . . must do our bit by conserving the supply of textiles. The manufacturers will help us to do this by using as little material as possible in their ready to wear garments. Skirts will be comfortably narrow, suit coats will be short, single breasted with small lapels and collars. Ornamental revers, patch pockets, and belts will be eliminated. Conservative styles will be in vogue because people will know that whatever they buy this year they must expect to wear much longer than usual.

paintings; he built up colors in layers, playing with the effects of light and transparency, printing and retouching to create textures and harmonies of color that were impossible to repeat (Fortuny 1981).

Fortuny drew upon the past and non-European cultures as inspiration for his designs. Among the most notable were ancient Greek styles that inspired his **Delphos** gown, probably his most famous design, and Renaissance and oriental motifs, which appear in many of his textile designs. (See *Color Plate 42.*) Just how he achieved the pleating for his Greek-inspired gowns is not known. The pleats would be removed by dry cleaning, and his clients returned garments to his atelier for cleaning and repleating.

His clients were dancers, actresses, and well-to-do women. Never part of the popular fashion market, he was ignored by the influential fashion press, but Poiret knew and admired his work, as did other designers. Museums and individuals, who sometimes still wear these garments, have collected his work. Late 20th century designers such as Mary McFadden are still inspired by his work. Jean-Michel Tuchscherer, Curator of the Textile Museum in Lyon, France, sees Fortuny's work this way:

As a creator, Fortuny remains an enigmatic figure isolated in his ivory tower, but his highly personal style infuses his creations with a stature and originality which make him a figure of far greater importance than most of his more avant-garde contemporaries (Fortuny 1981).

ORIENTAL INFLUENCES ON ART AND FASHION

Art movements and fashion trends are often connected. Influences from Japanese art on Impressionist painters and other European artists of the latter part of the 19th century probably had their roots in the opening of Japan for trade in the 1850s. It is likely that the Japanese, Chinese, and generalized Far Eastern influences that can be observed in women's clothing, especially in the years after 1907, derive from late 19th century fine and decorative art trends. (See *Figures 15.5* and *15.6*.)

The style connections to the Far East were plentiful. Kimonos became popular for leisurely at-home wear for both men and women. The cut of women's clothing grew less structured. Fabric designs and colors showed Oriental influences, as did the design of the haute couture. Kim and De-Long (1992), reporting on an analysis of women's fashions of the 1910s and 1920s, noted that "Virtually every category of garment type eventually was influenced, from morning jackets to afternoon frocks and evening gowns."

The Changing Social Roles of American Women

Although increasingly larger numbers of women were entering the work force (more than 5 million in 1900), most men and women considered the woman's place to be in the home. Concessions to the more active life that women were leading were evident in styles, as skirts grew somewhat shorter and the shirtwaist blouse and skirt were widely adopted. Business was employing increasing numbers of women, especially as "typewriters."

But even the more affluent married lady who saw her role as wife and mother was getting out of the house more. Women's clubs increased in membership to more than one million by 1910. These groups focused on self-improvement or good works such as helping the poor.

The woman's suffrage movement stepped up its campaigning for women's rights, but President Grover Cleveland spoke for many men, and women as well, when he declared "The relative positions to be assumed by man and woman in the working out of our civilization were assigned long ago by a higher intelligence than ours."

By the second decade of the century women were becoming even more adventurous. They drove cars, went out to work in increasing numbers (7.5 million in 1910 and a million more were added to the work force by 1920) and engaged in a variety of active sports from swimming to bobsledding. The clothes required for these active, competitive sports helped to modify the prevailing styles.

As women became more emancipated, support for the vote for women grew. After 1910 a series of public marches and rallies were held, and each one was larger than the last. The War caused a decrease in the activism of the suffragists and, at the same time, dramatized the place of women in American society as women moved in to fill jobs that the soldiers had left behind. Women worked in factories, delivered ice, and directed traffic. Women became auto mechanics and operated elevators. On June 4, 1919, after the War had ended, Congress passed the 19th Amendment, which guaranteed that the right to vote could not be restricted on account of sex.

The Automobile

The role of the automobile in American society is so thoroughly established that it is difficult to imagine what life must have been like before it came upon the scene. In 1900, the auto was a toy of the rich. Automobiles, or "bubbles" as they were sometimes called, cost upwards of $3,000 at a time when the average weekly wage was $12.00.

At first they were used for sport. Auto racing became a social event and in 1905, when the second Vanderbilt Cup Race was held, Manhattan society turned out in force. The newspapers reported the event as they would have reported a hunting party with descriptions of the crowds and their clothing. They reported that Mrs. Belmont wore tweed, a fairly sensible choice, while another dowager "dripped pearls" and yet another wore a large Gainsborough picture hat (Lord 1965).

Drivers of automobiles had no problems about what to wear. A long cotton or linen duster, a cap with a visor (worn backwards at high speeds to prevent its being blown off), and goggles became customary automobiling costume for men. Ladies wore face veils, green was preferred, and their coats sometimes had a more stylish cut, but like those of the men they covered the costume beneath completely. Cars were open and roads unpaved, so the term **duster** was appropriate. (See *Color Plate 43*.)

In 1908 Henry Ford made the first Model T, which sold for $850. The car was no longer a toy for the rich. By the end of the next decade Americans had purchased more than four million Model T Fords and the age of the automobile had arrived.

American High Society

Although the average woman in small-town America had no direct contact with the wealthy and socially prominent, she could easily be kept abreast of their doings through the press, particularly through the many magazines that were sold across the nation. Around the turn of the century, mass circulation magazines in the United States were available at low prices and in great variety. Their cost was kept low by the increasingly large quantities of advertising they carried.

Fashion magazines and women's magazines, which carried a good deal of fashion information, frequently printed photographs and drawings of the wealthy and stories of their latest escapades. The balls and weddings of the socially prominent were described in minute detail in *Vogue,* and a drawing of the bride's wedding dress often accompanied the article. From these photographs, articles, and drawings, fashion-conscious women across the country could keep up with the latest fashions in "society." By selecting similar styles from the growing number of pattern catalogs and ready-to-wear items, women of more limited means were able to obtain less expensive versions of the most popular styles.

THE PRODUCTION AND ACQUISITION OF CLOTHING

The ready-to-wear industry in America expanded and by 1920 was a mature industry. Athough some women kept on sewing their own dresses and other women and men continued to patronize custom dressmakers and tailors, almost all Americans purchased at least some elements of their wardrobes ready-made. The patterns of mass production and sale of ready-to-wear clothing in the United States established in the first two decades of the 20th century continued to dominate middle class American clothing comsumption practices throughout the century.

SOURCES OF INFORMATION ABOUT COSTUME

Clothing dating from the period, photographs, magazines, and an enormous variety of mail-order and store catalogs are readily available for study. To all these was added a new medium of communication, motion pictures. Fashion shows and exhibitions were filmed and shown as part of newsreels. Fashionable clothing was worn by heroines in the popular serial films. One serial attempted to combine fashion and adventure. The action of this film was interrupted periodically to describe the gowns; however, this was apparently not a successful idea, as only one of these serial films was made (Leese

1991). While filmed fashion shows and feature films showed high fashion worn by actresses and actors, newsreels of current events provided views of ordinary individuals.

COSTUME FOR WOMEN: 1900–1920

Between 1900 and 1920, women's fashions in Europe and America changed with remarkable rapidity. Examination of daytime and evening styles from this period is, therefore, simplified by subdividing the examination of women's dress into the following phases:

- Edwardian styles or styles with emphasis on an S-shaped silhouette.
- Empire revival and the hobble skirt.
- 1914–1918: World War I.
- 1918–1919: Postwar styles.

Costume Components for Women: 1900–1908

GARMENTS

Frilly, decorative petticoats and drawers continued to be popular. Eyelet insertion with ivory, pink, or blue ribbon threaded through was a popular trim for all kinds of underclothing, as were ruffles and lace edging.

The bust supporter of the 1890s was modified to make it more suitable for supporting the fashionable silhouette of the new century. The name **brassiere** seems to have appeared first in 1904 when the Charles R. De Bevoise Company used the name in promoting its product. The following year, Gabrielle Poix filed a patent in which she called her design a brassiere (Farrell-Beck and Gau 2002.) The brassiere gradually became a basic item of underwear for adult women.

See *Illustrated Table 15.1,* for examples of undergarments from the period 1900–1920.

Dresses were generally one piece, with bodices and skirts sewn together at the waistline, although some dresses were princess line as well. The shape of dresses seemed to be based on an S-shaped curve. (See *Figure 15.1.*) Typical dresses had high-boned collars, full pouched bodices (see *Figure 15.2*), and skirts that were flat in front and emphasized a rounded hipline in the back. After hugging the hips, skirts flared out to a trumpet shape at the bottom. (See *Figure 15.3.*)

Except for tailor-mades and shirtwaist styles made in imitation of men's shirts, the emphasis on frilly and much-decorated clothing required soft fabrics. Decorations included tucking, pleating, lace insertions, bands of applied fabric, lace, and embroidery. The popular white, frilly cotton or linen dresses with this decoration were referred to as

FIGURE 15.1

Two garments depicted in pattern book of 1903. The pleated jacket on the right has the straight, loose cut seen on some styles of jackets from this period, while the dress on the left follows the S-shaped curved silhouette that is more typical of the Edwardian styles.

FIGURE 15.2

This high school graduate of 1904 wears lace-trimmed, ruffled white "lingerie" dress with high, boned collar. (Photograph courtesy, Melissa Clark.)

lingerie dresses, probably because the fabric and decoration so much resembled women's undergarments or lingerie of the period. (See *Figure 15.2.*)

It is in this decade that the first advertisements for ready-to-wear maternity dresses appeared. In earlier periods women or their dressmakers adapted current styles to accommodate their expanding figures.

Bodices were often quite complicated in construction. The full-bosomed cut was almost universal. Most bodices closed with hooks and eyes or hooks and bars. High-boned collars predominated. Other styles were square cut, V-shaped (with or without collars), or sailor collars. Frilly jabots were often placed at the neck. In the first half of the decade, sleeves were generally long and made in either close-fitting or bishop style. The **bishop sleeve** was gathered into the armseye and full below the elbow with fabric puffed or pouched at the wrist. In the last half of the decade, sleeves were shorter (often three-quarter length). Some sleeves were wide at the end and finished with either ruffles or attached under sleeves. Japanese influences were evident in kimono-style sleeves.

The shape of skirts was achieved by goring. From waist to knee, skirts fit closely, and from that point on were full and flared to the hem. Some skirts had pleats at center back. Lengths varied with some skirts ending several inches off the ground, while others had trains. (See *Figure 15.3.*)

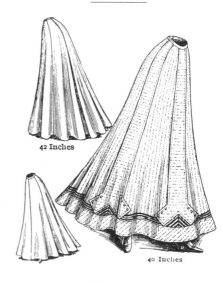

42 Inches

40 Inches

FIGURE 15.3

Gored skirt pattern, 1907. Skirt patterns were generally made in varying lengths ranging from those short enough to show the shoes to those that reached to the floor. (*McCall's Magazine,* October 1907.)

Illustrated Table 15.1

SELECTED UNDERGARMENTS FOR WOMEN, MEN, AND CHILDREN: 1900–1920

Lady's corset cover and drawers, 1907[1]

Lady's petticoat, 1905[2]

Lady's corset, 1907[1]

Ladies' corsets, 1917[3]

Children's corsets, 1917[3]

Cambric brassiere, 1917[4]

Man's union suit and drawers, 1914[5]

Lady's corset cover and drawers, 1914[5]

Petticoat combination, 1917[3]

[1]Courtesy, *McCall's Magazine*, October 1907.
[2]Courtesy, *The Delineator*, April 1905.
[3]Courtesy, Fairchild Publications.
[4]Courtesy, *Women's and Children's Fashions of 1917: The Complete Perry, Dame & Co. Catalog.* 1992. Mineola, NY: Dover, pp. 68, 142.
[5]Courtesy, *In Home Pattern Company 1914, Fashions Catalogue.* 1995. Dover, pp. 63, 73.

FIGURE 15.4
At a church outing of about 1901, young ladies wear cotton dresses or shirtwaists and skirts; young men wear white shirts and bow ties. Almost all of the women have arranged their hair in a pompadour. (Photograph courtesy, Almeda Brackbill Scheid.)

The **tailor-made** was an important item of clothing for women. Jackets varied in length ending anywhere from the waist to below the hip. Shorter jackets were generally fitted; long jackets were sometimes loose and sacquelike. (See *Figure 15.1*.) Many tailor-mades imitated the cut of men's jackets.

Separate blouses (shirtwaists) came in great variety and displayed features much like the bodices of daytime dresses. (See *Figure 15.4*.) Mail-order catalogs advertised a wide range of skirt styles with which these blouses were worn. Pictured were skirts that incorporated pleating, decorative stitching, applied braid trim, and ruffled hems.

More affluent women wore soft, less fitted **tea gowns** in the late afternoon. The gowns created by Fortuny were often worn as tea gowns. (See *Color Plate 42*.)

Evening dresses followed the same silhouette as daytime dresses. For evening, necklines were generally low and square, round, or V-shaped. Some had lace or sheer fabric scarves at the neck. Ruffled decorative sleeves covered the upper part of the arm. There were also sleeveless styles with shoulder straps. Skirts were full, extending to the floor. They were often trained, and were made from soft fabrics.

OUTDOOR GARMENTS

Outdoor garments consisted chiefly of cloaks and capes with high-standing (Medici) collars and wide revers, and coats that were fitted or unfitted and made in many different lengths. Some coats were fitted at the back, loose in the front. Capes were especially popular for evening wear. Oriental influences were evident in kimono-style coats. (See *Figure 15.5*.)

FIGURE 15.5
The caption for this pattern for a "Ladies Single or Double-Breasted Kimono Coat" shown in *McCall's Magazine* of October 1907 reads, "Fashions in Japanese effect are some of the most popular of the season's modes, and among these nothing is prettier than the new kimono coat."

HAIR AND HEADDRESS

See *Illustrated Table 15.2*, for some examples of hairstyles and hats from 1900 to 1920.

Arranged full and loose around the face, hair was pulled into a chignon or bun at the back of the neck. An important style, the **pompadour,** had hair built high in front and at the sides around the face. The first permanent wave was given in London in 1904.

Large in scale, popular hat styles included brimless toques and large-brimmed **picture hats.** Decoration was lavish with artificial flowers, lace, buckles, feathers, and bird wings. In 1905, a single page of the Sears Roebuck catalog showed 75 different styles of ostrich feather decorations. The slaughter of birds for feathers to decorate hats resulted in the near extinction of many birds. In 1906, Queen Alexandra of England tried to set a good example by refusing to wear any hats decorated with wild bird feathers. By the second decade of the century, some countries were banning the importation of most kinds of feathers. Fortunately for the birds, the fashion for large hats subsided after about 1914.

Hair ornaments worn for evening included feathers, jeweled combs, and small skullcaps of pearls called Juliet caps, after the heroine of *Romeo and Juliet.*

FOOTWEAR

See *Illustrated Table 15.3, page 376,* for some examples of footwear from 1900 to 1920.

Generally stockings of dark or neutral cotton lisle were worn for daytime and silk for formal wear. Some were decorated with colored clocks (designs knitted into the stocking) or lace insertion.

Shoes had pointed toes, long slender lines, and heels about two to two and a half inches high that were curved in the so-called "Louis" style. Boots were less fashionable than shoes, but when worn were high and buttoned or laced to close.

ACCESSORIES

See *Illustrated Table 15.4, page 380* for some examples of popular accessories.

Among the important accessories were large, flat muffs and suede or leather daytime handbags or beaded evening bags. Decorative lace or silk parasols were trimmed with fringe or lace. The less decorative and more serviceable umbrellas were made of oiled silk. For evening women carried long folding fabric fans or ostrich fans. The most popular belts were triangular shaped. **Swiss belts** were revived from the 1860s. Ruffles, boas, ribbons, or cravats were worn around the neck.

JEWELRY

The most worn types of jewelry included clasps, brooches, pendants, necklaces, chains, dog collars and long necklaces, and pendant or single stone earrings. Jewelry was often made in the Art Nouveau style. Such items were available in all qualities and price ranges.

Costume for Women: 1909–1914

GARMENTS

The quantity of underclothing worn decreased. Most women continued to wear corsets, even though Paul Poiret claimed that his designs liberated women from corsets. The new brassiere was especially suitable, when combined with a straight corset, for the revival of the empire line in dresses. Many women wore combination underwear, ornamented with lace and embroidery rather than drawers (frequently referred to as **knickers**) and a chemise. A narrower silhouette after 1909 required narrower petticoats, and the princess petticoat, which combined a camisole-type top with a petticoat into a single princess-line garment, became popular. See *Illustrated Table 15.1,* for examples of undergarments from the period 1900–1920.

Dresses were likely to be one piece, although skirts, blouses, and tailor-mades had also become a permanent part of women's daytime wardrobes. By 1909 the S-shaped curve of the Edwardian period was being replaced by a straighter line. The size of the full, pouched bodice decreased, and the location of the waistline moved upward. Skirts narrowed and grew shorter. The high-boned collar gradually went out of fashion. This collar had been part of women's costumes for such a long time that the clergy were outraged that women would show their necks, while health experts expressed fears for the women's health and predicted an increase in pneumonia and tuberculosis.

An Empire revival led to the use of a silhouette with an elevated waistline as well as a number of details that were considered to have originated during the First Empire. (See *Figure 15.6.*) These included military collars, ruffled jabots, and wide revers or lapels. As is true with most costume revivals, these latter details were only very loosely based on men's costume of the early 1800s. Oriental influences had also become evident in the cut and draping of some styles.

Although some vestiges remained of the frilliness of the Edwardian period, bodice styles gradually simplified. Front-buttoned closings were used for many garments. Sleeves tended to be tight-fitting, ending below the elbow or at the wrist, with cuffs of contrasting colors. Some shorter, kimono-style sleeves showed the impact of Japanese styles.

From 1909 to 1911 a narrow, straight skirt predominated (see *Figure 15.6*), but by about 1912 a number of different skirt styles of more elaborate construction had become popular. (See *Figure 15.7.*) But whether the skirt was single or multi-layered, it maintained an exceptionally narrow circumference around the ankles. Women could barely take a full step in the most extreme of these skirts, which were called **hobble skirts.** Some were so tight that a slit had to be made at the bottom

FIGURE 15.6

Dress of 1911 combines empire-style lines with oriental-influenced kimono-style sleeve. (French fashion magazine, *L'Art de la Mode*, 1911.)

to enable women to walk. **Peg-top skirts,** with fullness concentrated at the hip then narrowing gradually to the ankles, were also popular. Tunics were worn over underskirts. Tunics varied in shape from narrow tubes to wide, full-bottomed styles, and even multiple layers of tunic skirts. Paul Poiret designed a number of very exotic styles including the **minaret tunic,** a wide tunic, boned to hold out the skirt in a full circle and worn over the narrowest of hobble skirts. He also introduced the harem skirt, a full Turkish-style trouser that did not attract any significant following.

Jackets of tailored suits were cut to below the hips, with an overall line that was long and slender. (See *Figure 15.8.*) Narrow skirts were slit at the side or front.

Man-tailored shirtwaist blouses, complete with neckties and high tight collars, were worn with separate skirts or tailored suits. (See *Figure 15.7.*)

For evening, both Empire revival and Oriental influences were evident. Most evening dresses had tunics or layers of sheer fabric placed over heavier fabric. Trains were popular. Sleeves were short, often kimono style and of sheerer fabric than the body of the dress. Decorative touches included wide cloth belts or sashes, gold and silver embroidery and lace, beading, and fringe. (See *Figure 15.9.*)

OUTDOOR GARMENTS

For daytime, coats were long or three-quarter length. Some closed at far left in a sort of wraparound style. Evening coats were looser, cut full across the back and often with capelike

FIGURE 15.7

Almost all of the fashionable variations of skirt styles can be seen on the members of the Gamma Phi Beta sorority at Michigan State University in 1914. These include tight hobble skirts, some plain and others with single and multilayered tunics, and peg-topped skirts. (Photograph courtesy, Marilyn Guenther.)

FIGURE 15.8

Suit styles of 1913 have elongated jackets. The coat (far right) is full at the back but narrow at the hem. (French fashion magazine, *L'Art de la Mode*, 1913.)

sleeves. Some elaborately ruffled capes were also worn for evening.

HAIR AND HEADDRESS

See *Illustrated Table 15.2*, for some examples of hairstyles and hats from 1900 to 1920.

Hair was less bouffant now. The hair was waved softly around the face and pulled into a soft roll at the back or toward the top of the head.

Large hats included those emphasizing height, the brimless toque style, or hats with turned-up brims. Face veils were popular. Hats were decorated with artificial flowers, feathers, and ribbons. The fashion press noted the revival of tricorne hats, which they identified as part of the Directoire styles. (In actuality, tricornes were worn not in the Directoire or Empire periods, but earlier.)

FOOTWEAR

No radical changes occurred.

Costume for Women: 1914–1918

GARMENTS

Brassieres were now widely available. They were worn with a corset that ended below the bust. A combination garment that put together a camisole with a skirt that buttoned under the crotch to form drawers was called **cami-knickers.** This garment was especially popular when skirts grew shorter. Wider skirts required fuller petticoats. See *Illustrated Table 15.1, page 368,* for examples of undergarments from the period 1900–1920.

One-piece dresses were still preferred over two-piece styles. Coat dresses, either single or double breasted and belted or sashed at the waist, were stylish. During the wartime years the silhouette of women's clothes grew wider, and skirts shorter. Hems rose to six inches from the ground in 1916 and

FIGURE 15.9

Evening dress of 1911 has short, sheer kimono-style sleeves, silver embroidery on the bodice and overskirt. The bodice shows some slight evidence of the fullness through the bustline, characteristic of the earlier part of the decade, but also has the straighter skirt that became fashionable after 1909. (Photograph reproduced from *The Ladies's Field*, October 14, 1911.)

Illustrated Table 15.2

SELECTED HAIRSTYLES AND HATS FOR WOMEN: 1900–1920

Hats, 1905

Hair, 1907

Hat, 1907

Hats, 1909

Hats, 1912

Hair, 1912

Hair, 1919

Hats, 1919

Reproduced from contemporary fashion and pattern magazines.

came very influential during the 1920s, is often given credit for being the first person to interest women in knitted pullover sweaters about the time of World War I.

The lines of daytime and evening dresses were similar, although waistline placement for evening tended to be slightly higher than the natural waistline. Skirts were full, with many having tiers of ruffles, floating panels of fabric, or layers of varying lengths. At the neck, the décolletage might be filled in with flesh-colored or transparent fabric. Sleeves were short or to the elbow. Sleeveless dresses had only narrow straps over the shoulder. Fashionable trimmings were made with beading, gold, and silver embroidery. (See *Figure 15.12.*)

OUTDOOR GARMENTS

Coats grew wider to accommodate wider skirts. One popular style had a full back, others were full but loosely belted. Three-quarter-length coats were popular in 1916 and after. Military influence was evident in some coats.

FIGURE 15.10

Coat, dress, and suit designed by Chanel in 1916 have shorter, fuller skirts that were part of the wartime styles. The dress and suit are of wool jersey. The coat is trimmed with sealskin.

as much as eight or more inches from the floor in 1917. Throughout the period the waistline was at normal placement or slightly above. (See *Figure 15.10.*)

The fit of bodices was easy, and waistlines were defined, often with loose-fitting belts. Necklines tended to be V-shaped or squared. Some necklines were edged with sailor collars. Sleeves were generally straight and fitted. Skirts were full, the fullness achieved through pleating, gathering, or with gores.

Tailored suits became even more popular during the wartime years, and some had a distinctly military look. Jackets were long and belted at or slightly above the natural waistline. (See *Figure 15.11.*)

Special features of the blouses that were worn with skirts or suits included sleeves and yokes cut in one, leg-of-mutton sleeves, and Medici or standing collars with necks that were open or round or square at the front. Knitted sweaters that pulled on over the head (**pullovers**) became popular after 1915. Pullovers had no discernible waist, were belted at the hip, and had long sleeves. Gabrielle Chanel, the designer who be-

FIGURE 15.11

Women's suits of 1915 show military influence in the cut of the jackets and the style of the cap on the left. (French fashion magazine, *L'Art de la Mode*, 1915.)

FIGURE 15.12

Evening dress of 1916 has the shorter skirt and more comfortable fit of the World War I period. The dress is described as being available in either "white or flesh net with a triple pointed skirt of net over taffeta. Taffeta pipings and rose garniture." (Bonwit Teller & Co. advertisement from June 6, 1916. Courtesy, Fairchild Publications.)

HAIR AND HEADDRESS

See *Illustrated Table 15.2,* for some examples of hairstyles and hats from 1900 to 1920.

During the wartime period, hair was worn closer to the face and shorter. More women tried permanent waves. Hats were high rather than wide, and were smaller than before the War. They were made with and without brims and were often worn with face veils.

FOOTWEAR

See *Illustrated Table 15.3,* for some examples of footwear from 1900 to 1920.

Stockings were dark for daytime, but pale for evening. Rayon (also called artificial silk) stockings were introduced as an alternative to silk. (See *page 391* for a more complete discussion of rayon.)

Shoes styles did not change radically, but shoes were more visible as hemlines rose. High-buttoned shoes or shoes with spats kept feet warm in cold weather.

Costume for Women: 1918–1920

The postwar period is really a transitional period from the wartime styles to the styles of the 1920s. By 1918, the War had the effect of curtailing the supplies of fabrics, and the silhouette grew narrower again. In 1918 and 1919, dresses with narrow hems had waistlines that were rather wide. This produced a silhouette described as "barrel shaped." In 1919 after the end of the War, fashion designers turned back to narrower skirts, and hemlines gradually dipped to the ankle again. The silhouette remained loosely fitted through the waist. Jeanne Lanvin, a fashion designer of the period, is credited with creating the chemise dress, a straight tube of the type that was to become so fashionable in the 1920s.

COSTUME FOR MEN: 1900–1920

GARMENTS

Wool was the primary fabric for men's underwear, although cotton was coming into use as well. Heavier knits were used for winter, lighter for summer. Union suits, with drawers and underwear in one, were popular. In summer, drawers had short legs; in winter, long. See *Illustrated Table 15.1, page 368,* for examples of undergarments from the period 1900–1920.

Suits, consisting of jacket, vest, and trousers and worn with a shirt and necktie were appropriate dress for professional and business employees during the workweek. Laboring men wore sturdy work clothes. All men wore suits for important social occasions. For informal social occasions or during their leisure time, men could wear sport jackets, trousers, and shirts of various kinds. Some active sports required special clothing, as did formal evening or daytime events.

Except for summer when lighter weight flannel and linen fabrics were worn, suit jackets and trousers were generally dark in color and dark blue wool serge was the most popular fabric. Jackets, whether they were part of a suit or a separate garment, showed some variations in cut. Both single- and double-breasted suits were made, the popularity of each varying from year to year. In the early years of the century, jackets and coats were cut long, buttoned high, and had small lapels. Their full cut through the torso gave men an almost barrel-chested appearance. (See *Figure 15.13.*) During World War I, jackets and coats gradually shortened. Silhouettes narrowed; shoulder lines became less padded and more natural. (See *Figure 15.14.*)

Types of jackets included frock coats, which were worn only by dignitaries on formal occasions or by elderly men, and morning coats, still seen for formal occasions during the day. Before the War, morning coats were worn as suits with matching coat and trousers or with contrasting waistcoat and striped trousers. After the war, wearing of morning coats was

Illustrated Table 15.3

SELECTED EXAMPLES OF FOOTWEAR FOR WOMEN: 1900–1920

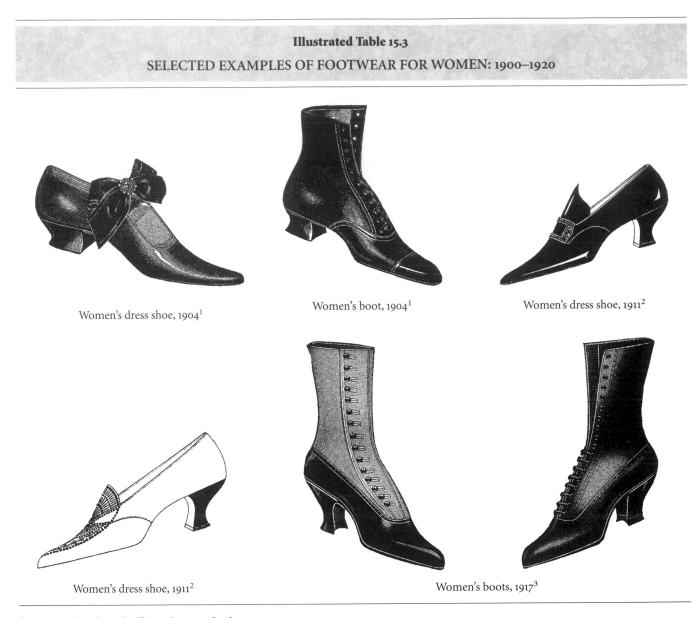

Women's dress shoe, 1904[1]

Women's boot, 1904[1]

Women's dress shoe, 1911[2]

Women's dress shoe, 1911[2]

Women's boots, 1917[3]

[1]*Chicago Mail Order and Millinery Company Catalogue, 1904–1905.*
[2]*The Ladies' Field,* October 7, 1911.
[3]*Women's and Children's Fashions of 1917: The Complete Perry, Dame & Co. Catalogue.* 1992. Mineola, NY: Dover.

limited to the upper classes or political leaders who donned them as formal dress for weddings, diplomatic receptions, or inaugurations. Formal occasions required a top hat; for less formal events a man might wear a derby or homburg.

Sack jackets became the standard suit jacket for men during the 20th century. They were worn for all occasions, and even appeared for leisure time wear as **sport jackets.** American tailors called these coats sack jackets and the British preferred the term **lounge coat.**

Vests were routinely worn as part of men's suits. Just after the turn of the century, vests were light or colored, but by the 1910s vests generally matched the suit with which they were worn.

When worn under coats and vests, shirts were visible only at the collar, above the vest, and at the end of the sleeves. Some shirts, particularly those for more formal dress, had stiffened fronts. Both white and colored shirts were worn, as well as patterns such as polka dots or stripes. (See *Color Plate 44.*) In the first years of the century, collars were high and stiff. The height of collars gradually decreased, and both soft and stiff collars were worn. Shirts worn by soldiers had softer collars. After the war men continued to prefer these less rigidly

Merwin, Inc.

FIGURE 15.13

Left to right: Evening wear of the tuxedo type, a chesterfield coat with velvet collar, and a business suit. (Courtesy, *Sartorial Arts Journal*, October 1911.)

starched shirt collars. Collars were either part of the shirt or detachable. The latter style made it possible to give the appearance of having on a fresh shirt by changing the collar and cuffs and the same shirt could be worn for several days.

Necktie varieties included bow ties, which could be purchased already tied to clip into place. These were considered unfashionable. Other styles were **four-in-hand** ties, today's standard necktie, and **ascots,** which were ties with wide ends that were worn with one end looped over the other and held in place with a tie pin. (See *Illustrated Table 15.4.*)

Trousers were generally cut loosely around the hips and narrower toward the bottom. Some had turned up cuffs;

FIGURE 15.14

Business suit with the narrower silhouette of the second decade of the 20th century, 1913. (Courtesy, Hart Schaffner & Marx.)

others had no cuffs. Trousers were worn with and without sharply pressed creases. Applied waistbands were becoming more popular.

Men's evening dress consisted of tailcoats or tuxedo jackets with matching trousers and a dark or white waistcoat. Dinner jackets were tuxedo style, sack cut, and were generally single breasted. Tail coats were double breasted, but worn unbuttoned, and had rolled lapels or notched collars and lapels. Most evening jackets had lapels faced in silk. (See *Figure 15.13*.) Trousers for evening matched the jacket, had no cuffs, and a row or two of braid placed along the outer seams.

Generally dress shirts had stand-up collars and were worn with white bow ties. Shirts closed with studs. After about 1910 shirt fronts were pleated and had wing collars. After 1915, black bow ties for evening were gaining acceptance.

OUTDOOR GARMENTS

Sweaters were generally worn by working class men, with available styles including collarless cardigans that opened down the front, V-necked pullovers, and high-collared styles similar to the modern turtleneck. (See *Figure 15.15*.)

Overcoats were full to accommodate the wide cut of men's suits in the first decade, then became more fitted in the second decade. Lengths varied, some being almost ankle length, others below the knee at mid-calf, and others were short. **Top coats** ended at the hip. The top coat was worn by

FIGURE 15.15

Young man of the turn of the century dressed (probably to play baseball or football) in a turtleneck sweater and padded knickers. (Photograph courtesy, Huntington Historical Society, Huntington, NY.)

affluent men who could afford more than one overcoat. Basic overcoat styles included:

- **chesterfields** and **raglan sleeve** coats, with versions for evening having velvet collars (see *Figure 15.13*).

- **ulsters** made with whole or half belts and, detachable hoods or capes.

- **inverness coats** with single or double capes.

- **mackintosh** was the name given to almost any kind of rainwear. The process patented by Charles Mackintosh for placing a layer of rubber between two layers of cloth was still a popular means of applying a waterproof finish to fabric. Other waterproof finishes were made by oiling fabric to make "slickers."

- **trench coat,** created by Thomas Burberry during World War I, was a belted twill cotton gabardine of very close weave that had a chemical finish that made the coat water repellent. Trench coats became fashionable for civilian wear after the War.

After the War military influences were especially evident in outdoor wear. Collars took on a military shape, high and fitted, and coats became shorter. Other postwar styles included fur coats. Raccoon was especially popular for motoring. Many coats had fur collars and fur linings.

In the early years of the period, jackets and casual coats were limited to working class men who wore heavy corduroy, leather, wool, and other utilitarian fabrics. Some jackets, such as lumber jackets, were associated with particular occupations. After the War interest in outdoor sports increased and, as a result, jackets for recreation were adopted by the public at large.

CLOTHING FOR ACTIVE SPORTS

Antecedents of the modern sport jacket, worn with unmatched trousers can be seen in the **blazer,** which was worn for tennis, yachting, or other sports. One story told of the origin of the bazer is this: In 1837 when Queen Victoria reviewed the crew of *Her Majesty's Ship Blazer,* the captain, lacking uniforms for his men, had them dress in dark blue jackets with shiny brass buttons when they took part in a parade in honor of the queen. The queen is said to have decreed that henceforth jackets of this style would be called "blazers" (Attaway 1991). Other sources claim the name came from the "blazing" red color of these jackets when they were worn for sports. The Norfolk jacket was an English style of belted jacket for golf, bicycling, and hiking. Knickers, long stockings, sturdy shoes, and a soft cap with a visor were often combined with these jackets. (See *Figure 15.16*.)

Outfits for riding differed from the traditional 19th century morning coat, breeches, and boots. Instead, a jacket with a flared skirt was worn with **jodhpurs,** a pair of trousers fitted closely around the lower leg and flaring out above the knee. Jodhpurs, another example of cross-cultural influ-

FIGURE 15.16

Golfing clothing, 1912. On the left, knickers and a Norfolk jacket; on the right, a plaid suit with a half belt at the back. (Courtesy, *Sartorial Arts Journal,* 1912.)

ences on Western dress, originated in India where they were adopted by British colonials and subsequently spread throughout the West.

In England swimming suits consisted of a pair of drawers, but men in the United States were more likely to wear either a knitted wool suit made up of fitted knee-length breeches and a shirt with short or no sleeves or a one-piece, short-legged, round-necked, sleeveless tank suit. Kidwell (1968) believes that bathing dress in the United States developed a more conservative character because men and women bathed together rather than, as was the custom in England until about 1900, separately.

Some men wore sport coats and flannel trousers for driving; however, placing long linen dusters or leather motoring coats over clothing was more practical. On their heads men wore goggles and peaked caps, which were worn with the peak at the back to avoid having them blown off.

Illustrated Table 15.4

EDWARDIAN AND WORLD WAR I, 1900–1920: ACCESSORIES

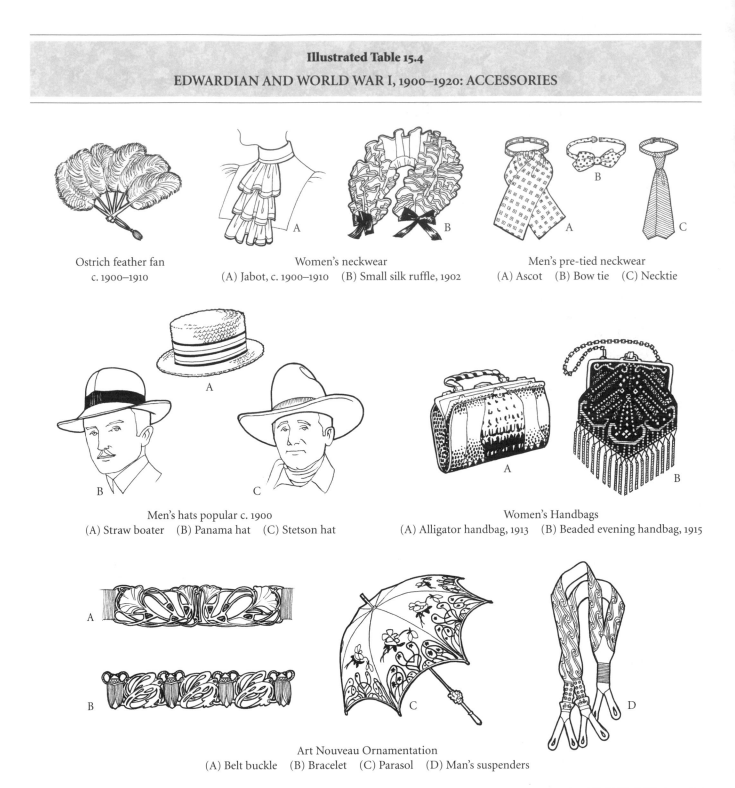

Ostrich feather fan
c. 1900–1910

Women's neckwear
(A) Jabot, c. 1900–1910   (B) Small silk ruffle, 1902

Men's pre-tied neckwear
(A) Ascot   (B) Bow tie   (C) Necktie

Men's hats popular c. 1900
(A) Straw boater   (B) Panama hat   (C) Stetson hat

Women's Handbags
(A) Alligator handbag, 1913   (B) Beaded evening handbag, 1915

Art Nouveau Ornamentation
(A) Belt buckle   (B) Bracelet   (C) Parasol   (D) Man's suspenders

LOUNGEWEAR AND SLEEPWEAR

Men's wear at home consisted of dressing gowns and smoking jackets, some of which had quilted lapels and were made in decorative fabrics.

Nightshirts were still worn by many men, but others wore pajamas.

HAIR AND HEADDRESS

Generally hair was short. The War helped to diminish the popularity of beards and mustaches, as they were more difficult to keep clean in combat zones and interfered with gas masks.

Hat styles remained much the same as those in the latter part of the 19th century, and included top hats, now only for formal occasions; soft felt hats with names as homburg or trilby; derbies; and caps for leisure. Western-style Stetson felt hats were worn in some parts of the United States. For summer, men used panama straw hats, straw boaters, and linen hats made in derby or fedoralike shapes. (See *Illustrated Table 15.4.*)

FOOTWEAR

Stockings were usually neutral colors. Some were made with a few stripes or in multicolored styles. Stockings had ribbed tops and were held up with elastic garters.

In the early part of the century shoes had long, pointed toes, and laced or buttoned to close. Many were cut high, above the ankle. For evening, black patent leather slippers were popular. After 1910, oxfords (low, laced shoes) increased in use. Some had perforated designs on the toes. Others were two toned. Some were made in white buckskin for summer. Sturdy, laced high shoes were still favored by many for every day. By the end of the decade, rounded more blunt toes were more popular.

ACCESSORIES

Walking sticks were popular until automobiles came into widespread use. Other accessories for men were gloves, handkerchiefs, and scarves.

JEWELRY

Jewelry was mostly limited to tie pins, shirt studs, rings, and cuff links. Wristwatches gained popularity as a result of their wartime use and because of the increased use of automobiles. The inconvenience of pocket watches to soldiers and drivers proved the value of wristwatches.

COSTUME FOR CHILDREN:
1900–1920

Throughout history, children's clothing shows clear similarities to that of adults. At times, particularly in the 20th century, the special needs of children for clothing that is reasonably practical have been recognized. In the first decade of the

20th century this recognition, while beginning, was not characteristic of all children's clothing. Moore (1953) calls the Edwardian period a time of transition in children's clothing as styles moved from impractical to more practical dress.

Costume for Girls

GARMENTS

Many girls of all ages wore white, light-, or cream-colored lingerie dresses (one of the less practical styles), cut with waistlines low on the hip. Decoration consisted of embroidery, smocking, and lace. Other styles had more natural waistline placement and full-bloused bodices similar to those of adult women.

For school navy blue serge was popular, as were sailor dresses and sailor hats (see *Figure 15.17*) and pinafores, which

FIGURE 15.17

Children dressed for cool weather around 1900. The girl at the left wears a coat with several shoulder capes, a style that appears frequently in mail-order catalogs of Sears, Roebuck and Company about 1900. Her hat is a wide-brimmed sailor style. The older boy at the center wears a turtleneck sweater and a cap with a visor. The girl at the right has a short jacket. Her hat is a tam-o-shanter under which one can see her large hair ribbon. (Photograph courtesy, Huntington Historical Society, Huntington, NY.)

FIGURE 15.18
Child from just after 1900 wears a checked pinafore over her lighter-colored frock. Even though the weather is warm enough for her to be outdoors without a coat, she wears heavy, dark stockings. (Photograph courtesy, Huntington Historical Society, Huntington, NY.)

were placed on top of other dresses to protect them. (See *Figure 15.18.*)

A style favored about 1910 had a large, cape collar; low waist; and sleeves full to the elbow, then tight to the wrist. After 1910 there was less white and more color in "best" dresses.

From 1914 to 1917 belts dropped low, to the thighs.

Throughout the period skirts for young girls were about knee length. For older girls they were longer, but still a practical length.

PHYSICAL EDUCATION UNIFORMS

Gym tunics, which were worn over blouses, had sleeveless yokes, square necks, and belted, full pleated bodices. This style remained popular in subsequent periods as well.

Costume for Boys

From 1900 to 1910, most small boys were still dressed in skirts until the age of three or four. These dresses followed the same lines as those for girls. From 1910 to 1920, little boys were more likely to be dressed in rompers and, when a little older, in knickers.

GARMENTS

Boys could choose from sailor suits, Eton suits, Norfolk jackets, and sack suit jackets, all with or without belts. Younger boys wore jackets with shorts or knickers and older boys wore them with long trousers.

OUTDOOR WEAR

Outside boys wore mackinaw coats in plaid or plain colors, Norfolk jackets, long cardigan sweaters, or turtleneck sweaters.

Costume for Boys and Girls

Innovative styles pictured in mail-order catalogs of 1914 included knitted tops and leggings for small boys and girls and sleeping garments with feet.

FOOTWEAR

High laced shoes were worn by either boys or girls. For dress wear, girls wore flat slippers with one or more straps across the instep or a flat shoe with an ankle strap. Stockings from 1900 to 1910 tended to be knee length. During the War these shortened for girls. Boys wore knee-length socks with knickers.

SUMMARY

THEMES

Many themes can be identified in the styles of the first two decades of the 20th century. Rapid FASHION CHANGE is seen in women's clothing and relative stability in styles of men's clothing. TECHNOLOGY in everyday life, as seen in the increasing use of automobiles, and SOCIAL CHANGES, such as the entry into the work force by more women both before and during World War I, probably helped to establish styles for women that were shorter, less confining, and more practical. The theme of PRODUCTION AND ACQUISITION OF TEXTILES AND APPAREL was evident in the growing availability of ready-to-wear clothing of all kinds. Mail-order catalog retailing helped to make fashionable clothing available in rural as well as urban regions.

The specific styles of this period can be related to themes such as THE RELATIONSHIPS BETWEEN COSTUME AND THE WORK OF INDIVIDUAL DESIGNERS such as Paul Poiret and Fortuny and also to CROSS-CULTURAL INFLUENCES from Asia. Furthermore, a new MEDIUM OF COMMUNICATION, motion pictures, not only served to spread styles but also added to SOURCES of INFORMATION ABOUT COSTUME for future costume historians.

POLTICAL CONFLICT was once again an important theme. World War I had an impact not only on the styles of the wartime period, when military influences were evident in the cut and colors of both men's and women's clothing, but also on styles after the war. Garments such as trench coats, sweaters, and jackets that had been part of military clothing were carried over into civilian use after the war.

SURVIVALS OF EDWARDIAN AND WORLD WAR I STYLES

Many of the revivals of Edwardian style have been in men's wear. King Edward VII of Britain had done much to popularize the homburg hat. American president Dwight Eisenhower brought the style to public notice again when he wore a homburg to his inauguration in 1952. The Teddy boys, British adolescents of the 1950s, adopted suits with styling similar to that of Edwardian men, and this narrower cut was adopted for mainsteam men's wear as well. (See *Figure 17.1.*)

In the 1960s mod styles again drew on Edwardian fashion for inspiration (see *Figure 18.3*), and in the 1990s the mod styles were themselves revived. Another repetition of early 20th century styles can be seen in the striped shirts with white collars that returned to men's wear in the early 80s.

The Edwardian lingerie dress and the frilly undergarments with embroidered and lace trimming that were worn under them also inspired fashions in outerwear and underwear in the 1980s. And in one of the most unusual revivals seen to date, women who had collected original Delphos gowns made by Fortuny about the time of the First World War, began wearing them. Designer Mary McFadden became known for her pleated gowns of the 1980s and 90s that derived from the Fortuny styles. (See *Figure 15.19.*)

FIGURE 15.19

The pleating used by Fortuny served as inspiration to designer Mary McFadden, who has used these pleats in designs from the 1970s up to the 1990s. Shown here is a design by McFadden from 1994. (Photograph courtesy, Fairchild Publications.)

Man: 1900–1920
Suits of jackets, vests, and trousers
worn with white, colored, or figured
shirts. Sack jackets predominate;
morning coats for formal occasions.

Man: 1900–1920
Until World War I, suits are cut
full through the torso. During and
after the war, silhouette narrows.
Norfolk jackets worn for daytime,
frock coats had limited use.

Woman: 1900–1908
S-shaped silhouette with full
bosom and morning glory
shaped skirt. Much use of frilly,
lacy fabrics. Many women wear
two piece tailor-made suits.

Woman: 1909–1914
Waistline moves higher
with Empire style revival. Skirt
lines become straighter. Hobble skirts,
very tight around the ankles, are
fashionable.

Woman: 1914–1918
Skirts shorten and grow wider.
Waistline is still slightly elevated.
Military influences are evident.

Woman: 1918–1920
Silhouette narrows, skirts lengthen.
Some dresses are barrel-shaped, wider
at the waist, more closely fitted at the
hem. An unfitted line begins to appear.

N O T E S

Attaway, R. 1991. "The Enduring Blazer." *Yachting*, October, p. 60.

Farrell-Beck, J. and C. Gau. 2002. *Uplift. The Bra in America*. Philadelphia, PA: University of Pennsylvania Press.

Fortuny. 1981. Catalog of an exhibition at the Galleries at the Fashion Institute of Technology, New York, April 14 through July 11, pp. 8, 28.

Kidwell, C. 1968. *Women's Bathing and Swimming Costume in the United States*. Washington, DC: Smithsonian Institution Press.

Kim, H. J. and M. Delong. 1992. "Culture Transfer: Chinese and Japanese Aesthetics in Early Twentieth-Century Western Women's Fashion." Costume Society of America: Symposium Abstracts: Exploring Our Cultural Diversity, May 27–30, San Antonio, TX.

Leese, E. 1991. *Costume Design in the Movies*. New York: Dover.

Lord, W. *The Good Years*. 1965. New York: Bantam Books, p. 108.

Lyman, M. 1972. *Couture*. Garden City, NY: Doubleday, p. 63.

Moore, D. L. 1953. *The Child in Fashion*. London: B. T. Batsford, p. 90.

S E L E C T E D   R E A D I N G S

Books and Other Materials Containing Illustrations of Costume of the Period from Original Sources

Fashion Magazines: *Vogue* and *Harper's Bazaar*

Women's Magazines: *The Delineator, Ladies' Home Journal,* and *McCalls'.*

Sears, Roebuck mail-order catalogs.

Battersby, M. 1974. *Art Deco Fashion: French Designers: 1908–1925*. New York: St. Martin's Press.

Carter, E. 1975. *20th Century Fashion: A Scrapbook—1900 to Today*. London: Eyre Methuen.

Men's Wear: 75 Years of Fashion. 1965. New York: Fairchild.

Mulvagh, J. 1988. *Vogue History of 20th Century Fashion*. London: Viking.

Schoeffler, O. E., ed. 1973. *Esquire's Encyclopedia of 20th Century Men's Fashion*. New York: McGraw-Hill.

Winter, G. 1975. *Golden Years, 1903–1913*. London: David and Charles.

Periodical Articles

Behling, D. and L. Dickey. 1980. "Haute Couture: A 25-Year Perspective of Fashion Influences: 1900–1925." *Home Economics Research Journal*, Vol. 8, No. 6, p. 428.

Behling, D. 1979. "The Russian Influence on Fashion: 1909–1925." *Dress*, Vol. 5, p. 1.

Feldkamp, P. 1972. "The Man Who Banned the Corset (Poiret)." *Horizon*, Vol. 14, Summer, p. 30.

Field, J. 2001. "Dyes, Chemistry and Clothing. The Influence of World War I on Fabrics, Fashions, and Silk." *Dress*, Vol. 28, p. 77.

Helverson, S. 1981. "Advice to American Mothers on the Subject of Children's Dress: 1800–1920." *Dress*, Vol. 7, p. 30.

Kearney, K. 1992. "Mariano Fortuny's Delphos Robe: Some Possible Methods of Pleating and the Permanence of the Pleats." *Clothing and Textiles Research Journal*, Vol. 10, No. 3, p. 86.

Kim, H. J. and M. Delong. 1992. "Sino-Japanism in Western Women's Fashionable Dress in *Harper's Bazaar*, 1890–1927." *Clothing and Textiles Research Journal*, Vol. 11, No. 1, p. 24.

Palmer, A. 1986. "Form Follows Fashion: A Motorcoat Considered." *Dress*, Vol. 12, p. 5.

Warner, P. C. 1988. "Public and Private: Men's Influence on American Women's Dress for Sport and Physical Education." *Dress*, Vol. 14, p. 48.

Daily Life

American Heritage History of the Confident Years.* 1988. New York: Random House.

Andrist, R. K. 1972. *American Century: One Hundred Years of Changing Life Styles in America.** New York: American Heritage.

Churchill, A. 1947. *Remember When (1900–1940).** New York: Golden Press.

The Clamorous Era, 1910–1920 (This Fabulous Century). * 1991. New York: Time-Life.

The Golden Interlude, 1900–1910 (This Fabulous Century).* 1991. New York: Time-Life.

Kennedy, D. M. 1980. *Over There*. New York: Oxford University Press.

Lord, W. 1960. *The Good Years*. New York: Bantam.

(*Also contains illustrations of costume from contemporary sources.)

CHRONOLOGY

1920
Warren G. Harding elected president
Passage of the 18th Amendment (prohibition)
United States ratifies the 19th Amendment, giving women the right to vote

1922
Fascist dictatorship established in Italy
Commercial radio broadcasting to the public begins

1924
Founding of the surrealist movement when André Breton releases his *Manifeste du surrealisme*
Department of Commerce establishes name rayon for regenerated
cellulosic fiber that had been called "artificial silk."

1925
L'Exposition Internationale des Arts Decoratifs et Industriels Moderns held in Paris
B. F. Goodrich registers the trademark "zipper"
Publication of *The Great Gatsby* by F. Scott Fitzgerald

1927
Charles Lindbergh makes first flight across the Atlantic Ocean
Sound comes to motion pictures in *The Jazz Singer*

1929
Stock market crash

1932
Franklin Delano Roosevelt elected president; the New Deal begins
First use of technicolor process in motion pictures

1933
Hitler comes to power in Germany
Repeal of prohibition

1934
The film *It Happened One Night* shows Clark Gable without an undershirt,
and men's undershirt sales drop sharply

1935
WPA is established and the Social Security Act becomes law
Italy invades Ethiopia

1936
Edward VIII abdicates to marry Wallis Simpson

1938
Germany annexes Austria and part of Czechoslovakia
Nylon fiber first marketed by DuPont

1939
Germany invades Poland, beginning World War II
Publication of *The Grapes of Wrath* by John Steinbeck
Film version of *Gone with the Wind* is released

1941
Japan bombs Pearl Harbor and the United States enters the war
Regulations restricting clothing manufacture and the rationing
of leather goods are imposed in the United States

1945
FDR dies and Harry Truman becomes president
United Nations Charter is signed
First atomic bombs are detonated
World War II ends

1947
Christian Dior introduces the New Look
Princess Elizabeth of England marries Prince Philip

CHAPTER SIXTEEN

THE TWENTIES, THIRTIES, AND WORLD WAR II

1920 – 1947

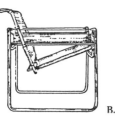

B.

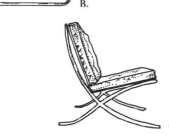

C.

D.

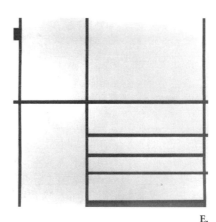

E.

A.

F.

A.

Chrysler building by William van Allen, 1930

B.

Wassily lounge chair by Marcel Breuer, c. 1926

C.

Barcelona chair by Marcel Breuer, 1929

D.

Painting by Pablo Picasso, *Girl Before a Mirror*, 1932

E.

Painting by Piet Mondrian,
Composition in White, Black, and Red, 1936

F.

Art Deco architectural detail, door

Figures A, F courtesy of V. R. Tortora. Figures B, C courtesy of J. Curcio in Federico, J. T., 1988. *Clues to American Furniture*. Washington, Starrhill, pp. 56, 57. Figures D, E courtesy of the Museum of Modern Art, New York, gift of Mrs. Simon Guggenheim (D); gift of the Advisory Committee (E).

HISTORICAL BACKGROUND

With the end of World War I, Europe and the United States hoped for "a return to normalcy." The American President, Woodrow Wilson, a strong proponent of the League of Nations, campaigned arduously for ratification of the Treaty of Versailles and membership for the United States in the League. These efforts cost him his health—he suffered a breakdown in 1919—and he was an invalid for the remainder of his 17 months in office. In the end, the Senate defeated the Treaty, and the United States never joined the League of Nations.

· Warren G. Harding was elected President of the United States in 1920. During his administration a separate peace resolution was approved and the "official business" of World War I finally was concluded.

The Twenties

In the wake of World War I, imperial monarchies in Austria–Hungary and Russia collapsed. Germany, reduced in size, became a republic; Austria–Hungary split into small, weak states. In Russia, following the fall of the Czar and the demise of a weak democratic government, the Communists, led by Vladimir Lenin, seized power in 1917 and established a centralized government with the Communists as the only legal party. To enforce its will, the Communist government established a secret police to persecute political opponents and maintain the tyranny of the party.

After Lenin's death, Josef Stalin emerged victorious in the power struggle. Stalin decreed forced industrialization and collectivization of agriculture. He then launched a purge of the people to break resistance to his policies and to eliminate all possible opposition. Millions of Russian men and women were killed or imprisoned, and millions more were shipped to slave labor camps in Siberia.

Italian parliamentary government succumbed in 1922 when the Fascist party, led by Benito Mussolini, came into power. In the meantime in the early 1920s the United States settled down to a period of unequaled prosperity. From 1923 to 1927 business was booming. A survey of the consumer goods that sold most actively provides a key to the interests and lifestyle that developed over the period. Leading the sales charts were automobiles. Radios (commercial broadcasting to the public began in 1922), rayon, cigarettes, refrigerators, telephones, cosmetics, and electrical devices of all kinds were sold in huge quantities. The purchasing power of the dollar increased twofold for most Americans. There was a boom in higher education, self-improvement books sold briskly, and travel abroad increased. In 1928, 437,000 people left the United States by ship to visit some distant place.

This prosperity, however, had a dark side. While business was thriving and most people were increasingly affluent, the American farmer was experiencing hard times. The demand for agricultural products was fairly stable and the export market dropped off, creating surpluses. Cotton went into decline as rayon, a manufactured fiber, became more popular.

Another cloud on the horizon of the population was Prohibition. The Eighteenth Amendment had been passed and the distilling, brewing, and sale of alcoholic beverages became illegal in 1920. In the long run, the Amendment was ignored by many, but in the process of violating the law a new institution, the speakeasy, a clandestine drinking club for drinking, dining, and dancing, replaced the saloon. When Prohibition was repealed in 1933, the speakeasy made a rapid transition into the nightclub.

Several other American institutions planted their roots firmly during the 1920s. One was the chain store. These national or regional chains of stores served to bring the prices of consumer goods down and increase purchasing power. Installment buying took a firm hold, too.

With the spectacular success of Charles A. Lindbergh's transatlantic flight in 1927, flying took on a new importance. Passenger service was beginning by the end of the decade. A cross-continent flight combined with rail transportation (it was too dangerous to fly at night, so by night passengers took the train) took two days. And the first airmail service was initiated.

Changes in the Social Life of the Twenties

After World War I had ended, the social climate in Europe and in the United States changed. This change was especially pronounced in the United States. Not only had the War left people wondering whether their efforts had been justified, but other disturbing notions such as the sexual theories of Sigmund Freud and the changing social roles of women resulted in a revolution in mores and values, especially among the young. Reactions varied. There were the romantic cynics like the novelist F. Scott Fitzgerald and his heroes and heroines, escapists who followed a ceaseless round of parties and pleasure, an increasing number of isolationists who saw America as having no important ties to Europe or the rest of the world, and, of course, there were the many average citizens who were increasingly bewildered by the antics of the pleasure-seekers.

Writers of the period speak of a revolution in morality. This was evident in the behavior of the young, particularly young women. Until World War I, there were certain standards of behavior expected of "ladies." They were not supposed to smoke, to drink, to see young men unchaperoned, certainly they were expected to kiss only the boy they intended to marry. By the 1920s, all this had changed. The "flapper" as she was nicknamed seemed free from all of the restraints of the past. She smoked and drank, she necked in parked cars, she danced the Charleston until all hours of the night, and what is more she looked totally different as well. She was caricatured perfectly by John Held Jr., whose drawings of flappers appeared often on the covers of *Life* magazine. (See *Color Plate 45.*)

> "*. . . the sensitivity of fashion to social problems provides a visible index of agitation and unrest. Drastic changes in clothing patterns are evidence of changes elsewhere*" (Horn 1975).

Women's costume of the 1920s provides the visible evidence of agitation and unrest of which Horn speaks. Never before in the history of costume in the civilized West had women worn skirts that revealed their legs. Except for a brief period after the French Revolution, women's hair had never been cut so short nor had flesh-colored stockings been worn. Trousers had heretofore been strictly a man's garment. (Earlier attempts to introduce bifurcated garments for women had utilized bloomers, which were cut differently from a man's trousers.) Rouge and lip color had not been used by "nice" girls. But during the 1920s all of these things became commonplace. These were visible changes in acceptable dress for women that paralleled changes in the social roles of women.

The Thirties

THE DEPRESSION

Toward the end of the decade the bubble of the 1920s prosperity burst. Business had been faltering after about 1927, but the stock market continued to rise to what astute financial observers felt were dangerous heights. On October 29, 1929, the stock market collapsed, the last of several drops that had each been followed by recovery, but this time the recovery never came. The United States and Europe sank into the period now known as "The Great Depression."

Unemployment was widespread. The American farmers who had never participated in the prosperity of the 1920s were affected even more sharply during the Depression and those of the Midwest were further devastated by natural disasters that included floods and dust storms.

The Labor Movement, which had made gains in the United States during World War I and shortly after, had no great successes in the 1920s, but during the 1930s unionization advanced. These advances were accompanied by violence and strikes, as industrialists did not capitulate to labor without resistance.

At the same time not everyone was poor. Many individuals and families retained their wealth. These were the group to which fashion magazines such as *Vogue* and *Bazaar* for women and *Esquire* for men turned for fashion news. They vacationed on the Riviera, in Palm Springs, or at Newport, Rhode Island. They made headlines in the gossip columns and socialized with movie stars. (See *Contemporary Comments 16.1* about the effect of the Depression on styles.)

INTERNATIONAL POLITICAL DEVELOPMENTS

In Germany democracy fell victim to the Depression when a government headed by Austrian-born Adolf Hitler, leader of the Nazi party, came into power in 1933 and established a one-party dictatorship. Soon Hitler began to rearm Germany, evading the restrictions of the Treaty of Versailles.

In 1935, fascist Italy invaded Ethiopia and in 1936, Italy and Germany formed the Rome–Berlin Axis. In 1938, Germany annexed Austria and part of Czechoslovakia. World War II began on September 1, 1939, with the German invasion of Poland. German forces overran Norway, Denmark, France, and the Low Countries in 1940, but the invasion of Russia in 1941 proved a disaster for Hitler's armies. The United States remained outside of the war but was clearly sympathetic to the British and French.

In the Far East the Japanese parliamentary government moved toward military dictatorship when Army officers precipitated a clash in an outlying province of China in 1931, and moved swiftly to occupy that province. China, lacking an effective central government, failed to stem Japanese aggression. In 1937, a clash between Japanese and Chinese forces turned into a full-fledged war.

Meanwhile Japanese leaders, convinced that the United States blocked their path to an empire in Asia, ordered the December 7, 1941, attack on Pearl Harbor. The United States became fully involved in the war in Europe following declarations of war against the United States by Germany and Italy.

Wartime industrial production brought the United States out of the Depression. In the late 1930s, recovery had begun, but this recovery was not complete as the war began.

World War II

Americans did not experience devastation of homes and communities during World War II, being outside of the zones of fighting. The war was brought home to noncombatants more directly by the drafting of young men and by military casualties. Scarce goods were rationed. These were largely foodstuffs and gasoline. Few clothing items were actually rationed except for shoes made of leather, which was in short supply. Guidelines called the "L-85 Regulations" were passed that restricted the quantity of cloth that could be used in clothing. Savings in fabric were made by eliminating trouser cuffs, extra pockets, vests with double-breasted suits, and by regulating the width of skirt hems and the length of men's trousers and suit jackets. Some garments such as wedding dresses and burial gowns were exempt from restrictions. (*Contemporary Comments 16.2* on *page 395*, summarizes these restrictions on women's styles as reported in *Women's Wear Daily*.)

Many fabrics available before the war were in short supply. Nylon, introduced at the New York World Fair in 1939, was diverted to military use. Wool was scarce. Silk supplies

CONTEMPORARY COMMENTS 16.1

Impact of the Depression on Paris Fashions

*The impact of the depression on Parisian fashions is noted on July 28, 1932
in the* New York Times *(page 2, column 6.)*

HARD TIMES HIT PARIS SOCIETY
MANY WEAR LAST YEAR'S GOWNS

By the Associated Press
Paris. July 20 (by mail)
Europe's smart set is feeling the pinch of hard times.

Summer soirees held in Parisian embassies, long famous for the brilliance of the women's costumes, this year reveal many gowns of last year's vintage worn with jewels worth hundreds of

thousands of dollars. The jewels remain as souvenirs of more prosperous days, while the price of a new frock is often lacking.

Many of the wealthiest women who have not yet felt the pinch are dressing more simply than last year, since they feel ostentatious costume is bad taste these days.

White satin gowns are favorites with many smart women for formal embassy functions, since they can be worn with different jewels and varicolored wraps and slippers. They follow somewhat classic lines, which have not varied markedly within the last two years and may be worn without appearing hopelessly out of date.

Courtesy of the Associated Press.

---

were disrupted because of the war in the Pacific. Natural rubber was unavailable for civilian use.

Because most able-bodied men enlisted or were drafted into the armed services, women entered factories and took on jobs that were formerly held by men. In the factories, women required specialized kinds of clothing, and coveralls, slacks, and turbans were generally adopted for jobs involving active physical labor.

The war in Europe ended in May 1945, but continued in the Pacific until September. With the cessation of hostilities the countries involved turned to rebuilding their devastated lands. The United States emerged from the fighting with its land unscathed and its economy intact, but millions of families had experienced the loss of one or more men in battle.

SOME INFLUENCES ON FASHIONS

The Movies

Silent films had, by the 1920s, become a part of everyday life. In addition to providing a diversion, the movies brought vi-

sions of glamorous actors and actresses into every small town across America. Life depicted in films helped to reinforce the hedonistic attitudes and helped to spread urban tastes, urban dress, and an urban way of living.

Film stars became fashion setters. Rudolph Valentino was the idol of millions of American women, and men copied his pomaded, patent-leather-look hair. In her first major film role the actress Joan Crawford personified the fast-living, shingled flapper of the 1920s and women across the country aped her makeup, hairstyle, and clothes.

With the beginning of talking pictures in 1927, films became more popular than ever. In the early 1930s reaction in the United States against some films that were thought to have too much nudity and sex led to a strict code of propriety as to what could or could not be shown on the screen. Many films of the 1930s did not at all reflect the bleak economic picture of the Depression. Women were lavishly gowned and houses magnificently furnished. Off screen the movie star was a fashion influence. Greta Garbo's broadshouldered, natural beauty was one ideal of feminine beauty of the era. Other women bleached their hair blonde in imitation of Jean Harlow. Thousands of mothers curled their daughters' hair into ringlets like those of Shirley Temple, the famous child star.

During the War movies stressed patriotic themes. Among the screen heroes of the day were the "clean-cut American boy" like Van Johnson, and the rugged individualist like Spencer Tracy. Teenaged girls wore page boy hair like June Allyson or draped a wave over one eye in the "peek-a-boo" style of Veronica Lake. Movie studio publicity offices printed "pin-up" pictures of actress Betty Grable in a backless bathing suit and high heels. Films were made in Technicolor, and Americans flocked to the movies throughout the War.

Royalty and Cafe Society

European royalty and ex-royalty as well as cafe society influenced fashion. During the 1920s and 1930s one important style-setter was the British Prince of Wales (later known as the Duke of Windsor). He ascended to the throne as King Edward VIII in 1936, but left it after a reign of 325 days to marry American divorcee Wallis Simpson. During the 1930s wealthy Americans and Europeans were photographed at fashionable resorts in the United States and abroad. The rich first wore much of the sportswear that became popular for tennis, riding, and skiing. Few others had the leisure and money to engage in these activities in the 1930s. Some of the debutantes of the late 1930s caught the imagination of the public, and gossip columns were full of news about coming out parties and cotillions and charity balls. Brenda Frazier, one of these "debs," helped to publicize a new style, the strapless evening gown.

Sports

The numbers of participants in both spectator sports and active sports increased. Attendance at sporting events in the 1920s broke all previous records. Baseball, college football, boxing, tennis, and golf were widely followed. Seeing women as leading sports figures was a new phenomenon. The interest in watching sports had the logical side effect of increasing participation in sports and the widespread prosperity made this participation easy for many. Sports stars appeared in films, so that a national audience that would otherwise have seen them only in photographs knew them through these films.

As active sports for everyone became more widespread, sports clothing became more important. Special costume was required for sports such as skiing and tennis. The move to expanded outdoor recreation reinforced the need for practical, casual dress and established sportswear as a separate category of clothing.[1]

[1]This new type of clothing, worn for leisure time but not dedicated to one particular sport, entered the vocabulary of fashion and also became a merchandising term. Henceforth in this text, the term "sportswear" will refer to clothing for men and women that is worn for leisure time or informal situations, while clothing for particular sports will be discussed under the heading of clothing for active sports.

The Automobile

Once the automobile had become practical transportation rather than a sport, special costume for motoring disappeared. As women began to drive routinely, the need for shorter and less cumbersome skirts was evident. Although daytime skirts did drop fairly low to just above the ankle in the early 1930s, and again in the 1950s, skirts have not reached all the way to the floor for everyday wear since 1910, and it is possible that the automobile has been, in part, responsible for this.

The automobile also may have been responsible for the abandonment of the parasol or sun shade. Women walked less and parasols were impractical in open cars and unnecessary in closed vehicles. Cars encouraged the use of wristwatches, which were easier to look at while driving than pocket watches, and probably made smaller hats preferable. Canes and walking sticks went out of style.

Cars allowed workers to live in suburban areas and commute to the city and made new recreational opportunities possible by carrying individuals and families out of the city and into the countryside. These recreational aspects of car use contributed to the growing use of casual sport clothes.

PRODUCTION AND ACQUISITION OF TEXTILES AND CLOTHING

Technological Developments Affecting Fashion

For centuries the fabrics available for clothing had been limited to those found in nature. Although people in a few parts of the world did use unusual local materials for garments, Western societies tended to utilize four fibers: cotton, linen, silk, and wool. As early as the 1880s, Count Hilaire de Chardonnet of France had manufactured a new fiber from cellulose. Called **artificial silk,** the fiber did not gain rapid acceptance, as it was too lustrous and did not wash well. Gradually it was improved, and by the 1920s, when the United States Department of Commerce established the name **rayon** for this material, it was used fairly widely. A second and quite different manufactured fiber came into commercial use after World War I. It, too, was called rayon until the 1950s when it was given a separate name, **acetate,** to distinguish it from rayon. Throughout the 1920s and increasingly in the 1930s, rayon fabrics (including acetate) were used, mostly in women's clothing.

The first nylon fibers were marketed by E. I. du Pont de Nemours Company in 1938. Shown at the 1939 World's Fair, nylon quickly gained favor for use in women's underwear and stockings. This strong, durable fiber was put to military use during World War II. No longer available to the general public, nylon was not readily available again until after the war. (See *page 433* for further discussion of nylon.)

Unless individuals were to wear only loose, unfitted clothing that could be put on over the head, some means of closure had to be used. Lacing and buttons were the chief means of fastening garments shut until the 19th century when a wide variety of metal hooks and eyes were developed.

Whitcomb L. Judson from Chicago had invented the **zipper** in 1891. He called this first version a clasp locker. An imperfect device (it kept falling apart), the design was improved by Gideon Sundback, who went on to manufacture **hookless fasteners** that were sold for use in corsets, gloves, sleeping bags, money belts, and tobacco pouches. In the 1920s, B. F. Goodrich bought hookless fasteners for closures on rubber boots. It was Goodrich who first used the term **zipper,** calling the boots "zipper boots." Goodrich registered the word zipper as a trademark in 1925, but zippers were so widely used in the 1930s and after that zipper became a generic term applied to any toothed, slide fastener (Berendt 1989).

By the mid-30s, the zipper was a well-known device, but was not universally used. Zipper manufacturers mounted a campaign to get men's trouser and suit manufacturers to use zippers in trouser fly closings. This objective, which took considerable effort to accomplish, was helped when the English Prince of Wales, his brother the Duke of York, and his second cousin started to wear zippered trousers.

Use of zippers in women's high fashion clothing grew after couturiers incorporated them into their collections. Charles James was the first major designer to use the zipper as a decorative element when in 1933 he "spiraled it all the way around one of his dresses." Schiaparelli put colored plastic zippers into her designs as decorative elements in 1935. Paquin, Molyneux, and Piguet used zipper closures in their 1937 collections (Freidel 1994).

By the early 1940s the zipper was well established as a closure, and appeared in clothing in all price ranges. After the beginning of World War II, the supply of zippers was curtailed because of metal shortages.

The French Couture

From 1920 until Paris was cut off from contact with England and America by the German occupation during World War II, the French couture maintained its position as the arbiter of style in clothing for women. Although the couture in general was influential, in each period certain designers stood out from the rest. Just as Poiret had occupied a special place among the designers of the late Edwardian Period and before World War I, so did the designs of Chanel typify the style of the 1920s, Vionnet the early 1930s, and Schiaparelli the later 1930s.

Gabrielle "Coco" Chanel began to work as a designer before World War I. During the War she had a small shop at Deauville, a seaside resort, where she had great success in making casual knit jackets and pullover sweaters. She designed comfortable, practical clothes, buying sailor's jackets

and men's pullover sweaters that she combined with pleated skirts. Soon she was having these garments made specially for her own clients.

After the War she returned to Paris and set up a salon that became one of the most influential in Paris. She is credited with making the suntanned look and costume jewelry popular, but her real genius lay in designing simple, classic wool jersey styles. (See *Figure 16.1.*)

FIGURE 16.1

Typical wool jersey suit from 1929, designed by Chanel. (*Harper's Bazaar,* June 22, 1939.)

In the late 1920s Chanel went to Hollywood briefly to design for films. It had been the practice to dress the film stars in the most elaborate possible costumes, even when these were not appropriate for the time of day. Chanel insisted that the costumes be appropriate for the action of the drama and in this way she was responsible for a new authenticity in film clothes. She continued to be a leading fashion designer throughout the 1930s. Chanel closed her shop during World War II, and she did not reopen after the War. In 1954 she came out of retirement and she surprised the fashion world by reentering the couture. She went on to have a highly successful second career as a leading couturier.

Madeleine Vionnet began to work as an apprentice in a dressmaker's shop at the age of thirteen. She worked at the important fashion house of Callot Soeurs, and later for Doucet. Her plain, unadorned but well-cut designs were not acceptable to Doucet where elaborate and lavish clothes were the mode, so she left in the years before World War I to set up her own shop. She was not especially successful until after the war in the early 1920s, at which time the house of Vionnet became part of the haute couture.

Her distinctive talent was in the cutting of dresses. She originated the **bias cut,** a technique for cutting clothing to utilize the diagonal direction of the cloth, which has greater stretch and drapes in such a way that the body lines and curves are accentuated. During the 1930s, when this cut was especially fashionable, she was one of the most sought-after of the French designers. She has been compared to an architect or sculptor. (See *Figure 16.2*.) She completely understood the medium of fabric and through cutting and draping created styles of such simplicity and elegance that they are still admired. She retired in 1939, and although she lived on until 1975, she never returned to the couture.

Elsa Schiaparelli, an Italian designer, worked in Paris in the 1930s where she began by creating sweaters in bizarre designs. Hers was a flair for the theatrical. By the end of the 1930s she was an exceedingly popular designer whose emphasis on color and unusual decorative effects was widely praised. She is credited with being among the first in the couture to use zippers—she put them on pockets in 1930 and in dresses in 1934 and 1936. Her other innovations included the first evening dress with a matching jacket and skirts to match sweaters. She worked with artists such as Salvador Dali (see **Surrealism,** *page 398* and *Color Plate 49*) who designed fabrics for her. She had a talent for gaining publicity for her work. In the mid-1930s Schiaparelli labeled a vivid pink color that she used "shocking pink." (See *Color Plate 50*.) When the war broke out, she came to the United States where she continued to work during and after the war.

Chanel, Vionnet, and Schiaparelli were only three of the influential Paris-based designers of the 1920s and 1930s. Other important couturiers of the 1920–1947 period are listed in *Table 16.1*.

FIGURE 16.2

Evening dress of 1931 designed by Vionnet and showing bias-cut features that she favored. Dress is describing as having "fine embroideries in beads, tiny spangles, jewel studs, of metal thread, on chiffon." (*Harper's Bazaar*, February 1931.)

Table 16.1

DESIGNERS OF THE FRENCH COUTURE: 1920–1947

Designer	Couture house and Date of opening	Notable Characteristics Designs or Career
Gabrielle Chanel (1883–1971)	Chanel, 1914	Simple and classic designs. (See pages 392–393.)
Fortuny (1871–1949)	Fortuny, 1906	Designed his own fabrics, originated a singular style of pleating. Timeless clothing styles worn by women who valued their uniqueness. (See pages 363–364.)
Alix Grès (1903–1993)	Alix, 1934	High level of craftsmanship, soft draped designs.
Jacques Heim (1899–1967)	Heim, 1923	Known for well-made clothes that reflected current trends.
Jeanne Lanvin (1867–1946)	Lanvin, began as milliner in 1890	Emphasized more ornate designs. Originated *robe de style,* popular gown of the 1920s.
Lucian Lelong (1889–1958)	Lucien Lelong, 1919	Not himself a designer, his house was "famed for elegant, feminine clothes of refined taste and lasting wearability." Among the designers who worked for him were Dior, Balmain, Givenchy.
Main Rousseau Bocher (1890–1976)	Mainbocher, 1929	American, opened Paris salon in 1929, moved to New York during World War II. Designed wedding dress for Duchess of Windsor. (See page 396.)
Edward Molyneux (1891–1974)	Molyneux, 1919	Known for "well-bred, elegant, fluid" lines.
Jean Patou (1887–1936)	Patou, 1914	". . . specialized in lady-like, elegant, uncluttered country-club clothes." In 1929 he led the way to longer skirt lengths, natural waistlines.
Robert Piguet (1901–1953)	Piguet, 1933	Used freelance designers, including Givenchy and Dior, who said that he "taught the virtues of simplicity."
Nina Ricci (1883–1970)	Nina Ricci, 1932; ceased designing in 1945 but the house continued with other designers	". . . graceful, with superb, detailed workmanship."
Marcel Rochas (1902–1955)	Rochas, c. 1924	Known for color, lots of decoration, and "fantastic" ideas in fabrics an designs.
Maggie Rouff (1897–1971)	Rouff, 1929	Characterized as "standing for refined, feminine elegance."
Elsa Schiaparelli (1890–1973)	*Pour le Sport,* 1929; Schiaparelli, 1935.	Original, with a flair for the unusual and for garnering publicity. (See page 393.)
Madeleine Vionnet (1876–1975)	Vionnet, 1912	Noted for bias cut, exceptional technical skills. (See page 393.)

All material in quotes from Calasibetta, C. M. (1988). *Fairchild's Dictionary of Fashion,* 2nd edition. New York: Fairchild Publications, and Stegemeyer, A. (1996). *Who's Who in Fashion,* 3rd edition. New York: Fairchild Publications.

📖

CONTEMPORARY COMMENTS 16.2

General Limitation Order L-85

On April 8, 1942, Women's Wear Daily *published the "General Limitation Order L-85, Restrictions on Feminine Apparel for Outerwear and Certain Other Garments." Reproduced here are some of the major items in the order.*

The fulfillment of requirements for the defense of the United States has created a shortage in the supply of wool, silk, rayon, cotton and linen for defense, for private account and for export; and the following Order is deemed necessary and appropriate in the public interest and to promote the National Defense....

(d) GENERAL EXCEPTIONS: The prohibitions and restrictions of this Order shall not apply to feminine apparel manufactured or sold for use as:

   (1) Infants and Toddler's Apparel, size range from 1 to 4;

   (2) Bridal Gowns;

   (3) Maternity Dresses;

   (4) Clothing for persons who, because of abnormal height, size or physical deformities, require additional material for proportionate length of skirt or jacket or sweep of skirt or width of sleeve;

   (5) Burial Gowns;

   (6) Robes or Vestments as required by the rules of Religious Orders or Sects

or when manufactured for or sold to the [armed forces.]...

(e) GENERAL RESTRICTIONS...

   (1) more than two articles of apparel at one unit price...

   (2) any garment of multiple units, any of which contains wool cloth to be sold at a unit price...

   (3) French cuffs on sleeves.

   (4) double material yokes.

   (5) balloon, dolman, or leg-of-mutton sleeves.

   (6) fabrics which have been reduced from normal width or length by overall tucking, shirring, or pleating, except for minor trimmings.

   (7) inside pockets of wool cloth.

   (8) patch pockets of wool cloth on a lined wool cloth garment.

   (9) interlinings containing any virgin or reprocessed wool.

The Order went on to identify specific restrictions for Women's Misses and Junior Misses sized coats, daytime and evening dresses, suits, jackets, separate skirts and culottes, slacks and playclothes, and blouses and also for teenage girls and children's apparel in the categories of dresses, coats, rainwear, slacks and playclothes, snow and ski suits, and nurses' and maids' uniforms. Specific limitations, identified in tables appended to the Order, were placed on length and circumference of skirts and width of jackets. Some notable restrictions included:

- No coats with "separate or attached cape, hood, muff, scarf, bag or hat."
- No daytime or evening dresses "with a separate or attached belt exceeding 2 inches in width"
- No evening dresses or suits or skirts and culottes "with a hem exceeding 2 inches in width."
- No jackets "with sleeves cut on the bias or with cuffs on long sleeves."
- No slacks "with a cuff."

American Designers

Although the French couture continued to work on a limited basis during the War, international press coverage could not be given to the designs created there. As a result, a number of talented American designers were featured in magazines like *Vogue* and *Harper's Bazaar* to an extent that might not have been possible had they been competing with the French Couture. Once established, these designers continued to have a substantial following—although the operation of the fashion industry in America was quite different from the operation of the French Couture.

A trade association called the *Chambre Syndicale de la Couture Parisienne* represents the French haute couture. This group defines the **haute couture** as firms that create models that may be sold to private customers or to other segments of the fashion industry who also acquire the right to reproduce the designs. In the period between the wars, the designs of the French haute couturiers were sold to private customers and to retail stores where they were resold or copied and sold to customers of the store. Through this system the designs originated by the couturiers influenced international fashions (Latour 1956).

In the United States, by contrast, fashion designers generally worked for ready-to-wear manufacturers. Although many of the fine department stores in large cities maintained custom dressmaking or tailoring departments, and smaller towns and cities had a number of local dressmakers, most American women purchased their clothing ready made in local stores.

The American fashion designer, therefore, usually worked for the dress manufacturer. He or she prepared a line of designs for a given season. Most dress firms produced clothing for four seasons: spring, summer, fall, and holiday. Some also had a resort line. These clothes were shown in New York to buyers for stores across the country. In lower-priced dresses, salesmen took samples directly to the stores. Buyers placed orders for items from the line. Those designs that did not receive an adequate number of orders were not put into production.

American designers for the most part worked in this system. Even the highest priced fashions of the 1930s and 1940s were produced in this way. One exception to this rule was **Mainbocher,** an American-born designer who went to Paris in the 1920s to work as a fashion editor. He opened his own couture house in Paris in 1929. He designed Wallis Simpson's wedding dress. (She married the Duke of Windsor in June of 1937.) When the War came, he left Paris and returned to New York where he continued to work as he had in Paris, following the practices of the French couture.

Among the American fashion designers of the period between 1920 and the end of World War II, certain figures stand out. **Claire McCardell** is one such figure. Sally Kirkland (1975), writing about McCardell in *American Fashion,* says, "Many think Claire McCardell was the greatest fashion designer this country has yet produced. Certainly she was the most innovative, independent, and indigenous of American designers."

Claire McCardell was born in Frederick, Maryland, in 1905. She studied at the Parsons School of Design and in Paris. Her first individual collection was done for Townley Frocks in 1931 when the head designer with whom she worked was killed accidentally. She remained with this firm until 1938 when it closed. She designed chiefly sportswear and casual clothes for Townley. After 1940, she designed under her own name. She had her greatest success in the 1940s and 1950s. Her clothing was considered radical at first and was difficult to sell, but when women found her designs fit them well and were comfortable, they looked for more of the same.

Some of the important styles and design features that she is credited as originating or making popular include: matching separates, a new idea at the time; dirndl skirts; the **monas-**

FIGURE 16.3

Some of the styles originated by Claire McCardell during her career: (a) the popover, c. 1942; (b) the draped bathing suit, c. 1944; (c) railroad-stitched denim with a bib front and low back, c. 1944; (d) string-tied empire line dress, c. 1944. (*Women's Wear Daily,* March 24, 1958. Reproduced courtesy, Fairchild Publications.)

tic, a bias cut, full tent dress that when belted followed the body contours gracefully; hardware closings; spaghetti or shoestring ties; the diaper bathing suit; ballet slippers; and the poncho. (See *Figure 16.3.*) She died in 1958.

Another prominent American designer, **Adrian,** gained his earliest recognition as a designer for films. Throughout the 1920s and 1930s he designed both for contemporary and period films, and the name Adrian became synonymous with high fashion and glamour. (See *Figure 16.4.*) In 1941 he

Color Forecast
by *Adrian* of Hollywood

Guatemalan pink linen jacket...
mauve sheer wool skirt...
eloquent colors punctuated
with vivid plaid

Exclusively at **NAN DUSKIN**
in Philadelphia

FIGURE 16.4

Tailored suit with large, square shoulder pads created by American designer Adrian in 1945 and typical of the sophisticated designs for which he was famous. (Courtesy, Nan Duskin.)

opened his own business, seeing that American design would become more important because Paris designs had become inaccessible as a result of the war. His work is known for its subtle details. He designed "in the round," thinking about how a woman would look from all angles, a result of his work in films (Horyn 2002).

The firm of Adrian Ltd. continued in business throughout the 1940s but had to be closed in 1952 when the designer had a severe heart attack. His recovery was long and slow. When he felt ready to return to active work it was to design costumes for the musical comedy *Camelot;* however, he died in 1959 before he was able to complete the project.

Two other American designers who came to prominence during the wartime period should also be mentioned. These are **Norman Norell** and Pauline Trigère. Norell was a native of the United States, **Pauline Trigère** was French and came to America in 1937. Although both Norell and Trigère were more influential in the period to be discussed in the next chapter, they were active in the 1940s as well. Both worked for Hattie Carnegie for a time. (See *Table 17.2, page 436.*) Then Norell joined with a fine tailor, Anthony Traina, to form the firm of Traina–Norell and later, in 1960, went off on his own. (See *Color Plate 50.*) Trigère formed her own business after leaving Carnegie in 1942 and showed her first collection in that year, a group of 12 dresses.

After the end of World War II, the French couture resumed its operation and its primacy as the center of international fashion design. American designers had, however, shown that they could create innovative and original styles, and had earned an important place in the world of fashion design. In recognition of the importance of American design in the postwar period, fashion magazines continued to give extensive coverage to American designers as well as featuring Paris design.

Théâtre de la Mode

Paris was liberated from foreign occupation in the autumn of 1944. To convince the world that the couture was once again ready to provide leadership in fashion design and to raise money for war relief, the *Chambre Syndicale* organized an exhibit of miniature mannequins, 27 inches tall, dressed in clothes designed by more than 40 of the leading French couturiers. Not only were dresses, suits, and coats included, but also shoes, hats, gloves, belts, and real jewelry. Shown in nine miniature stage sets, the almost 200 small-scale figures traveled throughout Europe and the United States. (See *Figure 16.5.*) From 1952 to 1983 they remained at the Maryhill Museum in Goldendale, Washington. In the 1980s, they were sent to Paris for refurbishing and once again sent on tour. When not on tour, they are exhibited at Maryhill Museum.

FIGURE 16.5

Twenty-seven inch tall mannequins from the *Théâtre de la Mode* of 1944 displayed on a miniature set showed the latest fashions from the *haute couture*. This traveling exhibit not only featured the work of more than 40 French couturiers but also raised funds for war relief. (Courtesy Mary-hill Museum.)

ART MOVEMENTS AND THEIR INFLUENCE ON FASHION

Art Deco

The term **Art Deco** derives from the *L'Exposition Internationale des Arts Decoratifs et Industriels Moderns,* the name of an exposition held in Paris in 1925. The term has been applied to art typical of that produced in the 1920s and 1930s. Geometric forms that could be derived from artistic expressions of the past or present characterized Art Deco styles. Egyptian and Mayan motifs can be seen in Art Deco, as well as designs related to modern art movements such as Cubism, Fauvism, and Expressionism.

Art Deco influences are especially notable in the fashions of the 1920s, when the geometric lines of many garments can be seen to echo Art Deco style lines. Art Deco style can be observed in many fabric prints, embroideries, beaded decorations, and jewelry. (See *Color Plate 46* and *Illustrated Table 16.4, page 411.*) Art Deco styles underwent a revival in the 1970s.

Surrealism

Surrealism, literally "beyond the real," was a literary and art movement that began in the 1920s, influenced by Freudianism. Artists such as the Italian Giorgio de Chirico, the Spanish Salvador Dali, and the French Rene Magritte painted nonconventional scenes and objects, drawing on the subconscious imagination. By the 1930s Surrealism could be seen as an influence on fashion (Martin 1987).

Elsa Schiaparelli was a friend of many Surrealist artists, and surrealist influences are especially pronounced in her work in the 1930s. Among the surreal aspects of her work were the use of body parts such as eyes, mouths, and hands in unexpected places on garments or in prints. One organza dress had a painted lobster on the skirt. Suits had butterflies or cicadas as buttons. A hat was shaped like a shoe. Not only Dali, but also Surrealist writer, film director, and artist Jean Cocteau, created fabrics and embroideries for Schiaparelli. (See *Color Plate 49.*)

Fashion photographers of the 1930s frequently used Surrealistic settings for their photographs of fashions. During and after the war, interest in Surrealism in fashion waned, but in the 1980s fashion designers such as Lacroix and Lagerfeld incorporated Surrealist motifs in their collections.

SOURCES OF INFORMATION ABOUT COSTUME

Photographs of fashions had been appearing in fashion magazines since the late 19th century. By the 1920s some fashion photographers were trying to create increasingly artistic effects. As a result some fashion photographs might be called fashion *art* photography and others fashion *information* photography. Fashion art photographs sometimes prevent the viewer from getting the maximum information about the details of clothing being shown. Fashion information photographs present a clear, undistorted view of items of dress.

The technology for reproducing color photographs improved sufficiently by the late 1930s that color photographs were extensively used. During the 20s and early 30s, when color illustrations were used in fashion magazines they had to be drawings.

COSTUME FOR WOMEN:
1920–1947

Costume for Women: 1920–1930

GARMENTS

As depicted in mail-order catalogs, undergarments came in a wide variety of styles. Items included brassieres, which had to first flatten and later, toward the end of the decade, uplift the bosom in order to provide the current fashionable shape. Drawers or knickers became **panties** in the 1920s. These were short, buttoned or elasticized at the waistline, and often very decorative.

An evolution of the combination was a garment alternately known as **cami-knickers, step-ins,** or **teddies,** a combination of the camisole and panties. A straight cut chemise or petticoat was renamed the **slip,** and was comparable to the garment called by that name today. Larger women wore corsets. These were boned or made with elastic panels, or both. Garters suspended from the corset held up the stockings; women who did not wear corsets wore garter belts or garters to hold up their stockings. See *Illustrated Table 16.1,* for examples of undergarments during the years between 1920 and 1947.

A figure with a flat bosom and narrow hips was the ideal. The fashionable silhouette was straight, without indentation at the waistline. When a dress had a belt, the belt was placed at the hipline. Most dresses were one piece. (See *Figure 16.6.*)

At the beginning of the period, skirts were long and reached almost to the ankle, tending downward in 1922–23, but gradually moving upward in 1924 and after. By 1925 they were about eight inches from the floor, by 1926–27, 14 to 16 inches and some even as short as 18 inches from the ground. Once the skirts reached this elevation, they remained relatively stable in 1928–29, then began to lengthen again (Richards 1983–84). The first move toward longer lengths was observable in a tendency to cut skirt hems unevenly with panels, flares, scalloped, or pointed segments of the skirt. By the end of the decade, skirt lengths had dropped. (See *Figure 16.7*

FIGURE 16.6

Styles of 1922 reflect the introduction of a new silhouette: narrow with a dropped waistline. In the postwar period hemlines had lengthened. (French fashion magazine, *L'Art de la Mode,* 1922).

for diagrammatic representation of skirt lengths throughout the 1920s.)

For daytime one-piece styles predominated. Some coat dresses had crossover, right to left, closings. Necklines usually ended at the base of the throat or lower, with round, V-shaped, bateau, or cowl styles. Round, high, and V-necklines often were finished with collars or bias ruffles. When dresses had sleeves, they were often long. Many dresses were sleeveless. Most bodices were plain and cut straight to the hip. Some had embroidered decorations or pleating. Skirts were more complex in cut than bodices, often utilizing bias cutting to produce interesting effects. Skirts had pleats and gathers placed off center, scalloped hems, godet insets, and paneled effects that achieved **handkerchief skirt** styles.

Separate blouses and sweaters were popular. Most were elongated, low-hipped, and straight, and worn over, not tucked into, the skirt. Middy blouses were fashionable. (See *Figure 16.8.*)

Tailored suits had matching jackets and skirts, with jackets ending at the hip or below. The Chanel suit, a cardigan-style jacket and skirt made from wool jersey (see *Figures 16.1* and *16.8*), was very popular. When suits were belted, the belt

Illustrated Table 16.1

SELECTED UNDERGARMENTS FOR WOMEN, MEN, AND CHILDREN: 1920–1947

Woman's brassiere, 1923[1]

Woman's corset, 1923[1]

Woman's step-in chemise, 1923[1]

Brassiere and girdle, 1930s[2]

Slip and panties, 1934[3]

Brassiere, World War II period; due to shortage of broadcloth, these brassieres were made of printed calico[2]

[1]Franklin Simon & Co. 1993. *Franklin Simon Fashion Catalog for 1923*, Mineola, NY: Dover, pp. 83, 88.
[2]Illustration courtesy of The Maidenform Museum, New York City.
[3]Fairchild Publications.

Illustrated Table 16.1

SELECTED UNDERGARMENTS FOR WOMEN, MEN, AND CHILDREN: 1920–1947

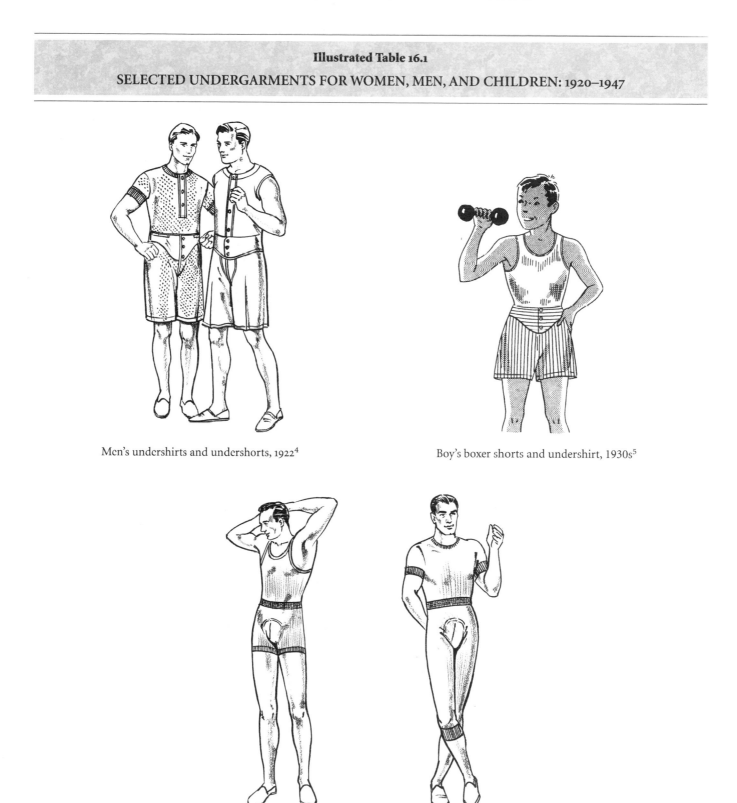

Men's undershirts and undershorts, 1922[4]

Boy's boxer shorts and undershirt, 1930s[5]

Men's jockey-type undershorts, undershirt, long underdrawers, and T-shirt, 1938–1939[3]

[4]Blum, S. 1981. *Everyday Fashions of the Twenties*. Mineola, NY: Dover, p. 190.
[5]Grafton, C. B. 1993. *Fashions of the Thirties*. Mineola, NY: Dover, p. 55.

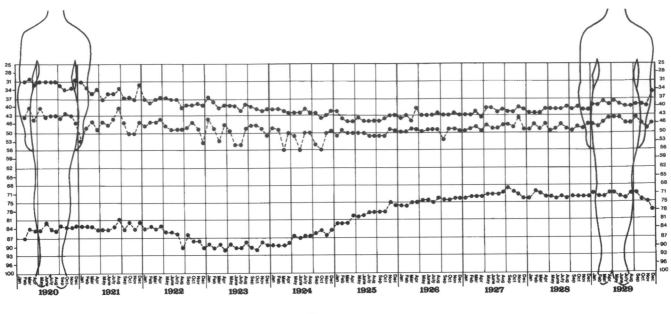

FIGURE 16.7

Location of the average waistline, hipline, and hemline during the 1920s as calculated according to percentage of total figure height. (Reprinted from Richards, L. 1983–84. "The Rise and Fall of it All: The Hemlines and Hiplines of the 1920s." *Clothing and Textiles Research Journal*, Vol. 2, No. 1, p. 47.)

FIGURE 16.8

Styles of 1927, including jodhpurs, which were worn by both men and women for riding, hats in the cloche style, and a suit of the type made famous by Chanel. (French fashion magazine, *L'Art de la Mode*, 1927.)

was placed well below normal waist placement. Some opened at the center front, closed on the left. Long lapels that rolled to a low closing were fashionable. (**Ensembles** were matching dresses and coats, or skirts, overblouses, and coats.)

Made in the same lengths as daytime dresses, evening dresses grew shorter as daytime dresses grew shorter. Generally sleeveless, with deep V- or U-shaped necklines, some evening bodices were supported over the shoulder by small straps. Skirts of evening dresses were often more complex in cut than for daytime dresses and used such effects as floating panels, draped areas, or layered skirts. In 1919 Jeanne Lanvin introduced a bouffant skirt, reminiscent of the crinoline period. An evening dress of this type with a dropped waistline and full skirt was a popular alternative to the tubular silhouette. It was called the **robe de style**. (See *Figure 16.9*.) As the decade progressed, the tendency to cut skirts unevenly also appeared in evening styles.

Beading was a popular means of ornamenting evening dresses and sometimes covered the entire dress. (See *Figure 16.9*.) Fashionable fabrics included chiffon, soft satins, and velvets (and for the robe de style garments, silk taffeta.) Geometric Art Deco designs were frequently used as fabric patterns. (See *Color Plate 46*.)

OUTDOOR GARMENTS

The most characteristic coats closed over the left hip, often with one large decorative button or several small ones. Some coats, known as **clutch coats,** had to be held shut as they had no fastening.

a   b

FIGURE 16.9

Evening dresses of the 1920s. The dresses in (a) follow the tubular silhouette and are decorated with beading. The dress in (b) was designed by Jeanne Lanvin and has the wide skirt she created in the *robe de style*. ((a) *Chic Parisien,* November 1926. Reproduced courtesy, Fairchild Publications. (b) Photograph courtesy, Wadsworth Atheneum, Hartford. Gift of Mrs. Frank W. Crocker.)

Young women (and young men) wore raccoon coats for motoring or to football games. Fur and fur-trimmed capes and wraps were popular among the more well-to-do. Sweaters, long and belted low, were popular as sportswear.

SLEEPWEAR

Night clothing consisted of either nightgowns or pajamas, both of which had long, straight lines.

HAIR AND HEADDRESS

See *Illustrated Table 16.2,* for some examples of hairstyles and hats from the period of 1920 to 1947.

Women's hairstyles of the 1920s were one of the more revolutionary developments in fashion. Except for the Empire period, in which short hair was fashionable, no other earlier costume periods can be cited in which women cut their hair short. Viewed at first as a radical style, by 1923 it had become accepted fashion and college girls across the country were singing (to the tune of *Jingle Bells*), "Shingle bob, shingle bob, cut it all away . . .". To have one's hair **bobbed** was to have it cut. The **shingle** was an exceptionally short cut in which the back hair was cut and tapered like that of a man. Although the most fashionable cut was short with the hair tapering off to the nape of the neck, many variations were seen.

Illustrated Table 16.2

SELECTED HAIRSTYLES AND HATS FOR WOMEN: 1920–1947

Woman's hairstyle, 1921

Bobbed hair, 1922

Woman's cloche-style hat, 1921

Woman's hat, 1926

Woman's hat, 1928

Women's hats, 1933

Woman's hat, 1937

Woman's "upsweep" hairstyle, 1941

Stocking cap, 1943

Flowered hat with face veil, 1943

Hat with a one-sided look, 1944

Some women cut their hair short, with bangs at the front and the hair turned under at the ends on the sides and in the back. Others followed the extreme **Eton crop,** a style in which hair was exceptionally closely cropped and dressed like that of the men. Frederick Lewis Allen (1964) pointed out the widespread nature of the style for short hair in the United States. "In the latter years of the 1920s bobbed hair became almost universal among girls in their 20s, very common among women in their 30s and 40s, and by no means rare among women of sixty."

Some women wore their bobbed hair straight, others with a **marcel wave,** a style made up of a series of deep waves all over the head. The old fashioned, open hairpin was replaced by the **bobby pin,** with its tight spring clip. By the end of the decade, however, women started to let their hair grow again and small curls began to appear at the back of the head. Of course, some women never did cut their hair, but even those with longer hair usually wore it dressed straight or waved close to the face with a tight bun at the back of the neck.

Because they were worn with short hair, hats could be fitted close to the head. Just as the bob was the prevailing hair style, a small, close fitting hat called the cloche became the predominant hat form. In general, cloches had small or larger brims that turned down around the face. Some larger summer hats with wide, down-turned brims almost hid the face entirely. Berets were popular for sports. Headbands were colloquially known as "headache bands." Some that were jeweled and others with tall feathers attached were popular for evening, as were turbans.

FOOTWEAR

See *Illustrated Table 16.3,* for some examples of footwear from the period of 1920 to 1947.

Short skirts caused women to focus greater attention on hosiery. In the early years of the decade, dark stockings or white stockings continued in use, but as skirts grew shorter, tan- or flesh-colored stockings replaced them. More luxurious stockings were silk, but rayon was coming into widespread use for less expensive stockings. Cartoons of George Held Jr. depict the "flapper" of the period in stockings rolled below the knee, skirt above the knee and rouge on the knees. (See *Color Plate 45.*)

Heels of shoes were two to two and a half inches in height, toes pointed or rounded. Commonly seen styles included pumps with a strap across the instep or T-shaped straps which crossed the instep and ran down the center of the foot. Oxfords were worn, especially for sports. Dressy evening slippers were made of fabric or gold or silver leather.

Women wore Russian-style wide-topped boots. (One photo of the period shows how neatly a flask of bootleg whiskey fit into the top of this boot.) Young women affected the style of wearing their overshoes for bad weather or galoshes open and flapping. It is to this practice that some have attributed the origin of the term flappers although a variety

of derivations are claimed for the word. Another suggested origin is the large hair bows worn by young girls in the post–World War I period, which flapped on the backs of their heads. Most dictionaries of word origins indicate the word derives from the flapping of the wings of young birds, making an analogy to the young, human "fledgling" of 15 or 16 who is "trying her wings." The term had been applied to young girls before the 1920s, and the use of the word probably received reinforcement from the flapping of the galoshes of the young girls of the 1920s. In the 1920s it was applied quite specifically to fashionable and "modern" young women in their late teens and twenties.

Costume for Women: 1930–1947

GARMENTS

In a change from the straight lines of the 1920s, undergarments of the 1930s and 1940s emphasized the curves of the figure. Brassieres of the 30s were cut to lift and emphasize the breasts. Corsets extended to slightly above the waist. Rigidly boned corsets were still worn by large women, but smaller women wore corsets in which the shaping was achieved by elasticized fabric panels. Terminology changed: panties became **panty briefs** and then **briefs** as they grew shorter in order to fit under active sportswear. Older women continued to wear fuller, looser "drawers" or "bloomers." Slips fitted the torso and were fuller in the cut of the skirt. Lower-priced underwear was made of cotton, rayon, or acetate; more expensive garments were silk. See *Illustrated Table 16.1, page 400,* for examples of undergarments during the years between 1920 and 1947.

One-piece dresses, skirts and blouses, and tailored suits remained the staples of women's wardrobes for daytime wear. The beginnings of a change in silhouette came in the late 1920s when hemlines began to lengthen and belts moved gradually closer to the natural waistline. The silhouette of the 1930s emphasized the natural form of the woman's body. Bosom, waistline, and hips were clearly defined by the shape of clothing. (See *Figure 16.10.*)

Hemlines fell early in the decade. They were about 12 inches from the ground for the first several years, and by 1932 went as low as 10 inches. Indeed, some illustrations of high-fashion garments show a hemline that comes almost to the ankle. By mid-decade, skirt lengths started upward again, 13 or 14 inches off the ground, and by the end of the period skirt lengths had reached 16 or 17 inches from the floor.

The wartime period, with its restrictions, essentially "froze" styles of the late 30s and 1940–41. By the beginning of the War, skirts had become shorter, ending just below the knee, and had grown fuller. Shoulders had broadened, and shoulder pads were inserted into all garments to provide greater width. Bias cut was rarely used.

Necklines for daytime were generally high. In the first half of the decade, cowl necklines, cape collars, and soft fin-

FIGURE 16.10

Daytime dresses of 1933 show the fitted line, bias cut, and interesting sleeve variations of the early 1930s. (*Women's Wear Daily*, Spring 1933. Reproduced courtesy, Fairchild Publications.)

ishes such as bows and jabots predominated. (See *Figure 16.10.*) Later, V-necklines and collared dresses were more important. Yoke constructions were common. Sleeve styles included those that were long and full and gathered to a wristband at the end. Others styles were short, many with a capelike construction. Full sleeves were cut in raglan style or as *magyar* or **batwing** sleeves. At the end of the decade, short, puffed sleeves came back into fashion.

Most skirts were cut with several gores. Some had bias-cut pieces set into a yoke that covered the hips to create a skirt that was narrow but flaring. Others were made with box pleats or shirred sections, and a few had layered tunic constructions. All these constructions continued to be used until the end of the period. Toward the end of the 30s, skirts became wider.

Suits remained a basic item of women's wardrobes. Made in firmer fabrics, their line was not so supple as that of most dresses. (See *Figures 16.4 and 16.11.*) Some styles were clearly modeled after men's suits. Except for some square, boxy jackets of the early 30s, suits curved in to fit closely at the waist. Styles were both single and double breasted; some were belted. Jacket lengths were shorter in the early 1930s, longer toward the end. Lapels were wide in the early years, narrower and longer later.

Wartime suit styles included bolero suits with short curving jackets that ended above the waist or **Eisenhower jackets,** based on military jackets that were slightly bloused above the waist and gathered to a fitted belt at the waist, and named after the Supreme Allied Commander Dwight Eisenhower, who wore this type of jacket. (See *Figure 16.19.*)

Both casual and dressy versions of blouses, sweaters, and skirts were available. Retailers classified the more casual versions into a new category of clothing called **sportswear.** Blouses were constructed in much the same way as dress bodices. Pullover wool sweaters were made in decorative patterns or plain colors with short or long sleeves. Sometimes belts were worn over sweaters. Matching short-sleeved sweaters and long-sleeved cardigans were popular in the early forties. In the mid-1940s adolescents wore large, loose pullovers called **sloppy joes.** Sweaters were especially popular during the war. Movie stars who were photographed in tightly fitting sweaters for "pin-up" pictures were called "sweater girls."

In the 1930s skirts were generally cut without much fullness. Construction details included gores, pleats that released fullness low and below the hip, top-stitching, and panel insets. In the 1940s, and during the war, skirts were fuller and shorter. About 1945, **dirndl skirts** (*dirn'del*) (full, gathered skirts) became fashionable.

Evening and daytime dress lengths were markedly different. Evening gowns always reached to the floor. Bias-cut styles were utilized until the late 1930s. Such dresses followed the body to the hips, where they flared out. Other common characteristics of evening dresses included bare-backed gowns cut low to the waist at the back, halter-type sleeveless bodices, and full, capelike or puffed sleeved styles. (See *Figure 16.2* and *Color Plate 48.*)

Toward the end of the 1930s, less ornamentation, less detail in construction and more severe lines were more common. Evening styles included blouses and skirts and evening suits with long skirts and matching jackets of plain, unclut-

Illustrated Table 16.3

SELECTED EXAMPLES OF FOOTWEAR FOR WOMEN: 1920–1947

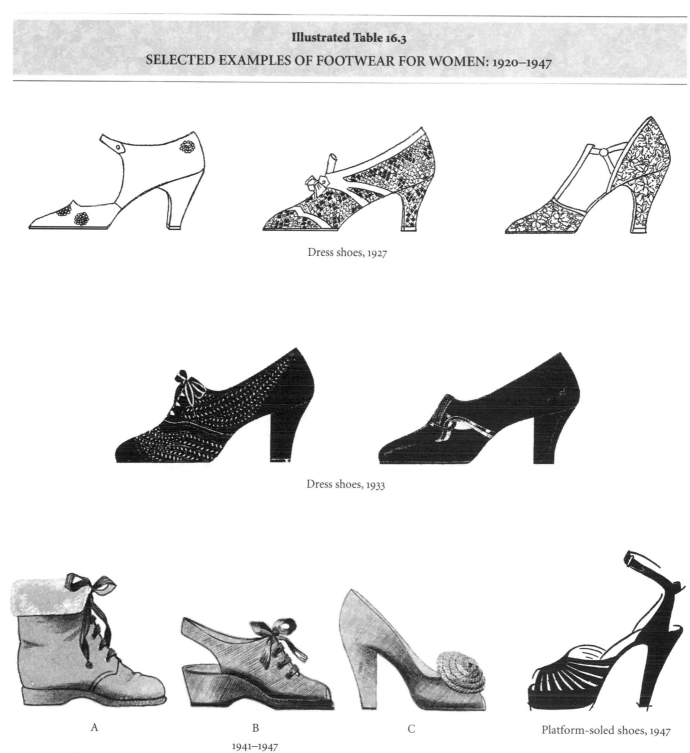

Dress shoes, 1927

Dress shoes, 1933

Platform-soled shoes, 1947

A   B   C

1941–1947
Wartime shoes made without leather (A) Jungle cloth, fleece lining, sisal soles
(B) Gabardine wedge-soled oxford with composition soles
(C) Gabardine open-toed pump with plastic soles

OUTDOOR GARMENTS

In the early 1930s many coats were cut with decorative detailing around the necklines and shoulderlines. Large collars were often made of fur. Some coats had leg-of-mutton sleeves. Closings tended to be at the left, often with only one button. Overall the line was slender until the latter part of the decade when more boxy, fuller coats, some in three-quarter length, some ending at the hip, and some in full length were popular.

Many coats of the 1940s had features such as large collars and revers, heavily padded shoulders, and raglan and dolman sleeve constructions. Some had plain, straight boxy shapes. Fur coats were popular and the increased affluence of Americans who worked in highly paid wartime industry brought these coats within the means of many more women. Military influence was evident in the war years, when the military trench coat was often seen.

SLEEPWEAR

Women could choose between nightgowns and pajamas.

HAIR AND HEADDRESS

See *Illustrated Table 16.2, page 404,* for some examples of hairstyles and hats from the period 1920–1947.

In the early years of the 1930s, hair was relatively short, softly waved, and with short, turned-up curls around the nape of the neck. As the decade progressed, fashionable hairstyles grew longer. Toward the end of the decade, the **page-boy bob** (straight hair turned under at the ends) and hair dressed on top of the head in curls or braids (the **upsweep**) were more fashionable. During the War some women arranged the hair in a high pompadour at the front and sides of the face while making a long, U-shaped roll at the back. Others wore a short, curly hairstyle called a **feather cut.**

In the early 1930s, hats were small in scale, of many different shapes and usually tipped either to one side, front, or back at an angle. In the later 1930s, there were berets and sailor hats and wider-brimmed styles. When upswept hairstyles were worn, higher hats and small hats with face veils were fashionable. Milliners found inspiration in many sources, including the Middle Ages, and some hats were shown with wimplelike scarves draped under the chin and attached to the hat at or above the ear. Hats and hair ornaments became fashionable for evening, especially turbans, decorative veils, artificial flowers, and ribbons. Snoods returned to fashion for the first time since the Civil War era, possibly as a result of the popularity of motion pictures such as *Gone With the Wind* and *Little Women.*

In the 1940s, hats tended to be small, among them pillboxes and small bonnets. Many women went hatless, but to be considered well-dressed a lady had to wear a hat. Women working in wartime factories covered their hair with turbans or wore snoods to protect hair from getting caught in the machinery.

FIGURE 16.11

Suit by Madeleine Vionnet, designed in 1931. Contrast the soft lines of this suit with the harder lines of the suit by Adrian from 1945 in *Figure 16.4.* (*Harper's Bazaar,* 1931.)

tered lines. Under these, soft, frilly, and often backless or sleeveless blouses or bodices were worn.

Strapless gowns appeared in Hollywood films of the late 1930s. The tops of these dresses fitted tightly and were held in place by boning sewn inside, along the seams.

FOOTWEAR

See *Illustrated Table 16.3* for some examples of footwear from the period 1920–1947.

Stockings were made in flesh tones of silk or rayon and seamed up the back. Cotton and wool stockings were for sportswear. Ankle socks were worn by young girls and for sports. In the 1940s teenaged girls wore ankle socks so constantly that adolescent girls came to be known as **bobby-sox ers.** Shortages of fabrics for stockings during the war led women to paint their legs with **leg makeup** to simulate the color of stockings. Some even went so far as to paint a dark line down the back of the leg in imitation of the seams. (See *Color Plate 51.*)

During the War, leather shoes were rationed. Each adult was entitled to two new pairs per year. Shoes made of cloth were exempt from restriction, and so cloth shoes with synthetic soles were readily available.

Costume for Women: 1920–1947

SPORTSWEAR

Throughout the period from 1920 to 1947, women were becoming more active participants in sports. As a result, women adopted both specific costumes for individual sports such as tennis, swimming, and skiing, and general informal dress for spectator sports and outdoor activities. (See *Figures 16.12 and 16.13.*) By 1928 such clothing was referred to as spectator sports styles by fashion magazines. By the 1930s, the clothing industry identified this new category of clothing as sportswear.

Except for basically unsuccessful attempts by dress reformers of the 1860s to introduce bloomers and the knickers worn by women for cycling, trousers for daytime wear had remained essentially a man's garment until the 1920s. Harem skirts had been introduced by Poiret in the preceding period. These exotic bifurcated garments were unlike men's trousers and were not widely worn. In the late 1920s, women began to appear in garments made like men's trousers for casual wear. The general term **slacks** was used to designate these garments. By the 1930s the style was well established, but slacks remained strictly a sportswear item. During the War many women found slacks a useful garment for working in factories.

In the 1930s jeans had a short run as a "fashion" item when *Vogue* magazine ran an advertisement depicting two society women in tight-fitting jeans, a look that they called "Western chic." Adolescent girls began to wear men's work jeans in blue denim for casual dress (Ratner 1985).

In the 1920s and on into the early 1930s, women wore beach pajamas. These were long, full trousers with matching tops, either separate or seamed together, that were worn for leisure activities. (See *Color Plate 47.*) Some even had large, matching hats.

FIGURE 16.12

Slacks, acceptable by 1934 as sportswear for women, and halter-top sundresses. (*Tres Parisian*, 1934.)

CLOTHING FOR ACTIVE SPORTS

White clothing was traditional for tennis. Like dress skirts in the 1920s, tennis dresses grew shorter, and remained shorter even when daytime dresses lengthened again. In the 1930s, bodices of tennis dresses were sleeveless and collarless; skirts were either short or divided culotte-style, and shorts were also commonly worn for tennis. No special costume was required for golf, but tweed skirts with pullover sweaters worn over a blouse seemed to be favored.

Costume for swimming altered radically. (See *Figure 16.14.*) In the early 1920s, a fairly voluminous two-piece tunic and knickers was a carryover from the 1910s. Gradually the knickers grew shorter, armholes grew deeper, necklines lower, and one-piece tank suits were adopted by women. Knee-length stockings were worn only in the first years of the 1920s. By the end of the 1920s, the modern concept of costumes in which women could really "swim" rather than

a

b

FIGURE 16.13 A AND B

Sportswear of the 1940s. (a) slacks and a crepe blouse, (b) a one-piece playsuit. (Photographs courtesy, Division of Costume, the American Museum of National History.)

"bathe" had been established. The first women to wear the more revealing tank suits were often arrested for "indecent exposure."

In the 1930s, bathing suits with halter tops or low-cut backs became popular. These lines were similar to those seen in some evening gowns. Bathing suits were made from knitted wool, rayon, acetate, and cotton. In the early 1930s, **Lastex**®, a fabric made from yarns with a rubber core covered by another fiber, was used to make bathing suits that had stretch and were more form-fitting and wrinkle free than other fabrics. It was also in the 1930s that two-piece bathing suits with either a brassierelike or halter-top and shorts made

their first appearance. Women could choose from an assortment of bathing suit styles including one-piece or two-piece styles with either shorts or skirtlike constructions.

Ski clothes consisted of full trousers and a sweater or, especially in the 1930s and after, matching jackets. Close-fitting ski clothing was not introduced until after World War II. Women wore jodhpurs with high riding boots, shirts, and tweed jackets for riding horses.

ACCESSORIES

See *Illustrated Table 16.4,* for examples of some popular accessories.

Illustrated Table 16.4

1920–1947: ACCESSORIES

Popular jewelry in the
1920s: Drop earrings, long
pearl or bead necklace,
and bracelet

Fur neckpiece, 1930s

Men's neckties, 1920–1947,
shapes varied, as did widths

Accessories showing
art deco influence
(A) Woman's neck scarf, 1930
(B) Art deco pendant
(C) Mesh handbag, c. 1920s, with
geometric pattern

(A) Man's black silk socks
with embroidered clocks, 1923
(B) Man's patterned golfing socks

Stocking styles for women, 1930
(A) Figured knitted stocking
for casual wear
(B) Long flesh-colored silk
dress stocking, seamed
up the back

Wrist watch, 1923

Umbrellas, 1937
(A) See-through plastic umbrella
(B) Oiled silk umbrella with decorative
handle

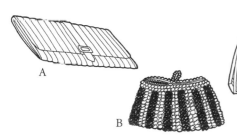

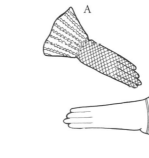

Handbags
(A) Envelope style handbag, 1923   (B) Wood bead handbag, 1938
(C) Cordé handbag, 1940s

Women's gloves, 1920–1940 (A)
Gauntlet styled glove
(B) Glove trimmed with ruffle

Sunglasses, 1939

FIGURE 16.14 A, B, C, AND D

Bathing suits show marked evolution in the period from 1920 to 1947. (a) A black wool knit bathing suit from 1925–1927, made in one piece, the trunks attached at the waist. This suit was made by Gantner and Mattern Company and worn in California. (b) "Trio of striplings," January 1, 1934. (c) "Swoon suit" from Cole of California, May 1, 1939. (d) "Perfect Form" bathing suit from June 1944. (Photograph of (a) courtesy, Division of Costume, The National Museum of American History; (b), (c) and (d) courtesy, *Vogue* magazine, Condé Nast Publications.)

Umbrellas were practical, rather than fashionable, with either long or short handles and were produced in conservative colors. (Parasols were hardly used.) Fans made of ostrich feathers were carried in the evening during the 1920s, but fans were not much used after this decade.

Handbags ranged in size from large leather bags to dainty, beaded evening bags barely big enough to hold a handkerchief and a lipstick. From a vast variety a few especially fashionable items stand out in each decade. In the 1920s, some fashionable evening bags were made from brocade, embroidered silk, glass or metal beads, or wire mesh in gold and silver. Daytime leather bags were often flat, envelope types held by small straps. In the 1930s, women carried bags that were mounted on frames and had straps and others that were pouch shaped. In the 1940s, shoulder strap bags became especially popular.

Throughout the period women were expected to wear gloves out-of-doors in the daytime. In the 1930s, long evening gloves appeared. During the war, cotton gloves replaced leather because of shortages. Gloves often matched dresses or hats and/or handbags in color or fabric.

An important accessory in the mid-1940s, scarves were made of fabrics that contrasted with dresses. Throughout the period fur scarves, stoles, and skins were worn around the neck; often the head and paws of the animal were retained for decoration.

JEWELRY

In the 1920s jewelry was plentiful, especially long, dangling earrings that looked well against short haircuts and long necks. Many brooches, bracelets, and shorter necklaces were made with Art Deco designs. Long strands of pearls or beads were popular accessories.

By the 1930s jewelry was more subdued, in keeping with the depressed economy, and included short pearl necklaces and jeweled clips in pairs placed at the neckline or on collars. Although earrings were generally worn in the evening, many fashion magazines showed women modeling daytime dresses without earrings.

Upswept hairstyles of the 1940s contributed to greater interest in earrings, many of which were large in scale. Rhinestones were popular for evening. Other jewelry included brooches for collars and lapels, short necklaces, and bracelets.

COSMETICS AND GROOMING

During the 1920s, cosmetics (popularly called makeup) became an accepted part of women's fashion. Prior to this time most women who used cosmetics did so in secret. In the 1920s, cosmetics became essential to achieving a fashionable look. This notation from *Only Yesterday* may serve to dramatize the magnitude of the change that took place. Back in 1917, according to Frances Fisher Dubuc, only two persons in the beauty culture business had paid an income tax; by 1927 there were 18,000 firms and individuals in this field listed as income tax payers (Allen 1964).

Fashionable ladies plucked their eyebrows into a narrow line, which was then emphasized with eyebrow pencil. Bright shades of rouge and lipstick were preferred. Lipstick in a round metal tube had been invented in 1915. Some flappers even went so far as to rouge their knees. Powder completed an almost masklike appearance that the most fashionable women attempted to achieve.

COSTUME FOR MEN:
1920–1947

No dramatic changes in men's costume took place from the 1920s through the end of World War II. Among the well-to-do, the English tailor retained his reputation as the best in the world. The English tailor was to men's clothing what the French couturier was to women's.

Fashion influences in England were also given a boost by the popularity of the youthful Prince of Wales. The Prince, who after his abdication from the throne was known as the Duke of Windsor, was always very much interested in clothing, and his adoption of a style was sure to give it importance throughout the menswear industry.

Hollywood leading men also influenced styles. The appearance of leading men on screen in unusual clothing was likely to start a new trend. Matinee idols known for their taste and style often ordered their clothing from British tailors.

Sack suits remained the basis of suits for almost every occasion. Vests, trousers, and jackets matched in color and fabric. Only wealthy and prominent individuals still wore morning coats, and then only for very formal occasions. Those who could afford variety in their wardrobes wore white suits for summer. F. Scott Fitzgerald's character, Jay Gatsby, was portrayed as wearing a white suit at his fabulous summer parties on Long Island, and the white linen or flannel suit became symbolic of an upper-class lifestyle.

GARMENTS

As underwear for more conservative men, one-piece knitted union suits were available with short or long sleeves or legs. Other underwear had no sleeves and ended at the knee or above. **Boxer shorts** were introduced in the 1930s. The shorts worn by professional boxers inspired this style. Other new styles of the 1930s included **athletic shirts** of knitted cotton that were adapted from the top of tank swimsuits, and fitted brief knit shorts, patented in 1935. The trademark name for these knitted briefs, **Jockey shorts®**, has since become an almost generic designation for this style of men's underwear. Made initially without a front opening, these shorts added a Y-shaped front opening in 1942. During World War II servicemen wore knit undershirts with short sleeves called

T-shirts. After the war civilian men continued to wear these undershirts and they eventually found their way into general sportswear, as well. See *Illustrated Table 16.1, page 401,* for examples of undergarments during the years between 1920 and 1947.

In the film *It Happened One Night* (1934) actor Clark Gable appeared bare chested and without an undershirt. *Esquire's Encyclopedia of Men's Fashion* credits this film with beginning a fashion for going without undershirts that severely affected the underwear industry. Other motion picture influences cited were the **Wallace Beery shirt,** a ribbed-knit undershirt with a buttoned vent at the front of the neck, worn by the character actor of that name (Schoeffler and Gale 1973). This shirt is more likely to be called a **henley shirt** today.

Business suits of the 1920s featured jackets with fairly natural shoulderlines, fairly wide lapels, and pronounced waists. Single- and double-breasted styles were worn and sleeves were short enough to show at least half an inch of shirt cuff. (See *Figure 16.15.*) During the 1920s, trouser legs widened. The impetus for wider trouser legs may have come from a fad that developed at Oxford College in England. Students at Oxford were forbidden by dress regulations from wearing knickers to classes. To be able to change quickly from the acceptable long trousers to knickers, the students took to wearing trousers with excessively wide legs that could be slipped on over the knickers. After classes, off came the **Oxford bags** (Schoeffler and Gale 1973). The style spread to other young people, and Oxford bags with legs as wide as 32 inches

tuxedo

business suits

polo coat

oxfords

formal vests

FIGURE 16.15

Men's wear fashions from 1920s. (*Men's Wear Review.*)

414

in diameter were soon seen in America, too. Although most men never wore Oxford bags, trousers grew generally wider and remained fuller in cut.

Shirts, manufactured in white and colors, had narrow collars. Some had button-down collars (a new form), other collars were designed to be pinned together under the tie with a tie pin, and some had a tab fastening points of the collar together under the tie. The Barrymore collar (named after actor John Barrymore) had long points. Four-in-hand neckties, bow ties, and ascots made up the repertory of neckwear.

Turtleneck jerseys, around for about 30 years as sportswear, gained popularity for a time as a substitute for shirts and ties when, in 1924, actor Noel Coward initiated the style.

In the 1930s, suits were made from such popular fabrics as lightweight worsted wools, gabardine, and linen. Rayon was the first manufactured fiber to gain widespread use. It was made into some suits, as well as other garments. After the Prince of Wales wore a plaid suit while on a visit to the United States, plaid suits became more popular, along with pinstripes and summer suits in light colors.

Jackets grew wider at the shoulders, more fitted at the hips. In the latter part of the decade a style known as the **English drape suit** was introduced and became the predominant cut for suits. This style, which was cut for comfort, fell softly with a slight drape or wrinkle through the chest and shoulders because it had more fabric in the shoulders and chest.

The width of trousers decreased in the 1930s. A major change occurred when manufacturers began to use zippers rather than the customary buttons for fly closings.

White was considered more traditional for shirts, but they were also made in colors and with stripes or checks. Collar styles included tab and button-down styles. **California collars,** seen on film actors such as Clark Gable, had shorter, wider points than the Barrymore collar of the twenties. Windsor or spread collars were worn with the larger Windsor tie knot. Some collars also had short, rounded shapes.

Wartime restrictions modified the English drape cut somewhat in the 1940s. To conserve wool fabric, which was in short supply, restrictions were imposed on the quantity of fabric that could be used in suits. The American War Production Board decreed maximum lengths for jackets and trouser inseams in each size, ruled out the making of suits with two pairs of trousers, eliminated waistcoats with double-breasted suits, cuffs, pleats in trousers, and overlapping waistbands. (See *Figure 16.16.*)

The **zoot suit** was thereby eliminated. This unusual fashion, one of the few that had originated at the lower end of the socioeconomic ladder, had been adopted by African American and other teenage boys in the early 1940s. It became a mark of status among some of the young, and was associated with the popularity of jitterbugging, an especially athletic type of dancing. The suit was an extreme form of the sack suit of this period. The jacket was long, with excessively wide

FIGURE 16.16

Drawing from June 1942 of a suit that conforms to the War Production Board regulations for men's suits. Specifications included shorter jackets with no patch pockets, belts, vents, pleats, tucks or yokes; no vests with double-breasted suits; and no pleats, tucks overlapping waistbands or cuffs on trousers. (Courtesy, Fairchild Publications.)

shoulders and long, wide lapels. The trousers were markedly pegged. (See *Figure 16.17.*)

Evening dress of the 1920 to 1940s underwent changes. Tail coats were reserved for the most formal occasions. For evening, jackets generally were of the tuxedo type, made in black or "midnight" blue. (See *Figure 16.15.*) Tuxedos had either rolled collars faced in silk or notched collars. Lines of jackets followed the lines of daytime business suits. In the

FIGURE 16.17

Zoot suit, 1942, has a loose jacket with wide shoulders, and high-waisted trousers that are narrow at the ankles. (Courtesy, BETTMANN)

1920s, single-breasted styles were preferred; in the 1930s, double-breasted. From the late 1920s on, some men substituted a **cummerbund,** a wide pleated fabric waistband, for the waistcoat. Waistcoats after the 1930s often had a sort of halter-type construction and no back. In the 1930s and after, white dinner jackets, especially for summer, were worn. (See *Figure 16.18.*) Wartime restrictions required that all dinner jackets be single breasted. Evening trousers followed the lines of daytime trousers but had no cuffs, and added a line of braid following the outer seam line.

White shirts with starched fronts that closed with two shirt studs were worn with tail coats throughout the period. With dinner jackets and tuxedos, soft-fronted shirts were acceptable after the late 1920s. Dark bow ties were worn with dinner jackets, white bow ties with tails. Except for more affluent men, most did not own evening clothes, but rented them for special events.

OUTDOOR GARMENTS

Generally outdoor garments followed the predominant jacket silhouette. Coat styles included chesterfields and raglan-sleeved coats, with either buttoned front closings or fly-front closing in which a fabric placket obscured the buttons.

In the 1920s, raccoon coats were popular among the young college crowd. Singer Rudy Vallee, a student at Yale in 1927, said "The raccoon coat was the true hallmark of the successful collegian." Men who could not afford these coats might "pool their resources and form syndicates" to buy one coat that they could share (Berendt 1988). Tweed and herringbone patterned fabrics were used for casual coats.

Polo coats made of tan camel's hair were worn by a British polo team playing exhibition matches in the United States and the style swept the United States and continued on into the 1930s. (See *Figure 16.15.*) The classic cut of this coat was double-breasted, with a six-buttoned closing, and a half belt at the back. Camel's hair coats included single-breasted box coats, belted raglan sleeved coats, and wraparound coats without buttons that tied with belts. Trench coats, slickers, and waterproof coats modeled after fishermen's foul weather gear were worn as rain coats.

In the 1930s many of the styles seen in the 1920s continued and some new styles were added, such as the **English guards' coat,** a dark blue coat with wide lapels and an inverted pleat in the back and a half belt. **Zip-in linings,** a new feature, made cold weather coats convertible to use in warmer temperatures.

Informal coat styles included short jackets with knitted waistbands and cuffs, **parka jackets** with hoods (copied from Eskimo cold weather wear), and **lumber jackets** or **mackinaws** (sturdy jackets made of heavily fulled wool). The affluent wore leather jackets.

In the 1940s, styles showed marked military influences and included **pea jackets,** which were the double-breasted dark box jackets of American sailors, and Eisenhower or **battle jackets,** which were short, waist length, bloused jackets the lower edge of which was attached to a belt of the same fabric. (See *Figure 16.19.*)

INFORMAL DAYTIME CLOTHING OR SPORTSWEAR: 1920–1947

During this period a whole new category of clothing for men, as well as women, developed. It is generally classified as sportswear, but would perhaps be more accurately termed "leisure" or "casual" clothing. It was worn not only for active sports but also during a man's leisure time.

Jackets without matching trousers, cut along the lines of business suit jackets and worn with contrasting fabric trousers were known as **sport** or **casual jackets.** (See *Figure*

FIGURE 16.18

Men's styles of the 1930s. (a) Sport jacket with contrasting trousers, 1935. (b) Double-breasted white dinner jacket, 1934. (c) Knitted polo shirt and sailor trousers, 1931. (d) Knitted bathing shorts, 1931. All from issues of *Men's Wear.* Reproduced courtesy, Fairchild Publications.)

16.18.) Sport jackets were made in more colors and fabrics than regular suit jackets and were worn with vests in matching or contrasting colors, pullover sweaters, or shirts. Some were cut with half belts or were belted all the way around. Golfers adopted Norfolk jackets with a pleat in the back. The Prince of Wales made tweed jackets popular. **Bush jackets,** short-sleeved tan cotton jackets with four large flapped pockets made to imitate styles worn by hunters and explorers in Africa, were popular for casual wear in the 1930s.

During the 1920s sport jackets were often combined with knickers or **plus fours** (a fuller version of knickers) and ar-

gyle socks. In the 1930s, trousers or shorts replaced knickers to some extent. **Walking shorts,** based on military costume of British Colonial soldiers, had been adopted by the well-to-do for vacation wear. They were worn with knee-length stockings and often had matching shirts. Trousers for sportswear were made in a variety of colors and patterns including plaid, checked, and striped designs.

Shirts for leisure, as opposed to those for wearing with suits, were a new development in men's wear. Styles included **polo shirts,** which were knitted shirts with attached collars and short, buttoned, neck vents. They usually had short

FIGURE 16.19

A two-year-old boy wears an "Eisenhower" jacket, a popular style modeled after the type of military jacket General Dwight Eisenhower liked to wear. (Photograph courtesy, UPI/Corbiss-Bettmann.)

Sweaters were popular for golfing and other sports. Multi-colored sweater patterns were worn in imitation of a sweater worn by the Prince of Wales in the 1920s. Turtleneck sweaters were popular in the 1920s and the 1930s.

CLOTHING FOR ACTIVE SPORTS: 1920–1947

For tennis, knitted white shirts worn with white flannel trousers were popular until the 1930s when some men substituted white shorts for the trousers. White was mandatory as a color on tennis courts. Many clubs forbade play to those wearing colors.

The **Lacoste® knit tennis shirt,** made along the lines of a polo shirt, was introduced in the 1920s. Rene Lacoste, a well-known player who had been nicknamed "the crocodile," designed a short-sleeved cotton knit shirt with a longer tail in back so it would not pull out when he was playing tennis. He marketed this shirt, using a crocodile as the logo. The shirt became very popular and was worn not only for tennis, but also as general sportswear.

Clothes for golf consisted mainly of shirts, sweaters, or jackets combined with knickers in the 1920s and slacks or shorts in the 1930s and after. (See *Figure 16.20.*)

In the 1920s, one-piece swim suits were held on over the shoulders with shoulder straps. As an alternative, sleeveless knit pullover shirts with or without sleeves were worn with short trunks. The pullover was worn either out, over the trunks or tucked into trunks that were belted at the waist. Upper sections of bathing suits often had deep armholes and straps across the armhole to maintain a snug fit. In the 1930s, tops decreased in size until eventually men stopped wearing any covering for the upper part of the body, and by the 1940s only bathing trunks were worn. (See *Figure 16.18.*)

Skiing was taken up by large numbers of people only after World War I. In the 1920s, skiers wore wool sweaters and plus fours. In the 1930s, wind-resistant jackets were adopted and worn with long trousers cut full and gathered into an elasticized cuff at the ankle. (See *Figure 16.21.*)

SLEEPWEAR

Pajamas had largely replaced nightshirts. The cut varied: in the 1920s, the jacket was long, below the hip, often belted. Russian influence was evident in the late 1920s and 1930s in styles that had standing collars, and closed far to the left. Some pajamas buttoned down the front; others slipped over the head. Robes ranged from kimono-style silk to ornately patterned flannels that buttoned down the front and tied shut with a corded belt.

HAIR AND HEADDRESS

Throughout the period hair was short. In the 1920s, many men controlled their hair with glistening hair dressings and pomades in imitation of the film star Rudolph Valentino, whose hair looked as if it were plastered to his head. Faces

sleeves. This style originated as costume for polo-players, but was adopted generally for informal wear in the 1920s and after. (See *Figure 16.18.*)

In the 1930s and after, men wore **dishrag shirts** of net fabric that were first seen on the Riviera; **basque shirts,** striped, wide crew-necked shirts; and dark blue linen sport shirts patterned after one worn by the Prince of Wales. In the late 1930s, men bought **cowboy shirts** in bright colors and fabrics with button-down pockets on the chest and pointed collars, and **Western shirts** in solid or plaid wool or gabardine with crescent-shaped pockets in front. About 1938, **Hawaiian shirts** printed in vivid colors entered mainstream fashion. (See *Color Plate 52.*)

High shoes went out of style in the 1920s and oxfords became the predominant style. White and two-toned shoes were worn in the summer. Moccasin-type shoes were introduced in the 1930s, adapted from shoes worn by Norwegian fishermen and nicknamed **weejuns.** Other 1930s styles included sandals, cloth shoes for summer, crepe-soled shoes, and higher shoes that ended at the ankle, closing either with laces (**chukka boots**) or a strap and buckle across the ankle (**monk's front**).

FIGURE 16.20

Golfing outfit; jacket from 1930, knickers from 1928. (Photograph courtesy, Division of Costume, The American Museum of National History.)

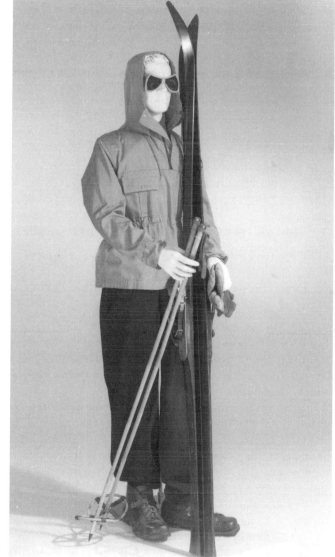

FIGURE 16.21

Ski outfit, the pants from 1940 and the jacket from 1937. The skis, goggles, gloves, boots, and ski poles all date from the same period. (Photograph courtesy, Division of Costume, The American Museum of National History.)

were generally clean shaven. Some men wore pencil-thin mustaches. In the 1930s, hair was worn waved and parted on the side. Mustaches were more likely to be worn by older than by younger men. Mustaches went out of fashion in the 1940s. Some authors attribute the decrease in popularity of mustaches in the 1940s to the fact that the German dictator Adolf Hitler wore a mustache.

Hat styles altered very little. Major forms continued to be fedoras (becoming more popular), derbies (becoming less popular), homburgs, straw boaters and panama hats, and sports caps. During the 1930s, the pork pie—a low-crowned, soft felt hat that could be rolled up—was used for sportswear.

FOOTWEAR

Stockings became more colorful as a result of the availability of machinery for making fancy patterned hosiery. In the 1930s, argyle, chevron, and diamond-patterned socks were popular. Elastic-topped socks were introduced and did away with the need for garters.

Wartime rationing made leather shoes and tennis shoes with rubber soles scarce. Composition soles were used to conserve leather.

Galoshes or overshoes and rubbers changed little over this period. Galoshes closed at the front with snaps or zippers. Synthetic rubber material was used during the war.

ACCESSORIES

Men used relatively few accessories, mainly gloves, handkerchiefs, scarves, umbrellas, and canes. Sunglasses were first manufactured at the request of Army Air Corps flyer Lieutenant John Macready, who wanted lenses for goggles that would absorb the sun. The manufacturer, Bausch and Lomb, went on to market them to the general public.

JEWELRY

As before, jewelry was largely functional: watches, tie pins, shirt studs, cuff links, and rings.

COSTUME FOR CHILDREN: 1920–1947

See *Illustrated Table 16.5*, for some examples of children's clothing from the period 1920–1947.

Costume for Girls

GARMENTS

Toddlers wore loose, smocklike dresses that often had a yoke at the neck. Many had matching bloomers that could be seen beneath the short skirts. Smocking and embroidery were favored decorations.

In the 1920s young girls' dresses, like those of adults, were unfitted. In the 1930s waistlines of dresses returned to anatomical placement. Older girls' dresses often had fitted bodices with skirts attached and a sash tied in the back. Skirt fullness varied according to whether adult skirt styles were wider or narrower. Puffed sleeves were commonly seen.

For school, skirts and blouses were common in the 1930s and 1940s. Some skirts had straps or suspenders. Once pants had been accepted for women, young girls wore pullover and cardigan sweaters and slacks for sportswear. The popularity of Shirley Temple, a child actress, influenced clothing styles for little girls in the 1930s.

OUTDOOR GARMENTS

In the 1920s, girls wore straight, narrow coats. Princess line coats, often with fur trimmed collars were popular in the 1930s, and in 1944 the Sears, Roebuck catalog shows a cross section of coats for young girls including princess line, single-breasted chesterfields with velvet collars, **boy coats** that were cut straight with patch pockets, and wrap coats that had tie belts. Leggings were available to match dress coats for cold weather.

Costume for Boys

GARMENTS

The custom of dressing small boys in skirts had ended. They wore romper suits or short pants instead. The custom of dressing small boys in blue and small girls in pink seems to have begun around the 1920s in the United States. Prior to this time, shades of red had been considered "masculine" colors, and were more likely to be worn by boys than girls. Indeed, this gender-related color assignment was not firmly established until around 1940 (Kidwell and Steele 1980). Although boys' styles showed some minor differences from decade to decade, a boy could expect to spend the first few years of his life in short pants, then graduate to knickers, and finally into long trousers.

For dress occasions in the 1920s, boys wore long belted jackets or Norfolk jackets. By the 30s and 40s, jackets were less likely to be belted, shorter, and cut like those of adult men. Some had matching vests.

In the 1930s, polo shirts were common for everyday dress. Cotton knit pullovers with napped under surfaces appeared in the early 1930s and by the 1940s this garment was being called a **sweatshirt.** Throughout the period boys wore sweaters of all types: cardigans, pullovers, and sleeveless pullovers. Turtleneck sweaters went out of fashion after the 1920s.

OUTDOOR GARMENTS

Dress coats followed the lines of men's dress coats in each decade. For everyday wear in the 1920s, mackinaws remained popular and a lumberjack jacket with knitted waistband ending just below the waist was worn. In the 1930s, fingertip length, boxy jackets were added, and in the late 1930s and early 1940s, poplin jackets and waterproof parkas. During the war years boys wore Eisenhower jackets.

Costume for Boys and Girls

GARMENTS

As athletic shorts and sleeveless undershirts became available for men and brief panties for women, they also were made for children.

Beginning in the 1930s and in subsequent decades, children wore jeans as play and everyday clothing. The rivets on the back pockets made holes in wooden school seats. Teachers complained, so this feature of jeans was discontinued (Ratner 1975). Overalls made of blue denim and pants of the

Illustrated Table 16.5

CHILDREN'S CLOTHING STYLES: 1920–1947

Girl's dress, 1926

Boys' clothing, 1926

Girls' clothing, 1933

Girls' dresses, 1938

same fabric appeared in the boys' section of the Sears, Roebuck catalog of 1923 with this caption "for work or play" and henceforth were a consistent feature of work or playclothes for boys, especially in rural areas. In the 1940s they also appeared as playclothes for girls.

Preschool boys and girls continued to wear sailor suits and dresses, respectively. Other items also appeared. In the 1920s, "Tom Mix" (a popular cowboy movie star) outfits were advertised. The same page of the Sears catalog advertised Indian suits, policeman suits, and other cowboy outfits. In the 1930s, cowboy and Indian suits remained popular and baseball players' suits and flyers' uniforms were added. The availability of space suits reflected the popularity of cartoons and films such as those about Buck Rogers. (See *Figure 16.22.*) Girls could wear nurses' uniforms and, sometimes, cowgirl or Indian dresses. In the 1940s, during the War, boys could choose from officers' suits from the army, navy, or marines, admirals' suits, aviators' suits, or sailors' suits, and girls from WAAC or WAVE uniforms with skirts, of course.

OUTDOOR GARMENTS

There was little difference between snow suits for preschool boys and girls other than color, pink being reserved for girls. For small children, there were one-piece snow suits; for older children, two-piece jacket and leggings. In the 1930s water-repellent fabrics were used. In the 1940s, hooded jackets were popular.

In the 1920s and 1930s rubberized cloth or oiled slicker material was used for rainwear. By the late 1930s, water-repellent fabric replaced oiled slicker fabric. For true waterproofing, rubberized fabrics were required. During the War when rubber was scarce, rainwear was made of synthetic rubber.

CLOTHING FOR ACTIVE SPORTS

Bathing suits followed adult styles.

SLEEPWEAR

From the 1920s on, much sleepwear for young children was in the form of pajamas with feet in them, sometimes called **sleepers.** Older boys wore pajamas almost exclusively, whereas girls wore either pajamas or nightgowns.

FIGURE 16.22

Page from Sears catalog, 1935. Interests of small boys of this period are reflected in the cowboy, Indian, aviator, and Buck Rogers space suits that could be purchased. (Illustration reproduced courtesy, Sears, Roebuck and Company.)

Costume for the Teenage Market

This market began to grow in the United States in the 1940s as a specialized segment of the fashion industry. Adolescent and college-age girls made skirts and sweaters into veritable uniforms. To skirts and sweaters they added white ankle socks, and either loafers or saddle shoes. The favorite hairstyle was a long, page-boy cut.

In the mid-1940s adolescent girls wore large, loose sweaters known as sloppy joes or put on cardigan sweaters backward.

SUMMARY

THEMES

A theme evident in any consideration of styles between the first and second World Wars is that of CHANGES IN SOCIAL BEHAVIOR, especially for women. Clothing styles for men continued the trends begun before the 1914 War. Wardrobes for men who were "white collar" office workers and for "blue collar" laborers offered relatively little choice. The former was confined to a suit with vest, white shirt, and necktie for business and the latter to sturdy, washable workclothes. In clothing for leisure, however, men were able to exercise a wider degree of selection from a broader range of styles.

Women's clothing in the 1920s incorporated elements that had rarely appeared in earlier historical periods and that provided visible evidence of CHANGES IN THE ROLES OF WOMEN. The radically shorter skirts, cropped hair, acceptability of cosmetic use, and adoption by women of traditionally masculine garments such as trousers showed that women had rejected patterns in feminine dress that had been established for hundreds of years, just as they were rejecting patterns of behavior for women that had confined them to more limited roles in society.

The importance of THE RELATIONSHIP BETWEEN COSTUME AND THE WORK OF INDIVIDUAL DESIGNERS continued to grow, as designers such as Chanel, Vionnet, and Schiaparelli had a great impact on styles that were copied by the American fashion industry at all levels. THE RELATIONSHIPS BETWEEN COSTUME AND DEVELOPMENTS IN THE FINE AND APPLIED ARTS can be seen in *art deco* design motifs on textiles of the 20s and in Schiaparelli's incorporation of surrealistic elements in her designs.

ECONOMIC EVENTS can be identified as another important theme, which was evident in the extremes of prosperity in the 20s and depression in the 30s. Clothing styles of the two decades contrast almost as sharply as economic trends, with the lavish, beaded gowns of the 20s giving way to the simpler, more subdued lines of the 30s.

TECHNOLOGY made new fibers available. Rayon was used throughout these periods, and nylon was introduced just before World War II. As always, the POLITICAL CONFLICT of World War II affected apparel, removing nylon from the consumer market, cutting off supplies of silk from the Far East, and leading to restrictions on the cut of clothing. The war also served to bring American fashion designers to the forefront of fashion design, as Paris was occupied by the Germans.

SURVIVALS OF STYLES OF THE 1920s AND 1930s

Fashion designers of the post–World War II period often turned to the past for design inspiration. In those periods when unfitted styles have been popular, the 1920s have often served as the source. The 1960s was such a period. (See *Figure 19.17, page 529.*) Other 20s revivals could be seen in the 80s and 90s. Art Deco design motifs came to prominence again in the 1970s after several art exhibitions focused attention on these styles of the 20s and 30s.

When Chanel reopened her couture house in the 1950s, she also revived her signature cardigan suit. (See *Figure 18.5.*) Although this suit has been "reworked" by subsequent designers at the house of Chanel, it has maintained its popularity. (See *Figure 19.16, page 528.*)

Both the platform soled shoes and the big shoulder pads of the 1930s have been seen again. Platform soles grew to extreme heights in the 70s, then returned again in the 1990s. Big shoulder pads reentered the fashion scene in the early 1980s and some form of these pads have continued in use into the mid-90s.

In their constant mining of the past, fashion designers have not overlooked the 1930s. Often these revivals followed the release of films set in the 30s. The first was in 1967 with 30s style sweaters and berets from the film *Bonnie and Clyde*. Some designs of the 80s and the 90s clearly came from bias cut styles of the 30s, as did some printed textile designs.

423

Visual Summary Table

1920–1947

Man: Business Suit, 1927/1928
Chief elements continue to be shirt,
vest, jacket, and trousers. Trousers
slightly wider in the 1920s than in
previous decade.

Man: English Drape Suit, 1938
English drape style jackets have
wider shoulders. Men wore sports
jackets for casual dress.

Woman: Dress, 1926
Typical style: flat bosom, unfitted
waist, and belt placed at the hip.
Skirts shortest c. 1926–27, longer
again by 1930. Pants seen for sports
and outdoors.

Woman: Dress, 1933
Garments now follow body curves.
Waist is again at anatomical
position. Bias cut often used.
Skirts, long at the beginning of the
decade, gradually shorten.

Woman: Dress and Jacket, 1941
The lines of dresses just before
the war are "frozen" by the war
at shorter lengths, somewhat
fuller skirts, and broad, padded
shoulders.

NOTES

Allen, F. L. 1931. *Only Yesterday*. New York: Harper and Row, pp. 87, 88.

Berendt, J. 1988. "The Raccoon Coat." *Esquire*, Vol. 109, No. l, January, p. 22.

Berendt, J. 1989. "The Zipper." *Esquire*, Vol. 111, No. 5, May, p. 42.

Friedel, R. 1994. *Zipper*. New York: W. W. Norton.

Horn, M. 1975. *The Second Skin*. New York: Houghton-Mifflin, p. 107.

Horyn, C. 2002. "Silver Screen or Mezzanine: His Designs Were for All." *New York Times*, April 30, p. B8.

Kidwell, C. K. and V. Steele. 1980. *Men and Women: Dressing the Part*. Washington, DC: Smithsonian Institution Press, p. 27.

Kirkland, S. 1975. *American Fashion*. New York: Quadrangle/New York Times Book Co., p. 211.

Latour, A. 1956. *Kings of Fashion*. London: Weidenfeld and Nicolson, p. 58.

Martin, R. 1987. *Surrealism and Fashion*. New York: Rizzoli. See this work for a complete discussion of surrealism and fashion.

Ratner, E. 1975. "Levi's." *Dress*, Vol. l, p. 3.

Richards, L. 1983–84. "The Rise and Fall of It All: The Hemlines and Hiplines of the 1920's." *Clothing and Textiles Research Journal*, Vol. 2, No. l, Fall/Winter, p. 48.

Schoeffler, O. E. and W. Gale. 1973. *Esquire's Encyclopedia of 20th Century Men's Fashion*. NY: McGraw-Hill, pp. 374–375.

SELECTED READINGS

Books and Other Materials Containing Illustrations of Costume of the Period from Original Sources

Fashion Magazines such as *Esquire, Harper's Bazaar,* and *Vogue.*

General women's magazines such as *The Delineator, Ladies' Home Journal, McCalls', Woman's Home Companion,* etc.

Catalogs: Pattern and mail-order.

Brunhammer, Y. 1969. *The Nineteen Twenties Style*. New York: Paul Hamlyn.

Howell, G. 1976. *In Vogue*. New York: Schocken Books.

Lynam, R. 1972. *Couture*. Garden City, NY: Doubleday.

Olian, J. 1990. *Authentic French Fashions of the Twenties*. New York: Dover.

Robinson, J. 1976. *Fashion in the Forties*. New York: St. Martin's Press.

———. 1976. *The Golden Age of Style*. New York: Harcourt Brace Jovanovich.

Schoeffler, O. E. and W. Gale. 1973. *Esquire's Encyclopedia of 20th Century Men's Fashion*. New York: McGraw-Hill.

The 10's, 20's, and 30's. Inventive Clothes 1909–1939. [N. D.] New York: Metropolitan Museum of Art.

Periodical Articles

Berendt, J. 1988. "The Raccoon Coat." *Esquire*, Vol. 109, No. l, p. 22.

———. 1989. "The Zipper." *Esquire*, Vol. 111, No. 5, May, p. 42.

Bryant, N. O. 1986. "Insights into the Innovative Cut of Madeleine Vionnet." *Dress*, Vol. 12, p. 73.

Cohen, R. H. 1979. "Tut and the 20's: The Egyptian Look'" *Art in America*, Vol. 67, No.2, p. 97.

Cunningham, P. 1986. "Swimwear in the Thirties: The B.V.D. Company in a Decade of Innovation." *Dress*, Vol. 12, p. 11.

de la Haye, A. 1993. "The Dissemination of Design from Haute Couture to Fashionable Ready-to-Wear during the 1920s." *Textile History*, Vol. 24, No. 1, p. 39.

Hall, L. 1972. "Fashion and Style in the Twenties: The Change." *Historian*, Vol. 34, No. 3, p. 485.

Paoletti, J., C. Beeker, and D. Pelletier. 1987. "Men's Jacket Styles 1919–1941: An Example of Coordinated Content Analysis and Object Study." *Dress*, Vol. 13, p. 44.

Richards, L. 1983-1984. "The Rise and Fall of it All: Hemlines and Hiplines of the 1920's." *Clothing and Textiles Research Journal*, Vol. 2, No. 1, p. 42.

Taylor, L. 1995. "The Work and Function of the Paris Couture Industry During the German Occupation of 1940–44." *Dress*. Vol. 22, p. 34.

Daily Life

Allen, F. L. 1931. *Only Yesterday*. New York: Harper and Row.

———. 1940. *Since Yesterday*. New York: Harper.

Andrest, R. K., ed. 1970. *The American Heritage History of the 20's and 30's*. New York: American Heritage.

Costello, J. 1987. *Virtue Under Fire: How World War II Changed Social and Sexual Attitudes*. New York: Fromm International.

Green, H. 1992. *The Uncertainty of Everyday Life: 1915–1945*. New York: HarperCollins.

Frank, M., et al. 1982. *The Life and Times of Rosie the Riveter*. Emeryville, CA: Clarity Educational Productions.

Hard Times, 1930–1940. This Fabulous Century. 1991. New York: Time-Life.

Jenkins, A. 1976. *The Thirties*. New York: Stein and Day.

The Roaring 20s, 1920–1930. This Fabulous Century. 1991. New York: Time-Life.

Terkel, S. 1970. *Hard Times*. New York: Avon.

Werstein, I. 1970. *Shattered Decade: 1919–1929*. New York: Scribners.

Women of Valor: The Struggle Against the Great Depression as Told in Their Own Life Stories. 1990. Chicago: I. R. Dee.

CHRONOLOGY

1947
Dior shows New Look collection
Nylon fiber becomes available again

1948
The United States and Britain airlift supplies to Berlin when Russians cut off access
Television becoming more widely available for use in the home

1949
NATO founded
Communist Peoples Republic of China established
Russia explodes its first atomic bomb
Alaska becomes the 49th state

1950
Korean War begins
Acrylic fibers synthesized

1952
Queen Elizabeth II ascends the British throne on the death of George VI
Dwight Eisenhower elected president

1953
The Korean War ends
Josef Stalin dies
Polyester fibers become available commercially

1954
School segregation declared unconstitutional by the United States Supreme Court
Chanel reenters the couture
American department stores sell copies of Paris styles

1955
Civil rights movement begins with bus boycott in Montgomery, Alabama

1957
European Common Market established
Jack Kerouac publishes *On the Road*, a novel considered to be the
"testament" of the "beat" generation
Russians launch *Sputnik*, the first space satellite

1958
Charles de Gaulle becomes president of France

1959
Castro comes to power in Cuba
Hawaii becomes the 50th state

CHAPTER SEVENTEEN

THE NEW LOOK

Fashion Conformity Prevails

1947 – 1960

A.

Guggenheim Museum by Frank Lloyd Wright, 1955

B.

Lounge chair by Charles and Ray Eames, c. 1946

C.

Chair, Bertoia, 1950

D.

Painting by Jackson Pollock,
One, (Number 31, 1950)

E.

Table and chair by Saarinen, 1956

F.

Sculpture by David Smith,
XI Books III Apples, 1959

Figures A, F courtesy of V. R. Tortora. Figures B, C, E courtesy of J. Curcio in Federico, J. T. 1988. *Clues to American Furniture*. Washington: Starrhill, p. 58. Figure D courtesy of the Museum of Modern Art, New York, Sidney and Harriet Janis Collection Fund (by exchange).

In the post–World War II period Parisian fashion turned in dramatic new directions. The fashion press labeled these changes **the New Look,** and these distinctive styles dominated fashion design until the mid-1950s when some members of the *haute couture* began the first movement away from the New Look toward another silhouette. The discussion of fashion in this chapter is divided between consideration of the New Look (1947 to about 1954) and the gradual emergence of a softer, easier style (1954–1960). In the period after World War II definitive style changes enter onto the fashion stage at various points in each decade; therefore some of the major trends in fashion may persist from one decade to another.

HISTORICAL BACKGROUND

With the rapid development of air travel in the post–World War II era, the almost instant transmission of news from one part of the world to another, and the transition from national to globally interdependent economies, the world became a much smaller place. It was no longer possible to understand the historical background of a period by examining developments only in Western Europe and North America.

International Developments: 1947–1960

EASTERN AND WESTERN EUROPE

The end of World War II found Europe devastated, with millions of people homeless, shortages of food, transportation wrecked, and cities in shambles. The political vacuum left in Central Europe following the defeat of Nazi Germany and its allies had been filled by the victorious Allied armies who, in effect, partitioned Europe into pro-Western and pro-Soviet spheres of influence. In Western Europe parliamentary governments and capitalist economies revived. In Eastern Europe, the states under Soviet occupation were compelled to follow the Soviet political and economic model, and to support Moscow's foreign policies. Divided Europe now became the center of the power struggle known as the Cold War.

European countries were vulnerable to Soviet domination because of their need to repair their war-damaged economies. To aid in repairing their economies the United States government instituted the Marshall Plan in 1948. Although the Soviet Union and its satellite states rejected the Marshall Plan, this aid restored the economic well-being of Western Europe. By 1952, as a result of Marshall Plan aid, industrial production in Western Europe had surpassed prewar levels.

By 1949 the western zone of a divided Germany had a new democratic constitution. Soon West Germany with a new economic policy began a period of sustained economic growth that made it an industrial power by the end of the 1950s.

In 1949 the United States and Canada joined the western European nations to form the North Atlantic Treaty Organization (NATO). In this agreement the members pledged to assist each other should there be an attack. In addition, in 1951 France and Germany joined the European Coal and Steel Community whereby German and French coal and steel production would be combined and supervised by an international authority. This agreement led to the creation in 1957 of the European Economic Community in which six European states, including France and Germany, pledged to gradually eliminate all restrictions on trade movements, capital, and labor.

In the postwar years, Europe underwent major social changes, including a spurt in population growth. Europe also experienced an exodus of people from the rural areas to the cities. As a result, the new society of Europe came to be dominated by the cities, and the new urban culture came to resemble that of the United States—white collar, middle class, and oriented toward a consumption economy. There was almost a class revolution in transportation. Before World War II only wealthy Europeans could afford automobiles. Most people traveled by streetcar or bicycle. In the 1950s, however, the number of automobiles more than doubled, and there was an increase in motor scooters. Highway systems were limited, and as a result the narrow, medieval streets were soon clogged with traffic.

THE MIDDLE EAST AND ASIA

In the Middle East and in Asia, World War II ended European imperialism. After the collapse of the Ottoman Empire at the end of World War I, Britain and France had dominated the successor states. But World War II undermined the Anglo-French influence in the Middle East. Radical changes came as a new generation, often led by young, radical army officers, seized power. Palestine, however, was divided between Arabs and Jewish refugees from European persecution. When the Arabs rejected a United Nations partition plan in 1948, the Arab states attacked the Jews and war followed. A truce came in 1949. The Jews, who had held off their attackers, at last established the state of Israel that had been approved in 1947 by the United Nations.

In Asia during World War II the fact that the Japanese had defeated the Western nations at the beginning of the war was not lost on the Asian people, and this undermined imperialism. Britain led the way by granting independence to India in 1947. Ultimately three separate states were created: India, Pakistan, and Bangladesh. The Netherlands gave Indonesia freedom in 1949. Only France attempted unsuccessfully to retain power in Indochina. China came under communist rule in 1949 after the government of Chiang Kai-shek had been forced to flee to the island of Taiwan.

THE SOVIET UNION

In 1953, the death of Soviet dictator Josef Stalin brought changes to the Soviet Union. Nikita S. Khrushchev, secretary general of the Communist Party, at last lifted a curtain on the crimes of Stalin in a speech in February 1956 to the Twentieth Communist Party Congress. Communists in Western Europe outside the Soviet bloc hoped that Khrushchev's speech meant a lessening of Soviet control over satellites. But in 1956 the new Soviet leadership would not allow Hungary to embark on a policy of neutrality in the Cold War or to hold free elections. Soviet troops put down the Hungarian rebellion and installed a puppet who would follow Moscow's desires. The Soviet Union still controlled its new empire.

The United States: 1947–1960

THE COLD WAR HEATS UP

Harry Truman had become president following the death of Franklin D. Roosevelt in 1945. One of Truman's first decisions was to order that the atomic bomb be dropped on Japan. In the immediate postwar era any hope that some type of international control could be established to deal with atomic power proved futile. Truman, however, along with many of the American people imagined that the United States had a monopoly on the "secret" of the atomic bomb. In 1949 Americans were shocked to learn that the Soviet Union had exploded an atomic device in Siberia. In 1950, frightened by the Soviet progress in producing atomic weapons, Truman ordered the development of a thermonuclear weapon—the hydrogen bomb. The first American H-bomb was exploded in 1952. Soviet authorities exploded their first hydrogen bomb in 1955. The arms race was under way.

The Cold War appeared to be heating up in June 1950 when Communist North Korean troops crossed the 38th parallel, the dividing line between North and South Korea. President Truman ordered American forces under the command of General Douglas MacArthur to defend South Korea. The conflict worsened when Chinese troops entered the war in support of their North Korean allies. Eventually the fighting came to a stalemate, and after protracted negotiations a truce was signed in 1953.

MCCARTHYISM

As the Cold War intensified many Americans wondered why after a victory in 1945 the United States now seemed to be a nation in peril. Some Americans blamed a communist conspiracy for the nation's troubles. The Truman administration had to set up a loyalty program to determine if foreign agents—communists—were undermining the nation's strength. No communist plot was uncovered. The crisis was ready for an unscrupulous politician such as Senator Joseph McCarthy from Wisconsin who, exploiting fears of a communist plot, issued charges that numbers of communist

agents were in the Department of State. A clever demagogue, McCarthy never attempted to prove his charges.

The election of 1952 was a victory for the commander of the Allied forces in Europe during World War II, Dwight Eisenhower. In the early years of Eisenhower's presidency McCarthy was riding high as his pursuit of alleged communists turned into a witch-hunt. He was too powerful even for the President of the United States. McCarthy went unchallenged until 1954 when he took aim at the army in a search for communist spies at Fort Monmouth, New Jersey. In a series of televised Army–McCarthy hearings—a new spectacle for the American viewing public—McCarthy's arrogance and lies, revealed on television, undermined his power. In December 1954 the Senate summoned up enough courage to censure McCarthy. He was no longer a force in American politics.

THE SILENT GENERATION

Veterans of World War II and the Korean War were entitled to educational subsidies, and many of them took advantage of these benefits by returning to college. The college students of the immediate postwar period and the generation of college students who followed after the veterans have been described as:

> . . . studious, earnest, rather humorless, bent on getting an education not for its own sake but because it clearly would, under the emerging national system, lead surely and inevitably to a good job and the solution to the youth problem of not so long before—economic security (Brooks 1966).

The postwar generation of young people have since been labeled the **silent generation.**

THE BEGINNINGS OF SOCIAL PROTEST

In the decade of the 1960s, the Silent Generation would give way to more vocal youth. The advance guard of the newly awakened young in the United States were the **Beatniks,** who appeared in the latter part of the 1950s. Beginning as a literary movement that included writer Jack Kerouac and poets Allen Ginsberg and Gregory Corso, the "Beats" adopted eccentric habits of dress and grooming—"beards, pony tails, dirty sneakers, peasant blouses" (Brooks 1966). They experimented with drugs, turned to Eastern mysticism, especially Zen Buddhism, and rejected the "square" world. Contacts with French existentialists led to the adoption of black clothes, especially turtlenecks and berets for men and leotards, tights, and ballet slippers for women. (See *Figure 17.1*.) Although the Beatnik phenomenon faded, it may be seen as a precursor of some of the youthful protest movements of the 1960s.

CIVIL RIGHTS BECOMES AN ISSUE

During the Eisenhower administration, the issue of civil rights came to dominate much of American life. During the Truman years, Congress had rejected civil rights legislation proposed by the president. The breakthrough came in the

FIGURE 17.1

French existentialist-influenced dress for male beatniks included dark clothes, turtleneck tops, berets, sandals, small pointed beards and moustaches.

---

unanimous Supreme Court decision in the case of *Brown v. the Board of Education of Topeka.* On May 17, 1954, the court overturned the doctrine of "separate but equal" in public education and held that "separate educational facilities are inherently unequal." A year later the Supreme Court directed that school authorities draft plans for desegregation of public schools and ordered action "with all deliberate speed."

The states of the Deep South took steps to avoid compliance with the orders of the Supreme Court. Resistance to the court's decision erupted in 1957 when a mob in Little Rock, Arkansas, threatened African-American students who were attempting to enter Central High School. A reluctant President Eisenhower ordered federal troops to restore order and to protect the African-American students.

Congress took some action by passing the first Civil Rights Act in 82 years that was designed to help African-

Americans to vote. In a series of decisions over the next few years, the Supreme Court struck down segregation in interstate commerce, buildings, interstate bus terminals, and airports. African-Americans themselves undertook personal campaigns aimed at ending segregation. In Atlanta, Georgia, a year-long bus boycott led by Dr. Martin Luther King helped end segregation on buses. In Greensboro, North Carolina, in 1960 four young African-American men remained seated at a lunch counter when a waitress refused to serve them. Thus began the first of a number of "sit-in" demonstrations against segregation. By 1960, however, only limited progress had been made in ending segregation in the United States.

INFLUENCES ON FASHION

The Silent Generation Moves to the Suburbs

The changing patterns of life in the United States and western Europe had a major impact on what people wore. Many American women had returned to full-time homemaking after working for pay during World War II. By producing a bumper crop of babies, families created a **baby boom.** The family orientation was emphasized as women's magazines stressed "togetherness." As the American highway systems expanded during the Eisenhower administration, many urban families moved to the rapidly growing suburbs. Family travel increased and camping became a popular form of recreation. Domestic help was scarce. All these changes helped to create an emphasis on more informal or casual styles. Department stores expanded sportswear departments for men, women, and teens. The proportion of leisure-time clothing in the suburban American's wardrobe increased, a tendency which accelerated as the period progressed.

The newly created suburbs had produced a changed lifestyle for large numbers of Americans. Part of that lifestyle was the suburban shopping mall. Shopping malls supplemented, and later replaced, downtown department stores; shopping had become almost another form of recreation. American adolescents found the shopping mall an especially appealing place to congregate.

Fashion Influences from the Young

Changes in the socioeconomic status of adolescents had begun during World War II. Before the War many young people became wage earners and members of the work force soon after they entered their teens. But the postwar socioeconomic changes kept many young people dependent on their families for a longer period of time—through high school and even beyond—and this accentuated the period of adolescence as a separate stage of development. The teen market in records and clothes grew rapidly and teen-age fashions and fads played an important role in the garment industry.

But it was in Britain in the late 1940s and 1950s that the **Teddy boys** created the first truly independent fashions for young people. Teddy boys were working class British adolescents who adopted styles in menswear that had a somewhat Edwardian[1] flavor: longer jackets with more shaping, high turned back lapels, cuffed sleeves, waistcoats, and well cut, narrow trouser. Teddy boys adopted an exaggerated version of these styles, somewhat akin to the prewar zoot suit, an earlier example of a style popular with less affluent youth. (See *pages 414–415*.) They wore elongated, loose jackets with wide, padded shoulders and, often, a velvet collar. Trousers were very narrow and tight, and short enough to allow garishly colored socks to show. They added narrow neckties. In the 1950s, flat, broad shoes were replaced by **winkle pickers,** shoes with exaggeratedly pointed toes. Their hair was somewhat longer, with sideburns and a duck-tailed shape cut at the back known as a **DA** (short for "duck's ass") (Ewing 1977). (See *Figure 17.2.*)

The female companions of Teddy boys wore long gray jackets over tight, high-necked black sweaters and black skirts. They combined dark stockings with a feminized version of the winkle pickers that had very high heels and pointed toes.

Ewing (1977) sees the Teddy boy phenomenon as having a threefold significance:

1. It was the first outfit to be promoted by the young, for the young.

2. It was the first fashion to begin among the lower classes.

3. It was the first fashion to be the outward evidence of a lifestyle cult.

Unlike the zoot suit, some elements of Teddy boy styles, such as the narrow-toed shoes and hairstyles, did penetrate mainstream fashion. Teddy boy styles were only the beginning of a new phenomenon that was to characterize subsequent fashion periods, that of the origination and adoption of style changes by a young, less affluent subgroup within the larger society.

The Impact of Television

Television became commercially available to the American public around 1948, but in that year only 20 stations were on the air and only 172,000 families had sets. According to the Census of 1950 five million families reported having a TV set in the house (Brooks 1966). As a medium for the spread of fashion information, television probably had an indirect impact on fashion. Influences on fashion from television were

[1]Teddy, a nickname for Edward, derives from these Edwardian influences.

FIGURE 17.2

Three British adolescent boys dressed in the Teddy Boy styles of the post-World War II period. (Courtesy, Corbiss-Bettman.)

more evident among the young. Styles directly attributable to television included the wearing of white buckskin shoes (called **white bucks**) after singer Pat Boone wore these shoe styles, Elvis Presley look-alike pompadours, a slick, combed-back hairstyle copied from a character named "Kookie" on a show called *77 Sunset Strip,* and a fad for Davy Crockett coonskin caps.

When Lucille Ball allowed the story line of *I Love Lucy* to incorporate her pregnancy into the format of the TV show, more attention was paid to maternity clothing. (See *Figure 17.3.*) But as Milbank (1989) points out, "For the most part, early television depicted a sanitized view of family life, with exaggeratedly middle-class housewives as the most prevalent female characters. Women wanting to emulate television fashions would have concentrated on the ball gowns and cocktail dresses worn by singers or those shown off by actress Loretta Young in the entrance scene to her weekly series."

FIGURE 17.3

During the "baby boom," even international couturiers designed lines of maternity clothing. Left to right, designs created in 1956 by Miguel Dorian of Spain, Givenchy of France, and Norman Hartnell of England. (Reproduced courtesy, Fairchild Publications.)

Internationalism

Air travel made it possible for people of the postwar period to move easily from one place to another. The relatively low cost of this transportation and its speed, as compared with ship travel, coupled with an increased affluence for many Americans, encouraged more of them to travel abroad. In 1929, 500,000 Americans travelled abroad. In 1958 the number of Americans who went abroad reached 1,398,000, and they spent an estimated two billion dollars in their travels (*The New York Times* 1960). Travelers returned with fashion goods from the countries they visited. They also became more receptive to imported goods sold in the United States.

The steady increases in imports were seen by labor and management in the American garment industry as a serious threat. These imports were at first chiefly from Western Europe, and tended to be high fashion and to command fairly high prices. Fashion promotions by the sophisticated Western European countries created a demand for fashionable Italian, French, and British goods. In the 1960s, the developing countries in Asia, Africa, and South America began to export goods. Imports from the Third World cost much less than European goods, and because they were sold at low prices they gradually came to dominate the low and midrange price markets. Retailers liked the imported goods because often they could take a higher mark-up on these items than on domestic goods.

High fashion design took on a more international flavor. The French position as the sole arbiter of fashion for women was challenged not only by American designers who had come of age during the war, but also by English, Italian, and even a few Irish and Spanish designers.

PRODUCTION AND ACQUISITION OF CLOTHING AND TEXTILES

The Fabric Revolution

Before World War II clothing was made from a limited number of fibers: the natural fibers (silk, wool, cotton, and linen) and the manufactured fibers (rayon and acetate). The successful marketing of nylon, invented before the war but not given wide distribution to the civilian population until after the war, touched off a search for other synthetic fibers. Many of these came onto the market in the 1950s. The major apparel fibers that appeared at this time included modacrylics (1949), acrylics (1950), polyesters (1953), triacetate (1954), and spandex (1959). Other fibers were also developed, but these either had limited use or were found mostly in household textiles or industrial applications. Many companies that had formerly been chemical companies began to manufacture fibers, which were chiefly derived from chemical substances.

One of the characteristics of most of the postwar fabrics was that they were easy to care for. With the more casual life style that had evolved, and with the virtual disappearance of servants from the middle-class household, these fabrics were easier to maintain and rapidly gained consumer acceptance. The expansion of travel helped to promote **drip dry** fabrics. In the late 1950s, there were **wash-and-wear** fabrics. In the 1960s, wash and wear was replaced by **permanent press.** These were chiefly cotton and cotton blended with polyester. Some wool fabrics were given special treatments to render them more readily washable. These new fibers may also have contributed to the popularity of the full skirts of the period which were held out by lightweight, permanently stiffened nylon petticoats.

With manufactured fibers, and especially with blends, American consumers experienced difficulty in identifying fibers and knowing how to care for these products. Congress passed the Textile Fiber Products Identification Act (TFPIA) in 1960. This legislation decreed that, as an aid to consumers, textile products had to be sold with labels that identified the fiber content.

The Changing Couture

Ever since the establishment of the haute couture in France in the 19th century, the designers who were members had been considered to be the primary source of major fashion trends. The French couture, as noted previously, had developed an organization and structure through which designers who were part of the *Chambre Syndicale* showed at least two collections a year. The haute couture is not a theoretical concept, but a business organization that serves to promote the products of designers. Membership in the *Chambre Syndicale* requires the development and showing of new style ideas several times each year. In the postwar period potential customers and the fashion press attended fashion shows presented by each couturier (designer).

The garments shown and sold by couture houses are called **originals.** The term original does not mean the garment is the only one of its kind, but only that it was made in the establishment of the designer. More than one original could be made of any style. Prices for originals were very high, but so were expenses. Most French couture houses did not make profits on their haute couture operations. Instead they established auxiliary enterprises such as perfume sales and "signed" accessory items, manufacture of which had much lower overhead costs. These more affordable items became the profitable part of their businesses and supported the costly couture.

PROMINENT DESIGNERS OF THE POSTWAR COUTURE

Some individual members of the French couture continued designing in Paris throughout World War II, but most had left Paris or closed their ateliers. Mainbocher and Schiaparelli had gone to New York, Balenciaga had gone to neutral Portugal. Chanel gave her last show in 1940. But once the war had ended, the couturiers began to plan for a revival of their businesses. This revival was given an enormous push forward by the collections of 1947 and the New Look, the name given by the fashion press to the collection mounted by Christian Dior.

Dior had worked before the war for Piquet and after, briefly, for the House of Lucien Lelong. (Lelong was not a designer but ran an establishment carrying his name.) In 1945 Dior was offered financial backing to open his own establishment, and in 1947 the House of Dior made fashion history. The new styles were successful overnight, and the House of Dior became one of the most influential of the houses in the haute couture. Dior remained a major designer until his death in 1957.

Another major designer of the postwar period was Cristobal Balenciaga. The Spanish-born Balenciaga opened his first Paris establishment in 1937. When he returned to Paris after the War, he became a favorite of Carmel Snow, the editor of *Harper's Bazaar* who featured his work often in the magazine. His work showed a mastery of almost sculptural forms and shapes and frequently his styles were well ahead of their time. A major force in the haute couture for the 1950s and on into the 1960s, he suddenly and unexpectedly closed his establishment in 1968. Balenciaga died in 1972.

Chanel did not reopen her *atelier* until 1954. Once again she became a major force in the couture, continuing to influence styles until she died in 1971.

The couture remained a vital, active force in fashion throughout the 1950s and early 1960s. Interest in the couture remained exceptionally high and many other Parisian couturiers were active in the postwar period. *Table 17.1* lists major French designers of the period between 1947 and 1960.

Table 17.1

INFLUENTIAL PARIS-BASED DESIGNERS, 1947–1960

Designer	Couture House and Date of Opening	Notable Characteristics of Designs or Career
Balenciaga (1895–1972)	Balanciaga, 1937	Innovative designer, major influence after World War II, considered a master craftsman. (See *page 433.*)
Pierre Balmain (1914–1982)	Balmain, 1945	"Known for wearable, elegant clothes . . . daytime classics, extravagant evening gowns."
Marc Bohan (1926–)	Chief designer and artistic director of Christian Dior, 1958–1989 after which he became head designer at Jean Patou.	Noted for the quality of his workmanship, "refined and romantic clothes."
Pierre Cardin (1922–)	Cardin, 1950	Created many innovative and exciting designs in the 1950s and 1960s for women; began designing for men, 1958.
Gabrielle Chanel (1883–1971)	Chanel, 1914; closed house during both world wars; first postwar collection, 1954. House of Chanel continued under various designers, most notably Karl Lagerfeld. (See Table *19.2*)	"Trademark looks included the little boy look, wool jersey dresses with white collars and cuffs, pea jackets, bell-bottom trousers, bobbed hair, and magnificent jewelry worn with sportswear. Other widely-copied signatures were quilted handbags with chain handles, collarless jackets trimmed with braid, beige sling-back pumps with black tips."
Christian Dior (1905–1957)	Dior, 1947. After his death the house continued with other designers: Yves Saint Laurent until 1960, Marc Bohan until 1989, Gianfranco Ferré until 1996; John Galliano, in 1997	Originated the New Look, spring 1947 (see *page 433;* with the sensuous line, loosened the waist, 1952; H-line, 1954; and Y-line, 1955.
Jacques Fath (1912–1954)	Jacques Fath, 1937. Closed in 1957, the company was reopened in 1992 and in March 1997 was bought by the group EK FINANCES and now produces a prêt-a-porter line.	"Designed elegant, flattering, feminine, sexy clothes."
Hubert de Givenchy (1927–)	Givenchy, 1952; sold to LVMH, 1988; announced his retirement, 1995, following presentation of his final haute couture collection; British designer, John Galliano, was named to succeed him; then Alexander McQueen, 1996; in 2001, Julien MacDonald.	"Noted for clothing of exceptional workmanship, masterly cut, beautiful fabrics."

All materials in quotes from Calasibetta, C. M. (1988 and 2003). *Fairchild's Dictionary of Fashion,* 2nd and 3rd editions. New York: Fairchild Publications and Stegemeyer, A. (1996 and 2004). *Who's Who in Fashion,* 3rd and 4th editions. New York: Fairchild Publications.

The American Mass Market

In the field of sportswear for the American market, designers in the United States were originating most of the designs as early as the 1930s and 1940s. The elimination of Paris as a design center during World War II had allowed American designers to flourish. Some, such as Mainbocher, Charles James, and designers such as Sophie and Castillo, who worked for department stores, created custom-made clothing for an exclusive clientele. Others working in the higher-priced ready-to-wear market, such as Claire McCardell, Norman Norell, Pauline Trigère, Arnold Scaasi, and James Galanos developed a strong following and influenced styles, making New York a postwar center of design. (*Table 17.2* lists major American designers of the postwar period.)

The American mass market was organized to originate, manufacture, and distribute clothing to retailers throughout the United States. The pre–World War II mass market designers generally seemed to draw their inspiration from styles presented by fashion designers in Paris. Initially the clothing was purchased by a fashionable, moneyed elite, a situation that continued for moderate and lower-priced ready-to-wear throughout the 1950s. However, especially in higher-priced lines, innovative and creative American designers also created new styles and their work was regularly reported by the fashion press.

Popular designs originated by couture and American ready-to-wear designers working in higher-priced lines were quickly copied by designers for lower-priced lines. These copies are known in the garment industry as **knock-offs.**

AMERICAN RETAILERS AND THE COUTURE

Some exclusive American retail stores purchased designer originals that they sold to their customers. These garments were very costly because import duties had to be added when prices were set. For example, the price of an original Chanel suit in 1958 at one American specialty shop for women in Philadelphia was $3500 (the cost of a mid-priced automobile at the time).

In order to make high fashion design available to American women, department stores such as Ohrbach's, Macy's, and Alexander's in New York City bought designer original garments and by arrangement with the designer made relatively faithful **line-for-line copies** which they sold at much lower prices than the originals could command. Around 1954 American stores began a type of design piracy of French designer styles. Low-priced copies were sold as copies of Monsieur X, Monsieur Y, or Monsieur Z. Knowledgeable customers were aware that Monsieur X was Dior, Monsieur Y was Jacques Fath, and Monsieur Z was Givenchy.

New Centers of Fashion Design

In the postwar era, a number of fashion design centers other than Paris also became important. When travel had been by ship or required lengthy and slow airplane trips, there was a certain practical aspect to having a single important center for fashion design. In the postwar period jet travel made reaching any of the major cities of the world faster and easier. The fashion press could cover shows in diverse parts of the globe with ease. By the 1950s Florence, Rome, and London had joined Paris and New York as important centers of fashion design. Nevertheless it was still Paris to which the fashion world looked with greatest interest. (*Table 18.2, pages 470–472,* lists important fashion designers of the 1950s from international fashion centers other than Paris.)

Design for men's clothing had no fashion center comparable to Paris and no organization comparable to the couture. As early as the 18th century, England had a reputation for fine tailoring, but a high level of interest in fashion was not considered to be manly. In the period from after World War II to the early 1960s this had begun to change, and the centers for design for men as well as for women were beginning to expand.

COSTUME FOR WOMEN: 1947–1960

Seldom does fashion change almost overnight, but in 1947 an exceptionally rapid shift in styles took place. After the war, the Western nations began to recover from the wartime devastation. World War II ended in August 1945. After a little more than a year in which there were no major fashion upheavals, the French designer Christian Dior caused a sensation by introducing a line of clothing at his spring 1947 show that deviated sharply from the styles of the wartime period and which came to be known as the New Look. (See *Figure 17.4.*) It was accepted rapidly and became the basis of style lines for the next ten or more years. *Contemporary Comments 17.1, page 439* reprints the description of the "New Look" Collection, from *Vogue.*

Style Features of the New Look

The major style elements of the New Look and the changes that it brought were:

1. Skirt lengths dropped sharply. Examination of fashion magazines of the preceding months shows that there was already a tendency toward somewhat longer skirts. Many other designers in the spring of 1947 also showed longer skirts, but to the woman on the street who had worn her skirts just below her knees for the preceding four or five years, the change was radical. Although there were pockets of resistance to the longer skirts (in the United States groups of women banded together and called themselves

Table 17.2

SOME MAJOR AMERICAN FASHION DESIGNERS WHO CAME TO PROMINENCE DURING WORLD WAR II AND WERE IMPORTANT IN THE 1950s

Designer	Firms with Which Designer Was Associated	Notable Characteristics of Designs or Career
Gilbert Adrian (1903–1959)	Known first as designer for motion pictures, entered retail business, 1941; switched to wholesale, 1953	Known for big-shouldered suits, dolman sleeves. (See *page 397*.)
Hattie Carnegie (1889–1956)	Opened Hattie Carnegie Inc., 1918	Designed custom-made and ready-to-wear for well-to-do and celebrities over a long period of time. Influenced many American designers who worked for her.
Anne Fogarty (1919–1981)	Designed for Youth Guild, 1948–1057 and Margot Inc. 1957–1962. Established Anne Fogarty Inc., 1962 until her death	Originated "paper doll" silhouette, 1951, with full skirt, small waist, known for empire dress revival.
James Galanos (1929–)	Opened own business in Los Angeles, 1951. He closed his business and retired in 1998.	"Known for luxurious day and evening ensembles" as well as other types of clothing. Designed both inaugural gowns for Mrs. Ronald Reagan.
Charles James (1906–1978)	Had salons in London and Paris in the 1930s, and a custom-made business in New York in the 1940s and 1950s	Considered to be among the most original of American designers. Known for lavish ball gowns, architectural shapes.
Tina Leser (1910–1986)	Designed for Edwin H. Foreman, Inc., 1943–1952. Opened own company, Tina Leser Inc., 1952	Especially known for sportswear with influences from Mexico, Haiti, Japan, and India. Used cashmere in dresses.
Claire McCardell (1906–1958)	Except for two years at Hattie Carnegie, did most of her designing for Townley Frocks, Inc.	"Specialized in practical clothes for the working girl." Considered one of most innovative and creative of all American designers. (See *page 396*.)
Norman Norell (1900–1972)	Worked for Hattie Carnegie from 1928–1940; a partner in Traina–Norell until 1960; then established Norman Norell Inc.	"Known for precision tailoring, ...purity of line, conservative elegance." First designer elected to Coty Hall of Fame in 1958. A major figure in the American fashion industry until his death in 1972. (See *page 397*.)
Mollie Parnis (1905–1992)	Active since 1939 when she and her husband founded Parnis-Livingston; then Mollie Parnis Inc., until 1984	". . . specialized in flattering, feminine dresses and ensembles for the well-to-do woman over 30."
Claire Potter (1903–1999)	Worked under name "Clarepotter" in 1940s and 1950s, as Potter Designs Inc. in 1960s	Known for sportswear designs, informal and more formal evening clothes.
Adele Simpson (1903–1995)	Adele Simpson, 1949–1991	"Known for pretty, feminine clothes in delicate prints and colors."
Gustave Tassell (1926–)	Opened own firm in Los Angeles, 1956; designed for Norell, Inc. after Norell's death from 1972 to 1976; then opened his own firm	"Known for refined, no-gimmick clothes with stark, clean lines..."
Pauline Trigère (1912–2002)	Worked for Hattie Carnegie, then opened own business in 1942, which she closed in 1993.	Highly regarded designer, with extensive licensing operation. Used unusual fabrics and prints, and "intricate" cuts. (See *page 397*.)
John Weitz (1923–2002)	Began with sportswear for Lord & Taylor, licensed designs in 1954 and opened his men's wear business in 1964.	One of the earliest to design both men's and women's apparel, and to begin licensing. Known for designs of practical sportswear.

All material in quotes from Calasibetta, C. M. (1988). *Fairchild's Dictionary of Fashion,* 2nd edition. New York: Fairchild Publications and Stegemeyer, A. (1996). *Who's Who in Fashion,* 3rd edition. New York: Fairchild Publications.

OUTLINES

OF NEW

• Left: Chic afternoon suit, "Bar," holds key to the new look, shape, ease in the natural waist, the longer pleated black wool skirt. Made to order at Henri Bendel; Marshall Field; Balance for the silhouette— the wide, bowed hat-line.

• Above: Pearls in chains, Christian Dior loops long strands of pearls over the bib of a natural linen coat. Again he drops the figure of a hat, and a big muff of leopard-skin, effective with pure monotone of...

FIGURE 17.4

Drawing from *Harper's Bazaar*, May 1947, of a suit from the Dior "New Look" collection of March 1947. (Reproduced courtesy, *Harper's Bazaar*, division of the Hearst Corporation.)

the "Little Below the Knee" Clubs, and declared that they would not lengthen their skirts), the change seemed irresistible and within a year the longer skirt lengths were widely adopted.

2. The square, padded shoulder that had been worn since the late 1930s was replaced by a shoulderline with a round, soft curve (achieved by a shaped shoulder pad).

3. Many designs had enormously full skirts. One of Dior's models had 25 yards of fan-pleated silk in the skirt.

4. Other designs had pencil-slim skirts.

5. Whether the skirt was full or narrow, the waistline was nipped in and small. The rounded curves of the body were emphasized. Many daytime and evening dresses

were cut quite low. The curve of the hip was stressed. In jackets with basques, sections that extended below the waist, the basque was padded and stiffened into a full, round curve.

Once established, the New Look influence permeated women's clothes throughout the greater part of the 1950s.

Costume for Women: 1947–1954

GARMENTS

To achieve the fashionable look, women returned to more confining underclothing than had been seen since before 1920. Fortunately for the comfort of women, many of the undergarments required to maintain the soft curves of the New Look were made of newer synthetic fabrics that pulled the body into the requisite shape without the rigid, painful bones and lacing of the early 20th century. See *Illustrated Table 17.1*, for examples of undergarments from the period between 1947 and 1960. The necessary underwear included brassieres. Nicknamed bras, these emphasized an "uplift." For wearing under some of the strapless evening gowns, strapless brassieres were available both in short lengths or constructed to extend to the waist. The longer version was known as a Merry Widow. These were boned (with synthetic materials). By the 1950s whalebone was no longer in use. However, the term "boning" had come to be applied to any kind of material shaped like whalebone and used to provide stiffening in undergarments, strapless evening gown bodices, or hoops, all of which were popular in this period. Although the sections between the bones were generally made of elasticized or synthetic power net fabrics, wearing these confining garments did occasion some degree of discomfort.

Many women wore waist cinches of boned or elasticized fabric to narrow the waistline to the desired small size. Garments that had been called corsets in earlier periods were now generally referred to as **girdles** or **foundation garments.** They usually extended well above the waistline in order to narrow the waist and were made of elasticized panels with some stretch combined with panels of firmer, non-stretching fabrics. Some closed with zippers, others had enough stretch to simply pull on over the hips.

In order to hold out the skirts of these dresses, full petticoats were required. Starched crinoline half slips (at this time crinoline was any open weave, heavily sized fabric) were used, but permanently stiffened nylon plain weave fabrics or nets were generally preferred for these garments because they required less maintenance and were lighter in weight. Beneath the full skirts, slips with full skirts, often with a ruffle around the hem, were worn while the narrower skirts required a straight slip. Under evening and wedding dresses a hoop petticoat might also be used.

This period was marked by what might be called a dual silhouette for daytime garments because both exceptionally

Illustrated Table 17.1

SELECTED UNDERGARMENTS FOR WOMEN, MEN, AND CHILDREN: 1947–1960

Waist cinch, c. 1946[1]

Girdles of the late 1940s and the 1950s with elasticized extensions above the waist for achieving the small-waisted silhouette of the period[2]

Full-skirted, permanently stiffened petticoat, late 1940s and 1950s[2]

I dreamed I was

WANTED

in my Maidenform bra

Advertisement for Maidenform brassiere; this "I dreamt I went walking . . ." series of advertisements was exceptionally popular in the 1950s.[3]

Maternity slip and panties, 1953

Slip, c. 1950–1953

Boy's knit athletic shirt and cotton knit briefs, 1950[4]

Men's T-shirt and boxer shorts

---

[1]Fairchild Publications.
[2]Stern's Department Store.
[3]Photograph courtesy of The Maidenform Museum, New York City.
[4]*Boy's Outfitter*, 1950, Fairchild Publications.

CONTEMPORARY COMMENTS 17.1

The New Look Collection as Reprinted by Vogue

Vogue reports on the New Look collection in 1947.

If there could be a composite, mythical woman dressed by a mythical, composite couturier, she would probably wear her skirt about fourteen inches from the floor; it might have, for its working model, a flower: petals of padding and stiffening sewn beneath the cup of the skirt; or it might be a long, straight tube beneath a belled and padded jacket. Her waist could be as small and nipped-in in cut as tight bodice and padded hips could make it. Her shoulders would be her own (or it would seem so);

her arms traced closely in cloth. Her hat engaging but not silly   a gendarme hat; a hat with a broken brim; a mushroom hat which at eye level would have an almost flat surface with crown slipping into brim; or a thicket of straw and flowers. She might wear a high-necked, boned-collar blouse, or she might wear a suit with a low-necked collar; there would probably be a fan of pleating somewhere about her; and she would, without question, wear opera pumps—pointed, high-heeled.

Reprinted courtesy of *Vogue* magazine, April 1947, p. 137.

full and narrow skirts coexisted. On these long, narrow skirts the length required the bottom of the skirt be slit or have a pleat of some type in order to allow a full stride. Fullness was achieved by goring, pleating, gathering, or cutting garments in the princess style, without waistline seams.

See *Figure 17.5* for a variety of dress styles. Necklines were plain, round, or square and ended either close to the neck or lower. Many dresses had small square or round peter pan style collars, larger round or square collars, and Chinese style or "mandarin" standing collars.

Most sleeves were close fitting, the most popular styles being short, cap sleeves just covering the shoulder; short, medium, and longer set-in sleeves that fit the arm closely; and "shirt sleeves" similar to those on men's shirts but fuller.

Some notable dress styles included summer jacket dresses, usually sleeveless and with small straps or halter tops and over this a short jacket or bolero; shirtwaist dresses with full skirts; and coat dresses with full skirts, some in the princess style, buttoning down the front. Some dresses of the early 1950s had dropped waistlines.

Although some full-skirted suits were worn, most tended to be made with narrow skirts. Jackets fit closely to the waistline, extending below the waist where they either flared out into a stiffened peplum (a short extension below the waist) or had a rounded, stiffened, and padded hip section ending several inches below the waist. (See *Figure 17.6.*) Suit necklines varied in placement, but tended to stand away from the neck somewhat. Collar styles included peter pan, rolled, notched, and shawl types.

MATERNITY DRESSES

Most maternity dresses were two piece, with loosely fitting tops over narrow skirts that had a stretch panel or open area to accommodate the expanding figure. (See *Figure 17.3.*) The baby boom of the 1940s and 1950s together with Lucille Ball's very public pregnancy on the *I Love Lucy* show focused attention on maternity clothes. Even so, maternity clothes for advertisements were photographed on non-pregnant women.

Dresses for day and evening were usually the same length. Evening dresses that were the same length as daytime dresses were referred to as **ballerina length** and these predominated. They were especially popular with high school and college students and were worn over stiff "crinolines." Paris designers continued to show some long gowns and pattern catalogs included patterns in both lengths. (See *Figure 17.7* and *Color Plate 53.*) Bridal gowns were generally floor length. Wide skirts were preferred for evening but some narrow-skirted styles had elaborate puffs of fabric at the hips or **fish tails** (i.e., wide areas around or at the back of the hem). Strapless bodices predominated and the bodices were often boned.

OUTDOOR GARMENTS

Coats either followed the silhouette, having fitted bodice areas and full skirts, or were cut full from the shoulders. Most fitted coats were cut in the princess line and belted; full coats had a good deal of flare in the skirt. Sleeve styles included kimono and raglan types. Some had turned back cuffs ending well above the wrist and long gloves were worn with these. (See *Figure 17.8.*) Fur coats were popular with affluent women.

6. Golf dress? Here is a classic, tailored in Irish linen, buttoned down the front. $23; from Best's.
7. A wool coat, light or bright, for cool snaps, for evening coverage. In tweed, $110; Lord & Taylor.
8. A breakfast-in-bed jacket. This one, of permanently pleated nylon net (another view, far left); nylon nightdress, of tricot and the pleated net; each $20. At The Dayton Co.; Strawbridge & Clothier.
9. Playing tennis? A dress short as shorts, in tucked white piqué. $30; Abercrombie & Fitch.

10. Bathing suit. (Make it two, one for morning, one for afternoon.) This halter-neckline suit, in gingham, $30. From Lord & Taylor.
11. A dressing gown, discreetly cut, that can be worn down to breakfast. Here, full-skirted, in sheer eyelet nylon. $85; Bonwit Teller.
12. For lunch or cocktails, in or out, a dress not too bare without a cardigan. In rayon-and-cotton pinwale cord, $45; Lord & Taylor.
13. An evening dress, short. Here, a strapless dress, sleeveless jacket, of embroidered Swiss organdie. $125; Bergdorf Goodman.
14. What to arrive and leave in. Could be this city-country silk Shantung, line-stitched, the sleeves coolly deep. $80; Bergdorf Goodman.
15. Beach pieces: dotted Swiss blouse and brassière; piqué shorts. $30; Lord & Taylor.
16. Bathing suit (see 10). This, all one piece, in cotton broadcloth. $11; Arnold Constable.

FIGURE 17.5

Vogue magazine, May 15, 1951, suggested these items be included in packing for a weekend in the country. Note especially the examples of both full-skirted dresses for day (number 12) and evening (number 13) contrasted with the slim skirt of number 14. (Reproduced courtesy, *Vogue* magazine, Condé Nast Publications.)

a   b

FIGURE 17.6 A AND B

Typical examples of suits from 1952 with nipped-in waistlines and shaped peplums. Suit in (a) has a pencil-slim skirt; suit in (b) has a wide, circular skirt. (Reproduced courtesy, *Harper's Bazaar*, division of the Hearst Corporation.)

If these followed princess lines they were generally made of less bulky furs.

Jackets, ending above the waist and called **shorties** or **toppers,** were a convenient way to accommodate wide skirts. Longer jackets, full and flaring from shoulder to hem, were also worn.

SPORTSWEAR

Casual garments worn during leisure time and in informal situations became an increasingly large part of the wardrobe. Retailers called such clothing sportswear. Skirts were either very full or narrow. Lines of blouses were shaped to follow body contours with darts or seams so that they fit smoothly through the bust and rib cage. They were similar in cut to dress bodices.

Sweaters, worn either tucked into the skirt or outside with a belt, fit close to the body. Many sweaters had smooth shoulderlines achieved by knitting sleeve and body in one. Variations included matching cardigans and pullovers, evening sweaters with beaded and/or sequin decorations, and in the 1950s bolerolike cardigans called **shrugs.**

In the early part of the period, shorts were upper thigh length and fairly straight. (See *Figure 17.5.*) Knee-length Bermuda shorts were adopted around 1954 and until the late 50s virtually replaced shorter styles. (See *Figure 17.9.*) Narrow pants fit the leg so closely that shoes had to be taken off in order to pull on the pants. (See *Figure 17.9.*) Pant lengths included those ending at the ankle, **houseboy pants** ending at the calf, and shorter, mid-calf length pants that were given the fashion name of **pedal pushers.** Other styles had names that changed from season to season, according to fashion advertising copywriters' whims. Loose printed or knit tops were commonly worn with pants.

FIGURE 17.7

Evening gowns by Balmain (1949). Left to right: in the popular short length a skirted, strapless ballerina-type gown, a floor-length gown with matching jacket, and a short, slim-skirted, satin dress. The sketch appeared in *Women's Wear Daily*, October 21, 1949. (Reproduced courtesy, Fairchild Publications.)

CLOTHING WORN FOR ACTIVE SPORTS

In Europe, a scanty, two-piece bathing suit called a **bikini,** smaller than any that had ever been seen before, was introduced. Designer Jacques Heim is credited as the originator of the style, which he called the atom. Soon there was a version that was advertised as "smaller than the atom." Eventually the name atom was changed to bikini. (Bikini was the small coral island in the Pacific where atomic tests were made from 1946 to 1956.) Although bikinis were worn on the beaches of Europe, American women did not adopt them, but continued to wear one- or two-piece suits that covered more of the body. Many bathing suits were cut with bottoms like shorts, while others had skirtlike constructions, and a few had full bloomers. Cotton, nylon, and Lastex® were the most popular fabrics. (See *Figure 17.10.*)

Shorts, trousers, or skirts and sweaters were worn on golf courses. Cotton golfing dresses were constructed with extra pleats of fabric at the shoulders to accommodate the golf swing.

FIGURE 17.9

Bermuda shorts and narrow slacks were important sportswear styles of the early 1950s. (Reproduced courtesy, Butterick Pattern Archives/ Library.)

FIGURE 17.8

A variety of coat styles from 1952. (Reproduced courtesy, Butterick Pattern Archives/Library.)

FIGURE 17.10

Even the relatively modest bikinis at the top of the drawing were not accepted by American women who, instead, wore bathing suits like those in the lower section, which displayed less skin. (Reproduced courtesy, The Tobe Report.)

As slacks narrowed, so did ski pants. Stretch yarns, used since 1956, made it possible to make ski pants fit the leg tightly. Closely woven nylon wind-breakers were worn as jackets, and ski wear was made in bright colors. (The rapid increase in the number of skiing enthusiasts in the United States made for greater variety in skiwear styles.)

Tennis clubs required players to wear white. Women's tennis outfits had short skirts (see *Figure 17.5*); however, players on public courts were likely to wear ordinary sportswear consisting of colored shorts with knitted tops.

SLEEPWEAR

Nightwear followed the trend toward fuller skirts and figure-hugging bodices, although tailored pajamas were also available. Advertising in fashion magazines and mail-order catalogs emphasized nightgowns, and a wide variety of sheer and full-skirted models were available. Toward the end of the 1950s pastel sleepwear was superseded by more colorful prints in floral and abstract patterns.

HAIR AND HEADDRESS

See *Illustrated Table 17.2,* for some examples of hairstyles and hats for the period from 1947 to 1960.

Short hair had become fashionable with the New Look. In the mid-1950s, longer hair was again in fashion.

Worn for all but the most casual occasions and especially when attending religious services, hats ranged from those that were small in scale, to large-brimmed picture hats. In the later 1950s, hats were consistently small and fit the head closely. Also seen were some turban styles in brightly colored prints or plain colors.

FOOTWEAR

See *Illustrated Table 17.3, page 446,* for some examples of footwear for the period from 1947 to 1960.

Terminology applied to stockings was somewhat confusing. Stockings and hosiery were generic terms, and included items ranging from long, sheer stockings, also called hose, to ankle-length, cotton stockings, often called socks or anklets. Women called their long, sheer stockings **nylons,** as these were inevitably made of nylon. Some were seamed (more popular), others seamless. Seams were often stitched in dark thread with reinforced heels made in dark yarn and extending several inches up the back of the ankle.

Through the 1940s and mid-1950s, rounded toes and very high heels and some open-toed, ankle-strap, sling-back, or sandal styles were worn for dress. Lower-heeled and flat shoes were also available. With more people living in the suburbs there was an increase in casual styles which included moccasins, loafers, ballet slippers, and canvas tennis shoes, called **sneakers.**

In the mid-1950s, toes of shoes grew more pointed and heels narrower. High-heeled shoes had "stiletto heels" made with a steel spike up the center of the heel to prevent the narrow heel from breaking.

ACCESSORIES

See *Illustrated Table 17.4, page 448,* for examples of popular accessories for the period from 1947 to 1960.

Gloves were worn as an accessory for many occasions, and were made from cotton and nylon knitted in a variety of weights and textures and colors, as well as leather. They ranged from very short to elbow-length styles that were worn with strapless evening gowns.

Handbags tended to be moderate in size, usually with small handles.

JEWELRY

Popular jewelry items included necklaces (usually fitting close to the neck), bracelets, and earrings. Rhinestones, col-

Illustrated Table 17.2

TYPICAL HATS FOR WOMEN: 1947–1960

Hats, 1948[1]   Small hat, 1853[2]   Wide-brimmed hat, 1954[3]   Small-brimmed hat, 1955[4]

[1] *Charm,* April 1948
[2] *Women's Wear Daily,* 12/9/55
[3] *Women's Wear Daily,* December 9, 1954, Fairchild Publications.
[4] *Women's Wear Daily,* December 9, 1955, Fairchild Publications.

ored stones, and imitation pearls in a variety of colors were used for costume jewelry.

COSMETICS

Women favored bright red lipstick, used face makeup in natural skin tones, mascara on eyelashes, and eyebrow pencil. After 1952, eye makeup became more pronounced, and some women drew a dark line around the eyes. About 1956 colored eye shadow began to appear in fashion magazines. Nail polish was available in many shades of pink and red.

Signs of Silhouette Changes: 1954–1960

The precise point at which the general public gave up the styles influenced by the New Look in favor of the unfitted look that became the predominant style of the better part of the 1960s is difficult to identify. Balenciaga had introduced the unfitted dress style as early as 1954 (his suits were unfitted from 1951 on) and Dior presented the **A**-line in his collection of 1955, but the unfitted look or **chemise styles** in dresses as they were called did not catch the public fancy immediately. (See *Figure 17.11.*) By 1957 most suits had shorter jackets, loosely fitted and ending shortly below the waist. Some blouson (full-backed) styles were shown and skirts had been growing gradually shorter and narrower. Coats

were straighter, and hair was longer and showing a tendency to be arranged in styles that were higher and wider around the face.

By 1958, some women had bought unfitted dresses of the **chemise**-type (see *Figure 17.12*) or the **A**-line **trapeze** (see *Figure 17.13*), but many others continued to resist the style. Even as late as the early 1960s, fashion magazines continued to show both new styles in the unfitted cut and dresses that followed the narrow-waisted full-skirted silhouette associated with the New Look. By the mid-1960s, however, the unfitted style was almost universally worn, and this style had become the dominant silhouette.

COSTUME FOR MEN:
1947–1960

The major elements of men's costumes immediately after the war showed no significant changes, and styles made no radical departures, from those of the wartime period and before. Over time, however, the wide-shouldered silhouette altered and styles for men became more diverse in the 1950s.

a   b

FIGURE 17.11 A AND B

Both Dior and Balenciaga showed unfitted silhouettes in their 1955 collections. Balenciaga (a) shows an unfitted, tunic dress. Dior (b) introduces a so-called A-line silhouette. (Reproduced courtesy, *Vogue* magazine, Condé Nast Publications.)

GARMENTS

Boxer shorts, jockey-type shorts, athletic shirts, and T-shirts remained much the same, but the variety of fabrics and colors in which these items were manufactured increased. See *Illustrated Table 17.1, page 438,* for examples of undergarments from the period between 1947 and 1960.

No postwar change in men's fashions occurred that equaled the radical New Look change in women's styles of 1947, although the men's wear industry tried to promote a different look for men. *Esquire,* a men's magazine with a heavy emphasis on fashion, introduced the term the **Bold Look** for men in October 1948 (a year after the New Look

made its appearance). This was not a radical change in fashion, but rather a continuation of the English drape cut with greater emphasis on a coordination between shirt and accessories and the suit.

Broad-shouldered jackets had lapels with a long roll. Double-breasted suits predominated. (See *Figure 17.14.*) Jackets were somewhat longer than during the wartime years. After wartime restrictions were lifted in the United States in 1945, most pant legs were cuffed.

Shirts tended to have wide collars. Cotton fabric had long been favored for shirts, but as nylon again became available to the civilian population some shirts were made of nylon.

Illustrated Table 17.3

SELECTED EXAMPLES OF POPULAR FOOTWEAR FOR WOMEN: 1947–1960

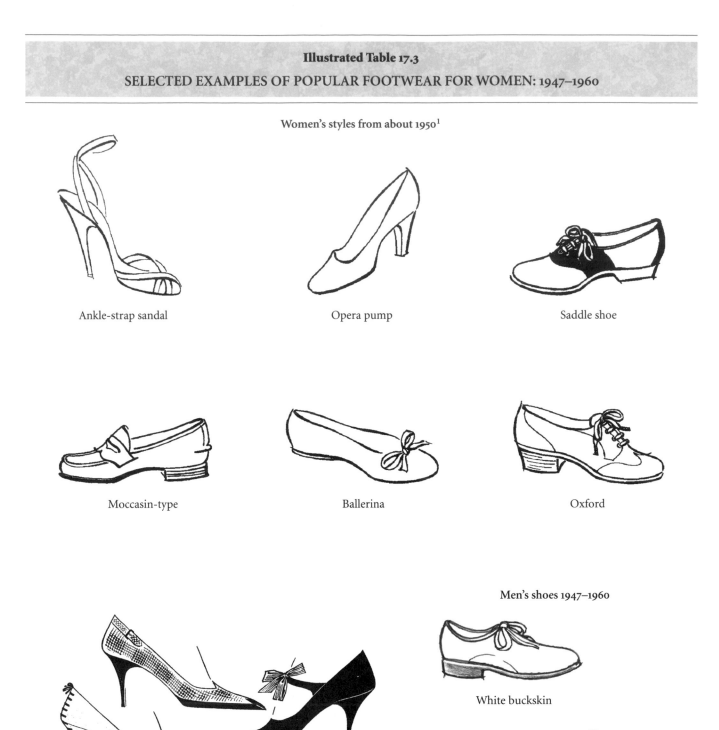

Women's styles from about 1950[1]

Ankle-strap sandal   Opera pump   Saddle shoe

Moccasin-type   Ballerina   Oxford

Men's shoes 1947–1960

White buckskin

Stiletto-heeled shoes with pionted toes, 1959[2]

Leather oxford

[1] *Department Store Economist*, October 1950.
[2] *Women's Wear Daily*, July 24, 1959.

FIGURE 17.12

A variety of unfitted "chemise" styles featured in *Women's Wear Daily* in late 1957. (Courtesy, Fairchild Publications.)

FIGURE 17.13

The A-line dress called "the trapeze" from 1959 was an example of the unfitted styles being introduced at this time. (Courtesy, Butterick Pattern Archives/Library.)

In the 1950s, the Edwardian influences, evident in the Teddy boy styles, moved mainstream menswear away from the English drape cut. The outcome was a suit with less padding in the shoulders, and a narrower silhouette. Single-breasted styles prevailed. (See *Figure 17.15.*) Dark gray (called charcoal) was the most popular shade. The title of a popular novel, *The Man in the Gray Flannel Suit,* and a film made from the book starring Gregory Peck, were indicative of the wide use of this suit for career-minded business men. The 1950s are sometimes nicknamed the era of the **gray flannel suit.**

It was the shirts worn with the gray flannel suits that provided touches of color—sometimes pink or light blue. Shirts most often had small collars either buttoned-down style, or they were fastened together under the tie with tie pins. Television helped to bring color to men's shirts. The early black-and-white television cameras caused white shirts, which were traditionally worn with business suits, to appear somewhat dingy. Men on television wore blue shirts, which appeared much more "white" to the camera. Shirt manufacturers started to produce colored shirts to wear with suits. This change met with resistance when some employers banned the wearing of colored shirts with business suits. As polyester fibers came into widespread use, they were blended with cotton to make "wash and wear" shirts that wrinkled less than all-cotton shirts.

Vests were also produced in bright colors for informal occasions.

Illustrated Table 17.4

1947 TO 1960: ACCESSORIES

A B C D E

Men's hats and hairstyles
(A) Driving cap for suburban wear (B) Pork pie hat, c. 1950 (C) Fedora, c. 1956 (D) Alpine hat, c. 1950 (E) D.A. or Duck tail hairstyle, 1950s

  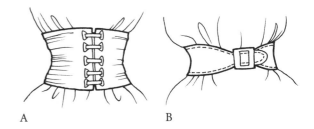

A B C A B

Women's handbags
(A) Clutch bag (B) Kelly bag (C) Bucket bag, c. 1955

Women's belts
(A) Cinch Belt, 1940s and 1950s (B) Contour belt

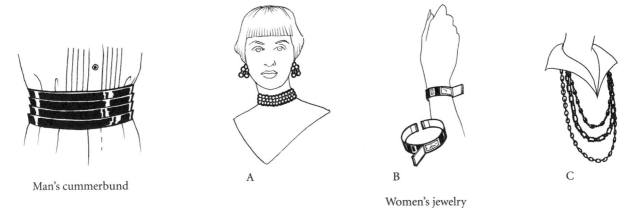

Man's cummerbund

A B C

Women's jewelry
(A) Pearl choker and earrings (B) Bracelet watch (C) Long chains and bead necklaces

FIGURE 17.14

A post–World War II double-breasted, wide-shouldered suit from 1950. (Courtesy, Fairchild Publications.)

FIGURE 17.15

Narrower lapels and single-breasted cut characteristic of the early 1950s. (Photograph courtesy, Hart Schaffner & Marx.)

Suits altered somewhat in cut in the late 1950s, as men abandoned the gray flannel suit. Fashion writers called the new suits with shorter jackets, a closer fit through the torso, and rounded, cutaway jacket fronts, **continental suits.** (See *Figure 17.16.*) These new styles continued into the 1960s.

Evening wear consisted of tuxedos or dinner jackets. Tail coats were rare, worn only for very formal occasions. The cut of jackets for evening followed the prevailing cut of jackets for daytime. White dinner jackets were worn in summer. About 1950 a light blue dinner jacket in a color called **French blue** was noted by *Esquire,* but otherwise evening styles remained quite conservative.

OUTDOOR GARMENTS

In the 1950s designers of outdoor garments turned away from the large scaled, broad-shouldered styles of the late 1940s and made coats with trimmer, narrower lines. The predominant line of overcoats in the 1950s had natural shoulders and more slender cuts. Some specific styles included tan polo coats; tweed, checked, and small-patterned fabric coats; and raglan-sleeved coats. In the late 1950s the wraparound, belted coat was revived.

Coats for casual wear were generally either hip or waist length, made in light- or sturdy fabrics, lined or unlined, had set-in or raglan sleeves, and either buttoned or zippered closings. The great variety of casual coats reflected an increased emphasis on leisure activities.

SPORTSWEAR

See *Figure 17.17* for some examples of men's sportswear.

The clothing favored by college students influenced some of the sportswear styles. Fashion promoters called this the Ivy League Look. Sport jackets reflected the cut of business suits. During the gray flannel era, sports jackets of tartan plaids were

449

FIGURE 17.16

Three popular suit jacket styles of 1958: left to right, the "ambassador," the "continental," and the "Ivy League" style. Illustration appeared in *Daily News Record,* November 4, 1958. (Courtesy, Fairchild Publications.)

popular. In the mid-1950s, sport jackets cut along the lines seen in continental suits (see *Figure 17.16*) had interesting textures achieved by using raised cord or slub yarns with thick and thin areas. Leather-buttoned corduroy jackets, checked and plaid and Indian madras plaids were also fashionable.

In the 1950s, casual trousers were slim and straight. Among the important Ivy League styles were **chinos** (khaki-colored, twill weave cotton fabric trousers) with a small belt and buckle at the back. These were generally combined with button-down shirts and crew-necked sweaters.

In the late 1950s, self-belts and beltless trousers were worn. Slacks tapered to the ankles and were cuffless. About 1954 Bermuda or walking shorts, a style of the 1930s, were revived for general sportswear. These were combined with knee-length stockings. Some attempts were made to incorporate Bermuda shorts into walking suits, which were business suits with Bermuda shorts instead of trousers, but these styles never captured any significant segment of the market.

In the immediate postwar period, sport shirts reflected the wide-collared styling of more formal shirts. They were made in bright colors; plaids were especially popular. In the 1950s, small-patterned fabrics in shirts with buttoned-down collars were preferred. Knitted shirts and sweaters of all kinds were worn throughout the period, including T-shirts and polo shirts.

CLOTHING FOR ACTIVE SPORTS

In the early 1950s, tailored trunks were preferred for swimming, especially medium-length boxer shorts. Men sometimes wore sets of matching sport shirts and trunks. By the end of the

1950s, varieties of trunks similar to Bermuda shorts, still-longer Jamaica shorts, and tailored trunks were all being worn.

SLEEPWEAR

In the postwar period, men preferred pajamas to nightshirts.

HAIR AND HEADDRESS

After World War II, some men continued to wear short crew cuts like those given to soldiers. When the hair was cut flat on top, it was called a flat top. In the 1950s, a contrasting longer hairstyle, inspired by the Teddy boys in England and singer Elvis Presley in the United States, had a curly pompadour in front and hair at the back brushed into a "DA," a point that resembled a duck's tail. While crew cuts and DA's were worn by younger men, older men tended to compromise somewhere between the two, with hair long enough to be combed back from the forehead.

During the 1950s, hats continued to be much the same as in the prewar period, with the fedora the staple of men's head wear. In 1952 President Dwight Eisenhower helped reestablish the homburg when he wore one to his inauguration rather than the customary top hat. Straw hats for summer followed the lines of the fedora, hat brims decreased in size. For businessmen in winter a narrow, Russian-style hat made of curled astrakhan fur or its imitation in synthetic fiber fabrics gained popularity among businessmen. Some of these hats were made with ear flaps that tucked inside the hat and folded out for use on especially cold days.

Sporty hats for suburban and leisure wear appeared. These included the Tyrolean hat with a sharply creased crown, a narrow brim turned up in back and down in front, and a cord band with a feather or brush decoration. Sports car drivers wore flat-crowned caps with visors and some men wore flat crowned, small-brimmed round pork pie hats. (See *Illustrated Table 17.4, page 448.*)

FOOTWEAR

Synthetic fibers made possible one size, stretch stockings. These were available in a variety of patterns and styles. Anti-static finishes were added to stockings to combat the tendency of synthetic fabric trousers to cling to synthetic fiber stockings.

By varying the type of leather used, the color, and style detailing, the same type of shoes could be used by manufacturers to make shoes for either dress or casual wear. Among the more popular styles were oxfords, brogues (a type of oxford with perforations at the tip and side seams), and moccasins. White buckskin shoes, known as white bucks, were part of the uniform of casual clothing for college students. Imported Italian shoes were fashionable, especially for dress, in the mid-1950s.

ACCESSORIES

For men accessories were limited to functional items: wristwatches, handkerchiefs, umbrellas, and jewelry such as rings, identification bracelets, cuff links, and tie pins.

FIGURE 17.17

Popular sportswear items ranged from sport and knit shirts to sport jackets, including many items made from manufactured fibers and/or blends. (*Daily News Record,* April 8, 1959. Reproduced courtesy, Fairchild Publications.)

COSTUME FOR CHILDREN:
1947–1960

As in all previous periods, styles for children displayed many elements of adult styles. The sociocultural events and technological changes that influenced adult clothing were also reflected in developments in children's clothing. For example, the synthetic and synthetic-blend wash-and-wear fabrics of the 1950s and, later, permanent press found a ready market in children's clothing.

In the 1950s, plaid vests and miniature gray flannel suits just like those for their fathers were made for boys, while most pattern companies of the period included several patterns for mother–daughter "look-alike" outfits. One is tempted to see in these styles a reflection of the emphasis on family togetherness that was characteristic of the United States in the 1950s. See *Illustrated Table 17.5,* for some examples of children's styles from 1947 to 1960.

Costume for Infants and Preschool Children

After the late 1950s, long pants up to about size three were made with gripper-snap fasteners up the inseam and around the crotch area to facilitate changing of diapers without having to take off the entire garment. For children at the crawling stage, knees were reinforced

Small girls, ages one to about four, were dressed in loose, yoked dresses. Boys wore romper suits or short pants. Both boys and girls wore long corduroy pants or overalls.

Costume Components for Girls

GARMENTS

Echoing the silhouette of adult women's styles of the 1940s and 1950s, girls dresses had full skirts and fitted bodices. Princess-line styles, full circular skirts, and jumpers all conformed to the predominant shape.

The most frequently seen styles for blouses and tops were tailored shirts, which often had rounded peter pan collars, knit polos, T-shirts, and other knit tops.

Girl's pants followed the cut of adult styles. For play or active sports, girls wore shorts or pants, including Bermuda or walking shorts, pedal pushers, and other lengths that carried the same fashion names as those for women.

HAIR

Hair tended to be short.

Illustrated Table 17.5

CHILDREN'S CLOTHING STYLES: 1947–1960

Toddlers' styles, 1955[1]

Princess-style coats, 1955[2]

Full-skirted dress, 1960[3]

[1] *Infants and Children's Review*, August 1955.
[2] *Vogue*, March 1, 1955.
[3] Butterick Patterns, courtesy, Vogue/Butterick Pattern Company Archives/Library.

Costume for Boys

GARMENTS

The practice of dressing young boys in jackets and knickers in the years prior to adolescence was abandoned after the war. Although suits with short pants were available for very young boys, most boys' suits had long pants and were like those of adult men. Younger boys wore Eton jackets; boys of all ages wore blazers.

Dress shirts were worn with suits and jackets. The most common casual shirt styles were knitted T-shirts that pulled over the head and polos with collars and buttoned vents at the front; woven sports shirts and plaid flannel shirts in cold weather. In the late 1940s, there were Western-style shirts with yoke and cuffs in contrasting colors to the body of the shirt.

HAIR

Usually hair was cropped short or cut in a "crew cut."

Costume for Boys and Girls

OUTDOOR GARMENTS

Dress coats were made in miniature versions of classic styles for men and women. The enormous variety of jackets available included buttoned and zippered jackets with knit waistbands and cuffs that were made in fabrics ranging from lightweight poplin to leather. Hooded parkas, boxy jackets, pea jackets, and melton (a dense, wool fabric) toggle coats with wood or plastic "toggle" closings were also popular.

NOTABLE YOUTHFUL FADS

Fads are styles of intense popularity worn by a large number of people for a very short time. Adolescents, especially girls, seemed to be prone to the adoption of fad styles. Fads no-

table in the late 1940s included long, full black skirts, worn with leg-of-mutton-sleeved plaid blouses and flat ballet slippers and denim jeans, worn with saddle shoes, and a large shirt with a loose tail. In the 1950s, fluffy bedroom slippers were a fad, as were **poodle skirts,** full-circle felt skirts with a poodle appliqué in a contrasting color of felt. Rhinestones were used for the eyes and to form a collar on the dog. Such skirts were generally worn together with ankle socks, two-tone saddle shoes, a white shirt, and a small scarf tied around the neck.

SUMMARY

THEMES

The importance of the theme of RELATIONSHIPS BETWEEN COSTUME AND THE WORK OF INDIVIDUAL DESIGNERS is evident as styles of the New Look, introduced by Christian Dior in 1947, signaled a sharp change in women's fashion and marked the beginning of the postwar styles. For another decade the silhouette of women's clothing continued to follow the pattern established by Dior in 1947. Throughout this period the PRODUCTION AND ACQUISITION OF TEXTILES AND APPAREL was much influenced by designers, as the French couture was followed closely by well-to-do women and celebrities who patronized the couturiers and by slightly less affluent women who bought line-for-line copies of Paris designs from American retail stores. At the same time a growing internationalism in fashion was reflected in the establishment of fashion design centers in other major European cities.

Themes related to SOCIAL GROUP MEMBERSHIP can also be identified in the dress that both the Teddy boys and the Beatniks used to set themselves apart and, at the same time, to express dissatisfaction with the broader society.

CHANGES IN PATTERNS OF SOCIAL BEHAVIOR were evident as more Americans moved to the suburbs, where their clothing needs changed, along with their lifestyles. The emergence of adolescence as an identified stage of development between childhood and adulthood was also reflective of changes in social behavior. Moreover, these changes were related to the theme of ECONOMICS, as adolescent purchasing power grew, allowing them to acquire popular fad items.

The new medium of COMMUNICATION, television served to spread fashion information rapidly, while TECHNOLOGY made a host of new fibers available for use in clothing.

FASHION was an omnipresent theme of the 1950s. The first stirring of change from the New Look–inspired silhouette had begun as early as the mid-50s when designers such as Balenciaga and Dior showed some unfitted dress styles as part

of their collections. By the end of the 1950s straight, shorter dresses were beginning to appear in retail stores. They met with little success, possibly they were too radical a departure from the established, figure-hugging shapes.

But these styles, like some of the social changes that were just beginning to simmer beneath the smooth-appearing sur-

FIGURE 17.18

In the 1990s, the corset of the 1950s was revived as the "bustier." Often it was ornately decorated and worn as outerwear, as in this example by Dolce & Gabbana in 1992. (Courtesy, Fairchild Publishers, Inc.)

Visual Summary Table

THE NEW LOOK: FASHION CONFORMITY PREVAILS

Man: 1947–1950

The prewar, full shoulder line double-breasted suits, with somewhat longer jackets and cuffed pants return.

Man: 1950–60

Lines slimmer, based on Edwardian styles of the Teddy Boys. Suits are often made in gray wool flannel. Some colored shirts begin to appear.

Woman: 1947–1960

As war restrictions end, the New Look appears with rounded shoulders, narrow waist, and longer skirts, either very full or very narrow and straight.

Woman: 1955–1960

First move toward different silhouette as less fitted garments, chemise, trapeze, and **A**-line garments appear in Paris.

face of the postwar society, were a harbinger of things that would come to occupy the attention of the world by the middle of the next decade.

Survival of New Look Styles

Of the New Look styles that have been utilized by fashion designers of the late 1980s and 1990s, probably the most notable have been the corsets. Although transformed with beading and other ornamentation and given the name bustier, the shape and structure of these garments is very like the "Merry Widow" of the New Look. (See *Figure 17.18.*)

Short, wide-skirted "mini-crinolines" had antecedents not only in the 19th century Crinoline period, but also in the New Look. Frequently they were strapless, an important feature of the longer but similarly shaped evening dresses of the New Look. (See *Figure 19.17A, page 529.*)

NOTES

Brooks, J. 1966. *The Great Leap.* New York: Harper and Row, pp. 162, 232, 236.

Ewing, E. 1977. *History of Children's Costume.* New York: Scribners, p. 156.

Milbank, C. 1989. *New York Fashion: The Evolution of American Style.* New York: Abrams, p. 179.

New York Times, January 17, 1960, cited in J. Brooks. 1966. *The Great Leap.* New York: Harper and Row.

SELECTED READINGS

Books and Other Materials Containing Illustrations of Costume of the Period from Original Sources

Fashion and general magazines and newspapers of the period such as: *Vogue, Harper's Bazaar, Glamour, Mademoiselle, Seventeen, McCall's, Good Housekeeping.*

Trade newspapers such as *Women's Wear Daily* and *Daily News Record.*

Catalogs: Pattern and mail-order.

Bond, D. 1988. *The Guinness Guide to 20th Century Fashion.* Enfield, Middlesex, England: Guinness.

de Pietri, S. and M. Leventon. 1989. *The New Look to Now: French Haute Couture 1947–1987.* New York: Rizzoli.

Dorner, J. 1975. *Fashion in the Forties and Fifties.* New Rochelle, NY: Arlington House.

Ewing, E. 1974. *History of Twentieth Century Fashion.* London: B. T. Batsford.

Gold, Annalee. 1991. *90 Years of Fashion.* New York: Fairchild.

Lee, S. T., ed. 1975. *American Fashion.* New York: Quadrangle/New York Times.

Milbank, C. 1989. *New York Fashion: The Evolution of American Style.* New York: Abrams.

Mulvagh, J. 1988. *Vogue History of 20th Century Fashion.* New York: Viking Penguin.

Schoeffler, O. E. and W. Gale. 1973. *Esquire's Encyclopedia of 20th Century Men's Fashion.* New York: McGraw-Hill.

The World of Balenciaga. 1973. New York: Metropolitan Museum of Art.

Periodical Articles

"Charles James: Architect of Fashion." 1983. *American Fabrics and Fashions,* No. 128, p. 19.

Coleman, E. A. 1982. "Abstracting the Abstract Gown." *Dress,* Vol. 8, p. 27.

Cooper, A. C. 1985. "Casual, But Not That Casual." *Dress,* Vol. 11, p. 47.

"It Was 25 Years Ago: Dior, the New Look." 1972. *Harper's Bazaar,* July, p. 32.

Martin, R. 1981. "'The New Soft Look': Jackson Pollock, Cecil Beaton, and American Fashion in 1951." *Dress,* Vol. 7, p. 1.

Scott, B. 1987. "Paris Pays Tribute to Christian Dior." *Apollo,* July, No. 126, p. 49.

Daily Life

Brooks, J. 1966. *The Great Leap.* New York: Harper and Row.

Cooke, A. 1989. *America Observed from the 1940's to the 1980's.* New York: Macmillan.

Crouzet, M. 1970. *The European Renaissance Since 1945.* New York: Harcourt Brace Jovanovich.

Dodds, J. W. [N. D.]. *Everyday Life in 20th Century America.* New York: Putnam.

Harvey, B. 1992. *The Fifties: A Women's Oral History.* New York: HarperCollins.

Lefebvre, J. 1971. *Everyday Life in the Modern World.* New York: Harper and Row.

Miller, D. T. and M. Nowak. 1977. *The Way We Really Were.* Garden City, NY: Doubleday.

This Fabulous Century. 1969. Vols. 5 and 6. New York: Time-Life. (Also contains illustrations of costumes from contemporary sources.)

CHRONOLOGY

1960

Food and Drug Administration approves
oral contraceptive pill

John F. Kennedy elected President

1961

Bay of Pigs invasion of Cuba

Berlin wall erected

Freedom rides begin in the American South

Russians put first man into space

Alan Shepard, American astronaut, makes
suborbital space flight in May

1962

Cuban missile crisis

Pop Art symposium at the Museum of Modern Art

John Glenn orbits the earth three times

Publication of Rachel Carson's book *The Silent Spring*

1963

Civil rights rally in Washington, DC

Assassination of President Kennedy

Betty Friedan publishes *The Feminine Mystique*

The Beatles have their first successful record:
"I Want to Hold Your Hand"

1964

Congress passes the Civil Rights Bill

Martin Luther King wins the Nobel Prize

1965

American sportswear manufacturer for men,
McGregor, introduces "mod" clothes to U.S. market

Designer John Weitz opens a boutique for men

1966

National Organization for Women (NOW) founded

1967

Demonstrations against the Vietnam War
in the United States

10,000 young people participate in "Be-in"
in Central Park, New York City

1968

Martin Luther King assassinated

Robert Kennedy assassinated

Student demonstrations in Europe
and the United States

American designer Ken Scott introduces
"hippie-gypsy look"

Richard Nixon elected president

1969

Apollo II lands on the moon

Woodstock music festival

1970

Four students killed in anti-war
demonstration at Kent State University

First celebration of Earth Day

1971

200,000 participate in anti-war march
on Washington, DC

1972

Nixon goes to China

Break-in at the Watergate

Nixon is reelected

1973

Peace treaty ending Vietnam War signed

U.S. Supreme Court rules that abortion is legal

Yom Kippur Arab–Israeli War

Arabs impose oil embargo

1974

Nixon resigns;
Gerald Ford becomes president

1976

Jimmy Carter elected president

1977

Treasures of King Tutankhamen exhibit begins
its tour of the United States

Fans of "punk" rock music introduce
punk fashions; British designer
Zandra Rhodes incorporates
these styles in her line of clothes

1978

Diplomatic relations opened between
the United States and China

1979

Camp David agreement between
Egypt and Israel is signed

Three-Mile Island nuclear power plant
failure occurs

The Shah of Iran overthrown by revolution

Soviet troops invade Afghanistan

THE SIXTIES AND SEVENTIES

Style Tribes Emerge

1960 – 1980

A.

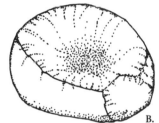

B.

E.

A.

Geodesic dome

B.

Bean bag chair, c. 1965

C.

Op Art Painting by Bridget Riley,
Current, 1964

D.

Pop Art Paintings by Andy Warhol
Campbell's Soup Cans, 1962

E.

Lincoln Center, 1966

C.

D.

Figure A courtesy of the New York Public Library Picture Collection. Figure B courtesy of J. Curcio in Federico, J. T. 1988. *Clues to American Furniture.* Washington: Starrhill, p. 65. Figures C, D courtesy of the Museum of Modern Art, New York, Philip Johnson Fund (C); purchase and partial gift of Irving Blum (D). Figure E courtesy of V. R. Tortora.

The years that encompassed the Vietnam conflict in the United States were marked by social upheaval and turmoil. Opposition to the war among the young, continuing efforts to right the wrongs of segregation and racial discrimination, the rise of feminism, and the budding environmental movement all contributed to a period of ferment that was clearly reflected in the fashions of the period.

HISTORICAL BACKGROUND

Europe and the Soviet Union

The Soviet Union launched the first satellite to orbit the earth in 1957 and the Space Age had begun. Americans were shocked at the gap in technology between the United States and Russia that this feat represented. In 1960 President Kennedy vowed that the United States would reach the moon by 1970. The first manned moon landing was made in 1969.

By the mid-1960s, the European Economic Community (EEC) had created a single market for their economic resources. The 12 member nations abolished all tariffs affecting trade among themselves and set up a common tariff on goods imported from other countries.

In contrast, the Soviet Union continued to keep a tight control over its satellites in Eastern Europe. In 1968, when the Czechoslovak Communist Party sought to grant freedom of press and expression to make the Party more popular, troops from the Soviet Union and other Communist states invaded Czechoslovakia and restored repressive Communist rule. Within the Soviet Union during the 1970s dissent continued to grow. Even the renowned Soviet writer and Nobel Prize winner Alexander Solzhenitsyn was exiled in 1974.

The Soviet people had been promised more consumer goods and greater investment in agriculture in the 1970s. These promises were never fulfilled because of crop failures and spending on heavy industry and defense. Dissatisfaction grew as a 10-year war in Afghanistan proved costly in Soviet lives and money.

The Middle East

On Yom Kippur, October 6, 1973, the holiest day of the Jewish calendar, Egyptian and Syrian troops attacked Israel. After some months of fighting in which Israel prevailed, Egypt accepted a cease-fire in November 1973; Syria in May 1974. Meanwhile the Organization of Petroleum Exporting Countries (OPEC) imposed a brief oil embargo on the United States and other nations supportive of Israel.

Tensions in the Middle East were lessened after a summit conference between President Anwar Sadat of Egypt, Prime Minister Menachem Begin of Israel, and President Jimmy Carter at Camp David in September 1978. The resulting Camp David Accords ultimately led to a 1979 Israeli–Egyptian peace treaty, the withdrawal of Israeli troops from the Sinai peninsula, and the establishment of diplomatic relations between Egypt and Israel.

Earlier that year the government of Shah Mohammed Reza Pahlavi of Iran, whose autocratic policies antagonized religious leaders, was overthrown. After the Shiite Ayatollah Ruhollah Khomeini established an Islamic fundamentalist republic in which all institutions, laws, and economic and social policies were based on Islam, Khomeini's followers seized the American embassy and took the American personnel as hostages, not to be released until early in 1981.

Africa and the End of Colonialism

In 1957 the Gold Coast became the first African state to be granted independence by Britain. It is now known as Ghana. By the mid-1960s Britain, Belgium, and France had freed most of their African colonies. The French government however, supported by French men and women living in Algeria, opposed independence for Algeria; a bitter war followed until Algeria became independent in 1962. Freedom, however, did not solve the problems of the African people. Coups, civil wars, and famines continue today.

The Emergence of Japan as an Economic Power

For many of the people of Asia, political freedom meant economic freedom as well. Led by Japan, many Asian countries experienced an industrial expansion. Much of Japanese industry, destroyed by bombings, was replaced by brand new plants often more modern than those to be found within the United States where too many factories were out of date and in need of replacement. Nevertheless the United States helped the recovery of Japan by providing technological information. Japan made significant increases in output thanks to weak trade unions, low wages, high savings rate, demanding schools, and lifetime employment. Soon South Korea, Hong Kong, Singapore, and Taiwan had followed Japan's example.

Japan created the economic model that set the pace for other industrialized nations and those who aspired to compete in the now worldwide market. The Japanese invested in new technologies to make their production cheaper and more efficient. As a result their products became noted for high quality and standards of performance. No longer was the prewar phrase "cheap Japanese import" true. Japan's quality products—computers, cameras, binoculars, radios, tape recorders, television sets, and automobiles—were sold throughout the world. By the 1990s Japanese automobile manufacturers had even built their own plants within the United States.

In textiles the Japanese pioneered new technologies in the synthesis of manufactured fibers. In the 1960s and 1970s, before higher costs of wages and production in Japan drove the Japanese to move the manufacture of textiles to lower-wage Southeastern Asian countries, the Japanese produced high-quality natural and manufactured textile fabrics that were utilized by American and European clothing firms.

It was also in this decade that some Japanese fashion designers gained international notice. Most worked in Japan, but Kenzo, who had come to Paris in 1965, opened his own ready to wear boutique in 1970.

The United States

THE KENNEDY ADMINISTRATION

The election of John F. Kennedy to the presidency in 1960 began a decade that contrasted markedly with the Eisenhower years. The United States and the Soviet Union went to the brink of war in 1962 over the Cuban missile crisis after American spy planes discovered that the Russians were installing nuclear missiles in Cuba. President John F. Kennedy ordered a naval blockade of Cuba, and eventually Soviet Premier Nikita S. Khrushchev agreed to withdraw the missiles, which avoided a nuclear conflict.

The assassination of President Kennedy in 1963 stunned the American public. Lyndon B. Johnson succeeded Kennedy.

THE CIVIL RIGHTS MOVEMENT

The issue of civil rights had become more pressing. As early as 1962 federal troops had been used to enroll an African-American student at the University of Mississippi. Similar action was taken in 1963 at the University of Alabama. To show their concern about civil rights, over 250,000 demonstrators had gathered on the Great Mall in Washington, DC in August 1963 to hear Dr. Martin Luther King say, "I have a dream that one day this nation will rise up and live out the true meaning of its creed: We hold these truths to be self-evident, that all men are created equal."

The assassination of President Kennedy in 1963 had shocked the nation, but it did not halt the civil rights movement. In the administration of Lyndon B. Johnson, the cause of civil rights became a major force in American life. After a Senate filibuster had been broken, Johnson was able to sign the Civil Rights Act of 1964, the most far-reaching civil rights law ever enacted by Congress. Another important law, the Voting Rights Act of 1965, ensured every American the right to vote and authorized the attorney general to dispatch examiners to register voters.

Despite the passage of these laws, riots broke out in American cities during the summers of 1965 (Los Angeles), 1966 (Chicago, Cleveland, and 40 other cities), and 1967 (Newark and Detroit). These riots had erupted because civil rights legislation alone could not change residential segregation in urban centers.

By the mid-1960s, among African-Americans dissatisfied with the nonviolent tactics of Martin Luther King, the new rallying cry became "Black Power." The most articulate spokesperson for black power was Malcolm X, born Malcolm Little. The "X" indicated his lost African surname. He rose from a ghetto childhood to a leadership position in the Black Muslim movement. Later Malcolm X broke with the Nation of Islam and established his own organization committed to establishing an alliance between African-Americans and the non-white people of the world. In 1965, Black Muslim assassins shot Malcolm X.

When Martin Luther King was assassinated on April 4, 1968, in Memphis, Tennessee, the civil rights movement lost its most charismatic leader; his death was mourned by both whites and African-Americans. Rioting followed in over 60 American cities, including Chicago and Washington, DC.

In the same year Richard M. Nixon was elected president. He tried unsuccessfully to undo the civil rights legislation enacted during the Johnson administration. The Supreme Court, however, ordered a quick end to segregation in schools. As a result, more schools were desegregated in Nixon's first term than during the Kennedy–Johnson administrations.

The revelation that President Richard M. Nixon had attempted to cover up White House involvement in the Watergate scandal led to Nixon's resignation under threat of impeachment on August 9, 1974. His successor, Gerald R. Ford, had to grapple with a domestic economy that was hit by a quadrupling of oil prices as a result of the Arab oil embargo following the Yom Kippur War.

Jimmy Carter, a former governor of Georgia, defeated Ford in the presidential election of 1976. Important events during Carter's single term included a treaty turning the Panama Canal over to the government of Panama by 1999 and the 1979 peace treaty between Israel and Egypt. Unemployment remained high, and inflation soared 10 percent in 1978. Another fuel shortage in 1979 forced motorists to wait in long lines at gasoline pumps.

WAR IN VIETNAM

Fearing the repercussions if another country came under Communist rule, President Kennedy had authorized more aid to the South Vietnamese government that was struggling against Vietnamese communists, the Vietcong. When President Johnson assumed office following Kennedy's death, he authorized the dispatch of American ground combat troops to Vietnam. By 1965 the United States was at war in Vietnam. This bitter struggle soon aroused widespread opposition across the nation and provoked violent antiwar demonstrations on many American college and university campuses. Students publicly burned their draft cards, and antiwar demonstrators blocked the entrance to army installations and draft headquarters.

THE THAW IN RELATIONS WITH CHINA

A major change in foreign policy occurred in the 1970s. Since 1949 Chinese-American relations had been in the deep freeze. The thaw began with the visit to Beijing by President Richard M. Nixon in February 1972, where he engaged in discussions with Chinese leaders over questions relating to Korea, Japan, and Taiwan. Nixon also offered trade concessions, credits, and technical assistance.

Nixon hoped there would be a trade-off: Chinese pressure on the North Vietnamese to be more conciliatory in discussing armistice terms. However, Chinese influence on North Vietnam had been overestimated, and it was not until January of 1973 that the United States finally signed an Armistice, agreeing to withdraw its troops from Vietnam by April of that year. Nixon's opening to China led to increased trade with the United States ranging from clothes to toys and beer.

ENERGY

Following the Yom Kippur War (1973–74), OPEC instituted an embargo on oil shipments to the United States. Imports of oil dropped and prices quadrupled—a signal that OPEC had taken control of output and pricing of oil. Although this first fuel crisis experienced by Americans had a relatively brief impact, it did serve to awaken Americans to the need to conserve energy. Higher oil prices also led to higher costs for synthetic fibers made from petroleum-derived chemicals.

A calm and stable oil market from 1974 to 1978 was followed by a crisis in 1979, when the fall of the Shah of Iran's government led to another oil shortage. Gas stations began to close early and on weekends. Gasoline lines often stretched for blocks. President Carter went on television, dressed in a sweater, and devoted one of his trademark fireside chats to energy in an effort to arouse public support for his new energy program, which he styled "the moral equivalent of war." Although his energy program fared poorly in Congress, Carter issued a presidential proclamation prohibiting commercial, government and public buildings from using air conditioning to lower temperatures below 78 degrees or using heating systems to raise temperatures above 65 degrees. Americans were urged to reduce heat and air-conditioning levels in their homes and offices. During the daytime those who lived or worked at lower temperatures wore more layers of clothing, including sweaters and jackets, that could be added or subtracted. Mail-order catalogs of the period showed more warm nightgowns, pajamas, and robes.

The oil shortage gradually ended as the demand for oil decreased because of world recession, energy-saving measures, and the installation of energy-saving equipment. President Reagan removed controls on oil prices in January 1981. During the subsequent years, as oil prices stabilized, the goal of energy independence was abandoned as the memories of the oil crises of the 1970s faded.

ENVIRONMENT

By the 1970s, public concern over environmental problems had increased substantially. Politicians were enthusiastic until they understood the impact of environmental policies on the economy. Cleaning up the environment was expensive and it could cost jobs. Nevertheless, steps were taken to safeguard the environment. The National Environmental Policy Act of 1970 had established the Environmental Protection Agency (EPA) and subsequent legislation addressed concerns about drinking water, nuclear waste, toxic waste site cleanup, and ocean dumping of sewage sludge.

CHANGES IN FAMILY LIFE AND THE ROLE OF WOMEN

The 1970s saw changes in the American family. The divorce rate doubled and the marriage rate dropped to a low of ten marriages per thousand people in 1976. Those who did marry delayed the wedding date. Consequently the birth rate slipped below the rate required to replace the population. Nevertheless, four fifths of those who were divorced remarried within three years. Frequent divorces combined with remarriage produced new so-called "blended" families. The change in traditional marriages encouraged a proliferation of couples who lived together without legal and/or ecclesiastical sanction. It was estimated that the number of unmarried couples who established households tripled to 1.6 million, and signaled a change in public opinion concerning cohabitation.

The number of households headed by women increased, which forced more women into the work force. By 1976 only 40 percent of American jobs provided enough income to support a nuclear family. This led more married women to seek paid employment. It was estimated that by 1976 one half of American mothers worked outside the home. Women not only suffered discrimination in income levels that did not equal male earnings, but also found opportunities for advancement limited.

The gradual addition of millions of women to the work force changed fashion. Merchandisers noticed the change in shopping patterns, as working women shopped in the evenings and on weekends. They bought clothing for work and for play. As more women entered managerial positions in the corporate world in the 1970s, they wore a feminized version of the man's business suit: a tailored jacket, a moderate-length skirt, and a tailored blouse. This style was being recommended for women who wanted to "dress for success."

SOCIAL PROTEST MOVEMENTS

To the consternation of their elders, and unlike the "Silent Generation," young people of the 1960s demanded to be heard. The advance guard of the new generation had been the "Beatniks" (see page 429) of the late 1950s. The Beatnik phenomenon faded, but as early as 1960 a college student association president was quoted in *The New York Times* as seeing greater concern among students with non-college affairs (Brooks 1966).

Some students became involved in the growing civil rights movement, which succeeded in ending the most blatant forms of discrimination against African-Americans through non-violent resistance and the courts. The civil rights movement itself continued to work toward full equality for all Americans. During the late 1960s and early 1970s other groups such as hippies, feminists, and environmentalists also made their dissatisfactions known.

College Student Protests   By the mid-1960s student unrest on college campuses was drawing more and more media coverage, particularly on television. Anti-war protests, demonstrations, and student strikes spread from campus to campus. *The New York Times* spoke of a student "revolt against conformity, boredom, and tediousness of middle-class life" and students began calling for a greater voice in college governance.

The Hippies   Another expression of youthful revolt against the values of the adult society, the hippie movement, surfaced in 1966. Young people, most of them from middle-class families, responded to the call from Timothy Leary, a proponent of the use of the drug LSD, to "turn on to the scene; tune into what's happening; and drop out of high school, college, grad school . . . ." Beginning in California in the Haight-Ashbury District of San Francisco, the movement, which became a drug-using subculture, spread across the country. The hippie philosophy stressed "love" and freedom from the constraints of "straight" society. On Easter Sunday, 1967, in Central Park in New York, 10,000 young people—not all of them hippies—gathered to honor love. In Philadelphia on May 15, of the same year, 2,500 hippies held a "Be-in," a gathering honoring the notion that everyone had the right to "be."

The Feminist Movement   The decade of the 60s saw the beginning of the feminist movement as many American women began to question traditional values. A call to action came with the publication of *The Feminine Mystique* by Betty Friedan in 1963. The author described the frustration of college educated women who were trapped in the routine of housework and child care. To Friedan the middle-class home was a "comfortable concentration camp" for women. Her book was a call for women to rethink their role in American life. The National Organization for Women (NOW), formed in 1966, announced a program calling for equal rights, equal opportunity, and an end to sex discrimination. In 1973 many women applauded the Supreme Court's decision in *Roe v. Wade* legalizing abortion on the basis of the "right to privacy." Earlier a sexual revolution had occurred when in 1960 the Food and Drug Administration had approved an oral contraceptive popularly known as "the pill."

The Environmental Movement   With the publication of Rachel Carson's book *The Silent Spring* in 1962, Americans became aware of the dangerous effects of the powerful pesticide DDT, which killed birds and wildlife as well as insects. Her book jolted American complacency about the environment and helped to ignite the environmental movement, which celebrated the first Earth Day in April 1970.

Environmentalists also recognized that hunting and loss of habitat through development posed a threat to a number of animal species. These animals were considered to be "endangered," and threatened with extinction. Among the animals that were considered to be endangered were American crocodiles, cheetahs, tigers, snow leopards, and Asiatic lions, all of which had pelts used for fashionable clothing and accessories. The United States passed the Endangered Species Act in 1973 to afford protection to such animals. International agreements were initiated in 1975. Taking advantage of the public awareness of the danger to wild animals posed by using their pelts for fur clothing, manufacturers of high pile synthetic fabrics created **fake furs** which were promoted as an environmentally sound alternative to real fur.

THE IMPACT OF SOCIAL CHANGE ON FASHION

Style Tribes and Street Styles

The notion of using dress to proclaim ideology or membership in a specific group did not originate in the 1960s. Throughout the history of dress some individuals have chosen to wear clothing that identifies them as members of a particular group. After fashion became a feature of Western dress, some groups deliberately avoided fashionable dress in order to show that they differed from the rest of society in religious or ideological beliefs (the Amish, the Quakers, and the Puritans), in artistic preferences (the Aesthetes), or in politics (the Sans Culottes of the French Revolution).

In the mid-20th century, subcultural dress was especially notable in the zoot suit of the 1930s and 40s (see *page 416*), in the late 1940s and 1950s with the Teddy boys in Britain (*Chapter 17, page 431*), and in the United States with the Beatniks of the 1950s and early 1960s (*page 430*). Most of these styles originated among the young who often congregated in groups on the street. As a result such fashions became known as **street styles.**

Writer Ted Polhemus (1994) in his book *Street Style*, labeled these sub-cultural groups **style tribes**. He says, "Style isn't just a superficial phenomenon. . . . encoded within its iconography are all those ideas and ideals which together constitute a (sub)culture. Like-looking is like-thinking and in this sense the members of a style tribe have a great deal in common."

This tendency for young people, especially adolescents, to identify with a particular group, and to try to set themselves apart from the mainstream culture through their dress

accelerated in the 1960s and 1970s. By 2003, street style and style tribes had become a major factor in fashion and significantly changed the way the fashion system operates. Although street styles were intended to make a statement about being different from the mainstream, these counter-cultural fashions also provided nourishment for the fashion industry, ever-hungry for new ideas. See *pages 504–508* for a discussion of style tribes of 1980 to 2003.

Some Style Tribes of 1960–1980

THE MODS

The **Mods** and the **Rockers** were groups of young people in Britain in the mid-1960s. Rockers were rough and tough, rode motorcycles, and wore black leather jackets. They vied with the Mods, who were "up for love, self-expression, poetry, and getting stoned." The Mod fashion statement was "elegance, long hair, granny glasses, and Edwardian finery" (McCloskey 1970). In the contest for dominance over the allegiance of young Britons, the Mods won, and the importance of the Rockers gradually faded away.

The center of Mod activities was on Carnaby Street and on Portobello Road in London. The Beatles, then rising to fame in the popular music field, adopted mod-influenced clothing and, in turn, helped to spread the popularity of the style. One of the ideas described as central to the mod fashion concept was the notion that males as well as females were entitled to wear handsome and dashing clothing. (See *Figure 18.16, page 489.*) In 1965 McGregor, an American sportswear manufacturer, produced and distributed mod styles in the United States. Mod styles had good success at first, and much positive press notice. But by 1967, a sort of anti-mod backlash seemed to have caused the styles to lose favor, at least for a time (McCloskey 1970).

THE HIPPIES

In the meantime, the appearance of the hippies in the United States was also causing ripples in the fashion industry. Following the 1967 hippie gatherings, media coverage made the colorful hippie costume familiar: long hair, to the shoulders or longer, for men and women; beards, headbands, and love beads for men; long skirts and gypsy-like costume for women. Hippies assembled imaginative costumes from used clothing purchased in thrift shops. By 1968 Ken Scott, an American designer, had already designed a collection that included what he had called a "hippie gypsy look." (See *Color Plates 57 and 58.*)

Many young people who were not themselves hippies adopted elements of these styles. The young gathered together at popular music concerts, such as the Woodstock Music and Art Fair attended by 200,000 in August of 1969. The "beads, feathers, and bandannas" that some of them wore were copied by others. *Newsweek* (1969) magazine described

Woodstock as "different from the usual pop festival, not just a concert but a tribal gathering, expressing all the ideas of the new generation: communal living away from the cities, getting high, digging arts, clothes, and crafts exhibits, and listening to the songs of revolution."

Some young people joined communes or became involved in mystical religions led by gurus, religious teachers from India. This interest in Indian religions may have been a factor in the widespread popularity among young people of styles inspired or influenced by clothing from India.

By the close of the 1960s, mod styles had a resurgence. Both mod and hippie styles stressed long hair for men and women and greater color and imagination for men's clothing. Both were adopted, first by young people, and slightly later for mainstream fashion. *Esquire* magazine proclaimed a Peacock Revolution for men, and fancifully colored and styled garments ranging from underwear to evening wear appeared in the stores. (See *Color Plate 59.*)

ANTI-WAR PROTESTERS
AND THE ADOPTION OF JEANS

In the 1960s young people protesting against the establishment adopted blue jeans as a symbol of solidarity with working people. Richard Martin and Harold Koda (1989), in tracing the history of jeans as a symbol, point out that as early as 1950 they were "associated with the American West and disestablishment behavior" and in the play and subsequent movie *Blue Denim* of 1955 they were "associated with youth and rebellion." The association with the counter-culture was dramatized for the American public in the 1960s when jeans became a sort of uniform for the young, anti-war protesters. Young people began to use jeans as a medium of self-expression. They embroidered designs on them, added patches and painted messages.

It was not long before the fashion industry had turned these work pants cum protest uniform into a hot fashion item. By 1970 jeans had become an international success. Young Americans traveling behind the Iron Curtain where Western goods were not available reported that they could trade their blue jeans for enormous quantities of local goods.

PUNK STYLES

Striving to dramatize their alienation through their garb, young devotees of so-called "punk" rock music in 1977 began wearing "messy, baggy, ripped up clothes." Boys generally wore black leather. Girls wore micro-minis with black fishnet stockings. Fabrics were purposely made with holes, tears, and stains. Accessories included safety pins, worn as earrings or through the skin, and razor blades. Punks wore black eye makeup, two-toned purple lips, and hair painted green, yellow, and red. (See *Color Plate 61.*)

British fashion designer Zandra Rhodes quickly incorporated punk ideas into her 1977 collection, bringing punk style to a wider audience. Punk styles never dominated mainstream fashion, but remained as a viable alternative among some young people even after the millennium.

The Women's Movement

Feminists in the 19th century supported dress reform because they viewed women's clothing as being a means of limiting their freedom. Some feminists in the 1960s also saw clothing as symbolizing oppression. To dramatize their liberation from social as well as physical constraints and to protest against the Miss America contest, which they saw as glorifying women for their beauty alone, a few feminists demonstrated and burned brassieres outside of the pageant in Atlantic City in the fall of 1968.

While the majority of women did not abandon brassieres, many women no longer wore corsets, and underclothing became much less confining. Many bra styles were less rigid, molded from knitted synthetic fibers rather than cut and sewn to produce maximum uplift, as in the 1950s.

Some of the fashion developments in the late 1960s and the 1970s have been viewed as symbolic of changes in women's roles. Examples cited are the acceptance, especially by young people, of garments for men and women that are similar such as blue jeans and T-shirts and pantsuits, which became an important component of women's wardrobes in the 1970s (see *Figure 18.1*), and the aforementioned changes in undergarments.

The Civil Rights Movement

Along with the accomplishments of the civil rights movement of the 1960s, came a new consciousness of African culture, traditions, and art that was expressed in the phrases "Black pride" and "Black is beautiful." Many African-Americans adopted styles in dress that reflected this interest in their African heritage, wearing traditional African garments such as **dashikis,** collarless, wide shirts with kimono-type sleeves, and caftans, similar garments in longer lengths. These and other garments were fabricated from textiles made in traditional designs, such as **kente cloth** (complex, elaborate, multicolored, woven designs made on narrow strip-looms by Ashanti men in Bonwire, Ghana, which is expensive and highly prized), mud cloth (in which mineral-containing earth is used to produce designs), tie-and-dye fabrics, and handsome embroideries. (See *Color Plate 66.*)

The **afro** hairstyle, full and fluffy and taking advantage of the curl natural to the hair of many African-Americans, was widely adopted by both men and women in the late 1960s and early 1970s and has remained a popular style ever since. Styles in afros have changed periodically. By 1976 afros were cut shorter, and closer to the head. **Corn-row braids,** a traditional African way of arranging the hair in myriad small braids, were worn by women in the 1970s and after. (See *Illustrated Table 18.2, page 476.*)

FIGURE 18.1

Example of "unisex" styles, 1968. (Courtesy, Corbiss-Bettman.)

Jewelry was constructed in traditional designs, much of it imported from Africa, and utilized materials native to Africa: amber, ivory, and ebony.

Initially those African-Americans who wanted to make a statement of their pride in being black wore African-inspired clothing both at home and on the job. By the mid-1970s, these clothes were more likely to be worn at home as leisure wear or for social occasions.

African-inspired fashions penetrated the mass market. In a film called *10,* white movie actress Bo Derek wore her hair in cornrow braids. (See *Illustrated Table 18.2.*) When black women had adopted the style in the 1970s it was said to take from two to six hours to arrange the cornrows, and cost $50. Later when this style was being promoted as a part of mainstream fashion around 1980, it was said to take up to 10 hours to arrange, and cost $300!

From the period of the civil rights movement of the 1960s onward, African-Americans have had and continue to have a strong impact on contemporary fashion. Black fashion models began to appear as models in high fashion magazines in the 1960s, and gradually, over time, newspapers and magazines have come to include greater racial and ethnic diversity in the presentation of fashion illustrations. Over the same period a number of African-American fashion designers have risen to the top levels of American fashion design. In 1992 Fashion Institute of Technology in New York City recognized their contributions in an exhibit of outstanding designs by African-American fashion designers.

OTHER INFLUENCES IN FASHION

See *Table 18.1* for a summary of media influences on fashion: 1960–1980.

The White House Influences Styles

Political leaders often become style leaders. This has been true of royalty for centuries, and is often true today for political leaders, especially if they are considered attractive. Media coverage has made it possible for personalities to be seen at work and at play. This was the case with the Kennedy family. John Kennedy went bare headed to his inaugural in 1961, after which hat use among men declined. Mrs. Kennedy became a major influence on styles. The press paid close attention to her inaugural ball gown. (See *Figure 18.2.*) Bouffant hairstyles, pillbox hats, A-line skirts, low-slung pumps, empire style evening dresses, and wraparound sunglasses were some styles associated with her. She remained a fashion leader in the years after she was no longer the First Lady. The Ford, Nixon, and Carter families were not seen as major influences on fashion.

Political Events

Political events, as well as political figures, may influence fashion. Among the influences from the Vietnam War were the adoption of jeans by youthful anti-war activists and some military-inspired clothing. *Newsweek* magazine published an article on July 12, 1971, that described a "Vietnam vogue" seen in St. Tropez, France, which consisted of army-style clothing. *The New York Times* reported interest in army fatigues in 1975

Table 18.1

SOME MEDIA INFLUENCES ON FASHION: 1960–1980

Media	Dates	Style Influences
Motion Pictures	1960s	French actress *Brigitte Bardot:* long hair, knee length boots.
	1970s	*The Last Picture Show, Grease, American Graffiti:* revival of 1950s styles.
Television	1960s	Television news shows pictures of hippies, anti-war protesters, and their (initially) unique clothing.
Popular Music Performers	1960s	*The Beatles:* long hair, mod style outfits worn for performances.
Popular music concerts and festivals such as Woodstock	1969	Opportunities to exchange fashion information.

and *Gentlemen's Quarterly,* a men's fashion magazine, featured United States navy-style pea jackets in the same year.

When Richard Nixon announced his intention to go to China in 1972, Chinese-influenced styles began appearing at once. These ranged from actual Chinese clothing to textiles, accessories, design motifs, and adaptations of Chinese styles. (See *Figure 18.3.*)

The Space Age

Some fashions of the 1960s reflected interest in the growing aerospace developments. After the Russian launching of *Sputnik* in 1957, the United States and other major industrialized nations moved quickly to develop their own space programs. Fashion design in the mid-1960s reflected these developments both directly and indirectly. Couturier André Courrèges showed what he called a "Space Age collection" in 1964. Fashion models wore helmets, and the lines were "precise and unadorned" and the shapes geometrical.

Designers used materials similar to those required for the technological advances that accompanied space exploration. New materials such as Velcro®, a nylon tape that was used for closures, appeared. Paco Rabanne made dresses of square pieces of plastic held together with metal rings; vinyl was used for rainwear and for outerwear. The most extreme of these styles were not widely adopted, but the clean, geometric lines, and plastic jewelry and accessories in geometric shapes were often seen.

FIGURE 18.2

Drawings from the Associated Press show three items of evening wear worn by Jacqueline Kennedy for the inaugural festivities in 1961. They are from left to right: a white silk ottoman gown designed by Oleg Cassini for the inaugural gala; a slim sheath for the Inaugural Ball of *peau d'ange* silk under chiffon, the silver-embroidered bodice visible under a transparent overblouse of white chiffon, designed by Bergdorf Goodman; and an evening wrap designed by Bergdorf Goodman; and an evening wrap designed by Bergdorf Goodman to be worn with the Inaugural Ball gown. This sweeping cape is made of *peau d'ange* completely covered with three layers of white chiffon, and the simple stand-up collar fastens with two buttons. (Courtesy, Fairchild Publications.)

The Fine Arts

Op art (short for optical art) and **Pop art** (short for popular art) entered the art world during the 1960s. Pop art featured glorified representations of ordinary objects such as soda cans and cartoon figures. Op art created visual illusions through largely geometric patterns. The op art designs translated readily into fabric, and soon appeared in fabrics for clothing. (See *Figure 18.4.*) Saint Laurent placed large, Pop art influenced designs on straight, black dresses.

The geometric lines were also evident in fashions that used the paintings of the early 20th century Dutch painter Pict Mondrian as inspiration. The most famous of these was Saint Laurent's 1965 "Mondrian dress," which was widely copied. (See *Color Plate 56.*) Both Art Deco and Art Nouveau designs were also revived.

FIGURE 18.3

Chinese-inspired designs for children's clothing, 1971. (*Women's Wear Daily*, September 20, 1971. Courtesy, Fairchild Publications.)

FIGURE 18.4

Op art printed fabric designs from the 1960s.

In the 1970s, museum "blockbuster" exhibitions excited designers and the public. The discovery of the tomb of the Egyptian King Tutankhamen in the 1920s had served as a catalyst for Egyptian-inspired designs. In the mid-1970s a major show of the treasures from the tomb of King Tutankhamen opened in London, then traveled around the world, and in its wake jewelry, makeup, and some clothing items of Egyptian derivation appeared. (See *Illustrated Table 18.4, page 484.*)

The 1970s also saw the origin of a combination of clothing and fiber art in what was known as **wearable art** that probably had its antecedents in the decoration of the textiles used for clothing by hippies. Artists who created wearable art used and often combined a variety of techniques such as crocheting, knitting, embroidery, piecing, special dyeing techniques, and painting on cloth. They used feathers, beads, layers, and slashing. Each garment created was a unique work of art. (See *Color Plate 65.*)

Ethnic Looks

Fashion designers seemed to be looking everywhere for design inspiration. Another source that they tapped was ethnic clothing. Design inspiration came from a variety of sources such as Native American dress, styles from countries such as India, from traditional Eastern European folk costume,

and from the aforementioned African-inspired styles. See *Color Plate 62.*

THE CHANGING FASHION INDUSTRY

How and why fashions change has been a matter of debate among scholars. One of the most widely accepted theories about fashion change is the so-called **trickle-down theory** in which, it is suggested, upper-class individuals initiate styles. These styles are then imitated by the next, lower class within the society. Their clothing, in turn, is imitated by a still lower class. As the highest class individuals see the styles they have originated being copied by those they consider inferior in social status, they change these styles, and the cycle of imitation begins again.

From the Medieval period, when fashion seems to have first become an important factor in the development of clothing styles in Western Europe, until the 1960s this explanation worked reasonably well. By the 20th century, a vast fashion industry had developed that expedited the design, manufacture, and distribution of clothing to all social classes except the abject poor or cultural subgroups that rejected modern, fashionable dress.

Increasing Variety in Fashion Segments

In the 1960s, some popular styles seemed to originate not with the well-to-do but with less affluent individuals and with style tribes or subcultures such as the hippies in the United States and the mods in Britain. Some have called this phenomenon the **bottom-up theory,** in contrast with "trickle down."

The explanation of the causes of fashion change is undoubtedly more complex than either the "trickle down" or "bottom up" theories would suggest. Even as early as the 1920s, clothing for men and women could be seen as becoming more diversified. In previous centuries, fashionable dress could fairly easily be divided between everyday dress and dress for special social occasions. By the 20th century, men and women had added clothing for active sports to their wardrobes. As more women entered the work force in larger numbers, they bought clothing suitable for work. Shortly before World War II, psychologists developed the concept of a stage of development that they called "adolescence," and clothing with certain unique features was manufactured for this age group. Adolescents were seen as prone to fad behavior in which an element or item of clothing had a short, very intense burst of popularity. *Seventeen* magazine reported in 1965 that teenage girls bought 20 percent of all apparel and 23 percent of all cosmetics sold in the United States, but represented only 11 percent of the population (Schnurnberger 1991).

After World War II, fashionable dress might be compared to a tree trunk that continually divided into more and more branches, each branch representing a different segment of the buying public. Until the mid-1960s, it was still possible to see a predominant fashion silhouette that influenced the various categories of clothing: daytime, evening, casual sportswear, outdoor clothing, underwear, and so forth. About 1970 the fashion press, led by the influential trade publication *Women's Wear Daily,* insisted that the midi skirt was destined to replace the miniskirt. The **midi skirt,** also called the **longuette,** was a mid-calf length skirt. Refusal to accept the proposed new

styles now spread to mainstream fashion consumers. Many women rejected the style. Groups such as GAMS (Girls Against Midi Skirts) held anti-midi skirt parades. Consequently retailers were able to sell only a small part of the large stocks of midi skirts that had been ordered. The fashion press spoke of a period when "anything goes" and declared that fashion was dead. (See *Figure 18.11, page 481.*)

Attempts to Curb Fashion Changes

Violation of established norms in dress can cause individuals or groups to feel threatened, especially if the "radical" new styles are adopted by groups that question existing social values or seek to challenge the *status quo.* Many of the changes in fashion that began in the United States in the 1960s did just that. Authority was being challenged by "kids" in long hair, African-Americans in dashikis and afros, women in pantsuits, and girls in short, short skirts.

In many offices, managers forbade women to wear pants to work. Women wearing pantsuits were not admitted to fashionable restaurants. (*Contemporary Comments 18.1* chronicles the attempts in 1966 of a *Women's Wear Daily* reporter wearing a pantsuit to be admitted to chic Manhattan restaurants.) Boys with long hair and girls wearing miniskirts and/or pants were expelled from school. African-American women who adopted afro styles were subjected to "humiliation and jokes from co-workers about the afro resembling a porcupine." Some employers insisted that women with afro haircuts wear wigs to work (Giddings 1990).

In one unemployment office benefits were denied in 1970 to men whose hair was below their ears and women who wore miniskirts because the unemployment office supervisor deemed them to be "unemployable" and therefore ineligible for benefits. A professional ball player was suspended because he had long hair, and a transit officer because he had a beard. One junior high school student, who wore a long maxi skirt to commencement instead of one of the miniskirts her classmates had selected, was denied participation in commencement (Klemesrud 1970).

Legal challenges overturned most such restrictions, and by the early 1970s the "radical" new styles had become mainstream fashion.

Changes in Fashion Design

In the 1960s, a group of young designers who had trained under men like Dior and Balenciaga left these established couture houses and opened their own establishments. The most successful of these young men were Yves Saint Laurent, Pierre Cardin, André Courrèges, and Emmanuel Ungaro. In the mid-1960s, after becoming established in the haute couture, most of these designers expanded in the direction of ready-to-wear (or as the French call it, **prêt-à-porter**). Both Cour-

CONTEMPORARY COMMENTS 18.1

Fashionable Restaurants Reject Pantsuits

In "Pants and Prejudice," published in Women's Wear Daily, *October 17, 1966,*
Toni Kosover recounts the difficulties of finding a fashionable New York City restaurant that would
allow her admission in her new pantsuit.

Women can wear the pants but they can't go very far. What's left when you can't eat at the Colony . . . can't dance at El Morocco, and you can't even get through the door at "21."

We tried and even though it hurts us to admit it, we failed. Even in a simple elegant black crepe pantsuit by Victor Joris of Cuddlecoat, we failed. Can you imagine nothing but rejection almost all night long. And just on the basis of appearance.

How sad.

How unsophisticated.

How downright prejudiced.

It starts the other night with our dinner reservation at the Colony. Gene Cavallero just takes one swift glance at the pantsuit.

"I'm sorry but we can't serve you."

"But we have a reservation."

"I am sorry but we can't serve any woman in pants."

"Not even if we sit at a table in the back?"

"No, I'm sorry, if we make an exception this time, we will have to do it all the time." . . .

Who would take us in? Offer us a bit of French cuisine? Perhaps La Cote Basque understands the Modern Woman. . . .

Raymond said, "no," so nicely.

"We don't want any part of it. No one ever tries to come in here in pants. It's not that we are worried about beatniks. To tell you the truth, I prefer women without pants."

And we move back into the night.

At this point we were willing to settle for a drink. Maybe the St. Regis would accept us. It looks hopeful. They watch us skeptically as we glide across the almost empty room. No problems. They serve our drinks. Only it's quiet here and we are still hungry.

. . . we drive up to La Caravelle . . . They are looking us over.

A man at one table smiles. "Oh! Look . . . she's wearing slacks."

And then the maitre d', "The kitchen is closed, now."

Is it really closed, or was it the pantsuit? "It is a little too late for service, and it is not the policy of the house to serve women in pants," says the man. . . .

Before going to El Morocco we stop at "21," where we can barely get in the door before Gary stands before us with his arms crossed and says, "No." . . .

El Morocco is really no better. Angelo has to confer with a couple of others. Finally we tell them we are doing a story . . . and they give us a table which just misses the door by an inch. "If we make an exception for you, we will have all sorts in pants. The drinks are on the house but, please, . . . no dancing and no pictures." . . .

Later on we all go to Yellowfingers, which welcomes us—pantsuit and all. . . .

Which only goes to prove the pantsuit does stand a chance if individuality and fun ever replace status symbols and staring.

règes and Saint Laurent designed lines of ready to wear in the mid-1960s. Cardin had opened a men's wear boutique in 1957 and turned his design expertise to a variety of other products as well. In the years since this radical alteration was made in the operation of some of the couture houses, the Paris pret-a-porter group has become so important that the fashion press goes to Paris not only for the regular shows of the haute couture but also for the opening of the pret-a-porter collections. The successful ready-to-wear industry in the United States had provided a model for a new business venture for the French couture designers. In turn, the prêt-à-porter pro-

vided a new source of fashion ideas for the American fashion industry.

By the late 1960s, franchised boutiques, a new aspect of merchandising of the ready-to-wear designs by couturiers, had emerged. These retail boutiques were either owned and operated by the couture house, or by independent merchandisers who purchased a franchise and the right to sell the designer's products in a store that carried the designer's name or trade name. For example, Saint Laurent opened the first ready-to-wear boutique in Paris in 1964 under the trade name *Rive Gauche*.

Ready-to-wear design had a long history in the United States, but except for some individual designers such as Hattie Carnegie, Claire McCardell, Norman Norell, or Pauline Trigere who gained a loyal following in the 1940s, 1950s, and 1960s, most American fashion designers had been anonymous, working for manufacturers whose trademarks were known to the public. By the 1970s, this had changed. Not only were designer labels a major factor in selling products, but designer-owned firms also became more common. Customers came to know and look for the clothing produced by individual designers whose styles they preferred.

In Italy after World War II, Rome, Florence, and Milan had organized couture houses that showed collections semi-annually. In the mid-1970s, the Italian ready-to-wear industry started to hold showings in Milan.

Except for some of the startling designs derived from punk styles by Zandra Rhodes around 1977, the 1970s had been a relatively quiet period for English design, with a return to classic tailoring and promotion of high-quality cotton products from firms such as Liberty of London and Laura Ashley.

See *Table 18.2* Influential Designers in Paris and Other Fashion Centers: 1960–1980.

Labeling and Licensing

In the late 1970s so-called **designer jeans** were produced by well-known designers. Almost twice as expensive as regular jeans, designer jeans prominently displayed the name of the designer on the posterior of the wearer. With the popularity of designer blue jeans and other logos such as the LaCoste alligator, labels or logos placed on the exterior of garments became a major selling point. The status element in designer labels led to counterfeiting of designer-labeled products.

As labels became more important in promoting products, the practice of **licensing** a designer's name for use on a wide variety of products also expanded. Licensing has been part of American business ever since the early 20th century when the cartoon character Buster Brown and his dog Tige became enormously popular. With the advent of TV, opportunities for licensing increased. Beginning in the 1950s and continuing into the new millennium, licensing has been especially prevalent in, though certainly not limited to, children's clothing. Cartoon characters and sports figures, team names, and other logos appeared on all kinds of garments.

Designers of Men's Clothing

Until the 1960s, internationally known fashion designers created women's clothing. Well-to-do men patronized custom tailors. Certain brand-name items and particular retailers were known for the quality of their merchandise and classic styling. But this was changing. Pierre Cardin had begun to design for men in 1957, and designer John Weitz opened a boutique for men in 1965. Soon others joined them. From this point onward designer styles for men became increasingly important. Throughout the 1970s the practice that had begun in the 1960s for well-known designers to produce a line of men's clothing accelerated, and designer clothes for men became a permanent part of men's fashion.

COSTUME FOR WOMEN: 1960–1980

For the first years of the decade of the 1960s, styles showed some uncertainty. Skirts shortened gradually, a trend that had begun in the late 1950s. The earliest examples of new styles were either straight and unfitted or princess style with a slight A-line in which the waist was loosely defined. The **skimmer,** a sleeveless, princess-line style was a popular example of the latter form. The empire waistline experienced a brief revival around 1960.

By 1964 the transition from New Look–influenced styles to an easy, unfitted line was well established. Gradually shortening skirts had climbed to as much as two inches above the knee in the United States in 1966. The term **miniskirt** was coined to describe these skirts, and the term **micro mini** was applied to the shortest of the short skirts.

All kinds of clothes for women and girls from dresses to evening dresses and outdoor clothing had unfitted, short silhouettes. By the end of the 1960s, the fashion industry introduced the **maxi,** a full-length style, and the midi, a skirt that ended about mid-calf. However, these styles were not widely worn, and the transition to a new length and silhouette was still several years away in the mid-1970s.

It was during this period that pants gained acceptability not only as appropriate garments for leisure, but also for all occasions. Blue jeans, first worn by the hippies, then picked up by the young, were adopted by mainstream fashion and by 1970 were being worn by both sexes and all ages. Pantsuits were worn for work and leisure, and soon after the fashion industry produced other types of pants: knickers, gaucho pants, and hot pants.

Costume for Women: 1960–1974

GARMENTS

Brassieres, underpants, slips, and girdles continued to be the most common items of women's underwear. They were made in solid colors and restrained prints in the first part of the decade.

Table 18.2

INFLUENTIAL DESIGNERS IN PARIS AND OTHER FASHION CENTERS: 1960–1980

Designer	Name of Firm and Date of its Opening	Notable Characteristics of Designs or Career
PARIS		
André Courrèges (1923–)	Courréges, 1961. Retired 1995. The firm continues.	Associated with "space-age" influences. Ideas included low-heeled white boots, industrial zippers, hard-line minidresses in the 1960s, more feminine styles in the 1970s.
Jules-François Crahay (1917–1988)	Chief designer for Nina Ricci, 1954–1964; head designer at Lanvin, 1964–1984 when he retired and started a ready-to-wear firm.	"Young, uninhibited, civilized clothes"; made glamorous evening pants, jeweled gaucho pants, lavish evening gowns.
Emmanuelle Khanh (1938–)	Especially known for inexpensive ready-to-wear in the 1960s. In 2002, the firm was bought by France Luxury Group.	Very influential in late 1960s among the young, continued to work in 1970s and 1980s in highly individual styles.
Guy Laroche (1923–1990)	Laroche, 1957	Most notice in the couture came in the early 1960s; "back cowl drapes, short puffed hems for evening . . ."
Paco Rabanne (1934–)	Rabanne, 1966. Relinquished creative control of his firm in 2000.	Known for garments made from geometric plastic shapes held together with metal rings. In the 70s combined other unusual materials.
Yves Saint Laurent (1936–)	Chief designer for Dior, 1957–1958; opened own house Yves Saint Laurent, 1962. Limited himself to couture after sale of the fashion house in 1993; retired in 2002.	Originated many innovative styles; trademark looks included the fisherman's shirt, 1962; trapeze, 1965; see-through blouse, 1968; longuette, 1970; tuxedo dress, 1978; and others. Sometimes called "The King of Fashion" for his preeminent place in the couture.
Emanuel Ungaro (1933–)	Ungaro, first couture collection, 1965; later entered ready-to-wear market as well. After 2001 he did only couture.	Known for geometric, straight and A-line shapes in the 1960s; 1970s and 1980s styles softer and "more body conscious."
Valentino (c. 1932–)	Valentino, first success, 1962; showed ready-to-wear in Paris from 1975 shows couture in Rome.	"Noted for refined simplicity, elegantly tailored coats and suits." Also designs men's wear.
ITALY		
Princess Irene Galitzine	First show, 1959; continued to 1968, then sporadically for several years in the early 1970s.	Introduced palazzo pajamas, 1960. Other noted designs include: "at-home togas, evening suits, open-sided evening gowns."
Rosita and Ottavio Tai Missoni	Missoni, c. 1953. Children continue to operate the business.	Especially known for timeless knits with distinctive colors and patterns.
Emilio Pucci (1914–1992)	Couture house called Emilio, 1950. Firm bought and reopened in 2002.	Noted for distinctive, colorful prints. Interest in the prints revived in 1990s. (See *Color Plate 60*.)
Mila Schoen	Mila Schoen, 1959 in Milan and Rome. Showed couture collection in Paris in 1991. Remained active after selling business in 1994.	Known for high-quality design and workmanship in women's clothing, men's wear, and swimsuits. Active in 1960s, 1970s, 1980s, 1990s.

Table 18.2
INFLUENTIAL DESIGNERS IN PARIS AND OTHER FASHION CENTERS: 1960–1980

Designer	Name of Firm and Date of its Opening	Notable Characteristics of Designs or Career
GREAT BRITAIN		
Jean Muir (1933–1995)	Worked for Liberty, Jaeger; under her own label Jane and Jane, 1962; Jean Muir Inc., 1967.	"Characteristics: soft, classic, tailored shapes in leathers or soft fabrics."
Mary Quant (1934–)	Opened boutique and began designing in late 1950s. Still active in 2003.	Influential designs in the Mod styles of the 1960s, the miniskirts of the later 1960s. A major factor in making London a fashion center in the 1960s.
UNITED STATES		
Adolfo (1933–)	Opened his own millinery firm, 1962; added then switched to apparel. Apparel design business now closed, but licensing continues.	Known for Chanel-inspired knits. Also does men's wear.
Geoffrey Beene (1927–2004)	Samuel Winston and Harmay, 1949–1957; Teal Traina, where his name was put on the label, 1958–1962. Opened his own business in 1962. Closed wholesale business in 2001, continued to sell to private clients.	"Simplicity, emphasis on cut and line, dressmaking details, and unusual fabrics." Expanded into accessories, men's wear, and licensing.
Bill Blass (1922–2002)	After World War II, became head designer for Maurice Rentner Ltd.; eventually became owner and changed the name to Bill Blass, Ltd. Continues under other designers.	"Noted for women's classic sportswear in men's wear fabrics, elegant mixtures" of patterns and fabrics, and very feminine, glamorous evening wear that contrasts with more mannish day wear. Has design interests in a wide variety of products carrying his name.
Bonnie Cashin (1915–2000)	Worked as freelance designer since 1953; started The Knittery for hand knits, 1967.	Specialized in functional clothing, innovative designs especially in outerwear, used knits, tweeds, canvas, and leather.
Oscar de la Renta (1932–)	After working in Paris and New York, opened own business after 1965. Designed for House of Balmain from 1992 to 2002, when he retired but continues to design a New York collection.	Created luxury ready-to-wear; known for "opulent fabrics" for evening wear and "sophisticated and feminine day wear." A variety of other products also carry his name.
Rudi Gernreich (1922–1985)	Worked in California.	Particularly known for sport clothes and for radical styling including a topless swimsuit, and see-through blouses, "no-bra" bras in the 1960s.
Roy Halston Frowick (1932–1990) Frowick	Designed under name, Halston. Opened own business 1968 for private clients, ready-to-wear in 1972. The firm name was revived in 1997.	"His formula of casual throwaway chic, using superior fabrics for extremely simple classics made him most talked about designer in early 1970s."
Charles Kleibacker	Started his own company, 1963.	Maintained a small business where he could keep control of the making of the bias cut styles for which he was especially known.

Table 18.2 (*continued*)

INFLUENTIAL DESIGNERS IN PARIS AND OTHER FASHION CENTERS: 1960–1980

Designer	Name of Firm and Date of its Opening	Notable Characteristics of Designs or Career
Anne Klein (1923–1974)	Formed Junior Sophisticates, (1951–1964); Anne Klein & Co., 1968. After her death other designers worked under her label.	Noted in the 1960s for "classic blazers, shirtdresses, long midis, leather gaucho pants, . . . and slinky hooded jersey dresses for evening."
Calvin Klein (1942–)	Calvin Klein Ltd., 1968. His "designer" blue jeans important in the 1970s. Markets a wide variety of products under Calvin Klein label. Company sold in 2002.	"Considered the foremost exponent of spare, intrinsically American style . . . refined sportswear-based shapes in luxurious natural fabrics such as cashmere, linen, and silk . . . color preferences are earth tones and neutrals."
Ralph Lauren (1939–)	Polo line of men's wear, 1967; for women, 1971; and other spin-off firms later. The Polo and Ralph Lauren names are licensed to a number of products.	Came to prominence with wide neckties, known for work with natural fabrics, Western influences, outdoor wear. ". . . classic silhouette, superb fabrics, and fine workmanship . . . attitude is well-bred and confident."
Giorgio Sant'Angelo (1936–1989)	Sant'Angelo Ready-to-Wear, 1966; di Sant'Angelo Inc., 1968. Licensing continued after his death.	"Noted for ethnic themes" and designs "a bit out of the ordinary."
Arnold Scaasi (1931–)	Did ready-to-wear in New York, 1960; switched to couture, 1963; returned to ready-to-wear, 1983 and closed it in 1994, concentrating on made-to-order designs.	"Known for spectacular evening wear in luxurious fabrics."
Diane Von Furstenberg (1947–)	Diane Von Furstenberg label.	Made major impact in 70s with jersey knitted wrap-around dress with surplice closing. Left the field from 1977 to 1985, then reentered, designing dresses and eveningwear. Moved into telemarketing, and again into design in 1997.

Information about designers already listed in Tables 17.1 and 17.2 (see *pages 434* and *436*), who continued to be active for all or part of this period is not included in this table.

All material in quotes comes from Calasibetta, C. M. (1988). *Fairchild's Dictionary of Fashion,* 2nd edition. New York: Fairchild Publications and Stegemeyer, A. (1996). *Who's Who in Fashion,* 3rd edition. New York: Fairchild Publications.

A new garment, part hosiery, part underwear, was introduced. Sheer, nylon **pantyhose** were first marketed about 1960 as an alternative to nylon stockings held up with a garter belt or girdle. (The Sears mail-order catalog carried them in 1961.) Structured in the same way as the opaque, knitted tights worn by dancers, these garments joined underpants and stocking into one garment, and became a virtual necessity as skirts became shorter. See *Illustrated Table 18.1,* for examples of undergarments from the period between 1960 and 1980.

With the advent of short skirts after styles changed in the 1960s, underwear took on a new importance. Wide legged panties were sometimes worn instead of a slip. Undercloth-ing was manufactured in vivid and striking colors and prints. (See *Color Plate 55.*)

The distinction between underwear, footwear, and outerwear became less clear as new garments appeared that combined outerwear and underwear and, sometimes, extended from neck to toe, eliminating the need for stockings. These garments included:

- **body stockings,** which were body-length, knitted stretch underwear.
- **body suits,** similar garments that usually ended at the top of the leg. Some extended from shoulder to toe. Of-

Illustrated Table 18.1

SELECTED UNDERGARMENTS FOR WOMEN, MEN, AND CHILDREN: 1960–1980

Designer Rudi Gernreich's "No-Bra" bra in nude tricot for Exquisite Form manufacturer, 1969[1]

Bikini pants and bra, 1969[2]

Bodysuits served as both underwear (1969) and outerwear (1973)[3]

Slip, underpants, and girdle, 1969[4]

patterned pantyhose, 1967[5]

Left to right: men in jockey shorts and T-shirt, boxer shorts and athletic shirt, long thermal underwear[6]

[1] *Women's Wear Daily,* December 10, 1969. Fairchild Publications.
[2] *Women's Wear Daily,* march 6, 1969. Fairchild Publications.
[3] Fairchild Publications.
[4] *Women's Wear Daily,* July 31, 1969. Fairchild Publications.
[5] *Women's Wear Daily,* December 14, 1967. Fairchild Publications.
[6] *Men's Wear,* January 9, 1968. Fairchild Publications.

ten body suits were designed to be worn with the upper section visible as or instead of a blouse. Said one fashion writer, the body suit "takes the place of bra, panties, panty girdle, pantyhose, and a blouse or sweater" (*The New York Times* 1971). (See *Illustrated Table 18.1.*)

The ancestor of many of these garments was the leotard, a two-piece, knitted, body-hugging garment worn by French acrobat Jules Leotard in the 19th century. Dancers and acrobats adopted this costume, but until a brief introduction of the garment by Claire McCardell in 1943 that did not catch on, it had never been part of fashionable dress.

Hippies and some radical feminists rejected brassieres. Some women ceased wearing bras, others bought the "no-bra bra," a design originated by Rudi Gernreich in 1964, which was the underwear manufacturers answer to the desire of many women for a brassiere that didn't appear to be there. (See *Illustrated Table 18.1.*) The use of girdles diminished.

Acceptance of a new line in suit styles had come earlier than for dresses. By the late 1950s, these were generally made with loosely fitted jackets. One of the more important suits of the 1960s was Chanel's braid-trimmed, collarless, cardigan-style jacket with three-quarter length sleeves, A-line skirt, and blouse with a bow tie at the neck and sleeves extending a little beyond the jacket sleeves. (See *Figure 18.5.*)

When the first chemises of the late 1950s had been introduced, dresses had a rather soft, draped appearance. (See *Figure 17.12, page 447.*) By the mid-1960s, many dresses tended to have a harder line. (See *Figure 18.6.*) Dresses with bodices joined to skirts were uncommon. Some notable silhouettes for dress styles included:

· empire waistlines (around 1960)
· A-line shapes with dresses flaring slightly from neck to hem
· dresses cut straight and loose from shoulder to hem
· dresses falling straight from a yoke at the shoulder
· dresses unfitted through the torso and with a flounce joined to the hem of the dress at the knee

The most fashionable length for skirted garments was above the knee, although more conservative women rarely wore knee-baring styles. Most garments were loosely fitted, without waistline definition. In the early 1970s, bright printed fabrics made from manufactured knitted fabrics were quite popular.

Long daytime dresses, known as **granny dresses,** were popular among the young in the early 1970s. They apparently derived from mod and hippie styles. Some had design elements that harked back to earlier historical periods, others were cut simply, with elasticized necks, waists, and sleeves. (See *Illustrated Table 18.5, page 493.*)

A fashion for sheer, see-through blouses and for dresses worn without underclothing was reported in the press. This had a limited following and did not spread beyond urban, cosmopolitan areas.

FIGURE 18.5

Chanel's classic cardigan-style suit which became very popular in the 1960s. Here worn by "Coco" Chanel. (Courtesy, Fairchild Publications.)

Illustrated Table 18.2

TYPICAL HAIRSTYLES AND HATS FOR WOMEN: 1960–1980

Pillbox, 1960

High-crowned,
hunter's cap, 1965[1]

A

B

Hats that revive earlier styles
(A) "Carole Lombard" head cap from the 1930s
(B) 1930s fedora style, 1969[2]

Brimmed velour hat
that ties under the chin, 1970,
worn over long, straight hair[3]

Knit ski cap, 1973[4]

Beret 1973[4]

[1] *Women's Wear Daily,* November 16, 1965. Fairchild Publications.
[2] *Women's Wear Daily,* January 1, 1968. Fairchild Publications.
[3] *Women's Wear Daily,* June 19, 1970. Fairchild Publications.
[4] *Women's Wear Daily,* May 5, 1973. Fairchild Publications.

A brief flurry of interest in **paper dresses** emerged in 1966. Scott Paper Company produced some paper dresses as part of a promotion of its other paper products. The manufacturer had no interest in manufacturing paper dresses, but the positive consumer response to the promotion was surprising, and other manufacturers quickly picked up on the idea. The uncomplicated, A-line, unfitted style lines and the vivid, colorful prints popular at this time made the production of acceptable paper styles possible. Interest was brief, however, and the demand for paper dresses declined quickly after 1968.

Matching pants and jackets were introduced just after the mid-1960s for daytime, business, and evening wear. Double knit polyester fabrics were often used for inexpensive pantsuits; wool double knits for more expensive versions. (See *Figure 18.1.*) By the late 1960s, pantsuits had surpassed skirted suits in popularity. At a time when controversy over skirt lengths was raging, wearing pants solved the problem of what length to wear very effectively!

Evening dresses were made in both long and short lengths, but short lengths were preferred. As the fitted styles

Illustrated Table 18.2 (*continued*)

TYPICAL HAIRSTYLES AND HATS FOR WOMEN: 1960–1980

Bouffant hairstyle, 1963[7]

Second half of the 1960s

Corn row braids, early 1960s

Soft, "natural" hairstyle,
1975–1980

Frizzy curls, late 1970s

Wedge, c. 1976

[7] *Vogue,* July 1963, drawing by Henry Koehler. Courtesy, *Vogue.* Copyright 1963 by Condé Nast Publications.

lost their popularity, elaborately beaded bodices or overblouses were worn with long skirts. (See *Figure 18.2.*) Trends included straight, short dresses, some in vivid prints (see *Color Plate 54*) and others made of metallic fabrics, or trimmed with sequins, paillettes of plastic, and/or beads. (See *Figure 18.7.*)

In the late 1960s, long evening dresses began to supplant shorter ones. Pantsuits of decorative fabrics with full-legged trousers were also worn for evening, as were wide-legged pants, made in soft fabrics, and given the fashion name **palazzo pajamas.** They vied with hostess gowns as appropriate to wear for entertaining at home, as well as for formal occasions. (See *Figure 18.8.*)

SPORTSWEAR

A gradual shift in skirt silhouettes occurred. Most tended to be A-line. Many had no waistband, but were finished with a facing instead. By the early 1970s, most skirts tended to be mini in length, in spite of heavy fashion promotion of the mid-calf length midi. A few midis were worn, and full-length maxis appeared occasionally for daytime wear, more often in the evening than for daytime.

In the early 1960s, knitted stretch pants with narrow legs were worn with straight or blouson tops, or knitted tops. Separate skirts and blouses were less important than in earlier decades, having been replaced to a large extent by pants and knit tops.

FIGURE 18.6

Styles from 1966 feature lengths well above the knee, and include designs by Hardy Amies, an English designer, for "five-seventh" length coat, and a dress and matching coat design that uses an op art-type pattern. A John Cavanaugh suit with a pleated skirt appears at upper right.

_____

Pants of all kinds, especially blue jeans were popular. The predominant style, called **hip huggers,** had wide, flaring or bell-bottom legs, fitted smoothly across the hip, and was often made with a facing rather than a waistband at the top. These pants were set lower on the hip than the anatomical waistline. The flared bottoms of bell-bottom pants derived from the shape of the pant legs of sailors' uniforms. These wide-legged trousers had been designed originally to make it easier for men who fell into the sea and needed to remove their clothing to swim, to pull off the trousers without catching them on their shoes. **Hot pants** (very short pants) were a feature of the early 1970s. (See *Figure 18.9.*)

Tight, figure-hugging, fitted blouses gave way to looser styles, many with straight lines. Turtlenecks were among the most popular separate tops. Their use corresponded with a general interest in knitted fabrics for easy-fitting tops worn over skirts and pants. Young women often wore turtlenecks with jumpers and tights that matched the jumper.

Popular sweater styles included **poorboy sweaters** or tightly fitting, rib-knit sweaters that looked as if they had shrunk. Matched cardigan and pullover sweater sets and mohair (the wool of the angora goat) sweaters were fashionable.

OUTDOOR GARMENTS

Coats tended to be straight and loose, with an easy fit through the shoulders and a rounded shoulderline. Some coats narrowed slightly toward the bottom or, alternately, had a slight A-shape. Up until the end of the decade, coats were short. Around 1970 midi, mini, and maxi lengths were all available. Long greatcoats in single- or double-breasted styles with belted and flared skirts in maxi lengths were inspired by the film *Doctor Zhivago* and its early 20th-century Russian styles. Coats in longer lengths were more successful than dresses or skirts. Some manufacturers made coats with horizontal zippers that allowed the wearer to zip off sections at each of the mini, midi, or maxi lengths.

Often coat sleeves had a slightly dropped shoulder, or were cut in one with the body of the coat. Most were wrist length or shorter.

Capes and ponchos, in short lengths, were popular in the late 1960s as were vinyl-coated fabrics for rainwear.

Emphasis on preservation of endangered fur-bearing animals caused some women and men to wear manufactured pile fabric imitations of fur. Such fabrics were called fake fur. Synthetic fibers were used in pile linings to add warmth. Zip-in linings remained popular, especially for rainwear.

CLOTHING FOR ACTIVE SPORTS

Women adopted leotards, long used by dancers for exercising, for aerobic exercises. The Danskin company had sold these garments for years at department store hosiery counters. Now sporting goods stores were carrying them in a variety of styles and colors and they were also being worn as tops with skirts. Terminology was not clear cut, and in the March 1979 issue of *Vogue* the editor noted that the terms body suit, maillot (a one-piece, knitted bathing suit), and leotard were being used interchangeably.

Leg warmers, loose-fitting footless stockings used by dancers to keep their legs warm during warm-up sessions, were worn for exercise sessions and also on the street, a sort of fad among young women.

For most of the 20th century, clothing has been manufactured that takes into account the special requirements of sports such as swimming, tennis, golf, and skiing. Considerable variety was evident in bathing suit styles. These ranged from two-piece bathing suits of relatively conservative cut to more scanty bikinis, which gradually became acceptable in the United States. Rudi Gernreich introduced a topless bathing suit in 1964 which he called a monokini. (See *Figure 18.10.*) Some one-piece bathing suits made in blouson, loosely fitted styles echoed the unfitted lines of dresses.

FIGURE 18.7

Typical evening wear from 1966 includes (left to right) white crepe dress with embroidered design down the front, white fox coat with white leather inserts and upstanding collar at the back, all-black velvet petals, bare-topped black silk organdy dress with tiered skirt, and high-necked, blue brocade dress with matching fox hem. (*Women's Wear Daily,* August 3, 1966. Courtesy, Fairchild Publications.)

FIGURE 18.8

Palazzo pajamas, c. 1968, in a distinctive print of the type originated by Italian designer Emilio Pucci.

More people took up downhill skiing. In the mid-1960s skiwear was made in bright colors and prints. By the late 1960s skiers were wearing warm-up pants and overalls with parkas. Synthetic and down fillings were quilted into ski jackets and other sportswear for warmth. Styles worn at the Olympic games influenced skiwear, and as Olympians looked for styles that enhanced speed, they adopted streamlined stretch knit ski pants. In 1968 Olympic skier Susie Chaffee wore a sleek, silver jumpsuit and began the trend toward one-piece **unitard** ski suits.

Knickers and knee-length socks, worn with sweaters and lightweight windbreakers, were appropriate for cross-country skiing, which was becoming popular.

On July 5, 1972, at the tennis matches at Wimbledon, England, Rosie Casals broke with the tradition of wearing white to play tennis. She appeared in a tennis dress decorated with purple scrolls. This marked the end of an era, and color entered professional tennis. From this point on, white tennis outfits required by tennis clubs were replaced with color-trimmed or colored garments. Tennis became an enormously popular sport, and in affluent suburban areas it was common to see women wearing tennis outfits for supermarket shopping.

By the late 1970s the quest for good health through fitness had led many men and women to jog, run, and work out. Manufacturers responded with new lines of warm-up suits, running and jogging clothing, and shoes, especially sneakers.

FIGURE 18.9

(a) Pantsuit by Gunter (left) and John Anthony (right), *Women's Wear Daily*, August 8, 1968. (b) "Midipants" that top at mid-calf (left) and knickers in suede with matching suede jacket (right), *Women's Wear Daily*, May 8, 1969. (c) Gaucho pants, *Women's Wear Daily*, May 7, 1968. (d) Various types of hot pants, *Women's Wear Daily*, October 15, 1970. (Courtesy, Fairchild Publications.)

FIGURE 18.10

Topless wool swimsuit called the monokini, designed for Harmon Knitwear in 1964 by Rudi Gernreich, whose designs were often startling. (*Women's Wear Daily*, December 10, 1969. Courtesy, Fairchild Publications.)

The popularity of professional sports led clothing manufacturers to feature famous athletes in endorsements, advertisements, and TV commercials for clothes and shoe styles based on sports uniforms.

SLEEPWEAR

The variety of sleepwear styles had increased in the late 1950s and 1960s. Short-legged pajamas, short nightshirts, and a wide range of colors and fabrics were added to more traditional styles. The varieties of sleepwear included colorful nylon nightgowns ranging in length from the floor to hip length, "shortie" gowns worn with matching panties, pajamas, and warm robes of synthetic pile fabrics and quilted nylon or polyester fabrics

HAIR AND HEADDRESS

See *Illustrated Table 18.2* for some examples of hairstyles and hats for the period from 1960 to 1980.

New, bouffant hairstyles, the fullness achieved by a technique of massing the hair called "backcombing" and/or the addition of artificial hair pieces became stylish in the early 60's. By the mid-1960s, girls and young women were allowing their hair to grow straight and long. Girls whose hair was not naturally straight pressed the curl out of their hair with clothes irons. The vogue for long, straight hair continued into the early 1970s.

French fashion designers Courrèges and Cardin and English designer Mary Quant had the hair of their models cut in almost geometric styles for their mid-decade collections. English hair stylist Vidal Sassoon also helped make the **geometric cut** a popular alternative to long hair.

More and more women elected to go hatless as a result of lifestyle changes. Bouffant hairstyles also discouraged the wearing of hats. Those hats that were worn included many with large crowns and small or no brims. Jacqueline Kennedy wore a pillbox hat designed by Halston to the presidential inauguration in 1961. The style was subsequently adopted by many women. However, hats never recovered the popularity they had before 1960 and, in general, were more used as practical head coverings for cold weather than as a fashionable accessory.

FOOTWEAR

See *Illustrated Table 18.3* for some examples of footwear worn in the period from 1960 to 1980.

Stockings without seams became popular after advances in technology for making nylon stockings made possible the construction of seamless stockings that fit the leg smoothly and without wrinkles. Pantyhose gained wide acceptance. Colored and textured stockings, pantyhose, or tights were worn with short skirts. Knee-length, colored socks were worn with miniskirts.

Heels lowered as skirts shortened. By the mid-1970s, toes were more rounded and less pointed. In the early 1970s, platform soles, ranging from small platforms to enormously high ones, were added to all kinds of shoes and boots. Clogs, with wooden soles, were especially popular over the period when platform soles were in vogue.

After the 1920s, women had worn boots as functional footwear for bad weather. During 1960s women went back to wearing boots as a fashionable part of daytime dress, as they had in the early 20th and 19th centuries. Shown first in the early 1960s, boots were quickly adopted for wearing in the colder months. They ranged from ankle-length, short boots worn with stretch pants to calf-high boots. Boots remained a basic item of footwear, showing annual variations, throughout the period.

ACCESSORIES

Notable among widely varying types and shapes were small tailored bags, very large bags with round handles and/or shoulder straps, shoulder bags. Materials included leather and plastic imitations of leather, fabric, and straw. (See *Illustrated Table 18.4* for examples of popular accessories in the period from 1960 to 1980.)

JEWELRY

Popular jewelry items included long strings of pearls or other beads similar to those worn in the 1920s, necklaces of brightly colored stones, earrings either small or long and hanging, and an enormous variety of costume jewelry at a variety of prices.

Increasing numbers of women had been piercing their ears since the late 1950s. This trend, led by adolescents, accelerated in the late 1960s and the early 1970s. The Montgomery Ward Christmas catalog of 1974 even featured a do-it-yourself ear-piercing device.

Colorful plastic jewelry in geometric shapes complemented the somewhat geometric forms evident in women's clothing. In the latter part of the 1960s large decorative wristwatches appeared, and gold-colored jewelry, especially multiple gold chains, overshadowed colored beads.

COSMETICS

For those who used cosmetics, bright red lipstick was replaced after 1966 by a variety of lighter, paler colors. Mascara, eye liner, and eye shadow were available in colors ranging from mauve to lavender, blue, green, and even yellow. False eyelashes were commonly used. For the first part of the 1970s makeup, though much used, was supposed to create an "unmade-up" or "natural" look. Lip gloss was first introduced in 1971.

The Introduction of the Midi:
1970–1974

Throughout this text it has been evident that fashionable clothing evolves gradually. Dramatic changes are rare. When the 20th century fashion industry has attempted to impose radical change, as with the first chemise-style dresses at the end of the 1950s, it has generally failed. This happened again around 1970 with the advent of the midi skirt, also known as the longuette. (See *Figure 18.11.*)

The longuette, coming to mid-calf length, was a sharp change from the mini and micro-miniskirts being worn at the time. Although the stores stocked large numbers of midi skirts, the majority of women either continued to wear short skirts and also some of the full-length skirts, called maxi skirts, or some version of pants. Long pants were worn as part of pantsuits, for casual wear, and for formal evening dress. Knickers were popular, as were gaucho pants. Some young women wore very short shorts, called hot pants by *Women's Wear Daily.* (See *Figure 18.9.*) The unfitted, straight, and short silhouette of the last years of the 1960s continued on into the early 1970s. But by August of 1971 *The New York Times* declared that women had the right to wear any length they chose.

By 1973, however, a fashion reporter for *The New York Times* was reporting that the midi skirt was getting a warmer reception, and by 1974 Paris couture houses were showing mid-calf length skirts with defined waistlines. Women seemed to take it for granted that skirt lengths could vary according to choice, although by mid-decade the very short

FIGURE 18.11

Sketch from *Women's Wear Daily,* September 1971, showing hemline lengths that range from "mini" (far left) to "midi" (center) to "maxi" (far right). (Courtesy, Fairchild Publications.)

miniskirt was no longer fashionable. *The Times* reporter noted from Paris in 1978 that "length was not much of an issue" and that most designers were covering the knee.

Contemporary Comments 18.2 (page 485) reprints excerpts from *Women's Wear Daily* and *The Wall Street Journal* that follow the progress of the midi from 1969 to 1973.

Changes in Costume for Women:
1974–1980

In spite of the resistance to the midi and the continuation of the mini as part of fashionable dress, mainstream fashions continued to evolve. The prevalent silhouette of the mid- and later 1970s has been described by fashion writers as "fluid," "an easier and more casual fit." At the same time the use of softer

fabrics molded the body and displayed body curves. An emphasis on fitness made the long, lean, trim, and well-exercised body the ideal of feminine beauty.

GARMENTS

Some women had abandoned brassieres and now went braless; most did not. Brassieres were molded from synthetic fabrics to eliminate unsightly seamlines, and provided a "natural" appearance under the clinging fabrics so much used during the latter part of the 1970s. Pantyhose with control tops took the place of girdles. See *Illustrated Table 18.1* for some examples of undergarments from the period between 1960 and 1980.

In 1973 fashion writers spoke of a "classic revival." Most dresses were belted or had clearly defined waistlines. Lines were soft, with shaping that followed and revealed body contours. (See *Figure 18.12*.) By mid-decade skirts had lengthened, and often flared gradually from waist to hem.

Natural fibers made in beige and neutral colors replaced the brightly colored manufactured fibers so often seen in the 1960s. Fabrics used were soft and drapable, many were knitted. Some examples of popular dress styles included:

- dresses that pulled over the head, had elastic or drawstring waistlines, and slightly bloused bodices
- cotton knit wrap dresses, the style originated by designer Diane Von Furstenberg, that tied shut with an attached belt

Pantsuits had become a staple in the wardrobes of all but the most conservative women. Made in fabrics such as knitted

FIGURE 18.12

Typical dress styles of late 1970s by Diane von Furstenberg illustrated in this sketch from *Women's Wear Daily.* (Courtesy, Fairchild Publications.)

Illustrated Table 18.3

SELECTED EXAMPLES OF POPULAR FOOTWEAR FOR WOMEN AND MEN, 1960–1980

Women's Shoes

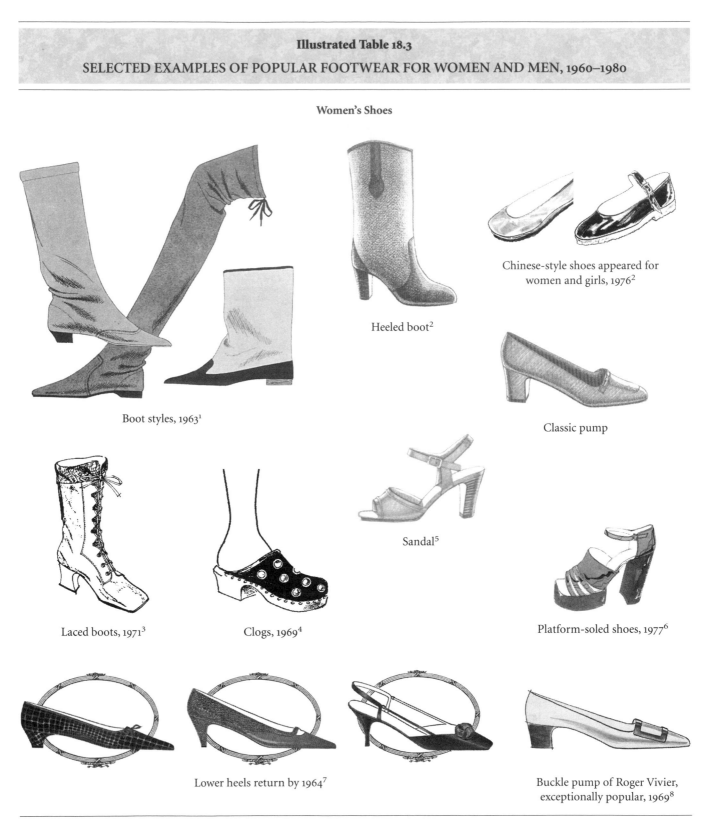

Boot styles, 1963[1]

Heeled boot[2]

Chinese-style shoes appeared for women and girls, 1976[2]

Classic pump

Laced boots, 1971[3]

Clogs, 1969[4]

Sandal[5]

Platform-soled shoes, 1977[6]

Lower heels return by 1964[7]

Buckle pump of Roger Vivier, exceptionally popular, 1969[8]

[1] *Women's Wear Daily,* August 25, 1963.
[2] *Footwear News,* Spring 1976. Fairchild Publications.
[3] *Footwear News,* March 11, 1971. Fairchild Publications.
[4] *Footwear News,* July 24, 1969. Fairchild Publications.
[5] *Footwear News,* July 20, 1978. Fairchild Publications.
[6] *Footwear News,* August 3, 1972. Fairchild Publications.
[7] *Harper's Bazaar* and Delman shoes at Bergdorf Goodman. September 1964.
[8] *Footwear News,* December 16, 1965. Fairchild Publications.

Illustrated Table 18.3

SELECTED EXAMPLES OF POPULAR FOOTWEAR FOR WOMEN AND MEN, 1960–1980

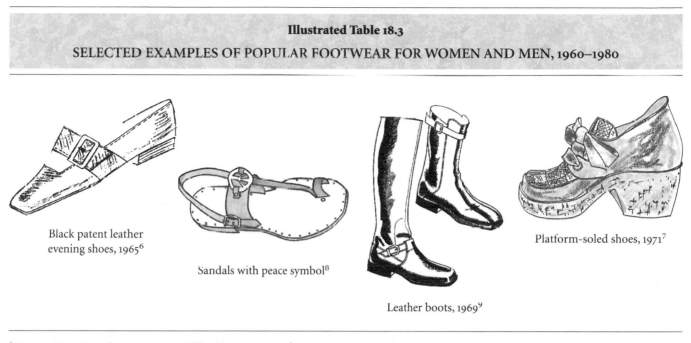

Black patent leather
evening shoes, 1965[6]

Sandals with peace symbol[8]

Leather boots, 1969[9]

Platform-soled shoes, 1971[7]

[6]*Footwear News,* December 23, 1965. Fairchild Publications.
[7]*Footwear News,* September 5, 1971. Fairchild Publications.
[8]*Footwear News,* September 18, 1969. Fairchild Publications.
[9]*Footwear News,* April 3, 1969. Fairchild Publications.

or textured polyester and wool gabardine and sold at widely varying prices, pantsuits were worn for work and during leisure time as sportswear and for formal evening occasions.

Women in managerial positions in the corporate world were advised in John Molloy's *Dress for Success,* published in 1977, to avoid pantsuits, and to wear a feminine version of the male business suit: a tailored jacket and skirt in a dark color with a blouse similar to a man's shirt. A small bow at the neck was permissible, a mannish-looking necktie was not advised. (See *Figure 18.13.*)

As discos replaced elaborate formal dances and parties, evening clothing was not so important as in previous periods. Clothing for discos was decidedly less formal; some women wore jeans. When skirts or dresses were worn, they tended to be floor length, having replaced the miniskirted evening wear of the 1960s. As with daytime garments, fabrics were soft, clinging, and often knitted. (See *Figure 18.14.*)

SPORTSWEAR

Pants were an alternative to skirts in almost all situations. By 1976 they had moved away from the bell-bottom shape and were narrower in the leg. By 1978, most were pleated or gathered into a waistband, tapering toward the ankle, and cuffed or rolled to ankle length.

Jeans were a virtual uniform for casual wear; designer jeans were very popular among all age groups. Some girls and

women, conforming to the body-conscious look of the period, wore exceptionally tight jeans. To get into them young women had to lie on the floor in order to be able to zip them.

By mid-1970s and after, skirts had more fullness, tended to flare out and covered the knee by at least several inches. (See *Figure 18.15.*) Skirts that wrapped around the body and tied into place and the **swirl skirt,** made from bias-cut strips of multicolored fabrics that were often from India, were part of the ethnic styles that appeared periodically.

For most of the 70s, blouses were of soft fabrics, often knit. Shoulder lines followed the natural curve of the shoulder. Many knit tops fell somewhere between a blouse and a sweater. Short or long-sleeved, made of narrow ribbed knits, they fit the body closely and ended a short distance below the waistline. Man-tailored shirts and other blouses that buttoned up the front were worn open at the neck by some women to show that they were braless. The wrap-style closing was popular in blouses as well as dresses. Toward the end of the 1970s and on into the early 1980s, large, loose shirts were worn over pants or skirts. The film *Annie Hall* (1978) had a strong impact on current fashion. It helped to popularize not only the combination of layers of separates, including the aforementioned large shirts worn with men's vests, but also pantsuits, and men's hats for women.

In 1975 *Vogue* magazine proclaimed the sweater as a basis for building a wardrobe. Often sweaters with round necks were worn over tailored blouses, the collar of the blouse vis-

Illustrated Table 18.4

1960–1980: ACCESSORIES

Accessories adopted by Hippies
(A) Headband (B) Hippie or love beads

Man's jewelry:
Chain and Maltese cross

Woman's necklace, 1972,
showing Egyptian influences
from museum exhibit about
King Tut

Handbags
(A) Women's Chanel bag (B) Woman's handbag in linen and leather
(C) Man's handbag, c. 1974

Long neckscarf with lettuce edging, 1977.

Digital wristwatch, c. 1976

Men's neckties and ascot
(A) Neckties grow wider in the 1970s. (B) Men also wore ascots

CONTEMPORARY COMMENTS 18.2

Reports from Women's Wear Daily *and* The Wall Street Journal *chronicle the promotion and resistance to the midi skirt*

Women's Wear Daily, July 7, 1969:
Here's the Lowdown . . . On the Lowdown.

The Lowdown Length is the big news for fall.

Paris says so . . . Rome says so . . . London says so.

So does New York.

Designers have been experimenting with lowered hemlines—from below-the-knee to ankle length—for the past five years. The Midi and the Maxi made it . . . mostly in coats worn over pants or short skirts.

The daytime Lowdown has had limited acceptance in New York fall collections. London says the Midi is old news to them . . . the Maxi is where it's happening there now.

Practically everyone agrees it's time for new lengths. It's an addition . . . another choice . . . another facet to the way fashion is moving today.

While the time is right for a new lowdown, it still needs that final stamp of approval from a designer like St. Laurent to make it happen.

And that's just what Yves will do on Monday when he shows his couture collection. St. Laurent has already down the Lowdown in his Rive Gauche fall collection. Now he strengthens his point by doing it for the couture.

Women's Wear Daily, January 14, 1970.
New York. It's just 10 days before the Paris couture collections open.

And the big question on everybody's mind is—what length?

But there's no question about what the news is. It's the Midi. It's the time for it. It's in today's newest mood.

Women's Wear Daily, February 2, 1970
New York—Hemline War is Escalating

The battle of the hemline rages on.

There are some who see it clearly. Skirts are on the way down.

There are those who are hemming the issue.

Some designers showed short for summer . . . and some buyers bought short.

Some of both are adding inches to the short skirts. And they're missing the point of the Longuette.

You can't add a few inches to a skirt that was designed short and expect to get a new look. The news is lengths are not around the knee. Some women never wavered from that length even at the height of the mini's popularity.

What is news is the skirt that drops a few inches below the knee—or longer still to Midi.

Women's Wear Daily, February 5, 1970
Longuette Placing SA in a Quandary
By Tom McDermott
New York—The Longuette look has raised more questions than it has answered, according to many SA [Seventh Avenue] dress manufacturers.

It has caused such confusion and doubt among store executives and resident office buyers, they maintained, that retailers are becoming stingy in placing early summer business and holding back on spring orders.

Everyone, it seems, is looking for direction—especially the direction that lengths will take for late spring and summer. The lowdown look has both retailers and producers in a quandary.

The Wall Street Journal,
October 2, 1970.

Moribund Midi
Woeful Retailers Say The Lower the Hem, The Lower the Sales

Women Call It Sleazy, Dowdy, Depressing; but Designers Say It Will Catch On Yet

Laughed Out of the Office

A Wall Street Journal News Roundup
Silence on the Set, please.

We've had months of buildup and lots of heated controversy, but now it's opening night. The notorious midi skirt, much-scorned but also much-promoted, is finally making its debut in thousands of boutiques and department stores across the country. Places everyone. Curtain . . . up!

Ker-plunk.

That's right, fashion fans, that's the sound of the star herself, entering the market place, tripping on her own hemline and falling flat on her face.

That, according to despairing retailers interviewed by *Wall Street Journal* reporters across the country is exactly how it's happening. With crisp weather bearing down and the traditional fall buying season already a couple of weeks old, women from coast to coast are trooping into the nation's retail clothing stores—and trooping right back out, sans midis.

Articles from *Women's Wear Daily,* reprinted courtesy of *Women's Wear Daily,* Fairchild Publications. Article from the *Wall Street Journal,* reprinted by permission of the *Wall Street Journal,* © 1970, Dow Jones & Company, Inc. All Rights Reserved Worldwide.

Among the most popular tops were T-shirts, especially those with messages. As the focus on fitness grew, sweatshirts in various colors were much worn. Leotards were worn not only for exercising, but also as tops with jeans or wrapped skirts.

As part of the emphasis on preppy-style clothing, single-breasted, tailored wool blazers were combined with pants or skirts and tailored blouses.

FIGURE 18.13

Conservative tailored suits often worn with blouses with a soft tie at the neck were recommended for business women who wanted to succeed in the corporate world.

ible at the neck of the sweater. The preppy look focused on Shetland wool sweaters. Hand-knitted sweaters were popular.

Long thigh-length cardigan sweaters usually had a matching tie belt and were worn over trousers or skirts. Another popular sweater style was the twin sweater set, with matching cardigan and belted pullover, and made from natural fibers. (See *Figure 18.15.*) Sweaters grew larger, looser in fit. In 1977 Japanese designer Issey Miyake combined oversized sweater tops with narrow leggings.

FIGURE 18.14

Evening dress of 1978 designed by Charles Kleibacker. The dress was described by the designer: "yards and yards of silk satin-striped chiffon fall from a yoke; a tiny bias string holds the silhouette close to the body in front, lets it float free in the back. Pale grey is the subtle color, with rows of skinny gold threads edging each stripe. Under dress of silk surah is cut to deep V in front, has no back." (Photograph courtesy, Charles Kleibacker.)

FIGURE 18.15

Belted twin sweaters set with a tweed skirt from the Anne Klein firm includes features characteristic of the latter part of the 1970s: natural fiber fabrics, longer skirts, and body molding designs. (*Women's Wear Daily*, May 16, 1974. Courtesy, Fairchild Publications.)

OUTDOOR GARMENTS

Coats, like dresses, followed body lines, flaring out gently below the waist. When sweaters and pantsuit styles featured tie belts of the same fabric, tie-belted coats, including trench-coat raincoats, became popular. Most coats ended below the knee.

Down or fiber-filled coats, which may have been inspired either by Chinese padded coats or down-filled ski jackets, gained great popularity for winter wear in the late 1970s. Restaurants reported problems in accommodating these large coats in their coatrooms.

CLOTHING FOR ACTIVE SPORTS

Tennis clothing was made in a wide array of colors. Bathing suits came in styles ranging from the tiny string bikini, a short-term fad of 1974, to empire style, skirted swimming

dresses of the same year. In 1975 Rudi Gernreich designed the **thong,** variously described as a "virtually bottomless bathing suit" or a "glorified jockstrap," cut to reveal as much of the buttocks as possible while covering the crotch. One-piece maillot suits were particularly popular around 1976 and after.

By 1976 the sleek, fitted jumpsuit was popular on the slopes. In 1977 a suit that had the appearance of a one-piece suit, but which could zip apart with a zipper at the waistline had been developed. Stretch pants with stirrups worn with puffy parkas were fashionable in 1979. Top fashion designers had begun to design skiwear in the late 1970s. Downhill outfits grew increasingly colorful and subject to seasonal style changes. Styles in cross-country ski wear did not change markedly.

SLEEPWEAR

Although both nightgowns and pajamas were available, nightgowns in short or long lengths predominated. In the winters of the later 1970s, when heating restrictions were imposed to save energy, warmer fabrics such as cotton flannels, brushed tricot, and all-in-one sleepers like those worn by children gained in popularity.

Robes often tied with a sash, were cut in kimono style or with notched or shawl collars.

HAIR AND HEADDRESS

See *Illustrated Table 18.2* for some examples of hair styles and hats for the period from 1960 to 1980.

By mid-decade hair was becoming shorter, and for the rest of the decade a soft, "natural" style was preferred. Media and sports stars helped some fashions in hair. Among the trends were:

- Toward the end of the 1970s, some women were wearing their hair in tight, "frizzy" curls, a style seen on movie star Barbra Streisand in the film *A Star is Born* in 1977.

- A short haircut called the **wedge** became popular in 1976 after Olympic medal-winner Dorothy Hamill wore the style at the Olympic games.

- Farrah Fawcett-Majors in the TV program *Charlie's Angels* had a full, streaked, blonde "mane," a style popular after 1977.

Although hats were not an important fashion item, berets and knit caps were used in colder regions in winter. Head scarves were featured in the fashion press in the mid-1970s.

FOOTWEAR

See *Illustrated Table 18.3* for some examples of footwear for the period from 1960 to 1980.

Pantyhose and/or tights had supplanted stockings for most women, and were available in colors and in a wide variety of textures and designs.

By the second half of the decade "slender, more graceful shoes with comfortable heels" had replaced the "clunky" platform soles. Boots remained an important item of footwear.

ACCESSORIES

Wide varieties of accessories of all kinds were available each season. Among those noted in the fashion press were handbags that included narrow rectangles fashionable around 1973; large tote bags after 1976; large, soft satchels with interesting textures around 1979. Throughout the period women carried small square quilted handbags with chain shoulder straps originally designed by Chanel. Women who "dressed for success" carried briefcases rather than handbags. The emphasis on natural materials led to a strong interest in real leather accessories. (See *Illustrated Table 18.4.*)

JEWELRY

Along with natural materials for garments came an interest in real gold and gemstones, in particular in gold chains, gold wire hoop earrings, and **diamonds by the yard,** designer Elsa Peretti's strings of gold chain with diamonds interspersed periodically. In 1973 snakeskin-covered bangle bracelets were something of a fad. Digital watches were first introduced in 1976.

COSMETICS AND GROOMING

In the mid-1970s women worked hard at using makeup to create a "natural" look. Major cosmetic companies developed and marketed complete lines of skin care products. As hairstyles grew in volume, more hair care products were required to hold the styles in place. By the end of the 1970s lipstick shades grew brighter and eye makeup more obvious.

COSTUME FOR MEN:
1960–1980

GARMENTS

Men's undergarments continued to include boxer shorts, knitted briefs, athletic shirts, and T-shirts. Some changes were evident.

In the late 1960s boxer shorts, already available in colors and small printed fabrics, were made in bright prints. The manufacturers of Jockey® briefs produced these garments in cotton mesh in 1970, and continued to make the bikini-cut shorts in bright colors. See *Illustrated Table 18.1* for examples of undergarments from the period between 1960 and 1980.

By the mid-1960s, continental suits were being supplanted by mod clothes: English styles with jackets padded slightly at the shoulders, wider lapels, moderate flare to the skirt, and pronounced side or center-back vents. Jacket fronts had a moderately cutaway shape. Suits with body shaping remained fashionable for the rest of the period. (See *Figure 18.16.*)

In the early 1970s, lapels were fairly wide and suits were fitted through the body. Double-knit fabrics in both manufactured and wool fibers were widely used and trousers tended to flare at the bottom. Suits were both single and double breasted, although single-breasted styles predominated.

In the latter part of the 1970s three-piece suits with vests, in decline since the 1930s, returned. Lapels narrowed and grew longer. The cut was looser. Men's suits were conservatively tailored, usually double breasted, made in dark colors and smooth-textured fabrics.

An upsurge of interest in fashion for men was accompanied by heavy press promotion and publicists began to speak of a "revolution in men's wear." *Esquire* in its *Encyclopedia of 20th Century Men's Fashions* declared, "from a gray flannel cocoon stepped a peacock." (See *Color Plate 59.*) A spurt in retail sales of men's clothing induced some famous designers of women's clothing to enter the men's wear market as well. Cardin was one of the first.

Suits with **Nehru jackets** appeared on the scene. Based on a traditional Indian jacket that buttoned all the way to the neck and had a small, stand-up collar, this garment was named after the Prime Minister of India, Jawaharlal Nehru, who wore the traditional jacket. (See *Figure 18.17.*) The style lasted about two years. After Lord Snowdon (then the husband of Princess Margaret, sister of Queen Elizabeth II of England) wore a formal evening Nehru suit with a white turtleneck, other men combined Nehru jackets with turtlenecks. Turtleneck shirts remained a fashionable item of men's wear even after the Nehru suit disappeared. The Nehru style had gained notice when, in 1966 after returning from a trip to India, French designer Pierre Cardin began to wear gray flannel suits made with Indian-style jackets.

Sweaters in the 1970s fit fairly close to the body, ending just below the waistline. In the late 1970s sweaters became larger and looser.

From the early 1960s on, turtlenecks were accepted as an alternative to the collared shirt. They were available in a wide variety of styles and colors. Even so, some restaurants refused admission to men without neckties.

Shirts cut and seamed so as to follow body lines and called **body shirts** were popular in the 1960s. In the early 1970s, many synthetic knit fabrics were used. Shirt collar sizes varied so that shirts would be in proportion to the lapel width of suit collars. Striped shirts were popular. (See *Figure 18.18.*)

An alternative to business suits developed for casual wear. Top and pants were usually made from the same fabrics. The unstructured tops had shirtlike collars or were collarless. Fashionable throughout the 1970s, **leisure suits** were out of style by the end of the decade. (See *Figure 18.19.*)

The Peacock Revolution had a major impact on tuxedos, which were cut with more body shaping and manufactured in a wide range of colors. Burgundy, green, and brown were especially popular. With these suits men wore shirts with ruf-

FIGURE 18.16

Mod influences note for men's wear in 1967. (*Daily News Record,* February 14, 1967. Courtesy, Fairchild Publications.)

fled fronts. (See *Figure 18.20.*) Evening jackets and trousers didn't always match in the 1970s.

OUTDOOR GARMENTS

As women's skirts grew shorter, so did men's outerwear. Fur and leather coats, and fur-collared coats appeared in the latter part of the 1960s.

By the early 1970s coats were made in a variety of lengths, paralleling the mini, midi, and maxi lengths in women's styles.

Casual outdoor garments included Western dress influences during the presidency of Texan Lyndon Johnson, campus or stadium coats that ended below the hip, shorter jackets for bicycling or motorcycling, quilted jackets filled with down or synthetic fibers.

SPORTSWEAR

In the mid-1960s tapered slacks were replaced by those with trouser bottoms that grew wider and included some flared pant legs and wide, bell-bottoms. They fit close to the torso without pleats. Blue jeans moved from being work clothes to fashionable dress by the late 1960s.

Sport jackets generally followed lines of suit jackets. Styles that were widely used included polyester knits in the

1960s and early 1970s and **safari jackets** and norfolk-style jackets in the late 1960s and 1970s.

Available in diverse styles, types of sport shirts varied with the seasons: For warm weather, men wore T-shirts and polo shirts. For cooler weather, turtlenecks, velour pullovers and shirts, jacquard-patterned knitted sweaters, and sweatshirts were popular.

CLOTHING FOR ACTIVE SPORTS

In the 1960s, the minuscule European knit bikini for men (or, as the European's called it the "slip") was appearing on American beaches. Synthetic knits were used for bathing suits because they dried quickly and were wrinkle free. In the 1970s suits were made of stretch nylon or of cotton in longer lengths called swim jams. The Olympics seemed to influence styles in bathing suits, and in 1972 the suit worn by Mark Spitz, American Olympic gold medal winner, was an important fashion. Throughout the period, men could choose among bikinis and trunks, with race-inspired bathing suits setting the styles.

Until the early 1970s, white predominated for tennis. After this, men as well as women were more likely to wear colored tennis clothes.

FIGURE 18.18

Striped shirts, many in polyester and cotton blends, were worn with the wide neckties popular in the early 1970s. (*Daily News Record,* March 15, 1973. Courtesy, Fairchild Publications.)

FIGURE 18.17

The Nehru suit, also called the tunic, which was often worn with a chain and pendant. (Courtesy, Fairchild Publications.)

Styles for ski clothes changed yearly, moving gradually toward a tighter fit and the use of fabrics designed to offer as little wind resistance as possible. For cross-country skiing, men, as well as women, wore knickers with knee-length stockings.

SLEEPWEAR

Pajamas continued to be the major form of sleepwear, but these were made with either short or long pants and in vivid solid or printed colors. In the late 1970s when velour fabrics were fashionable, men wore velour robes.

HAIR AND HEADDRESS

Radical changes in hair length came in the 1960s, and at the beginning were seen as a protest by the young against middle-class values. Longer-than-shoulder length hair was chiefly limited to high school and college-age youth or older men wishing to dramatize a personal protest against some aspect of contemporary society. Moderately long hair, beards, mustaches, and sideburns had become accepted styles for all segments of society by the close of the 1960s. The longer hairstyles are often said to have been inspired by the British music group The Beatles. Fashion-conscious men began to patronize "hair stylists" rather than "barbers." Longer hairstyles persisted until the late 1970s when shorter styles returned.

John F. Kennedy did not wear a hat to his inauguration in 1961. Hat sales dropped, and consequently hats became a much less important part of men's wardrobes. When hairstyles grew longer, hats became even less important.

FOOTWEAR

See *Illustrated Table 18.3* for some examples of footwear from the period, 1960 to 1980.

FIGURE 18.19

Leisure suits, worn as casual wear, were noted in *Daily News Record* on October 1, 1974 as "market leaders" for spring, 1975. (Courtesy, Fairchild Publications.)

In the 1960s the classic styles were supplemented by high shoes and boots, seen for the first time since the 1930s for street wear. By the end of the decade most shoes had somewhat squared toes. As platform soles were added to women's shoes, they were also seen on some, especially younger men's, shoes. After hippie men wore work shoes and sandals, these entered mainstream men's fashion.

ACCESSORIES

Ralph Lauren made three-inch wide ties popular in 1967, and ties remained wide until the late 1970s when ties became narrow again. (See *Figure 18.18.*) Ralph Lauren came to prominence in 1967 as a designer of men's neckties. He then moved into menswear design, and in 1971 into ready-to-wear for women, and eventually even entered the home products market. Lauren provides an illustration of the increasing tendency of successful designers to move easily from one market into another, although more designers have moved from women's design into men's design than vice versa.

JEWELRY

New jewelry styles appeared. With turtleneck sweaters and shirts men began wearing necklaces. Bracelets and earrings were also seen. The trend seems to have begun with the hippies who wore beads and other decorative jewelry. (See *Illustrated Table 18.4.*)

COSMETICS

With longer hair, products for hair care for men expanded.

1960 basic garments for infants, stretch, all-in-one, footed terrycloth outfits, were introduced, and these became a staple in infants' wear. Disposable diapers were introduced in 1960.

As child development experts increasingly stressed the importance of allowing children freedom from physical restraint in clothing, garments for toddlers took into account factors of comfort and safety. Most dresses tended to be loosely fitted, hanging from the shoulders. One-piece or two-piece tops and pants that fastened together at the waist were made for boys. Children at the crawling stage wore corduroy overall-type pants with reinforced knees.

Preschool and School-Age Children

Throughout the decade children's clothing inevitably displayed the same trends that were evident in adult styles. Current events were reflected in children's clothing. As the American involvement in Vietnam grew, *The New York Times* children's fashion supplement of August 14, 1966, featured clothes with military influences. Mod- and hippie-derived styles appeared in the latter part of the 1960s. Fabrics that were washable and required little ironing were preferred, leading to the widespread use of nylon, polyester, acrylics and blends of synthetics with cotton.

The Garan Corporation developed a new marketing technique for mid-price level children's clothing in 1976. They produced clothing for children two years or older that had animal labels. Children could then select coordinated outfits by matching, for example, blouses with monkeys on the label with pants with monkeys on the label, or lions with lions, and so forth. This promotion was successful until well into the early 1980s.

See *Illustrated Table* 18.5 for some examples of children's styles for the period from 1960 to 1980.

Costume for Girls

GARMENTS

When the full-skirted New Look styles for women began to be replaced by loosely fitted lines in the early 1960s, girl's dresses also gradually took on a looser fit. Slightly A-line, princess-cut "skimmers" were popular as dresses in summer and jumpers in winter. Skirts shortened, ending well above the knee. With the short skirts in cool weather, girls wore long tights in matching or contrasting colors and in a variety of textures. For the duration of the unfitted line, most girls' dresses were either straight, unfitted, sometimes with a wide ruffle around the hem, or gradually and slightly flared from shoulder to hem. When maxi skirt lengths were introduced for adult women, versions for girls were seen as well, especially for party clothes. In the late 1970s hems lengthened, the silhouette became more fitted, and more belts were used.

FIGURE 18.20

Tuxedo from 1973 showed mod influences in its cut, velvet collar, ruffled shirt, and was available in a wide variety of colors. (*Men's Wear*, August 13, 1973. Courtesy, Fairchild Publications.)

COSTUME FOR CHILDREN:
1960–1980

Infants and Toddlers

Clothing for children in this age group tends to change less than for older children. Many of the basic styles of infants' dresses might be called "classic," with styles that continue for many decades. This is particularly true of styles produced for the so-called "grandmother" market, consisting of embroidered and/or smocked dresses or suits in cotton or cotton-blended with manufactured fibers in pastel colors. Around

Illustrated Table 18.5

CHILDREN'S CLOTHING STYLES: 1960–1980

Back-to-school advertisement of clothing for small girls, 1961[1]

Boy's clothing for fall, 1961[1]

Children's outerwear, c. 1966; on the left, a modacrylic parka and knit tights, on the right a melton togglecoat and blue jeans

Poncho styles, popular in the late 1960s[2]

A-line styles, the predominant line for girls' dresses and tunics[3]

Dresses from McCall's Pattern Catalog, April 1977

Leisure suit with bell-bottom pants for boys[4]

Long "granny" dress, a style which appeared for girls in the early 1970s[5]

[1]Courtesy of Saks Fifth Avenue, New York.
[2]*Women's Wear Daily,* December 1, 1969. Fairchild Publications.
[3]Butterick Pattern Illustration, 1970, courtesy of the Vogue/Butterick Pattern Archives Library.
[4]*Women's Wear Daily,* March 15, 1971. Fairchild Publications.
[5]*Women's Wear Daily,* January 1, 1972. Fairchild Publications.

Various pants styles were popular. In the 1960s young girls wore stretch nylon pants with narrow legs. At the beginning of the 1970s, pants were more often seen than dresses. Comfort in clothing for girls had clearly become important, as blue jeans and overalls were worn for school and for play. Girls also wore pantsuits. The fashion of pants for girls is another instance of the parallels between adult and children's styles. Whereas in earlier periods pants had been worn for play by girls, they were not generally worn for school until the late 1960s or early 1970s, the period during which adult women began to wear pants to their jobs.

In the early 1960s, a fad developed for adolescent girls to wear **"Go-go" boots,** which were calf-length and white.

HAIR

Hairstyles for girls were like those for adult women, including long straight hair and for African-American girls, afros.

Costume for Boys

GARMENTS

Suits for boys were miniature versions of suits for men, and included Nehru-style suits and mod-influenced suits. They were often made of polyester. In the 1970s some boys wore three-piece suits, some of which had an Edwardian cut. Sport jackets were worn with short pants by younger boys and with long pants by older boys. These were often collarless blazers.

Knitted T-shirts and polo shirts, sometimes with white collars, and often made in bright horizontal stripes were the preferred garment for play. Shirts worn with jackets and suits were like those for adult men.

HAIR

The change to longer hair for males was much influenced by the music group The Beatles. Adolescent boys quickly adopted similar styles, and some school authorities suspended boys with long hair. As longer hair became the predominant style in the latter part of the 1960s, boys of all ages, like men, wore their hair in a wide variety of lengths.

Costume for Boys and Girls

Probably the most important fashion item for both boys and girls was jeans. Jeans and other pants were made with bell-bottom legs from the late 1960s through the mid-1970s. Message T-shirts and clothing bearing licensed logos or other art began to gain importance in the 1970s and their use accelerated throughout the decade.

OUTDOOR WEAR

Among the more distinctive items of outdoor garments were those made from manufactured fiber pile fabrics, some of which simulated fur. Boys and girls wore quilted and down-filled jackets, hooded sweatshirts, and vinyl slicker raincoats.

SUMMARY

THEMES

Almost all of the themes that were identified in *Chapter 1* are to be found in the 1960s. But those that stand out most strongly relate to **POLITICS, POLITICAL CONFLICT** and **SOCIAL CHANGES.** Politics, for example, influenced fashions when the young and popular Kennedy family entered the White House. The 1960s was a period of upheaval in the United States. The civil rights movement, student unrest, women's liberation, and growing dissent over the escalation of the American military commitment in Vietnam were accompanied by changes in fashion that contrasted markedly with the styles of the 1950s. Skirts for women came to be shorter than in any previous period in the history of Western dress. Trousers for women were accepted for daytime and evening wear in place of skirts. Some young men adopted shoulder-length hair for the first time in almost 200 years. Men began wearing more colorful and varied clothing for business and leisure than had been seen since before the 19th century.

Those who study clothing as it relates to social change have pointed out that marked changes in dress often accompany social unrest. The decade from 1965 to 1975 was a period of social upheaval, especially in the United States. It also appears to have been the catalyst for radical changes in attitudes toward fashion that affected not only subsequent styles but also, in the decades to come, would cause profound changes in the organization of the systems for originating, producing, and merchandising fashionable clothing.

Visual Summary Table

1960–1980

Man: 1960–1970
Greater variety in color and pattern,
more decorative mod-influenced styles
appear. Turtleneck shirts worn with suits
and Nehru suits provide alternatives.

Man: 1970s
Color and pattern continue to be
one option for men, along with more
traditional business suits. Leisure suits
are worn as casual dress in the 1970s.

Women: 1960–1970
By mid-60s dresses are very short
and unfitted. The Chanel suit becomes an
important style. Street styles are incorporated
into current fashion.

Woman: 1970–1980
Mid-calf length skirts introduced
c. 1970 are unsucessful. Women retain
short skirts, and adopt pantsuits as
part of daytime wear.

Woman: 1970s
By mid-70s, skirts lengthen,
and a softer, fitted line replaces
the straight, short styles. Punk and
African-inspired styles appear.

Survivals of Styles of 1960–1980

The miniskirt, first seen in the early 60s and characteristic of most of the rest of this period, was revived again in the 80s. It had become one of the many skirt alternatives from which designers could choose.

In the 90s fashion designers were also reaching into this decade to borrow ideas from mod styles, op art, and the sleeveless A-line shift. Bell-bottoms returned again after the millennium.

Blue jeans, not a new style in the 60s but one that was ubiquitous in this period, never left their prominent position in fashion. They became a fashion staple. With a trend in the 90s toward casual wear in the white collar workplace, jeans took on even greater importance.

FIGURE 18.21

Pantsuits, introduced in the second half of the 1960s, were revived by designers in the 1990s. The example here was designed by Giorgio Armani in 1994. (*Women's Wear Daily,* January 25, 1994. Courtesy, Fairchild Publications.)

NOTES

"Age of Aquarius: Woodstock Music and Art Fair." 1969. *Newsweek,* August 25, p. 88.

Brooks, J. 1966. *The Great Leap.* New York: Harper and Row, p. 232.

"Fashions of The Times." 1971. *The New York Times,* August 29.

Giddings, V. L. 1990. "African American Dress in the 1960's." In B. Starke, et al., *African American Dress and Adornment.* Dubuque, IA: Kendall Hunt, p. 153.

Klemesrud, J. 1970. "They Like the Way They Looked—Others Didn't." *The New York Times,* September 4, p. 22.

Martin R. and H. Koda. 1989. *Jocks and Nerds.* New York: Rizzoli, p. 47.

McCloskey, J. 1970. "The Men's Fashion Report: Aquarius Rising." *Gentlemen's Quarterly,* March, Vol. 4, No. 2, p. 109.

Schnurnberger, L. 1991. *Let There Be Clothes.* New York: Workman, p. 380.

SELECTED READINGS

Books and Other Materials Containing Illustrations of Costume of the Period from Original Sources

Fashion and general magazines and newspapers of the period such as *Vogue, Harper's Bazaar, Mademoiselle, Seventeen, McCall's, Good Housekeeping, W.*

Catalogs: Pattern and mail-order.

Bernard, B. 1978. *Fashion in the 60's.* London: Academy Editions.

Bond, D. 1988. *The Guinness Guide to 20th Century Fashion.* Enfield, Middlesex, England: Guinness Publishing.

Connike, Y. 1990. *Fashions of a Decade: The 1960s.* New York: Facts on File.

De La Haye, A. 1988. *Fashion Source Book.* Secaucus, NJ: Wellfleet Press.

de Pietri, S. and M. Leventon. 1989. *The New Look to Now: French Haute Couture 1947–1987.* New York: Rizzoli.

Ewing, E. 1974. *History of Twentieth Century Fashion.* London: B. T. Batsford.

Lee, S. T., ed. 1975. *American Fashion.* New York: Quadrangle/New York Times.

Lobenthal, J. 1990. *Radical Rags: Fashions of the Sixties.* New York: Abbeville Press.

Martin, R. and H. Koda. 1989. *Jocks and Nerds.* New York: Rizzoli.

Milbank, C. 1989. *New York Fashion: The Evolution of American Style.* New York: Abrams.

Mulvagh, J. 1988. *Vogue History of 20th Century Fashion.* New York: Viking Penguin.

Periodical Articles

Dewhurst, C. K. 1988. "Pleiku Jackets, Tour Jackets, and Working Jackets: 'The Letter Sweaters of War." *Journal of American Folklore,* Vol. 101, p. 48.

McCloskey, J. 1970. "The Men's Fashion Report: Aquarius Rising." *Gentlemen's Quarterly,* Vol. 4, No. 2, March, p. 106.

Palmer, A. 1991. "Paper Clothes: Not Just a Fad." In P. A. Cunningham and S. V. Lab, eds., *Dress and Popular Culture.* Bowling Green, OH: Bowling Green State University Popular Press, p. 85.

Ratner, E. 1975. "Levi's." *Dress,* Vol. 1, No. 1, p. 1.

Daily Life

Cooke, A. 1989. *America Observed from the 1940's to the 1980's.* New York: Macmillan.

Cuminini, T and N. Shumsky. 1988. *American Life: American People.* 2 vols. New York: Harcourt Brace Jovanovich.

Feinstein, S. 2000. *Decades of the 20th Century The 1970s. From Watergate to Disco.* Berkeley Heights, NJ: Enslow.

Hoobler, D. and T. Hobbler. 1981. *An Album of the Seventies.* New York: Franklin Watts, 1981.

Leonard, T. 1988. *Day by Day, the Seventies.* New York: Facts on File.

Obst, L. R., ed. 1977. *The Sixties.* New York: Random House/Rolling Stone Press Book.

O'Neill, W. 1971. *Coming Apart. An Informal History of America in the 1960s.* New York: Quadrangle.

Powe-Temperly, K. 2000. *20th Century Fashion The 60s: Mods & Hippies.* Milwaukee: Gareth Stevens.

This Fabulous Century. 1969. Vols. 5 and 6. New York: Time-Life. (Also contains illustrations of costume from contemporary sources.)

CHRONOLOGY

1980
Ronald Reagan elected president

1981
Wedding of Prince Charles and Lady Diana Spencer

1983
Japanese designers show their designs
at the Paris prêt-à-porter shows

1985
Mikhail Gorbachev becomes Soviet premier

1987
Christian Lacroix opens new couture house in Paris

1988
George Bush elected president

1990
East and West Germany reunited

1991
War with Iraq in the Middle East
Government of the Soviet Union collapses
Croatia and Slovenia declare their independence
Fighting breaks out in Bosnia

1992
United States troops land in Somalia
Bill Clinton elected president

1993
Maastricht Treaty goes into effect in Europe
North American Free Trade Agreement
(NAFTA) becomes law
White House meeting between Palestinian
Yasser Arafat and Israeli Yitzak Rabin
Terrorist attack on World Trade Center

1994
U. S. troops land in Haiti
Republicans win majorities in both houses of Congress
First custom-fitted clothing produced through
computer imaging sold at retail by Levi Strauss
Three million computers connected to the Internet

1995
Yitzak Rabin assassinated
Bombing of federal building in Oklahoma City
Dayton Agreement signed and NATO
troops enter Bosnia
Federal government shutdown

1996
Russia makes peace with Chechyna
Ten million computers connected to the Internet
Congress overhauls the welfare system
Bill Clinton reelected president
British designers chosen for houses of
Dior and Givenchy

1997
China assumes control of Hong Kong
NATO expands

1998
Bill Clinton impeached

1999
Vladimir Putin named Acting President of Russia

2000
George Bush elected president
Vladimir Putin elected president of Russia

2001
Terrorist attacks on the World Trade Center
in New York
War in Afghanistan

2002
The Euro becomes the currency
for most of the European Union
605.60 million computers connected
to the Internet

2003
Invasion of Iraq
Capture of Saddam Hussein

CHAPTER NINETEEN

THE EIGHTIES AND NINETIES

Affluence, Information, and a New Millennium

1980 – 2003

A.

D.

B.

E.

A.

Postmodern architecture, Queens College Library

B.

Bronze sculpture by Botero, *Man on Horseback*

C.

Painting by Julian Schnabel, *The Wind*, 1985

D.

Sheraton side chair by Robert Venturi, 1984

E.

Mandarin chair by Ettore Sottsass, 1987

F.

Environmental art, pattern in grass
by Kadishman, *Suspended*, 1977

C.

F.

Figures A, B, F courtesy of V. R. Tortora. Figure C courtesy of the Art Institute of Chicago, gift of the Society for Contemporary Art (1998.91). Figures D, E courtesy of J. Curcio in Federico, J. T. 1988. *Clues to the American Furniture*. Washington: Starrhill, p. 59.

HISTORICAL BACKGROUND: INTERNATIONAL

The Cold War Ends

By the 1980s, the strain of the Cold War had begun to undermine the Soviet system. Mikhail Gorbachev, Soviet premier in 1985, proposed a policy of *glasnost* (openness) and *perestroika* (economic reform) in the hope of saving the communist system. The idea of *glasnost* spread to the unhappy satellite states in Eastern Europe. Moscow could no longer keep them in line without war, a course rejected by Gorbachev. Consequently in 1989, the Soviet control of Eastern Europe collapsed and noncommunist governments seized control. The Berlin Wall fell in 1989, and East and West Germany were reunited in 1990.

After hard-line communists attempted a coup in 1991, the Soviet government collapsed. The Soviet Union ceased to exist when the Russian Republic under President Boris Yeltsin joined with other republics to form the Commonwealth of Independent States. The Cold War was over.

The Russian Republic was passing through a crisis as it stumbled from communism toward a capitalistic democracy. A faltering economy, inadequate services, and strikes made the situation worse. Law enforcement suffered because of low pay and inadequate staffing.

One bright spot in Russian political life was the first popular democratic election of a president, Boris Yeltsin, in 1996. Yeltsin pushed through needed economic reforms but could not halt corruption and a fall in living standards. A civil war broke out in the republic of Chechnya in southwest Russia where the Chechens, who were Sunni Muslims, had declared their independence. In 1994 Russian forces launched a full-scale invasion only to suffer a humiliating defeat by 1996.

In August 1999, Yeltsin appointed Vladimir Putin prime minister. When Yeltsin resigned as president, Putin, a former KGB colonel, succeeded him. Putin cracked down on the independent press and curtailed the freedom of television and radio. He also took aim at the oligarchs, wealthy Russian business tycoons, whenever they displayed any signs of interest in politics. Putin ordered a resumption of the Chechen war in 1999. The rebels continued their rebellion and this conflict continues.

Progress Continues Toward European Union

The European Community (EEC) continued to develop and expand its functions. Steps were taken to encourage trade and investment among Community members. Barriers to the movement of capital and curbs on financial services were reduced. European passports were issued.

Austria, Finland, and Sweden joined the European Union (EU) in 1995, bringing the total membership up to 15 nations. On March 26, 1995 all border controls were removed between Portugal, Spain, France, Belgium, Luxembourg, Germany, and the Netherlands. Citizens of these countries could cross borders without any passport checks.

The Maastricht Treaty, effective November 1, 1993, set tough economic standards that each member of the EU had to meet in order to join the European Monetary Union, which established one currency, the **euro.** Beginning January 2, 2002, euro coins and notes were used in the 12 countries that met the standards and chose to use the Euro. Three EU countries—Britain, Denmark, and Sweden—did not adopt the currency.

The European Union expanded again in May 2004 when Poland and other Eastern European and Mediterranean countries joined the Union.

War and Peace

After the fall of communism, Yugoslavia began to split apart as various ethnic groups sought to establish sovereign states. In 1991, Croatia and Slovenia voted to declare their independence. Serb-controlled Yugoslav army units began to battle the new states. When Bosnia-Herzegovina followed with a declaration of independence, fighting broke out. By the summer of 1992, reports of death camps for Muslim and Croat populations controlled by the Serbian army and the first reports of "ethnic cleansing" led to the establishment of the Hague International War Crimes Tribunal, which was charged with investigating war crimes in the former Yugoslavia.

The conflict continued unabated until diplomatic talks in late 1995 led to a cease-fire and, finally, an agreement between the warring groups.

The Middle East

Turmoil continued in the Middle East. Iraq and Iran clashed in a war that dragged on for eight years.

War came again in the Middle East in 1990 when Iraqi armies invaded and conquered Kuwait, a neighbor of Saudi Arabia and a major source of oil for the United States. After Iraq ignored a United Nations resolution sanctioning the use of force, coalition forces, headed by the United States, began hostilities in January 1991, retaking Kuwait and entering Iraqi territory in February. The Persian Gulf War ended after 100 hours of fighting.

After a positive start toward peace between the Israelis and the Palestinians in 1993, the peace process once again began running into roadblocks. On November 4, 1995, a religious right-wing Israeli assassinated Rabin as he left a peace rally in Tel Aviv. From this point on, the peace process continued with alternating periods of agreement and disagreement. Conflict intensified, and by 2003 peace was nowhere in sight.

United States forces, with the support of British troops, invaded Iraq on March 20, 2003. The invasion was launched after the American and British governments had failed to obtain authorization from the United Nations for their actions. The announced aim of the invasion was to disarm Iraq because it was believed that the Iraqi leader, Saddam Hussein, held massive supplies of chemical and biological weapons and that he had developed weapons of mass destruction. In addition, the allies sought to overthrow Saddam Hussein's government and free the Iraqi people.

On May 1, 2003, from the deck of the USS *Abraham Lincoln*, President George W. Bush announced the end of the campaign and the defeat of the Iraqi forces. Allied forces had been unable to locate the weapons of mass destruction. In the days following Bush's announcement of the end of the war, American and coalition troops suffered almost daily attacks resulting in more casualties than were suffered before May 1. Saddam Hussein was captured in December 2003.

Japanese Economic
Influences

It was not until the 1980s that the American people became fully aware of the growing power of the Japanese economy. By the 1990s, Japanese competition in automobiles and electronic products had forced American producers to renovate their plants, cut their payrolls, and introduce new technologies, including robotics. Some American plants producing these goods were moved outside the country in search of cheaper labor. Many companies moved their garment manufacturing operations to areas such as the Pacific Rim.

Japanese fashion designers opened couture houses in Paris and ready-to-wear houses in Paris, New York, and other major cities throughout the world. Japan had become a world economic power and had emerged as the major competitor to the United States in world markets.

In the 1990s, the once formidable Japanese economy suffered a severe deflation. Retail and wholesale prices dropped drastically, real estate prices collapsed, retailers had to compete with cheap imports, and stocks dropped drastically in value. Consumer prices have dropped but so have wages. In March 2001, the Japanese finance minister announced that Japan's financial situation was close to catastrophe.

There were some benefits to Japan's deflation. Housing became cheaper. Tariffs dropped and consequently imported food became cheaper. Discounting has become more prevalent and discount stores have multiplied. Shoppers are not buying as in the past but are waiting for a further fall in prices. Deflation has been the force in transforming Japan's economy.

HISTORICAL BACKGROUND:
UNITED STATES

Political and Economic Developments

Ronald Reagan, the former governor of California who was elected to the presidency in 1980, accepted the "supply-side" or "trickle-down" economic theory, which held that cutting taxes for corporations and wealthy individuals would benefit those lower down on the economic scale and revive the economy. Reagan advocated reduced government spending, increases in the military budget, and lower tax rates. These lower tax rates did not produce enough revenue, however, resulting in unbalanced budgets and an enormous increase in the national debt.

George Bush, elected in 1988, was handicapped in fighting a recession because of Reagan administration borrowing. Notable foreign policy events were an invasion of Panama and the Persian Gulf War, following the invasion of Kuwait by Iraq. Rising unemployment and economic recession helped Arkansas governor Bill Clinton defeat Bush in 1992.

Passage of the North American Free Trade Act (NAFTA), which reduced tariffs between the United States, Canada, and Mexico, was an early legislative victory. This agreement established the world's largest free trade zone.

The Republicans swept to victory in the Congressional election of 1994, capturing both houses of Congress for the first time in 40 years. For the first time in 60 years, the welfare system was overhauled and the federal guarantee of cash assistance for the poor ended. Arguments between the President and the Republicans over the budget, however, led to the federal government being shut down twice, an event that influenced national elections in 1996.

Helped by a booming stock market, low unemployment, and low interest rates, Bill Clinton won a second term. The Clinton presidency, however, was plagued by scandals about his personal life, which resulted in his impeachment. The votes for impeachment were not sufficient to remove him from office.

Gore–Bush Presidential Campaign

The 2000 presidential campaign ended with Vice President Al Gore ahead in the popular vote and Governor George W. Bush of Texas holding a slim lead in the electoral vote. The outcome of the national election hinged on the final vote in Florida. Because of the closeness of the vote, Florida law required a mandatory recount of the ballots. Problems soon developed in those counties that used punch cards, resulting in questions about the accuracy of the counts.

The Bush campaign appealed the case to the United States Supreme Court. The court, by a five to four majority, ruled in favor of Bush, basing its decision on the equal protection clause of the Fourteenth Amendment of the Constitution. George W. Bush became president of the United States.

The first terrorist attack within the borders of the United States came on February 25, 1993 when a bomb under the World Trade Center in New York City killed five people and injured more than a thousand. Then on April 19, 1995, a bomb wrecked the federal building in Oklahoma City, killing 168, many of whom were children.

But the worst was yet to come. On September 11, 2001 terrorists highjacked four jet liners. Using these planes as bombs, they flew two of them into the twin towers of the World Trade Center in New York City and one into the Pentagon. The fourth was deflected from its target when passengers overcame the terrorists. This plane crashed in rural Pennsylvania en route to Washington, DC. President Bush declared a "War on Terrorism" and the nation adopted a broad array of new security measures.

Energy and Environmental Issues

In 1990, Congress passed the Clean Air Act. Dangers to the environment continue to grow. Depletion of the ozone layer over the Antarctic and a small ozone hole over the Arctic have been observed. Many scientists believe that global warming is increasing, but international agreement on steps to combat these potential problems has not been achieved.

The environmental movement was probably responsible at least in part for a preference for natural fibers evident in the late 1970s and 1980s. On March 25, 1990, *The New York Times* published a front-page story with the headline, "The Green Movement in the Fashion World," which described efforts of manufacturers and designers to publicize to consumers their efforts on behalf of the environment.

Consumer support for environmentally sound products led to the cultivation and sale of naturally colored cottons that did not require dyeing, to the use of "organic cotton" grown without the use of pesticides, and fabrics dyed with natural dyes from plants, insects, and minerals. (See *Color Plate 69*.) Polyester fibers made from recycled soda bottles began to appear in such varied products as T-shirts, baseball caps, and fleece fabrics for active wear for cold weather sports.

Animal rights activists began to campaign against the wearing of fur in the 1980s. Interest increased in synthetic pile fiber fabrics made to simulate furs because of aggressive tactics of the anti-fur protesters such as spraying women in fur coats with paint. In 2003, animal rights activists presented a fashion show of synthetic fur fashions in the hope of encouraging women to wear imitation rather than real fur. But none of these activities eliminated fashion interest in fur. (See *Color Plate 72*.) The importation of products such as tortoise shell, ivory, crocodile skin, and other products on the endangered species list was banned.

Babies' diapers came in for environmental scrutiny. Many mothers used disposable diapers, which had been available since 1961. Debate raged over the impact of disposing of massive numbers of disposable diapers in landfills, and some environmentally conscious mothers switched to cloth diapers.

Disposal of used clothing in landfills, especially those from synthetic fabrics that are not biodegradable, was another issue that caused some environmentalists to stress recycling of used clothing. There were consumers who did shop at second-hand clothing stores but this was often because of fashion interest in antique clothing or a desire to save money, rather than out of concern for the environment.

The Changing American Family

By 2002 46.5 percent of women over 16 were in the labor force. The Bureau of Labor Statistics reported that women held 50.5 percent of managerial and professional positions, but far smaller numbers (only 5 percent in 1996) were in senior management positions (Dobrzynski 1996).

The peak childbearing years for the baby boom generation came in the 1980s. As a result children's clothing sales increased. The economic good times of the early 1980s were reflected in the willingness of affluent parents to spend lavishly for what *Newsweek* magazine called **kiddie couture** as some designers of adult clothing started producing lines for children. This trend continued into the new Millennium, when increasing numbers of manufacturers of adult clothing entered the children's clothing market.

Changes in the Roles of Women

After the late 80s, men's and women's garments for business were called **power suits.** In the 1980s the fashion press noted a dichotomy in women's clothing, with conservative, tailored clothing for working hours and glamorous, feminine, and sexy clothing for leisure time.

Many observers saw changing gender roles as the reason for the appearance of many items of clothing for men and women that were interchangeable in appearance. The fashion press called such items **unisex clothing.** Examples include blue jeans, tailored shirts, T-shirts, sweatshirts, sweaters, blazers, running suits, and sneakers. Some women shopped in men's wear departments for clothing, although most manufacturers distinguished men's and women's clothing sizes even in items that were visually identical. Along with major changes for women in career and lifestyle options and with a more diffuse view of the social roles of men and women had come a breakdown of the taboo against wearing clothing styles traditionally assigned to the opposite sex and an erosion of the social norms that required clear differences in men's and women's clothing.

The Computer Revolution

Since World War II nothing has so affected life in the United States as the computer revolution. The uses of computers range from helping engineers to design automobiles, buildings, airplanes, clothing, and textiles to enabling astronomers to develop theories about galaxies. Extensive computer applications in the fashion design and manufacturing areas aid designers and make it possible for manufacturers to respond to or create changes in styles almost instantaneously.

Computers have made it possible for retailers to work more efficiently with manufacturers through **quick response**, the name given to computer-based systems that permit rapid ordering, manufacture, and delivery of goods. Computers also provide retailers with innovative sales techniques through computer imaging. Using this technique, consumers can see themselves in different fashions or hairstyles. The first custom-fitted clothing produced through computer scanning was sold in November 1994 by Levi Strauss. Computer software transmitted customers' body measurements to a factory where patterns were cut by robots to the individual's exact measurements, and the garments assembled. Orders were filled in about three weeks (Rifkin 1994).

In the 90s the potential of the computer increased when Americans discovered the Internet, an obscure communications system or network of computers used chiefly by academics and military researchers, which became an important communications tool. By September 2002 it was estimated that 605.60 million computers were connected to the Internet.

The Internet also serves as a source of information about fashion. And it provides opportunities to purchase apparel. The computer revolution and the Internet are new chapters in the history of the Industrial Revolution which are changing profoundly the way business, government, and industry function.

The New Immigrants

A 1965 change in the immigration law had eliminated racially based barriers to immigration. There followed a surge of immigrants from Asia, Latin America, and especially from Korea and the Philippines. The end of the Vietnam conflict brought immigrants from Laos, Cambodia, and Vietnam. After the Cold War, immigrants came from Eastern Europe and the former Soviet Union. The 2000 Census showed that the Hispanic population of the United States had grown to 35.5 million. As a result, many retailers were trying to increase their appeal to Hispanic consumers. In 2003, Kmart introduced a new line of fashions named for Thalia, a popular Mexican singer. A line of fashions by Jennifer Lopez, a Latino star, is featured in the teen department of many stores, and fashions for spring of 2003 included Latino-influenced styles that featured bright colors and ruffled trims.

After the attacks of 9/11, the United States immigration authorities became concerned about the possible immigration of terrorists. As a result, they rigorously enforced existing immigration laws and sought out individuals who were in the country illegally. In the future it is likely that immigrants will face stricter admission policies, especially if they immigrate from countries or regions associated with terrorism.

Between 1980 and 2003 ethnic influences appeared sporadically as fashion designers incorporated design elements from various cultures in their collections. The focus on multiculturalism evident in the United States was not the inspiration for these designs, which often originated with Paris designers such as Yves St. Laurent. (See *Color Plate 62*.)

AIDS

Medical researchers of the 1980s were grappling with what soon amounted to an epidemic: AIDS—acquired immune deficiency—a deficiency of the immune system resulting from infection with human immunodeficiency virus (HIV). By 1984 French and American researchers had identified the HIV virus.

It is now believed that AIDS originated about 1959 in what was then the Belgian Congo and that the virus, HIV, evolved from a disease found in chimpanzees. Somehow the virus crossed the barrier between species.

The disease is transmitted through sexual contact, blood transfusions, needles shared by drug addicts, accidental needle injuries, and from mother to unborn child. The spread of AIDS to epidemic proportions was the result of dramatic changes in sexual mores, increased use of drugs, and increase in international travel.

In the 1980s AIDS became the leading cause of death in New York City among men aged 25 to 44. The National Institutes of Health reported in 2002 that about 850,000 to 950,000 U.S. residents were living with HIV infection. As of 2003, more than 42 million people have now been infected with AIDS, making it probably the greatest worldwide epidemic of the 21st century.

By 1996, tests of a new combination of drugs were proving successful in forcing the AIDS virus into remission and giving patients a rebound in health. In tests using these drugs, some patients appeared to be entirely free of the virus for almost a year. The expensive new multidrug treatment is not yet proven to be a cure for AIDS.

The AIDS epidemic has had a devastating impact on the fashion industry. By 1996 a number of top designers (Halston, Angel Estrada, Perry Ellis, Willi Smith) as well as colleagues who were unknown to the public, but worked in supporting roles in the fashion industry, were known to have died of AIDS, and there were rumors about the cause of death for still others.

The AIDS plague also resulted in economic problems for the industry. Investors were reluctant to provide backing for firms that they saw as vulnerable to disruption from the loss of key personnel. This led the financial community to look more favorably on some of the firms with women designers who are viewed as less likely to succumb to AIDS.

Because of the effect on business, the fashion industry had at first been reluctant to speak out about AIDS; however, this has changed. The Design Industries Foundation for AIDS (DIFFA) assists sufferers, and well-publicized benefit events have been held to advance the work of DIFFA.

THE FASHION INDUSTRY UNDERGOES CHANGES

The idea that that the fashion industry could no longer dictate styles to its customers had been growing for some time. Developments in the fashion industry between 1980 and 2000 ratified this proposition. Before the 1970s, scholars who wrote about fashion had generally agreed that fashion trends tended to begin with adoption of styles by an upper-class elite, after which the styles "trickled down" to the less affluent. Often the affluent individuals that began fashions were themselves patrons of the designers of the haute couture. By the 60s, when mainstream fashion began co-opting the styles of hippies and the young protesters, the notion was taking hold that some fashion influences came from the "bottom up."

Initially the number of influential street styles and the young style tribes who originated them (see *Chapter 18, pages 462–463*) were relatively few. But over the next four decades, style tribes proliferated. Analysis of these groups for an exhibit of street style fashion at the Victoria and Albert Museum in 1996 showed that almost half of the groups came together as a result of an interest in some kind of music, sometimes music of a particular ethnic group. The second most important interest bringing groups together was sports. Race, ethnicity, social class, political affiliation, ecological interests, sexual orientation, and drug habits united other groups. As their numbers increased, members easily recognized each other by the clothing they wore. Over time, some new style tribes grew out of other groups in a complex interconnected evolution (Crane, 2000, p. 188). See *Table 19.1*, which describes some of the better-known style tribes and *Figure 19.1* for depictions of the dress of some style tribes.

By 2000, the variety of acceptable options in dress available to consumers was enormous. Clothes could be bought from sources ranging from the haute couture to thrift shops. The style tribes described by Polhemus and others were mostly adolescents and young adults. Steele (2000) pointed out that affluent adult followers of certain fashion designers (often called **fashionistas**) could also be seen as members of style tribes. This concept can be extended to many other segments of the consuming public, for example, devoted catalog customers for merchants such as L. L. Bean and Land's End, or those who confine their shopping to particular television networks or Internet sites.

The fashion industry, which has always been a perilous business because of the unpredictability of fashion changes, found it was no longer possible to simply copy new trends originating with the top designers. Instead, manufacturers tended to focus on niche or specialized markets aimed toward persons from particular geographic areas, ages, social classes, ethnicities, or lifestyles.

Postmodernism

Some scholars believe that this movement away from a single predominant fashion ideal toward a variety of fashion segments can be explained by postmodernism. **Postmodernism** is the name given to the culture of the present period by some artists, philosophers, and social scientists. Morgado (1996, pp. 41–42) explained that this term has been applied to (1) theories about the nature of present-day society, (2) a style of expression in the arts, and (3) certain cultural values and sensibilities. The following examples may serve to illustrate a few of the ways that contemporary fashions can illustrate some of the elements of postmodern culture.

- *Rejection of authority* The rise of street fashion as an influence on mainstream fashion, the absence of a single dominant fashion silhouette, and the wearing of casual dress in almost any situation are all said to illustrate the rejection of the authority of both social mores and the fashion establishment.

- *Cultural or ethnic groups with irreconcilable differences* Styles based on ethnic and subcultural dress in both mainstream fashion and within subcultures play an increasingly important role in fashion.

- *The appropriation or juxtaposition of elements from different styles* Examples cited include the tendency to combine items such as hiking boots with sheer dresses or the turning of functional objects such as safety pins into ornaments.

- *The use of symbols without reference to their traditional meanings* Couturiers have designed high fashion clothes based on the traditional dress of nuns, monks, and Orthodox Jewish groups.

Elements of the Fashion System

A brief review of the elements of the system of design, production, and distribution of fashions and the changes they have undergone from 1980 to 2000 may help to clarify how the fashions available to consumers are determined in the 21st century. Crane's (2000, p. 135) analysis of the fashion system

FIGURE 19.1 A, B, C, D

Dress adopted by some of the more widely known style tribes. a. Hippie, 1960s. b. Punk, 1970s and after. c. Goth, 1980s and after. d. Hip-hop, late 1980s and after.

Table 19.1

SOME STYLE TRIBES AND THEIR IMPACT ON MAINSTREAM FASHION

Style Tribe	Dates Active	General Dress Characteristics	Impact on Mass Fashion
Zooties	Late 1930s into early 1940s	Long jackets, high cut baggy trousers, bow ties. Mostly adopted by young African Americans.	Disappeared as a result of World War II clothing restrictions. Revived in the early 1980s by some musical groups.
Beatniks	1950s	Originated with poet Jack Kerouac and friends, who wore casual clothes: workshirts, sweatshirts, jeans. Later, Americans followed French existentialists' preference for black. Women wore black tights under black skirts with ballet slippers, black knit blouses or striped knit shirts. Men wore black turtlenecks; grew small beards. Berets a preferred head covering.	Saint Laurent incorporated Beatnik style ideas in 1963 and Ralph Lauren used them as a basis for some designs in 1993.
Teddy boys	1950s	Elements cut in style somewhat like men's suits of the Edwardian period (1900–10).	Later Mods adopted similar types of styles for men.
Mods	1960s to early 1970s	Also known as neo-Edwardians. (See discussion in *Chapter 18, page 462.*)	In 1990s influenced Tom Ford for Gucci, 1995–96; Mark Jacobs, Anna Sui, Helmut Lang, Gianni Versace, Ralph Lauren, and Calvin Klein.
Hippies	1960s	Also incorporated psychedelics and body painting.	1993 Dolce and Gabbana collections included hippy-style beads, patchwork, fringes, shawl. Kenzo and Saint Laurent also revived.
Skinheads	1970s	In Britain, started as fans of Jamaican music. Shaved heads, heavy boots, clothes associated with manual labor. In U.S. skinheads associated in the public mind with racism, conflict and aggression. Evening Clothes were influenced by Mod styles.	Revival of interest in 1976. Dress clothes of skinhead women revived by "purist group of skinheads" in the early 1990s.
Rasta	1970s	Jamaican believers in Rastafarian religion wore large knitted tams; red, gold, and green shirts in the colors of the Ethiopian flag, hair worn in dreadlocks. Reggae musicians helped spread the styles. Bright-colored, tight clothing, worn with flashy accessories and fake gold jewelry.	Dreadlocks adopted by many African-Americans and some Caucasians as hairstyle in the 1990s and after. Designer Rifat Ozbek used Rastafarian dress as basis for clothes in 1991.
Glam	1970s	David Bowie and other musicians adopted androgynous costumes with ornate decorations and fabrics, accessories such as feather boas and platform shoes, dramatic makeup.	Fans of Glam rock stars copied their dress when attending concerts. Glam eventually branched into New Romantics and Goths.
Punks	Mid to late 1970s up to present	Originated with fans of punk rock music. Early punk followers dressed in original ways. Media stereotype developed of their dress as black leather and metal, ripped, safety pins as jewelry, brightly colored hair.	Designer Vivienne Westwood originated designs for early punk musicians and their followers. Has retained its popularity among a segment of young people. Punk revival evident in 1993. Designers Helmut Lang, Thierry Mugler, John Galliano, Jean Paul Gaultier, and Alaia all showed punk influenced styles in mid-90s. Punk surfaced again in late 2003.

Table 19.1

SOME STYLE TRIBES AND THEIR IMPACT ON MAINSTREAM FASHION

Style Tribe	Dates Active	General Dress Characteristics	Impact on Mass Fashion
New romantics	Late 1970s and early 1980s	Styles often derived from idealized and elegant view of earlier historic period styles in luxurious fabrics.	An offshoot of glam styles. Certain elements of the more decorative aspects for men's glam clothing were somewhat similar to typical new romantic styles. Vivienne Westwood's Pirates Collection in 1981 drew on new romantics style.
Goths	1980s	Dress derived from literary and art versions of characters in gothic novels and stories, in which vampires dress in black gowns and accessories. Charles Addams and *The Addams Family* TV show were especially influential.	An off-shoot of Glam and new romantics. John Galliano showed Goth inspired clothes in his 1992 collection. Influenced Gaultier and Gucci styles.
Preppies	1979 to early 1980s	Based on styles worn at famous preparatory schools: chinos, LaCoste polo shirts, blazers, D-ring belts, deck shoes.	As a conservative style, it caught on and became popular with both the young and young adults.
Fashion fetish or pervs	1980s and early 1990s	Stereotypical ideas of dress worn by those involved in sado-masochistic sex led to introduction of leather, rubber, and vinyl clothes, and tightly laced corsets, stiletto heels.	Previously an underground group, some of these styles were incorporated into punk styles and later into goth styles. Couture designers such as Gaultier, Versace, Mugler, Alaia, Westwood used as inspiration for collections.
Grunge	Late 1980s; early 90s	Originated as clothes worn by laborers in Seattle (plaid shirts, T-shirts, blue jeans–casual and unkempt); picked up by musicians, surfers. This look of "put on poverty" was adopted by grunge fans, who liked shapeless print dresses, torn jeans, faded denim vests, and plain shirts.	Designers, Jacobs for Perry Ellis, Anna Sui, and others picked up styles c. 1993.
Hip-hop	Late 1980s and after	Origin in the South Bronx with an athletic street solo dance style, break dancing. Boys were called B-boys (break boys) and girls, Fly girls. Associated with rap music. Men wore baggy pants and football or baseball shirts, baseball caps turned backward, and high running shoes with untied shoe laces. Clothes were oversized, pants worn low on the waist. Jeweled clips were worn on the teeth.	Hip-hop inspired styles especially popular among the young. Most of the young wore baseball caps backward or do-rags. Designers such as Tommy Hilfiger did well with these design ideas. A number of popular hip-hop musicians branched out into designing and/or merchandising their own lines of clothing. Galliano used do-rag headwear in 2003.
Ravers	Late 1980s and 1990s	Huge dance parties held outdoor or indoors in large spaces, called "raves." Drug ecstasy became associated with some raves. Dancers wore T-shirts with smiley faces, or tie-dyed, psychedelic prints, hippie-like elements. Or functional clothes: T-shirts, shorts, sneakers, baseball caps.	Rave influences show up in designs of late 90s done by German designer Walter Van Beirendonck.
Cyberpunks	1990s	Clothing uses leather, rubber, PVC, and incorporates technical hardware devices, cables, circuit boards, etc.	Gaultier, 1992–93, incorporated cyberpunk ideas in collection.

Sources: De la Haye, A. and C. Dingwall. 1996. *Surfers, Soulies, Skinheads, & Skaters*. Woodstock, NY: The Overlook Press. Polhemus, T. 1994. *Street Style*. New York: Thames and Hudson. Takamura Z. 1997. *Roots of Street Style*. Tokyo: Graphic-Sha.

at the turn of the millennium is useful. She states that haute couture as a source of fashion inspiration has been replaced by three major categories of styles, which she calls luxury fashion design, industrial fashion, and street styles.

Luxury fashion, in this categorization, includes the firms that are part of the haute couture and some of the more innovative and expensive ready-to-wear designers. Luxury fashion is not limited to Paris, but can also be found in fashion centers such as New York, Milan, London, Tokyo, and other cities. American luxury fashion is rarely made-to-measure. But often it is sold, Crane says, via designer trunk shows. Trunk shows are held in various cities, attended by wealthy clients who see and can try on the clothes, and they are hosted by the designer who can use these opportunities to build a sense of the needs and wants of this market. Bill Blass before his retirement was famous for his use of trunk shows. Michael Kors is a designer who has continued the practice.

Crane defines industrial fashion as fashion "created by manufacturers, which sell similar products to similar social groups in many different countries, as well as by smaller companies that confine themselves to a particular country or continent." Firms such as Ralph Lauren, Liz Claiborne, and Tommy Hilfiger would fall into this category.

Street styles are the styles originated by urban subcultures or style tribes. Media attention helps to spread styles that seem to arise spontaneously or that are adopted by a small group. For example, urban youth in places such as the South Bronx were wearing certain kinds of clothes for street performances of break dancing and rapping. These styles were copied by teens in other places, especially after hip-hop music became popular. In the 1990s Tokyo became known for constant innovation in street styles. Young Japanese avidly participated in fashion that appeared on the street and was quickly manufactured and sold by small producers. Japanese newsstands sold weekly newspapers that reported "as seen on the street" fashions. By 2000, Western fashion entrepreneurs were visiting Tokyo to observe the fashion scene.

The interconnections between luxury fashion, industrial fashion, and street styles cannot be ignored. With the rapidity of communication in the 21st century, ideas can move easily from one area to another. As a result, ideas originating in Tokyo street fashion may show up on the runways of Paris haute couture shows or in clothes produced by industrial fashion firms. Crane (2000) effectively summarizes how and why fashion in the new millennium is so diverse: "Different styles have different publics; there are no precise rules about what is to be worn and no agreement about a fashion ideal that represents contemporary culture."

THE ROLE OF THE HAUTE COUTURE IN THE 80s AND 90s

Until the 1960s, the Paris *haute couture* was the undisputed pinnacle of made-to-measure clothing. Its designs set the style trends. (See *Chapter 17, page 433,* for a description of the structure and functions of the *haute couture.*) This position had been challenged during the social revolution of the 1960s when *prêt-à-porter* (ready-to-wear) designs became more influential. Fashion pundits proclaimed the death of the couture. Morris (1982) summarized this viewpoint, saying "During the era of miniskirts, T-shirts, and blue jeans, a couture designer seemed as obsolete as a blacksmith."

The couture did not disappear, although its influence waned in the 1970s. By the early 1980s, the couture had made something of a comeback. Wealthy women from the oil-producing countries provided a new clientele able to afford couture clothing, although because of Moslem dress restrictions many women from Arab states wore these couture creations only in the privacy of their homes.

The good economic times of the Reagan years (1980–88) made affluence socially acceptable, and lavish clothing, especially for evening wear, was prominently featured in the fashion press. Designer Christian Lacroix opened a new couture house in 1987. But even though the affluent were patronizing the couture, the emphasis of couture designers had shifted. In their shows couturiers did not try to compete with prêt-à-porter, but rather focused on suits, dresses, and evening dresses.

Although fashion no longer proposed only one way of dressing, the reaction of fashion designers to this change differed enormously. It was almost as though two divergent schools of thought had developed about design. Some designers came to be considered as classicists. Others saw fashion as a plaything, available for people to use. (See *Figure 19.2.*) Most couturiers participated in both the couture and ready-to-wear. As Spindler (1996) commented, "The client list [of couture houses] has dwindled drastically, and most see high fashion only as an engine to drive the other businesses at couture houses: ready-to-wear apparel, perfumes, and makeup licenses."

Changes in the way the business of luxury fashion design is organized also affected fashion. The two most important transformations were the acquisition of couture and ready-to-wear houses by large businesses (conglomerates) and global marketing. In the new world of fashion, it is often most important for a design firm to gain media attention that will help to promote not the designs shown on runways, but a wide variety of auxiliary products sold worldwide. As Koda (2001) observed, "While many of the most elaborate idea-driven designs are never seen on the street, they are invariably crucial to the promotion of a more diluted 'realistic' product." (See *Figure 19.3.*)

READY-TO-WEAR

Much of the action in fashion between 1980 and 2000 came from the ready-to-wear segment of the fashion industry.

The United States Americans had, by the 1980s, become accustomed to buying ready-to-wear clothes designed by famous American as well as foreign designers, many of whom

a
b

FIGURE 19.2 A AND B

The contrast in designer attitudes toward fashion is evident in the differences in these two designs for men's suits. On the left (a), the "classic" style favored by Armani (1996); on the right (b), a "theatrical" three-piece, striped suit by Gaultier (1994). (From *Daily News Record*, Armani suit from Fall 1996; Gaultier suit from July 7, 1994. Courtesy, Fairchild Publications.)

had their own businesses. Department stores organized sales floors according to designers or manufacturers, so that customers could easily find the clothes from their favorite fashion houses. *Table 19.2* lists some of the major American designers active from the 1980s up to 2003.

France The prêt-à-porter firms established in the 1960s thrived. Many were connected with established couture houses and the couturiers designed the lines. Franchised boutiques sold these ready-to-wear products in cities around the world. Manufacturers purchased licenses to use the couture

name on such diverse items as handbags, jewelry, and household linens.

Other designers and firms emerged who created only prêt-à-porter lines. Many of these firms were not French but participated in the French shows because of the attention paid to the two showings each year in Paris. French firms also took part in trade shows in other countries.

Italy Italians continued to be a strong presence in ready-to-wear and in the couture. Firms such as Biagiotti, Gianfranco Ferré, Versace, Krizia, Missoni, Dolce and Gabbana, Prada,

FIGURE 19.3

Many runway styles, like this Dior garment by Galliano from the 2002 haute couture show, were not likely to appear on the street as shown. (Photo courtesy of Fairchild Publications.)

and Soprani in women's wear; Giorgio Armani in men's and women's wear; Fendi in furs; and Ferragamo and Gucci in leather products developed international reputations for fine design, quality, and workmanship.

London In the 1980s British fashion diversified and unconventional and innovative styles, many derived from street fashions, once again appeared along with the classics. Princess Diana and Sarah Ferguson, the Duchess of York, helped to draw attention to British fashion designers through their patronage. British design got attention in 1996 when British designers were selected as head couturiers at Dior and Givenchy.

Japan In the 1980s Japan emerged as a major fashion center. A number of Japanese designers, some already internationally known, others relatively unknown outside of Japan, showed their lines at the 1983 Paris prêt-à-porter show. Many of the Japanese designs were radically different from other

contemporary fashions and immediately stimulated interest and wide press coverage. (See *Figure 19.4.*) *Gentlemen's Quarterly* noted in May 1984, "Japanese fashion is different. These are clothes that conform to no fashion standards. They seek to abolish form. They hang loosely on the body in oversized, unusual silhouettes. The colors are almost always monochromatic or black."

The best-known designers were Issey Miyake, Yohji Yamamoto, Mitsukiro Matsuda, and Rei Kawakubo. Kawakubo called her firm *Comme des Garçons* (French for "like the boys") and reactions to her designs and those of other innovators ranged from enthusiastic endorsements of the "new wave" to derisive labeling of the loose, dark, unfitted clothes as "bag lady styles."

FIGURE 19.4

Cotton blouse with a floppy collar and a matching skirt from the 1982 line of Japanese designer Rei Kawakubo for *Commes des Garçons.* (*Women's Wear Daily,* October 8, 1982. Courtesy, Fairchild Publications.)

Throughout the 1980s and the 90s the Japanese continued to garner attention for both men's and women's wear. After initially showing extreme styles, many firms became more conservative and more commercial, with *Daily News Record* reporting in 1988–89: "Many Japanese designers who recently showed collections in Tokyo moved away from idiosyncrasy in favor of a more wearable and classic approach to design." At the same time, designers such as Miyake continued to innovate truly individual styles. (See *Color Plate 68*.)

Table 19.3 lists some major foreign ready-to-wear and couture designers active in the period from 1980 to 2003.

Changes in the Production and Retailing of Apparel

MANUFACTURE

Although some American manufacturers were using computer technology to cut the costs of apparel manufacturing, many were responding to increasing globalization of industry by having their merchandise assembled in Third World countries. This practice has changed apparel manufacturing for those large companies that rely heavily on offshore manufacturing. In the past, companies would manufacture only those styles that were ordered in quantity by retail store buyers. Under the foreign production system, orders must be placed before manufacturers know which styles will be most popular, so it becomes especially important for the company to research its customers' preferences carefully. A representative of Liz Claiborne (Daria 1990, p. 139) explained, "If we have a sweater on the line and we own ten thousand units of that sweater, and people want to buy fifty thousand units, we can't supply it. We're stuck. On the other hand, if everyone hates it, we're in big trouble."

Changes made in 1994 in the GATT treaty that regulates imports led to a gradual termination of all quotas for imports. Predictions were that domestic apparel production would decline from 60 percent to 50 percent in the period from 1994 to 2004, when the treaty was fully implemented. American apparel manufacturers also expected to see Mexico increase its share of ready-to-wear clothing manufacturing at the expense of domestic production as a result of the North American Free Trade Agreement (NAFTA); however, China has taken much of the business expected to go to Mexico.

By 2003 it was evident that both the apparel and the textile industries in the United States had already suffered severe economic losses. In order to meet foreign competition, some American manufacturers in the 1990s exploited workers, often immigrants, who worked in sweatshops in metropolitan areas of the United States. Protesters have also made the abusive working conditions and low pay of some foreign workers an issue, especially targeting those firms selling high-priced merchandise.

MERCHANDISING

Merchandising practices were as diverse as apparel styles by 2003. Beginning in the 1960s and early 1970s small boutiques opened to sell craft and creative fashions. Other boutiques with specialized style orientations appeared in towns and cities across the country. This led many department stores to organize sales floors into small boutiques that featured the clothing of one designer. American consumers also purchased clothing from "off-price" retailers (fashion apparel discounters), factory outlets for particular manufacturers, and an ever-increasing number of mail-order outlets.

Vintage Clothing   Used clothing stores had first been patronized by hippies in the 1960s, and later by other shoppers who sought out "vintage" clothing. Sometimes fashion trends were begun when shoppers found designer styles in resale clothing stores that were, in turn, manufactured in new, contemporary versions. Some customers who valued quality and excellent workmanship shopped for vintage designer clothes, often paying prices of over $1,000 for garments in good condition. Stores selling used clothing ranged from these expensive boutiques to low-cost thrift shops.

An active, overseas market for used blue jeans had developed. A *Vogue*, April 1995, article described the trade in Levi's 501 jeans. (The number 501 was the lot number given to jeans in 1890 by the manufacturer.) Depending on quality and type, used 501's commanded prices that might go as high as $2,000 in Japan for a pair of "hidden rivets" in good condition. Hidden rivets jeans are those with rivets hidden inside the pockets, and were made between 1937 and about 1960. By 2002, specialty manufacturers were making replicas of well-worn jeans. All of the worn spots, tears, repairs, stains, and so forth, on an authentic pair of used jeans were reproduced on a new pair of jeans and sold for around $150 to $200. These sales of "new vintage jeans" represented about three percent of the jeans market, but mass market retailers such as Gap soon started selling distressed jeans for under $50 (Bunn 2002).

New Methods of Selling   By the 1990s competition from off-price, discount, and factory outlet stores, together with ill-advised financing and management decisions, led to the disappearance of many old and well-established department store chains. Catalogs proliferated. They accounted for about five percent of apparel sales in the United States. Television shopping channels and the Internet were other sources of apparel. One research study done at New York University's Stern School of Business (Pastore 2000) predicted that by the year 2004, at least 60 percent of those having access to PCs in the United States will have bought over the Internet. But these projections are for all Internet shopping, not just apparel. Researchers at Cotton Incorporated do not expect apparel sales on the Internet to exceed about 5 percent of garment sales (Messura 2003). It may be that Internet apparel sales will be most appealing to rural residents who live far from stores and those who prefer to remain anonymous, such as cross-

Table 19.2

SOME PROMINENT DESIGNERS WORKING IN PARIS AND OTHER FASHION CENTERS: 1980–2003

Designer	Working in:	Notable Characteristics of Designs or Career
Italian Designers		
Giorgio Armani (1934–)	Ready-to-wear: Showed his own men's wear collection: 1974; women's wear in 1975.	Known for fine tailoring, easy, comfortable designs. A retrospective exhibit of his work was done at the Guggenheim Art Museum in New York in 2000.
Gianfranco Ferré (1945–)	Ready-to-wear: Established his own firm: 1974. Couture: served as designer for Dior from 1989 to 1996.	Brought background in architecture to his designs; high standard of tailoring. Continues to produce ready-to-wear in Italy.
Domenico Dolce (1958–) and Stefano Gabbana (1962–)	Ready-to-wear: opened their own business in 1982, added knitwear in 1987 and lower-priced collection called D&G.	Described as combining modern styles with romantic and historic references.
Miuccia Prada (1950)	Ready-to-wear: first showed in 1989.	Clothes said to be "supremely comfortable," and "coming to life on the body."
Gianni Versace (1946–1997) and Donatella Versace (1956–)	Ready-to-wear. First men's wear collection: 1979; women's wear later. After his death in 1997, his sister Donatella took over the firm and has continued to be very successful.	Known for innovative designs in leather and other fabrics. His sister works "in the Versace mode of bold prints and forthright sexiness."
French Designers		
Azzedine Alaïa	Ready-to-wear: Shows only sporadically.	Known for clinging, sexy styles. Helped initiate this trend in early 80s. Is considered a highly innovative designer.
Jean-Paul Gaultier (1952–)	Ready-to-wear, until he joined Hermès in 2003 where he will do couture.	Shows non-conformist, exaggerated designs. Bustier styles of mid-80s especially notable. Designs of 2000 and after seen as more classical.
Nicholas Ghesquière (1972–)	Couture: Named head designer at Balenciaga in 1997.	Considered to be a young designer to be watched, a "leader of the avant-garde."
Christian Lacroix (1951–)	Couture: Designer for Patou 1981-87; opened own house in 1987. Also does ready-to-wear and was named creative director for Pucci in 2002.	Introduced wide-skirted short gowns in mid-80s, known for theatrical styles.
Karl Lagerfeld (1939–)	Couture and ready-to-wear: designs for Chanel (from 1982) and also under his own name.	Tremendously versatile designer. Also designs furs of Italian firm, Fendi.
Claude Montana (1949–)	Ready-to-wear: freelance until opening his own firm.	"Characteristics: bold, well-defined shapes."
Thierry Mugler (1946–)	Ready-to-wear: designed under own label after 1973. Retired from fashion design in 1999; the firm closed in 2002.	First known for designs with very broad shoulders, narrow waists. His fashion shows often were considered outrageous.
Sonia Rykiel	Ready-to-wear: opened own boutique, 1968.	Especially well known for sweater-like designs. Later added men's wear and children's wear.

Table 19.2

SOME PROMINENT DESIGNERS WORKING IN PARIS AND OTHER FASHION CENTERS: 1980–2003

Designer	Working in:	Notable Characteristics of Designs or Career
English Designers		
John Galliano (1960–)	Ready-to-wear: London in the 1980s Couture: Chief designer at Givenchy for couture and ready-to-wear 1995; moved to Dior in 1996.	Initially known for uninhibited, avant-garde styles; evolved to more sophisticated clothing made with great skill.
Alexander McQueen (1970–)	Ready-to-wear: London. Couture: named to succeed Galliano at Givenchy in 1996. By 2001 he had left Givenchy and was showing under his own name.	Known for provocative shows and linear tailoring.
Zandra Rhodes (1942–)	Ready-to-wear: began making own designs 1969.	Known for original and sometimes eccentric designs. Incorporated punk designs in mid-70s.
Vivienne Westwood (1941–)	Ready-to-wear: around 1970.	Often working with street style and clothes such as Punk, New Romantic, Fetish styles.
Belgian and German Designers		
Martin Margiela (1957–)	Ready-to-wear: beginning in the 1980s.	Belgian "fashion iconoclast" who makes unconventional clothes. Became head designer at Hermès from 1997 to 2003. Known for superb tailoring skills; "deconstructionist" styles with seams on outside, etc.
Jil Sander (1943–)	Ready-to-wear; first collection under own label in 1973. Firm bought by Prada in 1999. She left firm a year later and returned in 2003.	German "minimalist" with emphasis on "design without decoration," "lines and cuts out of the ordinary," and high quality.
Japanese Designers		
Rei Kawakubo (1942–)	Ready-to-wear: Showed in Tokyo-1975, Paris-1981. Firm called *Comme des Garçons*.	One of Japanese designers to make major impact in Paris in early 80s. (See *page 510.*)
Kenzo (1945–)	Ready-to-wear: Notable in Paris from early 70s. He retired in 1999 and his firm continues with new designer.	"Designs based on traditional Japanese clothing; spirited combinations of textures and patterns."
Issey Miyake (1938–)	Ready-to-wear: Opened own firm in Tokyo, 1970 after studying in Paris; first showing in Paris, 1973. In 1999, he appointed another designer to do men's and women's collections.	"Combines Japanese attitudes of fashion with exotic fabrics of his own designs."
Hanae Mori (1925–)	Couture and ready-to-wear: well-established in Japan before showing couture collection in Paris in 1977. the firm suffered from the economic downturn in Japan and filed for bankruptcy in 2001.	Notable aspects of her designs are "unusual and beautiful" fabrics with "Japanese feminine motifs. . . evening and at home wear."
Yohji Yamamoto	Ready-to-wear: first collection shown in Tokyo in 1976 and in Paris in 1981.	One of Japanese designers to make major impact in Paris in early 80's.

Information about designers already listed in Table 18.2 (see *pages 470–472*), who continued to be active for all or part of this period is not included in this table.

All material in quotes comes from Calasibetta, C. M. (1988). *Fairchild's Dictionary of Fashion,* 2nd edition or Calasibetta, C. M. and P. Tortora (2003), 3rd edition New York: Fairchild Publications and Stegemeyer, A. (1996 and 2004) *Who's Who in Fashion,* 3rd or 4th editions. New York: Fairchild Publications.

	Table 19.3	
	SOME AMERICAN DESIGNERS WHO BECAME PROMINENT IN THE PERIOD 1980–2003	
Designer	**Name of Firm and Date of Its Opening**	**Notable Characteristics of Designs or Career**
Liz Claiborne (1929–)	Established Liz Claiborne Inc. in 1976. Retired from the company, which continues, in 1989.	Orginally focused on sportswear; expanded to dresses and children's wear. "Philosophy: Simple and uncomplicated designs of mix-and-match separates" in moderate price range.
Perry Ellis (1940–1986)	Perry Ellis Sportswear established in 1978; Perry Ellis menswear in 1980. Name continues to be licensed in United States and abroad.	Designs described as "young, adventurous, spirited; use of natural fabrics." Designed wide variety of apparel and household textiles.
Tom Ford (1962–)	After working at Perry Ellis and other firms, he joined Gucci in 1990 and brought clothing design to this firm, which had been mostly leather goods. In 1999 he added the post of Design Director at Yves Saint Laurent. Ford left these positions in 2003.	In positions at Gucci and Saint Laurent, Ford was responsible for overseeing design, product development, choosing designers, and the advertising campaigns. Seen as having revitalized the Gucci brand.
Carolina Herrera (1939–)	Established firm in 1981; did her first fur collection for Revillon in 1984, did lower priced ready-to-wear called CH in 1996.	Makes clothes to order for some private clients. Known for elegant clothes. She designed Caroline Kennedy's wedding dress.
Tommy Hilfiger (1952–)	Entered fashion design from retailing, beginning to design in 1979 and showing under his own label in 1984.	Beginning with styles for men, he gained a loyal following among rap and hip-hop musicians and their fans. He expanded into clothing for women, children, and plus sizes.
Marc Jacobs (1964–)	Managed own firm beginning 1986–88; joined Perry Ellis from 86-83; showed under his own name after 1994 and continues in 2003. In 1997, he became the designer for Vuitton.	Considered a "design prodigy" who was immediately successful in building a reputation as a highly original young designer.
Sean Puffy Combs (1979–)	Created Sean John label in 1998. Continued to expand the types of products he produces.	Sean Puffy Combs, a musician and music entrepreneur, who entered design with clothes geared to teens and young adults. Between then and 2003, he earned a number of fashion awards, and has become very successful.
Betsey Johnson (1942–)	Designed for various firms; opened boutique with friends, Betsey, Bunky & Nini (1969); Betsey Johnson Inc, 1978.	Unique and original styles, in particular is known for "Basic Betsey," described as "a limp, clinging T-shirt dress in mini, midi, and maxi lengths."
Norma Kamali (1945–)	Established boutique and company called OMO in 1978.	Produces innovative designs for wide variety of prices and markets. Especially known for bathing suit designs and garments made of sweatshirt-type fabric.
Donna Karan (1948–)	After designing for Anne Klein, established her own firm and showed first independent collection in 1985.	Influential designer in the 80s and after, made particular impact with clothes for successful professional women. Designs own accessories. Expanded to less expensive line DKNY in 1988.
Mary McFadden (1936–)	Formed Mary McFadden, Inc. in 1976.	Known for designs that utilize unusual fabrics, fine pleating reminiscent of Fortuny, quilting.

Table 19.3

SOME AMERICAN DESIGNERS WHO BECAME PROMINENT IN THE PERIOD 1980–2003

Designer	Name of Firm and Date of Its Opening	Notable Characteristics of Designs or Career
Isaac Mizrahi (1961–)	Worked at Perry Ellis, Jeffrey Banks, and Calvin Klein before forming his own business in 1985. Closed his business in 1998, worked in TV and theater, and reentered fashion design in 2003 doing a lower priced line for Target stores.	Specialized in luxury sportswear for women and beginning in 1990 for men also. Designs were considered inventive, using unexpected colors and fabrics, while also being comfortable.
Willi Smith (1948–1987)	WilliWear Men, 1978.	Quoted as saying about clothes, "People want real clothes, I don't think people want to walk around looking like statements with their shoulders out to there." Introduced graffiti-art inspired designs.
Anna Sui (1955–)	Stylist and designer in 1970s, her own line marketed first in 1980. First runway show in 1991.	Clothes described as a "mixture of hip and haute, romance, and raunch." Prices clothes moderately so that young customers can afford them.

Information about designers already listed in Table 18.2 (see *pages 470–472*), who continued to be active for all or part of this period is not included in this table.

All material noted comes from Calasibetta, C. M. (1988). *Fairchild's Dictionary of Fashion*, 2nd edition or Calasibetta, C. M. and P. Tortora (2003), 3rd edition. New York: Fairchild Publications and Stegemeyer, A. (1996 and 2004) *Who's Who in Fashion*, 3rd or 4th editions. New York: Fairchild Publications.

dressers, transvestites, and those who comprise very specialized markets, such as members of style tribes, individuals who require very large or small sizes, or handicapped persons with special needs.

Television stations devoted to shopping provide another means of selling apparel. The traditional way for shoppers to make such purchases has been by telephone; however, technology is being developed to permit interactive television purchases using special electronic devices. Some potential customers for Internet shopping and television shopping are reluctant to make electronic purchases because they cannot view the merchandise closely, or handle it. Delays necessitated by shipping merchandise and the inconvenience and expense of returning unsatisfactory products by mail are other reasons given for resistance to electronic shopping.

The Growing Teen Market By 2000 it was evident that the teen market, and a new segment of the children's market that they called **tweens** (approximately 7–14 years of age), were playing an increasingly important role in retailing. In 1995 there were 4,000 stores aimed exclusively at teens. By 2003, this number had increased to about 10,000. The teen market (for all products) was estimated to be about $70 billion a year (Rozhon 2003). Trying to capture this market was not easy. Teens tended to be fickle and capricious in their tastes. They got their fashion information from celebrities such as rappers and athletes, magazines, television, and music—most

notably MTV—and from peers. Their loyalty to brands fluctuated, although labels associated with pop music stars did well. Price was important. With 31.6 million shoppers between ages 12 and 19 and a market estimated to grow to 33.9 million in 2008, retail concentration on teens will obviously continue (Scardino 2002). (See *Contemporary Comments 19.1*.)

THE PROMINENCE OF LABELS

Designers' labels for men's clothes had become a selling point by the 1980s. Italian styles, especially those by Giorgio Armani, were widely copied. Japanese designers created men's as well as women's fashions in the early 1980s. By the 1990s, lines of clothing for men carrying designer labels were available in everything from suits and coats to active sportswear and accessories.

Whole stores were being devoted to licensed goods from individual companies, such as Disney. Licensing and logos were so important in children's clothing that trade magazines devoted monthly sections to news about licensed goods. (See *Illustrated Table 19.5. page 545.*)

Loyalty to brands had diminished by 2000. With a downturn in the economy and availability of larger quantities of lower cost imported apparel, consumers were paying more attention to price than to brand names. Market share of many popular brands had dropped substantially by 2003.

CONTEMPORARY COMMENTS 19.1

Tween Shopping

by RUTH LA FERLA

CHANTAL WILLIAM, the owner of the G. C. William boutique on Madison Avenue near 85th Street, looked on in amusement the other day as Romy Schreiber breezed in, her fashion antennae twitching. As Ms. William recalled, no sooner had her client crossed the threshold than she made a beeline for a rack of little black dresses, pleading to try on a sleeveless model sparkling with bead. "I picked it out myself, it was my style," Ms. Schreiber said later.

Pressed to define that style, she fumbled for the right word, setting on "cool," an adjective she applied to other items on her most-wanted list, which ran from twin sets and pendant chokers to long skinny skirts, bell-bottoms and tiny kilts like one she had just acquired by Burberrys. Ms. Schreiber also obligingly listed her favorite makes and models—Calvin Klein, DKNY, Kate Moss and Cindy Crawford—chanting their names in the sing-song rhythm of a small girl skipping rope.

Ms. Schreiber is 9. At an age when many of her contemporaries are decked out in overalls and box-pleated skirts, her own hyper-hip fashion choices conjure up an image that's two parts Posh Spice, one part Diana, the Princess of Wales.

She would recognize a kindred spirit in Kristina Obermeier, 10, who was spied perusing the racks in Saks Fifth Avenue's girls' department. With her blond hair pulled back in a chignon like her idol, the Olympic figure skater Tara Lipinski, Kristina streaked toward the DKNY rack, leaving her mother in the dust. She gazed Frisbee-eyed at a calf-length column-shaped jumper that could easily pass muster at her parochial school but flirted with fashion just the same. "It's black and I love to wear black," she said, with the authority of a budding style maven. "It goes with everything."

Both girls cultivate a look poised at fashion's cutting edge. Only a few years ago, it would have marked them as members of a hip elite, their tastes outside the mainstream. But to hear the experts tell it, youngest fashion consumers, age 10 and under, represent a huge market, whose profile is rapidly shifting, said Traci Mitchell, the executive editor of Children's Business, a fashion trade monthly.

"The majority of little girls want to look grown up and fashion-conscious—it's a big trend," Ms. Mitchell said, adding that although parents hold the purse strings, their style-savvy offspring are increasingly making the buying decisions.

Copyright © "Ex/Chic Little Numbers: The Hipless Elite." 1998 by The New York Times Co. Reprinted with Permission.

THE FASHION INDUSTRY IN THE NEW MILLENNIUM

In spite of the fragmentation of the fashion market, the affluent 1980s had seen the rise of a number of very successful designers and manufacturers. By 2000 a number of these firms were in serious financial difficulty. In *The End of Fashion, Wall Street Journal* reporter Teri Agins (1999) chronicled the difficulties experienced by many leading fashion industry firms. She identified four trends as contributing to the changes that had come about in the fashion industry. These were the movement of women away from fashionable dress and toward clothes that were practical for their work and lifestyles, the trend toward more casual dress, the devaluation of designer labels, and the success of some designers and manufacturers in focusing on clothes that customers would be willing to buy.

THE ORIGINS OF MAJOR FASHION TRENDS OF 1980–2003

Retro Fashions

Retro, short for retrospective, styles took their inspiration from the past. Many designers of the 1980s and 90s looked back and not ahead. Milbank (1989), catalogued revivals in the decade of the 80s of bustles and crinolines; turn-of-the-century camisoles and petticoats; long hobble skirts; Jazz Age dropped-waisted chemises, Depression-era looks; World War II large shoulders; 1950s bustiers, toreador pants, and off-the-shoulder stoles; and sheath dresses and minis in Day-Glo colors from the 1960s. In 1995 mod styles returned, designers of 1996 created flapper dresses and empire waistlines. (See *Figure 11.8, page 276.*) Some 2000s styles were based on mod, punk, 1950s and 1970s styles, and on miniskirts and op art prints.

Various Social Groups Influence Fashion

Both trickle-down and bottom-up origins for fashion can be seen in the 1980s and 90s.

THE AFFLUENT AS CONSUMERS OF HIGH-PRICED FASHION

Political and Social Elites For centuries, royal families had influenced fashions. Such individuals continued to capture the imagination of the public, especially when romance was involved. The engagement and 1981 wedding of Prince Charles of England to Lady Diana Spencer served to thrust "Princess Di" into the fashion spotlight. Not only did imitations of her wedding dress become instant best sellers in bridal wear, but also the press kept up a running commentary on her wardrobe throughout the 1980s. When British Prince Andrew married Sarah Ferguson in 1986, the bride wore a dress with back fullness, a feature that then became fashionable.

After Ronald Reagan's election as President of the United States in 1980, social activities at the White House provided a stage for the display of lavish fashions. Like Jackie Kennedy before her, Nancy Reagan was much criticized for the amount of money she spent on clothing. Neither Barbara Bush nor Hillary Clinton caught the imagination of the fashion press. In 1996 at least one fashion writer noted that Mrs. Clinton had "no clear image," while Laura Bush's preferences might be characterized as simple and understated.

Yuppies and Preppies The booming economy of the early 1980s made the acquisition of high socioeconomic status both desirable and possible for many young people. Until the stock market crash of 1987, **yuppies** (the nickname applied to young, upwardly mobile professionals who worked in fields such as the law and business) strove to acquire high-status possessions. Male yuppies wore Italian double-breasted "power suits" to work, and female yuppies donned similarly cut women's versions.

Affluent students in Ivy League colleges who would become yuppies after graduation and their imitators wore **preppy** styles, a name derived from the private preparatory schools these students had attended before entering college. The preppy look stressed classic tweed blazers, conservatively cut skirts or trousers, tailored blouses or shirts, and high quality leather loafers, oxfords, or pumps.

STREET STYLES INFLUENCE FASHION

African-American Style For a time the African-inspired fashions that had made headlines in the 1960s were out of the news. In the late 1980s African-influenced styles were back in the news with much of the impetus for these fashions coming from African-American inner-city youth and from the rap musicians they saw on MTV. They began the practice of wearing Adidas® sneakers or high tops with the laces untied, oversized T-shirts, huge gold earrings, and gold chains. They originated the **fade,** a hairstyle in which the hair was cut very short on the sides, and long on top, and began to have names, words, or designs shaved on the scalp. When the rock group Public Enemy introduced a song called "Black is Back," there was a return to black consciousness, and young African-Americans began wearing African-inspired round, flat-topped crown hats and leather medallions with maps of Africa in the colors of African or West Indian countries that were layered four or five at a time over T-shirts.

Kente cloth, a traditional, colorful African fabric became enormously popular. The African fabric had a woven design, but many printed imitations were made and used in items ranging from dresses to umbrellas. (See *Color Plate 66.*) By the 90s, hip-hop music fans, both white and black, were wearing oversized, baggy pants, matching football or baseball shirts, baseball caps that were put on backward, the aforementioned untied running shoes, and carrying leather knapsacks. **Dreadlocks,** long hair arranged in many long hanging twists, were worn by Rastafarian (a religious sect) reggae musicians from Jamaica, and during the period from 1980s to 2003 some young African-American men and women and some Caucasians adopted these styles. (See *Illustrated Table 19.2, pages 532–533.*)

Body Piercing and Tattooing Some of the aforementioned style tribes incorporated body piercing and/or tattooing as elements of their dress. Other individuals called themselves modern primitives and chose to adopt these forms of ornamentation as a kind of tribute to "traditional peoples." By the 1990s and after, body piercing and tattooing had become fashionable for both women and men. The scale of tattoos ranges from small decorations that are not visible when the person is fully dressed to tattoos covering almost all of the body. For those who wanted to participate in the style temporarily, removable imitation tattoos were available. (See *Color Plate 76.*)

In the 1990s, many young people were wearing several earrings in several piercings in the same ear. Addition of jewelry to other parts of the body (tongue, nose, lips, navel, nipples, and private areas) required that these areas be pierced. Jewelry worn in these areas is known as **body jewelry.** (See *Figure 19.5.*) In 2003, while midriff baring styles were very fashionable, body jewelry for the navel was particularly popular. (See *Figure 19.24, page 537.*) Those reluctant to be pierced might wear simulated body jewelry that clipped into place or was held together with magnets.

The Persistence of Blue Jeans and the Importance of Denim Jeans continued to be a staple in people's wardrobes. Even haute couture designers used denim fabrics. Denim was used for jackets, for skirts, and for entire suits. For those who preferred jeans that looked used, textile manufacturers developed techniques for dyeing and finishing that produced a faded or streaked look and a soft texture. Called pre-washed, stone-washed, or acid-washed, these and other jeans were produced in a wide variety of colors.

FIGURE 19.5

Young men and women began wearing several earrings in several piercings in the same ear in the 1990s and after. Other facial ornaments were also added, as the fashion for body jewelry grew. (Photograph courtesy of Matt Templeton.)

FIGURE 19.6

Jeans with tears became an important style for young people in the late 1980s. (*Women's Wear Daily,* May 22, 1986. Courtesy, Fairchild Publications.)

Old jeans were cut off at the knee and worn as shorts. Manufacturers picked up on this development and sold them as **cutoffs.** By the late 1980s young people were wearing jeans that were purchased with large horizontal tears on the legs. (See *Figure 19.6.*) The style became a Paris street fashion in 1985 and, aided by a 1987 revival of interest in 1960s protest clothing in the United States, was brought to a wider audience in a 1988 music video, by British rocker George Michael. After young people began appearing in jeans that they had slashed themselves, manufacturers began to manufacture and sell them.

This phenomenon might be seen as an illustration of a type of status symbol described by Quentin Bell (1973) in *On Human Finery.* Social scientists had accepted that conspicuous consumption and conspicuous leisure were symbols of wealth. Bell suggested that a third type of status, which he called **conspicuous outrage,** be added. He argued that economic status could be demonstrated by purchases so outrageous that they showed the buyer had money to invest in something nonfunctional or, as in the case of torn jeans, something contrary to expectations for "new" and high priced garments.

Current Events

Current events often inspire particular fashions or clothing practices. The impact of the tragic events of September 11, 2001 on fashion was largely economic. Demand for clothing dropped sharply and many manufacturers had to lay off significant numbers of workers. Clothing with American flags and red, white, and blue ornamentation appeared everywhere, providing a means of making a patriotic statement. See *Figure 19.7,* and *Color Plate 71.*

As the United States went to war, military influences appeared in civilian dress. Cargo pants were fashionable, especially among the young. Trench coats and battle jackets appeared on Paris runways. Styles ranging from cargo pants to women's sheer blouses were made from fabrics decorated with camouflage prints. At first these prints were made in the traditional camouflage mixes of tans, browns, greens, and grays, but by 2003, they also appeared in mixes of vivid colors, with no pretense that these patterns would blend into any natural background. (See *Color Plate 73.*)

FIGURE 19.7

After the terrorist attacks on the United States of 9/11/2001, many items of clothing were decorated with patriotic symbols. (Author's photo, model: Rosemary Perry.)

FIGURE 19.8

Interest in the Far East was evident in garments such as this kimono designed by Valentino. (Photo courtesy of Fairchild Publications.)

The transfer of Hong Kong to China on July 1, 1997 stimulated interest in Chinese-influenced styles, including kimonos and the traditional cheongsam dress. (See *Figure 19.8.*)

Clothing has been worn in protest against politics and the social milieu in many historic periods. But by 2000, it was difficult to engage in clothing-based protest against the current establishment. The disappearance of widely accepted norms of dress has robbed protest clothing of its ability to shock or startle. Almost the only way to really get a message across, Givhan (2002) concludes, is to wear a T-shirt with a clearly printed message.

The Media as a Fashion Influence

Motion pictures and television continued to influence fashion. Sometimes films or TV shows or personalities inspired a general look, and other films helped to make a particular garment popular. Films with period settings helped to contribute to the focus on retro fashion. *Table 19.4* provides some specific examples of influences on fashions from various media in the period from 1980 to 2003.

ROCK MUSIC GROUPS

From the 1970s to the 1990s, rock bands and stars such as Michael Jackson, Madonna, Grace Jones, Annie Lennox, and others had followers who copied their style of dressing. Some music groups have their own designers, others hire stylists who shop for the clothing they wear during performances. Still other performers, like Madonna, change designers often so their look does not become predictable. Designers who work for performers also design for the retail market or operate their own boutiques. In discussing the influences of music on fashion, Conlin (1989) observed, "Teen fashion trends

Table 19.4
SOME MEDIA INFLUENCES ON FASHION: 1980–2003

Media	Dates	Style Influences
Motion pictures	1981	*Raiders of the Lost Ark:* gives men's Stetson-type hats brief popularity.
	1983	*Flashdance:* made gray sweatshirt fabric dress: a popular fashion.
	1985	*Top Gun,* with Tom Cruise, started a fashion for cropped hair and a military look.
	1986	*Sid and Nancy:* Film about punk rock stars helps to maintain interest in punk styles.
	1990s	Disney film productions such as *Pocahontas* and re-release of earlier Disney animated films related to growth in use of logos of cartoon characters on children's clothes.
	1996	Three films made from Jane Austen novels contribute to a revival in empire styles.
	1999	The coats worn in the film *The Matrix* helped make trench coats popular in subsequent couture collections.
	2000	In *Erin Brockovitch,* actress Julia Roberts wore special bra that gave a natural look and cleavage to flat-chested women.
	2001	*Moulin Rouge* contributed to a fashion for lace, Edwardian clothing, and bustiers.
Television	1978–91	*Dallas:* creates interest in Stetson hats and Western attire.
	1984–89	*Miami Vice:* star Don Johnson with unshaven look, no socks.
		Dynasty: program spun off a line of clothing bearing its name.
	1990s	*Barney:* dinosaur on PBS children's programs becomes popular logo on children's clothing.
Popular music and popular music videos	1980s	Michael Jackson wore one sequined glove on his right hand, was imitated by teens.
		Madonna wore sexy outfits, including such items as off-the-shoulder bra straps, torn fishnet stockings, leather and chains, and imitated Marilyn Monroe's look from the 50s.
		Rock group *Public Enemy* with the song *Black is Back* helped to begin revival of African-influenced styles.
	1990s	Teens who followed hip-hop, grunge, reggae, or other music groups adopted the styles worn by these musicians.
	Late 1990s	Spice Girls music group's skimpy bustiers, bare-midriff halter tops were copied by fans.
		Britney Spears becomes major fashion influence for pre-teens.
	Late 1990s to 2000s	A number of successful musicians (Sean Combs, Jennifer Lopez) start their own clothing lines.

owe much to the music world. Kids pick up styles from concerts and videos and quickly take them to the street." Styles from the street may circulate among the young fans or penetrate the mainstream. The enormous diversity of these styles helped to contribute to the many fashion trends that coexisted in the 1980s and 90s.

With the growth in the Internet, even those fans living in rural areas could obtain information easily about where to buy clothing like that worn by their favorite musicians and other fans. Some musicians branched out into fashion design.

Hip hop musicians were represented by Russell Simmons' *Phat Farm,* Jay Z's *Rocawear,* Jennifer Lopez' line called *J. Lo,* and Sean Combs, whose *Sean John* label won a number of menswear fashion design awards between 2000 and 2003.

Influences from the Fine Arts

Diana Vreeland, retired from her position as editor of *Vogue* magazine in the early 1980s, joined the staff of the Metropolitan Museum of Art in New York City, and presented a number of major costume exhibitions. Among the exhibitions that helped to stimulate designs were those based on the costumes of India, China, and the 18th century.

Retro fashion revived not only styles from previous fashion eras, but also drew inspiration for garments and textiles from the work of such artists of the past as Picasso, Velasquez, Klimt, and from such art movements as Surrealism of the 1930s and op art of the 60s. At the same time, contemporary art had an impact when Willi Smith utilized graffiti art, spray-painted on New York subways, in his designs in 1984.

Artists working in the medium of fiber and apparel continued to produce striking wearable art designs.

Demographic Changes

White (1996) pointed out that demographic changes appear to have affected the fortunes of the fashion industry negatively. Apparel spending peaked in 1978 when the baby boomers, some 75 million individuals born between the end of World War II and 1964, were between 15 and 32 years of age. In 2003, 24 million of those "boomers" were over 50 years of age and 27.5 percent of the population consisted of baby boomers. Since 1978, spending on apparel has declined and spending on services increased. Furthermore, as women age, their bodies change. The trend toward increased use of casual clothing may also be related to demographics. The baby boomers grew up wearing jeans and casual clothes. It is probably not surprising that they also welcomed the opportunity to wear those casual clothes to work.

The North American Association for the Study of Obesity (2000) reports that some 64 percent of Americans are overweight or obese. Large size or "plus size" apparel is available not only for adults, but also for children. It is estimated that plus size clothing sales bring retailers around $17 billion a year. One result of these demographic changes has been the opening of apparel stores that cater to larger women

Overweight women and the boomers moving toward middle age feel that they have little in common with the hyper-thin fashion models they see in fashion magazines. During the mid-90s fashion models appearing on runways and in magazines looked almost anorexic, and many women wrote to magazines to protest illustrations they felt might be setting a dangerous precedent for impressionable adolescents, who admired these "supermodels." (See *Contemporary Comments 19.2, page 526.*)

The widespread use of models in advertising and fashion magazines who appeared emaciated, pale, with unkempt hair and large circles under the eyes was inspired by the work of influential fashion photographers. This trend of the 1990s coincided with an increase in use of hard drugs by celebrities, which the media started to call "heroin chic" in 1995. Eventually the name was applied to this style of fashion photography, and concerns were raised that the elevation of **heroin**

chic models to high fashion status would encourage the use of drugs among young people.

The Trend to Casual Dress

The movement of population to the suburbs after World War II and the concurrent growth of casual sportswear had contributed to an increase in informality in daily life and dress in the United States. Young people of the 60s with their protests against "the establishment" had adopted jeans and other casual clothing as dress for school and for play. Adults followed their example, and sportswear became the major style worn during leisure time. Formal occasions requiring people to "dress up" became fewer; however, the business world still required a certain standard of decorum in the office.

By the 1990s, a number of businesses had instituted policies whereby employees could dress casually on Friday. In 1996, 90 percent of all companies had at least one casual dress day each week. Spokespersons for the apparel industry felt that the casual dress trend posed a threat to the nylon hosiery industry (Sara Lee 1996), to necktie companies, and suits (Adler 1995). At the same time, sales of men's casual wear increased. From 1990 to 1996, sales of men's shirts, sweaters, and knit tops increased by 31 percent, while khakis, casual dress slacks, jeans, and golf pants were up 36 percent (Steinhauer 1997). (See *Figure 19.9.*) But as the economy weakened in the new millennium, casual dress for business seemed to be declining somewhat. In May 2003, David Wolfe of The Doneger Group, a fashion merchandising consulting firm, noted that top managers in Fortune 500 companies, some major law firms, and financial institutions were dressing in a more traditional manner (Gordon 2003).

Fabrics Old and New

In the 1980s and 90s new, so-called **high-tech** fabrics made possible the design of clothing for active sports that took advantage of the unique properties of these fabrics. Waterproof but breathable fabrics were used for running, biking, backpacking, camping, and hiking. Ultra fine **microfibers** (see *Color Plate 70*) made of nylon and polyester were used to make high-performance, water-resistant, soft fabrics for skiwear and other active, outdoor sports. Fabrics made from blends of natural fibers or manufactured fibers and spandex, a high stretch synthetic fiber, appeared in bathing suits, bicycling pants, and skiwear. (See *Figure 19.10.*) Manufacturers developed special fabrics for racing swimmers that, when warmed by body heat, clung closely to the body, minimizing drag. A silicone finish repelled water, which helped to move the swimmer ahead in the water. Polypropylene, a manufactured fiber that dried quickly and carried the moisture of perspiration away from the body, was made into socks and thermal underwear for winter sports.

FIGURE 19.9

Examples of causal business dress for men, 1996. (Photograph courtesy, Levi Strauss & Co.)

Although these materials were designed for active sports, designers of high fashion and sportswear were soon utilizing some of these fibers and concepts. Stretch fabrics became a major factor in fashion. Body-hugging, knitted leggings, leotards, and body stockings were included in many couture and ready-to-wear collections beginning in the late 1980s. Eventually fabrics for classic garments such as tailored blouses and shirts, blazers, fitted skirts, and pants incorporated stretch yarns to ensure a better fit.

As the apparel industry moved into the new millennium, some technologically enhanced fabrics were beginning to be available. Teflon-coated fabrics that resisted staining were marketed. Other advanced fabrics were beginning to appear, such as those that store and release heat in order to maintain body temperature. One Japanese firm showed a prototype of a jacket with a computer screen in the sleeve.

The manufacture of rayon, an important fiber for clothing since the 1920s, produces substantial levels of water pollution. A variant of rayon, given the generic name of lyocell, was developed that is more environmentally friendly, and by the 1990s garments made from Tencel® and other trademarked lyocell fibers were widely available.

High tech and manufactured fabrics contributed to new ideas in fashion, but it was a natural fiber that was one of the most important fashions of the 1990s. Cashmere has long been used for luxury knits and woven fabrics. Pashmina is cashmere; it is the name that cashmere is called in the Kashmir region. Fashion promotion of brightly colored shawls of fine quality cashmere as "pashmina shawls" gave this accessory an elite status. By 2000, pashmina shawls had become mass fashion, and many of the shawls sold by street vendors in large cities as "pashmina" were made of ordinary wool and even of manufactured acrylic fiber.

Fabrics fueled other fashion trends. These included voided velvet, a fabric in which sheer background alternated with designs in raised velvet pile; op art prints; and animal prints, especially leopard, wild cat, tiger, cow, and zebra designs.

FIGURE 19.10

In the 1990s, clothing for active sports and working out, called activewear, utilized stretch and microfibers. Bare midriff styles were especially popular for women. (*Sportstyle*, February 1996. Courtesy, Fairchild Publications.)

Sports

Interest in fitness continued to stimulate the growth of clothing for running, jogging, and exercising. The distinctions between clothing for active sports and sportswear for non-sports activities blurred.

In the past, one pair of athletic shoes or sneakers had been sufficient for almost any kind of sport activity and for casual wear. It is almost impossible to overestimate the importance of sneakers in the 1980s and 90s. Sneakers became **high-tech footwear.** In 1980, when New York City experienced a transit strike, young women walking to work wore sneakers and carried their more dressy work shoes, changing once they got into the office. When the strike ended, the practice continued, and throughout the 1980s and after, many women wore sneakers as they traveled to work.

Expensive sneakers became a status symbol among poor, inner-city youth, and incidents were reported in which sneakers and other high-status garments were stolen and their owners killed to obtain the prized items (Berkow 1990).

By 1995 retro fashion had taken hold even in sneaker styles with revivals of sneaker styles of the 50s and 60s. In addition to a huge variety of sneakers, there were also tennis shoes, running shoes, jogging shoes, walking shoes, and hiking boots. After 2000, high, stiletto-heeled shoes with uppers of canvas sneakers appeared.

Recognition of the important place of active sportswear in the fashion industry came in the mid 1990s as well-known designers began designing lines of active sportswear. The Sporting Goods Manufacturing Association reported that 86 percent of Americans owned sports apparel, and but that only 8 percent of the population wore sports apparel *exclusively* for athletic activities (Schiro 1996). (See *Color Plate 64*.)

Costume Components for Women: 1980–1995

Several schools of design emerged in the 1980s. Although these designs did not appeal to the average consumer, they did have an impact on other designers. Japanese influences, for example, were evident in the popularity of blacks and grays, and the innovative cuts typical of the Japanese were reflected in the work of other designers. Martin Margiela, a Belgian designer, became one of the best-known of the **deconstructionists,** designers who made clothes with seams located on

FIGURE 19.11

In the early 1980s, designers such as Thierry Mugler shortened women's dresses and added broad, exaggerated shoulder pads. (*Women's Wear Daily*, October 4, 1982. Courtesy, Fairchild Publications.)

the outside, linings that were part of the exterior, or fabric edges left unhemmed and raw. As with the Japanese, these designs had an impact on mainstream design in subtle ways.

A few trends were identifiable within the many varying fashion segments. The 1980s had begun with an indication of change. Shoulders and sleeves were larger, with shoulder pads being added to everything from daytime dresses to sweaters for casual wear and evening dresses. (See *Figure 19.11*.) The fashion for large shoulders continued into the early 1990s, after which shoulder lines became smaller and more natural.

The 1980s ushered in a period of greater interest in the body that continued into the new Millennium. Skirt lengths gradually decreased. Tightly fitting dresses were made from spandex stretch fiber blends. (See *Figure 19.12*.) Not only were many items made with cutouts or bare midriffs, but through-

FIGURE 19.13

Sheer styles of the 1990s were shown by designers with little or no underwear beneath or, as in this dress with tights and a short jacket by Anna Sui, as part of a "layered" look. Women generally wore such styles over some other garment. (*W* magazine, January 1997. Courtesy, Fairchild Publications.)

FIGURE 19.12

In the mid-1980s and later, short, tight dresses made of fabrics that blended stretch fiber spandex with other fibers were one of the available style options. (*Women's Wear Daily*, August 3, 1988. Courtesy, Fairchild Publications.)

out the 90s lace and sheer fabrics were fashionable. (See *Figure 19.13*.) Designers showed these garments with little or nothing underneath; however, most women wore these transparent dresses as an outer layer over a more opaque garment and stores ordered these items with linings.

Short skirts and miniskirts reappeared in the 80s. Throughout the 90s these were seen side-by-side with skirts

FIGURE 19.14

By the 1990s, dresses and skirts were being made in a wide variety of lengths ranging from (a) short to (b) medium to (c) long. All of these different styles appeared in 1992. (*Women's Wear Daily:* (a) Complice, October 12, 1992, (b) Evan-Picone, March 18, 1992, (c) Kors by Michael Kors, October 20, 1992. Reproduced courtesy of Fairchild Publications.)

---

of many different lengths. (See *Figure 19.14.*) The most common choices were between very short skirts and those that reached to below the calf. Long, straight skirts had long slits. Many dresses, skirts, and pants were fitted and tight until the early 1990s. By the mid-90s pant legs had became wider, and short, full skirts appeared.

UNDERWEAR

While the same general repertory of undergarments continued in use, frilly, feminine underwear made a comeback. Victoria's Secret, a national chain of stores, was quite successful, selling colorful lace and ribbon-trimmed undergarments and sleepwear.

When clothing became more form-fitting in the 90s, undergarments provided more support and shaping, with modern versions of corsets and even bustles. The latter were padded panties with trademarks such as Rear Riser™ or Butt-booster™. See *Illustrated Table 19.1* for some examples of undergarments from the period between 1980 and 2003. When bodice styles were cut low and intended to show cleavage, special bras were designed to provide the needed uplift.

GARMENTS

While no one silhouette or skirt length predominated and the range of fabrics used was very wide, a few trends in fabric use were evident. Rayon fabrics, out of fashion since the end of World War II, returned to popularity in the 1980s and 1990s. Bright floral-patterned rayons, many reminiscent of fabrics of the 1930s, were popular. Printed rayon dresses often had empire waists and buttoned down the front. Although natural fibers were preferred over synthetics by many people, Lycra® spandex was used extensively in blends with other fibers for stretch fabrics. Very fine polyester microfibers were made to look and feel like silk.

CONTEMPORARY COMMENTS 19.2

Readers Object to Extremely Thin Models

Some readers of fashion magazines took exception to the exclusive use of fashion models who were extremely thin. The following are excerpts from letters to the editor of W, a monthly fashion magazine published by Fairchild Publishing Company.

February 1996
"I am absolutely appalled by the pictures in the December edition.

. . . All the models appear to be anorexic at best and like refugees from concentration camps at worst. With cases of anorexia in adolescents and young women increasing dramatically, I find it almost criminal for this magazine to glamorize girls and women who look like this."

April 1996
"Varied theories and opinions have been offered by celebrated designers regarding the 'depressed' state of fashion today. I would like to offer another.

Much designer fashion does not target a major market: 'plus size' or 'full figure.' . . .

Affluent large-size women attend fashion shows. They shop. They are eager to see how a fashion ensemble could be interpreted for them. As fashion consumers, they are involved in a never-ending quest to find quality, stylish clothes. . . .

. . . In our country, more women wear dresses sizes 12–16 than 0–8."

May 1996
". . . And if the models in those spreads were animals, you can bet the Humane Society would fine you for starving them and depriving them of exercise. . . ."

Diverse dress styles from which women could choose included classic shirtwaist dresses or long, dresses unfitted through the bodice and joined to gathered skirts at a dropped waistline (a 1920s revival). Sweater dresses; T-shirt dresses; sweatshirt dresses; and short, tight dresses made with spandex stretch fibers could be found, as could chemise or shift dresses, usually sleeveless, and ranging from fitted to full tent-like styles. Young women wore delicate, sheer dresses over other garments and combined them incongruously with hiking boots or sturdy sandals. Coordinated ensembles of dresses worn with short to almost full length jackets or coats were also seen.

Tailored suits worn with a tailored blouse were considered appropriate wear for women pursuing active careers in business, although by the latter part of the 1980s these suits were somewhat less uniformlike and more diverse. Some were collarless, cardigan style. As skirts grew shorter, working women were cautioned against wearing their skirts too short. Around 1987 when skirts were growing very short, the length being recommended for the office was "just above the knee." When skirts continued to shorten, some women switched to pants suits which made a comeback in the 90s. (See *Figure 18.21, page 496.*)

After 1987, when the style was introduced by Giorgio Armani, a suit consisting of shorts and a matching tailored jacket called the **shorts suit** was worn as an alternative to the skirted suit. (See *Figure 19.15.*) In the mid-80s, the traditional Chanel suit was revived by designer Karl Lagerfeld, who became designer for the Chanel firm after 1982. Lagerfeld took the basic Chanel formula and updated it imaginatively with vivid colors and his own individual touches. Some versions were made more for the fashion show runway than for the street. (See *Figure 19.16.*)

By 1990 jackets were long. With them women wore short, slim skirts or pants.

EVENING WEAR

Dresses for evening were among the most interesting of the designs produced in the 80s by a revived French couture. These designs influenced ready-to-wear formal clothing as well. The glamour of evening clothing contrasted with the conservative clothing recommended for daytime wear for career women. Evening dresses had a great deal of glittering embroidery, sequins, and beading. Colors were bright and fabrics ornamented with vivid woven or printed designs.

Around 1985 Christian Lacroix, designing for Patou, produced a design nicknamed **Le Pouf.** It had a wide, puffy skirt with a light airy appearance. Shown in both short and longer styles by Lacroix, it was copied widely, especially in shorter lengths. Other wide-skirted, short styles were

Illustrated Table 19.1

SELECTED UNDERGARMENTS FOR WOMEN AND MEN: 1975–1996

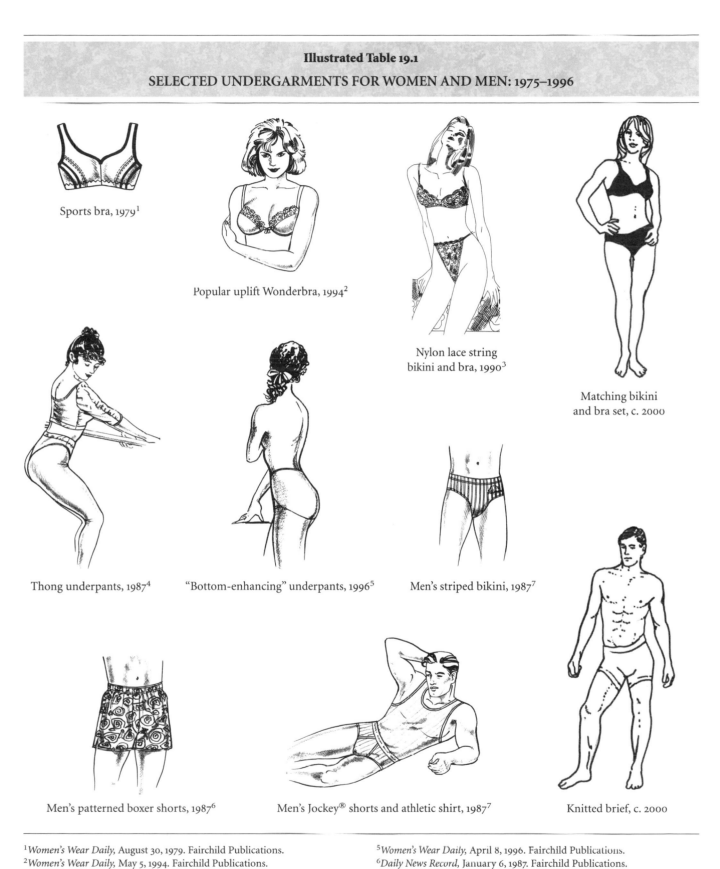

Sports bra, 1979[1]

Popular uplift Wonderbra, 1994[2]

Nylon lace string
bikini and bra, 1990[3]

Matching bikini
and bra set, c. 2000

Thong underpants, 1987[4]

"Bottom-enhancing" underpants, 1996[5]

Men's striped bikini, 1987[7]

Men's patterned boxer shorts, 1987[6]

Men's Jockey® shorts and athletic shirt, 1987[7]

Knitted brief, c. 2000

[1] *Women's Wear Daily,* August 30, 1979. Fairchild Publications.
[2] *Women's Wear Daily,* May 5, 1994. Fairchild Publications.
[3] *Women's Wear Daily,* May 10, 1990. Fairchild Publications.
[4] *Women's Wear Daily,* November 11, 1987. Fairchild Publications.

[5] *Women's Wear Daily,* April 8, 1996. Fairchild Publications.
[6] *Daily News Record,* January 6, 1987. Fairchild Publications.
[7] *Daily News Record,* January 7, 1987. Fairchild Publications.

FIGURE 19.15

The shorts suit, shown here in a version by Giorgio Armani, was an alternative to the skirted suit in the latter part of the 1980s. (*Women's Wear Daily,* October 16, 1990. Courtesy, Fairchild Publications.)

known as **mini-crinolines.** By the late 1980s the wide-skirted evening dresses were superseded by tightly fitting, short evening dresses that were either strapless or had tiny shoulder straps and were made from stretch fibers. Simple, slip dresses of soft, crepe fabrics were often worn in the 90s and maintained their popularity after the Millennium. (See *Figure 19.17a* and *b.*)

By the mid-90s the full-skirted, short, strapless evening dress was back again. Lace or elaborately decorated bustiers were worn for evening in the 90s. (See *Figure 17.18.*) So, too, were long, fitted evening dresses. Black was a popular color. These long gowns might be strapless, sleeveless, with one covered shoulder, or with "peek-a-boo" cutouts. Some

dresses of the mid-90s had interesting details that were visible at the back. In 1996, Galliano, designing for Givenchy, showed flapper-style beaded evening dresses. (See Figure *19.17c* and *d.*)

OUTDOOR GARMENTS

By the end of the 80s, longer down coats were replaced by short, casual down jackets. Both real and imitation fur coats were worn throughout the period. In the 90s furs became less

FIGURE 19.16

After Karl Lagerfeld became head designer for Chanel, he included "updated" versions of the classic Chanel suit in his collections. Some seemed to be designed more for the fashion show runway than for street wear. (*Women's Wear Daily,* October 18, 1994. Courtesy, Fairchild Publications.)

FIGURE 19.17 A, B, C, AND D

Between 1985 and 1996, evening dresses included a wide range of styles. (a) short, wide-skirted mini-crinoline dresses from the Paris collections of Patou, 1987. (*Women's Wear Daily,* January 28, 1987). (b) Short, bare evening dresses, this one by Donna Karan, were popular in the late 1980s. (*Women's Wear Daily,* November 7, 1989.) (c) Long gowns with cutouts or bare shoulders; the one depicted is by Donna Karan and worn by Hillary Clinton, wife of U.S. President Bill Clinton, in 1993. (d) Retro fashions, based on beaded dress styles of the 1920s, were created by Galliano in 1996. (*W* magazine, September 1996. All photos reproduced courtesy, Fairchild Publications.)

bulky and some were brightly colored. Large oversized coats, perhaps inspired by Japanese design, were worn over narrow dresses and suits in the early 80s, but by the mid-decade many coats were neat and not over-wide. Lengths varied. Some were quite long, and shorter lengths were also available. By the late 1980s shorter coats were being worn especially with pants.

Throughout the 90s, wrap coats and trench coats were popular. In 1996, the idea of "between season" coats was revived, and a design originated by Chanel in the 1960s was widely copied.

SPORTSWEAR

pants and skirts: Culottes or divided skirts were worn on and off throughout the 80s. Toward the end of the decade of the 80s, spandex was used to make tight-fitting, stretch tights or leggings. Some of these covered the entire leg including the foot, others extended to the ankle, and still others ended at mid-calf or around the knee. Some were made in bright prints such as those designed by Emilio Pucci. These were worn with large, loose T-shirts, sweaters, or under miniskirts.

Pants were slender at the beginning of the 90s, then started to widen. By 1994 some pants had grown quite wide and had large cuffs.

blouses, sweaters, and other tops: Early in the 1980s sweatshirts became a big fashion item. American designer Norma Kamali originated a line of clothes inspired by the knitted fabric used in sweatshirts and characterized by fanciful colors. The styles included not only traditional sweatshirt design features, but extended to skirts, dresses, and even evening wear. (See *Figure 19.18*.)

Blouse styles of the mid-80s ranged from tailored designs used with business suits to blouses and sweaters with standing collars finished with a ruffle at the top and sleeves gathered into the armscye and with puffed sleeve caps that looked as if they owed their inspiration to the Gibson Girl. Other notable styles of the 80s and early 90s included shirts cut large though the shoulders and full through the body, which were often worn as overblouses with pants or skirts. T-shirts ranged from basic cotton tees to those made in handsome fabrics and with embroidered, sequined and beaded decorations. Fine gauge cotton or silk knit T-shirts were being worn with suits as distinctions between work and play clothes broke down.

Fair Isle patterns and knitted pictures appeared on sweaters in early and mid-80s, but after this sweaters were more likely to be plain or have overall patterns.

One of the most popular blouse styles of the early 90s was a frilly, white blouse with large sleeves. Sometimes it was worn with slim, black pants for evening. Sweater sets were similar to those of the 1950s: a pullover and matching cardigan. More expensive versions were made from cashmere. Some T-shirts and knit tops were made to fit tightly. Turtlenecks, never altogether abandoned, became more important again.

FIGURE 19.18

Norma Kamali's sweatshirt fabric designs, here in an oversized turtleneck worn by Ms. Kamali (left), and a blouse with a short, full skirt were exceptionally popular. (*Women's Wear Daily*, November 11, 1980. Courtesy, Fairchild Publications.)

CLOTHING FOR ACTIVE SPORTS

As a result of the promotion of fitness, running suits, warmup suits, jogging and exercise suits proliferated and were worn as casual streetwear as well as for exercising. In the early 1980s sweatshorts were worn over sweatpants or tights. Spandex blended stretch fabrics were used for everything from brightly colored leotards to bathing suits and ski suits. Synthetic fleece fabrics provided good insulation in cold weather for outdoor activities. Making polyester fleece from recycled soda bottles was seen as an ecological advantage.

swimming: A new bathing suit style appeared, cut with a high, inverted **V** at the sides over the hip, the cut reaching almost to the waistline. (See *Figure 19.19*.) Often this high side was combined with a deep V in front and/or in the back of the suit. Bikinis, including those with thong bottoms, continued to be an option, as did more conventional one-piece suits. Holly Brubach, writing in *The New Yorker* (1991), noted, "Those days of consensus, in swimsuits as in fashion, are gone. Today all the options exist simultaneously."

skiing: Olympic skiers used skin-tight, hooded skisuits in vivid colored fabrics made from high tech fibers that minimized wind resistance. Styles for recreational skiers utilized some of these ideas, but were more fashion-oriented with bright Day-Glo colors dominating until the late 1980s when softer, more pastel colors were preferred.

In the 1990s, ski clothing styles also reflected the trend to retro fashion. Ski styles of the 60s and 70s were revived. Ski styles included tight knit sweaters with racer stripes, quilted down parkas, flared stretch pants, and short, snug jackets. At

FIGURE 19.19

A new "high-thigh" cut for bathing suits, originated by Norma Kamali, influenced bathing suit styles of the 1980s. (*Women's Wear Daily*, February 27, 1985. Courtesy, Fairchild Publications.)

the same time, there was a fad for wearing ski goggles pushed up on the head.

tennis: Women wore knitted tops (often white) with either skirts and shorts in white or colors. In 1985 Anne White wore a skin-tight, white jumpsuit to play her first match at the Wimbledon tennis tournament, and was banned from wearing the garment for subsequent matches. The authorities said the garment was "not traditional tennis attire."

SLEEPWEAR

Choices for sleepwear ranged from all-in-one sleepers with feet to frilly, feminine nightgowns in fabrics ranging from silk to brushed nylon tricot. In the mid-80s and 90s both short and long T-shirts were being worn as nightshirts.

Robes included long or short fleece styles made from colorful, high pile or velour knits made from manufactured fibers and long and short quilted robes.

HAIR AND HEADDRESS

See *Illustrated Table 19.2* for some examples of hairstyles and hats for the period from 1980 to 2003.

hair: ". . . hairstyles reflect diversity of current fashion" noted *The New York Times* on April 6, 1980. This comment had been true for the latter part of the 1970s and continued to be true throughout the 1980s and the 1990s.

Both long, full, curly hair and frizzy, curly hair in both longer and shorter lengths continued.

By 1984 shorter hair was being seen more often, and by the close of the decade women wore hair either short or long. In 1986, those who wanted to experiment with punk styles could use erasable post-punk colors to color their hair. By the end of the 80s some women were wearing their hair very short and in some cases men and women wore the same hair cut. The 1990s saw a return to popularity of long, straight hair, another 60s revival.

Beginning in the mid-1980s, hat sales rose as much as 15 percent each year. Young people were more likely to wear hats than were older persons. Hats were still being used more to keep the head warm than as a fashion statement. With publicity about the need to protect the skin from ultraviolet light, hats were also worn as protection against the sun. Nevertheless, a variety of ways of decorating the hair could be observed. In 1985, headbands appeared in summer; in the late 1980s, hair bows; in 1988, scarves were tied around the hair or small elastic bands with ribbon or fabric decorations attached; and after Bill Clinton's election in 1992, some women wore headbands like those worn by Hillary Clinton. Elastic bands covered with fabric, for confining ponytails, were called **scrunchies.**

FOOTWEAR

See *Illustrated Table 19.3, page 538* for some examples of footwear for the period from 1980 to 2003.

Illustrated Table 19.2
TYPICAL HAIRSTYLES AND HEADCOVERINGS FOR WOMEN AND MEN: 1980–2003

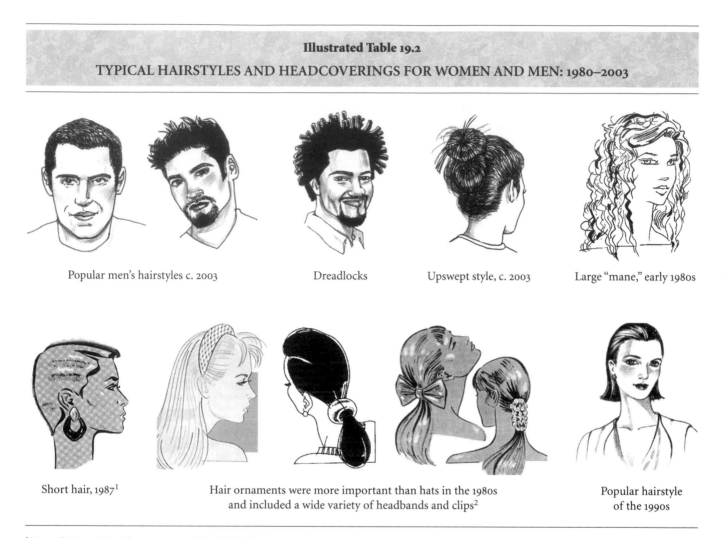

Popular men's hairstyles c. 2003   Dreadlocks   Upswept style, c. 2003   Large "mane," early 1980s

Short hair, 1987[1]   Hair ornaments were more important than hats in the 1980s and included a wide variety of headbands and clips[2]   Popular hairstyle of the 1990s

[1] *Women's Wear Daily*, February 27, 1987. Fairchild Publications.
[2] *Women's Wear Daily* Accessories, October 23, 1987, January 1989, October 1988. Fairchild Publications.

Pantyhose were either opaque or sheer. Some were patterned and others had beaded, sequined, or other decorations applied. By the mid-1990s opaque stockings without texture or pattern were more fashionable.

shoes: As skirts grew shorter toward the end of the 80s, lower heeled shoes were worn. Throughout the 1980s sneakers of all kinds were worn for sports and leisure time. In the 1990s sneaker styles from earlier decades were being revived.

The 90s provided considerable variety in footwear. Many of the styles were revivals of earlier styles. They included platform-soled shoes revived in 1992 that had wedgie or large, square heels, stiletto heels, two-tone, spectator-style shoes that were often black-and-white. In the 1990s, boots made a major return. Important styles ranged from thigh-high boots to hiking boots.

Many young people wore Doc Martens laceup boots, which had first been made in 1946 for physician Klaus

Maertens who, after hurting his foot skiing, had shoes made for himself with air pocket soles to ease pressure on his feet. The style, licensed to R. Griggs & Co. in 1959, first came to the notice of the fashion world when they were adopted by skinheads and punks in the 60s and 70s.

JEWELRY

Small diamond solitaire ear studs were very popular in the 1990s.

ACCESSORIES

See *Illustrated Table 19.4, page 539* for examples of popular accessories from 1980 to 2003. Among the most notable of the many fashionable accessories of the decade of the 1980s were shawls and large scarves, often worn over coats. In 1983

Illustrated Table 19.2
TYPICAL HAIRSTYLES AND HEADCOVERINGS FOR WOMEN AND MEN: 1980–2003

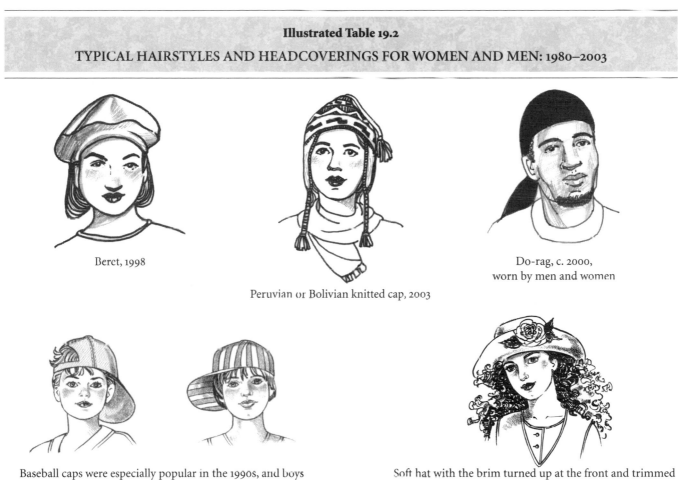

Beret, 1998

Peruvian or Bolivian knitted cap, 2003

Do-rag, c. 2000,
worn by men and women

Baseball caps were especially popular in the 1990s, and boys
and young men often wore them with the bills turned backward[1]

Soft hat with the brim turned up at the front and trimmed
with a flower or a bow was a popular hat style of the 1990s[1]

[1]Simplicity Pattern Catalog, Fall 1995.

Swatch® watches became a fad and maintained their popularity in the ensuing years. Quilted leather handbags remained popular in the 90s and after. Small duffel back packs replaced handbags for some women. As cell phones became more popular, handbags and business cases had special compartments for them.

COSMETICS AND GROOMING

The natural look of the 1970s was replaced in the 1980s by more obvious makeup. Lipstick was darker, often with a still darker outline at the edges of the lips. In order to have the full, pouty lips popular in the 80s, models and some women had silicone injections to make their lips larger. Pale, powdered skin was preferred to a tanned look. The connection pointed out by physicians between sun exposure and skin cancer was probably responsible for making suntans unfashionable.

Fingernail polish came in a host of colors. Some young women followed a fad for coloring each nail a different color.

A variety of hair care products were needed to maintain the fashionably tousled hairstyles, and as a result hairstyling mousses, gels, and sprays proliferated.

Street fashion focused interest on tattooing and body piercing for the attachment of ornaments. To participate in these fashions without making permanent changes in their bodies, one could buy clip-on rings for the navel and the nose and decal tattoos that would wash off.

Costume Components for Women:
1995–2003

Many of the trends of the early 1990s continued into the last half of the decade and on into the 2000s. During the 1990s, it had become more and more difficult to identify any one "look" or predominant silhouette. Individuals were likely to dress in styles acceptable to their peers. If the peer group was attuned to current fashion trends for that group (as adolescents, media stars, or avid followers of high fashion were likely to be) fashionable styles came and went quickly. For other women, the same basic, classic styles might be worn year-after-year, with more current fashions showing up in clothing for special occasions or in hems moving slightly up or down from one year to another. By 2003, dressy dresses often had uneven hemlines. As fashion moved toward and entered the new Millennium, not only did the variety of available fashions increase, but at the same time, customers could find almost any variation they wanted in these garments. If one skirt length was not to their taste, shoppers could find another.

The following section presents a brief summary of developments in women's dress in the late 1990s until 2003 that differ from those of the 1980s to mid-1990s.

GARMENTS

By the latter years of the 90s, influential designers who were called **minimalists** were making styles in neutral or darker tones that had little ornamentation and good lines. (See *Figure 19.20B*.) After the turn of the millennium, the minimalist tendencies declined, although some examples remained, and more colorful and dramatic styles could be seen.

Overall, trends seemed to be more evident in the fabrics and materials that were used than in particular silhouettes or designs. Certain printed designs continued to be fashionable throughout the period. Examples include camouflage prints, which by the early 2000s were made in colors not traditionally associated with army camouflage cloth; prints that simulate animal fur; and brightly colored stripes. Leather was much in use for garments ranging from skirts to coats. Asian influences appeared, showing up in typically Asian banded collars, dresses and jackets cut like the Chinese cheongsam dress, and beautifully embroidered silk kimonos. Retro styles continued to emerge. In 2003 fashion writers spoke of the strong showing of 1950s influences in "ladylike" dresses and also of 1960s revivals.

Undergarments did not change much, but Playtex, manufacturers of brassieres, announced that they would begin to make brassieres in half sizes as well as in the traditional even numbered sizes. Because dresses and blouses were being made with a wide variety of necklines, brassiere manufacturers advertised specially constructed bras suitable for halter necklines, strapless necklines, and tank tops. Some garments were made with built-in brassieres. (See *Color Plate 74*.)

The many different necklines of both dressy daytime dresses and evening dresses included strapless dresses, halter tops, dresses with one bare shoulder, off-the-shoulder necklines, camisole tops, and draped necklines. (See *Figure 19.21*.) Minimalist slip dresses in satin appeared often.

In previous decades, maternity dresses had been loosely fitted, but by the late 1990s and after, maternity clothes followed the body curves of pregnant women. (See *Figure 19.22*.)

Tweed was a particularly popular fabric around 2000. Daytime dresses were made from this fabric, as were suits, skirts, and coats. Skirts often had a row of lace, fringe, or some other ornamental fabric attached to the hem. (See *Figure 19.23*.)

Evening dresses glittered and shone. Many were ornamented with sequins and beading, others were made from rich fabrics or from ornamental brocades. Many evening dresses were bare and low cut.

The bare midriff styles that had started in the 1980s, continued and blouses were cut high and pants or skirts low, so that the navel was visible. Young women, especially, wore body jewelry in pierced navels. (See *Figure 19.24*.)

In addition to classic blouses and tops, there were ultra feminine blouses in peasant style, some of which were ornamented with ruffles and frills. A popular neckline style was the funnel neck, similar in appearance to a turtle neck, but wider. Tops cut like men's athletic shirts were nicknamed "**wifebeaters,**" the term coming from the costume worn by Marlon Brando when he played a violent working class husband in the play and film *Streetcar Named Desire*.

Cashmere and angora were popular for sweaters. By the millennium, and especially after Christmas 2001 when a video by Robbie Williams and Nicole Kidman showed her in a patterned sweater, Fair Isle sweaters and other patterned sweaters were again fashionable, although they were "smaller, shorter, neater and less baggy" than in 1980s.

Skirts could be found in almost any length. Some were A-line; some were short, tight miniskirts; others were long, slender skirts, called pencil skirts. Latina-inspired ruffled skirts were also evident.

Like skirts, pants showed considerable variability. Bell-bottoms revived from the 1960s were often made with a dropped waist. Other styles included spandex-containing tight-fitting pants, tailored pants with legs of moderate width, and in 2003, a style of pants made with ties or a belt at the bottom hem. Throughout the period, but especially after the invasion of Iraq, cargo pants, popular throughout this period, were often made in camouflage printed fabrics. The large cargo pockets on these pants and on other garments were popular, in part because they made a convenient storage place for cell phones, which had become ubiquitous. (See *Figure 19.25*.)

OUTERWEAR

Cloth coats had, by the 2000s, generally been cut in slender, classic styles of varying lengths. Trenchcoats were popular, interest in them probably stimulated by the costumes of characters in the 1999 film *The Matrix*. Fur coats and outerwear trimmed in fur were very popular in the 2000s. New techniques for handling fur had made these coats lighter. One popular means of constructing these coats was knitting. Furs

a

b

FIGURE 19.20 A AND B

Among the innovations in design of the 1990s and early 2000s were the introduction of (a) deconstructionist designs like this one by Martin Margiela from Fall, 2001, in which parts of the garment are left unfinished or (b) simple, unadorned but well-cut minimalist styles like this white dress by Jil Sanders from 2003. (Photos courtesy, Fairchild Publications.)

were being dyed in bright colors. (See *Color Plate 72.*) Synthetic imitations of fur were very close in appearance and feel to the real thing. Often such coats were made in lively colors. Coats and jackets made of leather were fashionable.

HEADWEAR AND HAIRSTYLES

See *Illustrated Table 19.2* for some examples of hairstyles and hats for the period from 1980 to 2003.

Hair could be either short or long. Often it was long and worn straight and sometimes it was curled and full in order to make the head appear bigger. Tousled hair was called "**bed hair.**" Young girls tied their hair into ponytails at the back of the head, purposely allowing wisps and strands of hair to escape.

Popular hat styles ranged from flower-decked picture hats, to fedoras, to Andean-inspired knitted caps for winter.

FOOTWEAR

See *Illustrated Table 19.3* for some examples of footwear for the period from 1980 to 2003.

Many shoe types were available. Stiletto and other high heels, such as cone heels, were used on dressy sandals, open-toed pumps, and boots. A fad for wearing flip-flops, inexpensive rubber sandals with straps that came from between the toes, led designers to make flip-flops with heels that ranged in height from moderate to high, and also some with wedge-shaped heels. Many high-heeled shoes had ankle straps or were sling backs.

a

b

c

FIGURE 19.21 A, B, AND C

Many women's garments of the years after 2000 had interesting necklines. (Photos courtesy of Fairchild Publications.)

FIGURE 19.22

Maternity clothing of the late 1990s and early 2000s made no attempt to hide the expanding figures of pregnant women. (Photo courtesy of Fairchild Publications.)

FIGURE 19.23
Skirts of the early 2000s were often edged with fringe, lace, or beads. (Photo courtesy of Fairchild Publications.)

FIGURE 19.24
The fashion for bare midriffs of the early 2000s provided a means of showing off body jewelry for the navel. (Photo courtesy of BellyJewels.com)

Backless shoes included clogs with no or low backs and high-heeled mules.

ACCESSORIES

By the 2000s belts had become an important accessory. Often they were heavily ornamented with metal studs or chains. Elaborate belt buckles were attached.

In the late 1990s and early 2000s, pashmina shawls became an essential item for women who followed current fashion. From the way that pashmina was promoted, it appeared that this was a new fabric. In reality, it was cashmere, a soft, lustrous and expensive fiber often used in high-priced knitwear and coatings.

Handbags were made with cell phone compartments. Certain classic handbags, such as the Chanel and the Grace Kelly bag were a status symbol if original, and were much copied at lower price levels. Women bought bags made to im-

FIGURE 19.25
By 2000, cargo pants had become an essential part of the wardrobes of most young people. (Photo courtesy of Fairchild Publications.)

Illustrated Table 19.3

SELECTED EXAMPLES OF POPULAR FOOTWEAR FOR WOMEN, MEN, AND CHILDREN: 1980–2003

Shoes worn with ankle socks, 2001

Flip-flops with heels, c. 2002

Suede moccasins with low backs came in many colors

Many women's shoes for 1989
were cut high across the instep[1]

Two examples of classic men's loafers,
often associated with "preppy" styles[2]

Athletic shoe styles for men, women, and children proliferated as "fitness" became more important[3]

Retro fashion extended to shoes in the 1990s with the revivals of interest in:

Boot styles[4]

Black-and-white
"spectator" shoes[5]

Platform-soles[6]

Stiletto heels[7]

[1]*FNM Viewpoints,* January 1989.
[2]*FNM,* February 1987.
[3]Buyer's Guide, *Footwear News,* September 22, 1975. Fairchild Publications.
[4]*Footwear News,* January 24, 1994. Fairchild Publications.

[5]*Footwear News,* July 31, 1995. Fairchild Publications.
[6]*Footwear News,* August 10, 1992. Fairchild Publications.
[7]*Footwear News,* July 26, 1993. Fairchild Publications.

Illustrated Table 19.4

ACCESSORIES: 1980–2003

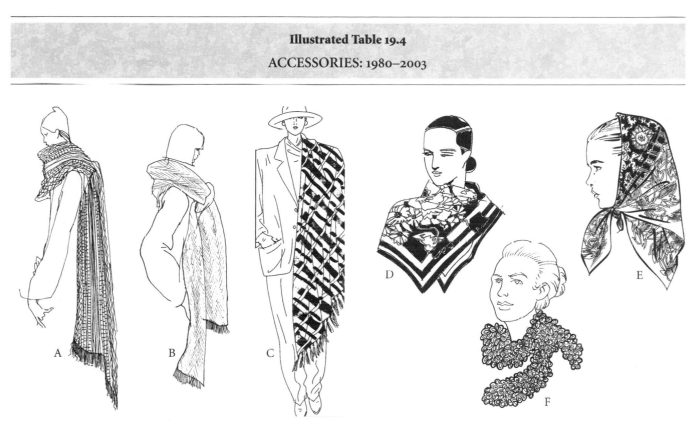

(A and B) Mufflers   (C) Large shawl-type scarf   (D) Neck scarf   (E) Silk head scarf   (F) Boa, made from yarn loops, c. 1999

Women's handbags
(A) Gym bag handbag   (B) Backpack   (C) Duffel bag   (D) Tote bag   (E) Pouch handbag

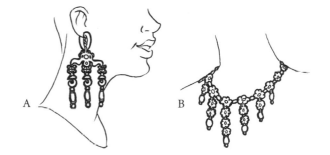

Women's jewelry, 1996–2003
(A) Chandelier earrings   (B) Bib necklace

Chain belt, c. 2003

itate bowling bags or gym bags. A variety of classic bag styles were also available.

JEWELRY

By the late 1990s, costume jewelry made in bright colors had become fashionable. Large, dangling earrings, called chandelier earrings, were especially popular. Necklaces made from cultured pearls strung on a transparent cord made it appear that the pearls were lying on the wearer's neck without any support. Chokers were also popular.

COSTUME FOR MEN:
1974–2003

Costume Components for Men

The so-called Peacock Revolution of the 1960s had focused attention on men's clothing and the menswear industry. From that time on, men, like women, had more choices among clothing options, and fashion segmentation increased. (See *Color Plate 67*.) While the corporate world still required traditional business attire in the 1970s and 80s, there was wide latitude in acceptable dress for social occasions and leisure activities. Then in the 1990s, the institution of casual dress policies made casual dress acceptable in many business settings, as well. Separates became more important. Ever since World War II the differences between clothing for active sports and sportswear had been lessening. Even dress clothing had become sportier.

Boutiques sold designer clothing for men, and more designers of women's clothing began to design lines for men. Men's styles also provided inspiration for women's clothing for work and for play in the 1980s and after.

GARMENTS

The same basic items of boxer shorts, briefs, and undershirts continued to be worn, innovations being evident in color and cut. In 1984, the classic brief was first made in colors. In 1990, Jockey® introduced a string bikini for men. Burberry plaids were so popular in the 2000s that they were even used for the waistband on some men's boxer briefs.

Interest in hiking and camping increased in the 1980s, and soon thermal underwear for cold weather was being produced in cotton, wool, silk, and polypropylene. These products were manufactured for both men and women.

See *Illustrated Table 19.1, page 527* for examples of undergarments from the period between 1980 and 2003.

A change in silhouette for men's suits came about with an emphasis on Italian styling, especially fashionable in the 1980s. These suits had wide shoulderlines; the fit remained easy. (See *Figure 19.26a.*)

a

b

FIGURE 19.26 A AND B

(a) More loosely fitted suit by Giorgio Armani from 1990 contrasts with (b) pinstriped suit of the early 2000s in which fit is enhanced by the use of spandex fiber in the fabric. (Courtesy of Fairchild Publications.)

The November 19, 1990, issue of *Time* magazine reported the loose-fitting sack suit, the staple of men's business suits in the medium price range for conservative American men for many years, was "fading fast." Citing large financial losses by American ready-to-wear men's suit manufacturers, author Jay Cocks also reported the rise of interest in English styling that was narrower at the waist, wide at the shoulders, and had side vents. Suspenders were being used to hold up trousers. French and Italian suits, with slightly softer tailoring, were also noted as fashionable. Color ranges were broadening, too. By 1996, a more structured line in suits was apparent. Some Italian suits even had stretch fibers incorporated to maintain a line that was closer to the body. (See *Figure 19.26b.*)

By 2000 suits tended to be dark, slim in cut, and had either three or two buttons. In summer men could wear unpressed linen suits, with a somewhat rumpled look.

Men could buy dress shirts in a wide variety of colors and patterns. In the early 1980s colored or printed shirts with white collars were especially popular. Collar sizes varied, their proportions suited to the proportion of jacket lapel widths. Striped shirts were being worn with patterned neckties in the 1990s. Around 2000 shirts in darker shades of colors were being worn with neckties in lighter shades and patterns of the same color. Asian influences showed up in men's shirts made with band collars. Striped and patterned shirts, including Hawaiian prints, were featured.

Italian designer Giorgio Armani showed some of his suits of the 1980s being worn with T-shirts. By the 1990s men working in informal settings or for leisure were wearing a variety of informal shirts with business suits. The trend toward increasingly casual clothing was evident in the denim suits, composed of matching denim pants and jackets, that were fashionable in the early 1980s.

SPORTSWEAR

Sport jackets generally followed lines of suit jackets, easy in the 80s, then more fitted again in the 90s. Some of the more popular styles included double-breasted blazers, wool tweeds, especially in the early 1980s when natural fibers were popular. These were often worn over a sweater or a fabric vest. Linen jackets were made in light or bright colors for summer in the 1980s and 1990s and tweed, checks, and plaids were popular in the 1990s.

Pants styles for casual wear ranged from blue jeans to tailored slacks. Along with traditional, conservative styles, some innovations can be identified. In the early 1980s some pants tapered to the bottom and closed with Velcro® fasteners at the ankle). (See *Figure 19.27.*) By the latter 1980s trouser fronts

a   b

FIGURE 19.27 A AND B

(a) Men's sportswear styles of the early 1980s were broad-shouldered, pants often tapered to the ankles to close with Velcro©, zippers, or tabs. (b) Sportswear designs of 1995 manufactured under the popular trademark of Tommy Hilfiger ranged from casual cotton madras anorak and shorts to a dressy linen/silk jacket. (Both from *Daily News Record,* (a) June 22, 1981; (b) November 11, 1995. Courtesy, Fairchild Publications.)

had pleated fullness and a loose, easy fit. A 1994 feature article in *GQ* showed a cross section of pants styles. All of these pants had pleats, although the style of the pleats was not the same for all trousers. Most had cuffs. The styles included:

- Slim, narrow at ankle
- Wide all the way to the hem
- Cargo style, with large patch pockets on the side
- Highwaisted and tapered to the ankle
- Casual with suspender buttons and no cuffs

By 1996, pleats were disappearing and dress trousers were tighter. Casual pants alternatives, however, picked up some style features from hip-hop style and were full, baggy, overlarge, and low on the hip. Cargo pants maintained their popularity.

The basic sport shirt styles continued to be T-shirts, polo shirts, and woven short-sleeved styles. Many T- and sweat shirts were decorated with "messages," cartoon characters, or sports logos. Summer wear included tank tops. For cooler weather, men wore turtlenecks, velour pullovers and shirts, jacquard-patterned knitted sweaters, and sweatshirts. In the 1980s, mesh shirts worn by football players were added to casual sportswear. Sweaters of the 1980s were loosely fitted and were made in a wide variety of handsome knits made from natural fibers in earth tones.

EVENING DRESS

Tail coats were worn by musicians and other stage performers and occasionally for weddings. Almost all other men wore tuxedos for formal evening dress. Their fit varied in much the same way as that of daytime suits. Evening dress colors were diverse. (See *Figure 19.28*.) By the mid-90s, white dinner jackets were being featured in men's fashion magazines.

The ruffled shirt fronts first adopted in the 1960s continued in use throughout the period.

OUTDOOR GARMENTS

Hemline lengths of coats for business and dress were similar to those of women. The fit of overcoats followed the fit of suit jackets.

Some of the more popular casual outdoor wear included leather motorcycle jackets, Western-style split cowhide with pile lining jackets (or simulated synthetic pile versions), down-filled vests and jackets. Parkas were also worn.

Polhemus (1994) cites black leather Perfecto motorcycle jackets, made by the Schott Brothers company, as examples of street fashions that "bubble up" into mainstream fashion. Such jackets had been symbols of rebellious youth ever since Marlin Brando wore one in the 50s film *The Wild One*. Gradually, through the 70s and 80s, these jackets became "normal" apparel, helped along by their adoption by rock musicians. By the 80s and 90s this jacket was appearing in shows by the

FIGURE 19.28

Evening wear of the late 1980s shows the large-shouldered, looser fit characteristic of much of men's clothing from this period. (*Daily News Record*, February 6, 1989. Courtesy, Fairchild Publications.)

haute couture and its transformation into mainstream fashion was complete.

CLOTHING FOR ACTIVE SPORTS

For swimming men could choose from a wide range of styles that included the extreme thong, bikinis, briefs, and boxer trunks. After the end of the 1980s stretch fabrics were used. As surfing got more attention, so did surfer shorts that were loose and long.

Warmup suits, popular as a result of jogging and running fads, were important garments from the early 1980s on. Gym shorts and sweatpants were being worn for athletics and as casual sportswear in the 1980s and 90s. From the mid-1980s through the 90s, spandex bicycling shorts were worn. The knee-length styles that were worn by competitors in the Tour de France set the styles.

By the 1980s colors were much in evidence in tennis clothing. Skiing styles changed yearly, with gradually tighter fit and fabrics designed to offer as little wind resistance as possible. Bob Ottum writing in the February 27, 1984 issue of *Sports Illustrated,* observed that the Olympic ski uniforms of that year were so tight that "The next step can only be to line up the racers naked at the starting gate and spray paint them." Cross-country skiing continued to be popular. Knickers or tightly fitted pants made of high tech synthetic fibers were worn for competitions, while amateurs wore wool or corduroy knickers with knee-length stockings. By the 1990s knickers had largely been replaced by manufactured fiber stretch pants.

Interest in snowboarding grew rapidly after 1990. Unlike skiers, snowboarders wore loosely fitted, well-insulated clothing. Most often it was two piece, and top and bottom were different in color. Popular colors varied from season to season. (See *Figure 19.29.*)

FIGURE 19.29

Snowboarders prefer loosely-fitted and more casual clothing than downhill skiers. (Photo courtesy of Fairchild Publications.)

SLEEPWEAR

Most widely used pajama styles tended to be either high-necked pullovers, V-neck pullovers, or shirt-collar tops with pants. Robes were made in collarless kimono styles. Other robes had shawl collars. In the 1980s, there were terry robes with matching shorts.

HAIR AND HEADDRESS

Shorter hair predominated throughout the 1980s, although hair of all lengths was still seen. Men's hair stylists in the late 90s and 2000s used hair care products to make men's hair stand up into a tousled effect. Very short hair was seen often in the 2000s, possibly a military influence. (See *Illustrated Table 19.2, pages 532–533.*)

Hats were not worn a great deal except in cold weather. For sports, men wore caps. In the 1990s baseball caps, worn backward by younger men, became exceptionally popular. In June 1993, *Fortune* magazine suggested that one reason for their popularity was that as male baby boomers were aging, their hairlines were receding. Traditional hat styles were not something they were comfortable with, but baseball caps could be related to their nostalgia for the past (*Fortune*, June 14, 1993).

Stetson-style hats experienced a brief revival during the popularity of the television program *Dallas,* set in Texas, and snap-brim felt hats in the early 1980s after the release of the film *Indiana Jones and the Raiders of the Lost Ark.*

FOOTWEAR

See *Illustrated Table 19.3, page 538,* for some examples of footwear for the period from 1980 to 2003.

Stockings were available in a wide variety of knit fabrics, colors, and patterns. When the leading character on the television program *Miami Vice* wore shoes without socks, some young men imitated him.

Boots remained fashionable throughout the 1970s. In the 1980s various types of sneakers, both high and low, were important, as were Western boots, hiking and walking shoes. The wide variety of shoes in the 1990s ranged from wing-tipped styles and two-tone shoes to sturdy hiking boots and included a vast array of sneakers. The casual focus was evident in shoes in 1994. One shoe company introduced a Casual Fridays line, and sales of loafers and sporty oxfords increased. Rock stars were responsible for the popularity of some casual shoe styles, such as driving shoes and foam-soled, suede laced oxfords.

ACCESSORIES

In the late 1980s floral ties gained popularity, and ties grew wider again, remaining wide into the 90s.

JEWELRY

Although more men were wearing jewelry, including gold chains and earrings, manuals of advice to men about appropriate attire for business generally counseled them to wear only wedding or signet rings, conservative watches with leather bands, tie clips or stickpins, and cuff links.

COSMETICS AND GROOMING

A billion dollars was spent on men's toiletries in 1987, 560 million of which was for fragrances and aftershave lotions, double that of 10 years before (*Vogue*, June 1987). More skin care products were also available.

Gentlemen's Quarterly of March 1990 printed a feature article about a session at a men's beauty salon in New York City. While men's beauty salons were not commonplace, the location of nine others elsewhere in the nation was noted for readers who might be interested. Many men had their hair "styled" at unisex beauty parlors rather than "cut" at barber shops.

Don Johnson, the leading man in *Miami Vice* generally appeared on that TV show of the 80s with several days' growth of beard. Soon fashion models, popular musicians, some fashion conscious students, and men whose jobs permitted were cultivating an "unshaven" look. Some men and boys imitated professional athletes who shaved their heads and wore goatees. After 2000, facial hair was still much in evidence. Some men grew mustaches, sometimes with goatees and a soul patch, a small patch of hair centered beneath the lip. Special razors could be used to maintain the stubble from several days' growth of beard.

COSTUME FOR CHILDREN:
1980–2003

Throughout the period children's clothing displayed clear reflections of adult styles in silhouette, hemline length, and preferred fabrics. As soon as a new style was introduced for adults, it was likely to be made in child-sized versions. High-priced, high-fashion lines of clothing for children of all ages were being made by many more firms as children dressed like small adults. (See *Contemporary Comments 19.1, page 516*, and *Color Plate 75*.) Retro fashions were designed for children as well as adults. In 1990 *The New York Times* noted a tendency for baby-boomer parents to dress their children in styles reminiscent of the 1960s, while 1960s style revivals were also being promoted for adults (Leinbach 1990). Trade magazines for the children's wear industry cited street fashion styles and retro styles, especially mod, as important influences in 1996. In November 2003, those same trade magazines were emphasizing "authentic urban looks" (i.e., cargo pocket styles, T-shirts, large and loose dress shirts and jackets) for boys that were like those being produced for adults.

The aforementioned *New York Times* feature went on to note the influence of television shows such as MTV and *Sesame Street* on children's fashions (Leinbach 1990). Film and TV cartoon and comic strip characters were extensively licensed to children's clothing manufacturers, and appeared on garments ranging from sweatshirts to sneakers. This trend accelerated during the 90s and continued in the 2000s.

Infants and Preschool-Age Children

For many decades it had been customary to dress very young children in soft pastel or light colors. Patterned fabrics had been made in small scale. The conventional wisdom had been that these colors best suited the delicate complexions of small children and that small-scaled patterns were better on small people. Children were rarely dressed in black. A major shift occurred in the 1980s when vivid, multicolored clothing styles were introduced for even the youngest children. (See *Color Plate 63*.) From this point one could find both bright colors and pastels for children. By 2000, children's clothes were also being made in black.

By the mid-1990s, newborn infants were wearing caps intended to reduce heat loss from their heads. As Austin (1995) pointed out, "... 21 percent of the newborn's body surface area is head, and 44 percent of the infant's heat production is done by the brain. Logic indicates that keeping the head warm would go far in assisting in heat regulation." Research indicated that the most effective of these caps were wool with cotton and gauze lining, polyolefin fiber, cotton with polyester fiberfill, and terrycloth. The most commonly used material, a plain knitted fabric, was rated as "surprisingly ineffective" even when made with double layers.

Among the more popular items for infants cited by retailers in the 90s were rompers for warm weather and one-piece outfits and coveralls for colder weather. Bubbles, one-piece outfits with extra width in the shaping that give them a rounded effect, were popular for infants and toddlers. When an early 1990s Public TV show for preschool children featured a purple dinosaur named Barney, the dinosaur logo appeared on preschoolers' clothing. By 1996 animal and vegetable prints were popular.

Toddler-sized versions of hiking boots appeared in the 90s and after, along with small scale versions of popular sneakers.

Since the 1970s the Flammable Fabrics Act has required that children's sleepwear sizes 0 to 14 meet certain flammability standards. To achieve a non-flammable fabric, manufacturers have had to use either certain manufactured fibers that are not inherently flammable or to give cotton and cotton blends special finishes. When one of the chemical finishes, TRIS, was found to possibly be mutagenic, the public became suspicious of flame-retardant finishes. As a result, some parents bought loose cotton T-shirts or other undergarments for children to use as sleepwear. These loose-fitting garments are

Illustrated Table 19.5

CHILDREN'S CLOTHING STYLES: 1980–2003

Plus sizes for overweight children
became available

Children's styles of the 1990s and 2000s
echoed adult styles

High fashion designer clothes
for tweens

Dresses from Simplicity Pattern
Catalog, March 1989

Licensed cartoon characters were an important part of children's
clothing. T-shirts and sweatshirts, often oversized and worn over
narrow tights, were popular for adults and children, 1985[1]

---

[1] *Women's Wear Daily*, September 3, 1985. Fairchild Publications.
[2] *Children's Business*, October 1985. Fairchild Publications.

Illustrated Table 19.5 (*continued*)
CHILDREN'S CLOTHING STYLES: 1980–2003

Many items of children's clothing reflected adult styles, 1985[1]

Through licensing agreements between Sears, Roebuck and Co. and the fast food chain McDonald's in 1987, a line of casual sportswear for children called McKids was produced[2]

Throughout the 1970s and 1980s jeans and other clothes made of denim, including stone-washed denim, were especially popular with adolescents[3]

Short and long garments, called "bubbles," with gathered pants were among the best-selling items for very young children in the 1990s[4]

Retro styles for adolescents included poodle-skirt revivals of the 1950s[4]

[1]*Children's Business,* October 1985. Fairchild Publications.
[2]*Women's Wear Daily, Youth,* July 27, 1987. Fairchild Publications.

[3]*Women's Wear Daily,* May 27, 1986. Fairchild Publications.
[4]Simplicity Pattern Catalog, Fall 1995. Fairchild Publications.

more likely to be flammable than tight-fitting sleepwear. In 1996 changes were made in this legislation and tight-fitting sleepwear for children was exempt from regulation. This was done in the hope that parents would purchase fitted sleepwear, which was safer. Sleepwear for children under six months of age was also excluded from the standard, based on the rationale that children so young are not mobile enough to come close to sources of ignition. By the millennium the technology for making fire retardant fabrics had improved and as a result manufacturers were producing more fashionable sleepwear styles that complied with the regulations.

School-Aged Children: Trends Affecting Boys and Girls

In the 1990s many schools across the United States reacted to problems, such as students wearing gang colors that led to in-school conflicts, and other issues of security and behavior by requiring that students wear uniforms. Some educators thought that discipline problems would decline as a result, and students would be more serious, paying more attention to classwork and less to competition over clothes. By 2002, participation in this experiment was waning as schools found that students resisted and it was difficult to get full participation by parents. When in 2003, pre-teen and adolescent girl fans of singer Britney Spears began wearing sexy and skimpy clothing, some schools imposed dress codes requiring that skirts be no shorter than a specified length (example: four inches above the knee) or disallowed tube tops or tops with spaghetti straps.

As more adult clothing became "unisex" in nature, so did clothes for children. Knitted fabrics were extensively used in clothing throughout the period, especially those made from manufactured fibers or blends that were easy to launder. Vividly colored fabrics with large-scale prints, stripes, and checks were used, especially during the late 1980s and the 90s.

GARMENTS

T-shirts remained a major clothing item for boys and girls. Interest in licensing and logos grew year by year, and by the late 90s and after sports and entertainment logos were everywhere. T-shirt messages reflected current issues such as global warming and ecology.

Both boys and girls wore pants for almost all occasions, and blue jeans continued to be enormously popular. Bell-bottom pants from the 1960s were revived in the early 1990s, and continued to be important as the fashion for bare midriffs spread to younger children. Spandex was used to make tight-fitting pants for girls. Boys adopted loosely fitted, large hip-hop styles.

As warmup suits became popular for adult wear, they also penetrated the children's market. Active sports clothing with spandex for stretch, such as bicycling pants, were popular, as were manufactured fiber fleece fabrics for outdoor wear.

Sometimes these fabrics were used as linings for warmth, or as the outer layer.

Bathing suits were like those of adults. When the high-cut bathing suits for women were introduced in the 1980s, suits for little girls also incorporated these lines. In the 90s, rumba suits, bathing suit styles from the 1950s with ruffles across the backside, were revived.

FOOTWEAR

In the 90s the most important types of footwear were boots and sneakers.

ACCESSORIES

By the 90s both boys and girls carried books to school in backpacks. Many backpacks had logos, and local fashions played a role in what type of backpack was most desirable. When violent incidents began to occur in some schools, pressure mounted to require students to bring clear plastic backpacks so that it would be evident if the bag contained any weapons.

Costume Components for Girls

GARMENTS

In the 1980s hem lengths were variable and included lengths from several inches above the knee to knee-length. By the late 1980s and 1990s some dresses ended several inches below the knee, others were short. In the 2000s, almost any length from short to well below the knee could be found.

In the 90s, pre-teen girls wore layers. Blouses hung out over skirts or pants, and vests over the blouses. Specific styles that appeared frequently included sweatshirt dresses, jumpers, and dresses with dropped waistlines. Many dresses for more formal occasions had lace or other decorative collars and trimmings. Prints were popular for summer, velveteen for winter.

Other popular items included a wide variety of shorts and longer pants, knee-length or longer tights worn with large T-shirts, jump suits, and jogging suits.

Costume Components for Boys

Influences from sports were strong in boys' clothing. Among the more important styles were baseball players' jackets and caps, rugby shirts, and fashions endorsed by sports figures. Sports logos appeared on clothing ranging from caps to jackets.

Among the adult men's styles that had a strong influence on boy's clothing in the 1980s were safari, and western styles, men's leisure suit styles, and natural-look fabrics. As men's wear became more casual in the 90s, boy's dress clothing reflected this trend and focused on blazers and jeans or chinos.

See *Illustrated Table 19.5,* for some examples of styles for children in the period from 1980 to 2003.

SUMMARY

Most readers of this book will have had direct, personal experience with many of the years reviewed in *Chapter 19*. Furthermore, detailed, day-by-day records of events in the period from 1980 to 2003 are readily available. For these reasons, it will be easy for readers to identify the many themes that appeared in the dress of these decades. Look at the themes identified in Chapter 1. One can find examples of many themes in the styles of 1980–2003: The impact of POLITICS through the influences on style of POLITICAL LEADERS and their families such as Nancy Reagan and Princess Di; the introduction of styles with military influences over the period when POLITICAL CONFLICTS such as the first Persian Gulf War, Somalia, Bosnia, Afghanistan, and Iraq took place; ECONOMIC EVENTS such as the GATT and NAFTA treaties and their impact on the American apparel industry, to mention only a few.

At the same time, when one has had so much direct experience of a period and when so much information is available, some overarching themes that have the most meaning for understanding the changes in dress over this period may be more difficult to explain. One such theme can be singled out for more detailed examination, the theme of FASHION.

The theme of fashion, broadly defined as a taste shared by many for a short period of time, first appeared in the Middle Ages when social and economic conditions in Western Europe provided fertile ground for its growth and development. With succeeding centuries, fashion change accelerated. By the 19th century, major fashion changes were coming about every 20 years. The development in the 20th century of a complex industry that to some extent manipulated the social phenomenon of fashion and a population that was economically well off enough to follow the latest styles resulted in still shorter fashion periods, lasting 10 years or less. Designer Karl Lagerfeld claims that today major fashion changes come every five or six years.

But compare fashion at the turn of the millennium with fashion in the period from just after World War II until the 1960s. Few choices were available for consumers who might want to purchase clothing that did not conform to mainstream fashion. With the 1960s, that began to change.

Fashion did not disappear. It should be noted that, as in previous periods, any consideration of styles in the decades since 1960 reveals that some generalizations can be made about similarities of clothing styles for women, men, and children. One is that when there is a trend that clearly predominates, that trend may be evident in the clothing of women, men, and children. For example, when an unfitted silhouette without a defined waistline was popular for women in the latter part of the 1960s, the same silhouette appeared in girls' clothing. Both men's and women's garments grew wide at the shoulders in the early 1980s. Men, women,

and children were all wearing clothing made of fabrics decorated with camouflage prints in the 2000s.

Hemline location is another general trend that has often been evident in clothing for both sexes and all ages. When women's and girls' hems were long in the 1940s, men's overcoats tended to be long, but as women's' and girls' hemlines grew short in the 1960s and early 1970s, men's overcoats also shortened, as did boys'. When almost any length of skirt was acceptable in the 90s for women, hemlines in men's overcoats and girls' dresses also became variable.

Popular fabrics are generally popular across age and sex lines. The polyester knitted fabrics of the 1960s showed up not only in women's and girls' dresses, pants, and sportswear, but also in men's and boys' suits, sport jackets, and trousers. Denim as a fabric and blue jeans as a garment were used by everyone throughout the period and when natural fibers returned to popularity in the 1980s and 90s, it was for all consumers. Hairstyles for adult women and for young girls tend to be similar, as do hairstyles for adult men and boys.

Influences from current events, the media, and new fashion designers usually appear widely. Some examples include the Western styles of the 1970s, designs inspired by the film *The Great Gatsby* in the late 1970s, Japanese designer ideas from around 1980, and retro fashions seen in the 1980s and 1990s. Many American and foreign designers produced both men's and women's lines. In the 2000s, some of these firms also entered the upscale children's market.

While these common threads that tie together clothing for all ages and both sexes continue to be evident, something happened to fashion in the late 1960s. Although American society was questioning many of its assumptions about issues as diverse as politics and government, race and ethnicity, the arts, and morality, fashion was also questioning the old rules.

The old world of fashion, in which conformity to the predominant silhouette and skirt length was a mark of sophistication disappeared. While fashion had never been totally predictable, the industry had developed a structure and a means of production and distribution that relied on customers who would, at least, follow the latest major trends from the international style centers. A more diverse, more segmented marketplace has replaced the fashion industry that once spoke with a single voice.

The fashion industry was far from dead. Instead it had been transformed. Entrepreneurs in the fashion industry are well aware that they must satisfy the preferences of their customers if they wish to survive. Consumers have gotten used to having a wide variety of fashion goods from which to choose. This, together with the development of new computer-based technologies that enable manufacturers to adapt more rapidly to style changes and the proliferation of spe-

Visual Summary Table

SOME MAJOR STYLES c. 1980–2003

Women: 1980–1995
Trends that influenced mainstream fashion included wide, padded shoulders and shorter skirts

Women: 1990s and after
Spandex added to many fabrics provided a tight, close fit. Shoulders narrowed somewhat.

Women: 1995–2003
Skirts of many lengths could be found. Often hemlines were uneven. A layered look was also fashionable.

A major feature of styles in the 1990s and after was a bare midriff.

Men: 1980–2003
Business suits had wide shoulders and an easy fit until the latter half of the 1990s when the incorporation of stretch fibers made for more fitted garments.

Men: 1990s and after
Casual dress for business became more widely accepted.

Men: 1980–2003
Emphasis on fitness made activewear an important part of men's wardrobes.

Men: 1980–2003
More colorful and decorative clothing continued to be an option for men.

cialized retail outlets, is likely to sustain the desire for and the availability of a wide variety of diverse styles from which to choose.

Fashion, with its dual elements of public acceptance and change, has long provided individuals with the opportunity to conform and express individuality at the same time. Fashion continues to fuel changes in dress in the Western World. In 2003, however, widely accepted styles tend to be segmented according to such diverse factors as age, social or economic class, ethnicity, occupation, recreational preferences, or musical tastes. To complicate the picture, specific fashions may move from one segment to another, movements facilitated by the fashion press or other media.

In the history of dress at the beginning of the 21st century, costume might be compared to a constantly moving river. This river divides into many narrower channels that separate, cross, come together, and separate again, and yet that river continually moves on.

NOTES

Adler, J. 1995. "Have We Become a Nation of Slobs?" *Newsweek,* February 20, p. 56.

Austin, P. 1995. *Science/Health Abstracts,* Vol. 15, No. 5. (Source: (MIDIRS Midwifery Digest 4(4)470-471, December 1994) http://www.tagnet.org/abstracts/v14n5.html

Bell, Q. 1973. *On Human Finery.* Philadelphia: R. West.

Berkow, I. 1990. "The Murders Over the Sneakers." *The New York Times,* May 14, p. C6.

Boynton-Arthur, L. Personal communication, October 14, 1996.

Brady, D. 1993. "Kids, Clothes and Conformity." *McLean's,* September 6, p. 44.

Brubach, H. 1991. "In Fashion." *New Yorker,* September 2, p. 72.

———. 1994. "Whose Vision Is It Anyway? *New York Times Magazine,* July 17, p. 46

Bunn, A. 2002. "Not Fade Away." *New York Times Magazine,* December 1, 2002, p. 60.

Conlin, J. 1989. "Gonna Dress You Up." *Rolling Stone,* April 20, p. 51.

Connelly, J. "The Meaning of Caps." *Fortune,* June 14, p. 12.

"The Denim Standard." 1995. *Vogue,* April, p. 372.

Crane, D. 2000. *Fashion and Its Social Agendas.* Chicago: University of Chicago Press.

Drobrzynski, J. H. 1996. "Study Finds Few Women in 5 Highest Company Jobs." *The New York Times,* October 18, p. 1.

Fairchild, J. 1989. *Chic Savages.* New York: Simon & Schuster, p. 43.

Givlin, R. 2002. "From Bellbottoms and Beads to Casual Friday Protest Apparel." *The Washington Post,* April 19, p. C1.

Gordon, K. 2003. "Ironing Out the Clothes Issue." *Workforce,* May 2003, p. 18.

"Inside Fashion." 1984. *Gentlemen's Quarterly,* May, p. 39.

Koda, H. 2001. *Extreme Beauty.* New York: Metropolitan Museum of Art.

Leinbach, D. 1990. "Trends in Children's Fashions." *The New York Times,* March 4, Part VI, p. 52.

Lord, S. 1987. "The Masculine Presence." *Vogue,* June, p. 187.

Mead, R. 1996. "The Last Designer." *The New Yorker,* September 16, p. 26.

Messura, M. 2003. Answer to question from the audience after presentation. Savannah, GA: International Textile and Apparel Association.

Milbank, C. 1989. *New York Fashion: The Evolution of American Style.* New York: Abrams, p. 264.

Moore, S. 1996. "The Body Politic." *The New York Times,* October 6, p. 73.

Morgado, M. A. 1996. "Coming to Terms with *Postmodern:* Theories and Concepts of Contemporary Culture and Their Implications for Apparel Scholars." *Clothing and Textiles Research Journal,* Vol 14, No. 1, p. 41.

Morris, B. 1982. "The Case for Couture." *Fashions of the Times, The New York Times,* March 7, p. 174.

North American Association for the Study of Obesity. "What Is Obesity?" data from the National Health and Nutrition Examination Survey, 1999–2000. http://www.naaso.org/information. (accessed Nov. 18, 2003).

Ottum, B. 1984. "Notable Triumphs, Wrong Notes." *Sports Illustrated,* February 27, p. 23.

Pastore, M. 2000. "Consumer E-Commerce Growth Expectations May Be Unrealistic." May 31, http://cyberatlas.internet.com /markets/retailing/article/0,1323,6061_383821,00.html.

Polhemus, T. 1994. *Street Style.* New York: Thames and Hudson.

Rifkin, G. 1994. "Digital Blue Jeans Pour Data and Legs into Customized Fit. *The New York Times,* November 8, p. A1.

Rozhon, T. 2003. "The Race to Think Like a Teenager." *The New York Times.* February 9. Section 3, p. 1.

"Sara Lee Hosiery Executive Tells Symposium Attendees 'Casual Dress Trend Poses Threat to Hosiery Industry.' 1996. *Southern Textile News,* October 21, p. 7.

Scardino, E. 2002. "Knows What's 'In,' and Spends Accordingly." *DSN Retailing Today.* December 16, 2002, p. 31.

Schatz, R. D. 1996. "Fashion World Discovers the Net is Not a Snood." *The New York Times,* January 21, p. 32.

Schiro, A. M. 1996. "Chic Scales the Heights, or Walks the Dog." *The New York Times,* December 3, p. B10.

Spindler A. M. 1996. "Investing in Haute Couture's Lower-Brow Future." *The New York Times,* January 22, p. D2.

Steele, V. 2000. "Fashion: Yesterday, Today, and Tomorrow." In N. White and I. Griffiths, eds. *The Fashion Business.* New York: Berg, p. 1.

Steinhauer, J. 1997. "What Vanity and Casual Fridays Wrought." *The New York Times,* April 9, p. A1.

White, C. R. 1996. "The Way of All Flesh Goes South." *The New York Times,* October 6, Section 4, p. 16.

SELECTED READINGS

Books and Other Materials Containing Illustrations
of Costume of the Period from Original Sources

Fashion and general magazines and newspapers of the period, especially: *Daily News Record, Ebony, Elle, Essence, Gentlemen's Quarterly, Harper's Bazaar, Mademoiselle, Mirabella, The New York Times (special fashion supplements), Seventeen, Vogue, Women's Wear Daily, W.*

Catalogs: Pattern and mail-order

Carnegy, V. 1990. *Fashions of a Decade: The 1980s.* New York: Facts on File.

———. 1990. *Fashions of a Decade: The 1970s.* New York: Facts on File.

De la Haye, A. and C. Dingwall. 1996. *Surfers, Soulies, Skinheads, & Skaters.* Woodstock, NY: The Overlook Press.

Martin, R. and H. Koda. 1989. *Jocks and Nerds: Men's Style in the Twentieth Century.* New York: Rizzoli.

McDonell, T. 1996. "Feedback." [fashion and rock and roll]. *Harper's Bazaar.* February, p. 45.

Periodical Articles and Other Readings

Barol, B. 1990. "Anatomy of a Fad." [torn blue jeans]. *Newsweek,* Special Issue, Summer/Fall, p. 40.

Bellafante, G. 2003. "The Littlest Clotheshorse." *The New York Times,* November 4, p. B11.

Berkow, I. 1990. "The Murders Over the Sneakers." *The New York Times,* May 14, p. C6.

Brubach, H. 1991. "In Fashion: On the Beach." *The New Yorker,* September 2, p. 70.

Carlsen, P. 1984. "Fashion's Breakdown." *Gentlemen's Quarterly,* September, p. 156.

"The Denim Standard." 1995. *Vogue,* April, p. 372.

Dickey, S. J. 1991. "'We Girls Can Do Anything—Right Barbie!' A Survey of Barbie Doll Fashions" In P. A. Cunningham and S. V. Lab, eds., *Dress and Popular Culture.* Bowling Green, OH: Bowling Green State University Popular Press, p. 19.

Gordon, B. 1991. American Denim: Blue Jeans and Their Multiple Layers of Meaning." In P. A. Cunningham and S. V. Lab, eds., *Dress and Popular Culture.* Bowling Green, OH: Bowling Green State University Popular Press, p. 31.

Kaiser, S. 1997. "Postindustrial Society and Postmodern Culture." In *The Social Psychology of Clothing,* revd, 2nd ed. New York: Fairchild, pp. 401–410.

Koda, H. 1985. "Rei Kawakubo and the Aesthetic of Poverty." *Dress,* Vol. 11, p. 5.

McDonell, T. 1996. "Feedback." [fashion and rock and roll]. *Harper's Bazaar,* February, p. 45.

Morgado, M. A. 1996. "Coming to Terms with *Postmodern:* Theories and Concepts of Contemporary Culture and Their Implications for Apparel Scholars. *Clothing and Textiles Research Journal,* Vol. 14, No. 1, p. 41.

Nordquist, B. K. 1991. "Punks." In P. A. Cunningham and S. V. Lab, eds., *Dress and Popular Culture.* Bowling Green, OH: Bowling Green State University Popular Press, p. 85.

Reed, J. "Hail to the T, the Shirt That Speaks Volumes." *Smithsonian,* Vol. 23, No. 1 (April, 1992), p. 96.

Sanders, S. 1992. "Calling the Shots: Purchasing Power of Mothers and Children in the 90s." *Earnshaws,* October, p. 70.

Daily Life

This Fabulous Century, Volume 7. New York: Time-Life Books, 1969.

Matthews, R. and T. Smart. *Eyewitness to the 1980s.* England: The Book People, 1990.

Prost, A. and G. Vincent, eds. *A History of Private Life, Vol. IV: Riddles of Identity in Modern Times.* [World War I to the Present]. Cambridge, MA: Belknap Press of Harvard University.

BIBLIOGRAPHY

A selected bibliography of books in English that deal with the subject of historic costume

Dictionaries and Encyclopedias

Calasibetta, C. and P. Tortora. 2003. *Fairchild's Dictionary of Fashion*, 3rd edition. New York: Fairchild.

Cassin-Scott, J. 1994. *The Illustrated Encyclopedia of Costume and Fashion: From 1066 to the Present.* United Kingdom: Studio Vista Books.

Cunnington, C. W., P. Cunnington, and C. Beard. 1960. *A Dictionary of English Costume, 900–1900.* London: A. & C. Black.

Davies, S. 1995. *Costume Language: A Dictionary of Dress Terms.* New York: Drama Book.

Fairholt, E. W. 1976. *A Glossary of Costume in England.* Wakefield, England: E. P. Publishing. (Facsimile of 1885 edition.)

O'Hara, G. and G. Callan. 1998. *The Thames and Hudson Dictionary of Fashion and Fashion Designers.* London: Thames and Hudson.

Planche, J. R. 1876–1879. *A Cyclopaedia of Costume or Dictionary of Dress.* London: Chatto and Windus.

Wilcox, R. T. 1969. *The Dictionary of Costume.* New York: Scribners.

Yarwood, D. 1978. *The Encyclopedia of World Costume.* New York: Scribners.

General References and Surveys

Arnold, J. 1977. *Patterns of Fashion,* Vol. 1: *1660–1860,* Vol. 2: *1860–1940.* New York: Drama Book.

Ashelford, J. 1996. *The Art of Dress: Clothes and Society. 1500–1914.* New York: Abrams.

Baines, V. B. 1981. *Fashion Revivals from the Elizabethan Age to the Present Day.* London: B. T. Batsford.

Batterberry, M. and A. Batterberry. 1977. *Mirror, Mirror.* New York: Holt, Rinehart and Winston.

Black, J. and M. Garland. 1990. *A History of Fashion.* London: Black Cat.

Boucher, E. *20,000 Years of Fashion.* 1987. London: Thames and Hudson.

Bradfield, N. 1997. *Historical Costumes of England, 1066–1968.* Quite Specific Media..

Braun, L., et al. 1982. *Costume Through the Ages.* New York: Rizzoli.

Braun and Schneider. 1975. *Historic Costume in Pictures.* Mineola, NY: Dover.

Breward, C. 1995. *The Culture of Fashion: A New History of Fashionable Dress.* New York: St. Martin's Press.

Brooke, I. 1973. *A History of English Costume.* New York: Theatre Arts Books.

Bruhn, W. and M. Tilke. 1991. *A Pictorial History of Costume.* London: Alpine Fine Arts Collection.

Clinch, G. 1975. *English Costume from Prehistoric Times to the End of the 18th Century.* London: Rowman and Littlefield.

Cumming, V. 1981. *Exploring Costume History.* London: B. T. Batsford.

Davenport, M. 1948. *The Book of Costume.* 2 Volumes. New York: Crown.

Gorsline, D. 1994. *What People Wore: One Thousand Eight Hundred Illustrations from Ancient Times to the Early Twentieth Century.* Mineola, NY: Dover.

Kelly, F. M. and R. Schwab. 1980. *Historic Costume: A Chronicle of Fashion in Western Europe 1490–1790.* London: Art Book. (Reprint of 1929 edition.)

Kemper, R. H. 1977. *Costume.* New York: Newsweek Books.

Kohler, C. 1963. *A History of Costume,* Mineola, NY: Dover.

Laver, J. 1985. *Costume and Fashion: A Concise History.* New York: Thames and Hudson.

Norris, H. 1924. *Costume and Fashion.* 5 Volumes. New York: Dutton.

Nunn, J. 1990. *Fashion in Costume*. New York: New Amsterdam Books.

Payne, B., G. Winakor, and J. Farrell-Beck. 1992. *History of Costume*. New York: Addison-Wesley.

Pistolese, R. and R. Horsting. 1970. *History of Fashions*. New York: John Wiley & Sons.

Racinet, A. 1988. *The Historical Encyclopedia of Costumes*. New York: Facts on File.

Ribeiro, A. 1986. *Dress and Morality*. New York: Holmes & Meier.

Ribeiro, A. and V. Cumming. 1990. *The Visual History of Costume*. New York: Drama Book.

Rothstein, N., ed. 1984. *400 Years of Fashion*. London: Victoria and Albert Museum.

Selbie, R. 1977. *The Anatomy of Costume*. New York: Crescent Books.

Squire, G. 1974. *Dress and Society, 1560–1970*. New York: Viking.

Stavridi, M. 1966. *The Hugh Evelyn History of Costume*. London: Evelyn.

Stibbert, F. 1968. *Civil and Military Clothing in Europe*. New York: B. Blom.

Tilke, M. 1990. *Costume Patterns and Designs*. New York: Magna.

Waugh, N. 1968. *The Cut of Women's Clothes, 1600–1930*. New York: Theatre Arts Books.

Wilcox, R. T. 1983. *The Mode in Costume*. New York: Scribners.

Yarwood, D. 1975. *European Costume: 4000 Years of Fashion*. New York: Larousse.

———. 1992. *Fashion in the Western World, 1550–1990*. New York: Drama Book.

Costume from Specific Historic Periods

Antiquity

Abrams, E. and Lady Evans. 1964. *Ancient Greek Dress*. Chicago: Argonaut.

Bonfante, L. 1975. *Etruscan Dress*. Baltimore, MD: Johns Hopkins University Press.

Brooke, I. 1973. *Costume in Greek Classic Drama*. Westport, CT: Greenwood Press.

Bruhn, J. A. 1993. *Coins and Costume in Late Antiquity*. Washington, DC: Dumbarton Oaks.

Croom, A. T. 2002. *Roman Clothing and Fashion*. Charleston, SC: Tempus.

Gullberg, E. and P. Astrom. 1970. *The Thread of Ariadne*. [Studies in Mediterranean Archeology, Vol. XXI.] Sweden: Goteborg.

Hope, T. 1962. *Costume of the Greeks and Romans*. Mineola, NY: Dover.

Houston, M. G. 2002. *Ancient Egyptian, Mesopotamian, and Persian Costume*. Mineola, NY: Dover.

———. 1977. *Ancient Greek, Roman, and Byzantine Costume and Decorations*. New York: Barnes and Noble.

Klepper, E. 1964. *Costume in Antiquity*. New York: Clarkson Potter.

Sebesta, J. L. and L. Bonfante. 1994. *The World of Roman Costume*. Madison, WI: University of Wisconsin Press.

Sichel, M. 1980. *Costume of the Classical World*. London: Batsford Academic & Education.

Vogelsang-Eastwood, G. 1993. *Pharaonic Egyptian Clothing*. Leiden, The Netherlands: E. J. Brill.

Wilson, L. M. 1924. *The Clothing of the Ancient Romans*. Baltimore, MD: Johns Hopkins University Press.

Middle Ages

Brooke, I. 1935. *English Costume of the Later Middle Ages, the 14th and 15th Centuries*. London: A. & C. Black.

Brooke, I. 1936. *English Costume of the Early Middle Ages, 10th–13th Centuries*. London: A. & C. Black.

Crowfoot, et al. 2004. *Textiles and Clothing: c. 1150–1450*. London: Boydell and Brewer.

Cunnington, C. and P. Cunnington. 1973. *Handbook of English Medieval Costume*. Northampton, England: John Dickens.

Evans, J. 1952. *Dress in Medieval France*. Oxford: Clarendon.

Goddard, E. R. 1973. *Women's Costume in French Texts of the 11th and 12th Centuries*. New York: Johnson Reprints.

Grew, F., M. de Neergaard, and S. Mitford. 2004. *Shoes and Pattens: Finds from Medieval Excavations in London*. London: Boydell & Brewer.

Harte, N. B. and K. G. Ponting, eds. 1983. *Cloth and Clothing in Medieval Europe. Essays in Memory of E. M. Carus-Wilson*. Brookfield, VT: Gower.

Houston, M. 1996. *Medieval Costume in England and France, the Thirteenth, Fourteenth, and Fifteenth Centuries*. Mineola, NY: Dover.

Koslin, D. and J. E. Snyder, eds. 2002. *Encountering Medieval Textiles and Dress*. New York: Palgrave Macmillan.

Newton, S. M. 1980. *Fashion in the Age of the Black Prince*. Totowa, NJ: Rowan and Littlefield.

Owen-Crocker, G. R. 1986. *Dress in Anglo-Saxon England*. Dover, NH: Manchester University Press.

Piponnier, F. and P. Mane. 1997. *Dress in the Middle Ages*. New Haven, CT: Yale University Press.

Piton, C. 1986. *The Civil Costumes of France of the 13th and 14th Century*. Watchung, NJ: Saifer.

Scott, M. 1980. *The History of Dress: Late Gothic Europe, 1400–1500*. New York: Humanities Press.

———. 1986. *Visual History of Costume: 14th and 15th Centuries*. London: B. T. Batsford.

Renaissance

Arnold, J., ed. 1980. *Lost from Her Majesty's Back*. Birdle, Bury, England: Costume Society.

Ashelford, J. 1983. *The Visual History of Costume: The 16th Century*. New York: Drama Book.

———. 1988. *Dress in the Age of Elizabeth I*. New York: Holmes & Meier.

Birbari, E. 1975. *Dress in Italian Paintings, 1460–1500*. London: John Murray.

Brooke, I. 1950. *English Costume in the Age of Elizabeth—16th Century.* London: A. & C. Black.

Cunnington, C. W. 1972. *Handbook of English Costume in the Sixteenth Century.* Boston: Plays.

Frick, C. C. 2002. *Dressing Renaissance Florence: Families, Fortunes, and Fine Clothing.* Baltimore, MD: Johns Hopkins University Press.

Herald, J. 1981. *Renaissance Dress in Italy, 1400–1500.* New York: Humanities Press.

Kelly, F. M. and A. Mansfield. 1976. *Shakespearean Costume.* New York: Theatre Arts Books.

LaMar, V. A. 1958. *English Dress in the Age of Shakespeare.* Washington, DC: Folger Library.

Morse, E. 1969. *Elizabethan Pageantry.* New York: B. Blom. (Reprint of 1934 edition.)

Vecellio, C. 1977. *Vecellio's Renaissance Costume Book.* Mineola, NY: Dover.

17th and 18th Centuries
Baumgarten, L. 2002. *What Clothes Reveal: The Language of Clothing in Colonial and Federal America.* Williamsburg VA: The Colonial Williamsburg Foundation.

Buck, A. 1979. *Dress in 18th Century England.* New York: Holmes & Meier.

Cumming, V. 1984. *A Visual History of Costume: The 17th Century.* New York: Drama Book.

Cunnington, C. W. and P. Cunnington. 1957. *Handbook of English Costume in the Eighteenth Century.* London: Faber and Faber.

———. 1972. *Handbook of English Costume in the Seventeenth Century.* London: Faber and Faber.

Delpierre, M. 1998. *Dress in France in the Eighteenth Century.* New Haven, CT: Yale University Press.

Gallery of Fashion, 1790–1822. 1949. London: B. T. Batsford.

Hart, A., S. North, and R. Davis. 1998. *Fashion in Detail: From the 17th and 18th Centuries.* New York: Rizzoli.

Klein, J. and E. Gordenker. 2002. *Van Dyck and the Representation of Dress in Seventeenth-Century Portraiture.* Turnhout, Belgium: Brepols.

Le Bourhis, K. 1989. *The Age of Napoleon: Costume from Revolution to Empire.* New York: Metropolitan Museum of Art.

Mackie, E. S. 1997. *Market à la Mode: Fashion, Commodity, and Gender in the Tatler and the Spectator.* Baltimore, MD: Johns Hopkins University Press.

Munns, J. and P. Richards, eds. 1999. *The Clothes That Wear Us: Essays on Dressing and Transgressing in Eighteenth Century Culture.* Newark, DE: University of Delaware Press.

Ribeiro, A. 1983. *A Visual History of Costume: The Eighteenth Century.* New York: Drama Book.

———. 1985. *Dress in Eighteenth Century Europe: 1715–1789.* New York: Holmes & Meier.

———. 1985. *The Dress Worn at Masquerades in England 1730–1790 and Its Relation to Fancy Dress in Portraiture.* New York: Garland.

———. 1988. *Fashion in the French Revolution.* New York: Holmes & Meier.

———. 1995. *The Art of Dress: Fashion in England and France 1750–1820.* New Haven, CT: Yale University Press.

Roche, D. 1994. *The Culture of Clothing: Dress and Fashion in the Ancien Regime.* New York: Cambridge University Press.

Sichel, M. 1977. *Costume Reference, No. 3: Jacobean, Stuart and Restoration. No. 4: The 18th Century.* London: B. T. Batsford.

19th Century
Beaudoin-Ross, J. 1992. *Form and Fashion: 19th Century Montreal Dress.* Toronto: University of Toronto Press.

Blum, S. 1974. *Victorian Fashions and Costumes from Harper's Bazaar. 1867–1898.* Mineola, NY: Dover.

———., ed. 1985. *Fashions and Costumes from Godey's Lady's Book.* Mineola, NY: Dover.

Bradfield, N. 1975. *Costume in Detail.* London: Harrap.

Buck, A. 1984. *Victorian Costume.* Carlton, Bedford, England: R. Bean.

Cunnington, C. and P. Cunnington. 1970. *A Handbook of English Costume in the 19th Century.* London: Faber and Faber.

Dalrymple, P. 1990. *American Victorian Costume in Early Photographs.* Mineola, NY: Dover.

Evolution of Fashion: 1835–1895. 1980. Kyoto, Japan: Kyoto Costume Institute.

Foster, V. 1983. *A Visual History of Costume: The 19th Century.* New York: Drama Book.

Gersheim, A. 1963. *Fashion and Reality, 1840–1914.* London: Faber and Faber.

Gibbs-Smith, C. H. 1960. *The Fashionable Lady in the 19th Century.* London: Her Majesty's Stationery Office.

Ginsburg, M. 1983. *Victorian Dress in Photographs.* New York: Holmes & Meier.

Goldthorpe, C. 1989. *From Queen to Empress: Victorian Dress: 1837–1877.* New York: Abrams.

The House of Worth: The Gilded Age in New York. 1982. New York: Museum of the City of New York.

Imperial Styles: Fashions of the Hapsburg Era. 1980. New York: Rizzoli.

Johnson, J. 1991. *French Fashions of the Romantic Era.* Mineola, NY: Dover.

Lambert, M. 1992. *Fashion in Photographs, 1860–1880.* London: B. T. Batsford.

Leich, J. 1995. *Who Wore What? Women's Wear 1861–1865.* Gettysburg, PA: Thomas.

Levitt, S. 1986. *Victorians Unbuttoned: Registered Designs for Clothing, Their Makers and Wearers.* London: HarperCollins.

———. 1992. *Fashion in Photographs, 1880–1900.* London: B. T. Batsford.

Newton, S. M. 1976. *Health, Art, and Reason: Dress Reform of the 19th Century.* New York: Schram.

Setnik, L. 2000. *Victorian Costume for Ladies.* Atglen, PA: Schiffer.

Severa, J. 1995. *Dressed for the Photographer. Ordinary Americans and Fashion 1840–1900*. Kent, OH: Kent State University Press.

Shep, R. L., ed. 2001. *Early Victorian Men*. Mendocino, CA: R. L. Shep.

Sichel, M. 1977/1978. *Costume Reference Series: No. 5: The Regency; No. 6: The Victorians*. London: B. T. Batsford.

Tarrant, N. [N. D.] *The Rise and Fall of the Sleeve, 1825–40*. Edinburgh: Royal Scottish Museum Collections.

Tozier, J. and S. Levitt. 1984. *Fabric of Society: A Century of People and Their Clothes*. New York: St. Martin's Press.

Walkey, C. and V. Foster. 1978. *Crinolines and Crimping Irons: Victorian Clothes. How They Were Cleaned and Cared For*. London: P. Owen.

20th Century

American Women of Style. 1975. New York: Metropolitan Museum of Art Exhibition Catalog.

Battersby, B. 1974. *Art Deco Fashion. French Designers 1908–1925*. New York: St. Martin's Press.

Benbow, Pfaltzgraf, T. 2002. (Editor) *Contemporary Fashion*. Detroit: St. James Press.

Bernard, B. 1978. *Fashion in the 60's*. London: Academy Editions.

Blum, S. 1982. *Everyday Fashions of the Twenties as Pictured in Sears and Other Catalogs*. Mineola, NY: Dover.

Bond, D. 1988. *The Guiness Guide to 20th Century Fashion*. Enfield, Middlesex, England: Guiness.

Bowan, S. 1985. *A Fashion for Extravagance: Parisian Fabric and Fashion Designers from the Art Deco Period*. New York: E. P. Dutton.

Byrde, P. 1986. *A Visual History of Costume: The Twentieth Century*. London: B. T. Batsford.

Carnegy, V. 1990. *Fashions of a Decade: The 1970's*. New York: Facts on File.

———. 1990. *Fashions of a Decade: The 1980's*. New York: Facts on File.

Carter, E. 1975. *20th Century Fashion: A Scrapbook*. London: Eyre Metheuen.

Cawthorne, N., et al. 1998. *Key Moments in Fashion: from Haute Couture to Street Wear, Key Collections, Major Figures, and Crucial Moments that Changed the Course of Fashion from 1890 to the 1990s*. New York: Hamlyn.

Clancy, D. 1996. *Costume Since 1945: Couture, Street Style, and Anti-fashion*. New York: Drama Book.

De La Haye, A. 1988. *Fashion Source Book*. Secaucus, NJ: Wellfleet Press.

de Pietri, S. and M. Leventon. 1989. *"New Look" to Now: French Haute Couture 1947–1987*. New York: Rizzoli.

Dorner, J. 1973. *Fashion in the Twenties and Thirties*. London: I. Allen.

———. 1975. *Fashion in the Forties and Fifties*. New Rochelle, NY: Arlington House.

Ewing, E. and A. Mackrell. 1992. *History of Twentieth Century Fashion*. London: B. T. Batsford.

Feldman, E. 1992. *Fashions of a Decade: The 1990s*. New York: Facts on File.

Friedel, R. 1994. *Zipper*. New York: Norton.

Glynn, P. 1978. *In Fashion. Dress in the 20th Century*. New York: Oxford University Press.

Lobenthal, J. *Radical Rags: Fashions of the Sixties*. New York: Abbeville Press, 1990.

Mansfield, A. and P. Cunnington. 1973. *Handbook of English Costume in the Twentieth Century. 1900–1950*. London: Faber and Faber.

Martin, R. 1987. *Fashion and Surrealism*. New York: Rizzoli.

———. 1997. *The St. James Fashion Encyclopedia: A Survey of Style from 1945 to the Present*. Detroit, MI: Visible Ink.

Milbank, C. R. 1989. *New York Fashion: The Evolution of American Style*. New York: Abrams.

Mulvagh, J. 1988. *Vogue History of 20th Century Fashion*. New York: Viking Penguin.

Nuzzi, C. 1979. *Parisian Fashion*. New York: Rizzoli.

Olian, J. 1990. *Authentic French Fashions of the Twenties*. Mineola, NY: Dover.

Owen, E. 1993. *Fashion in Photographs, 1920–1940*. London: B. T. Batsford.

Peacock, J. 1993. *20th Century Fashion: The Complete Sourcebook*. London: Thames and Hudson.

Polhemus, T. 1994. *Street Style*. New York: Thames and Hudson.

Robinson, J. 1976. *Fashion in the Forties*. London: Academy Editions.

———. 1976. *The Golden Age of Style, 1909–1929*. New York: Harcourt Brace Jovanovich.

———. 1978. *Fashion in the Thirties*. London: Oresko Books.

Rolley, K. and C. Aish. 1992. *Fashion in Photographs, 1900–1920*. London: B. T. Batsford.

Sichel, M. 1979. *Costume Reference Books: The Edwardian's Costume; No. 7; 1918–1939, No. 8; 1939–1950, No. 9; 1950 to Present*. London: B. T. Batsford.

Steele, V. 1985. *Fashion and Eroticism: Ideals of Feminine Beauty from the Victorian Era to the Jazz Age*. New York: Oxford University Press.

Thompson, P. 1979. *The Edwardians in Photographs*. London: B. T. Batsford.

American Costume

De Marly, D. 1990. *Dress in North America*. New York: Holmes & Meier.

Earle, A. M. 1970. *Two Centuries of Costume in America*. 2 Volumes. Mineola, NY: Dover.

———. 1974. *Costume of Colonial Times*. Detroit: Gale Research Company.

Gummere, A. M. 1968. *Quaker: A Study in Costume*. New York: B. Blom. (Reprint of 1901 edition.)

Hall, L. 1992. *Common Threads: A Parade of American Clothing*. Boston: Bulfinch Press.

Modesty to Mod: Dress and Undress in Canada, 1780–1967. 1967. Toronto: Royal Ontario Museum.

Routh, C. 1993. *In Style: 100 Years of Canadian Fashion.* Toronto: Stoddart.

Warwick, E., H. Pitz, and A. Wykoff. 1965. *Early American Dress.* New York: Bonanza Books.

Wilcox, R. T. 1977. *Five Centuries of American Costume.* New York: Macmillan.

Worrell, E. A. 1975. *Early American Costume.* Harrisburg, PA: Stackpole Books.

Wright, M. 1990. *Put On Thy Beautiful Garments: Rural New England Clothing, 1883–1900.* Montpelier, VT: Clothes Press.

Children's Costume

Brooke, I. 2003. *English Children's Costume: 1775–1920.* Mineola, NY: Dover.

Cunnington, P. and A. Buck. 1965. *Children's Costume in England, 1300–1965.* London: A. & C. Black.

Ewing, E. 1977. *History of Children's Costume.* London: B. T. Batsford.

Garland, M. 1963. *The Changing Face of Childhood.* London: Hutchinson.

Guppy, A. 1978. *Children's Clothes. 1939–70.* Poole, Dorset, England: Blandford.

Macquoid, P. 1925. *Four Hundred Years of Children's Costume.* London: Medici Society.

Martin, L. 1978. *The Way We Wore: Children's Wear, 1870–1970.* New York: Scribners.

Moore, D. L. 1953. *The Child in Fashion.* London: B. T. Batsford.

Olian, J. 1993. *Children's Fashions, 1860–1912: 1,065 Costume Designs from "La Mode Illustree."* Mineola, NY: Dover.

Rose, C. 1989. *Children's Clothes.* New York: Drama Book.

Sichel, M. 1990. *History of Children's Costumes.* Oxford, UK: Chelsea House.

Worrell, E. 1981. *Children's Costume in America. 1607–1910.* New York: Scribners.

Men's Costume

Byrde, P. 1979. *The Male Image: Men's Fashion in England 1300–1970.* London: B. T. Batsford.

Chenoune, F. 1993. *A History of Men's Fashion.* Paris: Flammarion.

Davis, R. I. 1995. *Men's Garments 1830–1900. A Guide to Pattern Cutting and Tayloring.* Studio City, CA: Players' Press.

DeMarly, D. 1985. *Fashion for Men: An Illustrated History.* New York: Holmes & Meier.

Harvey, J. 1996. *Men in Black.* Chicago: University of Chicago Press.

Herald, J. 1997. *Men's Fashion in the Twentieth Century.* London: Chrysalis Books.

History of the Men's Wear Industry, 1790–1950. 1950. New York: Fairchild.

Hochswender, W. 1993. *The Golden Age of Style from Esquire.* New York: Rizzoli.

Martin, R. and H. Koda. 1989. *Jocks and Nerds: Men's Style in the Twentieth Century.* New York: Rizzoli.

Schoeffler, O. E., ed. 1973. *Esquire's Encyclopedia of 20th Century Men's Fashion.* New York: McGraw-Hill.

Walker, R. 1989. *Saville Row, An Illustrated History.* New York: Rizzoli.

Waugh, N. 1964. *The Cut of Men's Clothes, 1600–1900.* London: Faber and Faber.

Zakim, M. 2003. *Ready-Made Democracy: History of Men's Dress in the American Republic: 1760–1860.* Chicago: University of Chicago Press.

Special Types of Costume

Accessories

Armstrong, N. J. 1973. *Jewelry: An Historical Survey of British Styles and Jewels.* Guilford, England: Butterworth Press.

———. 1974. *A Collector's History of Fans.* New York: Crown.

Black, J. A. and M. Garland. 1974. *Jewelry Through the Ages.* New York: Morrow.

Cartlidge, B. 1985. *Twentieth Century Jewelry.* New York: Abrams.

Colle, D. 1972. *Collars, Stocks, Cravats.* Emmaus, PA: Rodale Press.

Corson, R. 1972. *Fashion in Eyeglasses.* London: P. Owen.

De Vere Green, B. 1976. *A Collector's Guide to Fans over the Ages.* London: F. Muller.

Ewing, E. 1982. *Fur in Dress.* London: B. T. Batsford.

Flower, M. 1973. *Victorian Jewelry.* Cranbury, NJ: S. Barnes.

Foster, V. 1982. *Bags and Purses.* London: B. T. Batsford.

Gere, C. 1975. *European and American Jewelry.* New York: Crown.

Haertig, E. 1983. *Antique Combs and Purses.* Carmel-by-the-Sea, CA: Gallery Graphics Press.

Hinks, P. 1975. *Nineteenth Century Jewelry.* London: Faber and Faber.

Jewelry Through 7000 Years. 1976. London: British Museum.

Mason, A. F. 1973. *Jewelry—An Illustrated Dictionary.* London: Osprey.

Mulvagh, J. 1988. *Costume Jewelry in "Vogue."* London: Thames and Hudson.

Newman, H. 1981. *An Illustrated Dictionary of Jewelry.* London: Thames and Hudson.

Raulet, S. 1988. *Jewelry of the 1940s and 1950s.* New York: Rizzoli.

Shields, J. 1988. *All That Glitters: The Glory of Costume Jewelry.* New York: Rizzoli.

Stera, D. F., ed., 1992. *Jewels of Fantasy: Costume Jewelry of the 20th Century.* New York: Abrams.

Von Boehn, M. 1970. *Ornaments: Lace, Fans, Gloves, Walking Sticks, Parasols, Jewelry, and Trinkets.* New York: B. Blom. (Reprint of 1929 edition.)

Cosmetics

Angeloglou, M. 1970. *A History of Makeup.* London: Macmillan.

Castelbajac, K. de. 1995. *The Face of the Century: 100 Years of Makeup and Style.* New York: Rizzoli.

Corson, R. 1981. *Fashions in Makeup: From Ancient to Modern Times*. London: P. Owen.

Gunn, F. 1974. *The Artificial Face: A History of Cosmetics*. New York: Hippocrene Books.

Footwear

Baynes, K. and K., Baynes, eds. 1980. *The Shoe Show: British Shoes Since 1790*. London: Crafts Council.

Brooke, I. 1976. *Footwear*. New York: Theatre Arts Books.

Farrell, J. 1992. *Socks and Stockings*. New York: Drama Book.

Grass, M. N. 1955. *History of Hosiery*. New York: Fairchild.

Lawlor, L. 1996. *Where Will This Shoe Take You? A Walk Through the History of Footwear*. New York: Walker.

Probert, C. 1981. *Shoes in Vogue*. London: Thames and Hudson.

Ricci, S. and E. Maeder. 1992. *Salvatore Ferragamo: The Art of the Shoe, 1896–1960*. New York: Rizzoli.

Smith, D. 2001. *Fashion Footwear: 1800–1970*. Atglen, PA: Schiffer.

Swann, J. 1982. *Shoes*. London: B. T. Batsford.

Walker, S. A. 1978. *Sneakers*. New York: Workman.

Wilcox, R. T. 1948. *The Mode in Footwear*. New York: Scribners.

Wilson, E. 1975. *The History of Shoe Fashion*. New York: Theatre Arts Books. (Reprint of 1900 edition.)

Hats and Headdress

Amphlett, H. 1974. *Hats: A History of Fashion in Headwear*. Chalfont St. Giles, England: Sadler.

Clark, E. 1982. *Hats*. London: B. T. Batsford.

Corson, R. 1971. *Fashion in Hair*. London: P. Owen.

De Courtais, G. 1973. *Women's Headdress and Hairstyles in England: A.D. 600 to the Present*. Totowa, NJ: Rowan and Littlefield.

Ginsburg, M. 1990. *The Hat*. Hauppauge, NY: Barron's.

Jones, D. 1990. *Haircults: Fifty Years of Styles and Cuts*. New York: Thames and Hudson.

Prober, C. 1982. *Hats in Vogue Since 1910*. London: Thames and Hudson.

Severn, B. 1971. *The Long and Short of It. 5000 Years of Fun and Fury over Hair*. New York: D. McKay.

Wilcox, R. T. 1959. *The Mode in Hats and Headdress*. New York: Scribners.

Underwear

Carter, A. 1992. *Underwear: The Fashion History*. New York: Drama Book.

Cunnington, C. W. and P. Cunnington. 1951. *The History of Underclothes*. London: M. Joseph.

Ewing, E. 1990. *Underwear: A History*. New York: Drama Book.

Farrell-Beck, J. and C. Gau. 2002. *Uplift: The Bra in America*. Philadelphia, PA: University of Pennsylvania Press.

Lord, W. B. 1993. *Freaks of Fashion: The Corset and the Crinoline (1868)*. Mendocino, CA: R. L. Shep.

Martin, R. and H. Koda. 1993. *Infra-Apparel*. New York: Abrams.

Probert, C. 1981. *Lingerie in Vogue Since 1910*. New York: Abbeville Press.

Steele, V. 2001. *The Corset: A Cultural History*. New Haven, CT: Yale University Press.

The Undercover Story. 1983. New York: Fashion Institute of Technology.

Waugh, N. 1954. *Corsets and Crinolines*. New York: Theatre Arts Books.

Armor

Blair, C. 1958. *European Armour*. London: B. T. Batsford.

———. 1962. *European and American Arms, 1100–1850*. London: B. T. Batsford.

Hewitt, J. 1975. *Ancient Armour and Weapons in Europe*. North Branford, CT: Arma Press.

Robinson, H. R. 1975. *The Armour of Imperial Rome*. New York: Scribners.

Wilkinson, F. 1973. *Arms and Armour*. New York: Bantam Books.

Clothing for Special Occasions

Ackerman, E. 1984. *Dressed for the Country: 1860–1900*. Los Angeles: Los Angeles County Art Museum.

Cunnington, P. and C. Lucas. 1972. *Costume for Births, Marriages, and Deaths*. New York: Barnes and Noble.

———. 1978. *Charity Costumes*. New York: Barnes and Noble.

Cunnington, P. and A. Mansfield. 1969. *English Costume for Sports and Outdoor Recreation*. New York: Barnes and Noble.

Ewing, E. 1975. *Women in Uniform Through the Centuries*. London: B. T. Batsford.

Kidwell, C. 1968. *Women's Bathing and Swimming Costume in the United States*. Washington, DC: The Smithsonian Institution Press.

McBride-Mellinger, M. 1993. *The Wedding Dress*. New York: Random House.

Mansfield, A. 1980. *Ceremonial Costume: Court, Civil, and Civic Costume from 1660 to the Present Day*. New York: Barnes and Noble.

Poli, D. D. 1997. *Beachwear and Bathing Costume*. New York: Drama Publishers.

———. 1997. *Maternity Fashion*. New York: Drama Publishers.

Probert, C. 1981. *Swimwear in Vogue*. London: Thames and Hudson.

Probert, C. and C. Lee-Potter. 1984. *Fashion in Vogue Since 1910: Sportswear*. New York: Abbeville Press.

Smith, A. M., et al. 1984. *Man and the Horse: An Illustration of Equestrian Apparel*. New York: Metropolitan Museum of Art.

Stevenson, S. and H. Bennett. 1978. *Vandyck in Check Trousers. Fancy Dress in Art and Life, 1700–1900*. Edinburgh: Scottish National Portrait Gallery.

Taylor, L. 1983. *Mourning Dress: A Costume and Social History*. Boston: Allen and Unwin.

Zimmerman, C. S. 1985. *The Bride's Book: A Pictorial History of American Bridal Gowns*. New York: Arbor House.

Occupational and Working Class Dress

Barsis, M. 1973. *The Common Man Through the Centuries*. New York: Ungar.

Copeland, P. E. 1977. *Working Dress in Colonial and Revolutionary America.* Westport, CT: Greenwood Press.

Cunnington, P. 1974. *Costume of Household Servants from the Middle Ages to 1900.* London: A. & C. Black.

De Marly, D. 1987. *Working Dress.* New York: Holmes & Meier.

Lansdell, A. 1977. *Occupational and Working Clothes, 1776–1976.* Alyesbury, England: Shire Books.

White, W. J. 1971. *Working Class Costume from Sketches of Characters (c. 1800–1815).* London: Victoria and Albert Museum.

Williams-Mitchell, C. 1983. *Dressed for the Job: The Story of Occupational Costume.* Poole, Dorset, England: Blandford Press.

Fashion Magazines, Fashion Designers, and the Fashion Industry

Blum, D. 2003. *Shocking: The Art and Fashion of Elsa Schiaparelli.* New Haven, CT: Yale University Press.

Carter, E. 1980. *Magic Names in Fashion.* Englewood Cliffs, NJ: Prentice-Hall.

Charles-Roux, E. 1975. *Chanel: Her World and the Woman Behind the Legend She Herself Created.* New York: Random House.

Coleman, E. 1982. *The Genius of Charles James.* New York: Holt, Rinehart and Winston.

De Marly, D. 1980. *The History of Haute Couture, 1850–1950.* London: B. T. Batsford.

———. 1980. *Worth-Father of the Haute Couture.* London: Elm Tree Books.

———. 1990. *Christian Dior.* London: B. T. Batsford.

———. 1991. *Worth: The Father of Haute Couture.* New York: Holmes & Meier.

Demornex, J. 1991. *Madeleine Vionnet.* New York: Rizzoli.

Derycke, L. and S. Van de Veire, eds. 1999. *Belgian Fashion Design.* Ghent, Belgium: Ludion.

Devlin, P. 1978. *Fashion Photography in Vogue.* London: Thames and Hudson.

Duncan, N. H. 1979. *History of Fashion Photography.* New York: Alpine Press.

Etherington-Smith, M. 1984. *Patou.* New York: St. Martin's Press.

Farber, R. 1981. *The Fashion Photographers.* New York: Watson Guptill.

Fashion Illustration. 1991. New York: Rizzoli, 1979.

Gaines, S. 1991. *Simply Halston.* New York: Putnam.

Holland, V. B. 1955. *Hand Coloured Fashion Plates, 1770–1899.* London: B. T. Batsford.

Jouve, M. and J. Demornex. 1989. *Balenciaga.* New York: Rizzoli.

Kellog, A., et al. 2002. *In an Influential Fashion: An Encyclopedia of Nineteenth and Twentieth Century Fashion Designers and Retailers Who Transformed Dress.* Westport, CT: Greenwood Press.

Kidwell, C. 1979. *Cutting a Fashionable Fit—Dressmaker's Drafting Systems in the U.S.* Washington, DC: Smithsonian Institution Press.

Kidwell, C. B. and M. C. Christman. 1974. *Suiting Everyone: The Democratization of Clothing in America.* Washington, DC: Smithsonian Institution Press.

Langley-Moore, D. 1972. *Fashion through Fashion Plates.* New York: Crown.

Lee, S. T., ed. 1975. *American Fashion.* New York: Quadrangle/New York Times.

Lynam, R., ed. 1972. *Couture.* Garden City, NY: Doubleday.

Mackrell, A. 1990. *Paul Poiret.* London: B. T. Batsford.

———. 1992. *Coco Chanel.* New York: Holmes & Meier.

Madsen, A. 1990. *Chanel, A Woman of Her Own.* New York: Holt.

Martin, R. and H. Koda. 1990. *Giorgio Armani: Images of Man.* New York: Rizzoli.

———. 1995. *Haute Couture.* New York: Metropolitan Museum of Art.

Milbank, C. 1985. *The Great Designers.* New York: Stewart, Tabori & Chang.

———. 1989. *New York Fashion: The Evolution of American Style.* New York: Abrams.

Miller, L. 1993. *Cristobal Balenciaga.* New York: Holmes & Meier.

Moffitt, P., et al. 1990. *The Rudi Gernreich Book.* New York: Rizzoli.

Osma, G. 1980. *Fortuny. His Life and Work.* New York: Rizzoli.

Pelle, M. 1991. *Valentino: Thirty Years of Magic.* New York: Abbeville Press.

Rhodes, Z. and A. Knight. 1985. *The Art of Zandra Rhodes.* Boston: Houghton Mifflin.

Steele, V. *Women of Fashion: Twentieth-Century Designers.* New York: Rizzoli, 1991.

Thornton, N. 1979. *Poiret.* New York: Rizzoli.

Trachtenberg, J. 1988. *Ralph Lauren—Image-maker. The Man Behind the Mystique.* Boston: Little Brown.

Walkley, C. 1985. *The Way to Wear 'Em: One Hundred Fifty Years of Punch on Fashion.* Chester Springs, PA: Dufour (P. Owen).

The World in Vogue. 1963. New York: Viking.

The World of Balenciaga. 1973. New York: Metropolitan Museum of Art.

Stage and Screen Costume History

Bailey, M. J. 1982. *Those Glorious, Glamour Years: The Great Hollywood Costume Designs of the Thirties.* Secaucus, NJ: Citadel.

De Marly, D. 1982. *Costume on the Stage.* New York: Barnes and Noble.

La Vine, W R. 1982. *In a Glamorous Fashion: The Fabulous Years of Hollywood Costume Design.* New York: Scribners.

Leese, E. 1976. *Costume Design in the Movies.* Bembridge, England: BCW Publishing.

McConathy, D. with D. Vreeland. 1976. *Hollywood Costume*. New York: Abrams.

Prichard, S. 1981. *Film Costume: An Annotated Bibliography*. Metuchen, NJ: Scarecrow.

Periodicals

Historic Costume and Dress

Costume Dress Fashion Theory: The Journal of Dress, Body, and Culture

CIBA Review (no longer published)

Fashion Magazines and Newspapers

Ackermann's Repository of the Arts. London: 1890–1929

Almanach des Modes. Paris: 1814–1822

La Belle Assemblee or Bell's Court and Fashionable Magazine. London: 1806–1818

Cabinet de Modes. Paris: 1785–1789

Daily News Record. New York: 1892 to present

Delineator. New York: 1873–1937

Demorest's Monthly Magazine. New York: 1865–1899

Ebony. Chicago: 1945 to present

Elle. Paris: 1945 to present

Esquire. New York: 1933 to present

Essence. New York: 1970 to present

La Galerie des Modes. Paris: 1778–1787

The Gallery of Fashion. London: 1794–1803

Gentleman's Quarterly (GQ). New York: 1957 to present

Glamour. New York: 1939 to present

Godey's Lady's Book. Philadelphia: 1830–1898

Harper's Bazaar. New York: 1867 to present

Journal des Dames et des Modes. Paris: 1797–1839

Le journal des Demoiselles. Paris: 1833–1904

M. New York: 1983–1992

Mademoiselle. New York: 1935 to present

Men's Wear. New York: 1890–1983

Mirabella. New York: 1989 to present

Les Modes Parisiennes. Paris: 1843–1875

Officiel de la Couture et de la Mode de Paris. Paris: 1921 to present

Peterson's Magazine. Philadelphia: 1837–1898

Petit Courrier des Dames. Paris: 1822–1865

Sir. Amsterdam: 1936 to present

Vanity Fair. New York: 1913–1936

Vogue. New York: 1892 to present

W. New York: 1971 to present

Women's Wear Daily. New York: 1910 to present

INDEX

Key terms, even when listed as sub-entries, and the pages on which their definitions appear are indicated in **boldface** type.

A

Abolla, 78

Accessories
  belts, jeweled, 32, 105, 181, 187
  canes, 274, 293, 320
  daggers, 128–129, 134
  fans, 77, 184, 186–187, 211, 217, 244, 245, 270, 341, 370, 380, 413
  feather boas, 347, 349, 370
  handkerchiefs, 75, 77, 187, 217, 220, 270, 293
  masks, 187, 211, 217, 244
  muffs, 217, 235, 244, 270, 272, 315, 317, 370
  parasols, 77, 244–245, 270, 290–294, 315, 317, 341, 370
  quizzing glasses, 274
  scarves, 215, 243, 413, 484, 539
  snuff boxes, 235, 293
  sunglasses, 411, 420
  Swiss belts, 315, 370
  umbrellas, 293, 320, 370, 411, 413
  walking sticks, 235, 350, 381
  watches, 235, 244, 270, 274
  See also specific time period (*e.g. Middle Ages*) and specific accessory; Gloves; Handbags; Jewelry; Purses

Acetate, 391

Acrylics, 433

Active sports clothing
  Bloomer costume, 258, 305, **307**
  for children, 547
  cycling clothing, 329, 345–347, 542
  fitness/jogging clothing, 477–478, 486, 542
  footwear, 341, 343, 443, 478, 523
  golf clothing, 409, 417–418
  Greeks, 52
  gym suits, 329
  high-tech fabric for, 521–522
  jersey fabric, 335
  knickerbockers (knickers), 318, 329, 345–346
  leotards, 477
  riding clothes, 244, 270, 379, 410
  ski clothing, 410, 418–419, 443, 478, 487, 530
  for snowboarding, 543
  swimwear. *See* Bathing suits
  tennis clothing, 335, 409, 418, 440, 443, 478, 487, 489, 531
  turkish trousers, 307–308, 347
  See also specific time period (*e.g. Bustle period*)

Adolfo, 471

Adrian, Gilbert, 397, 436

Aesthetic dress movement
  characteristics of, 331
  and children's clothing, 351–352

Afiche, 114

African Americans
  fashion trends of, 463, 517
  hairstyles, 463–464, 476, 506, 517

Age, dress as designation of, 3

Aiguillettes, 182, 187–188

Air travel, impact on fashion, 432

Akkadians, rise and fall of, 16

Alaia, Azzedine, 506–507, 512

Alb, 98

Alexander the Great, 11, 16–17, 48

A-line dresses, 444–445, 447, 474, 476

Amice, 98

Amish, 3

Amorites, 16

Amulets
  Egyptian, 26, **35**
  Romans, 77

Anakalypteria, 57

Ancient civilizations, 11–80
  costume terminology, 12*n*
  Egyptians, 11–12, 24–40
  Etruscans, 11–12, 64–67
  Greeks, 47–60
  Mesopotamians, 11–12, 16–23
  Minoans and Mycenaeans, 11–12, 44–47
  Romans, 11–12, 67–80

Anglomania, 230, 232

Anglo-Saxons, 99–100

Animal skins
    barbarian tribes' use, 95
    cloth simulations of, 30
    Egyptian use, 30, 35
    and garment construction, 2
    See also Furs
Ankle socks, 409, 453
Anklets, Egyptian, 35
Appliqué, Egyptians, 27, 31–32
Apprenticeship, Middle Ages, 102
Aprons, 217, 313
    Egyptian, 27–29, 32
    Minoans, 45–46
Arena, The, 339
Arkwright water spinning frame, 196
Armani, Giorgio, 510, 512, 526, 528, 540,
    541
Armlets
    Egyptian, 27, 35
    Empire period, 270
    Mesopotamian, 23–24
Armor
    Greeks, 58
    Middle Ages, 114–115, 140
    Romans, 78
    See also Military dress
Artificial silk, 391
Arts
    impact on clothing, 5–6
    as information source, 6–7
Ascots, 377
Asian influence
    Edwardian fashion, 365, 369, 371
    Eighties/Nineties, 518, 534
    Rococo fashions, 234, 243
    Sixties/Seventies, 464, 482
    World War I era, 371
Assyrians
    rise and fall of, 16
    See also Mesopotamian civilizations
Athletic shirts, 413, 438, 473, 527, 534
Automobiles
    dress for driver, 365, 379, 448
    as fashion influence, 365, 379, 391

B

Baby boom, 430, 521
Babylonian civilization
    rise and fall of, 16

See also Mesopotamian civilizations
Back packs, 533, 539, 547
Balagny, 206
Bald/shaved heads
    Egyptians, 25, 29, 32, 35
    Mesopotamians, 19
    Nineties, 544
Balenciaga, Cristobal, 433–434, 445
Ballerina length, 439
Balmain, Pierre, 434, 442
Balmorals, 343
Balteus, **72**
Bangs, 335
Banyans, 234, 273
Barbarian tribes
    hose, 95
    trousers, 95
Barbettes, Middle Ages, 108, 113, 130
Barege, 309
Baroque period, 193–222
    accessories, 211, 217
    children's dress, 217–220
    cosmetics, 217
    evidence related to dress, 204
    fashion revivals of, 220, 222
    footwear, 206, 208–210, 213, 215, 217
    hairstyles, 206, 208–209, 212, 215
    hats, 206, 208–209, 211–212, 220
    historical view, 200–202
    hose, 207, 210, 217
    jewelry, 217
    men's clothing, 206–210
    outdoor garments, 206, 208, 210, 215
    Spanish dress, 202–203
    textile production, 203–204
    undergarments, 210, 213
    women's clothing, 210–217
Barrymore collars, 415
Baseball caps, 533, 543
Bases, 174
Basques, 203, 212, **311,** 333
Basque shirts, 418
Bathing shoes, 335
Bathing suits
    bathing gowns, 244
    bikini, 442–443, 489
    bloomers/trousers/knickers, 308, 335,
        341, 346
    high performance fabrics, 521
    high-thigh cut, 530–531

Lastex, 410, 442
    men's trunks, 450
    tanks suits, first, 409–410, 412
    thong, 487
    topless, 477, 479
    two-piece for men, 379, 418
    two-piece for women, 410, 412,
        442–443
Battle jackets, 416
Batwing sleeves, 406
Bavolet, 287, 289
Beach pajamas, 409
Beadwork
    Egyptian, 26–27, 31–32
    Twenties, 402
Beak, 291
Beards
    Baroque era, 206
    Byzantine era, 91
    Egyptians, 32, 35
    Etruscans, 65
    false, 32, 35
    feudal era, 103
    Greeks, 53–54
    Merovingian and Carolingian, 96
    Mesopotamians, 19–20, 23
    Middle Ages, 106, 112
    Renaissance, 161, 185
    Romans, 76–77
Beatnicks, 429–430, 506
Bed hair, 535
Bedroom slippers, Romantic era,
    293
Beene, Geoffrey, 471
Belgium, fashion designers
    (1980–2003), 513
Bell-bottom pants, 477
La Belle Epoque. *See* Nineties (1890s)
Bell-shaped sleeves, 311, 316
Belts
    Byzantine era, 92
    Egyptian, 32, 35
    Eighties/Nineties, 537, 539–540
    Greeks, 57
    jeweled, 32, 105, 181, 187
    Merovingian and Carolingian, 96
    Mesopotamian, 19
    Middle Ages, 104–105, 127–129, 134,
        136, 141
    Minoans/Mycenaeans, 46

New Look, 448
  Renaissance, 181, 187
Berets, 286, 405, 408, 423, 475, 487, 533
Bergere, 239, 241
Bermuda shorts, 450
Berthas, 212, 287, 300, 313, 315
Bias cut, 393, 399, 406, 424
Bicornes, 234, 272, **274**
Biggins, 219
Bikini, 442–443
Bikini-cut undershorts, 488, 527
Birrus, 74
Bishop sleeves, 287, 367
Blass, Bill, 471
Blazers, 379
Bliaut, 105, 110
Bliaut gironé, 105–106
Bloomer costume, 258, 305, **307**
Blouses
  Bustle period, 333, 354
  Edwardian era, 369
  Garibaldi blouse, 311, 313, 316
  Gibson Girl, 345, 355, 530
  Nineties, 344
  see-through, 474
  shirtwaists, 344–345, 369, 371
  Sixties/Seventies, 474, 483
Blue jeans
  for children, 420, 422
  designer, 469
  Eighties/Nineties, 517–518
  as fashion staple, 496, 517
  Levi's, 305–306, 323
  Sixties/Seventies, 462, 469, 483
  Thirties, 409
  vintage, 511
Blue war crown, Egyptians, 35
Bobbed hair, 403–405
Bobbin-and-flyer spinning wheel, 172
Bobbin lace, 172–173
Bobby pins, 405
Bobby-sox, 409
Body jewelry, 517, 537
Body piercing, 517–518, 533
Body shirts, 488
Body stockings, 472–473
Body suits, 472–474
Bohan, Marc, 434
Bold Look, 445
Bombast, 177–178

Bonnet rouge, 262
Bonnets
  Crinoline period, 314–315
  Empire period, 270–271, 274
  Romantic period, 286, 288–289
Boot cuffs, 231
Boots
  ancient, 23, 55
  ankle, 295, 315, 321
  for children, 295, 321
  Congress-style, 342–343
  cuffed, 134
  go-go, 494
  jack boots, 209, 211, 235
  laced, 270, 341–342
  lower behind knee, 274
  military names for, 274
  open-toed, 93
  Russian-style, 405
  Sixties to Nineties, 480, 482–483, 491,
    532, 538, 543
  spats, 375–376
  zipper boots, 392
  See also footware of specific time
    periods (*e.g. Romans*)
Bottom-up theory, 467
Bouffant, 476, 479
Bourgeoisie dress, Middle Ages, late,
  124
Bourrelet, 139
Bowl crop, 133
Bowlers, 293, 317, 320, 350
Bow ties, 348, 377, 416
Box coats, 292
Boxer shorts, 401, 413, 438, 473, 488,
  527
Bracelets
  bracelet watch, 448
  Egyptian, 27, 35
  Greeks, 56
  ID for men, 450
  Mesopotamian, 23–24
  Sixties/Seventies, 488
Braces, 318
Braids
  ancient use, 32, 65, 77
  Middle Ages, 108, 113, 130
  Renaissance, 159
Braies, 102, 104, 109–110, 174
Braless, 474, 483

Brassiere
  bust improvers, 344
  Greek breast support, 52
  modern era, 372, 399–400, 405, 437
  Nineties breast supports, 344
  "no-bra" look, 473–474, 481
  origin of, 366, 368
  Roman breast support, 74
  strapless/halter conversion, 534
  Wonder Bra, 527
Breast support. *See* Brassiere
Breeches
  Baroque, 206–207, 219
  Empire period, 273
  petticoat breeches, 205, 207–208
  Renaissance, 175, 177–179, 189
  Rococo, 231, 233–234
  Romantic period, 292
  Venetians, 175, 177, 179, 221
Breeching, 3, 217
Bridal clothing. *See* Wedding clothing
Bridal knot, 57
Briefs, 405, 488
Brocade, 90, 123, 153
Brooches
  Bustle period, 343
  Empire period, 270, 274
  Greeks, 55
  Merovingian and Carolingian,
    96–97
  Middle Ages, 114, 141
  Renaissance, 187
  Romantic period, 293
Brummel, George "Beau", 266–267
Buckles, shoes, 134, 209, 217, 235, 244
Buckram stiffening, 231
Bulla, 77–78
Bum rolls, 179, 183, 186
Burberry, Thomas, 379
Burnous, 289, 313
Bush jackets, 417
Busks, 179
Bustle period, 328–343
  accessories, 341, 343, 349
  active sports dress, 335
  aesthetic dress movement, 331,
    351–352
  children's clothing, 350–352
  cosmetics, 343
  evidence related to dress, 332

fashion revivals of, 330–331, 353, 355
footwear, 341–343, 350
hairstyles, 335, 340, 350
hats, 335, 340–341
historical view, 328–332
hose, 341
jewelry, 343, 350
men's clothing, 347–350
mourning clothes, 352–353
outdoor garments, 335, 348, 350
ready-to-wear, 329–330
textile production, 329
undergarments, 332–333, 336–337, 347
women's clothing, 332–343
Bustles, 282, 284
types of, 332, 336, 354
Butterick, Ebeneezer, 330
Buttoned closures, Renaissance, 153
Buttons, jeweled, 293, 320, 350
Byrnie, 114
Byzantine period, 88–94
evidence related to dress, 89–90
footware, 93
hairstyles, 92
headdresses, 91, 93
historical view, 83–84, 88–90
hose, 91, 93
jewelry, 93
men's clothing, 90–91
military dress, 93
royal dress, 91–93
social organization, 88
textile production, 89–90
undergarments, 90, 92
women's clothing, 92–93

C

Cabochon stones, 315
Cafe society, 391
Cage crinoline, 309–311
Calamancos, 234
Calashes, 236, 241
Calasiris, 27, 29, 34, 38
Calico, 195
California collars, 415
Calves, artificial, 235
Camel hair coats, 416

Cameos, 315
Camicia, 154, 158–163, 165
Cami-knickers, 372
Camisole
Crinoline period, 309–310
Nineties, 344
Camouflage print, 518, 534
Canes, 274, 293, 320
Canezou, 285, 313
178–179
Canons, 207
Capes and cloaks
Baroque, 206, 212, 215
Bustle period, 345
Byzantine era, 93
coat-capes, 319, 335, 348–349, 379
Crinoline era, 319
Directoire period, 268
Edwardian era, 369
Egyptian, 30–32
Etruscan, 65–66
Greeks, 50, 52, 56, 59
Merovingian and Carolingian, 96, 98
Mesopotamian, 19
Middle Ages, 107–108, 110–111, 113, 128, 132–133, 136
Minoans/Mycenaeans, 46
Nineties, 345
Renaissance, 158–159, 178, 180
Rococo, 243
Romans, 72, 74, 78–79
Romantic period, 293
Sixties/Seventies, 477
Capotes, 286, 289
Caps
Crinoline period, 312, 314–315, 321
Empire period, 270–271
Rococo, 234–235, 236–237, 239
Romantic era, 286–287
Caraçao, 241
Cardin, Pierre, 434, 467–469, 488
Cargo pants, 518, 534, 537
Carmagnole, 262
Carnaby Street, 462
Carnegie, Hattie, 397, 436, 469
Carolingian dynasty. *See* Merovingian and Carolingian dynasties
Carriage dresses, 283
Carriage parasols, 290

Carrying frocks, 219
Casaques, 206
Cashin, Bonnie, 471
Cashmere, 256, 522, 537
Cassocks, 206
Castles and court, Middle Ages, 99, 101
Catholicism, clerical dress, 98
Catogans, 234
Caul, 139
Cavalier-style hat, 208, 211–212
Chainse, 107
Chains, gold, 176, 181, 187
Chaldeans, rise and fall of, 16
Chambre Syndicale de la Couture Parisienne, 304, 395, 397, 433
Chanel, Gabrielle "Coco," 6, 392–394, 433–434
handbags, 484, 488, 537
suits of, 374, 392, 399, 402, 423, 474, 526, 528
Chapeau bras, 234, 274
Chaplets, 130
Chasuble, 98
Chatelaines, 290, 294
Chausses, 115
Chemise
Baroque era, 213
Bustle period, 332, 337
Crinoline era, 309–310
Directoire period, 267
Middle Ages, 102, 104, 110
New Look, 444, 447
Renaissance, 159, 179–180
Rococo era, 237
Romantic period, 282, 284
Chemise dresses, 375, 444, 447
Chemise a la reine, 240, 242
Chemisettes, 285
Chesterfield, 292, 319, 345, 348, 377, 379
Chignon
Baroque era, 212
Bustle period, 335
Byzantine, 92
Greeks, 55
Mesopotamians, 19, 21
Romantic era, 287
Children's clothing
active sports clothing, 547

American slaves, 296
ancient, 18, 24, 35, 67, 77–78
blue jeans, 420, 422
breeching, 3, 217
carrying frocks, 219
christening clothing, 219
corsets, 368
costumes, 422
distinctive, first use of, 217–220
Eton suit, 295, 322, 350
gender-related colors, 420
going frocks, 220
gym clothing, 382
hats, 321–322, 352
infant bodysuits, 451, 492
infant caps, 321
infant heat regulating caps, 544
kiddie couture, 502
knickerbocker suits, 322
knickers, 350, 352
layette, 219
leading strings, 218
miniature adult style, 137, 164–165,
    187–188, 350, 451
pajamas with feet, 382, 422, 487
pants for girls, 493–494
pinafores, 218, **220,** 381–382
pudding, 220
rainwear, 422
ribbons of childhood, 218–219
robes, 217–218
Rousseau's influence, 246–247
sailor suits, 322, 381, 422
skirts/dresses for boys, 295, 321, 350,
    352, 382
snow suits, 422
swaddling clothes, 55–56, 77,
    136–137, 219
teething rings, coral, 220
tunic suit, 295
undergarments, 337
See also specific time period (*e.g.
    Romantic period*)
China
    Mongol rule, 84–85
    Polo expeditions, 84–85
à la Chinoise, 285, 288
Chinos, 450
Chintz, 195

Chitons
    Etruscans, 65
    Greeks, 12*n*, **50**–52, 54–60
Chlamydon, 52, 54
Chlamys, 52, 54, 59
Chlanis, 58
Chopines, 163–164, 167, 187, 203
Christening clothing, 219
Chukka boots, 419
Circlets, Middle Ages, 105
Cities, Middle Ages, 101
Claiborne, Liz, 508, 514
Clavi, 67 **68,** 90, 92
Cloaks. *See* Capes and cloaks
Cloche, 404–405
Clogs
    Baroque era, 213
    Middle Ages, 104, 122, 128, 141
    Rococo era, 243
    Sixties/Seventies, 480, 482
Closed mantles, 103, 105
Clothing
    earliest evidence of, 1
    early functions of, 1
    as social communication, 4
Clothing making
    buttoned closures, 153
    cutting machines, 330
    by draping, 2
    foreign production, 511
    hookless fasteners, 392
    patterns, 330
    piecework concept, 330
    sewing machine, 306–307
    sewn clothing, early, 27, 45, 95
    steam power, 330
    tailors, 124, 153, 204, 228–229
    Velcro, 464
    zippers, 392, 415
    See also French couture; Ready-to-
        wear
Cloth production. *See* Textile
    production
Club wigs, 234, 245
Clutch coats, 402
Coal tar dyes, 309
Coat-dresses, 285, 372
Coat of plates, 140
Coats, outdoor

box, 292
chesterfield, 292, 319, 345, 348, 377,
    379
clutch, 402
coat-capes, 319, 335, 348–349
curricle, 292
down-filled, 487, 489, 494
English guards', 416
evening, 316, 371–372
frock overcoats, 319
fur, 146, 379, 403, 408, 439, 441, 489
greatcoats, 273, 292, 477
kimono, 369, 439
mackinaws, 382, 416, 420
mackintosh, 292–293, 319, **379**
for men, 206, 208, 210, 231, 273,
    292–293, 318–319
military-style, 374, 408
pardessus, 289, 313, 316
pelisse, 269–270, 289, 335
polo, 416, 449
Raglan capes, 319
raglan sleeve, 379, 408, 439
reefers, 347
surtouts, 208, 234
toggle, 453
top, 378–379
trench, 379, 534
ulster, 335, 345, 350, **379**
for women, 215, 243, 313, 335
wraparound, 371, 449, 530
See also outdoor garments for
    specific time period (*e.g.Baroque*
    period)
Code of Hammurabi, 11, 16
Codpiece, 131, 161, 174–175, 178
Coif, 106, 112, 133, 164, 174, 182, 185
Coleman, Ann, 7
Collars
    Barrymore, 415
    California, 415
    Egyptian, 27, 31, 35
    jeweled, 27, 35, 93, 187
    Medici, 184, 190, 330, 369
    Middle Ages, 134
    Renaissance ruff, 175, 178–186
Combinations, 332, 337, 368, 370
Combs, Sean Puffy, 514
Commode, 211, 215

Conch, 184
Congress boots, 342–343
Conspicuous outrage, 518
Constantinople, 79, 83–84, 88, 94
Consumer revolution, and fashion, 196–197
Continental suits, 449, 488
Cope, 98, 110
Copotains, 185, 208, 211–212
Coral, teething rings, 220
Cornettes, 111–**112**
Cornrow braids, 463–464, 476
Corselets
    Egyptian, 30, 35, 39
    Mesopotamian, 23
    Romans, 78
Corset covers, 309–310, 336
Corsets, 128
    Baroque era, 213
    Bustle period, 332, 337
    for children, 368
    Crinoline era, 309–310
    Directoire period, 267
    Edwardian era, 368
    forerunner of, 178–179
    New Look, 437
    Nineties, 344
    Renaissance, 179
    Rococo era, 235
    Twenties, 399–400
    See also Stays
Cosmetic procedures, 533
Cosmetics
    eyebrow darkening, 77, 217, 244, 413
    eye makeup, 30, 35, 444, 488
    home remedies, 315–316
    lipstick/lip color, 35, 77, 187, 217, 413, 444, 488, 533
    men's use of, 35, 274
    nail polish, 24, 30, 35, 217
    night treatments, 217, 244
    patches over flaws, 77, 217, 244
    plumpers, 217
    powdered/whitened skin, 77, 281, 290, 343, 413
    Puritan view of, 187
    rouge, 114, 187, 244
    toxic types, 77

See also specific time period (*e.g. Romantic period*); specific types of cosmetics (*e.g. Eye makeup*)
Cossacks, 273
Costume history
    ancient civilizations, 11–80
    clothing as art form, 5–6
    cross-cultural influences, 5
    economic events/trade in, 4
    evidence, sources of, 7–8
    fashion-related terms, 7
    fashion in Western dress, 6
    folk dress, 6–7
    geographic/environmental influences, 5
    information sources about, 7–8
    politics/political conflicts in, 4
    production/technology in, 4
    revivals, 6
    social context of dress, 2–4
    themes across time, 2–7
    See also specific historical eras
Cote-hardie, 126–127, 129–130, 132, 143
Cotes, 108–110, 113, 129, 135, 143
Cotte, 110
Cotton
    and Assyrians, 21
    Egyptian use, 26
    industrial production of, 228
    in Middle Ages, 101–102
    Roman use, 69
    trade with India, 195
    United States cultivation, 281
    washable, 309
    and World War I, 364
Cotton gin, 267
Coul, 111
Courrèges, André, 464, 467, 470
Courtesans, Greek hetairi, 49
Cowboy clothing. *See* Western dress
Cowl, monastic dress, 98
Crackowe, 128, 130
Crahay, Jules-François, 470
Cravat pins, 293, 320
Cravats, 208, 211, 230–231, **270, 291,** 294, 316, 319
Crete, Minoan civilization, 11–12, 44–47
Crew cuts, 450, 452
Crinoline, 323

Crinoline period, 304–324
    accessories, 315, 317, 320
    active sports dress, 307–308
    Bloomer costume, 258, 305, **307**
    children's dress, 320–322
    clothing production, 306–307
    cosmetics, 315–316
    evidence related to fashion, 308–309
    fashion revivals of, 323, 455
    footwear, 315, 317, 320
    hairstyles, 314–315, 319
    hats, 314–315, 317, 320
    historical view, 304–308
    hose, 315
    jewelry, 315, 320
    men's garments, 316–320
    outdoor garments, 313–316, 318–319
    textile production, 309
    undergarments, 309–311
    women's garments, 309–316
Cross-cultural influences
    cultural authentication, 5
    mixtures, 5
Crowns
    Byzantine, 91, 93
    Egyptian, 36–37
    Etruscans, 67
    Mesopotamian, 19–20
    Middle Ages, 130
    See also Diadems
Crusades
    historical view, 84, 88
    influence on dress, 101
Cuff links, 350, 420
Cuirass, 58
Cuirass bodice, 332, 334
Culots, 177
Culottes
    Eighties, 530
    Minoans, 45
Cultural authentication, 5
Cummerbund, 416, 448
Curling irons, ancient era, 23
Curricle coats, 292
Cutoffs, 518
Cutting machines, 330
Cutwork, Renaissance, 172
Cyberpunks, 507
Cyclas, 111

Cycling clothing, 329, 345–347, 542
Cyrus, Persian king, 16

D
DA (duck tail), 431, 448, 450
Daggers, 128–129, 134
Dagging, 127
Dalmatic, 79, 92
Dashikis, 463
Day caps, 270
Day dresses. *See* Dresses
Deconstructionists, 523–524, 535
Decoration, as function of clothing, 1
Deerstalker caps, 349–350
Delphos gown, 364, 383
Demi-gigot, 284
Denim, Levi's, 305–306
Derby hats, 293, 348, 350
Designer jeans, 469
Diadems
    Byzantine era, 91, 93
    Egyptian, 35–37
    Romans, 77
    See also Crowns
Diamond ear studs, 532
Diamonds by the yard, 488
Diapers, 219
Dimity, 101
Dior, Christian, 433–434, 437, 445, 510
Diplax, 52
Directoire period
    fashion extremists, 263
    hairstyles, 263
    historical view, 262–263
    men's clothing, 270–274
    outdoor garments, 268
    time span of, 262–263
    undergarments, 267
    women's clothing, 267–269
Dirndl skirts, 406
Dishrag shirts, 418
Ditto suits, 232–233
Doc Martens, 532
Doge, dress of, 163–165
Dolce and Gabbana, 506, 509, 512
Dolman mantles, 335, 339
Dolman sleeves, 117, 408
Do-rag, 533

Dorians, 11, 44
Double knits, 475, 488
Double mantles, 104
Doublets
    Baroque, 206–207, 221
    Middle Ages, 123, **126,** 131, 143
    Renaissance, 156–157, 161, 166,
        174–175, 189
Down coats/jackets, 487, 489, 494
Draped garments, 2
    Egyptians, 27, 29, 30–33, 39
    Etruscans, 65–66
    fasteners, 12, 51, 55, 114, 130, 180
    Greeks, 49
    Mesopotamians, 20, 22
    Romans, 3, 12*n*, 69–72, 79
    See also Capes and cloaks;
        Loincloths; Shawls; Tunics; Veils
Drawers, 154, **174,** 213, **230**–231, 267,
    309–310, 316, 336–337, 347
Draw loom, 204
Drawn bonnets, 289
Dreadlocks, 506, 517
Dress down days, 521
Dress elevator, 316
Dresses
    accessory garments for, 285, 313
    A-line, 444–445, 447, 474, 476
    ballerina length, 439
    bias cut, 393, 399, 406, 424
    Bustle period, 333–334
    carriage, 283
    chemise, 375, 444, 447
    coat-dresses, 285, 372
    Crinoline era, 311–313
    Edwardian era, 366–367
    Egyptian sheath, 27, 29, 31–32, 34,
        38–39
    granny, 474
    lingerie, 367, 381, 383
    monastic, 396–397
    morning, 283
    New Look, **444**–445, 447
    Nineties, 344–345
    paper, 475
    princess, 313, 333–334
    promenade, 283
    Romantic era, 282–287, **283,** 285–286
    skimmer, 469, 492

sleeveless, 399
tea gowns, 333
Thirties, 405–406
Twenties, 399, 402
V-necked, early, 32, 34, 135, 143, 163,
    180
walking, 283
World War I era, 374
World War II era, 405–406
wraparound, 31, 481
See also Evening dresses; Gowns
Dressing gowns
    banyans, 234, 273
    Crinoline era, 318
    New Look, 440
    Romantic era, 292
    smoking jackets, 318, 381
    World War I era, 381
Drip dry fabric, 433
Driving clothes, 365, 379, 448, 450
Dropped shoulder, 311
Duckbills, 185–186
Dusters, 365, 379
Dyeing of textiles
    ancient era, 26, 45, 57, 69
    coal tar dyes, 309
    Middle Ages, 102
    mordants, 26, 45
    Renaissance, 153

E
Earrings
    Egyptian, 27, 35
    Eighties/Nineties, 532, 539
    Greeks, 55–56
    male use, 35
    Mesopotamian, 23–24
    Minoan, 47
    Renaissance, 187
    Sixties/Seventies, 480
    Twenties, 411, 413
East India Company, 195–196
Economic events, impact on dress, 4
Edwardian period, 366–370
    accessories, 370
    evidence related to dress, 366
    fashion revivals of, 383, 462, 506
    footwear, 370

French couture, 363–365
hairstyles, 370
hats, 370
historical view, 362–366
hose, 370
jewelry, 370
outdoor clothing, 369
ready-to-wear, 366
undergarments, 366, 368
women's clothing, 366–370
Egyptians, 24–40
children's clothing, 35
cleanliness, 25
cosmetics, 24, 30, 35
entertainer's clothing, 31, 38
evidence related to costume, 25–26
family in, 25
fashion revivals of, 40, 466, 484
footwear, 29, 32
hairstyles, 29, 32, 35, 37
headdresses, 32, 36–37
historical view, 11–13, 16–18
jewelry, 26, 27, 32, 35
kingdoms/dynasties of, 16–17
men's garments, 27–35
military costume, 35
religious dress, 29, 35, 38
royal dress, 25–27, 30, 32, 35
social structure, 24–25, 27
textile production, 26–27
women's garments, 31–35
wrapped garments, 30–33
Eighties and Nineties, 523–547
accessories, 532–533, 537, 539, 543
active sports clothing, 523, 530–531,
542–543
children's clothing, 544–547
cosmetics, 533, 544
designers' labels, 515
fashion industry, 504–511
fashion merchandising, 511, 515
footwear, 532, 535, 537, 538
hairstyles, 531–532, 535, 543
hats, 531, 533, 535, 543
historical view, 500–504
hose, 532, 543
influences on fashion, 517–523
jewelry, 532, 540, 543–544
men's clothing, 540–544

outdoor garments, 528, 530, 534–535,
542
retro fashion, 516, 521
sleepwear, 531, 543
sportswear, 530, 541–542
undergarments, 525, 527, 534, 540
women's clothing, 523–540
Eisenhower jackets, 406, 416, 418, 420
Ellis, Perry, 514
Embroidery
Egyptians, 27
Mesopotamians, 23
Middle Ages, 103, 108, 132
Minoans, 46
Renaissance, 160, 163, 172–173, 182
Spanish work, 172, 182
Empire period
accessories, 270, 272, 274
children's dress, 274–275
cosmetics, 274
fashion revivals of, 275–276, 370
footwear, 270, 274
hairstyles, 269–271, 274
hats, 270, 272, 274–275
historical view, 264–265
jewelry, 270, 274
men's clothing, 270–274
outdoor garments, 273
time span of, 262
undergarments, 267–268
women's clothing, 267–269
Empire waistline, 60, 265, 269, 277,
370–371, 384, 474, 525
En cour, 287
Engageants, 239, 311–312
English drape suit, 415, 424
English guards' coats, 416
Ensembles, 402
Entertainer's clothing
Egyptian, 31, 38
Greeks, 50, 58
Renaissance, 187
Environmental activism, 502
Epaulettes
Crinoline period, 312
mancherons, 283
Nineties, 344
Eschelles, 239
Eton crop, 405

Eton suit, 295, 322, 350
Etruscans, 64–67
children's clothing, 67
evidence related to costume, 64
footwear, 67
garments, types of, 65–66
hairstyles, 65
hats, 66–67
headdresses, 67
historical view, 11–13, 64
jewelry, 67
social and family life, 64
undergarments, 65
Evening clothes, men
capes and cloaks, 293, 318, 345,
371–372
cummerbund, 416, 448
dinner jackets, 416, 449
dress shirts, 348
shoes, 315, 341–342
tail coats, 348, 378, 415
top hats, 350, 381
tuxedo, 348, 350, 377, 414–416, 449,
488, 492, 542
white dinner jackets, 416, 542
Evening dresses
bare-backed, 406
Bustle period, 333–335
Edwardian era, 369
evening suits, 406, 408
halter-top, 406, 409
Le Pouf, 526, 528–529
New Look, 440, 442
Nineties, 345–346
off-the-shoulder, 313, 315, 333, 345
robe de style, 402–403
Romantic era, 285
short, 475–476, 478
slip dresses, 528, 534
strapless gowns, 408, 528
Twenties, 402–403
World War I era, 371, 374–375
Exomis, 51, 59
Eyebrows
darkening, 77, 217, 244
plucking, 130, 244, 413
Eye makeup
Egyptians, 30, 35
modern era, 444, 488

F

Fabric
earliest evidence of, 1
production. *See* Textile production
Facial hair
soul patch, 544
unshaven look, 544
See also Beards; Mustaches; Shaving
Factory system, 196, 255–256
Fade, 517
Fake furs, 477, 494
Fall, 231
Falling bands, 206, 211
False rumps, 240
Fans, 184, 186–187, 211, 217, 244, 245, 270, 290, 315, 341, 349, 370, 380, 413
Romans, 77
Fashion
and consumer revolution, 196–197
historical development, 6, 85., *See also* Costume history
as social phenomenon, 6
Western dress, 6
Fashion information
fashion babies, 229
fashion dolls, 197, 229
fashion plates, 204, 282, 287
and magazines. *See* Fashion magazines
motion pictures, 359, 366
of photographs, 7–8, 282, 308, 332
Renaissance dissemination of, 171–172, 197
See also specific historical era (*e.g. Romantic era*)
Fashionistas, 504
Fashion magazines
color photos, 399
early, 282, 308
fashion art photography, 398–399
high society profiles, 366
and ideal versus real, 7
photographs versus drawings, 332
Fashion terms, changes over time, 7
Fasteners. *See* Clothing making
Fath, Jacques, 434
Feather boas, 347, 349, 370
Feather cut, 408
Feathers

fans, 187, 217
hat trim, 128, 178, 181, 185–186, 206, 335, 370
Fedoras, 347, **350,** 419, 448
Feminists
Bloomer costume, 258, 305
braless, 474, 483
and dress reform, 258
Fendi, 510
Fermail, 114
Ferragamo, 510
Ferré, Gianfranco, 509, 512
Ferroniere, 159, 161–162, 167, 187
Fetish/perv styles, 507
Feudalism, 99, 101
Fez, Mesopotamian, 23
Fibula, 12, 51
Fichu pelerine, 285
Fichus, 313
Filet, 172
Fillets
ancient use, 19, 21, 35, 46, 55, 66, 77
Middle Ages, 108, 113, 130
Filling yarns, 26
Films
as fashion influence, 390–391, 420, 423, 464, 520
as information source, 359, 366
Fish-tails, 439
Fitchets, 111
Flammeum, 78
Flappers
origin of term, 405
See also Twenties
Flax, linen production, 18, 26
Flip-flops, 535, 538
Flying shuttle, 228
Fogarty, Anne, 436
Folk costume, 6–7, 197
influence on fashion, 466
Fontange, 211, 215–216
Footwear
makers of, 69, 124
origin of, 20–21
See also specific time periods (*e.g. Romantic period*); Boots; Sandals; Shoes
Ford, Tom, 506, 514
Forehead

high, plucking hair for, 130, 136, 154
jewelry for, 21, 159, 161–162, 167, 187
Foretop, 234
Fortuny, 363–365, 369, 383, 394
Foundation garments, 437
Four-in-hand ties, 377, 415
France
prêt-á-porter, 467–468, 509
See also French couture
French blue dinner jackets, 449
French bonnet, 174, 185
French couture
designers (1920–1947), 394
designers (1947–1960), 434
designers (1960–1980), 470
designers (1980–2003), 512
founding of, 304, 346
haute couture, 395–396, 433
originals, 433, 435
French farthingale, 183
Frescos, 70
Frets, 130
Frock coats, 232, 291, 299, 316, 318, 347–348, 375
Frock overcoats, 319
Frocks, 136, 232
Fulling, 49, 101
Furs
coats, 379, 403, 408, 439, 441, 489
fake, 477, 494, 502, 535
mantles, 104, 108, 127
Middle Ages use of, 104, 108, 111, 124, 127, 129, 132
neckpiece, 411
raccoon coats, 403, 416
Renaissance use of, 158
tippets, 243
World War I era, 379

G

Gabled, 185
Gaiters, 289, 293, 320
Galanos, James, 436
Galitzine, Princess Irene, 470
Galliano, John, 506–507, 510, 513, 528
Gallygaskins, 177
Galoshes, 208, 289, 293, 420
Gambeson, 140

Gardcorps, 110–**111,** 116
Garibaldi blouse, 311, 313, 316
Garment industry, development of, 330
Garnache, 110–112, **111,** 113, 116, 128
Garter belts, 399–400
Gauls, trousers, 78–79
Gaultier, Jean Paul, 506–507, 512
Gay Nineties. *See* Nineties (1890s)
Gender differences, dress as
    designation of, 2–3
Geography, influence on dress, 5
Geometric cuts, 476, 480
Germanic tribes and kingdoms, 84, 94,
    99
Germany
    fashion designers (1980–2003), 513
    Renaissance. *See* Renaissance,
      Northern Europe
Gernreich, Rudi, 471, 474, 477, 479,
    487
Ghesquière, Nicholas, 512
Gibson, Charles Dana, 344
Gibson Girl, 344–346, 355, 530
Gibus hats, 293
Gigot, 284
Gilet corsage, 287
Gipon, 126
Girdles, Middle Ages, 105
Girdles, undergarment, 399–400,
    437–438
Givenchy, Hubert de, 434, 510
Glam styles, 506–507
Gloves
    Baroque era, 217
    Bustle period, 341
    Crinoline era, 315, 320
    Egyptians, 31
    Empire period, 270, 274
    fingerless, 290, 294, 315
    Middle Ages, 114, 129–130, 134, 136
    mittens, 244, 290
    New Look, 443
    Nineties, 347, 350
    Renaissance, 163, 186, 187
    Rococo era, 244
    Romantic period, 289–290, 293–294
    Twenties/Thirties/World War II era,
      411, 413
Godey's Lady's Book, 282, 308, 332

Go-go boots, 494
Going frocks, 220
Golf clothing, 409, 417–418
Goodman of Paris, 124
Goodrich, B. F., 392
Goring, 367, 406
Goth look, 505–507
Gowns
    Baroque, 210, 212–215
    with bum rolls, 179, 183, 186
    chemise a la reine, 240, 242
    cotes, 108–110, 113, 129, 135, 143
    Directoire period, 268
    empire, 265, 269, 274, 277
    Empire period, 263, 268–269, 274
    houpplelande, 127, 129, 131–135, 143,
      166
    layered, 159–160, 166, 179
    mantua-style, 213, 215, 221, **237**
    Middle Ages, **129,** 131, 135–137, 143
    pet-en-lair, 237, 239
    petticoats with, 181–182, 239,
      267–268
    polonaise, 240–241
    Renaissance, 159–160, 163, 166, 176,
      179–184, 189
    robe à la Française, 237, 239, 249
    robe à l'Anglaise, 239, 241, 246, 249
    Rococo, 237–243, 249
    rocs, 136–137
    ropa, 172, 182–**183**
    round, 240, 265, 268
    sacque, 237–238, 335
    skirts with, 212–215
    with Spanish farthingale, 181, **183,**
      210, 237
    and stomachers, 174, 179, 183, 210,
      213, 221, 239, 249, 268
    surcotes, 108–111, 113, 115, 126, **129,**
      143
    Watteau back, 239
    See also Dresses; Evening dresses
Granny dresses, 474
Grave goods/clothing, Egyptian, 25–26
Gray flannel suits, 447
Great Britain
    fashion designers (1960–1980), 471
    fashion designers (1980–2003), 513
Greatcoats, 273, **292,** 477

Great Depression, 389, 390
Greaves, 57–**58,** 78
Grecian bend, 268
Greeks, ancient, 47–58, 47–60
    athletic clothing, 52
    cosmetics, 55
    evidence related to costume, 49–50
    fashion revivals of, 55, 60, 270, 364
    footwear, 55
    hairstyles, 52–53, 55
    hats, 52–53, 56
    historical view, 47–48
    jewelry, 55–56
    men's garments, 51–55
    military dress, 57–58
    social organization, 48–49
    textile production, 49
    theatrical costume, 58
    undergarments, 52
    wedding clothing, 57–58
    women's garments, 51–55
    See also Minoan and Mycenaean
      civilizations
Greenway, Kate, 351
Grès, Alix, 394
Group membership, dress as
    designation of, 3
Guardaroba, 153
Guardinfante, 203
Gucci, 510
Gym suits, 329, 382
Gypsy hats, 270

H

Habit shirt, 268
Hair care products, 488, 492, 533, 543
Hair dye
    Middle Ages, 114, 130, 136
    Renaissance, 163–164, 185
    Romans, 77
    Thirties, 390
Hair nets
    Crinoline era, 315
    Middle Ages, 113, 130, 136
    Renaissance, 181
Hair ornaments/fasteners
    bobby pins, 405
    combs, 286

fillets, 19, 21, 35, 46, 55, 66, 77, 108, 113, 130
frets, 130
headbands, 405, 484, 531–532
jeweled, 244
scrunchies, 531
snoods, 312, 314–**315,** 408
Hairstyles
bald for men, 19, 25, 32, 35
bangs, 335
bed hair, 535
bobbed, 403–405
bouffant, 476, 479
bowl crop, 133
braids, 32, 77, 108, 113, 130, 159
chignon, 19, 21, 55, 92, 212, 287, 335
à la Chinoise, 285, 288
cornrow braids, 463–464, 476
crew cuts, 450, 452
DA (duck tail), 431, 448, 450
dreadlocks, 506, **517**
dyed hair. *See* Hair dye
Eton crop, 405
fade, 517
feather cut, 408
fontange, 211, **215**–216
frizzy look, 476, 479
geometric cuts, 480
Gibson Girl, 346
hair nets with, 113, 130, 136, 181, 315
hedgehog, 241–242
horned, 162–164
lock of Horus, 35, 37, 39
long for men, 46, 106, 158, 208, 484, 490, 494
loose, 24, 92, 103–104
love lock, 206
mane "Farrah Fawcett" look, 487, 532
marcel waves, 405
neoclassical, 263, 269–271
page boy cut, 133, 391, 408, 422
peek-a-boo style, 391
permanent waves, 375
piled high, 183, 185, 215, 236, 239, 241
pompadour, 346, 369–**370,** 408
sausage curls, 287–288, 312, 315
shingle, 403
short for men, 53, 76–77, 273–274, 319, 350, 381, 418–419, 532, 543

short for women, 271, 373, 375, 403–405, 408, 476, 480, 487, 531–532
side-whiskers, 319
straight/long for women, 479, 531
tete de mouton, 239
tiered arrangements, 76–77
toupee, 234, 239
tutulus, 66–68, 75
upsweep, 404–405, **408,** 413, 532
à la victime, 269, 271
wedge, 476, **487**
wide for women, 129–130, 136, 139
wigs, 25, 32, 77, 208, 234
See also specific time periods (*e.g. Romantic period*), and specific styles (*e.g. Chignon*)
Halston, 471
Halter-top
bathing suits, 410, 412
evening dresses, 406, 409
Hammurabi, Babylonian king, 16
Handbags
early. *See* Purses
Edwardian era, 370, 380
Eighties/Nineties, 533, 537
Empire period, 270, 272
men's, 245
New Look, 443, 448
Nineties, 349
Sixties/Seventies, 480, 484, 488
Twenties/Thirties/World War II era, 411, 413
Handkerchiefs
Baroque era, 217, 220
Crinoline era, 315
Empire period, 270
Renaissance, 187
Romans, 75, 77
Romantic era, 293
Handkerchief skirts, 399
Handlebar mustache, 344
Harem skirts, 371, 409
Hats
Andean-style, 533, 535
baseball caps, 533, 543
berets, 286, 405, 408, 423, 475, 487, 533
bergere/shepherdess hat, 239, 241

bicornes, 234, 272, **274**
bonnets, 270–271, 274, 286, 288–289, 314–315
bowlers, 293, 317, 320, 350
caps, 234–235, 236–237, 239, 270–271
Cavalier-style, 208, 211–212
chapeau bras, 234, 274
cloche, 404–405
coif, 106, 112, 133, 164, 174, 182, 185
copotains, 185, 208, 211–212
deerstalker caps, 349–350
derby hats, 293, 348, 350
driving caps, 448, 450
with face veils, 375, 404, 408
feather trim, 128, 178, 181, 185–186, 206, 241, 286, 335, 370
fedoras, 347, 350, 419, 448
fez, 23
French bonnet, 174, **185**
gibus, 293
hennin, 123, 136, 138
homburgs, 348, **350,** 450
of Jews, 103–104, 112
Panama, 419
petasos, 52–54, 59
Phrygian bonnets, 52–53, 91, 103
picture, 370, 373
pillbox, 408, 475, 480
pork pie, 315, 419, 448
sailor, 352, 381, 408
scented cones, Egyptians, 24, 30
Stetson, 320, 380–381, 543
straw, 239, 315, 320, 341, 347, 381, 450
straw boaters, 347–348, 350, 381, 419
top, 234, 274, 293–294, 320, 348, 350
tricornes, 209, **234,** 245, 372
turbans, 20, 93, 154, 163, 174, 270–271, 288
wide awake, 320
See also specific types of hats (*e.g. Bonnets*); specific time periods (*e.g. Middle Ages*)
Haubergeon, 140
Hauberk, 114
Haute couture, 395–396, 433
Nineties replacements for, 508
See also French couture
Hawaiian Island, Empire period influence, 275–276

Hawaiian shirts, 418
Headbands, 405, 484, 531–532
    See also Fillets
Headdresses. *See* Caps; Crowns; Hats;
        Hoods; Veils
    See also specific time periods (*e.g.*
        The Late Middle Ages, etc.)
Hedgehog hair style, 241–242
Heim, Jacques, 394, 442
Helmets
    Egyptian, 35
    Greeks, 57–58
    Mesopotamian, 19–20, 23
    Middle Ages, 112, 115, 140
Henley shirts, 414
Henna, 35
Hennin, 123, 136, 138
Herigaut, 110–111, 113, 116, 128
Heroin chic, 521
Herrera, Carolina, 514
High-heeled shoes, Renaissance, 187
High stomacher dress, 268
High-tech fabric, 521–522
Hilfiger, Tommy, 507–508, 514
Himation
    Etruscans, 65
    Greeks, 51, 54, 56, 59
Hip-hop style, 505, 507, 517
Hip huggers, 477
Hippies, 462, 469, 474, 484, 490–492,
        505–506
Hobble skirts, 363, 370–371
Holoku, 275–276
Homburgs, 348, 350, 450
Home attire, Rococo era, 234
Hoods
    Baroque era, 212
    Middle Ages, 103, 106, 112, 128, 130,
        133, 136
    Rococo era, 236–237, 241
Hookless fasteners, 392
Hoops
    cage crinoline, 309–311
    paniers, Rococo era, 235, 237, 239,
        249
Hose
    with artificial calves, 235
    barbarian tribes, 95
    and codpiece, 131, 161, 174–175, 178

cotton lisle, 370
footed, 126, 133, 159, 161
with foot strap, 126
knitted, 133, 172, 178, 217, 282, 293
lingerie makers, 124
nylon stockings, 443
opaque/tights, 480, 487, 532
pantyhose, 472–473, 480–481, 487
parti-colored, 124, 128, 133, 142,
    158
patterned stockings, 341, 370, 411,
    473, 532
rayon, 375, 405
seamed nylons, 443
and short skirts, 405
stockings, women's, 243, 245, 289,
    315, 341, 411
stockings with seams, 411
stretch stockings, 450
tights, 131, 142, 144
trunk hose, 175, 177–178, 189
upper and nether stocks, 175–176
woven, 133, 156
    See also specific time periods (*e.g.*
        Baroque period)
Hot pants, 477, 480
Houce, 128
Houpplelande, 127, 129, 131–135, 143,
    166
Houpplelande a mi-jamb, 128, 132
Houseboy pants, 441
House of Worth, 304, 363
Housse, 128
Hukes, 132–134, 154, 159
Hussar front, 291
Hyksos, 17

I
Identification (ID) bracelets, 450
Imbecile sleeves, 284
Incroyables, 263
India
    cotton trade, 195
    textile imports, 18th century, 256
Indispensibles, 270
Industrial fashion, 508
Industrial Revolution, 196, 255–256, 267
    and women's roles, 281

Infants. *See* Children's clothing
Innocente, 237–238
Internet shopping, 511, 515
Inverness cape, 319, 348–350, 379
Iridescent fabric, 309
Islam
    founding and spread of, 84, 88, 94
    See also Muslims
Italy
    ancient inhabitants of, 64
    fashion designers (1960–1980), 470
    fashion designers (1980–2003), 512
    Venetian dress, 163–165
    See also Renaissance, Italian

J
Jack boots, 209, 211, 235
Jackets
    Baroque era, 212
    battle, 416
    blazers, 379
    bush, 417
    Crinoline era, 318
    Eisenhower, 406, 416, 418, 420
    lumber, 379, 416, 420
    mackinaw, 382, 416, 420
    Middle Ages, 132–133, 143
    morning coats, 318, 347, 375–376
    motorcycle, 542
    Nineties, 347
    Norfolk, 333, 347, 417
    parkas, 416, 420
    pea, 318, 416
    Renaissance, 156–158, 161, 163, 166,
        174–175
    Romantic period, 291
    sack, 318–319, 347, 376
    safari, 489
    shorties, 441
    smoking, 318
    spencers, 268–269, 273
    sports, 375–376, 416–417, 449–450,
        541
    stadium, 489
    tailor-mades, 345, 369
    toppers, 441
Jacobs, Mark, 506–507, 514
Jacquard, Joseph Marie, 267

James, Charles, 436

Japan
- fashion designers (1980–2003), 513
- influence on fashion, 331
- Perry's opening of, 257

Jeanette, 290

Jeans. *See* Blue jeans

Jerkin, 174

Jersey, 335

Jet jewelry, 315

Jewelry
- **aiguillettes, 182,** 187–188
- **amulets,** 26, **35,** 77
- anklets, 35
- armlets, 23–24, 27, 35
- Art Deco, 411, 413
- Art Nouveau, 370, 380
- belts, jeweled, 32, 105, 181, 187
- **body jewelry, 517,** 537
- cabochon stones, 315
- cameos, 315
- collars, 27, 35, 93, 187
- cravat pins, 293
- crowns, 19–20, 35–37, 67, 91, 93
- cuff links, 350, 420
- enameled, 93, 97
- forehead ornaments, 21, 159, 161–162, 167, 187
- glass, 27, 315
- jet, 315
- pectorals, 27, 35
- rhinestones, 413, 443–444
- semi-precious stones, 27, 93
- sets, 244
- shirt studs, 293, 320, 350
- shoe buckles, jeweled, 244
- tie studs, 348, 350, 381
- *See also* specific time period (*e.g. Renaissance*), and specific types (*e.g. Earrings*)

Jews
- anti-Semitism and dress, 112
- dress in Middle Ages, 103–104, 112

Jockey caps, 270

Jockey undershorts, 401, **413,** 473

Jodhpurs, 379, 402, 410

Johnson, Betsey, 514

Judson, Whitcomb L., 392

Jumps, 237

Jumpsuits, 487

Justacorps, 208

K

Kamali, Norma, 514, 530

Karan, Donna, 514, 529, 536

Kashmir shawls, 256

Kate Greenway styles, 351

Kaunakes, Mesopotamian, 19, 21, 39–40

Kawakubo, Rei, 510–511, 513

Kente cloth, 463, 517

Kenzo, 506, 513

Khanh, Emmanuelle, 470

Kickups, 334

Kiddie couture, 502

Kilt, 12*n*, **28**

Kimono coats, 369, 439

Kimono-style sleeves, 370–372

Kleibacker, Charles, 471, 486

Klein, Anne, 472, 487

Klein, Calvin, 472, 506

Knickerbockers (knickers), 205, **318,** 323, 345–346, 350–352

Knickerbocker suits, 322

Knights
- Middle Ages, 99, 101
- Roman, 68

Knitting
- hand knitting, 172
- knitted hose, 133, 172, 178, 282, 293
- knitting machine, 172, 282

Kohl, Egyptian use, 30, **35**

Kors, Michael, 508

L

Lace
- **bobbin lace,** 172–173
- forerunners of, 172
- machine-made, 282
- **needlepoint lace,** 172–173
- **pillow lace, 173**
- **Renaissance,** 172–173

Lacerna, 74

Lacis, 172

Lacoste knit tennis shirt, 418

Lacroix, Christian, 398, 508, 512, 526

Laena, 74

Lagerfeld, Karl, 398, 512, 526, 528

Lang, Helmut, 506

Langtry, Lillie, 335

Lanvin, Jeanne, 375, 394, 402

Lappets, 174, 185, 215, 237, 315

Laroche, Guy, 470

Lastex, 410, 442

Latchets, 187, 206

Laurel wreaths, Greek wedding, 57

Lauren, Ralph, 472, 491, 506, 508

Laver, James, 4

Layette, 219

Leading strings, 218

Leather, Egyptian use, 27, 29

Leg bandages, 104

Leg coverings
- **leg-makeup, 409**
- military, 58, 115, 150
- *See also* Hose; Socks

Leggings, 530

Leg-of-mutton sleeves, 283–284, 300, 331, 344, 347, 408

Leg warmers, 477

L-85 Regulations, 389, 395

Leisure suits, 488, 491

Lelong, Lucian, 394

Leotard, Jules, 474

Leotards, 474, 477, 486

Le Pouf, 526, 528–529

Leser, Tina, 436

Levi's
- fashion revival, 323
- origin of, 305–306

Licensing, **469,** 515

Line-for-line copies, 435

Linen
- Byzantine era production, 89
- Egyptian production, 26, 29
- Greek use, 49
- Merovingian and Carolingian production, 95, 97
- Mesopotamian use, 18, 22
- Roman use, 68–69
- washable, 309
- and World War I, 364

Lingerie
- lingerie makers, 124
- use of term, 124*n*

Lingerie dresses, 367, 381, 383
Lipstick/lip color
   Egyptians, 35
   modern era, 413, 488, 533
   Renaissance, 187
   Rococo era, 244
   Romans, 77
Liripipe, 111–**112,** 128
Little Lord Fauntleroy suits, 222,
   351–352
Livery, 124
Loafers, 538, 543
Lock of Horus (youth), 35, 37, 39
Loincloths
   Egyptians, 27–29
   Etruscans, 65–66
   Greeks, 50, 52
   Mesopotamian, 20
   Minoans/Mycenaeans, 45
   purpose of, 13
   Romans, 72, 74
Longuette, 480–481
Looms, Middle Ages, 102
Lorum, 91
Louis heels, 330
Lounge coats, 376
Love locks, 206
Lumber jackets, 379, **416,** 420
Lyocell, 522

M
Mackinaws, 382, **416,** 420
Mackintosh, 292–293, 319
Mackintosh, Charles, 379
Magazines. *See* Fashion magazines
Magyar sleeves, 109, 111, 117, 406
Mail garments
   Mesopotamian, 23
   Middle Ages, 114–115, 140
Mail-order catalogs
   first in U.S., 330
   modern, 511
Mainbocher, 394, 396, 433
Makeup. *See* Cosmetics
Mancherons, 283
Mannerism, 200
Mantilla, 202–203
Mantles

Crinoline era, 313, 316
dolman, 335, 339
Etruscan, 65–66
Middle Ages, 103–108, 110–111,
   113–114, 127, 129, 136
Renaissance, 159
Romantic era, 289
Mantlet, 289
Mantua, 213, 215, 221, **237**
Mappa, 77
Marcel waves, 405
Margiela, Martin, 513, 523
Marie sleeves, 284
Marital status, dress as designation of,
   3
Mascara, 444
Masks, 187, 211, 217, 244
Mass market, 435
Mass production, and sewing machine,
   4
Maternity clothes, 432, 438, 439, 534
Matsuda, Mitsukiro, 510
Maxiskirt, 469, 476, 480–481
McCardell, Claire, 396–397, 436, 469,
   474
McFadden, Mary, 364, 383, 514
McQueen, Alexander, 513
Media, impact on dress, 4–5
Medici collars, 184, 190, 330, 369
Medieval period. *See* Middle Ages,
   early; Middle Ages, late
Mental illness, and clothing, 2
Mercerizing, 329
Merovingian and Carolingian
   dynasties, 94–97, 96–97
   evidence related to dress, 95
   footwear, 96
   hairstyles/headdresses, 95–96
   historical view, 84, 94–95, 99
   hose, 95, 97
   jewelry, 97
   men's garments, 95–96
   religious dress, 97–98
   royal dress, 95–97
   textile production, 95
   women's clothing, 96–97
Merry Widow, 437
Merveilleuse, 263
Mesopotamian civilizations, 16–23

children's clothing, 18, 24
evidence related to costume, 19
family, 18
footwear, 20–21, 23–24
hairstyles/headdress, 19–21, 23–24,
   40
hats, 20, 23
historical view, 11–13, 16–18
jewelry, 19–21, 23–24
men's garments, 19–20, 22–23
military dress, 20, 23
and modern fashions, 40
religious dress, 21
royal dress, 20–23
social structure, 18
status and dress, 22–23
textile production, 18
women's garments, 19–21, 23–24
Microfibers, 521–522, 525
Micro mini, 469
Middle Ages, early, 83–117
   accessories, 114
   Byzantine period, 88–94
   cosmetics, 114, 130
   evidence related to dress, 89–90, 95,
     102, 114–115
   fashion, development of, 6, 85
   fashion revivals of, 117, 408
   footwear, 104, 106, 112
   hairstyles, 104, 106, 108, 112–113
   hats, 103, 106, 112
   historical view, 83–85, 88–89, 99–102
   hose, 91, 93, 95, 97, 102, 104, 111–112
   influences on clothing, 101–102
   jewelry, 104–105, 114
   men's clothing, 102–106, 108–112
   Merovingian and Carolingian
     dynasties, 94–97
   military dress, 99, 103, 112, 114–115
   religious dress, 97–98, 104
   textile production, 89–90, 95,
     101–102
   undergarments, 102, 104, 110
   women's clothing, 104, 107–108, 113
Middle Ages, late, 121–144
   accessories, 128–129, 134, 136, 141
   bourgeoisie dress, 124
   children's clothing, 136–137
   evidence related to dress, 123–125

fashion change in, 125–126
fashion revivals of, 142–143
footwear, 128, 130, 133, 136
hairstyles, 123, 128–130, 133, 136
hats, 128, 130, 133, 136, 138–139, 141
historical view, 122–124
hose, 124, 126, 128, 130–131, 133, 136
jewelry, 130, 136, 141
men's clothing, 126–129, 131–134
military dress, 140
mourning clothes, 137–138
peasant clothing, 122–123
royal dress, 123–124, 129–130
student dress, 138, 140
textile production, 124
undergarments, 134
women's clothing, 129, 134–136
Middle-East fashion influence
    Crinoline, 307
    Renaissance, 153–154, 163, 172, 183
    Rococo, 234
Midi skirts, 469, 476, 480–481, 485
Military dress
    armor, 58, 78, 114–115, 140
    boots, Empire style, 274
    helmets, 19–20, 23, 35, 57–58, 112, 115, 140
    influence on civilian clothing, 126, 175, 274, 313, 315, 374, 379, 406, 416, 518
    leg protection, 58, 115, 150
    mail garments, 23, 114–115, 140
    padded clothing, 126, 140
    See also specific time period (*e.g. Romans*), and specific clothing items
Miller, Elizabeth Smith, 307
Minaret tunics, 371
Mini-crinolines, 528–529
Miniskirts, 4, **469,** 476, 480–481, 496, 524–525
Minoan and Mycenaean civilizations, 44–47
    children's clothing, 47
    cosmetics, 46–47
    evidence related to costume, 45
    footwear, 46–47
    hairstyles, 46
    hats, 46

    historical view, 11–13, 44
    jewelry, 46–47
    men's garments, 45–47
    religious dress, 45–46
    social structure, 44
    textile production, 45
    women's garments, 45–47
Mi-parti, 124
Missoni, Rosita and Ottavio Tai, 470, 509
Mittens, 244, 290
Mixtures, cross-cultural influences, 5
Miyake, Issey, 510, 513
Mizrahi, Isaac, 515
Mob caps, 237, 241
Moccasins, 264–265, 419, 446
Modeste, 212
Mods, 462, 506
Mod suits, 488–489
Molyneux, Edward, 394
Monastic, 396–397
Monks, dress of, 98, 104, 111, 113, 155
Montana, Claude, 512
Montgomery Ward catalog, 330
Mordants, 26, 45
Mori, Hanae, 513
Morning coats, 318, 347, 375–376, 413
Morning dresses, 283
Morning gowns, 234
Mother goddess, Minoan, 44
Motorcycle jackets, 542
Mourning clothes
    Bustle period, 352–353
    Middle Ages, 137–138
    Romans, 68–69, 75
Muckinder, 220
Muffs, 217, 235, 244, 270, 272, 290, 315, 317, 341, 370
Mugler, Thierry, 506–507, 512, 523
Muir, Jean, 471
Mules, 187, 211, 217, 243, 342
Music, pop, impact on fashion, 464, 519–520, 543
Muslims
    textile production, 101
    veiled women, 4
Muslin
    children's clothing, 247, 269
    Directoire period gowns, 268–269

    as import, 101, 195, 256
Mustaches
    Baroque era, 206
    Crinoline era, 319
    Nineties, 344, 350
    Renaissance, 185
    Twenties/Thirties, 419

N

Nail polish
    Baroque era, 217
    Egyptians, 24, 30, 35
    modern era, 533
    Rococo era, 244
Nappies, 219
Native Americans, influence on clothing, 229, 264–265, 466
Natural fibers, 481, 486, 488
Necklaces
    chains, gold, 176, 181, 187
    chatelaines, 290, 294
    diamonds by the yard, 488
    Greeks, 55–56
    Jeanette, 290
    Mesopotamian, 21, 24
    Middle Ages, 136, 141
    neck bands, 21, 105
    pearls, long strands, 411, 413, 480
    Renaissance, 162, 187
    Rococo era, 244
    Sixties/Seventies, 484, 491
    Twenties, 411
Neckties
    Baroque era, 207
    Eighties/Nineties, 348, 349, 543
    four-in-hand ties, 377, 415
    Sixties/Seventies, 484, 491
    Twenties/Thirties/World War II era, 411, 416
    World War I era, 380
Neckwear for men. *See* Ascots; Bow ties; Cravats; Neckties
Needlepoint lace, 172–173
Negro cloth, 296
Nehru jackets, 488, 490
Neoclassical style. *See* Empire period
Nether stocks, 175–176
New Look, 433–455

accessories, 443, 448, 450
active sports clothing, 442–443, 450
children's dress, 451–452
cosmetics, 444
fashion revivals of, 455
footwear, 443, 446, 450
hairstyles, 443, 450
hats, 443–444, 448, 450
historical view, 428–432
hose, 443, 450
jewelry, 443–444
maternity clothes, 432, 438, 439
men's clothing, 444–450
outdoor garments, 439, 441, 449
sleepwear, 443
sportswear, 441–442, 449–450, 450
textile production, 433
undergarments, 438–439, 445
women's clothing, 435–444
Newmarkets, 291, 318
New Romantics, 507
Nightgowns, 408, 443, 479, 487
Nightshirts, 381
Nile River, 16
Nineties (1890s), 343–355
accessories, 347, 349–350
active sports dress, 345–346
cosmetics, 347
fashion revivals of, 355
footwear, 347, 350
Gibson Girl, 344–346, 355
hairstyles, 346, 350
hats, 346–347, 350
hose, 347
jewelry, 347, 350
men's clothing, 347–350
outdoor garments, 345
undergarments, 343–344, 347
women's clothing, 343–347
Nineties (1990s). *See* Eighties and Nineties
Nineveh, 16
Norell, Norman, 397, 436, 469
Norfolk jackets, 333, **347**
Nuns, dress of, 98, 108, 155
Nylon, 389, 391
Nylon stockings, 443
Nymphides, 57

O

Occupation, dress as designation of, 3
Opaque stockings, 480, 487, 532
Open breeches, 177
Open mantles, 103, 105, 113
Orange blossoms, Greek bridal dress, 78
Orarium, 77
Originals, 433, 435
Orphrey, 98
Outdoor garments. *See* Capes and cloaks; Coats, outdoor; Jackets; Mantles; Shawls
Overalls, 205
Oxford bags, 414–415
Oxfords, 343, 350, 381, 405, 446, 450
Ozbek, Rifat, 506

P

Paenula, 74, 93
Page boy cut, 133, 391, 408, 422
Pagoda sleeves, 311
Pair of bodys, 178
Paisley design, 256
Pajamas. *See* Sleepwear
Palazzo pajamas, 476, 478
Paletot, 289, 292, **313,** 319, 335
Palla, 74–75, 77–78, 80, 92, 95
Pallium, 72, 78, **91, 98**
Paltock, 174
Paludamentum, 74, 78, 93, 95
Panama hats, 419
Panes, 175
Paniers, 235
Pantalettes, 267–269, 321
Pantaloons, 205, 263, **273**
Panties, 399–400
Pantofles, 211, **217**
Pants, 205
See also Trousers
Pantsuits, 469, 475–476, 479, 481, 483, 496
Panty briefs, 405
Pantyhose, 472–473, 480–481, 487
Paper dresses, 475
Parasols, 244–245, 270, 272, 290, 294, 315, 317, 341, 349, 370
Romans, 77
Pardessus, 289, 313, 316

Parkas, **416,** 420
Parnis, Molly, 436
Parti-colored, 124, 128, 133, 142, 158
Pashmina, 522, 537
Patent leather shoes, 350, 381, 483
Patou, Jean, 394
Pattens, 134, 136, 164, 243, 270
Patterns, clothing, 330
Pea jackets, 318, 416
Peasant clothing
folk dress, 6–7, 197
Middle Ages, late, 122–123
Peascod belly, 175, 178–179
Pecadils, 175
Pectorals, 27, **35**
Pedal pushers, 441
Peg-top skirts, 371
Pelerine-mantlet, 284, **289**
Pelisse, 7, **269**–270, 289, 335
Pelisse-mantle, 313
Pelisse-robe, 285
Pellison, 111
Peplos
Etruscans, 65
Greeks, 50–51, 59
Peretti, Elsa, 488
Perfume
Baroque era, 217
of designers, 363
Egyptians, 35
Empire period, 274
Greeks, 55
Middle Ages, 114
pomander balls, 187, 217
Rococo era, 235, 244
Romans, 77
Perizoma
Etruscans, 65–66
Greeks, 50, **52**
Permanent press fabric, 433
Petasos, 52–54, 59
Pet-en-lair, 237, 239
Peterson's Magazine, 282
Petticoat breeches, 205, **207**–208
Petticoats
as overgarment, 181–182, 239, 267–268
undergarments, 213, 237, 282, 309–310, 337, 344, 368, 437–438

Photographs
  carte de viste, 308, 312
  daguerreotypes, 282
  as information source, 7–8, 308, 332
Phrygian bonnets
  Byzantine era, 91
  Greeks, 52–53
  Middle Ages, 103
Picture hats, 370, 373
Piecework concept, 330
Piguet, Robert, 394
Pillbox hats, 408, 475, 480
Pillow lace, 173
Pilos, 55
Pinafores, 218, **220,** 381–382
Pinners, 237
Pins, Merovingian and Carolingian,
  96–97
Placard, 129
Plaid, men's suits, 415, 449–450
Plastron, 129
Platform shoes
  Greeks, 58
  modern, 407, 423, 480, 482–483, 532,
    538
  Renaissance chopines, 163–164, 167,
    187, 203, 491
Playsuit, 410
Pleats
  Egyptian dress, 24, 26, 28, 30–31
  Etruscan dress, 65
  Fortuny, 364
  Greek dress, 49, 52
  medieval garments, 107, 131–132, 135
  men's trousers, 542
  Romantic era dress, 287
  skirts, modern, 399, 406
Plumpers, 217
Plus fours, 417
Pockets
  in-garment pockets, 287
  precursor of, 244
  tie pocket, 244–245, 284
Points, 126, 131
Poiret, Paul, 6, 363, 370–371
Political conflict, impact on dress, 4
Politics, impact on dress, 4
Polo coats, 416, 449
Polo, Marco, 84–85

Polo shirts, 417–418, **420**
Polonaise, 240–241
Polyesters, 433, 447, 475
Pomander balls
  Baroque era, 217
  Renaissance, 187
Pompadour, 346, 369–**370,** 408
Ponchos, 477
Poodle skirts, 453
Poorboy sweaters, 477
Pork pie hats, 315, 419, 448
Porte jupe (dress elevator), 316
Postmodernism, 504
Potter, Claire, 436
Poulaines, 128, 130, 134, 141
Pourpoint, 125–**126,** 143
Powdered wigs, 208, 234, 246
Power suits, 502
Prada, Miuccia, 509, 512
Preppy look, 486, 507, 517, 538
Prêt-á-porter, 467–468
Priests, dress of, 98, 155
Princess dresses, 313, 333–334
Princess polonaise, 333
Promenade dresses, 283
Prostitutes
  Greek, 49
  Mesopotamian, 24
  Roman, 70
Protection, as function of clothing, 1
Pucci, Emilio, 470, 530
Pudding, 211, 218, **220**
Pullovers, 374, 378, 406, 420
Punk styles, 462–463, 469, 505, 506, 531
Puritans, dress of, 202
Purses
  Baroque era, 217
  Crinoline era, 317
  Middle Ages, 114, 129, 134, 136, 141
  Renaissance, 187
  Romans, 77
  See also Handbags
Putting out system, 124
Pyramids, Egyptians, 16

Q
Quakers, dress of, 229
Quick response, 503

Quant, Mary, 471
Queues, 234
Quizzing glasses, 274

R
Rabanne, Paco, 470
Racoon coats, 403, 416
Raglan cape, 319
Raglan sleeve coats, 379, 408, 439
Rain coats
  mackintosh, 292–293, 319, **379**
  slickers, 422, 477
Rain shoes
  clogs, 104, 122, 128, 141, 213, 243
  galoshes, 208, 289, 293, 240
  pattens, 134, 136, 164, 243, 270
Rasta, 506, 517
Rationals, 329
Rave style, 507
Rayon, 375, 391, 525
Ready-to-wear
  Bustle period, 329–330
  department stores, 330, 509
  Edwardian period, 366
  1980s-2000, 508–511
  Empire period, 267
  mail-order catalogs, 330
  prêt-á-porter, 467–468, 509
  Renaissance, 153
  Romans, 69
  and sewing machine, 306–307
Redingotes, 230, 240
Reefers, 318, 347, 351
Religious dress
  Egyptians, 29, 35, 38
  functions of, 4
  Merovingian and Carolingian,
    97–98
  Mesopotamian, 21
  Middle Ages, 97–98, 104
  Minoans/Mycenaeans, 45–46
  Romans, 69, 78–79
Renaissance, Italian, 147–167
  children's clothing, 164–165
  evidence related to clothing, 154
  fashion revivals of, 167
  footwear, 159
  hairstyles, 158–159, 162

hats, 159, 162–163
historical view, 147–154, 170–171
hose, 156–157, 161, 166
jewelry, 159, 165, 167
men's clothing, 154–161, 163
Middle-Eastern influence, 153–154, 163
textile production, 153
undergarments, 154, 159, 163
Venetian dress, 163–165
women's clothing, 154, 159, 162–163
Renaissance, Northern Europe, 169–190
accessories, 187
children's clothing, 187–188
cosmetics, 187
evidence related to costume, 173
fashion change, phases of, 173–174
fashion information, dissemination of, 171–172
fashion revivals of, 190
footwear, 185, 187
hairstyles, 181, 185–186
hats, 174, 176, 178, 185–186
historical view, 170–171
hose, 174–178
jewelry, 181, 187
men's clothing, 174–178
Middle Eastern influence, 172, 183
textile production, 172–173
undergarments, 178–179, 181
women's clothing, 178–184
De la Renta, Oscar, 471
Reticules, 270, 272, 290, 294
Retro fashions, 516, 521, 534, 538
Revivals, in costume history, 6
Rhinegraves, 205, 207
Rhinestones, 413, 443–444
Rhodes, Zandra, 462, 469, 513
Ribbons of childhood, 218–219, 244
Ricci, Nina, 394
Riding clothes, 244, 270, 379, 410
Rincinium, 75
Rings
Greeks, 55
Merovingian and Carolingian, 97
Renaissance, 187
Romans, 77
Robe à la Française, 237, 239, 249

Robe à l'Anglaise, 239, 241, 246, 249
Robe battante, 237–238
Robe de style, 402–403
Robes
children's, 217–218
Middle Ages, 103, 110, 131, 143
Renaissance, 158, 163–165, 174–175
Robe volante, 237–238
Rochas, Marcel, 394
Rockers, 462
Rococo era, 226–250
accessories, 235, 244–245
active sports dress, 244
children's dress, 244, 246–247
cosmetics, 235, 244
evidence related to clothing, 229
fashion revivals of, 248, 250
footwear, 235, 243–244
hairstyles, 234, 236–237, 239, 241
hats, 234–239, 241
historical view, 226–228
hose, 235, 243
jewelry, 235, 244
men's clothing, 230–235
outdoor garments, 243
outer garments, 237
rural dress, 229, 232
textile production, 228–229
undergarments, 230–231, 235, 237
women's clothing, 235–243
working class dress, 229
Rocs, 136–137
Rollers, 219
Romans, 67–80
children's clothing, 77–78
cosmetics, 77
evidence related to costume, 69–70
footwear, 68–69, 77
hairstyles, 68, 76–77
headresses, 76–77
historical view, 11–12, 64, 67–68, 83, 94–95
jewelry, 69, 77
men's garments, 70–74
military dress, 78
religious dress, 69, 78–79
royal dress, 68–69
social class and dress, 68, 74–75
textile production, 68–69

toga, 3, 12*n*, 69–72, 79
undergarments, 70, 72, 74
wedding clothing, 78
women's garments, 74–75
Romantic period, 280–300
accessories, 289–290, 293
children's clothing, 295
cosmetics, 290
evidence related to dress, 282
fashion revivals of, 300, 506–507
footware, 289, 294
hairstyles, 285, 287–288, 293
hats, 286–289, 293
historical view, 280–282
hose, 289, 293
jewelry, 290, 293–294
men's clothing, 290–293
outdoor garments, 289, 292–293
slaves (American) clothing, 295–298
textile production, 282
undergarments, 282, 284, 290
women's clothing, 282–290
women's garments, 282–290
Ropa, 172, 182–**183**
Rotonde, 313
Rouff, Maggie, 394
Rouge, 114, 187, 244, 274, 413
Round gowns, 240, 265, 268
Round hats, 234
Royal dress
Byzantine period, 91–93
Egyptians, 25–27, 30, 32, 35
Merovingian and Carolingian, 95–97
Mesopotamian, 20–23
Middle Ages, late, 123–124, 129–130
Romans, 68–69
Ruchings, 287
Ruff
Baroque era, 210, 212
Renaissance, 175, 178–186
Ruffles
Baroque era, 207, 213
Edwardian era, 367, 369–370
Rural dress
blue jeans, 305–306
Rococo era, 229, 232
Rykiel, Sonia, 512

S

Sack jackets, 318–319, 347, 376
Sacque, 237–238, 335
Saddle shoes, 446, 453
Safari jackets, 489
Sagum, 78
Sailor hats, 352, 381, 408
Sailor suits, 322, 350, 381, 420
Saint Laurent, Yves, 465, 467–468, 470, 506
Sandals
  ankle-strap, 446, 482
  Egyptians, 25, 30, 32, 34
  Empire period, 272
  Etruscans, 67
  flip-flops, 535, 538
  Greeks, 55–57
  Mesopotamian, 20–21, 23–24
  Romans, 77–78
Sander, Jill, 513
Sand, George, 2
Sans culottes, 262
Sant'Angelo, Giorgio, 472
Santon, 285
Sargon, Akkadian ruler, 16
Sashes, Egyptians, 32
Sassoon, Vidal, 480
Satin, 153, 213
Scarab, 26
Scarves, 215, 243, 413, 484, 539
Scassi, Arnold, 472
Schentis, 28–30
Schiaparelli, Elsa, 393–394, 398, 433
Schoen, Mila, 470
Scrunchies, 531
Seams, 27
Sears, Roebuck, and Co. catalog, 330
Secret, 212
Segmentae, 90, 92
Selvage, 26
Seventies (1970s). *See* Sixties and Seventies
Sewing machine, 306–307
Sewn clothing
  Egyptians, 27
  Merovingian and Carolingian era, 95
  Minoans, 45
  See also Tailored clothing

Sexual attractiveness, enhancement and dress, 3–4
Shaved heads. *See* Bald/shaved heads
Shaving, Romans, 77
Shawl-mantle, 313
Shawl-mantlet, 289
Shawls
  Crinoline era, 319
  Egyptians, 30–32, 34
  Eighties/Nineties, 522, 532, 537
  Etruscans, 65–66
  Greeks, 50, 54
  Mesopotamian, 20, 22, 24
  Minoans/Mycenaeans, 45–46
  Rococo era, 243
  Romans, 74, 79
  Romantic era, 289
Sheath dress, Egyptians, 27, 29, 31–32, 34, 38–39
Shepherdess hats, 239
Sherryvallies, 205
Shingle, 403
Shirts
  Baroque, 206–207
  Crinoline period, 316
  Eighties/Nineties, 541
  Empire period, 270
  men's sportswear, 417–418
  New Look, 445, 447
  Nineties, 348
  Renaissance, 154, 174
  Rococo, 230–231
  Romantic era, 290–291
  Sixties/Seventies, 488, 490
  Twenties, 415–416
  as undergarments, 230–231, 310
  World War I era, 376–378
Shirt studs, 350, 416, 420
Shirtwaists, 344–345, 355, 369, 371
Shoemakers, Romans, 69
Shoes
  ancient, 20–21, 23–24, 47, 55
  athletics/sports, 341, 343
  balmorals, 343
  bathing, 335
  bedroom slippers, 293
  buckles, 134, 209, 217, 235, 274
  chopines, 163–164, 167, 187, 203
  chukka boots, 419

  clogs, 104, 122, 128, 141, 213, 243, 245, 480, 482
  cloth, 407, 409
  crackowe, 128, 130
  curved toe, 20–21, 67
  decorated, 93, 206, 208
  Doc Martens, 532
  duckbills, 185–186
  evening, 315, 341–342
  flats, 270, 272, 289, 294, 382, 443, 446, 482
  gaiters with, 289, 293, 320
  galoshes, 208, 289, 293, 420
  high-heeled, 187, 206
  latchets, 187, 206, 243
  loafers, 538, 543
  Louis heels, 330, 370
  moccasins, 264–265, 419, 446
  monk's front, 419
  mules, 187, 211, 217, 243, 342
  oxfords, 343, 350, 381, 405, 446, 450
  patent leather, 350, 381, 483
  pattens, 134, 136, 164, 243, 270
  platform, 58, **163**–164, 407, 423, 480, 482–483, 491, 532, 538
  pointed-toed, 106, 128, 134, 136, 141, 341–343, 370
  poulaine, 128, 130, 134, 141
  pumps, 482
  rubber-soled, 293, 341, 350
  saddle, 446, 453
  slap soles, 206, 211
  sneakers, 443, 478, 523
  spatterdashers (spats) with, 235, 293, 320
  spectator-style, 532
  square-toed, 185–186, 235, 289, 293, 315
  stiletto heels, 443, 446
  straight soles, 206
  tie closing, 93, 134, 274, 320
  T-straps, 405, 407
  weejuns, 419
  white bucks, 431, 446, 450
  winkle pickers, 431
  See also footware of specific time periods (*e.g. Baroque era*)
Short gown, 229
Shorties, 441

Shorts
for men, 450, 526, 528
for women, 441–442, 477, 480
Shorts suit, 526, 528
Shoulder pads, 405–406, 408, 423, 424, 524
Shrugs, 441
Siamoises, 204
Silk
Baroque production, 203–204
blends, 309
Byzantine production, 89–90, 117
draw loom, 204
Egyptian use, 26
Greek production, 49, 90
industrial era production, 196
Merovingian and Carolingian use, 97
Renaissance use, 153
Roman use, 69
weighting, 329
and World War I, 364
Silk damask, 101
Silk stockings, 289, 315, 341
Simpson, Adele, 436
Singer, Isaac, 306–307
Sinus, 70–72
Sixties and Seventies, 469–496
accessories, 480, 488, 491
active sports clothing, 477–479, 487, 489–490
children's clothing, 492–494
cosmetics, 480, 488, 491
fashion industry, 466–469
fashion revivals of, 496, 544
footwear, 480, 482–483, 487, 491
hairstyles, 475, 479, 487, 490
hats, 475, 480, 487, 490
historical view, 458–459
hose, 472, 480, 487
influences on fashion, 461–466
jewelry, 480, 488, 491
men's clothing, 488–491
outdoor garments, 477, 487, 489, 494
sleepwear, 479, 487, 490
sportswear, 476–477, 483, 486, 489
undergarments, 469, 472–474, 481, 488
women's clothing, 469, 472–488

Skeleton suit, 247
Ski clothing, 410, 418–419, 443, 478, 487, 531, 542–543
Skimmers, 469, 492
Skinheads, 506
Skirts
Baroque, 212–213
Bustle period, 333, 354
dirndl, 406
Egyptian, 27–28, 31, 35, 39
fish-tails, 439
goring, 367, 406
handkerchief-style, 399
harem, 371, 409
hobble, 363, 370–371
maxi, 469, 476, 480–481
Mesopotamian, 19–22
Middle Ages, 105, 129, 135
midi, 469, 476, 480–481, 485
mini, 469, 476, 480–481, 496, 524–525
Minoans/Mycenaeans, 45–47
Nineties, 344
peg-top, 371
pleated, 399, 406
poodle, 453
Renaissance, 159, 181–183
shorter, 372, 374–375, 384, 391, 399, 402, 405
swirl, 483
and tailor-mades, 345, 369
World War I era, 370–371
wrapped, 28
Slacks, 409
Slap soles, 206, 211
Slashings, 175–176, 181, 187, 189
Slave dress, United States, 295–298
Sleepwear
nightgowns, 408, 443, 487
nightshirts, 381
pajamas, 381–382, 403, 408, 418, 450, 479, 490, 543
pajamas with feet, 382, 422, 487
T-shirt nightshirts, 531
Sleeves
batwing, 406
bell-shaped, 311, 316
bishop, 287, 367
en bouffant, 287

Byzantine era, 92
dolman, 117, 335, 339, 408
imbecile, 284
kimono-style, 370–372
leg-of-mutton, 283–284, 300, 331, 344, 347, 408
magyar, 109, 111, 117, 406
Marie, 284
Middle Ages, 102–103, 106–107, 109, 111, 116–117, 127, 130–132, 134–136
Pagoda, 311
raglan, 379, 408
Renaissance, 157–158, 165–166, 174, 180–182, 189
en sabot, 287
undersleeves, 287, 311, 317
Victoria, 287
virago, 212
Slips, 399–400, 437–438, 473
Sloppy joes, 406, 422
Slops, 177, 205
Smith, Willi, 515, 521
Smock, 134, 229
Smock coats, 232
Smocking, 232
Smoking jackets, 318, 381
Sneakers, 443, 478, 523
Snoods, 312, 314–315, 408
Snowboarding clothes, 543
Snow suits, 422
Snuff boxes, 235, 293
Soccus, 77
Social class, and fashion, 85
Social communication, clothing as, 4
Social context, functions of dress in, 2–4
Socks
ankle socks, 409, 453
bobby-sox, 409
elastic-topped, 419
knee-length, 480
patterned, 419
Solae, 77
Soul patch, 544
Spandex, 433, 521, 524–525, 530, 547
Spanish cape, 293
Spanish farthingale, 181, 183, 210, 237
Spanish work, 172, 182
Spats. *See* Spatterdashers (spats)

Spatterdashers (spats), 235, 293, 317, 320, 375–376
Spencers, 268–269, 273
Spindle and distaff, 102, 124
Spinning mule, 196
Spinning wheel, 102, 124, 172
Spinny jenny, 196
Sports and athletics
    dress for. *See* Active sports clothing
    sports star influences, 391, 479, 487, 489
Sports jackets, 375–376, 416–417, 449–450, 541
Sportswear
    active sportswear, 523
    men's, 416–418, 449–451, 489, 541–542
    women's, 406, 409, 441–442, 476–477, 483, 486, 530
Stadium jackets, 489
Status, dress as designation of, 3
Staybands, 219
Stays, 178–179, 219, 237, 267, 282, 309
    See also Corsets
Steam power, 228, 330
Steinkirk, 230–231
Stephane, 57
Step-in chemise, 399–400
Stetson hat, 320, 380–381, 543
Stiletto heels, 443, 446
Stockings. *See* Hose; Socks
Stocks, 270
Stola, 68, 74–75, 80
Stole, 98
Stomachers, 174, 179, 183, 210, 213, 221, 239, 249, 268
Straight soles, 206
Strapless gowns, 408
Straw boaters, 347–348, 350, 419
Street styles, 461
    See also Style tribes
Stretch pants, 443, 476, 494
Strophium, 74
Student dress, Middle Ages, late, 138, 140
Style tribes, 461–462, 542
    names and impact of, 506–507
Subligar, 73
Sudarium, 77

Sui, Anna, 506–507, 515, 524
Suits for men
    boy's suits, 295, 322, 351–352, 382, 452
    business suits, 377, 414, 424
    continental, 449, 488
    Crinoline era, 316, 318–319
    ditto suit, 233
    Empire period, 273
    English drape suit, 415, 424
    gray flannel, 447
    leisure, 488, 491
    mod, 488–489
    Nehru, 488, 490
    New Look, 445, 447, 449
    Nineties, 347–348, 354
    Rococo, 232–233
    Romantic era, 291–292
    three-piece, precursor of, 207–208
    tuxedo, 348
    Twenties, 413–414
    with vests, 376, 488
    walking suits, 450
    white, 413
    World War I era, 375, 377
    World War II era, 415–416
    zoot suits, 415–416
Suits for women
    business suits, 483, 486, 502, 526
    Chanel, 374, 392, 399, 402, 423, 474, 526, 528
    elongated jackets, 371–372
    evening suits, 406, 408
    men's suits as influence, 406, 483, 486
    military-style, 374, 406
    New Look, 439, 441, 447
    pantsuits, 469, 475–476, 479, 481, 483, 496
    power suits, 502
    Romantic period, 287
    shorts suit, 526, 528
    tailor-mades, 345, 369
    undergarments, 399, 402
Sumerians
    rise and fall of, 16
    See also Mesopotamian civilizations
Sumptuary laws, 3, 7, 85, 129, 202
Sundback, Gideon, 392
Sunglasses, 411, 420

Sudarum, 77
Supportasse, 184–185
Surcotes, 108–111, 113, 115, 126, 129, 143
Surtouts, 208, 234
Suspenders, 318, 541
Swaddling clothes
    ancients, 55–56, 77
    end of practice, 247
    Middle Ages, 136–137
    swaddling bands, 219
Sweaters
    loose, 486, 488
    patterns/pictures, 530, 534
    poorboy, 477
    pullovers, 374, 378
    shrugs, 441
    sloppy joes, 406, 422
    thigh-length, 486
    turtleneck, 418, 420, 488, 491, 530
    twin sets, 486–487, 530
Sweatshirt fashions, 530
Sweatshirts, 420, 486, 494, 542
Swimwear. *See* Bathing suits
Swirl skirts, 483
Swiss belts, 315, 370
Swoon suit, 412
Synthesis, Roman, 78
Synthetic fibers, types of, 433

T
Tabards, 111, 113
Tablion, 93
Taffeta, 309, 313
Tailclouts, 219
Tail coats
    Crinoline era, 316
    Empire period, 273–274
    evening use, 348, 378, 415–416
    Romantic period, 291–292, 299
Tailored clothing, 2
    early sewn clothing, 27, 45, 95
Tailor-mades, 345, 369
Tailors
    Baroque era, 204
    English tailor, 413
    Middle Ages, 124
    Renaissance, 153
    Rococo era, 228–229

Talma-mantle, 313
Tank tops, 542
Tapestries, Byzantine era production, 90
Tarbush, Mesopotamian, 23
Tassell, Gustave, 436
Tattoos, 517, 533
Tea gowns, 333, 369
Tebenna, 65–66, 68
Technology
    and cloth making. *See* Textile production
    impact on dress, 2, 4
Teddies, 399
Teddy boys, 431, 450, 506
Teenage clothing
    Eighties and Nineties, 515–516
    fads, 453
    Sixties and Seventies, 494
    Teddy boys, 431, 450
    World War II era, 415–416, 422
Teething rings, coral, 220
Television
    impact on fashion, 431, 447, 464, 520, 544
    shopping networks, 515
Tencel, 522
Tennis clothing, 335, 409, 418, 440, 443, 478, 487, 489, 531
Tete de mouton, 239
Textile decoration. *See* Appliqué; Beadwork; Cutwork; Embroidery; Lace; Slashings
Textile production
    acetate, 391
    cotton gin, 267
    drip dry fabric, 433
    fabric dying. *See* Dying of textiles
    factory system, 196, 255–256
    flying shuttle, 228
    high-tech fabrics, 521–522
    and Industrial Revolution, 196, 255–256, 267
    knitting machine, 172, 282
    lace, machine-made, 282
    lyocell, 522
    mercerizing, 329
    microfibers, 521–522
    natural fibers, 481, 486, 488

nylon, 389, 391
permanent press fabric, 433
putting out system, 124
rayon, 391
steam power, 228
synthetics, types of, 433
trade guilds, 102
wash-and-wear fabric, 433
water power, 196, 228
weighting, 329
and World War I, 364, 395
and World War II, 389–390
See also specific time period (*e.g. Romantic period*), specific types of fabric (*e.g. Linen*); Weavers and weaving
Textiles
    impact on dress, 4
    See also specific types (*e.g. Silk*)
Théatre de la Mode, 397–398
Themes, in history of costume, 2–7
Thermal underwear, 473
Thirties
    accessories, 411, 413, 420
    active sports dress, 409–411, 418
    art and fashion, 398
    children's clothing, 420–422
    fashion information of, 398–399
    fashion revivals of, 423, 475
    footwear, 407, 409, 419–420
    hair styles, 404, 408, 418–419
    hats, 405, 408, 419
    historical view, 388
    hose, 409, 419
    influences on fashion, 390–391
    jewelry, 413, 420
    men's clothing, 413–420
    outdoor garments, 408, 416
    sleepwear, 408, 418
    sportswear, 406, 409, 416–418
    textile production, 391–392
    undergarments, 400, 405, 413–414
    women's clothing, 405–413
Thong swim suit, 487
Thong underpants, 527
Thread and money system, 195
Thutmose III, Egyptian pharaoh, 17
Ties. *See* Neckties
Tie studs, 348, 350, 381

Tights, 131, 142, 144
Tigris and Euphrates Rivers, 11, 16
Tippets, 111, 135, 243–244
à la Titus, 269–271
Toga, 3, 12*n*, **68**–72
    for children, 77–78
    decline of, 79
    draping, 71
    predecessor of, 65–66, 68, 70
    types of, 69–71
Toga with folded bands, 72–73
Toggle coats, 453
Tom Mix outfits, 422
Top coats, 378–379
Top hats, 274, 293–294, 320, 348, 350
    precursor of, 234
Topless bathing suit, 477, 479
Toppers, 441
Toques, 270, 341
Tortoise shell combs, 286
Toupee, 234, 239
Tower of Babel, 11
Trade
    ancient civilizations, 17
    impact on dress, 2, 4
    with India, 195–196, 256
    with Japan, 257
    and textiles, 18, 26, 69
Trade guilds, 102
Traina, Anthony, 397
Trench coats, 379, 534
Triacetate, 433
Trickle-down theory, 466–467
Tricornes, 209, 234, 245
Trigère, Pauline, 397, 436, 469
TRIS, 544
Trousers for men
    barbarian tribes, 95
    for boys, 247, 321, 350
    chinos, 450
    Crinoline era, 318
    Empire period, 273–274, 277
    evolution of, 205
    Oxford bags, 414–415
    pleated, 542
    Romans, 78–79
    Romantic era, 291–292, 299
    World War I era, 377–378

Trousers for women
  beach pajamas, 409
  bell-bottomed, 477
  blue jeans, 409, 462, 469, 483
  cargo pants, 518, 534, 537
  hip huggers, 477
  houseboy pants, 441
  palazzo pajamas, 476, 478
  pants for girls, 493–494
  pedal pushers, 441
  pleated, 483
  slacks, 409–410
  stretch leggings, 530
  stretch pants, 476
  turkish trousers, 307–308, 347
Trunk hose, 175, 177–178, 189
T-shirts, 414, 438, 486, 541
Tuckers, 285
Tunics
  Byzantine era, 90–92
  Egyptians, 27–31, 35, 39
  feudal era, 102–104
  Greeks, 12n, **50**–52, 54–59
  Merovingian and Carolingian, 95–97
  Mesopotamian, 20, 22–24
  Middle Ages, 104–105, 107, 110
  Minoans/Mycenaeans, 46
  monastic use, 98
  Renaissance, 163
  Romans, 70–72, 74–75, 78–80
Tunic suit, 295
Turbans/turbanlike headdress
  Byzantine era, 93
  Empire period, 270–271
  Mesopotamians, 20
  Renaissance, 154, 163, 174
  Romantic era, 286, 288
  Thirties, 408
Turkish fashion. *See* Middle Eastern
    influence
Turkish trousers, 307–308, 347
Turtleneck jerseys, 415, 488
Turtleneck sweaters, 418, 420, 491, 530
Tutankhamen, Egyptian king, 25–27,
    31, 35, 40
Tutulus, 66–68, 75
Tuxedo, 348, 354, 377, 414–416, 449, 488,
    492, 542
Tweens, 515–516

Twenties
  accessories, 411, 413, 420
  active sports dress, 409–411, 418
  art and fashion, 398
  children's clothing, 420–422
  cosmetics, 413
  fashion information of, 398–399
  fashion revivals of, 423, 528–529
  footwear, 405, 407, 419
  hair styles, 403–405, 418–419
  hats, 405
  historical view, 388–389
  hose, 409, 411
  influences on fashion, 390–391
  jewelry, 411, 413, 420
  men's clothing, 413–420
  outdoor garments, 402–403, 416,
    420
  sleepwear, 403, 418
  sportswear, 409, 416–418
  textile production, 391–392
  undergarments, 399–401, 413–414
  women's clothing, 370–375, 399–405

U
Ulster, 335, 345, 347
Umbo, 70–72
Umbrellas, 293, 320, 370, 411, 413
Undergarments
  athletic shirts, 413, 438, 473, 527
  bikini-cut, 488, 527
  body stockings, 472–473
  body suits, 472–474
  bottom-enhancing, 355, 527
  boxer shorts, 401, **413,** 438, 473, 488,
    527
  braies, 102, 104, 109–110, 174
  breast support. *See* Brassiere
  briefs, 405, 488
  bustles, 282, 284
  camica, 154, 158–163, 165
  cami-knickers, 372
  chemise, 102, 104, 110, 159, 179–180,
    213, 237, 267, 282, 309, 332, 337
  combination, 332, 337, 368, 370
  corsets, 128, 179, 213, 235, 237
  drawers, 154, 174, 213, 230–231, 267,
    309–310, 315, 347

garter belts, 399–400
girdles, 399–400, 437–438
half slips, 437–438
henley shirts, 414
jockey undershorts, 401, **413,** 473
leg garments. *See* Hose
long thermal, 473
long underdrawers, 401
Merry Widow, 437
modern, development of, 102
pantalettes, 267
panties, 399–400, 405
panty briefs, 405
perizoma, 52, 65
petticoats, 213, 237, 282, 309–310, 337,
    344, 437–438
Roman indutus, 70
to shape body, origin of, 178–179
to shape outer garments, 179, 181,
    183, 186, 203, 210, 235, 237
shirts, 230–231, 310
slips, 399–400, 473
stays, 178–179, **219, 237,** 282
step-in chemise, 399–400
subligar/subligaria, 72, 74
teddies, 399
thong, 527
T-shirts, 414, 438
undershirts, 347, 401
union suits, 347, 368
waist cinches, 437–438
Wallace Beery shirts, 414
See also specific time period (*e.g.
    Middle Ages*)
Undershirts, 347, 401
Undersleeves, 287, 311, 317
Ungaro, Emanuel, 467, 470
Union suits, 347, 368
Unisex, 463, **502**
Unitard, 478
United States
  colonial dress, 202, 229
  fashion designers (1920–1940s),
    396–397
  fashion designers (1940–1950s), 436
  fashion designers (1960–1980),
    471–472
  fashion designers (1980–2003),
    514–515

garment industry, 330
  mass market, 435
  slave dress, 295–298
Upper stocks, 175–176
Upsweep, 404–405, **408,** 413, 532

V
Valentino, 470
Van Beirendonck, Walter, 507
Veils
  Byzantine, 92–93
  Catholic nuns, 98
  conch, 184
  face veils on hats, 375, 404, 408
  Greeks, 48, 54–55, 57
  mantilla, 202–203
  Mesopotamians, 24, 40
  Middle Ages, 104, 108, 113, 130, 136,
    139
  Muslims, 4
  Nineties, 347
  Renaissance, 184
  Romans, 75, 78–79
Velcro, 464, 541
Velvet
  Renaissance, 153
  voided, 522
Venetians, 175, 177, 179, 221
Venice
  Doge, dress of, 163–165
  garments of, 163, 173
Verdugado, 202–203
Verdugale, 179, 181, 183
Versace, Donatella, 512
Versace, Gianni, 506–507, 509, 512
Vests, 207–208, 210, 221, 376, 488
à la victime, 269, 271
Victorian era, morality and sexuality,
  257–258
Victoria sleeves, 287
Vintage clothing, 511
Vionnet, Madeleine, 6, 393–394, 408
Virago sleeves, 212
Vitta, 75
V-necked dress, 32, 34, 135, 143, 163,
  180
Voided velvet, 522
Von Furstenberg, Diane, 472, 481

W
Waist cinches, 437–438
Waistcoats, 207–208, 273, 277, 291–292,
  299, 318–319, 348, 416
Walking dresses, 283
Walking shorts, 417
Walking sticks, 235, 350, 381
Walking suits, 450
Wallace Beery shirts, 414
Wallets, Middle Ages, 114
Ward, Aaron Montgomery, 330
Warp yarns, 26
Wash-and-wear fabric, 433, 447
Wash balls, 244
Watches, 235, 244, 270, 290, 293
  bracelet watch, 448
  watch chains, 293, 309, 320
  watch fobs, 274
  watch pins, 347, 349
  wristwatches, 381, 391, 411, 484, 488,
    533
Water power, 102, 228
Watteau back, 239
Wearable art, 466
Weavers and weaving
  ancient, 45, 49–50, 69
  as cottage industry, 196
  Egyptians, 26
  horizontal looms, 26, 102
  knitting by hand, 172
  Mesopotamians, 18
  Middle Ages, 95, 101
  organized. *See* Textile production
  spindle and distaff, 102, 124
  spinning wheel, 102, 124, 172
  vertical looms, 26
  women weavers, 18, 26, 49–50, 69, 95,
    101
Wedding clothing
  Greeks, 57–58
  Romans, 78
  synthesis, 78
  waistcoats, 292
Wedge haircut, 476, 487
Weejuns, 419
Weft, 26
Weighting, 329
Weitz, John, 469
Weiz, John, 436

Western dress, 418, 452, 489
  cowboy suits, 418, 452
Westwood, Vivienne, 506–507, 513
Whalebone
  corsets, 332–333
  hoops, 237, 309–311
Wheel farthingale, 179, 183, 210
Whisk, 213
White bucks, 431, 446, 450
Wide awake, 320
Wifebeaters, 534
Wigs
  Baroque era men, 208
  Egyptians, 25, 32
  powdered, 208, 234, 246
  with queues, 234
  Rococo era men, 234, 245
  Romans, 77
Wilde, Oscar, 331, 351
Wimples, Middle Ages, 108, 113, 130
Winkle pickers, 431
Winter mantles, 104
Women
  social roles and dress, 74–75, 281
  in sport/athletic activities, 305, 307,
    335, 391
  tailors, 204
  as weavers, 18, 26, 49–50, 69, 95,
    101
Wonderbutt, 355
Wool
  blends, 309
  Byzantine production, 89
  Crinoline period, 309
  Egyptian prohibition, 26, 29
  English, 102
  Greek production, 49
  Merovingian and Carolingian
    production, 95
  Mesopotamian production, 18–19, 21
  Renaissance, 153
  Roman production, 68–69
  and World War I, 364
Working class dress
  Rococo era, 229
  rural dress, 229
  sans culotte dress, 262
World War I era, 370–382
  accessories, 380–381

active sports dress, 379
children's dress, 381–382
footwear, 375–376, 381
hairstyles, 372 373, 375
hats, 372–373, 375
hose, 375
jewelry, 381
loungewear/sleepwear, 381
men's clothing, 375–381
outdoor clothing, 371–372, 374, 378–379
outdoor garments, 374, 378–379
textile production, 364, 395
undergarments, 370, 372
World War II era
    accessories, 411, 413, 420
    active sports dress, 409–412, 418
    children's clothing, 420–422
    footwear, 407, 409, 419–420

hairstyles, 408, 414, 418–419
hats, 404, 408
historical view, 389–390
hose, 409
influences on fashion, 391
jewelry, 413, 420
men's clothing, 413–420
outdoor clothing, 408, 416
sleepwear, 403, 408, 418
sportswear, 409, 416–418
teenage clothing, 422
textile production, 389–390, 391–392
undergarments, 400, 405, 413–414
women's clothing, 405–413
Worth, Charles Frederick, 304, 363
Wraparound coats, 371, 449, 530
Wraparound dresses
    Egyptians, 31
    Sixties/Seventies, 481

Wrapped clothing, ancient. *See* Draped garments
Wrapped skirts, Egyptians, 28
Wrappers, 333
Wristwatches. *See* Watches

Y
Yamamoto, Yohji, 510, 513
Yuppies, 517

Z
Zeitgeist, impact on dress, 5–6
Zip-in linings, 416, 477
Zippers, 392, 415
Zooties, 506
Zoot suits, 415–416
Zouave, 313, 316